ENCYCLOPEDIA
OF CRIMINOLOGY

Edited by

VERNON C. BRANHAM, M.D. & **SAMUEL B. KUTASH, Ph.D.**

Chief, Outpatient Section, Neuropsychiatric Division, Veterans Administration • Editor, Journal of Criminal Psychopathology • Formerly Superintendent, Woodbourne Institution for Defective Delinquents and Deputy Commissioner, New York State Department of Correction.

Chief Clinical Psychologist, Newark Mental Hygiene Clinic, Veterans Administration • Lecturer in Psychotherapy, Brooklyn College • Formerly Psychologist, New York State Department of Correction and Department of Mental Hygiene.

PHILOSOPHICAL LIBRARY • **NEW YORK**

COPYRIGHT, 1949, BY

THE PHILOSOPHICAL LIBRARY

15 East 40th Street

New York 16, N. Y.

TO THE MEMORY OF

COLONEL DAVID MARCUS

WHO DIED IN THE BATTLE OF JERUSALEM

JUNE 10, 1948

ENCYCLOPEDIA
OF CRIMINOLOGY

PREFACE

IN THE COURSE of their work in the field of Criminology, over a period of years, the editors had occasion to work closely with police officers, criminal lawyers, judges, prison officials, social workers, probation and parole officers, educators, religious personnel, sociologists, psychologists, psychiatrists, physicians, college instructors and students, crime prevention workers as well as the families of offenders. They were often called upon to recommend a single compact volume which would give a reasonably thorough view of the entire field of Criminology with all important viewpoints and disciplines represented. Similar requests were received from educated laymen who, like the students, were at a loss as to where they could begin their exploration of the many-faceted aspects of criminality. Out of these requests grew the plan for this book.

Like most editors, with a limited amount of space allotted by the publishers, we were faced with the almost insurmountable obstacle of what to include. A committee was organized representing the various professional groups that were interested and this was gradually expanded into the full list of sixty-one contributors who have made this volume possible. We were motivated by the idea that only the collaboration of many specialists could adequately bring together, in one volume, the variety of divergent points of view in a field in which are found strongly entrenched such disciplines as Psychiatry, Psychology, Medicine, Anthropology, Sociology, Law, History, Penology, Religion, and Philosophy.

Every effort was made to cover all basic concepts and theories that have contributed to the development of Criminology as a science. Wherever possible, controversial issues within each topic were dealt with from all acceptable points of view. No attempt was made to pass final judgment on anything. Each student of a particular discipline will expect from a publication such as this professes to be in miniature, a full and detailed exposition of the best-known laws and hypotheses of his chosen subject. This Encyclopedia cannot be a substitute for original sources since most of the topics covered could justify a volume by themselves. The editors have endeavored to steer a mid-course between detailed discussion and journalistic notation. Every article, however, concludes with a bibliography enabling the reader to continue his interest in a particular subject as far as he wants to go. The new type of index provides at a glance a list of related subjects covered in the same volume.

Some topics of seeming importance of necessity had to be omitted. In the majority of instances these did not relate to the broad general scope of criminality to any important extent, for frequently the omitted topic was too controversial, purely hypothetical or of casual interest to the general reader.

Because of the large number of contributors and various factors beyond our control, such as the intervention of World War II, this volume took almost five years to complete. In the case of two of our collaborators, Warden Lewis E. Lawes, who wrote the entries on *Capital Punishment* and *Prison Management*, and Dr. Caroline B. Zachry, who prepared the article on *Adolescence*, this volume contains their last contribution to fields in which they pioneered.

It is our fond hope that the ENCYCLOPEDIA OF CRIMINOLOGY, by having brought together in one volume some of the leading exponents of a variety of divergent points of view, will enable those interested in this field to make a beginning toward developing that breadth and flexibility of view which alone can provide some understanding of the complex phenomena of criminal intent and behavior which run the gamut from the misdeeds of the greatly honored general and the statesman to the eleven-year-old child who calmly murders his playmate and thinks no more of it than a game of marbles. Primarily, the editors are hopeful that the service which has been rendered to the thousands whose needs this volume may serve, may justify the effort expended by the participating specialists to whom the editors are greatly indebted.

VERNON C. BRANHAM, M.D. and SAMUEL B. KUTASH, Ph.D.

CONTRIBUTORS

NICHOLAS ATLAS
Assistant District Attorney, County of New York, New York City.

LLOYD V. BALLARD
Chairman, Department of Sociology, Beloit College, Beloit, Wisconsin.

HON. FRANCIS BERGAN
Justice of the Supreme Court, State of New York, Albany, New York.

VERNON C. BRANHAM, M.D.
Chief Outpatient Section, Neuropsychiatric Division, Veterans Administration, Washington, D. C.

AUGUSTA F. BRONNER
Director Emeritus, Judge Baker Guidance Center, Boston, Massachusetts

HERMAN G. CANADY
Professor of Psychology, West Virginia State College Institute, West Virginia.

NATHANIEL CANTOR
Professor of Sociology, University of Buffalo, Buffalo, New York.

HERVEY CLECKLEY, M.D.
Professor of Neuropsychiatry, University of Georgia School of Medicine, Augusta, Georgia.

MARSHALL B. CLINARD
Associate Professor of Sociology, University of Wisconsin, Madison, Wisconsin.

WILLIAM E. COLE
Head, Department of Sociology, University of Tennessee, Knoxville, Tennessee.

RAYMOND CORSINI
Senior Psychologist, Guidance Center, San Quentin Prison, San Quentin, California

VICTORIA CRANFORD
Psychotherapist, Neurophychiatric Institute, Baltimore. Maryland

HON. THOMAS C. DESMOND
Senator, State of New York, Newburgh, New York.

EDGAR A. DOLL
Director of Research, The Training School, Vineland, New Jersey.

WLADIMIR ELIASBERG, M.D.
Psychiatrist, New York City.

ARTHUR N. FOXE, M.D.
Associate Editor, Psychoanalytic Review and Journal of Nervous and Mental Disease, New York City.

EMIL FRANKEL
Director, Division of Statistics and Research, Department of Institutions and Agencies, Trenton, New Jersey.

FREDERICK J. GAUDET
Associate Professor of Psychology, Director, Department of Psychological Studies, Stevens Institute of Technology, Hoboken, New Jersey.

GEORGE GENN
Lecturer, Sociology and Psychology, University College, Rutgers University, New Brunswick, New Jersey.

G. I. GIARDINI
Superintendent, Parole Supervision, Pennsylvania Board of Parole, Harrisburg, Pennsylvania.

CLARENCE E. GLICK
Professor of Sociology, Tulane University, New Orleans, Louisiana.

DORIS L. GLICK
Assistant Professor of Sociology, Tulane University, New Orleans, Louisiana.

ELEANOR T. GLUECK
Research Associate, Harvard Law School, Cambridge, Massachusetts.

[ix]

SHELDON GLUECK
Professor of Criminology, Harvard Law School, Cambridge, Massachusetts.

IRVING W. HALPERN
Chief Probation Officer, Court of General Sessions, New York City.

HON. GARRETT HEYNS
Member, Parole Board, State of Michigan, Lansing, Michigan.

LELAND E. HINSIE, M.D.
Professor of Psychiatry, College of Physicians and Surgeons, Columbia University, New York City; and Assistant Director, N. Y. Psychiatric Institute and Hospital.

JOHN D. HOLSTROM
Chief of Police, Berkley, California.

HON. ALEXANDER HOLTZOFF
United States District Judge, District of Columbia, Washington, D. C.

HON. J. EDGAR HOOVER
Director, Federal Bureau of Investigation, Washington, D. C.

CARL E. JOHNSON
Associate Professor of Sociology, University of Wisconsin, Madison, Wisconsin.

SAMUEL B. KUTASH
Chief Clinical Psychologist, Mental Hygiene Clinic Veterans Administration, Newark, New Jersey; Lecturer in Psychotherapy, Division of Graduate Studies, Brooklyn College.

HON. LEWIS E. LAWES †
Former Warden, Sing Sing Prison, Ossining, New York.

V. A. LEONARD
Professor of Police Science, Head, Department of Police Science, State College of Washington, Pullman, Washington.

ROBERT M. LINDNER
Chief Psychologist, Haarlem Lodge, Catonsville, Maryland.

LEONARD LOGAN
Professor of Sociology, University of Oklahoma, Norman, Oklahoma.

EDWIN J. LUKAS
Executive Director, Society for the Prevention of Crime, New York City.

† Deceased.

ALFRED MANES
Professor of Economics and Insurance, Bradley University, Peoria, Illinois.

ELIO D. MONACHESI
Professor of Sociology University of Minnesota, Minneapolis, Minnesota.

ALBERT MORRIS
Professor of Sociology, Boston University, Boston, Massachusetts.

O. HOBART MOWRER
Research Professor of Psychology, University of Illinois, Chicago, Illinois.

WINFRED OVERHOLSER, M.D.
Superintendent, St. Elizabeth's Hospital, Professor of Psychiatry, George Washington School of Medicine, Washington, D. C.

MICHAEL J. PESCOR, M.D.
Mental Hygiene Consultant, Department of Public Health, Atlanta, Georgia.

C. T. PIHLBLAD
Chairman, Department of Sociology, University of Missouri, Columbia, Missouri.

HARRIS PROSCHANSKY
Research Historian, New York City.

WALTER C. RECKLESS
Professor of Social Administration, Ohio State University, Columbus, Ohio.

ORLANDO F. SCOTT, M.D.
Director, National Detection Laboratories, Chicago, Illinois.

ROBERT V. SELIGER, M.D.
Instructor in Psychiatry, Johns Hopkins University Medical School, Chief Psychiatrist, Neuropsychiatric Institute, Baltimore, Maryland.

LOWELL S. SELLING, M.D.
Formerly Director, Psychopathic Clinic, Recorder's Court, Detroit, Michigan.

ENVOY J. STANLEY SHEPPARD
Director, Men's Prison Bureau, The Salvation Army, New York City. .

HERMAN K. SPECTOR
Senior Librarian, California State Prison, San Quentin, California.

REV. A. W. STREMEL, D.D.
Protestant Chaplain, Western State Penitentiary, Pittsburgh, Pennsylvania.

CONTRIBUTORS

EDWIN H. SUTHERLAND
Professor of Sociology, Indiana University, Bloomington, Indiana.

NEGLEY K. TEETERS
Professor of Sociology, Temple University, Philadelphia, Pennsylvania.

LOUIS P. THORPE
Professor of Education and Psychology, University of Southern California, Los Angeles, California.

JOSEPH G. WILSON, M.D.
Director, Mental Hygiene Bureau, State Hospital, Trenton, New Jersey.

FRITZ WITTELS, M.D.
Psychiatrist, New York City.

MARTIN L. WOLF, L.L.D.
Former Trial Judge Advocate, Defense Counsel, Senior Military Law Instructor, United States Army Air Forces.

ARTHUR LEWIS WOOD
Associate Professor of Sociology, Bucknell University, Lewisburg, Pennsylvania.

CAROLINE B. ZACHRY †
Late Director, Bureau of Child Guidance, Board of Education, New York City.

GREGORY ZILBOORG, M.D.
Psychiatrist, New York City.

† Deceased.

Edwin H. Sutherland,
Professor of Sociology, Indiana University,
Bloomington, Indiana.

Negley K. Teeters,
Professor of Sociology, Temple University,
Philadelphia, Pennsylvania.

Louis P. Thorpe,
Professor of Education and Psychology,
University of Southern California, Los
Angeles, California.

Joseph G. Wilson, M.D.,
Director, Mental Hygiene Bureau, State
Hospital, Trenton, New Jersey.

Fritz Wittels, M.D.,
Psychiatrist, New York City.

Martin L. Wolf, LL.D.,
Former Trial Judge Advocate, Defense
Counsel, Senior Military Law Instructor,
United States Army Air Forces.

Arthur Lewis Wood,
Associate Professor of Sociology, Bucknell
University, Lewisburg, Pennsylvania.

Caroline B. Zachry,†
Late Director, Bureau of Child Guidance,
Board of Education, New York City.

Gregory Zilboorg, M.D.,
Psychiatrist, New York City.

†Deceased.

INDEX

*Articles are arranged in alphabetical order according to the principal terms in the titles. Main titles are in bold face type while topics which are covered by articles bearing other titles are in light face type.

A

Abandonment
See Classification of Crime.

Abduction
See Criminal Law.

Abortion
See Classification of Crime, Criminal law.

Abreaction
See Therapy.

Accessory
See Criminal Law.

Accidental Criminal
See Capital Punishment, Criminal Psychology.

Accidents
See Police Administration, Traffic Violator, University Training.

Accomplishment Ratio
See Defective Delinquent.

Accusation
See Criminal Law, Jury System.

Acquittal
See Military Criminology.

Acromegaly

Addict
See Drug Addiction.

Adjective Crime
See Criminal Law.

Adjustment
See Frustration and Aggression.

Adjustment Counseling
See Psychological Services.

Administration
See Medical Service, Police Administration, Prison Personnel, Prison Systems, Statistics, University Training.

Administrative Crimes
See Classification of Crime.

Administrative Office of the U. S. Courts
See Organizations.

Admissions
See Evidence.

Adolescence
See Sociological Aspects.

Adult Correction Authority
See Prison Systems, Youth Correction Authority.

Adultery
See Criminal Law, Primitive Society.

Affirmation
See Criminal Law.

Age and Crime
See Sociological Aspects.

Agencies
See Prevention.

Aggression
See Alcoholic Criminal, Criminal Law, Frustration and Aggression, Psychoanalysis.

Alcohol
See Alcoholic Criminal, Traffic Violator.

Alcoholic Criminal
See Criminal Psychology, Homosexuality, Medical Service, Traffic Violator.

Alcoholics Anonymous
See Medical Service.

Alibi
See Criminal Law.

Alien
See Civil Rights of Criminals.

Allocution
See Sentencing Procedures.

Alloeroticism
See Mental Mechanisms.

[xiii]

INDEX

Death Penalty
  See Sentencing Procedures.
Deception, Scientific Detection of
  See University Training.
Defective Delinquent
  See Classification of Offenders, Mental Deficiency, University Training.
Defendant
  See Criminal Law.
Defense Counsel
  See Criminal Law, Jury, Military Criminology.
Defenses
  See Criminal Law.
Definite Sentences
  See Release Procedures, Sentencing Procedures.
Degradation
  See Prison Systems.
Degrees of Crime
  See Criminal Law.
Delinquency Areas
  See Segregation, Social Disorganization, Sociological Aspects.
Delinquency Control
  See Prevention, University Training.
Delinquency Rates
  See Segregation, Sociological Aspects.
Delirium Tremens
  See Incompetent Persons.
Delusions
  See Incompetent Persons, Mental Mechanisms, Schizophrenia.
Dementia Praecox
  See Schizophrenia.
Dental Services
  See Prison Personnel.
Deportation
  See Civil Rights of Criminals
Desertion
  See Military Criminology.
Desertion from Military Service
  See Civil Rights of Criminals.
Destructiveness
  See Homosexuality.
Detainers
Detection of Crime
  See Criminal Law, Criminalistics, Deception, Police Administration.
Detectives
  See Insurance Crimes, Police Administration.
Detention
  See Criminal Law, Penology, Prison Systems, Segregation, Statistics, Youth Correction Authority.
Deterioration
  See Alcoholic Criminal, Mental Tests.
Determinism
  See Criminal Psychology, Prevention.
Developmental History
  See Defective Delinquent.
Device
  See Criminal Law.
Diagnosis
  See Alcoholic Criminal, Behavior Clinics, Control, Defective Delinquent, Mental Deficiency, Prison Systems, Therapy, Youth Correction Authority.
Direct Examination
  See Criminal Law.
Disbarment
  See Civil Rights of Prisoners.
Discharge
  See Youth Correction Authority.
Discipline
  See Frustration and Aggression, Prison Systems, World Penal Systems.
Discussion Method
  See Prediction.
Dishonorable Discharge
  See Civil Rights of Criminals, Military Criminology.
Disorderly Conduct
  See Classification of Crime.
Displacement
  See Frustration and Aggression, Mental Mechanisms.
Disqualification
  See Evidence.
Distributive Analysis and Synthesis
  See Alcoholic Criminal.
Divorce
  See Civil Rights of Prisoners.
Dreams
  See Mental Mechanisms.
Duress
  See Frustration and Aggression.
Drug Addiction
Drunken Driving
  See Classification of Crime.
Dualism
  See Criminoses.
Duress
  See Criminal Law.
Dutch Criminology
  See Classification of Offenders.

Maconochie, Capt. Alexander
  See Parole, Penal Reform, Prison Systems.
Macrophotography
  See Photography.
Magistrate's Court
  See Criminal Law.
Maiming
  See Criminal Law, Prison Systems.
Malicious Mischief
  See Criminal Law.
Malingering
  See Deception.
Manic-Depressive Psychosis
  See Mental Mechanisms.
Manikin Test
  See Mental Tests.
Manslaughter
  See Classification of Crime, Criminal Law,
    Homicide, Psychoanalysis, Suicide.
Manuals, Police
  See University Training.
Mare and Foal Test
  See Mental Tests.
Marihuana
  See Drug Addiction.
Mark System
  See Penal Reform, Prison Systems.
Marshal
  See Police Administration.
Martial Law
  See Military Criminology.
Masochism
  See Mental Mechanisms, Perversion,
    Sodomy.
Masturbation
  See Perversion.
Maturation
  See Follow-Up Studies, Mental Deficiency.
Maximal Age
  See Mental Tests.
Maximum Security
  See Prison Systems.
McNaughton Rule
  See Criminal Psychology, Incompetent
    Persons, Mental Mechanisms, Schizo-
    phrenia.
Mean Square Contingency Coefficient
  See Prediction.
Medical Examination
  See Defective Delinquent.
Medical Service in Prisons
  See Defective Delinquent, Prison Per-
    sonnel, Prison Systems.

Medications
  See Traffic Violator.
Medium Security
  See Prison Systems.
Megalomania
  See Homosexuality.
Mens Rea
  See Criminal Intent, Criminal Law.
Mental Age
  See Intelligence Quotient, Maturation,
    Mental Deficiency.
Mental Deficiency
  See Defective Delinquent, Prevention, Psy-
    chiatry and Law, Psychological Services,
    Traffic Violator.
Mental Element in Crime
  See Criminal Law.
Mental Examination of Defendants
  See Maturation, Psychiatry and Law.
Mental Hygiene
  See Alcoholic Criminal, Mental Mecha-
    nisms, Psychological Services.
Mental Mechanisms
  See Psychopathic Personality, Schizo-
    phrenia.
Mental Tests and Measurements
  See Maturation, Psychological Services.
Mexican Criminology
  See Penal Reform, Segregation, University
    Training, World Penal Systems.
Military Criminology
Military Government
  See Military Criminology.
Military Law
  See Military Criminology.
Minimum Security
  See Prison Systems.
Minnesota Mechanical Assembly Test
  See Mental Tests
Minority Groups
  See Negro in Crime, Social Disorganiza-
    tion.
Minor Offenses
  See Military Criminology.
Misdemeanor
  See Civil Rights of Criminals, Classifica-
    tion of Crime, Crime, Criminal Law,
    Felony.
Mob Violence
  See Criminal Law.
Morality
  See Frustration and Aggression.
Moral Turpitude
  See Civil Rights of Criminals.

Objective Psychology
See Expert Testimony.
Obscenity
See Indecency, Perversion.
Obsessive Neurosis
See Perversion.
Occasional Criminal
See Causation.
Oedipus Complex
See Criminoses, Mental Mechanisms, Perversion, Psychoanalysis.
Opinions
See Evidence.
Opium
See Drug Addiction.
Oral Eroticism
See Criminoses, Perversion.
Ordeal
See Criminal Law, Jury System.
Ordinance of 1670
See Napoleonic Code.
Organization of Crime
See Changing Concepts, Sociological Aspects.
Organizations
Osborne Association
See Organizations.
Osborne, Thomas Mott
See Prison Systems.
Otis Self-Administering Test
See Mental Tests.
Outlaws
See Segregation.

P

Palm Prints
See Finger Prints.
Panel
See Jury.
Panic
See Homosexuality.
Paranoia
See Mental Mechanisms, Schizophrenia.
Paranoid Schizophrenia
See Schizophrenia.
Paraphrenia
See Schizophrenia.
Parasympathetic Nervous System
See Frustration and Aggression.
Pardon
See Appeal, Civil Rights of Criminals, Release Procedures.

Parent-Child Relationship
See Behavior Clinics.
Parole
See Control, Detainers, Follow-Up Studies, Maturation, Mental Deficiency, Penal Reform, Penology, Prediction, Prison Systems, Probation, Release Procedures, Statistics, Youth Correction Authority.
Parties
See Criminal Law.
Pathological Liar
See Psychoanalysis.
Patrol
See Police Administration, University Training.
Patrolman
See Police Administration, University Training.
Patterns
See Sociological Aspects
Paul, Sir George O.
See Penal Reform.
Pederasty
See Perversion, Sodomy.
Pedicatio
See Criminal Law.
Pedophilia
See Mental Mechanisms, Perversion.
Peel, Sir Robert
See Mental Mechanisms, Penal Reform.
Peeping Tom
See Mental Mechanisms, Perversion.
Penal Code
See Criminal Law and Procedure.
Penal Colonies
See Prison Systems, Segregation.
Penal Reform
See Criminal Law, Prison Systems, Prison Visiting, Psychoanalysis, Segregation, World Penal Systems.
Penalties
See Criminal Law, Military Criminology.
Penitentiary System
See Prison Systems.
Pennsylvania Prison Society
See Organization, Parole, Penal Reform.
Pennsylvania System
See Penal Reform, Prison Systems, World Penal Systems.
Penology and Corrections
See Criminal Law, Education, Prison Management, Prison Personnel, Prison Systems, Psychoanalysis, World Penal Systems.

INDEX

People's Case
  See Criminal Law.
Performance Tests
  See Mental Tests.
Perjury
  See Changing Concepts, Classification of Crime, Psychoanalysis.
Personality
  See Adolescence, Alcoholic Criminal, Behavior Clinics, Control, Maturation, Psychological Services, Sentencing Behavior.
Personnel Therapy
  See Education, Follow-Up Studies, Police Administration, Psychological Services, University Training.
Perversion, Sexual
Petit Larceny
  See Criminal Law.
Petty Jury
  See Jury.
Peyote
  See Drug Addiction.
Pharmacology
  See Therapy.
Philippine Criminology
  See World Penal Systems.
Photography
  See Ballistics, Fingerprints.
Physical Defects
  See Traffic Violator.
Physical Examination
  See Behavior Clinics.
Physician
  See Prison Personnel.
Pickpocket
  See Criminal Law.
Piece-Price System
  See Prison Industries, Prison Personnel.
Pinel, Philippe
  See Psychoanalysis.
Plaintiff
  See Jury.
Plea
  See Criminal Law, Criminology.
Pleasure Principle
  See Frustration and Aggression.
Plundering
  See Military Criminology.
Police
  See Penology, Photography, Police Administration, Statistics of Crime, University Training.

Police Academy
  See Police Administration, University Training.
Police Administration
  See Criminal Psychology, Statistics, University Training.
Police Chief's News Letter
  See Organizations.
Police Offenses
  See Classification of Crime, Statistics of Crime.
Police Research
  See University Training.
Police Science
  See University Training.
Policy Games
  See Gambling, Lotteries.
Political Offenses
  See Classification of Crime.
Polygraph
  See Deception.
Polymorphous Perverse
  See Psychoanalysis.
Pornography
  See Indecency, Perversion.
Poroscopy
  See Criminalistics, Fingerprints.
Porteus Maze
  See Mental Tests.
Positive School
  See Penal Reform.
Possession as a Crime
  See Criminal Law.
Possession of Burglar's Tools
  See Criminal Law.
Possession of Firearms
  See Criminal Law.
Precipitating Factors
  See Prevention.
Prediction of Criminal Behavior
  See Follow-Up Studies, Parole, Penology, Sentencing Behavior, Statistics.
Predisposing Factors
  See Prevention.
Pre-Parole Training
  See Release Procedures.
Pre-Sentence Investigation
  See Probation, Sentencing Procedures.
Presentment
  See Jury System.
Presumptions
  See Evidence, Prison Management.
Pre-Trial Procedure
  See Military Criminology.

INDEX

Sanctuary
See Criminal Law.
Scandinavian Criminology.
See Prison Systems, World Penal Systems.
Schizophrenia
See Medical Service, Mental Mechanisms, Perversion, Psychopathic Personality.
School Clinics
See Behavior Clinics.
Schools
See Adolescence, Behavior Clinics, Prevention.
Scopalomine
See Criminalistics.
Scopophilia
See Perversion.
Scotch Criminology
See Sentencing Behavior.
Secret Service
See Police Administration.
Seduction
Segregation
See Defective Delinquent, Prison Management, Prison Systems, World Penal Systems.
Seguin Form Board
See Mental Tests.
Selection of Prison Personnel
See Prison Personnel.
Selective Migration
See Segregation.
Selective Service Violations
See FBI.
Selective Training and Service Act
See FBI.
Self-Defense
See Criminal Law.
Semantics
See Therapy.
Sentencing Behavior of the Judge
See Detainers, Sentencing Procedures, Youth Correction Authority.
Sentencing Board
See Prison Management.
Sentencing Procedures
See Criminal Law, Criminology, Detainers, Follow-Up Studies, Jury, Military Criminology, Prison Management, Prison Systems, Sentencing Behavior, Youth Correction Authority.
Sergeants
See Police Administration.
Servitude
See Prison Systems.

Sex Crimes
See Classification of Crime, Criminal Psychology, Negro and Crime Perversion, Sentencing Behavior, Sociological Aspects.
Sex Differences
See Medical Service in Prisons, Sociological Aspects.
Sex Education
See Adolescence.
Sexual Aberration
See Perversion.
Sheriff
See Police Administration.
Sherman Anti-Trust Law
See White Collar Criminality.
Shock Therapy
See Therapy.
Shoplifting
See Perversion.
Sick Call
See Medical Service in Prisons.
Significance of Differences
See Prediction.
Situational Criminals
See Criminal Psychology.
Slums
See Prevention.
Social Age
See Maturation, Mental Deficiency.
Social Case Worker
See Behavior Clinics, Court Clinics, Medical Service, Prison Personnel, Prison Systems, Probation.
Social Class
See Sociological Aspects.
Social Climate
See Therapy.
Social Competence
See Maturity, Mental Deficiency.
Social Disorganization and Crime
See Causation, Changing Concepts, Disorganization and Crime, Segregation, Sociological Aspects.
Social Handicaps
See Negro in Crime.
Social History
See Behavior Clinics, Control, Defective Delinquent, Probation.
Social Hygiene News
See Organizations.
Social Integration
See Frustration and Aggression, Negro in Crime, Social Disorganization.

INDEX

Witness
See Criminal Law, Evidence, Jury System,
Napoleonic Code.
Women and Crime
See Medical Service in Prisons, Prison
Systems.
Women's Prison Association of N. Y. and the
Isaac T. Hopper Home
See Organizations.
Work Camps
See Prison Systems, World Penal Systems,
Youth Correction Authority.
Workhouse
See Prison Systems, Statistics of Crime.
World Penal Systems

Y

Young Men's Vocational Foundation
See Organizations.
Youth
See Criminal Law, Follow-Up Studies,
Juvenile Delinquency, Prevention, Youth
Correction Authority
Youth Bureaus
See Prevention.
Youth Correction Authority
See Follow-Up Studies, Juvenile Delin-
quency, Prison Systems, Sentencing Pro-
cedures.

ENCYCLOPEDIA
OF CRIMINOLOGY

A

ABANDONMENT. This term is applied to a number of specific criminal offenses involving the desertion of minor children by their parents or guardians, of animals by their owners or custodians, or of pregnant women by their husbands. For example, the following provisions are included in the Penal Law of the State of New York:

(1) A parent, or other person charged with the care or custody for nurture or education of a child under the age of sixteen years, who abandons the child in destitute circumstances and willfully omits to furnish necessary and proper food, clothing or shelter for such child, is guilty of a felony, punishable by imprisonment for not more than two years, or by a fine not to exceed one thousand dollars, or by both.

(2) A parent, or other person having the care or custody, for nurture or education, of a child under the age of fourteen years, who deserts the child in any place, with intent wholly to abandon it, is punishable by imprisonment in a state prison for not more than seven years.

(3) A person being the owner or possessor; or having charge or custody of an animal, who abandons such animal, or leaves it to die in a street, road or public place, or who allows it to be in a public street, road or public place more than three hours after he receives notice that it is left disabled, is guilty of a misdemeanor.

(4) A man who abandons his wife, while she is pregnant and in destitute circumstances or liable to become a burden upon the public, is guilty of a felony.

BIBLIOGRAPHY

Gilbert, F. B., *Criminal Law and Practice of the State of New York,* Matthew Bender and Co., 1935.

ABDUCTION. The term *abduction* covers a number of specific criminal acts, all of which include the taking or carrying away of a child, ward, wife, etc., by means of fraud, persuasion or open violence. For example, the following specific offenses are classified as *abduction* under the Penal Law of the State of New York:

(1) Taking, receiving, employing, harboring, or causing or procuring to be taken, received, employed or harbored, a female under the age of eighteen years, for the purpose of prostitution or extra-marital intercourse, or for the purpose of marriage without the consent of her parents or legal guardian.

(2) Inveigling or enticing an unmarried female, of previous chaste character, into a house of ill-fame or elsewhere, for the purpose of prostitution or sexual intercourse.

(3) Taking or detaining a female unlawfully against her will with the intent to compel her, by force, menace or duress, to marry or be defiled.

(4) As parent or legal guardian of the person of a female under the age of eighteen years, consenting to her being detained or taken by any person for the purpose of prostitution or sexual intercourse.

The crime of abduction is a felony in most states and is punished as such. For example, the punishment in New York State is imprisonment for not more than ten years, or a fine of not more than one thousand dollars, or both. Most statutes provide that no conviction can be had for abduction or compulsory marriage upon the testimony of the female abducted or compelled, unsupported by other evidence.

BIBLIOGRAPHY

Waite, J. B., *Criminal Law in Action,* New York, 1934.

Abortion

ABORTION. The term *abortion* is applied to the criminal offense of causing or procuring a miscarriage or the production of young before the natural time, or before the fetus is perfectly formed. An abortion may be legally performed by a physician only if it is necessary to preserve the life of the woman or of the child with which she is pregnant. According to the Penal Code of the State of New York, the crime of abortion is deemed to have been committed when a person, with intent thereby to procure the miscarriage of a woman, either:

(1) Prescribes, supplies or administers to a woman, whether pregnant or not, or advises a woman to take any medicine, drug, or substance; or

(2) Uses, or causes to be used any instrument or other means.

In New York State, abortion is punishable by imprisonment in a state prison for not more than four years, or in a county jail for not more than one year. The woman upon whose body a criminal abortion is performed is also guilty of abortion and subject to punishment. Also, a person who manufactures, gives or sells any instrument, medicine, drug, or other substance, with intent that they be unlawfully used to procure miscarriage of a woman is guilty of a felony.

There is no way of knowing how many abortions are performed annually nor is it possible to determine how many physicians perform abortion operations illegally. Careful students of the subject have estimated that there are annually in the United States between seven hundred thousand and two million abortions. Many of these are performed by the women themselves by the most harrowing devices. A sizable minority are performed by unethical medical practitioners who usually operate clandestinely. It is estimated that a minimum of ten thousand deaths each year result from abortions and that many other thousands of unfortunate women are made invalids for life as a result of this practice.

Most authorities agree that our current efforts to punish those who perform abortions fail miserably. It is frequently almost impossible to secure the necessary witnesses to effect a conviction in these cases.

BIBLIOGRAPHY

Cooper, C. R., *Designs in Scarlet,* Little, Brown, & Co., 1939.
Gilbert, F. B., *Criminal Law and Practice of the State of New York,* Matthew Bender and Co., 1935.

ACROMEGALY. This is a glandular disorder and is considered one of the endocrinopathic states which may bear some relationship to psychopathic personality and criminality. Acromegaly is the result of overactivity of the anterior lobe of the pituitary gland if such overactivity takes place after puberty. The oversecretion causes changes in bodily structure such as great enlargement of the hands and feet, projection and overgrowth of the lower jaw, enlargement and widening of the nose, thickening of the tongue and separation of the teeth. The chin becomes prominent and the face has a gorilla-like appearance. According to some authorities, individuals suffering from this condition are more frequently psychopathic and antisocial.

BIBLIOGRAPHY

Henderson, D. K., *Psychopathic States,* W. W. Norton & Co., New York, 1939.
Jung, C. G., *Psychological Types,* Harcourt, Brace & Co., New York, 1923.
Kahn, Samuel, *Sing Sing Criminals,* Dorrance & Co., Philadelphia, 1936.
Lichtenstein, P. M., *A Doctor Studies Crime,* D. Van Nostrand Co., New York, 1934, pp. 167–186.

ADOLESCENCE. Adolescence properly represents a period of the flowering of the human organism. During this period the body and personality of the individual are assuming the configuration of adulthood. Physical growth ceases; there are assimilation and replacement, but neither fundamental change nor development. The parallel between physical growth and growth of the personality does not completely hold, however, for in the healthy individual growth continues throughout life, or to senility or death. The mature adult has achieved a certain emotional balance. Fluctuations in basic drives, interests, attitudes and attachments may occur, but these will be far less extreme than during childhood or adolescence. The mature individual is likewise emotionally independent; his personality is integrated through work and he is a responsible and socially conscious human being.

Correspondingly the unhealthy organism has usually shown certain definite signs of weakness. Physical malformation, stunting, distortion, or overdevelopment will always be evident, as will predispositions to certain diseases. Weaknesses in personality are also apparent, often to the layman, invariably to the trained observer. Tendencies toward criminality, which is merely a name for a particular manifestation of personality disorder practically always appear before the close of the adolescent period.

Personality disorders can, of course, be successfully treated in adulthood, but to delay treatment until this period entails waste, pain, and suffering, both to the individual and to society. For this reason adolescence is considered by many authorities to be the most important period of human life. It is further so considered because it is the most critical period, the period when the individual is subjected to the heaviest strain, experiences the most intense conflict. In the light of real understanding of the nature of growth, however, it is apparent that this is not the case. For growth is a process of steady, smooth progression; its stages are not isolated segments; each one prepares the individual for the stage which follows.

The common conception of the age span of adolescence as extending from the fourteenth to the eighteenth year is a mistake. Its limits are more accurately set as the twelfth and the twenty-first years, though the period may begin a little earlier and end a little later. And individual variations in the rate of development are striking. Girls are generally well advanced over boys.

The rapidity and unevenness of growth during adolescence explains its stresses and strains. Puberty, which ushers in this period brings an upsurge of growth. The body lengthens, broadens, and becomes heavier. The chest of the boy becomes both deeper and wider, his shoulders expand, the muscles in his arms and legs develop, his voice begins to change. The figure of the girl assumes the softness and contours of womanhood: her hips widen, her breasts become round. The genital organs mature, glandular changes take place; the girl begins to menstruate; pubic hair makes its appearance, secondary characteristics develop. The first pubertal changes start at ten or eleven in some girls, at fourteen in others, in still others at all ages between. In boys they usually begin between twelve and sixteen. There is evidence that the beginning spurt in body growth and the genital development of puberty always occur at a certain point in bone development. While there are wide individual differences, the median girl begins to grow rapidly in height and weight at about eleven, is taller and heavier than the boy at twelve or thirteen, and by fifteen has reached virtually full stature. The boy's spurt in height and weight is more likely to begin at about thirteen; it carries him past the girl at fourteen or fifteen, and he is still gaining height and a good deal of weight at seventeen. Physical impairment, malnutrition, glandular disturbance, or disease interferes with growth during this period as at any time. Rest, fresh air, and exercise are most important to the adolescent.

Changes in personality are no less rapid and marked during adolescence. In fact their rapidity makes it seem to the boy or girl that only yesterday he was a child. Though normally he was steadily gaining independence, and was finding security among his own peers in age, he depended to a great extent upon the love, protection, and guidance of his parents, teachers, and other adults; he turned to his parents in large and small crises. He was passionately curious about the world, but could understand only its outer semblance; inner meanings were beyond him. He investigated the where and how; the why concerned him little. He could see his way. Black was black, white was white; he himself, his gang, his town, his nation, these were on the side of the right, and the right would always win.

But adolescence brings a sudden deepening of comprehension and with it a resistless urge to response. Indeed a comparison might be drawn between the way in which reality presses upon the developing personality of the adolescent and the impinging of the material world upon the senses of the new born infant. In neither instance are limitations fixed, in both there is a drive to absorb the whole. The panorama of the adolescent includes science, government, economics, politics, music, art, literature. Nor must he only find out, he must also act. The urge is forward, and it is insistent, compelling. Happenings at home or in school are ignored as trivial; he must go out into the real world of men and women and must establish himself there. Furthermore he must be as good as or better than the best, for his emotion is permeated with the childhood longing for perfection. Since the body symbolizes the self, he must prove himself physically competent. The boy wants to assert his manhood by strength, speed, and agility; the girl wants to be lovely, graceful, and attractive. Both feel a necessity to assert themselves; to shake off forever the authority of adults, and to think and act for themselves. Both must be sure of economic independence, both want to find a good job, to make a large income, and to be sure of rapid advancement. They seek to find a husband or wife who is not only ideally suited to them, but whom others admire, and to found a family of their own. And both want to be respected citizens of their community, and to work for the common good.

But the urge toward adulthood continually comes into conflict with another, the urge to remain a child. And the result of this conflict between strong and opposing tendencies is strain and tension, anxiety and fear. Nor does the adolescent have the background of experience to give him perspective or the ability to make sound judgments. Thus he is disturbed about his rapidly developing body. Studies have shown little causal connection between the anxieties of the adolescent and the physical imperfections which give rise to them. They magnify small blemishes, feel that slight variations of feature mar their entire appearance. Acne, a common affliction of adolescents, adds further to their humiliation. And they worry because, unable as yet to manage their rapidly growing bodies, they are ungainly and clumsy. And the boy or girl tries to make his declaration of independence of adult authority, then hesitates and reverts to childish dependency. Often he dreads to meet the challenge of sexual maturity; is disturbed by erotic sensations which are strange and new; fears he cannot attract members of the opposite sex. Similarly he doubts his ability to become successful economically, he may even wonder if he can ever find or hold a job. And though he longs to take part in community life, he shrinks from the responsibility of actually doing so. For he doubts the world as himself. He has lost his childish certainty, the old standards of value no longer hold. At times the sense of disillusionment seems almost everwhelming.

Variations in the development of adolescents and in the mental, physical, and social growth of the individual add still further to the conflict. A boy or girl who is either much taller and more mature looking than his friends or classmates and one who is shorter and more childish in appearance feels "queer," and "different." And often the one who is well developed physically may be immature emotionally; the adolescent who matures physically very slowly may have the mental development of an adult.

This conflict, a normal accompaniment of adolescence, produces emotional disturbance which explains the behavior characteristic of this age period. The adolescent tends to be moody, vacillating, unstable, introspective, to go to extremes. Sometimes the struggle to free himself from emotional dependence leads him to show open hostility and to defy adult authority. Because he is most attached to his parents, and has depended on them most completely, he may deliberately turn from them, and seek counsel and advice from some adult outside of the family. Often he idealizes this person as he idealized his childhood heroes. The adolescent may withdraw within himself and take refuge daydreaming, in which, also as in childhood, he creates an ideal world.

Again, feeling sure of himself in one sphere of life the adolescent may overemphasize that and neglect the others; thus he may overwork in school, or devote himself almost wholly to sports or to social life. He may exaggerate his social responsibilities, and really feel he was born to set the world right. Nearly always he longs to be "like the rest," meaning others of his own age; he wants to look like them, dress like them, behave like them. Ill health adds to the emotional difficulties of the adolescent because physical and emotional growth are closely related. And, in turn emotional strain may have untoward effects on health.

This strain and tension are found among adolescents who come from homes of all income levels, they are found where family and school and neighborhood conditions are wholly favorable. And periods of social stress invariably aggravate them. It is as though adults in these times viewed the adolescent through a pair of field glasses, with a resulting distortion, a dwarfing or magnification of the image. In periods of depression the image is dwarfed. Then, because the labor market is glutted and work is hard to find, the pressure on boys and girls is to remain children, to stay at home, to continue with their education, and to postpone the idea of marriage indefinitely. This procedure blocks independent behavior but not the urge to independence; consequently its effect is to intensify strain and conflict. The adolescent, normally unsure of his own competence and questioning the ethical standards in which he has been brought up, suffers still further loss of confidence in himself and in society. Boys and girls who are more or less seriously disturbed and for whom no solution can be found either enter upon a seemingly interminable period of hopeless waiting, or commit such overt acts as running away from home and even turning to open vagrancy.

In times of war the image of the adolescent is magnified. For then man power is short, and his services are urgently needed, both on the fighting front and in industry. Boys are given the opportunity to enter the armed forces; both boys and girls are offered positions in industry. Here they are often expected to do the work of adults and to assume adult responsibilities; as a rule the financial value of their work is greatly inflated. Similarly economic and social conditions accelerate the process of sexual maturity. The adolescent boy feels he will soon be able to marry and support a family. Furthermore the early marriages of young men and women influence adolescents, who tend to imitate the behavior of the next older group. In many ways the position of girls is more difficult than that of boys. They feel a sense of unworthiness because they are not allowed to fight for their country. Permission to enter the armed forces is a help to them, but as they mature earlier than boys, they resent being forced to wait two years longer before doing so. Girls are also disturbed by the departure of boys for the front; many of them try to face the fact that their friends may never return, or may have outgrown them, and that consequently they will have to go through life without marrying and having homes and children of their own. Added to these pressures are the general anxiety of and the prevalence of the aggressive psychology of war.

There is no question that war is less injurious for the adolescent than depression. For though he finds himself being driven, at least he is driven in the direction in which he himself is already moving. But the disturbed adolescent is driven too far. He is too immature to accept the responsibilities which are thrust upon him. His image of himself is even more distorted than that of society. He considers himself a man or woman, and while still needing adult guidance, refuses to accept it. Thus during war time there is a general increase in restlessness and hostility among young people, a tendency to neglect school work or to drop out of school, and to spend money unwisely. A rising delinquency rate is but one evidence of the emotional disturbance of adolescents at this time.

Normally the adolescent should pass this final and most severe test of early growth. He should have the strength even to weather the strains entailed by depression and by war. A certain proportion of adolescents do achieve maturity. But numbers of them do not, and it is from the members of this group that the unadjusted, frustrated, neurotic, as well as psychotic adults are drawn. And the determining factor in growth is not the individual himself, but his environment. Nor is it only his present environment, for, as has been said, growth is a process of steady progression, and the years which lie behind the adolescent are quite as important as his present and his future.

It is essential that the adolescent should

have felt, from the time of birth, the strong and abiding love of his parents. It is his mother, and later his father, who are the first persons he knows, and on whom he is dependent, whose love gives him faith in himself and in the world, the faith which is the foundation of his security. When, in infancy, he gradually becomes aware of the difference between himself and other human beings, it is through returning his mother's love that his emotional drive begins to turn away from himself. It is because of his strong attachment to his parents that he gains a conception of the masculine and feminine roles, and learns to play his own; through identification with them he sets standards of behavior, and tries to live up to them.

It is also important that the adolescent should have felt the continued affection of his teachers. For they are closer to him than any adult except his parents; they share with the latter the responsibility for guiding his growth. He must have been allowed to make a place for himself with others who are of the same age or nearly the same age as himself. If his father and mother show more affection for a brother or sister than for him his security is undermined, for he believes himself unworthy, since he cannot hold his own. He can only develop socially as he enters into a cooperative relationship with his peers, and can establish himself with them by making his special contribution to the life of the group.

The adolescent must have been given the opportunity to achieve, for achievement is the second fundamental growth need. He was born with an insatiable curiosity about the world, also with an overflowing energy, an impelling urge to act in relation to that world, to make and to do, to master his environment. He will be able to achieve only if he is given an environment in which he can function, if experiences have meaning for him, if he is allowed enough freedom to make his own adaptation to that environment, and is not compelled to conform to a rigid pattern of behavior. He also needs the kind of guidance (using the word in its generalized sense) which means assistance, and not domination.

The child who has grown up in such home and school environment, and where neighborhood conditions are favorable, will approach adolescence with an inner strength. Though he will be somewhat conflicted, anxious and uncertain, he will be fortified both by his past achievements and by the fact that he has both given affection and received that affection from others. He will not be too dismayed by the responsibilities of approaching adulthood because he has been accustomed to accept responsibility in proportion to maturity. And he will be disciplined because he has learned to discipline himself, to delay present gratification for future and more important ends, whose importance he could understand, to subordinate personal desires for the common good since his own interests have been identified with those of others.

Though now the individual is seeking to free himself wholly from his home, this is still the basic influence in his life. His greatest need is that his parents should understand the nature of the struggle he is making and give him the right kind of assistance. It is essential that they appreciate both his continued need for guidance and his urge to independence, and be ready to help him when he needs help, while respecting the fact that he is increasingly trying to think and act like an adult. They should also understand and neither criticize nor ridicule his idealism, his often groundless anxieties, his vacillations, his sometimes bizarre behavior. They should respect his vocational choice even though it might not be their own. And they must steadily encourage his attempts to become emotionally independent of them, through widening his social interests, through deepening attachments to other adults, and to other adolescents of his own and the opposite sex.

The school which meets the adolescent's needs is one where the teachers also understand him and respond to him warmly and affectionately. In this case his tendency to turn to someone outside of the family will cause him to seek their advice naturally with his personal problems. Where he needs more intensive help than they can give, he should have adequate service from a skilled guidance counsellor or psychologist. To meet the adolescent's need for greater self-assertion he should be given definitely more responsibility than was accorded him in elementary school for planning courses of study, classroom organization, and methods of discipline. The curriculum of the high school should include practical cooperative undertakings as well as academic work, in order to meet the adolescent's need to function in the world of reality. Courses of study should be vital and deal with subjects of pressing, immediate concern to the students. They should induct him into the larger life of the community by giving him the opportunity both to study it and to assist in promoting its welfare. Sex education should be a part of almost all subjects, and should deal with the emotional as well as with the biological aspect of sex. Vocational education should be realistic, in order to meet the adolescent's economic need, and there should be adequate vocational counselling. Ample opportunity should be given for emotional expression through painting, music, sculpture, and dancing. The student should be helped to acquire skill in the use of his body through sports in which all are encouraged to participate. And the high school should provide for wholesome recreation by programs which are sufficiently varied to allow for the unevenness of development during this period.

The adolescent's community should also provide the right kind of recreation programs, should abolish undesirable forms of commercial recreation, and should provide adequate health, family, and other social agencies. It is important that members of the community should promote racial understanding, and social and economic equality between members of various minority groups.

Under these conditions the adolescent can achieve maturity. Where they are absent, where parents, themselves immature seek personal fulfillment through their children, where they cling to them emotionally, exert pressure upon them to follow a course of behavior simply because it seems to them desirable, resist their attempts to lead their own lives and to choose their own friends— then adolescents have difficulty in growing up. And schools which are remote from the real world, whose teachers are cold, distant, and formal, where learning is regimented, and the students are subjected to harsh and repressive disciplinary measures, these also block growth. And among the untoward community factors are lack of organized recreation, the prevalence of a spirit of intolerance, congested housing, marginal incomes, and unfavorable adult influences. When to these factors are added the strains and dislocations which accompany general periods of social stress, as depression or war— the adolescent too frequently finds himself wholly unable to accommodate himself to his environment. Lacking the strength to face the demands of reality, he finds increasingly that his fears about himself were not groundless, that he is unable to make up his mind, to establish himself economically, to make the right marriage, to find his place in the community.

The result of this inability to make a satisfactory adjustment to the environment with adolescents, as with individuals of any age, is emotional disturbance. Exactly as rising temperature or pain are symptomatic of an untoward physical condition, so the behavior of these persons is symptomatic of personality disturbance. The individual responds in one of two ways, depending on his nature. If he feels he has the strength to do so, he stands his ground and opposes the environment; if he doubts his strength, he withdraws from it. Those adolescents who oppose the environment openly defy adults, parents, teachers. Others refuse to do their school work, truant, quarrel and fight with their brothers, sisters, and classmates, or bully younger and weaker boys and girls. These adolescents are seeking to gain a false security in place of the real security which has been denied them. Since the world has seemed wholly unwilling to accord them love, or attention or a chance to count, they are trying, at least to force it to notice them by the trouble they cause. They are also "getting even," trying to assert themselves against domination. And where they are bullies, they are trying to prove themselves by attacking the weak since they cannot measure themselves against the strong.

The adolescent who withdraws from the world may shrink into himself and be timid, or cold or reserved. Or he may be what adults call "good," be polite, well behaved, and docilely obedient. Often these withdrawn individuals commit acts of surreptitious hostility also against those weaker than themselves. Sometimes these adolescents indulge in excessive daydreaming, trying, through exaggerated phantasies to create an environment which meets their great needs. Though they often do not appear so to the layman, these boys and girls are quite as disturbed as those who manifest their condition more openly, and are quite as in need of help.

In neither instance do emotional disturbances manifest themselves suddenly. Since the environments of home, school, and community have as a rule been long exerting pressures upon the boy or girl, he has usually presented difficulties earlier, possibly even in infancy. These difficulties have simply increased with the added strains of adolescence. If he does not receive assistance, the behavior of the boy or girl will clearly reflect the growing seriousness of his condition. The one who was aggressively hostile becomes openly, bitterly antagonistic. In some cases hostility toward the authority of adults, parents, teachers, and others becomes hostility toward the final authority, which is the state, and he commits delinquent acts. And the behavior of the withdrawn boy or girl becomes increasingly neurotic or psychotic. And it is a fact, though by no means generally appreciated, that the acts of surreptitious hostility committed by this adolescent, may be quite as socially injurious as those of the delinquent. For he too is trying to "get even," and his subtle domination or his attempts to prove his superiority at the expense of others may cause untold suffering and damage to personality. It is also not appreciated that delinquency is by no means largely confined to the so-called depressed areas of our communities. Certainly such conditions as marginal incomes, bad housing, and lack of play space contribute to emotional disorders. But frequently adolescents from more privileged sections commit these acts, but do not appear before the juvenile court for the reason that their parents can afford to settle their difficulties out of court.

Before the development of modern psychology the young person who committed unsocial acts was held to be culpable. The delinquent was branded as a criminal and was punished by the state. At a later period delinquents were believed to be mentally defective and an attempt was made to meet the problem through segregation. Though the modern position, based on psychological knowledge, views them, neither as culprits nor defectives, but as patients in need of treatment, the older points of view—particularly the theory of crime and punishment—still prevail among large portions of our population. Delinquents continue to be branded as criminals and to be made outcasts from society.

Punishment and ostracism as methods of handling emotional disturbance have had most deleterious effects, both on the adolescent and on society. For the cause of the disturbance is a belief, on the part of these boys and girls that the world is against them, that they can never find a place in it. They have no conception of the reason for this, but vaguely associate it with their own unworthiness. Though they appear to glory in their behavior, they secretly fear, both it and society's attitude toward it. Thus to inflict further suffering and humiliation merely confirms them in their belief, and consequently aggravates the disorder and the unsocial behavior. Outward conformity may be a temporary result, but since authoritarian control is weakening to personality as it does not teach self-discipline, but only submission to superior force, when that force is removed the adolescent is at the mercy of his increased antagonism.

The adolescent should be viewed neither with harsh criticism nor with sentimental pity, but with objective understanding. Adjustment can only be achieved through treating, not the behavior, which is merely symptomatic, but the underlying condition. Emotional disorders are complex in origin, their proper handling requires a variety of skills. The method of the bureau of child guidance illustrates the rounded approach. A thorough study of the case is made. The psychiatrist studies the adolescent's personality; the pediatrician reports on his health, the social worker visits his home and school and describes conditions there, the findings of the psychologist disclose his mental capacity, interests, and special aptitudes. On the basis of these combined reports a diagnosis is made, and a course of treatment recommended. Treatment may include, in addition to consultations with the psychiatrist, medical care, service to the family and to the school by the social worker, special tutoring, change of grade or of school, referral to a social or recreational agency, and so on. The service to the adolescent himself and to his family forms a most important aspect of treatment. His "transference" to the psychiatrist, whose attitude toward him is uncritical, sympathetic, and understanding develops a foundation of security, on his own maturity level. He unburdens his mind; the techniques of the psychiatrist bring subconscious attitudes and feelings to the surface and conflicts and difficulties are seen in their true light. In the meantime, with the help of the social worker, his parents, gaining new insight into his nature and needs, change their attitude toward him, and become less overbearing, or exacting, or overprotective.

The importance of the school environment should not be overlooked. Teachers should also become less critical, show more confidence and friendliness. The adolescent is increasingly able to find himself in work, to make a place with his classmates. Gradually he responds to treatment. He becomes less openly hostile, or less withdrawn. Adjustment is effected rapidly or slowly, depending on the nature of the adolescent, the environmental changes, and the seriousness of the disturbance.

Since the early treatment of emotional disorders is important, parents, teachers, and other adults serving adolescents should be trained to recognize symptoms of disturbance in their initial stages and to refer them to sources of treatment. Milder cases can be successfully treated by specialists who have had psychological training, as psychologists, social workers, or guidance counsellors, who frequently work under the supervision of the psychiatrist.

Society should make adequate provision for the treatment of all emotionally disturbed adolescents. Free treatment or treatment at low cost should be available to all those whose parents cannot afford to pay for it at any or at regulation prices, in public psychiatric clinics or bureaus of child guidance. All school systems should have bureaus of child guidance. These bureaus should do more than render a clinical service to the school. Their work should be closely integrated with the system as a whole and with every department in it. They should be centers from which knowledge as to mental hygiene and the dynamics of human behavior reaches the classroom. They should not only help to coordinate all guidance work in the school, but, through educational programs and consultative services should assist teachers in the handling of pupils and in the selection and presentation of subject matter. They should also carry on educational programs for parents, and school and community work.

The organization and procedure of the juvenile court should be thoroughly in harmony with modern psychological principles. The adolescent referred there is no more properly a "delinquent" who is being punished than is a patient who needs to seek medical aid. Institutions for the care of these adolescents should be staffed and equipped with all facilities for proper psychiatric and physical care. And their programs should be so related to those of high schools and colleges that the adolescent can take his place there with as little loss of time as possible. Absolutely no stigma should attach to him before, during, or after his stay in the institution. Every community should have an adequate number of well trained probation officers.

Necessary as are the proper treatment and care of emotionally disturbed adolescents, the greater responsibility of society is to prevent disturbances from arising. This means providing the kind of environment in home, school, and community which is suited to the growth needs of the individual from early infancy through adolescence. To provide this environment involves both extension and modification of many of our social institutions. It will require the conduct of adult education programs in the field of mental hygiene, far reaching changes in our educational system, increased community health, recreation, and welfare facilities, also improved housing and standards of living in many sections of this country.

Authorities on human growth believe these changes are imperative, that they are fundamental to the welfare of a democratic social order. For they hold that most of society's serious problems—class antagonisms, exploitation, racial intolerance, autocracy in government, and wars between nations have their roots in the blocking of emotional growth during the period of childhood and adolescence. For the mature adult is so emotionally secure that he does not need to prove his competence through self-aggrandizement, through reducing other human beings, be they members of other races or classes, or nations to a state of subjection. He is continually growing, continually attaining personal fulfillment through the contribution which he and he alone can make to the common good.

CAROLINE B. ZACHRY,
Late Director,
Bureau of Child Guidance,
New York City.

BIBLIOGRAPHY

Hollingworth, Leta S., *The Psychology of the Adolescent,* New York, Appleton, 1928.
Jersild, Arthur T., *Child Psychology,* New York, Prentice-Hall, 1933.
Symonds, Percival M., *Psychological Diagnosis in Social Adjustment,* New York, American Book Co., 1934.
Williams, Frankwood E., *Adolescence; Studies in Mental Hygiene,* New York, Farrar & Rinehart, 1930.
Zachry, Caroline B., *Personality Adjustments of School Children,* New York, Scribner, 1929.

ADULTERY. Adultery may be defined as the voluntary sexual intercourse by a married person with some one other than her or his husband or wife. Under the English common law, adultery is not a crime but is a subject of ecclesiastical censure. In most parts of Europe, adultery may involve either a husband or wife and an unmarried participator. The offense is called *single adultery* when only one party is married, and *double adultery* when both are married. Under the Roman law and the Jewish law, to constitute

criminal adultery, the woman must be the wife of another. In some states of the United States, adultery is made a crime by statute for both parties regardless of whether they are married or not; while in other states, it is a crime only on the part of the married person; and in still others, only when one of the wrongdoers is a married woman.

The Penal Law of the State of New York defines adultery as "the sexual intercourse of two persons, either of whom is married to a third person. The offense is deemed a misdemeanor and is punishable by imprisonment in a penitentiary or county jail, for not more than six months or by a fine of not more than two hundred and fifty dollars, or by both." Conviction cannot be had on the uncorroborated testimony of the person with whom the offense is charged to have been committed.

Adultery is also a civil injury for which damages may be recovered from the correspondent by either wife or husband. It is a common ground for divorce.

BIBLIOGRAPHY

Gilbert, F. B. *Criminal Law and Practice of the State of New York,* Matthew Bender and Co., 1935.

ALCOHOLIC CRIMINAL. Does alcohol *inhibit* or *release* aggressive drives and damaging activities against society that result in criminotic behavior? This problem has been studied and discussed intensively by many investigators, but the evidence to date is insufficient for the conclusions to be clear cut or definitive. In general it has been our experience that criminal offenses against society are committed by individuals with poorly integrated personalities, emotional instability, conflicts with the environment and frustration; these are also found in many alcoholics whose drinking is symptomatic of their inability to adjust themselves realistically to the environment and its demands upon them.

One factor is clear, however; alcohol, pharmacologically, acts as a depressant on the nervous system resulting in relaxation (to varying degrees and extents) of judgment and control so that underlying forces—the personality dynamics—find a more direct mode of expression. While such underlying forces may be of a passive, laissez-faire nature as well as an aggressive, disruptive one, the general result of the loosening of conscious control is the release of id urgings, in themselves amoral in tenor. Both practically and theoretically the response of the individual to alcohol is the response of the total personality, comprising the emotional maturity level and intellectual and physical endowment—equipment functioning in a specific environment and stimulated by specific environmental situations that activate internal re-action behavior patterns. This applies just as pertinently to the non-criminal as the criminal alcoholic but in contrast to the case of the social drinker, the effects of even slight loss of control are a hazard to the criminal (prison inmate, the parolee, or the released convict).

The individual who has a criminal record will, if he faces reality, one of the prime objectives of modern penology, recognize that "rightly or wrongly" society has judged not interpreted his behavior. Society rarely accepts legal justice, trial, incarceration and release at the end of the sentence as completely cancelling the initial provocation and crime. It would be most unrealistic to expect such an attitude. Moreover, and as unrealistically, the criminal rarely seeks any deeper solution to his behavior, past and future, than that imposed by the prison sentence and thus on release frequently becomes recidivistic. Objectively, both society and the criminal are at fault in this shallow understanding of psychological factors involved in their mutual conflict. Because the results of the conflict affect the individual more painfully, one of the objectives of scientific minded and enlightened prison personnel should be a more than superficial insight into his difficulties with the end result that the criminal will develop a better understanding of the motivations that led to the commission of his unlawful acts and come to the blunt realization that he must in the future expect more of himself than of others and not feel that the world is to blame if he does not do his full part.

Modern students of criminology in their stress on the part that society plays in crime causation, would seem to be on the wrong track as far as the rehabilitation of the individual criminal is concerned. No matter how right or wrong society is, the delinquent must recognize that the majority of people do not commit crimes and that his criminal behavior is definitely indicative of underlying personality difficulties, characterized in part by an immature approach to life. The prisoner must be made to accept the fact that fundamentally it is his personality mal-integration and attitudes that need correction; so long as he inwardly feels persecuted and belligerent, so long will his ultimate conduct continue to bring him into open conflict with the laws of society. The basic situation remains the job of becoming a respected and self-respecting individual and this can only be done by the active cooperation of the individual. When he realizes that the job can be done and is worth doing then he has traveled the most difficult part of the road to rehabilitation.

The prisoner, and those working with him, must be aware of and accept these facts if he is to succeed in reintegrating himself with the community. He must understand that he will be on probation for a considerable period of time; that his actions will be closely scrutinized; that society will rebuff him, and in some instances be frankly unjust, primarily because society still fears that he may regress to criminal actions.

The individual who has engaged in criminal behavior must, as a consequence, be prepared to meet with hostility and be taught how to meet this situation without becoming embittered and relapsing into earlier patterns of defensive aggression. He must become emotionally mature, or more mature than he was. If he fails to accept this, or if in a childish reaction of unthinking rage he strikes back at real or imagined provocation, it is he who will suffer.

So far as drinking is concerned, the prisoner should understand the far-reaching effects of alcohol. If he drank before incarceration, if drinking was in any way associated with the planning or perpetration of his criminal acts, he should never drink again. Old habits of reaction die hard and under the influence of alcohol previous aggressive asocial forces may find easy expression. Once he makes a misstep under the influence of liquor, even if his conscious intentions were of the best, he finds himself back where he started from and burdened with intensified feelings of failure and self-destructive emotions.

Drinking at any time, even for the social, controlled drinker who can stop at will, always leads to a temporary relaxation of judgment, discretion, and control. We do not need scientific research to acquaint us with this fact. Alcohol as stated, acts as a depressant on the nervous system: the quantitative and qualitative results depend on factors that vary between individuals and in the same individual at different times due to fatigue, sugar metabolism, and psychological state including mood, thought, and specific stimuli. Physiological changes of functioning include poorer coordination of thought and muscular action; diminished sharpness of sensory perception; and delayed and weaker motor performance with accompanying increase of error. Disregarding individual personality dynamics of alcoholism as a psychiatric illness symptom, the physical effects of alcohol are not conducive to controlled behavior, nor are its effects in any way predictable.

Alcoholism as a psychiatric abnormality is symptomatic of an underlying personality illness or disorder and must be treated as a psychiatric problem. That the alcoholic does not stop drinking in spite of painful experiences which include loss of job and prestige, physical torment and other related miseries should be adequate evidence that underlying factors are literally driving him to drink and that he is psychiatrically ill. No emotionally healthy individual deliberately does that which causes him to suffer provided that he is aware that suffering will result from such behavior. The alcoholic is, therefore, either unaware, not sufficiently aware, or does not want to be aware of the serious harmful consequences of his drinking to do anything constructive about his addiction. The reasons for this lack of insight are to be found in the unconscious and may be associated with such defined psychiatric groups as the feeble-minded, the organic, the psychopath, the psychotic and the neurotic. Physiological factors involved include cell changes and lowered resistance to the drug.

Alcoholism, uncontrolled drinking, leads to the following reaction types: acute pathological intoxication with stupor, excitement or convulsions; acute and chronic alcoholic hallucinosis; delirium tremens; marked paranoid development; Korsakow's psychosis; mental deterioration. There may also be encephalopathies (brain lesions and organic changes) and neuropathies, including polyneuritic features and also, with the above named reaction types, associated with avitaminotic conditions resulting from inadequate nourishment while drinking.

In general, alcoholics may be classified into the following distinct groups: (1) Those who because of constitutional inadequacies (genogenic) are unable to meet life responsibilities and in addition to their drinking habits have other poor life habits. These individuals may eventually become deteriorated or asocial, requiring permanent mental hospitalization. (2) Those who are not too strongly endowed intellectually and emotionally and who suffer psychic frustration with underlying psychiatric disorders (manic depressive swings, schizophrenic reactions) which cause them to seek escape from life reality by means of alcohol. (3) Those who drink to flee from unpleasant life situations they cannot or do not wish to face and meet —the neurotic or psychogenic personality. (4) Those who drink to relieve various combinations of feelings of inadequacy, self-consciousness, sexual maladjustment, etc. (5) Those who drink to narcotize physical or psychic pain. (6) Those who as a result of habit plus time and body changes and added strains and griefs of life develop from social drinkers into alcoholics.

The dynamics of personality motivation which may be found in any of these groups are summarized as self-pampering tendencies illustrated by a refusal to tolerate at all any unpleasant state of mind; a drive for self-expression without the resolve to take the practical steps to attain it; a more than usual craving for excitement and pleasure of the senses; a habit of sidestepping duties and obligations leading to the habit of substituting the rosy anesthesia of alcoholic daydreams; a definite insistent need for the feeling of self-confidence, self-importance, calm and poise that some temporarily obtain from alcohol.

It is also the conviction of the authors that alcoholism is evidence of latent or overt homosexuality as medically defined, or of self-destructive tendencies and deep-lying anxieties, hostilities, and tensions stretching far back to infantile formation of attitudes, sentiments, and interpersonal relationships in which identification and imitation play a decisive role. Contrary to popular opinion, science has no proof that alcoholism is hereditary, although some individuals with an alcoholic ancestry may have lowered resistance or be more sensitive to alcohol. Social inheritance involving the identification and imitation mechanisms would seem to be the basic factors, not heredity as such.

Narcotization of anxiety is a major factor in the misuse of alcohol. In some cases this anxiety is the result of traumatic experiences in early childhood which the personality was unable to assimilate, while in others it may be due to unresolvable conflicts. Other types of personality makeups that seem to require the narcotization escape device include the tense, perfectionistic, worrisome individual; the individual who has a vague inner restlessness and feels himself to be a bystander, not a participant in life; the emotionally immature individual; and the individual who is consistently inconsistent, whose main characteristic is that of unreliability—the total or partial psychopath.

Individual alcoholic therapy should begin, therefore, with a careful examination to determine the "type" of drinker, the personality makeup, and the presence or absence of serious psychiatric or neurologic reactions in order to determine whether the patient should be placed in a mental hospital, a health farm, or treated by regular office visits. The acutely intoxicated individual should, obviously, be placed in a mental hospital until the toxic condition has subsided and the patient is accessible to psychiatric examination. Psychiatric therapy consists of five separate but interrelated steps: examination and diagnosis; placement (hospital,

farm, office); medical and psychiatric treatment; reeducation; continuous lifelong follow-up.

With all except the acutely intoxicated patient the usual psychiatric procedure is employed including complete life history, neurological and mental status surveys, and personality and intelligence tests. It is well to obtain objective data from a friend or relative of the patient to provide factual information about the nature and extent of the drinking and resultant behavior changes. Personality and intelligence tests are of definite value in diagnosis and personality evaluation especially when individuals are unaccompanied and no objective data can be immediately ascertained. Of these tests the Rorschach Examination is the most useful and reliable in making a differential diagnosis, gauging the level and quality of emotional maturity, and in profile sketching of the personality makeup of the individual.

Therapy and reeducation of the alcoholic patient, regardless of his place of treatment, is conducted along the following lines: Regular visits or interviews in which distributive analysis and synthesis allows the patient to ventilate and learn how to objectify his underlying stresses and tensions, interpersonal relationships and attitudes, goals and strivings; while at the same time following a regular daily routine (self imposed or controlled by the environment) and, through discussion and observation develop new insight, views, and values. In this respect the benefits of socializing in the farm or hospital group are very important suggestive factors.

The goal of treatment is total permanent abstinence and therapy is organized to achieve this by reeducating the individual, helping him to establish new habits of living, thinking, action, and reaction to excitement, disappointment, or out and out frustration. The nature of his drinking problem is explained to him and discussed by using specific examples chosen from his own life history and including dream material, present conflicts, etc. Simultaneously, certain fundamental psychological facts are reviewed to help the patient acquire enough knowledge to help himself.

Every patient presents an individual problem and the treatment is approached from this angle. One of the greatest factors in successful rehabilitation of the alcoholic lies in the interpersonal relations of the patient and the physician, with general principles subordinated to the individual needs of the patient. Other necessary factors are the careful selection of voluntary patients with undamaged nervous systems; the personality of the therapist who should be kind but firm; time; suggestive influences and full cooperation of friends and family; lifelong follow-up. It must again be stressed that the alcoholic is a sick person and that his addiction and its causes extend over a long period of time. Thus his cure must be thought of as similar to the healing of tuberculosis scars, depending on his keeping in good mental and physical health. It is sound, practical, common sense for the ex-T. B. patient to periodically check with his physician and it is just as sound for the ex-alcoholic to do so. The crucial part of the treatment is to help the individual reach a level of emotional maturity which will enable him to live a relatively efficient, productive, and contented life with kindly, tolerant, interpersonal relations, and an inner poise and stability.

Sociological factors play a definite part in the production of the anxieties, hostilities, and frustrations which apparently produce a need in some individuals for the narcotizing effects of alcohol. America has never been known as a nation of teetotallers and alcoholism is certainly not unique in our time. Records dating back to early colonial times show that many people were even then seriously alarmed by the alcohol problem which they felt was directly connected with mental illness and crime. By the early part of the nineteenth century alcoholism had come to be recognized as a serious moral and cultural problem and gave rise to a temperance movement that was for a long while overshadowed by the problem of slavery but burst into full bloom after the war between the states.

England, to name but one country, during the 18th Century had an almost universal problem of alcoholism of the worst sort due to economic pressures of the industrial revolution resulting in wide-spread pauperism, rapid urbanization, and cruel economic inequality. We should not blind ourselves with the thought that mankind has always suffered in various ways and that nothing under the sun is new. America was not settled by the ruminative inaction of the alcoholic, rather was it settled in spite of the near universal drunkenness of the Frontiersman. The distillery and the saloon were the invariable accompaniments of the frontier settler (cf. the whiskey rebellion), and they in turn called forth their inevitable accompaniment of the revival meeting and the temperance pledge.

Within the last quarter century the trend toward the more moderate use of alcohol has been definitely reversed and there is a marked increase of alcoholism in all groups and ages. Some statistical surveys set the figures currently at 600,000 chronic alcoholics (this does not include those who have not been admitted to hospitals), 2,000,000 heavy drinkers and about 38,000,000 social drinkers. Excluding the non-scientific experiment of Prohibition which blossomed from the work of various sincere and well intentioned groups, we have never until recently made any organized attempt to attack this problem on a medical or coordinated basis, in spite of the thousands of arrests, admissions to city psychopathic and state mental hospitals, of accidents due to alcoholism, and the testimony of social workers and reformers as to the damage to life, health, and property due to alcoholism.

In England where social problems were attacked publicly for many years, Fleming reported in 1937 an eighty per cent decrease in arrests for alcoholism over a 25 year period due, he felt, to:

1. Social Legislation.
2. Labor receiving equal rights and responsibilities with capital and management.
3. Legislated restricted hours of sale of alcoholic beverages.
4. More diversion on an active participating level of the white collar and working groups.
5. Temperance societies, active social service work with the individual and the family unit.

While Fleming's reasons are a patent over-simplification of an England ruled by the Tory party, racked by the great depression, housed in horrible slums and honeycombed with slowly dying blighted areas it is interesting to contrast his analysis with the present American scene:

1. Large mobile population groups with little family cohesion, tradition of residence, or homogeneity.
2. No marked social legislation until recently; no marked public disapproval of drunkenness.
3. Labor receiving "equal rights" but, as yet, *not equal responsibilities* and little or no political respresentation.
4. No restricted hours of sale of alcoholic beverages except in some states.
5. Fewer socially utilized opportunities for diversion or creative recreation.
6. Due to Prohibition, temperance societies are held either in contempt, ridicule, or fear, while our social service groups have, for the most part, limited their work to curative measures with acute alcohol problems.

Several states have now set up commissions to study and deal with the alcohol problem, and we feel the results reported in England, Scandinavia and Switzerland should be considered in the overall approach. Mental illness, juvenile delinquency and criminality are, like alcoholism, partly derived from environmental situations, and also, like alcoholism, they are on the increase. We are not likely to see any decrease of the social tensions within the next few years. We are entering an era which will probably be more chaotic, disruptive, and emotionally disturbing than we have ever known. Violent changes and dreadful physical and emotional conditions throughout the world will have to affect us in many ways.

Retrospectively we understand the effects of our national expansion, restlessness, heterogeneity, industrialism and historical growth on the incidence of alcoholism to be enormous due to mass and individual insecurity and change in nearly all spheres of life, plus quantity and quality of mobile living.

Preventive measures on a broad basis should definitely, therefore, incorporate ways and means of helping to modify or change our social environment so that it will not tend to stimulate the production of anxiety and tension but rather will tend to provide relative security and support through healthy community living. Opportunities for such now exist in the medium of PTA groups, adult education centers, civic organizations, etc., but the general public is either uninformed or does not utilize these to the fullest extent. It is up to the leaders in all fields to act more vigorously to help bring a deeper participation and interest in such groups. Preventive measures must of necessity stress the recognition of early signs of emotional illness and provide facilities for prompt examination and treatment, as well as prophylaxis.

In specific reference to the problem of alcoholism, from the immediate practical point of view, we need to train more workers to treat the individual alcoholic; we need to set up more, and more adequate facilities, such as hospital wards, psychiatric hospitals, reception centers associated with mental hygiene clinics at which patients and relatives could receive help through diagnostic, placement and treatment services.

We are on the road to achieving these goals and with the cooperation of all groups having the same purposes and with community and individuals' support and work, we would accomplish some of our aims within the coming years.

Meanwhile it is definitely the obligation of all workers and educators to explain the fundamental facts of alcoholism to the community and to drive home over and over again that alcoholism is a symptom of a psychiatric disorder, illness or maladjustment; that the alcoholic cannot stop drinking at will and is different from other, social drinkers; that he can be helped, treated and rehabilitated; that the alcoholic in contemporary America is partly a product of our culture and its inherited and present strains and tensions, and that in addition to treating the alcoholic individual, we must help reorient our culture and social ways of thinking and living to a more decent, vital and spiritually productive level.

In brief summary, the non-psychotic non-deteriorated prisoner who sincerely desires to rehabilitate himself has, we feel, a splendid opportunity to take advantage of modern scientific psychological knowledge that will enable him, practically, to help himself and others in understanding that criminal behavior and alcoholism are not only waste products of a society that does not care about the individual's welfare but also of *individuals who do not care about society's welfare.*

If he wants to, the prisoner can by his behavior do much to stimulate sound reforms in thinking about these very similar personality reactions—criminality and alcoholism, and to support sound ways of helping prevent their incidence in such large numbers; for, since truth is never hackneyed to those who desire truth, "Actions speak louder than words" and "As we would have others be and behave so should we behave and be." Therefore the prisoner who understands that his criminal acts were the result of emotional instability and poor integration of his personality assets that precluded his feeling and being a part of the social group, should understand that the use of alcoholic beverages would definitely reactivate these disruptive conditions; and he should for his own sake keep in mind that:

1. His period of being on trial extends beyond the prison sentence and parole: he must be prepared to meet with rebuffs in a mature manner of tolerance and forgiveness.

2. He, as an individual, has physical, intellectual and emotional drives which he must learn to control if he is to have any measure of "happiness" or inner security.

3. The use of alcoholic beverages (including beer and wine) always tends to relax self-control and to set free any underlying forces. Whether or not he feels that he has an alcohol problem, he should never drink again. From the down to earth point of view, he should recognize that the average man or woman naturally tends to be over critical of the criminal and a discharged criminal who is known to drink will necessarily be thought of with less confidence and more distrust than the non-

drinker. Conversely, the discharged prisoner who does not drink is given more moral support by the community and life is made considerably easier for him. There is here a definite choice the prisoner himself can make between the relatively easy and the relatively hard way of readjusting to and being accepted by the community.

In conclusion, alcoholism in America is a serious national health problem; the problem of criminality is closely associated in the personality field with alcoholism; neither the alcoholic nor the criminal (provided there are no organic or deterioration changes) should be viewed as hopelessly beyond rehabilitation. Society must assume its responsibilities on a realistic basis to help provide environments that do not tend to produce retarded or warped personalities; and individuals themselves must take some responsible purposive action along these lines and not, in an infantile manner, expect the community or the state to administer to all their wants and desires.

ROBERT V. SELIGER, M.D., *Chief Psychiatrist.*
VICTORIA CRANFORD, *Psychotherapist.*
Neuropsychiatric Institute, Baltimore, Md.

BIBLIOGRAPHY

Seliger, Robert V., The Problem of the Alcoholic in the Community, *American Journal of Psychiatry,* vol. 95, no. 3., 1938.

Seliger, Robert V., Recent Psychobiological Approaches to Patients with Alcohol Problems. *The Southern Journal,* vol. 32, no. 10, 1939.

Seliger, Robert V. Do You Dare Take This Liquor Test? *Your Life Magazine,* December, 1939.

Seliger, Robert V. The Problem of Chronic Alcoholism and Its Treatment. *Medical Annals of the District of Columbia,* vol. 3, no. 2, 1939.

Seliger, Robert V., The Psychiatrist's View of the Alcohol Problem. *The International Student,* vol. 37, no. 5, 1940.

Seliger, Robert V. and Rosenberg, Seymour J., Personality of the Alcoholic. *Medical Record,* December 3, 1941.

Seliger, Robert V., The Psychiatric Treatment of the Alcoholic Addict. *The Journal of Criminal Psychopathology,* vol. 3, no. 1, 1941.

Seliger, Robert V. Understanding the Alcoholic. *Southern Medicine and Surgery,* vol. 104, no. 10, 1941.

Seliger, Robert V. and Cranford, Victoria.
The Role of Psychiatry in Alcoholism, *Virginia Medical Monthly*, vol. 71, April, 1943.
Cranford, Victoria and Seliger, Robert V.,
Alcohol Psychopathology in a Family Constellation, *The Journal of Criminal Psychopathology*, vol. 5, no. 3, 1944.
Seliger, Robert V., Cranford, Victoria and
Goodwin, Harold S., Alcoholics Are Sick
People, *Journal of Clinical Psychopathology
and Psychotherapy*, vol. 6, no. 1, 1944.
Cranford, Victoria and Seliger, Robert V.,
Understanding the Alcohol Patient: The
Practical Use of Projective Techniques:
Part I—The Rorschach Analysis, *Journal of
Clinical Psycho-Pathology and Psychotherapy*, vol. 6, no. 1, 1944.
Seliger, Robert V. and Cranford, Victoria,
Social Pathology in Contemporary Alcoholism in America, *The Councillor*, Baltimore
Council of Social Agencies, vol. 9, no. 4,
1944.
Seliger, Robert V. and Cranford, Victoria,
The Rorschach Analysis in the Treatment
of Alcoholism, *Medical Record*, vol. 158,
no. 1, 1945.
Seliger, Robert V., Is a Diagnostic Center For
Alcoholics a Necessary Part of a Sound
Community Health Program? *Journal of
Clinical Psychopathology and Psychotherapy*, vol. 6, nos. 4 and 5, 1945.

ANARCHY. *Criminal anarchy* is the doctrine that organized government should be overthrown by force or violence, or by assassination of the executive head or of any of the executive officials of government, or by any unlawful means. In most states it is a felony. The New York statute is typical and according to the New York Penal Law, the advocacy of criminal anarchy either by word of mouth or writing is a felony. The organization of, membership in, or assemblage with any group of persons formed to teach or advocate criminal anarchy is also a felony. In New York, criminal anarchy is punishable by imprisonment for not more than ten years, or by a fine of not more than five thousand dollars or both.

The owner, agent, occupant, etc., of any place, building, or room, who willfully and knowingly permits therein any assemblage of persons for the purpose of advocating or teaching the doctrines of criminal anarchy, is guilty of a misdemeanor, and punishable by imprisonment for not more than two years, or by a fine of not more than two thousand dollars, or both.

Editors or proprietors of any publication in which criminal anarchy is advocated are liable unless they are able to show in their defense that the matter complained of was published without their knowledge or fault and against their wishes.

BIBLIOGRAPHY

Gilbert, F. B., *Criminal Law and Practice of
the State of New York*, M. Bender and Co.,
1935.

APPEAL. An appeal is a proceeding by which a cause is brought from an inferior to a superior court for reexamination or review and reversal, retrial, or modification. Provision is made by the statutes of the United States and of the various states for taking appeals in criminal cases from the courts of original jurisdiction to a higher court for review. Thus, convicted persons are afforded every opportunity to rectify any errors that may have been made. The defense must file the application for appeal with reasons, within a short time after conviction.

When an appeal is taken, the party appealing is known as the *appellant*, and the adverse party as the respondent. In New York State an appeal to the supreme court may be taken by the defendant from the judgment on a conviction after indictment, except that when the judgment is of death, the appeal must be taken direct to the court of appeals, and upon the appeal, any actual decision of the court may be reviewed.

Every person convicted in a criminal action or proceeding has the right to have such judgment of conviction or order reviewed on appeal by an appellate tribunal, but there can only be one such appeal and the decision of the appellate court is final except that a further right of appeal to the court of appeals can be granted when a judge of the court of appeals or a justice of the appellate division of the supreme court where the conviction was had, certifies that a question of law is involved which ought to be reviewed by the court of appeals.

In New York State (which is typical) an appeal must be taken within thirty days after the judgment was rendered. It must be taken by the service of a notice in writing on the clerk with whom the judgment-roll is filed, stating that the appellant appeals from the judgment.

An appeal taken by the people, in no case stays or affects the operation of a judgment in favor of the defendant, until the judgment is reversed. However, when the appeal is taken by the defendant, a stay in executing the sentence pronounced by the judge is effected by the appeal even if it is denied.

While appeals to higher courts are numerous, the proportion to the number of criminal trials is small. The percentage of cases upheld by the appellate court differs in various states and at different times but, generally, most decisions are sustained. When a convicted offender is denied a new trial by the appellate court, he can still appeal to the governor or pardon board for a *pardon* or *commutation of sentence*. In rare instances, his case may be taken to the Supreme Court of the United States but usually only when, in the judgment of the U. S. Supreme Court, the *due process* clause has been infringed or some peculiar set of happenings brought about a situation where a fair and just trial was not possible.

BIBLIOGRAPHY

Gilbert, B. F., *Criminal Iaw and Practice of the State of New York*, M. Bender and Company, 1935.
Glueck, Sheldon, *Crime and Justice*, Little, Brown, 1936.
Tannenbaum, Frank, *Crime and the Community*, Ginn, 1938.

ARREST. Arrest may be defined as the taking or detainment of a person in custody by authority of law. In the common law, the power of arrest was almost equally invested in the police and the ordinary citizen. Arrests could be made on written orders of the court (warrants), by any person authorized to serve them. Arrests could be made without such warrants when a crime was known to have been committed, and when the crime was either committed in the presence of the person making the arrest, or, in case the crime was a felony and was not committed in the presence of the arresting officer, he had good reason to suspect that the person arrested was guilty. Thus, according to Sutherland, "a person committing a misdemeanor could not be arrested, except on warrant, by anyone, police officer or other, not present when the offense was committed; a person suspected of having committed a felony might be arrested by one who was not present when the felony was committed, provided that he had positive knowledge that a felony had been committed by someone and had good reason to suspect that this was the guilty person." This general law of arrest has been somewhat modified by statutes in the various states.

Arrests by Warrant. A *warrant* is a written order in the name of the people, signed by a competent magistrate, and calling for the arrest of the person named and on grounds stated therein. If the person to be arrested is not known by name, the law permits the insertion of a fictitious name in what is known as a "John Doe" warrant. A warrant may be issued by the magistrate if he is satisfied, from depositions of the witnesses and prosecutor, that the crime complained of has been committed and that the matter is within the jurisdiction in which the magistrate is functioning. The magistrate must issue a warrant if he is satisfied from the depositions that the crime complained of has been committed, and that there is reasonable ground to believe that the defendant has committed it The defendant arrested must in all cases be taken before the magistrate without unnecessary delay, and he may give bail at any hour of the day or night.

An arrest may be, by a peace officer, under a warrant; by a peace officer, without warrant; or by a private person. Every person must aid an officer in the execution of a warrant, if the officer requires his aid and is present and acting in its execution (New York State Penal Law).

When and How an Arrest Can Be Made. If the crime charged is a felony, the arrest may be made on any day, and at any time of the day or during any night. If it is a misdemeanor, the arrest cannot be made on Sunday, or at night, unless by direction of the magistrate indorsed upon the warrant. An arrest is made by an actual restraint of the person of the defendant, or by his submission to the custody of the officer. The defendant must not be subjected to any more restraint than is necessary for his arrest and detention. The defendant must be informed by the officer that he acts under the authority of the warrant, and he must also show the warrant, if required. If, after notice of intention to arrest the defendant, he either flees or forcibly resists, the officer may use all necessary means to effect the arrest. The officer may break open an outer or inner door or window of any building, to execute the warrant, if, after notice of his authority and purpose, he is refused admittance, or for the purpose of liberating a person, who, having entered the building for the purpose of making an arrest, is detained therein, or when necessary for his own liberation.

Arrest by an Officer Without a Warrant. A peace officer may, without a warrant, arrest a person, (1) for a crime, committed or attempted in his presence; (2) when the person arrested has committed a felony, although not in his presence; (3) when a felony has in fact been committed, and he has reasonable cause for believing the person to be arrested to have committed it. When arresting a person without a warrant, the officer must inform him of the authority of the officer and the cause of the arrest, except when the person arrested is in the actual commission of a crime, or is pursued immediately after an escape. A peace officer may take before a magistrate, a person who, being engaged in a breach of the peace, is arrested by a bystander and delivered to him.

Arrest by a Private Person. A private person may arrest another for a crime, committed or attempted in his presence, or when the person arrested has committed a felony, although not in his presence. The private person before making an arrest, must inform the person to be arrested of the cause of the arrest, and require him to submit, except when he is in the actual commission of the crime, or when he is arrested on pursuit immediately after its commission. The private person, who has arrested another for the commission of a crime, must, without unnecessary delay take him before a magistrate, or deliver him to a peace officer.

BIBLIOGRAPHY

Hall, Jerome, Legal and Social Aspects of Arrest Without a Warrant, *Harvard Law Review,* 49:566–592, April 1936.
Sutherland, E. H., *Principles of Criminology,* J. B. Lippincott Company, 1939.
Waite, J. B., Some Inadequacies in the Law of Arrest, *Michigan Law Review,* 29:448–468, February 1931.

ARSON. Arson is defined as the malicious burning of a dwelling house of another person and is a felony by common law. However, the definition of this crime is varied by statutes in different jurisdictions, and generally it has been widened to include the similar burning of other property, as of churches, factories, ships, or of one's own house. In most states of the United States, various degrees of arson are distinguished and defined by statute and different punishments are provided depending upon the degree of the crime committed.

The Penal Law of New York State defines *arson in the first degree* as the willful burning, or setting on fire, in the nighttime of a dwelling-house in which there is, at the time, a human being; or of a car, vessel, or other vehicle, or a structure or building other than a dwelling-house, wherein, to the knowledge of the offender, there is, at the time, a human being. This offense is punishable by imprisonment for a term not exceeding forty years.

The crime of *arson in the second degree* constitutes the willful burning, or setting on fire, in the night time, of a dwelling house, in which, at the time, there is no human being; or of an uninhabited building, which adjoins or is within the curtilage of an inhabited building, in which there is, at the time, a human being, so that the inhabited building is endangered, even though it is not in fact injured by the burning; or of a car, vessel, or other vehicle, or a structure or building, ordinarily occupied at night by a human being, although no person is within it at the time; or of a vessel, car, or other vehicle, or a building, structure or other erection, which is at the time insured against loss or damage by fire, with intent to prejudice or defraud the insurer thereof. A person who commits an act of burning in the day time, which, if committed in the nighttime, would be arson in the first degree, is also guilty of arson in the second degree. This offense is punishable by imprisonment for a term not exceeding twenty-five years.

The willful burning, or setting on fire of a vessel, car, or other vehicle, or a building, structure, or other erection, under circumstances not amounting to arson in the first or second degree, constitutes *arson in the third degree* and is punishable by imprisonment for a term not exceeding fifteen years.

BIBLIOGRAPHY

Gilbert, F. B., *Criminal Law and Practice of the State of New York*, Matthew Bender and Co., 1935.

ASSAULT. An assault is an apparently violent attempt or seriously intended threat to do bodily harm to another, without the actual doing of the hurt threatened. The actual doing of the hurt constitutes a *battery*. Assault and battery are frequently linked together because they usually occur together. The term, *assault,* is often loosely used to include the battery. Assault is both a civil and criminal offense and in most statutes it is defined in such a way as to include battery. The punishment prescribed in the statutes for assault varies with the degree of the offense.

The Penal Law of the State of New York distinguishes and defines three degrees of assault. Thus, a person is guilty of *assault in the first degree,* who, with intent to kill a human being or to commit a felony upon the person or property of the victim, or someone else:

(1) Assaults another with a loaded firearm, or any other deadly weapon, or by any other means or force likely to produce death; or,

(2) Administers to or causes to be administered to or taken by another, poison, or any other destructive or noxious thing, so as to endanger the life of such other.

This offense is punishable by imprisonment for a term not exceeding ten years.

A person is guilty of *assault in the second degree* who, under circumstances not amounting to assault in the first degree,

(1) With intent to injure, unlawfully administers to, or causes to be administered to,

or taken by another, poison, or any other destructive or noxious thing, or any drug or medicine the use of which is dangerous to life or health; or,

(2) With intent thereby to enable or assist himself or any other person to commit any crime, administers to or causes to be administered to, or taken by another, any intoxicating narcotic or anesthetic agent; or,

(3) Willfully and wrongfully wounds or inflicts serious bodily harm upon another, either with or without a weapon; or,

(4) Willfully and wrongfully assaults another by the use of a weapon, or other instrument or thing likely to produce grievous bodily harm; or,

(5) Assaults another with intent to commit a felony, or to prevent or resist the execution of any lawful process or mandate of any court or officer, or the lawful apprehension or detention of himself, or of any other person.

This offense is punishable by imprisonment in a penitentiary or state prison for a term not exceeding five years, or by a fine of not more than one thousand dollars, or both.

A person is guilty of *assault in the third degree,* who

(1) Commits an assault, or an assault and battery, not such as is specified in assault in the first and second degrees, or,

(2) Operates or willfully permits anyone subject to his commands to operate or drive any vehicle in a culpably negligent manner, whereby another suffers bodily injury. This offense is punishable by imprisonment for not more than one year, or by a fine of not more than five hundred dollars, or both.

Certain instances of the use or attempted use of force or violence toward another person are not unlawful as in the following examples drawn from the Penal Law of New York State:

(1) By a public officer in the performance of a legal duty.

(2) By any person in arresting one who has committed a felony, and delivering him to a public officer competent to receive him in custody.

(3) By a party about to be injured or by another person attempting to aid or defend him, in preventing or attempting to prevent

an offense against his person, or a trespass or other unlawful interference with real or personal property in his lawful possession, if the force or violence used is not more than sufficient to prevent such offense.

(4) By a parent or the authorized agent of any parent, or by any guardian, master, or teacher, in the exercise of a lawful authority to restrain or correct his child, ward, apprentice or scholar, provided that the force or violence used is reasonable in manner and moderate in degree.

(5) By a carrier of passengers or his authorized agents in expelling from a carriage, railway car, vessel or other vehicle, a passenger who refuses to obey a lawful and reasonable regulation prescribed for the conduct of passengers, if such vehicle has first been stopped and the force or violence used is not more than sufficient to expel the offending passenger, with a reasonable regard for his personal safety.

(6) By any person in preventing an idiot, lunatic, insane person, or other person of unsound mind, from committing an act dangerous to himself or another, or in enforcing such restraint as is necessary for the protection of his person or for his restoration to health.

BIBLIOGRAPHY

Gilbert, F. B., *Criminal Law and Practice of the State of New York*, Matthew Bender and Co., 1935.

ATTEMPT TO COMMIT CRIME. Under penal law, a person who unsuccessfully attempts to commit a crime, is indictable and punishable. Also, a person may be convicted of an attempt to commit a crime, although it appears on the trial that the crime was consummated, unless the court, in its discretion, discharges the jury and directs the defendant to be tried for the crime itself. According to the provisions of the Penal Law of the State of New York, the person convicted of the attempt to commit a crime punishable by the death of the offender or life imprisonment, is punishable by imprisonment for not more than twenty-five years. In any other case, he is punishable by imprisonment for not more than half of the longest term, or by a fine not more than one-half of the largest sum prescribed upon a conviction for the actual commission of the offense attempted, or by both such fine and imprisonment. The above provisions cannot be construed as protecting a person who, in attempting unsuccessfully to commit a crime, accomplishes the commission of another and different crime, whether greater or less in guilt, from suffering the punishment prescribed by law for the crime committed.

BIBLIOGRAPHY

Gilbert, F. B., *Criminal Law and Practice of the State of New York*, Matthew Bender and Co., 1935.

B

BAIL. Bail is a method of the release of an accused person before trial by means of having him post financial security for his appearance for trial. The right to bail is guaranteed in the constitutions of thirty-five of the states in all cases except capital crimes. In early English law an accused individual could be released if a friend agreed to be responsible for him and act as surety for his court appearance. The person who acted as surety was then liable for the punishment if the prisoner was not delivered. Later the friend pledged his property such as his house or land, but still remained the prisoner's actual keeper. Thus arose the custom of using pledges of property as bail for prisoners. The real estate of friends is still used as security in small towns and to some extent in cities, but in the city many defendants do not have friends who own property which could be used for bail. Thus, professional bondsmen and surety companies have been called upon by many defendants to provide surety. According to *Sutherland,* 40 to 50 per cent of the criminal bonds in New York City are provided by surety companies. The percentage is much lower for other cities.

In New York State, when a defendant is held to appear for examination, bail for such appearance may be taken either by a magistrate, a judge of the supreme court, or any judge of the court of general sessions. For minor charges arrangements for bail can generally be made with a police officer. The *taking of bail* consists in the acceptance, by a competent court or magistrate, of the undertaking of sufficient bail for the appearance of the defendant according to the terms of the undertaking, or that the bail will pay to the people of the state a specified sum. A defendant cannot be admitted to bail either before or after indictment except by a justice

of the supreme court or by a judge of the court of general sessions or a judge of the county court where the defendant is charged with a crime punishable by death or the infliction of a probably fatal injury upon another under such circumstances that, if death occurs, the crime would be murder. The same provision applies in cases of felonies or certain misdemeanors when there is reason to believe that the defendant has either previously been convicted of a felony or has been twice convicted of any of certain designated misdemeanors such as illegally using a dangerous weapon, etc. Before a person can be admitted to bail, his fingerprints must be taken to ascertain whether he has previously been convicted of crime. In all cases but those specified above the defendant may be admitted to bail before conviction as a matter of right in misdemeanor cases and as a matter of discretion in all other cases.

After conviction and upon appeal, a defendant may be admitted to bail if the appeal is from a judgment imposing a fine only, on the undertaking of bail, that he will pay the fine, or such part of it as the appellate court may direct, if the judgment is affirmed or modified or the appeal dismissed. He may also be admitted to bail if the judgment of imprisonment has been given, stipulating that he will surrender himself in execution of the judgment, upon its being affirmed or modified, or upon the appeal being dismissed.

The Bail Bond Racket. According to most criminologists, the professional bondsman is an evil because of the bail bond racket which has grown up around him. According to *Barnes* and *Teeters,* "professional bondsmen are usually parties to a questionable, if not downright corrupt, political system and usually have no appreciable assets with which to go to bail for those who must later appear for another hearing. They offer what is called a *straw bond*, that is, they present evidence that collateral exists which is non-existent or is insufficient for the purpose." Other irregularities in bail-bond practice are pointed out in most texts on Criminology.

S. B. KUTASH.

BIBLIOGRAPHY

Beeley, Arthur L., *The Bail System in Chicago,* Chicago, 1927.
Barnes, H. E. and Teeters, N. K., *New Horizons in Criminology,* Prentice-Hall, Inc., 1943.
Sutherland, E. H., *Principles of Criminology,* Lippincott, 1939.
Tannenbaum, Frank, *Crime and the Community,* Ginn, 1938.

BALLISTICS, FORENSIC (FIREARM EVIDENCE).

Forensic ballistics, strictly speaking, means the scientific study of projection and projectiles employed criminalistically. The popular use of the term, however, limits the meaning to the use of firearms. Since the entire procedure from the observation of the projectile at its point of impact and its recovery to its final identification as to the type of weapon and the particular weapon from which the projectile was fired is a complete entity and involves evidence other than the study of the mere projectile and weapon themselves, a better term than "forensic ballistics" would be "firearm evidence." The practical procedure of tracing the ownership of a lethal weapon or a fired projectile therefrom may be outlined as follows:

The investigating officer will see to it that photographs of the body are taken from various angles so as to show the exact relationship of the body to the surrounding fixed objects of the environment. Precise notes are to be made accompanied by sketches which will confirm the factors indicated by the photographs and measurements of the exact distance of the body with relation to surrounding objects will be indicated thereon. Questioning of by-standers should be made to determine if the body or any object has been moved or tampered with in any way and the notes should make a record of such observations. These matters are of very great

concern in establishing the probable line of flight of the projectile. Quite frequently near the body, in the event that an automatic pistol has been used, one or more discharged cartridge cases will be found. In the event that a revolver has been used, the case is usually carried away with the revolver. Quite frequently the murderer in his flight will get rid of the lethal weapon and a careful search of the ground and nearby environs will give to the investigator the weapon and probably the discharged cartridge as well. Investigator should make a mark upon the side frame or back strap of the weapon for purposes of later identification during cross-examination. Marks should never be made upon the stocks since these are readily removable. The coroner or examining physician will determine if death has taken place and will note especially the position of the body before it is removed to the morgue.

Recovery of the bullet must be done with the utmost care. First, a probe is introduced into the wound in such a way as to give a clear idea of the course of the bullet into the body. This factor, of course, will be correlated with the evidence given by the officer making the initial investigation. The point of entrance of the bullet into the body is carefully examined as to size, shape and possible powder markings on the skin. Due to the fact that the skin is taut by the pressure of the bullet, wounds at the point of entrance are likely to appear much smaller than the actual caliber of the bullet itself. The tissues return to their original position before impact. Points of exit, on the other hand, are much larger than the bullet and are usually torn and ragged due to detritus being carried through the body ahead of the missile. Often shreds of tissue will exude from exit wounds. If possible, the probe should be passed entirely through from entrance to exit which will indicate clearly the line of passage and also notes will be taken as to what structures are encountered by the bullet on its way through the body. Bullets removed from the body or from any object in which they have imbedded themselves must be recovered with the utmost care as the marks of any instrument used in such recovery may seriously hinder the process of identification. The examining physician will then put his identifying mark upon the nose of the bullet rather than upon its base or sides since those portions of the bullet are factors of great importance in the examination of marks of identification. If the lethal weapon is held directly against the body as is so often the case in suicides—this is especially true with contact wounds of the head—the point of entry is likely to be quite torn and to give somewhat the effect of the point of exit type of wound. Pressure of the muzzle of the weapon against the skin, the undermining of the tissues immediately beneath due to impedence of expanding gases from the muzzle and other factors will indicate readily the nature of the wound. If the wound is made within a range of 2″ to 18″, the skin becomes "tattooed" by powder grains being projected into the surface of the skin. Accompanying this is smudging especially if black powder has been used. The caliber of the bullet and the type of powder used give valuable evidence as to the distance the gun was held at the time of firing. Tattooing and smudging are usually not present when the muzzle of the gun was above 18″ distant from the point of entrance. The powder grains must be embedded in the skin to constitute tattooing.

When the bullet, the expended cartridge case and possibly the lethal weapon itself are recovered, they must be transported to the science laboratory with the utmost precaution. Much valuable evidence can be destroyed through carelessness at this point. The gun should not be cleaned in any way for possible fingerprints might be removed in this way. This is particularly true of automatics which frequently show fingerprints on the magazine clip. Individuals who take great pride in the use of firearms are quite likely to take these down for cleaning and oiling the internal mechanism. Not infrequently fingerprints may be discovered on the inner workings of a gun where the outside has been wiped clean of prints. The gun should be wrapped in waste or loosely in rags and shipped in a wooden box properly addressed. Fired bullets must be handled with extreme care because even minute scratches made after recovery of the bullet might interfere with proper identification.

No wire or tag of any kind should be attached to the body of any bullet. Identification mark is made upon the nose and the bullet is to be shipped in a strong cardboard box or container wrapped in absorbent cotton. The fired cartridge case should be treated just as respectfully. In the event that the gunshot wound was made with a shotgun, the wad usually can be recovered. This should be sent along in a cardboard box as a separate package.

A knowledge of the various types of weapons, particularly hand guns, and their mode of action is absolutely necessary for proper identification of fired projectiles. This technical knowledge is usually quite outside the experience of the ordinary officer and investigator and, therefore, work of this kind should be undertaken by ballistic experts only. Considerable laboratory apparatus of a specialized kind is also needed. The four types of weapons most commonly used by criminals in this country in their order of frequency are pistols, revolvers, shotguns and machine guns. Common usage makes no distinction between pistols and revolvers. An automatic pistol, however, is a firearm in which the case of a fired cartridge is automatically ejected from the weapon and a new cartridge is fed into the barrel from a magazine clip during the recovery from recoil. Single shot pistols have no revolving cylinder. A revolver is a weapon in which the cartridges are placed in a revolving cylinder. Each chamber of the cylinder is aligned with the barrel and the firing-pin by the cocking of the hammer. This may be done singly by means of the thumb or it may be done, in double-action revolvers, by the automatic advance of the cylinder a chamber at a time through trigger pressure. The criminal sees in the pistol a weapon that is flat and, therefore, easily carried in an arm holster under the armpit with a minimum of bulging of the coat to show its presence. In the case of a heavy automatic the weapon provides an excellent instrument for slugging the victim into unconsciousness. Furthermore, the magazine clip of an automatic will hold half again as many bullets as could be contained in the cylinder of a revolver. Most favored of all, of course, is a machine gun which can be "sprayed" over the victim with little need for accuracy or skill on the part of the operator.

The most frequently used weapons by criminals, which are of domestic manufacture, are the 25 Automatic Colt (especially useful in carrying in the pocket or handbag because of its small size and its lethal power), the 32 Automatic Colt, 38 Colt Revolver, and 38 Smith & Wesson Revolver, both of regular and special sizes, the so-called Police Positive which is a standard weapon used by policemen and is of 38 caliber, the Detective Special which is the same type as the Police Positive except for a short barrel which facilitates its being carried with minimum visibility and the 45 Colt Automatic Pistol. Those of foreign make most favored by criminals in this country are the 7.65 Luger Automatic, the Mauser 7.63 caliber, the Ortegies, and a flood of Spanish guns of crude make especially prevalent among Porto Ricans, Mexicans, and other Spanish-speaking individuals. Not infrequently the 41 Remington Derringer is found throughout the West. This is an over and under 2-shot pistol and can be carried relatively easy in the vest pocket. It is an old-time weapon much used in the early history of this country but has never lost its popularity entirely and quite frequently can be picked up in pawn shops even today. The old frontier 45 and 44 caliber revolvers so popular in the movies and in western stories are seldom encountered among criminals because of their great bulk, the difficulty of concealment, and the fact that most of them are single-fire weapons except counterparts made in modern times of double-action variety. Many of them are models that do not have the cylinder swung wide of the frame for easy loading.

When a bullet is submitted to the scientific laboratory to determine by the markings thereon the make of the weapon from which it was fired, and if possible, the identical weapon itself, a certain well-defined line of procedure is followed. The bullet is carefully observed with respect to distortions caused by impact and a note is made of all details so noted. The diameter of the bullet is ascertained to 1/100th of an inch by means of a Vernier Micrometer. This determines the caliber of the bullet and the entire range of bullets are so classified. The actual diameter of the bullet does not correspond exactly with this caliber, however. Thus, a 45 Colt Automatic measures .4505 and a 38 Smith and Wesson Special measures .3585. In reloading by hand the bullet is usually cast to full size and then sized down to the indicated diameter by means of a sizing die. The weight of the bullet in grains is next taken and then a note is made as to the type of bullet, whether it be metal-cased, lead or, if a rifle bullet, whether it had a gas check on the base, is hollow-pointed, or has other peculiarities distinguishing it from the usual rounded and somewhat stub-nosed type of bullet found in automatic and revolver ammunition.

The next problem is the determination of the measurement and number, as well as the direction, of the so-called lands and grooves which are markings found on all bullets fired through rifled barrels. The interior of rifles, pistols and revolvers is cut into grooves so that the bullet in traversing the barrel will be given a spinning motion along its long axis thus stabilizing the bullet in its line of flight after leaving the muzzle. The raised portion of the barrel between the groove-cuts is known as the land. Obviously, the bullet records the lands as grooves and the grooves appear as raised surfaces on the bullet in exactly reversed order as in the barrel of the weapon itself. Various methods as to measuring the width of the lands and the grooves, as well as the depth of the grooves, have been employed over a number of years. In the early years of the analysis of bullet-markings, it was the custom to roll the bullet firmly over carbon paper or a sheet of wax or of soft lead to record the markings thereon and to measure them as closely as possible. This exceedingly crude process has been replaced in more modern days by more accurate methods. The lands on the bullet can be measured by a Vernier Caliper to 1/1000th of an inch. Since the diameter of the bullet is known, the circumference can be calculated and the number of lands multiplied by their respective width can be deducted from that circumference, thus giving the total area of the grooves. This divided by the number of grooves gives the average width of each groove. In general grooves are much wider and more irregular than lands and, therefore, are more difficult of measurement. This is due to the fact that the cutting knives with which the barrel of the weapon is rifled become worn and are not always replaced at the proper time. Rifling at best is a crude procedure and many marks are made in the gun barrel during the process of manufacture that are not at all uniform so that each barrel has its individual markings in its totality and differs from any other barrel put out by that manufacturer or by any other manufacturer of that type of weapon. An even more precise type of measurement of lands is afforded by the use of a microscope with oculars scaled to 1/1000th of an inch, or some multiple thereof. The direction which the lands and grooves take with respect to the longitudinal axis of the bullet are of considerable importance since their deviation either to the right or to the left may be one of the factors determining the make of the firearm through which the bullet was fired. The number of lands on the bullet is likewise of considerable value in determining the make of the weapon.

There are additional marks on the bullet that yield valuable information. Thus, the base of the bullet almost invariably is depressed into a small cup. Lubricants, burned and unburned powder granules, and other detritus may be recovered from this depression and should be examined microscopically, as well as grossly, and filed for future reference. Each bullet for purposes of lubrication has what is known as a cannelure encircling the bullet at right angles to its long axis. This is usually near the base and consists of a groove filled with a lubricant. Smaller accessory cannelures are to be noted farther up on the bullet, especially in the case of hand-loaded ammunition. These contain smaller amounts of lubricant. Old-fashioned bullets, particularly for obsolete types of rifles, may contain quite a number of these cannelures. The modern ammunition for hand guns, however, contains only one main cannelure. In addition to this, the bullet is encircled with knurls parallel with the long axis of the bullet, giving the same effect as the milling of the edge of a coin. The combination then of the number of lands and

grooves with their width, and the depth of the grooves, combined with the direction of the twist, as well as the diameter of the bullet, its weight, and size of cannelures and knurls give a picture that is distinctive of one type of bullet only.

Tables can be consulted which indicate immediately the type of gun from which the bullet was fired. Since there are a large number of makes of hand guns throughout the world, obviously a short-cut to identification must be made. Tables of groups of leading types of bullets with their markings are prepared in the order of the size of the caliber of the bullet. Thus, a limited number of makes of guns may be of 32 caliber having six lands with the rifling or pitch directed to the right. This simplifies the classification of the bullet to a relatively small number of weapons from which it could have been fired.

The next object for analysis is the expended cartridge case. Certain markings are imparted thereto through the process of loading and firing the cartridge. This is especially true of automatic pistols. A knowledge of the action of an automatic pistol is necessary to determine the significance of the markings it imparts to a case upon firing. The cartridge of an automatic is held in the barrel by its seating against the conical portion of the forward part of the chamber. Its seating is not determined by a rim as is the case of revolver cartridges. The rim of an automatic cartridge is flush with the body of the cartridge itself but is separated therefrom by a deep groove into which a spring clip called an extractor is fitted. When the cartridge is fired in an automatic, the expansion of the gases causes a recoil so that the case is projected backward against the breech face in the center of which is a hole through which the firing pin operates. A small metallic projection at the breech face known as the ejector and which is located for purposes of efficiency diametrically opposite the extractor, impinges on the head of the cartridge case in its recoil in such a manner as to flip the empty case through the top opening of the weapon, thus freeing the mechanism for the introduction of another cartridge into the barrel. The slide which has been thrown backward by the recoil is then shot forward by the action of a compressed spring so that it catches the top of a fresh cartridge in the clip and projects it into the chamber of the barrel.

In this process certain distinct markings are made upon the case and the empty case itself is thrown in a characteristic direction and to a definite distance distinctive for each type of automatic pistol used. It is possible to plot distances and directions from the point at which a cartridge is located so as to determine the exact point at which that cartridge has been fired if it has not rolled to any extent or otherwise has not been disturbed. The examination of the fired cartridge case after ejection is next in the order of examination. The extractor leaves a mark on the forward surface of the rim. The ejector leaves a mark on the rear surface of the rim. The introduction of the fresh cartridge into the chamber may leave a chamber rim marking on the circumference of the shell. Impact of the shell upon the breech face leads to distinctive markings which are identical for that gun and which form the chief source of identification as to the individuality of the weapon used in contradistinction to the markings of the bullet which are likely to determine chiefly the type of bullet used. Exceptions to this are where some special deformity of the barrel such as mutilation of the muzzle or rust spots within the barrel itself or other markings which give characteristic impressions to the bullet can be noted.

Most of these markings upon the cartridge case are not visible to the naked eye nor to the uninitiated. In the hands of an expert, however, especially with resort to the microscope very significant deductions can be made. It can be readily understood that these markings are not constant nor may all of them be present in any given case. Such information as can be gained by the examination of a cartridge case must be correlated with the bullet findings and all other data so that a final deduction and evalution can be made on the basis of the total picture rather than any single group of data. With respect to the value of cartridge case markings, the extractor may make a mark on the forward surface of the rim in one of four basic positions covering about one-quarter of the circumference on the right side. This may be in the form of a sharp corner indentation above or below the horizontal axis of the head of the shell or may be a full imprint of the extractor in the one or three o'clock position. The exact location of the extractor mark, especially in its relationship to ejector marks, is of extreme importance in determining the particular make of weapon from which the cartridge was fired. About two-thirds of the various kinds of pistols on the market are equipped with special ejectors and the remaining third employ the firing-pin as an ejector. The ejector marks are usually opposite the extractor marks for purposes of efficiency in supporting the flipping action of the mechanism during the process of ejection. Ejector marks are small indentations of the right-angled variety. Where the firing pin is used as a portion of the ejector mechanism, a small oval depression can be noted to the left of the firing-pin depression in the primer itself.

Most characteristic of the markings on cartridge cases are those imparted by the impact of the case upon the breech face. When the frame of the pistol or revolver has been cast by the manufacturer, a considerable amount of machine work must be done upon the breech face to put it into usable condition. In America the workmen do this by careful filing so that the breech face is flush throughout and the markings are inclined to be fine lines. Nevertheless the head of the case may pick up these markings upon the recoil. In foreign countries much less attention is given to perfect machining of the face. German automatics are likely to have a sunken breech with concentric rings. This, of course, cannot be touched by the file. Milling off is done in a vertical plane only so there are parallel tool marks in the vertical plane. Breech face marks, therefore, can be classified into three categories; namely, those with a straight parallel tool marks, those showing concentric rings about the firing pin hole as a center and those showing irregular file marks produced by hand as opposed to the rough tool marks.

Most characteristic of all are the markings on the breech faces of Spanish makes of hand guns. This is due to the method of manufacture. The manufacturer makes rough castings and in many cases turns the gun over to private individuals for final finishing. They are usually interested in production and do a very crude and rapid hand filing of the weapon. The weapon is then turned over to an importer who puts his own trade mark on the gun. These are cheap guns, very crudely machined, and in many cases dangerous to use. Quite a flood of these cheap Spanish guns came on the market following the first World War and were used widely by Latin-American criminals in this country.

The firing-pin aperture may likewise make an impression upon the shell head. This will occur, of course, on the primer itself. It is a distinctive marking because the primer is made of a softer metal than the rest of the cartridge. If a cartridge has high gas pressure, the primer is often bulged. If the firing-pin is used as the ejector, there is often a small oval bulging to the left of the firing-pin depression in the primer. About one-third of automatic pistols use the firing pin as an ejector. In some cases the edges of the firing-pin aperture are beveled which, of course, gives a less uniformity to the impress on the primer. This is particularly true if brass primers are used because it is a harder metal. Nevertheless even these can be detected by the measuring microscope in which the photograph is enlarged ten times and projected on illuminated ground glass. Cellophane paper spread thereon and marked with concentric rings enables the expert to measure within 5/100th of a millimeter the diameter of the firing-pin aperture mark. Lateral lighting brings this out into relief to best advantage. (Slit lamp.) This is also true of most markings on cartridge cases. Fired shells may be classified into main groups the same as bullets. Bullets are classified according to caliber with sub-divisions of classifications in accordance with the number of grooves and lands and the direction they take either to the right or to the left. Shells are grouped primarily on caliber with sub-classification according as to whether the markings are of a separate ejector or of a firing-pin type.

The third class of markings to be found on cartridges is that of the chamber rim. Three basic types are noted as a concentric inden-

tation extending from the extractor marks in accordance with whether it is in the three o'clock, two o'clock, or twelve o'clock position respectively. These are subject to groupings the same as with markings of the breech face in accordance primarily with the caliber of the shell and sub-classification in accordance with basic forms 1, 2, or 3 as indicated above. Comparison with a test shell fired from the lethal weapon may be made under the comparison microscope as indicated under the topic *Photography*.

Examination of the suspected weapon itself is relatively simple due to a recently-invented device which gives exact measurements of lands and grooves in the rifling of the gun barrel, as well as its caliber and any characteristic peculiarities. The weapon to be examined is fixed in a proper vise at one end of a lathe bed. Upon this bed a lathe-like instrument resembling very much the tailstock of a lathe can be advanced precisely by means of a rotary screw. On the head of this is a detachable push rod to which is affixed a soft lead disc 1/16″ in diameter. The disc is pushed into the rifling for a distance of exactly 1″. A reading is made on the Vernier Scale at the other end of the push rod. The micrometer dial is calibrated to 1/1000″. The amount of rotation imparted to the recording scale which gives readings to 3 minutes of angle provides the means for computation of the distance required for a complete revolution of the rifling. The disc is then advanced through the entire length of the barrel, is withdrawn and measured with Vernier calipers or otherwise to determine the exact width of the grooves and lands and the depth of the grooves, respectively. The exact caliber, of course, is readily notable by the diameter of the disc. This procedure gives a much more precise measurement than pushing a blank bullet through the barrel. Dies are provided with the rifling meter so that different size discs may be punched out for the different calibers of weapons to be examined.

A more time-honored method of determining these measurements is to fire several test shots through the weapon under examination. For this purpose a specially-devised firing box insures the quick recovery of the fired bullet without any distortion whatsoever. Originally, test bullets were fired into water but it was found that no matter how carefully this was done, some distortion of the bullet took place. The present system, then, is to take a square box into which frames or sections of stuffed cotton batting are inserted serially. The cotton batting is stuffed between the cloth attached to each side of the wooden frame so that it is readily removable for purposes of recovering the spent bullet. Experts are able to estimate within a frame or two the exact location of the spent bullet after firing. Paper patches can be pasted to the holes in the cloth in each frame and the box can be used repeatedly for test firing. The spent bullet is then put under the comparison microscope and matched against the bullet recovered from the body. If the matchings are relatively exact, the deduction is made that the suspected weapon is the one from which the lethal shot was fired. Its ownership can then be traced as the suspects are materially narrowed by this information.

The comparison microscope likewise affords means for examining the spent cartridge shell found at the scene of the crime with that obtained by firing test shots into the firing box. Exact duplication of all markings cannot be expected nor can identification be secured on the matching of one or two markings only. The general pattern throughout, however, is studied, the markings are photographed and are superimposed upon each other in such a way as to produce evidence of identity. It is in this form that presentation of the case is made before the jury during trial. Some experts will mark with red crayon or with arrowpoints the identifying comparative marks but usually these are so obvious as to necessitate such procedure. The projection of photographs with ten to twenty enlargements serves to bring out comparative points all the more readily.

In the study of shells obtained from revolvers, the markings on the cases are much less notable than those obtained from automatic pistols. There is no extractor in a revolver, of course, and the cartridge cases or unfired cartridges are ejected by hand after the cylinder is swung away from the frame.

There is no impinging, therefore, of the cartridge against the ejector at the time of firing. Also, there are no chamber rim markings inasmuch as the revolver cartridge is held in place in the cylinder chamber by means of the flange of the rim on the head of the cartridge. In many types of revolvers the cylinder chamber is recessed to accommodate the cartridge rim. In the case of the automatic, seating of the cartridge is made by the conformation to the forward portion of the chamber in the barrel of the automatic itself. Identification, therefore, in revolvers is limited somewhat to breech face markings, the marking of the firing-pin, and of the firing-pin hole and occasional shaving of bullet by faulty alignment of chamber cylinder with barrel. Usually a very thorough examination made by a ballistic expert is necessary to classify revolver cartridges.

Machine guns are great favorites as lethal weapons for use by criminals but on account of the marked restrictions placed by the government upon the ownership of these weapons, few of them were available to the underworld during past years; however, the cessation of hostilities during World War I and to a greater extent at the end of the second World War has led to the bringing in of large numbers of machine guns into this country by returning veterans. These are brought in a souvenirs and, of course, the veterans being accustomed to handling the weapon prefer them in perfect working condition. They are potentially a source of great harm to the community since they may readily find their way into the hands of criminals.

The most extensively-used machine gun is the so-called Thompson Machine Gun (Tommy Gun) because it is easily dissembled, the parts are easily accessible and capable of being cleaned, and ammunition is plentiful and easily secured. The Thompson Machine Gun uses a 45 caliber automatic ammunition which is interchangeable with a 45 caliber Automatic Pistol. It weighs only ten pounds and its overall is only 4″ short of a yard in length. When the butt stock is removed, the gun measures only 24″ in length and is capable of being readily concealed about one's person, particularly if he is wearing an overcoat. The gun is capable of delivering approximately 700 shots per minute and holds a 20-shot clip. Drum magazines holding 50 shots are available but have never been of much favor. Operators of this gun have found that carrying several 20-shot clips separately about the person is much easier than to use a 50-shot drum. Despite the popularity of this weapon, a new one has just come on the market from the Ordnance Department which is capable of being carried in a brief case. This, apparently, is equivalent to the German Schmeisser Machine Pistol and the British Sten gun. Machine gun pistols are far better known on the continent than in this country. For example, there was available before World War II a Mauser Automatic Pistol, caliber 7.63. This shot a steel-nosed bullet with high velocity and considerable penetrating power. Its impact and shocking power, of course, were considerably less than that of the 45 caliber bullet used in the Thompson Gun. The magazines in these types of weapons are forward of the trigger guard; just as the same is true of the Thompson Machine Gun. In rapid automatic fire this may be grasped by the left hand for steadying purposes but the recoil is so terrific that accuracy with a machine pistol of this type is quite out of the question. In order to stabilize this, a skeleton stock is fitted into the slot of the back strap of the pistol so that it can be used as a light rifle. In this combination the gun, in effect, becomes equal to that of a rifle in accuracy, and is so compact upon dissembly that it can be stored about one's person without attracting attention. It is quite likely that machine pistols of this kind will make their entry into this country in fairly large number within the next year and at the present time the government has not been able to secure sufficient control of this menace.

VERNON C. BRANHAM, M.D.
Chief, Outpatient Section, Neuropsychiatric Division, Veterans Administration, Washington, D. C.

BIBLIOGRAPHY

Federal Bureau of Investigation, *Firearms Identification,* Government Printing Office, 1941.
Hatcher, J. S., *Textbook of Firearms Investigation, Identification and Evidence,* 1935.

Inbau, F. E., Scientific Evidence in Criminal Cases, *Journal of Criminal Law and Criminology,* 24, 4, 825–845.
Snyder, Lemoyne, *Homicide Investigation,* C. C. Thomas, 1944.
Wilson, C. M., The Identification of Extractor Marks on Fired Shells, *Journal of Criminal Law and Criminology,* 27, 5, Jan.-Feb. 1939, 724–730.

BARRATRY. Common *barratry* is defined as the practice of exciting groundless judicial proceedings and is classified as a misdemeanor. No person can be convicted of common barratry, except upon proof that he has excited actions or legal proceedings, in at least three instances, and with a malicious or corrupt intent to annoy or vex. Upon a prosecution for common barratry, the fact that the defendant was himself a party in interest or upon the record to any action or legal proceeding complained of, is not a defense.

BIBLIOGRAPHY

Gilbert, F. B., *Criminal Law and Practice of the State of New York,* M. Bender & Co., 1935.

BEHAVIOR CLINICS. I. DEFINITION. Behavior clinics are clinics to which are referred for expert study and treatment what formerly were called "problem children," now better designated children and adolescents presenting problems of behavior. These problems include delinquency of various degrees of seriousness, from mild to chronic offenses, problems of personality development, of persisting unfavorable habits, of school and general educational or vocational difficulties. However manifested, these difficulties are today conceived to be largely of emotional origin and for the most part derived from interpersonal relationships.

II. RATIONALE. a. *Diagnosis before Treatment.* Initially the behavior clinic was established as an adjunct of the juvenile court which had preceded the clinic by about ten years. Its purpose was exemplification of the common-sense principle that diagnosis should offer the foundation for treatment, a principle generally accepted in medicine, but completely absent in social treatment in the early years of the twentieth century. The character of the functioning of the court at that time is well illustrated by two statements, one by a juvenile court judge, the other by a ward of another court. The former said, "My job is to make a guess in each case, that's what I'm here for." The latter said to the judge who had just committed her to a correctional school, "Of course you mean to do what's right, but you just don't understand me."

The clinic was set up as a center to make a study of the individual that should offer a diagnosis and prognosis in the light of which, ideally at least, a plan not only for immediate disposal of the case but for rational treatment could be formulated. Today when therapy is the province of many clinics, especially those not exclusively for court delinquents, diagnosis remains the guide for all subsequent treatment procedures.

b. *Behavior Seen as Symptomatic.* The clinic, adopting the attitude that scientific study of behavior is possible, views behavior as symptomatic, the outward evidence of causes and conditions susceptible of determination. It places emphasis not on the behavioral act but on the urges behind the act. Thus it is not stealing or running away or truancy that constitute the real problem; these are but symptoms that something is going wrong in some sphere of the individual's life. They indicate the need for discovery of the meaning which the misconduct has for the individual, for knowing the environmental pressures that may be playing upon him, the forces that in any way have been impeding his normal social growth, in particular the influences of early life that have tended to create his asocial trends. Whatever theories in these days of diverse psychiatric interpretations may be held concerning these causative factors, there is general belief in the necessity for delving beneath the surface of the behavior to discover the roots whence the actions stem.

c. *Individualization of Treatment.* This belief leads to a third principle, namely the necessity for individualization of treatment. If the study of the individual reveals individual differences in personality and in needs it follows that treatment must vary to meet these differences. In line with this, in relation to delinquency, emphasis has shifted from the specific misdeeds or offenses committed to the offender himself. Treatment can not be routinized, e.g., probation for a first offense, so many months of institutional commitment for a second or for a particular offense and so on. These had been and still too largely are the criteria for determining prescriptions for types of treatment. In the view of the clinic, however, it is not the offense, its severity and its frequency of repetition that are most meaningful, either for diagnosis or as criteria for treatment, but rather the needs, conscious and unconscious, that are best known by clinical study.

The great aim of the law, namely the protection of society, is inevitably and inextricably tied up with this principle. For since the vast majority of offenders will ultimately be returned to community life, it follows that the best planning for their reformation is the best hope of society's protection.

d. *Prevention.* From the beginning the reasoning seemed justified that if treatment were based on scientifically determined needs, the outcome would be more hopeful. Recidivists, understood and properly treated would have their careers of crime checked; first offenders might not become recidivists. Later, as clinics broadened the scope of their activities, it was hoped that if signs of difficulty were noted early, diagnosed and adequately treated, delinquency itself might be forestalled.

III. HISTORY. The first behavior clinic was established at Chicago in connection with the Chicago Juvenile Court in 1909 under the direction of Dr. William Healy. Privately supported through the interest and generosity of Mrs. William F. Dummer, it had its headquarters in the Detention Home and confined its efforts very largely to the study of severely delinquent offenders, recidivists who by the fact of repetition of offense indicated the failure of past attempts at treatment.

Begun as a five year experiment and having during that period proved its value, in 1914 the clinic was taken over by Cook County and in 1917 by the state of Illinois. Later named The Institute for Juvenile Research it has developed into a large organization functioning in various communities and institutions of the state though its main center remains in Chicago.

From its inception the clinic aroused attention and it was widely visited by judges and other professional workers. Dr. Healy through his writings, lectures and college courses created an ever-increasing interest in the clinical study of youth. Some measure of psychiatric service began to be sought by various courts, but it was not until about 1917 that new clinics, full time and with adequate staffs, began to come into existence. The Judge Baker Foundation (later The Judge Baker Guidance Center) was opened in Boston in April, 1917. In that year clinics were started in Detroit, Los Angeles, New York, Philadelphia and White Plains, N. Y.

It is probable that psychiatric services both to courts and other social agencies might have continued steadily to increase, but it was not until 1922 when the Commonwealth Fund sponsored a program under the direction of the Division on the Prevention of Delinquency of the National Committee for Mental Hygiene that the movement gained great momentum. Under the name of child guidance clinics, demonstration clinics were set up in eight cities. Most of these were later maintained by the communities and during the five years of support by the Commonwealth Fund it is reported that guidance clinics in the United States increased fourfold. Similar clinics patterned on American methods were gradually established abroad, notably in London, Paris, Oslo and Warsaw. Some of these had to be abandoned during the war years but it is interesting that in England not only was the London clinic then maintained but other clinics were founded under appropriations made by the English parliament.

Today the fairest estimate one can make is that there are approximately 500 full-time and part-time clinics giving psychiatric service to children and youth.

IV. Types of Clinics and Types of Problems. a. *Court and Institutional Clinics.* The earliest clinics, as we have said, were established in connection with juvenile courts, to study offenders, to offer diagnoses and recommendations for treatment. Such clinical services continue in some places. Some

of these serve largely a single court, as in Toledo; some serve courts in a whole area— a county or group of towns and cities, the latter often when the social agencies of the district or area are under a single Community Fund or Council of Social Agencies. Thus The Judge Baker Guidance Center of Boston, begun as an aid to the juvenile court of that city, now, among other types of cases, studies offenders for a half dozen or more communities that comprise Greater Boston and its suburbs. The Institute for Juvenile Research in Illinois while rendering service to the Chicago Juvenile court and to certain correctional institutions, through an ambulatory staff, covers many sections of the state. The same plan of a state-wide, ambulatory service ready to give aid to the juvenile courts has more recently been set up in Michigan, New York and Connecticut. The Ohio plan is different because it utilizes a residence center at Columbus; over the years from various courts throughout the state many hundreds of delinquents have been committed there for study and recommendations for treatment, the latter being undertaken by the courts themselves, by state agencies or by the institution itself.

Even from the start of clinical study of young people, parents and social workers outside the court sought such help. It was soon manifest that by no means all delinquents appear in the juvenile court or are even apprehended by the police and that the delinquencies of these non-court offenders are often quite as serious as those with which the court is called upon to deal.

Where private funds support them, clinics are apt to change their rôle as being sole adjuncts of the court and to become community clinics. The trend in the Judge Baker Guidance Center, one of the oldest clinics, illustrates this. In the first three years of its existence, the proportion of court cases constituted 81%, 69%, and 49% respectively of its total case loads. This trend was exemplified in the demonstration clinics. Initiated as a prevention of delinquency program, only the first of these clinics, that in St. Louis, devoted the major part of its efforts to offenders; 74% of its accepted cases were referred by the court. In the second such clinic of the project the proportion dropped to 32%; thereafter the clinics were definitely oriented away from the official delinquent if not from delinquency itself.

Clinics that now serve delinquents exclusively or very largely are either part of the court administration or are clinics serving correctional institutions; sometimes these latter are called "classification clinics." Among the most interesting of these latter are those attached to the Youth Authority of California. Karl Holton, the Director, stated in 1946 that in the very beginning the Youth Authority established a diagnostic clinic for all the older boys while service was given to selected cases in correctional schools for younger boys and for girls. Two other diagnostic reception centers were then under way, one in northern and one in southern California. On the basis of their findings allocation to the school, camp, or boarding home best equipped to meet the individual's needs will be made. While other state correctional schools have clinical features, California with its richer resources for allocation probably offers the most forward-looking plan. This is similar to and largely modeled on the celebrated and effective English Borstal system where after a month of observation and study at a reception center youths are allocated to the correctional institution the program of which seems most constructive for the individual.

b. *Community Clinics.* We have seen how readily clinics that were originally set up to be study departments for a court became broadened in their activities. This was partly due to the hope that early attack on problems of behavior might be rewarding in delinquency prevention. Indeed, it became the policy of the demonstration child guidance clinics to stress more and more the desirability for community clinics under private support which should center activities on those children and youth not yet overtly delinquent. Thus Stevenson and Smith in their book, "Child Guidance Clinics" say, ". . . many of the children coming into court were past the stage of prevention," and again, "The clinic bore just as large a relationship to social service agencies and to schools as to juvenile courts; it was seen as a center for clinical child guidance rather than as merely a service for the delinquent. But it appeared that the prevention of delinquency was furthered rather than diminished by this changed emphasis: the pre-delinquent rather than the early delinquent was affected—and the psychiatric approach to the prevention of delinquency was no longer focused on the courts."

This is an interesting statement because it has not yet been proved to be true. No follow-up study of these demonstration clinic cases has ever been made and hence the statement is based on belief rather than on evidence. Follow-up studies of the Judge Baker Guidance Center indicate that selected court delinquents have as favorable outcome as non-court delinquents when treated by the clinic itself. As for non-delinquents there is no proof either that these young people would ever have become delinquent, even without clinical help. There is no indication, for example, that neurotics, untreated, become delinquent—neither the shy, introverted nor even the definitely non-delinquent aggressive.

While some community clinics accept for service all youth problems, including those of delinquency, others reject the latter and confine their work to personality and educational problems. Inability to get on normally within the family group or the school group or with one's own age group, expressed in a wide variety of ways; speech or learning disabilities; fears, anxieties, extreme phantasy—all these claim the attention of those clinics that have either a specialized interest (as in the case of one that is primarily concerned with so-called psychosomatic problems) or those who believe the delinquent beyond the hopeful stage for clinical treatment.

The child guidance clinic of the present can be more selective in its case load than the court clinic; it accepts those cases where it considers there is at least fair possibility for successful outcome of therapy. It may reject the feebleminded, those with gross physical handicaps, such as neurological disorders, even those where social pathology looms large. It may select only those delinquents who seem clearly able to profit by psychotherapy.

In 1921 the first "habit clinic" with Dr. Douglas A. Thom at its head undertook the helping of children 2 to 5 years old who were developing undesirable methods of meeting daily situations, revealed largely by asocial habits—temper tantrums, enuresis, thumb-sucking and the like. Although this particular clinic later raised its age limits and enlarged the scope of the problems accepted, its early purpose has been copied with more or less variation. The most recent offshoot of this venture is the nursery school clinic which attacks problems of behavior at an even earlier age and in the setting of the nursery school.

c. *School Clinics.* The school clinic is an integral member of the school organization. It has a reciprocal relationship with the other personnel in the system; it is itself interested in the school's point of view; in turn it interprets to the school staff its findings, including the meaning of the school's regulations and interrelationships for the emotional life of the child. Usually the functioning of the clinic is not limited to strictly school problems but rather is concerned with the better adjustment of children to any feature of their environment. It learns and interprets not only the facts concerning problems arising from pupil-teacher and pupil-pupil interrelationships, but also concerning those emotional difficulties which the child brings to school from previous home and other non-school experiences. Just as the community clinic includes in its range of effort many educational difficulties, so the school clinic concerns itself with misbehavior of all kinds. Indeed many see in the school clinic one best possible means for combatting delinquency at an early stage.

Such school clinics exist in various cities; the largest development of them is in New York City, there being at present no less than eight well-staffed such clinics under its Board of Education.

d. *Hospital Out-patient Clinics.* A good many hospitals, especially those for the mentally disturbed, seek to promulgate the principles of mental health by offering out-patient services, sometimes ambulatory, not limited to any one type of problem, indeed often dealing with delinquency. With staff recruited from the hospital or with a special staff of its own, the clinic usually serves the community as a whole, carrying on the regular clinic

procedures. In a number of states rural needs are thus met, the so-called "traveling clinic" sometimes functioning with a social worker residing in a given district or with a local social agency co-operating.

V. METHODS AND PROCEDURES. a. *General Point of View.* In his writings Dr. Healy tells how, when the first behavior clinic was projected in 1908, he journeyed over the country consulting professional authorities concerning how to make "well-rounded studies of young human individuals." Everywhere the answer was the same: no such studies were afoot nor was there any concerted opinion about methods to pursue; he would have to blaze a trail. Thus he became the pioneer in the field.

It is an evidence of Dr. Healy's wisdom that he realized this is a task in which several "disciplines" must be co-ordinated. So from the very beginning medicine, psychiatry, psychology and social work played their part. This four-fold approach has remained the pattern of methodology in behavior clinics. The scientific development in the different fields has been immense, but the general structure of the program has altered little.

b. *The Physical Examination.* Through studies of the physical make-up and the developmental history of the individual the aim has always been to discover past and present physical handicaps that may have bearing upon his behavior tendencies. Gradually there have been definite accretions to our knowledge. When the first clinic began functioning in 1909 there was throughout the scientific world great emphasis on possible biological bases of delinquency and crime. Dr. Healy has told of the theories of that period purporting to explain misconduct—enlarged tonsils causing "air-hunger," focal infections, intra-cranial pressure, especially upon the hypothetical "moral center" of the cortex, impacted teeth, refractive errors of vision, etc. More generally held was the theory of atavism; the seriously misbehaving individual frequently represented a throw-back to primitive ancestors and proofs of this were to be found in the stigmata of degeneracy, misshapen ears, hard palates, skull contours, and what not.

Lack of substantiation has caused these

theories to pass into oblivion, for the most part, but it has ever been necessary to determine by thorough studies the physical status of the individual, both because from the standpoint of treatment he should be helped to be as physically fit as possible and because certain physical findings are definitely related to the mental, emotional and social life of the growing child. We have come to know much about the meaning not only of deformities but of seemingly insignificant deviations of physical structure and functioning for the feeling life of the child and adolescent.

Then, we have learned of various pathological conditions that have bearing upon misbehavior. Very notably there is encephalitis lethargica which was unknown until 1920, and since then other encephalopathies and their effects have become known. Through the development of endocrinology light has been thrown upon personality and behavior manifestations. The electroencephalogram has its story to tell in many cases as well as studies of metabolic functioning.

c. *The Psychological Examination.* Likewise advances have been made with regard to the psychological aspects of the study of the individual. First there was recognition of the values of knowing the child's intelligence in terms of rough age-level concepts, later the more accurate determination of this by means of age-level tests and rated as an intelligence quotient or its equivalent. Later still came development of the concept of the importance of special abilities and disabilities. Today there is wide-spread acceptance of the need to determine—and the possibility of so-doing with a high degree of accuracy—capacities of many kinds, notably ability to deal with ideas and with things—manual skills and dexterity—, to reveal talents and defects, and to interpret the results of such testing as they bear specifically on educational and vocational success or failure and more generally on behavior, social and antisocial. In some instances there is great value in unearthing disabilities since the program for treatment may include remedial efforts, say in reading or speech disability.

Beyond even this, psychological tests now make their contribution to the study of personality structure and functioning and they offer clues to the content of the ideational life. Through use of the newer tests of the projective techniques light is thrown not only on composition of the personality but on all the individual's emotional involvements, to say nothing of deviations and abnormalities that indicate aberration or psychosis.

The battery of tests used varies from clinic to clinic, depending on the point of view concerning the value of their use. Projective tests may play a small role, for example; or Rorschach and Thematic Apperception Tests may be relied on almost entirely for all desired psychological data.

d. *The Psychiatric Interview.* Although direct communication of one's experiences, attitudes and emotional reactions must always have been part of social relationships, it was the emphasis placed on the "Own Story" of the child in the first behavior clinic and the use of this material for gaining insight into motivations of behavior that attracted immediate attention and came to make psychiatric interviewing more stressed and valued in all study of conduct. As dynamic psychology has become enriched, the interview has reflected this in the skill with which the psychiatrist has by various methods elicited the subtler aspects of the feeling life. It is the function of the interview to provide a vehicle for expressing those desires and feelings that are the core of the problem that brought the child to the clinic. If right relationship has been established with the therapist, there is revealed directly or symbolically the material from which can be interpreted satisfactions and dissatisfactions, loves and hates, gratifications and frustrations, fears and guilt. These usually have not been expressed heretofore; often they have been so deeply repressed that they lie largely in the unconscious mind.

Various techniques are employed in this revealing and unburdening process: conversation, free association of thought and phantasy, projective methods as in play and art work with younger children, drama and autobiography with older ones.

e. *The Social History.* While the child or adolescent is being studied in and of himself, the environmental situation is also scrutinized

—environment including not only school and neighborhood, recreational and church affiliations but even more importantly home life, especially parental and child-parent relationships. The now prevalently held belief that the early years are the all important ones has brought into the focus of attention the parents, their goals and the achievement or frustration of them. What their children mean to them in the light of these facts, the early relationships and upbringing of the children, the children's reactions and responses—all these are usually regarded as highly significant data that are the province of the social worker, especially the trained psychiatric social worker.

There is some disagreement in the coverage of the data that are sought. Those clinics that adhere to belief in the early psychogenesis of problems seek to capture as fully as possible the picture from even the antenatal period, whether the child was wanted or unwanted. This leads to the correlated facts of possible rejection or overprotection of the child, usually on the part of the mother. Other clinics hold to the theory that one accepts both the child and the family situation as it is at the time of referral of the case making then little effort to procure from the parent any facts that antedate the referral except as these are spontaneously given. Not the parent's own difficulties but his concern about the child's problems is stressed.

A very clear statement of a currently widely accepted psychoanalytic point of view is to be found in a recent book by Dr. Kate Friedlander of London, "The Psychoanalytic Approach to Juvenile Delinquency." In her discussion she distinguishes between what she considers the "primary" and the "secondary" factors operative in delinquency. She states "The primary factors which lead to anti-social behavior are to be found in the relationship of the mother, later the father, to the child and in those other emotional factors which constitute early family life." It is in the first five years of the child's life that the anti-social character is formed," she believes—as do many others—and whether delinquency or other difficulties later become overt is dependent upon the secondary factors that, during the subsequent years through adolescence either enable the individual to find socially acceptable outlets or, contrariwise, push him into expression of overt delinquent or neurotic behavior.

Others consider as primary those inimical influences that arise from the more conventionally termed environmental sources; poverty, crowded homes, poor neighborhoods, bad companionships, etc. What any or all of these mean in terms of the attitudes and feelings of the various members of the family, what philosophy of life they engender, what values they develop and how they are met may then be considered secondary factors in the evolution of the delinquent. But after all it is both the personality that has been formed and the external circumstances and the interplay of these that go to form the total picture.

To obtain knowledge of these forces and facts as they contribute to the study of the child is, then, the task of the social worker.

f. *The Staff Conference.* The interpretation of all gathered data is a vital part of the function of the clinic. The staff conference for this purpose has become largely standard procedure. Interpretations vary in keeping with the school of thought to which the staff adheres, but medical, psychological, psychiatric and social data are usually important as they illuminate the problem to be solved, as they lead to the formulation of the diagnosis and etiology, and based on these, to the plan for treatment. Secondarily, the conference since it is attended by those not on the clinic staff but who play a part or carry some responsibility in the therapeutic process, serves as a means of reaching common understanding for co-operative effort. Even more broadly the conference may be a tool for spreading in the community the mental health point of view of the clinic.

g. *Treatment.* The strictly diagnostic behavior clinic outlines the program it recommends as meeting individual needs and leaves its carrying out to the probation officer, should the plan meet with approval of the judge, and to the social case-work agencies. It may have a continuing relationship with the agency, restudying and rediscussing the case in the light of new facts, from time to time. It may go a step further and point out cases that in its judgment require psycho-therapy.

In clinics not limited to diagnostic services —and this constitutes today the majority of those not officially attached to courts and correctional institutions—treatment is the major purpose of the clinic. The techniques used in various settings and by various therapists are highly diversified, from the nursery school setting of the pre-school age clinic to the more recently used, psychiatrically staffed resident home where the goal is not merely observation of the child but rather psychotherapy. Some indication of this range in types of therapy, which at one time or another have been in use is suggested by the following incomplete list of terms: Active therapy, passive therapy, relationship therapy, non-directive therapy, attitude therapy, release therapy, psychoanalytic therapy, group therapy, hypnosis, hypnoanalysis, psychodrama, manipulative therapy.

This is scarcely the place to discuss the basic differences between these various treatment methods; some differences are suggested by their appellations. Distinction is made between psychotherapy and psychoanalysis as a special form of psychotherapy, the latter referring to any of the now fairly numerous techniques all of which seek to bring to light unconscious motivations that lie back of symptomatic behavior, delinquent or neurotic. Psychotherapy, on the other hand, though it may or may not utilize psychoanalytic concepts, applies to any method that on a conscious level seeks to help the individual through the revelation of his feelings about himself in his relationships with others.

The common feature of all these forms of therapy, individual and group, lies in the fact that a relationship is set up between the patient and the therapist, a relationship which the therapist uses for therapeutic ends and in which the child as an active participant is able to "work through" his problems. (The therapist is usually a psychiatrist, but may be a specially trained clinical psychologist, or more rarely a phychiatric social worker.) This relationship may be called "transference," with all this term connotes technically to the analyst, or "rapport," indicating recognition by the child of the sympathetic, non-judging, understanding attitude of the therapist, or the "permissive," "accepting" relationship of the non-directive method. The goal of the treatment may be "catharsis," or the gaining of insight, or the chance to work out a new plan of behavior. Or as in "manipulative" therapy, environmental changes may be inaugurated. With children and adolescents often both external and internal modifications may be sought. In all treatment, wherever the emphasis is placed, modification in the feeling life of the individual is the aim, just because it is the feeling life that lies immediately back of behavior.

One other aspect of therapy in behavior clinics needs mention. In most clinics the parents, frequently only the mother, maintain an active part in the process. The nursery school clinic not only demonstrates through its day by day activities what it considers psychologically sound procedures in dealing with the child, but through regular interviews re-educates the parent. When older children are the patients, the parent may be the focus of intensive treatment as in attitude therapy, or there may be less concern about the parent's own emotional difficulties, but only rarely is the parent merely an onlooker or passive agent. The most usual exception is in the case of the adolescent who is ready, perhaps, struggling, for emancipation.

Witmer in a recent book, "Psychiatric Interviews with Children," which gives a detailed discussion of the processes in psychiatric therapy, says, "The therapist-patient relationship is usually the focal point of a larger process that is concerned with the reorganization of certain emotional aspects of family life."

VI. OTHER ACTIVITIES OF BEHAVIOR CLINICS. a. *Training.* As in the training of all medical specialties it is necessary for those who become professional workers in behavior clinics to have clinical experience under competent supervision and teaching. This is true for psychiatrists, clinical psychologists, and psychiatric social workers. After their general training they must have extended periods of dealing with individuals and their problems in order to gain professional skills. In 1927 the advisors of the Commonwealth

Fund so appreciated the need for trained personnel to develop more behavior clinics that the Fund was induced to establish the Institute for Child Guidance in New York which functioned for five years under the strong leadership of Dr. Lawson Lowrey and Dr. David Levy and was entirely devoted to the training of the three groups who form such clinic staffs. Many of these trainees hold important positions in the field.

The behavior clinics, nowadays, many of them, afford the opportunities for such field service. The demand for trained personnel has been great for years and at present is acute. Earlier the Rockefeller Foundation and later the Commonwealth Fund has been offering psychiatric fellowships for such training. Under the National Health Bill it is hoped that still more fellowships for child psychiatry will be available. Psychologists with adequate prior training are often able to obtain modest stipends while developing skills in clinical service. After attending a school for social work, field placements in a considerable number of clinics are open to those who want to become psychiatric social workers; these last spread out over the country in various social service agencies and carry with them certain techniques and the psychiatric point of view of trying to understand and deal with the factors that underlie behavior patterns.

b. *Research.* Research should be regarded as an essential aspect of clinic projects. In such a complicated field, research is necessary for advancing knowledge, for amassing and comparing observations, and for continual testing of theories and, in general, for wholesome growth. There is by now a very considerable literature on the general topic, on particular problems involved, on case material, and on the etiological aspects of behavior problems. Books by Stevenson and Smith, by Allen, Plant, Witmer discuss the child guidance movement; Healy's "The Individual Delinquent" was the first and still is the classical work on the clinical approach to the study of juvenile offenders. Burt of England followed some years later with "The Young Offender." Other books deal with some part of the subject; Levy's "Maternal Overprotection" and "Studies in Sibling Ri-

valry" are illustrations. Articles too numerous to mention are to be found in various journals, particularly the American Journal of Orthopsychiatry.

Less has been done by way of research on accomplishments of behavior clinics. The follow-up study of the work of the Bureau of Children's Guidance of New York by Lee and Kenworthy has a chapter on the "leading results" of the clinic's efforts. "Delinquents and Criminals, their Making and Unmaking," "New Light on Delinquency and Its Treatment," "Treatment and What Happened Afterwards" by Healy and Bronner deal with outcomes of cases seen in the several clinics they have directed. The first of these books deals with cases seen diagnostically, the other two with cases treated by the clinics. The books by Sheldon and Eleanor Glueck, "One Thousand Juvenile Delinquents" and "Juvenile Delinquents Grown Up," are follow-up studies on groups of offenders given diagnostic service at the Judge Baker Guidance Center and treated by the Boston Juvenile Court. The Ohio Bureau of Juvenile Research has published extensively, including reports on the outcome of cases and a number of student theses on this topic have appeared in the Smith College School of Social Work journal. Then there are the reports of a small but very interesting venture, the Institute for Scientific Treatment of Delinquency in London.

c. *General Education.* In the very considerable but still too limited measure of public education concerning the background causes of misconduct, the behavior clinics have been playing their part. Public lectures and articles in other than strictly professional journals have been their media for the dissemination of information about the prevention and treatment of delinquency and other problems. Sometimes these principles are set forth under the caption of mental hygiene especially when local and state mental hygiene societies sponsor such educational schemes. The periodical, "Understanding the Child" was begun in this way. The National Committee for Mental Hygiene, always active in the endeavor to educate the public, now publishes this magazine. Some clinicians have produced simply phrased books on the upbringing of children. The Federal Children's Bureau has distributed many pamphlets written by such authorities. All those who have a professional interest in young people—pediatricians, teachers, ministers, leaders in so-called character building agencies—have had their thinking and professional standards influenced by psychiatric knowledge; indeed to a certain degree such knowledge has reached a goodly number of laymen.

VII. PRESENT STATUS AND OUTLOOK FOR THE FUTURE. It seems certain that behavior clinics of all the types discussed are now firmly rooted. New ones are steadily being established and the inauguration of still others only awaits the training of more personnel. To cite one proof: of the thirteen panels that participated in the National Conference on Prevention and Control of Juvenile Delinquency called in 1946 by the United States Attorney General, six—all that dealt with non-administrative features—recommended the establishment of child guidance clinics as a vital part of a preventive program.

In spite of only moderate statistical proof of specific achievements, the general principles underlying the clinical approach to problems of behavior are so much a matter of common-sense and it is so logical to apply scientific knowledge to the problems of human conduct that their development in the future is likely to be even more rapid than it has been up to the present. In the less than forty years of their existence clinics have already added much to the understanding of the motivations of conduct and the development of personality. In relation to delinquency they have helped to change emphasis from punishment of the offender to re-education and rehabilitation.

Even the diagnostic clinic has an honorable function to perform; with enrichment of concepts, diagnostic terminology has greater interpretative significance both for etiology and treatment. The simple thesis that diagnosis is essential to determine the most promising type of therapy is not yet universally accepted and hence clinics must widen their influence further to mold public opinion. In all behavior problems, delinquent and neurotic, as Witmer suggests, the determination of the

nature and extent of the emotional ill health and its causative factors or the purposes the behavior serves are especially required.

At present, explanations of the dynamics of human conduct are many and in line with this there are great diversities in therapy. Probably this is a valuable asset in the situation; much experimentation with critical evaluation remains for the future. More and more the clinic as it grows in maturity, will make its positive contribution, in co-operation with other social agencies, towards the making of better human beings and the betterment of human interrelationships.

AUGUSTA F. BRONNER,
Director Emeritus,
Judge Baker Guidance Center,
Boston, Massachusetts.

BIBLIOGRAPHY

Cabot, P. S. de Q., *Juvenile Delinquency, A Critical Annotated Bibliography,* New York, The H. W. Wilson Co., 1946.
Friedlander, Kate, *The Psycho-Analytical Approach to Juvenile Delinquency,* London, Kegan Paul, Trench, Trubner & Co., 1947.
Healy, William, *The Individual Delinquent,* Boston, Little Brown & Co., 1915.
Lowrey, Lawson G., Evolution and Present Status of Treatment Approaches to Behavior and Personality Problems, *American Journal of Orthospychiatry,* Oct. 1939.
Stevenson, George and Geddes Smith, *Child Guidance Clinics,* New York, The Commonwealth Fund, 1934.
Witmer, Helen L., *Psychiatric Clinics for Children,* New York, The Commonwealth Fund, 1940.
Witmer, Helen L., *Psychiatric Interviews with Children,* New York, The Commonwealth Fund, 1946.

BIGAMY. The act of ceremonially marrying one person when already legally married to another who is still alive, constitutes bigamy. Originally it was only an ecclesiastical offense in England but, in 1603, it was made a felony under the law. At present, it is considered a criminal offense in all civilized countries. To constitute a crime punishable under the law, the act of bigamy must have been committed willfully and with full knowledge of the existence of a prior legal marriage. The term is generally applied to the offense no matter how often it is repeated although in the strict sense, bigamy is a species of polygamy.

Under the provisions of the New York State Penal Law, a person who marries another person, although she or he has a husband or wife living, is guilty of bigamy and is punishable by imprisonment in a penitentiary or state prison for not more than five years. A person who knowingly enters into a marriage with another, which is prohibited to the latter by the above provisions against bigamy, is also punishable by imprisonment in a penitentiary or state prison, for not more than five years, or by a fine of not more than one thousand dollars, or both.

The provisions with regard to bigamy do not apply in the cases of: a person whose former spouse has been absent for five successive years without being known to him or her within that time to be living, and believed by him or her to be dead; or a person whose former marriage has been pronounced void, or annulled, or dissolved, by the judgment of a court of competent jurisdiction, for a cause other than his or her adultery; or a person who, being divorced for his or her adultery, may be permitted to marry again under the provisions of the domestic relations law; or a person whose former husband or wife has been sentenced to imprisonment for life.

BIBLIOGRAPHY

Gilbert, F. B., *Criminal Law and Practice of the State of New York,* Matthew Bender and Co., 1935.

BLACKMAIL. Blackmail is the extortion of money from a person by threats of public accusation, exposure, or censure. An example would be the blackmail of a merchant by threatening to expose alleged or actual fraud. Frequently, blackmail is committed by a woman with a male accomplice. The woman places her victim in a compromising position and the male accomplice then turns up to effect the squeeze.

In the Penal Law of the State of New York, blackmail is punishable by imprisonment for not more than fifteen years. A person who, knowing the contents thereof, and with intent, by means thereof, to extort or

gain any money or other property, or to do, abet, or procure any illegal or wrongful act, sends, delivers, or in any manner causes to be forwarded or received, or makes and parts with for the purpose that there may be sent or delivered, any letter or writing, threatening:

1. To accuse any person of a crime; or,
2. To do any injury to any person or to any property; or,
3. To publish or connive at publishing any libel; or,
4. To expose or impute to any person any deformity or disgrace,

Is guilty of blackmail.

Blackmail can be distinguished from *extortion* on the basis of the type of pressure used. In extortion there is implied or threatened bodily harm while in blackmail it is threatened exposure.

BIBLIOGRAPHY

Gilbert, F. B., *Criminal Law and Practice of the State of New York,* Matthew Bender and Co., 1935.

BRIBERY. In general, bribery is the act or practice of giving or taking bribes or of influencing the action of another by corrupt inducements. Bribery of public officials is a crime both for the bribe-taker and the bribe-giver while bribery of private persons is not a crime, from the legal point of view, but is closely allied to it in effects and attitudes. Most authorities state that bribery is an extremely prevalent crime for which arrests are seldom made. In most jurisdictions, bribery of judicial officers, jurors, arbitrators, referees, public officers, witnesses, labor representatives, and participants of professional games, is made a penal offense.

Thus, the Penal Law of the State of New York contains provisions relating to a number of different types of bribery. Bribery of a judicial officer, juror, referee, arbitrator, appraiser, or assessor, or any other person authorized by law to hear or determine any judicial matter, with intent to influence his decision, is punishable by imprisonment for not more than ten years or by a fine of not more than five thousand dollars or both. The same penalty is provided for the officer accepting the bribe. The conviction of the officer also forfeits any office held by the offender, and forever disqualifies him from holding any public office under the state.

A juror, arbitrator, or referee, who makes any promise or agreement to give a verdict for or against any party or willfully receives any communication or converses, or attempts to converse with any person, in relation to a matter pending before him; except according to the regular course of proceeding upon the trial or hearing of that matter, is guilty of a misdemeanor. If he actually receives the bribe upon the understanding or agreement that his vote, opinion, action, judgment or decision, shall be influenced thereby, he is punishable by imprisonment for not more than ten years, or by fine of not more than five thousand dollars, or both.

A *trial juror* who takes a gift or gratuity, in order to render a verdict favorable to the briber, forfeits ten times the sum, or ten times the value of that, which he took or received, to the party to the proceeding, aggrieved thereby. He is also liable to that party for his damages sustained thereby, besides being subject to the punishment, prescribed by law.

A person who influences or attempts to influence improperly, a juror, arbitrator or referee, in respect to his verdict or decision, is guilty of *embracery,* a misdemeanor. A person communicating or attempting to communicate in any manner with a juror concerning a matter pending before him, is also guilty of a misdemeanor. An *embraceor,* who procures a juror to take gain or profit, forfeits ten times the sum, which was so taken, to the aggrieved party; is liable to that party for his damages; and is also subject to the punishment prescribed by law.

A person who bribes or attempts to bribe a public officer with intent to influence him in respect to any act, decision, vote, opinion or other proceeding, in the exercise of the powers or functions which he has or may have, is punishable by imprisonment for not more than ten years, or by a fine of not more than five thousand dollars or by both.

A *witness* or prospective witness upon any court proceeding or trial, who receives or agrees to receive a bribe with the understanding that his testimony shall be influenced thereby, or that he will absent himself from the trial or proceeding, is guilty of a felony.

Bribery of labor representatives is a misdemeanor while bribery of participants in professional games is punishable by imprisonment for not less than one year, nor more than five years and by a fine of not more than ten thousand dollars.

BIBLIOGRAPHY

Gilbert, F. B., *Criminal Law and Practice of the State of New York,* Matthew Bender and Co., 1935.

BURGLARY. Under the common law, burglary is a crime which consists of breaking and entering the dwelling house of another, in the night time, with the intent to commit a felony, whether or not the felonious purpose is accomplished. In most states of the United States, the definition of the crime has been variously modified, or a statutory burglary has been created in addition to that of the common law, to cover such offenses committed by day, such as entering of shops, factories, warehouses, etc. Various degrees of the crime have been created.

The Penal Law of the State of New York, which is typical of statutes in other states, defines three degrees of burglary. A person who, with intent to commit some crime therein, breaks and enters, in the night time, the dwelling-house of another, in which there is at the time a human being:

1. Being armed with a dangerous weapon; or,
2. Arming himself therein with such a weapon; or,
3. Being assisted by a confederate actually present; or,
4. Who, while engaged in the night time in effecting such entrance or in committing any crime in such a building, or in escaping therefrom, assaults any person,

Is guilty of *burglary in the first degree.*

A person who, with intent to commit some crime therein, breaks and enters the dwelling-house of another in which there is a human being, under circumstances not amounting to burglary in the first degree, is guilty of *burglary in the second degree.*

A person who:
1. With intent to commit a crime therein, breaks and enters a building, or a room, or any part of a building; or,
2. Being in any building, commits a crime therein and breaks out of the same,

Is guilty of *burglary in the third degree.*

Burglary in the first degree is punishable by imprisonment in a state prison for an indeterminate term the minimum of which shall not be less than ten years and the maximum of which shall be not more than thirty years. In burglary in the second degree, the term shall not exceed fifteen years, and for the third degree, not exceeding ten years.

In New York State, possession of burglar's tools or the making or mending of such tools, is a misdemeanor, and if the offender has been previously convicted of any crime, is a felony. Also, a person who, under circumstances or in a manner not amounting to a burglary, enters a building, or any part of it, with intent to commit a crime, is guilty of a misdemeanor.

BIBLIOGRAPHY

Gilbert, F. B., *Criminal Law and Practice of the State of New York,* Matthew Bender and Co., 1935.

C

CAPITAL PUNISHMENT. Capital punishment is probably the oldest type of punishment inflicted upon criminals.

As late as a century and a half ago, most felonies were punishable by death. The widespread, indiscriminate use of the extreme penalty was a logical expression of the time, for it was thought that a criminal deliberately chose to do wrong and was, therefore, entitled to no mercy. In harmony with this attitude, executions were conducted before huge throngs so as to deter others from crime.

Gradually, some countries, including the United States, began to limit the number of capital offenses. In 1788, for example, Ohio made murder the only crime punishable by death. Today that crime is subject to the extreme penalty in all states utilizing capital punishment; rape in some southern states; and burglary, robbery, arson, treason, kidnapping, and train wrecking in other states. And after New York abolished public hangings in 1835, executions began to be held privately throughout the United States. However, in a few southern states, those convicted of rape are still publicly executed.

During the middle of the nineteenth century, the humanitarian spirit impelled many to seek the abolition of capital punishment altogether. Michigan was the first to do so in 1847. In the years that followed, a great many people, realizing that crime is a result of social and economic forces, sought similar legislation.

The following states did away with the death penalty but later reinstated it: Kansas, Iowa, Colorado, Washington, Oregon, Arizona, Missouri and Tennessee.

The following states (in addition to Michigan) no longer inflict the death penalty; Rhode Island, since 1852. (In 1882, an amendment provided that a convict, serving a life sentence for murder, who should be convicted of making a murderous attack on a prison official should be put to death. However, there has never been an execution under this statute.) Wisconsin, since 1853. Maine, since 1876. (Due to the attack of an insane convict on a keeper, capital punishment was restored in 1882, only to be abolished again in 1887.) Minnesota, since 1911, and both North Dakota and South Dakota since 1915. (In 1939, capital punishment was restored in North Dakota, but the act did not appropriate funds for an electric chair. When that was finally done in 1942, restrictions on vital materials due to the war, made it impossible to construct the "chair." Consequently, South Dakota, is technically a state with no death penalty.)

Many European countries likewise abolished capital punishment: Belgium in 1863, Portugal in 1867, the Netherlands in 1870, Switzerland (15 cantons) in 1874, Norway in 1905, Sweden in 1921, Lithuania in 1922, Spain in 1932 (The Franco government revived it for some offenses), and Denmark in 1933. The countries which did away with the extreme penalty but reinstated it are Italy, Austria and Roumania.

Most of the countries of Central and South America have no capital punishment. It was abolished by Brazil in 1891, Ecuador in 1895, Colombia in 1910, Argentina in 1922, Costa Rica, Peru, Uruguay, and Venezuela, all in 1926, Mexico in 1929, and Chile in 1930. New Zealand abolished it in 1941.

The advocates of capital punishment urge its retention for the following principal reasons: (1) the need of eliminating those who menace the life and security of society; (2) retribution; (3) murderers sentenced to life imprisonment will win their freedom through political intervention; (4) those who don't, will be troublesome behind walls; (5) deterrence. In other words, people, knowing that the death penalty exists, will not commit murder or other capital crimes.

The argument that capital punishment is necessary as a process of elimination is faulty, for it is completely unscientific in application. About 7000 persons commit murder each year, but only about 150 are executed. How can it possibly be said that the "worst" are eliminated from our midst? As a matter of fact, the defendant of wealth—*no matter how heinous his crime*—seldom goes to the chair. Through astute counsel, he manages to escape death, while the man who is destitute too often pays the extreme penalty, even though, in some cases, he pulled a trigger in a moment of blind fury, and was never in conflict with the law before.

As for retribution: the idea of punishment of any type solely "to get even" is gradually disappearing, together with other of the older, unscientific criminological concepts. This idea is yielding to the more modern and progressive attitude, that retribution is not justification for any system of punishment nor are its results beneficial. It is repressive, not reformative; it ignores social responsibility and disregards the possibility of reformation.

Murderers make the best prisoners. They are least troublesome to any warden, and often they accomplish a great deal behind bars. I know of none released during my wardenship at Sing Sing who reverted to crime. Furthermore, it is not true—at least in New York State—that a murderer whose death sentence is commuted to life imprisonment can easily obtain his freedom. The average period of incarceration among those who receive the second commutation is about twenty years. Granted that other states are too lenient, that would be an argument for a better administration of justice, not for putting people to death. Furthermore, if some murderers (the accidental types, particularly) gain their freedom, after competent officials are certain that they will never again menace the community, certainly that is far more sensible than keeping them behind bars.

Now does capital punishment really deter crime? Statistics, for one thing, show that it does not. Many of the states that do not inflict the death penalty have much lower murder rates than those that do. (The murder rate did not decrease when Kansas reinstated the death penalty.)

Other statistics show that few murderers are even arrested. How can it be said then that capital punishment is a threat to the potential murderer? And even if arrests were more frequent, the situation, in my opinion, would not be changed.

Roughly speaking, murderers fall into three classes: 1) the psychopathic; 2) the emotional or accidental; 3) the professional.

A psychopath, or for that matter any individual with some mental affliction does not think of the chair, and the same can be said of those who commit crimes of passion. The latter certainly are in no position to think beyond brooding over a presumed wrong inflicted upon them. The jealous lover who kills his sweetheart, the disillusioned husband who murders a faithless wife, the enraged patron who brains an absolute stranger in a barroom brawl—these individuals, all of them, are rash, impulsive and inflamed beyond control. Their minds have become glutted with but one thought—to do away with the other person. Only after the act has been perpetrated do they reflect upon the futility and enormity of their behavior. And, it is such people, incidentally, who contribute many more to the ranks of murderers, each year, than any other group. The underworld, my surveys show, commit only about 15% of all murders.

Do so-called professional criminals or those who seek divorce by murder fear the chair? Hardly. When they plot their crimes, they concentrate on one thing only: how to avoid detection. They don't speculate upon the punishment awaiting them if they fail, because they don't expect to fail. Should they ever think of punishment—and that is very improbable—they are not fazed; they are confident of evading the law through a successful getaway or legal chicanery. And, as I pointed out, most murderers do. That is one of the reasons why the threat of capital punishment lacks the deterrent force many people believe it possesses. If anything would be a deterrent, it would be swift, sure, justice—detection, an immediate but fair trial, followed by a period of imprisonment, long enough to fit the needs of society and the particular offender. This would also reduce the number of acquittals. For, too often, juries, reluctant to send a man to the chair, grant him his freedom. Knowledge that the defendant would not be put to death—an abhorrent idea to so many—would result in many more convictions of the guilty.

But there is another objection to capital punishment. It is the possibility that innocent men may be executed. During my wardenship, there have been some inmates convicted of offenses other than murder who were later discovered to be guiltless. As they walked jubilantly into a free world, my thoughts turned to others—murderers—shuffling languidly into an unknown world not of their own choosing. Had perjury, a mistake in identification, or a stony conscience also brought about their conviction?

About twice a month, at Sing Sing, the chief clerk or I received calls from police officials, wanting to know whether certain inmates were still in prison. Usually, we were not told the reasons for these queries, but once in a while, a little private sleuthing uncovered some disconcerting facts. It seemed that careless witnesses, thinking they recognized in the Rogues Gallery the perpetrators of recent crimes, picked out photographs of felons still confined in Sing Sing. (Though the police records showed that the suspects were confined, the calls were made as a double check.)

Many years ago, an inmate about whom such an inquiry was made had been "positively identified" as a murderer's confederate. I have often wondered what would have happened to him had he been free or on parole. What chance would he have had without the protection of prison bars?

Laying aside, therefore, all arguments for or against capital punishment, this important fact must be considered: If an error is made, and a man—an innocent man—is put to death, nothing in the world can be done to rectify the mistake—even if it be an honest mistake.

But if a man is alive, even though he had been confined behind bars for fifty years, and his innocence has been established, compen-sation, far from sufficient can nevertheless be made. He can be released, and rewarded materially for his suffering. And, at least, he can be grateful for one blessing. He is still alive.

LEWIS E. LAWES,
Former Warden,
Sing Sing Prison,
Ossining, New York.

BIBLIOGRAPHY

Calvert, E. Roy, *Capital Punishment in the Twentieth Century,* Putnam's, 1927.
Johnson, Julia E., Editor, *Capital Punishment,* H. W. Wilson Company, 1929.
Lawes, Lewis E., *Meet the Murderer,* Harper and Bros., 1940.
Lawes, Lewis E., *Man's Judgment of Death,* Putnam's, 1924.
Vold, George B., Can the Death Penalty Prevent Crime? *Prison Journal,* October 1932.

CAUSATION OF CRIME. With the development of the sciences relating to human behavior, there has been a steady trend away from single, specific, explanations of behavior in the direction of multiple explanation. This trend has been especially true of the rapidly developing field of Criminology. As the researchers in Criminology and in allied fields have probed for explanations of criminal behavior, we have more and more been forced to concede that criminal behavior, or any form of behavior for that matter, is a complex phenomenon. Nevertheless, for our purpose we must consider some of the attempts to postulate relatively narrow explanations of criminal behavior.

Cesare Lombroso (1836–1909), who is sometimes credited with being the father of Criminology, and whose name is famous because of the Lombrosian doctrine of crime causation, held that the habitual criminal, particularly, is an atavistic being who produces in his person the ferocious tendencies of human beings and inferior animals. Such criminals are by birth a distinct type. Being born with a nature favorable to criminal behavior, they may only escape criminal careers if the social milieu in which they develop and in which they circulate during their mature years is unusually favorable.

In addition to "born" criminals, Lombroso classified other criminals as "criminals by passion," "insane criminals" and "occasional criminals." In discussing these classes he recognized the part that social conditioning plays in criminal behavior, although his peculiar experience as physician in the Italian Army, led him into hereditary and psychological explanation of criminal behavior even in these classes. Habitual criminals were held to be not only physically insensitive but also morally insensitive.

Enrico Ferri (1856–1929), who held for a period a professorship in Criminal Law at the University of Rome, gave more breadth to his explanations of causes of crime than did Lombroso. He recognized three groups of causative factors, first, those inherent in the physical environment; secondly, those inherent in the constitution of the individual and, thirdly, those inherent in the social environment, such as the density of population and the nature of the economic and political organization.

Ferri was one of the first criminologists to popularize the recognition of the criminal insane and to develop knowledge conecrning them. He, like Lombroso, recognized a class of criminals which he called "born criminals." Ferri, however, is most noted for his criminal sociology, and for his "equivalents of punishment" which were in reality preventive measures designed as substitutes for punishment. He held that punishment is limited in its possibilities to combat and prevent crime and that it is the duty of the criminal sociologist to seek other preventive measures. These are his equivalents of punishments. Among them are free trade, freedom of emigration and immigration, tax systems based on ability to pay, public improvements, better care of neglected children and the suppression of the glamor of vice and crime such as is currently featured in the Press.

The French scholar, Gabriel Tarde, who is best known for the development of his theories of imitation, held that criminal behavior originated in the upper classes and that criminal behavior in lower classes was due to the imitative process extending from the upper to the lower classes. (See: Tarde, Gabriel, *Penal Philosophy,* Boston, Little, Brown &

Company, 1912.) Tarde opposed the idea of a constitutional criminal type holding strongly to the theory that crime has a social genesis which operates especially through what he called "laws" of imitation and suggestion.

From time to time students of criminal behavior have attacked bitterly the existing economic system as a factor in crime causation. Such a theory was advanced by W. A. Bonger, a Dutch criminologist, toward the capitalistic system. He held that criminal behavior was produced by such factors as poor housing, illiteracy, poverty and inadequate institutions and that these were in turn offshoots of the capitalistic economy. (See: Bonger, W. A., *Criminality and Economic Conditions,* translated by Henry P. Hauton, Boston, Little, Brown & Company, 1916.)

Turning our attention more specifically away from the statements relating to causes of crime, advanced by scholars in the field of criminology abroad, we have an important contribution on causes of crime advanced by William Healy, who for a number of years was head of the Juvenile Psychopathic Institute of Chicago and who made an outstanding contribution to the case study method for the study of delinquent behavior. Healy held that mental abnormalities and peculiarities led the list in causes of delinquency, whereas unfavorable home conditions and bad companions are second in importance. Healy held that influences causing crime first affect the mental life and attitudes of the individual and those, in turn, determine the nature of behavior.

One may say that this nation was founded by individuals who rebelled against law. While most of us would hold that this rebellion was necessary, it was the beginning of an American heritage and frontier philosophy of disregard for law. As the nation expanded westward beyond the reach of established courts and law, each man became a law unto himself. Thus there was established a tendency which is still fairly strong in American life and this is the tendency for citizens to choose what laws they wish to obey. This means that the disregard for law is, in the view of some authorities, for example, Truslow Adams, a national folkway or attitude of mind. One, however, cannot explain away the causes of crime in America on this theory. It is merely one conditioning factor of importance.

Inherent within the social processes taking place within American society and the characteristics of this society, are important causes of American crime. The bigness and complexity of American society; the machine, mass-production, dollar-income-urban economy; the rapid social mobility, with its attendant relaxation of social controls, and the competition, restlessness and marginality of it are forces which help to set the stage for criminal activity. Added to these processes have been two recent Wars and one depression. In this society, crime becomes big business and this becomes organized and protected. Minorities are sometimes deprived of civil rights and become the victims of discrimination, prejudice, conflict and inadequate systems of legal procedures.

In spite of the fact that the American standard of living is usually adjudged the highest in the world, bad housing, poor home conditions, bad neighborhoods, inadequate community resources, especially for the young, displays of wealth on the one hand, and low economic status on the other, tend to feed the juvenile courts daily with fresh delinquency which improved conditions might prevent. These delinquents frequently find themselves in the hands of inadequate and untrained officials and personnel, equipped with inadequate treatment and remedial procedures and facilities. Thus there is channelled up from these sources into reformatories, detention homes and adult penal institutions a constant stream of delinquents. Those released to free society frequently are done so without adequate supervision and treatment, later to find themselves repeating old offenses or committing new ones.

There is no question but that the American crime volume is aggravated by inadequate law enforcement, archaic legal machinery and procedures in some communities and inadequate probation, detention and parole procedures and facilities. The very great percentage of recidivists among adult offenders bears evidence to the critical need for improved treatment and release procedures and more adequate staffing of those responsible for administering these procedures.

WILLIAM E. COLE,
Head, Department of Sociology,
University of Tennessee,
Knoxville, Tennessee.

BIBLIOGRAPHY

Clemmer, Donald, *The Prison Community,* Boston, Christopher Publishing House, 1940.
Glueck, Sheldon and Eleanor T. Glueck, *500 Criminal Careers,* New York, Alfred Knopf, 1930.
Healy, William, *The Individual Delinquent,* Boston, Little, Brown & Co., 1929.
MacDonald, C. R., *Crime Is A Business,* Stanford, California, Stanford University Press, 1939.
Shaw, Clifford R., *The Jack Roller,* Chicago, University of Chicago Press, 1930.
Sutherland, E. H., Ed., *The Professional Thief,* Chicago, The University of Chicago Press, 1937.
Von Hentig, Hans, *Crime: Causes and Conditions,* New York: McGraw Hill Book Co., 1947.
Washington, D. C., *Reports* of the National Commission on Law Observance and Enforcement and the many excellent texts and works in Criminology.

CHANGING CONCEPTS OF CRIME. "Crime" is a broad term of variable and often uncritical usage. Its definition may be approached at several semantic levels.

All societies recognize and distinguish between behavior believed to be harmful to the group and behavior believed to be beneficial and respond emotionally with blame or approval proportioned to the assumed importance of the behavior. The acceptance and evaluation of any particular behavior as harmful is dependent upon the total organization and culture of the group.

The line between crimes, defined as public wrongs, and other wrong doing cannot be sharply drawn. Probably no harmful act, whether directed towards another individual as a tort, or towards a deity as a sin, or towards the individual himself as a vice, is without some unfortunate effect upon the group as a whole. Conversely, whatever harms the group inevitably harms each individual member of it. In principle, crimes are acts that are considered by those in authority to be sufficiently inimical to the general welfare as to warrant official interdiction and punishment.

In small, homogeneous, culturally isolated societies where a common store of knowledge and belief and similar problems of survival support generally accepted customs, crimes may be defined by consensus. In populous and complex societies, in which the social consequences of behavior are more difficult to assess and the state of public opinion more difficult to determine, and where political authority is delegated to or assumed by a socially remote minority, the definition of crime may not in the same measure reflect the protective emotional response and the moral disapproval of the total group.

The law of custom, strong in more stable and simple societies, has inherently a measure of flexibility that permits its modification to deal with the unique circumstances of each individual case. Statutory law, made necessary by the rapidity of social change and the need for predictability under conditions where custom has not matured, is inherently rigid and may offend the public sense of justice in particular cases. Furthermore, it is not self-defining. There is therefore need and pressure to define the statutory criminal law to conform to strong currents of public opinion, and the tendency of the courts to so define the law permits the interpretation to reflect the conscious or unconscious bias of the interpreter.

This being so, the authority which defines and punishes crime may reflect only the judgment of a segment of the population (a majority in a democracy, a handful in a dictatorship), as to what behavior is socially harmful. Harmful might, under some circumstances, mean contrary economic or political views, or it might even include any behavior in opposition to the interest of those in power however publicly beneficial. From the standpoint of the lawbreaker, then, his crime could appear as socially desirable conduct while official behavior might appear to him morally wrong if not technically criminal.

The common denominator of crime is recognition by those in political authority that an act is of such a nature and is sufficiently dangerous to the solidarity of the group as to warrant interdiction and punishment. Whether an act will seem to threaten group survival will depend upon the cultural-evaluative frame of reference within which it has its setting.

There is probably no type of specific act which has not under certain circumstances been given official approval. Deliberate killing is not always murder; sexual intercourse by force and without the victim's consent is not always rape; the taking of another's property without his consent is not always theft; as witness the legally justifiable killing of a condemned criminal by an executioner, the exposure of Australian aboriginal women to sexual attack for violation of the sexual code, or the seizure of an allegedly immoral book by a custom's officer.

The assumed mental state of the actor and his alleged purpose may therefore be quite as essential as the act itself in the determination of whether in any specific circumstance an act is a crime. Modern criminal law generally recognizes that a guilty mind intending to commit an act that is criminal is essential to conviction. However, since under the criminal law legally responsible adults are held to the standard of a "reasonable" man, it is quite possible for the individual to have a legal criminal intent while being entirely clean of conscience. In primitive societies, however, the element of intent as a factor in crime may be entirely absent.

Necessarily, therefore, the acts that have at some time been recognized as crimes are numerous and varied, and the content of the criminal code in the form of specific acts tends to change roughly in proportion to the rapidity and extent of cultural change in general, although with something of a lag.

Many of the simpler and more primitive societies handled theft, rape, arson, murder and other secular offenses, not as crimes, but as private wrongs to be settled by the direct action of families or clans rather than by tribal authority. Crime was more nearly synonymous with sin and consisted of acts considered offensive to the spirit world and dangerous to the entire group because they invited punishment by supernatural powers. In Ashanti the historian who made an error in the ceremonial recitation of the titles of the great ancestral spirits would have been executed. In Polynesia the violation of a tabu might be punished by the community if not directly by the gods. Among Eskimos the eating of seal and caribou at the same meal is an offense to the supernatural and is regarded as a crime. Among the Ifugao one who breaks the tabu on asking the relative of a dead man if he is dead would be fined.

In the Western world the centralization of authority in the kingship was accompanied by the extension of the king's protection beyond the limits of his immediate household to the entire kingdom. As a result, many acts that had been private wrongs became violations of the king's peace to be dealt with by the state as crimes.

The persisting idea of divinity associated with the kingship and the existence of theocratic states continued to give to violations of the king's peace the connotation of an affront to the supernatural and hence of something more than a breach of public order. As a consequence of the dominance of a theological interpretation of the universe and the limitations of scientific knowledge, witchcraft, sorcery, sacrilege, heresy and blasphemy were serious crimes frequently punishable by death. In England the offense of witchcraft, punishable by death, was not repealed until 1736. Blasphemy is still forbidden both at common law and by statutes in many states of the United States and in several foreign countries.

In England, and in Pennsylvania, New York, Connecticut, Delaware and Massachusetts, Christianity has been judicially declared to be part of the law of the land. The crime of perjury involves the wilful giving under oath of false testimony material to the issue at hand. The common requirement that testimony be given under oath has been defined as "a religious act by which the party invokes God not only to witness the truth and sincerity of his promise but also to avenge his imposture or violated faith, or, in other words, to punish his perjury if he be guilty of it." (Bouvier.)

Since the Renaissance, the extension and secularization of knowledge and belief about man and the universe, and the attendant development of technology, have necessarily affected the social consequences and the related evalution of behavior. The relations of men to one another were altered and new political, economic, and social organizations and interests required support and protection. The spread of rationalistic philosophy was accompanied by a decline in the scope and prosecution of religious offenses.

The decline of a feudal caste system led to a limitation of the crime of treason. The English Statute of Treasons in 1351 defined petit treason as the killing of a master by his servant, of a husband by his wife, or of a prelate by a priest owing him obedience. In 1828 these acts were made simple murders and the crime of petit treason vanished. High treason, of which there were seven forms in 1351, has been much restricted, and in the United States includes only two acts: levying war against them, or adhering to their enemies giving them aid and comfort.

The rise of towns and cities brought new problems of sanitation, housing and transportation. Mumford notes that "in France the stage-coach introduced in the seventeenth century killed more people annually than the railroad that followed." Official notice was taken of the increased dangers of pestilence and riot. Laws with reference to the disposals of refuse, the keeping of livestock, the quarantine of strangers, and the use of streets, and the construction of buildings reflected these public dangers.

The displacement of populations attendant upon the breakdown of the feudal system left multitudes of people in poverty and resulted in hordes of wandering vagrants and beggars. With feudalism had gone a measure of responsibility of the lords for their serfs, but no well-established system of social responsibilities accompanied the rise of the newly rich, and the gap between wealth and power on the one hand and poverty and weakness on the other was great.

In 1552 a group of prominent London citizens besought the Privy Council to help them control the troublesome poor and the multitudes of petty thieves, gypsies, beggars and vagabonds. The countries of the continent faced a similar problem. Paris, alone, in the late seventeenth century had in the neighborhood of fifty thousand beggars.

The great social gap between the powerful privileged few and the common man encouraged petty crime and general maladjustment among the dispossessed and politically helpless masses. Crime, as an expression of mass misery, consisted predominantly of behavior disturbing to those in authority. Houses of correction during the sixteenth to the eighteenth centuries were filled with unlicensed beggars and peddlers, lazy and disobedient children, refractory apprentices, and idle, frivolous and insolent men, while thousands of petty thieves and vagabonds were exiled or executed. In England during the reign of Henry VIII alone some 72,000 offenders were executed.

It is during periods of rapid social change that the gap between the legal and the popular conception of crime is apt to be greatest. Since the law finds its ultimate support in public attitudes, these exert a pressure leading to the definition of new crimes or the redefinition of old ones where new public interests are inadequately protected, and to the modification by direct or indirect means of old laws that seem, under new conditions, to work with undue severity.

The great changes in finance, industry and transportation that accompanied the development of foreign colonies and the invention and utilization of power machinery profoundly affected the structure of Western society and created extensive new interests to be protected, and so new crimes. As Jerome Hall demonstrates (Theft, Law and Society), the law of theft is largely a development of the eighteenth century and an accompaniment of the rise of the factory system, mass production, distant bulk shipments, more complex business organizations, and new impersonal trade relations.

The establishment of the Bank of England in 1694 followed slowly by the organization of provincial banks led to the embezzlement acts of 1742, 1751, 1763 and 1799, which first recognized and defined embezzlement in the modern sense. Public disturbances over losses suffered through investment in joint stock companies led to a demand for protection against misrepresentation. The Anglo-Saxon concept of property, as consisting of movable goods, sufficient when cattle were the chief objects of larceny, became inadequate with the possibility of appropriating such items as electricity, gas, news, trademarks, patents, copyrights, or the use of labor and machinery. In some instances the courts have extended the concept of property to include gas and electricity as subject to larceny. By statutes the willful infringement of trademarks, patents, and copyrights has been made a criminal offense. A systematic revision of the criminal law with reference to the subject matter of larceny under modern conditions has not yet, however, been brought to fruition.

That the concepts of crime and punishment reflect the nature of the societal structure is seen in the former practice of excusing ecclesiastics from liability under the secular law, permitting even murder with no more serious penalty than thumb branding until 1547. The so-called benefit of clergy was extended in 1350, by statute and judicial interpretation to all who could read, and in 1706 to everyone, regardless of literacy. What had formerly been a class privilege, extended in varying degrees to the clergy, peers and peeresses and male commoners (women commoners having no benefit of clergy), was made available to the masses. However, an accompaniment of this democratization of procedure was an increase in the number of offenses excluded from benefit of clergy so that, in spite of it, during the sixteenth and seventeenth centuries England experienced its greatest severity of punishment.

The four-fold increase in the volume of criminal laws attendant upon the industrial changes of the eighteenth century was not based upon any careful analysis and classification of offenses and their social sources and effects but was simply a patch-work extension of the law to cover new types of behavior. The lack of discrimination in the law which assessed capital punishment alike for poaching, simple theft, and a wide range of petty offenses, as well as for murder and other crimes of violence, was contrary to the evolving public sense of fitness.

As the humanitarian movement of the eighteenth century developed, it affected the practices of the courts, which, in the absence of adequate legislative revisions, brought the practice of the law more nearly into line with public sentiment by evasive judicial technicalities and by jury findings that in thousands of cases obviously avoided the facts by what Blackstone called "a kind of pious perjury" in order to avoid capital punishment for offenses committed without violence. Modifications in the severity of punishment more formally introduced into the criminal law by nineteenth century legislation represented primarily a more precise formulation of what the courts had long been accomplishing by administrative practice.

The transformation of modern Western society is a consequence of an intricate interplay of many factors among which the successful application of science to the understanding of the physical world and the resulting changes in technology are merely the most concrete and obvious. The tremendous increase in population during the nineteenth century, the rise of vast urban agglomerations, the economic interdependency of individuals, the decline in family size and authority, the mobility of population, the factory system and mass production for distant markets, and the emphasis on money and credit, are aspects of the great social changes associated with the final displacement of the landed aristocracy by the capitalistic bourgeoisie.

The need and opportunities for large concentrations of capital, and for the sharing of risks, favored corporate organization for business purposes and led to increasing concentration of economic, and related political, power in the managers of capitalistic enterprises. The development of effective mass communication and control of the media of communication by those possessing the necessary wealth helped them to build an ideology favorable to the principles and practices associated with wealth getting. The resulting emphasis upon secular and sensate values, supported in part by the ethos of Protestantism and, in turn, permeating even the church itself, has given rise to a new hedonistic morality.

The increased variety and impersonality of human interrelations in an aggressive competitive society is associated with selfishness and a minimum degree of social morality.

The effects of conduct are diffused and concealed. Impersonality in business relations tends to acceptance of the letter of agreements, rather than the spirit. The power of organization is often used to achieve desired ends with little regard for the general welfare. Associations whose activities are socially acceptable seek to obtain privileges from the state which they may, in some instances, rival in power.

Wage earners reacted to the weakness of their economic bargaining position in the new industrial society by attempts at organization also, and these have become increasingly successful under the pressure of industry-created wants. The democratization of education, the pooling of financial resources, and the utilization of effective techniques for exploiting the economic power of the strike and the political power of the vote have contributed to that success.

Inevitably in a society undergoing profound technical, organizational and ideological changes, moral codes established under simpler and more stable conditions are inadequate as guides to conduct. The difficulty of assessing the social consequences of much of contemporary behavior contributes to a lack of moral consensus and to a weakening of social controls over behavior.

Many traditional crimes such as unorganized murder, rape, robbery, burglary, arson, and larceny, in its more direct and obvious forms, are clearly disapproved. Organized crime, however, while not new, as witness the early and continued group activities of bandits, brigands, pirates and smugglers, or the organizational activities of such men as the notorious eighteenth century Jonathan Wild, has developed a new dimension through the application of modern organizational techniques to criminal enterprises.

Modern rapid bulk transportation facilitates the wholesale theft of furs, silks, cigarettes, liquor and other merchandise from warehouses, freight cars and trucks in amounts of many millions of dollars annually. As early as the International Congress on the Prevention and Repression of Crime held at London in 1872, Edwin C. Hill read a paper on "Criminal Capitalists," which, though limited in conception, indicated the growing significance of crime as an organized business requiring the cooperation of real estate owners, investors and manufacturers of the implements used by criminals and other "honest" people.

The mobility and concentration of urban populations under conditions of relative anonymity and freedom from social control are favorable to a ready market for opportunities for gambling, prostitution and the consumption of alcoholic beverages. Lack of agreement as to the social consequences and the morality of this demand is reflected in the sporadic prohibition or legalization of gambling, prostitution and the sale of alcoholic liquor or the frequent non-enforcement of criminal laws forbidding these activities. The demand for illegal services in connection with vice is not limited to criminals by vocation but comes from the general population and is extensive enough to require and to support major organizations which rely upon corruption of law enforcement authorities, and upon public ignorance and apathy, for the continuance of operations not subject to concealment.

The passage of the Eighteenth Amendment and the National Prohibition Act, in 1920, which forbade the general manufacture, sale, transportation or possession of intoxicating liquors throughout the United States was followed by widespread refusal to obey the law. Public hostility to prohibition found expression in patronization of bootleggers, speakeasies, roadhouses and other sources of supply, and in home-brewing of alcoholic beverages, rather than in acceptance of the law until it could be repealed or modified by legal means.

The tremendous demand for illegal liquor created a business for organized criminals of more than two billion dollars and led to concentrations of illicitly acquired wealth that was used to corrupt police administrators, judges, political office holders, real estate operators, and others, or to remove those who could not be corrupted. The Capone syndicate alone had an annual gross income of $27,000,000 and Capone's personal fortune from his combined ventures in prostitution, gambling and bootlegging was estimated by internal revenue agents at $20,000,000. Be-

fore 1930 gangsters anticipating a modification of the National Prohibition Act were beginning to extend their interests to the organization of workers and tradesmen, through terrorism, into unions upon which the racketeers levied fees, fines, and dues, and the most publicized aspect of crime was the internecine warfare among the business enterprises of the organized underworld.

The maturing of sociology brought an increasing measure of objectivity to the analysis of the contemporary social structure that has been reflected in a new valuation of the relative consequences and importance of specific patterns of behavior upon the social welfare. The economic depression of the 1930's dramatized in concrete fashion the effects of a socially inadequate economic philosophy. The attendant revelations of criminal behavior among those engaged in occupations, in themselves legitimate, made almost inevitable the crystallization of such concepts as that of "upperworld crime," suggested by Morris (Criminology, 1934), and of "white-collar crime," suggested by Sutherland (American Sociological Review, February, 1940), to refer to criminal behavior among respected, socially accepted and trusted members of society. These terms helped to bring into focus a grist of earlier and later writings which gave evidence of extensive violations of the criminal law by those whose social authority and position has largely protected them from exposure, prosecution, or conviction. Representative of such writings are:

L. Steffens, *The Shame of the Cities*, 1904.
G. Myers, *The History of Great American Fortunes*, 1907.
E. A. Ross, *Sin and Society*, 1907.
H. Asbury, *The Gangs of New York*, 1928.
J. Flynn, *Graft in Business*, 1931.
A. Reeve, *The Golden Age of Crime*, 1931.
Kallett and Schlink, *100,000,000 Guinea Pigs*, 1936.
E. A. MacDougall (Ed.), *Crime for Profit*, 1933.
M. Josephson, *The Robber Barons*, 1934.
J. McConaughy, *Who Rules America*, 1934.
F. Allen, *Lords of Creation*, 1935.
F. Schlink, *Eat, Drink and Be Wary*, 1935.
M. Mooney, *Crime Incorporated*, 1935.
C. Cooper, *Here's to Crime*, 1936.
L. Huberman, *The Labor Spy Racket*, 1937.

A. Winthrop, *Are You a Stockholder*, 1937.
D. Loth, *Public Plunder*, 1938.
H. Seidman, *Labor Czars*, 1938.
M. Shadid, *A Doctor for the People*, 1939.
J. MacDonald, *Crime is a Business*, 1940.
C. McWilliams, *Prejudice*, 1944.
G. Myrdal, *An American Dilemma*, 1944.

That the economic importance of upperworld crime far exceeds that of the conventional underworld is indicated by the history of great American fortunes, by the reports of various official, semi-official, and private organizations concerned with the regulation of business practices, and by the trial reports of convicted upperworld offenders such as Kreuger, Musica-Costa, Insull, Fall, Whitney, Sinclair, and others of prominence. The amount stolen by Ivar Kreuger, the Swedish match king, alone, was estimated at $250,000,000.

The full extent of upperworld criminality, ranging from the occasional or frequent petty thefts and frauds practiced by tradespeople upon customers, by customers upon tradespeople, by workers upon employers, by employers upon workers, to organized and persistent criminal dishonesty on a national or international scale can only be surmised. Its enormity is suggested by the demonstrated frequency of fraudulent bankruptcies; the falsification of income tax returns; fraudulent investment schemes; the illegal exploitation of labor unions and trade associations by their officers and agents; the adulteration and misbranding of foods, drugs and cosmetics; bribery and corruption among public office holders, policemen, and judges; insurance frauds, fee splitting, illegal abortions, illegal sales of alcohol and narcotics, involving physicians and others; frauds in fulfilling manufacturing and construction contracts; and the violation of the rights of racial groups. In all of these instances it must be recognized that reference is made to actual violations of existing criminal laws.

Recognition of the existence of extensive criminality among respected business and professional people has led to criticism of theories of crime causation and control based upon the assumption that criminal behavior is predominantly a function of low socioeconomic status and inferior biological constitution. It has led also to increasing aware-ness of the inadequacy of conventional police methods for the detection and prosecution of upperworld crimes which stress fraud rather than violence and which have a low social visibility. Moreover, it suggests an uncomfortably close relationship of example, imitation, and justification between organized underworld crime and the criminal acquisitive practices of the upperworld. Since, as Sutherland has made clear, white-collar crime involves a violation of public confidence and trust in one who is presumed to be honest, it has the effect of destroying social morale and of promoting social disorganization.

As modern technology has moved towards the creation of One World in which the fortunes of men and of nations are inextricably interrelated there has come about a resurgence and extension of ethical sensitiveness to territorial aggression, to imperialistic expansion, to the exploitation of colonial peoples, and to war. This ethical sensitiveness, dulled or absent during the modern period of expansion by the Western sovereignties, is not new, for both ancient and medieval states found it necessary to seek justification for their aggressions.

The greatly increased effectiveness and range of communication and transport during the nineteenth century led to such international agreements as those regulating the traffic in drugs and other commodities, and those restricting slavery and warfare. Insofar as it was concerned with ethical situations, so-called international law represented the extension of public sentiment into the field of international relations. In many respects, the growth of international law is comparable to that of the English common law, since it was not enacted by an international legislative body. Because it has rested upon the consent of sovereign states to abide by its provisions, the question has been raised as to whether there is an international law in a strict legal sense.

The First World War (which, however immoral, was not a crime at law), with its enormous destructiveness and the extension of its direct effects to neutrals and noncombatants, intensified the moral reaction to war and led presently to the Paris Pact of

1928, in which the major nations of the world renounced the right to make war as a means of solving international controversies. The Geneva Protocol of 1924, the Eighth Assembly of the League of Nations in 1927, and the Sixth Pan-American Conference of 1928 all specifically declared that a war of aggression constitutes an international crime.

Although an adequate definition of a war of aggression was not found and attempts to implement the provisions of the Paris Pact had been unsuccessful, the mass miseries of the Second World War, with its global dimensions, its total destruction, its bombing of civilian populations, its indescribable tortures and deliberate sadistic killings of millions of non-combatant men, women, and children, made it seem necessary to find some way of dealing with such behavior that would accord with the principles of law and the moral sense of the world's peoples.

Pursuant, therefore, to an agreement signed in August, 1946, by the governments of the United States, Great Britain, the Union of Soviet Socialist Republics and the provisional government of France, an International Military Tribunal was established to try and punish the war criminals of the Axis power for *Crimes against peace:* namely planning, preparing or conspiring to wage a war of aggression or a war in violation of international agreements; *War crimes:* namely, violations of the customs or laws or war; and *Crimes against humanity:* namely, inhumane acts and persecutions on religious and racial grounds committed against civilian populations before or during the war.

The Charter of the International Military Tribunal provided that official position, even as heads of state, should not free defendants from responsibility or punishment, nor should the fact that a defendant acted on the order of his superiors. Provision was also made for declaring entire organizations guilty.

In accordance with the Charter, on October 18, 1945, twenty-four German leaders and seven organizations were indicted and charged with conspiracy to wage aggressive war, with war crimes, and crimes against humanity. Twenty-one of these defendants were found guilty in a trial, unique in history, in which Justice Robert H. Jackson,

Representative and Chief Counsel for the United States, called aggressive war the greatest menace of our times and asserted that "the common sense of mankind demands that law shall not stop with the punishment of petty crimes by little people. It must also reach men who possess themselves of great power and make deliberate and concerted use of it to set in motion evils which leave no home in the world untouched."

Following the convictions of political leaders, charges were brought against Germany's military and industrial leaders as war criminals.

Although the power and the glamour once associated with German political, military and industrial leadership has made it difficult to think of them, and their counterparts in other countries, as criminals in the same sense as the racketeers of the underworld, the detailed evidence of their crimes has done much to demonstrate that it is rather in the breadth and complexity and ultimate power of their operations than in their moral stature that those who commit genocide and who conspire to wage aggressive warfare differ from underworld criminals.

The concept of upperworld crime, as applied either to the more or less frequent or habitual violations of the criminal codes of a nation or to violations of an embryonic international criminal code, has seemingly not been well assimilated by the public. In part, this may be due to the fact that many upperworld crimes, usually non-violent and non-frightening, are but elaborations of offenses of which, at a petty level, probably all adults are occasionally guilty. The inclusion of them in the criminal code, to cope with the more extreme instances of injurious behavior, may represent a public ideal rather than a workable standard.

The psycho-somatic-sociological approach to the study of man, as distinct from the pre-scientific or theological, tends to view the interacting factors in human behavior, including the role of the individual organism, in an impersonal and non-moralistic manner. This does not preclude recognition of the fact that the personality is, itself, a vital factor in interaction. It does, however, tend to minimize concern with the guilt or moral responsibility of the individual and to emphasize, instead, the personal and social consequences of behavior evaluated in the light of what seem to be currently accepted or desirable human values. The objective of treatment would then be social protection and the social readjustment of the offender, rather than punishment.

This tendency may lead towards a reduction in the use of the generalized, omnibus, changing, concept "crime" as unserviceable for the purpose of scientific research and to a concern with the more precise analysis and definition of the nature and social consequences of specific types of socially injurious behavior.

ALBERT MORRIS,
Professor of Sociology,
Boston University,
Boston, Massachusetts.

BIBLIOGRAPHY

Barnes and Teeters, *New Horizons in Criminology,* 1943.
Barton, R. F., *Ifugao Law,* Vol. 15, University of California Publications in American Archaeology and Ethnology, 1919.
The Bible: Old Testament.
Boas, F., *The Central Eskimo,* Bureau of American Ethnology, 6th Annual Report.
Cherry, R. R., *Lectures on the Growth of Criminal Law in Ancient Communities,* 1890.
Frazer, J. G., *Folk Lore in the Old Testament,* 1918.
Frazer, J. G., *The Golden Bough,* 1922.
Goldberg and Rosamond, *Girls on City Streets,* 1940.
Hall, J., *Theft, Law and Society,* 1935.
Hopkins, E. J., *Our Lawless Police,* 1931.
Jackson, R. H., *The Case Against the Nazi War Criminals,* 1946.
Landesco, J., *Organized Crime in Chicago,* Illinois Crime Survey, 1929.
League of Nations, *Report of the Special Body of Experts on Traffic in Women and Children,* 1927.
Loth, D., *Public Plunder: A History of Graft in America,* 1938.
MacDougall, E. D. (Ed.), *Crime for Profit,* 1933.
Maine, H. J. S., *Ancient Law,* 1861.
Malinowski, B., *Crime and Custom in Savage Society.*
Morris, A., *Criminology,* 1934.
Murdock, G. P., *Our Primitive Contemporaries,* 1934.
Myers, G., *History of Great American Fortunes,* 1907.
Pike, L. O., *History of Crime in England,* 1873.
Powell, H., *Ninety Times Guilty,* 1939.
Ross, E. A., *Sin and Society,* 1907.
Rusche and Kirchheimer, *Punishment and Social Structure,* 1939.
Seidman, H., *Labor Czars,* 1938.
Stephen, J. F., *History of the Criminal Law of England,* 1883.
Sumner, W. G., *Folkways,* 1907.
Sutherland, E. H., White Collar Criminality *American Sociological Review,* February, 1940.
Westermarck, E., *Origin and Development of the Moral Ideas,* 1907.

CIVIL RIGHTS OF CRIMINALS. At common law a person convicted of a felony became an outlaw. He lost all of his civil rights and all of his property became forfeited. This harsh rule no longer prevails. Under modern jurisprudence the civil rights of a person convicted of a crime, be it a felony or a misdemeanor, are in nowise affected or diminished except insofar as express statutory provisions so prescribe.

In many States, either by constitution or by statute, a person convicted of a felony loses certain civil and political rights, the most important of which is the right of franchise. Some times it is loosely said under these circumstances that he loses his citizenship. This is an inaccurate statement of the law. No one loses his citizenship as a result of a conviction of a crime—that is, no citizen of the United States ceases to be a citizen by reason of a conviction of a crime—except in the exceptional instances later referred to. The loss of rights consequent upon a conviction of a crime may be the loss of certain rights of citizenship, but not of citizenship itself. There are some States in which the convict is deprived of the right of franchise only during the period of his incarceration and resumes that right automatically upon his release from imprisonment. There are other States in which right of franchise is not affected by a conviction, except insofar as the prisoner may be physically prevented from exercising that right by reason of the physical restraint concomitant on the imprisonment.

In many States there are certain other rights that are lost as a result of a conviction of a crime, particularly if the offense is a felony or other crime involving moral turpitude. In many States deprivation of the right to hold public office and of the right to serve on a jury follows such a conviction, because of an express constitutional or statutory provision. In many States a person convicted of such an offense is not permitted to pursue certain callings, for which a license is required. For example, it is quite common to bar the granting of a license to sell liquor to such a person. In some States, such a person may not even be employed in a place where liquor is sold. Such a conviction may preclude a person from being admitted to practice a profession. Thus, in many States, a person convicted of such an offense may not be admitted to the bar or licensed to practice medicine or dentistry. A conviction of such a crime may be grounds for disbarring a lawyer from practice, or precluding a physician or dentist from pursuing his professional calling.

The civil rights of a convicted person may be restored to him by a pardon granted by the Governor, or other agency clothed with the pardoning power. In many jurisdictions it is a common routine to grant pardons for the purpose of restoring civil rights to a person, who having been convicted of a crime, has served the sentence imposed on him and has conducted himself as a law abiding person for a number of years.

In some jurisdictions, a conviction of a serious offense followed by a sentence of imprisonment for a term of not less than specified duration, if it is wholly or partially served, constitutes a ground for divorce or dissolution of marriage at the option of the other spouse. In New York a sentence of imprisonment for life automatically dissolves the convict's marriage without any judicial proceeding for that purpose.

In respect to the loss of civil rights, the position of a person convicted in a Federal court is somewhat anomalous except in the few instances hereinafter mentioned. Such a conviction does not often operate as a deprivation of any rights under the Federal Constitution or Federal statutes. This is due to the fact that most of the civil rights that accompany citizenship are derived from State constitutions or laws, rather than being founded on the Federal Constitution or laws.

It is due to the further fact that, with a few exceptions, Federal statutes do not deprive a convict of those civil rights which are based on the Constitution or laws of the United States. Under the laws of most States, however, the consequences of a conviction in a Federal court are the same as those of a conviction in a State court. Consequently, the extent to which a person convicted of a crime in a Federal court loses his civil rights depends very largely on the law of the State in which he happens to live. For example, if under the State law a person convicted of a felony loses the right of franchise, the same consequence follows, irrespective of whether the conviction took place in a Federal or State court. By the same token, if no such consequence attaches under the laws of a particular State, a person convicted in a Federal court does not lose his right of franchise. In case of persons convicted in a Federal court, the consequence of a conviction may be wiped out by a pardon granted by the President of the United States. With that end in view, the President frequently grants pardons for the purpose of restoring civil rights. This is done after the expiration of the sentence, if the person involved applies for such a pardon and an investigation conducted by the Federal Bureau of Investigation of the Department of Justice, shows that he has been conducting himself as a law abiding person for a specified number of years. The Federal Government has well established machinery and procedure for the granting of pardons. In such cases, the President acts upon the recommendation of the Attorney General. One of the officials of the Department of Justice of the United States, who is known as the Pardon Attorney, reviews all applications for pardons and causes the necessary investigations to be made. He then makes an appropriate recommendation to the Attorney General, who in turn makes a recommendation to the President. The result is that the granting of Federal pardons is based on a well established procedure and routine, governed by a set of rules approved and promulgated by the President.

In most States a Presidential pardon of a Federal conviction operates to restore the defendant's civil and political rights. There are some States, however, in which only a pardon granted by the Governor or other pardoning power of the State, as the case may be, has the effect of restoring rights guaranteed by the State constitution or laws. In other words, in its ultimate analysis, both the deprivation and restoration of civil rights consequent upon a conviction in a Federal court, is a matter governed entirely by State law.

As stated above, a person convicted of a crime in a Federal court rarely loses any civil rights derived under the Federal Constitution and laws. There is an exception, however, in that a person convicted of treason or of bribery of any Federal judicial official, or of accepting a bribe while being a Federal judicial official, becomes disqualified to hold any office of honor, trust, or profit under the United States. The same consequence attaches to a Member of Congress who is convicted of receiving unlawful compensation.

The foregoing discussion so far has dealt with the loss of certain rights of citizenship as a consequence of conviction of a criminal offense. In addition, there are two situations in which a person convicted of a crime loses his citizenship. In other words, he ceases to be a citizen of the United States and presumably becomes a Stateless person or a man without a country. He not only loses his citizenship, but he ceases to be a national of the United States, which is a concept that is broader than citizenship. This consequence attaches as a result of conviction, either by a court-martial or by a court of competent jurisdiction, on a charge of treason or on a charge of attempting by force to overthrow the Government of the United States or bearing arms against the United States. The same penalty also follows a person who deserts the military or naval forces of the United States in time of war, provided he is convicted thereof by court-martial and as the result of such conviction is dismissed or dishonorably discharged from the service. If, however, he is restored to active duty in time of war, or re-enlists or is inducted in time of war with the permission of competent military or naval authority, his nationality and citizenship and all of his civil and political rights are automatically and immediately re-

stored. The foregoing appear to be the only two instances in which a person loses citizenship of the United States, or his status as a national of the United States as a result of a conviction of a crime.

This discussion has so far been devoted to the subject of the loss of civil rights and nationality status on the part of citizens of the United States as a result of conviction of a crime. While in the nature of things, an alien who is convicted of a crime is not deprived of citizenship or nationality or of any right of citizenship, for he has none to lose, nevertheless, he forfeits certain civil rights. One of the requirements for naturalization is that the applicant shall have been a person of good moral character for at least five years preceding the date of filing the petition for naturalization. A person who during the five-year period has been convicted of a crime involving moral turpitude is not regarded as a person of good moral character. Consequently, conviction of a crime involving moral turpitude disqualifies an alien from naturalization for five years thereafter.

An alien who is convicted in the United States of a crime involving moral turpitude committed within five years after his entry into the United States, and is sentenced to a term of imprisonment for one year or more, is subject to deportation. This is also true of any alien who is convicted at least twice of crimes involving moral turpitude and is sentenced to terms of imprisonment for one year or more, irrespective of when the crimes may have been committed. The court sentencing the alien may, however, at the time of imposition of sentence, or within thirty days thereafter, make a recommendation to the Attorney General of the United States that the alien is not to be deported, in which event deportation may not take place. The same consequence attaches to an alien who is convicted of certain violations of the narcotic laws or of attempting unlawfully to enter the United States after having been deported therefrom as a result of a conviction on a charge of importing into the United States any alien for the purpose of prostitution or other immoral purpose. Thus, as a result of conviction of a crime under the circumstances above summarized, an alien may lose his right to remain in the United States and become subject to deportation.

Hon. ALEXANDER HOLTZOFF,
United States District Judge,
Washington, D. C.

BIBLIOGRAPHY

U. S. Code, Title 18, Sections 2, 237, 238.
U. S. Code, Title 8, Section 801.
Various State Constitutions and Statutes.

CLASSIFICATION OF CRIME. Attempts to classify crimes have been made for both practical and theoretical purposes. In terms of the gravity of the offense, and for the purpose of assessing penalties, crimes have been legally classified as treason, felony and misdemeanor. For the purpose of orderly arrangement and codification, criminal statutes have been organized into categories based on type of crime or in terms of individual or social interest affected. For administrative and statistical purposes classificatory systems have been designed by police, courts and institutional agencies. Theoretical systems of classification, in terms of feelings or sentiment violated by criminal acts, or in terms of drives, impulses or sentiments leading to criminal acts have been attempted by earlier writers on criminology and criminal law. In this paper we shall be concerned with the first three of these aspects of crime classification.

LEGAL CLASSIFICATIONS

Probably the most familiar as well as the oldest classification of crimes is the one found in the common law. Here, crimes, from early times, have been divided into treason, felony and misdemeanor. These categories seem to have had their origin during the centuries immediately following the Norman Conquest and to be an outgrowth of the social, political and legal changes of that period which saw the extension of the authority of the Crown and the establishment of the principle of "King's peace." Distinctions gradually came to be drawn between offenses which were matters for local settlement by compensation between offender and victim, and those for which appeals to the Crown might be had

and which could not be settled by compensation to the injured or his kinsmen (*wer* and *bot*) or through fines to the King (*wite*). The principle came gradually to be established that certain offenses were unemendable and non-compensable. Included among these were high and petty treason, and felony, offenses for which only the severest penalties, death and confiscation of estates, were appropriate. Thus, by the end of the 12th century, a category of the more serious offenses had come to be recognized in the law to which the word felony had come to be applied. Pollock and Maitland, in their History of the English Law, point out that although the origin of the word felony may not be entirely clear yet. . . ." At all events this word expressive to the common ear of all that was most hateful to God and man, was soon in England and Normandy, a general word name for the worst, the utterly 'bootless crimes.' " (Vol. II, p. 464.) The increasing substitution of the death penalty for mutilation and other less severe forms of corporal punishment also seems to have been an accompaniment of the multiplications of crimes defined as felonies. Some historians of the English law also suggest that the development of the concept of felony may have stimulated the increasing use of death as the principal punishment for crime. At least it is clear that the increase in number of felonies accompanied the growing use of the death penalty.

At first it appears that treason was regarded as one of the felonies. In time, however, it came to be distinguished as a special class of offense directed against the life and safety of the sovereign, for which death alone was hardly a sufficient penalty. The concept of treason was further extended to cover a lesser degree of that offense, petty treason. This designation was applied to acts directed against the life of a superior or person in authority by an inferior or subject. Thus murder of a husband by wife or of a master by a servant are examples of petty treason.

Gradually, in the 12th century, the number of crimes to which the punishment of death and forfeiture could be applied increased. To most of these the term felony came to be applied. Sir James Stephens has pointed out, however, that punishability by death and forfeiture was not entirely adequate as the criterion of felony.

"It is usually said that felony means a crime which involved the punishment of forfeiture, but this definition would be too large for it would include misprision of treason which is a misdemeanor. On the other hand, if felony is defined as crime punishable with death, it excludes petty larceny which was never capital, and includes piracy which was never felony." *History of the Criminal Law in England.* Vol. II, p. 192.

It would appear, therefore, that from the beginning the distinction between felony and misdemeanor was somewhat arbitrary in that certain offenses of minor nature, not punishable by death and forfeiture, were declared felony. Other offenses, which did carry the extreme penalty, were not defined as felony.

It has been suggested that the principle of forfeiture came to be associated with felony as a result of the influence of Norman law. Here the concept of *felonia* seems first to have been applied to offenses involving breach of trust between lord and man. Such offenses called for forfeiture of fees and land. In England forfeiture was a penalty associated with most felonies, which tended to be expanded in number by the willingness of the lords to surrender to the Crown the power to punish crime in return for the forfeitures of lands of those convicted of felony in the royal courts. Thus Pollock and Maitland say:

"The specific effects of the words of felony when they were first uttered by appellors who were bringing charges of homicide, robbery, rape, etc., was to provide that, whatever other punishment the appellees might undergo, they should at all events lose their land. The magnates saw no harm in this, though in truth the extension of felony, if it might bring them some accession of wealth, was undermining their power." *History of the English Law.* Vol. II, p. 465.

By the end of the 13th century, according to Pollock and Maitland, felonies appear to have had the following characteristics: (1) they were crimes which could be prosecuted on appeals to the Crown; (2) lands and chattels were forfeit on conviction; (3) the convicted might be punished by loss of life or member; (4) the accused would be outlawed if he fled. Classified as felonies were certain crimes against the person; murder, manslaughter, rape and wounding. Mayhem, originally a felony, was later reduced to a misdemeanor, as was also false imprisonment. Crimes against property, classed as felonies, were arson, larceny, burglary and robbery. All of these offenses were unemendable, deserved the punishment of life or member and worked a disherison. In addition to the distinction drawn between felonies and lesser offenses in terms of penalties a good many differences in criminal procedure also existed. Among these were: (1) those accused of felony could be arrested without warrant, which was not true of disdemeanants; (2) felonies were not bailable while misdemeants might be admitted to bail; (3) the right to peremptory challenge was permitted persons accused of felony but denied those charged with misdemeanor. Survivals of those differences in procedure may be found today in many jurisdictions. The classification of crimes, thus came to depend on the penalties and other legal consequences, which, as Pollock and Maitland point out, involved the impossible logical position of making the definition of crime turn on its legal consequences and, at the same time, determining the consequences by the definition.

With the evolution of the common and statute law in England, from the late middle ages down through the 18th century, the number of crimes classed as felonies appears to have multiplied steadily. In large measure this was probably due to the increasing use of the death penalty as the principal punishment for all but the most petty breaches of the law. With the possible exception of the 17th century, when imprisonment in the workhouse was a common form of punishment for lesser offenses, the number of capital offenses appears to have multiplied until they exceeded 200 by the end of the 18th century. To the common law offenses Parliament added numerous other felonies by statute.

During the 18th century in England we

begin to find other forms of punishment supplementing and supplanting the death penalty as punishment for even more serious types of crime. Transportation to the colonies, during the 18th and early part of the 19th century, came to be the penalty imposed for an ever growing list of offenses or as a mitigating substitute for the death penalty. The 19th century saw the development of the penitentiary and imprisonment as punishment for all except a few most heinous offenses. Forfeiture of land and property had also fallen into disuse. With the growing disuse of the death penalty, and discontinuance of confiscation, the basis for distinguishing between felony and misdemeanor almost entirely disappeared. As statute law gradually superseded common law, the more heinous offenses came specifically to be denominated felonies while lesser crimes were defined as misdemeanors. In addition to the death penalty, long terms of imprisonment were prescribed for the former while the latter carried punishment of fine or short prison term. As in earlier centuries final jurisdiction over felonies remained a prerogative of the royal courts. Since the latter part of the 19th century the death penalty has been applied only to a relatively small number of offenses, and the primary distinction between felony and misdemeanor has become the duration of imprisonment which might be imposed.

In the American colonies the traditional common law distinctions between felony and misdemeanor prevailed down to the end of the 18th century. After 1790, however, most of the states, following the lead of Pennsylvania, reduced the number of felonies punishable by death and substituted imprisonment as the major penalty. As a consequence the primary criterion for distinguishing felony from misdemeanor disappeared. The problem was solved by defining felonies as crimes punishable by death or imprisonment in a state prison, while misdemeanors were lesser offenses for which fines or imprisonment in local jails or workhouses were assessed. In addition, the common law differences in procedure, mentioned above, also continued to distinguish felonies from lesser offenses.

The legal classification of crimes as treason, felony and misdemeanor has long been criticized, from both a legal and social point of view. In his *History of the Criminal Law in England* (1883), Sir James Stephen rejects the classification as illogical, arbitrary and without value. Why, asks Stephen, should embezzlement be a felony while fraud by agent is a misdemeanor? Why should bigamy be felonious while perjury is a misdemeanor, or certain forgeries be defined as felonies when obtaining goods under false pretenses remains a misdemeanor? Stephen suggests that the very existence of the classification has not only become useless but that its continuance is pernicious both as an encouragement to hasty legislation and as leading to mechanical treatment of the offender in the courts. As mentioned earlier, the tendency to lump together an increasing number of offenses as felonies tended also to swell the number of crimes punishable by death. Although publishing more than half a century ago, Stephen anticipates many of the criticisms of the legal classifications of crime found in modern textbooks on the criminal law and criminology. In his insistence on focusing attention on the offender rather than the offense, Stephen anticipates the position of the modern criminology and penology. He suggests that the only defensible criteria for classification must be found in differences in judicial procedure provided for different classes of offenses, in penalties or consequences or in privileges and rights properly granted to different classes of offenders. Each of these criteria, however, involves a different problem so that the same offense might be differently classified depending on which criterion is selected. For example, Stephen cites the crime of perjury, an offense for which, from the point of view of social injury, the severest penalties might be justified. The common law of his day, however, defined the crime as a misdemeanor. At the same time perjury might not be an offense for which summary arrest would be advisable although in some cases the desirability of bail might be doubtful. Whether or not an offense is to be considered a grave crime, to be dealt with by the superior courts, to call for severely repressive measures and to deprive the accused of his right to bail or to cause his arrest without warrant cannot be decided by whether or not the crime falls nicely into a legal definition which may be labeled felony or misdemeanor. Rather, procedure should be determined in terms of the conditions surrounding the offense, and the character of the offender. Thus, to use Stephen's example, burglary might be a trifling offense of entering a kitchen and stealing a loaf of bread or it might be the entry into a house by an armed intruder with the intention of committing robbery, rape or murder. Robbery, under one set of circumstances might be akin to murder; under another set more closely related to common assault. Only the circumstances of the offense, and the characteristics of the offender, are likely to throw much light on the present injury caused or the potential future menace to the community. Only such knowledge is likely to give insight into what the legal consequences of an offense ought properly to be, or with what means and devices the offender might best be dealt. Stephen concludes that: "A classification . . . which might be made out of the various distinctions mentioned would be extremely intricate and technical. A classification which did not recognize them would be of little use. Hence the most convenient course in practice is to have no classification at all."

With the growth of the criminal statutes in the laws of our states, the distinctions between felony and misdemeanor have become ever more confused and arbitrary. In most states the original felonies, defined as such in the common law, are still felonies. In addition also most states define any offense punishable by death or state prison sentence as felony. On this point, however, there exists a great deal of confusion and the criterion of a state prison sentence is by no means an infallible index of felony. Thus in Delaware the penalties for some misdemeanors are more severe than those for some felonies. Examples of crimes which are *misdemeanors* by definition but punishable by state prison sentence for from two to ten years are embezzlement by the state treasurer, incest, prize fighting and throwing missiles at a railroad train. In Michigan, mutilation or destruction of state records, or fraudulently obtaining signature to a note are misdemeanors but may

be punished by penitentiary sentence up to ten years. In Pennsylvania, keeping a bawdy house is a misdemeanor, but the penalty may be a state prison sentence up to two years. On the other hand, there are states in which offenses are declared felonies but the punishment is something less than state prison sentence. In Mississippi assault with a deadly weapon may be a misdemeanor and punished by *either* jail or prison sentence. The same is true of child abandonment.

Again, in some jurisdictions, the statutes define crimes punishable by sentence to the state prison as felony but provide as a penalty for many felonies *either* fine and/or jail sentence, or sentence to state prison. In such cases the option of the heavier or the lighter penalty is left to the court. Only after sentence has been imposed, therefore, can it be determined whether or not the crime was a felony. In other states the test of felony is "imprisonment at hard labor" and in still others the issue depends on whether or not the crime is "infamous." Frequently the test of infamy is "imprisonment at hard labor" or occasionally whether or not conviction is followed by loss of civil rights. But we have one state, Maryland, where only those crimes are felonies which were so at common law or have been declared such by statute. The penalty has nothing to do with the classification of the offense, nor does the fact that the crime is infamous make it a felony. In North Carolina if a misdemeanor is infamous or is done "with secrecy" it may be punished by prison sentence up to two years but this does not make it a felony. In New Jersey no distinction is made between felony and misdemeanor. Offenses are classified as "misdemeanors" and "high misdemeanors" carrying alternative penalties of fine or imprisonment.

We find, thus, that individual states show no clear-cut or consistent pattern with reference to the definitions of classes of crime. Neither is there any consistent agreement between the various states as to the classification of the same crime. For example, in a number of states involuntary manslaughter is punishable as a misdemeanor by fine or jail sentence; in others as a felony by state prison sentence up to ten years. The possession of burglar's tools is a felony in about half the states, a misdemeanor in the rest. Examples of sex offenses which are misdemeanors in some states and felonies in others are: abortion, a felony in most states, but a misdemeanor in Nebraska and Oklahoma; bigamy, a felony in most states, but a misdemeanor in New Mexico and Pennsylvania; sodomy, usually a felony, but a misdemeanor in New Mexico; keeping a bawdy house, usually a misdemeanor, but a felony in South Dakota.

The lack of consistency between the states is further illustrated in the distinctions drawn between grand larceny (usually a felony) and petty larceny. In Missouri, theft of money or property with a value of thirty dollars or more, or the theft of a horse, mare, colt, cow, sheep or hog, constitutes a felony and carries a prison sentence. Theft of other property, with value less than thirty dollars is a misdemeanor. But there is one important exception to this generalization. Theft of a fowl or fowls in the night time, if stolen from messuage, a dwelling or premises thereof, is a felony, irrespective of the value of the property. Presumably, if stolen from premises, other than those of a dwelling, or if stolen during the day time, the theft of fowl would not be a felony unless the value was in excess of thirty dollars. The value of the property stolen, which distinguishes misdemeanor from felony in the several states, varies from five dollars in the lowest state to $500 in the highest. The distinction, hence, between grand and petty larceny (felony and misdemeanor) may depend on the nature of the property, its value or the time and place of the theft. The pressure of special business groups on legislatures to give protection to their economic interests tends to multiply the number of crimes classed as felonies by increasing the severity of punishments provided. In part, it is this process which leads to much of the confusion described.

The legal distinctions drawn between felony and misdemeanor would be of little social significance, and of little interest to the criminologist, were it not for the consequences both to the offender and to the community which rise out of the distinction. The assumption is commonly made that felonies are grave offenses, seriously injurious to the community, and the felon a dangerous public menace. A misdemeanor, on the other hand, is an offense of less serious import and the offender rather a nuisance than a public enemy. The safety of the community can be secured only through the intervention of the state authority and a prison sentence in the case of the felon, while the misdemeanant may safely be left to local authorities and the deterrent and reformative effect of the city or county jail.

That there is little foundation for such assumptions has already been demonstrated by the lack of consistency between states in their definitions of major and minor offenses earlier described. The fact that a person convicted of felony in one state would, for the same offense, be defined as a misdemeanant in another state, is the best evidence that there exists little difference between the two classes of offenders. If punishment or treatment of crime is designed primarily to protect the community, or if it is to be suited to the special nature of the offender, it cannot be determined by sterile legal distinctions between felony and misdemeanor.

Familiarity with the characteristics of prisoners in prisons and jails throws further doubt on the wisdom of distinguishing between felons and misdemeanants either in terms of the authority which should be responsible for their care or the institutions best suited to their needs. In an early study of county jails Queen found that there were few respects in which the inmates of the county jails differed from the supposedly more serious offenders confined in state prisons. A later study in Massachusetts seems to show that while a somewhat larger proportion of prison inmates (75%) had served previous sentences in penal institutions than was true for jail inmates (63%), the number of previous commitments averaged three for inmates of penitentiaries as compared with five for jail inmates. Other studies also seem to indicate that a greater degree of recidivism, measured in terms of number of previous commitments, prevails among jail prisoners than among persons confined in penitentiaries. The greater amount of recidivism among jail inmates may be due to the tendency for the jail population to contain a relatively larger number of defective and deteriorated types than are to be found in the prisons. The notoriously ineffective policy of repeatedly committing alcoholics, vagrants, sex offenders and other similar types to the jail or workhouse instead of to state institutions equipped to care for such types is in part a consequence of our antiquated system of crime classification and the differentiation in treatment growing out of it. This point is excellently illustrated in a recent article on the sexual psychopath. The writer points out that widely different kinds of offenders are convicted of sex offenses. Thus the sex murderer and rapist will frequently show a history of repeated jail commitments for indecent exposure or improper advances toward small children. Because his offenses have been misdemeanors in the eyes of the law his case may never have gone beyond the minor courts. He may never have been under the observation of experts competent to diagnose the nature of his disorder and to provide for the prolonged detention which his symptoms indicate to be necessary. On the other hand, the youthful offender who has had relations with a girl just under the age of consent may, and often is, sent to the penitentiary convicted of rape, even though his offense would be a misdemeanor, or no crime at all, had his partner been a few weeks or days older.

The meaningless nature of the distinction between misdemeanor and felony is further demonstrated by the fact that a very large per cent of offenders are convicted of offenses other than those of which they were originally charged. It is a matter of common knowledge that a great number of persons accused of crime plead guilty to some lesser offense than that originally charged in order to take advantage of the milder penalties provided. As a consequence, the penalty or treatment policy (prison sentence, jail commitment, fine or probation) tends to be determined by the specific legal definition of the offense (whether felony or misdemeanor) instead of on the basis of the character of the offender. In this connection it may be noted that in the laws of some states probation is limited to persons convicted of misdemeanor. The absurdity of such restrictions is obvious in light of the prevailing confusion

in the distinctions drawn between felony and misdemeanor. The very existence, however, of the distinction encourages the kind of hasty legislation which results in the restriction.

One further legal distinction drawn between classes of crime deserves brief attention. This is the distinction drawn between minor offenses contravening state law and those which are in violation of local ordinances, police regulations, etc. In some jurisdictions the latter are offenses over which the minor courts have exclusive summary jurisdiction for which fines and/or short terms of imprisonment in city jails or workhouses may be assessed. The addition of such a classification reminds one of the distinction drawn in the French criminal code between *crimes, delits* and *contraventions,* where the latter are trivial offenses punishable through summary procedure by small fines, or short terms of confinement. In the United States many courts have held that the violation of city ordinances are not crimes at all, since they do not contravene public law, but rather are in the nature of public torts than crimes. Other courts, however, have held violations of ordinances to be crimes on the ground that a municipal ordinance is the creation of a proper public authority (created by legislative statute) and designed to secure the general welfare as much as is a statute passed by the state legislature. The only distinction between the two is that the ordinance seeks to protect the municipality while the statute applies to the public of the entire commonwealth. These distinctions are probably of greater interest to the students of the law than they are to criminologists, although again it is significant that the violators will be dealt with in terms of the class of offense of which they may be found guilty.

CLASSIFICATION FOR PURPOSE OF LEGAL CODIFICATION

So far in this article we have been concerned primarily with the traditional common law classification of crimes in terms of their supposed gravity. The problem of classification, however, has also interested students of the criminal law who have sought to reduce the criminal statutes of the various states to some semblance of order by devising a logical basis for their classification. Freund, in 1915, for the American Law Institute, investigated this problem. Later studies were published by Lester in 1924 and by J. W. MacDonald for The Committee on the Simplification of the Penal Law of the New York State Commission on the Administration of Justice. Pound has also dealt with this problem in his penetrating studies of American criminal jurisprudence. Among the criminologists Parmelee in 1918 and Gillin, somewhat later, have attempted to devise classifactory systems. The results of these studies indicate that the states fall into three groups. There are those in which no attempt has been made to classify the criminal statutes, a second group which classify crimes alphabetically, from abortion to usury, and a third group in which various schemes and plans of organization have been adopted.

Most of the classification schemes are organized in terms of the *type* of crime committed and in terms of the interest violated. The simplest plan is to divide the criminal statutes into three classes: those designed to protect the person, those protecting property and those in the interest of preserving the state or other public interest. There are few crimes which do not violate one or the other of these broad interests, but the categories are so general and all-inclusive as to be of little value. More detailed schemes of classification have been attempted in many states of which that in Missouri is a good illustration. Here crimes are classified as follows:

1. Offenses against the government and the supremacy of law.
2. Offenses against the administration of justice.
3. Offenses by persons in office, or affecting public trusts or rights and concerning elections.
4. Offenses against the person or lives of individuals.
5. Offenses against public or private property.
6. Offenses against record, currency, instruments and securities.
7. Offenses against public law and peace.
8. Miscellaneous offenses.

9. Miscellaneous provisions and definitions.

After examining the criminal codes of American states and those in European countries Professor Freund suggests a classification in terms of the interests violated, viz: safety of the state and maintaining the authority of government; the conformity to legislative policy; purity of justice and administration; maintenance of peace, security and good order; purity of sex relations; ordinary safety of the person and property. In terms of these interests the following classification is suggested:

1. Political offenses
2. Statute violations
3. Administrative crimes
4. Police offenses
5. Crime against morality
6. Ordinary or common crimes.

Professor Freund, however, doubts the practical value of his own classification and believes that it would present too many controversial problems and involve too complete a reorganization of the criminal law to make it of immediate significance for legislative consideration. Freund concludes that any worth while system of classification must take into consideration the relevant elements which throw light on the conditions which lead up to a crime and the character of the perpetrator, and thus aid both in the determination of guilt and the punishment to be provided. In reaching such a classification he feels that the legislator must turn to the trained criminologist. If such classification could be reached it might be possible to avoid the alternative between excessive, inappropriate or futile punishment and absolute acquittal. A program of this kind would involve a much greater degree of individualization of treatment than the present law permits but, Freund believes, would be the only kind of crime classification which would be of value.

In 1933 MacDonald undertook the problem of exploring the possibility of the classification of the criminal statutes for the New York State Commission on the Administration of Justice. MacDonald suggests five criteria for such classification: it must be sufficiently flexible to include all offenses; it must rest on some uniform principle; it should determine the social necessity for continuing penal sanction; it should be of value in reconstructing an all-inclusive penal statute; it should be of assistance to statisticians, criminologists and other experts. MacDonald believes that a modification of a classification suggested by Pound best fills these criteria. This classification includes five major groups, as follows:

1. Crimes against the person of individuals
2. Crimes against general morals
3. Crimes against general security
4. Crimes against the security of social institutions
5. Crimes against the security of social resources.

Professor Sutherland has pointed out that legal classification of the criminal statutes have value for the purposes for which they were intended, but for the criminologist or for those interested in a theoretical analysis they can be of only limited interest.

CLASSIFICATION FOR STATISTICAL PURPOSES

Discussion of the classification of crime would not be complete without some reference to classifications made for statistical purposes. Public agencies, such as the police and the courts, are concerned with the recording of law violations. State and federal penal and correctional institutions record offenses committed by inmates. Certain private institutions, such as life insurance companies and newspapers, also have attempted to gather and organize criminal statistics. One of the major difficulties confronting all attempts to tabulate and organize criminal statistics has been the varying definitions of crimes contained in the criminal codes of our states. As pointed out earlier, the labels attached to various offenses often conceal more than they reveal about the nature of these crimes. No assumption can be made that even such common words as murder, manslaughter, larceny, rape, or assault mean the same thing in different states.

The pioneer work in the United States in the classification of crime for statistical purposes was undertaken by the International Association of Chiefs of Police. In 1927 this Association appointed a committee to conduct studies of crime reporting, police records and statutory classification of offenses in various states. This Committee, under the chairmanship of Bruce Smith, published in 1929 a complete report and guide entitled *Uniform Crime Reporting: A Complete Manual for Police.* In this manual were set forth standardized categories of offenses which were later adopted by the *Federal Bureau of Investigation* as the basis for crime reporting in its quarterly, now semi-annual bulletin, *Uniform Crime Reports.*

In the preparation of a standard classification the Committee was faced with two alternatives. It might, on the one hand, make an effort toward persuading the several states to adopt a uniform criminal code. The other alternative, was to analyze the criminal codes of the states and by a process of comparison and elimination establish a standard set of categories which would minimize the statistical effects of existing differences. The latter alternative was adopted in light of the slight possibility of securing any substantial alteration of the criminal code in the states.

Following the pattern laid down in the police manual, *Uniform Crime Reporting,* crimes reported for statistical purposes are divided in two divisions, Parts I and II. Part I contains a list of seven major offenses which commonly come to the attention of the police and for which it was possible to establish a fairly uniform standard for definition. Part II contains a list of fifteen other offenses which were not included in Part I, either because they were crimes for which violations frequently are unknown to any official agency, or because the definitions of the offenses varied from state to state to such degree as to make impossible any uniformity in tabulation. Part I contains the group of offenses in terms of which crimes known to the police are reported. Part II classes are used only for the purpose of compiling facts about persons arrested and charged. The seven major crimes included in Part I are:

1. Criminal homicide
   a) Murder and nonnegligent manslaughter
   b) Manslaughter by negligence
2. Rape

3. Robbery
4. Aggravated assault
5. Burglary-breaking or entering
6. Larceny-theft
   a) $50 and over in value
   b) Under $50 in value
7. Auto theft.

Part II, other offenses, includes: other assaults, forgery and counterfeiting, embezzlement and fraud, buying, receiving or possessing stolen property, carrying and possessing weapons, prostitution and commercialized vice, sex offenses, offenses against family and children, violations of narcotic laws, violations of drug laws, driving while intoxicated, drunkenness, disorderly conduct and vagrancy, gambling, traffic violations, arrests on suspicion and a category of "all other offenses."

According to the bulletin for the first six months of 1947 statistical data, classified as described above, are being reported and tabulated for 2,437 cities with 68,500,000 population and 1,605 rural jurisdictions containing more than 34 million persons. For a much more complete account of the topic of criminal statistics see article entitled *Criminal Statistics*.

In addition to the classification of crimes adopted by the Federal Bureau of Investigation in its *Uniform Crime Reports* a somewhat similar system of classification is found in the annual Census Bureau reports entitled *Judicial Statistics*. Since 1931 the Bureau of the Census has been gathering data from criminal courts of general jurisdiction in about half the states. This volume contains information concerning the procedural outcome of cases handled in the courts as well as the disposition of all cases convicted of crime. The classification of crime adopted in this report is substantially the same as that used in the *Uniform Crime Reports*. Attention, however, is called to the fact that the problem of classification has been a difficult one and that comparisons of crime rates as between the states based on court data should be made only with the greatest care. One problem rises out of the fact that court jurisdictions over the same offense often differ between the states. The other difficulty is the fact that different states often do not use the same title for the same offense or use the same title to describe different offenses. This is especially true of such categories as larceny, robbery, burglary and forgery. The classification adoped, however, probably contains more uniformities than differences, and while subject to some margin of error, still makes possible some interstate comparisons.

CONCLUSION

The problem of crime classification no longer occupies a position of great importance in the literature of criminology. The traditional common law classification of felony and misdemeanor may have significance because of the consequences in terms of punishment, but in light of the prevailing confusion with which these concepts are used in different jurisdictions, and recognizing the fact that no real differences prevail between felons and misdemeanants, one cannot but agree with Sir James Stephen that we had better have no classification at all. Attempts by earlier criminologists to classify crimes in terms of the individual or social interest violated, or in terms of the drives or impulses of the perpetrator have only historical interest and have proven to be of little use either for practical administration or theoretical analysis. Classification for purposes of codification of the criminal law is useful to the degree to which it furthers the objective of a logical and systematic organization of the criminal code. It may be observed, however, that this interest seems on the wane among legal scholars. It is not of paramount importance to criminologists.

Classification for statistical purposes has been of great importance in the United States since 1930 and has greatly aided in the development of uniform criminal statistics. As the area in which such uniform system of classification is adopted increases we may expect to see an increasing trend to uniformity in the criminal statutes and the recording of criminality.

In conclusion a word might be said about recent attempts to attack the problem of crime classification from a sociological point of view. Most of this work is the result of the research of a few scholars, notably Sutherland, Thrasher, Shaw, McKay Hall and others. Here the objective of classification is to define and describe criminal behavior systems in terms of the development of a common habit systems, ideology, esprit de corps, techniques and vocabulary. As Sutherland points out, the development of a sociological system of classification and the defining and describing of such behavior categories must await the results of further research.

C. T. PIHLBLAD
Chairman, Department of Sociology
University of Missouri
Columbia, Missouri

BIBLIOGRAPHY

Durkheim, E., *De la division du travail social,* Alcon, Paris, 1902.
Freund, Ernst, "*Classification and Definition of Crimes*" *Jou. Crim. Law and Criminology,* 5:807–826, March, 1915.
Gillin, J. L., *Criminology and Penology,* 3rd ed. New York, 1945.
Hall, Jerome, *Theft Law and Society,* Boston, 1935.
International Association of Chiefs of Police, *Uniform Crime Reporting,* New York, 1929.
Lester, Hugh, Classification of Crimes, *Jou. Crim. Law and Criminol.* 14:593–596, 1924.
Miller, Justin, *Handbook of Criminal Law,* Hornbook series, St. Paul, 1934.
McDonald, J. W., "*The Classification of Crimes,*" *Cornell Law Quat.* 19:524–563, June, 1933.
Parmelee, M., *Criminology,* New York, 1918.
Pollock and Maitland, *History of the English Law,* London, 1923.
Pound, Roscoe, *Criminal Justice in America,* New York, 1930.
Pound, Roscoe, "The Scope and Purpose of Sociological Jurisprudence," *Harv. Law Rev.* 29:489–516, Apr. 1912.
Queen, S. A., *The Passing of the County Jail,* Menasha, Wisc. 1920.
Reynolds, Jas. Bronson, Criminal Justice, Its Simplification, Clarification and Better Adaptation, *Jou. Amer. Judic. Soc.* 6:173–176, Apr. 1923.
Stephen, Jas. F., *A History of the Criminal Law in England,* London, 1883.
Sutherland, E. H., *Principles of Criminology,* 4th ed., New York, 1947.
Spalding, W. F., The Legislative History of a State Prison sentence as a Test of "Felony" and "Infamous Punishment" and the Practical Results in Mass, *Mass. Law Quat.* 7:91–108, Jan. 1922.
Tulin, L. A., The Role of Penalties in the Criminal Law, *Yale Law Rev.,* 37:1048–1069, June 1928.
United States Bureau of the Census, *Annual Reports of Judicial Statistics.*
U. S. Department of Justice, *Uniform Crime Reports,* Semi-Annual Bulletins.

CLASSIFICATION OF OFFENDERS. It is impracticable and also unnecessary for present purposes to more than casually review the history of penal classification prior to about 1920. (The classification procedures dealt with here are those which have developed in the last twenty-five years.) Penal classification in general, of course, probably dates from the earliest times when presumably at least there was a classification of accused and condemned. There has also presumably always been some grouping of prisoners according to type of crime, if not also according to age and sex.

By the days of John Howard there was a definite classification of prisoners according to sex, age, and degree of criminality at least in Holland if not elsewhere. As early as 1838 at least, Holland's convicted offenders were separated from the merely accused. Prisons for convicted persons were even then divided into six classes.

The individual study of the offender, however, is generally considered as having begun with Lombroso's "The Delinquent Man" published in 1872, which was followed by his "The Criminal Man" in 1889. Lombroso's early work dealt chiefly with the anthropological characteristics of individual criminals and his later work with their mental and social characteristics. Lombroso's work was subsequently expanded by an entire school of Italian criminologists.

This comparatively recent emphasis on the individual offender was felt in England where the Borstal institutions reflect the most recent trend, and also in the classification of adult offenders. In this country these tendencies were reflected in the separate treatment of the criminal insane and defective delinquents.

Classification as we know it in this country today is much more systematic and extensive than was the case prior to about 1920. Healy's work on the individual delinquent, the development of mental tests (especially the Binet-Simon scale, and the rise of clinical psychiatry in the decade preceding 1920) were forerunners of the subsequent developments. The more immediate development of the formal classification procedures of today dates, however, from the report of the Prison Inquiry Commission in New Jersey in 1917.

As a result of that investigation, a commission headed by Dwight Morrow recommended a welfare program of far-reaching proportions for the State of New Jersey. This culminated in the creation in 1918 of the State Board of Institutions and Agencies in New Jersey, with Burdette G. Lewis as the first Commissioner. Concurrent with these events, Dr. Henry A. Cotton had urged the establishment of a department for the criminal insane at the Trenton State Hospital. Dr. Cotton also recommended the mental examination of all men committed to the New Jersey State Prison. Prior to this time mental tests of delinquents and criminals had been made by Dr. Henry H. Goddard, and as early as 1912 Dr. Frank Moore was employing individual methods of classification at the New Jersey Reformatory with the assistance of Dr. George Lee Orton. At about the same time Dr. Guy Fernald in Massachusetts, Dr. Jean Weidensall of New York, Dr. Walter N. Thayer, and others were following along the lines similar to those laid down by Dr. William J. Healy assisted by Dr. Augusta Bronner.

When Burdette G. Lewis assumed office as Commissioner of Institutions and Agencies in New Jersey, that state department had been organized for the central coordination of all institutions in the state. The law creating the Department gave broad powers for utilizing the resources of all institutions in relation to each other and afforded considerable freedom of transfer from one to another of like institutions as well as among institutions of different kinds. This created a situation highly favorable to the classification of offenders in state institutions already established for different types of wards. Mr. Lewis brought wtih him to New Jersey the late Calvin Derrick as Director of Education and Parole. One of Mr. Derrick's first undertakings was to prepare a procedure for the classification of offenders supplemented by a credit marking system designed to create an effective system of preparation of offenders

for parole. This procedure was subsequently elaborated by Dr. Edgar A. Doll who became Director of Education and Classification in 1920. Able assistance to this preliminary movement and continuing later support were given by Mr. E. R. Johnstone whose long experience in the individual classification of the mentally deficient and his acquaintance with general institutional programs were invaluable.

With this background Dr. Doll promulgated the classification program within the correctional institutions of New Jersey, elaborating the procedure and extending its scope, and winning the cooperation of the superintendents and managing boards of the state's correctional institutions. In this work he was ably assisted by William J. Ellis, who later succeeded Mr. Lewis as Commissioner of Institutions. The work was further extended through a considerable number of research studies regarding the intelligence, educational attainments, occupational skills, and the like of the populations of the several correctional institutions in the New Jersey system. Excellent liaison was effected with the medical, psychiatric, disciplinary, training, religious, and other groups involved in the procedure. Particularly adequate psychological service was established supporting an equally adequate program of field investigation. Within the space of three years the classification system was solidly established in each of the correctional institutions, and programs for the further development of institutions in terms of classification needs were under way.

Movement of personnel within the New Jersey program subsequently led to the development of other young leaders in the field. Research studies and numerous publications advertised both the feasibility of the procedure and the administrative value of its results. Effective exposition of these experiences in public and professional addresses, and particularly in the professional literature, served to extend the method to other states. Many of these states, notably New York and Massachusetts, already were employing classification programs of their own, but in the course of time the programs of different states became amalgamated in a general consolidation of procedures largely patterned after the New Jersey plan.

Special credit is due to the American Prison Association for the readiness with which its membership received and extended the classification idea. The enthusiastic support of Edward R. Cass, Secretary of the Association, was an important factor, and the energetic persistence of Dr. V. C. Branham, for several years Secretary of the Association's Committee on Casework, finally won wide-spread action. Special credit is also due Dr. F. Lovell Bixby who succeeded Dr. Branham as Chairman of the Committee on Casework, and to the various members of that committee, for the earnest and competent way in which what easily might have been a fad became a genuinely successful method. It was largely through Dr. Bixby's efforts, with the effective support of Sanford Bates, then Commissioner of Federal Prisons, that classification became well established in the federal system. The success with which classification was found to "work" in federal prisons and reformatories has removed the remaining doubt as to the practicability and value of this plan.

The system for the individual classification of offenders has been most fortunate in winning to its support able leaders in the field of correction in this country. The obvious merits of the plan have always been a factor in its success, coordinating as they do all agencies for the welfare of the offender. But even more important is the effectiveness of the plan in simplifying institutional administration and increasing its effectiveness. Yet the real promise of classification is its economy and efficiency from the point of view of the public in protecting society and at the same time caring for offenders in a more constructive manner than has ever been done in the entire history of penology.

The future of classification continues promising. The literature has already moved into younger hands with the earlier workers giving generous aid and comfort. Scientific classification of offenders is indeed a product of the vision and imagination of recent leaders in penology. It affords the means of continuing modern progress in the correctional field at a high level and in the right direc-

tion. It is in accord with the declaration of principles of the American Prison Association written in 1870 and subserves all four of the major objectives of that Association. Although devoted principally to the study of the individual offender and the improvement of means for dealing with him, it is obvious that the results in the direction of prevention of crime and the treatment of the offender are best served in this way. Systematic study of the individual offender must continue to be the principal clue to the causes of crime, the improvement of laws, the improvement of treatment, and the ultimate success of correctional rehabilitation.

EDGAR A. DOLL,
Director of Research,
The Training School,
Vineland, New Jersey.

BIBLIOGRAPHY

Bixby, F. Lovell, Classification Technique, *Proceedings,* American Prison Association, 1936.
Doll, Edgar A., Principles and Methods of Individualized Penal Treatment, *Proceedings,* American Prison Association, 1935.
Doll, Edgar A., Handbook of Casework and Classification Methods for Offenders, *Report of Committee on Casework (V. C. Branham, Chairman),* American Prison Association, 1934.
Ellis, William J., Practical Results of the Classification Program, *Journal of Criminal Law and Criminology,* May-June 1941.
Yepsen, Lloyd, Classification—The Basis for Modern Treatment of Offenders, *Prison World,* May-June 1940.

COERCION. Coercion is the application to another of such force, either physical or moral, as to induce or constrain him to do against his will something he would not otherwise have done. A person coerced by another to perform an act is not legally liable for the act performed.

Coercion is, however, one of the elements in the orthodox definition of law and the method of coercion is threat or application of punishment. A law which does not provide a penalty that will cause suffering is regarded as quite impotent and in fact no law at all. The *coercion of the law* differs from that of the lynching mob in that it is applied decently by representatives of the state in such manner that it may win the approval of the cool judgment of impartial observers (Sutherland).

Certain types of coercion constitute violations of the law and are specifically prohibited by statute or common law. Thus, under the provisions of the Penal Law of New York State, coercing another person is a misdemeanor. A person who with a view to compel another person to do or to abstain from doing an act which such other person has a legal right to do or to abstain from doing, wrongfully and unlawfully,

1. Uses violence or inflicts injury upon such other person or his family, or a member thereof, or upon his property or threatens such violence or injury; or,

2. Deprives any such person of any tool, implement or clothing or hinders him in the use thereof; or,

3. Uses or attempts the intimidation of such person by threats or force,
Is guilty of a misdemeanor.

Coercion of an employee by employers to compel the employee to enter into a written or verbal agreement not to become a member of any labor organization, as a condition of such employee or person securing employment, or continuing to be employed by the employers, is a misdemeanor, the penalty for which is imprisonment in a penal institution for not more than six months, or a fine of not more than two hundred dollars, or both.

A person who by force, menace or duress, compels a woman against her will to marry him, or to marry any other person, or to be defiled, is punishable by imprisonment for a term not exceeding ten years, or by a fine of not more than one thousand dollars, or by both. No conviction can, however, be had for compulsory marriage upon the testimony of the female compelled, unsupported by other evidence.

BIBLIOGRAPHY

Gilbert, F. B., *Criminal Law and Practice of the State of New York,* Matthew Bender and Co., 1935.
Sutherland, E. H., *Principles of Criminology,* J. B. Lippincott Company, 1939.

COLONIAL CRIME. Any description of colonial crime must be etched against the background of the history of the New World and England's imperial policies. In the sixteenth and seventeenth centuries, England was embarked on a mercantilistic policy, whose express aim was to export as much as possible, in return for which England was to accumulate as much gold and silver as possible.

It was in line with the mercantilistic conception to encourage the transportation of criminals and incorrigibles to America. As Charles M. Andrews states, "The criminal, the incorrigible and the hopelessly indolent they would ship off to America, in vague expectation that another country would transform these people into useful laborers and artisans and make them profitable members of society."

In England, instead of the galleys, it was deemed advisable to find a substitute. Hence in 1597, the first law authorizing transportation of criminals to America was passed. An order of the Privy Council in 1617 extended the amount of transportation, and confirmed it as a policy of England.

Naturally, the American colonies resented the fact that their territory constituted a dumping ground for England's criminals and "ne'er do wells." As Harry E. Barnes remarks, "As early as 1670, Virginia passed an act prohibiting the importation of criminals, and as a result of the vigorous agitation by the colonists, Great Britain confirmed the act and extended it for a brief period to other colonies. In 1717, however, it authorized the transportation of convicts for seven years and in cases where the penalty for the crime was death, for fourteen years."

Charles M. Andrews, one of the leading authorities on the colonial period, believes that the act of 1717 was intended both to rid England of its criminals and to benefit the colonies by an increase in their supply of labor. Harry E. Barnes, however, properly advises that, "At the outset, the movement for transportation appears to have been motivated by the desire to rid England of criminals, including political prisoners, paupers, and common felons, rather than to provide the colonies with manpower, one of its later functions."

By 1775, however, England's policy of transportation did provide a sorely-needed supply of labor for the colonies since about 2000 colonists annually were arriving in America, mostly as indentured servants. Barnes states that conservative estimates place the number of criminals transported to America at about 50,000 with Maryland receiving about 20,000. Naturally, the advent of the Revolution put a stop to this practice.

Against this background of England's policy of transportation of criminals in line with her mercantilistic policies, we must sketch our picture of colonial crime.

Let us first look at the methods of punishment of offenders. The colonial codes of punishment were based largely upon England's penal code, which was characterized by a free employment of capital punishment for offenses that today are considered minor in nature. As Dr. Lewis remarks, "Even at the close of the eighteenth century, the English penal code still retained the death penalty for 160 offenses. And the policy of England had been to superimpose upon the Colonies her own methods of punishment." The colonies, following the example of England, originally punished offenders with mutilation, branding, ear-cropping and the like.

Unoffending women, usually elderly and perhaps suffering from senile dementia, accused of witchcraft, were hung in many colonies. The colonists followed the Old World in believing in the power of so-called witches, who were regarded as being in league with the devil. Lest we blush at the superstitions and follies of our colonial ancestors, we must not forget the Spanish Inquisition of the 15th and 16th centuries, or the fact that witches were hung all over Europe during the colonial period. Nevertheless, we cannot condone this barbarous practice.

A famous example of the witchcraft craze in the colonies occurred in Salem in 1692. Mr. V. F. Calverton remarks in his "The Awakening of America" about the Salem tragedy that the colonists "believed that witches could change the course of things, exercise and exorcise curses, create calamities, cause death. This belief was not confined to the ignorant, it was shared also by the intellectuals of the day. The leading preachers, physicians, judges and writers believed in witchcraft. It was an accepted, undisputed phenomenon. Sir Thomas Browne, Boyle, Cranmer, More, never doubted for a moment that witchcraft existed and influenced the affairs of men. It was natural, therefore, that the American settlers should believe the same thing."

The witchcraft craze must also be judged in the light of the limited knowledge of disease that people possessed in those days. Since they didn't have a scientific explanation for disease, "it was not unnatural for them to blame illness upon individuals instead of upon germs, bacteria and microbes."

While awaiting punishment, the so-called witches and others accused of crime remained in the county jail. The county jail was a grim structure, bleak, barren and bare and was an importation from England. Every colony had its county jails.

However, through the growing realization of the enlightened and more public-spirited members of the community that barbarous punishments didn't lessen crime or solve the problems of crime, steps were taken in individual states to put the punishment of criminals on a more humanitarian basis.

An interesting example of reform in the methods of punishing criminals is provided by Pennsylvania. In the Great Charter drawn up by Penn, an interesting feature was the fact that capital punishment for all crimes except homicide was abolished. Penn's Great Charter was a striking example of humanitarianism, especially when we compare it with the harsh system of punishments in force in England at the time. Penn abolished tortures and bloody punishments, and he believed in the idea of reforming criminals through labor, since he had visited the workhouses of Holland and was deeply impressed by their industrial features.

The progress exhibited by Pennsylvania stands out clearly when compared with the criminal laws in force in Rhode Island. As Andrews remarks, "Rhode Island criminal laws were modeled after the English statute book. . . . In Rhode Island, the death penalty was imposed for high and petty treason, murder, manslaughter, robbery, burglary, arson, witchcraft, and unnatural sexual practices."

Let us look also at the methods of treating criminals in some of the other colonies to get a better picture of colonial crime. Connecticut is another example of the harsh treatment of criminals. For the most part, the criminals came from the ranks of the apprentices and servants transported from England.

We do not wish to imply that all the men transported to America as indentured servants were criminals. The large majority of them proved to be honest, law-abiding decent men and women, who proved to be a great asset for America. The great majority of the inhabitants of the various colonies were also honest, energetic, and law-abiding. Of the small percentage of colonists who were criminals, the major portion, nonetheless, came from the indentured servant class. Andrews points out that "As was the case in other colonies, most of those hanged for wanton dalliance, fornication, lying, drunkenness, blasphemy, robbery and breaking the laws of the colony were apprentices and servants, of whom there were many in Connecticut as elsewhere bound to labor for a term of years. But some of these delinquents were clearly of the better classes, good men, ministers, and esquires. Among them were those charged with contemptuous words and insolent carriage toward court and commonwealth, threatening and malicious speeches, defiance of authority and laws, and the slighting of court orders. Some twenty or more cases of witchcraft or familiarity with the Devil are recorded for Connecticut and New Haven before 1663, with at least ten hangings."

Equally harsh was the State of Delaware in punishing what it regarded as criminals. As V. F. Calverton remarks in his "The Awakening of America," in regard to Delaware, "Throughout the Counties any persons guilty of sodomy, buggery, rape or robbery were put to death. In the case of Negro slaves, the death penalty was meted out with ruthless expedition, and the owner was refunded by the county treasury two-thirds of the value of the slave executed. Negroes convicted of rape were pilloried, their ears being nailed back to the structure and then cropped off close to the head. Negro slaves—not white slaves or white freemen—who were condemned to death for theft could be spared the penalty, "in Mercy to the said owners," if the latter would inflict such corporal punishment upon the culprits "as may be requisite for a Terror to others of their colour." For lesser crimes, black slaves were led to a bridge "with their arms extended and tied to a pole across their necks, a cart going before them," and for three successive days were harshly whipped as they passed, and afterwards were put in irons and confined to prison. For blasphemy, whites as well as blacks were pilloried for two hours, branded with the letter B, and given thirty-nine lashes before the eyes of neighbors and friends."

Georgia was also very harsh in its treatment of culprits, even for minor offenses. Slaves especially were severely punished for any type of offense. As in Georgia, offenders among the Plymouth colonists in Massachusetts were harshly punished, but especially harsh punishments were meted out to those guilty of moral offenses. Adultery was severely punished and considered a crime of the first magnitude, in contrast to our modern standards.

As V. F. Calverton remarks in reference to the Plymouth Colony, "Woman was viewed not only as a more evil creature than men, but also as definitely inferior in economic, social and psychological status. It was a despotic, patriarchal ethic which the New Englander transported from the old to the new country." Hence, women were more harshly treated than men for similar offenses. "In the case of bastardy, the man had only to appear before the parish church and admit his guilt, whereas the woman involved was often subjected to a public lashing."

Finally, we have to examine the methods of punishment used by the Indians. While the common conception prevalent at all times was that the Indian was fierce, cruel and treacherous, he was in some respects more gentle than the colonists. For instance, V. F. Calverton points out that "The absence of prisons among the tribes stands out in sharp contrast to the prisons built by the settlers. Punishments were meted out by the nearest kin with great expedition and effectiveness."

The colonists imitated the English in establishing a county jail, which was later replaced by the prisons of the modern day. In general, the colonists had their share of crime but the amount was relatively small since the energies of the colonists were directed towards the end of creating a civilization out of the wilderness that was then America. Capital offenses were relatively small in amount.

We can consider the colonists on the whole as law-abiding, decent citizens, subject of course to the usual human frailties, weaknesses and passions of homo sapiens. There were bright rays of sunshine on the colonial horizon, such as Penn's Great Charter, which was a noble humanitarian gesture; there were also dark flecks on the colonial escutcheon, such as the witchcraft craze, the harsh treatment of criminals, especially of women offenders, and the treatment of crime among the indentured servants.

But, nevertheless, when we examine colonial crime against the background of the political, social and economic conditions prevalent at that time, especially in Europe, we can rest assured that the colonists were struggling in their own heavy, clumsy way to a more humanitarian conception of the nature of crime and how to punish crime.

In conclusion, may we state that the present day study of criminology, especially in its historical aspects, would be greatly enriched by a more extensive knowledge of colonial crime.

HARRIS PROSCHANSKY,
Research Historian,
New York, New York.

BIBLIOGRAPHY

Andrews, Charles M., *The Colonial Period of American History,* Vol. I–IV, Yale University Press, 1938.
Encylopaedia of the Social Sciences, Articles on Transportation of Criminals, Criminology, Punishment, Humanitarianism, 1935.
Lewis, Dr. Orlando F., *The Development of American Prisons and Prison Customs, 1776–1845,* 1922.
Calverton, Victor F., *The Awakening of America,* John Day Company, 1939.

COMPOUNDING CRIME. The voluntary concealment or compounding of a crime, or the willful withholding of evidence concerning it, as well as the purposeful failure to prosecute or deliberate delaying of the prosecution of a crime, in return for money or other reward, actual or promised, are all considered as violations of the law in most jurisdictions. The Penal Law of New York State, for example, provides that a person who accepts money or other reward, or a promise thereof, to compound or conceal a crime or legal violation, or to abstain from, discontinue, or delay, a prosecution therefor, or to withhold any evidence thereof, except in a case where a compromise is allowed by law, is guilty: (1) of a felony, punishable by imprisonment in a state prison for not more than five years, where the agreement or understanding relates to a felony punishable by death or life imprisonment; (2) of a felony, punishable by imprisonment in a state prison for not more than three years, where the understanding or agreement relates to another felony; (3) of a misdemeanor, punishable by imprisonment in a county jail for not more than one year, or by fine of not more than two hundred and fifty dollars, or both, where the agreement or understanding relates to a misdemeanor, or a minor statutory violation.

Thus, compounding a felony constitutes a crime in itself. It is not compounding of a felony for the holder of a forged paper to accept payment of the same and surrender it up, although he knows it to be forged, no proceedings having been taken against the forger. In general, upon the trial of an indictment for compounding a crime, it is not necessary to prove that any person has been convicted of the crime or violation, in relation to which an agreement or understanding prohibited was made.

BIBLIOGRAPHY

Gilbert, F. B., *Criminal Law and Practice of the State of New York,* M. Bender and Co., 1935.

CONSPIRACY. A conspiracy is any agreement, manifesting itself in words or deeds, by which two or more persons confederate to commit an unlawful deed, or to use unlawful means to do a lawful act.

In New York State, the Penal Law specifies exactly what types of conspiracy are punishable. Thus, if two or more persons conspire:

1. To commit a crime; or,

2. Falsely and maliciously to indict another for a crime, or to procure another to be complained of or arrested for a crime; or,

3. Falsely to institute or maintain an action or special proceeding; or,

4. To cheat and defraud another out of property, by any means which are in themselves criminal, or which, if executed, would amount to a cheat, or to obtain money or any other property by false pretenses; or,

5. To prevent another from exercising a lawful trade or calling, or doing any other lawful act; or,

6. To commit any act injurious to the public health, to public morals, or to trade or commerce, or for the perversion or obstruction of justice, or of the due administration of the laws,

Each of them is guilty of a misdemeanor.

Conspiracy Against the Peace of the State. If two or more persons, being out of the state, conspire to commit any act against the peace of the state, the commission or attempted commission of which, within this state, would be treason against the state, they are punishable by imprisonment in a state prison not exceeding ten years.

Punishable Conspiracies. No conspiracy is punishable criminally unless it is one of those enumerated above. The orderly and peaceable assembling or cooperation of persons employed in any calling or trade for the purpose of obtaining an advance in the rate of wages or compensation, or of maintaining such rate, is *not* a conspiracy. Associations, corporate or otherwise, of farmers, gardeners or dairymen, engaged in making collective sales or marketing for its members or shareholders, are not conspiracies, nor are contracts or agreements made by such associations or their members in making collective sales.

No agreement except to commit a felony upon the person of another, or to commit arson or burglary, amounts to a conspiracy, unless some act beside such agreement be done to effect the object thereof, by one or more of the parties to such agreement.

BIBLIOGRAPHY

Gilbert, F. B., *Criminal Law and Practice of the State of New York,* Matthew Bender and Co., 1935.

CONTEMPT OF COURT. Contempt of court is the willful disobedience to, or open disrespect of, the valid rules, orders, or process, or the dignity and authority of a court of justice, whether by disorderly, contemptuous, or insolent language or behavior, or other disturbing conduct, in presence of a court, or by mere failure to obey its orders. Contempt may also be an offense against a legislative body. The power of punishing for contempt is incident to all superior courts. Inferior courts are usually restricted to the punishment of contempts done in the presence of the court.

Under the Penal Law of New York State, for example, contempt of court of any of the following kinds, is a misdemeanor:

1. Disorderly, contemptuous, or insolent behavior, committed during the sitting of the court and directly tending to interrupt its proceedings or to impair the respect due to its authority;

2. Behavior of like character, committed in the presence of a referee, while actually engaged in a trial or hearing, pursuant to the order of the court, or in the presence of a jury, while actually sitting for the trial of a cause, or upon an inquest or other proceeding authorized by law;

3. Breach of the peace, noise, or other disturbance, directly tending to interrupt the proceedings of a court, jury, or referee;

4. Willful disobedience to the lawful process or other mandate of a court except in cases involving or growing out of labor disputes;

5. Resistance willfully offered to its lawful process or other mandate except in cases involving or growing out of labor disputes;

6. Contumacious and unlawful refusal to be sworn as a witness, or, after being sworn, to answer any legal and proper question;

7. Publication of a false or grossly inaccurate report of its proceedings.

A criminal act is not the less punishable as a crime, because it is also declared to be punishable as a contempt of court.

BIBLIOGRAPHY

Gilbert, F. B., *Criminal Law and Practice of the State of New York,* Matthew Bender and Co., 1935.

CONTROL OF DELINQUENCY AND CRIME.

Many vocal but uninformed individuals have supposed that institutionalization in state schools is the most effective method of dealing with juvenile delinquents and potential criminals. But, as has been pointed out, there is little logic in expecting the state to be successful in preventing or correcting antisocial behavior in instances where the family, the school, and other community organizations have previously been unsuccessful. This seems especially true when it is realized that public correctional institutions actually provide, for any given inmate, an essentially delinquent or criminal culture. Many studies have demonstrated the limited value of institutions, as well as of parole and probation, as agencies for the correction of delinquent behavior. This is probably because all of these efforts at reform have been made on the assumption that the individual can be understood and revamped apart from the social setting or culture in which he must make his adjustments. That this is an impossible outcome, based on wishful thinking, has been amply demonstrated.

Institutionalization. There is an adage which states that criminals come out of prison worse morally than when they went in. That this is true, or at least that many continue in careers of delinquency or crime, is borne out by the facts. Shaw and McKay, for example, found in a study of boys confined in Cook County (Illinois) correctional institutions that 82.6 per cent of one group and 69.2 per cent of another had subsequently continued their criminal activities. Similar figures have been reported for men five to ten years after being released from state prisons and reformatories. Incarceration in penal institutions is evidently not an effective method in the treatment of either young or confirmed criminals, especially in instances

where hundreds of them are forced into close and intimate contact.

Parole and Probation. The case for parole and probation appears to be equally inadequate. Glueck's study of criminals showed that approximately four-fifths of a group of 500 offenders had recommitted crimes upon being released. Other data paint a similar picture in the case of young delinquents. One pair of investigators found that of those who had been in court once ten to twenty years before, 52.0 per cent now had adult crime records; of those who had been in court twice, 66.2 per cent had such a record; for those who had been apprehended three times the percentage was 73.5; and for four times (or more) offenders, 89.7 per cent. In instances where probation has shown a high percentage of successes, it is believed that the parolees were for the most part mild offenders, non-recidivists, and "accidental" offenders. Apparently, little improvement can be anticipated from parole or probation as long as the individual is returned either to a community in which former delinquency-producing situations remain unchanged or to a conflicting culture in which he is unable to find status, companionship, recognition, and other essential personal satisfactions.

It should be clear that the usual procedure in granting parole is psychologically unsound. It is customary to make a decision on the basis of a so-called case report or "social picture" of the offender. Such a statement may include much concerning the individual's home background, economic status, vocational experience, former friendships, and the like, but it provides *no diagnosis of the individual's personality organization or state of mental health.* A sociological survey of the criminal or delinquent may provide a picture of his external symptoms and mechanisms but it does not explain the behavior deviations noted and their probable functions as auto-corrective adjustment processes. There is usually little in the case report that indicates *why the offender has turned to crime for his ego satisfactions* or how the perpetration of criminal acts is enabling him to avert threats to his psychological integrity.

Guidance Clinics. Even institutes for juvenile research and readjustment have been relatively ineffective in the treatment of delinquency. This is probably because they, too, endeavor to work with the offender apart from his social setting and the many forces which daily either thwart or satisfy his fundamental psychological needs (status, feeling of adequacy, etc.). The roots of crime are inseparably intertwined with conflicts in the home and with frustrations or repressions leading to resentment and a variety of emotional stresses conducive to antisocial behavior. A guidance clinic is not in a position to control many of these factors and cannot, thus, be expected to be successful in regulating the offender's conduct. It is therefore not surprising that a follow-up investigation of juvenile delinquents who had been examined by the Institute for Juvenile Research (Chicago), showed that 70.2 per cent continued to pursue criminal careers. The same may be said for the finding reported by the Gluecks, that 88.2 per cent of 1000 Boston juvenile delinquents, studied by the Judge Baker Foundation Child Guidance Clinic, showed no improvement in behavior five years after such examination and assistance. Guidance clinics have been able to bring about improvement in many children and youths suffering from severe personal maladjustments and psychoneurotic conditions, but there is not a great deal of a permanent nature that they can do for the rank and file of relatively normal delinquents whose living conditions are not under their (the clinic's) control.

Proposals for the control of delinquency and subsequent crime have recently come to be based upon psychological as well as sociological principles and findings. They tend, thus, to be more in harmony than formerly with the findings of analyses of the psychodynamics of behavior. Concrete suggestions usually take the form of (1) a program of community action and (2) the psychological diagnosis of individual delinquents.

A Program of Community Action. Since delinquency and crime, like other forms of behavior, are apparently outcomes of human associations and group living as these affect the attitudes and personal morale of individuals, it is evident that the successful prevention of such behavior must be sought in programs of adequate community action. The rehabilitation of delinquents and criminals can be anticipated only to the extent that they become assimilated into cultural groups which make possible the fulfillment of dynamic psychological needs and in which socially acceptable standards of behavior prevail. It is essential to eliminate from a community frustrations to normal and acceptable social expression, quasi-criminal groups who provide conflicting values, and other influences which stimulate criminal careers. It is for these reasons that modern criminologists advocate area projects or neighborhood action plans in which local residents pool their resources in an effort to provide satisfactory physical equipment, make available adequate recreational facilities for children and youth, cooperate with the programs of community schools, and bring about improved methods of handling children.

There is increasing realization that the local community is the fundamental unit in the control of antisocial behavior and that the responsibility for formulating positive programs designed to promote respect for law and order should rest with its citizens. It is apparently essential that all responsible members of a community cooperate with their energies, interests, special abilities, and common purposes in providing conditions necessary to the provision of security, status, recreation, education, and physical well-being for each child and youth. It is to these ends that local schools, churches, courts, service clubs, social agencies, civic bodies, youth organizations, business groups, and other neighborhood institutions must coordinate their efforts in providing new facilities where needed and in attacking, in a concerted fashion, all conditions known to be conducive to delinquency and to stresses of insecurity in general.

As an example of efforts to carry out such a coordinated series of community activities may be mentioned recent developments in the city of Los Angeles, where a Youth Activities Committee and a similar division in the District Attorney's office have been set up. A sociological report, designed to provide a basis for more specific recommendations as the work proceeds, indicates that the attack on delinquency and crime is to be made from the following four directions:

1. *The Strengthening of Community Home Life.* The incidence of broken homes, excessive family conflicts, lack of economic security, physical and mental abnormality, cultural differentiation, moral laxity, and lack of parental supervision is to be ascertained and dealt with in every way possible. Every effort will also be made to educate parents, to place responsibility on them for the conduct of their children, and to make certain that young children are not neglected because of employment outside of the home.

2. *The Development of Citizenship Through Organized Recreation, Religious Instruction, and Education.* In view of the fact that delinquency rates are known to be highest in areas where there is a minimum of supervised recreation and playground facilities, it is proposed to provide (a) adequate youth leadership, (b) expanded public and school playgrounds the year around, (c) special facilities for coping with the "drifter girl" problem, (d) leisure hour recreation for working youths, and (e) more opportunity on the part of youths for experience in self-government.

3. *The Control of Community Conditions.* The community is expected to cope with slum conditions, destructive gangs, and undesirable commercial amusements, as well as to deal intelligently with excessive mobility, minority groups, cultural conflicts, child labor problems, and maladjusted individuals. Singled out for special attention are inter-social problems, the improvement of living conditions, and deleterious commercialized amusements.

4. *Law Observance and Enforcement.* Because of widespread contempt on the part of juveniles for law and law enforcement officers, it is proposed to enlist strong public support for equitable but firm treatment of offenders who endanger the safety and morals of others. The program is not designed merely to frighten youths, but to control them through the agency of Junior Auxiliary Police and Delinquency Prevention programs designed to reach into local areas with a view

to providing wholesome activities where these do not at present exist.

The Psychological Diagnosis of Individual Delinquents. It should be apparent that careful study needs to be made of individuals who for one reason or another have already developed antisocial tendencies. As community conditions exist today, many children and youths will encounter sufficient frustrations, rejections, and criminal patterns to lead them to become delinquent in either the moral or legal (or both) sense of that term. Such young people need careful diagnosis and a modification of the conditions which have brought about their maladjustment, be it an internal conflict or one with the sanctions of society. The former notion that only cases of an emotionally or mentally pathological (psychoneurotic or psychotic) nature required study and disposition has given way to the realization that since delinquents and criminals are for the most part relatively normal individuals struggling with problems of an emotional nature, they, too, are in need of psychological help.

However, the individual help described here is not the type to which criminologists and sociologists have been objecting as being relatively futile. The latter scientists have reference to institutionalization, parole, probation, and the type of clinical or case study in which a great deal of background material concerning the offender is gathered, but in which he is ultimately studied apart from the social forces and inter-personal stresses which brought about, not only his delinquency status, but also his *personal maladjustment.* It is not always recognized that delinquent and criminal behavior are apparently often but auto-corrective mechanisms by means of which the individual maintains his sense of personal worth and competence.

It seems essential thus that the delinquent be dealt with either as an individual who has encountered conflicting cultures and is, as a result, more or less confused morally, or as an emotionally maladjusted person who is in need of a thorough psychological or clinical analysis *in relation to all of the home and community factors which have constituted his syndrome of experience and which have led to the internal stresses from which he is*

seeking relief through antisocial behavior.
As society leaves behind the unscientific age
of coercion, condemnation, and condonement
in which antisocial individuals were regarded
as being constitutionally inferior or as being
the victims of "weak wills," it is coming to
realize that deviate behavior serves the individual in some satisfying way in relation to
his need for self-esteem that is not always
apparent on the surface.

Therapy in the delinquency field often involves enabling the individual to gain insight
into his mechanisms and the factors which
apparently brought about their appearance.
Its objective is that of leading the antisocial
or otherwise maladjusted person to secure
his satisfactions and fulfil his dynamic needs
through socially acceptable channels. The
delinquent has been prevented from realizing
the advantages of the socialized or mutual
way of behaving. The goal is to provide him
with a social environment in which the
absence of conflicting cultures or defeating
ego-frustrations, together with the presence
of constructive conditions and agencies,
makes lawful behavior more or less spontaneous. It can thus be concluded that *overt
aggressive or defiant behavior is one form of
adjustment to the frustration of fundamental
needs*, and that home and community conditions which may appear to an observer to be
adequate for the satisfaction of these needs
frequently are so thwarting as actually to
result in the development of antisocial tendencies.

LOUIS P. THORPE,
Professor of Education and Psychology,
University of Southern California,
Los Angeles, California.

BIBLIOGRAPHY

Burgess, E. W., et al., *Environment and Edu-
cation,* Chicago, University of Chicago
Press, 1942.
Freeman, Max J., Changing Concepts of
Crime, *Journal of Criminal Psychopathology,*
4, 290–305, 1942.
Glueck, S., *500 Criminal Careers,* New York,
Alfred A. Knopf, 1930.
Glueck, S., and Glueck, E., *One Thousand
Juvenile Delinquents,* Cambridge, Harvard
University Press, 1934.
Neumeyer, Martin H., Preliminary Report to
the Executive Committee of the Los An-
geles Youth Activities Committee, *Unpub-
lished Manuscript,* 1943.
Shaw, Clifford R., and McKay, Henry D.,
Juvenile Delinquency and Urban Areas,
Chicago, University of Chicago Press, 1942.
Schwebel, G. A., Reymert, M. L., et al., *Re-
port of the Coordination Committee,* De-
partment of Public Welfare, State of Illi-
nois, 1943.

CONVICTION. Conviction is the act of
proving, finding, or determining an individual
or number of individuals to be guilty of an
offense. Specifically, it is the act of finding
or the state of being found guilty of a crime
before any legal tribunal, such as a jury. Any
punishments prescribed by law can be inflicted only upon a legal conviction of the
defendant in a court having jurisdiction.

In most states, like New York, a prisoner,
upon the trial of an indictment, may be convicted of the crime charged therein, or of a
lesser degree of the same crime, or of *an
attempt to commit* the crime so charged, or
of an attempt to commit a lesser degree of
the same crime.

The manner of prosecuting and convicting
criminals is regulated by the codes of criminal procedure of the various jurisdictions.
No conviction can be had for *abduction* or
compulsory marriage, upon the testimony of
the female abducted or compelled, unsupported by other evidence. Similarly, a conviction for *adultery* cannot be had on the
uncorroborated testimony of the person with
whom the offense is charged to have been
committed. No conviction for *rape* can be
had against anyone who was under the age
of fourteen years, at the time of the alleged
act, unless his physical ability to accomplish
penetration is proved as an independent fact;
beyond a reasonable doubt.

BIBLIOGRAPHY

Gilbert, F. B., *Criminal Law and Practice of
the State of New York,* Matthew Bender
and Co., 1935.

COURT CLINICS. After the World War
of 1914–1918, it was obvious that legal institutions in themselves did not have the ability
to solve the problem of crime. The ordinary
policeman and judge of that day acted in a

mechanical fashion, picking up the offenders as fast as they could be detected and by due process of grand jury investigation, arraignment and the other legal steps, trying them and, if found guilty, sentencing them either to probation or to a corrective institution.

Probation was seldom used, but in the early twenties probation departments were established in the courts with the idea of studying the offender as much as possible so that a reasonable sentence could be given to him in order to make him law-abiding rather than merely to take out the vengeance of society against him. It was realized that if the policy of *lex talonis* were to be carried out and legal sentences were purely to be a matter of the expression of society's hostility against one who failed to conform, then crime probably would, as it had in the past, increase and that increase would be even more rapid in cities because of the rapidly developing anonymity of the city dweller.

Juvenile courts in Chicago and elsewhere had already established laboratories for the study of juvenile offenders and in the Chicago Municipal Court, such a laboratory was set up in 1919. The Institute for Juvenile Research was established in the same year which undertook the scientific study of problem children, of offenders in corrective institutions and took over Dr. William Healy's laboratory in the Cook County Juvenile Court, all to be under the authority of the State Criminologist.

It was early found that a probation investigation and treatment consisting simply of reporting to a probation office were not the solution of the problems of crime. The first type of cases which were obviously not readily solved by simple probation were those of the insane and the psychopathic personalities. Laws were provided in some states for the hospitalization of the criminal insane because they were felt not to be sufficiently responsible to be able to stand trial. The public beheld the dubious spectacle of psychiatrists apparently testifying on either side of a murder case, for it did not believe there could be two honest viewpoints to such trials. But, of course, the reason for contention lies in the fact that the prosecution strictly defines insanity in the law while the defense brings in expert medical testimony to explain or even justify the offense upon the grounds of complete medical and psychiatric evaluation transcending pure verbal criteria of mental health or illness.

The first clinic was the Municipal Court Laboratory in Chicago and in 1921 the Psychopathic Clinic of the Recorder's Court in Detroit was established. At first these clinics were found to be useful in evaluating the insane. The insane were brought out of the welter of court cases and current laws were invoked to hospitalize them. In many instances they were hospitalized by means of the Clinics and were not brought to trail. In other instances the judges requested interpretation of the offenders who exhibited bizarre behavior and who might be insane.

Out of this rather elementary application of psychiatry came the development of a broad psychiatric viewpoint. This broad viewpoint developed parallel to the use of psychiatry in child guidance and prisons after 1920 and to a lesser extent in the Armed Services during the war of 1914–1918.

Psychiatry in the 30's, particularly in those communities where there was a court Clinic, was called in to explain and interpret why the offender got into trouble and to suggest treatment for him. Prior to this time the Supreme Bench of Baltimore had acquired a psychiatrist. The Municipal Court of Philadelphia added psychiatric services to its Clinic, which is primarily a medical Clinic, but after 1930, clinics were set up or strongly supported in Cleveland, New York, and Pittsburgh, and a second clinic was set up in Chicago in the Criminal Courts. Since that time consulting psychiatrists have been brought into many courts, which do not have a formal clinic. For instance, the penal services in Illinois and Michigan will send out a psychiatrist to advise a judge in any case where he wishes an examination.

Court Clinics have developed in two ways: one, in which the clinic has its own social workers to take case histories and to investigate the past of the offenders, and the second is when the Clinic utilizes the probation department as historians and as therapists. In both types of clinics, a thorough history is taken, appropriate psychological tests are given to the offender, with particular reference to his intelligence, and a physical examination and a psychiatric examination are made. Usually these clinics have a meeting in which the whole staff discuss the cases when a diagnosis is made and, finally a report is sent to the referring judge, informing him as to the probable reason why the offender has committed the offense, the appropriate treatment if any is necessary, and the probable outcome of the case if the treatment procedures recommended are carried out. The majority of the cases coming through these clinics are classed as psychopathic personalities. The hospitalization of insane eliminates some of the contention which was so offensive in the early decades of the century, and, in the case of misdemeanors, the mentally sick are hospitalized or otherwise given psychiatric treatment, after the court proceedings are quashed. Medical treatment is advised where it has a bearing on the case and penal treatment where it is available exists in all degrees from a lecture from the bench, or supervision with reporting (probation) or even a suspended sentence to the most drastic form of incarceration where the patient is permanently segregated in the penal institution because no known therapy will make him into a law-abiding citizen.

The general policy of these clinics is to make an investigation for the judge that he would make himself if he had been especially trained in medicine, psychology, psychiatry, and education, and if he had the time to make a thorough study before sentence. Such a study, taking usually a minimum of four hours, suggests means of treatment to the judge about which in the past he might have had no conception whatsoever, but which at the present time he usually utilizes to make the administration of justice more of a therapeutic procedure than an act of public vengeance.

LOWELL S. SELLING, M. D.

Formerly Director,

Psychopathic Clinic,

Recorder's Court,

Detroit, Michigan.

BIBLIOGRAPHY

Alchorn, August, *Wayward Youth,* Viking Press, 1936.
Alexander, Franz and Healy, William, *The Roots of Crime,* Knopf, 1935.
Alinsky, Saul D., Philosophical Implications of the Individualistic Approach in Criminology, *Proceedings,* American Prison Association, 1937.
Selling, Lowell S., *Diagnostic Criminology,* Ann Arbor, 1935.
Wood, Arthur and Waite, John Barker, *Crime and Its Treatment,* American Book Company, 1941.

CRIME, CRIMINAL ACT. A "crime" is any act or omission forbidden by law and punishable upon conviction by: death, imprisonment, or fine, or removal from office, or disqualification to hold any office of trust, honor or profit under the state or by other penal discipline. Crimes are classified into *felonies* and *misdemeanors.* An act done with *intent* to commit a crime and tending but failing to effect its commission, is "an attempt to commit that crime." Persons who attempt to commit crime may be arrested and charged with an attempt. This carries a lesser punishment than if the crime itself has been completed.

The parties to a crime are designated either as principals or accessories. A person concerned in the commission of a crime, whether he directly commits the act constituting the offense or aids and abets in its commission, and whether present or absent, and a person who directly or indirectly counsels, commands, induces or procures another to commit a crime, is a *"principal."*

A person, who *after the commission of a felony,* harbors, conceals or aids the offender with intent that he may avoid or escape from arrest, trial, conviction or punishment, having knowledge or reasonable ground to believe that such offender is liable to arrest, has been arrested, is indicted or convicted, or has committed a felony, is an "accessory" to the felony.

There are no accessories in misdemeanor cases. A person who commits or participates in an act which would make him an accessory, if the crime committed were a felony, is a principal and may be punished as such if the crime committed is a misdemeanor.

Crimes are divided into degrees in some cases and the purpose of degrees is to regulate the amount of punishment which may be inflicted. A crime declared to be in the first degree carries more punishment than second or third degrees.

A person who takes money, property or other reward to conceal a crime or to abstain from or delay prosecution is guilty of *compounding a crime.*

Misdemeanors may be compromised civilly before a magistrate through agreement to settle costs and damages and the criminal charges may be withdrawn. Felonies cannot be so compromised.

BIBLIOGRAPHY

Sutherland, E. H., *Principles of Criminology,* J. B. Lippincott Co., 1939.
Barnes, H. E. and Teeters, N. K., *New Horizons in Criminology,* Prentice-Hall, Inc., 1943.
Gilbert, F. B., *Criminal Law and Practice of the State of New York,* Matthew Bender and Co., 1935.

CRIMINAL INTENT. Every crime consists of two elements—the criminal intent and the *criminal act.* They must concur in point of time and the act must be the result of the intent. The act without the intent is innocent; and the intent if carried into effect without the act, is only a *cheat.* The criminal intent is a condition of mind upon the part of the accused in consequence of which the criminal act was performed. *"Actus non facit reum, nisi mens sit rea."* Every crime committed does not as a consequence, contemplate the existence of a guilty mind (*"mens rea"*) for the mental elements may differ widely. In the case of murder the "mens rea" means malice aforethought; and in the case of theft, an intention to steal; in some cases, a mere inattention, etc. If the mental element of any conduct alleged to be a crime is proved to be absent in any given case, the crime so defined is not committed.

The idea is fallacious that criminal intent includes an intent to do wrong, to violate the law. A criminal intent is generally an element of crime, but every man is presumed to know the necessary and legitimate consequences of what he knowingly does.

Therefore, while criminal intent is a state of mind of the accused at the time the crime is committed and is essential to criminality in the particular case, that intent must be distinguished from the *motive* which induces him to do the act, or the belief in its propriety or wicked character. This intent varies so much in the different crimes that no precise and definite statement can be made as to what particular intent must exist in general.

The existence of a criminal intent is presumed by law from the commission of the act. Thus, in a prosecution, the state need offer no evidence to prove the existence of the intent, unless the person accused attempts to show incapacity or restraint. Of the various possible conditions recognized by law for *incapacity* or *restraint,* one is mistake. The proof of any one of these conditions successfully counteracts the presumption of criminal intent and shows that, though the act was committed, the person who did it has not perpetrated a crime.

Generally speaking, men are held criminally liable for their conduct according to the facts known to them at the time they did the alleged act or which by reasonable diligence they might have known—and if, without negligence on their part, they are mistaken in the facts, and do an act which would be a crime if done with a knowledge of the facts, they are held only according to the facts they knew. An exception to this rule is noticed in cases of those statutory crimes in which the legislature has deemed it best to require all persons to act at their peril.

Further, in general terms, mistake or ignorance of the law, is no defense to a criminal charge. This is a rule of necessity.

BIBLIOGRAPHY

Frank J., *Law and the Modern Mind,* New York, 1930.
Levitt, A., The Origin of the Doctrine of *Mens Rea, Ill. Law. Rev.,* 17:117–137, June 1922.
Levitt, A., Extent and Function of the Doctrine of *Mens Rea, Ill. Law Rev.,* 17:578–595, April 1923.

CRIMINALISTICS is a word coined by *Hans Gross* which is defined as the science of *crime detection*. It is based upon the application of psychology, physics, chemistry, physiology, and other sciences to the "running down" of criminals and is a highly complicated field calling for the collaboration of various specialists. Thus, it involves *fingerprinting*, the analysis of bloodstains, extended and technical photography, comprehensive physical measurements of criminals, *lie detectors*, the study of handwriting, *ballistics*, the use of dictaphones, the psychology of testimony, and other refined techniques.

The identification of criminals is an integral part of criminalistic science. The system of identification known as the *Bertillon system* is worked out on the assumption that an individual's physical measurements are constant after maturity is attained. Such measurements include height, span of arms, sitting height, length of head, width of right ear, length of left foot, length of left middle finger, length of left little finger, and length of left forearm. The Bertillon system also records photographs (front and profile), hair and eye color, complexion, scars, tattoo marks and any asymmetrical anomolies. The system is in many ways more effective than fingerprinting methods.

Some other fields in which scientific techniques of crime detection and investigation have been applied, are the following: *poroscopy*, the examination of sweat pores for investigation; identification of bullets, cartridges and traces of burglars' tools; metric photography and fingerprints; analysis of questioned documents; examination of blood, hair, stains, dust particles, and poisons; detection of counterfeit coins and bills; *dactyloscopy*, or identification by means of fingerprints.

Forensic ballistics is the scientific identification of bullets fired from a gun. *Moulage* is the making of plaster casts for use in identification. *Scopolamine* or *"truth serum"* is a drug which is often suggested as a lie detector but its use is unconstitutional and its scientific infallibility is not clearly established. Many other scientific techniques have been developed to aid in the apprehension of criminals and the detection of crime.

BIBLIOGRAPHY

Inbau, Fred E., *Lie Detection and Criminal Interrogation*, Williams and Wilkins, 1942.
Morrish, Reginald, *The Police and Crime Detection Today*, Oxford University Press, New York, 1940.
Perkins, R. M., *Elements of Police Science*, Foundation Press, Inc., Chicago, 1942.

CRIMINAL LAW AND PROCEDURE.

Law, generally. As with definitions of law so too with definitions of criminal law, writers have greatly struggled, and this article cannot undertake a task at which the glorious have failed or seemed to fail. One of these writers (Pollock) has indicated that no complete answer to the question, "What is law" will be possible without a complete theory of the nature of the functions of human society. But we cannot wait for such a theory. "We are born into a social and political world from which we cannot escape," he says. "We have to abide the law whether we will or no; and to abide it on the whole in obedience rather than in resistance." But in regarding this whole so described and with which we have to abide, some generalizations at least must be set down, generalizations as to what the law is, descriptive, if not successfully definitive.

We know that the law has an object—the object of providing and enforcing a pattern for uniform practices and habits of life in a society, and that this is so no matter who may be the creator, imposer, and enforcer of that law. The words 'imposer' and 'enforcer' suggest the picture: 1) The law is put upon people (sometimes by themselves, sometimes by imposers of its own choice, sometimes by its masters, sometimes through the reported revelation by the Divinity which it acknowledges); and, 2) The Tenets, mandates, dictates and demands of the law are to be enforced, which is to say that some sanction is to be inflicted, some gain, property, personal movement, delimited, or subtracted from, some intrusion into these to be carried out, if and whenever people, and, of course, each one of them, will deviate from the pattern imposed by the law. Such inflictions, delimitations, subtractions, intrusions, are called *sanctions*.

Criminal Law. The formulation that we have just made applies both to civil and to criminal law and is general enough to include the mention of the sanctions which each imposes. But the sanctions of the criminal law are so different that they become an intrinsic part of any attempted definition of what the criminal law is. Everybody has tried to define criminal law but what it really is, how it is to be recognized, seems most succinctly to be in these words, the words of Professor Jenks. "Perhaps the best answer is to say that any offense which in the opinion of the community deserve *punishment* as distinct from the mere award of compensation to the injured party should be regarded as criminal and be made the subject of the criminal law." (Italics Jenks'.) Now it is this description, for we will not call it a definition, which is to be found in the penal codes. Of these, for example only, we quote Section 2 of the Penal Law of the State of New York, which says: "A crime is an act or omission forbidden by law and punishable upon conviction by: 1) Death; or, 2) Imprisonment; or, 3) Fines; or, 4) Removal from office; or, 5) Disqualification to hold any office of trust, honor or profit under the State; or, 6) Other penal discipline. There we have the calendar of the dire consequences which an infraction of the criminal law will bring.

The Concept of Crime. Of course, this has nothing to do with where the concept of crime came from, the concept of what *is* criminal. If one were to look at a mere codification of penal laws, and mere is intentionally used, the conclusion would be forced that every crime is only evil prohibited and an evil because prohibited. But such codes are in fact drawn from, based upon, and cannot be made without thought, experience, usage, beliefs that exist in society, just as grammar cannot be made except on the basis of what language already is. So in the criminal law will be found expressions of public views and mores; epitomizations of religious, social, economic, cultural pressures and emotions of the people; taboos; thought going back to a past so far away man cannot remember it nor remembering, wholly reconstruct it; prejudices, otherwise unspoken, made articulate in an edict, weapons of defense for the society for which it has been formulated, weapons of offense against evils that threaten that society.

Now, if the provisions for punishment is the gauge of whether a law and the act it describes, are criminal, then the absence of such a provision will take a law and offense out of the criminal category. Many crimes that we know now have had different punishments in different times. Larceny was once punishable by death (imagine the death penalty for stealing a lady's handkerchief from her person); so was highway robbery. Again, many offenses that were once punishable are now no longer so and have been lifted out of the category of criminal law. Acts once wholly innocent, even now morally so, have been made punishable and have become crimes. These mirrorings of the public attitudes toward a given act or omission are eloquent proof that the dynamics of living will in the long run, and it is long, affect the concepts of crime.

Crimes that have come down to us from antiquity, crimes that we learned from the Bible and other books of religious revelation, crimes that we have learned to know from the ancient days of the English-speaking peoples, from the practices as well as codifications of the ancients, the so-called common-law crimes, are not the only ones. (The Common Law precedes our Statute Law. It is the total of maxims, doctrines, decisions, precedents, reasonings, practices comprising the legal heritage of Anglo-American law and the well-spring of our legal thinking.) Acts can be made criminal by legislation and edict. In that sense, to use the words of a contemporary writer (Seagle), the criminal law is "a list of acts against ever-rising emergencies." Criminal law is thus filled with statutes that we put there to guard against particular acts and omissions which are revealed in the processes of living, acts or omissions, the reprehensibility of which could only be revealed in the actual business of living, in the actual contact between humans. The criminal law decries them, expresses our sense of outrage over them, and imposes a punishment. Other complexities of our modern life have evoked much legislation and there are now innumerable crimes which have been so called, so designated because they are outrages to standards which we have reached dynamically because we have lived together.

Criminal law is thus a necessary attribute to government. It designates the abnormal, what should be avoided. (Sometimes what is designated as abnormal may be the normal thing done under abnormal circumstances, but in the eyes of the criminal law it is abnormal, wrong and punishable.) It reflects the social and economic status and movement of the society for which it is written. It shifts crimes in the category of their importance. It is expressive of the State's monopoly of vengeance as well as of control of the evils. To say that the State, that is to say, the Sovereignty, has an interest in such or such an act is another way of saying the State intends to mantain its control over that act no matter how private its implications are. Of course, the law contains many a fossil of folklore and even superstition.

Purposes of Punishment. If, then, the criminal law is distinguished by the fact that it imposes punishment for acts and omission, we must ask, "What is the purpose of punishment?" Of course there is, basically, the purpose of reminding the individual of the sovereignty, the power of the State, the fact that he does not live alone, the fact that the State, theoretically at least, expresses the disapproval of all of its constituents. Once upon a time the tribe did the same thing to enforce its power, but the tribe also would punish because punishment was propitiatory, an offering to heaven, an offering to divert the vengeance of the gods from the tribe itself. Some element of that is still in punishment today, some effort, conscious or unconscious, but usually conscious, of correlating the gravity of an offense with those things upon which religion frowns, with determining the gravity by the outrage to the religious, to the moral, and to the ethical standards of the community let alone the governmental desirabilities. All of this, to say that whether the offender is punished by his heaven or not, punishment is, the long and short of it, vengeance. "The desire for vengeance imports an opinion that its object is

actually and personally to blame. It takes an internal standard, not an objective or external one, and condemns its victim by that" (Holmes). True, we moderns, and the term is used without boast, have other explanations for punishment. We say that we are moving away from the idea that punishment shall be retribution; we speak of segregating the offender to where he can no longer harm society; we speak of "correcting" the offender, thus suggesting that punishment is a cure; we speak of the deterrent qualities of punishment, suggesting that punishment is a warning. We trust that these are not rationalizations. Certainly the wholehearted sincerity of thousands of students of penology, probation and prison reform, has been expended in seeking to make these explanations truthful. But we are far from perfect. Punishment is still vengeance commingled with self-protection on the part of the State, and mollified in recent years by an interest in the welfare of the punished.

Responsibility and the Mental Element in Crime. There is responsibility in crime—the responsibility of the offender, himself. It is a notion that has taken a long time to evolve. An eye for an eye, as Hammurabi would have explained it, would have meant that if X put out the eye of Y's son, Y would put out the eye of X's son. That seemed justice then. Our concept of law is different. The offender, himself, must be responsible. He must have committed the offense or made the omission and no one other than he can be punished for his act. This refers not only to the physical act or omission, to the action of the crime, but also to the question of the mental element in it. What were the intentions of the offender? Was his crime knowing? Did he act with *animus furandi*, a mind set for stealing? Did he have *mens rea*, an evil mind? Did he wilfully commit an offense? Was the purpose of his blow with intent to inflict grievous bodily harm?

This mental state of the defendant, this mental element will contribute either to exculpating the offender entirely or to alleviating the consequences of punishment, or in the reverse, to convicting him. Where, as in some jurisdictions, it must still be proved that the mind was evil, or where, as in others, it is only necessary to prove an intent to do wrong, or even only wilfulness, the mental element cannot be ignored. It is part of the act. There are, however, some crimes where lack of knowledge, intent, does not matter, as, for example, the crime of statutory rape, in which the law does not recognize the fact that the defendant did not know the girl involved was under the age of consent. But juries have been known to cure such things upon trial. (Crimes in violation of regulatory provisions [see below] rarely require intent—deviation from the rule is of itself the crime).

There are, therefore, exemptions from responsibility. He who lacks the intent, if intent is required, to commit a crime is exempt from responsibility; he who was insane so that he did not know at the time of his act, its nature and quality and that it was a crime, is exempt from responsibility; he who is too young to commit a crime is exempt from criminal responsibility though he may by his act become the subject of control in a juvenile court; he who was under compulsion or, who, like a sleepwalker or epileptic, lacked volition, would be exempt. The bulk of crimes *not* requiring intent are misdemeanors, but there are also such felonies.

Parties. Now, who are the parties to a criminal action? In the first place, there is the State, the primal and the final accuser. Sometimes the crime will hurt no one individual but will still be hurtful to the State and be so regarded. Most often a crime is directed against an individual rather than against the State as such. Although this latter may be satisfied, if he could get it, with compensation for the injury inflicted upon him, the State is not satisfied and proceeds to exact punishment. The offended against thus becomes, willingly or unwillingly, the complainant. The offender becomes the defendant.

He may be alone in his offense. What he has done is the *substantive* crime, the crime as such, the crime in itself, the crime as an entity. On the other hand, he may not be alone. He may have contrived the crime with the advice of another. He may have

been incited to it. He may have been aided in it. He may have, to use an old word, abetted in it. He may have divided its execution with another. He may have done it for the benefit of another. He may have whispered silently in secret places planning its execution. In each of these cases he will not be, alone, the defendant. His advisors, inciters, aiders, co-planners will have a responsibility with him. In some jurisdictions the responsibility is known as that of an accessory either before the crime is committed or afterwards; in other jurisdictions, wiser in their methods, the responsibility is as of the principal offender himself.

Crimes in Aid of Crime. Not only is the substantive crime to be complained of and to be punished, but even the planning together to commit the crime, the conspiracy, the nefarious scheme is a crime, an adjective crime, a crime in preparation for and defining the activity and scope of the substantive crime. Kenny calls such crimes inchoate crimes—incitement, conspiracy and attempt. For an attempt, too, is a crime. Though the evil act fall short of its mark, if it had a likelihood of reaching its mark, the law forbids and punishes an effort to make it reach its mark. Though it be interrupted by the defense of the person it threatens or by physical interference or other interference or by the intervention of the police or other agencies of government, to have tried to execute the substantive crime is a crime, too. It is an *attempt.* Most jurisdictions do not think of an attempt to commit a crime as an inchoate crime for the attempt, itself, is a complete crime—the crime of attempting.

Degrees of Crime. The criminal law makes a difference between degrees of crime, that is, it considers one crime less offensive to the public mores, less grave than another. This is no new concept. One may argue that the establishment of cities of refuge in the Bible was an indication that then, too, in that antiquity for which we can fix no date, it was already discernible that not all kinds of homicide were the same. The wilful killer could be taken from the altar for punishment. The accidental killer was given a city of refuge to which to flee, in which to find sanctuary during the life of the then High

Priest, so that he could escape from tribal or family vengeance. Isn't this a differentiation between the degrees of crime? So, likewise, the criminal law of today differentiates between degrees of crime. Stealing so much is a larceny of one degree; stealing less is a larceny of another degree. Premeditated murder is punishable in one way; murder designed though not premeditated in another way, homicide committed in rage, by recklessness, in yet another way. Sometimes the differences made in degree cannot be explained upon some rationale, for example, the differences in the degrees of forgery. But they are there to represent the conscious effort on the part of the law in justice and humaneness to establish differences in the gravity of crimes. In this, the mental element in crime plays a large part.

CLASSIFICATION OF CRIMES

We will now proceed to speak of particular crimes. Generally, crimes are classifiable as treasons, felonies and misdemeanors. Of the first, it is necessary only to say that they are crimes which consist of a personal conflict between the offender and the State as such, the sovereignty. (In days of yore, in feudal and patriarchal society, what was murder of the suzerain lord or of the father, but treason!) They are offenses against the sovereignty of so grave a nature that they jeopardize its safety or conceivably can jeopardize its safety. Not all offenses against the State and its machinery are treason. Some of them are ordinary felonies or misdemeanors for which the punishment is prescribed. But treason is a breach of the loyalty which the sovereignty exacts of its constituent, the person.

It would be hard to define the differences between felonies and misdemeanors. Generally one might say that felonies are graver crimes than misdemeanors, but, if this is so, that gravity is established by law, practice and attitude and not by any philosophical rationale. Ethically, philosophically, the misdemeanor of petit larceny involving the stealing of property valued at less than so much is no different from the felony involving the stealing of property worth so much more. But the law makes this difference. Once

upon a time a felony was a crime for which an offender not only could be punished but for which his property could be confiscated. Of course, a crime involving capital punishment, the punishment of death, is a felony. Some crimes are misdemeanors in one jurisdiction, felonies in another, and vice versa. One kind of perjury is a felony and another kind is a misdemeanor but both are lying under oath, an offense to both man and God. Divulging the contents of a letter is a misdemeanor, but getting a company employee to divulge the contents of a telegram is a felony. Impairing the morals of a child under the age of 16 is only a misdemeanor though having intercourse with that child is a felony. Giving a man a blow which will result in grievous bodily harm, if the grievous bodily harm was not intended is only a misdemeanor, but if the grievous bodily harm was intended it is a felony. These tenuous distinctions, however, are not for us. A misdemeanor, a felony, is anything so called by the law. It is sufficient merely to know that crimes are divided into treasons, felonies and misdemeanors.

Procedurally, too, crimes are divided, first, in the way they can be charged. A felony in most jurisdictions is charged by an indictment obtained before a Grand Jury, of which more later, whereas a misdemeanor may be charged by an information filed by a prosecutor. Again, procedurally, crimes may be classified on the basis of what the object of the crime was or what the wrong committed was. Thus, there are crimes against bodily security, crimes against property, crimes against religion and morality, and crimes against the reputation. And, there are also crimes against the State, the public order, and in defense of regulative institutions which the State has established.

SPECIFIC CRIMES

A bird's-eye view of most of the named crimes may be gotten from a study of the table of contents of almost any codified penal law and a somewhat closer examination of almost any code of criminal procedure. In the latter too, tucked among prescriptions for judicial process, may be found many a command and prohibition for the violation of which punishment is provided. And in the volumes of law dealing with specialties, such as labor laws, corporation laws, general business laws, election laws, etc., and (in the Federal system) laws relating to the army, navy, revenue, tax, customs, etc., trusts, bankruptcy, postal service, food and drugs, etc., there are again sections directing methods of administration, stating standards, and directing policy provisions for conduct, violations of which are crimes and punishable as such.

To such as, on the basis of fiction read, seen and heard in books, cinema and radio, are accustomed to picture "crime" as a welter of stealth and violence, pilfer and bloodshed, rape and browbeating, it will be startling to note that the vast majority of provided crimes deal with acts or omissions contravening or tending to contravene the purposes of the State in its regulatory and administrative functions, and protective of public order in government. Of course, in a strong sense, these crimes are by implication and in effect also in many cases crimes against bodily security, property, religion and morality, reputation. And of course crimes against bodily security, property, religion and morality, reputation, are also crimes against the State and its functions and against the public order. Again, under the heading religion and morality, by broad definition may be considered many wilful acts with respect to another—violence against a fellow creature, sexual acts, stealing and deprivation of property, trick, cheating, discrimination, and fraud, lying (certainly lying under oath), among others, and the establishment of methods and devices for accomplishing these are, however else they may be classifiable, also crimes against religion and morality. Our cries of outrage over what we have been taught by religion, ethics, the mores of our day and of the days of our forebears where these survive (and they do often enough), are expressed in crimes such as murder, kidnapping, robbery, abduction, perjury, stealing and the like—crimes of man against man, in which the State, protector of the weak and unwary, has an interest. In the crimes for the enforcement of public regulations and the maintaining of public order, may be found expression of the cautions of living in a complex society. All are punishable as the law may prescribe for each, though the soul may be revolted by homicide and only grieved or disappointed by a violation of rules relating to prizefighting, passage tickets, disguises, pawnbrokers, or ice.

Crimes Against the State's Regulatory Functions. Now, bearing all this in mind let us at least name some of the crimes in the category of those against the State and the regulation of public order. In naming them, we will omit crimes better included in the other categories, however they may relate to the public order. (Examples—Abortion, Frauds and cheats, perjury, etc.) Alphabetically, we find (this is by no means an all-inclusive calendar of such crimes), crimes arising out of and dealing with Advertising, Agents, Anarchy (and out of its order, Treason, both crimes against the safety of the State as sovereign, crimes even against its existence), Animals, Attorneys and Barratry (dealing with acts of those licensed among other things to appear in courts and plead, and designed to maintain the dignity of the courts and the Bar, the latter a prohibition against the instigation of groundless judicial proceedings), Banking, Billiards, Bills of Lading, Business and Trade, Bribery and Corruption (designed to maintain the integrity of public officers, to prohibit the taking of illegal fees, to secure fair dealing in the fora to which the citizen must resort for the obtaining and protection of the rights given him by law), Canals, Civil Rights and Discrimination (to protect the citizen's equality before the law and socially in all his acts and doings within the society of which he is a part—a volume of law steadily increasing under the impact of libertarian thought), Communication (safeguarding the channels of information), Contempt of Court (providing punishment for contemptuously resisting the fair impositions of constituted justice), Convicts and Convict Made Goods, Corporations, Disguises, Disorderly Conduct, Dueling, Elective Franchise (important to safeguard the efficiency of the vote in a democracy), Exhibitions, Ferries, Gambling and its sisters Horse Racing and Lotteries, Husband and Wife, Ice, Incompetent Persons (who may also by proper proceedings be made wards of the court at Civil Law), Indians, Insolvency, Insurance, Intoxicating Liquors, Juries and Jurors (to make unassailable what is yet the bulwark of criminal justice), Labor, Legislature, Logs, Marriage and Divorce (solemnizing unlawful marriages, advertising to procure divorces, etc.), Meetings (protection of public assembly), Military, Navigation, Negotiable Instruments, Nuisances, Oysters, Passage Tickets, Pawnbrokers, Peddlers, Platinum Stamping, Poor Persons, Prisoners, Prize Fighting, Public Health, Public Justice, Public Offices and Officers, Public Safety, Quarantine, Railroads, Real Property, Records and Documents, Riots and Unlawful Assemblies, Salt Works, Sepulture, Societies and Orders, Taxes, Trade Marks, Trading Stamps, Tramps (this too, punishment at hard labor being provided), Usury (providing against an interest of more than a permitted per cent on certain types of property—there are other laws making it a crime to engage in banking without license), Witnesses, Women (under this heading may be found in some jurisdictions crimes relating to compulsory prostitution, living off the proceeds of prostitutes, the crime of concealing birth or death of issue) and, last but not least, Wrecks.

It would seem that the State has overlooked nothing. Yet there are acts and omissions to be seen and experienced in our everyday living that cry for regulations concerning which there is no regulation, no law, no punishment provided. They may hurt or outrage but they are not crimes. And though they may have been the subject of legislation, if no punishment regarding them has been provided, they are still no crimes. No crime without punishment. This is of course not to be construed as a call for the creation of more crimes.

Crimes Against the Reputation. Of the crimes against reputation there is usually to be found but one, which is Libel. The crime consists of the publication, in any manner other than mere speech, of matter exposing the living or the memory of the dead, to hatred, contempt, ridicule, obliquy, or causing a person to be shunned, or tending to injure a person or association of persons or a corporation in his or their business.

Why uttering by word of mouth any such matter is, in most jurisdictions, not a crime admits of no juridical explanation. Practically spoken language can hurt as much as the printed word—but, practically, too, a case based on a spoken utterance would be more difficult of proof. This crime cannot exist unless the matter is in writing or print, or in the form of an effigy or sign. The crime as defined is broad enough to include publications of false statements about business stability, though there is the question whether such a false statement calculated to induce another person to do or not to do an act or make an investment or part with money is not rather a crime of a larcenous nature.

CRIMES AGAINST BODILY SECURITY

Man has a right to call himself his own, says our law, and it means him to be free as far as that may be, from the physical contacts of other men which he does not permit. Man is also a part of the society for which the State and the law are made and, mingling in that society, the law means him to be free from *wilful* unpermitted physical contacts, malevolent and whimsical, whatever the case; to be protected against the aggression of his fellows. To that end, then, the law prohibits certain acts and establishes crimes against his bodily security.

All of these crimes contain the basic element of assault, unpermitted physical contact, the violent laying of hands on the body of another. Other laws provide punishment for threats of assault or physical injury. Sometimes though the contact is permitted by the person assaulted, it is prohibited by the State because special considerations make this desirable. Thus in Abduction, Abortion, intercourse with a girl under the age of consent (Rape—in most jurisdictions Rape in the Second Degree), Seduction and Crimes against Nature (a term comprising Sodomy, both fellatio and pedicatio, Bestiality, Necrophilia), crimes against children in the impairment of their morals, the "victim" may be willing or may have no will, but the law prohibits and punishes the act and regards it as a crime—in *Abduction,* for the purpose of protecting family ties and chastity, in *Abortion* to conserve the fruit of reproductive unions and in response to religious interdiction against the slaying of unborn life, in *Rape* of the underaged, because the victim is deemed not yet to have reached the capacity to consent, in *Seduction,* to protect the virgin against the blandishments of the deceitful suitor who dangles the promise of marriage, in *Crimes against Nature,* to deter men from engaging in acts which are an abomination to the religious and irreligious alike. It will be noted, of course, that all of the crimes mentioned are crimes, too, against religion and morality, in their strictest definition.

It should be added here that the law has created safeguards against unjust and invented accusations which in some of these crimes can be so readily made. So, in Abduction, Rape and Seduction, no conviction may be had on the testimony alone of the woman defiled. Her testimony must be corroborated in every essential of the crime, including the penetration, the minimum proof of an act of intercourse. In Crimes against Nature, if the "victim" was in fact a willing participant, he (or she) is an accomplice and his testimony requires corroboration—but if in fact he *was* a victim and resisted to the utmost (a very elastic word, as the decisions of the courts amply show), then no such corroboration is required.

The crimes against bodily security are Abduction (taking, receiving, harboring, using a female under a given age for purposes of sexual intercourse, or to marry her without the consent of her parents or guardian or against her will), Abortion (in short, inducing miscarriage where the life of neither mother nor child is at stake), Assault, Crimes against Children (including sexual crimes and impairment of morals), Crimes against Nature, Hazing (what collegians think a pastime is a crime in most states and a felony if it results in tattooing or permanent disfigurement), Homicide, *Kidnapping* (the definition is the same in law as in literature —it is a capital offense if the victim is not returned alive prior to the opening of the trial—the sending of a ransom note or threat of kidnapping is a crime too, severely punished), *Lynching* and *Mob Violence* (the

record of convictions for this crime is, alas, not impressive), *Maiming* (the old Mayhem in modern spelling—the crime of wilfully injuring another in a bodily member, or destroying that member, first established, it would seem, to keep the King's soldiers fit for his service and punished by the law of retaliation, membrum pro membro, a member for a member), Rape, *Robbery* (in which the bodily security is jeopardized by the seeker of property), Seduction, and, still in some jurisdictions, *Suicide.*

Convicts and prisoners, too, are protected in their bodily security by prohibitions carrying the sanction of punishment.

Threats of bodily injury are crimes when used to cause the victim to do an act which he has a right not to do (*Coercion*) or to exact from him something of value (*Extortion*).

A special word now about Assault, Homicide, Rape and Robbery.

We have already defined Assault, over and over again, for it is that very unpermitted and violent contact of which we have been speaking. There are various degrees of Assault, usually three. The difference between them is predicated (1) on the intent with which the Assault is committed and (2) on the extent of the injury done. Assault in the First Degree is an Assault with intent to kill, an assault with a firearm or deadly weapon or any force likely to produce death or by the administration of a poison or noxious thing endangering life. It is, in effect, a homicide which has fallen short of the mark. Assault in the Second Degree is an assault accomplished by wilful and wrongful wounding or the infliction of grievous bodily harm with or without a weapon, or an assault with a weapon or instrument likely to produce such harm, or with drugs dangerous to health, or an assault (laying on of hands) with intent to commit a felony (as, for example, an assault with intent to commit rape), or in resisting process or arrest. All other assaults, ranging from a tap on the head to the blackening of an eye, are simple or third degree assaults. In some jurisdictions it has been held that though grievous bodily harm may have resulted, if such harm was not intended, the assault is a simple assault. This last is a misdemeanor. First and Second Degree Assaults are felonies.

Self Defense. Here we advert to "Self Defense." The law does not require a man meekly to submit to attack. He may resist an assault. Nor need he wait till his back is to the wall, to begin his resistance. He may from the outset use all the force reasonably necessary to repel his attacker, but he must use no more. Use of more force than is reasonably necessary may make him in his turn an assailant. He must not resist blows with bullets. He may even, if he is in fear of imminent attack, having, because of his adversary's bad reputation or threats made against him adequate reason for such fear, attack himself to avert an attack upon him. But he must never use more force than is reasonably needed to accomplish this purpose. It should be added that oral provocation is *not* an excuse for attack. "Sticks and stones, etc.," is more than folklore.

Homicide. Homicide is the killing of a man by the act, procurement or omission of another. It may be either murder or manslaughter or it may be excusable or *justifiable homicide.*

Homicide is excusable when committed by accident or misfortune, while doing a lawful act, lawfully, with lawful intent and with ordinary caution.

Homicide is justifiable when committed in obedience to the judgment of a competent court (the executioner commits no crime in killing the condemned), or in overcoming resistance to legal process or in the discharge of a legal duty. It is justifiable, too, when committed in the defense of self, spouse, child, sibling, master or servant where there is reasonable ground to apprehend a design on the part of the slain to commit a felony or a great personal injury to the slayer or the persons named, *and* there is imminent danger that such design will be carried out. There is even still one jurisdiction left where killing an unfaithful spouse and the paramour, caught in flagranti delicto and before the parties have separated, is justifiable homicide.

The distinction between the degrees of murder is so tenuous as to have troubled even the luminous and illuminated Cardozo, who once expressed a doubt that juries could really assimilate it. Generally speaking, Murder in the First Degree (nearly everywhere still a capital offense, an offense punishable by death) is killing from a deliberate and premeditated design to effect the death of another; Murder in the Second Degree, a killing with design to effect death, but without deliberation and premeditation. Since both deliberation and premeditation may be present, however briefly the accused may have engaged in them, it may well be imagined how much struggle the Courts and juries have had with their findings in this regard.

Murder in the First Degree may also be committed when death results even without premeditated design from an act imminently dangerous to others, evincing a depraved mind and disregard for human life. And it may be committed, even without a design to effect death, by a person engaged at the time in the commission of, or the attempt to commit a felony. This is known as Felony Murder, a means by which a person who in the process of robbing a man kills, even if he does not intend to kill, either the victim of his felony or another there, is guilty of Murder in the First Degree. Likewise, one committing Arson commits Murder in the First Degree if someone dies as the result of his act. And the loosener, remover, displacer of a railroad track whose act results in the death of another commits the same crime.

All homicides not Murder in the First or Second Degree or Excusable or Justifiable are Manslaughters.

One who kills while engaged in committing or an attempt to commit a misdemeanor, or in the heat of passion in a cruel and unusual manner or with a dangerous weapon or kills an unborn child by injuring its mother or kills a mother or her unborn live child while committing abortion, is guilty of *manslaughter*, usually in the First Degree. Killing while engaged in trespass, in the heat of passion not in a cruel or unusual manner and without a dangerous weapon, by culpable negligence, by causing one's own miscarriage, by one's mischievous animals, by the negligent use of machinery, overloading passenger vessels, oversteaming ships and steam engines, by physicians while intoxicated, by keeping explosives contrary to law are all Manslaughter, usually in the Second Degree. Ignorance, recklessness, gross neglect are in most of these instances no excuse.

Rape. As to Rape, it is the perpetration of an act of sexual intercourse with a woman not one's wife against the will of that woman, whether her will was overcome by force or fear, or drugs, or intoxicants, or where through lack of mental capacity she had no will or is for any reason unconscious of the nature of the fact or when she is in the custody of the law. This is Rape in the First Degree (so-called in many jurisdictions) and is the gravest form of this crime, in some states still a capital offense. Rape in the lesser or Second Degree has already been mentioned. In this connection the age at which a girl is deemed by law to have the power to consent has varied with time and place. It has been as low as ten years old and as high as 18 (now so, in New York). The rule that such an intercourse is Rape is based upon the reasoning (rationalization, perhaps) that a girl beneath the age of consent has no capacity to consent and independent proof that she has such capacity, did consent, nay, lured the defendant to the act, that the defendant did not know her age, that she looked above the age of consent, will not avail as a defense, though it may be mitigative in the punishment. The act is the crime.

Of course, as already pointed out, the testimony of the female in these cases requires corroboration. No conviction for rape against boys less than a certain age (variously fixed) may be had unless the defendant's capacity to perform penetration is proven.

Robbery. Robbery is the unlawful taking of property, from another against his will, by force, violence or fear of present or future injury to him or his property or to the person or property of a relative or one in his company at the time of the act.

This crime, severely punished everywhere (in New York for Robbery in the First Degree by a mandatory sentence of 10 to 30 years for a first offender) at Common Law (the uncodified ancestor of our legal ideas) by death, is also regarded in various degrees,

depending on the manner of its commission. Fear or force in any degree must be employed in its commission. Fear or force used to effect escape does not constitute robbery.

Robbery committed with a dangerous weapon, or with an accomplice actually present, or aided by use of an automobile or motor vehicle, or when its perpetrator inflicts grievous bodily harm on the victim, his spouse, servant, child or an inmate of his family or one in his company, is the gravest form of this crime and usually called Robbery in the First Degree. Robbery committed, not under these circumstances, but nevertheless with violence or by the use of fear of immediate injury, is a lesser form, usually Robbery in the Second Degree. And there is still a lesser form, usually Robbery in the Third Degree, which is an act within the general definition of Robbery, but lacking the circumstances which would amount to Robbery in the First and Second Degrees.

CRIMES AGAINST PROPERTY

Our society is organized on the basis of private property and the Criminal Law occupies itself greatly with the protection of such property and the prohibition of the deprivation, by stealth, duress, device, damage, of property owned and property possessed, and even the rights to property and possession. This deprivation may generally be described as appropriation to one's own use without the intent to return it, of a thing of value. There was a time when the deprivation or appropriation of the mere rights to property and possession were not crimes. Modern codes have remedied this.

The crimes against property are—(1) *those by stealth*, Burglary (of which more later), and stemming from it the Possession of Burglar's Tools, *Forgery* (not merely the simulation of a victim's handwriting, but the keeping of false entries, the invention of names in writing, the counterfeiting and invention of documents), Fraud and Cheats and False Representations (of which more later, under the heading of Larceny), Larceny itself and the Receiving of Stolen Goods, Usury (already discussed above), and by Weights and Measures (a form, to be sure of deceit, and false representations); (2)

those, *by duress*, Robbery, Coercion, Extortion (all already mentioned); (3) those *by device*, using the word "device" to include trick and play of fear, schemes for the unlawful obtaining of property, *Bucket Shops* (relating generally to the seeming purchase of evidences of property and credit without intending a real purchase—a method of controlling fraudulent margin buying, fraudulent reports of sale and purchase on a market reactive to such reports), *Coercion* and *Extortion* (methods of obtaining property by fear and threats; the essential ingredients, too, in *Rackets*, which are organized crimes for large depredation chiefly relying on coercive and extorsive methods), and (4) those *by damage*, Arson (a wilful burning or setting on fire of property, the degrees of which are determined by the time—day or night—manner and circumstances of the burning and firesetting, one of the gravest of crimes) and *Malicious Mischief* (the wilful damage or destruction of valuables, a felony or a misdemeanor depending on the value of the property damaged or destroyed).

Kidnapping (already discussed), of course, is a method of obtaining property unlawfully—money—but it is essentially a crime against bodily security. The labor of convicts is protected against exploitation and slave labor by appropriate provisions of the criminal law as is the property of incompetent persons.

Burglary. Burglary is the breaking and entering of another's close. It may be, in certain circumstances opening an entrance, obtaining an entrance by collusion with a person in the close, entry through a chimney or opening, or it may be violent by excavating or actual breaking of walls, or the detaching of parts. Walking through an open door of a close with intent to commit a crime there, where by definition these acts do not constitute burglary itself, is a crime, though the intent is not carried out or frustrated. It is an unlawful entry. The type of close which may be broken is broadly defined and includes not only buildings, dwelling houses but railway cars, vessels, tents, and even a garden.

Burglary is divided into degrees, depending on the time—day or night—manner and circumstances at and under which it is com-

mitted. A burglar entering at night a close in which there is a human being, being armed, or later arming himself in the close he has broken, or assisted by a confederate, or assaulting any person while entering or leaving or in the commission of his crime is guilty of Burglary in its highest (or First) Degree. One who enters a close in which there is a human being, with the intent to commit a crime there, under circumstances not amounting to Burglary in its highest degree, is guilty of Burglary in the Lesser (or Second Degree). Finally one who breaks and enters with intent to commit a crime in a close or part of a close, or being in one, commits a crime and breaks out of it is guilty of the third or least degree of Burglary. The distinctions are, here again, sometimes tenuous, but we must do with them for want of better.

Possession of burglar's tools is also a crime, if the intention to use them unlawfully can be shown. Since, what constitutes a burglar's instrument can, in almost all instances, be determined only by the intention with which it is possessed, the use to which it is to be put if the opportunity serve, it will be seen that the title of this crime (which is also its definition) is largely a begging of the question. When does a chisel, innocent carpenter's tool, become a burglar's tool? Only in the hands of an actual or would-be burglar. All too often, the possession of a "jimmy" (a "jimmy" is only a small crowbar, whatever flavor of stealthy enterprise and clandestine prying the word "jimmy" may have acquired in fiction and melodrama) can be entirely innocent. It is the intention that counts.

Larceny. Larceny must be discussed a bit before it can be defined. And one cannot here resort to saying that larceny means stealing, because stealing too must be discussed. Perhaps we ought to begin with some questions. Who can steal? What can be stolen? When can it be stolen? What are the acts which constitute stealing? They are all idle questions.

If Jack and Joe are in partnership and Jack withdraws all the money in the partnership intending to deprive Joe, is it stealing? No. He is merely taking his own, since as a partner he owns all of the partnership property, just as does Joe. His act in withdrawing the money is indeed a wrong to Joe but not a crime, and Joe's remedies are elsewhere than in a criminal tribunal. But if Jack is the president of a corporation and the sole person with authority to sign its checks, and he withdraws its moneys intending to deprive it and take them for himself, he is stealing, for he is one person, the corporation another, though artificial, person and Joe if he be a stockholder, yet another person. Whatever the implications of their relationship, their property in the money is, by law, different. Now, change the facts a bit, and say that Joe, an employee of the corporation, has in his possession the cash box of the corporation for the custody of which he is solely and exclusively responsible, and access to which has been delegated solely and exclusively to him. Jack takes this box to keep it for himself. He has stolen not only from the corporation, but he has stolen from Joe who had the right to possession of the box. We see, then, that (1) a man cannot steal from himself, his own, (2) he can steal from the person who has the property right in, the title to an object, (3) he can steal from the person entitled to its possession.

At common law only personal property could be stolen and personal property meant movables. In addition, this meant only personal property already in existence. Thus crops already cut and harvested could be stolen—growing crops and trees could not; the actual proceeds of a suit-at-law could, the right to sue could not (i.e., a note, which is a promise to pay and a suable claim, a so-called thing-in-action, an actionable claim, could not be the subject of larceny). Wild animals could not be stolen. All this is in varying degree, however, not so today. Almost anything which can be owned or possessed can be stolen, movables, evidences of debt, control, right and title (documents, things-in-action, money). Finders are no longer keepers (a duty of inquiry and search for the true owner is imposed almost everywhere). A tramp or prowler or an acquisitive but otherwise honest man may steal, commit larceny when he carries away a pipe, a bolt, a piece of metal or stone, from rubble

lying where there has been demolition, and not actually abandoned. The object stolen may be of extrinsic or only intrinsic value. The value can have bearing only on the degree of crime. Ideas and language cannot be stolen though stealing them is a wrong for which remedies are provided at civil law, but the paper on which they are written may be stolen.

We can see, that with such a diversity of stealable property, one cannot, in a word, indicate the actual moment when larceny has occurred. There are in larceny, elements which must be present before we can say that it has been accomplished. There is, of course, the taking, there is the carrying away (asportation, a stuffy latinate word), there is the withholding from the true owner, there is the resolve to keep for oneself or another, there is the intention not to return. In the act of a pickpocket all these elements coincide in time and place. His larceny is in one fell swoop an accomplished fact. But what of the man to whom a watch has been given to repair, or money to invest, or to hold or use in a given way, or property to keep? The taking, the carrying away, may be lawful, even the withholding may in circumstances be lawful, and it is only with the resolve to keep for himself or another, not to return, to divest the true owner or the one entitled to possession, that the larceny is completed. It is another kind of larceny, but stealing none the less, and in the case of money entrusted, it even has a name of its own, "embezzlement" (another word about this last, below).

This brings us to the acts which may constitute larceny. We already have noted the simple taking and carrying away (such a larceny if from the person, the very body, of its victim is usually of the highest degree, though some jurisdictions have sought in the case of pickpockets a less severe method of dealing by establishing the "offense" of jostling, usually a frustrated larceny from the person, and granting their lowest criminal courts jurisdiction to try and punish this crime summarily). We have also noted the larceny of those entrusted for one purpose or another with property, other than money, who expropriates the true owner or person entitled to its possession. A clerk, agent, officer of a bank or corporation, employee or other person to whom money is given, or by whom it is received for the transaction and purposes of its owner's business, who appropriates it to his own use commits larceny by embezzlement. There is larceny by trick and device, by artifice, by issuing fraudulent check, by the unauthorized use of another's vehicle (taking a car, even for a joyride, is larceny), by obtaining property or credit with the use of a false statement, by fraudulent use of a slot machine (slug in the telephone box, etc.), by appropriating lost property, by bringing stolen goods into a jurisdiction, by conversion of property held in trust or by virtue of office, by the failure to turn over deposits in renting or business transactions, or appropriating deposits for faithful performance of contracts, by a general contractor who fails to pay subcontractors from funds given him on his general contract with a view that he do so, by conversion of materials given for manufacture, by appropriation of funds in one's custody for the purchase of real property.

Larceny by false pretenses requires a special word. In this crime the true owner of property or the one entitled to its possession parts with it voluntarily. His will is swayed by false representations of the perpetrator that certain facts exist, that certain conditions are as he states them. These representations must be as to existing facts, may not be as to what will be in the future, otherwise the crime has not been committed. The victim believes the representations, though they are false, relies upon them, and parts with his property because of this reliance. In our complex business world, this type of larceny is not infrequent.

In the discussion of larceny the words and concepts, title, ownership, custody, possession are always important, but there can be no place here for an extended discussion of their juridical meaning.

Indeed, the questions raised by these words and the questions raised by the various types of larceny described have deeply perplexed the courts. In most jurisdictions the pleadings (the formal charges) have yet to be made with an eye to the differences in method

shown and the circumstances of ownership and possession, upon pain of having the prosecution fail.

New York has sought to meet these difficulties by virtually abolishing the distinctions. There larceny is defined (it is a very good definition and therefore given here) as follows:

"A person who, with intent to deprive or defraud another of the use and benefit of property or to appropriate the same to the use of the taker, or of any other person other than the true owner, wrongfully takes, obtains or withholds, *by any means whatever*, from the possession of the true owner or of any other person any money, personal property, thing in action, evidence of debt or contract, or article of value of any kind, steals such property and is guilty of larceny." (Italics ours.)

With this excellent statute the manner of obtaining the property in the first place, questions of title and possession, purpose of parting with the property, are no longer material in a defense to a prosecution for larceny in New York. Stealing is stealing. This statute should be widely copied.

The degrees of larceny, grand larceny in the first and second degrees and petit (pronounced petty—the spelling is a remnant of the French in early English law) are determinable only upon the value of the property stolen. Usually petit larceny is theft of $100 or under, grand larceny in the second degree of $500 or under, grand larceny in the first degree of property valued above $500, or of any value if taken from the person in the nighttime, or of $25 if taken from a dwelling-house, etc., at night. But these distinctions vary with the jurisdictions, some of which have no such designation as grand.

Receiving Stolen Goods. Buying, receiving, concealing or withholding stolen goods is a crime. The accused may not be the thief, must have bought, received, concealed and withheld the property *knowing* the same to have been stolen, must have done so intending to appropriate it to his own or another's use and to deprive the true owner (or the person entitled to its possession) of this property. According to some decisions a thief may also be guilty of concealing and withholding what he has stolen.

So much space and time have been taken to treat larceny and its forms and offshoots because in our society, large with business and property, this is one of the most important (and, alas, one of the most frequent) of crimes.

CRIMES AGAINST RELIGION AND MORALITY

In every section of the criminal law can be seen the touch and hope of religious striving, the implementation, so far as we may implement it, of our religious and ethical standards—distinctly so among us, in America, where Christian, Jew and Mohammedan inherit the same ethic from their respective faiths, where the common Anglo-American culture has made the Bible and its law a part, however at times unfelt, of our daily thinking.

In a sense every crime is a crime against religion and morality. Even the crime of violating a regulatory provision, being against the will and welfare of the State may be a breach of religion and morality. Here, however, we address ourselves to those perpetuative of virtues, rebuking failings, approved of or forbidden, respectively, by religion and morals themselves. Most of these crimes deal with those things which are said to be *mala in se*, evils in themselves, not evils merely because they are *mala prohibita*, evils prohibited. Almost all are associated with dogma, ancient or more recent, and are in our law because it mirrors us.

These crimes are *Abandonment* (the desertion in destitution of a child beneath a certain age by the person responsible for his maintenance—a law echoing with the protective duties imposed on the parent by religion and our morality); *Abduction* (already discussed as protective of parental authority and chastity); *Abortion* (surely grown of religious injunction against the taking of life, the killing of even the unborn already quick with life); *Adultery* (the injunction of the Decalogue enacted into statute); *Blasphemy*; Crimes in the treatment of animals (our duty's to God's creatures, a religious con-

cept); *Bigamy* (in keeping with our religious concepts of marriage—of course the crime is protective of our family, therefore also of our economic and social structure); Crimes against children (already discussed); Crimes against nature (already discussed); *Prostitution* (in defense of public order to be sure, but, nevertheless, in keeping with our standards of chastity as enjoined upon us by religion); *Incest* (a Biblical crime, the crime of sexual relationship with one who is within certain degrees of consanguinity [blood relationship], which the law has modeled on if not wholly copied from the Biblical Law); *Indecency* (in furtherance of our ideals of the fitting and pure, laws prohibiting and punishing displays, utterances, acts offensive to the public mores, the enforcement of which often enough requires a determination of what those mores are, for they do change from time to time); Crimes relating to marriage, divorce, married women (already discussed); Perjury and its subornation (again the Decalogue enacted into law—a law all too often broken; its effective enforcement the despair of prosecutors and courts); Rape (already discussed); Crimes against religion itself (the misdemeanor of wilfully preventing another by threats or violence from performing a lawful act enjoined upon or recommended to him by the religion he professes, the disturbing of religious meetings by rude or profane talk or act, or noise, or by promoting gambling or racing within certain distances from a religious meeting, or obstructing passage to such a meeting, Sabbath violation, and in many places the depiction of Deity, divine or person, in public performances.

As long as religion is part of our lives, as long as we have ethics, be they derived from religion or philosophy, these will among other factors and facets of our living find their expression, implicit or explicit, in our law.

CRIMES RELATING TO CRIMES

Crimes relating to crimes are those which owe their being to exigencies in the fixing of criminal acts and the enforcement of criminal law. We have already spoken of the crimes of attempting to commit a crime and of conspiracy to commit a crime. Two others should be mentioned—(1) *Compounding a felony,* the act of compromising the differences between an accused and the person whom he has injured upon a corrupt agreement that the latter will abstain from, desist or default in his duty to aid the State in its prosecution, and (2) *Bail Jumping,* the act of an accused who has been admitted to liberties under a bond guaranteeing his appearance before the tribunal to hear his case at certain times, in avoiding the limits of his liberty, failing to appear and defaulting in his obedience to the directions of the court in this regard. Before the establishment of the latter crime an absconding defendant could defeat justice in his case by evading capture long enough for the witnesses against him to forget, or be unavailable. Now, even if this last should occur, he may upon recapture be tried for the crime of bail jumping.

POSSESSION AS A CRIME

Elsewhere we have spoken of the possession of burglar's tools as a crime. There the commission of the crime is conditioned on the intention to use the tools unlawfully. There are other instances where possession is itself a crime. One of them is in the case of firearms, concerning which there has been much legislation in many states. Not all states view such possession alike. The firearm, possession of which is usually prohibited is the pistol or revolver, though sawed-off shotguns are also largely under ban. A distinction is made between possession of a loaded and unloaded pistol. In some jurisdictions if a pistol was used in the commission of a crime the court may upon conviction for that crime impose additional punishment because the pistol was used. Similar prohibitions exist against the carrying concealed or dangerous weapons (daggers, swordcanes, etc.). Again in the case of narcotics (heroin, morphine, etc., and in recent years marijuana) mere possession is illegal and is a crime. This prohibition applies also to possession of a hypodermic needle and other utensils in the taking and administration of drugs.

Of course, permits are issued to appropriate persons for the carrying of pistols, and peace officers carry them without permits.

And, of course, physicians, druggists, etc. may, under registration, possess narcotics.

PROCEDURAL MATTERS

In the procedure for the enforcement of the criminal law, which is to say, for the proving of the defendant's guilt and the application of the punishment prescribed, the accused, whom we shall hereafter call the defendant, himself is the most important person. His presence is required at every stage of the proceedings (except upon applications relating only to questions of law made outside of the trial) and he must hear (and see) the evidence produced against him, have the right of confronting his accusers, the right of denying his guilt (should he choose to do so —he may stand mute, i.e., say nothing), and he must be available for all these purposes and, in the event of his conviction, also for the judgment of the court and its execution.

He is, therefore, when first accused taken into custody, apprehended and dispatched through the formalities of arrest. This done, he is at the disposal of the court to await trial. He may have been arrested on a simple complaint by his victim, and brought before a court of limited jurisdiction, namely, a magistrate's court or a justice's court, to determine his rights pending trial. Or he may have been more formally accused by information or indictment (forms which we shall presently examine) issuing from the court before which he will stand trial, and be brought before that court. In either case, unless his crime be murder in the first degree or treason, he is entitled at least to ask for bail pending the time of his trial or other action by him to test his detention.

Bail. Bail is security. It is security furnished to the court (usually by the bond of a surety company duly accredited) for the appearance of the defendant when his presence is needed whether for trial or any command of the court. Upon furnishing it the defendant may be at liberty within the conditions of his bail. The court fixes these conditions and it alone can alter them. He may be required to remain within certain areas (jail limits) or, on the other hand, in the court's discretion, may be allowed to go where his legitimate business may take him.

By constitutional requirement bail may not be excessive, but excessive is a word which must be determined in each case by its circumstances. In some jurisdictions inferior courts may grant no bail at all to an habitual criminal. If a defendant feels his bail is excessive he may make application for its reduction again and as often as he wishes to the court about to try him and also to the highest court of general jurisdiction in the county where he is held. This last he will usually do by the ancient writ of *habeas corpus*.

Habeas Corpus. There is nothing mysterious about this writ. It must be issued upon request. It requires the authority holding a person in custody to bring that person before the tribunal issuing it so that the legality of his detention may be tested. "Let you have the body" (habeas corpus) of so-and-so before the court, is the direction to the detaining authority. If the detention is legal, the writ is dismissed, if illegal sustained. Upon such a hearing bail may be reduced, or the defendant let go.

Initial Steps. Now a defendant may be arrested at the scene of the crime which he appears to have committed. Even if this is so, he cannot be held except on a formal complaint. Sometimes this complaint is only a makeshift to provide sufficient time for the making of a full complaint by the person he has aggrieved. Such a makeshift complaint is usually by a police officer. Its value is limited and it must be within a specified time, usually forty-eight hours, replaced by a full complaint. Upon the full complaint the defendant is entitled to have an inquiry into his detention. He may hear the witnesses against him, may cross examine, may testify himself or not as he wishes, may waive the inquiry after hearing witnesses against him or even before hearing them. As the inquiry is only to establish whether his detention should continue and he be held for the action of the court having jurisdiction to try the crime of which he is accused, the testimony is sparse. At the close of the hearing the court either dismisses or holds for such action. If the defendant waives the hearing at any stage the court will hold him forthwith.

The Accusation—The Grand Jury. Now accusations in the court having jurisdiction over the crime of which he is accused may be made independently or as a result of this hearing, in two ways. The first, is by information. This is a formal paper in which the prosecuting officer accuses the defendant of crime and its filing by that officer is sufficient to commence the proceedings leading to trial. Also it becomes the basis of a warrant for the defendant's arrest. The other way is by indictment. The indictment is a much older form, but like the information, it is an accusation, only the accuser is not the prosecutor but the *grand jury*. This is a body of citizens sworn to make, in secrecy, inquiry into the commission of crimes in the county for which they are appointed. Their names for this service are drawn by lot. Their usual number is twenty-three. (This number may have got into our system from the number of the lesser courts in the ancient Jewish State—the provincial Sanhedrin, which consisted of twenty-three). Their proceedings are secret. They hear the evidence against the defendant. He, too, may be heard by their permission, or, in certain states, by absolute right accorded him by law. But he need not be heard. He need not appear. His witnesses are not heard, but may be, upon his request, if granted. If the grand jury is satisfied that the evidence before it, if not contradicted or rebutted, is sufficient to convict him of crime, they vote a so-called true bill, an indictment. This form, usually drawn for them by the prosecutor, is then filed with the court and based upon it a warrant is issued for the defendant's arrest.

Thus the defendant may be arrested preliminarily and have a hearing on the question of whether he should be held for action leading to an information or indictment. Or he may not be arrested until after such action. But after the filing of an information or indictment he is always arrested again and arraigned (brought to bar) in the very court in which he will be tried.

Usually informations are used to charge misdemeanors and indictments, felonies. But some jurisdictions have abolished the indictment and proceed only by information. On the other hand, there is nothing to preclude the grand jury from charging misdemeanors.

Arraignment and Preliminary Applications.
Upon his arraignment the defendant pleads
for the first time to the accusation. His plea
may be guilty, but this is rare. He may plead
"not guilty," thereby setting in issue every
element of the accusation. A general denial,
so to speak. In some jurisdictions he may
plead "non vult" or "nollo contendere" signifying his unwillingness to defend; the effect
of such pleas is no different, practically, than
that of a plea of guilty.

After his plea of not guilty he awaits a
trial of the issues he has thus created. His
right is to put the people to the proof. But
he may also apply to the court (by motion)
for other relief before his trial is reached. He
may ask for an inspection of the grand jury
minutes, to see if the grand jury was properly constituted, its action legal, the evidence
against him sufficient in law to sustain the indictment. Upon this application, the usual
thing is for the court to read the minutes
itself. If, upon such reading, they are found
sufficient the motion of the defendant is denied—if insufficient, the motion is granted
and is usually accompanied by a dismissal of
the indictment. Rarely is the inspection alone
granted. It is most usual for the defendant's
application to be for an inspection and dismissal. Upon such a motion, too, all legal objections to the prosecution may be raised.
The defendant may also move (apply) for
particulars of the accusation so that he might
prepare himself to meet it—dates, times,
places, persons, etc. Among legal objections
to the prosecution he may assert that the Statute of Limitations has run against it. This
means that the time limit in which the prosecution might have been brought has expired.
(Usual limitations are for misdemeanors two
years from the commission or discovery of
the crime, for some felonies five years, others
twenty, murder, none). Or he may assert
that his case is before the wrong court, in
the wrong jurisdiction. (A crime, with few
exceptions and these all specified in the statutes creating them, must be tried in the
county in which it occurred). Or he may,
complaining that he cannot get a fair trial
in the county in which he is, ask for a change
of venue, a change of forum to another
county. He may make other motions (appli-

cations) which it is unnecessary to discuss
here.

Resolving the Accusation. An indictment
or information once filed can be disposed of
(resolved) in the following ways: (1) By the
defendant's plea of guilty (2) By dismissal
by the court for insufficiency in law (this may
be before or during trial) or upon the recommendation of the prosecutor certifying the
possibility of reasonable doubt (of which
more below) other failing of fact and law, or
the impossibility of obtaining a conviction
(justice defeated is justice lost), and (3) by
trial followed by conviction or acquittal.

The Trial. Having entered his plea of "not
guilty" the defendant is ready, at least in a
technical sense, for trial. He is entitled by
law to a speedy trial. The prosecution must
not delay, unreasonably, leaving him under
the cloud of accusation, or worse, in jail
awaiting his day in court. Time may be had
in appropriate circumstances by either side
for preparation, for the preliminary applications already described, for the preliminary
examination of witnesses. The defendant
may take depositions of witnesses far away
from the tribunal in which his case is. This
privilege is not usually accorded to the prosecution which must produce its witnesses in
court. No witness belongs to either side—
either side has a right to confer with all the
available witnesses to learn what they will
say. It would be folly, indeed, to call any
witness to the stand, when what he will say
is not known to the side calling him. And
the defendant is entitled to counsel. Recent
decisions of high courts including the United
States Supreme Court have wrathfully set
aside convictions where it appeared that the
defendant either in pleading guilty or in defending himself, was without counsel; had
even rejected the court's proffer of counsel.
This does not mean to say that the defendant
may not try his own case, but he does it at
his own peril. "A man who is his own lawyer
has a fool for a client," the saying goes. Even
so the court must be vigilant to see that his
rights are not diminished, or nullified even
by his own ignorance.

Counsel for the State, "the people," the
Commonwealth is the prosecutor, district attorney or attorney general.

Anyone who has attended trials will sooner or later have heard judge or counsel refer to the trial as, a search for the truth. The truth has been searched for, variously, in our legal history. Once upon a time it was searched for by ordeal—ordeal by fire, in which the accused was not burned by live coals if he was innocent; ordeal by water, in which he did not drown if free of guilt; trial by combat, in which he never, never lost, if he was not guilty. In the last, he was given the privilege of not fighting himself—he could choose a champion. The king (the crown, in our case, the State) had his champion too.

If the modern trial at the criminal bar, is an ordeal too, it is only one of nerves. It is a search for the truth, but that search is conducted upon facts adduced, and by the ascertainment of what conclusions could in human experience, acting by the law of probabilities, be drawn from them. The Court (and the jury in trials of felonies) cannot say what, in very deed, happened; they can only declare what, in the greatest probability, happened.

The parties, the State (accuser) and the defendant (accused) have, also today, their champions, respectively the prosecutor and defense counsel. While these are to assist with their learning the conduct of the trial and the search for the facts, and with loyal and noble partisanship to defend each his client's rights within the law and the canons of ethics, it cannot be gainsaid that their struggles all too frequently veer the trial from its best purposes and assume the aspect of personal contest, in which the parties are periodically all but forgotten.

The Jury. The vaunt and glory of this struggle, too, is increased because in the forum in which they appear they have not only the judge for audience, but also a warm segment of the population at large, laymen, the jury. In ancient days the jury was really an assembly of witnesses called to testify to the facts of a matter. They were called to speak sooth —*verum dicere.* Today they have developed into judges of the facts—they hear the evidence, are guided by the arguments of counsel, instructed in the law by the judge, and then called upon to speak sooth—to bring in the *ver-dict,* verdict. In ancient days they spoke what they knew of their own knowl-

edge. Today they report their conclusions from what they have been told in properly admitted evidence.

The jury usually most frequently number twelve. The Federal Courts, bound constitutionally, may not use other than twelve. The States have taken some liberties with this. There has been much guessing as to why this number was chosen. The earliest juries were not twelve, were both less and more than twelve. There are today juries of less than twelve in many courts and jurisdictions. Many crimes are tried without juries, misdemeanors almost always, felonies rarely, depending on the jurisdiction. Is there in the number twelve a reminder of the Apostles? Twelve, in any event, has long been one of the magic numbers. In some jurisdictions one or two alternates may be chosen to serve in the event of the disqualification or disability of a chosen juror during trial. If no such disqualification or disability occur the alternates will not participate in the deliberations of the jury. They are replacements who sit by (and listen) to await such an event. Before this system was instituted, disqualification or disability of a juror would render the trial of no effect, i.e., a mistrial. They are drawn from a panel assembled by lot. Before they are chosen they may be questioned, usually by both counsel, in some jurisdictions by the court, with a view to learning if they harbor any prejudice, if there is an obstacle to their impartiality as judges of the facts. If such an obstacle is shown they may be challenged for cause. But the parties have, too, challenges of a peremptory nature, for which no reason need be offered, which they may exercise in response to intuitional reactions to a given juror. The number of such peremptory challenges is limited according to the nature of the crime to be tried and its punishment, more or less as the case might be. The first juror chosen is the foreman who presides over the jury's deliberation and eventually reports its verdict.

The functions of the court (i.e., the judge) and those of the jury are rigorously divided and neither may intrude upon the functions of the other. The jury are the judges of the facts. These they are to determine solely upon the evidence adduced, using their worldly experience in considering it, and its significance, the credibility of the witnesses testifying before them, all that they see and hear in the courtroom. They may not go outside of the evidence, may not bring in facts known to them as persons when such facts have not been brought out in the trial, may not, except as part of the whole court, visit the scene of any occurrence, may not conjecture or guess about the facts, may not, so far as they can control (they are *so* human) allow themselves to be swayed by emotion (love, hate, aversion, etc.), prejudice, sympathy, thought of what punishment might await the defendant, or reluctance to do a disagreeable duty. In their work they are sheltered against influences outside of the trial. The court, itself, in almost all jurisdictions may not indicate its opinion as to a fact, nor comment upon any. The notable exception to this rule is in the Federal courts, where comment is allowed. But even Federal judges sitting in districts within State jurisdictions where the prohibition obtains, will not, as a rule, comment. The court's function, is to conduct the trial, see that it follows the procedure prescribed for it by law and usage, rule according to law upon the admissibility and sufficiency of evidence, decide whether, in law, such a case has been made out as may be submitted to a jury for its findings, instruct the jury on the law it must apply in determining the facts, and finally, in the event of acquittal, discharge the defendant, in the event of conviction, pass judgment upon him (sentence him). The verdict of the jury is not the judgment. Sentence is the *judgment* of the court. The court may also, upon appropriate application, or on its own motion, set aside a verdict which is contrary to law or unsupported by evidence. Since, before a verdict is brought in, the court has already had ample opportunity to rule on law and evidence, such an occurrence is very rare.

To pursue its deliberations a jury is given privacy. Court attendants charged to preserve their privacy and sworn to this duty, guard the quarters in which they deliberate. Modern courthouses even have soundproofed or almost soundproofed rooms for jury rooms. If the jury is perplexed, they may ask the court for supplementary instructions, on the law and their function, or, may have reread to them portions of the evidence on which they wish to refresh their minds. They may ask to have sent to them corporeal evidence (documents and objects exhibited to them during the trial) to examine it again. To sending them such evidence the consent of the defendant is usually required. When they are agreed upon a verdict they dispatch an attendant to inform the court. So, too, if they cannot agree.

Verdicts in a *criminal* case cannot be rendered except upon unanimous agreement of the jury. This is important to remember as in *civil* cases, in some jurisdictions a verdict may be arrived at by a 10 to 2 vote of the jury. If the jury has agreed unanimously their verdict is reported to the court. If they cannot possibly agree, after a reasonable time, they are discharged. In this event, the case is where it started, and the whole weary process of trial must be gone over again. The prosecutor, however, may after considering how the jury stood in its disagreement and the state, quality and quantity of the evidence to be presented upon a new trial, conclude that no better result could be obtained by retrying the case. Such a conclusion may lead him to recommend to the court dismissal of the indictment. If the jury stood heavily in favor of conviction such a recommendation is not likely, if heavily in favor of acquittal very likely. It should be added, that while the jury's deliberations are secret, they may after their discharge (it is their own choice) discuss how they stood. It is not unusual for even the court, after a disagreement, to ask them about this, quite informally of course.

What goes on in a jury room, what a jury will do, no one knows. Even the oldest lawyer's guess is vanity in face of the unexpected. Jurors are human and have emotions and failings. A strong charactered juror may sway the rest, an obstinate or ignorant one complicate the deliberations. Jurors have been known to wait messages from another world, refuse to join in deliberations, trot out prejudices they failed to mention when questioned, remember their own old wrongs, weep for the defendant or his wife or child, or, on the other hand, call for his swift conviction. With all that, the jury is still the best of fact finders even in complicated cases, still the best defender of the unjustly accused, the best judge of the rightness of an accusation. The mistakes of juries shock us. That shock, however, makes us forget the innumerable times when they are quite right. The jury is after all a true segment of the people at large, who accuse, and try, make mistakes and are so often right.

The Steps of the Trial. Now, these are the steps of the trial. After the jury is chosen, the prosecutor makes his opening, in which he is required to state what he will prove, how, and by whom. He must make an opening. In this way the defendant may know what he is to expect, what he needs to meet. The defendant may or may not open, as he chooses. He has no burden in the trial. The state is put to its proof and has all the burden of proving the defendant guilty beyond a reasonable doubt. The defendant need not say a thing at any time, nor produce a witness.

Direct Examination. When the openings are done the time to offer proof has come. The State calls its witnesses, one by one (a wise trial lawyer will have well considered his order of proof before the trial begins). These are questioned to bring out their testimony. This questioning is called direct examination. They do not make narrative statements, as in continental European courts. Direct narratives would be impossible under our rules of evidence.

Rules of Evidence. These rules are made to keep a trial strictly on the issues presented. Questions may not be "leading" (feeding the answer to the witness in the question). They may not incorporate within themselves facts not proven, or assume such facts. The testimony must be of the witness' own knowledge. Hearsay (with few exceptions, among them the declarations made by the dying in contemplation of death) is inadmissible. The operation of the witness' mind, his conjecture, reasoning, argument, are not admissible. Nothing may be brought out in the testimony which is irrelevant (unrelated to the issue), incompetent (from sources or of a nature prohibited by law) or immaterial (having no

bearing or effect on the issue). Collateral issues may not be pursued (i.e., in a trial for larceny, the question of the defendant's membership in a union may not be pursued, though proof to contradict his denial of such membership may exist). All is calculated to bear upon the defendant's guilt or lack of guilt and the acts and factors making for one or the other. The rules mentioned here are given for illustration. They are not to be regarded as a full catalogue of evidentiary law.

Circumstantial Evidence. Circumstantial evidence has a bad reputation among those who do not reflect and are full of the slipshod criticism of this form of evidence by maudlin writers who themselves do not reflect. Neither side in a trial can offer direct eye and ear evidence of everything. The jibe to those who unconscionably demand this used to be—"what do you want, a movie?" Modern methods of detection have come to the stage, where moving pictures and recordings, the first not as frequently as the second, can be provided. But often enough, an occurrence, an act can be proven only by circumstances all pointing one way. If all the stalks in a field bend north, it is proper to conclude the wind is blowing that way. When circumstantial evidence points to the guilt, unequivocally and exclusively when no other conclusion is possible it is acceptable proof.

Cross Examination. When the witness has, under the guidance of counsel, concluded his direct examination, he may be cross-examined. The right to do this is so essentially a right of the defendant that interference with or obstruction of it vitiates a trial and any conviction based upon it. But the right to cross examine need not be exercised. It may be waived, either by affirmative spoken waiver (all of the trial is oral, though the proceedings are carefully recorded by a shorthand writer) or by deliberate failure to exercise it.

The purpose of cross examination is, to *test* the veracity of the witness, his *credibility*. It is designed to bring out faults in the quality and nature of the testimony, motives for it, if any, faults in the witness himself, and to expose him if he is lying. The questions and their form must therefore be accommodated to this purpose. Now the witness may be asked a "leading" question. It is his to resist the implications. He must answer "yes" or "no" if he is able to. If unable to he must say so and be prepared to answer questions designed to show that his professed inability is indeed an evasion. If the question contain an innuendo, he may resist it by not answering "yes" or "no." Facts already proven may be incorporated in the question. The question may be framed to suggest a certain answer. It is for the witness to resist the suggestion, not to make that answer if it is not so. Cross-examination will search to see if the testimony the witness has already given, is, indeed, of his own knowledge, to see if the witness could have had such knowledge, could have seen and heard what he professes to have seen and heard. It may challenge his memory. It may show changes in his statements. It may prove infirmities in his senses. It may bring out his inability to understand what he saw or heard, or, his inability accurately to report it. It may show preparation and memorization of the testimony. Such generally are the functions of this difficult art, and it is an art, calling upon every skill in thinking and language.

Regrettably, many who try cases, forget these functions. They do not address themselves to saliencies in the testimony. They do not attack where they discern weakness, lacunae, hiatus, anachronism and inconsistency. As a result, they flounder and blow hard, but all in vain. Under their questioning, like as not, the witness will only repeat what he has said on direct examination. This, so far from impugning his testimony, usually serves only to reinforce it. Probing into the witness' motives and acts, such examiners may even ask the most dangerous of questions which is "Why?" Now, "Why?" goes into the operation of the witness's mind which, as we have already said, is not testimony. But the question "Why?" asked on cross-examination opens the gates. The witness may now give the operation of his mind, asseverations of his honesty, his motives (usually self-justification), hopes, aspirations, yearnings, even hates and prejudices, all the gamut of human emotion articulately explained in answer to this unguarded but provocative "Why?"

Witnesses and Their Credibility. Anyone of sound mind and the ability to understand the nature of an oath or affirmation may be a witness—that is any such person may be called, sworn and heard by the court. Children of tender age unable to comprehend the nature of swearing may testify, but not under oath. Their testimony requires corroboration. In our law there is no disqualification of witnesses by reason of station in life, occupation, previous bad or even criminal record, race, religion. Other systems, and our own in the remote past, provided for such disqualifications. (The ancient Hebrews would not hear a gambler—he was disqualified.) The defendant may, if he chooses be a witness. He had not always this right.

Witnesses testify under oath or affirmation. A witness with moral or religious objections to swearing may not be forced to swear; he may affirm and this is in law as binding as an oath. The oath or affirmation, one or the other, are in the same form for all witnesses and this form may not be varied. (This too was not always and everywhere so—witness the struggle [joined by Macaulay] to eliminate the English parliamentary oath, the invocation of the witness's faith as a Christian, and in France the battle [led by Crémieux] to abolish the humiliating oath *more judaico*.) Both oath and affirmation contain the solemn promise that the witness will in the case in which he testifies tell "the truth, the whole truth and nothing but the truth."

Whether the witness actually does this is tested by cross-examination and by all the elements in the case. The credibility (believability) of a witness is for the jury. How are they to judge this? By the witness's testimony, his appearance, his manner of testifying and answering questions, his statements and behavior under direct and cross-examination, by what they have learned of him as a man and of his background, and in the light of the general worldly experience of the jury itself. To bring them information of these last, certain questions are permitted on cross-examination—questions, asked in good faith, as to immoral or illegal act he may have committed; questions addressed to bringing out that the witness has been convicted of crime. It must always be remembered that the jury must consider the answer not the questions. Questions are not evidence and the jury may form no conclusions from them for which there is no evidence. A denial by the witness of the commission of immoral or illegal acts is binding on the questioner and he is foreclosed from proceeding with further questions in this regard. Some cases however have held he may proceed, by confronting the witness with a prior contrary statement under oath. A denial of prior conviction does not foreclose the questioner and he may proceed to offer evidence of such conviction. If such questions do bring out the commission by the witness of immoral or illegal acts or his conviction of crime, these are elements, too which the jury may consider in judging the witness's believability. The testimony of such a witness must be specially scrutinized. But the jury is not precluded from believing all or part of what he says. Likewise, if it be shown that the witness has lied about a material fact, the jury may cast all he says aside, but they need not do so, may accept what they deem true. In short, the jury is the sole judge of the credibility of witnesses.

All that has been said here of witnesses generally applies of course to the defendant himself if he elects to take the stand in his own behalf.

The People's Case. With the calling of all the witnesses available to the people and appropriate to proving it there is an end to the "people's case." Either side may of course call any witnesses supporting its contentions. Witnesses are called by a process called *subpoena* and this process is available to both. For this reason neither side may complain that one or another witness hasn't been produced unless it can be shown that such witness is solely in the control of the side failing to produce him. When the "people's case" is ended the people (the State or Commonwealth, Crown or Government as the case may be) "rest."

Now this direct case of the prosecution must contain all the proof legally necessary to sustain the indictment or information. It is not as yet challenged or contradicted (except in cross examination) by anything the defendant has produced. This, however, is no matter, since the defendant is not required to produce, or offer any evidence, or even to

defend. The burden of proving guilt, and that beyond a reasonable doubt, is on the people. The case of the prosecution must, therefore, in and of itself have at its close *proved* the case. Whether it has or not now becomes a question of law for the Court. This question comes to the Court upon the motion of the defendant to dismiss upon the ground (variously couched in various jurisdictions) that the case has failed of proof in law. If, indeed, it has, the Court will dismiss at the end of the "people's case." Upon such dismissal the defendant is free of the charge and may not be tried upon it again. If it has not the Court will deny the motion. This denial is in effect a ruling that enough has been proven to merit the consideration of the jury as to guilt or lack of guilt.

The Defendant's Choice. At this point the defendant must make an election—whether to defend or not to defend. He may rest forthwith, without calling a witness, thus putting the prosecution to its proof in fact as well as in law. He needn't defend and no implications may be drawn from his failure to do so. The burden is always the State's.

But he may elect to defend. In this event he, like the prosecution, may call witness to give his version or to contradict the prosecution's witnesses or to establish one or another affirmative defense in his behalf. He may choose to testify himself. No one can force him to do so. He need not take the stand. He cannot be called to it except by himself. But if he takes the stand he submits himself to all the hazards of the trial, all the dangers of cross-examination. While he may otherwise never be forced to incriminate himself, he may, if he takes the stand, upon cross-examination be asked questions the answers to which would incriminate or degrade him. He may not, as other witnesses may, refuse to answer these upon the ground that they do so. His answers, like those of any other witness become evidence and a factor in the jury's determination of the facts. In no event may any conclusion be drawn from his failure to take the stand, nor may it be commented upon.

Defenses. If the defendant elect to proceed rather than rest what will be his defenses? He may confine himself to evidence purely contradictory of the evidence produced against him. He may adduce testimony to support his denial. He may make a flat denial or a denial qualified by evidence explanatory of his actions. He may admit the acts charged against him and deny they are a crime or, if a crime, that they are the crime with which he is charged. He may admit them and then set up affirmatively that he was forced to do them; that, where intent is required, he lacked intent; that he was so insane at the time of their commission that he did not understand their nature or quality, did not understand that they constituted a crime. He may plead *alibi*. Alibi means "otherwheres." It is a simple declaration by the defendant that he was not at the scene of the crime and its action and therefore could not have committed it. In itself it is the best of defenses. If believed it is a complete defense. He may say the court has no jurisdiction territorially or of him because he is of nonage, has immunity, etc. He may say that by statute the time in which he could be tried has expired. (This is the so-called "statute of limitations"—a time limit to the prosecution of crimes—for misdemeanors, usually, two years, for most felonies, five years, for some felonies twenty years, for capital offenses, no limitation.) All or any of these defenses (the above is by no means a full catalogue of them) are, depending upon the facts and circumstances, his for the using. He will be wise to avoid inconsistent and incompatible defenses. Seemingly compatible defenses may sometimes destroy or weaken one the other. (There is the case of the defendant charged with rape who, pleading alibi, injected also the defense of impotence —inability to commit the crime. He said in effect, "I wasn't there, but if I had been, I couldn't have done it." When cross-examination showed he had been taking aphrodisiacs for only a functional impotence, his alibi, though well sustained, was discredited and the jury convicted. No doubt they felt that he, preoccupied with his failing and full of love philtres, was just the one to have committed the crime.

Character Evidence. There is no such thing as "character evidence." So-called "character evidence" is really evidence of reputation. The defendant may call persons, who know him and know others of his acquaintance to testify that his reputation for morality, placableness, honesty, etc. is good. This is not only hearsay, it *must* be hearsay. The witness may not give his own opinion. His own opinion is inadmissible, must be stricken out and the jury must be told to disregard it. He may only report the opinion of others, the defendant's reputation.

In and of itself evidence of good reputation may be accepted by the jury as sufficient to raise a reasonable doubt of the defendant's guilt. But it need not be. The jury may disregard it, or regarding it may yet experience no such doubt.

Rebuttal. The defendant having concluded and rested the prosecution may rebut. This means that evidence to meet issues raised by the defense, and only such issues, may be offered. The defendant may surrebut, that is, offer yet other evidence to meet the rebuttal. Of course, this may not continue forever, and the court will put an end to any such abuse. But this must be done with care for the rights of both sides.

Motions. Again, now, upon the whole case, the defendant may move to dismiss. Once again the court will consider, now with both sides heard, if the case as it stands has been made out in law. If yes, it is ready for submission to the jury. If no, it may be dismissed and the defendant may not be retried for the crime in issue.

Summings Up. In passing on these motions at the close of the whole case the Court has examined all of it as an entity, but that, upon the law, and to see if the evidence adduced is sufficient to comply with the requirements of the law.

Now, it is the jury, which must view the case as a whole in preparation for deliberating on its verdict. Part of this viewing and preparation are the summings up of counsel. (Summings up are also called summations or closing statements). Each of the lawyers in turn addresses the jury. The prosecutor, who it will be remembered opened first, closes last. Summings up need not be made. They may be waived.

What is the function of these addresses? To "organize" the evidence for the jury, we will be told. True, they "sum up," tell the jury what, on the question of the defendant's guilt or lack of guilt, all this evidence adds up to. But they do a great deal more. They are the vehicles of partisan argument. If they are not, in the sincerest but fairest sense, partisan, they fall short of what, in the modern trial, is expected of them. They are the medium of expression for the lawyers, long confined during the trial proper, to questions. They argue the meaning of the evidence. They urge upon the jury an approach to its consideration of the facts. They direct its attention to the points where the questions have exposed testimony or witnesses which (so they may now argue) should not be believed, or, in reverse, should be believed. They may comment for the first time on the faults which their cross-examination has succeeded in eliciting. They may discuss the probabilities in the case, call attention to the impossibilities as well as improbabilities. They may collate and mention and argue the human experience of the issue involved. They should not, but very often do, however guardedly, advert to punishment and the emotional involvements in the case. Counsel should not express personal opinions as to guilt or innocence. If defense counsel does it, it is unethical, if the prosecutor, it is an error for which a judgment of conviction may be reversed. But either counsel may urge that from certain facts certain conclusions including the conclusion of guilt or innocence, are inescapable.

Much language and oratory, skill in argument, logic and exhortation go into a summing up. For it is in the summing up that we see the final flourish in the battle of champions to which we have earlier alluded. A wise and eloquent (and it may be eloquent though most gently spoken) summing up has been known to carry a case from defeat to victory. Sad words these, defeat or victory, in what started out as was cautiously planned by law and the rules of evidence to be, only a search for the truth. But the human aspects of the trial are intense, and humans calculate success by victory. And after all the verdict here is to be one of "guilty" or "not guilty."

Charge. The atmosphere created by the summings up, may, however, be dispelled by the "charge of the court." This is that portion of the trial in which the court, as sole source of the law in the case, instructs the jury in those legal guides which they must follow in their function. It is of such importance that when it is delivered the court room is shut off from ingress or egress. Nothing may disturb the jury's attention.

Actually the court has been charging the jury from the very first, piecemeal, of course, and as the occasion arose. Some judges are in the practice of making a brief charge to the jury at the outset of the trial, defining their functions and explaining the procedure that is to unfold before them. At each recess of the trial the court must, by law, warn them against discussing the case with anyone, even with one or more of their own number, against visiting alone or with another the scene of the crime, against searching for information regarding the evidence outside of the courtroom and when they are together, against forming any conclusion or judgment before the moment they retire to deliberate.

But, at the close of the case, the court instructs them on the law applicable to it. They are taught the definition and the elements at law of the crime charged, what evidence is necessary, what facts have probative value. The defenses are explained and defined. Sometimes the evidence as a whole is reviewed (most jurisdictions require the judge to keep his own minutes), or it is used illustratively in discussing the law, but in each case, for fear such review and use may appear as comment, with the injunction that no matter what it is for the jury alone to say what the facts are. The jury is alerted to the limitations upon its functions, to matters it may not consider, punishment, sympathy, conjecture, comment and language inadvertently heard, matter not in the evidence. It is instructed in the methods of testing the credibility of the witnesses (see above), and the evaluation and effect of reputation evidence, how to judge exhibits which have been produced. It is told how to report its verdict. Especially it is instructed in the standard of proof which must be applied.

Reasonable Doubt. In civil cases as a rule, that side is entitled to succeed which can prove its case by a preponderance of credible evidence. This is not the standard in criminal cases.

We have already learned that *all* of the ultimate burden of proof in the criminal trial is on the prosecution. This burden is the heavier since the defendant enters the trial cloaked in innocence. He is presumed to be innocent, and that throughout the trial to the very last. This presumption is his even as the jury retires to deliberate. It can be upset by one thing only—the belief of the jury that upon the facts he is as the saying goes "guilty beyond a reasonable doubt."

Now what is "reasonable doubt"? The courts in numberless charges have defined it as a doubt for which a valid, not a whimsical or wanton, reason is given. The word "reason" as used is not to be considered synonymous with "argument" as one would say "I can give you an argument for it." It means a reason grown from the evidence, related to the action, evolved by the processes of reasoning the facts in common sense and logic (not formal logic necessarily). A reasonable doubt is not surmise, nor reluctance to yield. Remembering that we have said that the search for "truth" in the trial is in fact a search for the probability, let us illustrate. Picture probability as a line graduated by percentage from 0 to 100. If in a civil case preponderance is the goal, probability at 51% is enough for the success of the side attaining it. In a criminal case the probability must be greater, must strain to the perfection of 100%, which is security, and which is so rarely attained in human experience, certainly in the trial. When probability has reached this highest degree (and that can be no higher than the facts allow) even then that probability cannot avail to support a verdict of guilt if a "reason" such as described can be advanced against it. There is a "reasonable doubt" and it must be resolved in favor of the defendant.

Verdict. The jury retires to its privacy to deliberate. It must be kept together so long as there is a possibility of its agreeing. It may not be coerced, or subjected to coercive hardships to make it agree. Its deliberations may be brief or very long. The jurors must listen to one another, weigh each other's argu-

ments. It ballots to ascertain its divisions if any. It discusses the case, reviews the evidence, examines the exhibits, has testimony reread (by request sent to the court) all in the effort of attaining unanimity. If, after all this unanimity cannot be attained, it advises the court of its disagreement. If a verdict is reached it likewise advises the court.

The verdict in a criminal case is either "guilty" or "not guilty." It is announced by the jury foreman. At the request of counsel the jury may be polled to see if the verdict announced is that of each juror. This is usually an empty proceeding but may bring out that some juror has only seemingly yielded for one reason or another, to a majority suasion for unanimity. If there is more than one count (item of accusation) in the indictment the verdict must be addressed to each count. A defendant may be found guilty on some, not guilty on others. He may not be found guilty on inconsistent or incompatible counts where such have been submitted to the jury to determine whether the facts support one crime or another.

With the announcement of the verdict the case is concluded. If it is "not guilty" the defendant is discharged and may never be retried on the issue. If it is "guilty" the defendant must await the disposition of the court. The verdict may be challenged by motion, but to this we have already alluded. The defendant may be detained (remanded) to await sentence or may be continued on bail (this very rarely) to await it.

Sentence. In most jurisdictions before imposing sentence the court causes investigation of the defendant's background to be made by a probation department. The work of probation has already been discussed elsewhere in this volume.

In sentencing the court may impose such punishment as the law provides, or part of it where this is not prohibited or suspend sentence (better said "suspend sentencing") or impose sentence of imprisonment and suspend its execution. In the last two instances the defendant is as a rule turned over to the supervisory function of probation. The court will set the rules and conditions of probation.

Appeals. The defendant need not rest with the verdict. He may, within prescribed limitations of time take it by appeal to a higher court (and in instances to the highest court) assigning error calling for reversal. In capital cases, it is usual, for the case on appeal to go to the highest court of the State. The decision of this highest court is final and will not be reviewed by the United States Supreme Court except where constitutional questions raised reasonably, appear to be involved.

Youth. Youth in crime has been discussed elsewhere in this volume. It need only be said here that the majority of all crimes (60% some say) is committed by youths between 16 and 20 years old. Impressed with modern trends in criminology and penology the courts have bit by bit taken cognizance of the special treatment youth before the bar, requires. Some states (New York and California) have Youthful Offender Acts calculated to treat with the young criminal and yet leave him untainted by conviction. More and more, criminal courts and penal institutions, have sought to segregate youth from adult and inveterate criminals and to implement new ways of approach to youth in crime.

Conclusion

It has been sought here to give a very large overview of Criminal Law and Procedure. The goal has been to provide such a view without effort to be inclusive of nuances and the legion of particularities with which the law and the procedure abound. Technicalities and technical words have been studiously avoided.

Why should we be technical in discussing the Criminal Law, since it is everybody's business? Nevertheless, accuracy, within the limitations of space and method, has been a constant aim.

NICHOLAS ATLAS
Assistant District Attorney
New York County

BIBLIOGRAPHY

Best, Harry, *Crime and the Criminal Law in the United States,* considered primarily in their present day social aspects, New York, The Macmillan Company, 1930. (By a sociologist and, though old, helpful as a guide to mastery of the subject from the criminological viewpoint.)

Holmes, O. W. Jr., *The Common Law,* Boston, Little, Brown and Company, 1881. (See Chapter II of this masterpiece of American legal literature, so sophisticatedly written one may overlook that it is a pioneer approach.)

Jenks, Edward, *The Book of English Law,* Boston and New York, Houghton Mifflin Company, 1929. (By the Professor of English Law and Dean of the Law Faculty at London University. Of charming style and clarity. See Part IV "The Criminal Law" (Chapters XIII–XVIII).

Kenny, Courtney Stanhope, *Outlines of Criminal Law,* based on Lectures delivered in the University of Cambridge, Fifteenth Ed., revised by G. Godfrey Phillips, Cambridge, University Press, 1936. (A classic brief exposition by an English scholar.)

Michael, Jerome & Wechsler, Herbert, *Criminal Law and Its Administration—Cases, Statutes and Commentaries,* Chicago, The Foundation Press, Inc., 1940. (Materials and Theory with the Philosophy behind them.)

A *sine qua non* is the perusal followed by the study of a *Penal Code* (or Penal Law as it is sometimes called) and a *Code of Criminal Procedure.* The jurisdiction would not matter. The differences between jurisdictions are for the most part shades.

Ploscowe, Morris, *Crime and the Criminal Law,* Volume 2, of The National Law Library (Roscoe Pound, Super Ed. & Nathan Isaacs, Ed.)—P. F. Collier & Son Corporation,New York 1939.

(This is a discussion and, in a high sense, criticism of Crime and the Criminal Law by the Former Deputy Commissioner of Investigation of New York City, the compiler of the Wickersham Report, now a N. Y. City Magistrate. It addresses itself to problems rather than subjects, though to both, and is sustainedly as lucid as provocative.)

CRIMINALLY RECEIVING. A person who buys, receives, withholds or conceals any stolen property is guilty of a felony. The purchaser or receiver must assume the burden of making reasonable inquiry to ascertain the right of the seller to dispose of such property. When stolen property is found in the possession of a person, such person must be able to prove that he made a reasonable inquiry. If such inquiry was not made, then he is subject to arrest.

Upon the trial of a person charged with criminally receiving stolen goods, the person selling, offering, or delivering such goods is not deemed an accomplice of the person charged with receiving them, and it is competent for the jury to consider the testimony of the person selling, offering, or delivering such goods, even though this person may have been charged with their theft, or convicted of their theft.

A "fence" is a person who illegally receives stolen goods from criminals and disposes of such goods. Very often the "fence", junkman, and other persons who are willing to purchase stolen commodities are also engaged in stimulating delinquencies. The "fence" or receiver of stolen goods is frequently consulted in advance of a crime, and a theft may be executed for the purpose of securing specific commodities desired by the "fence." Somewhat permanent relations are often established between a group of criminals and a particular "fence." "Fences," likewise, are organized in a network which sometimes covers the principal cities of America.

BIBLIOGRAPHY

1. Thrasher, F. M., *The Gang*, Chicago, 1927.
2. Gilbert, F. B., *Criminal Law and Practice of the State of New York*, Matthew Bender and Co., 1935.

CRIMINAL PSYCHOLOGY. The term *criminal psychology* may have a number of definitions, equally valid and differing in range of inclusion. If by psychology we take in all human action and thought under the caption "behavior," then there is little under the heading of criminal and penal processes that falls outside of the field of criminal psychology, including the dynamic development of laws, the factors in sentencing, the factors leading to criminal behavior within and without the individual, the immediate motivations of different psychological types of individuals in committing various types of crimes, the processes involved in penology and in the rehabilitation processes, and finally, the post-penal period of life.

In this article we shall attempt merely a brief over-view of the field with emphasis on various psychological types of criminal. It must be remembered that criminal psychology does not at this period have a compact mass of observational and experimental material such as is possessed by child and adolescent psychology. It can be compared with the psychology of senescence which is beginning to be examined critically, but which has not as yet emerged as a full-blown and clear-cut discipline.

Historical. Crime is a physical action done by man. This is termed *actus reus* in legal language. In the early days of English common law all that was the concern of the law was the *actus reus;* its existence and perpetrator were questions of fact. Any mental and emotional concomitants of illegal acts were unimportant from the point of view of the law; and in theory, children and animals were capable of crimes. Finally, however, possibly through the influence of the church and its concept of the soul and the conscience, the law began to take cognizance of the mind, and eventually for conviction it was necessary to establish the guilty mind as well as the guilty act as expressed in the legal principle: *actus non facit reum nisi mens sit rea.*

This principle opened up, from the historical point of view, the numerous questions about motivation and intent and responsibility which forms such a large part in present determination of guilt and punishment.

The question of responsibility is one that has not been, and probably never will be, settled; each case is a new challenge to the law. An infant is obviously not capable of conceiving or perpetrating a criminal act and therefore any action on its part which may result in a consequence which would be criminal were it to have been done by an adult is surely not punishable. But where should we draw the line of responsibility, in terms of mental and social maturity? Where should we draw the line in terms of intellect? Where should we draw the line in terms of mental diseases?

A rough blueprint has been prepared by the well-known McNaghten rules, which form the operating principles of criminal responsibility. The essence of these rules is that at the time of committing the criminal act "the accused was laboring under such a defect of reason, from disease of mind as not to know the nature and quality of the act he was doing; or, if he did know it, that he did not know he was doing what was wrong." As can be readily seen, this is an all-or-none rule. Such is the nature of the law, but it is not the nature of man, since every human attribute has an extension from little to much. Lawyers and psychiatrists have continually talked of degrees of responsibility, and while in practice this partial responsibility is taken into account, the general rule of all-or-none is still basic legal reality.

It would be difficult to find a point to begin the history of scientific attitudes towards criminal psychology. The thin tenuous thread of the subject can be traced throughout history, but for convenience we can start off with Lombroso, whose conclusions were that criminals were biologically determined, being atavistic throwbacks, who were possessed of various stigmata and psychological quirks, such as low foreheads, lobeless ears, propensities for tattooing, insensibility to pain and so forth. In an attempt to substantiate or rebut Lombroso, the discipline of criminal psychology began. Nowadays, except for some as yet undecided points, Lombroso's theories are discredited. This particular historical development was paralleled also in pure psychology and psychiatry with the generally erroneous but stimulating theories of Gall and Mesmer.

Crime as a Social Phenomenon. It is the individual who is made responsible for the criminal act by law. Law assumes that if a person is not insane, his crime was in his mind, and that the individual is guilty of committing an act against the social good, and consequently is guilty of a reprehensible and punishable action. Nevertheless, it is obvious that crimes in the mass are affected in number and quality by phenomena outside the individual, such as wars, migrations, famines, depressions and other social upheavals. The individual is affected by these things as well as by his immediate environment—his parents and siblings, his neighborhood and acquaintances, his teachers and school mates. The individual, from the day of his birth, is subjected to countless small and great impacts which help to determine his personality. For each person these environmental contacts have great importance. They help mold him for good or for bad, and there is little that the individual can do in the important formative years about modifying this environment.

These environmental influences upon individuals appear to determine the course of individual lives. Sociological studies indicate clearly that the amount and kind of crime can be predicted to close limits of errors for any particular environment.

Crime as a Psychological Phenomenon. An accretion of evidence that is almost overpowering indicates clearly that the infant, not the child, is the father of the man. This means that the host of early influences on the person that is unknown to the mature adult—his own babyhood—are of supreme importance in determining the adult and his behavior. All investigations of minor and major abnormalities indicate that the genesis of such pathological behavior lies in early infancy and childhood. Psychotherapy, of the Freudian type, always leads back to the young child and early forgotten experiences. Criminal actions, as an example of personal pathological behavior as well as of a social behavior, is in some measure determined for each individual by the outside experiences of the child.

Free Will. Throughout history philosophies have struggled with the problem of materialism versus vitalism. We have seen this in many areas; in art it is functionalism versus abstraction; in psychology it is behaviorism versus gestalt; and in crime it is determinism versus free will. In essence the question is this: are we determined by the myriad external and internal forces beyond our control, or are we capable of determining our own directions? To what extent, if any, can we assume that we are captains of our destiny?

From the point of view of law as it operates, free will is the essence of its philosophy. Responsibility is fixed on the individual.

This is an issue that will forever be a problem challenging the best thought of all thinkers. Psychology as a science takes no stand on this issue, preferring to gather and to organize data from all sources until an answer emerges. We can at this period put forth as a hypothesis that the ability of man to decide his course of action is itself determined to some degree, if not entirely, by forces beyond himself. Evil, according to the sociologists, is not a constant, but a variable, changing with the society. The concept of an act "evil in itself" has given way to the act "evil in society."

Criminal Types. In trying to bring order out of confusion, one of the first acts of the social scientist is to break down the mass of data into orderly arrangement. Such arrangements are arbitrary and decidedly artificial but serve the excellent purpose of systematizing the material for further extensive study.

In attempting to subdivide criminals we could proceed from the crime, but psychologically this makes no sense, since any particular criminal act, such as arson, may have a number of causes. Proceeding from the psychological criminal type appears to be better. Now, there are no criminal types, per se, psychologically. Criminals are people who break the law, and from this premise we are all criminals, since the law in any civilized jurisdiction is so complex and pervasive that it is the rare active portion of our society that does not run counter to the rules at more or less frequent intervals. But if we take, as point of departure, as a definition of criminals, that relatively small segment of law breakers who go to penal institutions, we see the emergence of some more-or-less definite types. These types listed below have nothing sacred about them, but serve the purpose of classification.

1. Accidental criminals.
2. Situational criminals.
3. Irresponsible criminals.
4. Neurotic criminals.
5. Psychopathic criminals.
6. Psychoid criminals.
7. Professional criminals.

The Accidental Criminal. The accidental criminal, according to popular opinion, is the person who commits a criminal act without intending to do so. An example is the man who drives a car in a reckless manner, perhaps under the influence of alcohol, and as a result of his wild driving kills someone. The responsibility of the individual not to act in a manner potentially harmful to others is definite. Nevertheless, there was in his mind

no intent to kill; and his action, while criminal in the old legal sense of the word, which did not take into account the mental aspects involved in a criminal act, is definitely not now considered in the same classification as a planned and willful homicide.

The accidental criminal from the legal point of view, may or may not be the accidental criminal from the point of view of psychology. Accidents are looked on with great suspicion because it is clearly evident at the present time that the "accidental" action of man, even against his own best interests, may actually be in harmony with his deep inner impulses. A good example of this is suicide. We accept as a common truth that people want to maintain their existence, nevertheless, we have those who kill themselves. Less obvious, but just as important are those who mutilate themselves, or who behave in a manner so as to harm themselves or others.

A father takes his family out in a rowboat. Through an accident he tips over the boat. He and his family perish. This particular act was an "accident." But what the unconscious motives of the individual were would establish whether or not it was an accident from the psychological point of view. This point will be made clearer in discussing the neurotic criminal, but we wish to establish it in considering accidental criminals: no matter how accidental a criminal act may appear, it may actually be a "true" criminal act from the point of view of psychology, if it is in accordance with hidden unconscious motives. Only when the act is not in harmony with these unconscious desires is the act accidental from our point of view. The reader is referred to Menninger's excellent book for further development of this point of view.

The Situational Criminal. The situational criminal is the person who commits a crime with full consciousness of the wrongfulness of the action and who rationalizes the rightfulness of his behavior due to the peculiar structures and press of circumstances. We have as the classic fictional example of this the crime of Jean Valjean who stole a loaf of bread to keep alive his starving nephew.

Pablo came to a southwestern state from Mexico to work as a fruit picker. When work petered out, he remained until his money ran out. In desperate financial need, hungry, without shelter, and not aware of the possibility of assistance from social agencies, Pablo broke into a house in search of money.

The psychology of the situational criminal may be complex, but the psychology of the crime is simple: it is merely a question of the lesser of two evils. On the one hand is the array of forces that keep a man in line: teachings, attitudes, world-view, morals; and on the other hand is the press of the environmental forces. It is the rare individual who will not willingly commit a crime without even attempting to evade punishment when circumstances place him in a position that to him the breaking of a law is the lesser of two evils. It becomes essentially a question of the first law of nature.

The evaluation of the individuals who commit situational crimes however, indicates that these people have enough in common to make them a type. They are generally inadequate in terms of the society they are in. The ignorant Mexican cited above is a good example. He was not capable of understanding how to manipulate his environment to achieve his aims in a socially acceptable manner. It was not that there were no other alternatives, but that he did not see any.

The statutory rape crimes may be another example of this sort. A man has intercourse with a female not his wife who is below the age of consent in that state and he automatically commits a crime. Were the female a year or two older the action would not be considered criminal, although always considered reprehensible from ethical standards. The more sophisticated roué who is cautious about the age of his paramour escapes punishment, but the more inadequate individual becomes a criminal.

It is perhaps a rare occurrence that an inadequate individual, in the sense that we are using the word, is *literally* forced to commit a crime due to the forces of circumstances, but the possibility cannot be discounted. Fortunately, the law in its practical applications often shows mercy in these cases.

Max, a paroled convict who had a record for forgeries, suffered some business set-backs. He received news one day that his daughter had fractured her arm. Hurrying home, a physician advised him that a certain specialist was needed to repair the damage. The specialist "demanded" payment immediately. Max made out a bad check and gave it to the specialist. When the check was cleared, the forgery was discovered. Max's parole was revoked and he was convicted of a new crime, but was given a minimum sentence. It was evident to all that Max had not had any intention of evading responsibility in this matter.

While most fathers would have done the identical action if necessary, the question that concerns us is the necessity. While to this individual at this moment no other recourse seemed possible, the situation as sized up by him was probably false. There may have been other possibilities of action. Essentially, it is an inadequate comprehension of the situation rather than real necessity. Psychologically, this may be called a situational crime, wherein a wrongful act is willingly committed with full acceptance of responsibility for reasons that are in the main altruistic.

The Irresponsible Criminal. Whether or not we considered the ament and the dement psychologically guilty in their criminal actions is manifestly a value-judgment. Legally, they are not considered guilty, and in all cases, culpability depends on the judgment of experts as to the degree of irresponsibility. Just as an infant who turns on the gas and kills its family can not be considered a criminal, so the idiot and the insane person can not be conceived as capable of realizing the nature of their asocial acts. We witness the distressing scene of opposing alienists giving each other the lie to realize the delicate questions of responsibility. We must admit that the irresponsible criminal may have had conscious and unconscious motivation in directions that he knew was wrong, but that from the point of view of control there was little. Following this point we come to the conclusion that a far greater number of people than might be expected can be relieved of responsibility because of this factor.

The Psychopath. Psychopathy is an unfortunate term, since it means so little, and so much, depending on the writer. As conceived here, the psychopath is an emotionally immature individual, who has intellectual knowledge of his asocial actions, but who is so completely at the mercy of his impulses that he continually acts in an irresponsible manner. Psychopaths make up the bulk of prisoners. They start young and continue in their asocial actions until finally an emotional maturity overwhelms them. The prison psychologist often sees the process of change where the uncontrollable psychopath finally becomes mature. There is a sudden influx of insight, remorse, and conscientiousness so different from the usual pattern of the individual that it should stand closer examination. Qualitatively this change is great and the forces that make it operate are unknown.

One particular inmate diagnosed as a psychopathic personality, explained that while engaged in a conversation with some prison associates he became suddenly aware that their conversation was distasteful. He realized in a flash of insight the consequences of his past actions and the nature of his present attitude. He backed away from the group, feeling a revulsion for them. He walked around the prison yard overwhelmed by the intensity of the insights he was experiencing. He literally changed overnight in his psychological make-up, becoming an earnest, seeking, conscientious, ambitious person.

Another explained this change as occurring while walking down a corridor. He felt peculiar, as though he did not have complete contact with reality, and as though coming out of a dream began to know himself in a new light.

The psychopath is least amenable to treatment at the present time. We know nothing of the etiology of this condition, it is hard to properly define it, nevertheless, the clinician can isolate the psychopath with ease. Only maturity appears to be the solution, and up to this date, we do not know how to hasten this process. Correctional institutions as they exist today are best of all for the psychopath it would seem, since we do not know how to deal with him, but it is quite likely that the nature of these institutions is such that this needed process of maturation is delayed by present penal practices.

The Psychoid. This group impinges on the psychopathic and the frank psychotic. It is composed of those "crazy" individuals, who have all the earmarks of the psychotic, with the bizarre actions, the poor affect, the lack of perfect contact with reality, who, nevertheless, manage to get along in society to an extent sufficient to keep them out of insane asylums.

If we conceive of the psychoses as having extension, instead of being all or none, we can then conceive of schizoid and paranoid individuals who are sick to an extent insufficient to label them legally or medically insane but to an extent sufficient to not make them completely responsible in the normal sense of free-will.

How large this group is said to be will depend on the writer. Some may deny its existence, others may place an unreasonably large number in this group. It remains more a semantic question than one of fact.

The earmarks of the psychoid personality in terms of criminality is the senselessness or lack of psychological necessity for the crime, the unemotional acceptance of punishment, the falling into monotonous routine plus the above described personality aspects of flatness of affect, resignation, attitude of being in a "world of their own," and in general, being isolated from close human contacts. This group does not appear to deteriorate psychiatrically any more than other groups, but does appear to remain in the layer of suspension between the normal and abnormal.

This group, which is often but unjustly called the pre-psychotic, appears to be characterized by a tendency to violent crimes, often with no prior indications, except a peculiar coldness and dispassionate disregard for conventional thinking. Violent sex crimes are perhaps committed more often by this group, than any other type of crime.

The Neurotics. The neurotic criminal belongs in a reasonably clear-cut group, and of all groups the neurotics are the most hopeful from the point of view of immediate psychological therapy.

The neurotic has a problem which he fights, and does not know what he is fighting, why he is fighting, nor even that he is fighting. In his struggle for victory over the unseen and unknown enemy he may punish himself by committing a crime.

The neurotic criminal may appear to most

casual observers as the most culpable of criminals: he knows what he is doing, and does it deliberately. But always the neurotic acts against his own best interests, which is surely not the common definition of crime. Whenever we see a senseless crime, a clumsy crime, one which does not make sense, which is committed by an overconscientious. intelligent individual, we can detect the neurotic who is demanding, according to his distorted logic, release of guilt through punishment.

A respectable clerk began to drink, was separated from his wife. In an alcoholic fugue, he broke into the room of his neighbor who was a policeman, stole his gun, held up two stores, stole and wrecked a taxicab, got on a night-liner and went to sleep, giving himself up in the morning. This at the age of forty-seven, after an uneventful life. In prison he was a model convict and determined to devote his life to helping others, to become a lay monk on release. Besides his alcoholism and peculiar crime we noted inability to urinate when he heard people stirring or talking, as well as a complex of phobias and compulsions.

The neurotics who commit crimes are readily amenable to psychotherapy. The therapy is usually clean-cut and hynotism can be used to discover the immediate motivation. One such neurotic, who became a gunman, under hypnosis, directed his aggressions against the bullies in the school, the adults on his block, and then the trail led to the father. Whether we go to the extremes of the psychoanalysts and compare the big gun in his hand to the big penis with which he overwhelms the father, or if we wish to declare that he had not worked out in an acceptable fashion his incestuous desires, or if we assume his gun-carrying was his reply to his inferiority or a sign of his will to power is immaterial. The fact is that he obtained an insight as to the significance of his gun-toting and showed strong signs of cure.

The neurotic criminal is a victim of his own sickness and his deep motivations in committing a criminal action are to relieve himself of a tremendous pressure.

The Professional Criminal. Perhaps the professional criminal is as clear-cut a type as is the neurotic. He may be a psychological neurotic, but not a neurotic criminal. The explanation of the professional criminal is probably not found in abnormal psychology, but in anthropology and sociology.

He is not found in prisons in proportions to his numbers. While a very high percentage of neurotic criminals go to prison and serve long terms, the professional rarely gets into prison and when he does, rarely stays long. Crime is his business. The reader is recommended to Conwell's fascinating book on this group, edited by E. H. Sutherland.

We find that the professional criminal is normal, psychologically speaking. He understands what he does, knows the social implications of his actions, takes few chances, operates in a business-like manner. Since he operates in a criminal environment, the romantic underworld of fiction, he takes his values and philosophy from this group, which is just as united and as distinct as the culture of the gypsies.

The professional criminal is a specialist, who makes his living from criminal activities. But he firmly defends himself and his values, whenever he will talk. He points to Robin Hood and to Janoschick. He mentions that Dismus was the only person whom Christ assured of heaven. He insists with ardor and reasonable logic that all men have larceny in their hearts, that you can't cheat an honest man, that merchants, lawyers, doctors, ministers, mechanics, landlords, and psychologists are crooks. He cites the ruthlessness of big business, the universal tax evasion, the constant smuggling, the eternal petty pilfering, all to indicate that stealing is universal. He is most bitter towards crooked policemen, "fixed" judges and venal district attorneys. He insists that all men are basically dishonest, that dishonesty should have no moral implications since it stems out of the first law of nature, and that those who are honest are either not brave enough, or have no need of being dishonest, or have been so conditioned against dishonesty that they won't even act in their own best interests.

He cites many cases of complete loyalty among thieves, of the higher virtues, of patriotism and is bitter in his excoriations of those who prey on him and still retain their respectability. He insists that moral judgments are perverted view points.

As an example of the thinking of a professional thief the following is a summary of a conversation with a man of fifty, whose life was just one crime after another, and who was now serving his fourth felony sentence.

"I befriended this man, gave him money. He was down and out and I helped him get on his feet. I introduced him to my friends. I taught him the trade. I always insisted that he get a good sized cut of the proceeds. He was quite happy. He was now well off. In one of the jobs he was caught together with several others. I escaped. All the others kept their peace. He squealed. He squealed on me. They arrested, tried and convicted me. He got away with a small sentence, which was suspended. How did I feel hearing him accusing me on the witness stand? I marvelled, that is just the word. I was really overcome with surprise. I even was envious of him. Why? Because he wanted freedom so much that he would turn on a pal. Such an action is almost uncomprehensible to me. Of course, he must die, there is no other way he can expect to be treated. He must know it. I still like him. I have no animosity towards him. I was just surprised."

This makes terrible logic if the reader can accept all the premises necessary to understand this type of individual. He truly belongs in a world of different values from those of our society.

Psychology of Treatment of Crime. Our concern with crime is to reduce it. We have two general classes of criminals, those who have not been institutionalized and have not had "treatment," and those who have had. The psychiatrist and sociologist together with the economists have given us clear indications of what to do to reduce this first type of crime, for crime is affected by various environmental factors. But a good deal of crime is committed by those who have been "treated" for their criminalism.

We have seen many methods of handling criminals: none have been too good. As far as can be told, our present methods are just as poor. Be it torture, identical treatment, banishment, death, institutionalization, isolation or rehabilitation, the sole purpose of correctional treatment should be to reduce the frequency and the degree of crime. Whether it be negative conditioning, work habits, insight, psychoanalysis or academic and social education that are used as crime reducing methods, the sole criterion of any method must be a pragmatic one.

No method of treating criminals has been proven good; although some methods have been proven bad. Centuries of punishment have taught us almost nothing about the relative efficiency of various systems of handling criminals. Changes are based on hypotheses and none has been evaluated in a comparative sense. The elementary principles of scientific measurement and evaluations as practiced in the physical and social sciences have not been practised with respect to crime. The mounds of research data, the mountains of case histories and volumes on crime show no final lesson. Never has a clear-cut, scientifically oriented investigation of the effectiveness of penal treatment been made. We appear to be as close to final truth in this matter as in the days when witches were burned.

Penal development has been unsystematic and based on temporal, cultural philosophies. The principles of separation of the sexes, of segregating the criminally insane from the sane criminal, and the juvenile from the adult are only products of recent periods. Such administrative classifications have only limited therapeutic possibilities. It is only when classification of treatment is done in terms of personality types that effectiveness can be expected in group treatments. We are proceeding on the assumption that group treatment can be effective, a doubtful premise, but one worth trying out.

Our present manner of classification and treatment appears to be conceived as being universally applicable: neurotics, psychoids, psychopaths, professionals, casuals, and accidentals can all be helped by academic education, vocational training, classes in social ethics, recreation and exercise, movies, radio, and the thousand and one "rehabilitating" factors in addition to time.

Psychology, as one of the disciplines that is steeped in the scientific traditions, views the modern prison as a makeshift. While all men have some things in common, and various treatments affect them multilaterally, criminal personality groups are not alike and criminality will not yield to identical treatment. This is absolutely no brief for humanitarianism, education, or psychological treatment. Espousing these would be an example of bias: what is needed in penology is not new, or "better," or more advanced "treatments," but comparative evaluations, and basic research. We must get away from the idea that something is good, because it is self-evident.

Operating on what are frankly hypothetical grounds, we must assume that since no universal treatment will produce good results, the problem is to classify criminals and to work on them in different manners. What these methods will be that will operate satisfactorily we do not know. But perhaps we can make some reasonably shrewd guesses.

The neurotic should yield best to psychotherapy, the kind and extent varying with the degree of neurosis.

The psychopath probably should react best to kindness, and love, the lack of which probably causes his lack of maturity. This is, of course, in absolute variance to all thinking with respect to psychopaths, and it must be admitted that the prospect of attempting such treatment is a frightening one.

The psychoids probably need chemical treatment and psychotherapy.

The professional criminal probably cannot be treated, and strong negative conditioning may be the answer.

For all these classes there must be a large number that will need extended treatment, or renunciation of all treatment as chronic cases. But treatment must be considered not as coddling, just the opposite. We must even admit the possibility of the therapeutic value of torture and complete isolation and operate on impartial and scientific hypotheses.

RAYMOND CORSINI
Senior Psychologist
Guidance Center
San Quentin, California

BIBLIOGRAPHY

Corsini, R. J., Criminal Conversion, *J. Crim. Psychopathology* 1945, 7, 139–146.
East, William & Hubert, W. H. deB., *The Psychological Treatment of Crime*, H. M. Stationery office, 1939.

Goddard, B. H., *The Criminal Imbecile.*, MacMillan, 1910.
Gross, H., *Criminal Psychology*, Little, Brown, 1911.
Hooton, E. A., *Crime and the Man*, Howard Press, 1939.
Lombroso, C., *Crime, Its Causes and Remedies*, Little, Brown, 1911.
Menninger, K., *Man Against Himself*, Harcourt, 1938.
Conwell, C., *The Professional Thief*, (Edited by E. H. Sutherland) University of Chicago, 1937.

CRIMINOSES. To the juristic mind, the average criminal is just a criminal upon whom justice should be rendered. To the religious man he is one who has sinned, a sinner. To the police he is a quarry, culprit, or lawbreaker. To the warden of a prison he is an inmate. To his mother he is someone to be forgiven and pitied, while to his partners he is a friend. In all of these relationships there are varying degrees of a sense of responsibility, danger, hate, and love. Theoretically, these are least so in the juristic point of view, undoubtedly largely present in the deliberations of a jury. Inasmuch as no social structure heretofore has shown any striking solution of the problem of crime, one may, without presumption, apply newer instruments. Science has made so many contributions to the current way of living that one is not necessarily foolhardy in attempting to apply a scientific method, or as close an approximation of the scientific method as is available, in order to secure a first understanding. The scientific method attempts to be as dispassionate as possible; much more so than a court of law.

The scientist is not a gullible, tenderhearted, pitying individual. The hallmarks of all great scientists are courage, perseverance, extensive and intensive effort, lack of concern for self, and devotion to the cause of discovering new knowledge. Great discoveries often have been made at moments of actual detachment from the scientific task at hand.

An essential tool in the hands of the scientist is a terminology that is free of emotional meaning and that most accurately describes the thing that is meant. The word criminal is of juristic origin and has become exceedingly weighted with emotional content in the human mind. The word delinquency is softer but its monetary implication and the obvious fact that crime generally is examined from its aggressive rather than omissive (delinquent) aspect, leaves this word highly inaccurate. The writer and others have for some years used the word criminotic to describe the individual who commits crimes, and the word criminosis to the condition of such an individual. The word brings to mind similar words in psychiatry such as neurosis (a mild to a moderate nervous illness) and psychosis (a severe nervous illness). One does not necessarily have to assume that the criminotic individual is ill but the term criminosis would imply *his* condition.

Psychoanalytic theory has posited that the motives as played out by Oedipus (Sophocles) are present in each individual from earliest childhood and that these tendencies persist in the unconscious throughout life. Fundamentally they consist of closer attachment of the boy to the mother and strong hostility to the father, with the reverse combination in the girl. Later these patterns play themselves out in society with various figures such as officials, teachers, etc., acting as surrogates. These tendencies pass through the vicissitudes of life and are altered, transformed, and converted, so that one later may be quite different from and unlike Oedipus; indeed, one may become civilized and with any such feelings and ideas so well buried, organized, disciplined, or what you will, as to make it seem unbelievable that they ever existed. Considering how close the child is to its parents and for how many years it has only its parents upon whom to express its feelings, the idea is not at all shocking. In that the story of Oedipus conforms to so much that is discoverable in human beings and since its ancient character leaves it emotionless to present society, it serves as a convenient framework or perhaps scaffolding to aid in study and building.

The libido is a term used in analysis to describe the emotional thread that binds child to parent, but also as a term to describe the dynamic driving quality (of a sexual or love nature) within the child and hence within the adult. Many psychologists, Freud among them, later gave up the tendency to view the libido or main drive as being essentially sexual. Among many writers the term libido was expanded to include a more general concept; this led to some confusion. This writer found it satisfactory to retain the term libido for the separate or sexual drive and to use the term vita for the dynamic life drive. Thus the instinct of self preservation would be closest to the call of life and its dynamic outgoing core would be the vita. The instinct of reproduction would have the libido as its central moving core. These two drives are present from birth, the libidinal for many years rather thinly present in infancy and later assuming a crucial role during certain maturational phases of life.

The libido is to the vita as the periscope is to the submarine (a rough analogy). The libido is most sensitive and like the periscope to the outside observer, gives a considerable clue as to the course and direction of life beneath the surface. Earliest infancy is characterized by the child conceived to be just a womb or intrauterine child, then being a born child who gasps for breath and seeks for warmth in the relatively cold world. Then it becomes a mouth and teething baby in its first and second years when feeding problems are most pressing. Soon in learning to control its excretions it becomes a urethral and anal baby. When it learns to walk and talk it is something of a skeletal or muscular baby, and finally when it reaches the age of five or six, becomes curious about the difference between the sexes and plays the doctor game, it is something of a sexual baby. These phases pass and the child goes to school to become the educated child, while after school hours it is all zest for play and social relationships. At puberty new things begin to happen. Influences may operate upon the individual at any time of life and fortunately so, or else law, religion, psychiatry or any technique to alter and mold character would be but mockery. The examination of an individual's life from earliest infancy does give the nature of the foundation that was laid and what materials were used to rear the edifice of the individual; hence what may alter him.

At once plastic and impressionable, the infant passes through these early phases with considerable difficulty. If the adult could re-experience the pain of being born or being weaned, it is doubtful if he would question the severity and profundity of his earliest experiences. Earliest training leaves its impress upon one's constitution and character and so it is not surprising that so many individuals in whom this training deviated considerably from average should still show strong marks of primitive infantile patterns; in some orality (the heavy drinker, the gourmand, the biting sadist), in some anality (the sloven or over-meticulous). That even crime should show such impression—the tooth-like dagger of the assaulter and the tooth-like sadistic pen of the forger, the anal explosiveness of the gun holding robber—is not at all remarkable.

Later life is largely a series of sublimations (refinements), reactions (conversions to usefulness) of many primitive infantile traits. The infantile activities are the liquid concrete, stone, and molten steel that form in time the foundation upon which the more attractive edifice of human life is built. One also can judge of the nature of the foundation by the height, durability, and massiveness of the overlying structure. Also one now may anticipate what sort of structure is likely to arise from the sort of foundation that parents help to lay in their children. Much study, therefore, has contributed to help us classify the criminoses on the basis of early structural development and early influences. It is only exceptional events such as desperate and prolonged diseases, unsuspected and great fortunes and misfortunes, or extensive psychiatric treatment (all powerful external influences) that have any possibility of altering rather than merely deflecting the earliest structural setting and its subsequent fatalistic effect. Lighter events may tinge, color, or conceal fundamental character, but not truly alter it in any degree.

A classification is nothing more than a rough summary, a topographical outline of much accumulated research and knowledge. A classification based on the above knowledge puts order and reason into much of the data of the penal code. The average individual hardly knows the difference between robbery and burglary. One may inquire as to why a criminotic individual follows such a sequence of crimes as this—larceny of a car, burglary, robbery. The reverse order of development has not been observed by the writer. The answer is found in sequential maturational development.

As a last formal element it may be helpful to indicate two types of crime—criminosis in action and criminosis in reaction. By criminosis in action is meant the condition of an individual who commits an open, forceful, active crime upon person or property. Examples would be burglary and assault. Society, as a rule condemns the entire act. By a criminosis in reaction is meant the condition of an individual who commits a crime in which the form is correct but where society condemns the degree of the act. Such crimes are forgery and swindling. The check is usually a negotiable instrument, not so the gun. Swindling often differs from legitimate business activity merely in the degree of profit involved. In the criminotic reaction one often finds many favorable influences throughout childhood and yet the career subsequently becomes criminotic.

Now although a great disturbance in early development may color and condition later behavior, it is not by any means the necessary cause of that later behavior. The individual largely fixed in an oral phase may become a gourmand, a drinker, or a burglar. These are all different from one another. Hence it is now necessary to examine further, for factors and influences which not only influence the form of crime but which may indicate why crime occurs at all.

As in other fields of science, psychoanalysis early recognized something of a dualism in human affairs by its concept of a sort of conscience—a super ego acquired during training in early childhood. In later years Freud saw more deeply and conceived of the dualism as a struggle between two instincts—the life and death instincts. He apparently began these studies too late in life to fully develop his ideas and their confirmation. His death instinct seems but a pale reflection rather than anything dynamic or singular enough to be called an instinct much less a death instinct. His theory is sketchy though broad and actually lacking in logical structure. He was not acquainted with such violent manifestations of life such as one observes in the criminotic individual. He was perplexed by such tendencies in an average office patient. He apparently was in no position to see, until his very last moments, the struggles between life and death such as our times offer. He was unacquainted with glaring emotional depth in connection with action and the primitive man laid bare. This is no criticism of a great man, but a guiding post to where the newer knowledge must be sought. The problem is obvious to one who has seen these things and there is all the difference in the world between the urban patient who may leave one's office in a huff and the criminotic individual who with complete and ironic sangfroid, may toss a previously concealed dagger on one's desk as he leaves at the end of a therapeutic hour.

A dualistic concept is not strange in the human economy. The heart beats show such regularity and pace by virtue of one set of nerves that makes the heart go more rapidly and another set that slows it down. If one or the other of these sets of nerves is interrupted, the heart beats very rapidly or very slowly, either of which conditions, in extreme form, may bring about what is called death. If both of these systems are interrupted the heart beats irregularly and chaotically. In the body there are two sets of metabolic processes, one set of which (anabolic) builds and the other of which (katabolic) breaks down. The stomach and other muscles of the body do not merely contract, but expand as well and bodily activity is nicely carried out by antagonistic pairs of muscles. The skin may blanch or become red. Each organ of the body is not merely a loose conglomeration of cells but has an enclosing envelope which keep the cells compact. Each cell not only has its cellular activity within, but is held in check by its active, alive, cell wall or membrane.

In our expanding age, a mental blindness makes us focus on the expanding quality of things rather than the contracting qualities. People prefer to speak of life rather than any limitation to life, although it is easily seen that both are equally necessary. The heart beating without restraint would soon

lead to death. Unchecked growth would lead mankind into something like a wild cancerous formation. The emotional bias of the times prevents the individual from seeing much valuable scientific data.

Above, the vita, whose tendency is to drive bodily processes at ever higher rates, has been mentioned. The words vita, vital, vitality all have the same origin. The vita is merely the dynamic core of what usually is considered to be vitality. Unchecked vitality may cause death and disease to the individual and incidentally to others as well. Anyone who has observed children has recognized how readily they play until very exhaustion. At some point or other, processes in the body have a tendency to check excessive vital drives. The chest may tighten, a muscle may go into a cramp, etc. As helpful as these latter processes are in preserving existence, people as a rule resent and dislike their effects, again the one-sided view of our age. In Egypt where the dead were not hidden but rather held before the public eye constantly, disciplines and restraints may have been less obnoxious than today. The tendency of the vita is to expand and expend itself. If the tendency of the vita were unchecked one would virtually explode and not exist for very long in the human state. As unpleasant as it may be, it therefore is necessary to recognize within the human being, a dynamic drive that opposes constantly the too ready tendency of the vita. The vita and its opposite usually are in pretty good balance. The sentinel must be ready either to spring or to hold back.

This second drive is called the fatum, the drive that limits. The fatum includes the inhibiting, disciplining, controlling forces within the human economy. This is the inherent drive, which when projected into the external world is called fate. Most individuals conceive fate to be something highly unpleasant to think upon, mysterious, suspect, and non-existent. The rage and resentment such a concept brings forth shows the underlying fear; from fearful people we may not expect a solution of such a great problem as that of crime. Those who disparage the concept of fate or a fatalizing force are usually at a loss to explain or define life, except by some humorous cliché. It is disturbing to vanity and ambition to learn one is not entirely in control of one's future. There thus are the comparable words fatum, fatal, fatality and fatalize. The hypervitalized person burns like kindling wood and does not live long although he may live brilliantly. The hyperfatalized person may be consumed from within.

In an automobile, one may set the gas intake for a rich mixture. The car may show a sort of vital drive, quick pick-up, speed, etc. It is to be expected that a car driven hard will not last as long as one driven with more discretion. Similarly some individuals are hypervitalized (and some hyperfatalized) in early childhood. There is a sufficiently large area to work with if we study what is inherited, the environment, rather than that about which we eventually may know more, heredity per se. There is sufficient experimental knowledge to show the effects of early environment on degrees of vitality and fatality. Force, unless it be crushing, stimulates vital drives; love may do so as well as when a mother leaps to save a child from falling.

The criminotic individual in his crimes shows a high degree of vitalization. At times he continually may show such effects. The sheltered and ignored child may become inhibited and moronic, truly hyperfatalized. Force applied to an individual who cannot subsequently act may leave him almost paralyzed in action, hyperfatalized. In examination, the economy involved shows several possibilities. If early environment is instrumental in this hypervitalization of the criminotic individual, one would expect it to show in searching through their childhood histories. Thus, we approach the problem of causation in crime more intensively. One should not expect the aggressive criminotic (not all are aggressive) to tell of violence done to him in early childhood. To one who is permitted to do violence, the violence done unto him does not necessarily bring about hate (if parents also provide food and shelter, or companionship) and the criminotic is no less loyal to his relatives, especially when he knows that his questioner may use the knowledge given in some injurious way. Half a dozen years in daily contact with criminotic

individuals and tested and trusted from all angles will yield data otherwise unobtainable.

The childhood of the aggressive criminotic is characterized by exposure to unusual degrees of force, compulsion and violence. He is not crushed by this exposure because he bounds outwardly and delivers his impact to the world, thus saving himself in a way. The following thus may be given as the three main causal factors in crime. They are: first, a severe trauma, injury or stimulation to life or to the vita (the vital drive) sustained in infancy or early childhood. To this would be added the continuance of the stage of the traumatic situation for a considerable time. The traumatic situation revealed, usually is one of violence. One person recalled being torn from his mother's arms by an irate father, never to see her again; he was two at the time. Another recalled a stepmother who viciously, in anger, and with a knife stabbed the two eyes of the only picture of his mother. Another recalled a violent beating and homosexual assault at the age of four. Another remembered a violent thrashing by a mother and three brothers for the theft of an old 50-cent paper bill, which later was discovered to have been stolen by one of the brothers who was most active in the thrashing. Another person recalled a vigorously playful mother who, in addition to her manual cuffings, once cut his penis with a breadknife. One remembered being chained up for a day by a choleric father. One recalled standing beside his father as the latter carried on a gun duel with a relative. One remembered a flight through a fire escape at the age of 13, his father in hot pursuit with a gun in his hand. One does not find such experiences in every childhood. The additional factor here is that one does not as a rule find any leaven in the family environment. It is excessively rigorous and harsh. The surface worker will find many broken homes in the history of criminotic individuals, but he cannot see the true causes. The criminotic is hypervitalized in childhood.

The second etiological factor is that of a real want or need that cannot be satisfied in the home but is otherwise satisfiable. The writer supposes you will expect him to say it is the economic factor. The writer wishes he could say this. It would be fortunate for mankind if this were so. By a real need, he means what follows from the foregoing—a lack of real human personal warmth, understanding, encouragement, feeling, balanced firmness, limited emotional sweeps and such like.

The third factor that is of great etiological significance, is the hidden participation of other members of the family and later of other members of the community in the criminotic behavior. This participation may be overt or merely consist of sanction in any number of possible ways. The bribe-taking judge, the sharing policeman, the seller of stolen goods, the gun-seller, down to the relative who takes a gift of extraordinary dimensions, not questioning the source or blinding himself to the source, all contribute to the crime. When a man who has stolen reads of the thefts committed by some distinguished

man he automatically gets sanction for his own crime. Healthful fatalization thus fails or may be avoided.

ARTHUR N. FOXE, M. D.
Associate Managing Editor, Journal of Nervous and Mental Disease; *Associate Editor,* Psychoanalytic Review.

BIBLIOGRAPHY

Foxe, A. N., Crime and Sexual Development, *The Monograph Editions,* 1936.
Foxe, A. N., The Life and Death Instincts, *The Monograph Editions,* 1939.
Foxe, A. N., The Life and Death Instincts, *Journal of Criminal Psychopathology,* 4:67, July, 1942.
Foxe, A. N., Critique of Freud's Concept of a Death Instinct, *Psychoanalytic Review,* 30: 417, October, 1943.
Foxe, A. N., The Massive Structure of Delinquency. *Psychiatric Quarterly,* 16:681, October, 1942.
Foxe, A. N., An Additional Classification of Criminals. *Journal of Criminal Law and Criminology,* 30:232, July-August, 1939.

D

DECEPTION, SCIENTIFIC DETECTION OF.

Important points along the road of physiological discovery, leading to the development of the Polygraph, date from the time of Galileo, who, as a boy of eighteen attending the University medical school (1564), stood staring one day, during divine services, intrigued by the swinging lamps in the cathedral of Pisa. His lips were moving; the fingers of his right hand were clamped to the pulse of his left wrist; he was counting. For untold years those lamps had swung, as worshipers by the hundreds of thousands had watched them idly and then gone their way never dreaming they had been brushed by the wings of a great mystery—for Galileo had discovered the law of the pendulum, made possible the clock, and devised a doctor's instrument to count the pulse accurately. Dr. Harvey some fifty-two years later first recognized and described the circulation of the blood; then a few years after Galileo's death (1642) his pupil Torricelli, continuing his researches, developed the manometer. Now the stage was set for the Reverend Stephan Hales, an Englishman (1741), to discover that there was a pressure to tree-sap. Groping a step further he deduced that man, and animals as well, must have a blood pressure. He demonstrated this by inserting a brass tube into the crural artery of a horse. It was more than a century later before the first estimation of blood pressure was made in man (1856) when Dr. J. Faivre, a French military surgeon, who had a patient requiring amputation of the arm at the elbow, connected up the main artery by means of a rubber tube to a manometer and found that the mercury column was forced upwards 120 millimeters. The blood-pressure in this soldier's case was 120 millimeters of mercury, or, as we say today, simply 120 systolic pressure. This method of taking blood-pressure as a routine would have proven cumbersome so the world had to await the advent of an Italian physician, Scipione Riva-Rocci, who, in 1896, developed the blood-pressure cuff which, with some modifications, is the same device we use today both in the doctor's office and the lie detector laboratory.

The next phase of the Science of Detection of Deception took place at the Harvard Psychology Laboratory where its head, Prof. Hugo Münsterberg (1908) accidentally discovered the phenomenon of detection while recording blood-pressure and respirations on a kymograph. Some of his student-subjects happened to prevaricate in answering certain questions. The experimenter soon noted the following physiological changes: (a) increased rise of blood-pressure, (b) quickening of the pulse beat, and (c) changes in the respiratory ratios. He tied them in with the Phenomenon of Deception. As soon as he ascertained by a follow-up inquiry that untruths had been uttered and that these characteristic changes had occurred because of fear-of-being-caught. The so-called blood-pressure "lie detector" was discovered, in this way, by Münsterberg. Like many professors of the old school, he made no practical application of this discovery. Consequently, the technique was forgotten until one of his students later made certain innovations in it.

Neither the student's adaptation of the Münsterberg technique, nor the Northwestern Crime Detection Laboratory's Polygraph recording device, developed later, was ever admitted in the courts, in any case where it was offered as evidence over objections. In both instances where it was presented, the high courts rejected its "findings." Up to 1935 laboratory lie detection was shackled to the uncertainties of a technique where there is, admittedly, an approximate working error of 25%.

There were five main reasons for the rejections of the polygraph as trial evidence before 1935:

1. No blood-pressure lie detector operator had apparently ever analyzed or established the medico-legal status of the device, as applied to persons qualified to be given this type of emotional test. No non-medical operator had realized that there were two "machines" to qualify—the measuring machine or blood-pressure lie detector, and the human "machine." Before any experienced court of record will even consider admitting this type of examination as evidence, both "machines" must be duly and properly qualified as being in good working order and as valid, reliable instruments.

2. The only way in which the human subject can be qualified to suit the requirements of a court is for that subject to be physically and mentally examined by a doctor of medicine, skilled in psychiatry and in giving detection tests. This is necessary in order to determine whether or not the subject is normal in body and mind, capable of being given such a physiological test based on emotional reactions.

3. There was need for a muscle-graph to record the minute changes that muscular movements will produce in one's blood-pressure. When a subject was measured on a polygraph, sans a muscle-graph, even by a qualified physician, an astute cross-examiner could question whether the full rise of blood-pressure was because of an uttered untruth or the movement of some body muscle. The muscle-graph was invented by the writer to anticipate this difficulty. The writer constructed a special chair for the testee to sit in during the lie test. This chair is inflated so that any muscular movement can be recorded immediately on the tape alongside the other graphs.

4. The instrument used for the lie detection test, must be certified as, recognized equipment assembled from standard scientific parts, in good working order, and accurate in its recordings at the time the graphs were made.

5. The expert must be familiar with the proper taking and marking of the graphs and skilled in the use of the particular lie detector. He must prove that he took, or made the graphs, or was present when the graphs were recorded. He must give a description of the body of the person and the juxtaposition of the machine when the graphs were made. He must establish beyond a shadow of a doubt that the graphs were always in his possession and had not been tampered with between the time they were made and the trial. The graphs must be clearly identified as belonging to the person whose responses were recorded. Evidence must be offered concerning the number of such graphs he had previously made and how many years he had been engaged in the field of lie detection. The expert witness must testify as to his interpretation of the lie detector graphs, the correctness and accuracy with which the graphs reflect emotional reactions, and the internal emotional condition of the defendant.

The examiner must prove to the satisfaction of the court that the physiological variations recorded on the graphs were caused by the questions asked and the answers given to them. He must introduce as evidence graphs made when the defendant responded to known truths to be compared with the answers presumably causing the blood pressure or other physiological changes.

The lie detector was introduced as evidence for the second time in 1935, before the Federal Employees' Compensation Commission, Deputy Commissioner Kenneth G. McManigal presiding. A colored employe had suffered a broken arm and brain concussion. When the graphs were shown him he quickly broke down. Going before the Commission the next day the man was placed on the witness stand and upon interrogation of Deputy Commissioner McManigal he stated for the record that the lie detector was "right." Whereupon the Deputy-United States Commissioner stated for the record that he considered this test a "scientific malingering test."

The third admission of the lie detector in medico-legal history was in New York State (August 1935). An employe of the Buffalo Waterfront Corporation, contended that he had a severe spinal injury sustained in line of duty. Having occurred on the water it automatically became a Federal Employe matter. The medical evidence offered for and against was so contradictory that the Deputy-United States Commissioner, hearing this case and remembering the results obtained in the recent Chicago hearing which he also presided over, continued the case and ordered a test. It showed the claimant had never been injured on the premises as claimed. The lie detector proved he had been injured working for an entirely different company months before. The lie detector thus clearly exposed the dishonesty of his claim and, although the claimant even told lies while on the lie detector to his own attorney, the lawyer objected to the lie-detector evidence the next day at trial but was promptly and properly over-ruled. The Commissioner found against this litigant, where, if he had been successful it would have cost the Company at least $15,000.00. The case was never appealed!

Since 1935 lie detector experts have been successful in obtaining admissions of such technique in evidence, over objections, of both the Polygraph and Psycho-Detecto-Meter (Electronic Lie Detector). The findings have cleared up a large number of litigated controversies.

No essay on psychological tests, whether utilized in Criminology or in other fields is complete without a full explanation of the newer electrical methods of carrying out brain-body measurements. It took many years of much experimentation before bio-electrcity, brain-body electronics were discovered and their present method of measurement made possible.

The human brain, says Prof. Edward Burge, University of Illinois physiologist, has an electrically positive cortex in sleep and is electro-negative during waking consciousness. A sleeper has 1/100th of one micro-ampere of current but on awakening has five times as much. There is greater positive charge on the scalp over the thinking areas of the human brain.

Emotions, whether caused by external stimuli which excite fear or rage, or by memory or imagination are brought about by a change in the electrical potential of the brain. Thal-amic-cortical conscious apprehension and perception bring about changes or fluctuations in electrical potential in the brain.

When one measures these fluctuations in electrical energy by proper contact, he can accurately determine it in terms of any particular human mind's electrical-change-reaction to a word stimulus, because in all living human beings there is this same bio-electrical change and it is reliably accurate in every rational individual. The fractional micro-amperes of fluctuation do vary somewhat, depending upon age, sex, and condition of health.

The efficiency of this technique, as compared to the Polygraph, now antiquated as an efficient lie detector technique, is quite apparent. With this newer electrical method one can discard costly preliminary medical tests of the subject. With the Psycho-Detecto-Meter all individuals, if rational, can be taken on for the test directly from the waiting-room. It is no difficult matter to determine whether or not the individual is rational because the preliminary discussion of the high lights of the case in question with the subject, occupying some 15-30 minutes. provides ample time to arrive at an opinion as to the normalcy of the mind under observation.

The development of a scientific method of measuring brain-body electrical changes produced by emotional stimuli definitely refutes the objections by Judge Wickham in the State vs Bohner, Wisconsin case as well as the earlier similar objection of Judge Van Orsdel in the Frye v United States the Court of Appeals for the district of Columbia affirming the decision of a lower court which had held inadmissible expert testimony in explanation of a blood pressure deception test. They based their objections on "the uncertain character of the test in view of the experiments carried on up to that time." Just when a scientific principle or discovery crosses the line between experimental and demonstrable stages is, of course, difficult to define.

Today blood-pressure deception tests have definitely "emerged from that twilight zone," are no longer experimental and are truly in the demonstrable stage, if the blood-pressure technique is handled under medical supervision and the subject is qualified prior to the test. With our widespread knowledge of the accuracy of other brain-body measurements, such as the Electrocardiograph, (which measures electrical potential differentials in the heart) and the Electro-encephalograph (which measures brain electrical potential change to detect brain electrical variations in certain types of suspected intra-cranial brain pathologies, such as Dementia Precox, Epilepsies and Brain Tumors), there is no logical medico-legal reason today for refusing admittance as evidence to the Psycho-Detecto-Meter, the writer's invention, or the Pathometer, developed by Father Walter G. Summers, whereby brain-body electrical potentials are mechanically recorded as they occur in rationals stimulated by answering definite psychometric questions. There is a characteristic electrical pattern when the truth is told, as well as one characteristic of the brain electrical change when a subject tells a lie and thereby undergoes the emotional reaction that always accompanies a "fear of being caught" stimulus under proper test conditions.

ORLANDO F. SCOTT, M. D., Director
National Detection Laboratories
330 So. Wells Street
Chicago 6, Illinois

BIBLIOGRAPHY

Inban, Fred E., *Lie Detection and Criminal Interrogation*, Williams and Wilkins, 1942.
Larson, John A., *Lying and Its Detection*, University of Chicago Press, 1932.
Trovillo, Paul, A History of Lie Detection, *Journal of Criminal Law and Criminology*, Vol. 29, March-April, 1939, 848–881.

DEFECTIVE DELINQUENT. Before the inception of scientific methods for the diagnosis, classification and treatment of offenders against society's laws, every institution or state school for the feebleminded contained a certain percentage of inmates with criminalistic tendencies. They constituted a problem far out of proportion to their numbers because of their inability to benefit from or adjust to the programs of these institutions. Similarly, most prisons included criminal offenders who were feebleminded and could not fit into the prison programs by reason of their mental defect. Experience and progress led to the recognition of these individuals who were both mentally defective and socially delinquent as a special group in need of segregation and specialized methods of treatment and control. At first they were known as "moral imbeciles." Now they are referred to as "defective delinquents" and constitute a most troublesome class of the socially maladjusted.

One of the pioneers in the treatment of the feebleminded, Dr. Walter E. Fernald, recognized the defective delinquent type as early as 1910 and later described the individuals of this group as seen in his institution as follows:

"Many of this class are defiant, abusive, profane, disobedient, destructive and incorrigible generally. They honestly feel that they are unjustly confined and do not become happy or contented. They frequently attack those who are responsible for their custody. They resent every effort to amuse or entertain them. They have a very bad influence on the ordinary defective who constitutes the legitimate problem of the school for the feeble-minded."

Most experts in the fields of criminology and mental defect now agree that these individuals constitute the greatest menace to society of all the mental defectives even though numerically they comprise slightly less than ten percent of the total feebleminded population. They frequently simulate the normal very closely and so most observers expect from them normal behavior and adaptation to life. At the same time, their limited mentality and inability to recognize their own limitations, difficulties and responsibilities, prevents their profiting from experience. Therefore, their supervision and guidance is a costly item to society.

Authorities agree that the defective delinquent is a person who is both criminalistic and mentally defective but some have gone further in defining the term. Dr. Butler, in his presidential address to the American Association on Mental Deficiency in 1942, states that "the diagnosis of a defective delinquent briefly is an individual of subnormal intelligence who has decided anti-social tendencies as well as psychopathic attributes." In other words, he is *subnormal, criminalistic* and *psychopathic*. According to this view, he must be all three in order to qualify as a defective delinquent.

Dr. Davies, in his classic work on the social control of the mentally deficient, applies the term defective delinquent to "those feebleminded in whom anti-social and criminal tendencies are found to be so deep-seated as to require care and treatment quite distinct from that of the usual mental deficiency institution."

From the legal point of view, a working definition of defective delinquency is provided in the 1928 amendment to the Massachusetts law which states:

"If on a hearing on an application for commitment as a defective delinquent, the court finds the defendant to be mentally defective and, after examination into his record, character and personality, that he has shown himself to be an habitual delinquent or shows tendencies towards becoming such, and that such delinquency is or may become a menace to the public, and that he is not a proper subject for the schools for the feebleminded or for commitment as an insane person, the court shall make and record a finding to the effect that the defendant is a defective delinquent and may commit him to such department for defective delinquents according to his age and sex, as hereinafter provided."

The guide of the American Prison Association regards the defective delinquent as "an offender, who because of mental subnormality at times coupled with mental instability, is not amenable to the ordinary custody and training of the average correctional institution and whose presence therein is detrimental both to the type of individual herein described and to the proper development of the methods of rehabilitation of other groups of delinquents. Further, the defective delinquent, because of his limited intelligence and suggestibility, requires prolonged and careful training, preferably in a special institution to develop habits of industry and obedience."

From the practical point of view applied by correction departments, a defective delinquent is simply a mental defective who has been convicted of a crime and committed by the court to an institution for defective delinquents or one who has been transferred to such an institution from a state prison after having been found to be mentally defective.

The accurate and thorough diagnosis of defective delinquency requires the joint application of psychological, psychiatric, medical and sociological techniques to the study of the individual. The diagnosis concerns itself with establishing the fact that the offender is a mental defective and determining the degree of mental defect, confirming the fact that he has well-defined delinquent tendencies which are concomitants of the mental defect and discovering any indications of mental instability which may be present. The first two of these fields of inquiry are essential to making the diagnosis and the third is of value in helping to solve the problem of management of the case.

In the cases of low grade defective delinquency of the idiot and imbecile types, there is little difficulty in diagnosis. Developmental history and present behavior may be sufficient to establish a diagnosis with psychometric results adding something to prognosis and medical examination helping to determine possible etiology.

However, the greatest percentage of defective delinquents fall into the moron and borderline groups of mental deficiency. Here, careful interpretation of data from psychological, social, educational, medical and other examinations is required and skillful differential diagnosis based on extensive clinical experience is necessary.

The *psychometric examination* should include at least one verbal test of intelligence and one non-verbal performance test. If possible, these should be supplemented by a variety of other tests. Performance ratios or I. Q.'s consistently below 60 on several types of intelligence tests are strong diagnostic evidence of mental defect. Consistent performances represented by ratios from 60 to 75 or 80 may indicate feeblemindedness but require strong supporting evidence to establish the diagnosis. Inconsistent performances on tests of different types must be interpreted only in the light of other data.

Educational examination through achievement tests, indicating school retardation of three years or more when there has been adequate opportunity for schooling, is very suggestive of deficiency. Accomplishment ratios of 100 or less in persons having I.Q.'s below 60 to 70 strengthen the diagnosis of feeblemindedness. If the accomplishment ratio is over 100, it would suggest that the subject's psychometric functioning is spuriously low. Since poor reading ability brings both intelligence test and achievement test performance down, the possibility of its influence should be eliminated.

In the *social history,* economic or vocational adjustment may be important. Frequent changing from one unskilled, ill-paid job to another suggests inability to make an economic adjustment. In the consideration of delinquencies as part of the social history, it is important to determine the type of offense and the circumstance under which it took place. Crimes committed at the instigation of another person may be evidence of suggestibility which may afford added weight to a diagnosis of mental defect.

The *developmental history* of the defective usually shows retardation in several directions. Locomotor behavior, talking, bowel and bladder control, habits of feeding and dressing and the like will frequently be established at significantly later ages than in normal individuals. Such findings are of value because they indicate that the retardation has been present at an early age and is not something of recent appearance.

The *family history* is valuable in bringing out its socio-economic pattern and may account in part for the social behavior exhibited by the patient. Evidence of nervous or mental disorder and defect in parents, grandparents, children, collaterals or other relatives of the patient may serve to indicate the presence of pathology possibly related to the feebleminded condition but such data cannot establish a diagnosis without strong clinical evidence.

Medical and physical examination is important in the lower grades of defect, especially for determining possible etiology. In the medical diagnosis are included investigation of anatomical abnormalities and physiological, endocrinological, and neurological dysfunction and pathology. Such data can-

not establish the fact of feeblemindedness but they may be corroborative.

Once the fact of mental defect is demonstrated, it is then necessary to establish that the individual is criminalistic. This is usually determined through clinical *psychiatric examination* and psychological study supplemented by an evaluation of the criminal history of the subject compiled by the sociologist or probation officer. The existence of psychopathy and mental or emotional instability is also determined through psychiatric examination and is important for prognosis, treatment and management of the case.

Most cases of defective delinquency must necessarily be treated by separate segregation in a specialized type of institution for defective delinquents for a prolonged period of time. A certain percentage of selected cases can later be paroled under adequate supervision after they have developed suitable habits of industry as well as some insight. After a period of adjustment or parole, a very small percentage can be discharged from supervision when they are in a particularly favorable and stable environment.

The need for a specialized type of institution for defective delinquents was first recognized in 1910, when Dr. Fernald formulated for the State of Massachusetts the first law in this country, providing for their separate segregation. This law was passed in 1911, but it was not until 1922 that it was actually put into effect with the establishment of a division for male defective delinquents at the Massachusetts State Farm.

By act of the legislature in 1921, New York State established a special state institution for male defective delinquents at Napanoch. That institution was opened June 1, 1921 and thus became the first separate institution of this kind in the country. The law relating to the Napanoch Institution provided that it is for the care, training and custody of male defective delinquents over sixteen years of age. Napanoch may receive both by direct commitments from the courts or by transfer from the state prisons. The Woodbourne Institution for Defective Delinquents was opened in 1935 to relieve overcrowding at Napanoch and receives inmates only by transfer.

Institutions for defective delinquents have been conducted both along the lines of a penal institution and of a mental deficiency institution. As an example, the Woodbourne Institution is a medium security prison with dormitory provisions such as prevail in the usual civil institution. There is an active program of training for the inmates, including industrial training in the various shops of the institution. Many of the inmates find occupation on the institutional farm.

The law permits the parole of any inmate, after expiration of minimum sentence, to the custody of a parent, relative, legal guardian or other person. Each year a certain number of inmates are paroled and a fair percentage are discharged from parole after a successful adjustment in society.

A recent study by MacPherson based upon analysis of the cases of over one thousand juvenile delinquents appearing before the Hartford Juvenile Court concluded that "mental defectives who are continually before the Court need institutional training, and could, if such were given, be paroled later with a fairly high expectancy of success." Butler, in his analysis of the admissions to a California institution for mental defectives from 1931 to 1941 found that 39% were defective delinquents and that 24% of the boys and 35% of the girls adjusted later on parole with at least fair success.

Several investigations (Dybwad, Hart, Andriola, etc.) have recently supported the view that the institution for defective delinquents offers at least a partial solution to the problems involved in the treatment of such offenders. So far, only in the states of Massachusetts, New York, Illinois and the federal penal system are feebleminded delinquents given special treatment.

SAMUEL B. KUTASH
Chief Clinical Psychologist
V. A. Mental Hygiene Clinic
Newark, New Jersey

BIBLIOGRAPHY

Andriola, J. P., Some Suggestions for Treating the Defective Delinquent. *J. Criminal Law and Criminology*, 1940, 31, 297-302.
Branham, V. C., The Classification and Treatment of the Defective Delinquent. *J. Criminal Law and Criminology*, 17:183-217, 1926.
Butler, F. O., *The Defective Delinquent,* American Journal of Mental Deficiency, 1942, 47, 7-13.
Davies, S. P., *Social Control of the Mentally Defective*, Thomas Y. Crowell Co., New York, 1930.

DETAINERS. A detainer may be defined as a warrant filed against a person already in custody with the purpose of insuring that, after the prisoner has completed his present term, he will be available to the authority which has placed the detainer. Wardens of institutions holding men who have detainers on them invariably recognize these warrants and notify the authorities placing them of the impending release of the prisoner.

Such detainers may be placed by various authorities under varying conditions. For instance, an escaped prisoner may be apprehended in another state for the commission of a felony there and be institutionalized. Upon receiving such information the warden of the institution from which the man escaped may place a detainer with the authorities in the prison where the man is currently being housed, requesting that he be informed so that he may return the prisoner upon completion of his term. Again authorities in charge of parole in one state may place such detainers against a man who has absconded from parole and has committed a felony while at large in another jurisdiction, the purpose being that they be informed when a man has finished his current sentence, so that arrangements may be made for his return, or for concurrent parole.

These are illustrations of the placing of detainers on men who have already been in custody and have illegally departed from jurisdictions having authority over them. Detainers may also be placed by sheriffs and district attorneys. Let us suppose that a man has committed a crime in one state and in escaping has stolen an automobile, crossed state lines, committed a crime in a second state or perhaps even in a third. He is apprehended somewhere along in his career of crime. Immediately there will be state civil authorities interested in returning him to their jurisdiction for trial; the federal government may be interested in trying him for violation of the Dyer Act. One of these various jurisdictions will try the man first and sentence him to a term of years in prison. Authorities in other areas where he has violated the law will place detainers and will very likely, upon notification of his having finished his sentence, return him for trial for the crime committed in their jurisdiction. The process will continue until he will have paid in full for each of the crimes in the series.

All of this appears reasonable. It would seem in order that authorities in quest of a violator of the law should have every assistance in returning him to their jurisdiction. However, this system of placing successive detainers has long been a problem to penologists. They have deplored the practice and its evils, have tried to do something about it, but have not been particularly successful.

The difficulties involved in this system affect the judges, the institutional officials, the paroling authorities and the individual himself. The judge faces a problem when he is called upon to fix the sentence of a man involved in a series of crimes. The specific offense for which the man has been tried in his court may not have been particularly serious, but the judge is aware of the fact that this is but one of a series. Shall he then take into consideration all of the crimes in a series and impose a sentence commensurate with the entire situation, or shall he weigh only the offense for which the man has been convicted and impose a sentence which might customarily be given if the case before him were an isolated crime? The prisoner, too, is in a state of confusion; he does not know when he will reach the end of the time to be served in successive sentences for all his offenses, for in all likelihood, one jurisdiction after another will try him and imprison him. Before the end of the series has been reached he will feel that injustice has been done him, for the total length of time he is serving for all of his crimes will seem far out of proportion to the demands of justice, or to fulfill the requirements of a program of rehabilitation.

The problem confronts the institutional officials when they are trying to map out a program for the man against whom a detainer has been filed. It is a tenet of modern penol-ogy that one of the aims of institutionalization is rehabilitation. Therefore, it is a function of the prison authorities to do their best to fit an inmate in attitudes and habits for life on the outside. Aside from helping him with his mental and personal problems they must seek to equip him for a useful job when once he returns to free life. However, such planners face a difficulty when they know that upon finishing the present sentence the inmate is likely to go to a prison in another state to do additional time. What, they will ask, are the facilities available for training in that institution. If the institution now holding him plans for the ultimate placement outside, possibly by the time he has finished his second or third sentence he will have forgotten all he knew about the trade which was taught him. And yet it may be a fair question to ask how well an institution may be said to acquit itself of its task if it does nothing to train this man, merely because he will have to do time after he leaves it. It may be added that the fact of a detainer usually places restrictions upon the program that will be followed in any one institution, for prison authorities rarely grant trusty status to an inmate who is wanted by another jurisdiction.

Again the likelihood is that the inmate himself will be little inclined to cooperate with the officials if he knows that he has a lot of time facing him elsewhere. What good will it do him to learn a trade or to establish an excellent record if it has no effect at all toward reducing his time. He is likely, therefore, to slip into habits of getting along as best he can, doing only what is required of him and failing to put forth any strenuous efforts toward self-help. His morale will be low and he may be permanently lost to any effective program of rehabilitation.

The placing of a detainer may also affect the man's parole. There are jurisdictions, of which the federal government is one, who will not consider a man for parole if a detainer has been filed against him. Aside from the question of the justice of such a policy, there is no doubt but that it has a detrimental effect upon the prisoner's morale. No matter how well he has performed he will have to serve his maximum sentence.

There is a wide difference in the attitude which the paroling authorities of the various states take toward detainers as effecting parole, the length of time which a man will have to serve, the question of concurrent parole, and insistence upon a man's return to stand trial on the offense for which the warrant has been filed. In the majority of states the placing of a detainer does not have any appreciable effect upon the time which a man must serve on the current sentence. Most states will decide the question of parole, using the same measuring stick they would use in cases of men who do not have detainers; they will "parole in custody," that is, they will parole him from the institution and notify the state filing the detainer that the prisoner will be turned over to them if they send the proper officials. In some states, however, the filing of a detainer means that the man will automatically be passed to serve his maximum sentence. In a few states such action is not automatic but is nevertheless the rule. There are also a few states in which a man with a detainer actually serves less time than he would normally, on the theory that the state who has the man last should have time and opportunity to plan a program for him, and that therefore the inmate should be turned over to this state as speedily as is consistent with justice.

Again there is a variation in the attitude of state parole authorities on the question of the return of the inmate against whom they have placed a warrant. Some states insist upon the return of every parole violator on the theory that their Parole Board members should interview the man before they grant parole. Others will accept the recommendations of the authorities of the state where the man is now being held and will agree upon a concurrent parole, thus permitting the man to serve his parole period on both sentences concurrently.

Numerous suggestions have been offered toward the solution of problems of detainers. It has been suggested, for instance, that in the case of a man who has committed a series of crimes covering several states, the judge who hears him first should communicate with all the other jurisdictions and impose a sentence that would be considered commensurate with all of his offenses. There are, of course, numerous difficulties to overcome. The first is securing the agreement of all the authorities concerned. Again it may happen that the last offense is the least serious and the law might not permit the imposition of sufficient time. Another suggestion offered is that the man be turned over to the jurisdiction where the most serious crime was committed with the proviso that the other states will then waive the detainer. Others have contended that the prisoner should be turned over to the state in which the first of his series of crimes was committed, particularly if that is his home state. He can then be tried in his home community and serve his time where his friends and relatives can visit him, and ultimately be returned to a job in his own locale.

As far as paroling authorities are concerned, those who are conscious of the evils inherent in the system of detainers contend that no state should automatically pass a man with a detainer to his maximum sentence. It would seem reasonable to suggest that states should not insist upon the return of a parole violator serving term in another state, but should accept the recommendations of the authorities there, and agree upon a concurrent parole. Laws which make service of the maximum sentence or the return of a parole violator mandatory under these conditions should be repealed and discretion given to the parole board.

GARRETT HEYNS
Member, Parole Board,
Lansing 13, Michigan

BIBLIOGRAPHY

A detailed discussion on detainers can be found in "Federal Probation," July-September, 1945, Vol. IX, No. 3.

DISORDERLY CONDUCT. This term is used to characterize a group of minor violations of various kinds. Thus, under the Penal Law of the State of New York, which is representative, any person who, with intent to provoke a breach of the peace, commits any of the following acts, shall be deemed to have committed the offense of disorderly conduct:

1. Uses of offensive, disorderly, threaten-

ing, abusive or insulting language, conduct or behavior;

2. Acts in such a manner as to annoy, disturb, interfere with, obstruct, or be offensive to others;

3. Congregates with others on a public street and refuses to move on when ordered by the police;

4. By his actions, causes a crowd to collect, except when lawfully addressing such a crowd;

5. Shouts or makes a noise either outside or inside a building during the night time to the annoyance or disturbance of any considerable number of persons;

6. Interferes with any person in any place by jostling against such person or unnecessarily crowding him or by placing a hand in the proximity of such person's pocket, pocketbook or handbag;

7. Stations himself on the public streets or follows pedestrians for the purpose of soliciting alms, or who solicits alms on the public streets unlawfully;

8. Frequents or loiters about any public place soliciting men for the purpose of committing a crime against nature or other lewdness;

9. Causes a disturbance in any street car, railroad car, omnibus or other public conveyance, by running through it, climbing through windows or upon the seats, or otherwise annoying passengers or employees therein;

10. Stands on sidewalks or street corners and makes insulting remarks to or about passing pedestrians or annoys such pedestrians;

11. Is engaged in some illegal occupation or who bears an evil reputation and with an unlawful purpose consorts with thieves and criminals or frequents unlawful resorts;

12. Carries or has in his possession a "stink bomb" under circumstances evincing an intent to use or employ it for the purpose of injuring, damaging or destroying the real or personal property of another; or of disturbing the public peace.

13. Secretly loiters about a building, with intent to overhear discourse therein, and to repeat or publish the same to vex or annoy or injure others.

The offense of disorderly conduct is punishable as follows:

1. By imprisonment in a county jail or workhouse for a term not exceeding six months, or by a fine not exceeding fifty dollars, or by both;

2. By placing on probation for a term not to exceed three years.

BIBLIOGRAPHY

Gilbert, F. B., *Criminal Law ana Practice of the State of New York,* Matthew Bender and Co., 1935.

DRUG ADDICTION. When we speak of a drug addict we generally mean a person who is addicted to the use of habit-forming narcotic drugs. The legal definitions of habit-forming narcotic drugs and addict are as follows:

"The term 'habit-forming narcotic drug' or 'narcotic' means opium and coca leaves and the innumerable alkaloids derived therefrom, the best known of these alkaloids being morphia, heroin, and codeine, obtained from opium, and cocaine derived from the coca plant; all compounds, salts, preparations, or other derivatives obtained either from the raw material or from the various alkaloids; Indian hemp and its various derivatives, compounds, and preparations, and peyote in its various forms.

"The term 'Addict' means any person who habitually uses any habit-forming narcotic drug as defined in this chapter so as to endanger the public morals, health, safety, or welfare, or who is or has been so far addicted to the use of such habit-forming narcotic drugs as to have lost the power of self-control with reference to his addiction."—Section 221, Title 21, Foods and Drugs. The Code of Laws of the United States of America.

A few people become addicted to narcotic drugs innocently. Cases have been reported illustrating that a baby may be born addicted to opium or its derivatives provided that the mother has used such drugs during her pregnancy. Before the rigid control over patent medicines went into effect it was not unusual for individuals to become addicted unwittingly to heroin or opium contained in cough medicines and tonics.

However, the vast majority of addicts are introduced to narcotic drugs knowingly. About half of this group take to drugs for the relief of some unpleasant physical or mental condition, e.g., pain or other disagreeable symptoms associated with physical diseases, insomnia, worry, fatigue, mental depression, alcoholic hangovers, grief, abnormal sexual impulses, and the like. The remaining half of the group resort to the use of narcotic drugs through simple curiosity. This curiosity may be aroused through association with addicts or it may be the expression of youthful enthusiasm for trying anything once especially if it is socially taboo and promises to give a new thrill or sensation.

According to the records of the U. S. Public Health Service Hospital at Lexington, Kentucky, morphine is the most commonly used narcotic drug, heroin, the second most common. Users of opium and marihuana (the American counterpart of Indian hemp) are in the minority. Up to the present time no patient indulging in peyote has been received at that hospital. A negligible number take such opium derivatives as codeine, pantopon, and dilaudid. A considerable number use paregoric when morphine or heroin is unavailable since paregoric is comparatively easy to obtain, but only a few confine themselves to the use of this opium preparation. Individuals addicted exclusively to cocaine are becoming quite rare.

Narcotic drugs may be taken into the body in a number of ways. Thus opium and marihuana may be taken by smoking. Powdered cocaine and heroin may be inserted into the nose like snuff. Opium in the form of suppositories can be introduced by rectum. Practically all drugs can be taken by mouth. However, the dyed-in-the-wool morphine or heroin addict prefers to take his drug by hypodermic needle injecting it either under the skin or directly into the vein thereby combining quick action with minimum wastage of drug. This method of administration has one draw-back. Most addicts become careless about sterilizing their syringes and needles before use, consequently they are prone to develop infections and abscesses which in turn leave unsightly scars. These scars together with fresh needle marks are

considered presumptive signs of addiction to one of the opium derivatives. Cocaine which may also be taken by needle, tends to produce a bluish discoloration of the skin at the site of the injection. When taken by the nasal route for prolonged periods of time cocaine has a tendency to cause perforation of the nasal septum.

Under the influence of OPIUM or its derivatives the individual's skin becomes slightly flushed, warm, and moist. The pupils of the eyes constrict and the mouth feels dry. There is usually an accompanying sensation of warmth and well being, a diminished sensibility to pain and discomfort, a dreamy state during which the imagination is given free play, and finally a feeling of drowsiness shading off into sleep. That is what the addict is so desirous of experiencing. Unfortunately the continued use of opium or its derivatives at the same dosage eventually fails to produce this feeling of euphoria. As a consequence the individual gradually steps up his dosage in an effort to recapture the desired effect. He is able to do this because he develops a comparative immunity to the toxic manifestations of the drug so that he can take quantities which would produce serious symptoms or even death in unaccustomed individuals. This phenomenon is known as tolerance. It is not peculiar to the opium family of drugs, but may be associated with the use of many other drugs.

The most characteristic phenomenon connected with addiction to opium or its derivatives is the development of physical dependence which results in very distressing symptoms when the drug is abruptly withdrawn. The initial symptoms are yawning, watering of the eyes, running nose, sneezing, and sweating. These are followed by loss of appetite, dilatation of the pupils, tremor, restlessness, and the appearance of goose flesh. At the peak of this trying period which occurs about the third day the individual develops rapid breathing, fever, marked restlessness, insomnia, elevated blood pressure, nausea and vomiting, diarrhea, marked weight loss, and generalized aches and pains. Sometimes death may occur. All this misery may be relieved by resuming the use of the drug.

Contrary to popular belief the continued

use of the opium series of drugs, per se, does not lead to insanity, criminality, or physical breakdown. If an individual has an unfailing source of supply for his drug and an income adequate to support his habit in addition to maintaining a good standard of living, he can live the life of a respectable, honored citizen in his home community. If he has sufficient means to buy his drug, but not enough to maintain a decent standard of living, he will neglect his nourishment to the detriment of his physical well-being. If he does not have the wherewithal to purchase drugs then he must resort to begging, borrowing or stealing. Many addicts become narcotic drug peddlers in order to support their own habits. The common practice is to keep half the supply for personal use. The remaining half is diluted with milk sugar in equal amount and sold to the next customer. He in turn may practice the same duplicity on another victim. In other words the average opium, heroin, or morphine addict is not inherently a criminal. He is forced by the necessity of keeping up his habit to engage in illegitimate pursuits. To be sure some criminals become addicts, but addiction is merely incidental in their careers. Three-fourths of the patients at the Lexington Hospital had no delinquency record prior to addiction.

COCAINE, marihuana, and peyote differ from opium and its derivatives in that they do not produce physical dependence. Cocaine brings on a feeling of calmness, increases endurance to fatigue and hunger, and stimulates both mental and physical activity. However, the pleasant effects of the drug are usually followed by disagreeable sensations and irritability. To counteract the latter some cocaine addicts learn to take morphine or heroin with the result that these drugs are substituted for the cocaine. Certain individuals prefer a combination of cocaine and morphine or heroin. This is known as a "speed ball."

MARIHUANA or Indian hemp tends to produce hallucinations and a peculiar distortion of the sense of time. The hallucinations are usually of a pleasant character, but may on occasion be quite disagreeable or even terrifying. Most characteristic is the seeming prolongation of time. One addict in describing his sensations stated, "it took me a hundred years to climb up a table leg." Another effect of the drug is a loss of the ability to discriminate between what is good and what is bad; a three piece honkey-tonk band may sound like a top-notch orchestra. This may be the reason why some musicians think they can play better under the influence of marihuana.

PEYOTE is derived from a species of cactus plant and its use is practically confined to Southwestern Indians who take the drug as part of a religious ritual. Its effect is somewhat similar to marihuana, but there is a greater tendency toward hallucinations involving all the senses.

Marihuana, cocaine, and peyote do not produce physical dependence hence they may be discontinued without any physical suffering to speak of. As a consequence there is not the extreme drive to get the drugs at any cost. These drugs may be considered in the same light as alcohol in that they release inhibitions thereby revealing the true character of the individual. If he is base, vicious, or criminally inclined, he will exhibit these traits much more readily when he is under the influence of the drugs than when he is not. The marihuana users who get into trouble are usually those who also engage in selling the drug or those who congregate in unsavory social centers where they are likely to be raided by the police during a marihuana party.

While only opium and its derivatives produce a physical dependence, all narcotic drugs engender a strong psychological dependence. It is this factor that makes drug addiction so difficult to treat. It is simple enough to treat the physical dependence. The two major requirements are a controlled, drug-free environment and a gradual reduction of the drug to minimize the withdrawal symptoms. But the removal of psychological dependence entails many empirical measures such as the correction of physical defects, vocational training, religious instruction, the establishment of healthy recreational outlets, psychological probing into mental conflicts, building up the habit of living without the aid of drugs, finding suitable employment and a home after institutional treatment has been completed, and anything else that may contribute to the rehabilitation of the individual.

Once an individual becomes addicted to a narcotic drug he may choose to remain an addict, but by so doing he runs the risk of conflict with the law. If apprehended he may be placed on probation provided that he submits to treatment for his addiction in a private sanitarium, a state hospital, or, in the case of federal offenders, at the U. S. Public Health Service Hospitals in Lexington, Kentucky and Fort Worth, Texas. Most convicted addicts are given definite sentences to serve in city, county, state, or federal penal and correctional institutions.

Motivated by a genuine desire for a cure, by pressure from relatives and friends, or by fear of eventual legal entanglements a narcotic drug addict may voluntarily choose to terminate his habit. He may attempt a self-imposed cure at home with or without the supervision of his family physician. In the case of individuals addicted to opium or its derivatives such self-imposed cures are almost invariably doomed to failure because the environment is not controlled. In other words the patient can secure drugs at will to alleviate the suffering of withdrawal. If the addict has money he can enter a private sanitarium for treatment, but this is generally unsatisfactory because he may leave whenever he wants to which is usually too soon. If the addict has no money he may in some localities commit himself to a state hospital for a cure or else commit a petty crime so that he may be jailed long enough to "kick" the habit. At the present time any narcotic drug addict is eligible for treatment in Lexington whether he is able to pay or not. If he is able to pay it costs him one dollar per day. If he cannot pay, he must submit three affidavits from citizens in his home community stating that the applicant is unable to pay. His treatment is then given free of charge. Applications for treatment must be submitted to the Surgeon General, U. S. Public Health Service, Washington, D. C. Voluntary patients sign an agreement to remain in the hospital for one year if necessary, but this agreement is not legally binding. They must be released if they insist upon it. Under the circumstances two-thirds of the voluntary patients leave against medical advice.

Experience at the Lexington Hospital has shown that the most ideal patient to treat is one who has been placed on probation on condition that he submit to treatment for his addiction. The medical staff can keep such a patient in the hospital until he derives maximum benefit from institutional care, usually a period of nine months. After leaving the hospital he still remains under the supervision of his probation officer to whom he must report at regular intervals until the expiration of his probationary sentence. As an added precaution the hospital has inaugurated a new service for probationer patients who live within a reasonable distance from the institution. They are called back every 30 or 60 days for a 24-hour check-up including a urine and blood analysis for alcohol and opium derivatives. The knowledge that this test will be made helps the probationer in his fight against the temptation to use narcotic drugs.

The consensus seems to be that once an addict always an addict and that therefore any treatment is futile. A follow up study of patients released from the Lexington Hospital in 1936 revealed that five years after discharge the addiction status was unknown in 32 percent of the cases, 12 percent had died, 47 percent had relapsed to the use of drugs and only 9 percent were known to be still abstinent. Practically all those who relapsed did so within the first two years after leaving the institution. Only 29 percent returned to Lexington for further treatment and 58 percent had no history of subsequent admissions to any institution. While the chances for permanent cure may not be good at least they are not entirely hopeless. Moreover, as the research in the field of drug addiction begins to bear fruit, the prospects for cure will become increasingly brighter.

MICHAEL J. PESCOR, M. D.
Mental Hygiene Consultant,
Department of Public Health,
Atlanta, Georgia

BIBLIOGRAPHY

Felix, Robert H., Some Comments on the Psychopathology of Drug Addiction, *Ment. Hyg.*, 23: 567–582 (October, 1939).
Himmelsbach, C. K., The Morphine Absti-

nence Syndrome, Its Nature and Treatment, *Annals of Int. Med.* 15: 829–839 (November, 1941).

Kolb, Lawrence, Drug Addiction as a Public Health Problem, *Scientific Monthly,* 48: 391–400 (May, 1939).

Kolb, Lawrence and Ossenfort, W. F., The Treatment of Drug Addicts at the Lexington Hospital, *So. Med. Jour.,* 31:914–922 (August, 1938).

Pescor, Michael J., A Statistical Analysis of the Clinical Records of Hospitalized Drug Addicts, Supplement 143, *Public Health Reports,* (1938).

Ibidem, Follow-up Study of Treated Narcotic Drug Addicts, Supplement 170, *Public Health Reports* (1943).

Terry, Charles E. and Pollens, Mildred, *The Opium Problem,* The Committee on Drug Addiction, Bureau of Social Hygiene, N. Y. (1928).

Walton, Robert P., *Marihuana, America's New Drug Problem,* J. B. Lippincott Company, Chicago. (1939).

E

EDUCATION IN PRISONS. Two conflicting viewpoints are involved in prison education. First is the prevalent idea that education is a panacea for many evils. Second is the notion that prisons exist primarily for the incarceration of law breakers. Current educational thought would condemn any attempts at coercion in education. Prisons are fundamentally coercive institutions. Sutherland says, "Prisoners cannot be expected to appreciate efforts to help them when the institution as a whole is designed to injure them and make them suffer." [19] Ideally the educators advocate procedures that facilitate the growth of an individual in becoming a relatively well informed, socially useful and well integrated person. This implies acquisition of basic academic tool subjects, vocational training, health education (mental and physical), education for citizenship (including how to get along with people), and education for leisure time. There many educators who doubt if the objectives named above are being successfully achieved by our public school system. Therefore the likelihood of attaining these goals in prisons becomes even more debatable.

Although many educational programs have been instituted in prisons, the changes wrought are relatively negligible. Sutherland states: "Many prison administrators and many prisoners have expressed a belief that prison schools are an excellent reformative influence. Few attempts have been made to measure this influence and most of these attempts have not been reliable." Visits to prisons by impartial observers may elicit favorable comments concerning the educational program, but prison employees know about the "window dressing" arrangements that are common in prisons for creating favorable impressions. Well meaning prison teachers and prison educational directors are forced to justify their positions, if they want to continue their employment, by deliberately, or unwittingly and unconsciously presenting the best features of their efforts and playing down the obstacles and the opposition with which they are confronted. Administrators, educational directors and prison staff members acquire a vested interest in the continuance of whatever educational measures are in progress, since their future security is involved and they are forced to defend the procedures that they helped institute. Innovators are frequently resisted by those having a vested interest in the continuance of extant methods.

The following are features of prison life that are educational: formal classrooms; shops for vocational education; library facilities; recreational activities (i.e. inmate theatrical productions, educational radio programs, discussion groups, inmate orchestras, glee clubs, athletic teams, prison newspapers, etc. . . .); religious programs; and correspondence courses.

Prison inmates generally have less educational background than the general population and this may be related to the fact that a large proportion of these individuals had difficulties adjusting to school situations. Maturation cannot be presumed to have a sufficiently favorable effect on attitudes toward education. The hostility aroused among prison inmates by the actual or assumed oppressiveness of prisons is a further deterrent to rapport. Contempt for prison officials for their real or fancied corruption and prisoners' awareness of the need for education among prison staff members augment the negative attitudes of prisoners. Inmates generally believe that self-respecting individuals would rarely accept employment in a prison. This is borne out to some extent by the fact that salaries are relatively low for desirable and qualified personnel, and the inmates use monetary success standards for the evaluation of people. Well paid prison positions are presumed to be dependent on political favoritism. Trained staff members with good intentions are frequently frustrated and have the choice of leaving prison work or doing the best they can under trying conditions.

A preponderance of prison employees are cynical about attempts to reform prison inmates, and they are hostile to the occasional well trained individual who attempts genuine rehabilitation. The debut of qualified personnel is deemed a threat to their security by the untrained prison staff members. Custodial employees might be impressed by prison educators if examples of rehabilitation could be readily demonstrated. But this rarely happens. Budgetary provisions for educational purposes are low because legislators and the general public would resent great expenditures for "criminals." Prison administrators are legally responsible for the custody of the inmates and educational endeavors disrupt "custody and security," thereby creating resentment. Prison inmates are occasionally sympathetic towards teachers, especially when they are aware of the hostility toward teachers that the custodial staff harbors. The modern penologist considers the prison's function to be the rehabilitation of individuals and prison a place that is therapeutic in its orientation. Occasionally prison inmates realize that this is the point of view of the prison teacher. The awareness of these occasional sources of rapport between educators and inmates is a further source of alienation between teachers and other staff members.

Prison education is generally a form of adult education. Those who undertake courses in adult education usually choose courses as a result of suitable motivation. Prisoners may take courses because class attendance is compulsory; they have much time to "kill"; they may create the impression of being desirous of rehabilitation; or they may really want to learn. In the few instances where good classroom procedures are attempted these problems are faced; movement of prisoners to and from classes requires changes in existing schedules; additional custodial personnel to watch the inmates en route are necessary; guards to unlock and lock cells are required; and men to count the prisoners while coming and going are needed. Data based on psychological testing are frequently ignored and are occasionally inaccurate so that inmates of varied mental status may be incompatibly grouped for teaching purposes. Greater age differentials; wider variations in scholastic proficiency; less motivation; greater deviation from customary behavior norms; greater frequency of unhappiness, pessimism, resentment and other unfavorable attitudes occur more frequently than in traditional classes.

Usual adult educational materials presuppose more background than is generally found in the prison population. Elementary school curricula are too boring and are considered childish, so that inmate resentment may be engendered. "Adultized" elementary subject matter suitable for prisons is usually necessary. Some of the materials used and developed for our armed forces may be helpful for teaching illiterates or those having very little education. The type of educational content that would be suitable in most instances is not available to any great extent and the prison teacher is largely dependent on originating curricular materials if he expects to be effective. Usually little time is provided for such a purpose and most of the teachers are not sufficiently trained or gifted.

Vocational education in prisons is handicapped by the previously mentioned classroom shortcomings, and additional hardships are encountered. Prisoners are aware of the futility of learning a trade that will not be useful to them in obtaining employment after release. Organized labor is generally hostile to attempts to train people for work in unionized industries. Many employers will not hire "ex-convicts." Some employers hire released prisoners only so that they can obtain less expensive employees. Despite favorable employment conditions, even veterans desiring trade training confront many difficulties, so that it is unlikely to expect prisoners to be cordially received after training in prison shops. Vocational education in prison is usually conducted by shop foremen, rather than by trained vocational teachers, partly as a result of the shortage of good shop teachers and partly because prison shops are usually concerned with benefits for the prison or state, and are conducted on a production basis rather than for educational purposes. The organization of suitable shop training programs requires facilities that are considered too expensive.

Education that fosters good mental health or improved social relations is difficult to institute in prisons because the negative aspects of prison life that have been mentioned heretofore militate against learning how to get along well with others or how to acquire desirable attitudes. Until such time as treatment rather than security is the paramount value little can be done to alleviate these aspects of prison education. Prisons have been described as institutions of post graduate training for criminal careers. Prison inmates do acquire more refined knowledge about crime commission in prison.

Prisons frequently provide adequate facilities for physical exercise and participation in athletics, but formalized health education is subject to the same frustrating conditions as the other structured prison curricula. The opportunity to obtain favorable public opinion and local publicity about the prison often accounts for provision of stadia and paraphernalia for athletic events. But concern for the individual inmate's physical health betterment on an organized basis is rare.

Many leisure time activities in prison are of the hobby variety. Prisoners make objects from match sticks, tooth brush handles, coins, plastics, wood, metal and cloth, but the skill or artistic creativeness involved is seldom the kind that will be indulged in after release and it would be difficult to demonstrate their educational benefits. They do tend to make prison sentences seem shorter and they may have therapeutic mental health values. Utilization of interest aroused by hobby activities as a source of motivation for other learning seems likely but does not occur frequently.

The use of prison libraries is hailed as an educational advantage. An examination of the titles of the books most popular in prison reveals the marked degree of interest in sex that is prevalent in such institutions. The

popularity of comic books in prison is a reflection of reading taste. (Comic books are not provided by prison libraries, but are sent or brought by prisoners' relatives.) The reading taste of prison inmates may be a reflection of that of the general public. The frequency of pornographic drawings and remarks in books in prison may be indicative of less respect for books among prison inmates than is common in the non-prison world. Reading for a desirable objective is largely dependent upon cumulative motivation resulting from previous education or as a result of guidance. Such motivation and guidance is infrequent in prison. Since libraries in many of our large cities are complaining of insufficient financial support, it is not surprising if prison libraries usually lack sufficient funds for the latest and best books.

Prison inmates frequently attempt correspondence course study. The unsophisticated individual is often misled by the glowing promise for the future that characterizes many correspondence school advertisements. Lack of appropriate educational achievement or of scholastic aptitude are limiting factors for the successful completion of the courses undertaken. Such deficiencies can be remedied in a face to face educational framework, since the teacher can readily detect one who markedly lacks aptitude or knowledge of basic tool subjects, but this is not common in the correspondence course business, since loss of fees may be involved. Correspondence courses may be beneficial at times, but it is tragic to see the disillusionment and the antagonism toward education that are a result of unwise selection of correspondence courses.

The educational efforts of chaplains are so varied that it is difficult to assay their value. Undoubtedly there are instances where prison inmates benefit educationally as a result of a chaplain's endeavors. It may be that prison doctors, psychiatrists, social workers, custodial officers, and other prison employees also help prisoners educationally, but no accurate evaluation is possible.

Prison newspapers, orchestras, glee clubs, dramatic presentations offer opportunities for the more gifted or the more aggressive or the more favored prisoners to acquire valuable informal education. But these features of prison life affect only a small proportion of the prison population. Prison newspapers offer a means of disseminating educational data that may be of some help.

Little organized educational activity is encountered in jails and workhouses, because the inmates' residence is deemed too short to warrant any extensive efforts.

Gillin says, "In the face of the social progress of the last hundred years—the progress in educational methods, in knowledge of human psychology and social relations, in methods of teaching students in our schools, in methods of character formation in children, and in knowledge of the roots of social conditions —the prison system stands out as an anachronism and an abomination." An antithesis between penological practice and modern penological theory exists. Any worthwhile educational program would constitute a part of the new penology. A possible solution of the dilemma is suggested by Taft in the following: "The treatment of convicted offenders, adult and juvenile, the new penology would place under the control of a hierarchy of treatment tribunals and departments. These organizations might well be divisions of a state or federal department of correction. The treatment tribunal would need be staffed by trained non-political specialists."

GEORGE GENN
Instructor, Rutgers University,
New Brunswick, New Jersey

BIBLIOGRAPHY

Akers, E. R., A Prison Trade School, *Journal of criminal law and criminology,* 35:311–323.

Barnes, H. E. & Teeters, N. K., *New Horizons in Criminology: the American Crime Problem* (revised edition), New York: Prentice-Hall, Inc., 1945.

Correctional education today, New York: American Prison Association, Committee on Education, 1939.

Farber, M. L., Suffering and time perspective of the prisoner, in Lewin, K. et al. *Authority and Frustration.* University of Iowa: University of Iowa Studies in Child Welfare, 1944.

Gillin, J. L., *Criminology and Penology,* (third edition) New York: Appleton-Century, 1945.

Healy, W. & Bronner, A., *Treatment and What Happened After,* Boston: Judge Baker Guidance Center, 1939.

Ingsam, C. P., *Education in Training Schools for Delinquent Youth,* Washington, D. C.: U. S. Office of Education Bulletin No. 5, 1945.

Kendall, G. M., *The Organization and Teaching of Social Studies in Correctional Institutions,* New York: Columbia University Press, 1939.

Levy, R. J., *Reductions in Recidivism Through Therapy,* New York: Thomas Seltzer, 1941.

Lindner, R. M., *Stone Walls and Men,* New York: Odyssey Press, 1946.

Lindner, R. M. & Seliger, R. V. (eds.) *Handbook of Correctional Psychology,* New York: Philosophical Library, Inc., 1947.

MacCormick, A. H., Resume of Progress in Correctional Education, in *First yearbook of the committee on education of the American Prison Association,* New York, 1939.

MacCormick, A. H. *The Education of Adult Prisoners,* New York: The National Society of Penal Information, 1931.

Morris, A., Criminals' Views on Crime Causation, *Annals American Academy of Political and Social Science,* 1941, pp. 217–238.

Objectives and Standards for Libraries in Adult Prisons and Reformatories, *The Prison World,* Vol. V, No. 4, Supplement.

Radzinowicz, L. & Turner, J. W. C., *Penal Reforms in England,* London, England: Macmillan & Co., Ltd., 1946.

Reckless, W. C., *Criminal Behavior,* New York: McGraw-Hill Book Co., 1940.

Slavson, S. R., *An Introduction to Group Therapy,* New York: The Commonwealth Fund, 1943.

Sutherland, E. H., *Principles of Criminology,* (revised) fourth edition, Chicago: J. B. Lippincott Co., 1947.

Taft, D. R., *Criminology,* New York: Macmillan Co., 1942.

The functions of the prison chaplain in penal and correctional institutions, Joint Statement of the National Conference of Catholic Charities and the Commission of Prison Chaplains of the Federal Council of Churches of Christ in America, *The Prison World,* Vol. V, No. 1

Von Hentig, H., *Crime: Causes and Conditions,* New York: McGraw-Hill Book Co., 1947.

Wallack, W. M., Kendall, G. M. & Briggs, H. L., *Education Within Prison Walls,* New York: Bureau of Publications, Teachers College, Columbia University, 1939.

Wood, A. E., & Waite, J. B., *Crime and Its Treatment,* New York: American Book Co., 1941.

Young, P. V., *Social Treatment in Probation and Delinquency,* New York: McGraw-Hill Book Co., 1937.

EMBEZZLEMENT. Embezzlement is the fraudulent appropriation of property by a person to whom it has been intrusted, as of an employer's money by his clerk, or of public funds by the officer having them in charge. Embezzlement differs from larceny that, in the former case, the property is already in the wrong-doer's possession.

Larceny is a common law offense and need not be statutory, but embezzlement must be statutory. When larceny is statutory, each such statute has followed the common law, possibly adding to it and broadening its scope by defining the property which may be the subject of the offense. Generally speaking, the distinction is between custody (larceny) and possession (embezzlement). Thus, if the property never would come into the possession of the owner except through the medium of a servant, clerk, agent or other individual mentioned in the statute to which reference is made, the conversion by such person is embezzlement. If such conversion occurs after the property has come into the possession of the owner, then it is *larceny*. The felonious taking of goods from the owners' shop by a clerk, who is not a salesman is larceny and not embezzlement. If a person, as a cashier, in charge of a cash fund takes some money therefrom and retains it for his personal use, he is guilty of embezzlement, since his employer has given him a relation of special trust to the property taken by him. On the other hand, if some other employee passes by the open drawer of the cashier, takes some money therefrom and retains it for his personal use, he commits larceny. If the clerk is paid some money on account and before he deposits it in the till, he places the money in his pocket with the idea of retaining it for his own personal use, it is embezzlement. If, on the other hand, this clerk deposits this money in the cash drawer and later appropriates it to his personal use, he has committed larceny.

In New York State embezzlement is known as *larceny by the bailee*. The *bailee of property* is a person who, although not the owner of such property, is entrusted with its care or safekeeping, such as servants, attorneys, agents, clerks, trustees, public officers, etc. These persons come into possession of the property lawfully and are presumed to keep such property for the use or benefit of its true owner. If they use or appropriate to their own use such property without the authority of the owner, they are guilty of larceny to the amount of the property so appropriated. Perhaps the most outstanding example is the clerk or cashier who collects funds for his employer and uses such funds for his own purposes.

Thus, embezzlement is distinguished from larceny in that the property is entrusted to the embezzler; in larceny the property was never legally in his possession.

BIBLIOGRAPHY

Gilbert, F. B., *Criminal Law and Practice of the State of New York,* Matthew Bender and Co., 1935.

EVIDENCE. (A) *Development of Technical Rules.* A very considerable body of American law has been built up around the subject of "Evidence." Much of it concerns itself with rules of exclusion. It deals with the conditions under which evidence will not be received. The rules are often extremely technical and sometimes obscure in purpose and function.

The *rules of evidence* are part of the pattern of growth of The English and American Common Law. To understand why the evidence of the law court follows its present direction and why there is such emphasis on exclusion, it should be recalled that the rules were evolved primarily for the trial of cases before a jury. It was supposed that the layman juror who decided the facts in controversy, inexperienced in deciding legal disputes, would be unable to separate the immaterial and unimportant from the matters really germane to the issue; that he would tend, as people naturally do in making up their minds, to weigh in gossip, rumor and diverse impression, the "hearsay" of the Common Law; that he would be unduly influenced by the emphatic "opinion" of witnesses; that he would not show an adequate judgment of the witness competent to testify concerning a given subject.

For these and some similar reasons, rules grew up in practice which excluded from the attention of the jury many kinds of evidence which might logically be regarded as helpful in ascertaining truth and which would ordinarily be considered in any well rounded inquiry into facts. In systems of law which do not function with juries, the rules of evidence are far more liberal and the officer who decides the issue is regarded as able to segregate those matters which ought to enter into his decision from matters that are unrelated or unreliable.

While American and English law in the treatment of "proof" have some points in common with other systems, notably in insisting upon relevance, and in rules governing the acceptance of documentary proof, there is no such emphasis upon exclusion of evidence in other systems. The trend in the United States before administrative bodies which receive and act upon "proof" to free themselves from the technical rules of evidence developed for jury trials is founded on the belief that limitations proper enough in jury trials would serve no real function in an inquiry conducted by a trained specialist in the subject, and would, indeed, hinder adequate investigation. Lawyers trained in common law methods of proof have found difficulty in adjusting to the marked liberalization of methods by administrative bodies and have tended to regard the procedure as open to capricious and arbitrary determinations not founded fully on "evidence" or founded upon unreliable evidence as weighed by common law standards. Hence there is a feeling that the new procedures do not afford due process of law.

Theoretically the rules in the law courts are simple enough. The function of the witness is to give to the jury the benefit of his senses in the situation. He relates what he saw, what he heard (contemporaneously, not later); what he felt (physically) and what he smelled. Theoretically, everything else is excluded. The jury, from this relation, tries to put itself in the place of the witness in the situation and from its experience and its judgment of the reliability of the witness decides what happened. This, fundamentally, is the relative function of the witness and the jury in the law court. The judge keeps the trial within the rules of evidence, largely deciding points of exclusion or inclusion of

evidence and instructing the jury upon the general rules of law in the case upon which the jury is to give its verdict.

While basically the system is simple, a great body of exceptions to the rules of exclusion has grown up in the course of centuries of experience with trying cases before juries. Many of the rules are technical, but all have, or at their inception had, some logical reason of judicial policy based on experience with the English common law jury. At times the rules of exception are extremely confusing and the logic often seems lost in antiquity, but they are necessarily part of the equipment of every lawyer and judge who tries cases in the law courts.

A few exceptions to the "hearsay" rule illustrate this process. The general rule is that a witness may not relate what another person said on the subject of the controversy. The rule is based upon the theory that if the jury is to consider what the other person said, he ought to testify personally, so that his reliability might be considered. The common law judges felt that a man about to die and knowing that fact would be under rather strong compulsion to tell the truth. So they admitted statements of a dying person in a homicide case on the subject of the identity of his assailant and of the facts relating to cause and circumstances of the homicide. Thus the rule of admitting "dying declarations" became an exception to the hearsay rule, surrounded and protected by many "safeguards" among which was the necessity that the imminence of death be brought home to the deceased. The exception arose, in part, from the great difficulty in obtaining direct evidence in homicide cases.

The judges also felt that when men admit a wrong, or say something self-accusatory, or put themselves by their statements in a bad light, they are apt then to be telling the truth. It was argued that it is against human nature to admit one is wrong unless it is the truth. Thus the rule of admitting admissions developed as an exception to the hearsay rule. The practice admitted "confessions" by the accused upon this theory, and in turn a whole series of rules grew up on the subject of "confessions," that they should be unforced and freely made.

In the same pattern of development the judges concluded that if a statement was made as part of the happening of an event, and so closely integrated with it as to be spontaneous and contemporaneous, and hence without time to dissimulate or fabricate, or to think about what would be expedient to say, it would be safe enough to assume that what was thus said would be true, and hence have a probative value. So an exception was made in favor of admitting such statements, as, for instance, the words of the driver of a car at the time of an accident. The judges called such evidence a "part of the *res gestae*," really a situation in which words were treated as a part of the event.

These exceptions illustrate the radical limitation on the scope of evidence which would result if the general rules of exclusion were uniformly operative and suggest that the exceptions developed really for the purpose of giving some flexibility to the rules and making them work practically. The nature of the process, working from general negatives to exceptional positives, gave to the system, however, its peculiarly technical direction.

(B) *Matters Assumed.* Every judicial inquiry under any system starts out with certain assumptions. It accepts certain things as being true without proof. In general the assumptions that are accepted by the courts in this way are the usual assumptions of social and business life in an enlightened community. They include matters of common knowledge and of general acceptance. These are the things of which the court is said to take "judicial notice." The court will take notice without proof of the facts of geography, of the seasons, of the course of time, of the area of states and political divisions, of weights and measures, of the qualities and properties of matter and of scientific facts when commonly accepted, of common beliefs of the people, of historical facts of general knowledge, of census reports, of the meaning of words and phrases and abbreviations.

These and similar matters need not be proved, and the rule is quite elastic and to a considerable degree is discretionary. The court also "knows" without proof the various departments of government; the Constitution of the United States and of its own state; the statutory law of the United States and of its own state; the Common Law, which is also called the "unwritten law" of the state, of the colony or territory which preceded the state, and of England before the establishment of the United States.

Certain other special assumptions are made arising from the facts of the case at hand i.e., when certain facts are shown other facts or conclusions are regarded as consequent without further proof. These are called "presumptions." A few are conclusive in that they cannot be controverted. Most of them may be answered and the presumption may in such cases be dispelled by proof. The presumption serves the purpose of establishing to the satisfaction of the court the consequent fact if nothing more is said about it. Its function is expediency.

The conclusive presumption is not, strictly speaking, a rule of evidence, but is logically to be treated as an absolute rule of law, a substantive rule. It means that when a fact is established the consequent fact is presumed absolutely and may not be controverted. Relatively few of these exist. In most instances the legal results of facts are treated as rules of substantive law. The statute of limitations on debts is a good example. When the time specified by the statute has run, the debt is presumed to be paid whether this is the fact or not. A simpler way, of course, would be to bar any remedy when the time has gone by, but the time limit has developed as a rule of evidence—the non-rebuttable presumption of payment arising from the passage of time. A child under seven years is conclusively presumed to be incapable of committing a crime in the practice common in most states. A few other conclusive presumptions have been created by statutes.

The general use of "presumptions" in the law courts is merely to deem the presumed fact to be consequent on the establishment of the proved fact. If no rebutting proof is given, the presumed fact is accepted. There are a number of such instances. Where a marriage ceremony is performed, it is presumed to have been legally performed. In some states a presumption of marriage arises from continued and open cohabitation and the reputation of being married—the "common law" marriage. It is a very strong presumption where the necessary facts are shown. One of the strongest rebuttal presumptions is the presumption of the legitimacy of children born during a marriage. It is founded upon principles of public policy, the husband or wife is usually not allowed to testify to non-access by the husband. Solvency and sanity are presumed. There is a presumption against suicide. Death is presumed after seven years continuous absence, the reasons for which are unexplained and unknown to close relatives. There is a presumption in favor of the due execution of instruments. Public officers are presumed to have done their duty according to law.

Possession of property usually presumes a rightful ownership, and on the other hand, possession of the fruits of a recent crime creates a presumption of guilty possession. Persons, objects, conditions or tendencies are presumed to continue as long as would be natural for them in a "presumption of continuance." The deliberate destruction of relevant and material evidence creates a presumption that it would have been unfavorable to the spoliator. Sometimes material evidence in the control of a party and withheld by him creates an inference, but it is not as strong as the presumption arising from destruction.

A number of presumptions arise from the usual course of business. The delivery of mail and of telegrams is one. The possession of a note by the maker creates a presumption of payment; negotiable paper is presumed to rest on consideration; goods sold are presumed to be payable on delivery. There is a presumption of identity of person from identity of name. In criminal cases the accused is presumed to be innocent. But this is rather a rule of law that the prosecution must establish its case or the accused will be acquitted, than it is a rule of evidence in the strict sense.

It will be observed that many of the presumptions are matters of practical expediency in proof. Some matters would be extremely difficult of direct proof. So, the thing usually to be expected is treated as having actually happened and the party seeking to show the contrary has the burden of proof in that respect.

(C) *Circumstantial Evidence.* Quite often it is not possible to obtain direct evidence concerning the matter in dispute. The issue may not relate to an object which can be brought into court and observed. The fact being tried may not have been observed by any available witness, or it may have been observed only in part by available witnesses. Reliance is then placed upon "circumstantial evidence." This reliance is not unique to the law courts using the Anglo-American system. Indeed, it is used more or less in every system of judicial investigation and in highly specialized forums inferences are sometimes drawn which would be inadmissible under the jury system.

Circumstantial evidence is proof by synthesis. Known facts are correlated with human experience to reach the conclusion that a further fact does or does not exist. It is the common, and usually the only way of proving facts which the actor in the situation is interested in concealing. Its use is rather frequent in criminal cases, especially in murder, arson and burglary. It is often quite impossible to prove these crimes by witnesses to the fact itself and necessity requires that they are to be established circumstantially.

A relevant circumstantial fact is said to be one which logically and reasonably leads to a persuasion that the further fact is true. An inference may not be drawn entirely based upon another inference. Hence the inference must be based upon established facts or a series of established facts. Sometimes such facts will be excluded, if they create undue surprise, would unduly prejudice a jury or would confuse the issue being tried. Exclusion for any of these reasons will rest in the discretion and sense of fairness of the judge guiding the course of the trial.

The character of the accused may be established in a criminal case by showing his reputation in the community, as a relevant circumstance on the probability of his guilt or innocence. This subject is carefully controlled and usually it may be introduced only by the accused, but may be controverted by the prosecutor.

Circumstantial evidence may be as varied

as the myriad character of events to be proved. There are some well recognized fields in which it is commonly available. Physical capacity and a person's skill or technical knowledge are circumstances considered upon the probability of his doing the act at issue. The possession of mechanical, technical or physical means is similarly treated. Habit or custom of the person may be considered under limited conditions. A motive to do a thing, as for instance the taking out of fire insurance shortly before a fire, or the certainty of inheritance upon the death of a relative, are examples of admissible circumstantial evidence. The acquisition of a gun or other instrument of violence before a crime and its disposal afterward are commonly treated as relevant circumstances to be considered by a jury.

In common human experience the previous commission of a similar crime would be an important circumstance to consider in judging the guilt of the accused. And because juries would tend too readily to accept such proof as controlling, it is characteristic of the Anglo-American system that such proof is rigidly excluded in theory. And it is characteristic of the system, too, that such proof often is allowed to get before the jury upon highly rationalized exceptions to the general rule of exclusion. But the proof of prior crime is never frankly faced for the implication it may have in the probability of the commission of the instant crime being considered by the jury, and the court is bound to instruct the jury that the commission of the prior crime is not to be regarded as any evidence of the commission of the one presently charged. Still the general effect of this proof, despite its restricted purpose, is well known both to judges and prosecutors.

The most common of the exceptions to proof of other crimes is in a case where motive or intent is an essential part of the crime charged, and the prior crime would be a logical indication of whether the motive or intent exists. Such proof is received also in cases where guilty knowledge is an essential to the possession of objects, notably in cases of forgery, passing counterfeit coin, obtaining property by false pretense and receiving stolen property.

Under very limited conditions proof of prior crimes is received to rule out mistake, as in cases of giving poison, and it is received to show a conspiracy or common plan, to prove identity, and in sexual crimes, evidence of similar crimes is received to show the disposition of the principals toward each other in proximate point of time. Perhaps the most radical departure from the rigid general rule of exclusion is that the accused, if he becomes his own witness, may be cross-examined upon the subject of prior crimes, similar or not to the one charged, on the theory that this subject affects his "credibility" as a witness, and it is commonly the rule that if he denies a prior conviction it may then be proved independently. The underlying theme is preserved, however, that the prior crime is not in itself evidence of the truth of the instant charge.

Conduct of the accused after the crime, his flight or nervousness or acts indicating knowledge of the crime; or upon his arrest, his resistance, or attitude toward the subject of the crime are received as circumstantial evidence relevant to the crime.

(D) *Hearsay.* Perhaps the strongest rule of exclusion in the law courts is that of hearsay evidence. The reasons for the rule have already been discussed together with some exceptions to it. Essentially hearsay is proof of the relation of a fact by a person other than the witness. In addition to the policy that the jury should see and hear the person making the statement and so be able to assay its value, the exclusion of hearsay is based on the further policy that a party is deprived of the valuable instrument of cross examination in testing the reliability of the hearsay statement. The English judges based the rule of exclusion and it probably had its beginning, upon the fact the hearsay statement was unsworn, but even if this objection were eliminated, and the statement be in affidavit form, it would not be received as evidence in a trial based on oral proof.

Necessity impelled some exceptions. Proof of oral or written statements of others on family pedigree are received on the subjects of relationship, descent, birth, marriage or death. The declarant must be dead, however, and related to the family, and the statement must have been made before any motive pertinent to the litigation could exist. It is under this exception that entries in a family Bible are received as proof of family history and relationship. Matters of public or general interest like the location of old highways, the use of a common or town boundaries are similarly received from the hearsay statements of deceased persons who knew the facts. A person may testify also to his own status—age, date and place of birth and legitimacy, although these can never be "known" except by hearsay. Another exception relating to written evidence which would fall within the hearsay rule is that book entries made in the regular course of business are usually admissible.

By far the most important exceptions to the rule against hearsay evidence arise from two sources: (a) spontaneous statements which are part of the event in controversy; (b) admissions by the party. The first is received upon the theory that it is not really conversation at all, but an unpremeditated and integrated part of the event; the second is received upon the theory that a man will not speak against himself unless truthfully. This theory has assumed high significance in the treatment of "confessions" in modern criminal law which are received in evidence because of the acceptance of admissions against interest under general, and very old, principles of law.

The thing said as "part of the event" may be an exclamation, or a statement coincidental in point of time with the event, or it may be the oral manifestations of pain and suffering, the cry, groan or statement showing physical condition. Also part of the event are conversations which are part of a developing scheme or enterprise. These are received because the conversations are part of the scheme itself, or the contract in civil matters.

Some other exceptions to the hearsay rule exist which are neither part of the event itself nor admissions. Where the intent, reason, motive or feelings of a person become an issue upon the trial, the statements or declarations of such a person on those subjects may be received, probably because this would

be almost the only way that such a subject could be probed.

And just as the homicide case has a true and marked exception to the hearsay rule in receiving the "dying declaration" of the deceased, so a true and equally marked exception to the rule exists in rape cases. In such a case proof may be offered that the complainant made a complaint promptly after the offense. It may be offered only if the complainant becomes a witness and it cannot include the details of the conversation. Robbery and larceny have somewhat similar rules.

Evidence that a party made some statement of a fact which would be unfavorable to his interest in the litigation is received. Evidence that a witness (whether or not he is a party) made a previous statement different from his present testimony is received only after the witness has denied the prior statement. Sometimes admissions are established without words by the conduct of a party toward the subject, or by a refusal to answer when ordinarily an answer would be expected, but this does not apply to a failure or refusal to answer a written communication. Sometimes the relationship in the subject between parties is such that the admission of one is received in the case of the other. An admission of a partner about the partnership is one example, and where a criminal conspiracy is proved the admission of one co-conspirator about the scheme is received in the cases of the others.

(E) *Confessions.* A confession in a criminal case is received upon the theory that it is an "admission" against interest. The theory that a man is unlikely to admit an incriminating fact unless it is true is the basis of the rule under which confessions are received as well as other "admissions." A "confession" may be an admission of guilt as such, or of a fact which in part may lead to the conclusion of guilt. It may be written or oral. It must be voluntary, and not induced by fear or threats, or by a promise of immunity authorized or apparently authorized by law. But sometimes a confession obtained by deception, not of coercive nature is received. There is a tendency in the courts to regard an unreasonably long detention of a prisoner without being brought before a judge for arraignment as itself such proof of coercion as to exclude a confession from evidence.

Certain other safeguards are thrown around confessions. There must be independent proof (besides the confession) that the crime has been committed. Hence it is not possible to "confess" to a crime the existence of which is not proved independently. This is regarded as a safeguard against confessions of non-existing crimes due to psychic disturbances; but it is not a safeguard against such a confession related to an actual crime not committed by the accused. At the trial the accused may discredit the confession by showing it was forced, or not made, and may show also that the crime was not committed or not committed by him, as proof discrediting the confession, entirely aside from the general issue of his guilt or innocence.

Where a case has once been tried, the testimony of a witness may be read at a new trial where the witness cannot be found in the jurisdiction—usually when he is dead or is evading process. It is essential, however, that the opportunity to cross examine him must have existed at the first trial before his former testimony will be read.

(F) *Qualifications of Witnesses.* An absolute disqualification to testify is imposed on some witnesses. Their testimony will not be received. Among those falling in this group are the insane, the very young and the intoxicated witness. In criminal cases the unsworn testimony of a child under 12 years of age will usually be taken if the child apparently has sufficient intelligence to justify receiving the testimony. The question rests in the opinion of the judge. The rule varies from state to state.

A disqualification to give testimony is imposed in certain relationships: (1) attorney and client; (2) physician and patient; (3) clergyman and parishioner; (4) husband and wife. The disqualification does not extend to all matters, but only to confidential matters concerned with and arising out of the relationship. It is the rule that the "privileged communications" arising from these relationships may not be disclosed. Subjects falling within and without this classification have

been technically elaborated and distinguished, but the rule somewhat simplified, is that where the communication is made confidentially and is pertinent to the relationship, the privilege will be protected. It is relatively easy to classify the subjects pertinent to a conference with a lawyer, physician or clergyman. It is not so easy to classify what are the "confidential communications" between husband and wife. Formerly neither could testify on any subject against the other. In some states now they may not testify to any "private" communications between each other, although they may testify against each other except as to such communications. The general rule now is, except in matrimonial cases, that they may not reveal those communications made in the confidence of the marital relation. There is a recognized difference between this and the exclusion of all "private" communications between the parties. For instance, a conversation between husband and wife about business, travel or public experiences would be treated as private, but as not being so connected with the marital status as to be a "confidential communication." Some difficulty has been experienced in actual application. In criminal cases the tendency in border line questions is to classify them as not strictly pertinent to the husband-wife relationship unless they appear directly to be concerned with that relationship, and hence as admissible.

(G) *Expert Opinion.* It has been seen that the function of the witness in a jury trial is to state his sensual observations without his conclusions, so that the jury could say what the "facts" are. But it is obvious this could apply only in the fields of experience in which the judgment of the ordinary run of men would have validity. Another way of putting this is that the opinion of a witness will not be received where the opinion of one person is as good as another i.e. in the fields of ordinary business and social intercourse.

But in technical fields the jury needs help, not only in elucidation of the subject but also in opinion of qualified specialists, and in such cases opinions are allowed to be given to the jury, and this is a well established exception to the rule excluding opinions. A good example is the explanation of the physician of physical phenomena and of his opinion of the result. Engineering, chemistry, mathematics, finger prints, shorthand writing and other special fields of knowledge are similarly treated. Non-expert witnesses may testify to opinions on ordinary observations which may not be broken into further components, like the smell of liquor, or the weight or size of an object or identity and general appearance of a person.

FRANCIS BERGAN
Justice of the Supreme Court
New York State

BIBLIOGRAPHY

Borchard, Edwin M., *Convicting the Innocent*, Yale University Press, 1932.
Callender, Clarence N., *American Courts, Their Organization and Procedure*, McGraw-Hill, 1927.
Cantor, Nathaniel, *Crime, Criminals and Criminal Justice*, Henry Holt and Company, 1932.
Glueck, Sheldon, *Crime and Justice*, Little Brown, and Company, 1926.
Kirby, James P., *Criminal Justice*, H. W. Wilson Company, 1926.
Moley, Raymond, *Our Criminal Courts*, Minton, Balch, 1930.
Sutherland, Edwin H., *Principles of Criminology*, Lippincott, 1939.
Train, Arthur, *Courts, Criminals and the Camorra*, Scribners, 1912.
Waite, John Barker, *Criminal Law in Action*, Harcourt, Brace and Co., 1934.

EXPERT TESTIMONY. In all human society that we know of feelings of guilt have been used as one of the strongest factors for social control. It is by creating such feelings of guilt that the group makes the individual conform. But only in the most advanced of the ancient societies and more so in modern societies was the need felt for objective proof of guilt.

Demands on persuasive, strict and verifiable evidence of an individual's guilt could be made only in a society where the individual and his rights matter. [1] Whenever in a

[1] In the Nuremberg trials the principle of guilty organizations has been established, however this is not identical with the metaphysical concept of the guilt of a group. In fact if the German Nazi SS or SA were declared criminal organizations that means only that a) belong-

primitive society a corpse was found showing signs of violence this had to be construed as murder and if there were no signs of violence this was taken to mean that the gods had meted out punishment. Someone must have acted in such a way as to cause the anger of the gods to be visited upon him. The society and the person who had caused through their wantonness such displeasure of the gods, had both acted criminally.

In such a society then, there would have been no place for an expert. The facts seemed to be plain and obvious so that everybody could judge them. The apprehended man was mostly willing to confess and if not so much the worse for him. Material facts that would have militated against the guilt were unknown in a double sense. Generally speaking objective causal relationships of scientific order were not sufficiently known and if there was a stock of such general knowledge none would have thought of applying it to the case at hand. A good instance is the trial of Socrates as described in Plato's *Apologia*. The whole trial concentrates on the proof of the criminal intent of Socrates and there is not even an attempt to prove that by causal connection with this intent the material effect was reached. We know very well that up to this day in certain causes célèbres outraged public opinion has such an influence on the bench that the apprehended man is already convicted before the trial. Here again we have a good example. It is the famous defense by Clarence Darrow in the Loeb-Leopold trial in Chicago.

In the English law it had, as Winfred Overholser points out, become the rule, by the time of Edward I (end of the 13th century AD) to grant a royal pardon to criminals convicted but found insane. It is also good to keep in mind that our present rule about calling in the jury from the vicinity where the crime had been committed dates back to a time where the jurors were supposed to have direct i.e. pre-trial knowledge of the facts.

ing to such an organization is to be construed as a primafacie evidence against the individual member and b) that such organizations are to be eliminated, and "their charter revoked mandatorily."

Also very early the habit developed that the judge should call in competent and honest persons to advise him in their capacity as friends of the court. (amicus curiae).

The early experts therefore as Overholser again points out had an honored position in the court. The more however, our present system of the trial, moving on by the actions of the parties, became complete the more, too, the expert worked on a retainer basis. We have to keep in mind again that this is a part of the general background toward which all criticism and reforms will have to be oriented.

Whether they deal with handwriting, compacts, wills, objective facts, documents, or the psychology of the deed or the perpetrator, all experts have in common a special orientation towards the humanities. What kind of a psychology is the humanistic psychology? [2] We will first show what kind of psychology needs must eliminate itself from the courtroom. In criticising a certain type of psychology, William McDougall quotes H. A. Carr, a contributor like himself to Carl Murchison's *Psychologies of 1930.* "We must avoid the naive assumption that the ulterior consequences of an act either motivate that act or serve as its objective."

It is quite obvious that such psychology has no common ground with the psychology that is at the basis of a verdict of guilt or non-guilt. As I have shown in my *New*

Theory of the Perpetrator (1939), any psychology that may be useful in the courtroom must be able to describe and analyze characters, describe secondly motivations, i.e. the relations of the character and its functions or attitude to actions and the outer world, to describe thirdly how motivation and motives influence, and are in turn influenced by unmotivated impulses. For the implementation of these psychological demands very often clinical psychiatric and even general medical knowledge is necessary.

All the misunderstandings between lawyers and psychological and psychiatric experts stem from the fact that basically the lawyer does not understand the biological orientation of the psychologist while the psychologist and psychiatrist, perturbed by the apparent "free-will" assumptions [3] of the lawyers, will go to such length as to say that there is no room in a biologically oriented thinking for such concepts as guilt, negligence, malice, premeditation, etc.

As the courtroom is not a philosophical seminar, these clashes could and should be avoided. The lawyers know exactly what they are talking about, viz. such motives and motivations as are well known from average situations in everyday life; and the task of the experts is in 99 out of 100 cases to contribute their refined clinical observations which in certain cases may be still more refined by laboratory experiments. In other words, the proposition that in matters humanistical everybody must be considered an "expert" is not wrong, but the experts in the narrower sense of the word must be supposed to be better acquainted with living psychology than those people who indeed from in-

---

[2] The thinker first to differentiate sharply human existence and its scientific categories from the knowledge of things, was Blaise Pascal in his *Pensées:* "Le coeur a ses raisons, que le raison ne comprend pas." (The heart has its reasons, which reason does not understand.) Later the German term *Geisteswissenschaft* (geisteswissenschaftliche Psychologie) as developed by Wilhelm Dilthey and his pupil Eduard Spranger and others, points to the same differentiation. Most recently there appeared an article by Leslie A. White where he opposes culture-logical to other interpretations of behavior whereby he most unfortunately calls these other non-human interpretations psychological. He, however, clearly differentiates the symbolism in human understanding from the forms of understanding things. It might be said that what we have in mind with human existence is—could it be otherwise?—manmade. Thus also the concept of human equality is obviously not nature-made, but manmade.

[3] Obviously social existence is impossible without a.) believed-in symbols, taboos, rituals, stereotypes, fads and fashions, b) fictions i. e. (sometimes) consciously false assumptions that are made for certain theoretical or practical purposes. Under the democratic constitution we assume that all men are born equal which is biologically false, but enables us to strive for the realization of equal opportunity and equal legal and political rights. The Free Will fiction and all the other fictions mentioned above in the text should be understood as such by both lawyers and psychiatrists, which would contribute towards avoiding much unnecessary and fruitless clashes.

fancy on and throughout life practice the immediate understanding of human contacts and human expressions within average situations.

An example will make clear what the expert can contribute over and above the average understanding. In a trial for depraving the morals of minors, the child witness had repeatedly changed her testimony from one that was apt to entirely shake the people's case to one that indeed burdened the defendant considerably. The prosecution (the setting was in a small town of Bavaria) had during the pre-trial hearings brought the witness in with her mother; there was a crucifix and there were two candles lit and the priest and the community nurse were present, but the defendant was not. Now then, mother and the prosecutor (they could do such things in Germany) asked the child to finally "confess" the truth. The child broke down and told the story as public opinion in the little town had rumored it all the time. In court the prosecutor asked the expert whether he thought that a child would dare to lie before the crucifix. The explanation advanced by the expert was the following: This child had found the peace of her mind, she had joined her natural groups, family, religion, school class, play mates, public opinion and she felt relieved: this had been a confession in the full meaning of the word, as the prosecutor had called it, rather than a testimony, the confession had enabled her to come out of the ivory tower, to overcome the social ostracism and to resume her normal relationships. This is incidentally what many testimonies amount to. In political trials, in politically excited times, the witness very often shapes his testimony to his group loyalties rather than to the actual facts. The same happens in backwood counties and townships, if e.g. public opinion is roused by the immenseness of a crime, (see Th. Dreiser's *American Tragedy*), or by racial issues and, as we have said above in discussing Clarence Darrow's defense in 1924, the same phenomenon took place in the non-backwoods city of Chicago.

The better knowledge of the expert enables him to introduce social-psychological viewpoints instead of the psychology of the isolated individual which is usually resorted to, in a very superficial way, though, by laymen.

Stressing in this way the importance of humanistic psychology, we have anticipated what we deem to be one of the important achievements of the expert in the courtroom. This should not, however, obfuscate other complications. Generally speaking, scientific criminology and scientific opinions on criminals and their character, etc., must be based on universal causalism, which, as we said before, has very little to do with the issue of the Free Will. Whether or not we recognize a chemical, hormonal, glandular, psychological, psychoanalytical determinism, we are asking for the core of the relationship between the evildoer and his deed and in certain clinical well determined cases also for the causal relationship between disease entities or such well determined psychological states like irresistible impulse, twilight states, etc., as well as the motivation of the evildoer.

The most recent development in science is that from absolute causalism to probability statistics. The facts, however, with which criminology and the experts have to deal do not seem to imply any particular importance for criminology, of this recent development in theoretical physics. The following factors seem to rule out such applications for the time being: The number of factors, known in criminology to be contributory in the commission of crimes is small as compared to that of the molecules of a gas or the electrons of an atom. Secondly while the expert's knowledge may refer to facts of material order the human order is at least as important. We do not deny, that inasmuch as the material order of things comes in, new causal problems may develop.

What we have been saying so far may be summarized thus: The whole world, by which we are surrounded, may be divided into a world of things and one of humanities. In making this statement, it is necessary to see that human beings may be composed of parts like anatomical parts, physiological functions or psychological functions that may be isolated and therefore be considered as things, while on the other hand documents or other material facts may participate in what we call human existence. Humanistic facts are also amenable to objectivation.

The question may be raised as to what type of facts the expert's activity refers to, if the lie-detector is used. In the lie-detector-procedures, isolated and not voluntarily adjustable reactions are offered in evidence. On the other hand the voluntary agreement of the individual and his continued cooperation in the procedure are necessary. While a defendant cannot be forced, according to the prevailing opinion, to submit to lie-detector test, he may be forced to expose his anatomy. It is less important to take a definite stand on the question whether this knowledge is human or material as it is to see the complication and the interplay of factors.

Recently there have been grossly exaggerated claims for the so-called truth-serums Mescaline, Marijuana and Sodium-Pentothal. Even though it is quite possible to use them successfully, the above mentioned difficulties and considerations would still hold.

These objections do not seem to come in in other methods used by experts, where the specimens may be secured without the consent of the individual. Foremost in this field is Handwriting Analysis. The objections against graphology may be roughly divided into unjust ones and those that are justified, the former being directed against graphology as a science, the latter against most of the graphologists. The technique of the latter is mostly poor, but more important is that owing to their lack of general training and education and unfamiliarity with the basic ideas of procedural law, they tend to assume in advance that the deed has been perpetrated as a criminal act and furthermore they judge the connection between the accused and the deed as if the former were already convicted. However, even with serious signs in the person's handwriting indicating lying, pretending, assuming of roles, someone else still may have committed the crime in question. The expert must not set himself up as a finder of fact. Most graphologists assume a far too close connection between the character as expressed in handwriting and crime. Is for instance a burglar the one who needs more will power than the one who commits a simple embezzlement or theft? To sum up: motivational dispositions, but never the perpetration of crimes may be reflected in hand-

writing. (See W. Eliasberg: *Forensic Psychology,* etc., p. 365.)

It is common knowledge that psychology, especially experimental psychology, has contributed very much toward the evaluation of the witnesses' testimony. No court in our time will object to admitting in evidence an expert's opinion purporting to show that on a certain day, with a given illumination, a certain person, at a certain distance, could not have been identified. The court and the jury, however, will not, on the whole, be willing to admit limitations in the memory, especially if the expert's opinion trespasses into abnormal psychology or the unconscious.

Lawyers instead will follow their own psychology on these grounds. They will believe in certain movements of the witness under oath; they will take an oath that if the witness points with the thumb down, he is perjuring himself. [4]

What is the cause of our Belief in Reality? William James in his *Principles of Psychology* has devoted a famous chapter to this problem and the upshot of his ideas is that we call real any single given, and especially any single new fact, if upon putting it to the test ground of any of our various systems of reality, we find it verifiable or otherwise trustworthy and fitting. Quite similarly the historian has this to say:

"The Ideas of the remote past are not, except in a figurative sense, remembered. The power of conceptual thought to transcend the limits of time and link together the past and the present is presupposed in all historical knowledge. Even physical science is called upon to explain events that are remote in time as well as distant in space. It is the distinguishing feature of conceptual thought that it can thus embrace and surmount the station and personal biography of the individual thinker. This means that the logic of the past must be embraced within the logic of the present. It is necessary to suppose that a more limited system of meanings can be contained identically within a more elaborate system of meanings."

[4] About this type of psychology of the expressive movements see W. Eliasberg, Forensic Psychology, p. 359. Bibliography also referring to experimental and measuring methods is given in this place.

The historian Ralph Barton Perry from whom the preceding lines are quoted goes on to say that the problem of the historical understanding is essentially the same as that of sharing the ideas of other contemporary minds.

The logico-psychological method which may be derived from that I have called objective psychology. It is that psychology which is at the same time explanatory and experimental. It will enable the expert to let the finders of facts partake in the generic thought process by which the expert himself arrives at some conviction. It will in this way establish the contact which is necessary between the expert and the finders of fact, viz. the contact of persuasion. [5]

In what way does objective psychology proceed? It uses criteria which, while of factual nature, stand diagnostically as parts for the whole. Thus, there are criteria used in the prediction of probation. There are criteria for the existence of certain disease entities. But there can of course be no criteria for formal constructs such as guilty attempt. Objective psychology is aimed at the proof of certain objective occurrences either in the mind of the perpetrator or in the outer world if the latter are in some way or other conditioned by psychological occurrences.

If we knew all the facts like the famous World Spirit of La Place, could we dispense with juries, judges, counsel for the parties, probation officers, agencies of all sorts, with the limitations of the law of evidence, the rules on hearsay and cross examination, indeed, any special procedure of administering justice? Is it conceivable that some day science will eliminate jurisprudence and the law? It is not, more than for any other reason because the administration of law is not the impassive after-image as Santayana once said of history: Law as much as reason has not come to repeat the universe but to fulfill it. A basic fact which again every expert called upon to cooperate in the administration of justice should keep in mind.

[5] In a scientific meeting we have to convince our peers; the most advanced and leading scientist can still talk to people who had the same training, and know the same basic facts. In the courtroom the expert has to persuade and convince people without scientific training.

II. *The Who is Who of the Expert.* There are, broadly speaking, two groups of definitions of the expert in court. The first relates to his knowledge; the second limits him as one appointed to serve in court for a fee and as one to whom certain procedural rules apply.

A definition of the first type is the following: The expert is one who transmits knowledge, or applies it, or gets at the facts, or unearths them, or demonstrates them, or does any of these things or all of them with skill and thoroughness. [6] A definition in the second type: one who legally, on the order of proper judicial authority and under oath, applies his knowledge to unearth and demonstrate facts, and/or to interpret them for the particular purposes of a trial. The latter type of definition prevails in the continental literature. It is in keeping with the fact that the expert, whether or not he is introduced by the parties, may function only after the court appoints him and only after a special expert's oath [7] has been administered to him. The American Law Institute steers the middle course between these two definitions, thus: "*Expert witness defined:* A witness is an expert witness and is qualified to give expert testimony if the judge finds that to perceive, know, or understand the matter concerning which the witness is to testify requires special knowledge, skill, experience, or training, and that the witness has the requisite special knowledge, skill, experience, or training." [8] This definition would be complete if the fol-

[6] Rogers, *Expert Testimony*, 2nd ed., 1891, calls an expert anyone who is skilled in any art, trade or profession, and possessed of peculiar knowledge concerning the same. We object that this is not the definition of the expert in court, but in any relation in life. *Cf.* W. Eliasberg, *Psychology and the Administration of the Law*, Berlin, Heymann, 1932, p. 86 ff.
[7] In the continental litigation and trial, as often as not, the experts are chosen by the court. They may be rejected by the parties, who, however, may question them through the presiding judge. *Cf.* G. Aschaffenburg, *Synopsis of the Position of the Experts in Court in Western Europe and in the United States.* (Mimeographed lecture at the 99th annual meeting of the American Psychiatric Association, Detroit, 1943.)
[8] Rule 402 of the "Model Code of Evidence," American Law Institute, 1942.

lowing words were added: "and if the judge, upon such finding, appoints the witness in the way described by the law, to be an expert."

Let us see some examples of the different functions of the knowledge of an expert witness in a criminal trial. It may matter to know what is the present knowledge about schizophrenia in general; or the expert may be asked whether the defendant at the time of the commission of an alleged crime was conscious of acting contrary to the law or whether he was laboring under any delusions [9] or was following an irresistible impulse or whether a confession is a normal or pathological one, or whether a plea of guilty in a pathological case should be accepted.

Getting at the facts is one of the most important achievements of the expert. Poisons may be imperceptible to the naked eye and the other senses. The expert will prove or exclude their presence. He will have to make the second step also, viz., make the facts demonstrable to the common sense of the lay judge of the fact. But it is not his task to impose upon the bench, to trick them into a certain theory, to marshal all his facts artfully in such a manner as counsel may do.

This difference, slim as it may seem at first, has important consequences. If the expert claims to be possessed of facts which he cannot find ways to demonstrate to the common sense of the jury, but which he can only foist or force upon them, he must not be admitted in court. This holds for any expert or occultist who tells or implies that he possesses and can demonstrate certain facts only because he has peculiar qualities or powers, powers or qualities that have been "given" to him. It is not admissible that there is any knowledge that is accessible only to supernormal intelligence or to privileged votaries. If there were such knowledge the trier of fact would either have to believe it blindly or reject it. In other words, the decision of fact would be taken away from the trier of fact and given to the expert.

If the question is raised as to whether a certain deed has been committed by the defendant in a state of temporary confusion, the expert might be tempted to say that the hab-

itual character of the perpetrator is sufficient to connect him with the act. This would be circumstantial evidence, inasmuch as a certain characterological type is brought into close connection with the case at hand. As is well known, the so-called hypothetical question has been developed to offset this danger. Under no circumstances should the expert's demonstration of facts of knowledge amount to a statement of guilt or include it or, indeed, anticipate any finding of the jury or the court.

The expert has a double existence, as it were, as incidentally very many people have. He is either in court or somewhere else, in any of the numberless entanglements of life. He is the father of a family which he supports and he is the member of a political party, he is an elk or a rotarian, he is a scientist by inner calling, or a golfer by hobby and what not. It is quite clear that he cannot just cut out everything else from his mind and personality when he enters the courtroom, although it is known to all and sundry that the jurors e.g. are constantly admonished to perform such mental surgery on their own brains or minds. Leaving it to the lawyers to decide upon such auto-operationism, we want to say that a realistic social psychology of the expert does not reckon with magic. The expert remains a human being in the fullest sense of the word, and in all modesty we want to say that human institutions that need angels or expurgated souls for their function do not seem to be worthwhile on this our earth.

There are skilful experts and those endowed with less skill. There are among them men whom lawyers could envy for their cleverness in marshalling their facts. One expert will feel that he is in no position to simply answer Yes or No because he knows that the facts are too complex for him to dare such simplification. Another will say: if they want it that way, let them have it. If the court admits something into evidence, the expert might still feel conscience-bound to say that he is not dealing with facts altogether. Not so long ago and so far away, experts who never had examined or indeed seen the defendant felt competent to testify in answer to a so-called hypothetical question, which

[9] Question 4 put to the judges in M'Naghten's case in 1843.

might have helped them in their conscience but did not further the finding of facts. We have seen above what difficulties may arise in the process of getting at the fact and how the facts by the very process of unearthing them, needs get distorted. One expert winces under this insight, another doesn't even surmise that there is such difficulty. One expert deals professionally with numbers, therefore he might be more particular about statistics, while another trained to adapt theories to individual cases will dwell on the particulars. The former keeping aloof, as it were, from the individual case will take no keen interest in the verification of the item at hand. Consequently, while the former will talk of probabilities, the latter focuses on reasonable certainty of proof.

There are differences not based on sources of knowledge or individual training. Who retains the expert? There are as we all know "testifiers" for the plaintives and there are experts for companies. The same holds true in criminal cases where certain doctors invariably appear for the prosecution and others as invariably for the defense and while prosecutors may later open their private offices, they do not seem to take their doctors along. A situation has developed in which the more experienced and respectable doctors take sides with the companies in litigation and the prosecution in criminal cases.

The differences mentioned so far, have their roots in what precedes the trial: In the expert's techniques, beliefs, mores, customs, folkways and affiliations. But the "jeer, sneer and leer" (G. W. Courtney), the to and fro of attack and counterattack of fanning and rooting, and intrigue among all those before the bar, these are the ingredients within the hearing room, of an atmosphere which is just the opposite of what it should be.

The expert, then, called in by a party to promote the purposes of justice by offering his knowledge intends to make a living for himself in this way: He knows that litigation and trial in our system are based on several principles which it is not always easy to bring into harmony: The principle of the sovereign disposition of the parties and the law of evidence. And it is furthermore limited by the availability and the cost of making available evidence and retaining the best man.

The rule developed in antiquity and taken up by the church, that services of a spiritual order should not be paid for but that what is necessary for a decent life must be tendered by society to its servants, is not entirely eliminated in our own time. That much is clear! It has not proven feasible to keep the professional groups aloof from the mechanisms and motives of industrial democratic, competitive civilization. The free lance professional may sell his services to the highest bidder—if he can get high bids. Experience shows that less than one per thousand members of the professions are interested in keeping up the absolute freedom of bargaining with the individual client. There is on the other hand, the fee schedule, which is the spine of every type of socialization of professional services. No professional man and no client has ever been fully satisfied with the principle of the fee schedule which consists in computing conventional measures such as pieces of time or space, or "cuts" of performance. The professional man may feel that in that one moment when the diagnosis or basic idea dawns on him, he does more for the client than the employee who spends eight hours and gets paid for eight hours. The professional man knows that such achievements in seconds are possible only because of his years of patient work, training, and abnegation. The client knows all this, too. In other words, there is a wrong factor of accountability introduced into the profession. Every case is an individual case, no matter how much it may resemble the other fellow's predicament. And with this feeling there dovetails the conviction in all service-rendering and counselling professions that there won't be repeats no matter how often you spin it. How then, could this be paid for according to fee schedules!

There is, thirdly, a middle way, which in the legal terminology is expressed in such words as decent fee, reasonable fee, etc. The viewpoints of decency and reasonableness refer not only to the amounts paid, but also the ways of reaching the consumers. Certain actions are illicit such as advertising in the business manner and fee splitting. This is not ridiculous, prejudicial, absurd, and antiquated pettifoggery. These forms are preserved in the interest of the clients, who, it is felt, call in the professional man not only on account of his skill but also because they want to confide in him. Such terms as described leave it to the discretionary powers to determine what in a certain civilization at a certain time is reasonable and decent, depending on how these services are estimated, how much they are in demand etc. This holds true for the expert, too. The law does not directly prevent him from selling a specific skill for the highest price to the party, although he is expected not to sell out to the highest bidder. Society, in the interest of justice may demand that the extraordinarily skillful expert be available at a reasonable fee, because it is generally supposed that the expert primarily aids the process of justice by giving his opinion, (H. L. Bomar, Jr.) and witnesses, expert or lay, are duty bound to such help. Along the same line one has argued that in a criminal trial the defendant may be in no position to pay the fees to which an extraordinarily skilled expert is entitled, but obviously it is in the interest of justice that the financial position of the defendant should make no difference. Where the gist of the reform runs toward making the expert the companion of court and justice, any private compensation is, of course, ruled out. But this solution, much as it seems to appeal at present to the reformers, leads in its consequences to infringements upon the party principle in trial and such suggestions should be thoroughly examined.

III. *The Expert and the Others.* The administration of justice can be the result of team work only and this has not yet been achieved. Teamwork sets in with the work of the police, is continued by the prosecution and defense before the trial, is furthered by the search for evidence and witnesses, by the pre-trial research and work of the experts, reports from agencies of all kinds and is brought to a peak in the hours of trial, when in the atmosphere of the courtroom, the court and jurors cooperate with all those mentioned before.

The expert has a part in "a cast." He plays a rôle. He, therefore, must have an understanding of the rôle, must know it, must embody it and act it out. While to a certain degree his rôle is contained in the playbook (procedural rules) it is up to him to transfer himself into what he has to play. In a real cast for a real play there is no rôle that outshines all other rôles. The perfect play, is an inter-play. To understand this, the single actor will not have to be taught by general ethics. Altruism does not make for good acting. On the other hand, haughty manners of the star toward the other parts can easily endanger the whole thing.

We will try and give a few examples culled from the experience of many years. How should the expert approach the testimony of the laywitness? How should he handle the facts which he learns from the testimony? First of all he *should* try and learn as much from the testimony as he possibly can. He would be ill-advised to assume that "res ipsa loquitur." He may on the contrary assume that wherever he has to deal with objects others before him have already dealt with the same objects, and have imparted to those objects their own longings and desires, and have in this way more or less put the stamp of their personalities on the facts.

The expert can learn very much about these "alloys" by listening carefully to the testimony. On the other hand he should, of course, not assume, before the finder of facts has explicitly said so, that what the witness says is the fact. The following problems may arise: 1.) To evaluate testimony or to judge the witness or the confessant in border line cases e.g. the child witness, the psychotic and psychopathic witness, the deaf-mute, the feeble minded, the senile, the woman in exceptional stages of the gestation cycle, the pathological confessant etc. 2.) To measure the testimony against the established theories. These are the more important cases and at the same time those which as we will see presently are unfortunately infrequent.

Theories in many fields are based on statistics. The expert should examine the contingency of the theory by assuming as long as possible that the testimony may contain something which the witness knows from his own experience and that such aspects should not be easily superseded by theoretical and general knowledge. In certain cases, however, theory must have the priority over what the witness says and erroneously thinks. For example: We believe that the earth is a ball although the eye does not show it; upon closer examination it is not perception that the theory contradicts, the correct theory being based on perception, too. What the modern theory discredits is the primitive perception; thus, while accepting the witnesses' perceptions as long as possible, the expert must have a right to see into what theory they fit best.

In a recent case, three witnesses, all of them employees of the same company told the court that they had seen the claimant walk upstairs and had not seen him come down. So he must have fallen from the roof. The company was not liable to damage for falling from the roof. The claimant maintained he had been bruised when a crate fell from the roof, a height of twenty feet. The expert, by applying a simple physical formula, computed the force which must have been brought to bear upon the skull as that of an eighty-three horsepower automobile traveling at a speed of twenty miles an hour against a stone wall.

From such an impact the claimant must have sustained severe fractures not only of the skull but also of the limbs, etc. Being grazed by the crate while in a standing position was the much more probable assumption because the forces in that case were much smaller. This is a case where the expert was forced to put aside the witness' testimony. It is at the same time a case in which the witnesses, all employees of the same company, gave only circumstantial evidence.

This is what really happened in this trial: Instead of being allowed to bring out the facts on direct examination, objections of opposing counsel were sustained and thus the basic fact in the first trial was kept from the finders of facts.

Relationships between the expert and the counsel of the own and the opposing party are often very sterile. Counsel often feel they have to rely on what they call courtroom psychology, psychology of the judges and the jurors rather than on the best facts, even if these are favorable.

"Doctor I want you to look at this and tell me whether there are on this sheet (of the case history) neurological findings. Here, Doctor, it says no bleeding from the nose, mouth and the eyesockets. If these findings are negative, would you say that there are no neurological findings whatsoever?

There were two tricks sprung in this case a.) to make negative findings stand out and to rely upon the poor memory of the expert b.) the expert's obligation to answer with Yes or No so that he was prevented from telling the finders of fact that on the other pages there were positive neurological findings.

If the expert is questioned about his opinion, opposing counsel will very often jealously prevent him a.) from giving general viewpoints in either the cross-examination or on direct re-direct b.) from developing the concrete bases of his judgment. In this way the opinion is made to dangle, as it were, and the expert's authority is in a very subtle way, shaken. Experts should be given the right to explain how they arrived at their opinion. This can be achieved only if our present way of building up a tapeworm of hypothetical questions at the end of which the expert has to say Yes or No, is combined with other methods of letting the experts talk in a sensible and connected way. At present we have no "clinical method" of handling the expert in court. We should develop such a method.

We have said above that admonition, exhortation and appeal to idealism and voluntary reform will not do in our field any better than in any other. With the change of the situations, motivations may change; not automatically though, but education and re-education must find their scope as much in the society as in the individual.

With this in mind we may now shortly turn to the "party" with which the expert must be concerned most, viz. the jurors and the court.

We have already mentioned the "tangible facts of extra-mural life" that go into the attitudes and decisions of all of us.

The expert who has to persuade the finders of fact, should know, in addition, about the "intra-mural" psychology of the jury. There has remained a glimmer of that mysterious not to say metaphysical secrecy that did shroud the juries in the beginning of the 19th century in France, where the jury was required to find the facts not according to the principles of a law of evidence but to their "Conviction intime." Thus, the jury of today is not required to offer any reasons for the verdict or indeed to keep records of its deliberations. But even in the stage where the public is admitted there are many irrationalities at work and the idola specus et fori (Francis Bacon) are not discarded. Suffice it to say that the expert who considers serving regularly should read up or still better gather experience for himself.

IV. *Suggestions.* The expert's problems have been discussed by many. In no field as L. P. Stryker points out have there been so many super-serviceable and ill-considered proposals for reform.

Suggestions [10] for the improvement of the situation should follow the advice that all legislators must take: that the reforms must grow from the soil of present experiences and must be devised to meet the present need or that of the immediate future. In other words, there can be no absolute or metaphysical norm and law.

At present, the rules, procedural or otherwise, most urgently needed, are the following:

Referring to the expert:

The right of the parties to present experts must be preserved. The court should prepare lists from which the parties may or may not choose. The fact that the expert was or was not so chosen should be mentioned either at the beginning of the trial or when the jury is charged.

The scientific and professional organizations should offer comprehensive courses on scientific and legal aspects of rendering expert opinions.

He should be appointed by the court for the case at hand and sworn in. Counsel should be held in contempt if he willfully attacks the honor or disinterest of the expert. The expert should be allowed to depose, i.e.

[10] The following suggestions are a slightly revised edition of the suggestions I have given in my previous publication: "Opposing Expert Testimonies" 1945.

to read or to narrate his opinion, which should be prepared in writing if possible. On cross-examination or re-direct, the expert may be asked hypothetical questions which he may answer either in essay or yes-no, true-false form.

In cases where there is doubt, the expert should be present, when the witnesses are examined.

Counsel should be allowed to ask for the expert's opinion on the witness' testimony. A discussion of the expert's opinion in connection with the testimony of the lay witnesses should be possible. On the whole we are now ready to liberalize the common law rules of evidence because we are ready to forget the older fears of the incompetence of the layman juror and to hold a new belief in the common man. (See J. Friedrich.)

The regulation of the expert's fee should be based on the idea that the best experts should be available even to the poorest defendant. In other words, there should be state and/or federal funds for this purpose.

Referring to the Court and the Jurors:

The court and the jurors should rid themselves of the idea that there is only one indivisible truth and that at best one, and at worst, none of the experts, tells the truth. The task of the court and the jurors is to examine the expert's opinion logically, psychologically, and sociologically, and by combining the different aspects, find a reasonable truth.

WLADIMIR G. ELIASBERG, M. D.
420 West End Avenue
New York 24, N. Y.

BIBLIOGRAPHY

Aschaffenburg, G., Synopsis of the Position of the Experts in Court in Western Europe and the United States,—Mimeographed lecture in the 99th *Annual Meeting* of the American Psychiatric Association, Detroit, 1943.

Bomar, H. L. Jr., Compensation of Expert Witnesses,—*Law and Contemporary Problems,* School of Law, Duke University; Vol. 2, No. 4, 1935.

Brown, Esther L., *Lawyers and the Promotion of Justice,* New York, Russell Sage Foundation, 1938.

Carr, H. R., *Psychology,* Longmans Green, 1925, p. 226.

Courtney, G. W., "Address to the Graduation Class," Boston, *Medical and Surgical Journal,* Jan. 3, 1916.

Darrow, Clarence. *For the Defense,*—A Biography by Irving Stone, Doubleday, 1941.

Dreiser, Theodore, *An American Tragedy,* Doubleday, 1925.

Eliasberg, Wladimir, *Rechtspflege and Psychologie,* Carl Heyman Verlag, Berlin, 1932.

——, The New Theory of the Perpetrator and the Duties of the Psychiatric Expert, *Journal of Criminal Law and Criminology,* Vol. XXX, No. 4, Nov.–Dec., 1939.

——, The Acute Psychosexual Situation, Legal Meaning and Diagnosis, *Journal of Criminal Law and Criminology,* XXXIII, 6, March-April, 1943.

——, Opposing Expert Testimony, *Journal of Criminal Law and Criminology,* Vol. 36, No. 4, Nov.-Dec., 1945.

——, Forensic Psychology, *Southern California Law Review,* Vol. XIX, No. 4, July, 1946.

——, Irresistible Impulse and Crime, *The Psychiatric Quarterly Supplement,* Vol. 21, pp. 108–122, part 1, 1947.

Federal Rules of Criminal Procedure, Preliminary Draft, U. S. Government Printing Office, Washington, 1943.

Friederich, C. H., New Belief in the Common Man, Boston, Little Brown, 1942.

Glueck, Sheldon, *Mental Disorder and the Criminal Law,* Boston, Little Brown, 1925.

James, William, *Principles of Psychology,* 2nd Vol., Ch. 21, Henry Holt, 1902.

McDougall, William, *The Hormic Psychology, Psychologies of 1930,* Clark Univ. Press, 1930.

Michael J. and Adler, M. J., *Crime, Law and Social Science,* Harcourt, Brace, 1933.

Model Code of Evidence, American Law Institute, Philadelphia, Pa., May 15, 1942.

Overholser, Winfred, Psychiatric Expert Testimony, *Mental Health,* p. 313, Science Press, 1939.

Perry, Ralph Barton, *Democracy and Puritanism,* New York, Vanguard Press, 1944.

Rogers, L., *Expert Testimony,* 2nd ed., 1891.

Rosenthal, Lloyd, Development of the Use of Expert Testimony, *Law and Contemporary Problems,* Law School, Duke University, Vol. II, Oct., 1935.

Spranger, Eduard, *Lebensformen,* 2nd Ed. Halle a.d. Saale Max Niemeyer.

Stryker, L. P., *Courts and Doctors,* N. Y., Macmillan, 1939.

White, Leslie A., Culturological vs. Psychological Interpretations of Human Behavior, *American Sociological Review,* vol. 12, No. 6, Dec., 1947.

EXTORTION. Extortion is the obtaining of property from another, or the obtaining of property of a corporation from an officer, agent or employee thereof, with his consent, induced by the wrongful use of force or fear, or under color of official right. The crime of extortion is similar to *robbery* except that the nature of the threat, force or fear employed to obtain possession of the property induces the person to part with the property *with the consent* in order to avoid the results of the force or threat. The threats made in a case of extortion may be either oral or written.

The Penal Law of the State of New York outlines what threats may constitute extortion. Fear, such as will constitute extortion, may be induced by an oral or written threat:

1. To do an unlawful injury to the person or property of the individual threatened, or to any relative of his or to any member of his family or to a corporation of which he is an officer, stockholder, employee, or agent; or,

2. To accuse him, or any relative of his or any member of his family, of any crime; or,

3. To expose, or impute to him, or any of them, any deformity or disgrace; or,

4. To expose any secret affecting him or any of them; or,

5. To kidnap him or any relative of his or member of his family; or,

6. To injure his person or property or that of any relative of his or member of his family by the use of weapons or explosives.

A public officer who takes illegal fees or other compensation for his official service, commits extortion.

New York State law differentiates, as far as punishment is concerned, between extortion via threats of bodily harm "under circumstances not amounting to robbery" and extortion involving threats of exposure and the like. The former is punishable by imprisonment not to exceed fifteen years and the latter by imprisonment for from five to twenty years.

BIBLIOGRAPHY

Gilbert, F. B., *Criminal Law and Practice of the State of New York,* Matthew Bender & Co., 1935.

F

FEDERAL BUREAU OF INVESTIGA-TION, THE. Established in 1908, the *Federal Bureau of Investigation* provides the United States Department of Justice with a permanent investigative agency under its immediate control. It is the duty of the FBI to investigate all violations of Federal laws and matters in which the United States is or may be a party in interest, except those matters specifically assigned by Congressional enactment or otherwise to other Federal agencies, and to perform other functions imposed by law.

The Honorable Harlan Fiske Stone, former Chief Justice of the Supreme Court who was then Attorney General, appointed J. Edgar Hoover to his present position as Director of the FBI in 1924. It was then that the present organization and working policies were put into effect. Two cardinal rules established at that time were that the FBI should be completely divorced once and for all from politics and that appointments and promotions should be based solely on merit.

Special Agent applicants must be 25 to 40 years of age and of excellent background and character. Furthermore, they must be graduates of accredited law schools and members of the Bar, or graduates of recognized accounting schools and have at least three years' experience in commercial accounting or auditing. They are required to complete successfully an intensive 16-week training course prior to going into the field to do investigative work. There presently are more than 4,700 Special Agents assigned to the FBI's 57 field offices located strategically throughout the United States and its possessions. They have investigative jurisdiction over more than 100 violations of Federal laws. During the war, of course, a vast proportion of their work dealt with wartime matters.

The nation's all-out program of preparedness on the home front, accompanied by a nationally recognized need for combating espionage, sabotage and related matters, constituted a direct challenge to the men of the FBI. In keeping abreast of the tremendous increase in its responsibilities, the FBI handled a total of 390,805 matters pertaining to the internal security of the nation during the 1943 fiscal year. This represented a substantial increase over the 218,734 matters of this type reported to the FBI during 1942 and was indeed significant when viewed in the light of the fact that in the five-year period prior to 1938 an average of only 35 such matters were handled annually.

In handling national defense matters, the FBI carefully avoids any tendency toward hysteria and vigilante action. In contrast to its fight against kidnaping, bank robbery and other similar types of crime, the effectiveness of the FBI's internal security work cannot be judged alone by the number of arrests and convictions. The preventive aspect of the FBI's wartime work must also be considered. By way of illustration, counterespionage becomes effective only when enemy agents are placed under surveillance so that their methods of communication and sources of information may be discovered and later controlled.

In 1939, the President of the United States designated the FBI as the clearinghouse and coordinating agency for all internal security matters. It was recognized that the local law enforcement officer, with his intimate knowledge of affairs in his home community, would have an important role in the internal security program. With this in mind, there was instituted the FBI Law Enforcement Officers Mobilization Plan for National Defense. Its purpose was to coordinate and train the local police and sheriffs to meet the problems presented by their new wartime responsibilities. This program grew to tremendous proportions and in 1943 a total of 1,792 conferences were held throughout the United States at which some 9,669 law enforcement agencies were represented.

Another factor which enabled the local law enforcement officer to work hand-in-hand with the FBI in safeguarding the home front was the FBI National Academy established in 1935. In keeping with the FBI's aim to improve not only its own organization but also to raise the standards of all law enforcement to a professional plane, the FBI National Academy provides specialized training for instructors and executives in police agencies throughout the country. To date, 854 graduates representing more than 100,-000 police officers have gone forth from the Academy to establish similar training courses for their fellow officers.

When the national emergency began, the efforts of the FBI were concentrated against those who would undermine the country's war program, but investigations of other criminal violations were by no means neglected. During 1943 the investigative activity of the FBI resulted in 10,294 convictions. It should be noted in this regard that convictions resulted in 95.8 percent of the cases investigated by the FBI which were brought to trial. Sentences resulting from these convictions aggregated 24,624 years, three months and six days, three life terms and seven death penalties. Fines totaling $1,409,-376 were levied, and savings and recoveries amounting to $27,820,372 were effected.

An important phase of the FBI's wartime activity was enforcement of the Selective Training and Service Act. As of May 1, 1944, there were 8,854 convictions since enactment of the Statute on October 16, 1940. These resulted in sentences of more than 21,-978 years and fines totaling $917,759. Approximately 357,000 cases were closed since passage of the Act, and as a result of the activity of the FBI and local law enforcement officers, the individuals were either made available to the military services under the provisions of the statute or otherwise disposed of by law. It should be noted, however, that one of the primary purposes of these investi-

gations was to secure compliance with provisions of the law rather than to take prosecutive action for technical violations. Not once has there been a repetition of the so-called "slacker" raids which resulted in so much controversy in World War I.

From the peak reached in the year 1932, there was a drop of over 92 per cent in bank robberies in the United States, largely as a result of the FBI's activity in this field. Through the 1943 fiscal year there had been a total of 970 bank robberies coming within the investigative jurisdiction of the FBI as a result of passage of the Federal Bank Robbery Act on May 18, 1934. Convictions in these cases in Federal Courts totaled 699 and resulted in sentences of more than 11,384 years, two death penalties, 14 life terms and $351,-100 in fines. In addition, 310 convictions for bank robbery occurred in state courts in cases investigated jointly by the FBI and local authorities. These resulted in sentences of more than 2,961 years, eight death penalties, 37 life terms and ten indefinite imprisonments. In 1943 61 fugitive bank robbers were located in the United States, among them several who had been sought intensively for several years.

Since passage of the Federal Kidnaping Act on June 22, 1932, there have been 261 kidnaping cases investigated by the FBI. Of this total, all but two have been solved and these are still under active investigation. During 1943 there were 29 kidnaping cases and all of these were solved. They resulted in 47 convictions, sentences for which totaled more than 461 years. Indicative of the fate which awaits kidnapers is the fact that since 1932 and through the 1943 fiscal year a total of 44 life terms and 12 death sentences was imposed for this crime. In addition, during this period eight kidnapers were killed while resisting arrest, seven were murdered by other gang members, nine committed suicide, two were lynched and one was declared insane.

Since enactment of the National Motor Vehicle Theft Act in 1919 making it a federal offense to transport a stolen motor vehicle in interstate commerce, a total of 72,106 motor vehicles valued at $40,814,782 had been recovered in cases investigated by the FBI through the 1943 fiscal year. Federal court action resulted in 2,171 convictions and sentences aggregated 6,410 years, with fines amounting to $8,671.

Among the cooperative functions of the FBI are those embodied in the Identification Division, which was created in 1924 through consolidation of criminal identification files maintained at the Federal Penitentiary at Leavenworth, Kansas, and those of the International Association of Chiefs of Police. From this nucleus of 810,188 fingerprints, there has been developed the world's largest depository of fingerprint and criminal record data. In 1944, there were over 88,000,000 fingerprint cards of all kinds on file with the FBI in Washington. They were received at a rate of approximately 30,000 a day with more than 12,000 contributing agencies being represented. During 1943, identifications were effected in 64.68 per cent of the criminal fingerprint cards received for search. Nearly 12,000 fugitives were identified through fingerprints during the 1943 fiscal year.

An important need for scientific examination of evidence is met through the FBI Laboratory. Not only does it conduct examinations for Special Agents of the FBI but it also makes its services available to other governmental agencies and law enforcement officers in all sections of the country. In the tremendous volume of national defense matters handled during the 1943 fiscal year, the FBI Laboratory had an important role. A total of 193,371 examinations involving 247,886 individual specimens of evidence were made during the 1943 fiscal year, as compared with 51,475 examinations the previous year. Assistance was rendered to other agencies of the Federal government in 532 instances and to municipal, county and state law enforcement agencies in 982 cases.

In another of its cooperative functions, the FBI has served since 1930 as a central clearinghouse for nation-wide police statistics. Nearly 5,000 cooperating law enforcement agencies throughout the nation submit monthly and annual arrest statistics for their particular communities. These are summarized by the FBI and published semiannually in the Uniform Crime Reports Bulletin. This service provides a means by which local law enforcement officers can evaluate the trends

and fluctuations of crime, both nationally and locally.

J. EDGAR HOOVER
Director, Federal Bureau
of Investigation
Washington, D. C.

BIBLIOGRAPHY

Federal Bureau of Investigation, United States Department of Justice, *Report: Ten Years of Uniform Crime Reporting, 1930–1939,* Washington, D. C., November, 1939.
Hoover, J. Edgar, *Persons in Hiding,* Little, Brown, 1938.
Hoover, J. Edgar, Bankruptcy Frauds, *Journal of Criminal Law and Criminology,* 23, 1073–1080, March, 1933.
Hoover, J. Edgar, White Slave Traffic, *Journal of Criminal Law and Criminology,* 24, 475–482, July, 1933.

FELONY. Crimes are classified according to their seriousness into felonies and misdemeanors. A felony is a crime which is or may be punishable by death of by confinement in a state prison. Usually no person can be sentenced to a state prison for less than one year. Every crime, not a felony, is a *misdemeanor* which is usually punishable by confinement in a local prison, such as a county jail or penitentiary, or by fines. Certain crimes may be *either a felony or a misdemeanor,* depending on the manner of their commission or the amount of money or property involved as the subject of the crime, such as, Larceny, Assault, Malicious Mischief, Carrying Weapons Unlawfully, etc. The powers of arrest by a peace officer are greater in felony cases than in those of a misdemeanor. No compromise of felonies is permitted.

Authorities, such as Sutherland, do not consider the classification of crimes into felonies and misdemeanors as very useful and also point out that it is often difficult to make a clear-cut distinction between the classes. The fact that many things which are classed as felonies in one state are classed as misdemeanors in nearby states shows how difficult it is to make a real distinction between them. Queen reports an investigation which shows that of 110 offenses in the laws of eleven states in 1918, 39 were punishable in some states as misdemeanors and in other states as felonies, from which he draws the conclusion that there is no inherent distinction between a felony and a misdemeanor.

BIBLIOGRAPHY

Sutherland, E. H., *Principles of Criminology*, J. B. Lippincott Co., 1939.
Queen, S. A., *The Passing of the County Jail*, 1920, pp. 75–82.
Gilbert, F. B., *Criminal Law and Practice of the State of New York*, Matthew Bender and Co., 1935.

FINGERPRINTS, CRIMINAL IDENTIFICATION OF. The science of the analysis and comparison of inked or other recorded impressions of skin areas. The term is usually limited to the study of those impressions made of the palmar surfaces of the terminal phalanx (fingertips) of the thumbs and fingers of each hand. Impressions, however, are made not infrequently of the plantar surfaces (soles) of the feet, especially in lying-in hospitals for identification of babies, and of palmar surfaces of the hands (palm prints).

The discovery of the fact that friction ridges exist in the form of patterns on the skin seems to date back into antiquity. According to Heindl, fingerprints were used for identification purposes during the Tang Dynasty (618–906 A. D.). Scientific study and reduction of these patterns to classifications for purpose of filing, study and comparison (Dactyloscopy) had its origin in the Far East through the studies of Sir William Herschel of India and Dr. Henry Faulds of Tokio, Japan, whose conclusions were arrived at simultaneously and independently. The English anthropologist, Sir Francis Galton, was largely responsible for the technique of ridge-counting and ridge-tracing. He had studied very carefully the proposed fingerprint classification made by Sir Edward Henry then Inspector General of Police in the lower provinces of India. The resultant was the Galton-Henry System of Fingerprint Classification which is the one most widely used today. Other systems include the Battley of the London Police which is especially adaptable to the classification of single fingerprints.

In brief, the friction ridges of the skin, particularly over the palmar surfaces of the fingers and palms, tend to arrange themselves in set patterns, which may be classified, registered and used for comparison at a later date with suspected fingerprints. These ridges are formed in the foetus about the fourth month of pregnancy and the ridges remain constant throughout the entire life of that individual. By taking an arbitrary number of characteristics of such a print (first chosen as twelve in number) that fingerprint may be so classified that no one else in the entire world will have an identical pattern. The permutations and combinations of twelve characteristics run into such a huge number that the possibility of duplication is entirely ruled out for all practical purposes. Furthermore these ridges can be worn down or eroded through the use of lye, hard manual labor, and other damaging forces but they quickly regenerate upon rest. Gross has compared the fingerprint pattern to the traceries of tough lacing. The lace may be twisted and pulled in every direction but will regain its shape when given the opportunity. Thus, warts and other excrescences merely push aside the pattern which regains its former position once the growth has been removed. Criminals have repeatedly endeavored to remove fingerprints through the use of acids and plastic operations but the print is readily identifiable nevertheless. So permanent is the fingerprint pattern that bodies recovered after days of submersion in water may still yield fingerprint impressions through the simple process of embalming.

Advantage has been taken of these characteristics of permanency and, specificity, in using the fingerprints as a method of identification. Thus, if a fingerprint is discovered at the scene of a crime, it may be photographed and comparison made with existing fingerprints on file at a central bureau where they are properly classified and grouped for ready comparison. Thus, at strategic points, such as the State Departments of Correction, City Police Departments, the Federal Bureau of Investigation, and other smaller and less well-known divisions an immense number of fingerprints are on file dealing with criminals of all classes who have been apprehended in the past. Any suspect that is picked up, immediately is fingerprinted and comparisons are made, especially through the Federal Bureau of Investigation. Large concerns have found it advisable to fingerprint their entire staff, this being particularly true of those working in the field of Correction. Insurance companies have found a complete system to be of great value, particularly in the matter of missing persons. Banks have utilized this system as an additional measure of safety where the depositor was illiterate and unable to write his name. The system has been recommended for the tracing of immigrants who have been deported from this country so that they may be readily identified upon illegal reentry. In fact, there are a large number of students in the field who believe universal fingerprinting should be resorted to as a measure of identification in cases such as catastrophes, flood, fire, train wrecks, mutilation in battle, etc. Federalization of fingerprinting on a national scale, however, has not yet received adequate backing.

Dactyloscopy (the technique of fingerprinting) requires an exactitude of knowledge and extensiveness of experience. There are phases, however, of this work which can be utilized in the ordinary jails and sheriffs' offices which may lead readily to identification of much wanted criminals. When a criminal is picked up, he should be fingerprinted and the prints sent simultaneously to the Federal Bureau of Identification at Washington, D. C., and to the State Bureau of Identification. The technique of making fingerprints should be known by everyone handling criminals. Briefly this consists of cleansing the fingers with benzine or ether, permitting them to dry, and then to roll each one over a glass surface upon which printers' ink has been rolled. Each finger is then taken between the thumb and forefinger of the hands of the operator, placed upon prepared cards in the proper space with the side of the finger opposite the operator. The finger is then carefully and firmly rolled toward the operator who stands parallel to the finger upon which the impression is being secured. The thumbs are taken last and then simultaneous impressions in the proper spaces on the card are made of all four fingers as well as simultaneous impressions of both thumbs. These combined impressions are plain and are not rolled. The usual mistake in the taking of impressions is the use of too much ink, leading to the running together of ridges and the obliteration

of the spaces between. An adequate impression should be light gray in color with complete clear spaces of paper showing between each ridge so that the ridges may be counted and traced in their entirety. Any coalescence of ridges by ink defeats identification. Another common fault in taking the impressions is to permit the finger to slip slightly, thereby blurring the image. It is obvious that two impressions should not be superimposed upon each other; that is to say, if a mistake has been made in taking the impression of a finger, that impression should not be attempted again over the same space but a new card should be used. Standard cards are provided by Identification Bureaus. These are distributed to Police Stations, Sheriffs' Offices, Penal Institutions, and other points at which criminals may be apprehended or held. In general, they follow the plan of having a simple data outline, such as the name, age, height, weight, etc., and a space for the affixing of a photograph. On the reverse side, space is provided for three rows of impressions, the first two of which are rolled. The first row includes the impressions of the thumb and fingers of the right hand in that order. The second row includes those of the left hand and these, of course, are rolled also. The third row is made up of plain prints and includes the simultaneous impressions of fingers of both hands, as well as the simultaneous impressions of the thumbs. Usually the signature of the person to be identified is written on this side of the card. The card is then forwarded to the proper Bureau of Identification.

In addition to these carefully-prepared prints, the Bureaus of Identification must deal with prints that are picked up at the scene of the crime. These chance or accidental prints left by the criminal are either visible prints, latent prints, or plastic prints. Visible prints are usually smudged and may often look like a stain, especially if blood is present. They are usually single prints and require an expert for identification. Latent fingerprints are scarcely visible to the naked eye although they sometimes may be seen by glancing at the surface in an oblique direction. The palms of the hands and fingers, as well as the soles of the feet and toes, do not contain oil glands. Hence, the popular idea that the oil from the hands leaves fingerprints is not borne out by fact. Even the sweat glands which are present are not sufficient to leave a fingerprint. The friction ridges, however, pick up oil from other portions of the skin, particularly the face and the hair. Criminals as a class are rather dirty in their habits and their hands are none too cleanly. In the cases of burglary the criminal is quite likely to be using tools that are greasy and some of this will come off on his hands.

Gloves are frequently used by criminals in committing a crime, of course, but these are cumbersome and are frequently discarded. The experienced criminal, unless he is too hurried in making a get-away, will be careful to wipe away all surfaces he has contacted in order to remove prints. Nevertheless he overlooks contact surfaces at times and thus valuable information is yielded to the Bureau of Identification. Once a visible print has been noted, it requires being brought out for purposes of photographing. Latent fingerprints can be discovered by searching for them in the darkened room by means of an electric flashlight. Breathing on the object and examining obliquely, the vapor film thus produced reveals the presence of the latent print. If these are on smooth surfaces, such as bottles, plates, glass windows, furniture and the bodies of motor cars, they are dusted with finely-powdered white lead or aluminum powder and are brushed off lightly with a camel's hair brush. A photograph is then made of the print and an enlargement of five or six times is made on glossy paper for purposes of introduction into court as evidence. If the background of the latent fingerprint is white instead of dark, then a black dusting powder must be utilized. These are likely to be found on papers and documents. Powdered metallic antimony is very useful for this purpose but cold iodine fumes are much resorted to. By this method the suspected area is exposed to a container with a small amount of cold iodine in the bottom. Five minutes' exposure is sufficient to bring out any latent prints. Frequently latent prints are to be discovered on bed clothing, shirts, collars, handkerchiefs, and other textiles. These, of course, are invisible to the naked eye. The material to be

tested is then immersed in a 10% solution of silver nitrate and then dipped into a 10% solution of acetic acid. The area is exposed to sunlight or ultra-violet light. The print comes up as a dark brown impression and should be immediately photographed. If the print is needed for permanent preservation, it should be photographed, then washed and fixed by treating with a 5% solution of ammonium hydrosulphide. It is washed in water, wrung out and dried in direct sunlight. Latent prints on metallic surfaces are best brought out by the use of powdered copper. If the print is on the smooth side of a frosted glass window, printer's ink is rolled over the frosting, whereby the print is ready for photographing.

The third class of chance impressions taken at the scene of the crime are plastic prints which occur in putty, tar, butter, soap, or in any other type of plastic material. They are readily discernible but offer some difficulty in photography. An effective method of preserving the print is through a specialized form of moulage; namely, the use of foils. Two celluloid foils with a layer of transparent paste between them constitute the method of transferring the print from its place of origin. One of these films is quite thin and is used only as cover and protection. The other, of course, is the backing for the paste. The cover celluloid is peeled off carefully and the paste is applied directly to the plastic print. Great care must be exercised in this procedure so as to avoid smudging and slurring of the print. When the foil is removed, the cover celluloid is replaced to prevent disturbance of the impression. Colored fingerprints, such as those made in blood, can likewise be treated by the foil method. Two types of foils are on the market; namely, transparent and black ones. The transparent ones are easier to handle inasmuch as they may be used directly as a photographic plate for enlarging and printing. The fingerprint, of course, is brought into relief by the dusting with black powder. If the fingerprint is on a black background, then the black foil is used for direct photography. Foils may also be used to transfer footprints in dust or linoleum and similar material.

The visible, latent or plastic prints may not occur as a solitary print. Not infrequently several finger impressions are left at the scene of the crime. Usually none of these impressions contains enough characteristics to be an identifiable print of itself. The whole group of prints must be considered in toto. In these cases the identification of the exact finger from which the print came is a matter of some difficulty. There are a few rules, however, that guide the investigator. The thumb print is notable for its size. The base of the impression, that is to say, the open end of the loop, opens to the right or to the left in accordance with whether or not it came from the right or left hand. If the pattern is a twin loop, the underloop opens to the right on the right-hand thumb and to the left on the left-hand thumb. If the pattern is an egg-shaped whorl, the "egg" slopes to the right or left according to which hand is used. In the ordinary whorl the turn of the spiral is to the right when made by right thumbs and to the left when made by left thumbs. The index finger has a curve to the right or left in accordance with the handedness of the individual. Middle fingers are likely to be longer than the others, whereas the little finger is the smallest of the group. Ring fingers may easily be confused with the middle finger if they are a single print. In addition to these peculiarities of the individual prints, the pattern or relation of the various prints to each other is of significance. Due to the prehensile quality of the hand, the most common combination of multiple prints is that of the index and middle finger or of the middle, ring, and small finger, according to whether or not the individual is grasping in a forward or backward direction. The whorls appear most frequently on thumbs and ring fingers, whereas the little finger nearly always presents an ulnar loop. Also, the general trend is that index fingers have a radial loop, whereas the other fingers have ulnar loops. (An ulnar loop points to the ulnar or inner side of the hand, whereas the opposite is true of the radial loop.)

Upon the arrival of a card upon which fingerprint impressions have been recorded, the Bureau of Identification checks the source of the card, stamps the print, and classifies it as to whether the subject is white or black or a female since these are sub-divisions in the Technical Section for identification. In the Technical Section the print is given thorough analysis according to the Galton-Henry System or the Renoe Extension. Its proper relative sequence is determined after a primary classification has been made. Experts do this rapidly and efficiently by means of the naked eye. In the case of "questionable" prints or those that are obscured by smudging, such as is encountered in the visible chance impressions, resort may be made to the Dactyloscope Outfit. This consists of a magnifier in the base of which may be set circular discs (dispositives or reticules) upon which lines are etched so as to facilitate counting and tracing. These circular glass discs are severally etched with concentric rings or with diagonals or parallel lines to facilitate spacing and counting. By this means, the Henry, Battley, Jorgensen, and Borne Systems can be utilized interchangeably.

Originally, twelve characteristics must be discerned in a print in order to establish identity. The expert, however, marks on the space in which each impression is recorded the general characteristic of the print as to whether or not it is a Loop, Arch, or Whorl. A slanted line will indicate whether or not the loop is radial or ulnar. One of the quickest methods of making identification is to note any peculiarities, such as the presence of a scar, an excresence mark, or a peculiar and unusual pattern. Often these are of more significance than the routine matter of ridge-counting and ridge-tracing. As noted above, the fingerprint pattern may be classified into loops, arches, or whorls. A loop is a single backward turn with no twist. It is open at its lower end. The loop may be further classified as being either radial or ulnar (sometimes spoken of as inner or outer) or twinned. Arches may be further sub-divided into simple and tented arches. In arches the ridges in the center run from one side to the other of the finger bulb without making any backward turn or twist. They are, of course, arched in the middle of their course. Whorls make a complete turn through at least one circle. The simple whorl may be combined with other types of patterns to form what is known as a composite. Composites are usually classified as whorls. Whorls most frequently encountered are of the egg-shaped or so-called "eggs," circular or double. Of great importance in the analysis of a print is the location of the core and of the delta. The core is the center of the pattern and usually is the top of the loop or the middle of the innermost circle or tip of the rod composing the center of the pattern. The delta so-named from the fancied resemblance to the Greek letter Delta is formed by the splitting of a ridge or through the wide separation of two ridges which up to that point have run side by side. While arches have cores, they do not have any deltas. Whorls on the other hand always contain at least two deltas. Twinned loops, of course, will contain two deltas. The delta may be a short, thick rod, an isolated island, or a mere point but is readily distinguishable by its being at the lower end of the loop.

In *ridge-counting* an imaginary line is drawn from the core to the delta and the number of ridges cut by this line is recorded. The Dactyloscope is needed in this work. The method is particularly applicable to loops and the counting begins on the ridge outer to the core in its relation to the delta.

Ridge-tracing is particularly applicable to whorl patterns. If the end of the ridge meets the delta head-on or within two spaces thereof, it is known as a meeting ridge and is designated by the capital M. If the ridge goes outside of the delta more than two ridges, it is known as an outer ridge and is designated by O and if two or more inside the delta, it is known as an inner ridge and is designated by an I. These are important designations in the building up of a formula necessary to characterize the fingerprint pattern. Along the line of the fingerprint ridge certain interruptions occur which are highly significant. As a matter of fact, the length of the angle at which they offset from the parent ridge, the distance between such interruptions merely constitute a better basis for identification than the tracing of the ridge itself. Thus, the ridge may bifurcate to enclose a small space or eye. There may be a short off-shoot from the parent ridge which is designated as the hook. The hook may turn backward, in which case it is known as a contra-hook. The ridge may bifurcate for a considerable dis-

tance constituting a fork or it may be interrupted by gaps.

It will be recalled in the earlier paragraphs of this article that a precise sequence was followed in the matter of recording fingerprints on the cards provided by the various Identification Bureaus. These begin with the right thumb and go through the right hand and onto the left hand in that order. For purposes of classification the digits are divided into pairs; for example, the right thumb and right index finger constituting the first pair. The original investigators found that there were sixteen various combinations with respect to relationships between the two paired impressions and, therefore, assigned a numerical value of sixteen. The second pair provided eight additional ones, the third pair four, the fourth pair two, and the fifth pair one, making a total of thirty-one combinations. Numerical value was not assigned to any pair unless it contained a whorl. The even numbered fingers in these pairs were put in the numerator and the odd numbers in the denominator (an alternative method was to take them in the order given, putting the first in the numerator and the second in the denominator and inverting the final fraction). The numeral one was added to the numerator and denominator after the summation of the total series. For purposes of classification originally, a pigeon hole system was devised whereby there were thirty-two spaces horizontally and thirty-two vertically so that the prints could be filed according to the numerical value just described. This constituted the original primary classification. There have been many changes in this and, of course, the pigeon hole system is no longer used. The "master" print section in any Identification Bureau is the one that contains the best known prints of each subject that is registered. The technician will carry his primary classification of the card for purposes of identification to this master print section. If the card is not readily obtainable in this way, further sub-classification or secondary classification is necessary. Ridge-tracing and ridge-counting may have to be resorted to in that case. Thus, a formula is built up for any particular series of prints. This formula is attached to all posters and circulars sent out on wanted or missing people throughout the land and enables the sheriff, police chief, or other officer to make a quick identification of any suspect that he may have on hand.

For purposes of presentation of fingerprints in court, it is necessary to photograph, to enlarge the original photograph about six times, and to mount the prints in the regular order of sequence so that they may be readily compared with the original ones on file in the Identification Bureau. Fine ink lines either in black or red are drawn from the periphery to the center of the characteristic of each print and a number is assigned to that. Obviously, the number of each characteristic must correspond between the suspected print and the one on file for basis of comparison. While a great number of comparative points may be thus outlined, there is a tendency to discount characteristics in the periphery of the print. The center of the pattern is the most vital portion to be analyzed. Prints, of course, may be examined underneath the comparison microscope and these may be projected for the benefit of the jury if it is found to be necessary.

The identification of single prints has been especially developed by Battley of the London Police Force. The fingerprint comparison microscope is particularly valuable in this connection since the two prints, namely, that on file and the suspected one, can be viewed side by side with matched objectives of like magnification. Each Identification Bureau contains a separate file of single fingerprints. Special classifications have been devised for this type of print.

Poroscopy was first discovered by the Dyctylist Locard. The friction ridges have pinpoint openings which represent sweat pores. These may occur on the top of the ridge or may open out from the side. The distance between the pores differs with different individuals but, in general, the pores have the same properties as other pattern details and, therefore, may be used for absolute identification. The shape, size, position, and number of pores in the skin pattern of an individual are unchangeable and exist from the fourth month of fetal life and are not subject to any changes thereafter. Pores are much smaller in women than in men. A special technique is required to bring them out for purposes of photography. Heindl recommends the rolling of a clean finger against a glass plate and developing and printing with iodine fumes. Söderman suggests a special ink used by the Police Laboratory of Lyons, France, composed of yellow wax, Greek resin, and tallow. This is allowed to solidify and the clean finger is rubbed against the surface and then impressed upon glossed paper or celluloid. The print is brought out by the use of oxide of cobalt. Poroscopy is especially valuable in the identification of fragmentary impressions where the number of characteristic details is insufficient for identification alone. Also, there are cases in which only a small portion of the pattern can be utilized, and here the pores have a certainty of identification not obtainable by the ridge method.

Palm prints often yield evidence that cannot be obtained in any other way. Since the entire palm is covered with friction skin, the elements of permanency and innumerable variations insure for a palm print the same background for identification as a fingerprint itself. Careful examination of the object from which the suspected print is obtained readily differentiates a palm print from a fingerprint. For purposes of registry the following technique is observed in obtaining a palm print. The Stokis Apparatus consists of a curved block of wood, half of which is covered with a copper plate and is inked in the same manner as in taking fingerprints. The other half of the curved surface is covered with a piece of white paper. The entire hand with fingers slightly spread is pressed against the inked surface and the impression is made therefrom onto the white paper. An inflated rubber pillow makes an excellent foundation for the taking of palm prints. Another method of taking palm prints which in some respects is a little more precise is the use of a small rolling pin upon which an 8" x 8" white card is affixed by means of rubber bands. A small amount of printer's ink is applied directly from an inked glass plate to the hand and fingers of the subject to be examined. The entire palm, as well as the entire length of the fingers, must be well inked. The heel of the palm of the hand is placed on the card at the lower edge and the roller is then rolled away from the subject, keeping the fingers stiff and outstretched in the process of rolling. The card may be reversed for getting the other print. The usual defect shown in the taking of palm prints is the failure to get the center of the palm recorded. The entire palm should be so clearly defined that the so-called "life line" and other palm lines show in their entire extent. The second defect is the failure to catch the bases of the fingers in the print. This is due to failure in keeping the fingers extended rigidly. In the Stokis method, pressure is exerted against the knuckles so as to insure obtaining a fingerprint in its entire length. The same technique must be observed with respect to inking as in fingerprint taking; namely, that too much ink is not used and that the resultant print is light gray in color, is complete throughout, and that ridges are not coalesced by any running of ink. The value of palm prints, of course, is obvious since it will be recalled that many times a suspect in committing his crime may grasp objects without the fingertips coming into contact thereof.

The question has been repeatedly raised as to whether or not fingerprints could be altered, duplicated, or otherwise malingered. It is well known that the felon Dillinger resorted to plastic surgery in order to eradicate a portion of the fingerprint patterns on every one of his fingers. He failed utterly in his purpose because there are many characteristics outside of the field of operation that will give identifying data. To make this method of skin-grafting effective, the entire finger must be desquamated through into the corium in order to secure results. This is not only expensive but is exceedingly painful and very few surgeons capable of doing such an operation can be obtained by underworld characters. It must also be recalled that if such a man is picked up, his fingerprints become all the more readily identifiable because of their mutilation. Attempts have been made to burn the fingerprints, to scarify them, to rub the patterns against bricks as in the walls of the cells, but in all these cases the ridges readily return to their normal condition after a short rest.

Attempts have been made to reproduce in rubber, fingerprint patterns so they could be used for the purpose of forgery. The methods by which ordinary rubber stamps are made would seem to indicate that a fingerprint pattern could be duplicated by a similar technique. One of the main difficulties, however, is the reproduction of the sweat pores which have such distinctive outlines and characteristics. They cannot be reproduced in rubber stamp form any more clearly than can the engraving on a genuine bank note be reproduced by the ordinary process of photo-engraving. The lack of clearness of definition is one of the main defects in this attempt.

In this connection, it is interesting to note that Locard, one of the most prominent continental dactyloscopists, has fairly recently come forth with the assertion that fingerprints are not positive means of identification; that is to say, in certain instances the papillary ridges upon which fingerprint identification is founded may be altered. He drew his conclusions in a communication given before the Academy of Medicine in Paris in 1934 in which he presented evidence of marked changes occurring in the fingerprint pattern of lepers. Leprosy, as is well known, is a malady characterized by gangrene and sloughing off of portions of the body, especially the fingers and the toes. Since these unfortunate individuals are segregated, are well known, and do not have the opportunity for committing crimes, the whole question is largely an academic one.

A further word should be spoken with respect to the use of tabulating machinery in identification bureaus. All of the data required for fingerprint identification can be outlined on a prepared card known as a "punch card." Each set of prints of an individual is punched out on the card and filed for reference. When any particular factor is required, the tabulating machine may be set in such a way as to throw down a whole series of cards having that particular factor. For example, if an individual has a certain primary classification and some factor in the secondary classification is to be sought, then all of the punched cards having that primary classification are run through the tabulating machine. Those having that particular sub-classification sought, since the machine is set for that particular purpose through a series of intricate wiring, are automatically sorted out from the general group. A second factor in the sub-classification may be untilized at that point for the purpose of still further reducing the number of individuals that would meet that particular combination. Thus, the tabulating and sorting machine may be utilized to segregate almost any factor that is indicated on the punch card. Not only can certain intricate identifications be made this way but the procedure lends itself to research investigation. The method, of course, can be used with equal facility for tabulating and searching out other identification data, such as the modus operandi, Bertillon information, or blotter record data, such as age, type of crime, etc.

VERNON C. BRANHAM, M. D.
Chief, Outpatient Section,
Neuropsychiatric Division,
Veterans Administration,
Washington, D. C.

BIBLIOGRAPHY

Beffel, John Nicholas, Fingerprints, *The American Mercury,* Feb., 1925.
Cummins, Harold, Counterfeit Fingerprints, *Journal of Criminal Law and Criminology,* 25, 666–671.
Perkins, Rollin M., *Elements of Police Science,* Foundation Press, Incorporated, Chicago, 1942.
Soderman, Harry and O'Connell, John J., *Modern Criminal Investigation,* Funk and Wagnalls Co., 1945.

FOLLOW-UP STUDIES: THEIR NATURE AND VALUE.

I. In most fields of human endeavor nobody would think it wise to keep on doing things as they had always been done before, unless a periodic inventory of the product showed that no change from customary practices was called for. In the administration of fair and effective justice—probably the most important single function of a civilized state—we have been much too content to drift along in the accustomed channels, without checking up on the direction or progress of our journey.

Is not the chief aim of criminal justice the reduction of crime? And if it is, have we been sufficiently concerned with discovering whether or not our existing methods bring about that result? "By their fruits ye shall know them."

A number of researches into the "after-conduct" of delinquents and criminals have been made in the United States during the past fifteen or more years, most of them by the authors of this report.

The authors are convinced that these check-up studies provide a highly useful instrument for the reform of several of the most crucial processes in the administration of criminal justice, particularly the sentencing function, the revision of sentences, and the paroling of prisoners.[1]

Any intelligent programs for reform of the administration of criminal justice, must be based on more than an examination of the decisions of courts and the enactments of legislative bodies. A fundamental weakness of past reforms, however, has been the overlooking of the most basic element in the situation—*the offender himself.* Law has been designated a "verbal science;" but it is human beings with whom the criminal law and its administrators have to deal, not merely legal abstractions. And it is the intensive study of the human beings who commit crimes that must precede programs of redesign and reconstruction of our criminal law, criminal courts, punitive practices, correctional establishments, rehabilitative instrumentalities.

II. What happens to the former inmates of our prisons and reformatories? What percentage of them become law-abiding citizens? How many return to a life of crime and vice? What portion of them change from aggressive and dangerous criminals to misdemeanants, vagrants, chronic alcoholics and the like? What *types* of offenders persist in serious criminality, what types become minor offenders, what types give up their lives of crime? And at what *ages* do these changes occur? Is imprisonment a preventive of recidivism? How, in the light of the human grist and human product of the mills of justice, can we improve our methods of peno-correctional treatment?

These are but a few of the fundamental questions which it was long impossible to an-

[1] Details of the methods employed in the assembling, verifying, organizing and tabulating of the materials that enter into a follow-up study have been amply set forth in our various works to which the interested reader can refer.

swer with any degree of reliability. This was so because no thoroughgoing researches had been made with the object of tracing down large numbers of former prisoners, studying their make-up and histories prior to and after incarceration, interviewing them and their families, and evaluating the penal institutions and corrective practices in the light of accurate facts and legitimate inferences. Hundreds of volumes have been written on the fascinating subjects of crime and criminals, in addition to the numerous traditional treatises on the criminal law and criminal procedure; but until a relatively few years ago not one has furnished a reliable estimate of the work and worth of sentencing and paroling practices, punitive and correctional instrumentalities.

What has been the contribution of our follow-up investigations to a better understanding of the characteristics and background of offenders against the law? What are the physical and mental traits, the social and economic conditioning forces of the many thousands of boys and young men constantly fed into and ground out of, the mills of Justice? [2] We say "boys and young men," because modern crime, both in volume and in the difficulty of the issues it presents, is essentially a problem of youth and young manhood. According to American statistics, the young-adult period of life contributes the highest incidence of crime. There are, of course, vast hordes of offenders of the older vagrant, alcoholic and drug-addiction types, who fill the jails, houses of correction and industrial farms. But at that stage in their careers, offenders are no longer aggressively dangerous; they are the flotsam and jetsam of the social stream. Their problems are essentially medical and psychiatric.

The gravest concern is unquestionably caused by the children, adolescents and

young-adults who crowd correctional schools, reformatories and prisons, and who, in large measure, sooner or later commit serious crimes and continue their criminal careers well into adulthood.

Our investigations into the outstanding characteristics of offenders, comprising a thousand boy delinquents and five hundred young-adult male criminals who had been under the control, respectively, of the Boston Juvenile Court with its related treatment agencies, and of the Massachusetts criminal courts and the Massachusetts Reformatory,[3] disclose a picture that seems crucial to any understanding of the problems which courts, correctional agencies, prisons and parole systems have to cope with.

Limitations of space prevent the presentation of even a synopsis of the findings of our various follow-up studies concerning the makeup and charactertistics of delinquents and criminals, and their vicissitudes over the years. Suffice it to say that in respect to family life the facts and relationships unearthed in these researches show a substantial incidence of poverty and dependency and all they mean in the way of unhygienic home and neighborhood situations and the employment of mothers outside the home; unskilled, incompetent bread-winners; illiterate parents; harmfully unhappy relations between husband and wife and between parents and children; unwise disciplinary practices; broken homes; immorality, alcoholism and criminalism of parents, brothers and sisters of delinquents. In respect to the delinquents and criminals themselves, these researches show mental defect, disorder and distortion; inadequate schooling; employment of children at early ages in hazardous street trades; unwholesome recreations and vicious companionships; early origins of tendencies toward delinquency; marked recidivism.

The mere enumeration of such factors and conditions is itself the best evidence that any simplistic theory of crime causation, such as the law's "criminal intent," or any oversimplified conception of the influence of punishment on human behavior is not only unscien-

---

[2] Though female delinquents and criminals resemble the male in many traits and in their general socio-economic background, we do not, in this article, go into their characteristics. Much of the anti-social expression of women is related to the sex impulse and to some extent presents special problems in law, procedure and correctional treatment. The subject is explored in most of its ramifications in Glueck, S. and E. T., *Five Hundred Delinquent Women*.

[3] Details will be found in *One Thousand Juvenile Delinquents,* and *500 Criminal Careers*.

tific but bound to be ineffective in practice. Some implications of this point of view will be discussed below.

III. A good follow-up study should, however, include a careful, detailed analysis of the constructive and deteriorative features of the *regime* the product of which is under investigation.

How is it possible to relate the regimes of penal and correctional institutions to outcomes in terms of the post-treatment behavior of offenders subjected to it? Considering the complexity of the motivations and conditioners of human conduct, one despairs of ever being able to solve such a problem. An inherent difficulty in all research concerned with human beings is that the numerous and subtle factors and forces involved in both the organism and its *milieu* are not subject to that strict scientific "control" which to a great degree is possible in the physical and chemical laboratories. The fact that a former inmate of a reformatory is now classifiable as a "success" or "failure" in his behavior does not, by itself, indicate whether there was some actual improvement in his case; nor does it throw much light on the probable *role of the reformatory or parole system* in the process. The good or bad result may have been due more to extraneous factors than to the efforts of the institution.

The difficulties involved may be illustrated by the fact that in interpreting such improvements as, for example, reduced recidivism, increase in good work-habits, in skill, in earning capacity, and the like, the fact cannot be ignored that both the innate make-up of the offenders and the mere passage of time with its accompanying biologic maturation of the youths whose careers we are considering probably played a part—perhaps a considerable part—in addition to whatever the reformatory and parole systems might be credited with. As to certain aspects of behavior it is indeed possible to conclude that the correctional regime must have had little to do with the outcome. For example, we found that there is a high association between the pre-reformatory economic responsibility of the offenders and their meeting of economic obligations to dependents during the post-parole period. The correctional system could

be credited with but little improvement in this respect, since the offenders who met their economic responsibilities in the post-treatment period, were, as a whole, the same ones who had been meeting their obligations before they were subjected to the reformatory or parole regimes.

Indeed, the actual correctional process is in many places so superficial as to raise a serious question whether it has any penetrating and lasting effect in the reorientation of attitudes, the redefinition of ethical values, the better management of instinctual and conditioned impulses, and the reformation of character. It is a challenging fact that the opinions, standards, and activities of fellow-prisoners frequently exert a much greater influence upon the future behavior of offenders than do the blandishments of judges or the efforts of wardens, probation and parole officers. In such a state of affairs, the *make-up of the offender* may be regarded as much more determinative of his behavior under one form of treatment or another, or of his ultimate reform or recidivism, than are the punitive or corrective "medicines" given him by the instruments of the law.

Despite these and other inherent difficulties in the determination of the actual influence of corrective regimes, any realistic attempt at evaluation of the complex forces at work in the changing of human character and conduct ought to be encouraged. Indeed, it is a chief value to be derived from follow-up studies.

In our various researches we have coped with the problem of determining the influence of correctional regimes by several methods, among which we may mention the following:

(a) Comparisons of successes and failures in respect to factors which presumably facilitated and those which evidently hindered a satisfactory response to the regime and for varying spans of time thereafter;

(b) In the study of juvenile delinquents, a comparison of the behavior of the young offenders in whose cases the juvenile court had followed the recommendations made to it by a child guidance clinic after study of the lads in question, with the behavior of the boys in whose cases the court did not put the clinic's recommendations into effect;

(c) Comparison of the self-imposed standards and alleged practices of a parole board, with actual practices, in respect to such matters as obtaining jobs for parolees, the intensity of supervision by parole officers, and the like;

(d) Comparison of outcomes in terms of success and failure of the charges of different parole agents and probation officers, to determine whether supervision by any particular worker resulted in appreciably higher success than oversight by others.

Limitations of space prohibit the exposition of these various methods of comparison (see Bibliography).

IV. The follow-up study has contributed to a number of *scientific attitudes and experiments* that are of prime significance in any basic reform of the administration of criminal justice.

We may set down as the first scientific value of the follow-up study, the conviction it gives that a *multiple-causal approach to the understanding, control and treatment of criminal behavior is called for in our era.* Such an attitude is in contrast to the oversimplified approach that either bases criminal responsibility upon unproved assumptions of mankind's freedom of will, or stresses the sterile quest of "blameworthiness," limiting criminal *ir*responsibility to extreme degrees of mental defect or disease and basing these upon unrealistic and unscientific "tests" of irresponsibility.[4] The change of attitude involved need not necessarily radically transform the definitions of crimes or the mechanisms for determining guilt; it does imply, however, a fundamental change in emphasis in the aims of punishment and a re-design of the techniques of treatment of the convicted offender.

A second scientific value derived from our follow-up studies, is the exploration of the concept of *maturation.* In our earliest works we gained a general impression that a substantial proportion of our offenders, both male and female, presented a picture suggestive of the delayed or persistent adolescent

—one mature in years, but immature in respect to emotional, intellectual and physical integration. In *Later Criminal Careers,* wherein a total follow-up span of ten years beyond completion of sentence to the Massachusetts Reformatory was involved, this impression of immaturity and lack of integration among a large number of offenders crystallized into a conviction.[5] In that work we sought to determine which factors could properly be credited with reformation in criminal behavior (and, incidentally, improvement in other conduct as well). The method employed to this end was to compare the incidence of non-criminals among the ex-prisoners during the first and second five year follow-up periods, in respect to each of 63 factors involved; and to contrast this, in every instance, with the *total* incidence of non-criminals in the entire group of cases. This indicated that *the possessors of certain characteristics* had contributed a greater proportion of non-offenders (i.e., reformed criminals) than had the group as a whole.

The second scientific implication of our follow-up studies, is then, the highly important conclusion that *not age, per se, but rather the acquisition of a certain degree of maturation regardless of the age at which this is achieved among different offenders, is significantly related to changes in criminalistic behavior once embarked upon.* Apparently, abandonment of criminalistic conduct does not occur at any specific chronologic age-level, but rather after the passage of a certain length of time from the point of first expression of definite delinquent trends. On the whole, if the acts of delinquency begin very early in life, they are abandoned at a relatively early stage of manhood, provided various mental abnormalities do not counteract the natural tendency toward maturation which gradually brings with it greater powers of reflection, inhibition, postponement of immediate desires for more legitimate later ones, the capacity of learning from experience, and like constituents of what is generally recognized as a mature, self-managing, emotionally-intellectually integrated, and therefore successfully adapting personality. If

[4] See Glueck, S., *Mental Disorder and the Criminal Law.* Other exemptions from responsibility, consisting of the well-known instances of justification or excuse, are not mentioned above because not relevant to the discussion.

[5] See Chap. X, "Ageing and Its Accompaniments."

on the other hand, the acts of delinquency begin in adolescence, the delinquent tendency seems to run its course into a later stage of adulthood, provided the natural process of maturation is not radically interfered with.

Growing out of the theory of maturation is a third scientific implication of our follow-up studies—the possible role of *experimentation* in the correctional process. Society's penal apparatus was originally designed to inflict painful punishment. This is true whether it be considered at a stage in its evolution when retributive suffering was the chief motive, or the stage of prevention or that of deterrence. The reliance has long been, and still is, upon *pain* as a reformer of attitudes and habits. This, in turn, is predicated upon an oversimplified notion of the causes of misconduct. Since we are beginning to learn that the causes of delinquency and criminalism are many and complex and that the concatenation of causes in one type of individual is different from that in another type, we are led to the conclusion that many types of *therapy* are necessary to bring about permanent changes in ethical attitudes and behavior tendencies.

In some cases, various techniques of psychotherapy—ranging from hypnosis to psychoanalysis (including the recently developed technique of hypnoanalysis) may be indicated and necessary before criminalistic behavior is abandoned. In other cases, different forms of physiologic or chemical or "shock" therapy may be called for. In still others, various forms of special education, vocational guidance, training in trades, and like approaches may be indicated. All this is not to say that such approaches to the redirection of human conduct today give immediate promise of high percentages of "cures." It is merely to indicate that, since follow-up studies have shown how important are various tangible causal sequences of a mental and environmental nature in determining behavior both while the offender is undergoing different forms of punishment and thereafter, there is no longer any excuse for not re-designing our correctional equipment to cope with causes rather than to punish symptoms and end-results. If, in many instances, we are dealing with persons whose process of matur-

ation is for one reason or another distorted or retarded, it is the part of wisdom to set up experiments designed to find ways of straightening out or speeding up the maturation process. With a redefinition of the aims of the criminal law must come a redesign of instruments for the achievement of such aims.

Further detailed research will be needed to establish these theories solidly or to disprove or modify them. Basic questions remain unanswered:

Do variations in ethnic origin, in intelligence, in temperamental equipment largely account for differences in the pace and pattern of maturation? Or may the explanation be found in still other variations, say those of the endocrine system? Can the maturation process be hastened? How? Much ingenious scientific research is necessary to arrive at any conclusive answers. All that we could do in the follow-up studies here described was to show that some basic differences between the juvenile court group and the reformatory group might well have accounted for the variation in the average age at which they first became anti-socially maladapted, thereby revealing symptoms of a lack of the degree of maturity requisite to a particular age.[6] However, these are but straws in the wind. To really get at the underlying facts regarding differences in the pace and pattern of maturation a specially planned, detailed analysis of numerous factors would be necessary.

As is so often true of findings of a scientific nature, the above-described major conclusions raise a great many more questions than they answer—questions which the materials so far at hand in our researches are unfortunately incapable of answering. Why,

[6] Thus, for example, the juvenile court group contained a higher proportion of persons of normal intelligence than the reformatory group (41.6%, 33%), and a lower proportion of definitely feebleminded (13.1%, 20.6%). So also, psychiatrically considered, the juvenile court group had a lower incidence of mental disease or marked personality distortions than the reformatory group (55.7% and 72.7%). On the whole, therefore, juvenile court delinquents seem to have had a better endowment than the reformatory offenders; yet it was the former, more than the latter, whose first manifestations of delinquency had occurred very early in childhood.

for example, did one group of offenders begin their criminal careers later than the other? Are we dealing here not only with the influence of a faulty process of maturation upon *recidivism or reform,* but also upon the *origin* of criminal careers?

V. By showing causal relations between various biologic and environmental traits on the one hand and criminalistic or law-abiding behavior on the other, follow-up studies are providing a solid basis for the reform of criminal justice. Changes in criminal law, procedure and administration have in the past been based largely on arm-chair speculation, on philosophic theories, on historic accidents, or on the influence of various specially privileged pressure groups.[7] A systematic *factual* basis of the results of different forms of punishment as related to the types of persons undergoing them has heretofore been lacking. Follow-up studies are supplying this fundamental need.

In several of our works we have shown which biologic and social factors tend to facilitate and which tend to hamper reformation of offenders. Careful analysis of the makeup and background of large and sufficiently varied samples of all offenders coming before the courts should unquestionably furnish the basis for the definition of what may be called *treatment types* or *conduct types.* A beginning along these lines was made in *Juvenile Delinquents Grown Up,* wherein are presented the results of a systematic recording, in chronologic order, of the behavior of our offenders under all forms of peno-correctional treatment to which each had been subjected from his earliest delinquency through the Boston Juvenile Court "treatment period" and during three five year follow-up periods. This basic work of distinguishing various treatment and behavior types as a means of more intelligent sentencing and releasing practices was given further refinement in *Criminal Careers in Retrospect.*

The following minimal features of an improved system of criminal justice appear to

be indicated by analysis of the existing sentencing and releasing practices in the light of their products as disclosed by follow-up studies: First, the sentence-imposing feature of criminal proceedings needs to be differentiated from the guilt-finding phase in method and, to a large extent, in personnel. Secondly, the decision regarding the treatment necessary for each offender needs to be left to a tribunal or board specially qualified in the interpretation and evaluation of sociologic, psychiatric and psychologic, as well as legal, data. Thirdly, the treatment program arrived at by study of each case in the light of hundreds of similar cases, needs to be modifiable as indicated by periodic check-ups on the offender's progress submitted to the tribunal by the various experts entrusted with carrying out its corrective mandates. Fourthly, the rights of the individual must be safeguarded against possible arbitrariness or other unlawful or unfair action on the part of the special sentencing-and-treatment tribunal.

To those genuinely interested in the progress of justice along both scientific and ethical lines, it is especially gratifying that ideas of the kind noted above which were long ago expressed by the writers have in recent years received implementation in model draft-statutes and enacted legislation.[8] These mark a highly significant, indeed an almost revolutionary, departure from age-old attitudes and practices. They have pregnant possibilities for the future. Indeed, if administered with discretion and the aid of truly creative psy-

---

[7] Illustrations may be found in Stephen's *History of the Criminal Law of England II;* Jerome Hall's *Theft, Law, and Society,* Boston; and S. Glueck's *Mental Disorder and the Criminal Law.*

[8] The American Law Institute has drafted a model bill providing for a "Youth Correction Authority" with a philosophy and an organization essentially similar to the one described in the text. Bills along similar lines, to govern sentencing procedures in the Federal Courts, are at present (1944) pending in both the House and Senate. They are the outgrowth of recommendations of a distinguished committee of judges of the United States courts. See report of the "Committee on Punishment for Crime of the Judicial Conference of Senior (Federal) Circuit Judges," U. S. Government Printing Office, Washington, D. C. California has actually enacted a Youth Correction Authority Act. For a recent appraisal of its modifications and accomplishments, see Chute, C. L., "California's Youth Authority," 33 **Probation** (1944), pp. 1–6.

chiatrists, psychoanalysts, psychologists, sociologists, anthropologists, and educators they may produce evidence which might throw a new flood of light into the darker reaches of the human psyche.

The crux of the new reforms in the administration of criminal justice is, therefore, *personnel*. If the Youth Correction Authority, the Disposition and Treatment Tribunal, or other-named complement to existing legal institutions is staffed with political henchmen or employees not thoroughly trained in psychopathology, psychology and other relevant disciplines, it will be but one more gadgetary addition to the existing cumbersome machine, adding little to whatever therapeutic possibilities there may be in a correctional regime, adding less to whatever deterrence there may be in punishment, but adding much to the opportunity for political and corrupt manipulation of the processes of justice. A Youth Correction Authority statute without specific standards of education and experience for the personnel may well do more harm than good.

Indispensable, also, is the fundamental work of redesigning and reshaping existing forms of peno-correctional treatment in such a way as to permit them to exert a more penetrating influence on offenders than follow-up studies show them to have at present. A check-up is needed on the efficacy of specific aspects of the correctional programs of reformatories, prisons, probation, parole and the like. For example, if an institution has a variety of programs for academic training or the teaching of trades, the correlation of various types of offenders with their mastery or failure to master different kinds of training or teaching, becomes important for future offenders; since it furnishes a method of applying the regime appropriate to offenders of different general capacities, special abilities or disabilities, and temperaments. In fact, follow-up studies might profitably be used for this purpose by school systems in general. Another use of follow-up studies in the internal regimes of correctional institutions is the correlation of different types of offenders with their behavior under different forms of psychotherapy, such as suggestion, hypnosis, psychoanalysis, "shock" therapies, and the like.

VI. Finally, what is the effect of the evidence presented by follow-up studies on the structure and functions of society's apparatus for the administration of criminal justice in general? First, it raises the fundamental political issue of determining how the sum total of society's legal power to deal with criminal aggressions shall be distributed among the agencies of justice in order to obtain the highest efficiency in repressing crime consonant with humanitarianism and the constitutional protection of individual rights. This problem has not been sufficiently recognized or systematically coped with, either in American codes or statutory compilations or in English criminal legislation. What part of this power had better be embodied in the legislatively enacted substantive law which defines crimes, defences to crimes, and punishments? What part of it can safely be entrusted to the discretion of judges or members of administrative boards; and what shall be the qualifications of such personnel? What part had better be left to administrators of correctional institutions and to what type of administrators? Shall some of the offenses and offenders today coped with by traditional criminal trial procedure be otherwise disposed of? For even under the most advanced system of public law concerned with maladjusted and socially dangerous human beings there will be need for some effective and fair method of separating the sheep (those whose acts are not really violative of the law, or who have some other legitimate defense) from the goats (those whose status as determined at the trial or hearing, renders them subject to social control and correctional treatment in the name of the state).

We are not yet ready to give considered answers to many of these and similar questions. We wish merely to stress that the answers will not be found exclusively in law books; the books recording the life histories of delinquents and criminals before and after their contact with society's legal agencies will also have to be pondered.

SHELDON AND ELEANOR GLUECK
*Professor of Criminology and
Research Associate*
Harvard Law School
Cambridge, Massachusetts

BIBLIOGRAPHY

Burgess, E. W., Workings of the Indeterminate-Sentence Law and Parole Systems in Illinois, in Bruce, A. A., Harno, A. J., Burgess, E. W., and Landesco, J., *Parole and the Indeterminate Sentence,* Illinois Board of Parole, Chicago, 1928.

Chute, C. L., California's Youth Authority, *Probation,* 33, 1–6, 1944.

Clark, W. W., Success Records of Prisoners and Delinquents, *Journal of Delinquency,* 6, 444 et. seq., Sept., 1921.

Committee on Punishment for Crime of the Judicial Conference of Senior (Federal) Circuit Judges Report, U. S. Government Printing Office, Washington, D. C.

Glueck, S., and E. T., *After-Conduct of Discharged Offenders,* Macmillan Co., London and New York, 1944.

Glueck, S., and E. T., *Criminal Careers in Retrospect,* The Commonwealth Fund, 1943.

Glueck, S. and E. T., *Juvenile Delinquents Grown Up,* New York, The Commonwealth Fund, 1940.

Glueck, S., and E. T., *Later Criminal Careers,* New York, The Commonwealth Fund, 1934.

Glueck, S., *Mental Disorder and the Criminal Law,* Boston, Little, Brown & Co., 1925.

Glueck, S., Principles of a Rational Penal Code, *Harvard Law Review,* 41, 453–475, 1928.

Glueck, S. and E. T., *500 Criminal Careers,* New York, Alfred A. Knopf, 1930.

Glueck, S. and E. T., *500 Delinquent Women,* New York, Knopf, 1934.

Glueck, S. and E. T., *One Thousand Juvenile Delinquents,* Cambridge, The Harvard University Press, 2nd edition, 1934.

Hall, Jerome, *Theft, Law, and Society,* Boston, Little, Brown and Company, 1935.

Lindner, R. M., *Rebel Without a Cause,* New York, Grune and Stratton, 1944.

Monachesi, Elio D., *Prediction Factors in Probation,* The Sociological Press, University of Minnesota, 1932.

Stephen's *History of the Criminal Law of England II.*

Vold, G. B., *Prediction Methods and Parole,* The Sociological Press, University of Minnesota, 1931.

FORGERY. Forgery is the crime of falsely and fraudulently making or materially altering any written instrument or document which, if genuine, might apparently be of legal efficacy or the foundation of a legal liability. It must carry with it the intent to deceive and defraud. Any instrument by means of which one person can become obligated to another—to pay money, to render service, to forego a right, to respond in damages, etc. —is a writing subject to forgery.

Any alteration in such an instrument, by which its legal effect is changed or varied, is sufficient to constitute a forgery. An alteration is false when made by a person who has no right to make it. It is fraudulent when made with intent that the false instrument shall be used or received as valid. The forgery is complete when the instrument in question is made or altered with intent to defraud, even though it never may be used and no one actually may be defrauded.

The Penal Law of New York State defines three degrees of forgery. A person is guilty of forgery in the first degree who with intent to defraud, forges:

1. A will or codicil of real or personal property, or the attestation thereof, or a deed or other instrument, being or purporting to be the act of another, by which any right or interest in property is or purports to be affected in any way; or,

2. A certificate of the acknowledgment or proof of a will, codicil, deed or other instrument; or,

3. A certificate, bond, paper writing, or other public security issued or purporting to have been issued by or under the authority of the state, or of the United States, or of any foreign government, etc.; or,

4. An endorsement, stock certificate, bond, bank note, bill of exchange, draft, check, certificate of deposit, or other obligation or evidence of debt; or,

5. Any endorsement or other writing, transferring or purporting to transfer the right or interest of any holder of such a certificate, bond, or other writing obligatory, or of any person entitled to such right or interest.

The crime of *forgery in the first degree* is punishable by imprisonment for a term not exceeding twenty years.

Lesser types of forgery are punishable in the *second degree* by imprisonment for a term not exceeding ten years, and in the *third degree* by imprisonment for not more than five years.

The uttering and passing of a forged instrument or a forgery or the offering of it as genuine is also a crime.

The forger often drifts into forgery as an

easy way to cover up discrepancies in accounts. He is often a person of education and frequently possesses or develops a certain facility of graphic mimicry. In many of the cases of suspected wills and other documents, handwriting experts are needed to say definitely whether a signature is forged or not. The good forger is generally a person of fair intelligence. He may or may not be a psychopath, but psychopaths are fond of forging.

BIBLIOGRAPHY

Soderman, H. and O'Connell, J., *Modern Criminal Investigation,* Funk & Wagnalls Co., 1934.
Gilbert, F. B., *Criminal Law and Practice of the State of New York,* Matthew Bender and Co., 1935.

FRAUD. Fraud has not been defined by the courts in unequivocal language. What amounts to fraud in one case may not be in another. The courts judge each case separately. Fraud may be defined as an intentional perversion of truth for the purpose of inducing another in reliance upon it to part with some valuable thing belonging to him, or to surrender a legal right. Fraud is a false representation of a matter of fact (whether by words or conduct, by false or misleading allegations, or by concealment of that which should have been disclosed) which deceives and is intended to deceive another so that he shall act upon it to his legal injury.

In equity law the term *fraud* has a wider sense, and includes all acts, omissions, or concealments by which one person obtains an advantage against conscience over another, or which equity or public policy forbids as being to another's prejudice; as acts in violation of relations of trust and confidence. This is often called *constructive,* or *legal,* or *equitable, fraud,* or *fraud in equity.*

Although the Law is quite clear on the required elements of fraud, the facts which will constitute fraud depend upon the particular circumstances of each case.

Any intentional misrepresentation or concealment of some past or present material fact by a party in interest, such material fact not being open equally to the observation of both parties in interest, or not to be discov-

ered through the exercise of ordinary care, and being relied upon by one party to a transaction, to his damage, constitutes a fraud.

Fraud may be said to consist of all acts, dishonest or deceitful, the object of which is to deprive some person or corporation of property, without knowledge or consent of the owner.

The concealment of assets by a bankrupt is a fraud upon his creditors. Overstating the profits of a business by a vendor in a sale contract is a material misrepresentation amounting to fraud. Another example is the utterance of a false statement of financial condition to induce credit.

The Penal Law does not define *FRAUD* but gives a list of more than forty acts of this category. Some of the most common are:

Obtaining credit or accommodation at any hotel, inn, boarding house, or lodging house by means of false pretense and refusal to pay for food or lodging or other accommodation upon demand.

Falsely impersonating a public officer or a policeman; assuming without authority any uniform or badge of office; wearing or displaying the coat of arms of the State of New York or the United States without authority and endeavoring to gain some special advantage thereby.

Falsely impersonating another or falsely representing himself to be an officer or agent of an organization and in such assumed character receiving money or property intended to be delivered to that organization and intending to convert the same to one's own use. The mere wearing of the uniform or the mere impersonation do not seem to constitute a fraud. Some advantage must accrue from its use that is diverted from the usual channels of disbursement. Thus, representing the President of the United States on the stage does not constitute a fraud.

Obtaining the signature of any person to a written instrument, or any money or property for any alleged or pretended charitable or benevolent purpose, by color or aid of any false token or writing or other false pretense.

Unauthorized use of seals, device of arms of United States or any political division thereof. Use or display of the words "Police

Department," "Police," etc., on a motor vehicle, motor bicycle not used by a duly organized police department.

Fraud is not in itself a crime by want of criminal intent though it may become a crime in cases provided by law.

BIBLIOGRAPHY

Gilbert, F. B., *Criminal Law and Practice in the State of New York,* Matthew Bender and Co., 1935.

FRUSTRATION AND AGGRESSION. I.
Systematic thinking and research concerning the frustration-aggression sequence have received their most powerful impetus from the writings of Sigmund Freud. Although Freud, at different stages in his long scientific career, took different points of view concerning the problem of aggression, the proposition that frustration leads to aggression stems from some of the most central premises of Freudian thought.

Whatever else it may or may not be, psychoanalysis was in the beginning and today remains a psychological system in which the concept of motivation, drive, tension, or "psychic energy" is fundamental. From the outset, the human organism, like organisms in general, has been thought of as a biological system capable of being thrown out of equilibrium by any of a wide variety of stimuli, external and internal. When such a disequilibrium is created, the result is subjectively experienced as an urge, or drive, and is commonly manifested externally by an activation of behavior—behavior which is likely to persist either until the disequilibrium is eliminated, or until the organism is exhausted or dead. It is this sequence of stimulation-reaction-satiation (or death) which constitutes one of the distinguishing attributes of living as opposed to non-living matter. Fechner, from whom Freud drew heavily in this connection, called this capacity for self-regulation the *constancy principle.* Since return from a state of disequilibrium to a state of equilibrium is ordinarily accompanied by an experience of pleasure, Freud often spoke of it as the *pleasure principle.* More recently, Cannon has stressed the physiological concept of *homeostasis;* Raup has written about what

he calls *complacency;* and a number of psychologists and social scientists have stressed the notion of *adjustment,* all of which imply much the same thing.

In all complex organisms and perhaps also in many simple ones, the stimulation-reaction-satiation (or S-R-S) sequence is complicated by a factor which can best be termed *appetite* or *desire.* An appetite is an emotion of zest, often coupled with an anticipatory image or images of ultimate gratification. Thus, a hungry dog or boy, while trying to get a desired morsel of food, is likely to imagine how "good" it will taste. Physiologically this appetitive state will be reflected by salivation ("watering mouth") and other preparations for eating; and it is experienced subjectively as an augmentation of motivation. It is as if to the primary, biological drive of hunger is added a secondary, emotional drive of appetite, zest, or desire, which acts as a "booster system," a system which intensifies the total motivation of the organism, makes its goal-seeking behavior more vigorous, and, presumably, increases the chances that this behavior will be successful.

This account may at first seem contrary to common sense in that appetites are often thought of as pleasurable, whereas here they are classified as secondary, or derived, drives, which increase the organism's over-all disequilibrium and goad it to more vigorous action, not relaxation. It is true that excited, appetitive states are often characterized by momentary bubbles of pleasure and may, on occasion, serve temporarily to counteract fear, guilt, or boredom, thus producing (through mechanisms to be described below) a welcome net effect. However, their basic action is clearly one of drive intensification. This fact has been demonstrated by objective laboratory methods, and everyone knows that a sexually aroused, excited organism—i.e., one in which the secondary drive of sexual appetite has been added to the relatively weak primary sex drive—will strive much more vigorously and recklessly for sexual satisfaction than will an organism with the same basic biological need but without the factor of appetitive arousal. Introspectively we usually feel "glad to have" appetites, for they show we are physically and emotionally healthy, interested in life; but this is not to say that they are intrinsically pleasant: an appetite which goes long unfulfilled or for which there is no hope of fulfillment is unmitigated torment.

Now it is against this psycho-biological background that we must begin our discussion of frustration and aggression. As every living organism soon discovers, the path from need to satisfaction is often a rough one. Obstacles, barriers, and difficulties of all sorts often spring up and prevent or threaten to prevent the hungry, thirsty, or lustful organism from reaching its goal. Such barriers are not only a threat to psychological satisfaction; they also imperil the very existence of the individual and the perpetuation of its species.

It is not surprising, therefore, to discover that there have evolved psychological and biological provisions for helping organisms to cope with barriers to their satisfaction and threats to their survival. Confronted by a barrier or a difficulty on the way to gratification, in short, when frustrated, living organisms tend to react psychologically with the familiar emotion of anger and physiologically with a generalized mobilization of resources which Cannon has called the "emergency reaction." As is well known, this reaction involves augmented pulse and breathing, heightened blood pressure, release of adrenalin into the blood stream (which counteracts fatigue, shortens the coagulation time of the blood, and produces other important consequences), inhibition of digestion and other assimilative processes, increased perspiration (so that the individual may cool more rapidly and, in the case of the anthropoids, hold more firmly with hand and foot), and still other effects such as erection of the body hair or feathers.

The experience of anger and the physiological changes just described are well calculated to prepare and prompt the affected organism to attack with redoubled energy the barrier which is impeding its progress toward the desired goal. If that barrier is another organism the attempt to overcome and remove it as a barrier is called an *attack* or *fighting*. And in any case, whether the barrier is animate or inanimate, we are likely to speak of

this intensification of behavior as *aggression*.

II. The biological utility of the capacity to become angry and aggressive in the face of frustration is self-evident: it is an important factor in promoting the satisfaction, survival, and reproduction of living organisms. However, it is an asset which is not without attendant disadvantages.

Earlier we spoke of appetites as serving to "boost" the intensity of primary drives, such as hunger, thirst, sex. And we have just mentioned the capacity to become angry and aggressive as a still more radical device for intensifying goal-directed behavior. From one standpoint the emotions which we designate, on the one hand, as appetites and, on the other hand, as anger serve much the same function: they both help insure that living organisms will go into action when their satisfaction and survival are at stake. But in one respect appetite and anger are importantly different. This difference can be well illustrated if we start, let us say, with the primary drive of hunger. Although the mechanism which mediates this drive is not precisely understood, we do know that it involves the parasympathetic divisions of the autonomic nervous system.[1] Thus the primary drive of hunger and the secondary drive, or emotion, of appetite are neurologically compatible.

But when we come to the emotion of anger, the picture changes radically. Anger, as we have seen, is a preparation, not for digestion, but for vigorous activity on the part of the skeletal musculature. It tends, in fact, to inhibit digestion (cf. the "dry mouth" of anger or fear); and we also know that this inhibition is accomplished by virtue of the fact

[1] It will be recalled that most living organisms have two major nervous systems, the *central* and the *autonomic*. The former mediates voluntary, skeletal behavior, and the latter mediates involuntary, physiological reactions. The autonomic, in turn, is divided into two parts, the *sympathetic* and the *parasympathetic*. The latter mediates the various assimilative processes and appetites; the former mediates the affects (fear and anger) and the concomitant "emergency reaction" of Cannon. Since the sympathetic and parasympathetic nervous systems act reciprocally, activation of one ordinarily results in inactivation of the other. Thus the powerful arousal of an appetite tends to nullify the affects and *vice versa*.

that anger (and the attendant emergency re-action) is mediated by the sympathetic division of the autonomic nervous system, which is antagonistic to the parasympathetic division (which mediates salivation and other digestive processes).

All of this may seem slightly involved, but the essential point is this: whereas the appetite based on hunger is neurologically and physiologically compatible with the hunger itself, the emotion of anger, provoked by frustration of the appetite-hunger complex, is incompatible with that complex. This is an arresting but by no means unintelligible state of affairs. Hunger and its appetitive concomitant are oriented toward the end state of incorporation and assimilation of food and the storing up of readily available energy—processes which are properly referred to as *anabolic* ("positive" metabolism). Anger, on the other hand, is oriented toward vigorous activity of the large muscles, and this activity involves the expenditure of energy, not its storing up, and is properly termed *katabolic* ("negative" metabolism).

By this route we come to understand the first paradox of the frustration-anger-aggression sequence. This paradox, most briefly stated, is that anger and aggression are reactions which are designed to overcome barriers to the satisfaction of primary drives and of their attendant appetites, and yet anger and aggression themselves are physiologically antagonistic to the appetites and consummatory processes generally. This paradox is resolved by noting that although anger and aggression may *temporarily* upset the appetitive-consummatory orientation of the organism, they tend to insure the organism's *ultimate* satisfaction and survival. Thus an organism may be frustrated and become so angry in securing food or a sex partner that it will be, for the time being, impaired as far as eating or copulation is concerned. However, once the source of conflict, or barrier, has been eliminated, the fruits of victory can be enjoyed at leisure. In other words, the frustration-anger-aggression sequence mobilizes the organism so completely for attack that little energy is left for the consummatory processes; but the fact remains that anger and aggression are in the service, or "employ," of the consummatory

processes and tend, in the long run, to aid and insure their occurrence.

This analysis has two implications which may be briefly noted in passing. It suggests the basis for at least certain types of psychosomatic (especially digestive) disorders which occur in chronically frustrated, emotionally tense human beings; and it usefully highlights a relationship which is often neglected in the discussion of frustration-aggression theory, namely, the relationship between appetite-arousal and aggression. It is doubtful if any primary drive is ordinarily strong enough alone to lead, when blocked or denied, to anger and aggression. It is only when there is appetitive involvement, and what may be called the *intent* to gratify the primary drive, that frustration can be experienced in full force. In other words, *privation* is not necessarily experienced as frustrating. If the sacrifice or suffering seems worthwhile, if the renunciation is made willingly, as the condition for the fulfillment of some other valued goal, the experienced sense of frustration is likely to be minimal. If, however, the frustration involves a *deprivation,* a taking away or withholding of something that has been accepted as a desired objective, with full appetitive arousal, then the frustration-anger-aggression sequence is fully activated. The symbolic machinery whereby this differentiation is made is undoubtedly complex and is at present only partially understood.[2]

III. The paradox which has just been discussed may be characterized as bio-physiological. We now turn to a second paradox, or dilemma, which may be termed psycho-sociological. So far we have assumed that the barriers which produce anger and aggression are "natural" ones, i.e., inanimate objects and organisms which may be classified as evils, rivals, enemies. But most living organisms have found that some measure of group or social organization of their species has impelling advantages as against solitary existence. Some species rely hardly at all upon

[2] This emphasis upon acceptance of and commitment to a given goal as a condition of frustration has been especially stressed in the writings of Dr. Saul Rosenzweig. One should also examine in this connection the concept of "ego involvement" which Professor G. W. Allport has elaborated.

the mutual support and protection of other members of the species, but other organisms have carried the group-life principle to extraordinary lengths. Of these latter organisms, human beings and the so-called social insects offer the most remarkable examples. However, social integration is achieved in the two cases by very different means. In the insects it is achieved largely by means of bodily specialization and inherent reaction dispositions called instincts, with individual learning and instruction playing only a minimal role. With human beings, on the other hand, social integration is achieved predominantly through learning, learning from the experience of others (i.e., from "the culture") and from one's own experiences, with organic specialization and instinct playing a negligible role. We shall henceforth confine our remarks to social integration achieved in this latter way.

The first thing to be stressed in approaching an analysis of social as opposed to solitary existence is the more assured satisfactions and securities offered by group life. Were there not enormous advantages in it, group life would never have been evolved or maintained. But it is an equally inescapable fact that the advantages of group life are paid for, often dearly. A social group implies organization, and organization means order, control, restraint, discipline. We therefore arrive straightaway at the realization that social as opposed to solitary existence involves, not only satisfactions, but also certain restraints, limitations, frustrations.

And with this emergence of the group-life principle and all it implies, a new type of psychological problem is created. In a primordial state of nature, an organism's rivals and enemies can be hated wholeheartedly; but with the advent of organized group life, the self-same individuals and institutions that impose limitations and frustrations also mediate protection and satisfaction.

Again it is Freud and his followers who have pioneered our understanding of the essentially ambivalent nature of our attitudes toward parents, teachers, authorities, and, in fact, toward the whole human enterprise. By virtue of the mixture of gratitude and resentment which children feel toward adults and which adults feel toward society in general,

we are all caught in a major conflict, one which has prompted some writers to conceive of human personality as a seething caldron of love and hate. Around this conflict Freud formulated some of his most daring and controversial theories; and every clinician, no matter whether Freudian or otherwise, knows how many personality disorders hinge upon the dilemma that comes of simultaneously loving (being dependent upon) and hating (wanting to destroy) the same persons and the same social institutions. However, as we shall later see, it is doubtful if the Freudians have offered the best possible guide for the resolution of this conflict.

IV. Thus far we have made only passing reference to the emotion of fear and its bearing on frustration-aggression theory. But we have now reached a point in our analysis beyond which we cannot go unless we make up for this omission. The psychology of fear is itself a large and interesting chapter in the total dynamic account of human personality, but we shall here have to deal with it, not comprehensively, but only as it bears upon our present discussion.

In the earlier pages we have spoken as if, in a state of nature, aggressive attacks upon frustrating objects and organisms were always successful, i.e., always overcame the barriers to gratification and thereby contributed to continued existence. Obviously we have omitted mention of the not uncommon situation in which aggression is met by *counter-aggression*. In this event attack may be followed by pain instead of pleasure; and if the attacker survives the counter-attack, fear will long remain as a reminder of this ill-fated venture.

For the non-social organism, the problem which results from being punished rather than rewarded for its aggressions [3] is, in principle, easy of solution. If it sees it is getting the worst of a fight, such an organism may turn and retreat; and one or at most two or three repetitions of this sequence will lead to

[3] Space does not here permit a discussion of the role of learning in the genesis and perpetuation of the frustration-anger-aggression sequence. It is, however, a fascinating problem and one which has as yet been approached experimentally by only a few investigators, although a number of workers have made interesting incidental observations concerning it.

relatively enduring avoidance of the too powerful adversary.

But for social organisms in general and for man in particular, the solution is not so easy. Many of the frustrations which children experience come from persons, notably their parents, whom they can neither successfully attack, escape from, nor avoid. Conflicts are thus generated which, according to Freudian thought, can be resolved in one of three ways, no one of which is entirely satisfactory.

If anger is aroused in a given individual by a parent or other authoritative person who can be neither attacked nor avoided, the individual's anger may be turned toward other, more or less irrelevant, innocent things or persons. This is the mechanism of *displacement,* or *transference* (of one type.)

The second possibility is that aggression, resulting from the experienced frustration, may be turned back upon the self. The individual criticizes himself as foolish, stupid, inferior, and undeserving, and may impose upon himself, consciously or unconsciously, punishments of considerable severity. This strategy of anger-management is called *introjection.*

Finally, it is assumed that if the individual is sufficiently fearful of the external consequences of aggression and sufficiently disapproving of even the subjective experience of anger, he may not even allow this emotion to come into consciousness, much less find expression in direct, overt behavior. In this event the individual is said to *repress* his anger.

The free, direct expression of anger toward the sources of one's frustration is obviously possible for human beings in only a limited number of situations. When an individual is being used and exploited, it is often a socially and individually appropriate thing to strike out at such usury and exploitation; but very often aggressive behavior is socially disruptive and cannot be permitted. Such aggression is termed "anti-social," and the aggressor is called an offender, a delinquent, a criminal. It is a deduction from Freudian theory that such a person may be quite healthy emotionally; for he reacts directly and openly to his frustrations, and his only concern is with

the possibility of more powerful counter-aggression, either from individuals or from constituted social authority. In the "pure" criminal, there would thus be very little internal conflict; the conflict is all "acted out," between the individual and others; and as long as the criminal game is played successfully, all is well, and even when the game is lost, there may be comparatively little personal involvement or sense of defeat or shame.

By contrast, the neurotic is said to be a person who expresses his anger, not too freely, but too little, typically introjecting or repressing his true emotions and, in consequence, experiencing "recurrent" feelings of depression, inferiority, shame, and anxiety. The normal person, by the same logic, is one who falls into the rather uneasy intermediate zone, wherein one avoids expressing his anger in such a way as to make the resulting aggression appear anti-social and thus bringing retribution upon himself but who at the same time does not turn inward or consciously deny his resentments and hostilities. To some degree a person may be able to *sublimate* his aggressive impulses, thus turning them from destructive to constructive channels; but this is usually a dubious procedure which may easily become indistinguishable from displacement. The Freudians have no very satisfactory solution to propose for the dilemma which man has created for himself by deciding to live socially; and Freud himself has written a brilliantly bitter book about this dilemma, called *Civilization and Its Discontents.*

If one accepts the Freudian premises, these conclusions about the nature of normality, neurosis, and criminality follow; but we now have reason to question certain of these premises. Freud, for all his versatility and brilliance, was a physician whose formal training was largely in the physical and biological sciences. It is not surprising, therefore, that his thinking about psychological matters, however original, should show the bias of his training and of his affiliation with the medical profession. The great need is to review the whole of his work and to re-evaluate it in terms of evidence and concepts from related fields of inquiry.

V. Here we shall attempt to deal only

with some of the broader and most crucial issues. Freud's biological preconceptions caused him to found psychoanalysis squarely on biological principles, some of which have been reviewed in the earlier pages of this article and which constitute the valid first principles of psychological and social science. However, it is a less fortunate circumstance that Freud never sufficiently extended his basic orientation to give us a valid theory of the individual and society. Specifically, Freud seemed to have erred in continuing to the end of his long life to look upon neurosis and human woe generally as deriving from the inescapable conflict between the wishes of the individual and the limitations imposed by his group. This conflict might be open and vociferous as in the case of the criminal or the revolutionary.[4] It might be tensely muted as in the neurotic; or it might be dealt with, as in the so-called normal person, on the level of conscious control. But the conflict, Freud thought, was essentially irreconcilable. And particularly in respect to sex and aggression did he feel that society erects barriers which must continue throughout the life of the individual as sources of more or less serious frustration.

For Freud the *id* was the great, primordial reservoir of biological needs and impulses, which knows no delay and no negation. Its accent is always upon action and gratification. But an organism which is blindly impulsive gets into trouble with the external world, and from this clash is painfully forged the *ego,* which attempts to control, guide, and coordinate the strident forces of the id. The id provides the psychic energy; and the

[4] In mentioning the criminal and the revolutionary in the same sentence, we do not mean to imply that they are to be lumped together in all respects. It is true that both are in conflict with the existing social order; but, in the pure case, the revolutionary accepts social organization in principle; he simply wants to change "the rules"; whereas the criminal, in the pure case, is not interested in social, political, or economic reform, since in any event he proposes to live outside and beyond the rules of his society. However, as Lenin and others have discovered to their sorrow, every revolutionary movement attracts large numbers of persons who are characterologically immature and who try to modify social reality instead of themselves "growing up."

ego serves as an executive and prudential agency. But for the picture to be complete we must add what Freud called the *super-ego,* which is roughly equivalent to "conscience." This Freud thought of as that part of the total personality which is superimposed upon the ego by the moral training of the individual. In early childhood the super-ego does not exist; instead authority reposes in parents and other adults. *They* are the watchmen, the policemen, the supervisors. But eventually—through *identification* (which is little more than a word, since the process itself is very incompletely understood)—external author and social control become internalized; and, as super-ego, this inner authority now functions as part of the individual himself, a part which, however, is always regarded as something of an imposition, an intruder, essentially unfriendly and foreign. Thus, the task of the ego becomes still further complicated, for it must not only serve the interests of the id and at the same time keep an eye on external reality; it must also perform these functions in such a way as not to offend the super-ego.

In terms of this conceptualization, we may divide human personality into three types. The criminal is a person with a weak or virtually non-existent super-ego and whose ego may or may not be relatively well developed. (In other words, as numerous studies have shown, the criminal may be a dull fellow, but he is not necessarily so.) He is, however, characteristically id-dominated. A neurotic, on the other hand, is said to be a person whose conscience is hypertrophied, overgrown, "excessively severe." The normal individual, then, falls somewhere in between, with an ego that is able to meet the demands of the id but at the same time avoids offending, but does not surrender its autonomy to, the super-ego (and society). This is a way of thinking about the three major personality types which has gained widespread currency; but it has left unresolved a number of basic problems and suggests a relatively pessimistic view of life in general. Both in theory and in practice, it leaves unresolved the problem of social frustration and the management of the resulting aggression. Perhaps the answer is that there *is* no resolution to this dilemma.

Perhaps it is the dilemma of life itself; but there is growing evidence to indicate that in many human beings this dilemma is actually resolved and that its resolution is, indeed, the hallmark of maturity and normality. Perhaps it may turn out that Freud's frustration-aggression dilemma is more a product of misplaced conceptual ingenuity than of the very nature of human destiny.

It is something of a paradox that although Freud was preoccupied throughout his life with the problem of neurosis, his conceptualization of normality and maturity remained, in certain important respects, immature and eccentric. His biological bias enabled him to have highly illuminating insights concernng the young child, the criminal, and the neurotic—all of whom may also be said to have a "biological bias," i.e., they are dominated by their biologically given impulses. But Freud failed to grasp the essence of personality normality, and with this failure came the indifferent therapeutic accomplishment of psychoanalysis and many unresolved conceptual problems, of which the frustration-aggression dilemma is a prime example.

What Freud apparently did not sufficiently recognize is that biological, or "instinctual," satisfaction is not the only or indeed necessarily the most powerful form of human satisfaction. It is perhaps his central fallacy that he placed so little store by the satisfaction which comes with the clearing of conscience or from the improvement in actual inter-personal relations.

VI. Persons with strong moral and religious preoccupations have usually opposed the type of thinking about personality and society for which Freud and his followers have stood. In order to understand this opposition, it is necessary for us to distinguish between two reasons for it. Theologians have been unfriendly to Freudian thought because it is strongly anti-religious. In his books, *The Future of an Illusion* and *Moses and Monotheism*, Freud has attacked the supernaturalistic premises of religion and has attempted to show that religious forms and functions have their roots in psychological and social facts. In other words, his approach to these problems is empirical and scientific. To this extent many modern thinkers follow Freud.

They agree that human nature can best be understood and controlled if we take a wholly naturalistic view of the world, including man.

But Freud has scarcely more enthusiasm for morality than he had for religion. Religion for him was frankly an illusion, a hoax, a self-deception; and morality was also an evil, though an admittedly necessary one. Morality is forced upon man by the exigencies of social existence, and while it is necessary for the survival of the individual and of society, its observance is a drudgery and a self-limiting experience. There is no pleasure in it, and happiness and joy are to be had, if at all, in spite of morality, not because of it. Freud has repeatedly said that society imposes its rules upon the individual, not because it is concerned with the happiness of the individual, but because these rules are essential, or thought to be essential, to the survival of society.

A clear perception of Freud's position in this connection is necessary if one is to understand either the strengths or the weaknesses of the system which he promulgated. It can be predicted that future generations will credit Freud with having laid the foundations for an empirical, scientific study of man's ethical sense. His concepts are in certain respects so powerful that we need never again resort to supernaturalism, for example, to account for conscience. Much remains to be discovered about the precise nature of identification and conscience-learning; but there is no doubt that psychological and social science are now well on their way toward these objectives. Many students of the psychology of learning are becoming interested in this type of problem, as are an increasing number of clinicians.

But it is a paradoxical and somewhat ironical fact that Freudian thinking has, at the same time, a powerful appeal for untold thousands precisely because it takes a skeptical and unenthusiastic view of the morally responsible way of life. Granted that it may provide the basis for a new kind of faith in morality for those who have renounced supernaturalism, Freudian thought also provides the immature and neurotic elements in a society with subtle self-justification. As Alexander and French have pointed out in their book, *Psychoanalytic Therapy,* both the theory and practice of psychoanalysis often encourage neurotics to take refuge in a "deep narcissistic regression," viewing themselves as the innocent victims of a too severe, stupid upbringing rather than as persons who have not yet learned what they need to know as mature adults. The traditional, age-old view is that if a person is good he will be happy. The Freudian contention is that wickedness cannot necessarily be counted upon to lead to happiness, but neither can goodness.[5]

These considerations are more closely related than they may at first appear to frustration-aggression theory. We have already seen the unsatisfactory and contradictory conclusions to which the Freudian premises lead us in regard to questions concerning the management of man's aggression. Aggressions, we are told, may be displaced, introjected, or repressed; or, by a process which is by no means readily understood, they may be sublimated. But in any event the results are unsatisfactory, and even the best of men lead lives characterized by dilemmas only half resolved. What Freud overlooked is that when, as a consequence of acceptance of group life, human beings become able to keep their primary drives well satisfied, they also become capable of deriving their principal satisfactions from social approval and from the type

[5] Thus, for Freud, human life as a whole became tragedic. Social existence, he felt, was necessarily frustrating and provided no satisfactory way of discharging the resulting impulses to aggression. But Freud seems to have missed the deeper significance of tragedy (and, by the same token, a valid understanding of happiness). Sophocles, Shakespeare, and the other truly great dramatists have known that tragedy, properly speaking, is experienced, not just because an individual is prevented from getting something that he wants, but rather when a pleasure which he might have been is renounced on the basis of moral principle and the principle is then abrogated, whether by other persons or by "fate." Thus, to take a prosaic but good example, it is by no means necessarily tragedic if a little girl wants a new dress but does not get it; but if a little girl has worked and made sacrifices for a dress and has been told that such work and sacrifice will result in a dress, and if she then does not get it (without adequate explanation), that is tragedy—and an inauspicious event for the development of good character.

of self-approval that comes from an harmonious relationship between ego and super-ego. Freudians have had a rather uniformly low regard for both conscience and organized society; and in this they appear to have made a major error, for it has caused them to miss the essential condition for human happiness and the goal of efficient therapy. Instead of happiness and normality springing from the devious, disguised, and incomplete form of satisfaction which is called sublimation, it seems that happiness is derived from a process which may more appropriately be termed *substitution.* Religious writers and practitioners have long recognized *conversion* as the basis for happiness and the beginning of personal maturity. This, they believe, is the necessary basis for "salvation," not necessarily in the sense of a Heavenly salvation, but in the sense of being saved from lifelong suffering and frustration on earth. Literally "conversion" means "change," and what it involves, in the development of human personality, is a shift in satisfactions, a shift from the biological, or animal, satisfactions of infancy and childhood to the social and ethical satisfactions of adult life. As many clinicians are now beginning to see, efficient psychotherapy involves a "conversion" of this kind. Such a conversion provides the resolution of many personal dilemmas and at the same time gives a theoretical explanation of how it is that man can be happy in his society. All of which was well understood by the Old Testament poet (and psychologist), David, when he said: "I delight to do thy will, O my God: yea, thy law is within my heart" (Psalms 40:8).

VII. The way of thinking about frustration and aggression which has been followed in the preceding pages, while far from complete and by no means entirely systematic, has a number of important implications. Of these the following may be mentioned as perhaps most significant.

1). The impetus which Freud gave to the study of the frustration-anger-aggression sequence was a valuable one, but the resulting research and theoretical formulations have veered off in a direction that now seems unpromising. Because this line of thought has been too preoccupied with the biologically given drives and does not take into sufficient account the socially determined aspirations and apprehensions of human beings it has led to an unsatisfactory formulation of problems; and many of the results of research in this field are therefore less meaningful than they would have been if the general frame of reference had been different.

2). Future thought and research may be expected to pay increasing attention to the concept of moral, or ethical, frustration. There is growing evidence to indicate that neurosis is a product, not so much of the individual's attempt to deny and inhibit such impulses as sex and anger, as of attempts to repudiate his own moral strivings and to evade the social responsibilities which these strivings (embedded in conscience) reflect. From this it follows that the neurotic is not usually, perhaps never, the individual whose biological impulses have been too severely subdued, but is rather the individual who has found special difficulty in the acceptance of authority, both inner and outer.

3). This analysis puts special stress upon the importance of research designed to indicate the conditions under which authority is or is not internalized and upon the conditions under which authority is internalized but not accepted. If authority is not internalized, there is no conscience and the resulting individual is a criminal or psychopathic personality. If authority is internalized but is not accepted, the resulting individual is a neurotic. By the same logic, the normal person is one in whom authority has been both internalized and accepted. In this way it becomes clear why the problem of therapy is more difficult in the case of the criminal or psychopath than in the case of the neurotic. Therapy in the case of the neurotic involves the difficult but usually not impossible task of reconciling ego and super-ego; but therapy in the case of the criminal—at least in the "pure" criminal, uncomplicated by neurosis —calls for the establishment of conscience *de novo*. As yet we know so little about the conditions of satisfactory conscience-learning in children that we may be said to be almost wholly ignorant of how it may be brought about, if at all, in adults.

4). If, in a healthy individual functioning in a healthy society, the social (ethical) drives are the predominant ones, and if these drives are capable of being frustrated (by the unethical, irresponsible behavior of others or oneself), then we may expect anger and aggression to result from this type of frustration. Too often it has been assumed that aggression is always and inevitably *anti-social*. Too often we have failed to see that much aggression is *pro-social,* and that it is this form of aggression which is essential in the discipline of children by their parents and other teachers and of adults by the authorized agents of society at large.

5). In recent years there has been much confusion in the minds of parents and teachers, as well as in the minds of those concerned with the correction and control of adults who behave irresponsibly, concerning the problem of discipline. Some have come to feel that all discipline is dishygienic and dangerous. This view overlooks the fact that it takes a lot of aggression to run a society. Human society is not something that holds together and functions automatically. It was only with great difficulty that human societies were initially developed (we are still trying to develop a world society), and they are held together only with constant effort. Discipline, which is aggression toward the immature, irresponsible, and deviant elements in a society, is unavoidable if a society is to survive. The question, therefore, is not whether discipline, as such, is good or bad, necessary or unnecessary: it is inevitable. Instead the question is: How can discipline be made wiser and more effective? How can authority be presented in such a way that it will (a) be introjected and (b) once introjected, also accepted? These are large issues for the educational theorist of the future.

6). In re-thinking the problem of discipline, we probably need to abandon the concept of punishment as a form of retribution and come to regard it in more naturalistic, i.e., in psychological and social, terms. Certain forms of conduct have been and often are still condemned because they are "wrong" in the sense that it is believed that they will keep the person manifesting them from "going to Heaven." Since everyone wants to go to Heaven, or at least *should* want to, then punishment must be administered as a means of making the individual experience pain measure-for-measure, i.e., to "pay for" the pleasure that was involved in this misconduct.

A more realistic view is that punishment is designed to function (a) as a means of producing *behavioral change* ("conversion") in the person to whom it is applied and (b) as a deterrent to misbehavior on the part of others. The naturalistic and the super-naturalistic philosophies of punishment need to be clearly differentiated.

7). Such a distinction seems especially promising as a means of clearing up the following dilemma. It is sometimes argued that if one takes a "scientific" view of human behavior, one must assume that all behavior is caused, that every individual is the product of his past experiences, and that, given those past experiences, no one could possibly be anything else but what he is. Therefore, it is unfair and inhumane to "blame" anyone for anything or to punish him for what he is or does. The supernaturalistic position does not get into this difficulty. It frankly assumes free will and holds the individual strictly accountable (save under certain mitigating circumstances). Is the only choice therefore, between scientific fatalism on the one hand and supernaturalism on the other?

Practically, the dilemma is resolved by the fact that discipline is a social necessity. Regardless of the philosophical justifications or lack of them, the fact remains that no society (or family) can get along without disciplining its recalcitrant members. And psychologically the paradox is eliminated if we keep in mind the view that punishment is administered, not as retaliation or atonement, but as an agency of behavioral change. If a person "misbehaves," it is "his fault" precisely and literally in the sense that he is a faulty, incomplete, immature, deficient person, and the punishment is administered in the expectation that it will correct this deficiency. That punishment often fails to achieve the desired goal (both from the naturalistic and supernaturalistic standpoints) represents no theoretical obstacle, but is instead due to the very practical difficulty of seeing to it that

discipline is always alloyed with love, that punishment is balanced by reward, that fear is tempered by hope.

8). Clinically, it is certainly true that neurotic persons are frustrated and often aggressive. They commonly experience what might be called "free floating anger," or generalized irritability, which has commonly been interpreted as the outcropping of pent-up hostility toward parents, employer, husband or wife, siblings, own children, or society generally. However, in many instances the anger is found to be self-anger, and once the individual learns to live up to, rather than try to deny and evade, his own ethical expectations of himself, this kind of inner fury abates.

Self-anger is likely to be "projected" in any of several forms, of which perhaps the most common is the tendency to ridicule and "run down" others for the reason (not consciously recognized) that this temporarily eases the individual's self-criticism. Then, too, the neurotic often behaves aggressively as a defensive measure, as when, in the therapeutic situation, he shows the well known phenomena of "resistance" and "negative transference." By attack he has learned to ward off personal change, and if, in attacking, he succeeds in eliciting a counter-attack, he can then usually also justify to himself his initial aggressiveness.

Thus we arrive at the suggestion that instead of human beings characteristically turning inward aggressions aroused by frustration imposed upon them by others, they are perhaps more likely to project, or turn outward, aggressions which are aroused by inner frustration—frustration resulting, not from failure to gratify instinctual needs, but from failure to satisfy the moral demands which they make of themselves.

This reversal of conventional clinical perception may be taken as typifying the pervasive change in basic assumptions and, one may even say, in philosophical orientation which is today taking place in the entire field of clinical thought and therapy. This field is in rapid transition; and the present essay can perhaps serve no better purpose than to indicate the nature of some of the issues which are under most active debate and to suggest what seems to be the over-all direction in which theory and practice are now moving.

O. H. MOWRER
Research Professor of Psychology
University of Illinois

BIBLIOGRAPHY

Allport, G. W., *ABC's of Scapegoating*, Central YMCA College, Chicago.
Barker, R. D., Dembo, T., and Lewin, K., Frustration and Regression: An Experiment With Young Children. *University of Iowa Studies: Studies in Child Welfare*, 1941, *18*, xv 314.
Collias, N. E., Aggressive Behavior Among Vertebrate Animals, *Physiological Zoology*, 1944, *17*, 83–123.
Dollard, J., Hostility and Fear in Social Life, *Social Forces*, 1938, *17*, 15–29.
Dollard, J., Doob, L. W., Miller, N. E., Mowrer, O. H., and Sears, R. R., *Frustration and Aggression*, Yale University Press: New Haven, 1939.
Freud, S., *A General Introduction to Psychoanalysis*, Boni and Liveright, New York, 1920.

Freud, S., *Civilization and Its Discontents*, The Hogarth Press, London, 1929.
Menninger, K. A., *Man Against Himself*, Harcourt, Brace and Company, New York, 1938.
Mowrer, O. H., Discipline and Mental Health, *Harvard Educational Review*, 1947, 17, 284–296.
Newcomb, T. M., and Hartley, E. L., (Editors), *Readings in Social Psychology*, Henry Holt and Company, New York, 1947. See especially Pact VI, Social Frustration.
Rosenzweig, S., Mowrer, O. H., Haslerud, G. M., Curtis, Q. F., and Barker, R. G., Frustration as an Experimental Problem, *Character and Personality*, 1938, 7.
Rosenzweig, S., An Outline of Frustration Theory, in *Personality and the Behavior Disorders* (J. Nev. Hunt. ed.), New York, Ronald Press, 1944.
Sears, R. R., *Survey of Objective Studies in Psychoanalytic Concepts*, Social Science Research Council, New York, 1943.
Strang, R., Education Against Aggression, *Harvard Educational Review*, 1946, *16*, 273–281.
Symonds, P. M., *The Dynamics of Human Adjustment*, D. Appleton-Century, New York, 1946.

G

GAMBLING is the act of playing or gaming for money or other stake. The law defines a *common gambler* as a person who is the owner, agent, or superintendent of a place, or of any device, or apparatus, for gambling; or who hires, or allows to be used a room, table, establishment, or apparatus for such purpose; or who engages as dealer, game-keeper, or player in any gambling or banking game, where money or property is dependent upon the result; or who sells or offers to sell what are commonly called lottery policies, or any writing, paper, or document in the nature of a bet, wager, or insurance upon the drawing or selection or the drawn or selected numbers of any public or private lottery; or who indorses or uses a book or other document, for the purpose of enabling others to sell or offer to sell, lottery policies, or other such writings, papers or documents. Such a person is guilty of a misdemeanor. (Penal Law of New York State)

Many specific sections of the Penal Law deal with gambling. Some of these are summarized below:

The sale of gambling implements and devices is prohibited and made punishable as a misdemeanor. It is also unlawful to keep gambling apparatus in certain places such as in or near courts of justice; religious, benevolent, charitable, scientific, or missionary societies; academies, schools, colleges, or other institutions of learning; libraries; loan companies; election and polling places; military establishments; fairs, exhibitions or open air meetings; and vessels. Keeping gaming and betting establishments is a misdemeanor and punishable as such.

Policy Games. Section 974 of the Penal Law of New York State states, "A person who keeps, occupies or uses, or permits to be kept, occupied or used, a place, building, room, table, establishment or apparatus for policy playing or for the sale of what are commonly called "lottery policies," or who delivers or receives money or other valuable consideration in playing policy; or who shall have in his possession, knowingly, any writing, paper or document, representing or being a record of any chance, share, or interest in numbers sold, drawn, or selected, in connection with 'policy'; etc. is a common gambler and guilty of a misdemeanor."

Possession of Policy Slips. The possession of "policy slips" is presumptive evidence of possession thereof knowingly and in violation of the provisions of section 974.

Tenants using premises for policy games may be removed on application of any person having information that the place is used for policy playing or for the sale of "lottery policies." The law authorizes, in addition to the arrest of gamblers, the seizure and destruction of gambling implements. Upon the conviction of the defendant in a gambling case, the district attorney may cause to be destroyed everything suitable for gambling purposes which he has in his possession.

Persuading a person to visit gambling places is a misdemeanor. A commander, owner or hirer of any vessel who knowingly permits any gambling for money or property on board such vessel, or if he does not, upon his knowledge of the fact, immediately prevent the same, is punishable by a fine not exceeding five hundred dollars. Keeping slot machines or devices is a misdemeanor and such slot machines may be seized and destroyed upon conviction of the person in possession. Other types of gambling which are punishable by law include pool-selling, book-making, bets, wagers, racing animals for stake, and lotteries.

The law further provides for forfeiture for

exacting payment of money won at gambling and **penalties for winning** or losing twenty-five dollars **or upwards. All** contracts on account of money or property wagered, bet or staked are void. Securities for money lost at gaming are void and property staked may be recovered. Losers of twenty-five dollars or upwards may sue for and recover the sums lost.

According to most authorities legal measures to combat gambling have been ineffective. According to Barnes and Teeters our opposition to gambling in its more overt forms led to the much more serious gambling in the economic essentials of the nation. "The pious attempts to drive gambling out of existence by directly hostile legislation have merely thrown it into the hands of racketeers and criminal gangs. Racetrack gambling has taken on a new scope and impetus under the recent development of what is called 'pari-mutuel' betting at the tracks and under the handbook system set up in city poolrooms and other gaming emporia. There are innumerable types of slot machines used by organized gamblers, most popular of which at present are the bagatelle, or pin-ball games."

BIBLIOGRAPHY

Barnes, H. E., and Teeters, N. K., *New Horizons in Criminology*, Prentice-Hall, Inc., 1944.
Bergler, Edmund, The Gambler: A Misunderstood Neurotic, *Journal of Criminal Psychopathology*, 4, 379–393, January, 1943.
Gilbert, F. B., *Criminal Law and Practice of the State of New York*, Matthew Bender and Co., 1935.
MacDougall, E. D., *Speculation and Gambling*, Stratford, 1936.

GOOD TIME LAWS. A *good time law* is one which allows a reduction in prisoners' sentences of a stated number of days for each year of good behavior while incarcerated. Prison boards are authorized to examine the conduct records of prisoners and to effect their release in accordance with the schedule of reductions before the expiration of their full court sentences.

A good time law was passed in New York State as early as 1817, which provided that first-term prisoners on sentences of five years or less could shorten their terms by one-fourth for good behavior. However, the law was not utilized. Later, many other states passed good time laws so that by 1868 twenty-four states had made such provision. The Federal system of the United States operates under a good-time provision at the present time.

The purposes of such laws were many. Thus, it was claimed that they mitigated the severity of sentences, solved the problem of prison discipline by providing incentives for good behavior, got good work from the prisoners and assisted in their reformation. However, many modern penologists and criminologists have criticized them adversely. Thus, Barnes and Teeters state that good time laws are "held over the inmate as a constant threat." They conclude that, "in the last analysis, they are merely another form of institutional repression." Other objections are that they are too mechanical, that there is little correlation between good conduct in prisons and good conduct outside, and that they make for outward compliance on the part of hardened criminals who want their freedom quickly. Sutherland states, "In general this method of release does about as much injury as good."

BIBLIOGRAPHY

Maconochie, Alexander, *The Mark System of Prison Discipline*, London, 1855.
Teeters, N. K., *They Were in Prison*, Winston, 1937.
Wines, E. C., Commutation Laws in the U. S., Report of Prison Assn. of N. Y., 1868.

H

HABITUAL CRIMINAL. Many states have statutes relating to the control of habitual criminals which subject them to special control and supervision. In New York, for example, a person who is convicted of a felony after having had a prior conviction for any other crime, or who is convicted of a misdemeanor after five previous misdemeanor convictions, may be adjudged to be a *habitual criminal* in addition to any other punishment inflicted upon him. The duty of determining whether one is an habitual criminal is left to the court.

The New York Penal Law provides that the person of an habitual criminal shall always be subject to the supervision of every judicial magistrate of the county, and of the supervisors and overseers of the poor of the town where the criminal may be found, to the same extent that a minor is subject to the control of his parent or guardian. The governor may grant a pardon which shall relieve from judgment of habitual criminality as from any other sentence, but upon a subsequent conviction for a felony of a person so pardoned, a judgment of habitual criminality may again be pronounced on account of the first conviction, notwithstanding such pardon.

BIBLIOGRAPHY

Gilbert, F. B., *Criminal Law and Practice of the State of New York*, Matthew Bender and Co., 1935.

HOMICIDE. Homicide is the killing of any human being by the act, procurement or omission of another. There are four different kinds of homicide: murder, manslaughter, excusable homicide, and justifiable homicide.

Murder may be divided into two degrees. *Murder* is the unlawful killing of a human being with malice aforethought. *First degree murder* is the killing of a human being, unless it is excusable or justifiable, when committed:

1. From a deliberate and premeditated design to effect the death of the person killed, or of another; or,

2. By an act imminently dangerous to others, and evincing a depraved mind, regardless of human life, although without a premeditated design to effect the death of any individual; or,

3. Without a design to effect death, by a person engaged in the commission of, or in an attempt to commit a felony, either upon or affecting the person killed or otherwise; or,

4. When perpetrated in committing the crime of arson in the first degree.

5. A person who wilfully, by loosening, removing or displacing a rail, or by any other interference wrecks or so injures any car, locomotive, etc., or part thereof, while moving upon any railway as to thereby cause the death of a human being, is guilty of murder in the first degree.

Murder in the second degree is the killing of a human being, when committed with a design to effect the death of the person killed, or of another, but without deliberation and premeditation. Murder in the first degree is, in most states, punishable by death. Murder in the second degree is, in New York State, punishable by imprisonment from twenty years to life.

Manslaughter is any homicide, not justifiable or excusable, which is committed without malice aforethought and may also be divided into degrees. *Manslaughter in the first degree* is a homicide committed without a design to effect death: by a person engaged in committing, or attempting to commit, a misdemeanor, affecting the person or property, either of the person killed or of another; or, in the heat of passion, but in a cruel and unusual manner, or by means of a dangerous weapon. The wilful killing of an unborn quick child, by any injury committed upon the mother of such child, is manslaughter in the first degree (N. Y. Penal Law). This applies also to the providing, supplying, or administering of drugs to a woman with intent to procure her miscarriage, in case of her death; or of the death of any quick child of which she is pregnant. The punishment for first degree manslaughter in New York is imprisonment for not more than twenty years.

Manslaughter in the second degree is homicide committed without a design to effect death: by a person committing or attempting to commit a trespass, or other invasion of a private right, either of the person killed or of another, not amounting to a crime; or, in the heat of passion, but not by a dangerous weapon or by the use of cruel or unusual means; or, by any act, procurement or culpable negligence of any person, which does not constitute any of the other types of homicide. Also, a woman producing her own miscarriage is guilty of manslaughter in the second degree if her unborn child is killed thereby. Other types of manslaughter in the second degree are human deaths caused by negligent use of machinery, by mischievous animals (owner is guilty), by overloading passenger vessel, by carelessness of persons in charge of steamboats and steam engines, and by the acts of physicians while intoxicated. Imprisonment for a term not exceeding fifteen years, or a fine of not more than one thousand dollars, or both, is the punishment for second degree manslaughter in New York State.

Excusable homicide is homicide committed by accident and misfortune, in lawfully correcting a child or servant, or in doing any other lawful act, by lawful means, with ordinary caution, and without any unlawful intent.

Justifiable homicide is homicide committed by a public officer, or a person acting by his command and in his aid and assistance: in obedience to the judgment of a competent court; or, necessarily, in overcoming actual resistance to the execution of the legal process or order of a court or officer, or in the discharge of a legal duty; or, necessarily, in retaking a prisoner who has committed a felony, and who has escaped or is fleeing from justice, etc. *Homicide* is also justifiable when committed in self-defense or in resistance of an attempt to commit a felony upon the slayer, in his presence, or upon or in a dwelling or other place of abode in which he is.

Proof of Death. No person can be convicted of murder or manslaughter, according to New York law, unless the death of the person alleged to have been killed and the fact of the killing by the defendant, as alleged, are each established as independent facts; the former by direct proof, the latter beyond a reasonable doubt. The direct proof of the death can usually be accomplished by the existence of the *corpus delicti* or body of the deceased. No person can be convicted of a felony unless the corpus delicti be first shown.

BIBLIOGRAPHY

Baker, Amos T., A Clinical Study of Inmates Sentenced to Sing Sing Prison for Murder First Degree, *American Journal of Psychiatry*, 91, 783–790, January, 1935.
Gilbert, F. B., *Criminal Law and Practice of State of New York*, Matthew Bender and Co., 1935.
Patterson, Ralph M., Psychiatric Study of Juveniles Involved in Homicide, *American Journal of Orthopsychiatry*, 13, 125–130, January, 1943.
Rymer, C. A., The Insanity Plea in Murder, *American Journal of Psychiatry*, 98, 690–697, March, 1942.

HOMOSEXUALITY. Homosexuality exists in men as an overt sexual practice and also in an unconscious (latent) form. The latter plays a more or less important part in men who might not even be aware of the fact that they are possessed by a substantial homosexual component.

Overt homosexuality is frequent; we cannot tell how frequent because we lack reliable statistics on it. Some speak of four per cent in the civilized nations of the West; this figure is probably understated. In the Orient and among primitive people, homosexuality is so frequent that we may call it endemic.

There is, however, a difference between primitive and the majority of civilized homosexuals. The Anatolian peasant, Arabs and other half-primitive people practice homosexuality according to stimulus and response, i.e., they accept a man as their sex object when a woman is unavailable. In this same sense the primitive shepherd has intercourse with his animals because being too poor or for other reasons he cannot have a better object. There is, however, no doubt in him that a specimen of the other sex would be preferable to any and all surrogates; he acts like a homosexual but is not necessarily so. It seems that we must regard homosexuality in ancient Greece in the same light, particularly before Plato. Pre-Platonic Greek literature hardly mentions homosexuality.

Homosexuality as a modern phenomenon among civilized people is different from its primitive appearance because as a rule it implies a rigid fixation on objects of the same sex. In their great majority our overt homosexuals have no use for objects of the other sex. They are either indifferent to them or—particularly when forced to practice intercourse with them—they feel fear of and repugnance toward them.

Homosexuality always has been a scientific enigma. Nature is full of the most complicated arrangements for safeguarding propagation. There is no end to propagative devices in the animal and vegetable kingdoms from the lowest to the highest species. Homosexuality runs counter to the aims of propagation involving for individual pleasure a stimulus which nowhere else in nature has any other aim than propagation. In this sense homosexuality is puzzling to biology.

Anatomy is a little closer to a solution of our problem, showing that rudiments of the other sex exist in all men: the male has nipples and other bisexual anatomical formations. Many males display feminine sex characteristics, such as feminine distribution of fat and females masculine traits like hairy legs and moustaches. One might suspect that homosexuality of men is attributed to a more feminine anatomy. This, however, is not always so, not even in the great majority of homosexuals. We see males looking "womanish" and females looking "mannish" who are not at all homosexual. On the other hand, we see homosexual men who look athletic and

women very attractive to normal men because of their feminine beauty, although they themselves have no use for men.

To the physician also homosexuality is a puzzle, because it looks like a disease—which it frequently is—but often the homosexual himself does not feel ill or ailing by any means but on the contrary, satisfied with his perversion without suffering except for his social inferiority and even that not in all cases. Let us add that the concept of ailing involves diminished efficiency. We know, however, that unusually efficient men—in the higher strata artists, writers, scholars among them—often are homosexuals. Hence it is difficult to call homosexuality a disease.

Quite unimpressed by the puzzle is the legislator when in his penal codes he brands the homosexual a criminal and punishes him accordingly. The laws of most civilized countries establish a difference between male and female homosexuals. Female homosexuals have a psychology different from the male's anyway. Woman because of her position as a potential mother is prepared to love both sexes, boys and girls. The primitive form of homosexuality as described above seems to be more frequent among Lesbians than among homosexual men. They are rather bisexual than homosexual and more frequently than men do they find their way back to accepting the other sex as mates.

For about fifty years attempts have been made to explain homosexuality by assuming a general bisexuality. It is presumed that components of both sexes exist in all men, in the psychological as well as the anatomical sense. The homosexual component comes to the fore under unfavorable circumstances intensified by undesirable training in the formative years, morbid interrelations in the family and —there is no denying it—by inherited characteristics. This hypothesis was strongly supported by discoveries of biochemistry. Feminine and masculine products of the sex organs (Estrogen and Androgen) could be found in the urine of men and animals of both sexes. However, the bisexuality theory does not quite harmonize with the statistics on homosexuality either. We come to the conclusion that homosexuality with the exception of a few extreme cases is a psychogenic phenomenon. Psychoanalysis has contributed considerably to the understanding of its origin. We must, however, refrain here from giving an account of these doctrines.

By far more interesting than overt homosexuality and more important for sociology is its latent aspect. Some of it has to be expected in all men, if we think the theory of bisexuality to its logical end. Actually, psychoanalysis could prove a homosexual component of which they are not conscious in all men. The differences in various individuals are not so much inherent in the mere existence of this ubiquitous component but in the varying degrees of fear of it and in the defense mechanisms in which men take refuge. Fear of unconscious homosexuality can reach enormous heights and then release a kind of panic which was discovered in soldiers during the first world war. Living together in close quarters and prolonged separation from the other sex are responsible for an advance of the homosexual component generating anxiety over some unknown danger. Men in this condition behave in such a way that in bygone days they were convicted because of cowardly conduct in battle. Nobody realized then that a phenomenon existed which about thirty years ago was given the name of "homosexual panic." This tremendous anxiety connected with latent homosexuality was never completely explained. A forcible switch from heterosexuality to homosexuality is actually a social danger. However, anxiety as expressed in homosexual panic by far surpasses the rational importance of this danger and probably is rooted in some fear of disintegration of the entire personality which actually occurs at the onset of certain psychoses. These psychoses are very often connected with an advance of homosexuality. Psychoanalysis sees a connection with the phenomenon of neurotic castration fear. It is perhaps not superfluous to emphasize here that the ·overt homosexual is free of homosexual panic; he has accepted his perversion as such, and therefore is not afraid of it any more. All other men are more or less exposed to the danger of homosexual panic. Overt homosexuals are usually harmless and friendly. However, when hunting sexual mates they often happen upon latent homosexuals who are at-

tractive to them while the unconscious homosexuals, not knowing of their perverted instincts, are afraid of the tempter and seducer. Relations of this kind frequently end with homicide and atrocities which are reported in our newspapers without the foregoing psychological interpretation.

* * *

The anxiety of latent homosexuals has produced a great number of defense mechanisms which play an important though not yet adequately appreciated part in our culture. We refrain here from speaking of complicated neuroses and psychoses arising from the conflict between unconscious homosexuality and defenses against it. One of the most important defenses is *cruelty* and *compulsive destructiveness*. Aggressiveness and lust for destroying seem to be rooted in the animalistic understructure of man, but are often enormously increased by fear of an inner feminine drive. Some men wish to give evidence that they are not feminine by any means because of their being capable of committing atrocities. Even little boys know of no more terrible disgrace than to be called a "sissy." A boy has to fight and to be "tough." This is inculcated in them from early childhood by their teachers and by other children of their own age who often feel like crying rather than fighting; but fight they must, in order not to be called feminine.

From here the road leads to the theory of the *superman,* of whom we do not have to say much because it has been sufficiently discussed in recent years. *Megalomania* and *persecution mania* belong to one another. A demi-god or whatever term he chooses as an expression of his megalomania, does not have to be afraid of his feminine component any more. But then one has to be afraid that actually he might not be a demi-god: a cause for persecution mania. Only a few people are quite free of persecution ideas. A mechanism is here at work which modern psychiatry since Freud has been calling a projection of an inner voice to the outside. Actually these people feel persecuted by their own feminine component (in women it is the masculine component) without being aware of it. By projecting the danger outside they build up an illusion that other people—individuals or groups of men—persecute them and by so doing they feel somewhat removed from their vexing internal problems. They could not possibly act against an unconscious voice within, but if they can denounce other people they secure for themselves a right to hit back, to persecute their persecutors.

Another defense mechanism is *erotomania,* known in the figures of Don Juan and his feminine counterpart Messalina. Don Juan proves by his apparently insatiable sexlife— and mind you: exclusively with women—that he is not feminine. It is, however, easy to expose his feminine trends, just as the aggressive "oversexed" woman betrays her identification with men. A real man or woman, feeling within the completeness and certainty of his own sex, does not have to play a mad erotomaniac. In contrast to normal men, Don Juan cannot keep the conquered woman. On the contrary he has to run away from her as if haunted by furies. The real Don Juan is comparatively rare. Much more frequently do we see his rudimentary edition traveling all over the land, so to speak, burning and ravaging without ever reaching his goal. This variety of Don Juanism has been called the "kissing menace."

There is a form of *jealousy* to be booked in the catalogue of our defense mechanisms. Jealousy is a normal phenomenon which so definitely belongs to love that we have a right to doubt the presence of genuine love if jealousy is completely absent. However, there are pathological forms of jealousy based on the fact that one man is in love with another man. The layman cannot easily grasp the idea that a man can be in love without knowing it; yet it is one of the most common occurrences—and he experiences his own latent homosexuality in such a way that he is jealous of his wife or his sweetheart as though she and not he were in love with that man: another form of projection. In this way strange triangles arise of one woman and two men, not at all in the sense popular with novelists and playwrights. In the triangles which we have in mind, the most important line is the one between the two men and the line leading from the men to the woman is unimportant.

In addition to individual defenses we have to consider collective measures offered the individual by the various civilizations in which they live. Here we have to mention all kinds of *organizations* (covenants) *of men.* Religious associations like monasteries, religious knights and soldiers of Christ and well-disciplined and, particularly, fanaticized armies belong here, as well as certain fraternities and also involuntary groups as in prisons, or explorers on trips of long duration. In such associations the homosexual component is intensified, but as a rule checked by the regulations and practices of the group.

There are two ways leading out of the hardships of latent homosexuality.

Either man withdraws from the sex struggle for a love object, dodging the difficulty by changing into a *Narcissus,* in love only with himself like the youth of the ancient saga. Then he is not interested in anyone, either of his own or the other sex, only in himself. We cannot call him an ordinary egotist because he avoids association with his fellow-men even if they offer him personal advantage. He lives a lonesome life and by renouncing social life gets away from a fight of which he is afraid. In this camp we meet eccentrics of all kinds, misers, collectors, book-worms, also exaggerating lovers and protectors of animals who prefer pets to men, because animals are no danger to them. Being a gregarious animal, man cannot be happy as a narcissus and often deplores his lonesome life, but is not able to change it. As the alternative to homosexual panic he chooses narcissism because it promises him peace.

The other escape from fear of the homosexual component is called *sublimation.* If we can sublimate a drive we do not have to suppress it any longer. On the contrary its permanent practice and enjoyment are made possible in such a way that society and hence also the individual who sublimates are satisfied. An example of this is genuine friendship which—as we know—is not far removed from erotic warmth. Another example is charity of any kind which always has been felt to be identical with love. Generally speaking, devotion to any social cause which is not quite egotistic satisfies a piece of libido which if suppressed and pent up might become a danger for the individual. Different nations and different times have produced different collective possibilities and the individual can become a gentleman by sublimation of his instincts according to the taste of the people in whose midst he lives.

It is not always easy to differentiate between sublimation and repression. Not only does hypocrisy play an important role, but even with an actual benefactor, it sometimes is doubtful whether he has sublimated his cruel drives into charity or has remained cruel underneath and occasionally shows it. As an example of this kind we mention the philanthropist who builds orphanages for children whose fathers would have survived were it not for the cruel business methods of the philanthropist. Consider the Grand Inquisitor who by burning heretics alive, pronounces himself a philanthropist because by tormenting them here he saves the souls of his victims from eternal flames in hell.

Extremely momentous is the flight of latent homosexuals into liquor. Drug addicts (morphin, opium, cocaine, etc.) present more sinister a problem than the alcohol addict, but the social importance of alcoholism is infinitely greater because of the tremendous number of alcoholics in many countries of which unfortunately America is one. Many a man is driven to drinking habits because of his fear of unconscious homosexual tendencies. When intoxicated people drop their inhibitions, often enough the latent tendency comes to the fore and shows its existence even to the untrained eye of the observer. The defense is double barreled by encouraging what it was supposed to overcome. In view of this danger the alcoholic continues to drink until he eventually passes out or incapacitates himself in some other way. He then exchanges his dreaded homosexual component for narcissistic loneliness.

To summarize, we have described four categories of defense mechanisms against latent homosexuality:

Morbid defenses such as cruelty, megalomania (the superman), persecution mania, erotomania, pathological (paranoic) jealousy, and collective defenses.

Regression to narcissism which terminates the struggle in its particular way.

Sublimation into desirable social activities. Borderline cases between sublimation and morbid reaction formations.

* * *

Almost all men who are afraid of their own feminine component have one characteristic in common: they hate and despise women. They rationalize their feelings about the female sex in various ways. Women who suffer under this persecution can avoid these men's hatred only by renouncing their prerogative as sex creatures and identifying themselves with men as much as possible. In this way a race of masculine women is fostered who deal with men, their jailers, as they deserve, i.e. they torture them and make them unhappy. Sometimes it looks as though education and national training—in past history as well as in present times—have produced men who cannot love their women Accordingly, an unhappy generation may ensue living in permanent restlessness who will not permit other nations either to pursue their natural and peaceful happiness. We reach the conclusion that there are not only economic but also psychological causes for good luck and aggressivity of peoples and those who undertake the job of educating and re-educating nations should consult psychologists.

FRITZ WITTELS, M. D.
Psychiatrist
New York City

BIBLIOGRAPHY

Allen, Frederick H., Homosexuality in Relation to the Problem of Human Difference, *American Journal of Orthopsychiatry*, 10, 129-135, Jan., 1940.
Bergler, Edmund, Eight Prerequisites for the Psychoanalytic Treatment of Homosexuality, *Psychoanalytic* Review, 31, 253-286, July, 1944.
Green, E. W., and Johnson, J. G., Homosexuality, *Journal of Criminal Psychopathology*, 5, 467-480, Jan., 1944.
Hamilton, Donald M., Some Aspects of Homosexuality in Relation to Total Personality Development, *Psychiatric Quarterly*, 13, 229-244, 1939.
Nunberg, H., Homosexuality, Magic and Aggression, *International Journal of Psychoanalysis*, 19, 1-16, 1938.

I

INCEST. Incest is the crime of cohabitation or sexual commerce between persons related within the degrees wherein marriage is prohibited by law. The Penal Law of New York State provides that "when persons, within the degrees of consanguinity, within which marriages are declared by law to be incestuous and void, inter-marry or commit adultery or fornication with each other, each of them is punishable by imprisonment for not more than ten years." This section does not extend to a marriage between an uncle and a niece. The crime is complete upon intermarriage. Proof of carnal knowledge is unnecessary.

Psychiatric research indicates that sex relations with adults among children (including incest) are not basically destructive since the recollection of these experiences is usually strongly repressed, although it may appear in later life in the form of neurotic complex. The child itself often unconsciously desires the act and becomes a more or less willing partner.

Anthropological literature is replete with instances of the disruptive influence of incest among adults and the dread with which it is viewed by primitive peoples. Incest between adults is not a common phenomenon among civilized people. Usually one of the participants is a child.

BIBLIOGRAPHY

Bender, L., and Blau, A., Reaction of Children to Sex Relations with Adults, *American Journal of Orthopsychiatry*, 7, 14, 1937.
Devereux, G., Social and Cultural Implications of Incest Among the Mohave Indians, *Psychoanalytic Quarterly*, 5, 510–533, 1939.
Gilbert, F. B., *Criminal Law and Practice of the State of New York*, Matthew Bender and Co., 1935.
Sloane, P., and Karpinski, E., Effects of Incest on the Participants, *American Journal of Orthopsychiatry*, 12, 666–673, October, 1942.

INCOMPETENT PERSONS. Most jurisdictions have statutes relating to incompetent persons, their irresponsibility for crime and their segregation and protection.

The question of the legal responsibility of incompetent individuals has led to varied interpretations of what constitutes moral and legal irresponsibility. The courts now generally recognize that if a person is suffering from some mental disorder or insanity, an essential element in the commission of a crime, the sense of responsibility is lacking. But, the legal tests for insanity are still in a state of confusion. Among the tests used are the *wild beast test* (which stipulated that the offender must be so totally deprived of his reason as not to know what he is doing to any greater extent than an infant, a brute, or a *wild beast*) and the *delusion test* (which stipulated that the person must be suffering from *delusions*). The *M'Naghten Rules*, which are abided by in twenty-nine states, stipulate that the accused is not responsible if he "was laboring under such a defect of reason, from disease of the mind, as not to know the nature and the quality of the act he was doing, or if he did know it, that he did not know he was doing what was wrong." Some of the states stick close to the *right and wrong test* while others use the *knowledge of nature and quality test*. The most recent test is known as the *irresistible impulse test* and is now used in the District of Columbia and seventeen states. The test is based on the idea that in addition to intellectual judgment there must also exist the possibility of doing what is considered right and to refrain from doing what is thought to be wrong.

In the State of New York, the Penal Law stipulates that an act done by a person who is an idiot, imbecile, lunatic or insane is not a crime. A person cannot be tried, sentenced to any punishment or punished for a crime while he is in a state of idiocy, imbecility, lunacy or insanity so as to be incapable of understanding the proceeding or making his defense. A person is not excused from criminal liability in New York (which is true of most other states) as an idiot, imbecile, lunatic, or insane person, except upon proof that, at the time of committing the alleged criminal act, he was laboring under such a defect of reason as: (1) not to know the *nature and quality* of the act he was doing; or, (2) not to know that the act was wrong.

A lunatic is responsible for a crime committed during a lucid interval but the prosecution must show that the crime was committed during a lucid interval. *Delirium tremens,* like insanity, if it deprives one of the capacity of knowing right from wrong, saves him from any criminal responsibility from his acts.

The laws for the protection of incompetent persons can be illustrated by those of the State of New York. A person who confines an idiot, lunatic or insane person, in any other manner or in any other place than as authorized by law, and a person guilty of harsh, cruel or unkind treatment of, or any neglect of duty toward any idiot, lunatic or insane person under confinement, whether lawfully or unlawfully confined, is guilty of a misdemeanor.

The maintenance of a private insane asylum, or institution for the care or treatment of persons of unsound mind, without a license issued and granted according to law, is a misdemeanor.

A person who: (1) wilfully causes or permits the life or limb of any person, who is, from any cause, incompetent to care for himself, to be endangered or his health to be injured, or (2) wilfully is guilty of harsh, cruel or unkind treatment of, or any neglect of duty toward any person who is incompetent to care for himself, is guilty of a misdemeanor.

BIBLIOGRAPHY

Gilbert, F. B., *Criminal Law and Practice of the State of New York,* Matthew Bender and Co., 1935.
Gillin, J. L., *Criminology and Penology,* Century, 1926.
Glueck, S., *Mental Disorder and the Criminal Law,* Little, Brown, 1925.
Paton, John, Lunacy and the Law, *The Penal Reformer,* London, October, 1934.
Weihofen, Henry, *Insanity as a Defense in Criminal Law,* Commonwealth Fund, 1933.
White, William A., *Insanity and the Criminal Law,* Macmillan, 1923.

INDECENCY. This general term covers a fairly large number of offenses against public decency. In most jurisdictions, such offenses as indecent exposure, participating in nudist colonies, and the like are punishable as misdemeanors. The Penal Law of the State of New York specifically defines thirteen types of indecency which are punishable as misdemeanors.

Indecent exposure—A person who wilfully and lewdly exposes his person, or his private parts, in any public place or place where others are present, or procures another to expose himself, is guilty of indecent exposure. The practice of nudism in a gymnasium is not an offense under this provision.

Immoral Plays and Exhibitions—The preparing, advertising, giving, directing, presenting, or participating in, any obscene, indecent, immoral, impure scene, tableau, incident, part or portion of any drama, play, exhibition, show or entertainment, which would tend to corrupt the morals of youth or others, or which deals with the subject of sex degeneracy, or sex perversion, or the use and leasing of real property for such presentations, are all punishable as misdemeanors.

Nudity and Nudist Colonies—A person who in any place wilfully exposes his person, private parts in the presence of two or more persons of the opposite sex whose private parts are similarly exposed, or who aids or abets any such act, or who uses or leases real property for such purposes, is guilty of a misdemeanor.

Obscene Prints and Articles—The selling, lending, giving away, manufacturing, or showing of any obscene article or print such as a book, picture, motion picture, slot machine, etc. is a misdemeanor. This statute is aimed at *pornography,* and a pornographic book is taken to be one where all other incidents and qualities are mere accessories to the primary purpose of stimulating immoral thoughts. The courts have strictly limited the applicability of the statute to works of pornography and they have consistently declined to apply it to books of genuine literary value. The exposure of indecent prints and pictures in public places is also a misdemeanor.

Indecent Articles—The sale, loan, distribution or advertising of any instrument or article, or any receipt, drug or medicine for the prevention of conception, or for causing unlawful abortion, etc, is punishable as a misdemeanor.

Advertisements Relating to Certain Diseases—The provision prohibits the publication, sale, distribution, of any advertisements which concern a venereal disease, lost manhood, lost vitality, sexual impotence, and the like. This section, however, does not apply to didactic or scientific treatises which do not advertise or call attention to any person or place where information, treatment or advice may be obtained. It is also inapplicable to advertisements or notices issued by an incorporated or a licensed dispensary or a board of health, etc.

Mailing or Carrying Obscene Articles and Prints except in the United States mail is punishable as a misdemeanor by the State and, if in the United States mail, by the Federal Government.

Physicians' Instruments—An article or instrument, used or applied by physicians lawfully practicing, or by their direction or prescription, for the cure or prevention of disease is *not* an article of indecent or immoral nature or use.

Disorderly Houses—The keeping or maintaining, leasing or renting, of a house of ill-fame or assignation of any description is punishable as a misdemeanor. An owner who knowingly permits his property to be used for immoral purposes is also guilty. The keeping or maintaining of any place of public resort at which the decency, peace or comfort of a neighborhood is disturbed is a misdemeanor.

Male Procurers—Every male person who lives wholly or in part on the earnings of prostitution, or who in any public place solicits for immoral purposes, is guilty of a misdemeanor. A male person who lives with or is habitually in the company of a prostitute and has no visible means of support, shall be presumed to be living on the earnings of prostitution.

BIBLIOGRAPHY

Gilbert, F. B., *Criminal Law and Practice of the State of New York*, Matthew Bender and Co., 1935.

INDEMNIFICATION FOR ERRORS OF JUSTICE.

Because of the assumption that the State cannot err, existing practice has always been to disregard the erroneous conviction of innocent individuals and the wrongful imprisonment of persons who should not have been detained. The majority of the states do not provide indemnities to such victims as a matter of right. Three states, California, North Dakota, and Wisconsin, have made provisions to indemnify persons wrongfully accused but the relief is spasmodic even in these states. A Federal law, passed in 1938, provides "relief to persons erroneously convicted in the courts of the United States." A person who can establish the fact that he was wrongfully convicted and sentenced for a crime may file suit in the Court of Claims for damages of not more than $5,000 against the United States Government. In most jurisdictions, a special legislative law is necessary to make possible restitution to a victim of miscarriages of justice. Many European countries have long had provisions for indemnification of those wrongfully convicted of crimes.

Many arguments have been advanced, particularly by E. M. Borchard, in favor of indemnification for financial losses as a result of erroneous conviction. There is a decided movement for state legislation to remedy the injustice of not compensating wrongfully accused persons. In favor of such legislation is the fact that when private property is taken for public use the owner is compensated. Also, when the state requires an individual to give his time or services to the state, he is compensated. The principle involved in indemnification is the same as that of workmen's compensation laws, namely, to distribute the loss on the public rather than to impose it on one individual.

Such eminent criminologists as Sutherland, Barnes, and Teeters, advocate some form of indemnification but most penologists, like Sutherland, agree that it should be limited to financial losses only, with a maximum limit such as $5,000 and with a brief *statute of limitations* such as six months. Also, it should only be granted to those whose conduct in the matter is exemplary. Thus, indemnification should not be granted to a person who has refused to testify, attempted to escape, or was drunk at the scene of the crime.

BIBLIOGRAPHY

Barnes, H. E., and Teeters, N. K., *New Horizons in Criminology*, Prentice-Hall, 1943.
Borchard, E. M., *Convicting the Innocent*, New Haven, 1932.
Borchard, E. M., European Systems of State Indemnification for Errors of Criminal Justice, *Journal of Criminal Law and Criminology*, 3, 686-706, January, 1913.
Borchard, E. M., *State Indemnity for Errors of Criminal Justice*, U. S. Senate Document 974, 62nd Congress, 3rd Session.
Sutherland, E. H., *Principles of Criminology*, Lippincott, 1939.

INDETERMINATE SENTENCE. When the time of release of a prisoner is determined by an administrative board and the court merely imposes minimum and maximum limits of the penalty, the sentence is known as an indeterminate sentence. Technically, the sentence is not indeterminate if the limits are fixed by the court or by the legislature, and it should be called *indefinite* rather than indeterminate. However, no state has sentences that are completely indeterminate and the general practice is to call these indefinite sentences indeterminate. The "indeterminate sentence" refers to the fact that the exact period of custody is not fixed before the custody begins. A person on an indeterminate sentence may be released either conditionally on parole or unconditionally and completely without parole.

Strictly speaking the indeterminate sentence is more accurately called the *indefinite sentence*. The philosophy behind it implies that no judge is in a position to know at the end of a trial just how long a man should be committed to a penal institution.

Most states in the United States have indeterminate sentence laws but they are guarded by many exceptions. In general, indeterminate sentences in the United States apply primarily to first offenders who commit the less serious crimes.

BIBLIOGRAPHY

Sellin, Thorsten, Indeterminate Sentence, *Encyclopedia of the Social Sciences*, Vol. 7, pp. 650-652, New York, 1932.
Sutherland, E. H., Principles of Criminology, Lippincott, 1939.
Indeterminate Sentence, by a Prisoner, *Atlantic Monthly*, 108:330-332, September, 1911.

INSURANCE CRIMES. Insurance is an object of criminal exploitation. From the beginnings of insurance experience we find insurance crimes. These early forms have persisted, and there have been added many new varieties from time to time as the field of insurance has broadened. Hence the field of insurance crime is as broad and complex as that of insurance itself.

The number of insurance crimes attempted and successfully carried out is much higher than the number discovered and punished. Many cases are camouflaged as pure accidents. There is no adequate reporting of insurance crimes or their frequencies.

The chief motive in all insurance crimes is financial profit. In order to receive it, the criminal may intentionally or unintentionally hurt or kill innocent people. The intentional harm to others occurs in life insurance when the insured person is murdered for the purpose of obtaining the amount to be paid at the time of his death. The unintentional harm may happen in property and casualty insurance when in destroying an insured property persons accidentally lose their lives.

Many insurance contracts make it relatively easy to obtain unjust profits. Often it is difficult to avoid over-insurance, that is, insurance on amounts higher than the real value of the property covered. It may happen that the seller of the policy promotes such practices, especially when his income depends upon the amount insured.

Insurance is complicated, and, to most people, more or less mysterious. To understand it, one must have some knowledge of economics, business, mathematics, statistics, and law. Therefore, it is not surprising that ignorance about insurance prevails not only among average people, but also among lawyers, judges, and legislators as well. So one often finds loopholes for fraud. As soon as one has been eliminated, new tricks are invented to obtain unlawful profits.

When men are reimbursed for the loss of their property, many will maliciously destroy their own in the absence of strong measures against such behavior. If accidental losses but not planned losses are indemnified, many people will try to make any intended loss appear to result from carelessness. This is the explanation of many frauds connected with liability insurance.

That marine insurance crimes predominated in the past is easy to understand when we consider that marine insurance was the mother not only of many branches of insurance but of insurance law as well.

A few examples will illustrate.

During the third quarter of the nineteenth century, dozens of grain-laden ships went down at the entrance to the harbor of Montreal. Such losses were insured and paid by marine insurance companies. To prevent these losses, the Canadian authorities issued rules for the loading of grain vessels with fines of $40.00 for each infraction. However, not until 1873, when the fine was increased to $800.00 did the sinkings diminish. Overloading no longer was profitable to the insured ship owners.

In property insurance most crimes are against fire insurance companies. It is true that an ocean marine insurance policy offers much more opportunity for criminal exploitation because of the far-reaching multilateral coverage guaranteed by the marine insurer in contrast to the very specialized coverage offered by the fire insurer. But it seems to require much less courage and criminal spirit to cause a fire than to cause the sinking of a ship.

A fire is caused by simple friction—to repeat an old story—the simple friction between a $3,000.00 stock of goods and a $10,-000.00 fire insurance policy. The era of the professional arson-rings and gangs in New York, Chicago, Philadelphia, etc., is ended. They were smashed after the arson laws were passed in the majority of states. The experts in firebug fighting, backed by the efforts of police and fire departments and the organized fire insurance companies, shared responsibility. In spite of all this, the incidence of

arson is still considerable. Fire is a ready consumer of unsalable goods. There is about $125,000,000.00 worth of property damage caused by incendiary fires in the United States each year.

Probably the most striking examples of fire insurance crimes are to be found in Latin America. To correct the situation, a Chilean law provides for the arrest of the proprietor of any house insured against fire as soon as the house burns. He must stay in prison until it has been proved that the fire is not due to arson. In a certain district in Brazil fire insurance was not known until recently. From the moment of its introduction; the number of fires increased enormously.

A typical example of a present-day fire insurance fraud is found in a certain New York store which closed one morning at 1 a.m. The fire department was called a half hour later. Some damage to stock occurred. The next morning, from some place in the upper part of New York City, stock that had been damaged by a former fire was put in the cellar, and later upon the shelves. While the stock was in the cellar, water was poured on it by the employees. This merchandise was included in the inventory on the loss adjustment, and all the evidence pointed to an incendiary blaze.

It is not always true that property alone will be destroyed by the burning of an insured house. As mentioned before it may be that, contrary to the intention of the arsonist, innocent persons may be hurt or even killed. In contrast, such loss of human life does not occur in the case of burglary insurance crimes. In this case, not even the property will be destroyed. The insured goods will disappear from their usual place only to appear elsewhere where they will be reclaimed later by the policyholder. It is well known that insurance companies are suspicious of fur shops in certain districts where theft by the shopkeeper himself is a possibility. An incident of this type took place in a small New York City haberdashery shop. The shop was covered by a burglary insurance policy. After a hold-up, while one clerk called the police, the other rang up amounts on the cash register. At first the loss was only $50. When the insurance adjusters arrived, the book loss had been fraudulently increased to $350.00, which was paid.

The following is an example of a crime against a plate glass insurer. Some time ago, in the early morning, the police in a small town discovered that the windows of several stores had been broken during the night. The perpetrator of the crime was the agent of a plate glass insurance company whose intention was to show the need for plate glass insurance and benefits. By breaking windows, the advantages of insurance were advertised effectively and without cost to the agent.

The record of life insurance frauds reads like fiction. It is difficult to say whether the crimes committed in the remote past, with the goal of getting money through the death of persons insured, are more or less dramatic than those committed in our times. As long as insurance legislation was in its primitive stage, what was called insurance was in reality nothing more or less than pure gambling or betting. It was easy to misuse an insurance policy which was a promise by the company to pay an amount in the case of the death of the insured. There were in almost all European states, from the sixteenth until the nineteenth centuries, laws which forbade criminal misuse of life insurance, or more correctly stated, forbade gambling in lives. One may well imagine that insurance did not prolong the life of a king, prince, or other man in power when it was permitted and usual for anyone to make a contract by which a large amount would be paid to the "policyholder" in the event of the death of the insured person. Undoubtedly, such speculation on the early death of the insured was dangerous to him. And so it came to be forbidden to insure the life of kings and other high ranking people.

It was forbidden, also, to wager high amounts on the date of death of poor fellows who had been brought from the continent to England where they became destitute and welcome objects of shameful speculation by gamblers in lives. It was not until 1774 that the life of every person was protected by the statute of King George III. From that time on "no life insurance contract was valid unless the beneficiary had a bona fide interest in the life of the person insured." However, 100 years later in America not even such a modest preventive measure existed in all our states.

Another type of life insurance crime was associated with issuing policies on the life of little children. What has been disclosed in this connection by parliamentary discussions and the Royal Commissions in England in 1845 and 1870 is almost unbelievable. One of the principal causes for the high infant mortality rate was found to be the insurance against the death of children. In 1884, the Society for the Prevention of Cruelty to Children was founded in London for the purpose of keeping insured children from becoming angels too quickly. The same idea prevails in the American regulations, whereby not more than the burial costs may be covered by insurance of children.

Of more recent date is speculation on one's own life: the insurance of intended suicides. This was promoted greatly by competition among companies which passed reasonable limits in offering highly favorable conditions in policies such as unconditional payment of the whole insured amount in the case of suicide and without any waiting period. It is unnecessary to say that modern legislation has stopped such practice in the companies' own interest. On the other hand, many persons die intentionally, under the camouflage of pure accidents, without being discovered as suicides. The progress of science, first of all, in transportation (automobile, airplane, etc.) has brought much progress in suicide methods.

To obtain statistics on the known false testimonies which have been given by the insured might prove to be enlightening. Among life insurance companies there is a certain organization for the communication of refused risks; all member companies being informed of the persons who were refused life insurance applications by each member company. The members of this organization are thus in a position to control every application entered, whether or not the applicant has mentioned former refusals—about which the application blank contains specific questions. With the object of gathering material, an investigation concerning these concealments was begun about twenty years ago by a group of European life insurance companies and in this way some statistical material was collected. It was discovered in the investigation that, on the average, out of 100 applicants who approached an agency, seven had already been refused. The investigation further showed that out of these seven, only four admitted the refusal, while the other three attempted to conceal it. Therefore, the rate of intentional concealment is 40%. Consideration of this figure leads to an unfavorable conclusion concerning the honesty of applicants for life insurance policies.

Consider a modern example of this type of crime. An officer of a life insurance company was attending a concert presented by the inmates of a tuberculosis sanitarium. The sanitarium encouraged patients to stage amateur theatricals to bolster the morale of the institution. The officers' attention was diverted from the stage to his program. He didn't know what it was, but something about the program fascinated him, so he took it home with him. A few days later he discovered that many of the actors were listed on the rolls of his insurance company, and they were collecting a monthly disability income. The situation was rather unusual. These actors were from all over the United States, but they had all bought insurance from this company, and they were now all at the same institution. They had all passed the company's strict physical examinations and then, in a very short time, all had contracted tuberculosis. After an investigation, one of the patients confessed. The patients spent only enough time—about six months—in the sanitarium to heal the lung lesions. This was also just about as long as their money lasted. When they returned home, they told no one where they had been, and since the usual stethoscopic examination of the chest will not detect an incipient case of tuberculosis nor a healed lesion, they bought life insurance with disability-income riders attached, denying any tubercular history. After waiting for the contestable period—usually a year—to expire, they claimed disability and returned to the sanitarium with a comfortable life income. This was one of the largest life insurance frauds ever carried on. There were about 160 cases in this one institution. It is a type of life insurance fraud that does not depend on real or faked death for its success.

In a small western town a business man had a friend who was an undertaker in a neighboring city. The undertaker had as one of his duties the disposal of the pauper dead. The business man "died" one night as his friend was driving him home. The undertaker stated that his friend had got out of the car to crank it, and when the undertaker looked for him, he was dead. The undertaker then put the body into his car and took it to his undertaking parlor. The body was cremated after the usual death notices were published. After this was done, the "widow" claimed payment of a life insurance policy for $25,000. The man who had burned the body was interviewed, and from his description there were marked differences between the weight and height of the man he had cremated and those of the supposedly dead business man. Finally, by watching the "widow's" mail, the "dead" husband was located alive in Nebraska. Both he and the undertaker were sent to prison. The body was discovered to be that of a pauper which was supposed to have been sent to a dental school for dissection.

The case of Mr. Tetzner, an Austrian, which occurred in Vienna about 15 years ago, proves the importance of the services of special detectives to insurance companies. Mr. Tetzner had a large life and accident insurance policy, which covered automobile accidents. One day, Tetzner's automobile was found burned after an explosion, and inside the car was found the dead body of the driver. It seemed without doubt that this was Tetzner's body, and he was buried. However, the appraiser of the company became suspicious and ordered the body to be exhumed and autopsy performed. It was discovered that Tetzner was still alive. He had killed a traveling workman, burned his body, and caused the explosion. The dead artisan was at the driver's seat. This incident shows also the importance of the policy condition which states that the insurance company must be notified of each accident immediately after it has happened. It is interesting for another reason: similar frauds were tried, probably successfully, in various other countries shortly after the case of Tetzner became known.

A modern specialty of insurance crimes occurs in automobile liability insurance. It is the fake accident claimant. For about thirteen years there flourished in Missouri a gigantic faked accident ring which was able to collect $100,000.00 in insurance claims. The leader of the ring was the former operator of benefit assessment insurance concerns and was general agent for several companies in Missouri. He was sentenced to five years in a Federal prison for having used the mails to defraud. The various members of the ring were sentenced to prison for shorter terms. They faked accidents by self-mutilation and by automobile crashes. Several of the people had limbs amputated. An osteopath was fined $500.00 for manipulating a smashed limb of a member so as to necessitate amputation. Even a sheriff was sentenced to the custody of the United States marshal. Some of the defendants against whom charges were dismissed died within a year of their indictment.

An example of fraudulent claims against insurance companies for automobile collision insurance was supplied by a supposedly reputable business firm in New York City. An adjuster was sent to a garage to estimate the damage done to a car of a holder of collision insurance. He found the damage considerable and recommended a sizeable amount in settlement. Later, while talking to another adjuster in his company who had handled this car in a former accident, he was asked if he noticed a scratch on the left door that had not been fixed after the first accident. He had not, and after talking the situation over, they examined the car. The result was that they discovered the company had three cars with identical identification numbers on the chassis and motor and that they switched the license plates when an accident occurred.

Adjusters are sometimes in collusion with claimants. An adjuster representing the company which insured the second car of a collision came to see the owner of the first car. He found him putting some second-hand and damaged mudguards on his old car. He suggested that he claim $350.00 and give him,

the adjuster, $50.00. The real damage was approximately $25 and the public would have been paying the extra $300.00.

Analysis of the preceding examples is concerned with crimes committed against insurance companies. These are the most frequent ones. But it is difficult to say whether the crimes committed by insurance companies against the people generally, although smaller in number and less frequent in our time, are not more pernicious. Such insurance crimes are typical white-collar crimes with all their far-reaching disturbances. One such crime may ruin the confidence of large parts of a nation, even of the world, in insurance. It is for just that reason that in most countries during the past decades, the legislators have been busy fighting against many methods of white-collar crimes, and with some success. The United States was a pioneer in insurance supervision laws, beginning as early as 1840 in Massachusetts. However, if the country had not had much experience with insurance company crimes, it would not have been the first to take away some of the liberty. Not only has the confidence in insurance companies been re-established, but insurance supervisory legislation also has developed morale and trust among the people.

The criminal behavior of insurance companies consists in violation of trust by making misrepresentations. They published false financial statements, erroneous statistics, incorrect advertisements; there was embezzlement and misapplication of funds, and bribery of public officials, and all these violations were at the expense of the policy-holders—the insurance consumers. By enforcing certain controls in accounting and calculations, regular audits by public accountants, and other measures to be found in the supervisory laws of most countries, many opportunities for fraud have been eliminated.

Insurance companies' assets should be considered inviolable and in need of the strongest protection. If there were no preventive devices the nature of insurance business would offer special possibilities and enticements for fraud. Stock companies, however, have not defrauded the public more than the so-called brotherhoods, lodges, friendly societies, etc.

England, in the 30's and 40's of the 19th century, was afflicted by insurance crimes by bogus companies. Parliament lacked the power to fight against them. Not until 1862 was the principle of limited liability recognized so that it was possible to invest property in an insurance company without risking all of it.

Several novels have popularized insurance crimes. Dickens' *Martin Chuzzlewit*, published in 1842, contains information about the bogus "Anglo-Bengales Disinterested Loan and Life Association Company." Thackeray's *The Great Hoggarty Diamond*, 1839, about the "West Diddlesex Fire & Life Insurance Company," contains many details of fraudulent insurance.

What happened even half a century later in the United States is reported by the Insurance Commissioner of Massachusetts. In his Annual Report in 1890 he said: "It is doubtful if, since the famous South Sea Bubble at the end of the eighteenth century, such a gambling mania has seized an intelligent people as that which developed in the spread of the assessment endowment and its natural and legitimate offspring, the bond investment insanity."

These associations were built up on mysteries. Their chief officers were called "Supremes," etc. They were experts in making people believe that they could make profits out of nothing. They hoped that many lapses would occur so that payments could be distributed among the others. About one million people paid in approximately 40 million dollars in a four year period to these associations and about 75% of it was wasted. It is unbelievable that many thousands of people would join these unsound companies, that they did so is shown in the Cyclopedia of Insurance in the United States and in States Reports, especially those prior to 1906. One astounding example of an epidemic in swindling is "Graveyards," 1879-1882. "The secretary individually took all money paid to the Association and divided the admission premiums among his fellow officers, paid the expense of carrying on the business, collected all assessments for deaths, and paid such claims as were paid, without keeping any account."

The fake life insurance company is chiefly a fly-by-night organization with its office in somebody's brief-case. It operates mainly by mail and though it has headquarters in one state, it operates in another. Therefore the Federal Government alone can punish their fraudulent activities, but even so they often escape through the many loopholes in the Federal statutes. In addition to using the mail, they have advertisements and radio broadcasts, and their contracts usually contain a clause that permits them to escape without paying when the beneficiary comes to collect. It has been estimated that $50,-000,000 is collected annually by these companies.

Insurance undoubtedly has brought many large and small crimes in its wake, but just as one would not condemn religion because it has caused terrible wars, so the shadows which stand opposite the bright side of insurance should not condemn the entire insurance system. There is no radical method of eliminating bad results. Criminal law alone can accomplish little. It must be supported by a good civil law, but above all by an insurance science which can be understood by all classes of people. Our duty is to exclude as much as possible all misuse of insurance. That can be achieved by:

1. Better insurance legislation; covering insurance contracts and supervision.

2. Better insurance education: the public should be instructed in the elements of insurance in schools and colleges.

3. Better preventive service by insurance companies in many countries: examination of the moral hazard of applicants.

It is by no means exceptional to find low opinions about the behavior of insurers due to which, at least in times past, insurance crimes were made easy. It is recently that insurance companies have discovered what a large stake in crime prevention they have, and that, in the long run, their former attitude toward criminal behavior of the insured was rather costly to the company itself.

The man in the street needs much more knowledge of the value of insurance to the community. Especially in a democracy everyone must have such knowledge. The common men make the laws.

ALFRED MANES
Professor of Economics and Insurance
Bradley University
Peoria, Illinois

BIBLIOGRAPHY

MacDonald, J. C. R., *Crime Is A Business,* Stanford University Press, 1940.

Manes, Alfred, Insurance Crimes, *Journal of Criminal Law*, Chicago, 1944.

Monaghan, Robert, Fake-Claim Racket, *Forum Magazine,* February, 1940, 87–91.

Sutherland, Edwin H., Crime and Business, *Annals of the American Academy of Political and Social Science,* September, 1941, 112–118.

INTELLIGENCE QUOTIENT OR I.Q.

This is the index of relative intellectual brightness or rate of mental development and is obtained as a result of administering a standardized test of intelligence to the individual. In the Binet type of intelligence tests, such as the Revised Stanford-Binet Scale, the I.Q. is calculated by dividing the *mental age* by the chronological age and multiplying by 100. The resultant index or number can then be interpreted as follows:

I. Q.	Descriptive term
above 150	near genius or genius
130-149	very superior
115-129	superior
85-114	average
70- 84	dull
60- 69	borderline deficiency
below 60	feebleminded

In adult scales of intelligence, such as the Wechsler-Bellevue Adult Intelligence Scale, the I.Q. is derived from the weighted scores by looking it up in the tables which have been worked out by the authors for different age groups. The subject is thus compared with his own age group rather than with children of 16, and the I.Q. has a somewhat different meaning from that of a Binet I.Q. The Wechsler-Bellevue I.Q.'s are classified as follows:

I.Q.	Desctrive term
128 and over	very superior
120-127	superior
111-119	bright normal
91-110	average
80- 90	dull normal
66- 79	borderline
65 and below	mental defective

The *intelligence quotient* or I.Q. is used frequently for the purpose of classifying offenders according to intellectual capacity in courts, classification clinics, prisons, reformatories, penal and correctional institutions, etc. It is taken into consideration by judges before sentencing, commitment as a mentally defective delinquent and to aid in the determination of moral and legal responsibility or culpability. The I.Q. is also used in prisons of all types to decide upon assignment of the inmate for educational and vocational training, his suitability for parole, his possibilities for rehabilitation, and his job placement in the institution. Recommitment of offenders under the law pertaining to defective delinquents may also be based in part on the subject's I.Q.

BIBLIOGRAPHY

Doll, E. A., The Comparative Intelligence of Prisoners, *Journal of Criminal Law and Criminology,* 191–197, August, 1920.

Terman, L. M., *The Measurement of Intelligence.* Houghton Mifflin Co., 1916.

Terman, L. M. and Merrill, M. A., *Measuring Intelligence,* Houghton Mifflin Co., 1937.

Tulchin, S. H., *Intelligence and Crime.* University of Chicago Press, 1939.

Wechsler, D., *The Measurement of Adult Intelligence,* Williams and Wilkins Co., 1944.

J

JURY SYSTEM. The jury connotes a system of jurisprudence a) in which a body of men is entrusted by law with the duty of determining for the courts disputed questions of fact; and b) in which questions of law in proceedings before the courts are to be determined, for the most part, by the presiding judge. Those who constitute a jury are to be laymen "summoned and sworn to ascertain, under the guidance of a judge, the truth, as to questions of fact raised in legal proceedings whether civil or criminal." Jurors are sworn to render a verdict consistent with the law and the evidence presented to them, that is, they must accept the law as it is laid down for them by the judge, but they may determine the facts as they deem proper. In other words, the jury is a judicial procedure designed to secure the judgment of peers with respect to the guilt or innocence of crime or to equity in contested claims.

ORIGIN OF THE JURY SYSTEM. Many theories have been advanced with respect to the origin of the jury system. Some writers hold that it descended from the Anglo-Saxon doomsmen who "found the judgment and declared the law and the custom in the communal courts" of their day. Others believe that it originated with the Anglo-Saxon compurgators. Still others have attributed it to that legal genius, Alfred the Great. Certain writers maintain that the jury was derived from Celtic tradition based on Roman law and adopted by the Anglo-Saxons and the Normans from the peoples they conquered. Some are convinced that the Norsemen brought it to England from Scandinavia; others that it came from Asia by crusaders. Some contend that it was derived from intercourse with the Danes; others that it was indigenous to England. It is prob-

able, of course, that forms of trial resembling the jury system of England are to be found in the earlier institutions of many peoples.

The most acceptable theory, however, appears to be that of Brunner whose researches traced the origin of the jury back to the early ninth century (829) when the Frankish Emperor Louis the Pious, the son and successor to Charlemagne, ordered that "for the the future the royal rights shall not be ascertained through the production of witnesses but by the sworn statement of the best and most creditable people of the district." In this earlier form the jury was "a body of neighbors summoned by some public officer to give upon oath a true answer to some question." (Maitland). As such it was effectively used by the Norman rulers of England as an administrative device to obtain from an unwilling people information desired by the government in determining its rights and prerogatives, especially in fiscal matters. This procedure was early designated as a system of "recognition by sworn inquest." The Norman rulers, more than the native overlords, were obliged to rely upon such "recogniters" to secure a clear and truthful account of disputed points.

This "recognition by sworn inquest" is probably "only another form of the same principle which shows itself in the compurgators, in the frank pledge, and in every detail of the action of popular courts before the Conquest." Its use may have "fostered the growth of those native germs common to England with the other countries out of which juries grew." This inquest of office was employed by the king's magistrates "to ascertain facts in the interests of the crown or the exchequer" in such matters as revenue due the king, disturbances of the king's peace, and relations with ecclesiastical bodies. To determine these interests, selected men of the community were placed under oath by the royal officers and an inquiry into the matter under dispute was held. This, however, was not a judicial process.

In his *Norman Institutions* Haskins presents evidence to show that this device was carried into Normandy from the Carolingians. From thence it was brought to England by William the Conqueror who used the inquest to obtain information concerning tax returns due the king. This information was recorded in the Domesday Book. For a time the inquisition was entirely a royal prerogative, but Henry I occasionally conferred the privilege of trial by inquisition upon powerful lords or favored church groups. He also sent his representatives about the country regularly "to hear complaints against those who had violated the king's peace." Because of the impartiality of the king's magistrates the people came to prefer their procedures to those of the local courts "where both the accused and the accuser could count on friendships." So effective was this means of establishing proof that soon private persons frequently sought "as a favor from the duke or king the privilege of having their rights ascertained by means of inquisition," as the procedure was then designated.

With the Assize of Clarendon (1166) Henry II decreed that "in case of a dispute over land, instead of a trial by battle, an inquest of neighbors acquainted with the facts in the dispute should be held." The use of such an inquest in disputes arising from violations of the king's peace followed naturally. Here, it is obvious, are found the roots of the grand jury. When Innocent III forbade participation of the clergy in trials by ordeal (1215) it became necessary to set up some other method of trial to determine the facts. Henry III recognized the decree of Innocent III and "advised" his justices who travelled about from county to county representing the king to instruct the sheriff to select a number of members of the several inquests (grand juries) to return a verdict for the accused." Thus the trial jury developed out of the grand jury.

The twelve men who were thus selected as members of the trial jury, in fact, also sat on the indicting jury. In 1352 a statute was passed which permitted the accused to challenge the jury on this ground. This led to a more precise definition of the role of witnesses as contrasted with that of jurors, and clearer delineation of the functions of the trial jury as distinct from those of the grand jury.

At first, trial by jury was optional. At least the accused had to consent to the trial. The only alternative was to keep the accused in jail and to pile iron weights on him until he consented to trial by jury or until he died. Many chose to die rather than forfeit their their lands and possessions to the king.

In his writ of Justice in Eyre (1219) Henry III had also advised his justices that, in their trial of disputed matters they were to be "guided by suspicion," that is, "to reach their conclusions as to the reasonableness of that suspicion solely from their own discretion." Apparently this meant that the justices were to experiment as they saw fit and gradually feel their way to a solution. But even before 1219 "cases are to be found of presentment juries giving what has been called 'medical judgment', that is to say, declaring what ordeal ought to be assigned, or sometimes giving a verdict upon the issue of whether an appeal was brought maliciously out of hate or spite."

The next step was easily taken when it was realized, after years of indecision, that "if a jury could by its verdict declare that an appeal was brought maliciously, there was no valid reason why it should not answer the straight question as to whether the person was innocent or guilty." Thereafter judges sometimes used no jurors at all or they might use as many as 84. These larger numbers were not assembled as a body but were "examined unit by unit." From the numerous verdicts thus secured judges rendered final decisions. Judges sometimes acted in a high-handed manner so that the jury trial virtually became another kind of ordeal.

In 1275 the Crown imposed jury trial by sheer force in all cases where felons were accused. In its earliest form the jury was composed of witnesses to the transaction out of which the controversy arose. The separation of the functions of witnesses from those of the jurors gradually developed during the century which followed. By 1352 it was possible for the jurors to be challenged; attempts were thus made to secure impartial jurors. During the next 100 years "the jury evolved into a body of neutral men who heard evidence in open court by witnesses under oath and then returned a verdict. The jury had now assumed its function as a judge of facts." As a consequence of experience during fifteenth and sixteenth centuries with corruption, juries came to be protected against all outside and improper influence. In the eighteenth century it became necessary to limit the independence of the jury by giving the judge power to set aside its verdict as being contrary to the weight of evidence.

In its beginnings the jury was often employed as a drastic means of compelling people selected by the government to testify under oath to royal rights and prerogatives. In the course of a thousand years this effective administrative device became an essential part of the judicial system. By adding to its representative character and preserving the integrity of its impartiality it "grew into a cherished safeguard of liberty." In fact the right of accused persons to trial by jury came to be regarded as "a constitutional bulwark of the public against the executive," and as one of the fundamental and inalienable rights of man under free government. As such the jury system was brought to America where it became a wall of legal defense protecting the rights of the individual.

The Juries. The Grand Jury is a body of men, varying from 12 to 23 in number, designated by the court to consider bills of indictment and to inquire as to serious violations of law. Its origin has been traced to the Articles of Visitation (1194) which established the rights of a private accuser to appeal. The inquest provided for was neither of accusers nor of witnesses but of persons who "gave voice to the public repute as to the criminality of the persons whom they represented." Both the grand jury of presentment or accusation and the coroner's jury developed from this form of inquest. The grand jury is usually selected by the court,

sometimes by the sheriff. The coroner has become an elected official.

From testimony given under oath by witnesses called in support of the indictment the Grand Jury "ascertains whether the suspicion of guilt is warranted and the evidence sufficient to bring accused persons to trial." Since it is not concerned with defense but with inquiry with respect to violations of the law, it does not hear the accused or his witnesses. Neither does it usually hear counsel for the prosecution; its primary function is to determine "whether there is a *prima facie* case against the accused justifying his trial." In so doing the grand jury in fact exercises a sort of veto in criminal prosecution since persons may not be tried for treason or felony without an indictment of the grand jury. It may also intervene in cases of misdemeanor. For the most part the grand jury operates with closed sessions. When it hands down an indictment the case must then go before a petty jury in open court.

In the United States, however, the information of the prosecutor is increasingly substituted for the indictment of a grand jury. Such substitution decreases the expense and the delays involved in jury procedures. It also speeds up the judicial process so that those innocently accused will not be held in jail or under bail for so long a period. Moreover, it has been found that the information of the prosecutor is likely to be as accurate and as adequate as the indictment of the grand jury—at least when the accused is being held for serious criminal behavior.

The *Coroner's Jury* consists of at least 12 and not more than 23 jurors summoned by the coroner "to hold an inquest *super visum corporis* in cases of sudden or violent deaths and to fix responsibility therefor." In some states the coroner alone may hear the evidence and make his report to the proper authority, but in most states the coroner is required by law to impanel a jury, to secure evidence and to return the jury's verdict. This jury is usually composed of persons living in the vicinity where the death occurred. Testimony is taken under oath from such persons as the coroner may summon or who may voluntarily offer evidence. However, a witness may refuse to answer any questions which he may regard as incriminating.

The coroner is required by law to hold an inquest 1) if there is reasonable grounds to suspect that the deceased died a violent or unnatural death or died suddenly from some unknown cause; and 2) if the deceased died in a prison, a lunatic asylum or an inebriates' retreat, or under circumstances which leave doubt or uncertainty as to the natural cause of death. The coroner's jury is under legal obligation to view the body of the deceased, to ascertain the cause of death and to name the probable author of the crime if the death is found to be the result of violence. Unanimity is not required of a coroner's jury but 12 must concur in its verdict. Under certain circumstances, such as obvious suicide, the law does not require the coroner to impanel a jury.

In the United States the findings of a coroner's inquisition may subject the accused person to arrest, but he cannot be tried without an indictment by a grand jury. Moreover, the findings of a coroner's jury may not be used against the accused at his trial for the suspected crime. This means that the coroner's jury does not function as a court of record. Its jurisdiction is hence inferior to that of a trial court. In those states where a medical examiner has been substituted for a coroner this official investigates deaths occurring under suspicious circumstances. Such a method is being proposed in a number of states. In any case, the verdict must be recorded and transmitted to the proper court which will try the issue of innocence or guilt before a petty jury.

The *petit, petty* or *trial* jury constitutes the core of the jury system both in England and the United States. Indeed it is the piece of judicial machinery which came to be regarded as the guarantee of liberty and free government, especially among English-speaking peoples. The colonists who had most influence in setting the patterns of American institutions came to this country with a background of experience with English juries which had staunchly upheld the rights of ordinary Englishmen against arbitrary governmental action. They came also with a deep-seated distrust of the English judges

who had played a conspicuous part in the political and religious prosecutions of the period. The conduct of some of the royalist, colonial judges had reënforced their conviction of the importance of the petty jury. It was inevitable hence that all the American constitutions of the eighteenth and nineteenth centuries should provide that every person accused of crime or inequity be entitled to have the facts essential to his liability "determined by a jury."

The selection of a petty jury is the first step in the trial of the accused. Twelve persons are chosen from a larger number of eligible persons known as "the panel." An officer of the court calls up twelve such eligible persons at a time. Counsel for plaintiff and for the defendant then ask questions for the purpose of uncovering any disqualifications such as relationship to the contending parties or to the counsel. Those who fail to satisfy both parties as to qualifications are "challenged for cause" and excused from duty.

In general all citizens between the ages of 21 and 70 are eligible for jury duty unless they belong to one of the exempt classes such as business men, professional men and teachers. In the five boroughs of the City of New York, for example, the following persons are exempt from jury service by law (Chapter 202, Laws of New York): clergymen, physicians, surgeons, surgeon-dentists, pharmacists, women, attorneys, embalmers, optometrists, members of the army, navy, marine corps, national guards, naval militia; firemen, policemen, officers of vessels and licensed pilots. These exemptions must be based upon affidavits filed with the county clerk and open to public inspection. Such persons are engaged in professional service of a type requiring continuous attendance upon occupational activities. Interruption of such service by jury duty would obviously involve serious consequences. Yet these are the persons who possess superior qualifications for such service.

In different jurisdictions the rules of law governing the selection of jurors from the general population of the community vary widely. A review of the statutes of several States, however, shows some unanimity in requirements. In most States jurors must have the qualifications of any elector; they must either pay taxes, be a taxable person or be on the assessment rolls. They cannot be public officials or an employee of any city, State, of Federal government, nor have served as a juror within one year. They may not be insane, or an idiot; they must not have been convicted of a felony in any State or Federal court or of any crime involving moral turpitude. In some jurisdictions jurors must be the owners of a small amount of property, be well-informed, and able to read and write the English language understandingly.

The panel from which trial jurors are finally drawn is usually selected by lot from those known to be eligible. The sifting of the panel with reference to intelligence, freedom from prejudice, relationship, etc., is accomplished in the process of selection in open court. In both civil and criminal cases either the prosecution or the defense may challenge the entire panel on grounds of partiality, fraud or wilfull misconduct on part of the sheriff or other officers by whom the jurors were summoned. Both parties may challenge any individual juror for cause, that is, as not qualified or as not impartial. Some jurisdictions also provide that in criminal cases the prosecutor as well as the accused may challenge a limited number of those who have been found eligible without giving any reason for the challenge. Provision is also made in some States for a special or "struck" jury of persons qualified to serve in complicated and difficult cases where specialized knowledge or experience is required to determine the facts of the case.

Attendance by the panel and the jury when selected is enforced by fines. Once selected the jurors sit throughout the trial of a given cause. The absence of a single juror automatically suspends the trial; the death or withdrawal of a single juror before a verdict is reached terminates the trial. A new jury must then be selected and the trial begun anew. Members of the panel receive no compensation but jurors when once sworn in become entitled to a *per diem*, that is, a stipend fixed by law for each day of actual service.

THE JURY TRIAL. When the jury has been selected and seated the trial opens with a statement from the counsel for the plaintiff as to what he expects to prove. This is followed by the calling and examination of witnesses for the plaintiff. The counsel for the defense is then given an opportunity to cross-examine these witnesses. Next the counsel for the plaintiff may redirect or recross-examine his witnesses. Exceptions to evidence and rulings by the judge occur from time to time as the trial proceeds. Usually the examination of witnesses for the plaintiff is followed by a motion of the defendant's counsel that the judge direct a verdict for the defendant on the grounds of insufficient evidence. This motion is usually denied if the plaintiff's counsel has presented a *prima facie* case. The defendant, of course, may take an exception to the ruling. This is usually a mere matter of form.

The trial moves into its second phase when the defendant's counsel takes over to outline his client's defense to the court and the jury. Witnesses for the defense are then called and examined for evidence in support of the accused. These witnesses are cross examined by the counsel for the plaintiff with opportunity given for re-cross examination by the counsel for the defendant. The defense then moves for a dismissal of the action which is usually denied. Summaries of evidence are next presented, first by the counsel for the defense, then by the counsel for the plaintiff. The trial judge follows with a charge to the jury in which he outlines their duties and explains the law which is applicable to the case. The jury then withdraws to conduct its deliberations in secret. At common law its verdict must be unanimous; this means that its deliberations must continue until such a verdict is reached. This verdict must be announced in open court. Sentence is then imposed by the judge and the jury is discharged without delay. Motions for a new trial may follow.

Except in the Federal courts and some State courts the trial judge is not permitted to express his personal opinion with respect to the weight of the evidence presented or to the conclusions which may be properly drawn therefrom. Moreover, he may not voice his own belief in a particular witness's credibility or as to the improbability of certain alleged facts. Nor may he venture an opinion as to the guilt or innocence of the accused party. In the Federal courts and in some State courts he may do all of these. But in any case he is under obligation to make it perfectly clear to the jury that the responsibility for the final verdict devolves upon them. They need not follow his opinion nor be influenced by it.

In many States the judge is forbidden to, in any manner, indicate his own opinion. Appellate courts frequently reverse the convictions of lower courts when it appears that the judge has let the jury know that he deemed the accused party guilty. Moreover if the counsel either for the defense or the prosecution finds that the judge has omitted to charge the jury on some pertinent point they may request him to do so. If the judge refuses to change the charge in compliance with the request sufficient grounds are furnished for either the reversal of a subsequent judgment against the client, or for a new trial. In the case of Hicks vs. U.S. (2 Oklahoma Cr. R 626) it was inequivocally stated that "trial courts cannot be too careful and guarded in their efforts to avoid allowing juries to discover the opinion of the judge as to the weight of evidence and the credibility of witnesses."

The trial judge does, however, have the power to set aside the verdict of the jury if it is manifestly contrary to the weight of evidence. He may also set aside the verdict for obvious prejudice toward the party against whom the verdict is rendered, or for bribery and other irregular or corrupt practices. In such instances it is not sufficient that his own opinion differs from that of the jury. "He must believe that reasonable men could not fairly have deduced guilt from the evidence presented." "When the jury's verdict is favorable to the accused, however, the judge cannot set it aside no matter how unreasonable or inaccurate it may be." With these exceptions the verdict of the jury is conclusive. Only when it is clear that the verdict has been induced by fraud on the part of the defendant can the judge override an acquittal and order a new trial.

EVALUATION OF THE JURY SYSTEM.

In earlier years the jury system was not only greatly favored, but much effort was made to protect it, especially from the control of the judge. At present the trial courts, both civil and criminal, are widely criticized and at times bitterly attacked. Perhaps this is inevitable in any system in which the people at large participate to a considerable degree. At any rate so much dissatisfaction has been expressed that equity cases are now rather commonly heard by a court without a jury. Only actions at law in superior courts and serious criminal cases are still given a jury trial. The jury is now rarely employed in probate or surrogate courts. "Even in common law courts proper, all questions of law and many questions of fact are decided by the court without the jury."

Limitation of the common law powers of a trial judge is the most characteristic feature of the development of the jury trial in America. As noted above their English experience with royal judges had developed in the American colonists a hearty distrust of the trial judge. So, when English legal institutions were adopted in other respects, the colonists departed radically from the English model in respect to the powers of trial judges. It is significant, however, that similar restrictions have not been placed upon equity judges or the judges of appellate courts. As a matter of fact, appellate judges have these powers and others with respect to legislation which other judges may not exercise. But the common law powers of the trial judges have been so greatly curtailed in the United States that they no longer possess the authority necessary to the effective administration of justice (Pound).

The jury's loss of prestige in civil cases and the increasing resort to the judge in matters formerly handled by the jury is symptomatic of fundamental social change. Formerly greatly popular and increasingly powerful, today the jury system is being modified or restricted on every hand or it is "becoming disused." Waiver of jury trial and reference of cases to referees or arbitrators is increasingly common. In England the jury trial in civil cases is almost obsolete. In the United States it is infrequently used unless it is expressly demanded. In some of the latter instances the party concerned is often required to advance a part of the expenses involved. Finally, the growth of administrative tribunals and the development of elaborate machinery for commercial arbitration indicate further a growing distrust of civil juries and the development of devices for avoiding them.

The continuous tinkering with the jury system, especially of the sort which provides for trial without a judge if both the defendant and the prosecution are willing, indicates, Pound believes, a moribund institution. The civil jury was an effective tribunal in earlier rural society where the jurors knew the litigants and the property involved in the controversy. But in the urban community the juror is seldom acquainted with his neighbors whose interests and activities, as well as his, are greatly specialized. More significantly however the civil jury is excessively expensive. "It wastes the time of jurors, parties and witnesses beyond what is justified by any advantage it may have . . . If for no other reason, the expense of the civil jury as a tribunal for ordinary controversies is likely to make it obsolete in the economic order of tomorrow."

Both in England and the United States the jury is still generally employed in criminal causes of a serious nature. Less specialized knowledge is required to determine the facts of crime than the facts of equity. Yet the functioning of the jury has been vigorously attacked in criminal, as well as in civil, cases. The employment of a trial jury in criminal cases is fully as, if not more expensive than, its use in civil litigation, but in addition it is condemned for other grave weaknesses, namely, 1) that qualified persons generally either escape or avoid jury duty; 2) that as a result jurors are, for the most part, incompetent for the service which they are to render; 3) that jurors are too sympathetic to render impartial decisions; and 4) that jurors are no match for the skillful attorneys employed in most litigation.

The intent of the statutes providing for exemptions from jury duty is not, of course, to exclude certain classes of intelligent citizens, but such is precisely the result. To these exemptions must be added those whom the court excuses for what are accepted as good reasons. Finally, challenges by the counsels for the prosecution and for the defense may eliminate most, if not all, of the better qualified persons remaining on the panel. Instances are reported where ninety-one days were necessary to select the jury for the case in hand; another where 9,425 persons were summoned for jury duty, 4821 of whom were examined before twelve were accepted. Such procedures not only greatly increase the costs of jury trial but they are bound to result in the selection of inferior jury personnel.

Moreover, the average citizen is usually ignorant of the law; he is unacquainted with legal procedures and frequently unaware of what is meant by legal terms freely employed by both the judge and the attorneys such as "sustained", "overruled", "reasonable doubt", "moral certainty", and "the presumption of innocence". Often jurors are unable to remember testimony let alone to analyze and evaluate it. Under such conditions, it is contended, legally naive jurors can not be expected to deal wisely with involved principles or with technicalities of the law, especially with respect to evidence. Such jurors as are eventually selected are further bewildered by the legal game which is played in the court room by lawyers who hold to "the sporting theory of justice." Of the 5541 jurors who served Cuyhoga County (Cleveland) Ohio in 1936 only 329 ranked as Grade A and 897 as Grade B jurors under the classification of the Jury Commission of that county.

Finally, it is claimed that the juror is at great disadvantage because court-wise lawyers are adept at confusing and beclouding the real issues. As one judge has put it "it is downright scandalous to expose twelve well-meaning but naïve citizens to the sharp, high-powered, battle-scarred lawyers who are masters of the art of appealing to human sympathies and prejudices." The counsel in any case is partisan. As such it is legitimate, he believes, to bewilder the jurors with meaningless sophistry and meaningful innuendo. "If by chance an intelligent group of men and women are 'stuck for jury duty'," it is argued, "even then justice and truth are elusive." The naïve juror is rarely a match for the shrewd and experienced attorneys in the case.

In cases of an exceptional nature the statutes of some states permit the selection of a jury from a "blue-ribbon" panel of persons having further qualifications than those of ordinary jurors. Such special juries, it is supposed, may be relied upon to return more intelligent verdicts because the jurors have been selected from persons having special knowledge and more than average mentality. From seven to ten per cent of the cases in the Grand Sessions of New York City have been tried before such special juries. However, these juries have been found to favor the prosecution since they are persons whose sympathies are not likely to lie with the defendant.

Such being the situation, it is maintained that "intelligent and desirable jurors who are called for jury service pull every possible wire in an effort to avoid service under existing trial conditions." Indeed, it is held that such conditions offer some excuse for not calling the abler type of person for jury service. To ask busy and successful business and professional men to spend weeks "sitting in boredom" through the trial of a single case by lawyers who employ every known device for "winning the game" irrespective of the justice in case, to lock them up as if they were criminals and to deprive them of all communication with their families is to ask more than these abler citizens are prepared to give, and hence to place a premium upon escape from jury service.

Despite these criticisms of the jury system as it operates in criminal cases the proposal to abolish it is probably out of order. The jury system is deeply rooted in the American philosophy of life and law. Its elimination hence would constitute a radical operation. The principles upon which its essential structure is based are socially sound. Its pathologies arise from misuse rather than from basic faults. Notwithstanding these abuses it remains a guarantee against the political prosecutions so widely practiced in totalitarian countries. It is also a form of insurance against the irrational prosecution of minori-

ties. In criminal cases, especially of the graver type, it is probably the best, although expensive, tribunal that could be devised. "No enthusiast pretends that juries are especially competent to ascertain guilt, but only that they are not likely to convict innocence." Before so venerable a system is eliminated, hence, efforts should be made to alleviate, and possibly correct its abuses. Such efforts should increase its effectiveness.

Since many of the undesirable features of the jury system are traceable to the judge's inability to control the trial process, it has been proposed that he be given power

a) to assist in and accelerate the selection of jurors since his examination of the panel is likely to be more unbiased than that of others and to eliminate fewer of the better qualified persons;

b) to "strip the courtroom of confusing side issues, keep the language understandable and restrict the lawyers in their befuddling techniques";

c) to participate in the deliberations of the jury—at least to answer questions that may arise and to clarify issues, if not to decide upon guilt.

Such powers will afford the jurors protection against the questionable tactics of lawyers. Juries are exposed to forensic skills of partisan attorneys; they should also be exposed to "the matter-of-fact commentary of an experienced and undeluded judge."

In retaining the jury system in criminal litigation it is proposed that effort also be made to improve the qualifications of jurors. "In the long run the value of the jury system depends upon the character of the persons who serve as jurors, of the judges who preside and the lawyers who defend and prosecute." Usually the law is simple enough; justice is diverted when lawyers are permitted to torture and distort issues. Certainly it is possible to prevent favored persons, professional jurors and unqualified persons from sitting on juries charged with a sober, civic duty. More of the abler persons might accept jury duty if trials were expedited, if terms of service were fixed for a definite period (say six months), and if they were given a short, but intensive, course in legal terminology, court procedures and the obligations and functions of the jury. Such courses might well be given by neutral representatives of the bar associations, the law schools and the court.

It is likely, too, that some of the malfunctioning of juries could be avoided if verdicts could be rendered by a majority instead of a unanimous vote of the jurors. "As the law now stands a single unprejudiced, fairminded, intelligent juror can save an innocent man from undeserved conviction. But for the same reason a stupid, biased or corrupted juror can save a guilty man from a deserved conviction." Frequently, the requirement of unanimity, it is claimed, becomes "nothing less than legalized coercion." It condemns honest differences of opinion; it makes jury service disagreeable and it may actually provide an incentive for the corruption of the jurors.

Moreover, it is believed that the disservice of an unqualified jury could be avoided if provision were made for trial by a judge without a jury when both the prosecution and the defense consent. Such a procedure would also involve less expense both to the state and to the parties to the litigation. In grave situations involving capital punishment, imprisonment for life or grievous impoverishment and disgrace, a panel of three judges would relieve any single justice from the sole and heavy responsibility of the verdict. Where juries are not trained to weigh the facts, and since they are so susceptible to emotional appeals, such provisions, it is maintained, offer an assurance of a fair trial and of more effective law enforcement under a jury system with a long and a significant social history.

LLOYD V. BALLARD
Chairman, Department of Sociology
Beloit College
Beloit, Wisconsin

BIBLIOGRAPHY

Brunner, H., *Entstehung der Schwurgerichte,* Berlin, 1872.
Callender, C. N., *American Criminal Courts, Their Organization and Procedure,* N. Y., 1927.
First Tentative Draft, *Code of Criminal Procedure with Commentaries,* American Law Institute, N. Y., 1928.
Haskins, C. S., Norman Institutions, *Harvard Historical Studies,* Cambridge, 1918.
Holdsworth, W. S., *A History of English Law,* London.
Moley, R., *Our Criminal Courts,* N. Y., 1930.
Morgan, E. M., Functions of Judge and Jury in the Determination of Preliminary Questions of Fact, *Harvard Law Review* Vol. 43 (1928–29) pp. 165–91.
Plunckett, T. F. T., *A Concise History of the Common Law,* Rochester, 1936.
Pound, Roscoe, The Jury System in the *Encyclopedia of Social Sciences,* Vol. 8.
Scott, A. W., Trial by Jury and Reform of Civil Procedure, *Hard Law Review,* Vol. 31 (1917–18) pp. 669–91.

JUVENILE DELINQUENCY. The term *juvenile delinquency* applies to young offenders whose thinking is immature and who are therefore not deemed responsible for their acts. The current climate of opinion is that children and adolescents should not be stigmatized as criminals. This reasoning has led to the creation of laws, procedures and institutions for the management of young persons whose acts would be considered criminal if performed by a presumably responsible adult. *Juvenile delinquency* is not a social science concept, but essentially a legal one. The legal definition of juvenile delinquency usually includes the following features: habitual truancy from home or school; conduct that injures or endangers the morals or health of others; infraction of laws, ordinances and regulations of governmental agencies; and habitual disobedience or waywardness that is uncontrolled by parent, guardian or custodian.

Instances of juvenile delinquency are increasing, but its exact extent is not known, because many juvenile delinquents are not apprehended. The actual depredations and social damage committed by delinquent juveniles cannot be estimated with any great degree of accuracy at present. A large proportion of known adult criminals began their careers as youthful offenders. Potential criminal careers may be aborted if today's delinquents can be reformed.

Many causative factors purporting to explain juvenile delinquency have been proposed,* such as: cultural conflict that affects immigrants and city dwellers who recently arrived from rural areas; the anonymity characteristic of urban life; maladjusted parents; inadequate family supervision; inadequate housing; poverty; lack of suitable recreation; maladjustment in school; association with anti-social individuals; movies and radio programs; emulation of the unscrupulous grabbing of money by many "successful" adults; rebellion against authority; inadequate intelligence; undesirable traits and attitudes; mental illness; improper values and goals; and biological inferiority. Dr. Martha M. Eliot estimated that there are ten times as many children who are affected by the same causal factors as those that come to the attention of the juvenile courts.†

The consensus of social scientists is that no single explanation of juvenile delinquency should be expected. A young person may live in a slum, have a drunken father and be exposed to several of the factors named above and yet not become a juvenile delinquent. Monistic explanations or explanations that stress one factor more than others have been advocated by economic determinists, the ecologically minded, the psychoanalytically oriented, the biological determinists, or by members of other schools of thought; however, most social scientists do not accept the explanation provided by any single school.

Available data does not reveal any marked differences between juvenile delinquents and other young people. No significantly greater extent of feeble-mindedness, mental illness, school retardation, biological inferiority, or any other measurable factor has been scientifically demonstrated to exist among wayward youth than among other children and adolescents. No scientific evidence has been presented that reveals any harmful effects of radio programs and movies on young people. Many well adjusted individuals do not be-

* The British criminologist Burt mentions 170 causative factors related to juvenile delinquency.
† From the testimony of Dr. Martha M. Eliot of the U. S. Children's Bureau, in Hearings on S.1160 (National Mental Health Act), U. S. Senate, 79th Congress, Mar. 8, 1946.

come juvenile delinquents, despite radio programs or movies. Similar reasoning may be applied to several of the other alleged causative factors to show inherent fallacies.

Group therapy programs; cottage types of institutional arrangements; detention homes; disciplinary measures; foster home placement; special classes similar to those for the physically handicapped or the mentally retarded; case work techniques; probation; supervised leisure time programs; and child guidance clinics are procedures that are used for treating juvenile delinquents. The total effect of all treatment programs is not leading to a marked decrease in the number of delinquent juveniles, or in recidivism. Only a small proportion of these young people are affected by treatment that is deemed adequate by social workers, psychologists, educators, religious leaders and psychiatrists. Some prosperous and enlightened communities have the benefit of suitable treatment procedures; only a minority of the known juvenile delinquents are in a position to be rehabilitated by such programs. Police inefficiency or carelessness; avoidance of official agencies by families of high socio-economic status; leniency of court officials; inadequate budgetary provisions; low salary schedules and the doubtful security available for trained people; and the unascertained number of child offenders that are not apprehended are features which prevent reduction in the extent of juvenile delinquency. The number of juvenile delinquents who will become criminals is not expected to decrease to any significant extent in the near future.

Although no universally satisfactory explanation of juvenile delinquency is available, many promising treatment techniques are known, but these techniques are not applied in a sufficiently large number of instances. It is questionable if adequately trained personnel can be recruited at present for a major offensive against juvenile delinquency.

The most promising attack on the problem of juvenile delinquency is the emphasis on prevention. Comprehensive community programs; improvement of educational practices; parent education, increased use of educational facilities for after school hours;

youth club programs; special budgetary provisions; federal aid for poor communities; planning for adequate living; raising the educational status of our people; changes in our concepts of criminal behavior; enlightenment in regard to sex problems; increased concern for the young person as an individual; increased civic-mindedness as opposed to the individualism that fosters selfishness and aggressiveness, wider adoption of the Youth Correction Authority Act**; increased coordination of all relevant activities by state and federal governments; enlistment of better qualified personnel; and an increase in the number of child guidance clinics are features that have been proposed for the prevention of juvenile delinquency.

Neglected, handicapped and dependent children are considered victims of circumstances beyond their control. To no less an extent the juvenile delinquent suffers from conditions beyond his control. Segregated treatment of youthful offenders appears to offer only limited benefits. A comprehensive program for the treatment of juvenile delinquency by coordinating agencies that care for dependent, neglected and handicapped children offers promise of success.

The utilization of graduate students of sociology, psychology, guidance, education, hygiene and recreation in all prevention and treatment programs for juvenile delinquency, if properly planned and supervised, should be beneficial to the adolescents and children and to the graduate students. Pre-legal and pre-medical students may be included in such a program. Greater public enlightenment would ensue, since the students, as potential leaders of society, would eventually influence future programs. Current public apathy concerning crime prevention and related problems may be diminished as a result of hearing about these matters from graduate students. A pool of potential workers with adequate training would be created. Lack of finances that precludes the hiring of sufficient personnel in carrying out the re-

** The American Law Institute (Phila., Pa., June, 1940) recommended and proposed a model law for the commitment of offenders under 21 to specialized state agencies for individualized correctional treatment, disposition, and diagnosis.

forms necessary in the field of juvenile delinquency would be mitigated to some extent by utilization of graduate students in field work courses or the creation of internships. Institutions of higher learning may need to increase their budgets for the curricular changes that are involved. Field work courses would alleviate the current overcrowded college classes and college libraries, while students may learn facts that they tend to ignore or misunderstand in conventional educational situations. Universities and colleges may become more interested in research in juvenile delinquency and related problems. A far greater number of potential young offenders would be treated than is otherwise possible. Greater individualization of prevention and treatment could be instituted by means of the proposed plan.

GEORGE GENN
Instructor
Rutgers University
New Brunswick, New Jersey

BIBLIOGRAPHY

Abrahamsen, D., *Crime and the Human Mind,* New York: Columbia University Press, 1944.
Baylor, E. M. H. & Monachesi, E. D., *The Rehabilitation of Children,* New York: Harper & Bros., 1939.
Carr, L. J., *Delinquency Control,* New York: Harper & Bros., 1941.
Carr-Saunders, A. M., Mannheim, H. & Rhodes, E. C., *Young Offenders,* Cambridge, London: Cambridge University Press, New York: Macmillan, 1943.
Dollard, J., Doob, L. W., Miller, N. E., Mowrer, O. H. & Sears, R. R., *Frustration and Aggression,* New Haven: Yale University Press, 1939.
Glueck, S. & Glueck, E., *Criminal Careers in Retrospect,* New York: Commonwealth Fund, 1943.
Harrison, L. V. & Grant, P. M., *Youth in the Toils,* New York: Macmillan Co., 1938.
Healy, W. & Alper, B. S., *Criminal Youth and the Borstal System,* New York: Commonwealth Fund, 1941.
Hunt, J. McV. (ed.), *Personality and the Behavior Disorders,* New York: Ronald Press, 1944.
Kvaraceus, W. C., *Juvenile Delinquency and the School,* Yonkers: World Book Co., 1945.
Lesser, E. K., *Understanding Juvenile Delinquency,* Washington, D. C.: U. S. Dept. of Labor Children's Bureau Publications, No. 300, 1943.

Levy, R. J., *Reductions in Recidivism Through Therapy*, New York: Thomas Seltzer, 1941.

Lewin, K. et al., *Authority and Frustration*, University of Iowa: University of Iowa Studies in Child Welfare, 1944.

Lewis, N. D. C. & Pacella, B. L. (eds.), *Modern Trends in Child Psychiatry*, New York: International University Press, 1945.

Merrill, Maud A., *Child Delinquency*, Boston: Houghton-Mifflin Co., 1947.

Osborne Association, *Handbook of American Institutions for Delinquent Juveniles.*

Reckless, W. C., *The Etiology of Delinquent and Criminal Behavior: A Planning Report for Research*, New York: Social Science Research Council, 1943.

Seliger, R. W., Lukas, E. J. & Lindner, R. M., (eds.), *Contemporary Criminal Hygiene*, Baltimore: Oakridge Press, 1946.

Shaw, C. R., McKay, H. D. et al., *Juvenile Delinquency and Urban Areas*, Chicago: University of Chicago Press, 1942.

Slavson, S. R., *An Introduction to Group Therapy*, New York: The Commonwealth Fund, 1943.

Sutherland, E. H., *Principles of Criminology* (revised), Fourth Edition, Chicago: J. B. Lippincott Co., 1947.

Thrasher, F. M., *The Gang*, Chicago: University of Chicago Press, 1927.

Thurston, H. W., *Concerning Juvenile Delinquency: Progressive Changes in Our Perspectives*, New York: Columbia University Press, 1942.

Tulchin, S. H., *Intelligence and Crime*, Chicago: University of Chicago Press, 1939.

Young, P. V., *Social Treatment in Probation and Delinquency*, New York: McGraw-Hill, 1937.

K

KIDNAPPING. A person who wilfully:

1. Seizes, confines, inveigles, or kidnaps another, with intent to cause him, without authority of law, to be confined or imprisoned, or in any way held to service or kept or detained, against his will; or,

2. Leads, takes, entices away, or detains a child under the age of sixteen years, with intent to keep or conceal it from its parents, guardian, or other person having the lawful care or control thereof, or to extort or obtain money or reward for the return or disposition of the child, or with intent to steal any article about or on the person of the child; or,

3. Abducts, entices, or by force or fraud unlawfully takes, or carries away another, at or from a place without the state, or procures, advises, aids or abets such an abduction,

Is guilty of *kidnapping,* which is a felony, and is punishable, if a parent of the person kidnapped, by imprisonment for not more than ten years and, if a person other than a parent of the person kidnapped, by death. The jury can, however, recommend imprisonment in lieu of death. (Penal Law of New York State)

Kidnapping is a legal entity which is not a sociological entity, according to Sutherland. As a legal entity kidnapping consists of taking possession of the body of another person, against his will, by force or fraud and in violation of the law. Kidnapping appears in at least ten forms which are socially distinct and which generally involve different causal processes:

1. Kidnapping was the basis of the slave trade; and all those who participated in the slave trade and in slavery were accessory to kidnapping.

2. *Impressment* was a form of kidnapping in which a sailor was forced to leave a ship in which he had a legal right to be, to board another ship and work there as a sailor.

3. Sailors were shanghaied by force and compelled to work as sailors in ships.

4. Girls were kidnapped and used for prostitution. This aroused attention in the period before World War I under the name of *white slavery.*

5. Underworld leaders were kidnapped by underworld criminals and held for ransom, especially during the prohibition period.

6. Kidnapping of wealthy persons in the upper world by members of the underworld for purposes of *ransom* developed extensively about 1930.

7. Offenders took possession of victims in connection with other crimes, such as robbery, as a means of security for themselves.

8. *Illegal arrest* is a form of kidnapping.

9. Children have been kidnapped by lonesome and probably psychopathic women in lieu of other methods of securing children of their own.

10. A parent has kidnapped his own children who have been assigned by the court to the other parent.

These ten forms are somewhat interrelated but their objectives are different. The first six types mentioned (slave trade, impressment. shanghaing, white slavery, underworld ransom cases, and upperworld ransom cases) all aim at financial returns while the last four do not.

BIBLIOGRAPHY

Gilbert, F. B., *Criminal Law and Practice of the State of New York,* Matthew Bender and Co., 1935.
Sullivan, E. D., *The Snatch Racket,* New York, 1932.
Sutherland, E. H., *Principles of Criminology,* J. B. Lippincott Co., 1939.

[217]

L

LARCENY. This is the most common gainful offense against property and may be defined as the unlawful taking and carrying away of personal goods or real property with intent to deprive the rightful owner of the same. It is commonly referred to as *theft* or *stealing*. To constitute larceny there must be a taking without the owner's consent. However, a crime may be committed under certain circumstances, where consent is actually given by the owner. The taking away must be unlawful or felonious. Every part of the property stolen must be removed, however slightly, from its former position and it must be, at least momentarily, in the complete possession of the thief. Ownership must be proven by reasonable identification and, in addition, the stolen property must have a market value.

The Penal Law of New York State states that, "A person who, with the intent to deprive or defraud the true owner of his property:

1. Takes from the possession of the true owner, or of any other person; or obtains from such possession by color or aid of fraudulent or false representation or pretense, or of any false token or writing; or secretes, withholds, or appropriates to his own use, or that of any other person other than the true owner, any money, personal property, thing in action, evidence of debt or contract, or article of value of any kind; or,

2. Having in his possession, custody, or control, as a bailee, servant, attorney, agent, clerk, etc., or as a person authorized by agreement, or by competent authority, to hold or take such possession, or control, any money, property, article of value of any nature, etc., appropriates the same to his own use, or that of any other person other than

the true owner or person entitled to the benefit thereof,

Steals such property, and is guilty of larceny."

The crime of larceny is usually divided into *petit larceny* which is a misdemeanor and *grand larceny* which is a felony on the basis of the value of the goods stolen. The line between the two grades is arbitrarily drawn and varies considerably from place to place.

Grand Larceny (Felony) may be committed in any one of the following ways:

1. By stealing any property of any value off the person of another (in this case the value is not to be considered but the taking must be actually off the person, i.e., the property must be on the person and be taken and carried away).

2. By stealing any property *valued at over $500* from any place (Grand Larceny—First Degree) or of the value of more than one hundred dollars, but not exceeding five hundred dollars (Grand Larceny—Second Degree).

3. By stealing property *valued at more than twenty-five dollars* in the *night time* from a *dwelling house, vessel* or *railway car.*

4. By stealing any public record or document filed or deposited by law with any public office or officer.

Petit Larceny (Misdemeanor) is any larceny not a grand larceny.

BIBLIOGRAPHY

Gilbert, F. B., *Criminal Law and Practice of the State of New York,* Matthew Bender and Co., 1935.
Sutherland, E. H., *The Professional Thief,* Chicago, 1937.

LIBEL. A malicious publication, by writing, printing, picture, effigy, sign or any other method than by mere speech, which exposes any living person, or the memory of any dead person, to hatred, contempt, ridicule or obloquy, or causes any person to be shunned or avoided, or which has a tendency to injure any person, corporation or association of persons, in his or their business or occupation, is *libel*. A libel by mere speech is not indictable. *Criminal intent* is a necessary element of the crime of libel. In New York State, a person who publishes a libel, is guilty of a misdemeanor.

The publication is justified when the matter charged as libelous is true, and was published with good motives and for justifiable ends. The publication is excused when it is honestly made, in the belief of its truth and upon reasonable grounds for this belief, and consists of fair comments upon the conduct of a person in respect of public affairs, or upon a thing which the proprietor thereof offers or explains to the public.

To sustain the charge of libel, it is not necessary that the matter complained of should have been seen by another. It is enough that the defendant knowingly displayed it, or parted with its immediate custody, under circumstances which exposed it to be seen or understood by another person than himself.

Every editor, or proprietor of a book, newspaper or serial, and every manager of a partnership or incorporated association, by which a book, newspaper or serial is issued, is chargeable with the publication of any matter contained in the book, newspaper or serial. But in every prosecution for libel the defendant may show in his defense that the matter complained of was published without his knowledge or fault and against his wishes, by another who had no authority from him to make the publication and whose act was disavowed by him so soon as known.

A prosecution for libel can not be maintained against a reporter, editor, publisher, or proprietor of a newspaper, for the publication of a fair and true report of any judicial, legislative or other public and official proceeding, or of any statement, speech, argument or debate in the course of the proceeding, without proving actual malice in making the report.

Privileged Communications. A communication made to a person entitled to, or interested in, the communication, by one who was also interested in or entitled to make it, is presumed not to be malicious and is called a privileged communication.

A person who threatens another with the publication of a libel, concerning the latter or his parent, spouse, child, or other relative, and a person who offers to prevent the publication of a libel for a valuable consideration, is guilty of a misdemeanor. Furnishing another with libelous information or with false information or the circulating of false statements concerning the financial responsibility of any person or firm, are all punishable as misdemeanors.

BIBLIOGRAPHY

Gilbert, F. B., *Criminal Law and Practice of the State of New York,* M. Bender & Co., 1935.

LOTTERIES. A *lottery* may be defined as a scheme for the distribution of property by chance, among persons who have paid or agreed to pay a valuable consideration for the chance, whether called a lottery, raffle, or gift enterprise or by some other name (New York State Penal Law). A lottery, as defined above, is unlawful in New York and many other jurisdictions. It is also made a public nuisance by statute.

A person who contrives, proposes or draws a lottery, or assists in so doing, is punishable by imprisonment for not more than two years, or by fine of not more than one thousand dollars or both (New York). Sellers or furnishers of lottery tickets are guilty of a misdemeanor. Advertising or publicizing a lottery in any way is also a misdemeanor. Offering property for disposal dependent upon the drawing of any lottery, keeping a lottery office, insuring lottery tickets or advertising to insure lottery tickets are all misdemeanors. Property offered for disposal in lotteries is forfeited. Money paid for lottery tickets may be recovered by legal action and prizes won in lotteries are forfeited. Also, any transfers of property made in pursuance of a lottery or contracts, agreements, and securities given on account of raffling, are **void.**

Lotteries

What constitutes a lottery has been subject to much litigation and consequent clarification by the courts. Thus, racing horses for stakes is not a lottery but is gambling. Playing *policy* is a lottery. The sale of "prize candy" in boxes, each box represented to contain a prize of money or jewelry, and the purchaser selecting his box in ignorance of its contents, was held by the courts to be a lottery.

BIBLIOGRAPHY

Gilbert, F. B., *Criminal Law and Practice of the State of New York*, M. Bender & Co., 1935.

M

MAIMING. A person who wilfully, with intent to commit a felony, or to disfigure, injure or disable, inflicts an injury upon the person of another which: (1) seriously disfigures him; or, (2) destroys or disables any member or organ of his body; or, (3) seriously diminishes his physical vigor by the injury of any member or organ, is guilty of *maiming* and is punishable by imprisonment for a term not exceeding fifteen years. The infliction of the injury is presumptive evidence of the intent. It is immaterial by what means or instrument, or in what manner, the injury was inflicted.

Maiming one's self to escape the performance of a legal duty or to excite sympathy or obtain alms and charitable relief, is a felony. (Penal Law of State of New York)

Where the injured person subsequently recovers so that he is no longer disfigured by the injury or disabled by it, the offender cannot be convicted for maiming but may be convicted of *assault* in any degree.

BIBLIOGRAPHY

Gilbert, F. B., *Criminal Law and Practice of the State of New York*, M. Bender & Co., 1935.

MATURATION. The concept of personal responsibility has been a major problem during the entire history of jurisprudence. For some centuries it has been recognized that legal and moral responsibility are functions of the mental capacity and mental soundness of the offender. Imbecility and insanity have long been recognized as conditions affecting legal responsibility, and more recently the moron degree of mental deficiency has been included among these and other forms of mental and social incompetence (see Mental Deficiency). The advent of psychological measurement in this field has shed new light on these considerations so that today the determination of mental and social competence are recognized functions of expert court witnesses.

Psychological appraisal of personal responsibility began about fifty years ago with the work of J. McKeen Cattell on the measurement of individual differences. This work was of chiefly academic interest from 1890 to 1910 during a period when the substantial foundations of the present techniques of mental measurement were being laid. The work of Binet in 1905 afforded the first satisfactory method of measuring intelligence and produced the popular concept of mental age as a ready means of mental test interpretation. Following the first World War extensive improvements have been accomplished in the measurement of intelligence so that today this area of applied psychology is substantially sound.

This interest in the measurement of intelligence has gradually promoted concern for other aspects of individuality related to total individual competence. Among these the measurement of personality is experiencing current expansion. These two major aspects of the person as a socially behaving organism are of the utmost importance in relation to legal and moral responsibility.

The fundamental problem, however, is not so much that of mental competence *per se* as it is of the social competence which results from these preconditions. The direct measurement of social competence independently of its intellectual and temperamental prerequisites has excited attention only recently. During the past ten years successful work in this direction has been accomplished through the formulation of the Vineland Social Maturity Scale which provides a practical instrument for the direct measurement of social competence in terms of its developmental maturation.

Personal responsibility as expressed in terms of social competence matures in bio-genetic parallelism throughout the developmental period of individual growth and declines correlatively with senescent involution. It expresses itself in individual differences throughout the developmental period as well as during the period of prime and senescence. Variation from the normal is evident as a result of mental deficiency, insanity, and other mental and physical abnormalities, and the effect of these conditions upon social competence can now be estimated by considering the specific influences which accelerate, retard or disturb the expression of social competence.

The Vineland Social Maturity Scale is designed as a direct measure of overt social responsibility, independence, and initiative. Successive levels of performance in terms of maturation and decline are measurable through consideration of the various component categories of social behavior. These categories as presented in the Vineland Scale include self-help, self-direction, occupation, communication, locomotion, and socialization. Social competence matures in each of these categorical aspects of self-expression through a variety of stages which more or less sharply distinguish one age level from another.

The scale consists of one hundred seventeen items which reflect progressive stages of social performance from birth to the prime of life, and these items may be used as well for the measurement of abnormal deviation due to mental or physical disturbances, or to the decline in social competence which may accompany senescence. These various items are expressed in homely terms and have been normatively standardized on representative children and adults from birth to thirty years of age. The items are organized in the form of a year-scale similar to the Binet scale for measuring intelligence so that the obtained scores may be expressed in terms of social ages comparable to mental ages. These in turn may be converted to social quotients which are comparable to intelli-

gence quotients. Since intelligence is the principal determinant of social competence, the concomitant measurement of each is essential for an understanding of social maturity, and consequently of social responsibility.

The items of the scale are designed to represent the habitual or customary performances of normal children and adults as detailed stages of maturation in respect to the categories which compose the scale. Information regarding the characteristic success of the individual under examination in satisfying these evolutional stages of social behavior is obtained by interviewing someone who knows the person intimately or by interviewing the person himself as his own informant. Although the former method of examination is preferable and was used as the standardization procedure, the latter method has been successfully employed. The essential information is obtained by skillful interview which permits recording the individual's habitual performance as satisfactory or unsatisfactory in respect to the normative items. In the course of such interviewing some accessory information is obtained which enables the examiner to interpret success or failure in terms of limiting circumstances such as restricted environmental opportunity or mental or physical handicaps.

Extensive investigation has confirmed the practicability of this method of measuring social competence. Not only has the scale been standardized on normal subjects, but growth studies over a period of years have been made by reexamining the same normal subjects, thus not only confirming the standardization, but also yielding scientific evidence on the timing and direction of individual social maturation. Effective results have also been obtained from applying the scale with such handicapped groups as the deaf, the blind, the insane, the feeble-minded, and so on.

Such studies reveal the extent to which social competence is influenced by limiting or stimulating influences. Thus, deafness imposes a limitation of approximately twenty per cent on normal social maturation, whereas the effect of blindness is about thirty per cent. Untrustworthiness and misconduct may be viewed as specific limiting influences, the effect of which depends on the nature and severity of the conditions encountered.

The scale has been used in preliminary studies of delinquents and young adult offenders with illuminating results. In the case of juvenile delinquency, one such study has revealed that the social incompetence of juvenile delinquents, parallels their mental capabilities, and this was found also, although at somewhat higher levels, for young adult offenders. The social scale in these respects has, however, certain advantages over the mental scales since it deals directly with behavior and only secondarily with its causes or preconditions. The measurement of social maturity has the further advantage of encompassing a larger view of the whole offender since it considers social competence in terms of the capitalization of social experience in relation to all his aptitudes and opportunities. Thus the scale reveals the significance of personality deviation in terms of its social outcomes as it does also for intellectual deviation, response to schooling, occupational attainments, initiative and judgment, and assumption of personal responsibility.

The Vineland Scale has further uses as a therapeutic instrument as has been demonstrated in a study of youthful offenders under institutional care. As a treatment procedure it is comparable to the biographical method of personal analysis which has had such significant development in recent years. By employing the offender as his own informant in the social maturity examination, the individual can be encouraged to systematically review his present aptitudes, and their antecedent circumstances. Likewise the scale suggests normative standards of social attainment to which the offender can aspire, or in respect to which his own shortcomings can be made analytically clear.

The primary interest in the scientific study of offenders is directed toward an understanding of the individual offender for purposes of determining his personal responsibility and the extent to which he should suffer the consequences of his acts. But scientific study affords as well a means of classification for the treatment and disposition of offenders and for the estimation of the outcome of such treatment with reference to readiness for parole or social readjustment. Since the Social Maturity Scale measures social competence as the composite end-result of inherent characteristics in relation to environmental opportunities, it provides a direct means for measuring the progress in social rehabilitation which may take place under conditions of correctional therapy.

It is possible then by this means to examine the individual as to his present and past performances, and to evaluate such evidence predictively and therapeutically with reference to their bearing on his probable future social success. Hence the measurement of social maturity, at least by means of the Vineland Scale, makes possible more accurate prediction of readiness for parole as well as preparation for it. This is not to say that other methods of examination should be discarded in favor of the measurement of social maturity alone, but rather that the direct measurement of social maturity reveals the social attainments, both actual and potential, ensuing from the constitutional aptitudes revealed by other systems of personality measurement. Such evidence might well be used in support of pleas in mitigation.

EDGAR A. DOLL
Director of Research
The Training School
Vineland, New Jersey

BIBLIOGRAPHY

Doll, E. A., Annotated Bibliography on the Vineland Social Maturity Scale, *Journal of Consulting Psychology*, 4:123–132, July-August, 1940.
Doll, E. A., The Vineland Social Maturity Scale: Revised Condensed Manual of Directions, *Publication of The Training School at Vineland, New Jersey, Department of Research*, Series 1936; No. 3, April, 1936.
Doll, E. A., and Brooks, J. J., The Therapeutic Uses of The Vineland Social Maturity Scale in its Application to Adult Prisoners, *Journal of Criminal Psychopathology*, 3:347–358, January, 1942.
Doll, E. A. and Fitch, K. A., Social Competence of Juvenile Delinquents, *Journal of Criminal Law and Criminology*, 30:52–67, May-June, 1939.

MEDICAL SERVICE IN PRISONS. A complete medical service should embrace sanitary supervision of the entire prison, including its water, milk and food supply, primary physical examinations of all newly arriving prisoners, frequent secondary examinations, the services of good laboratories, an adequately equipped and staffed hospital, the employment of women nurses, a good working library, a consultant staff in all the specialties, provisions for autopsies, and an adequate system of records and filing.

With the above assumptions in mind certain psychiatric aspects of the medical service will be stressed not only as they apply to the prisoner himself, but also to the medical staff and other departments of the prison with which it must cooperate if it functions successfully.

A man behind the walls has the same alimentary tract, the same genito-urinary system, the same nose and throat, the same eyes, and the same brain and spinal cord as the man who is on the outside. Therefore, it would seem that medical service in prisons would have nothing essentially different about it from medical service in the general population. This is true, in the sense that the medical service in prisons should be equipped to render whatever is needed in taking care of whatever may happen to the prisoner's body, calling for medical or surgical treatment.

But when it comes to the mind—the influence of mental states over bodily complaints, and *vice versa*—we have an entirely different situation to confront. Even in the best of prisons the inmates, whether male or female are entirely wrapped up in the idea of getting out of prison as soon as possible. Every pain and ache they have, every mental upset, even their constipation and their diarrhoea, is either consciously or subconsciously tinctured with the longing to be free.

Thus, it happens that the medical staff must be thoroughly imbued with the idea that the mental aspects of physical complaints of the prisoners should be given the greatest possible consideration.

Gastric ulcers in male prisoners, ovarian and uterine complaints in women prisoners are cited as examples which need psychiatric consultation before they are turned over to the tender mercies of the surgeon.

Other examples could be cited, but these suffice to illustrate the general principle that the practice of medicine in prisons calls for special care to prevent unnecessary operations and unnecessary attention to such things as "gastric ulcers", "chronic constipation", "headaches", "eye strain", and a host of other psycho-somatic complaints that fill the daily routine of the physician in private practice and clutter up the daily sick line in prison.

The sick line in prison seems to be a necessary evil. Many have tried to dispense with it and allow the prisoner to have access to the doctor in precisely the same way he has on the outside. But we have found this impossible, because such free access for trivial complaints at any time of the day the prisoner chooses would seriously interfere with work details and custodial supervision. But we have found that the "sick line" can be made to serve a useful and constructive purpose, provided, we adhere to certain fixed rules for its operation.

After a careful study in 1937 of the uses and abuses of the "sick line", which at that time was held daily at the U. S. Penitentiary at Leavenworth, Kansas, the Psychologist, G. S. MacVaugh and J. G. Wilson came to the following conclusions:

The daily "sick call' in prison is the time when any prisoner has the right to visit the physician's office without seeking special permission from the custodial force. All he needs to do is to proceed to the designated place when the bugle blows the "sick call". The presumption is that he is sick, or, if not actually sick or disabled, at least in need of medical advice.

The "sick call", sometimes called the "sick line", is an invention of prison physicians to take care of the routine medical needs of large prison populations as expeditiously as possible. In one form or other it combines the functions of the drug store and family physician. The constipated patient, who needs, or thinks he needs, a purgative, "hits the sick line" and asks for laxative number so and so on the pharmaceutical list, in the same nonchalant way that the citizen outside the walls goes to the drug store for Sal Hepatica or Ex-Lax. If the prisoner has a headache he asks for an aspirin. If he has corns he seeks a corn plaster or the doctor's authority to obtain special shoes instead of the regular stock issue. For trivial ailments he seeks to pre-scribe for himself like the average citizen outside the walls. In some prisons the "sick line" is presided over by an inmate who hands out simple remedies as does the average drug clerk and refers only those to the doctor who insist on seeing him. This last procedure is not allowed in any Federal prison. There, one or more of the U. S. Public Health Service physicians on the med-ical staff "hold the sick line", and actually see every patient and assume every respon-sibility for his treatment, even though it be simply to grant him permission to prescribe for himself.

There are many objections to this whole-sale and necessarily rapid method of treat-ing ailments of any description. The greatest single abuse which may arise from the prac-tice is oversight of serious complaints. This danger is reduced to a minimum by putting aside all doubtful cases for a more intensive examination after the regular sick line is over and by admitting the obviously ill to the hospital for further study and treatment. On the other hand, almost every kind of prison sick line technique yet invented en-courages attendance at this function not only by those in actual need of medical services but also by those who do not need it, but utilize the opportunity to kill time and evade work. Even though such prisoners may fail to convince the doctor that they should re-main on the idle list for a day or two, the morning sick call at least guarantees idle-ness for the time spent in attending it and affords an opportunity to meet and con-verse with other prisoners while waiting in line. It also permits them to "connive" and to "make connections" for all sorts of illegal ends and ulterior motives.

Thus it happens that the sick line is the *bete noir* of every prison doctor. How to make it serve its legitimate ends without wasting

the time of the medical staff and abusing institutional time by the designing prisoner is an ever present problem.

Although the problem is not easy, there is one fundamental psychological principle which, if rigidly adhered to, will go a long way towards its solution. That principle is simply this: *require that sick line be held at a time when a well man would rather be some place else.*

So far as women in prison are concerned the sick line or sick call does not seem quite so practical as for men. Women in prison do not subscribe to routine as well as men. They seem to require more individual treatment for their special aches and pains. As a matter of fact it is extremely doubtful whether women should ever be sent to prison under any circumstances. The great majority of them are there for so-called crimes related directly or indirectly to their sex life, and imprisonment *per se,* has no specific influence in their reformation.

Prisoners whose social maladjustment has been dependent upon gland disturbances, actual psychosis, or other physical or men-tal disease do undoubtedly occur, and a well-organized medical service will be alert to this possibility. However, the medical service should not overstress the importance of any one factor and should remember that in terms of permanent social rehabilitation it has but little more to offer than the Educators, the Sociologists, and the Chap-lains.

Inference is not made of course that the Medical Service in Prisons has no special values of any kind. Outstanding examples of these are Research, and Group Psycho-therapy. Prison hospitals should be Research Laboratories for the study of the causes of crime and its prevention. A great opportu-nity for determining the significance of the psychopathic personality as a cause of crime is knocking at the doors of prison physicians and their staffs. Electroencephalographic studies should be useful in making differen-tial diagnoses between the neurotics and the psychopaths, and further psychological and sociological studies should help in evaluating their symptoms, until we are able to describe them in clinical terms as clear cut and definitive as we now define dementia praecox or involutional melancholia.

Group psychotherapy, intelligently administered, is exceedingly valuable. This is a comparatively new departure from the old line of placebos (both mental and physical) handed out by the prison physician, the chaplain and the educational director.

Group psychotherapy has for its aim the helping of each man or woman in the group to understand himself. Working and talking together in a group with the psychiatrist brings, as a general rule, more promising results than conferences with him alone. The psychological reasons for this are many but are beyond the scope of this article. Perhaps a careful perusal of William James' "Varieties of Religious Experience" will help to elucidate them.

An outstanding example of the benefits of group psychotherapy is to be found in the results accomplished by "Alcoholics Anonymous" in the permanent reformation of Alcoholic Addicts. This a specialized form of Buckmanism (The Oxford Movement) and when the alcoholic prisoner addict is carefully selected he or she often receives a new outlook on life.

When this form of group psychotherapy is practiced in prisons it is necessary to exclude carefully those who are not really alcoholic addicts, but who are simply curious, and seeking diversion to while away the tedium of prison life. In Prisons for women this precaution is especially necessary.

Although group therapy techniques would naturally seem to be the administrative responsibility of the Medical Service, the head of this service should not be too insistent upon his professional rights. He should know that he has seen many a psychiatrist who could properly diagnose and classify a person in accordance with the nomenclature of the American Psychiatric Association, but who was a flat failure in helping his patient toward recovery from his mental illness. He should also know whether the psychologist on his staff is capable of making the prisoner understand himself as well as simply determining his mental age and I. Q.

The same holds for the Social Worker, Chaplain, Educational Director, the Warden and all the Custodial Staff. The psychological atmosphere of the prison can be hopelessly contaminated if any of the key men in any department are hostile, or indifferent.

The medical aspects of imprisonment are not concerned solely with the diagnosis and treatment of diseases of prisoners. Medical rehabilitation means much more than that. It means not only the correction of physical and mental ills as they are found but the inculcation of those principles of living which insure a sound mind and healthy body. No one or two members of the medical staff, however proficient they may be in their specialties, can accomplish this by working alone. All must work together to the end that values may be properly balanced and individual enthusiasms or predilections for certain forms of treatment not given too much nor too little weight.

If the medical staff has coordinated the activities of its individual members in a sane and practical manner, there still remains the important duty of fitting this end result into the institutional machinery for social rehabilitation. This has to do, first, with making the medical staff itself more efficient, and second, with promoting a friendly and cooperative spirit with other departments of the prison.

To accomplish the first object there should be a daily short staff conference which all members of the medical staff attend. This daily conference should deal primarily with administrative problems. The noon hour in most penal and correctional institutions is longer than is actually necessary for lunch and this is a good time for each one of the staff to drop into the office of the chief medical officer. This daily practice obviates many misunderstandings and promotes smooth running of the hospital. The chief nurse, administrative assistant, and dental officer should also attend these daily meetings.

At least every two weeks and preferably every week a clinical conference should be held. This should be devoted primarily to the consideration of professional subjects. Case histories should be presented as well as an occasional formal paper. It should be the aim of the chief medical officer to have every member of his staff prepare and publish at least one paper or case report each year.

Members of the local medical profession who have been appointed as consultants should be invited to the weekly or semimonthly staff conferences and be encouraged to take an active part in them.

Every member of the staff should affiliate himself with the local medical society, taking an active part in its discussions, and striving to arouse a general interest in the medical aspects of prison work.

The medical library should be carefully supervised, as frequent additions made to it as finances will allow, and medical journals to meet all reasonable needs subscribed for. An inmate prisoner can be appropriately put in charge of the library, giving him a desk and typewriter, and requiring him to type manuscripts and perform other clerical duties appropriate to the position. Rigid rules regarding the loan and return of books should be made and strictly enforced.

If the institution is located in a city which boasts a university or medical college, opportunity should be afforded them for utilizing the facilities for teaching abnormal psychology and psychiatry to small, carefully selected student groups.

Finally, the hospital should be so organized and conducted that it may receive high rating by the American College of Surgeons.

All the foregoing procedures tend to raise the professional standards of the individual members of the medical staff and at the same time enhance the prestige of the medical service in the community.

No matter how good the organization or how high the standards of the medical staff it will fail in performing its proper functions if it does not work on a friendly and cooperative basis with the other departments of the prison. Probably the first and most important step toward this end is a clear understanding between the warden and the chief medical officer as to the relationship which should exist between them. For this purpose a good organizational chart tends to clarify the situation and prevent misunderstandings. Broadly speaking, the relationship should be similar to that of the medical department to the

line officers in the army. But whatever this relationship may actually be in any particular institution, it is exceedingly important to have a clear understanding as to the proper lines of communication. When the official channels for these are once established, they should be strictly adhered to by the members of the medical staff, even though there may be occasional deviations from it by other departments.

Staff conferences are frequently held by the warden to which the chief medical officer will be invited. He should take an active part in the deliberations at these conferences, not hesitating to express his opinion freely on any subject, provided he feels that he has a worthwhile contribution to make to the common good. While doing this he should never forget that many of the non-medical men in these general staff conferences are possessed of just as good qualities of leadership as the psychiatrist and equally alert to the psycho-somatic elements in personality problems.

While it is highly desirable to maintain friendly relations with all departments of the prison, there are some of them with which such relations are absolutely essential. This is notably the case with the deputy warden whose office controls the movement of individuals within the institution. Scarcely a day will pass which does not require consultation between him and the chief medical officer and if personal relationships between them are strained, it hampers smooth administration for both.

Next in importance is the relationship which should be maintained between the medical staff and the chaplain. The latter will be a daily visitor to the hospital and is often in possession of information which will be very helpful in the treatment of patients. Moreover, his visits should have a decided therapeutic value and every effort should be made to secure his friendly cooperation.

The aid of the chief of the social service department, as well as that of his assistants, should also be solicited and cordial relations established between the two offices.

Finally, in an institution where all these functions are properly coordinated, the warden and the chief medical officer will be perfectly in rapport, exchanging mutual confidences with the complete assurance that they will not be violated.

Joseph G. Wilson, M.D.
Director, Mental Hygiene Bureau
State Hospital, Trenton, N. J.

BIBLIOGRAPHY

Barnes, H. E. and Teeters, N. K., *New Horizons in Criminology,* Prentice-Hall, Inc., 1943.
King, M. R., The Medical Center for Federal Prisoners at Springfield, Missouri, *Prison World,* May-June, 1941.
Wilson, J. G., Medical Service in Penal and Correctional Institutions, *Prison World,* September-October, 1940.

MENTAL DEFICIENCY. The feeble-minded are those persons who are socially inadequate because of gravely subnormal mental development. The condition obtains at maturity but may be evident from birth or an early age according to the degree and type of deficiency. It is of constitutional origin, being essentially attributable to imperfect or incomplete cerebral development. It is incurable except as its social manifestations may be ameliorated temporarily or under favorable conditions by social disposition and training.

"Feeble-mindedness" and "mental deficiency" are commonly used as synonymous terms in traditional legal and scientific practice. The terms "imbecility" and "idiocy" are sometimes used as legal equivalents, although technically they represent specific degrees of mental deficiency. These terms all imply a state of mental and social incompetence of such degree as to constitute absence of legal responsibility comparable to legal insanity. The condition is consequently sometimes confused at law with insanity. Feeble-mindedness is a state of incomplete or arrested mental and social development, while insanity is a state of mental disturbance or deterioration from quondam normality; the former involves mental *sub*normality, while the latter reflects mental *ab*normality. Both conditions are seldom present in the same individual. Insanity occurs infrequently in the juvenile years, but mental deficiency always arises prior to normal mental maturity (about fifteen years) and continues ordinarily without amelioration thereafter.

Modern scientific methods make it possible to satisfy these distinctions in the majority of cases, although the condition requires skillful diagnosis since high-grade mental deficiency is easily confused with low-grade or dull normality, and the clinical subdivisions include many different varieties.

The conventional classifications of mental deficiency fall into three major divisions. The first of these deals with grade or degree of deficiency, the second with clinical variety or symptom-complex, and the third with form or etiology.

After the feeble-mindedness has been established in terms of the several diagnostic criteria, the gradation by degree includes: (a) idiots as the most severe degree, represented by mental and social ages below three years, (b) imbeciles, the middle grade, represented by mental ages from three to seven years inclusive, and by social ages from three to nine years, and (c) morons, the highest grade of deficiency, represented by Binet mental ages from eight to eleven or twelve years, approximately, and by social ages of approximately ten to eighteen or twenty years. During the developmental period these gradations are sometimes expressed in terms of IQ's (intelligence quotients) and SQ's (social quotients), but this practice is not dependable since (a) these quotients show individual variability with age, (b) require supplementation by other data, (c) may not hold constant at maturity, and (d) are calculated on different maturation "ceilings" (e.g. approximately fifteen years for the Binet scale and twenty-five years for the Vineland Social Maturity Scale). In the best technical usage these classifications of idiot, imbecile and moron are not merely gradations of mental and social age, but include multiple considerations because of the different patterns of traits for these three degrees of mental deficiency. Within each grade it is customary to use subdivisions of low, middle and high.

The classification by clinical varieties or symptom-complexes of mental deficiency includes (a) the familial, hereditary or endogenous cases, and (b) the pathological, non-hereditary or exogenous categories. The latter encompass such types as mongolism, intracranial birth lesion, microcephaly, hydrocephalus, cretinism, and other relatively unusual neuropathological syndromes.

The classification by etiology includes primary, secondary and mixed forms. These are closely allied to clinical variety. The primary form includes particularly those persons with inherited subnormal germinal endowment. Some authorities include in this group germinal impairment which results in pathological morphology of the embryo. In recent practice the term endogenous has been used for the primary form, and is most commonly reserved for the familial type as opposed to the pathological impairment of germ potentiality. The secondary or exogenous form includes causes which may be grossly grouped as traumatic, defective, degenerative, or deprivative. In recent practice these groups have been incorporated under the term exogenous. The tendency to merge classification by form with classification by clinical variety results from the essentially similar symptom-complexes corresponding to their respective etiologies, thus constituting approximations to clinical entities. Broadly speaking the endogenous cases may be described as simple mental deficiency, which is distinguished from normality by generalized retardation of development and is essentially subnormal rather than abnormal in kind. The exogenous cases are more readily recognizable from specific physical characteristics and significantly associated patterns of behavior.

Conservative estimates of the prevalence of mental deficiency in the general population indicate that this condition is present in about one per cent of unselected samples of the total population. The percentage varies with standards of determination, and with environmental or social-economic selection, as well as with age and by types and degrees of deficiency. These variables account for differences in estimates of incidence, with some as high as two or three per cent, or even higher.

The proportion by grade of defect is roughly one to three to six for institutionalized idiots, imbeciles and morons respectively, and one to four to sixteen for those at large.

The idiots and imbeciles are rather readily detected, while the morons require careful technical study. Since the morons constitute the largest proportion of all the feebleminded, and since their detection requires expert skill, the variations in estimates are largely attributable to difficulties inherent in recognizing persons in this grade. Less than ten per cent of all feeble-minded are cared for as such in state and private institutions; whereas at least one person per hundred of the general population is feebleminded, fewer than one per thousand are institutionalized. Some are found in correctional institutions, especially as juvenile delinquents. Many others are enrolled in special classes in the public schools while living at home. A relatively large number receive incidental community aid and supervision through state and local social agencies.

The proportions by etiology are most simply conceived as one-half endogenous and one-half exogenous. These proportions, however, are rendered difficult of estimate because of the considerable number of either mixed or unknown etiologies. At least one-third of all cases are considered familial, and most authorities place this proportion at two-thirds or even higher. Probably one-third of all cases are clearly non-familial, although some authorities place this estimate lower. Perhaps one-third are of mixed or undetermined etiology, and the assigning of these cases to either the endogenous or the exogenous form influences the estimates. These percentages are further influenced by the previously mentioned difficulty of detection in the case of the high-grade morons who are chiefly of the familial type. Broadly speaking, the familial cases are of moron and high imbecile grade, while the exogenous cases are of idiot and low imbecile grade.

The proportions by clinical variety are at present inexactly determined. In round numbers, about ten per cent of all institutionalized feeble-minded cases may be classed as intracranial birth lesions, and from five to ten per cent as the mongolian type of mental deficiency; each of most of the other exogenous types represents appreciably less than one per cent of all the feeble-minded.

Most of what is known about the feebleminded applies to those who have been studied as wards of public and private institutions or in field studies of subcultural family strains such as the Jukes, the Kallikak Family, the Win Tribe, the Pineys, and many other so-called degenerate stocks. Educational experience and research have revealed that the feeble-minded are gravely handicapped in scholastic learning but may succeed fairly well in simple occupational pursuits. Their social success is materially enhanced through habit training and well-considered supervision.

In the field of jurisprudence mental deficiency may be an important issue in either civil or criminal action. For example:

(a) Moral and legal responsibility with regard to the nature and quality of such acts as homicide, assault, rape, carnal abuse, arson, larceny, homosexuality.

(b) Social and economic competence, such as financial responsibility, inheritance of property, administration of business and personal affairs, guardianship, dependency.

(c) Marital and parental relationships, such as compatibility, cruelty, bigamy, promiscuity, cohabitation, legitimacy, incest, abandonment, child abuse and neglect, domestic relations.

(d) Testimony, such as competence and credibility as a witness, perjury, false accusation.

(e) Civil litigation, such as recovery for damages in cases of malpractice, accident, defamation.

Mental deficiency in relation to jurisprudence may also be related to specific legislation, such as laws relating to marriageability, sterilization, social and legal guardianship, institutional committability, educational privileges.

Or mental deficiency may be a consideration in the disposition of offenders through juvenile court procedures or the sentencing of offenders following trial and conviction as well as in relation to the consequent measures for social restraint, correctional custody, regimen, social rehabilitation and parole.

Many studies have been made of the intelligence of offenders, and particularly of the incidence of mental deficiency among offenders. These studies are frequently at odds in respect to their results because of the problems of selectivity according to age, sex, race or nationality, social-economic status, locality, type of offense, and other variables. The resulting estimates on incidence are specially related to the timing of the examination, from the stage of initial apprehension to that of final disposition. Such studies are further embarrassed by variations in the standards of definition, methods of detection, and techniques of examination. Thus the percentages of mental deficiency for juvenile delinquents have ranged from nearly zero to one hundred per cent. Most such studies, however, show at least one-third of juvenile delinquent boys mentally deficient, and about an equal number of girls. Among youthful and young adult offenders the proportion has been found to be somewhat less, perhaps only half as great as among juvenile delinquents, or about fifteen per cent. Similarly among adult offenders the incidence is again reduced by about half, amounting to eight or ten per cent. Most of the variations in such percentages can be accounted for on the basis of the variables already mentioned. Other things equal, the percentage of mental deficiency is appreciably higher for recidivists than for first offenders.

On the other hand it is not very clear that the feeble-minded as a group fail notably in success on parole as compared with the non-feeble-minded paroled offenders, or that feeble-mindedness of itself is a major cause of crime or delinquency. The social situations commonly surrounding mental defectives must be considered as well as the lack of judgment which reduces resistance to such situations. This in part accounts for the reduction in percentages with increase of age from the juvenile delinquent to the adult offender. And this in turn is reflected in the more serious types of offenses encountered as one goes up the age scale of offenses. It is notable that mentally deficient juveniles enrolled in special classes show a much lower incidence of delinquency than is found among those not so enrolled.

As a rule the percentages on incidence of mental deficiency in relation to crime and delinquency are based principally on the endogenous or familial defectives of relatively high mental grade. It is unusual in correctional institutions, or even the courts, to encounter exogenous or low-grade defectives. As a rule, the latter lack the aggressive initiative and behavioral conflicts which predispose toward serious misconduct. They also are more likely to have the advantages of favorable home environment, close supervision, ready recognition and constructive disposition than is the case with the familial type.

Are all the feeble-minded potential offenders? Such a question implies that the feeble-minded are peculiarly susceptible to crime and delinquency because of suggestibility, lack of foresight, poor judgment, and such influences as may induce either active or passive types of offenses. It does not necessarily mean that the feeble-minded are more aggressively antisocial than the normal person. Such generalizations, moreover, are more applicable to juveniles than to adults.

The feeble-minded are easily led and feebly inhibited. They are naive rather than vicious. One may think of the mentally deficient offender, therefore, not so much as an aggressor toward society as a victim of social circumstances. Constructive legislation and the sound administration of justice can do much toward improving the protection of society by well-advised concern for the welfare of its mentally deficient members.

EDGAR A. DOLL
Director of Research
The Training School
Vineland, New Jersey.

BIBLIOGRAPHY

Branham, V. C., The Classification and Treatment of the Defective Delinquent, *Journal of Criminal Law and Criminology*, 17,183–217, August, 1926.
Burt, Cyril L., *The Subnormal Mind*, New York, Oxford University Press, 1935.
Davies, Stanley P., *Social Control of the Mentally Deficient*, New York, Thomas Y. Crowell Co., 1930.
Doll, E. A., The Feeble-Minded Child, Chapter 18 in Carmichael's *Manual of Child Psychology*, New York: John Wiley & Sons, Inc., 1068 pp., 1946.
Murchison, Carl, *Criminal Intelligence*, Clark University, Worcester, Mass., 1926.
Tredgold, A. F., *Mental Deficiency*, London: Balliere, Tindall and Cox, 1936.
Tredgold, A. F., *A Text-Book of Mental Deficiency* (6th ed.) Baltimore: William Wood & Co., 556 pp., 1937.
Tulchin, Simon H., *Intelligence and Crime*, Chicago, University of Chicago Press, 1939.

MENTAL MECHANISMS.

The mind has organization and structure as other organs of the body do. It has its own peculiar ways of acting, that is, it has functions to perform. The term *mental mechanism* refers to the functioning of the mind. Before describing the functions, however, it is desirable first to gain a conception of the structure.

The mind or psyche is not the brain, but it is the resultant of brain participation. In early infancy stimuli from the environment (warmth, moisture, pain) and from the infant's body (intestinal cramps, bitter food) reach the brain where they are stored up as "organic memories". There is as yet no mind by which these stimuli are compared with past ones in order to form judgment as to how to act toward them. The infant must rely upon nature to handle these stimuli; that part of nature assigned to this task is called the instincts and we say the infant withdraws from pain instinctually.

The instincts are the composite of man's automatic behavior, derived from the distant past and ingrained in the body, perhaps with the brain as a central receiving and distributing center. The experiences of the distant past are racial and they are subsumed under the heading *phylogenetic*. A little later in infancy the child reacts automatically to favorable and unfavorable stimuli, from within and without, in a more complicated way, though the reaction is still automatic or instinctual or phylogenetic. He begins to act like a human being, not simply like organic tissue. That is, the human element enters, not, however, because of training by the mother but in virtue of the repetitious training through which mankind has gone. The mother of the race, so to speak, takes over control before the mother of the child does. This racial image of humanity is securely implanted in the infant's tissues, perhaps, especially in the brain, and cannot be separated from it. The human embryonic mind or mind-body, if you please, is called the *Id* by Freud and is further defined as the storehouse of the instincts. In adult development it occupies a position between the tissues of the body and the mind; it is the bridge between the two, securely anchored in both.

Stimuli from the body cross this bridge to reach the environment; and the first essential part of the environment that they contact is the mother, whose first duties with the child are in the nature of training the infant how to use its body, how to eat, to evacuate, to keep away from danger, to dress, to keep clean, etc., etc. In other words, the developing mind of the infant is now made up of a code of physical behavior, with special emphasis on the care of the infant's own body. Technically, this code of physical training constitutes what is called the somatogenic or autogenic sector of the mind. Stimuli from the infant's body, and to a lesser extent from without, that is, from the mother, pass over the bridge (Id) from the brain side to meet and mix with the newly developing part of the mind known as the somatogenic development.

The infant's mind is body-minded, so to say. Training in body-mindedness is almost the exclusive training that the child gets for approximately two to two and one-half years. But, it is a form of activity that is never abandoned, for the adult must continue to pay attention to his physique right up to the last day of living. Many human beings never give up this attention to any wholesome extent, living through childhood, adolescence, adulthood and senescence with their own body and body functions as the paramount issues of their lives. This perpetuation of body-mindedness into later life as a principal focus of interest is known as hypochondriasis. We sense in the hypochondriac a childishness; we think of him as part animal and part child, and we are right because he is little more than an instinctual child. Too, he leans upon the environment in a childish way. When later he marries, his wife becomes essentially a mother, for she has to watch over his food, clothing, and health to about the same extent that his own mother did.

Among normal infants there is a gradual relinquishment of body-mindedness in favor of mind-mindedness. In this transitional period the infant (infancy extends from birth until about the fifth year) begins to get praise and adulation for behavior that issues from the mind and brain. The first word spoken by the infant brings great joy to all, but the first sentence is a *cause celebre*. The infant is impressed with his accomplishments. Never again in life will he get so much for so little. To him the recitation of the alphabet is a remarkable achievement; praise is affluent when he learns to dress himself, when he behaves well in school, when he does his homework alone, when he shares his toys with others, when he learns the social amenities of his age. There are hundreds of other acts that go to make up a grand frame of mind and the aggregate takes the name *narcissism* (from Narcissus, the beautiful boy of Greek legend, who was forced by Nemesis to fall in love with himself and pine away in self-admiration). Nemesis has never ceased to exert her power; she still sees to it that anyone who is too uplifted by his prosperity is reduced and punished. When we carry into later life the self-glorification of our infancy, the goddess of divine retribution metes out punishment. The goddess today appears in the form of the child's mother, aided by the father, the siblings, then other children, teachers, employers, the social codes, the law, the police and courts—each of whom has his or her own set of "don'ts" that are designed to curb unbridled egotisms, inconsiderate narcissism. There is a set of "do's" also to encourage the expression of self-interests in the form of altruism.

Mind-mindedness replaces to a given extent body-mindedness. In infancy and for some time thereafter it is a valuable asset to the growing child. Too often, however, it persists without substantial change into late childhood, adolescence and adulthood. When it does it gives rise to abnormal expressions of the personality, sometimes in the shape of hysteria or other mental afflictions, sometimes in criminal careers, sometimes in just plain ordinariness. There is plenty of opportunity, however, for the normal extension of narcissism through the later years of life in forms of accomplishments that are not only beneficial to the self but to others as well. When the latter is seen, it is called sublimated narcissism.

The instinctual impulses, as we have seen, issue from the brain, then occupy that structure called the Id, which is part-brain and part-mind. Then the impulses enter into the somatic structure of the mind, whence they go into the mental organization to which the name *narcissism* is given. The architecture of the mind is well under way; the foundation has been completed and upon it has been erected the subcellar (the pristine instincts) and the cellar (the Id); the first (somatogenic) and second (narcissistic) floors have been completed. Nothing has been said about equipment of the rooms and very little can be said about it in this short space.

The rooms are equipped in the early years from two principal sources, namely, from the experiences of the race and from those of the mother (and father). Father is given parenthetical mention, because by and large mother is more important to the child's infancy. The early experimental life of the child, that is, the early organization of the child's mind, is largely a reflection of the codes of discipline implanted in the child's mind by the parents; which is but another way of saying that the child is the behavioristic image of the parents. It acts, feels, thinks as the parents do, but it acts, feels, thinks also as the instincts do. The early mind of the child is thus a blend of nature (instincts) and nurture (training). Instincts are first nature; discipline is second nature. Freud gave a special name to second nature; he called it the *Super-Ego*.

These two sets of equipment, the Id and the Super-Ego, comprise the principal articles of furniture in our mind-house. In the subcellar is the furnace (Id), in the cellar (basement to you) is the kitchen. When the house is well-run and well-manned, the tenants seldom know these two floors; they know the results of activity from below and they act accordingly. This is but another way of saying that the adult mind has structures and functions of which it has little detailed knowledge, but which are absolutely

essential for living. Freud was the first one to inventory the subcellar and cellar comprehensively; he gave it a name, the unconscious. Without the equipment on these floors we would starve or freeze to death. With it we are not too much at ease, though most of us appear contented with what the furnace man and the chef send up. Too much or too little lead to diseasedness, to disease of the mind, to a mental affliction.

In the mind-house of the child there are as yet no living rooms. They are gradually constructed over a period, called the latency period, extending from the end of infancy (5th year) to the beginning of puberty (about the 13th or 14th year). Because boys' emotional affiliations are largely with boys, and girls' with girls, the latency period is replete with experiences connected with the same gender. This is the phase of suigenderistic (of one's own gender) growth. Nature places great emphasis upon the relationship of males to males and females to females, for she provides physiologically some eight or nine years for what we may call the introductory exchanges between members of the same gender. Man has found by experience that even so long a time is too short, for in enlightened states we cannot bind ourselves to the opposite gender for about another five-year period. But, in nature's latency period boys move freely with boys, girls with girls.

Sometimes the relationships are particularly intimate and the suigenderism takes the form of homosexuality. Some individuals cannot break away from this prolonged affiliation; they go through the rest of life with accentuation on suigenderism or on some of its other manifestations. After all, to prefer one's own gender is not far removed from the preference of one's own self. The motive is the same; only the object to which the motive is attached is different. Suigenderism is but projected narcissism. Homosexuality and self-centeredness are close partners.

There is still another floor to our mind-house. Its construction begins in a very modest sort of way in early childhood, but the provisional contract for construction is not signed until puberty. It is at this later age period that the boy begins to make love to the girl. It is the phase of "puppy" love.

Among healthy individuals who are not too strongly fixed to the past, there is a succession of trials and errors, trials and successes, until marriage is achieved. This state of transferring interests to the other gender is known as *altrigenderism* (the other of two genders); supposedly it makes up the rest of one's life. From the standpoint of nature it ends at the climacterium, the end of the reproductive career, but from the standpoint of the individual efforts are made to prolong it. When the flesh is weak, the spirit is still strong. We end wherein we begin—in phantasy.

Genuine love for a member of the other gender demands relinquishment of much narcissism. This very valuable possession is difficult to externalize upon another, because it leaves one without much energy for other purposes. It is at once energizing and devitalizing. The longer it is perpetuated in an extreme degree, that is, the longer the intensive love, the less will the individual be able to accomplish in other matters of living. Therefore, as a rule, normal partners, after a varying period of years, pool much of their narcissism in something else, best of all in their children, or if there are no children, in their home, career, recreations, etc.

It is more or less characteristic of some people including the mentally sick, that they cannot give up enough of their narcissism or suigenderism to ensure harmonious married life. The failure to divert their interests to the other gender is almost the common denominator of unhappiness and is a very frequent precipitating cause for morbid mental states.

This altrigenderistic floor of our mind-house is the main living floor. When we first move in there is very little furniture, that is, for the average individual there is little, or comparatively, little, earning capacity with which to furnish the living floor.

The individual had started in childhood to seek a work goal, a career of industry of one type or another. He began it the day he started in school. Then he started to sublimate his earlier energies in what may be called essentially impersonal objectives— play, hobbies, sports, earning career. The energies that go into the service of impersonal reality have no special name; they are sub-

sumed under the general heading *alloerotism*. This is the final floor of our mind-house. Perhaps as the lower floors were under construction provision was made for a separate staircase eventually to lead to the *alloerotic* floor. Indeed, as each floor was completed so was the stair-case up to that floor. As the individual grows up he puts a certain quantity of energy in work, play, career.

Some people put an inordinate amount of their energy in the stair-case and the floor to which it goes. The living room is relatively bare, while the work room is richly furnished. Under such conditions the mind-house is poorly constructed, top-heavy, so to speak. The result is unhappiness, often manifesting itself in the form of mental deviation.

The floors of this mind-house above the level of the cellar or basement have a tenant who supervises the activities on the floors. The tenant is the (conscious) ego. He decides, when and if he is capable of it, what the furnishing of the floors will be and how they shall be arranged. He selects his guests and entertains them according to his wishes. If he is unschooled in equipping his home or untrained in entertaining guests, others may come in and run the place for him. When he is sick and medical help is unavailable, the furnace man and the chef take over. A weak ego succumbs to the forces of the unconscious.

Thus far we have spoken chiefly of structure. The mind-house has been erected and furnished. It remains now to have activity going on. The variety of activity that goes on in the mind constitutes what are called *mental mechanisms*.

1. *Identification.* In early infancy the child confines his activities exclusively to the nursery, the Id-room of the house. There there are no responsibilities on the part of the infant. The mother takes care of all the child's activities, sees that he is kept warm, clean, fed and safe. Only the autonomic, vegetative nervous system and its organs are active. Whenever a painful stimulus, such as bright light, heat or cold, or disagreeable food, or intestinal gas, irritates the child, the mother is there to remove the stimulus. In the early months there is no mind as such.

The child lives through the influences of mother nature and mother nurture.

When the sense organs—eyes, ears, nose, mouth, skin—begin to function outwardly towards the environment spontaneously, the infant begins to appreciate, to be aware of its environment. The energies of the infant now begin to be drawn from the phylogenetic zone, that is from the Id, to things outside of itself by way of the sense organs. The "environment" of the infant is remarkably restricted, being essentially the mother. The mother acts in a special way towards the child. For months she trains the child to recognize and do things with its arms, legs, head, eyes, mouth, etc. Thus, the newly developing mind is largely filled with ideas and feelings relating primarily to the infant's body. The movements of the infant are directed by the mother, that is, the movements are imitative and are the earliest manifestations of what is called *identification*.

After long training in the use of the body, but long before the body-training period is over, the infant is introduced to mind-training. Again, this mind-training is imitative of the mother and to a lesser extent, as a rule, of the father and others in the family. The child becomes the mirror-image of its parents, learning how to conduct itself, first in the family circle, later outside of the family. An extensive code of behavior and of ways of thinking and feeling is implanted in the child by way of the mental mechanism called identification. The code is known scientifically as the *super-ego*. Therefore, it might be said that the child's suger-ego is first in the parents; second, after the child learns sufficiently well what the parents want it to do, it moves to the child's own mind, the conscious part; third, and finally, after it becomes second nature by repetition, the code or super-ego goes into the unconscious part of the child's mind, whence it continues to operate, often without losing much of its original force, though further training and experience through the extra-familial years frequently reduces the force appreciably. The code or super-ego is also known as inner conscience.

Some children never get very far away from the nursery stage, meaning that they never get away from identification with or imitation of their parents. They go through life as children emotionally; they are child-adolescent, child-adult, child senescent, quite apart from intellectual and physical achievements.

Others are able to make the transition from parents to substitutes in the environment. The school teacher may be such a substitute, such a mother-imago; a boy classmate may "pinch-hit" for the father. Still later the girl classmate takes the mother's place to an ever-increasing degree until at the time of marriage identification she has led the boy from the parents (super-ego) to others (ego-ideals). New women take the mother's place, new men the father's.

If, as often happens, the shift from parents to others is transacted mainly through intellectual channels, with only a little sprinkle of emotions, adaptation to society will most likely be poor and insecure. It is relatively easy to buy a job with intelligence. Intelligence is the pin-money of living. But, marriage, for example, costs more than pin-money can buy. Even from the definitional point of view pin-money is a tenuous medium of exchange; as Addison put it, "they have a greater interest in property than either maids or wives and do not hold their jointures by the precarious tenure of portions or pin-money." Compatible marriage is purchased and held by the gold coins of living—compatible emotions.

From the criminological standpoint identification as a mental mechanism is often of extreme importance. For example, a son may grow up in close affiliation with a criminal father; the son's inner conscience may be largely antisocial; with his super-ego modeled after the father, it is not difficult for him to lead an antisocial career. The old expression "like father, like son" may well have experiential as well as hereditarial background. When the two exert their influences, maladjustment is the rule.

Each super-ego has its own particular composition, being dependent upon the training and experience implanted by the parents. Of course, the super-ego is influenced in part from within (from the instinctual sphere) and from without (from the environment).

A young man, separated from his parents, may identify himself with others. If he does so with criminals, then his career is as theirs. There are perhaps more aspirants for sadistic than for masochistic ways of living. Racketeers are notoriously emulative.

An important fact connected with identification is the relative weakness of the person's own ego. He acts as if he were someone else, not altogether unlike the patient with hysteria, who is usually so intimately identified with her own mother that, as she puts it, "I cannot think for myself or form judgments; I keep doing what something inside tells me to do and I don't like it. I wish I were myself."

Identification is responsible for many varieties of maladaptation—simple dependency, antisocial conduct, psychiatric adjustment. Identification is a natural, normal, physiological mental mechanism at all periods of life. The perpetuation of infantile identification into adolescence and adulthood is a mark of inferiority.

2. *Sublimation.* The normal, healthy solution for the disposition of impulses and experiences that are no longer appropriate and for those that are abandoned because of their undesirability is to relegate the experience to the unconscious and to put the energy into the service of conscious thoughts and actions that are personally and socially agreeable. This mental mechanism is called *sublimation.* Infantile exhibitionism is transformed, so to say, into stage-acting. The original motive is not changed, but the object to which it is attached is changed. The impulse to peep, to search into the unknown, to examine may be redirected along channels of scientific research. Infantile sadism is converted into healthy, competitive athletics.

Each instinctual component may undergo the same fate. Nature, however, seldom forsakes its primitive tendencies. It compromises, much against its own will, by relinquishing full claim to the instinctual component, always, though, retaining some of the energy of the infantile component. In almost all individuals there is a conflict between conscious and unconscious forces as regards the distribution of the energy. A healthy person is one whose energies are sufficiently mobile

to shift from one sphere to another as occasion warrants. When the energies are inordinately bound to the one or to the other, conflict ensues which may be severe enough to represent a morbid state. The old adage, "all work and no play, makes Jack a dull boy," is an understatement. He is certainly dull to the playgirl, but he is also intensely unhappy with himself. The glamor boy is no less comfortable with society in general or with himself, for the moral codes of man are often as implacable as the instinctual codes of nature.

3. *Repression.* While the infant is being taught to identify its interests with the mother, it is also taught, if it is the mother's disposition, to "forsake" earlier habits. It is taught new bed habits as regards evacuation of body contents; it is taught to be secretive in a given sense about those matters; it is taught to be neat and clean, to be properly dressed for comfort as well as for propriety, to be considerate of others; the training goes on and on until the transition is made from animalism to civilization.

Several courses are offered, so to speak, to the child. It may take one or all, in whole or in part. Let us follow one trait to see the possibilities. That trait is exhibitionism. In early infancy exhibitionism (the display of the uncovered body) is genuinely natural; indeed, it is out of the field of awareness of the infant for months, if not for a year or two. Depending upon many factors, personal and societal, exhibitionism may persist into adulthood with little modification. It may be severely repressed into the unconscious and be replaced by modesty (see *reaction-formation*). It may be repressed and while in the unconscious be deprived of its energy (see *undoing*) to the extent that it is no longer an urge, nor is it known ever to have been an urge. It may take other ways of expressing itself (see *sublimation*), such as display of attire, of physical prowess, of intelligence, of stage acting, etc., etc. It may be *displaced* (see *displacement*) upon others, that is, looking at may be substituted for being looked at. It may be projected (see *projection*) in the sense that the individual has the delusion that others spy upon him while he is in his privacy. It may appear as a physical symptom (see *conversion*), say, stomach trouble, that "requires" frequent examination.

The foregoing represent some of the destinies which an infantile impulse may finally achieve. The important consideration here lies in the fact that infantile, instinctual impulses, called *instinctual components*, last a life-time in one form or another. The law known as the conservation of energy is as applicable to mental as it is to physical energy.

Repression as generally understood means the forceful rejection of an impulse by consciousness into the unconsciousness. There are other forces, for example, the super-ego, that participate in repression, but for our present discussion the mere concept of repression meets our needs.

From the criminological aspect the absence of repression may gain great significance. Exhibitionism in the legal sense, for example, is not at all a rarity. But, other instinctual components may be equally as antisocial. We may mention such acts as peeping (Peeping Toms), as rape, pedophilia, homicide and suicide.

The absence of repression may be occasioned by disease, injury, or drugs (such as alcohol, morphine, etc.) in a person who in the absence of such agents handles his instinctual impulses in accordance with the requirements of the state. Alcohol is the great solvent. Apparently it can also dissolve the super-ego, thus freeing the crude, primitive impulses.

4. *Reaction-formation*. Reaction-formation, if not expressed too intensively and if not carried over too long a period, is one of nature's answers to the repression of infantile impulses. It is the substitution in consciousness of an attitude the opposite of that repressed. This mental mechanism normally begins in the infantile period, gains its greatest strength in the latency period (from the 5th year to puberty); it is retained in later age periods but not as extensively as in the earlier ones, save in states of mental illness. When reaction-formation (also called reversal formation) is at its peak modesty takes the place of (repressed) impropriety, timidity of pugnacity, taciturnity of loquacity, love of hate, etc.

Some people are able to go through a whole lifetime on the basis of reaction-formation. Others who "try" to make it their preferred personality succumb to a mental illness, such as manic-depressive psychosis. Still others break out into violent anti-social conduct. Not a few shy, modest paragons of virtue have faced the judicial system with very serious charges against them. Nature never intended man to function more or less exclusively on the reaction-formation basis, save as a temporary expediency during the time that primitive impulses are being repressed in favor of other means of outlet.

5. *Undoing*. After an impulse and the experience to which it is attached are repressed, the experience may be divested of its energy (affect) and remain in the unconscious realm as abolished. The energy of the experience attaches itself, under normal conditions, to an experience that is not hurtful and thus regains the sphere of consciousness. For example, a young lady was shocked in childhood when a sexual assault was made upon her. Subsequently she forgot entirely about the experience. Undoing is said to be related to amnesia. Sometimes, however, the energy reappears in consciousness as what used to be called "free-floating" anxiety. This is a pathological state often requiring psychotherapy.

6. *Isolation*. A painful experience (or a painful impulse), upon repression, may have a different fate. The experience and its painful affect may part company in the unconscious. The experience may then return to consciousness, but with its affect gone, it is not at all troublesome to the individual. Among normal people the affect stays repressed for a time, finally gaining the level of consciousness through less disturbing experiences. When *isolation* involves a number of experiences, the quantity of energy released in the unconscious usually cannot be easily released. It may then attach itself to incongruous ideas in consciousness, yet constitute a neurosis. For example, fear of disease in an otherwise healthy person or fear of enclosures may be the expression of the energy released from the unconscious, repressed experiences.

It appears that *isolation* neither by name nor by experience gains much significance in forensic psychiatry. The management of it is by way of psychotherapy.

7. *Displacement*. It appears that affect has autonomy, that it can, for example, shift from one set of experiences to another. When we do something that is intensely disagreeable and painful to us, for which we condemn ourselves, the sense of guilt may be alleviated in part, if we shift the sense of guilt to some experience that is less significant to us. For instance, a father felt extremely guilty for punishing his son. He blamed himself for having made a terrible error. Later that day he shifted the sense of guilt, almost in its entirety, to a trivial error he made in his office.

Clinically the mental mechanism *displacement* is observed in clear relief in the obsessional neuroses, in which inordinate guilt is placed upon otherwise indifferent ideas. A patient was beset with the idea that he had committed an unpardonable error because he had failed to be courteous to a guest.

Casper Milquetoast solves his problems through servility to all. This is a second possible response noted in *displacement*.

8. *Symbolization*. The displacement of affects is the essence of symbolization. The process takes place in the unconscious. Usually a symbol has such slight resemblance to what it stands for that the individual can see no relationship between the two, until his attention is called to it.

Practically all psychogenic symptoms are symbols. Among them are hallucinations, delusions, obsessions, compulsions, the many conversion phenomena, etc.

9. *Condensation*. It is more or less characteristic of symbols that they express in highly condensed form something of a much broader scope. The national flag stands for the nation; in it is put an exceptionally large and varied quantity of energy. A single word may convey the emotions of an extended experience. The affects of several experiences may be crowded into an obsession or compulsion.

10. *Conversion*. During infancy emotional bonds between the child and the parents are almost inseparable. For present purposes we will not consider the rejected or frustrated child. The union of parents and child often gains in intensity as the end of the infantile period is neared. It is common for the child to prefer the parent of the opposite gender. And the parent likewise takes preferentially to the child of the opposite gender. It is not within our scope to mention the several variations of this theme, called the Oedipus complex, but rather to stress the general fact that the emotions of the child and parents shuttle back and forth, often turbulently. The child prefers the mother, then the father, then both. Mother shifts from child to father; father moves from mother to child. It's a great life, but many weaken. Final settlement is often made by the child in the form of identification with both parents. This arrangement, if pursued too diligently, makes the child both of his parents, but leaves him as a nonentity. He may and often does try to meet the requirements of childhood, adolescence and adulthood by being someone that he isn't, by being a peculiar blend of both parents. He has no "self," no ego of his own.

One or more of several courses are "open" to him. He may go through life just that way without too much trouble, though usually he is recognized as different or eccentric. Or, he may eventually reject one or both parents and meet the world with his impoverished personality. He is equally as famished when he rejects one and remains more or less completely with the other. Or, through illness, mentally or physically determined, he may retain one or both.

Mental illnesses are purposeful. They are compromises, troublesome ones, to be sure, that serve to release irrepressible urges from the unconscious. The release is gained only on condition that it dress itself up, so to speak, in unrecognizable attire. The prisoner can escape detection by the guards and gain freedom if he dresses, for instance, as a tradesman, but never in his striped prison garb. But, being back in society, he is less at ease than he was in prison, because he is beset on all sides with threats of capture, with dread of capitulation. Neuroses are escaped prisoners.

Among the disguises by which neurotic unconscious trends escape is the mental mechanism known as *conversion*. Conversion refers to the investment of unconscious troubles in the garb of physical ailments. Mental symptoms are converted into physical phenomena. A girl marries, not out of love, but to get away from an unhappy home. From the day of marriage she regrets the change; like a stoic, she pretends not to be hurt. Indeed, she goes further; she pretends to enjoy her new lot. Over the succeeding months and years, if the marriage lasts that long, she disciplines herself to sacrifice, to the extent that she no longer looks upon her marriage as a fault; it becomes a virtue to her unwittingly deceiving mind. She may be able to go through life on that slender balance; many do; many do not. The troubled unconscious may gain ever-increasing pressure until finally it bursts out. It could not burst through the over-virtuous conscious barrier, but it did break into one or more organs of the body. It was not especially difficult for the emotions to get into the flesh because that is their natural outlet in health or disease. Since her conscious mind has for a long time been completely shut off from the unconscious; she, of course, cannot understand that her stomach, for example, is sick because it is flooded with emotions. All that she knows is that she is a sick woman physically. Because of her invalidism she loses the role of wife and becomes a patient. It is all a form of psychological divorce in the guise of organic sickness.

11. *Rationalization*. In the beginning of courtship and during the earlier years of marriage the young lady, mentioned in the foregoing paragraph, found it difficult to conceal her dissatisfaction with her mate. She found herself doing many things that betrayed her unhappiness in courtship and marriage, but she always caught herself up quickly with explanations that negated the betrayals, making the latter appear as simple acts or thoughts of inattention. More than once she "forgot" to keep an appointment with her fiance, but she always gave what to him were plausible reasons for her non-appearance, though she knew that at the time there was no "good" reason at all for the error. As courtship advanced errors increased in frequency, but she soon learned how to master them with reasoning that was as convincing to her as to him. She did not exactly live a

full life of rationalization with him; still hardly a day passed without an instance. Rationalization is the process by which inadvertent errors are explained away as negligible.

12. *Idealization*. Rationalization is a part of the mental mechanism called *idealization*, which refers to the exaggerated investment of love in a love-object. In idealization there is an impoverishment of love in favor of the loved one, or rather, in favor of the mental image of the loved one. When idealization is greatly accentuated the love does not go out in large measure upon the loved one, but centers mainly upon the image of the lover. In other words, idealization is essentially self-love, or, as it is more gently expressed, the lover is in love with love. We can easily see that our patient (of the foregoing paragraph), unable to love her husband, but having a great need for expressing love, bestowed it upon her mental ideal. Lovers usually sense this arrangement quickly, feel that it can eventually be corrected ("I'll learn to love him when we're married." "She'll learn to love me when she knows me better."), but generally they are disillusioned.

13. *Transference*. Our young married woman was unable to love her husband, save in the manner indicated, because she had never lived out a satisfactory love life with her own father. He had been a cold father emotionally, though warm in material provision. Her childhood with him was almost loveless, though she craved attention from him. Nature abhors a mental as it does a physical vacuum. We are always seeking to fill the voids of our childhood. Often, as in the case of the young married woman, there is an incessant, though usually fruitless search for the lost object. She kept looking for her father, imagined she saw him in this or that person. She reacted to men as if they were her father. Indeed, she made her husband her father, which is another way of saying that she transferred upon her husband the impulses that she would have given her father, had he been receptive to them.

A love object is not only what he really is; he is what we make him out to be. This latter situation involves *transference*.

Transference may thus be of a positive

(tender) or negative (hostile) nature. A daughter may come to hate her father, a son to hate his mother, as a defense against the expression of impulses that are forbidden between parent and child. When a daughter marries a man who to her (unconscious) is little more than the image of her father, the equivalent of a father-daughter relationship is set up. Her reaction to this unholy alliance may be expressed in one or more of several ways. She may resent the intimacies of married life, may become frigid sexually, personally, socially. She does not know why but she may hate her child and show it up to the point of infanticide. The child is the product of psychological incest. Not a few family discords, not a few desertions, not a few murders are based upon this theme.

The law, however, does not recognize the culpability of the unconscious in such matters except in the vague sense of irresistible impulse or of the provisions of the M'Naghten rule. Even then it places the responsibility in the conscious part of the mind. But, a capable lawyer plays the theme without full recognition of it. He describes the loveless life of his client's childhood, her unpreparedness for love or marriage, the ghastliness of intimacies, the weakness of her mind, the great emotional confusion at the time the child is born, the growing mental agitation leading up to the murder. He describes the loving, though perplexing, utterly confusing role that she played with her husband.

The jury saves her from execution, but removes her from society for a time. It all seems to come out psychologically true, for the guilt, stemming from symbolic incest, is atoned for in a prison sentence.

Some day mental hygiene will make its influences felt more widely than it does today and the parent-child relationship will be less tragic.

14. *Projection.* The instincts are merciless in their claims for conscious recognition and action. Reenforced by the experiences of childhood, in particular, they often cause anxiety in the individual as a defense against their intrusion into consciousness. The hope to keep the impulses repressed without trouble is often futile. Nor does the individual know what he is working against; he does not know the source of his anxiety. The forces from the unconscious sometimes get so close to consciousness that they can be driven off only by casting them out of the unconscious onto other people. Then, when they seem to belong to, to emanate from another source, they are subjected to condemnation. The projection mechanism, therefore, is the mental process by which the other fellow is blamed for what is in truth our faulty, though unknown, impulse.

This mechanism, like many of the others, is used by normal as well as abnormal people. It is natural for a child to throw upon another a responsibility that is really his. This method preserves his narcissism and its omnipotence. However, when later he finds out that he is not omnipotent, he projects the omnipotence upon others, usually the parents, who by word or gesture can drive bogey men away or evoke their presence, who can cure ailments, cause magnificent gifts to appear, etc., etc.

While there are many manifestations of the projection mechanism, its fullest development is observed in patients with the paranoid form of schizophrenia. In this clinical disorder there is, among other things, an especially strong, but latent, that is, unconscious homosexual set of impulses. The patient tries to keep the impulses repressed in the unconscious, yet they are so strong as to require more than repression. The unconscious arranges, so to say, that they gain the level of consciousness by placing the consciously unwanted homosexuality upon other people. Now from its new location the patient can fight it out in the open, without knowledge that he put it there. He believes he is being persecuted, debased, that men are seeking to lure him into unnatural sexual practices. The persecutors, he says, talk about him in derogatory ways, their conversations with him (though innocent) he believes are gross innuendoes; radio broadcasts are interpreted by him as only subtle references to his alleged immorality; newspapers convey in the guise of news bad stories about him; the height of their persecution is seen in advertisements of men's underwear. These mental falsifications are delusions.

His persecutors do more than torment his mind. They torment his body, particularly through the sense organs. Hence, he develops hallucinations of persecution. He hears his enemies talking ill of him; they surround him with bad odors; they put nasty stuff in his food; they play electricity upon his body, especially around his privates; on occasion he sees them, but that is not common. He knows many of them, he says.

The patient becomes a real menace to society when he believes he knows the arch conspirator and lays plans to "get even" with him, in fact to kill him. It was a paranoid patient who started things that led to the framing of the M'Naghten rule. Under the influence of delusions of persecution M'Naghten shot and killed Drummond, private secretary to Sir Robert Peel.

Paranoid patients usually fight or flee. Fortunately for others the majority flee, flee more deeply into their psychosis. When they pursue the latter course they usually end in a psychology of omnipotence, in the role of Christ. They are the paranoid individuals who have fought and won all the battles of iniquity. See *schizophrenia*.

15. *Introjection*. The loss or the threatened loss of a loved one causes considerable turmoil in the mind of the loser. When the loved one is lost the loser strives vigorously to maintain his full love but there is only the mental image of the loved one to love. This love of the image, preceded by love of the real object, involves the mental mechanism called *introjection*. It is described as psychic assimilation.

Grief is occasioned by the loss. It may be the principal and perhaps only reaction. Among those, however, who cannot adjust normally to the loss, there creeps in a certain amount of criticism of the lost one or, what is commoner, of the introjected mental image of the lost one. It is as though the patient said, "It was mean of you to leave me. Now that you have left me all alone I am beginning to hate you." The grief, originally directed upon the lost one and its image, now is turned upon the bereaved one himself, or, at least, it appears that way. So, too, is the criticism directed upon him, giving rise to intense self-condemnation and feelings of worthlessness. When severe, the clinical picture is called the depressive phrase of manic-depressive psychosis. The expulsion of the introjected object is connected with the manic stage.

From the standpoint of criminology *introjection* gains importance especially when there is threatened loss of a loved one, which loss the potential loser refuses to brook. His grief period is very short and is quickly covered up by hostility, which may in extreme cases consummate in the murder of the girl he is about to lose. Usually such murderers show, long before the murder, a puerile type of emotional adaptation to people. It is said that they are of the leaning type. They are not altogether unlike the beggar who snarls at or injures the person who denies alms to him. The murderer begged and lost.

16. *Unconscious Phantasy*. Man is born with certain instinctual tendencies that remain unconscious a lifetime, unless he succumbs to a mental disorder. The tendencies themselves do not normally achieve the level of consciousness, though they are often mirrored in the overt behavior of the individual in the guise of "socialized" acts. Examples of unconscious phantasies are the Oedipus and the castration complexes.

17. *Dreaming*. Dreaming is regarded as a form of mental activity taking place in the unconscious part of the mind under conditions of sleep. The dream material is usually presented as pictures, that is, the language of the unconscious is largely pictorial. In fact, dreams are often primitive representations of unconscious impulses, though also often current material provides the vehicle for the conveyance of the impulses.

Dreams are said to have a latent and a manifest content. The unraveling of the latent content is known as dream-work; it is accomplished through the use ordinarily of several of the mental mechanisms mentioned in this article.

LELAND E. HINSIE
Assistant Director
New York Psychiatric Institute
and Hospital
New York City

BIBLIOGRAPHY

Freud, Sigmund, *Collected Papers*, London, 1924–25.

Hinsie, L. E. and Schatzky, J., *Psychiatric Dictionary*, New York 1940.

Hinsie, L. E., *Understanding Psychiatry*, New York, 1948.

Masserman, Jules H., *Principles of Dynamic Psychiatry*, Philadelphia, W. B. Saunders Co., 1946.

Noyes, Arthur P., *Modern Clinical Psychiatry*, Philadelphia, W. B. Saunders Co., 1935.

Sadler, William S., *Theory and Practice of Psychiatry*, St. Louis, C. V. Mosby Co., 1936.

Strecker, E. A. and Ebaugh, F. G., *Practical Clinical Psychiatry*, Philadelphia, P. Blakiston's Son and Co., 1940.

MENTAL TESTS AND MEASUREMENTS IN CRIMINOLOGY. This article presents an explanation of the applications of mental measurement in the field of criminology, the limitations of psychological testing, and a description of the types and varieties of practical psychometric techniques. While the emphasis is on intelligence testing, for it is in this area that psychometrics has thus far found its widest use in criminology, some attention is paid to techniques for the study of other phases of personality in which clinical psychology promises to make its most useful contributions. For the reader who wishes to go into the subject of mental testing more thoroughly there are presented references to sources of further information.

APPLICATIONS OF MENTAL TESTS IN
CRIMINOLOGY

Mental tests, in the field of criminology, have been applied in a variety of ways and for a number of specific purposes. They are utilized in court psychiatric clinics, penal institutions, reformatories, child guidance clinics, parental and reform schools, school attendance bureaus, criminological research institutes, crime prevention agencies, police laboratories, and a host of other institutions and agencies which deal with criminals and potential criminals.

A valuable aid in the understanding of the adult criminal, the juvenile delinquent, the child behavior problem, or the prison inmate, is the appraisal of his mental level or intellectual capacity. In the court psychiatric clinic, intelligence tests are often administered to determine each offender's intellectual status prior to sentence, so that the judge may be aware of those individuals who are mentally defective and should be committed to special institutions for the custody and treatment of defective delinquents. In the state prison or reformatory, psychometric tests are of use in the classification of the inmate and the determination of his suitability for certain types of schooling and training.

Psychological tests are utilized in child guidance clinics in helping to solve childhood problems of behavior and learning difficulties which may be the forerunners of juvenile or adult delinquency. It is often necessary to evaluate the child's intelligence in order to decide whether his misbehavior or school failure results from mental deficiency or to help plan his subsequent education and to aid in elaborating a suitable program of activities for the child in line with his capabilities. The intellectually gifted as well as the dull child may show special, and very perplexing behavior patterns as well as delinquent acts.

In school systems, the administration of mental tests are of service in helping to solve many problems which, if neglected, could lead to delinquency or truancy. One of the most prevalent problems is the child with reading difficulties. When a careful examination of vision and hearing reveals no organic explanation of the difficulties, often the administration of intelligence tests and specialized diagnostic tests of reading ability points to the source of the problem and suggests treatment.

Frequently, in connection with courts and legal cases, it is necessary to evaluate the ability of an individual in administering his own affiars. The question arises whether the subject is legally responsible for his acts. The psychological tests will aid in determining the mental capacity and responsibility of an individual.

While psychometrics alone does not at present claim to be able to accomplish differential diagnosis of the various psychoses and neuroses, there are certain psychological testing instruments which are useful in measuring the intelligence of abnormal individuals and indicating the extent of deterioration when it is present. Tests and procedures are available which help supplement or substantiate psychiatric findings concerning personality aberrations and in many instances are crucial in enabling a diagnosis to be made.

TYPES OF PSYCHOMETRIC TESTS

Psychological testing makes possible the study of a cross-section or sample of human behavior. The individual being tested is asked certain questions, or given certain tasks to perform or problems to solve. His responses, or his performances, are compared to those of other individuals under comparable circumstances. The results of the test are a basis for estimates and predictions.

Psychological tests are designed to be administered in various ways depending upon the content of the test, the ability being measured, and the individual being tested. Some tests are so made that they can be given to only one individual at a time. Other tests may be given to ten, twenty, or almost any other number of persons at once. The first type is called *individual tests;* the second, *group tests.* In both kinds, some tests may require a high degree of language facility both in understanding directions and in the subjects' response. Others require a minimum of language; the directions may be given verbally or in pantomime, and the response require only manual performance, marking, or the like. The first in this classification are called *verbal tests;* the second are called *performance tests,* which may be further subdivided into non-verbal when directions are given by language, and non-language when the directions are given in pantomime.

Tests may be *oral* or *written.* Oral tests usually consist of questions read aloud or memorized and spoken to the patient. The tester records the answers on a scoring blank, and the whole procedure in evaluating intelligence by this method may require an interview with the subject of several minutes to perhaps an hour, depending upon the test. The test is scored and interpreted later at the examiner's leisure. Written tests are often preferred because they are easily administered. The subject is given a printed form with numbered spaces for his replies. Many group intelligence tests are written tests which require the supervision of a tester and consist of strictly factual questions, arithmetical problems, and complex problems requiring reasoning. The necessity for lengthy written notes by the examiner is avoided and such tests are conveniently scored and interpreted after the testees have left.

In deciding whether a subject should be given a verbal or performance test, a written or oral test, an individual or group test, and which particular test is most appropriate, the psychologist is influenced by a number of important considerations such as the ease of scoring, administration, and interpretation, the intrinsic value of the test in living up to its aim, its consistency in measuring a certain type of ability, and the problems involved in the particular case.

FACTORS AFFECTING TEST RESULTS

It is important for all persons connected with criminology in some way to be aware of a number of cautions in evaluating and interpreting test results. The judge, the probation or parole officer, the prison administrator, the social worker, the criminological researcher, and the host of other workers in this field will inevitably have occasion to utilize the results given to them by psychologists as an aid in their handling of offenders.

Tests give only an approximate measure of an individual's performance at a particular time and in terms of comparison with others. Each test is made to measure one particular thing such as intelligence, aptitude for mechanical work, emotional stability, etc., and must not be held responsible if it does not measure everything. In the testing of delinquents and criminals the results are particularly likely to be affected by subjective factors in the attitudes of the subject, the subject's physical and mental condition, disturbing stimuli in the environment, interruptions during the examination, language difficulties of the subject, emotional disturbances, language handicaps, etc. Only the most experienced examiners can be relied upon to secure valid results. Some of the attitudes of criminal offenders which affect performance on tests are deliberate deception, recalcitrancy, sportiveness (lack of seriousness), emotional disturbances (including general depression, anger, or resentfulness, fear, guilt feelings and shame, shyness, homesickness, mental conflict, psychopathy, and the like), general nervous excitement, lack of confidence, and suspiciousness.

The offender who has just been convicted of a crime may be uncooperative or emotionally upset or embittered and aggrieved so that suitable rapport cannot be obtained for adequate and valid testing. He should only be tested for intelligence when he is relaxed and cooperative so that he can put forth his best efforts. A skillful examiner will often succeed in securing good rapport under even the most adverse circumstances.

Validity, Reliability, and Norms

There are a bewildering array of mental tests available. In choosing a suitable test or tests, the validity, reliability, and norms, must be considered. A test standardized on children should be used with caution in testing adults and a test based upon samplings of college students can not be used with adults of no educational achievement.

Validity—Does the test measure what it purports to measure? Every test is accompanied by a manual which tells how the test was set up, how it is to be given, and how it is to be interpreted. This manual should contain a statement as to how the author established the validity of his test. The first thing one asks of an intelligence test is therefore some proof that it actually measures intelligence.

Reliability—Does the test always measure the same thing? Can the test be repeated on the same individual and still give the same results? The test manual should contain information concerning the reliability of the test.

Norms—This term refers to the kind and size of population upon which the test was standardized. Were the original trials of the test conducted on a suitable sample of the kind of people for whom the test is intended and were there enough of them? Obviously, an intelligence test based upon the testing of two hundred fourth grade school children

would not be safe or accurate enough to use on an adult illiterate criminal of rural background.

Representative Tests

Students of criminal behavior and practical workers in criminology need to be acquainted with those psychological tests and procedures which have found wide application in criminological work. The brief description of specific tests that follows is obviously not intended to meet the needs of those who actually are concerned with testing and must know tests but rather of those in the criminological field who should know *about* tests. With the multiplicity of tests available, the ones mentioned here are merely representative having been selected because of their usefulness in the study of delinquents and criminals.

Tests of Intelligence

Revised Stanford-Binet Intelligence Scale— This is the oldest and probably most widely used individual intelligence test and is available in two editions. The first Stanford Revision, that of Terman, was published in 1916 and was replaced after 20 years of very wide application by the Terman and Merrill revision published in 1937. The scale consists of a large number of test items ranging in difficulty from the two-year level to the superior adult level. It is standardized mainly on children of school age. A printed blank is provided for the verbatim recording of replies to oral questions and instructions and at the lower age levels for children this material is supplemented by a case containing various concrete objects to be manipulated and named by the subject. This scale is preferred by most examiners for children while another battery of tests is chosen for measuring adult intelligence. Many courts, clinics, hospitals, prisons and reformatories still use it for adults although there is now available an adequately standardized scale for those over sixteen years of age.

The scale provides a variety of tasks at each age level. For the younger children such tasks as putting wooden beads on a string, building block towers, and identifying objects and parts of the body are given.

Tests of immediate memory span for digits and words are found throughout the scale. At the higher levels, items are presented which depend upon abstract verbal and arithmetical reasoning. For example, absurd situations are described and the subject is required to detect the absurdity. Other items consist of defining abstract words, giving similarities and differences between common objects, drawing designs, and repeating digits in reverse.

The test items in the scale are arranged according to age level. The age level at which the subject passes all items is known as the *basal age*. Testing is continued until the individual fails all the items at an age level and this is known as his *maximal age*. Each item successfully completed receives a certain number of months credit depending upon the age level it is on and the number of items on that level. The total of these credits in terms of months when added to the basal age gives the *mental age*. The subject's mental age corresponds to the average ability of normal individuals of that age. Thus, a subject with a mental age of seven, has the mental capacity of an average seven year old child. The ratio of the mental age to the chronological age or actual age of the subject when multiplied by 100 gives the *Intelligence Quotient* or *I.Q.* Thus, a subject with a mental age of seven years and a chronological age of seven years would have an I.Q. of 100. However, if he had a mental age of five years with a chronological age of seven, his I.Q. would be 71. On the other hand, if he scored a mental age of ten years, six months and had a life age of seven, the I.Q. would be 150.

Wechsler-Bellevue Intelligence Scale — This scale is planned for the measurement of the intelligence of adults and adolescents. It consists of 10 tests, five of which are of a verbal nature and five of a performance type. The five verbal tests compose the *Verbal Scale* while the five non-verbal tests can be scored as the *Performance Scale*. A vocabulary test is provided as an alternate item. The verbal part of the scale contains the following tests: Information, Comprehension, Arithmetical Reasoning, Memory Span for Digits, and similarities. The per-

formance scale has the following tests: Picture Arrangement, Picture Completion, Block Design, Digit Symbol, and Object Assembly.

Simple directions are given orally by the examiner to the individual subject. The subtests are scored on the basis of speed, accuracy, comprehension, ability to analyze and discriminate, according to the nature of the task. The points accumulated for each subject are weighted and totaled to obtain the Full Scale Intelligence Quotient from tables provided in convenient form by the author. Verbal and Performance I.Q.'s are separately computed.

This scale is especially appropriate for use in testing adults and adolescents since it has been standardized on older subjects rather than on school children. The test material is particularly interesting to older subjects and the scale is increasingly being used in state prisons and court clinics. Qualitative analysis of the subtest patterns may bring out temporary losses of efficiency, mental deterioration, or impairment due to mental illness, all of which is valuable in work with adult prisoners. Such pattern analysis can also be of value in psychiatric diagnosis.

Kent's Emergency Test—Many workers in the criminological field have felt the need for an instrument for appraising intelligence which might be very quickly given without special preparations in the way of assembling materials. The Revised Emergency Test fills this need. It consists of ten simply-expressed questions to be given and answered either orally or in written form. The test is not intended to take the place of the full psychiatric or psychological examination. The test in its present form takes approximately one minute to administer and is useful in busy travelling clinics, draft boards, and large prisons for quick screening and segregation of prospective subjects for more intensive and specialized testing.

Otis Self-Administering Test of Mental Ability—This short, convenient intelligence scale is perhaps the most widely used of the many group tests available. It is of value in securing a rough estimate of an individual's mental level. It can also be used individually and is a self-administering paper-pencil scale. The test consists of the *Intermediate Exam-*

ination for grade four to nine and the *Higher Examination* for high school students and adults. There are four alternate forms for each of the examinations. Seventy-five problems compose the test: information, arithmetic, number-series completion, recognition of opposites, analogies, understanding of proverbs, logical inferences, and practical judgment items, arranged in random fashion for content but roughly in order of increasing difficulty.

Either a 20- or 30-minute time limit is allowed and from the raw score and equivalent standard score, Binet Mental Age, Otis I.Q., and Centile Rank may be read from tables. A low score on the test indicates the need for further testing of the subject with an individual scale such as the Stanford-Binet or Wechsler-Bellevue.

Arthur Point Scale of Performance Tests— This test serves as a non-verbal scale for measuring intellectual capacity and is often used to supplement verbal intelligence test results. In many cases of offenders or prison inmates with foreign language handicap, speech or hearing defects or reading disabilities, verbal tests are inadequate and this type of performance scale is utilized. It also brings out certain features in the intelligence of inmates in whom verbal and non-verbal abilities are markedly unequal in their development.

There are nine sub-tests, each measuring a different aspect of intelligence. The *Knox Cube Test* consists of five one-inch cubes. Four are placed in a row two inches apart and with the fifth cube the examiner taps the four cubes in a certain order. The subject is to copy the performance. Twelve different tapping patterns are given. The *Seguin Form Board, Two-Figure Form Board, Casuist Form Board,* are all boards with geometric figures cut out which the subject has to re-assemble as quickly as possible. The *Manikin* and *Feature Profile* tests are also in the Wechsler-Bellevue Scale and require the assembly of six pieces which fit together to form a man and four pieces forming an ear as well as three pieces giving a profile which together with the ear give a complete face. The *Mare and Foal Test* consists of a board on which is pictured a

farm scene. Seven pieces have been removed and are placed above the board and the subject is to fit them into the board as quickly as possible. The *Healy Picture Completion* consists of a board on which there is a picture of people doing various things. Parts of the picture are left out and the subject is required to fill in the most sensible solutions for each of the omissions. The *Porteus Maze* consists of 11 different mazes of increasing difficulty on paper. The subject is to start at the beginning of each maze and find his way out by the use of a pencil. The Porteus Maze Test has been used widely in its standardized form as a separate supplementary test and can give scores from five years to adulthood. The test yields much valuable information on the subject's personality traits. The *Kohs Block Design Test* which can also be used as a separate supplementary test since it has independent norms, completes the Arthur Point Scale battery. It consists of simple and attractively painted cubes, with different colors or combinations of colors on each of the six sides. The subject is required to arrange the blocks in a series of increasingly difficult and complex patterns of color and form.

Raw scores are obtained for each of the tests in terms of the time taken to complete each task, the number of correct performances, or both. These are then converted into points and into approximate mental ages by means of a table. The sum of the points for each test may be translated into a Performance Age. This P. A. indicates the subject's capacity level for manipulating concrete materials.

Deterioration Tests

The estimation of mental deterioration is often necessary to help determine a prisoner's parolability and his capacity for rehabilitation. Studies of decline in mental efficiency have shown that it occurs more slowly in certain abilities than in others. The abilities involved in vocabulary tests hold up much better than do those called for by tests of functions like immediate memory, the learning of new associations, adaptive response to complex situations, etc. The subject's vocabulary test score may represent, therefore, his original capacity before any decline had begun to set in. The results from the other tests may indicate the present level of the subject's mental functioning. Comparison of the vocabulary score with those resulting from the other tests yields an index of the individual's mental efficiency or how nearly his present functioning approximates the maximum he was ever capable of. Babcock and Levy have devised a test for the purpose of estimating mental deterioration. The *Babcock-Levy Examination for Efficiency of Mental Functioning* has proved useful to prison psychologists and others in the field of mental testing in criminology. Wechsler advocates the use of his intelligence scale as a measure of mental deterioration. The *Wells Memory Test* is a method for the detection of memory disturbances found in certain disorders. Shipley has devised a test of mental deterioration which he regards as still in the experimental or research stage.

Vocational Aptitude Tests

Minnesota Mechanical Assembly Test—This is an example of the type of aptitude tests used by psychologists as a basis for counseling individuals in the choice of an occupation. It is frequently given to prison inmates to determine their suitability for certain types of mechanical training in the institution. The test consists of 33 mechanical articles which are to be assembled by the subject in a specific period of time. Some of the articles are a bicycle bell, a die-holder, an expansion nut, etc. The subject gets a score of 10 for each contrivance assembled within the time limit and partial credit is given in proportion to lesser amounts of work correctly completed. Good performance on this test is considered an indication of aptitude for such mechanical trades as machinist, woodworker, ironworker, toolmaker, automobile mechanic, and the like.

Strong Vocational Interest Inventory—To supplement knowledge concerning an individual's capacities and special aptitudes, it is often important to have insight into his interests especially vocational interests. The Strong Inventory consists of a test blank of 400 verbal items on which the subject is asked to indicate his like, dislike, or indifference to each item. Two forms are available, one for men and one for women.

Personality Tests

Bernreuter Personality Inventory—This is a widely used instrument which consists of a printed questionnaire asking 125 questions to be answered by "Yes", "No", or "?". It is intended for individuals of high school age and adults. Its purpose is to uncover certain serious personality problems as shown by such traits as general abnormality, neuroticism, self-sufficiency, introversions, and dominance. Scores obtained on this inventory supposedly differentiate between the normal and the abnormal, between the emotionally stable and the unstable individual. However, in the field of criminology the test is seldom considered conclusive because the offender will not often truthfully reveal all the facts about his personality.

Bell Adjustment Inventory—This is a printed questionnaire quite similar to the Bernreuter Test. It has two forms, one intended for high school and college students and one for adults. Both forms measure adjustment in the home, in health, in social life, and in the emotional sphere. The adult form also measures vocational adjustment.

Projective Techniques

In contrast to the ubiquitous questionnaire and self-rating procedures, the various standardized personality tests, and the direct clinical interview, projective techniques enable the clinician to get away from static descriptive characteristics like neurotic tendency, self-sufficiency, introversion-extroversion, dominance-submission, *et al,* and to reveal latent strivings, images, and sentiments which the subject would be *unwilling* or *unable* to express in a direct communication. In projective techniques, the actual behavior of the subject is sampled and the individual often reveals himself even beyond his own conscious knowledge. These methods are therefore especially useful in evaluating the personalities of criminals and psychopaths who are uncooperative or deceitful in tests like the Bernreuter or Bell inventories.

Rorschach Psychodiagnostic Test—This consists of a series of 10 ink-blots, some in black and white and some in color. The subject is asked to look at the blots one at a time and mention anything he sees in them, what they remind him of, or what they could represent. The subject's responses and his replies to certain questions about them afterwards, furnish the bases for the scoring and interpretation. Notes are also made of card turning and reaction time, etc. The responses are scored according to total number of responses, apperception mode, qualities perceived, and the content of the responses. The apperception mode refers to whether the whole or parts of the blots are utilized by the subject in his responses. The qualities perceived include form, color and movement and the content refers to the specific objects which are recalled, such as animals, trees, landscape, and human beings, as well as whether the responses are popular or original.

The various scoring factors in the Rorschach are interpreted as signifying different functions of the personality. Special notice is taken of the way in which the different factors are related to each other as an expression of the total personality. According to certain norms arrived at from extensive research with subjects in various well-defined groups, an individual's pattern of responses can be interpreted as belonging to one or another of the groups such as normal personality, neurosis or psychosis of a certain type, etc.

Thematic Apperception Test—This consists of a series of photographs or pictures, which have been carefully selected in groups appropriate for children, male adults, and female adults. The subject is told that his imagination is being studied and is asked to make up a story for each picture, to say what the people in the picture are feeling and thinking, and to tell what the result will be. The subject reveals his personality through these stories. The stories are analyzed in terms of the relationship of the main story themes to each other after the major themes of each story have been determined, e.g., social status, vocational ideals, love relationships, ambitions, family conflicts, etc. Hidden or repressed conflicts, complexes, and trauma are often revealed in the stories. The endings and outcomes are often important. Considerable clinical skill is required for making valid interpretations.

BIBLIOGRAPHY

Arthur, G., *A Point Scale of Performance Tests*, (2 volumes), New York: Commonwealth Fund, 1930.

Babcock, H., *Time and the Mind*, Cambridge: Sci-Art Publishers, 1941.

Bell, H. M., *Adjustment Inventory*, Stanford University Press, 1934.

Bernreuter, R. G., The Theory and Construction of the Personality Inventory. *J. Soc. Psychol.*, 1933, 4, 387-405.

Garrett, H. E. and Schneck, M. R., *Psychological Tests, Methods and Results*, New York: Harper and Brothers, 1933.

Greene, E. B., *Measurements of Human Behavior*, New York: Odyssey Press, 1941.

Kent, G. H., Emergency Battery of One-Minute Tests, *J. Psychol.*, 1942, 13, 141-164.

Klopfer, B. and Kelley, D., *The Rorschach Technique*, New York: World Book Company, 1942.

Murray, H. A., *Thematic Apperception Test*, Cambridge: Harvard University Press, 1943.

Otis, A. S., *Otis Self-Administering Tests of Mental Ability*, New York: World Book Co., 1922.

Paterson, D. G., et al., *Minnesota Mechanical Ability Tests*, Minneapolis: Univ. Minnesota Press, 1930.

Strong, E. K. Jr., *Vocational Interests of Men and Women*, Stanford University Press, 1943.

Terman, L. M. and Merrill, M. A., *Measuring Intelligence*, Boston: Houghton Mifflin, 1937.

Wechsler, D., *The Measurement of Adult Intelligence*, (2d ed.) Baltimore: Williams and Wilkins, 1941.

Wells, F. L., *Mental Tests in Clinical Practice*, N. Y., World Book Company, 1927.

SAMUEL B. KUTASH
Chief Clinical Psychologist
Mental Hygiene Clinic
Veterans Administration
Newark, New Jersey

MILITARY CRIMINOLOGY. *Purpose.* In view of the vast numbers of men and women who submitted themselves to the Articles of War in World War II, and in the light of subsequent efforts of veterans' organizations and military authorities to maintain substantial peacetime forces, a survey of the field of criminology cannot be complete without inclusion of an analysis of the purpose, history, procedure, and operational effects of the system of military jurisprudence.

The foundation of the massive structure of military law consists of a group of 121

Articles of War, setting forth simply, briefly and completely the types of courts, qualifications of members (judges), rules of procedure, definitions of crimes and punishments, and allied pertinent matter. These articles are designed to maintain, to as great a degree as possible, the discipline of military personnel of all grades, consistent with the location, mission, and general past behavior of any unit or organization, and they afford swift, publicized punishments as precedent-setting factors in controlling the conduct of troops, to all of whom the results of trials are promptly made known through official channels.[1]

The speed employed in preparing a military crime for trial, the continual readiness of court personnel to sit in judgment, the brevity of the average military trial, and the apparent severity of punishment imposed upon the convicted accused (defendant), as compared to the endless procrastination, ponderous preparation, technicalities of defense, and average-to-minimum penalties which generally characterize the procedure in civil tribunals of criminal jurisdiction, are justified by the office of the Judge Advocate General of the Army on the basis of immediacy of purpose (particularly in time of war), recognition of the effects of unpunished misconduct upon troops local to the situs of the offense, and prevention of commission—rather than prevention of an untried backlog—of crimes calculated as deterrents to the efficient functioning of an organized warring force.

History. The development of military law as a creature of authority equals in excitement and fascination that of any segment of civilization's advancement. It is considerably older than the Constitution of the United States, and while the constitution represents a precise, cloven departure from old world law, designed to enhance the new type of existence desired by the colonists, military justice carries directly through a long line of trial and error employed by armies throughout the ages, in utter disregard of civil

statutes in the various nations of the world. It would appear, consequently, that while countries differ in systems of government and jurisprudence, there is a universality attached to the creation, maintenance, and purpose of armies to the end that the military law of any given nation is not radically different from that of any other. Since the law governing discipline of soldiers is indirectly, but essentially, as important as their combat ability, the military law of the successful army very often constitutes the standard after which that of other armies is patterned.[2]

While the use of Military Law (control by a nation of its own soldiers) is as ancient as war itself, and, as a matter of fact, considerably older than any country now using it, certain related branches dealing with actual combat conduct are comparatively new, having come into being with international recognition of the needlessness for savagery, pointless carnage, vicious suppression of defeated peoples, and devastation of conquered territory where pure military necessity did not so require. These newer offshoots, including *Military Government* (jurisdiction exercised by a belligerent occupying an enemy's territory), *Rules of Land Warfare* (covering treatment of prisoners of war, privileges of war correspondents, use of poison gas, dumdum bullets, etc.), and *Martial Law* (temporary control over the civil population of a locality by military forces without authority of written law, as necessity may demand) are interesting, but tangential to the subject, and further gleanings upon them may be had by reference to various War Department manuals and international treaties.[3]

[1] Usual course pursued is the posting of Court-Martial Orders on organization bulletin boards, citing accusation, findings, and sentence, or reading such orders to troops at a required formation.

[2] German military law in World War II was almost identical to that of the U. S. Even the age-old Prussian law permitting an officer to shoot a soldier in ranks for disobedience was eliminated in apparent deference to the successful operation of the Articles of War of the U. S. Army.

[3] War Department FM 27–10, Rules of Land Warfare. War Department FM 27–5, Military Government and Civil Affairs. Navy Department OpNav 50E–3, Military Government and Civil Affairs. Geneva Convention July 27, 1929, Treaty Series 846 & 847, 47 United States Statutes at Large, 233 & 286, Volume IV, 5209, 5224. Hague Convention October 18, 1907, Treaty Series 538 et seq., 36 United States Statutes at Large 2259 et seq., Malloy, Treaties, Volume II.

Any endeavor to establish the true origin of military law would result only in despair, for, in one form or another, it was probably used by primitive tribes. Prominent among early written codes is the brief but comprehensive *Ordonnances of Richard I, A.D. 1190*, undoubtedly calculated by that master of intrigue to eliminate the characteristic jealousy between the members of his army and navy in the crusade to Jerusalem. The complete text follows:—

"Richard, by the grace of God, King of England, Duke of Normandy and Aquitaine, and Earl of Anjou, to all his subjects about to proceed by sea to Jerusalem, greeting. Know ye that we, with the common consent of fit and proper men, have made the enactments underwritten. Whoever shall slay a man on ship-board, he shall be bound to the dead man and thrown into the sea. If he shall slay him on land he shall be bound to the dead man and buried in the earth. If any one shall be convicted, by lawful witnesses, of having drawn out a knife with which to strike another so as to draw blood, he shall lose his hand. If, also, he shall give a blow with his hand, without shedding blood, he shall be plunged into the sea three times. If any man shall utter disgraceful language or abuse, or shall curse his companion, he shall pay him an ounce of silver for every time he has so abused him. A robber who shall be convicted of theft shall have his head cropped after the manner of a champion,[4] and boiling pitch shall be poured thereon, and then the feathers of a cushion shall be shaken out upon him, so that he may be known, and at the first land at which the ship shall touch, he shall so be set on shore. Witness myself, at Chinon."

Observe the broad scope encompassed in these comparatively few words! The ordinance provides punishments of a specific nature (too specific, perhaps, from the point of view of the offender) for the crimes of murder on land or sea, striking by hand or weapon, stabbing, threatening, profanity or other verbal abuse (apparently including in-

subordination, disobedience, etc.), and theft of any type in any amount.

This code, it will be seen, relates only to the conduct of the troops as between themselves, and while it is to be assumed that such crimes as treason, desertion, and mutiny were omitted because of inclusion in other statutes, or perhaps for the reason that Richard's faith in his men did not presuppose such offenses, it is of notable interest that no provision was incorporated which defined or punished the offenses of plundering, rape, or intoxication. Whether these items were overlooked, or whether they were specifically omitted with a view toward having their commission serve as inducements for early entry into enemy territory is purely speculative. However, a study of the policies and tactics of some victorious armies in recent years lends credence to the latter possibility.

Intentional or not, these omissions remained conspicuously absent from the army law of England until introduction of the *Articles of War of Richard II* in 1385 and subsequent military codes [5] which prohibited plundering (Article VII), forcing of women (Article III), taking of servants (Article XXIII), and allied offenses, under the diverse penalties of forfeiting body and goods, losing horse and armor, drawing and hanging, hanging by the arms, loss of the left ear,[6] and others of varied and detailed account.

Sweden is found to have had a complete, effective compilation of military laws in the *Code of Articles of King Gustavus Adolphus*, adopted in 1621.[7] This codification of the most effective of all pre-existing army laws was characterized by its frequent allusion to religion and prayer, along with continual reference to the penalties imposed upon

---

[4] "Champion" was the term applied to men hired to fight legalized duels, and, in cases of murder or homicide, their hair was clipped close to their heads.

[5] *Articles of War of Richard II*, reprinted in full in "Military Law and Precedents," by Winthrop, pages 904–906, Second Edition, 1920; *Rules and Ordonnances of War of Henry V* appear in Upton's "De Studio Militari." The classic *Military Code of Henry VIII* is said to be preserved in manuscript form in the College of Arms, London.

[6] Never does removal of the right ear appear as a punishment; inaccurate physiological value placed upon the left ear at that period may have been the cause.

[7] Translated and printed in Ward's "Animadversions of Warre," London, 1639.

atheistic personnel and violators in general. Among the vast number of prohibitions and requirements (exceeding the number of articles in effect at the present time in the United States) were restrictions against all conceivable manner of misbehavior, as well as liberal use of such phrases as "idolatry, witchcraft, and inchanting of armes is forbidden," "God's name is not to be dishonored upon pain of death," "death to him, drunk or sober, who blasphemes the name of God," "publike prayer is to be said each morning and evening," and other references to religious conduct with which the articles are replete.[8]

It was English military law, however, that served as the broadest source of American army discipline, and the present military code of the United States consists of extractions from the *Articles of War of James II,* 1686 and 1688, the *British Articles* in force at the start of the Revolutionary War, the *Massachusetts Articles of War,* and the *American Articles of War* of 1775, corrected in 1776, 1786, 1806, 1874, 1892, 1895, 1916, 1921, 1928, and 1943.[9] Accordingly, the present United States Articles of War cannot possibly reflect a set of rules drawn together at a single sitting, nor a bill introduced to and enacted by Congress, nor the copied pattern set forth by any one nation or army. It is a code that grew by the side of international hostility through the centuries, its provisions carefully weighed by wide experience, its workability determined by its amenability and efficiency to each recurring mission at hand, and its retention or acceptability evaluated by the success or failure of the armies controlled by it. Briefly, military law may be said to be exactly that which experience through the exigencies of war have made it.

The value of the Articles of War of the United States can best be judged, of course, by the fact that the enormous test posed by World War II was consummated by victory. Nevertheless, while individual and collective complaints against the army's legal system could not receive detailed attention during the course of the conflict, the relaxed tempo of post-war military activity brought forth a veritable surge of denunciatory criticism. So great was the volume of execration, despite the fact that it was definitely not an organized movement, that the War Department saw fit to conduct hearings, appoint investigators, review a mass of trials, and throw itself open to corrective suggestions from the entire American population. Many newspapers took up the cry, and asked their readers to submit, on furnished blank forms, opinions and recommendations.[10] Much of the excitement and confusion attendant upon this controversy may be allayed by a study of the present Articles of War, the reasons for their respective inclusion, and the method of their operation.

The Military Courts. The Articles of War provide for three tribunals, known as courts-martial. The court of least jurisdiction is the *Summary Court-Martial* which may sentence the accused, for specified minor offenses, to a maximum of one month in confinement at hard labor. There is but one member sitting in judgment and he, as in the case of members of all courts-martial, must be a commissioned officer. Generally, there is no defense counsel representing the accused, although the member is required to explain understandably to the accused his rights before and during trial.

Next in order of power and composition is the *Special Court-Martial* which may, *inter alia,* sentence the accused to six months in confinement at hard labor (imprisonment must *always* be at hard labor, probably for the reason that confinement at leisure might well prove more attractive to some than the hard work and peril to which the average law-abiding soldier is subject). Three or more members constitute those sitting in

[8] Religion in the modern army is pursued, consistent with the allowances of time, location, and combat situation, and many dispensations are granted by the various denominations in order that practical fidelity to military duties may not be hampered by certain religious observances cumbersome to the demands of training or combat.

[9] Primary correction in 1943 was elimination of maximum punishment for AWOL, rendering any penalty. except death, allowable.

[10] The readers' remarks were categorized and tabulated, and then forwarded for consideration at the War Department hearings on the changes, if any, to be incorporated into the Articles of War.

judgment, and the accused is defended by counsel.

Concluding the group is the *General Court-Martial,* consisting of five or more members.[11] This tribunal has unlimited discretion in awarding of punishments (except in the case of crimes calling for specific, mandatory sentences), and it may impose death,[12] any

[11] Special and General Courts require respective minimum memberships of three and five. The *"or more"* provision guards against loss of jurisdiction, and members are appointed in excess numbers for the reason that illness, temporary duty elsewhere, transfer, or other absence of some would still leave the court with its essential minimum. Consequently, the usual Special Court has about six members, and the usual General Court, approximately ten.

[12] When imposing the death penalty, the court must specify the manner of execution—by hanging or by a firing squad. This custom is a carry-over from English law which set forth dozens of types of execution, each to fit the crime. Today, a crime of brutality (as murder) calls for hanging, whereas a purely military, or "honorable" crime (as spying) calls for the firing squad.

[13] The law member rules conclusively upon all questions concerning admissability of evidence, since he is presumed to be the only member present familiar with the technical rules of evidence. His rulings on all other interlocutory questions are subject to objection by any member of the court, and upon such objection, the members vote on the issue in closed court. In a Special Court, the president (ranking officer) undertakes the duties of the law member, and in this court, *all* rulings by him are subject to objection by any member.

[14] It would appear—for better or worse—that a Special Court may convene, judge, and sentence without the necessity for a single lawyer or legally-trained person in the room. This possibility is eliminated in a General Court by the presence of the law member, who nevertheless has but one vote on finding and sentence. Moreover, the law member may be challenged for cause by either side.

[15] Manual for Courts-Martial 1928, Article of War No. 8. Lesser authorities (although, in all cases, commanders) appoint Special Courts.

[16] All or in part by a General Court; in part only (usually 2/3rds) by Special or Summary Court.

[17] Enlisted man sentenced to any confinement must be reduced to private; an officer cannot be sentenced to reduction in grade, but may be sentenced to reduction in rank (delay in promotion).

[18] Manual for Courts-Martial, 1928, pages 97–101.

period of confinement up to and including a life sentence, dishonorable discharge, and forfeiture of all pay and allowances. The accused is defended by counsel and, as in the case of the Special Court, the highest ranking officer among the members is the president of the court. This is the only military court employing the legal abilities of a law member (usually an officer in the Judge Advocate General's Department) whose duty it is to rule on certain interlocutory questions of procedure arising during the trial.[13] There is no requirement that any other member, prosecutor, or defense counsel of any military court be a lawyer, or possessed of any legal training or experience.[14]

The members of General Courts-Martial are appointed to that post from their usual military duties by the President of the United States, Superintendent of West Point (except where the accused is a commissioned officer), and the commanding officers of various echelons,[15] and the appointment usually remains in force for a period during which the membership remains intact for a number of trials. As a rule, however, the Summary Court officer is permanently assigned to his task.

The rule requiring commissioned officers only as members of courts-martial is unwavering, with the result that non-commissioned officers, warrant officers and flight officers are ineligible, although officers in the Army Nurse Corps and the WAC are not only eligible, but at least one WAC officer must be a member at any court-martial in which a WAC officer or enlisted woman is the accused. Where possible, no member of a court should be junior in grade to an accused officer, and in any case, no officer should be appointed as a court-martial member unless he has had a minimum of two years' service.

Punishments. In addition to the punishments generally set forth above, all three courts have such miscellaneous powers as directing forfeiture of pay,[16] reduction in grade to Private,[17] restriction to a specified area without guard, admonition, and reprimand. *The Table of Maximum Punishments* [18] of the military justice system sets forth in detail the penalties which may be awarded for all crimes, and a careful examination of this "price list" will disclose, in the light of disciplinary requirements and organizational efficiency, that the widespread belief of excessiveness and severity is largely without foundation. This table developed along with military law through many years and many wars, and it is now presumed to represent the most expeditious and just treatment of offenders from all points of view, including consideration of their potential value to the service and their amenability to the army's rehabilitation program. Particular attention is directed to the fact that the courts, in a vast number of cases, impose substantially *less* than the maximum provided.

All nature of cruel, unusual, or corporal punishment is prohibited.[19] Nor may military duties, such as sentry work, drills, manual of arms, carrying of loaded knapsacks, or sounding of calls be degraded by having them imposed as punishments;[20] nor may

[19] This prohibition includes flogging, branding, marking or tattooing the body, wearing of irons, shaving the head (compare with Ordonnances of Richard I, *supra,*) and the use of the pillory or stocks.

[20] More than "degrading," these duties would not be undertaken as normal training in the proper spirit by faithful troops if known to serve as criminal penalties. This provision is flagrantly violated by many commanding officers, particularly when awarding punishments under Article of War 104, *infra.*

[21] This rule is aimed at placarding, primarily, which entailed the wearing of a "sandwich sign" by a soldier, reading "I went AWOL," or "I am an asset to the enemy," or "I am a goldbrick," etc.

[22] Manual for Courts-Martial, Article of War 104, & pages 103–106.

[23] Whether or not an offense may be considered "minor" depends upon its nature, time and place of its commission, and the person committing it. Generally speaking, the term includes derelictions not involving moral turpitude or any greater degree of criminality or seriousness than is involved in the average offense tried by Summary Court-Martial. Brief period of AWOL, as first offense, would be an illustration of a minor offense.

[24] While no portion of an enlisted man's pay may be forfeited under this authority, a commissioned officer, under Article of War 104, may be fined a maximum of one-half of one month's base pay (excluding allowances), *provided* the commanding officer imposing such penalty is a brigadier general or higher, and the offense occurred in time of war.

any punishment be awarded which, in its essence, subjects a soldier to humiliation or ridicule, or exposes him to public curiosity.[21] The reason for this limitation is obvious, for to cause a soldier to appear foolish before his comrades would mean the hopeless defeat of the very purpose of constructive correction for which the penalties in most cases are intended.

Military law possesses one aspect of disciplinary treatment, the inclusion of which, in operation and effect, far exceeds in wisdom and consequence the criminal procedure of the federal government as well as that of any state in the United States. It is the "fourth court" or power known technically as the *Disciplinary Powers of Commanding Officers under Article of War 104,* popularly referred to by army personnel as "company punishment." [22] Under this authority, a soldier may be punished *without* trial, for the commission of any minor offense,[23] by his immediate commanding officer. All minor crimes may be disposed of in this fashion, and no permanent record of the offense or penalty is made or maintained. Nor does the local and informal entry of such offense in the company or squadron books accompany the soldier to his new organization in the event of subsequent transfer, and he is affirmatively advised of this "blotting out" of his past, for valuable psychological reasons based upon his knowledge that he is enabled to make a fresh start in his new unit. Post-war inquiries into his army record will not reveal that he was the recipient of company punishment, nor is the type of his discharge certificate in any way affected. Various rules and limitations must be observed by the commander availing himself of this power, and particularly with respect to the punishments allowable thereunder, which include extra fatigue duty or restriction to specified limits for one week, or admonition or reprimand. Confinement (imprisonment under guard) is forbidden as a punishment under this authority, as are loss of pay [24] and reduction in grade. Prior to the imposition of company punishment, the commanding officer awarding it *must* offer to the offender his choice of a court-martial instead, and the subject soldier, after receiving explanation of the procedure, invariably elects to receive company punishment, principally because of his knowledge of the limitations on punishing power [25] and his desire—guilty or innocent—to preserve a clean army record.[26]

The value of this provision is incalculable, for statistics (numerical only; names are unavailable) disclose that more than eighty percent of all military offenses fall within the purview of Article of War 104. Nor is the entire benefit local to the offender himself, who maintains a spotless military history despite early indiscretion, for although he is saved—as well to his own self-respect as to the army which has expended huge sums in feeding, clothing, equipping, paying, and training him—the army is further spared the loss of time (the one priceless commodity in time of war) involved in drawing officers from their assigned duties and requiring them to sit as members, investigators (treated in detail, *infra*), prosecutors and defense counsel at military trials. True, Article of War 104 may be perverted, or deviously employed in the hands of the wrong commander, who may avail himself of its punishing powers for petty, personal, or insufficient reason (the average soldier will not choose a court-martial as an alternate, even

[25] As discussed, *infra,* the provisions of Article of War 104, along with other specified Articles of War, must be read and explained to all enlisted personnel within six days after entering the service, and at least once every six months thereafter.

[26] However, it is mandatory that the commander, upon explaining to the soldier his rights, describe further his privilege to appeal from company punishment to the next higher officer above the commanding officer, in the event the soldier feels the penalty to be unjust, or disproportionate to the offense. The officer to whom the appeal is directed may confirm the punishment, reduce it in time, or wipe it out *in toto.* Inasmuch as he cannot increase or alter the penalty, nothing is lost by the appeal.

[27] Article of War 110:—"Certain Articles to be Read and Explained.—Articles 1, 2, and 29, 54 to 96, inclusive, and 104 to 109, inclusive, shall be read and explained to every soldier at the time of his enlistment or muster in, or within six days thereafter, and shall be read and explained once every six months to the soldiers of every garrison, regiment, or company in the service of the United States." Purely procedural articles are omitted.

though innocent), or, conversely, in the hands of a shrewd wrongdoer who calculates mathematically that a choice under Article of War 104 will be afforded him, and that the comparatively light penalty allowed by this article might well justify a few days of unauthorized absence. By far and large, however, this power identifies military law as possessing one of the most magnificent items of human understanding in the entire world of jurisprudence.

Crimes. Every offense conceivable to the mind—observed through experience or conjured in the imagination—is set forth directly or indirectly in the Articles of War, and as such, is punishable upon discovery, apprehension and conviction. In accordance with the dictates of law,[27] the substantive articles must be read and explained to all enlisted personnel within six days after commencing their military careers, whether by induction or by enlistment, and at least once every six months thereafter for the entire duration of their service in the armed forces. While it would appear at the outset that this procedure is designed to prevent an accused soldier from pleading ignorance of the law generally, it possesses a more pointed and generous purpose. No man has to be taught that it is wrong to kill or to steal, for these matters, if not perceived through the universal teachings of the natural law, certainly must have come to his attention in hundreds of ways during the course of his existence in organized society. However, it is essential that a man, new to army life, understand that certain acts he could perform casually and frequently in civilian life (very often as admirable manifestations of American freedom of action and enterprise, such as demanding an increase in salary, departing impulsively on a vacation, or quitting one job to take another) are actually *crimes* in the military service, the commission of which would render him a *criminal* in the full sense of the word! Thus, the early indoctrination of a soldier on the matter of the regulations surrounding his sudden metamorphosis from one type of existence into another totally different, through the media of books, lectures, and films, orients him literally through shock on the things of normal life he can no longer do, regardless of many of his rights and powers granted under the constitution and laws of his government and state.[28]

He is acquainted with the so-called "purely military offenses," that is, words and deeds allowable by all civil law but prohibited by military law;[29] he is taught that all of his time—24 hours each day—belongs without reservation to the army, since he is subject

[28] Freedom of speech, freedom of petition and assembly, and trial by jury are prominent among the constitutional rights invaded by military law.

[29] Includes AWOL, desertion, disrespectful language to or about high authorities (even in banter), cowardice, misbehavior before the enemy, use of provoking speech, and the group dealing with insubordination of superiors.

[30] Such recall occurs when shipping orders affecting a unit are received without warning, and upon the occurrence of a surprise mass attack by the enemy or a large-scale military reversal. All furloughs, passes, and leaves were recalled almost immediately following the attack on Pearl Harbor in 1941, despite the proximity of Christmas and the resultant loss of morale.

[31] Articles of War 75 through 82, commonly called the War Offenses. These crimes are not listed in the Table of Maximum Punishments (considered *supra*, and footnote 18), allowing, thereby, vast latitude to the courts-martial convened for such trials.

[32] All property captured from or abandoned by the enemy belongs to the United States Government, except for casual souvenirs retained with consent of commanding officers.

[33] Includes enlisted personnel, officers, warrant and flight officers, cadets, persons serving in the field, such as Red Cross workers and war correspondents, and others. Article of War 2.

[34] Four-page document, corresponding somewhat to the indictment in state and federal courts, identified as War Department, Adjutant General's Office, Form No. 115.

[35] An official character, as notary public or Summary Court Officer, states that the accuser made proper oath before him to the effect that he is a person eligible to prefer charges (that is, subject to military law), that he personally signed the Charge Sheet, and that the charges are true to the best of his knowledge and belief. No person can be tried on unsworn charges without his consent, but consent of accused is sometimes given, as in "whitewash" cases, to establish innocence; or in cases where trial is desired to prevent subsequent trial in civil court of concurrent jurisdiction (use of double jeopardy prohibition, Article of War 40) as, where MP kills a fleeing prisoner in line of duty.

to recall from pass or furlough in accordance with the compulsion dictated by emergency as related to the mission of his organization;[30] he is taught that the army comes first in all respects, and that his business, home, family, and personal life are, without exception, subordinated to the demands of his new employer, the army; he is taught to live in harmony with close neighbors he cannot choose; all with the purpose that the great team which makes up a fighting force, actual or potential, will have its combat ability enhanced immeasurably if a demeanor of discipline, obedience, and cooperation prevails from the highest ranking generals down to the newest recruits.

Included in this orientation is careful identification and description of the common law crimes, with stress placed upon the wide scope of punishments allowed in most cases. This discussion considers murder and rape (either of which is punishable *only* by life imprisonment or the death penalty), burglary, larceny, embezzlement, forgery, etc. In addition, there is a section of the Articles of War concerned exclusively with conduct in the theatre of operations [31] and these are re-read and explained immediately prior to departure for overseas duty. Embraced in this classification are the crimes of casting away arms or ammunition, abandoning post or inducing others to do so, quitting post to plunder or pillage, occasioning a false alarm of danger, subordinate compelling a commander to surrender, using a countersign improperly, dealing in captured or abandoned property,[32] corresponding with the enemy (treason), and spying, almost all of which carry the death penalty upon conviction, in the discretion of the court.

Pre-Trial Procedure. Any person subject to military law [33] may prefer charges against any other, although in the great majority of cases the launching of charges is commenced by the immediate commanding officer of the accused. This is accomplished by completion of the *Charge Sheet* [34] which recites the identity of the accused, brief history of his enlistment or induction, data as to witnesses and documentary evidence for and against the accused, and sworn signature [35] of the accuser. The most vital items on the Charge

Sheet, however, are the charge(s) and specification(s), immediately preceding the signature of the accuser. Each charge identifies the Article of War alleged to have been violated, by insertion of the precise number of such Article of War,[36] and each specification describes briefly the time, place, and manner in which the Article of War was so violated.[37] Specifications are necessarily brief, for the reason that each item contained therein must, by law, be affirmatively proven by the prosecution.

After executing the Charge Sheet, the accuser forwards it through military channels to the commander of a higher echelon [38] who appoints an investigating officer to examine into all possible aspects of the accusation. The investigating officer performs a function not generally found in the preparatory pro-

[36] Typical charge:—Charge: Violation of the 64th Article of War.

[37] Typical specification:—Specification: In that Pvt. John Doe, having received a lawful command from Lt. Richard Roe, his superior officer, to appear for military drill, did at Maxwell Field, Alabama, on or about October 29, 1947, willfully disobey the same.

[38] Varies in the different structures of the armed forces. See Article of War 70 and Manual for Courts-Martial, pages 21 & 24.

[39] No confession is subsequently admissible into evidence unless the investigating officer testifies, and substantiates under cross-examination, that it was acquired by purely legal measures and that it was given as a completely voluntary and uninfluenced gesture by the accused. The claim of duress, fear of refusal through inequality of grade, or threat of retaliation will usually strike out the confession as evidence.

[40] Witnesses may be questioned by the investigator only in the immediate presence of the accused, who has the right of cross-examination. Private questioning by investigator is disallowed.

[41] Conviction requires proof of guilt beyond a reasonable doubt, for the accused enters the courtroom with a presumption of innocence.

[42] A commissioned officer may be tried by a General Court-Martial only, and sentence to any period of confinement (even for one day) requires dismissal from the service, which is tantamount to dishonorable discharge of an enlisted man. Non-commissioned officers cannot be tried by Summary Court (usually reserved for trial of Privates and Privates First Class) without their consent.

[43] Receives pay, whether civilian or military; Army Regulation 35-4120.

cedure of the state courts, and his duties involve a visit with the accused (who may have been placed in restriction or confinement pending trial, according to the seriousness of the charge), explanation to the accused of the precise nature of the charges, advice to him regarding his right to have defense counsel of his own choice, the taking of a confession from the accused,[39] questioning of witnesses and obtaining their written statements,[40] examination of evidence, and in general, determining, insofar as possible, exactly what happened and whether, in his opinion, a trial shall be held. If, upon completion of his mission, he determines that the accused is innocent, or that adequate evidence is lacking, he will recommend that no trial be held. And since he is probably better aware of the situation at this point than any other person connected with the pending affair, his proposal will be accepted, the accused will be released from restraint (with no recourse permitted him), and the charges will fall by the wayside. He may, as an alternate recommendation, suggest that the matter be referred back to the unit for disposition under Article of War 104, by reason of the minor nature of the offense, and thereby spare all concerned the necessity for needless expenditure of the time required for a court-martial. If, however, the investigating officer is convinced not only of the guilt of the accused after a just appraisal of the entire picture, but also of the sufficiency of the evidence,[41] he will recommend trial and state which of the three courts, in his opinion, is best suited to the case by reason of the nature of the crime and the grade of the accused.[42]

Upon receipt of the investigator's report recommending trial, the commanding officer authorized to appoint court-martial of that type orders the court to convene, appoints the trial judge advocate (corresponds to prosecutor, or district attorney in civilian courts, and is usually a permanent assignment) and his assistant, and the defense counsel and assistant. The detailed outfitting of the court is completed by the trial judge advocate who furnishes a court reporter [43] and an orderly. The defense counsel is afforded an opportunity to confer with the

accused in private with a view toward arrang-
ing the strategy of the defense, and it is
his unqualified duty to defend the accused
to the utmost of his ability, regardless of
any reluctance on his part to engage in the
case, and despite his personal beliefs concerning the guilt of the accused.

It is the duty of the trial judge advocate
to accomplish justice in the swiftest fashion
possible, and this duty distinguishes him from
the average state or federal prosecutor who
often seeks convictions for political purposes
in disregard of the facts. If, upon revelation
of the accused's evidence, it becomes apparent to the trial judge advocate that conviction is improbable under fair prosecution,
or that the accused may be innocent, he is
required to halt the proceedings and request
that the president dismiss the charges. This
occurs more frequently than is generally
supposed.

It is mandatory that the accused be made
to understand his right to have defense
counsel *of his own selection* (there is no
exception to this rule) and that if he be
dissatisfied with the counsel provided, he
may ask for and receive others. As in the
case of members, it is not requisite that the
defense counsel be a lawyer; any officer asked
by an accused to defend him should accept,
and military tradition frowns upon arbitrary
refusal. If the accused desires a civilian
defense counsel, he is required to bear the
burden of paying such civilian attorney's fee.

The Trial. The members seat themselves
in order of descending grade and rank from
the middle to the ends of the bench, with
the law member occupying a position directly
to the left of the president, who is seated in
the center. The prosecution and defense
tables, reporter's desk, and spectators' section
are similar to those in the usual state or
federal courtroom.

At the outset the accused is asked whether
he is satisfied with the defense counsel appearing with him, and by this time, of
course, he is, since he had previously been
advised of this right,[44] although he may still
voice objection at this time. Unfortunately,

in most cases the accused cannot evaluate
the merit of his counsel until after the trial
is under way, when it is too late to make a
change. The reporter, members, and trial
judge advocate are then sworn to do their
respective duties in accordance with law [45]
and it is interesting to note that the defense
counsel is the only person present who takes
no oath to truth, fidelity to office, or anything else. Here, obviously, is an advantage
to the accused for, within the limits of civilized conduct, no restraint is placed upon the
defense.

Preceding the taking of oath by the persons subject to it, the accused is offered his
right to challenge the members peremptorily
or for cause,[46] and this privilege is another
reason for the appointment of personnel to
the court in excess of the minimum requirements.

The accused is then arraigned by the trial
judge advocate who reads aloud the charges
and specifications contained in the Charge
Sheet and asks the accused for a plea to
the general issue [47] on each charge and each
specification individually. If he pleads guilty,
the court nevertheless proceeds to trial and
proof without the characteristic process of
"copping a plea" and receiving a sentence
without trial that prevails in most state
courts; if he pleads guilty and it is apparent
that such plea was made without full understanding of the arraignment, or that it was
ill-advised under the circumstances in the
case, the president is empowered to (and
often does) strike out the plea of guilty,
even over the objection of the accused, and
enter in its stead a plea of not guilty. The

[44] By the investigating officer and by the
assigned defense counsel, during the pre-trial
procedure.

[45] All witnesses are sworn to speak the
truth; the trial judge advocate and reporter
to perform their duties in accordance with the
demands of the law (Articles of War 17 and
115); the members to "duly administer justice
without partiality, favor or affection," etc.
President administers oath to trial judge advocate and assistants; trial judge advocate administers oath to members, reporter, and all
witnesses. If accused elects to make a sworn
statement (*infra*) he takes the same oath given
to witnesses.
[46] Each side is limited to one peremptory
challenge, but there is no limitation on the
number of challenges for cause. The law member may be challenged for cause only.
[47] Guilty or not guilty.

reverse, however, is not true, and an original plea of not guilty cannot be disturbed. If the accused refuses to plead one way or the other, but persists in standing mute, a plea of not guilty is automatically entered with the same force and effect as if he had affirmatively stated such plea. Special pleas in bar and in abatement [48] are allowed under military law as they are under state and federal law.

The trial proceeds in a manner substantially similar to that found in federal district courts. The rules of evidence are the same; opening and closing statements are heard in the same order; the prosecution submits its case first, with witnesses and evidence in support; all witnesses must expose themselves to cross-examination (and to re-cross, if new testimony is elicited on cross-examination); and in almost all respects, a spectator would believe himself to be observing a civil trial. A few matters, however, depart from convention. While in most non-military trials all witnesses are in the courtroom throughout, each witness at a court-martial is in the room for his own testimony only, and must leave immediately upon concluding. This,

[48] Double jeopardy, lack of jurisdiction of the court for any competent reason, statute of limitations, etc. Articles of War 39 & 40.

[49] Where the accused has a "tight" story that will probably withstand the attack of cross-examination, or where the accused is the type of person who can be steadfast and formidable in the witness chair, the sworn statement is advisable, for this choice carries the greatest aspect of sincerity and truth. The unsworn statement is to be avoided, since it bears but little weight, and would indicate that there is something to hide. To remain silent is more effective than to render an unsworn statement, because the members are aware that reasons other than guilt often motivate this election; reasons perhaps based upon poor power of expression, upon timidity, upon the fact that the prosecution's case is weak, and might be fortified by the accused as he is drawn out, or upon the desire of the accused—as a matter of pure principle—to refrain in dignity from what he believes to be a beseeching plea or entreaty.

[50] Among these are desertion in time of war, striking or wilfully disobeying a superior officer ("superior" interpreted to mean a commissioned officer only; these offenses against noncommissioned officers covered elsewhere: Article of War 65), mutiny (concerted pre-arrangement to defy lawful authority), and a sentry drunk or sleeping on his post.

it is believed, prevents collusion to a degree, and discourages the influencing—by design or accident—of one witness by the testimony of another. Many inconsistencies emerge by reason of this practice, and evidence that is a degree closer to the truth is adduced.

Upon the close of the prosecution's case, the law member (in a General Court) or the president (in a Special Court; or in a General Court wherein the law member was challenged for cause) advises the accused of his rights with respect to the making of a statement to the court in his defense. He is made to understand, simply and effectively, that he may pursue one of three courses: (1) Make a sworn statement, in which case he takes an oath as did each witness, and upon concluding he must submit to cross-examination by the trial judge advocate and by any member or members of the court, or (2) Make an unsworn statement without taking an oath, and cross-examination is forbidden, or (3) Remain silent, which choice raises no presumption as to the truth or falsity of any matter brought out at trial, and the trial judge advocate is precluded from commenting upon the fact that the accused desires to preserve silence. The accused then announces his choice which, of course, he and his defense counsel had determined long before trial.[49]

Findings and Sentence. Upon completion of the defense each side may sum up, the court is closed, and the members alone remain to discuss and vote upon the finding of guilt or innocence. It is notable that any evidence of previous convictions of the accused is carefully concealed throughout the trial, and at the time of the vote upon conviction or acquittal the members *know nothing* of the accused's criminal history, if any. In order to convict of a crime which calls for mandatory death penalty (as spying), the vote on the finding of guilty must be unanimous, and on all other matters the conviction may be determined by a vote of two-thirds of all members present.

There are about a dozen discretionary capital offenses contained in the Articles of War, that is, crimes for which the death penalty may or may not be awarded in the discretion of the court,[50] and if the conviction in any such case is obtained by less than unanimous vote, the court has thereby deprived itself of imposing the death sentence.[51]

Upon reaching their determination, the members reopen the court, but do not disclose the findings. The president asks the trial judge advocate at this time if there is any evidence of previous convictions, and the asking of this question establishes that the accused has been found guilty on one or more counts, for had the finding been not guilty on all charges and specifications, the accused would have been so advised immediately upon reopening of the court. After listening to the history of previous convictions, and miscellaneous information concerning the age, military background, and pay and allowances [52] of the accused, the members again close the court, this time to vote upon the sentence to be awarded. Again, the death penalty requires unanimity of vote; sentence to imprisonment for more than ten years requires a vote of three-fourths or more, and all lesser sentences, two-thirds or more.

The method of voting upon sentence is a highly novel and interesting one. Each member suggests a sentence by writing it upon a slip of paper and these are collected by the junior member who delivers them to the president in the center.[53] The president arranges the slips in the inverse order of severity, reads aloud the lightest sentence recommended, asks for a vote upon it, and requests the junior member to collect the ballots. If the necessary fraction or proportion is obtained to impose that sentence, *the court can proceed no further,* and such becomes the official sentence of the accused.[54] If the re-

quired three-fourths or two-thirds is not obtained on that ballot, the president reads to the members the next higher sentence recommended, and the same procedure is followed. If, after balloting upon the entire group, none of the sentences is approved by proper vote, the original process is reinstituted, with each member again recommending a sentence in writing. By this time, a more acceptable set of suggestions will undoubtedly be forthcoming, since each member has a better understanding of the attitudes of his colleagues. It is obligatory that every member vote upon sentence, including those who may have insisted upon acquittal during the earlier ballot on the findings. After reaching a determination in accordance with the above proceeding, the court reopens and the president apprises the accused of the findings and sentence, and as the accused is removed in custody of a military policeman, the court is closed until convened for the next trial.

Confinement. The place of imprisonment varies with the type of crime, severity of sentence, and age of the accused. Any sentence which carries more than six months in confinement *must* include dishonorable discharge from the service, and the soldier is known as a *general prisoner.* A sentence to six months or less renders the offender a *garrison prisoner,* and his time is usually served in the guardhouse or stockade on the post to which he is assigned, after which he resumes his military duties. Conviction after trial for common law crimes requires imprisonment in a federal penitentiary, as does conviction for the purely military offenses of mutiny, desertion in time of war, or repeated desertion in time of peace. Other general prisoners are confined at army disciplinary barracks. At the federal penitentiaries (Atlanta, Leavenworth, etc.), army general prisoners are separated from those incarcerated as non-military offenders.

The Review. Comparable to the appeal taken by the defendant after conviction by a civil tribunal of criminal powers, is *the review,* or "automatic appeal" which is a requirement after every military conviction, whether the accused desires it or not. Whereas the "appeal" from company punishment [55] under Article of War 104 is discretionary with the misdemeanant, and is initiated by him, the review after trial by court-martial is

[51] Article of War; Manual for Courts-Martial, 1928.

[52] To determine the extent to which forfeiture may be imposed.

[53] The junior member (lowest ranking officer present) arises from his place at the end of the bench to collect the ballots after every written vote, and assists the president in counting and tabulating them. On all votes taken orally (certain interlocutory matters) the junior member must vote first, to prevent influence by the discussions and votes of the higher ranking members.

[54] Subject, however to action taken by the reviewing authority, *infra.*

[55] See footnote 26, *supra.*

a *mandatory* procedure.[56] Upon preparation of the minutes of trial by the reporter, the trial judge advocate forwards the entire record to the authority who appointed the court, for his examination and possible action.[57] The reviewing authority is permitted to disapprove the proceedings of the court-martial (which nullifies the trial and sentence, with no provision for re-trial), or to approve all that transpired (in which case the findings and sentence stand as directed by the court-martial), or to order a new trial (where the court lacked jurisdiction,[58] was improperly conducted, in any serious manner prejudiced the accused, or committed reversible error), or, without explanation, reduce substantially or moderately the sentence. Certain limitations govern the action taken by the reviewing authority. For instance, he cannot alter or increase the punishment; he cannot order a new trial where the accused was found not guilty; he cannot order re-trial as to any charge or specification under which the accused was found not guilty; and he cannot order the same members to re-hear the case in the event of an allowable re-trial. Thus,

[56] No sentence by court-martial is considered binding until action by the reviewing authority is taken, made known, and complied with, although (except in cases involving the death penalty) the convicted soldier is required to serve his sentence (being credited with the time) pending the outcome of the review, which often takes many months. The brevity with which the huge machinery of pre-trial procedure is accomplished, compared to the length of time taken for the simple purpose of reading the record of trial is indeed a paradox in military law.

[57] Any sentence which includes dismissal of an officer from the service (see footnote 42, *supra*) must be reviewed personally by the President of the United States.

[58] A special plea in bar, based upon double jeopardy, will not be entertained in such eventuality, since under military law there has not been a trial (the first jeopardy) until after the reviewing authority has acted. Thus, the re-trial ordered for lack of jurisdiction will constitute the first jeopardy once again.

[59] All military prisoners remain subject to military law while in confinement, in consequence of this regulation.

[60] A bulging stockade is a direct reflection upon the general ability and leadership of the commanding officer.

[61] War Department, Adjutant General's Office Form No. 56.

the accused suffers no threat of detriment through the review, since at the worst, his original sentence will be approved.

Miscellaneous. Time is remitted for good behavior, and frequent hearings are conducted to determine the rehabilitation value, if any, of all military prisoners. Since the dishonorable discharge accompanying a term of imprisonment does not take effect until completion of the term,[59] many offenders who exhibit salvage possibilities are removed from prison and sent to rehabilitation camps for renewed military training. If found conformable, they are awarded fresh enlistments for a specified period of time, their dishonorable discharges are remitted, they are assigned to normal military organizations and duties with no record of the conviction and sentence, and upon subsequent separation from the service, are awarded honorable discharge certificates.

In view of the frequent convening of rehabilitation and clemency boards, to adjudge the reclamation value of military prisoners, it is clearly seen that few are required to serve out the full limits of their sentences as approved or adjusted by the reviewing authorities. In many military organizations, clemency boards meet semi-monthly for the purpose of releasing from confinement every garrison prisoner who has had an uninterrupted two weeks of good behavior, and while this practice may bear suspicion as originating with the desire of a post commander to show a small number of actual prisoners in his command,[60] motives of justice and army advantage likewise prevail, and regardless of the underlying psychology, the ultimate good inures to the individual prisoner.

Psychiatry in the Military Service. Many chronic offenders, whose infractions of the law operate as factors which undermine the discipline of a unit, are not punished by court-martial, but are awarded the *discharge without honor* (popularly known as blue discharge[61]). This certificate is issued in cases of undesirability through certain habits, repeated offenses of a minor nature, and general absence or failure of qualifications requisite to army training, usually within the control of the offender. This type of discharge does not deprive the subject soldier of separation benefits under the so-called "GI Bill of Rights" as does the *dishonorable discharge* (yellow [62]) which can be issued only after conviction by a General Court-Martial, and which burdens the soldier with incisive disadvantages through life. In keeping with the army's broad policy of not punishing for acts beyond the control of the soldier, it awards the *honorable discharge* (white [63]) to all servicemen completing a period of loyalty, and to those exhibiting inaptitude, lack of adaptability, phobias, complexes, neuroses, and other psychiatric disturbances immiscible with military training and warfare.

Army recognition of the problems of psychiatry has improved remarkably. The treatment of its numerous cases compares favorably with that of state medical and judicial processes in this field, and with respect to the choice of imprisonment or hospitalization in doubtful cases of criminality and/or mental disease, the army has made gratifying strides. Sodomy, for example, which is a crime invariably treated with imprisonment by the states (which imprisonment, ironically, affords the "criminal" a greater opportunity than ever to pursue his inclinations) is regarded for the most part as an ailment in the military service, with medical treatment, hospitalization, and discharge (white or blue) as the usual disposition. Any indication of a psychiatric quirk will result in immediate cessation of trial by court-martial, and the accused will be referred to medical authorities, completely eliminating the possibility of a dishonorable discharge from the service. In addition to this consideration, the soldier in question will be granted a pension based in amount upon his proportion of disability, if it is determined that his failing, mental or physical, was service-induced or service-aggravated.

*   *   *

Evaluation. The critics of military justice are many, and their arguments are sincere. Nor is this group confined to disgruntled

[62] War Department, Adjutant General's Office Form No. 57.

[63] War Department, Adjutant General's Office Form No. 55.

[64] From a trial practitioner's point of view, contrarily, speed in preparation and trial does the greatest damage to the prosecution, which carries the affirmative burden of proof.

prisoners or their families, who sustained the direct brunt of the swift, methodical force of the Articles of War, for numerous disinterested individuals and accredited veterans' organizations have expressed concern.

One of the complaints centers about the speed of preparation and trial [64] which the War Department explains away, justifiably or not, on the basis of the military necessity concomitant upon a warring unit, and the utter impossibility of individual coddling in known cases of criminality. In favor of the critics, however, it must be said that the leisurely opportunity afforded to state and federal defendants (a matter of common knowledge) may lull the accused into a state of false security which would operate to his detriment in securing witnesses, measuring the prosecution's case, and constructing his defense generally. This is true despite the prompt furnishing of defense counsel, for although the accused is quickly advised of his right to counsel of his choice, his subordinate grade and fear of reprisal often prevail upon him to refrain from demanding this, and other of his rights, with the inevitable result that inefficient counsel often damages his defense. In response to this contention, the authorities might well claim that a backlog of untried cases cannot be tolerated because of the continual shifting of personnel under army orders, affecting investigators, witnesses, prosecutors, and others concerned with the preparation and trial of cases. True as that may be, it sets forth a purely practical argument only, and one definitely not founded in justice to, or interest in, the accused as an individual, seeking individual justice and not the expedient convenience of his accusers.

The critics cite the fact that while the great preponderance of trials involve enlisted men as the offenders, no enlisted man is permitted to sit in judgment, and that this practice deprives the accused of consideration by those best equipped, through equality, to understand the position and problems of the accused, along with his compulsion for having committed the crime. This argument, which is perhaps the strongest on the complaint list, is basically sound, and particularly in view of the fact that many members of courts-martial, sitting in the judgment of enlisted men, were never enlisted men themselves, having received appointments to the officer ranks directly from civilian life. Consequently, it is difficult for this type of officer, to whom the court-martial duty is usually a distasteful one, to offer the capability of perception that is so necessary in rendering a decision that may deprive an individual of his liberty, or even his life, after a few short hours, or, in many cases, minutes of deliberation. Moreover, many officers who came up "through the ranks" are incapable of full and free exercise of judicial temperament by reason of their training in officer candidate schools, some of which taught them that they are superior to enlisted men, and that they must cease thinking and acting as such. While most officers endeavor to give the utmost in ability to their court functions, it cannot help but be apparent through simple logic that some are incompetent, by reason of extreme youth,[65] lack of interest in legal assignments, over-enthusiastic training in OCS, and because of the hasty mustering of an enormous officer corps, the great and immediate need for which resulted in the overlooking of many important details in personality and officer ability. While seasoned officers make every effort to reduce the newcomers' faults to a minimum, this assistance cannot satisfy the demands of court-martial functions, since the voting by members on findings and sentence is presumably accomplished by secret ballot, and the disclosing of any one member's vote is forbidden by law. The inclusion of enlisted men as partial constituents of courts-martial membership where enlisted men are the accused might well produce the desired result, and the selection of capable, responsible men from the enlisted ranks would prove a comparatively simple matter.

A point of strong controversy finds its crux in the fact that almost all military trials result in conviction, with acquittals being but rare exceptions to the rule. Many persons, including soldiers, fallaciously believe that under military law the accused is presumed guilty until he establishes his innocence, and that every trial must, of necessity, culminate

[65] In the early days of World War II, it was not an uncommon sight to observe officers of 17 years of age and younger; this was particularly true in the infantry.

in conviction. Nothing could be farther from the truth. While it is true that the proportion of convictions at military courts is tremendously greater than that of other criminal courts, the disparity is definitely not caused by deprivation of rights, presumption of guilt, "railroading" of offenders, or stereotyped inclinations by members toward conviction. The answer is found in the functions of the investigating officer (*supra*), whose prime duty it is to recommend a trial, or to recommend that no trial be held, in connection with the case he has investigated. If it appears to him that the accused is innocent, or that a reasonable doubt as to his guilt exists, he will recommend that no court be convoked on the case. Likewise, even if it is apparent to him that the accused is guilty, but that evidence sufficient to convict is lacking, he will again dissuade the holding of trial, since it would serve no purpose to gather the court when an acquittal is obvious from the start. This investigating process is a creature of military law, and in state cases this screening function is generally not employed, with the result that only at or after trial does it appear that no trial should have been held at all, and in consequence of this wasteful procedure, the state courts boast a greater percentage of acquittals.

Complaint is frequently voiced regarding politics, and the "fixing" of trials to the end that the conviction of every accused soldier is a foregone conclusion. True, the court-martial personnel of a military installation, including members, prosecution, and defense, is occasionally instructed by higher authority to award maximum punishments in all cases, because of poor discipline of the local units and ridiculously light sentences in the past which served to invite the commission of offenses. It must be understood in this regard that military compulsion dictates the subordination of individual considerations to the mass welfare of the army structure as a giant entity. Although a heavier-than-usual sentence is sometimes imposed upon one man because of widespread misconduct and the need for example-setting, it must be remembered that it is not an innocent man who is arbitrarily selected as the guinea pig, but rather, a soldier who has actually committed a crime, and who, nevertheless, cannot receive a penalty greater than that allowed by law. In addition, the power of reduction always remains with the reviewing authority, who often employs it. Instruction by higher-ups may "suggest" strong punishments, but can never breathe even the hint of conviction without overwhelming proof of guilt, as in each and every case brought to trial.

* * *

Immediately prior to publication of this encyclopedia, and subsequent to the composition of this chapter on Military Criminology, vast changes in court-martial procedure were proclaimed by the President of the United States in his capacity as Commander in Chief of the Armed Forces. This action, service officials promised, would make sweeping improvements in the administration of military justice.

The Army described the changes as far-reaching, and stated that they embodied certain basic conceptions called for in a rider to the Selective Service Act, formally known as The Title II. The purposes sought are: added legal protection to enlisted men and other accused persons, elimination of possible discriminations between enlisted men and officers, and administration of military justice in such a manner as to support the maintenance of a disciplined army.

In practice, the new Manual for Courts-Martial (1949) attempts to assure fulfillment of these concepts by making coercion or unlawful influence in obtaining a confession a criminal offense.[66] The procedures are also revised to emphasize the innocence of the accused person until he is conclusively proved guilty.

Officers, hitherto triable only by general courts-martial, are now subject to special courts in the new manual for 1949, and disciplinary powers of commanding officers (punishment without trial) under A.W. 104 are substantially enlarged. At the same time, limitations upon the punishment of enlisted personnel are made generally applicable to officers.

The most important changes, however, entail the inclusion of enlisted men as members of future courts-martial,[67] the requirement that the law member be a qualified military lawyer, and the provision for a final appellate court of review to consist of military legal specialists with long and active experience in that field.

This new army manual of 1949, effective February 1, 1949, represents the first major change in court-martial procedure since April, 1928, and it is contemplated that a uniform code of military justice for all three services will soon be issued. This, if enacted, will be the greatest "democratizing" document ever to appear on the scene of military law. At present, the new manual governs both the Army and the Air Force.

* * *

The foregoing revisions do not, by any measure, constitute an admission of failure error, oversight, or other shortcoming in the structure or administration of army justice. True, they were wrought through the wail and woe of those who felt most sharply the inadequacy of the former methods. But law is a strange, ever-belated creature of this world, always following upon, and never preceding the situation of apparent injustice demanding its enactment. Thus, in that period —sometimes brief, too often protracted—between recognition of the old as insufficient, and the effective inception of the new, there are bound to be those who feel that the only crime they committed was in committing it too soon, suffering under procedures acknowledged to be outmoded, but as yet unrefined by the slow, ponderous machinery of legislative change. Nevertheless, were it not for these comparatively few interim cases, most of which receive commensurate clemency, it is highly probable that the system's faults would rarely come to light.

It is said philosophically that law is one thing and justice another, far removed. True,

[66] Coercion has always been forbidden, but the penalty is now specifically a crime.
[67] This, it will be remembered, was the point of greatest dissention and complaint in the various surveys made following World War II. While specific provisions are not yet available, it may be presumed that a trial of an enlisted man will be judged by a combination of officer and enlisted personnel, but an officer's trial will still find officers alone sitting as the members. In all cases, however, the members will undoubtedly be senior in grade to the accused.

perhaps, but no code of laws, military or otherwise, is perfect, and no law meets with the unanimous approval of all for whom it is legislated. It is the purpose of any judicial enactment to meet the precise need for which it is intended, effecting the greatest possible good for the largest number of persons. Law, like medicine, cannot remain static and remain good, for the continually changing scene of local, national, and world politics, economy, and intrigue demands addition, deletion, and alteration in the rules under which we exist as communal beings. Military law is no exception, and it must be tried and analyzed at every opportunity in contemplation of improvement, for the strength of the Articles of War is the strength of our army; and the strength of our army is the strength of our nation.

MARTIN L. WOLF

Former Senior Instructor,
Military Law, U. S. Army Air Force
250 Montgomery Street
Brooklyn 25, New York

BIBLIOGRAPHY

Digest of Opinions of the Judge Advocate General of the Army, 1912–1930, with supplements.
Manual for Courts-Martial, 1928, War Department, corrected to 1943.
Military Justice for the Field Soldier, Col. Frederick B. Wiener, 1943, Infantry Journal.
Military Law and Precedents, Winthrop, War Department Document 1001.
Military Laws of the United States (annotated) 8th Edition, Judge Advocate General of the Army, 1939; Supplement I to same, 1940; Supplement II to same, 1942.
War Department Training Manual No. 27-255, Military Justice Procedure, 1945.
Manual for Courts-Martial, 1949, U. S. Army.

NAPOLEONIC CODE. Any discussion of the development of modern concepts of criminology and criminal punishment would not be complete without an analysis of the Napoleonic Code. Properly speaking, the Napoleonic Code includes a Civil Code which has had profound influence on the development of modern civil law. For the purposes of this article, however, we propose to examine only the Code of Criminal Procedure drawn up in 1808 and the Criminal Code published in 1810, both of which, because of various delays, did not go into effect until January 1811.

We cannot properly understand the Code of Criminal Procedure without knowing something of the Ordinance of 1670, drawn up under Louis XIV. The Ordinance was a codification of the criminal procedure that had gradually developed over three centuries in France prior to the reign of Louis XIV. It represented "the culmination of the process of transition from the oral and public accusatory system of the feudal period to the written and secret inquisitorial procedure of the early modern period." It was in effect until the period of the French Revolution and included cruel and unnecessary punishments, secret processes and all types of tortures.

The Code of Criminal Instruction of 1808 was the result of a long discussion carried out by the leading jurists and by the Council of State of the Napoleonic period. Napoleon himself contributed to the discussion but it is interesting to note that despite the popular impression, Napoleon was overruled on many important points and couldn't impose his will on the framers of the Code. The Code of Criminal Instruction embodied various concepts and forms of criminal procedure contained in the Ordinance of 1670 and earlier criminal legislation. It also incorporated the results of the thinking of the reformers and philosophers of the eighteenth century who agitated for more liberal and humane criminal procedure.

The influence of the earlier period (Ordinance of 1670 etc.) is reflected in the provisions for the preliminary and secret examination by the magistracy, the severity of the restrictions on the defendant in a criminal case, and the system of written testimony and instruction. On the other hand, progressive features advocated by the reformers and philosophers embodied in the Code included public trial and jury decision, the recognition of the Courts of Cassation and of Assize, and the provision for allowing the accused person better facilities for defense.

From the viewpoint of modern criminal thought, the fact that trial by jury was embodied in the Code was a great step forward since this Code served as a pattern after which the other Continental countries drew up their own codes. Great homage must therefore be paid to the framers of the Code who insisted on trial by jury in opposition to Napoleon's desires on this subject.

Let us examine in more detail the provisions of the Code of Criminal Instruction to see exactly what the person accused of committing a crime or misdemeanor had to face. If he were accused of a crime, it was mandatory for him to go through a preliminary examination. However, if he were accused of a misdemeanor, the preliminary examination was optional. The preliminary examination of the Code of Criminal Instruction was modeled after the Ordinance of 1670 and hence was of a harsh and arbitrary nature.

First of all, witnesses were heard secretly, and the person accused of crime or misdemeanor was not confronted with witnesses.

The witnesses testified secretly and in the presence of only the judge and his clerk. One difference may be pointed out in this respect between the Ordinance of 1670 and the Code of Criminal Instruction. The judge had a discretionary power to hear witnesses nominated by the accused, but it was not mandatory for him to do so. Under the Ordinance of 1670, the accused was not permitted to nominate witnesses in the preliminary examination.

In regard to the interrogation, the accused was examined in secret. The accused was ignorant of what had been testified against him previously by the witnesses except what the judge saw fit to reveal to him. Furthermore, during the whole course of the preliminary examination, with minor exceptions, the accused was detained and there were harsh restrictions regarding release on bail.

Once the preliminary examination was concluded, the judge submitted the results to the Chamber of Accusation which served as the arraignment branch. Here also the proceedings were secret. "The judges see neither the accused, nor the witnesses for either side." The attorney-general then drew up the indictment and the case was remitted to the Court of Assizes for trial and final judgment. The liberalizing tendencies of the eighteenth century philosophers were clearly reflected in the privileges allowed the defense in the actual trial.

As Esmein observes so succinctly in his brilliant work, *A History of Continental Criminal Procedure,*

"When, after the proceedings before the tribunals of examination, we consider the trial before the tribunals of judgment, the contrast is complete. We pass from obscurity into the full light of day. There the procedure was secret, written, and always favorable to the prosecution, not leaving to the defense even the right of confrontation; here everything is publicity, oral trial, free defense, and full discussion. . . . Whatever may be the tribunal before which appearance is made, the examination is public, otherwise void (Articles 153, 190, and 309); the rights of the defense are the same in every respect as those of the prosecution; it can produce its witnesses, and even the last heard, just as the defending counsel

and the accused are the last to address the court. The accused may always have the assistance of the defending counsel; the law officially assigns one to those accused."

Finally, one of the outstanding features of the Code of Criminal Instruction, namely, public trial by jury for the accused, was a monumental achievement. As previously mentioned, it has had profound influence on world systems of criminal law. Our brief examination of the Code of Criminal Instruction of 1808 points to the enormous progress in criminal procedure resulting from enactment of the Code. Many Continental countries followed France's example and adopted many of its provisions.

Turning from the Code of Criminal Procedure of 1808 to the Criminal Code of 1810, we find it equally remarkable in its humane aspects. We are all familiar with the harsh and arbitrary punishments existing in France prior to the French Revolution. The reformers of the eighteenth century directed their ire and scorn against these cruel punishments and attacked them as feudal relics. Similar to the discussion preparatory to the framing of the Code of Criminal Instruction, there was a widespread debate in France as to the general principles governing the punishment of criminals.

For the purposes of this article we will center our attention on the general principles of criminal punishment embodied in the Criminal Code. The Criminal Code of 1810 consisted of a codification of previous criminal laws and was based largely on the Criminal Law of 1791, which introduced many progressive concepts in the field of criminal punishment.

One of the most important principles established was the abolition of arbitrary punishments. As Hans von Hentig remarks, "The maxim nulla poena sine lege" (no punishment except in conformance with the law) "was established as the fundamental premise of the criminal law. Barriers were erected against the discretion of the judge." In addition to the fact that crimes were to be punished in accordance with law, humane principles were to govern the laws punishing criminals. Cruel and unnecessary forms of punishment were eliminated.

Another important principle laid down by the Criminal Code referred to the equal treatment of criminals before the law, no matter what their rank or position in society. Under the French monarchy, noblemen and those of higher rank had special privileges under the criminal laws then in force. The growth of the concept of democracy was thus powerfully reinforced by the application of this maxim. While the death penalty, deportation and confiscation of property were still continued in the Criminal Code, the remainder of the punishments mentioned in the Code were to be applied in connection with the principle of the maximum and minimum penalties. The judge had latitude to punish more or less severely the criminal within certain limitations prescribed by the Code.

This principle of the maximum and minimum with regard to punishment was of profound influence in the criminal systems of Europe and America. The flexibility that it introduced, coupled with the limits set on the judge's power of sentence, was a progressive, democratic step.

In conclusion, may it be noted that in the annals of criminology, the Napoleonic Code will forever be remembered as a mighty bulwark against the forces of tyranny and oppression. It gave a great impetus to men of good will throughout the world to organize programs for the reform of the criminal and to protect his rights and his dignity as an individual. From the historical point of view, the scientific study of criminology cannot be fully appreciated without a knowledge of the principles of the Napoleonic Code.

HARRIS PROSCHANSKY
Research Historian
New York, New York

BIBLIOGRAPHY

Esmein, Adhemar, *A History of Continental Criminal Procedure with Special Reference to France,* (translated by John Simpson), Boston, Little Brown and Company, 1913.
Loire, Vols. XXIV, XXV, Paris, 1808.
Boitard, Joseph Edouard, *Lecons sur les Codes Penal et D'Instruction Criminelle,* Librairie de Jurisprudence de Cotillon, fifth edition, 1851.
Codes de L'Empire Francois, P. J. Voglet, Paris, 1811. This contains the original texts of the Code d' Instruction Criminelle and the Criminal Code.
Encyclopaedia of Social Sciences, 1934, Articles on Criminology; Crime; Punishment; Imprisonment; Humanitarianism.
Van Kan, J., *Les Efforts de Codification en France, Etude Historique et Psychologique,* Librairie Arthur Rousseau, Paris, 1929.

THE NEGRO IN CRIME. The intention of this paper is to examine critically the evidence upon which many generalizations rest regarding *The Negro in Crime.* It does not seem worthwhile to summarize the whole literature on the topic. Extensive reviews have been made by McCord, Reid, Sellin, Johnson, Johnson and Kisner, Myrdal, Reuther, Johnson, and others. Our main concern will be with those portions of the material which throw light upon the present state of affairs.

Meaning of Race. Since there is a prevailing notion as to a predisposition of various races to different types of crimes, as well as to crime in general, it is important at the outset to define just what is actually meant by the term *race.* Although physical anthropologists do not agree upon an exact definition of race, the following statement would probably be accepted by most of them: namely, that race is a large subdivision of mankind the members of which are distinguished by possessing in common (a) certain distinctive physical characteristics (*e.g.,* pigmentation of skin, eyes, and hair; type of hair; skull index; length of body; nasal form) which are (b) determined by heredity. Only when both of these facts can be demonstrated do we have a true race. The term has its origin in biology and should not be used in any other sense as, for example, to refer to language and national groupings. Moreover, it is of the greatest importance to emphasize the second fact (determined by heredity) explicitly. Without it one cannot speak of race.

The difficulty in race classification is that the complexity of physical characteristics from one race to another are so great, and the individual differences within the same race so tremendous, that no race can be said to be sure. This problem (race mixture) has led some students of the problem to the assertion that there is but one race—the human race. Any view of race as a sort of permanent entity is mythical, for the evidence is incontrovertible that races are in constant flux and interaction. For readable accounts of many of the difficulties of race classification, see Huxley and Haddon, also Herskovits.

The Negro Race. Perhaps we should also stress the fact that as it concerns the American Negro, the word race is a sociological concept. Herskovits has shown that this group constitutes a population which is "probably less than one-fourth unmixed Negro descent." Thus, in the United States any degree of African ancestry classifies an individual as a Negro. Biologically, he may be a white person with one Negro great-great-grandparent; yet old patterns of racial prejudice tend to persist, and those suspected of possessing the slightest strains of "Negro blood" are classified sociologically as Negro. Incidentally, it is only in the United States that we find Negroes with blond hair and blue eyes—Strange Fruit indeed.

Thus the scientific concept of race is inapplicable to the American Negro since his origin is mixed and his physical type varied. A word, however, is not only defined by what it should mean, but by what people have come to use it to mean as well. The average American certainly has a definite idea of what he means by the "Negro race." And so, without attempting to account for the historical origin of the social definition of the Negro, we shall use the concept because it has a psychological reality for many people. But the reader should understand that it is being used in a social and conventional, not a biological sense. This point should be kept in mind as we proceed with our discussion, since before we can accept crime statistics on the Negro we ought to know how accurate the racial listings are.

The crime statistics do not differentiate between the full-blooded and the various degrees of mixture of Negroes. All of them are labeled "Negro." This procedure may cause a spurious difference in the actual Negro crime rate. If, for instance, the mulatto's rate is higher than the rate for the full-blooded Negro, by lumping them into one statistical category we thereby increase the Negro crime rate, and vice versa.

Finally, we should like to point out that crime is not a physical characteristic like the possession of dark skin, straight hair, blue eyes, and so forth. If this were so, then criminality would appear in all the individuals of a certain race and none in another race. The truth is, naturally, that crime occurs in all races and is committed by a limited number of individuals in each race.

Definition of Crime. Legally, crime is behavior prevented by the criminal code. It is not a fixed and static concept since every change in social philosophy, in methods of political and economic control, in attempts of government to manage our competitive system, bring with it changes in the content of the criminal code. The state has punished criminals for thousands of years, but crime is still with us on a large scale. This is because (a) the type of behavior regarded as criminal varies from place to place and from time to time—ethnological material is rich in examples of this variation; and, (b) it is not the individual who creates crime but society or, in other words, the individual merely behaves and society defines certain types of his behavior as criminal. It follows, as Michael and Adler have pointed out, that a crime is any act which violates the behavior code as defined by a particular society. Such behavior, however, is relative and pretty much like the violating behavior found in other social groups as, for example, the church, the school, the family, the lodge, the labor union.

Statement of the Problem. Granted some physical variations between the races, is it possible to find parallel differences in intelligence, temperament, emotionalism, inclinations, inhibitory capacities, and other psychological characteristics upon which one might erect a theory of inborn racial tendency toward types of criminal behavior? Specifically, is there acceptable evidence tending to show a psychological endowment in the Negro race different, qualitatively or quantitatively, from that of all other races thus making its members more predisposed to crime? Or, if there are differences between the criminality of the Negro and others, do they have little to do with race and can they be explained in terms of the position of the Negro in the

American social order? This is the problem of this study.

Although crime is behavior forbidden by law, and an act regarded as criminal in one society may be unobjectionable in another, nevertheless, many people believe that races differ in innate criminal propensities. Thus the large percentage of crime in the United States has been attributed by some to the influx of certain classes of immigrants into our country. Similarly, many Americans firmly believe that the Negro is a born criminal because statistics can be quoted to "prove" that he is much more likely to commit crime than whites.

Even capable and honest scientists have used available statistics to "prove" Negro criminality. For example, Baur, Fisher, and

TABLE 1

DISTRIBUTION OF ARRESTS ACCORDING TO RACE AND TYPE OF OFFENSE (EXCLUDING THOSE UNDER FIFTEEN YEARS OF AGE): 1946 *

	Per Cent Negro of Total in Each Offense	Rate Per 100,000 Population[a]	
		Negro	White[c]
Criminal homicide	44.3	35.0	4.3
Robbery	38.5	89.1	13.9
Assault	42.2	263.8	35.3
Burglary-breaking or entering	28.0	119.3	30.2
Larceny-theft	31.5	217.6	46.5
Auto theft	14.9	37.1	20.8
Embezzlement and fraud	13.5	21.1	13.3
Stolen property; buying, receiving, etc.	32.0	12.5	2.6
Arson	23.0	2.0	0.6
Forgery and counterfeiting	14.9	11.6	6.5
Rape	27.8	28.2	7.1
Prostitution and commercialized vice	36.3	46.4	7.7
Other sex offenses	17.2	34.1	16.1
Narcotic drug laws	32.2	11.0	2.4
Weapons; carrying, possessing, etc.	49.8	73.3	7.2
Offenses against family and children	15.1	20.9	11.6
Liquor laws	38.1	33.0	5.2
Driving while intoxicated	8.5	32.0	33.9
Road and driving laws	19.5	15.6	6.3
Parking violations	22.0	b	b
Other traffic and motor vehicle laws	25.4	17.8	5.1
Disorderly conduct	26.5	43.1	38.9
Drunkenness	14.2	261.5	152.6
Vagrancy	21.8	100.0	34.1
Gambling	51.2	81.1	7.3
Suspicion	28.3	148.4	36.9
Not stated	22.7	12.7	4.2
All other offenses	20.2	72.6	28.1
Total	24.7	1,938.7	578.6

* *Sources:* Federal Bureau of Investigation, U. S. Department of Justice, *Uniform Crime Reports,* Annual Bulletin, Vol. 17, No. 2, 1946, p. 124; and *Sixteenth Census of the United States: 1940,* population.
  a Population bases taken as of 1940
  b Less than one-tenth of one percent
  c White includes both foreign-born and native-born

Lenz, noting that there is much more crime among Negroes in the United States than among whites, conclude that this is "obviously due to the fact that Negroes have less foresight, and they have less power of resisting the impulses aroused by immediate sensuous impressions." Moreover, as Myrdal says, "at all times the stereotyped notion has prevailed that Negroes have a criminal tendency, which manifests itself in acts ranging all the way from petty thievery by household servants to razor-slashing homicide"; and, finally, social-pathological phenomena of race prejudice and discrimination dominate the whole subject.

The Criminal Record of the Negro. In order to answer the questions just raised the usual procedure has been, until recently, to turn to criminal statistics which, as we shall later show, are about the most difficult to interpret accurately because of a number of spurious factors. Nevertheless, let us look at a few such statistics from reputable sources.

Table 1 deals with arrests only. We see from it that 1,938.7 out of each 100,000 of the Negro population were arrested in 1946. Per 100,000 white population, the arrests were 578.6. Though rates in all cases except one (driving while intoxicated) are higher than for whites, they are *relatively* low when measured by arrests data for rape, embezzlement and fraud, arson, other sex offenses, buying and receiving stolen property, narcotic drug laws, forgery and counterfeiting; and *noticeably* high for assault, larceny, drunkenness, suspicion, burglary, robbery, vagrancy, gambling, carrying and possessing weapons. Strikingly are the Negro's low rates for rape and other sex offenses. They tend to explode a persistent myth that he is especially responsible for these crimes.

Table 2 deals with felony commitments to State and Federal prisons and reformatories. It shows that Negro males made up 32.8 per cent of the total commitments for the year 1945. The corresponding figure for Negro females was 32.2. We also see that these groups constituted 48.4 per cent and 56.00 per cent, respectively, of the commitments for the Southern states. Other interesting comparisons can easily be made by referring to the table.

Now let us look at Table 3 which shows the number of felony commitments of the native-born and foreign-born whites, and the Negroes, according to offenses, with the per cent distribution of the different offenses. It reveals that among the native white, the greatest proportions were committed for larceny, burglary, and auto theft. The three offenses for which the greatest proportions of Negroes were committed were burglary, larceny, and robbery. It is also interesting to note that the commitments figures re-enforce those concerning arrest data in showing that (a) sex offenses, including rape, among Negroes are relatively unimportant; and (b) Negroes do not tend to commit "white collar" crimes.

Explanations of the Criminal Behavior of the Negro. Given the greater criminality of the Negro, we now come to the explanation of it. Novices approaching the problem are eager for simple explanations, and feel more comfortable when race inferiority, ignorance, prejudice, poverty, inherited depravity, and the like are stated emphatically to be major causes. The fact is, however, that the causes of crime among Negroes, as well as other elements in our population, are legion. This is so true that certain recent writers, e.g., Cantor and Riemer, take the view that it is futile to discuss the causes of crime. Most criminologists, however, seem to be satisfied at present with a description of the conditions favorable to the commission of crime, without contending that they will inevitably cause crime. It is hoped that from a study of the factors associated with, or contributing to, crime, an effective scheme will evolve for the solution of the crime problem. This point should be kept in mind as a first step to a better understanding of *The Negro in Crime.*

Explanations of the Negro's excessive crime rates have come from three general directions: (a) racial differences in psychological qualities; (b) general social handicaps of the Negro; and (c) inequality of justice, that is, greater willingness on the part of the administrative machinery to suspect, arrest, and convict a Negro. Studies of Negro crime have accepted as a starting point one or more of these explanations.

A. *Race Differences in Psychological*

TABLE 2

PERCENTAGE DISTRIBUTION OF FELONY PRISONERS RECEIVED FROM COURTS BY RACE, NATIVITY, SEX, AND GEOGRAPHICAL AREAS: 1945 *

Race and Nativity	Total		Northeastern States		North-central States [a]		Southern States [b]		Western States	
	Male	Female	Male	Female	Male	Female	Male	Female	Male	Female
Total	100.0	100.0	100.0	100.0	100.0	100.0	100.0	100.0	100.0	100.0
White	66.3	65.9	69.5	74.6	76.2	80.2	51.2	43.1	83.0	79.1
Native	64.3	64.0	66.2	71.1	74.6	79.2	50.4	42.5	79.0	75.4
Foreign-born	2.0	1.9	3.3	3.4	1.6	1.0	0.8	0.6	4.0	3.7
Negro	32.8	32.2	30.2	25.1	22.6	18.8	48.4	56.0	14.6	18.2
Other races	0.9	0.9	0.3	0.3	1.2	1.0	0.4	0.9	2.4	2.7

* Source: U. S. Department of Commerce, Bureau of Census, "Prisoners in State and Federal Prisons and Reformatories, 1945." Government Printing Office, Washington, 1947, prepared under the supervision of Dr. Leon E. Truesdell—Table 14, adapted. ^a Michigan did not report. ^b Georgia and Mississippi did not report.

TABLE 3

MALE FELONY PRISONERS RECEIVED FROM COURTS, BY RACE AND NATIVITY, BY OFFENSE: 1945*

Offense	Total	Native White	Foreign Born White	Negro	Other Races	Percentage Distribution			
						Native White	Foreign Born White	Negro	Other Races
Total	40,852	26,249	1,662	12,428	513	100.0	100.0	100.0	100.0
Murder	1,281	488	41	737	15	1.9	2.5	5.9	2.9
Manslaughter	1,001	397	26	555	23	1.5	1.6	4.5	4.5
Robbery	3,479	2,007	38	1,420	14	7.6	2.3	11.4	2.7
Aggravated assault	2,403	1,036	63	1,265	39	3.9	3.8	10.2	7.6
Burglary	7,168	4,537	122	2,454	55	17.3	7.3	19.7	10.7
Larceny, except auto theft	7,009	4,628	107	2,210	64	17.6	6.4	17.8	12.5
Auto theft	3,114	2,580	28	466	40	9.8	1.7	3.7	7.8
Embezzlement and fraud	1,130	942	58	124	6	3.6	3.5	1.0	1.2
Stolen property	424	259	16	148	1	1.0	1.0	1.2	0.2
Forgery	2,373	1,936	33	374	30	7.4	2.0	3.0	5.8
Rape	1,868	1,181	54	603	30	4.5	3.2	4.9	5.8
Commercialized vice	242	177	6	57	2	0.7	0.4	0.5	0.4
Other sex offenses	1,060	832	76	138	14	3.2	4.6	1.1	2.7
Violating drug laws	990	568	96	238	88	2.2	5.8	1.9	17.2
Carrying & possessing weapons	190	91	6	91	2	0.3	0.4	0.7	0.4
Nonsupport or neglect	419	349	10	55	5	1.3	0.6	0.4	1.0
Violating liquor laws	2,062	1,240	76	735	11	4.7	4.6	5.9	2.1
Violating traffic laws	92	62	2	28	..	0.2	0.1	0.2	a
Violating Nat'l Defense laws	2,303	1,659	182	412	50	6.3	11.0	3.3	9.7
Other offenses	2,244	1,280	622	318	24	4.9	37.4	2.6	4.7

* Source: Ibid., Table 32, p. 45. Note: these figures are for 1945. Michigan, Georgia and Mississippi did not report.
a Less than one-tenth of one percent.

Qualities.—Perhaps the oldest theory advanced to explain the Negro's high crime rate is that of an innate tendency toward types of criminal behavior, as well as toward crime in general. However, when one consults the literature of anthropology, sociology, and psychology, it appears that the foundation for this theory is exceedingly weak. No attempt will be made here to give a review of all the studies on the problem as excellent summaries are readily available. We shall limit ourselves to a few resolutions and manifestos to illustrate the present trends in this area.

In 1930, Thompson circulated a questionnaire among "competent scholars in the field of racial difference" which revealed that only 4 percent of the respondents believed in "racial" superiority or inferiority. He concludes:

". . . The data reveal unmistakably that it is the general conclusion of scholars engaged in the field of racial differences and closely allied fields that experimentation to date has neither demonstrated that there are any *inherent* mental differences between American Negroes and American whites, nor corroborated the "mulatto hypothesis"—that Negroes with more white blood are *inherently* mentally different from Negroes with less white blood—which is a fundamental corollary of the racial-difference thesis."

At the 1938 annual meeting of the American Anthropological Association, a resolution was unanimously adopted in part as follows:

"(1) Race involves the inheritance of similar physical variations by large groups of mankind, but its psychological and cultural connotations, if they exist, have not been ascertained by science . . .

"(3) Anthropology provides no scientific basis for discrimination against any people on the ground of racial inferiority, religious affiliation, or linguistic heritage."

Recently, a group of psychologists prepared a protest against the "non-scientific interpretations" of "racial" psychology which "Fascists are using to justify persecution." The protest was prepared by psychologists who are specialists on "racial" psychology and was issued officially by the council of the Society for the Psychological Study of Social Issues. It reads, in part, as follows:

"In the experiments which psychologists have made upon different peoples, no characteristic inherent psychological differences, which fundamentally distinguish so-called 'races' have been disclosed. . . . There is no evidence of an inborn Jewish or German or Italian mentality. Furthermore, there is no indication that the members of any group are rendered incapable by their biological heredity of completely acquiring the culture of the community in which they live. This is true not only of Jews in Germany, but also of groups that actually are physically different from one another."

From the point of view of American anthropology and specialists on racial psychology, then, the very general assumption that the Negro is criminal by nature and particularly inclined to crime of violence is without basis in fact.

B. *General Social Handicaps of the Negro.* —The situation in scientific race psychology is not very encouraging at present for those who hold the theory of inborn racial proclivity to crime. We are thus forced to turn to a consideration of the Negro's social setting for an explanation of his excessive criminality.

Causation research since about 1915 has taken into consideration the complex process of personality development and, therefore, has gradually broadened its emphasis to include the cultural situation and its relations to and influence upon the development of personality, criminal and non-criminal. Nearly all factors favorable to criminality are found disproportionately among Negroes. Several investigations have revealed that most American Negroes are the products of a narrow and circumscribed world; of poor home conditions; of poor recreational facilities; of an impoverished social and cultural environment outside the school; of extremely inadequate schooling; and of a poor economic environment, with all that this implies in regard to nutrition and health, subordination, frustration, aggression, economic insecurity, and incomplete participation in the American society. Envisaged in these terms, one would expect some variations in crime rates between Negroes and whites, since there are also variations in every condition considered a handicap to successful social adjustment in our dynamic industrial society.

C. *Inequality of Justice.*—According to the American Creed, Negroes are *entitled* to justice with all other people. In reality, one finds inequalities either in the law, or the administration of the laws, or both. They are found in all the states in the Union; however, the Negro gets more legal justice in the North largely because (a) it is further removed from the memories of slavery; and, (b) there he can vote, thus sharing in the ultimate control of the legal system. As a consequence, the main problems of justice for the Negro are found in the South. But the South's race problem has been gradually moving North and West during the past thirty-five years because of several reasons among which are (a) The Great Migration, starting in 1915 and continuing in waves from then on, numerically significant during World War I and II; and, (b) increasing displacement of Southern workers by mechanical farm implements, and new job opportunities for Negroes in the North and West.

Practically all of the migrants have gone to the cities and almost all to the big cities. In 1940, 90.1 per cent of all Negroes in Northern and Western states outside of Missouri lived in urban areas. In the last sixteen years, Detroit's Negro population has increased 75 per cent (to 210,000). Los Angeles' 133,000 Negro population has more than doubled since 1940. Between 1930 and 1945, New York's Negro population has increased 67 per cent (to 547,000); Chicago's by 50 per cent (to 350,000); San Francisco's by 741 per cent (to 32,000). In Portland, Oregon, Negroes increased from 2,100 in 1940 to 11,000 in 1946.

Recent socio-economic dislocations, then, have started an exodus of Negroes from the South into the overcrowded cities of the North and the West. While the migration may well mean an eventual improvement in their status in both areas, nevertheless it presents a social situation of increasing danger. For example, somebody shoves somebody on a crowded bus; there is a brawl at a picnic park; somebody moves into a white neighborhood, or wants a job, or takes an extra drink; a rumor starts; and soon a lot of people are slugging each other. As students of race riots would say—"that's the pattern." Remember Chicago and Detroit.

Criminal statistics, therefore, reflect socio-economic conditions, police, legislative, and court practices as much as they do crime. Among the factors to be noted here are: (a) the structural characteristics of our judicial system which operates against all poor and uneducated groups as, for example, securing legal aid, and the bond and bail system; (b) the inequality of arrests and convictions among Negro-white groups; (c) Negroes are more likely than whites to be arrested under any suspicious circumstances; (d) justice often depends upon popular opinions and beliefs regarding Negroes; (e) white criminals are more likely than Negroes to have political "pull" protecting them from arrest and conviction; and (f) some Negro "crimes" are often merely violations of the extra-legal caste rules and customs.

It appears on looking over the present state of affairs that the summary of the situation given by the research committee of the National Interracial Conference in 1928 is substantially as true today as it was then. It covered the following points:

1. It is difficult to secure dependable data on Negro crime, because (a) general crime records are poor and comparative figures less dependable, and (b) racial factors enter, influencing the agencies of law enforcement most frequently to the disadvantage of the Negro and the Negro records of crime.

2. The Negro crime rate as measured by all comparative records is greater than that of the white.

3. The difference varies widely and according to geographical location and population ratios; it also varies by types of offenses.

4. There is a much higher Negro rate for homicides than white, even when the emotional factors referred to are taken into account.

5. Negro arrest rates are higher than white for petty offenses and lower than white in commitment to prison for serious offenses.

6. There is obvious discrimination in the administration of laws on the part of the police, magistrates, judges, and pardon boards, which explains an undetermined degree of the disparity between white and Negro rates.

7. It is possibly true that Negro rates of crime are more nearly actual crime rates of Negroes than white recorded rates are of crimes committed by whites.

8. Illiteracy, unfavorable environment, age distributions, and unfamiliarity with city and urban life, are factors to be seriously studied in relation to present Negro crime. (From Johnson.)

It should be obvious by now that a number of cultural factors must be given consideration in judging the Negro's present status in the criminal world. These factors tend to cause his *recorded* crime record to greatly exaggerate his *actual* criminal behavior. A large but indeterminable deduction should therefore be made from the statistics of Negro crime. Moreover, when we compare the crime record of Negro and white groups, we can draw no inference as to the criminal propensities of the groups, because we have no means of equating or weighing cultural factors.

Conclusion. Our critical discussion of the materials on *The Negro in Crime* makes clear at least some of the difficulties in the way of evaluating his comparative criminality by use of statistical records. As we look at the situation we are impressed by the great complexity of the picture. The statistics on which many generalizations have been based are not scientifically valid inasmuch as they are weighted by inaccurate racial listings (no distinction is made between the full-blooded and various degrees of mixture of Negroes) and a number of other spurious selective factors, the most important of which are: (a) the Negro's social-historical conditions, (b) his present position in the American social order, and (c) inequality of justice. Until and unless crime statistics are corrected for these and other weighing factors, we are not justified in claiming that race as such plays any significant part.

More precisely, the following statement may with some safety be made at this time. The Negro's excessive criminality is in all probability to be explained in terms of a disease in our society—unequal social privileges, economic and educational opportunities—rather than regarded as evidence of any innate racial proclivity to crime. It fol-

lows, then, that the task of American society, if it is to give effect to its democratic profession, is to work to correct the cultural inequalities which cause the present inequalities in behavior considered criminal. This concept of "society as the patient" or the "sick society" has recently been analyzed by Frank. HERMAN G. CANADY
Professor of Psychology
West Virginia State College
Institute, West Virginia

BIBLIOGRAPHY

Anastasi, A., *Differential Psychology: Individual and Group Differences,* New York, Macmillan, 1937.

Barnes, H. E., and Teeters, N. K., *New Horizons in Criminology,* New York, Prentice-Hall, 1944.

Baur, E., Fischer, E., and Lenz, F., *Human Heredity,* New York, Macmillan, 1931 (trans.).

Bonger, W. A., *Race and Crime,* New York, Columbia University Press, 1943.

Brearley, H. C., "Race as a Sociological Concept," *Sociol. and Soc. Resch.,* 1939, 23, 514–518.

Canady, H. G., *Test Standing and Social Setting: A Comparative Study of the Intelligence-Test Scores of Negroes Living Under Varied Environmental Conditions.* (Northwestern University, unpublished doctor's dissertation, Evanston, Illinois, 1941).

———. "The American Caste System and the Question of Negro Intelligence," *J. Educ. Psychol.,* 1942, 33, 161–172.

———, "The Problem of Equating the Environment of Negro-white Groups for Intelligence Testing in Comparative Studies," *J. Soc. Psychol.,* 1943, 17, 3–15.

———, "The Methodology and Interpretation of Negro-white Intelligence Testing," *Sch. and Soc.,* 1942, 55, 569–575.

———, "The Psychology of the Negro," In *Encyclopedia of Psychology,* P. L. Harriman (Ed.), Philosophical Library, 1946, 407–416.

Cantor, N. F., *Crime and Society.* New York, Holt, 1939.

Chicago Commission on Race Relations, *The Negro in Chicago, A Study of Race Relations and a Race Riot,* Chicago, University of Chicago Press, 1922.

Davis, A., and Dollard, J., *Children of Bondage,* Washington, D. C., American Council on Education, 1940.

Davis, A., Garder B., and M., *Deep South,* Chicago, University of Chicago Press, 1941.

Dollard, J. N., *Caste and Class in a Southern Town,* New Haven, Yale University Press, 1937.

Dollard, J. N., et al., *Frustration and Aggression*, New Haven, Yale University Press, 1939.

Doyle, B., *The Etiquette of Race Relations in the South*, Chicago, The University of Chicago Press, 1937.

Finot, J., *Race Prejudice* (Translated by Florence Wade-Evans), London, Constable, 1906.

Frank, L. K., "Society as the Patient," *Amer. J. Sociol.*, 1936, 42, 335–344.

Frazier, E. F., *The Negro Family in the United States*, Chicago, The University of Chicago Press, 1939.

Frazier, J. G., *The Golden Bough: A Study in Magic and Religion* (one volume, abridged edition), New York, Macmillan, 1940.

Garth, T. R., *Race Psychology: A Study of Racial Mental Differences*, New York, McGraw-Hill, 1931.

Grant, M., *The Passing of the Great Race*, New York, Scribner's, 1916.

Herskovits, M. J., *The American Negro: A Study in Racial Crossing*, New York, Knopf, 1928.

———, *Anthropometry of the American Negro*, New York, Columbia University Press, 1930.

Huxley, J. S., and Haddon, A. C., *We Europeans: A Survey of Racial Problems*, London, Jonathan Cape, 1935.

Johnson, C. S., *The Negro in American Civilization*, New York, Holt, 1930.

———, *Patterns of Segregation*, New York, Harper, 1944.

Johnson, G. B., "The Negro and Crime," *Ann. Amer. Acad. Pol. and Soc. Sci.*, 1941, 217, 93–104.

Johnson, G. B., and Kiser, L. K., "The Negro and Crime," (unpublished manuscript prepared for *"The Negro in American Life"* study directed by Dr. Gunnar Myrdal and deposited in the Schomburg Collection of the New York Public Library).

Klineberg, O., *Social Psychology*, New York, Holt, 1940.

———, *Race Differences*, New York, Harper, 1935.

———, *Characteristics of the American Negro*, New York, Harper, 1944.

Laughlin, H. H., "Analysis of America's Melting-Pot," *Hearings before the Committee on Immigration and Naturalization, House of Representatives*, 67th Congress, November 21, 1922.

Lee, A. M., *Race Riots Aren't Necessary*, Public Affairs Pamphlet No. 107, 1945.

Lee, A. M., and Humphrey, N. D., *Race Riot*, New York, Dryden Press, 1943.

Mangum, Jr., C. S., *The Legal Status of the Negro*, Chapel Hill, N. C., University of North Carolina Press, 1940.

McCord, C. H., *The American Negro as a Dependent, Defective, and Delinquent*, Nashville, Tenn., 1924.

McDougall, W., *Is America Safe for Democracy*, New York, Scribner, 1921.

McEntire, D., and Powers, R. B., *Police Training Bulletin—A Guide to Race Relations for Police Officers*, Department of Justice, State of California, 1946.

Michael, J., and Adler, M. J., *Crime, Law and Social Science*, New York, Harcourt, 1933.

Myrdal, G., *An American Dilemma: The Negro Problem and Modern Democracy*, New York, Harper, 1944 (2 vols).

National Survey of the Higher Education of Negroes, Federal Security Agency, U. S. Office of Education, Washington, D. C., 1942.

Powdermaker, H., *After Freedom: A Cultural Study of the Deep South*, New York, Viking, 1939.

Reckless, W. C., *Criminal Behavior*, New York, McGraw-Hill, 1939.

Reid, Ira de A., "Notes on the Negro's Relation to Work and Law Observance," *National Commission on Law Observance and Enforcement, Report on the Causes of Crime*, Washington, D. C., Government Printing Office, 1931, I, 221–255.

Reuter, E. B., *The American Race Problem*, New York, Crowell, 1938.

Riemer, S., "Theory and Quantitative Analysis in Criminological Research," *Amer. J. Soc.*, 1942, 48, 188–201.

Sellin, T., *Culture Conflict and Crime*, New York, Social Science Research Council, 1938.

———, "The Negro Criminal," *Ann. Amer. Acad. Pol. and Soc. Sci.*, 1928, 140, 52–64.

———, "The Negro and the Problem of Law Observance and Administration in the Light of Social Research," in Johnson (27, pp. 443–452).

———, "Race Prejudice in the Administration of Justice," *Amer. J. Sociol.*, 1935, 41, 215–217.

Sterner, R., *The Negro's Share*, New York, Harper, 1944.

Time Magazine, July 28, 1947, p. 16.

The New York Meeting of the American Anthropological Association, *Science*, 1939, 89, 20–30.

Thompson, C. H. (ed.), "The Physical and Mental Abilities of the American Negro." *J. Negro Educ.*, Yearbook Number III, July 1934, 3, 317–564.

———, (ed.), "A Critical Survey of the Negro Adolescent and His Education." *J. Negro Educ.*, Yearbook Number IX, July 1940, 9, 275–534.

———, (ed.), "The Health Status and the Health Education of Negroes in the United States." *J. Negro Educ.* Yearbook Number VI, July 1937, 6, 261–587.

Van Waters, M., "Race Psychology," *Science* (Supplement, Dec. 30), 1938, 88, 7–8.

White, W., and Marshall, T., *What Caused the Detroit Riot?* New York, National As-

sociation for the Advancement of Colored People, 1943.
Willcox, W., "Negro Criminality," *J. Soc. Sc.* (Dec., 1899) pp. 78–98.
Woofter, T. J., Jr., "The Status of Racial and Ethnic Groups," in *Recent Social Trends*, N. Y., 1933. Vol. 1, Chap. II: pp. 553–601.
Young, D., *American Minority Peoples*, New York, Harper, 1932.

NUISANCES. Under this heading are grouped a number of criminal offenses all of which have in common the fact that they constitute a *public nuisance*. A "public nuisance" is defined as a crime against the order and economy of the state, and consists in unlawfully doing an act, or omitting to perform a duty, which act or omission:

1. Annoys, injures or endangers the comfort, repose, health or safety of any considerable number of persons; or,

2. Offends public decency; or,

3. Unlawfully interferes with, obstructs, or tends to obstruct, or renders dangerous for passage, a lake, or a navigable river, or other body of water which has been dredged or cleared at public expense, or a public park, square, street or highway; or,

4. In any way renders a considerable number of persons insecure in life, or the use of property.

Criminal intent as applied to the crime of maintaining a public nuisance, does *not* mean that one charged with the offense should be shown to have consciously and positively intended to interfere with the comfort and repose of any considerable number of persons. His criminality is independent of any positive purpose of annoyance and may arise from his very failure to think of anybody but himself.

According to New York State Penal Law, a person who commits or maintains a public nuisance, the punishment for which is not specially prescribed, or who wilfully omits or refuses to perform any legal duty relating to the removal of such a public nuisance, is guilty of a misdemeanor. Examples of maintaining a public nuisance are such offenses as permitting the use of a building for a nuisance such as opium smoking, or the operation of a moving picture theatre on Sundays under certain circumstances. Ticket speculators are guilty of maintaining a public nuisance.

BIBLIOGRAPHY

Gilbert, F. B., *Criminal Law and Practice of the State of New York*, Matthew Bender and Co., 1935.

O

ORGANIZATIONS.

ADMINISTRATIVE OFFICE OF THE UNITED STATES COURTS (1940)

Washington (13), D. C. (Supreme Court Building)

Upon the establishment of this Office, the probation service was transferred from the Department of Justice, Bureau of Prisons. The probation service in addition provides investigation service for the Bureau of Prisons as well as pre-parole planning. In addition the federal probation officers supervise for the Parole Board all individuals under conditional release and parole. Publishes quarterly magazine—*Federal Probation*.

AMERICAN ACADEMY OF POLITICAL AND SOCIAL SCIENCE (1889)

3457 Walnut Street, Philadelphia, Penna.

Provides a national form for discussion of political and social questions; administers funds providing for research fellowships. Publishes—*Annals*—bi-monthly. Each issue is devoted to one subject, for example: *Prisons of Tomorrow* (1931), *Administration of Justice* (1933), *Crime in the United States* (1941).

AMERICAN INSTITUTE OF CRIMINAL LAW AND CRIMINOLOGY

504 Lee Street, Evanston, Illinois

To further the scientific study of crime, criminal law, and procedure; to formulate and promote measures for solving the problems connected therewith; and to coordinate the efforts of individuals and organizations interested in the administration of certain, speedy justice. It has now (1944) surrendered its charter, and ceased to exist as a separate organization. Publishes *Journal of Criminal Law and Criminology*.

AMERICAN LAW INSTITUTE (1923)

3400 Chestnut Street, Philadelphia, Penna.

An incorporated organization of judges, practising lawyers, and law teachers, established "to promote the clarification and simplification of the law and its better adaptation to social needs, to secure the better administration of justice, and to encourage and carry on scholarly and scientific legal work." The work planned by this Institute gives it a position of public importance and significance. Two main projects have been undertaken: a restatement of the substantive law, and a model code of criminal procedure. Very instrumental in creating the Youth Authority Act.

AMERICAN LEAGUE TO ABOLISH CAPITAL PUNISHMENT

124 Lexington Avenue, New York (16), N. Y.

AMERICAN PRISON ASSOCIATION (1870)

135 East 15th Street, New York (3), N. Y.

The objects of the Association are as follows: 1 The improvement of the laws in relation to public offenses and offenders, and the modes of procedure by which such laws are enforced; 2 The study of the causes of crime, the nature of offenders and their social surroundings, the best methods of dealing with offenders and of preventing crime; 3 The improvement of the penal, correctional and reformatory institutions throughout the country, and of the government, management and discipline thereof, including the appointment of boards of trustees and other officers; 4 The care of, and providing suitable and remunerative employment for paroled and discharged prisoners and probationers, and especially such as may have given evidence of reformation.

The Association, the duly qualified medium for the registration of the opinions of prison administrators in the United States, holds an Annual Congress in some city on this continent. At this Congress, which is the great yearly forum for the discussion of all problems relating to delinquency, there come together many hundreds of persons dealing with or directly interested in the problems of crime, delinquency, and abnormal behavior. Maintains a free clearing house, prepared to furnish advice and information on prison, reformatory, workhouse, and jail administration, construction of penal and correctional buildings, and in general on the treatment of the offender both inside and outside the institution. Publishes annual proceedings of its Congress. Publishes *The Prison World.*

AMERICAN SOCIAL HYGIENE ASSOCIATION (1914)
1790 Broadway, New York (19), N. Y.

Joins with federal and other official agencies and with voluntary groups in the promotion of social hygiene activities, which include: informing the public about syphilis and gonococcal infections, aiding medical and public health authorities to provide early diagnosis and proper treatment for all infected persons, and encouraging sound medical and general social measures for preventing these diseases; providing ample environmental safeguards for youth and mentally incompetent persons against commercial exploitation of sex; providing wholesome and constructive public entertainments for youth and adults as substitutes for vice; and providing sound sex education in its broadest sense for childhood and youth as part of character training, and adequate training for marriage and family relations. Publishes *Journal of Social Hygiene,* and *Social Hygiene News.*

ASSOCIATION OF JUVENILE COURT JUDGES OF AMERICA, SEE NATIONAL COUNCIL OF JUVENILE COURT JUDGES

CENTRAL HOWARD ASSOCIATION (1901)
608 South Dearborn Street, Chicago, Ill.

Activities include prevention of delinquency, by adoption of social legislation, such as juvenile courts, adult probation, etc.; protection, by eliminating political administration of prisons, adequate employment of prisoners, classification, and individual study and treatment of prisoners; aftercare service in behalf of released prisoners, employment, parole supervision, etc.

CHICAGO CRIME COMMISSION
79 West Monroe Street, Chicago, Illinois

Purpose: to help correct inadequate laws and procedures, uncover and punish crime and corruption, work with and encourage all good and honest public servants, help correct conditions that breed crime and make criminals. Recognizes as fundamental, just laws—fair, simple and easy to understand. Publishes an *Information Bulletin*—facts, analysis, comments of its activities.

CITIZENS COMMITTEE ON THE CONTROL OF CRIME IN NEW YORK CITY
50 Lafayette Street, New York (13), N. Y.

Purpose: to study and seek means of dealing with the problems existing in connection with the prevention, suppression and punishment of crime, and to educate the public with respect to such problems; to assist in the maintenance of the activity and efficiency of all agencies of the City of New York and its various counties for the administration of criminal justice.

COMMUNITY SERVICE SOCIETY OF NEW YORK—COMMITTEE ON YOUTH AND JUSTICE
105 East 22nd Street, New York (10), N. Y.

Primarily concerned with a program of research which has the objective of introducing into the criminal justice system of New York improved procedures for the social rehabilitation of offenders. The studies of the Committee have led it to suggest new administrative machinery which would provide more effective methods of dealing with youth offenders who fall into the hands of the law. The recommendations of the Committee are presented in four reports: *Preventing Criminal Careers* (1941), *Prisons Cost Too Much*

(1942), *Chaos in Sentencing Youth Offenders* (1943), *Correctional Treatment of Youth Offenders* (1944).

COUNCIL OF STATE GOVERNMENTS (1933)

1313 East 60th Street, Chicago (37), Ill.

A joint governmental agency established by the states, and supported by the states. It is the secretariat for the Governors' Conference, the National Association of Secretaries of State, and it acts as a clearing house and research center for legislators, legislative reference bureaus. It is a medium through which many federal-state and interstate problems have been resolved and a forum for the consideration of the increasing number of problems growing out of the war emergency. Publishes *State Government*, and reports on special problems, such as crime control.

INDUSTRIAL AREAS FOUNDATION

8 South Michigan Avenue, Chicago, Ill.

Purpose: survey and analyze the character and problems of the industrial areas of the nation with the objective in mind of lending aid towards the solution of such problems. Will assist communities in organizing their life. Fundamentally, its purpose is to restore the democratic way of life to modern industrial society.

INTERNATIONAL ASSOCIATION OF CHIEFS OF POLICE (1893)

918 F Street, Washington (4), D. C.

Now preparing a complete review of the police responsibility in juvenile delinquency, defining possibilities in the post-war period that will require special police action. Works to advance police profession, science of prevention and detection of crime and apprehension of criminals, advises on preparation of police reports concerning crime. Publishes *Police Chiefs' News Letters*, and *Yearbook* . . . of their annual proceedings.

INTERSTATE COMMISSION ON CRIME (1935)

Essex County Courthouse, Newark, N. J.

Purpose: to obtain better cooperation between the states and with the federal government in the field of crime control, both through the interaction of such governments themselves and of such government with the citizenry. As an official body, it represents every state and the federal government. Legislative, administrative, and judicial work for a series of statutes—model ones—and administrative measures by various states. The staff of the Council of Governments serves as the secretariat of this commission. Issues special reports on various aspects of crime, from an interstate point of view.

JUDGE BAKER GUIDANCE CENTER (1917)

38 Beacon Street, Boston, Massachusetts

Conducts scientific investigations and treatment of personality, conduct, and educational problems of childhood and youth. Cooperative therapeutic work is carried on with agencies, and also direct therapeutic work with individuals and families.

NATIONAL COMMITTEE FOR MENTAL HYGIENE (1909)

1790 Broadway, New York (19), N. Y.

Works for the conservation of mental health, reduction and prevention of mental and nervous disorders and defects, improved care and treatment of persons suffering from mental diseases, special training and supervision of the feebleminded, and the acquisition and dissemination of reliable information on these subjects and on mental factors involved in education, industry, delinquency, dependency, and others related to the broad field of human endeavor, behavior. Publishes *Mental Hygiene*.

NATIONAL COMMITTEE ON PRISONS AND PRISON LABOR (1916)

1102 Sixteenth Street, N.W., Washington, D. C.

Purpose: unite and concentrate the efforts of all persons interested in prison reform, to conduct investigations and make recommendations, to formulate and make effective a system for penalizing crime which will be just to the state, the prisoner, the prisoner's family, and the free workingman. To study the problems of labor in prisons and correctional institutions for the sake of obtaining legislation providing for the employment of all prisoners in such a manner as to prevent unfair competition between prison-made goods and the products of free labor, and to obtain a fair proportion of the rightful earnings of prisoners for the use of their dependent families.

NATIONAL CONFERENCE OF JUVENILE AGENCIES (1921)
State Colony, Woodbine, New Jersey

Purposes: to afford an opportunity for study and discussion to those interested or engaged in the administration or supervision of public and private agencies caring for children and youth; to encourage and otherwise stimulate progress in these agencies along with practical humanitarian lines; to diffuse reliable information with a view to their constant improvement and the advancement of the highest ideals in their administration; to confer respecting practical methods of work and principles and philosophy of administration; to sponsor and promote studies in the field of juvenile delinquency, dependency, and neglect, which may be useful to agencies dealing with these problems and of educational value to the general public. Publishes *Proceedings* . . . , issued quarterly.

NATIONAL CONFERENCE OF SOCIAL WORK (1873)
82 North High Street, Columbus, Ohio

Purposes: to facilitate the discussion of problems and methods of human improvement, to increase the efficiency of agencies and institutions devoted to this cause, and to disseminate information. Platforms are not formulated. Conference is now organized in four continuous sections—social case work, social group work, community organization, and social action. Publishes *Bulletin*, and yearly *Proceedings*. . . .

NATIONAL COUNCIL OF JUVENILE COURT JUDGES
Juvenile Court House, Toledo, Ohio

Purpose: to promote, organize, and develop juvenile courts throughout the United States, to interpret the philosophy of the juvenile court and to secure uniform legislation in the various states so that the courts will function both effectively and efficiently, to foster

studies and surveys in the field, and to cooperate and coordinate child welfare services.

NATIONAL JAIL ASSOCIATION (1938)
135 East 15th Street, New York (3), N. Y.

Is a continuation, in permanent form, of the former Committee on jails, of the American Prison Association. Its object, as embodied in the Constitution is: to band together all those concerned with or interested in the custody and care of persons awaiting trial, serving sentence, or otherwise confined in jails, with a view to improving the conditions and systems under which such persons are treated. Conducts regional conferences, annual meetings and other sessions from time to time, and is equipped to counsel and advise on problems pertaining to jails and other short-term institutions. Publishes, in collaboration with the American Prison Association, the official professional journal *The Prison World*.

NATIONAL PRISONERS' AID ASSOCIATION (1910)
322 Shops Building, Des Moines, Iowa.

Aids in the development and extension of work for prisoners, including the visiting of prisoners, fosters cooperation and exchange of ideas between local prisoners' aid societies.

NATIONAL PROBATION AND PAROLE ASSOCIATION (1907)
1790 Broadway New York (19), N. Y.

Purposes: to study and standardize the methods of probation and parole work, both juvenile and adult, by conferences, field investigations and research; to extend and develop the probation system by legislation; publication and distribution of literature, and in other ways; to promote the establishment and development of juvenile courts, domestic relations or family courts and other specialized courts using probation; and to cooperate with local, state, and national organizations to bring about the prevention of delinquency and crime. Publishes *Probation*, and yearly proceedings of their meetings.

Organized to improve parole service and legislation referring to it, to interpret parole to the public, to act as clearing house for information and advice as to new and improved processes in parole, to hold national and regional conferences, and to assist various state jurisdictions in working out parole programs. Publishes a quarterly informational bulletin of national interest, special reports. Formerly the American Parole Association (1931).

OSBORNE ASSOCIATION (1933)
114 East 30th Street (16), N. Y.

Combines the National Society of Penal Information, and the Welfare League Association, both established by the late Thomas Mott Osborne. Is supported by individual contributions and foundation grants. Makes nation-wide surveys of prisons, adult reformatories, institutions for juvenile delinquents, and other agencies and activities in the penal correctional field. Some of the volumes containing reports of its surveys, which began in 1925, have covered the whole country, but the Association's present procedure is to report on the institutions of a single geographical area—at the request of the authorities or a civic group. These reports are based on actual field studies, made by trained staff members and not on questionnaire material. Publishes a series of volumes under the title *Handbook of American Prisons and Reformatories*, and another series under the title *Handbook of American Institutions for Delinquent Juveniles*. Maintains an employment and aid service for released prisoners under a director of vocational placement. This service gives ex-prisoners assistance and guidance in securing employment and gives temporary financial aid, if necessary.

PENNSYLVANIA PRISON SOCIETY (1787)
311 South Juniper Street, Philadelphia (7), Penna.

Offers a casework service on a professional level to adult offenders in prison and after release. This includes such services as counselling, parole planning, financial assistance, sponsorship, and service to families as it relates to delinquent behavior of some member. The Society is interested in social action, looking toward the improvement of penal conditions in such matters as personnel, the promotion of public understanding, the ad-

ministration of penal and correctional institutions, and crime problems. The Society's primary interest in the field of social action is in reference to improvement in individualized service, extension of classification, and a centralized state administration. The abolition of the death penalty is another of the Society objectives. Publishes the *Prison Journal*.

PRISON ASSOCIATION OF NEW YORK (1845)
135 East 15th Street, New York (3), N. Y.

Works with men and boys on probation or parole from courts or institutions of the City or State of New York. Special referrals from courts or institutions out of the state. Works with families of men in prison, and consults with men and boys awaiting trial. Offers vocational guidance, employment and relief. Maintains educational activities for promoting public understanding of crime problems and the administration of penal and correctional institutions. Carries on legislative information and activity, and inspections as authorized by law. Conducts special surveys on related subjects and maintains an extensive information service.

SALVATION ARMY (1865)
120 West 14th Street, New York (11), N. Y.

Prison welfare department. Conducts prison visitations, has supervision of paroled men, seeks and obtains employment for ex-prisoners, and brings relief to their families. Publishes weekly *War Cry*.

SOCIETY FOR THE PREVENTION OF CRIME (1878)
122 East 22nd Street, New York (10), N. Y.

The Society is dedicated to research in all of the phases of crime prevention, with special emphasis upon the causative factors in juvenile delinquency and adolescent crime. It publishes pamphlets embodying its reports on special studies, and conducts a news service for newspapers, interpreting for the laity the studies and views of criminologists, penologists, and sociologists upon delinquency and crime problems. Engages in other diverse activities having to do with the penal and correctional institutions to which youthful offenders are committed, and with the promotion of proposed legislative and administrative improvements in the system of criminal justice.

UNITED STATES—DEPARTMENT OF JUSTICE, BUREAU OF PRISONS (1930)
Washington, D. C.

Purpose: to supervise, under the Attorney General, the administration of the federal penal and correctional institutions, including a social service program; to oversee the development of a system of classification of prisoners and the individualization of treatment; to make provisions for the care and custody of federal prisoners committed to jails and other local institutions; and to promote the efficient administration of the parole and probation system and the enforcement of the probation laws in all United States courts. (See Administrative Office of the United States Courts.) Publishes *Federal Offenders*—annual report of the Bureau. (Beginning with the 1943 fiscal period, ending June 30th, these reports will be titled—*Federal Prisons*.)

UNITED STATES—DEPARTMENT OF JUSTICE, FEDERAL BUREAU OF INVESTIGATION
Dept. of Justice Bldg., Washington, D. C.

Charged with the duty of investigating violations of the laws of the United States and collecting evidence in cases in which the United States is or may be a party in interest. Some of the major violations over which the Bureau has investigative jurisdiction: espionage, sabotage, violations of the neutrality act, impersonation of government officials, larceny of goods in interstate commerce, theft, embezzlement of government property, robbery of national banks, crimes in connection with the federal penal and correctional institutions, etc. Publishes *F.B.I. Law Enforcement Bulletin, Uniform Crime Reports,* special reports.

VOLUNTEERS OF AMERICA (1896)
34 West 28th Street, New York (1), N. Y.

The foremost aim of the organization is its mission to needy souls, especially to those hungering for spiritual food. In addition to the mission services it maintains homes for children, homes and clubs for working girls, emergency homes for stranded families, maternity homes, homes for the aged, day nurseries, and industrial homes for men.

WELFARE COUNCIL OF NEW YORK CITY
44 East 23rd Street, New York (10), N. Y.

The most inclusive federation of welfare and health agencies in New York. It embraces public and private agencies; carries on its work under all major sectarian and nonsectarian auspices. Maintains a central body of knowledge; serves as community's chief information center; promotes coordination between agencies in related fields; eliminates duplicating services; mobilizes community leadership; promotes growth of neighborhood councils; keeps watchful eye on appropriations and budgets of public funds for social purposes; improves general standards of social work practice. Publishes *Better Times*.

WOMEN'S PRISON ASSOCIATION OF NEW YORK, AND THE ISAAC T. HOPPER HOME
110 Second Avenue, New York (3), N. Y.

Case work with delinquent girls and women of any religion or color. Emphasis on social adjustment, medical and mental problems, vocational guidance, placement and subsequent supervision. Prison visiting. Cooperation with Departments of Correction, Probation, Parole, and Police, and social service agencies. Interest in developing broader understanding of the problems of women delinquents and in advancing the standard of administration of correctional institutions.

YOUNG MEN'S VOCATIONAL FOUNDATION
122 East 22nd Street, New York (10), N. Y.

Private social agency. Provides vocational guidance and job placement for probationers and parolees from correctional institutions and training schools, age limit 16–21 inclusive.

HERMAN K. SPECTOR
Senior Librarian
California State Prison
San Quentin, California

P

PARDON. The modification of penalties by the executive may take the form of pardon, commutation of sentence, or amnesty. A *pardon* may be defined as an act of mercy or clemency, ordinarily by an executive, by which a criminal is excused from the penalty which has been imposed upon him. The courts have frequently held that a pardon removes guilt and restores the person to his status before conviction. Pardon may be either conditional or absolute. The *conditional pardon* is one in which the offender's guilt is wiped away on condition that he conform to certain specified requirements. These requirements may involve performing certain acts or refraining from certain acts such as abstaining from intoxicating liquors or leaving the state. The conditional pardon becomes void if its beneficiary fails to perform the required acts. He may then be returned to prison for the remainder of his original term.

Commutation of sentence is a reduction of the penalty and is granted by governors or the president by executive order. Such reductions are granted in view of extenuating circumstances warranting leniency. The guilt of the prisoners is not thereby denied. A sentence is frequently commuted so that it expires at once. A commutation of sentence does not restore civil rights as does a pardon.

Amnesty is a pardon applied to a group of offenders, as, for instance, all who have violated a specific law. A King may, on the eve of a royal event or a holiday, grant amnesty to a group of convicts. In America, amnesty has now been almost entirely abandoned.

A *reprieve* or *respite* is a temporary postponement of the execution of a sentence, generally for the purpose of further investigation of the guilt of the prisoner. It is used in connection with the death penalty.

The pardoning power is variously placed. For federal prisoners it rests with the President. In 30 states it is in the hands of the governors, advised in 25 of them, by a board of pardons. In 18 states the governor and council together have pardoning power. Mayors occasionally have limited authority to pardon offenders against municipal ordinances.

Pardons were originally used as a means of rectifying errors in justice. Innocent persons convicted of crimes which they did not commit could thus be restored to freedom and citizenship. In practice pardons have become a means by which mercy may be exercised toward those who seem to have had sufficient punishment. Under a system of fixed sentences pardons are often necessary to relieve injustices. They are always most numerous where sentences are most severe. The pardoning power has often been abused for sentimental or political reasons. It is felt by most authorities that as fixed sentences are replaced by those of variable length, such as indeterminate sentences, the use of pardons may decrease. Many pardons are granted in some states after the period of imprisonment has ended and for the sole purpose of restoring the civil rights of the offenders.

BIBLIOGRAPHY

Jensen, Christen, Pardons, *Encyclopedia of the Social Sciences*, Vol. 11, p. 571, New York, 1933.

Neal, Ann, and Hager, Beatrice, Summary of the Provisions of the Constitution and Statutes of the Several States relating to Pardons, *Journal of Criminal Law and Criminology*, Vol. 20, p. 364, 1929–1930.

Sutherland, E. H., *Principles of Criminology*, J. B. Lippincott Co., 1939.

Wines, E. C., Commutation Laws in the United States, *Report of Prison Association of New York*, 1868, pp. 154–170.

PAROLE. Parole is a method of conditional release of persons sentenced or committed to penal or correctional institutions after serving a portion of the sentence or term imposed by the court. The usual conditions attached to this form of release are that the person will maintain good conduct and that he will remain under the custody of the paroling or some other designated authority, subject to reincarceration upon violation of the conditions of the release. The same principle of release is applied to persons released from institutions for the feebleminded and the insane.

Parole, as a phase of penal treatment, grew out of the shift in emphasis in penal philosophy from punishment to reformation. It is the logical outgrowth of the now generally accepted principle that the ultimate aim of penology is the protection of society, and that this aim can be best achieved by the rehabilitation of the offender.

The origin of parole, at least in the United States, may be traced to two movements in prison reform. One movement was fostered by the view that good conduct in prison should be rewarded by shortening of the sentence. The second step in this movement was that release should be made conditional, not only upon conduct in prison, but upon continued good conduct on the outside, with final discontinuance of custody after a period of time. The principle of conditional release was used in the prison colonies of Australia as early as 1790. In this country the first "good-time" law, designed to shorten sentences as reward for good conduct in prison, was passed in the State of New York in 1817. Later, as leading penologists felt the need for a more flexible sentence to permit greater individualization of treatment, the indeterminate sentence idea gained ground. The first indeterminate sentence law was enacted in New York in 1869, when the Elmira Reformatory was established.

The other important movement was the establishment of philanthropic societies, both in America and abroad, whose interest it was to aid criminals, both in the institutions and after release. It seems that the first of these societies was established in Philadelphia in 1776 and is still in existence under the name of the Pennsylvania Prison Society. As early as 1822 this Society, then known as the Philadelphia Society for Alleviating The Miseries of Public Prisons, recognized the importance of the problem of care for discharged prisoners, and considered the opening of an "asylum" for those not in position to obtain work upon release. But a suitable place could not be obtained. In 1851 the Society was able to appoint an agent to work with and for discharged prisoners, and in 1871 the Society succeeded in obtaining an annual appropriation from the State Legislature for the care of discharged prisoners. But as the appropriation was insufficient, the proposal of opening a home for discharged prisoners was revised, and an "Industrial Home" was opened in 1889 which has continued to this day, although it is now no longer connected with the Society.

The work of the Pennsylvania Prison Society was closely emulated by such other organizations as the Boston Prison Society, founded in 1826, and the New York Prison Association, organized in 1845. The interest of these organizations in the care of released prisoners supplemented the movement for shortening of sentences by "good time" allowances and for conditional release, and gave us the basic elements of parole as we know it today.

The principle of conditional liberation seems to have had its origin in the British Colony of New South Wales in Australia, in 1790, when Governor Phillips was given the power of conditional pardon over the criminals transported there from England. This method of release later became known as ticket-of-leave system, under which the prisoners were set free with grants of land. In 1840 Captain Alexander Maconochie introduced the ticket-of-leave system at Norfolk Island, combining it with a system of probation in which the prisoner passed through a series of stages from strict imprisonment, through conditional release to final and complete restoration of liberty. Promotion from one stage to another was based on a system of marks. Maconochie's system was adopted later in England by Joshua Jebb and continued by Sir Walter Crofton. The latter seems to have introduced the provision that, in case of violation of the conditions of release, the parolee was subject to reincarceration. The ticket-of-leave system was legally sanctioned in the English Penal Servitude acts of 1853 and 1857.

Elements of modern parole made their appearance in different countries throughout the first half of the 19th century. In this country, a form of conditional release was used in the indenture of juvenile delinquents as early as 1825 when the first House of Refuge was established in New York. In 1832 young delinquents at La Roquette in France were granted conditional release. In 1835 Montesinos in Spain reduced the length of sentence of prisoners under his charge by one third on condition of satisfactory conduct. Obermaier in Munich, Germany, developed a system of supervision in 1842. In 1846 Massachusetts appointed an agent to assist released prisoners in obtaining employment, tools, clothing and transportation with the aid of public funds. All of these were sporadic attempts, none of which resulted in the development of a permanent and thoroughgoing system of parole. On the other hand, the work of Maconochie, Jebb and Crofton resulted in something sufficiently permanent to give tangible proof that the principle of conditional release, combined with supervision and retention of legal control over the parolee for a period of time after release, is workable.

Although the first parole system was developed in Europe, parole, outside of England, has found wider acceptance in this country. It has been little used in Continental Europe. The first parole law for adults in the United States was passed in 1884 in Ohio, although conditional release legislation had been enacted in Massachusetts as early as 1837. Today there is not a single state that does not have a parole law.

In spite of the widespread legislation that has gone on in behalf of parole, there is a wide difference in the extent to which it is used in different states and the financial support it is receiving. The proportion of prisoners released on parole ranges from zero to almost 100 per cent. The states that make wider use of the indeterminate sentence, make also wider use of parole as a method of release.

The financial support that parole is receiving can be measured by the size of the personnel and salaries paid. There are states where parole legislation has been passed that do not hire a single parole officer. In others we find a highly developed system with a considerable number of parole officers and supervisors. The salaries of persons with the title of parole officers, parole agents, parole counsellors or probation and parole officers range from $1000 to $3600 annually. Supervisors and certain executives in certain states receive as much as $4000 to $12,000 annually. Salaries for parole board members run up to $12,000 a year.

The agencies vested with the power to grant parole differ in different states. In general we may group these agencies under three categories. The Governor of the state was for a long time the sole parole authority. There are still some states where the power to parole is vested in the Governor by the constitution, although the Governor may delegate the power to subordinates. Later the power to parole was given to the boards connected with the institutions. In many states these boards still have this power, but frequently their action must have the final approval of the Governor before parole becomes valid. In recent years the trend has been toward the establishment of central boards. In about 40 states parole is administered by such boards. In about one third of the states, the District of Columbia and New York City there are independent parole boards that have both the power to parole and the responsibility of supervising those paroled. In five states the pardon boards act as paroling agencies with the power to parole and supervise. In three states the institution boards perform these functions. Hence, about half of the states combine paroling and supervision under one agency. In six states and the Federal Government release and supervision are under two agencies. Twenty-two states and the Federal Government combine parole and probation under one agency.

It is believed that the central independent board type of agency is most suitable for parole administration. In most instances such boards are appointed by the Governor of the state, and not infrequently persons are appointed purely for political reasons and not because of any qualifications for the position. On the other hand, appointments of able persons have been made in a number of states, and tenure has not been dependent upon political affiliation alone. There are at least three states where the selection of board members is made on the basis of civil service examination.

Although parole systems vary in organization, there are certain desired goals toward which all parole agencies are striving with varying degree of success. Certain practices have been rather widely accepted. In practically all states preparole investigation is required before parole is granted, but only in a dozen states is the preparole investigation adequate. Some states make very elaborate investigation of the parolee's background, past history, personality development, as well as of his future home and employment. The majority of states make little more than a gesture in this direction.

In all jurisdictions the law provides that parole applicants be given hearings. With some parole authorities the hearing consists merely of the meeting of the board to discuss the case or to pass on someone's recommendation to parole or not to parole. The parolee never appears before them. In most places the parolee appears before one or more members of the paroling agency, even though it may be for a very short time. Parole laws in some states require that the parole applicant be heard by at least one member of the paroling agency. Some parole agencies hold "open hearings," at which, not only the parole

applicant appears, but the right to appear is granted also to his relatives, friends and counsel. In some instances the press is permitted to attend.

The conditions under which parole may be granted, of course, differ widely in different states. In seven states and the District of Columbia the applicant must have a sponsor before he can be paroled. A number of other states make use of sponsors, although they are not required to do so by law. The sponsor must be a person of good standing in the community who is willing to act as adviser to the parolee during the period of parole and will keep the parole officer informed of his behavior. Thirty-two states require that the parole applicant have employment to go to as a condition of release. In 28 states the law requires that the paroling agency notify the sentencing judge and district attorney of its intention to parole a prisoner and request their opinion in the matter.

Practically all parole agencies make use of parole rules which are given to the parolee usually in written form. These rules are quite similar from jurisdiction to jurisdiction. Parolees are not permitted to move from place to place or from one job to another without permission of the parole officer. They must be at home by a certain hour. They must refrain from drinking. They cannot apply for marriage or driving or other licenses without permission. They must report to the parole officer at certain intervals. They must not associate with other parolees or ex-convicts. Of course, a parolee must not commit any new crimes. Parolees who violate the terms of their parole are subject to return to the institution to complete their sentence. In some jurisdictions a violator is subject to reparole; in others he must serve the remainder of the sentence in prison.

The requirements on the form of report that must be submitted by parolees while on parole range all the way from no reports at all to written reports counter-signed by employer, sponsor or parole officer. As a rule reports are required monthly, but as the parolee approaches the end of his parole period supervision may be relaxed and he may be required to report quarterly, semi-annually, or only annually, depending upon how well he is adjusting and the length of his sentence.

Women parolees are treated quite differently in different states. In 27 states there are no women parole officers. In eight states there is only one, and in thirteen other states there are from two to seven women parole officers. In some states the law forbids the supervision of a woman parolee by an officer of the opposite sex.

Statutory provisions vary greatly on the length of time that a parolee must remain on parole. In a number of jurisdictions the length of the parole period is determined by the length of the sentence imposed by the court. When the sentence expires the parolee is automatically off parole. But in some jurisdictions parole may be terminated prior to the date of maximum expiration. In a third group of states the parole agency may continue a person on parole as long as it seems necessary. In a few states, parole given under certain conditions, cannot be terminated except by a pardon, or what is equivalent to a pardon, by the Governor.

In those jurisdictions where the statutes provide that a parolee cannot be kept under parole custody beyond the expiration of the sentence imposed, the statutes sometimes make provision for "good time" deductions. "Good time" is time usually deducted from the maximum length of the sentence imposed. Such deduction may apply either during imprisonment, or during the parole period. The amount of time deducted from prison time is usually fixed by law and is based on the period of time served with a clear record. Time deductions from the parole period is usually determined by the parole agency.

In the execution of policies and enforcement of regulations set up by parole agencies, the parole officer plays a very important role. As a rule, he is called upon to make preparole investigations, supervise anywhere from 75 to several hundred parolees, investigate offenses and breaches of parole rules committed by parolees while on parole, prepare all sorts of

reports and make recommendations for revocation of parole, return to prison, or reinstatement on parole. In some instances parole officers make investigations for the classification clinics in the institutions at the time the prisoner is received there.

As a rule, parole officers have the power of arrest under the law and, therefore, play the part of police officers on certain occasions. This has given rise to the controversy of whether a parole officer can be an effective case worker and exercise police authority at the same time. There seems to be agreement among practicing parole officers and parole administrators that police power can be used as an effective tool of parole case work if the parole officer is properly trained. The view is steadily gaining ground that a parole officer should have college training or the equivalent and that he should have experience in some branch of applied social or psychological science.

Students of crime have for some time been occupying themselves with the problem of developing a scientific technique for the selection of candidates for parole. It is argued that at the present time the selection of persons for parole and probation is done on the basis of hunches, or at best, subjective judgment. The situation is aggravated by the free play of personal biases and prejudices of the frequently untrained personnel making up parole boards. The problem of selecting candidates for parole is so complex that even the best trained and the most conscientious board can be expected to do only a haphazard job. To increase accuracy in parole selection, therefore, a group of workers has developed prediction tables involving a principle similar to that used in the development of actuarial tables of insurance companies. The advocates of these tables claim that, if the life history of a prisoner is known, it is possible to analyze it into its component factors. Each factor can be evaluated and weighted in terms of certain criteria, as either favoring or not favoring future criminal conduct. The positive and negative factors can then be added together and the differential score will be indicative of whether the prisoner will be a good or poor risk for parole. Unfortunately prediction tables have not been widely adopted. Only one state parole board has been known to use them to any extent, namely, in Illinois. More widespread adoption of prediction tables has been prevented partly by the fact that they have not been tested sufficiently Furthermore, their preparation and use require trained personnel. Adoption seems to have been further discouraged by the study on parole selection and parole outcome presented in the Attorney General's Survey of Release Procedure, which showed rather convincingly that the current parole agencies do a surprisingly good job of selecting prisoners for parole without the aid of prediction tables.

As state parole systems have developed, the need for interstate cooperation in parole matters has grown apace. In 1934 Congress passed a law permitting the states to enter into agreements or compacts with each other to promote mutual assistance in the supervision of parolees and in the prevention and control of crime. In 1935 the Interstate Commission on Crime of the Council of State Governments was organized to promote uniform state legislation covering the pursuit and arrest of criminals fleeing from one state to another, and supervision of parolees of one state by another. In the same year that Congress passed the law referred to above, Massachusetts, New York, New Jersey and Pennsylvania entered into an informal agreement to supervise each others' parolees. Since that time all four of these states have passed legislation enabling them to enter into formal compact with other states relative to parole matters. At the present time 44 states are members of the compact.

So far, we have said little about parole in countries other than in the United States. England, before World War II, was probably doing a better job than any other country in the preparation of prisoners for parole, but parole supervision has always been the task of private societies aided by limited state subsidies. The same situation prevails, more or less, in the British Dominions and Colonies. In the Latin speaking countries of Europe we have the same division, with the power to parole under state authority and supervision under private agencies with varying degree of supervisory control and occa-

sional subsidy by the government. In Belgium and France parolees are supervised by the societies of patronage. In Italy, under Mussolini, there were the Councils of Patronage, the members of which were appointed by the Ministry of Justice, and whose function it was to aid released prisoners. Spain and Portugal seem to have made little or no provision for supervision, although some form of conditional release is practiced. Nazi Germany has paid little attention to penology. Before Hitler very important experiments had been undertaken in Thuringia, Prussia and Bavaria relative to penal treatment and release. But these came to an abrupt end with the coming of Naziism. Communist Russia has no parole in the sense we understand it. Industrial colonies and camps may be said to have replaced both the traditional prison and parole. In these camps self-government is used, and life goes on much in the same manner as outside. Under certain conditions and at certain stages, the prisoner is permitted to have his own family with him. He is paid wages on the same scale as in the open market. In brief, the aim of these camps is education and training for communistic life. However, we are told that in recent years Russian penology has been reverting to more traditional forms.

The Latin American countries, for the most part, have followed the penal philosophy of the Italian School of Criminal Anthropology. A conditional form of release from confinement is used in nearly every country. But the problem of supervision after release remains largely unsolved. In a number of countries the patronage system of Latin Europe is used. The information available relative to the use of parole in other countries is sketchy, but we may say that the notion of conditional release from prison is rather widespread. On the other hand, provisions for supervision of parolees after release are nowhere as adequate as they are in the more progressive States of the American Union.

In conclusion it seems safe to state that parole is here to stay, in spite of the criticisms that are raised against it from time to time. Parole, as a method of release of offenders from penal and correctional institutions, affords the maximum protection to society and to the offender the fullest opportunity for rehabilitation. The advantages of parole can be realized if the paroling agency is permitted to function free of political interference and if it is adequately staffed with professionally trained personnel selected by civil service examinations.

Parole is now accepted as a form of case work with a legally sanctioned authoritative aspect. Its principal function is to help the offender bridge the gap between the relatively abnormal environment of the penal or correctional institution and the social environment to which he is to be returned so that he may gradually exercise his rights and assume his duties and responsibilities as any other well adjusted citizen. As case work, parole will come in contact with many agencies in the community that are concerned with the welfare of human beings. It will overlap especially with family case work. The parole officer, to do effective parole work, must be familiar with the resources in his community and must be able to coordinate community services and focus their resources and influences upon the parolee in order to bring about optimum results in rehabilitation.

G. I. Giardini
Superintendent, Parole Supervision
Pennsylvania Board of Parole
Harrisburg, Pennsylvania

BIBLIOGRAPHY

Attorney General Survey of Release Procedures, Volume IV, *Parole*, U. S. Government Printing Office, Washington, D. C., 1939.
Teeters, N. K., *They Were In Prison*, John C. Winston Company, Philadelphia, 1937.
Teeters, N. K., *World Penal Systems, a Survey*, Sponsored and Distributed by the Pennsylvania Prison Society, Philadelphia, 1944.
Wines, Frederick H., *Punishment and Reformation*, Thomas Y. Crowell, New York, 1919.

PENAL REFORM. Crime is behavior considered so harmful to the general welfare as to be prohibited by the politically organized group for those over whom it has authority. Punishment, in criminology, is the penalty imposed, in the name of the sovereign, upon those, within the group, who have been found guilty of committing crimes.

Punishment may be regarded as a means of restoring social balance. Sociologically, punishment is a reaffirmation of accepted social values and consequently of social solidarity. Its ultimate objective is the assurance of social survival. In practice it may serve many subsidiary and even incidental purposes, such as giving the group an approved outlet for the emotional tensions induced by the offender and, no doubt at times, for tensions arising from other frustrations. In primitive societies punishment has primarily served as a means of social purification and of protection through appeasement of the spirits; a use suggested by the Greek root "pu," meaning "to cleanse."

What acts shall be punished; how they shall be punished; and by whom they shall be punished are culturally defined in terms of the frame of reference which the group accepts. The types and conditions of punishment are, therefore, related to the social structure and reflect the values, beliefs, philosophy, knowledge and technical capacity of the group.

When labor to man the galleys was scarce, convicts were pressed into service, and the use of capital punishment for a time declined. As medical knowledge reduced human suffering and physical punishment declined in home, in school, in mine and field, and aboard ship, the flogging and mutilation of convicts became inconsistent with changes in the general pattern of culture. The rise of democracy, the minimizing of social class differences, and the increased range of social contacts has tended to develop social understanding and sympathy and consequently to reduce the severity of punishment.

Such changes in penal methods are an aspect of social change in general and may only, in part, be due to deliberately planned attempts to bring about social improvement.

Efforts consciously directed towards penal reform are most likely to occur during periods of rapid social change when individuals or groups more readily become convinced that existing methods of punishing criminals are harmfully inconsistent with a rational philosophy of crime and punishment. Since convicted criminals are socially marginal, uninfluential, and relatively inconspicuous; thoughtful and far-sighted attention is not apt to be given to their treatment until penal methods become seriously, even dramatically, out of harmony with the general trend of culture. The most far-reaching and persistent efforts purposefully directed towards penal reform have, therefore, found expression in Western civilization during the last two hundred years as a minor and lagging phase of the fundamental changes in Western culture that have developed since the Renaissance.

In smaller, primitive, relatively homogeneous, culturally isolated societies, both ancient and contemporary, the behavior apt to be most disturbing to the group as a whole was that considered displeasing to the spirit world. Crime was synonymous with sin, and punishment seems to have been grounded in fear of the supernatural and primarily designed to purify the groups and appease the spirits through expiation or through dissociating the group from its offending members. In more populous and complex theocratic societies under both Judaism and Christianity the church has sought to punish immoral conduct as an affront to the Deity and as a means of protecting the entire group from the wrath of God.

On the other hand, secular offenses, such as murder, arson, rape, and theft were more commonly handled as private wrongs or torts. Although the tribal group as a whole might disapprove such conduct, it did not attempt to arbitrate those disputes nor to punish the behavior as criminal, but left such matters to the family or clan subdivisions whose behavior was limited only by the force of custom. The common result was continuous family or inter-clan blood feuds in which the object was retaliation rather than judicially determined and limited punishment, since no family or clan would consider the aggression of its members upon outsiders to be criminal.

The social costliness of endless blood feuds eventually brought about less destructive substitutes in the form of pecuniary compensation, such as the complicated Anglo-Saxon system of graded "wergild" and the utilization of peace-making arbitrators. The substitution of monetary penalties was accompanied by a tendency to limit responsibility to the actual offender. With the rise of the kingship and a strong central government the peace-maker became invested with the greater authority of a judge, while the secular offenses, themselves, ceased to be private wrongs and, instead, came to be considered breaches of the sovereign's peace, to be dealt with by the state as crimes.

The theoretical justification for punishment by the state was the prevailing assumption that every man was possessed of a free will that enabled him to choose any course of action from among the opportunities for behavior with which he might be confronted, uninfluenced by his past experiences. The criminal, therefore, as a being completely responsible for his crimes, should be punished as an offset to the physical and psychical damage which he had caused in the community; as a means of inducing him not to repeat his offense by making it too painful and unprofitable; and as a deterrent example to others who might contemplate criminal behavior.

Such a frame of reference supported and encouraged severe penalties because of their presumably greater deterrent effects. Execution, exile, flogging, torture, mutilation, and social degradation, often in ingenious forms and combinations, were the common types of punishment for crime. Imprisonment, as a method of punishing offenders, was seldom, if ever, used in the Western world until the 13th century.

Three major, interrelated aspects of social change were most obviously influential in stimulating penal reform in modern Western civilization: the intellectual-scientific-technical revolution with its remarkable extension of human knowledge and control of the physical world; the humanitarian-charitable-social welfare movement grounded in the value system of Christianity and finding expression in concrete efforts at social amelioration; and the socio-economic reorganization of Western society associated especially with changes in technology.

The rise of science and the scientific method, reintroduced into Europe by the Arabs and developed there by such men as Galileo (1564–1642), Giordano Bruno (1550–1600), and Francis Bacon (1561–

1626), began to provide a new frame of reference within which penal reform could take place. Utilization of the inductive technique, in preference to the deductive and metaphysical techniques of the church, provided an effective method of furthering knowledge about the physical world and began to raise doubts about the validity of prevailing theological interpretations of the nature and processes of the physical universe.

As the observations of the scientists came to be extended to the entire realm of nature, including man, the implications of their theories became the object of serious speculation and discussion, especially in England and France, in the writings of such men as Locke, Hume, Bentham, Voltaire, Montesquieu, Rousseau and others who developed a new rationalistic philosophy concerned with the possibility and the means of social reconstruction and improvement. It was the dawn of new knowledge about the nature of man, himself, and its continuing emergence in the still developing sciences of biology, psychology and sociology, catalyzed by the humanitarian, reformist zeal of the Rationalists, that provided the framework within which the modern phase of penal reform began.

Disturbed by apparent injustices in criminal procedure involving secret accusations, inadequate defense, arbitrary exercise of judicial power and the imposition of barbarous penalties, and influenced by his study of the French and British Rationalists, especially Montesquieu, a young Italian nobleman, Cesare Bonesana, Marchese de Beccaria (1738–1794) wrote and published in 1764 a work, "Trattato dei delitti e delle pene" (An Essay on Crimes and Punishments), which came to have far-reaching effects upon the reform of criminal jurisprudence.

Beccaria's views, which became the basis of the so-called Classical School of Penology, accepted the doctrine that men follow that course of action which they believe will bring them the greatest pleasure and the least pain. Crime is an injury to society that should be prevented. It may be prevented by making the punishment just severe enough to overbalance the pleasure derived from the act.

The essential purpose of punishment being deterrence rather than social revenge. Therefore, it should be proportional to the crime and the least possible to obtain the desired result.

The emphasis of the Classical School upon deterrence as the purpose of punishment and as a basis for determining penalties, offered a rational principle to humanitarians interested in penology and led to a reduction in the severity and arbitrariness of penalties and to simplification of the sentencing process.

Beccaria's ideas were put into practical effect in the French Penal Code of 1791, and they were reflected in reforms in criminal procedure throughout Europe and in the United States, especially in Austria, Italy, England and Pennsylvania. In England the efforts of the great utilitarian theorist, Jeremy Bentham (1748–1832), ably supplemented by such leaders of social action as Sir Samuel Romilly (1757–1818), Sir James Mackintosh (1765–1832), Sir Thomas Buxton (1786–1845), and Sir Robert Peel (1788–1850), resulted in a major modification of penalties and an extensive revision of the British criminal code in accordance with the emerging humanitarianism.

The application of classical theory, however, made its limitations apparent. They grew chiefly out of its complete disregard of the criminal, himself. Since the type and amount of punishment were determined by the nature of the crime, first offenders and habitual criminals were treated alike and without regard to their age, sex, health or other conditions and circumstances under which their offenses were committed. Since such differences, however, existed as realities that had to be dealt with, it presently became apparent that a theory of prevention through the prospect of punishment was inoperative upon children, lunatics, and others who were limited in their ability to make rational choices. Gradually, therefore, the concept of limited responsibility of the individual and extenuating circumstances emerged and found expression as a basic principle of Continental and English law.

Humanitarian opposition to the death penalty and the rise of conditions unfavorable to transportation of convicts led to an increased use of imprisonment as a means of punishing serious offenders. However, the existing jails and houses of correction were not well suited to this purpose. The jails had originated as places of detention for those awaiting trial or punishment, and the houses of correction had been established in the late 16th century to care for the idle poor who seemed unwilling to work. By the 17th century both of these institutions had come to be used as places of confinement for petty offenders and on rare occasions for incorrigible rogues. The buildings, however, were often of flimsy construction, small and insecure, and not designed for the purpose of imprisonment. Almost any type of building or part of one might serve as a jail.

Conditions in them were about as bad as one could imagine. Men and women, young and old, those awaiting trial and those found guilty, debtors, prostitutes, vagabonds and thieves were lodged together. Untrained and unsalaried jail keepers earned their living by charging the prisoners fees. No adequate provision was made for feeding or clothing inmates. Prisoners made their own rules and formal discipline was absent.

Against these conditions the Society for Promoting Christian Knowledge began in the late 17th century to protest with sufficient vigor to bring about periodic jail inspections. Others, especially among the Quakers, had been moved to express their concern about the need to improve existing methods of dealing with prisoners. In America, the Quakers of West Jersey and Pennsylvania introduced in 1681–1682 the workhouse prison, free as to fees, food and lodging.

Outstanding in its practical influence for reform was the work of John Howard (1726–1790), started as a consequence of his treatment in French prisons following his capture by a French privateer as he was traveling to Portugal to aid the victims of the Lisbon earthquake. Appointed sheriff of Bedfordshire in 1773, Howard was shocked by the abuses he discovered. Thereafter he devoted his energies to prison reform. For the remaining sixteen years of his life Howard worked with untiring industry to replace the evils of the jail system with improved methods of jail management. He made four detailed inspections of the prisons of England and Wales, recording with the objectivity of an engineer the numbers, age and sex of the prisoners, the quality of food and water, the manner of sewage disposal, the methods of securing prisoners, the fees required of them, and other pertinent data. In addition, Howard made two journeys to observe conditions in penal institutions and lazarettos in Europe, traveling altogether some 42,033 carefully recorded miles before he was fatally stricken with jail fever at Kherson, in the Crimea.

In 1777 Howard had published some of his data in a classic monograph on *The State of the Prisons*, a tremendously influential volume made singularly impressive by the sheer weight of fact piled upon fact within it. Even before its publication Howard had been called to testify before Parliament.

As a consequence of Howard's efforts, Parliament abolished the fee system and took steps to improve the sanitary conditions of jails and bridewells. With the assistance of Sir William Blackstone and William Eden, Howard drafted the Penitentiary Act of 1779, providing for the establishment of clean and sanitary penitentiary houses, subject to regular inspections, with a rigorous reformatory plan designed to improve offenders by maintaining them in good health, protecting them from harmful associations, subjecting them to religious instruction, and exercising them in profitable labor, to be followed by assistance in obtaining employment upon their discharge.

The government moved so inefficiently that it never built the prisons authorized by the Penitentiary Act. However, some experimentation along the lines of the Act was attempted in the local jails; perhaps most thoroughly in the new institutions at Wymondham in Norfolk under the superintendency of Sir Thomas Beevor and at Gloucester, due largely to the leadership of an energetic and persistent magistrate, Sir George O. Paul.

On the Continent the penitentiary idea applied to the reformation of offenders had already appeared in church institutions as an adaptation of the long established system of cellular seclusion, reflection and penitence. About 1670, Filippo Franci was using cellular isolation combined with religious instruction in his home for vagrant and wayward boys in Florence, Italy, to correct the more headstrong among his charges and bring them to repentance. In 1704 Pope Clement XI established a papal correctional prison for juveniles at Rome as part of the great charitable hospice of San Michele. In 1735 he added correctional quarters for women. In place of the usual common room, individual cells were provided in the juvenile quarters. In these the boys were housed in solitary confinement at night, but they worked together in silence during the daytime. Reformation was the avowed aim of the régime at San Michele. In its shop were inscribed these words: "It is of little advantage to restrain the bad by punishment unless you render them good by discipline."

San Michele actually housed only about fifty delinquent boys; its discipline was mechanical; its moral training formal; and its immediate results probably very limited. Although John Howard visited and described the papal reformatory, it did not become widely known, and it seems to have had little direct effect upon succeeding prison experiments. Nevertheless, it was probably the first cellular penitentiary and one of the earliest attempts to make a positive reformatory use of imprisonment.

Of more influence upon the modification of penal methods was the system developed seventy years later by Hippolyte Vilain XIII at Ghent. There, in response to requests by the Deputies of the Estates in Flanders, Vilain attempted to devise satisfactory measures for dealing with the hordes of wandering vagabonds that emerged in Europe attendant upon widespread changes in its socio-economic structure. Vilain suggested and developed a reformatory prison which, though never completed, received its first occupants in 1773. In architecture and program it anticipated the essential features of the 19th century American prison.

Inmates were classified and separated on the basis of age, sex and seriousness of offense. Medical care was provided and an institutional chaplain appointed. Prisoners worked together in the prison shops but were housed in separate cells at night. Useful work combined with vocational instruction that would enable men to earn a living upon discharge was considered most likely to bring about their reformation. As a stimulus to industry, prisoners were paid a wage proportional to the value of their production. Vilain believed that both excessively short and excessively long sentences limited the opportunities for reformation, and he sought to obtain instead a minimum sentence of one year and the right to recommend convicts for pardon.

Although the opposition of free laborers and the intervention of Emperor Joseph the Second of Austria virtually destroyed Vilain's work, it was not before the ubiquitous John Howard had examined it and commended its features in his writings.

Apart from the isolated and somewhat abortive experiments of Pope Clement XI and Hippolyte Vilain XIII, the origin and earliest development of the penitentiary system occurred in the United States. In Pennsylvania and West Jersey the Quakers had long been active in their opposition to severe and barbarous punishments, preferring, instead, imprisonment at hard labor. In 1787 a group of influential citizens organized the Philadelphia Society for Alleviating the Miseries of Public Prisons, later called the Pennsylvania Prison Society. From its inception, this organization actively concerned itself with examinations of the penal system, and, influenced by its knowledge of the work and views of John Howard in England, it presented its findings and recommendations from time to time to the Pennsylvania legislature.

Goaded by the new society, the legislature provided in 1790 for a new penal code based upon the principle that the most suitable punishment for crime is imprisonment at hard labor. It converted the old Walnut Street Jail into a state prison, and ordered the erection therein of a special cell block or penitentiary house for the separate confinement in solitude of the more dangerous offenders. During the next twenty-five years several states, including New York, Massachusetts, Maryland and Virginia, built their prisons on the model of the Walnut Street penitentiary house; but their experience with confinement in idleness led Pennsylvania, which was then in process of building new penitentiaries at Pittsburgh and Philadelphia, to review its policies. As a consequence, it provided in its eastern penitentiary, called Cherry Hill, for confinement with labor and exercise in solitude in individual and completely separated cells and exercise yards; an arrangement that came to be known as the Pennsylvania system.

Meanwhile, New York, as a result of experimenting with three groups of prisoners in its penitentiary at Auburn, established a system of confinement of prisoners in separate cells at night with common meals and congregate work in silence during the day.

Both schemes became the object of examination and comment by commissions from abroad, as well as by prison reform societies within the United States. The Philadelphia Society for Alleviating the Miseries of Public Prisons, favoring the Pennsylvania plan, carried on a vigorous and sometimes bitter controversy with the Prison Discipline Society of Boston and the New York Prison Association, which urged the merits of the Auburn system. In general, European observers were favorably impressed by the Philadelphia system; and it was adopted and has been kept in continuing use, sometimes in modified form, by Belgium, Sweden, Norway, Denmark, Holland, France and England. In the United States, the Auburn system met with more ready acceptance, perhaps because of its seeming economies, and it eventually became the general pattern for prisons throughout the United States, including Pennsylvania.

The years following the establishment of cellular prisons have witnessed a succession of changes in their administration in accordance with increasing understanding of the sources and control of human behavior gathered by the developing social and biological sciences. The abolition of the silent system, the discarding of convict stripes, the establishment of libraries and courses of instruction, however limited and inadequate, and the rise of such extra-curricular prison activities as orchestras, debating teams and outdoor sports are evidences of a changing penal philosophy.

It was perhaps inevitable that the humanitarian movement that had led to an increasing substitution of imprisonment for the death penalty should also extend its interest so as to bring about a reduction in the length of prison sentences. As prisoners were earlier and more usually restored to freedom there developed a realization that imprisonment must come to be a positive factor in reformation for social protection and not merely a repressive punitive program. The rise of human biology, psychology and sociology as sciences and their increasing application in the fields of mental hygiene and social work began to build a new frame of reference within which changes in penology might occur. The lesser seriousness of juvenile offenses, the more general recognition of the limitations of children, and the greater hope of improvement fostered by their immaturity provided the point at which the new philosophy could find a foothold.

Over the doors of the juvenile wing at the papal institution of San Michele these words had been carved: "For the correction and instruction of profligate youth, that they who when idle are injurious, may when taught, become useful to the state." During the early nineteenth century a number of reform societies on the continent and in the United States became interested in correctional work with juveniles. The first juvenile reformatory in the United States was opened in New York in 1825 as the New York House of Refuge. Boston opened a House of Reformation in 1826 and Philadelphia a House of Refuge in 1828. In all of these institutions, founded by reform societies and supported by private funds, a definite correctional program of work, study and religious instruction was instituted, supplemented by a scheme of rewards and punishments. At Boston, corporal punishments were forbidden and a limited form of self-government was set up.

The application of reformatory principles to adult prisoners seems to have been first made in Europe. As early as 1828 the French penologist, Lucas, had urged the importance of a constructive program of reformation in prisons, and such programs were successfully introduced by Obermaier in the Bavarian prison at Kaiserslauten between 1830 and 1842, and later at Munich. In Spain, Colonel Montesinos, made governor of the prison of Valencia in 1835, established a progressive régime which included the opportunity to attend school and learn a trade. Convicts were also given the powerful incentive of a chance to reduce their sentences as much as one-third for good conduct.

Captain Alexander Maconochie of the Royal Navy, appointed superintendent of Britain's penal colony at Norfolk Island in 1840, was another pioneer in establishing a reformatory system for adults. Maconochie had pondered the possible application of the mark system as used in education for some years before he took charge at Norfolk Island. He knew that the existing arrangements of a fixed sentence offered a man no incentive to improve his conduct, since nothing he could do would alter the duration of his imprisonment. Maconochie therefore sought to make conditional freedom and privileges within prison dependent upon good behavior and the satisfactory completion of tasks. To achieve this end he debited each prisoner, upon arrival, with a number of marks proportional to the seriousness of his offense and made them redeemable in terms of good conduct and efficiency in labor; the scheme being designed to develop self-control and self-management in prisoners rather than compulsory obedience to external authority. Under Maconochie's plan prisoners, by acquiring the necessary marks, might move towards freedom through a definite series of stages, beginning with full imprisonment, to be followed by labor in government work squads, freedom within a restricted area, ticket of leave or parole accompanied by a conditional pardon, and, finally, complete freedom and release from all supervision. In practice Maconochie could only give his prisoners local privileges, since he lacked authority to release them from Norfolk Island, regardless of their behavior. Nevertheless, out of Maconochie's work at Norfolk Island and later at Birmingham came two of the most significant penological inventions of the nineteenth century, the indeterminate sentence and parole.

Meanwhile, the logic of making sentences of indeterminate length, implied as early as 1787 in the writings of Dr. Benjamin Rush of Philadelphia, was being set forth by the English prelate, Richard Whately (1787–1863), by the Scotsman, George Combe (1788–1858), by Frederick Hill, Inspector of the Prisons of Scotland, by his brother, Matthew Davenport Hill, Recorder of Birmingham, and others; while in France M. Bonneville de Marsangy, in his "Essay on the Institutions Complementary to the Penitentiary System" (1847) and his "Improvement of the Criminal Law" (1864), emphasized the advantages of permitting early conditional release of prisoners on parole and the right to return violators to prison.

Maconochie's ideas were introduced into the Irish prison system by Sir Joshua Jebb (1793–1863) and developed by Sir Walter Crofton (1819–1897), who became Chairman of the Directors of Irish Convict Prisons in 1854. To the general scheme of successive stages, progression by earned marks, and parole, Crofton added another level in the form of an Intermediate Stage, comparable to honor camps, in which groups of not more than a hundred prisoners lived at least six months in unlocked portable camps while they worked on land reclamation projects; this semi-freedom having the dual purpose of rewarding convicts for demonstrated improvement and of giving the public concrete assurance of their readiness for release into the community.

Gaylord Hubbell, Warden of Sing Sing prison, visited Ireland in 1863 to observe Crofton's work and was greatly impressed by it. He, together with Sanborn, Wines, Dwight, Brockway and others who had been aroused by the possibilities of the Irish system, began to favor the application of its principles in the United States. One consequence of their efforts was the passing of legislation by the state of New York in 1869, providing for the establishment at Elmira of the first adult penal institution in the United States for the specific purpose of reformation rather than penitence. The Elmira Reformatory was intended for first offenders between the ages of sixteen and thirty and the program centered around education and utilization of a limited indeterminate sentence.

Other states followed New York in establishing reformatories for young adults, but their achievements have been limited and their administrations have become similar to those in the penitentiaries. European visitors were impressed with the personality of Brockway, who became the first superintendent at Elmira, but they were irritated by the advocacy of the Elmira system by the United States at Brussels in 1900 and unconvinced of its value or its newness.

The short-comings of the reformatories were in part due to inadequacies of plant and personnel, but a major factor was their failure to receive the youthful first offenders for which they were designed. This, in turn, was due to the haphazard sentencing practices of judges, the difficulty of determining who were first offenders, and the increasing use of probation for those who were thought to have no previous criminal record.

A promising variant upon the American reformatory is the English Borstal System for offenders between the ages of 16 and 21, originated by Sir Evelyn Ruggles-Brise as a result of the impression made upon him by a visit to the reformatories at Elmira, New York and Concord, Massachusetts in 1897. The distinctive features that have emerged in the Borstal schools are the quality of the staff personnel, provision for close relationships between house-masters and boys, individual treatment in a graded system of walled and unwalled institutions, and good after-care by competent paid personnel and intelligent public-spirited volunteers in the Borstal Association and the Borstal Voluntary Associates.

In the United States probation has come to be a common substitute for reformatory commitment. A tendency to suspend the execution of sentences had long been used in the courts as an informal and probably illegal means of extending clemency when judges felt that circumstances warranted it. In 1844 a Boston boot-maker, John Augustus, began to persuade judges to release certain offenders in his care. Presently Father Rufus W. Cook, Chaplain of the Boston jail, and other volunteers, following the example of

Augustus, began to act as friendly counselors to arrested men and women, placed in their charge. A law passed in 1869, authorizing the Massachusetts State Board of Health, Lunacy and Charity to undertake the investigation, care and placement of juvenile offenders, in effect provided for probation. In 1878 Massachusetts added the word "probation" to the vocabulary of criminology in an act providing for a probation officer for Suffolk County and defining his duties. Since then, probation has come into general use in the United States, Canada, Europe, Japan, and to some extent in Latin America and South Africa, as a voluntary arrangement between the state and a defendant, intended to reestablish him as a law-abiding citizen in the community without the necessity of committing him to an institution. The purpose of probation has not been well understood by the general public, and its administration has been adversely affected by lack of a rational technique for selecting those to be placed on probation, and often by probation staffs inadequate in numbers and in professional qualifications. Probation is nevertheless generally considered to be a useful device of some present value and of greater promise as it comes to be better understood and as its administration is influenced by a general trend towards professionalization in penology.

The reformatory movement in America crystallized in the organization in 1870 of the National Prison Association, which adopted a Declaration of Principles proclaiming reformation to be the aim of all penal treatment and setting forth the conditions, similar to those of the Irish system, under which it might be accomplished. Renamed the American Prison Association, this organization has continued, through its Annual Congress of Correction and its journal, the Prison World, to act as a forum for the discussion and dissemination of ideas designed to bring about the improvement of penal, correctional, and reformatory institutions.

Similar efforts have been made by other national organizations, of which one of the most influential has been La Société Générale des Prisons, established in 1877 in France. Its journal, "Revue pénitentiare et de droit pénal," has been an effective organ for fostering an international exchange of views on penal problems.

Since 1846 a series of international congresses for prison reform have been held at intervals. Following a resolution passed by the U. S. Congress in 1871, a permanent international organization, supported by the governments of twenty nations, was established, whose first meeting was held in London in 1872, followed by others at more or less regular intervals since then. The early congresses of the International Penal and Penitentiary Commissions were concerned chiefly with the problems of prison management, but since the Stockholm meeting of 1878 consideration has been extended more broadly to problems of penal legislation, crime prevention, and the biological and sociological factors associated with criminal behavior. These Congresses have led to a healthy conflict and interchange of ideas and to awareness of differences in international problems and viewpoints, such as Europe's use of the indeterminate sentence for social defense through lengthening imprisonment as compared wtih America's emphasis upon its use as an incentive to reformation.

The rise in the late nineteenth century of the positive or Italian school of penology, based upon the work of Cesare Lombroso (1836–1909), Enrico Ferri (1856–1928), and Raffaele Garofolo (1852–1934), directed attention to the criminal rather than to the crime, denied the doctrine of free will and individual moral responsibility as the basis of criminal behavior, and instead sought the causes and cure of crime in the scientific study and treatment of the offender and the bio-social factors involved in his development. The positive school finds no ethical justification for punishment, but grounds its treatment of offenders in the need for social protection. The methods used are based upon the principle of protecting the group from the harmful effects of criminal behavior with such minimum restrictions upon human freedom as are consistent with the social good and the development and utilization of the acceptable personal assets of the criminal to the highest point consistent with the primary aim of social protection and social efficiency.

In accordance with the positive theory, the principle of scientific study and treatment of offenders has come to be generally accepted, although in practice its use is limited by lack of understanding of its meaning and implications, by the traditionalism of the law, by the existence of costly and substantial physical facilities such as prisons designed in accordance with classical penal theory, and by adherence to concepts inconsistent with those of the positive school but grounded instead in belief in freedom of the will and individual moral responsibility.

In accordance with the idea of scientific study and treatment of offenders there have arisen training programs for prison officers, the utilization of psychiatrists, psychologists, social workers, chaplains and other professional personnel, the use of case work procedures, programs of education and vocational rehabilitation, and the classification of offenders and their commitment to specialized institutions of appropriate types. These changes have occurred sporadically and in piecemeal fashion wherever Western civilization has penetrated. They have been limited, even in the best systems, by inadequate budgetary provision for new staff positions. In the United States they have perhaps found their fullest expression in the federal prison system; although individual institutions in a number of states are noteworthy. Of these the Massachusetts State Prison Colony at Norfolk, the New Jersey State Reformatory at Annandale, the Missouri Intermediate Reformatory at Olgoa Farms, and the New York State Prison at Walkhill are, or have been among the most frankly experimental in discarding the traditional prison architecture and the punitive-repressive régime in favor of social rehabilitation through the utilization of individual treatment programs under conditions more or less approximating normal community life.

In Europe and in Latin America, as in the United States, penal programs range from the punitive-repressive to the reformative-rehabilitative, under conditions frequently dissimilar to those in North America and including the use of family prison colonies and furloughs in Russia, community volunteers in England, Poland and Czechoslovakia, and the work-pay-restitution program and conjugal visiting in Mexico.

Shaped largely by the prevailing trend of knowledge, belief and technology, movements of varying strength are now pointed towards the improvement and extension of probation and parole services with an accompanying reduction in the use of imprisonment, especially for sentences of less than one year; complete abolition of the death penalty; abolition of the county jail and even of the penitentiary; limitation of the sentencing power of the courts; extension of the indeterminate sentence; the establishment of receiving and diagnostic centers; determination of individual, flexible treatment programs by a professionally staffed correctional authority; the development of diversified types of correctional institutions; classification of prisoners for assignment to institutions and within institutions; development of individual case work programs; and professionalization of staffs.

It is difficult to prove that penal reform has resulted in continuous reduction in crime or recidivism. Nevertheless; reform is essential to keep penal methods consistent with, and in effective adjustment to, the total civilization in which they have their setting. Apart from an undetermined and doubtful increase in social protection through deterrence and rehabilitation of offenders due to penal reforms, society may benefit from more economical methods of dealing with offenders, from increased duration of social protection, from reduction of disease, and from progress in understanding human behavior.

Since the scientific approach to the problem of dealing with convicted offenders implies diagnosis and treatment rather than punishment, its acceptance would make the term "penal reform" itself inapplicable. The scientific method is not, however, generally accepted because there is a fundamental conflict between the deterministic explanation of behavior inherent in scientific humanitarianism and the presently more popular explanation of behavior in terms of free will and moral responsibility. The consequences of this conflict are serious but not readily observed because the difference of viewpoint does not so commonly affect the types of

treatment as it does the vital decision as to how, when, and to whom they should be applied. It is possible that further fundamental improvements in applied criminology await the extension of a common, scientifically-based philosophy of crime causation and control to all of the interconnected public and private agencies dealing with criminal behavior.

ALBERT MORRIS
Professor of Sociology
Boston University
Boston, Massachusetts

BIBLIOGRAPHY

American Prison Association, *Yearbook of the Committee on Education*, New York, 1939. The Annual Congress of Correction, *Proceedings*, New York.
Barnes, Harry E., *The Evolution of Penology in Pennsylvania*, Indianapolis, 1927.
Barnes, H. E., and Teeters, M. K., *New Horizons in Criminology*," 1943.
Bates, Sanford, *Prisons and Beyond*, New York, 1936.
Beccaria, Cesare, *An Essay on Crimes and Punishments*, Albany, 1872.
Bentham, Jeremy, *The Works*, John Bowring, Ed., Edinburgh, 1838–1843.
Boston Prison Discipline Society, *Annual Reports*, Boston, 1827–1841.
Brockway, A. Fenner., *A New Way with Crime*, London, 1928.
Brockway, Zebulon R., *Fifty Years of Prison Service*, New York, 1912.
Brown, James B., *Memoirs of John Howard*, Boston, 1831.
Caldwell, Robert G., *The Penitentiary Movement in Delaware, 1776 to 1829*, Wilmington, 1946.
Commons, Yakhub and Powers, *The Development of Penological Treatment at Norfolk Prison Colony*, New York, 1940.
de Beaumont, Gustave and de Tocqueville, Alexis, *On the Penitentiary System in the United States and its Application in France*, Philadelphia, 1833.
Dix, Dorothea L., *Remarks on Prisons and Prison Discipline in the United States*, Boston, 1845.
Ferri, Enrico, *Criminal Sociology*, Boston, 1917.
Gillin, John L., *Taming the Criminal*, New York, 1931.
Healy, William and Alper, Benedict, *Criminal Youth and the Borstal System*, New York, 1941.
Howard, John, *The State of the Prisons*, Everyman's Library, New York, 1927.
The International Penal and Penitentiary Congresses, *Proceedings*, London.

Ives, George, *A History of Penal Methods*, London, 1914.

Lewis, O. F., *The Development of American Prisons and Prison Customs, 1776–1845*, Albany, 1922.

Maconochie, Alexander, *The Mark System of Prison Discipline*, London, 1855.

Mannheim, Herman, *The Dilemma of Penal Reform*, London, 1939.

McKelvey, Blake, *American Prisons*, Chicago, 1936.

National Probation Association Yearbooks, New York.

Phillipson, Coleman, *Three Criminal Law Reformers: Beccaria, Bentham and Romilly*, New York, 1923.

Ruggles-Brise, Sir Evelyn, *Prison Reform*, London, 1921.

Rusche, George and Kirchheimer, Otto, *Punishment and Social Structure*, New York, 1939.

Tannenbaum, Frank, *Osborne of Sing Sing*, Chapel Hill, 1933.

Teeters, Negley K., *They Were in Prison*, 1937.

Teeters, Negley K., *World Penal Systems*, Philadelphia, 1944.

Webb, Beatrice and Sidney, *English Prisons Under Local Government*, London, 1922.

Wines, Frederick H., *Punishment and Reformation*, Revised Edition, New York, 1910.

PENOLOGY AND CORRECTIONS. Penology can broadly be defined as the study of the methods of dealing with offenders. Originally Penology was mostly engrossed with measures of punishment. As capital punishment dwindled, as whippings, stocks and pillories, and punishments of public spectacle ceased, as institutional care was substituted for corporal and capital punishments, and as probation replaced some sentences and parole released men from institutions, Penology began to take a different direction. It became committed to efforts at reconstruction of the lives of offenders who were no longer hung or punished in public. At this juncture Penology in the United States became corrections. Corrections represented the provisions the state made for the care and handling of offenders. It was merged with public welfare. Board of Charities and Corrections was the title of many late 19th Century Public Welfare Departments of state government. The label of Corrections for the work of handling offenders at public expense stuck and superseded the older label of Penology, which seemed to recall to mind its close connection formerly with punitive measures.

At present there is the Annual Congress of Corrections which is sponsored by the American Prison Association and several affiliated organizations such as the National Probation Association, the American Parole Association, the National Prison Association, and so forth. Several states have departments or divisions of corrections. New York City even has its special department of corrections.

In the United States, Penology is still a sort of text book subject, which is taught in many departments of sociology in universities and colleges. The courses in Penology as now offered only touch lightly on the origin and philosophy of punitive measures and concentrates on an overview of correctional work. Outside the United States, where the methods of dealing with offenders has not developed along correctional lines, Penology is still very much in vogue.

Corrections as it has grown in the United States is an accumulation of practice of dealing with offenders plus the accumulated philosophy in back of such practice. As in the case of many similar fields of human engineering, corrections should be presented as a subject of study mainly in terms of its most recently approved good practices rather than its outmoded practices, although such good practices may only have a very limited circulation as yet. But the so-called good practices define the field at any one time.

Due to the child welfare movement and several allied social welfare movements in the United States, the juvenile offender has been separated in the handling process from the adult offender. At first, separate juvenile institutions were established. Later separate facilities for detention of children and separate courts for juveniles were erected. This separatist movement has led many to believe that the handling of the juvenile offender does not fall in the field of corrections but rather in the field of social work and child welfare. Corrections would thus be limited to the methods of dealing with the adult criminal.

There was ample justification for the establishment of separate facilities for the handling of the juvenile apart from the adult offender. But there is no justification for limiting the field of corrections to the adult and for excluding the juvenile. There is no good practice in juvenile probation, juvenile parole, juvenile training schools which would not be good practice in and applicable to adult probation, parole, and correctional institutions. And the reverse is true. Correctional workers need often to handle both kinds of cases, as in the case of federal probation officers. The border line between older juveniles and men and women is not easily discernible. Correctional workers need to be flexible enough to be able to deal with juvenile as well as adults.

The separatist movement went so far in the United States that the National Probation Association holds its principal meetings with the National Conference of Social Work rather than with the Annual Congress of Corrections and there was a split in the organization of training school workers, one group meeting with the National Conference of Social Work and the other meeting with the Annual Congress of Corrections. The thought behind this schism in the correctional field in the United States is that corrections is too much dominated by adult prison administrators whose philosophy is more penal than rehabilitative. Study would show that there are just as many adult correctional institutions as there are training schools for juveniles which display good practices. Likewise good practice is not the sole possession of juvenile probation officers. The point is, therefore, that corrections is corrections and applies equally to juveniles as adults rather than being limited to work with adult offenders.

The main correctional agencies in the United States today consist of the police, detention facilities, probation service at courts, institutions for short sentences, training schools, reformatories, prisons, and parole service (including parole boards).

While the police have concentrated on law enforcement, detection and investigation, arrests, and other protective measures, they must deal with offenders in the first instance. They have decisions to make as to whether to hold or arrest. They operate lockups and jails. They provide special services in many

departments for the handling of women's cases and juvenile cases. Police women are part law enforcement officer and part social worker or correctional worker. Officers assigned to the crime prevention bureaus or the juvenile squads, for the handling of juvenile cases, are more case investigators than law enforcement agents. They must decide what to do about the complaints and which juveniles to turn over to the juvenile court. Some police departments attempt to do something with cases they do not refer to the juvenile court. And this something is correctional work. If police departments could deal with men's cases as well as they deal with juvenile cases, the police would become much more of a correctional agency than a law enforcement agency. Police departments need to be both a law enforcement agency and a correctional agency—that is, a place where offenders can get service and help. The big task before the police is proper screening for detention and for court procedure and proper diversion of cases to special services inside the department or to social agencies outside the department. The average police department needs to act more and more as an intake department of a well organized social agency: screen, divert, and hold cases.

Separate facilities for detection of juveniles is still not possible in small towns, where the adult jail is the only facility. In larger cities, juvenile detention homes have been erected. But they have acted as collecting stations for a lot of children to influence one another for a few days. It has been difficult to get a detention home program (support it financially) which could counteract the interaction of child on child. Some detention homes are now acting as child study institutes, which try to use the time the child stays in detention for diagnosis and initiation of treatment. Such institutes require well trained staffs. Many juvenile courts have attempted to divert children from detention homes and allow them to remain in their own homes until their cases are ready to be heard in court. This practice can be followed in the instance of children who do not need custody and whose families are responsible. In a few cities, diversion from detention homes is attempted in some cases by the use of boarding homes. Such facilities can be used by juvenile courts in cases of younger boys and young and older girls who are not custodial problems but yet whose family and community situation is bad.

Adult detention has made some strides, especially as a result of federal and state jail inspection programs. But in general the adult jail or lockup is still by and large a woefully lagging institution. Its custodial service is low grade and its rehabilitation service is practically nonexistent. There are a few bright spots and the future for the jail would be good if key persons really took an interest in it and if it could attract jailers and wardens who were interested in good jail practices. The jail still needs sanitary control of living quarters, toilets, food and kitchen. It needs better medical service and disease control. It needs time occupying programs and space to carry them out. It needs better classification and segregation of prisoners and facilities to carry out good classification and segregation practices. It needs personnel which can consult with and render personal help to prisoners. Efforts are being made to find ways and means of reducing jail population by diversion to other facilities such as city or country hospitals for the acute alcoholics and the actually-ill prisoners. Bail of course has been misused and is not in reach of the persons who merit bail. Placing a person on his own recognizance without bail, could be used in meritable cases where bail is out of question. Justifiable substitutes for and diversions from jail, in order to reduce jail population to the minimum, are just in their infancy but they will assume a very important part of good correctional practice in the future.

The institutions for serving short sentences (those under a year) consist of county jails, city workhouses, road camps, and state operated misdemeant farms. There is no question but that the adult who is sentenced to a reformatory or prison is presented with a very much superior program than the adult who is sentenced to a short-term institution. The short-term institutions have most of the shortcoming of the jails and lockups—the places of detention while awaiting disposition. Apart from physical care, there is the grave problem of providing services and program which can offset the ravages of an institutional society of poorly occupied prisoners and which can also be helpful rehabilitation-wise to those prisoners who can be helped. Such a program requires budget and good personnel. Some states have taken the short-term institution out of the hands of local county and city government and have established regional farms, camps and other types of institutions where a productive work program is possible and where in some instances educational and recreation and health services are available. Short-term rehabilitation is a more difficult task than long term rehabilitation of prisoners in institutions. It would seem that the short-term institutions would need the most flexible and most abundant facilities and personnel to aid in short-care treatment. However, the institutions of longer terms have been the ones to make the greatest progress in developing a rehabilitation program. State operation of district or regional short-term institutions for misdemeants is one of the most obvious solutions for the advancement of the correctional work for short-term prisoners.

Probation service in the United States has developed much more extensively in juvenile courts than in adult courts. Some courts use probation without having a full-time probation officer, by placing persons on probation to the sheriff, the constable, or other court officer. It is generally accepted that there cannot be very much in the way of probation service without a full-time paid probation staff. In general, probation service divides itself into two allied parts: investigational and supervisory. From the standpoint of the court, the investigations are supposed to contain the information which enables the judge to determine whether the case can be placed on probation, that is, whether it merits probation and is a good probation risk. From the standpoint of adjustment of the case on probation, the investigation should contain information which gives good insight into the case, including the person's inner life, so that diagnosis, prognosis, and a workable treatment plan can be made. Supervision of cases placed on probation has graduated out of the checkup detective service, to see whether the probationer is abiding by the terms and conditions of his probation. It is becoming more of an adjustment service, whereby the probation officer assists the probationer in working out a better life situation. The probation officer is attempting to be a counsellor rather than a snooper and he is also attempting to use his legal authority of recalling a probationer to court with good discretion. The formulation of a probation plan with the probationer taking as much responsibility and initiative as possible for its execution and revision is becoming one of the major procedures of good probation practice. The legal restrictions on the class of offender who can be placed on probation are still made by state legislatures. Usually speaking the first offenders of crimes not involving aggression against the sanctity of the individual are accorded the right of probation by law. The best informed probation workers believe that restrictions should be taken off and that the state should place faith in the pre-sentence investigation as the best means of screening out unprobationable cases, thereby assuring the best protection to society.

The training schools for juvenile delinquents, the reformatories for younger men and women generally, and the prisons for adult men are veering toward good program facilities. These correctional institutions have had a long uphill fight to get a program which could combat the workings of a congregate inmate society and the many problems of tension which arise from persons being confined. Some institutions have won this fight and are now at the level where they are attempting to emphasize the rehabilitation of inmates according to individual treatment programs. This sort of procedure requires excellent facilities of work, education, recreation, health and so forth and excellent personnel to deal with the many phases of an individual human being's life. Individualized treatment is only possible in correctional institutions after the ordinary problems of institutional control have been solved and after budget permits ample facilities and specialized personnel.

The principal objective of the correctional institution is to prepare cases for release back into society, with the purpose in mind of returning the persons with greater strengths to handle his own affairs. The secondary objective of correctional institutions is to keep unimprovable and serious cases out of circulation—that is, to protect society. Institutional administrators realize the merits of having specialized institutions to perform these two functions. In larger state correctional systems, it is possible to have an institution or special facilities for cases needing lifetime care and for cases needing close custody. And institutions have developed for medium and minimum custody, in which the program can be somewhat different. Such specialization in institutions has mainly taken place in men's institutions. At best there is usually only one women's reformatory in the average state. What specialized custodial facilities are needed here must be worked out inside the institution.

Correctional institutions are gravitating toward the smaller sized institution rather than the large institution. And where custody permits, the cottage plan rather than the cell block plan is growing in favor. Small flexible units for housing and for program are indicated at the present time.

The best practice now dictates a reception program, in which the newly admitted prisoner or inmate is studied and oriented; a classification program, in which the professional personnel attempts to make the best assignments in the institution and to build an individualized treatment plan for the newcomer; progress review before this same professional staff, to determine what revisions in program are needed and to determine gains and readiness for release; preparation for release to a free world under parole supervision.

Finally, parole service is one of the very important agencies of corrections. States have various legal machinery to place inmates of correctional institutions on parole. In many instances, this is done by an independent parole board, which also recommends cases for pardon and commutation. In other instances, the parole release is made by the governor or persons acting for him. In still other instances, the parole is granted by institutional authorities or a board of managers of the institution. The main thing is to insure adequate selection of cases for release and to surmount pressure and influence in behalf of certain cases. Parole boards have also had to surmount a tendency on the part of members to retry cases before it. The main thing for the releasing agency to determine is the merit of the case. Is the case ready for release? Is it safe to return such a case to the community again?

When the person is released on parole, he is placed under the supervision of a parole agent. Heretofore, the parole officers have known so very little about the cases paroled to them, prior to their being placed on parole. This defect is being surmounted by having parole officers make pre-parole investigations and by having them verify parole plans which the prisoner has been projecting inside the institution. An institutional parole officer, who can prepare cases for release, work up parole plans with the individual inmate, and coordinate the efforts of the field parole officer, is growing in favor. Such a worker is already being used in federal institutions and a few state institutions.

Most state laws have required that a parolee have a job before he can be released. Parole work has recognized the importance of a job in the readjustment of cases. But usually the parolee has indicated where he can get a job and the person who can sponsor him on this job. Where this has not been so, it has been up to the parole officer to help find the parolee a job. This method of job finding has not always been satisfactory. With the tremendous development of prison industries and a vocationally oriented work program, inmates have been trained to do some very skilled tasks. It seems to be a definite industrial waste to turn a man back into any sort of available job with skill in two operations on shoes. Consequently, some federal institutions have created a new post, namely, that of employment placement officer. He develops contacts with high grade industries requiring skilled workers. He interviews the parolee and works up his industrial life history. He attempts to place a prospective parolee with such and such skills and experience in industrial plants which can use this skill and experience. This employment placement work will assume greater importance in the near future. If an institution goes to the expense of retraining a man and making him skilled in certain tasks, it is all the more necessary to see to it that this skill is well placed. And the average parole officer in the field is not always able to make such placements.

The problems of supervision of parolees are pretty much the same as those of supervising probationers. The use of authority and hounding a parolee by unskillful periodic checkups are to be kept to a minimum. Good use of discretion is needed, in allowing a parolee to work out his life's adjustments on parole. Allowing the parolee to take as much initiative and to assume as much responsibility in his own rehabilitation is in line with best parole practices today.

In conclusion, it can be said that corrections in the United States as judged by the best practices which are coming into operation represents a form of rehabilitation for the most part. In some part, corrections must include measures for protection of society, especially for screening out unprobationable cases and unparolable cases and for determining the degree of custody needed in institutional commitment. The premium in rehabilitation work is placed on individualized treatment, whereby the offender is able to share and cooperate to his fullest extent in determining his program of adjustment. The overuse of authority easily stifles the effort of the offender to help himself and to take the initiative. In a program of rehabilitation of offenders, it is very essential that competent personnel, who have knowledge of good practices, be placed in charge. The field of corrections has been slow to attract personnel who could carry out the best practices which are now understood and known. It is definitely hampered by the lack of high-grade, qualified personnel. The remuneration and the methods of selection of personnel in correctional work have been very poor indeed. The field will not advance very far until the personnel problem is solved. Recruitment for correctional service from the colleges and universities by a system of temporary appointment may be the best means by which to upgrade the service. Young persons with an interest in the work and pertinent college courses in criminology and penology could then be trained on the job for replacements as they occur in correctional service. Inservice training programs are also being used to upgrade correctional workers. Travel to conferences and educational leaves of absence are still other methods of fostering staff growth.

The field of corrections in the future may be influenced greatly by two trends which are coming from the scientific disciplines associated with criminological study. The one is the prior determination of outcome on parole and probation by prediction methods. The other is the establishment of prognostic or treatment types. What kinds of cases are poor probation and parole risks and what kinds are good risks? There have been one or two attempts to put prediction methods into actual operation. The state of Illinois had for several years a parole actuary, a person of sociological training. He worked up the actuarial statement on each prospective parolee for the parole board to consider along with all other information it had on the case. Probation and parole outcome prediction has gone very far in actual research work. It remains for key administrators to develop confidence in it. Some resistance to it might naturally come from the prisoners themselves who wish to get all the "breaks" they can. The establishment of prognostic or treatment types comes as a result of expert practitioners' pooled experience. As a result of wide experience with different sorts of offenders, it should be increasingly possible to tell that such and such type of offender will not respond well to such and such type of handling. Prognosis aims at the same thing prediction does—control over cases. The latter comes out of the actuarial approach which is statistical. The former emerges out of the observation of individual cases under treatment, that is, from the experience of practitioners. Both prediction and prognosis can be of great aid to correctional work, in implementing rehabilitation as well as protection. They can help ferret out the improvable as well as the unimprovable cases.

WALTER C. RECKLESS
Professor of Social Administration
Ohio State University

BIBLIOGRAPHY

Barnes, Harry Elmer and Teeters, Negley K., *New Horizons in Criminology*, New York, 1943.
Doering, Carl Rupp (ed), *A Report on the Development of Penological Treatment at Norfolk Prison Colony in Massachusetts*, N. Y., 1940.
Halpern Irving W., *A Decade of Probation*, New York, 1937.
Handbook of American Institutions for Delinquent Juveniles, The Osborne Association, Inc., 1st edition, vol. 4, New York, 1943, pp. 18–66.
Handbook of American Prisons and Reformatories, The Osborne Association, Inc., 5th edition, vol. 2, New York, 1942.
Pigeon, Helen D., *Probation and Parole in Theory and Practice*, New York, 1942.
Proceedings of the American Prison Association, 1870–1944, New York.
Robinson, Louis Newton, *Jails; Care and Treatment of Misdemeanant Prisoners in the United States*, Phila., 1944.

PERJURY. *Perjury* may be defined as false swearing or the voluntary violation of an oath either by swearing to what is untrue or by omitting to do what has been promised under oath. Perjury is punishable as a crime in all jurisdictions since the entire system of court procedure and trials is dependent upon the keeping of oaths and true testimony.

The New York State provisions with regard to perjury are cited here as typical of similar laws elsewhere. "A person is guilty of perjury who: (1) Swears or affirms that he will truly testify, declare, depose or certify, or that any testimony, declaration, deposition, certificate, affidavit, or other writing subscribed by him is true, in connection with, any action, proceeding, hearing or inquiry, or on any occasion in which an oath is required by law or is necessary for the prosecution or defense of a private right or for the ends of public justice or may lawfully be administered, and who in such action or proceeding, etc., willfully and knowingly testifies, declares, deposes or certifies falsely, or states in his testimony, declaration, deposition, affidavit, or certificate, any matter to be true which he knows to be false; or (2) Swears or affirms that any deposition, certificate, affidavit, or other writing by him subscribed, is true, and which contains any matter which he knows to be false affecting the title to any real or personal property, including the assignment or satisfaction of a mortgage, and upon which reliance is placed; or (3) Having been appointed or designated to be an interpreter in any judicial action or proceeding knowingly and willfully falsely interprets any material evidence, matter or thing between a witness and the court or a justice thereof in the course of an action or special proceeding."

Two degrees of perjury are distinguished. *Perjury in the first degree* is perjury committed as to any material matter in connection with any action or special proceeding, civil or criminal, or any hearing or inquiry involving the ends of public justice or on an occasion in which an oath or affirmation is required or may lawfully be administered. *Perjury in the second degree* is perjury committed under circumstances not amounting to perjury in the first degree.

Swearing falsely in any form is perjury and irregularities in the manner of administering an oath is no defense to a prosecution for perjury. Also, it is no defense to a prosecution for perjury that the defendant was not competent to give the testimony, deposition or certificate of which falsehood is alleged; or that he did not know the materiality of the false statement made by him; or that it did not in fact affect the proceeding in or for which it was made.

An unqualified statement of that which one does not know to be true is equivalent to a statement of that which he knows to be false. Witnesses who have committed perjury may be summarily committed by the court to answer an indictment for perjury and documents necessary to prove such perjury may be detained by the court and directed to be delivered to the district attorney.

Subornation of Perjury is the willful procuring or inducing of another to commit perjury and may also be committed in the first or second degree.

Both perjury and subornation of perjury are felonies and punishable as such. In the first degree, they are punishable by imprisonment for a term not exceeding five years while, in the second degree, for a term not exceeding two years, or by a fine of not more than five thousand dollars or both. (New York.)

BIBLIOGRAPHY

Gilbert, F. B., *Criminal Law and Practice of the State of New York,* Matthew Bender and Co., 1935.

Larson, J. A., *Lying and its Detection,* University of Chicago Press, 1932.

Münsterberg, Hugo, *On the Witness Stand,* Clarke Boardman Co., 1925.

Taft, H. W., *Witnesses in Court,* Macmillan, 1934.

PERVERSION, SEXUAL. The generalized psychiatric acceptance of the term perversion has broadened to that which includes any deviation of the normal heterosexual act of coitus which tends to be fixed and exclusive in its nature. Freud has attempted a somewhat more specific designation by dividing perverted acts into those which take place as an anatomical transgression from parts of the body designated by nature for sexual union or a deviation from a normal sexual aim. Thus, perversions of the first class would be fellatio, cunnilingus, anilingus, whereas those perverted sexual acts which use a substitutive object from the normal one would include fetishism, necrophagism, coprophilia, and kleptomania. It will be noted, therefore, that one of the essential elements of the definition of perversion implies the existence of a love object. The love object may be phantasied or be inanimate as in necrophagia or be a substitutive object as in fetishism. Masturbation without phantasy, therefore, is not a perversion, whereas with exhibitionism, it becomes such an act. This distinction is of importance inasmuch as failure to consummate the sexual act is a frustration of the race propagation of the community, whereas otherwise it becomes merely an offense against the individual himself.

Much confusion exists among sexologists as to the delimitations of the various perversions. There is a constant tendency to broaden the scope of each designation. The Law itself is quite vague in this matter and in many states penalties are laid down for a wide number of perverted acts coming under a common designation. Thus, Sodomy has been designated by law in several states to include unnatural acts between human beings, whereas its original designation limited the act to one between an animal and a human being. In the forepleasure of normal coitus, modified forms of sexual perversions may occur. If these do not pervert the participants from the consummation of the normal act and if these abnormalities in themselves do not become fixed and do not become the prime object of satisfaction, then they are not to be considered perversions. A great many forms of perverted sexual acts are known but those of chief interest from the point of view of culpability in the eyes of the law are as follows:

Anilingus, the commission of a perverted sexual act by the use of the mouth on the anus. Individuals so indulging have regressed to the anal erotic level of development. It is essentially an infantile act.

Cunnilingus, the commission of a perverted sexual act by the use of the mouth upon the external genitalia of the female. This frequently occurs between homosexuals of the female type. Not infrequently it is one of the perverted acts found in the forepleasure of normal intercourse. Individuals indulging in this perversion have regressed to the infantile oral erotic level. Emotionally, they are sexually fixated on the primary oral erotic zone.

Exhibitionism (see Indecent Exposure). The exposure of the genitalia to one of the opposite sex constitutes, in general parlance, the perversion of exhibitionism. Usually this offense is committed by the male in the presence of one or more females. Socially accepted sublimated acts of exhibitionism, however, occur among females in Terpsichorography, in burlesque shows, and in choruses, as well as in diving, swimming and bathing, while among males well-recognized forms are oratory, acting, boxing and wrestling. Psychogenically, the perversion of exhibitionism seems to have its origin in a failure to resolve thoroughly the elements of the oedipus situation. The victim through attachment to one of his parents identifies the love object with his own body (Narcissism). Tensional states are built up frequently by masturbation. The compulsion arises to exhibit the genitalia to the opposite sex but in so doing the individual hopes that the woman, in turn, will likewise expose herself.

Even the phantasy of being approached sexually for the purpose of intercourse is indulged by the male but unconsciously he revolts against this idea, does not desire it and in some instances would even flee if such an attempt were made upon him. Castration fear is deep in these cases. As a boy he has been unconsciously in love with his mother and fears revenge from the father whom he fears might deprive him of sexual competition through his castration. Through exhibitionism he attempts to eliminate this fear by reactivating the unconscious phantasy he had as a child of being a woman with a penis. Thus, self-identification of the exhibitionist with his love object becomes affirmed. The compulsive nature of tensional releases through exhibitionism is well known and has caused many investigators, notably Freud himself, to believe that there is a constitutional component compelling the individual toward a repetition of this act. Other investigators, such as Fenichel, deny the constitutional element of the act. There is no doubt that the act itself is a substitutive one and is a compromise of the individual with himself for the consummation of the normal heterosexual act of which he is usually incapable. The personality of these individuals is characteristic. There is little evidence of aggressive tendencies and the men tend to be shy and timid. They frequently come from puritanical homes where sex discussion is avoided and a very proper attitude toward sex problems is maintained. Such an individual may have the highest type of ideality and pursue many idealistic avocations. The Law, however, treats the offense with considerable severity. There is an increasing tendency on the part of the judiciary to refer these cases to psychopathic clinics for observation and report back to the court. This perversion is frequently allied closely to that of pornography, obscenity, voyeurism, toucherism.

Fellatio, carnal knowledge of an individual by or with the mouth. Freud explains the origin of this perversion by stating that it arises from a fixation of the psychosexual development of the individual at the so-called oral erotic level. During the normal development of an individual certain areas of the body, known as erogenous zones, become stimulated. These are primarily the mouth, the urethra and the anus. The zone about the mouth is stimulated by suckling of the mother's breast. The anal zone becomes stimulated through the process of defecation. The third zone is that of the urethra, which is stimulated through urination. All these processes have intense interest for the developing infant and, therefore, these three zones become highly emotionalized. As the development of the child proceeds, a large part of this emotionalized interest becomes diverted into other channels. Some individuals, however, are so conditioned to this emotional response that the zones become highly erotic and it is then a frequent and simple matter for the individual in his adult life to regress to the level in which these zones seek stimulation. The courts affix judgments of this act as an act of sodomy.

Fetishism, a compulsive perversion of the substitutive type in which an object possessed by the loved person replaces the love for that person herself. Thus, the fetishist employs the art of magic in investing an intimate object with the attractive evaluation of the individual himself. The object which serves as a fetish is a symbol. It embodies mysterious qualities which are considered by the victim to emanate from the loved one. By over-evaluating an object, such as a shoe or a stocking, the hair or any other portion of the loved one's body, the fetishist relinquishes the aim of accomplishing the normal heterosexual act and accepts a mystical substitute which to him offers even more miraculous qualities. A perverted sense of smell frequently accompanies the perversion of fetishism. The odor is often that of a portion of the body of the love object.

Psychogenically, an individual suffering from this perversion has a fear of being rejected by the love object and thereby being humiliated by the opposite sex. Through a symbolical possession of a portion of the love object, he magically assumes control of the whole individual without fear of rejection. Often there is a strong tendency toward self-degradation in this process. These individuals are usually quite masochistic. Anthropological literature is replete with instances whereby an object assumes all the magical powers of its possessor. Primitive extensive use of totem

and taboo arise from the magical use of symbolical objects which are considered to be surcharged with power, authority, ability to exact revenge and above all, the most desired qualities of the original owner. The fetishist is enabled through the use of a symbolized over-evaluated object to carry on all of his love-making with the exception of the actual heterosexual experience itself. He no longer desires this since he can accomplish everything else without fear of rejection.

In those cases in which the object sought by the fetishist has a symbolic equation with the female genitalia, such as velvet, fur, and underclothing, the basic perversion of the fetishist becomes most apparent. He fundamentally has an aversion to real female genitals on the basis that there is no evidence of a phallus, thereby symbolizing a fear of castration and so he turns to substitute objects for the genitalia. This permits him both a denial and assertion of the fact of castration and the avoidance of rejection if heterosexual advances were to be made to the female.

Fetishists often annoy the police through their breaking into houses and the stealing of unusual objects therefrom. The objects removed often seem to be of no value and the conduct seen is bizarre and inexplainable to the police. The same residence may be burglarized frequently and usually the same type of article is removed or despoiled. These may be shoes, lingerie, stockings or other female wearing apparel. Sometimes lingerie put out on the clothesline in the backyard for drying is thus despoiled during the night. Seminal emissions are frequently noted on such wearing apparel. The law considers the fetishist as a misdemeanant and is inclined to refer the case to a psychiatric clinic for further observation.

Kleptomania (Cleptomania). The uncontrollable compulsion to steal. This perverted act has a close resemblance to that of fetishism. The object stolen has symbolic meaning to the offender. It is the act, however, rather than the object which invests the offense with a value to the offender. In fetishism the object becomes magically invested with all kinds of authority and promise to the lover. In kleptomania the objective is revenge instead of adoration. The Freudian concept is that the stealing is associated with penis envy. The stealing from someone in authority or more powerful than the offender himself deprives that superior one of an object of power and authority. The object therefore symbolizes the penis and, the stealing is an act of castration of the father. This offense is nearly always a female offense. The woman in stealing, therefore, castrates her father and limits his power and authority over the mother.

Punishment of these individuals is singularly ineffective inasmuch as the punishment emotionalizes the act and, therefore, makes it all the more exciting to the doer. It is well known that pathological stealing occurs very frequently in cases of wealthy women who could afford to buy the object stolen ten times over. It is the act of stealing itself which invests the situation with exciting satisfaction rather than the object taken. Franz Alexander and Karl Abraham believe that the roots of kleptomania reach back to the first source of pleasure to the infant; namely, the mother's breast. The withdrawal of the nipple from the child has brought about a sense of frustration which has never been entirely overcome. The act is an obsessive one and, therefore, the individual is a psychopath. Lorand believes that, in addition to the penis envy and the loss of the mother's breast, another factor in this perversion is defective critical appreciation of the factors of reality. He found in all of his studies of such cases that there was an instinctual drive which crowded the function of the critical faculty. While these cases are of great interest to the student of abnormal pathology, they are relatively rare and from the point of view of the police do not constitute a great source of annoyance. For every case of true kleptomania there are perhaps fifty cases of outright shoplifting where the motive is pure greed and gain.

Masturbation. Genital excitation caused either psychologically or by mechanical manipulation which leads to ejaculation. The act without phantasy may be purely automatic and, therefore, does not constitute a perversion. Habitual masturbation is not a disease of the mind in itself but is a symptom of an underlying conflict of the personality or an actual neurosis. A well-known fact is that masturbation may be a bridge in the psychosexual development of the individual between narcissism and the divergence of the libido into more socialized channels. The period in question occurs about the age of puberty and such act should not be classified as a perversion.

The practice is very common in groups of men who are removed from association with the opposite sex for long periods of time. It is doubtful that such a method of sex expression should be classified as a perversion. Mutual masturbation in which the act is performed by two individuals, usually of the same sex, simultaneously upon each other is a perverted act inasmuch as the possibilities of normal heterosexual relationships are transgressed to a deviated abnormal method of expression. Here again the offense is against society more than against the individual himself. The practice of masturbation is so universal at some time in the course of the life of the individual, both male and female, that many theories and legends have grown up regarding self-abuse. The most prevalent of these is that the act engenders insanity. This belief has largely been discredited, but the fact is well recognized that excessive masturbation leads to moodiness, periods of depression and a chain of symptoms closely resembling neurasthenia. The mental reaction of the individual himself to the act and his feeling of guilt with respect to his committing something which he recognizes as being condemned by society and the extensiveness of the phantasy accompanying the act, are the most potent sources of injury to the individual. There is a certain compulsion to the act, but it does not have the elements of incurability that many of the obsessive, compulsive perversions exhibit. Psychic masturbation which results in ejaculation without mechanical excitation of the genitalia is often associated with other perverted tendencies, especially that of fetishism and toucherism.

The initial phase of the masturbatory act is one of phantasy. The phantasy-life in connection with this act is of more psychological importance than the act itself. A certain amount of dissociation of the personality occurs during phantasy and this in itself may become the basis of schizoid tendencies of some duration. Many schizophrenics are known to have a prolonged and continuous history of masturbation, although this must be construed as a symptom rather than a cause of schizophrenia itself. The fixation of the libido at a narcissistic level obviously is an obstacle in the psychosexual development of the individual toward the ultimate goal of heterosexuality. The length to which this goal is deferred becomes an increasing detriment to the individual. He tends to become more withdrawn in his personality, more inclined to avoid social contacts, and has a deeper feeling of guilt as time goes on. Such individuals may continue their practices throughout life and are generally known to be inadequate in their personality, vacillating with respect to decisions, and lacking in firmness of character necessary for leadership. The individuals recognize these deficiencies thoroughly with a consequent deepening of the feeling of inferiority so that a vicious circle is thus established. Castration threats frequently made by parents upon children addicted to masturbation may be carried into adult life as the roots of an anxiety neurosis and the castration fear.

Sometimes the child resorts to a substitutive act, namely enuresis, particularly of the nocturnal sort. Masturbation in itself is considered by adults to be a childish manifestation. The police are usually concerned with this in connection with exhibitionism. Conviction is usually for a misdemeanor, and in many instances the case is referred to a psychiatric clinic for observation.

Necrophilia, copulation with a corpse. This revolting act probably is more frequent than the paucity of scientific literature on the subject would indicate. Courts and juries are usually so horrified with these revelations that much of the confidential material dealing with acts of this kind does not become public or even available to the reporters themselves. History plainly indicates that the perversion was well known to antiquity and there are many allusions to the practice in the literature of ancient Greeks. Certain perverted acts of mutilation upon dead bodies as exhibited by the Axis Power during the recent World War II indicate that the perversion is

by no means a rarity. The sadistic feature of the act is clearly realized.

A certain parallelism is to be noted between necrophilia and bestiality. In each instance the love object is defenseless, and incapable of resisting maltreatment. A peculiarly revolting feature is the nature of the love object itself with associated odors. Coprophilia which is a perversion of the sense of smell is closely associated with necrophilia. In some instances where corpses are not available the necrophiliac requests prostitutes to dress up and act as corpses. Associated with this also is the perverted act of permitting the body to be saturated with execratory material or in the case of some types, particularly those who are psychotic, the ingestion of feces. The peculiarly revolting nature of these perverted acts has led many investigators to conclude that the offenders are degenerates. Certainly the incidence of psychosis is much higher in this group than in almost any other type of perverted offender.

Almost all investigators are inclined to the belief that a constitutional factor is involved, in addition to certain psychogenic elements. These cases manifest unusually perverse desires at an early age. Many seem to be totally devoid of superego development, so that the question of guilt and the feeling of having transgressed the tenets of the community are almost non-existent. Almost all the cases show a marked generalized development of erotic sensitization over the entire skin area instead of localized erogenic zones as in the normal individual. Many of the cases seem to be lacking entirely the sense of smell or they may have a perverted sense of smell in which the stench of decomposition or the odor of the products of defecation becomes pleasant rather than repulsive. The judiciary is inclined to consider such individuals essentially psychotic, and reference to a State hospital for prolonged observation is commonly the disposition.

Pederasty. Coitus per anum. The individual who indulges in this act is considered to be psychosexually fixed at the anal erotic level. The anus is a primary erogenous zone as explained in the topic under the heading of Fellatio. The law deals with this act as one of sodomy and imposes penalties accordingly.

Pedicacio, sexual excitation incurred only through the love of children. The sexual act usually engaged in is that of pederasty and fellatio. Individuals of this type are usually sexually impotent and cannot derive any sexual satisfaction except with young children. Individuals indulging in these practices are usually psychopaths and show many mental abnormalities in addition to their sexual perversions. *Carnal abuse of a female child* brings severe reprisals on the part of the law. Any adult who abuses the body of a female child under the age of ten years is adjudged to have committed a felony. If the child is between the ages of ten and sixteen, according to the New York State law, the offender is guilty of a misdemeanor for the first conviction, and for a felony for the second conviction. Carnal abuse includes not only attempted intercourse but the indulging in any indecent or immoral practice with the sex parts or organs of a female child. A sentence not to exceed ten years may be imposed by the court for the commission of such a felony.

Pornography, the expression of lewdness and obscenity through written language, pictures, or other forms of images. The distribution or possession of obscene books, pictures, literature or other objects frequently approaches the status of a cult among many individuals of high culture, good intelligence, and often high social status. The practice may be quite esoteric. Thus, a small, highly-gifted and cultivated group of individuals may collect and exchange pornographic literature and objects with the same keenness shown by a collector of vases of the Ming dynasty, for example. On a lower social scale the interchange of crude and exceedingly lewd pictures of the so-called "French photographs" may occur. Of greatest interest perhaps is the wide distribution of pornographic literature in thinly disguised forms, such as nudist magazines, so-called art studies, salacious literature and highly ambiguous paintings.

Distributors of these pornographic articles are highly organized to secure a wide market and are frequently subjected to legal prosecution. The difficulty with which they are brought to judgment indicates the cleverness with which the pornographic nature of the articles is thinly but effectually disguised legally. Furthermore, the existence of a large quantity of this material is indicative of the great number of consumers ready to receive it. The true pornographic pervert is likely to be either a frigid woman or an impotent man. A history of disastrous attempts at the heterosexual level is often revealed. The turning to the lewd article thus becomes, in effect, a securing of sex satisfaction through a symbolic object. The motivation thus becomes somewhat like that of fetishism without, however, having quite as strong an obsessive component. Psychosexually these individuals seem to be fixated at the early erogenous zone stages of development. Many of the lewd scenes depicted have elements of cruelty traits, revenge, horror, and other primitive emotional attitudes. There is very little subtlety of erotic expression. Closely allied to the perversion of pornography is that of obscenity making itself known through the repetition of lewd stories or the exhibitions of a lewd nature which are commercialized, and are presented to limited audiences. Finally there is the so-called "poisoned pen" writer who exhibits sadistic impulses through hurting others by means of letters written anonymously.

The law is inclined to group pornography with the perversion of exhibitionism. Each is classified as a misdemeanor and is so punished, but the courts usually refer the exhibitionist to a psychiatric clinic for observation, study, and report, whereas the individual addicted to pornography is dealt with more directly by the law as an offender. Undoubtedly, the crime of blackmail has its roots in the same level of psychosexual development with frustration of the kind found in the case of pornography.

Sado-masochism. Because of the close linkage between these ambivalent tendencies, sadism and masochism should always be considered coincidentally. Sadism is the sexual excitement engendered by inflicting cruelty and punishment on another individual. Masochism is the pleasure derived from suffering pain, ill-treatment, and humiliation either at the hands of a sadist or through other sources.

In many instances the two states are intermingled or there is a quick and sudden swing from one state to the other. It is doubtful that either state exists in its true form in complete absence of the other. The term sadism, as is well known, was derived from the name of Marquis de Sade, a French writer who gave voluminous and detailed descriptions of the infliction of cruelty upon others. It is obviously a source of intense sexual satisfaction to all concerned. Sadism during the course of love-making may take almost any kind of violent action toward the love object. The most frequent perhaps are biting and scourging with whips. Religious cults, known as the Flagellants, exhibit a mass form of sadism. The greatest exhibition of mass sadism is encountered, of course, during war. The violent forms of sadism are highly perverted sexual deviations but mild forms occur regularly in almost any kind of human relationship whether on an erotic or other level. One of the most devastating, although little known, forms is that of mental cruelty often exhibited toward the love-object itself.

Without exception these cases are obsessive neurotics. They possess the anal sadistic character. In the second or third year of the life of these individuals intense curiosity is manifested in the excretory processes. According to Freud, children of this type will resort to retention of excrement for the purpose of deriving greater pleasure at the moment of defecation. Also, the act of defecation is utilized as an expression of pleasure toward the person whose admiration was sought. The whole act of defecation thus becomes emotionalized. Also, the child by means of controlling the process of defecation through his own will is able to frustrate the desires of his parents who are attempting to establish normal toilet training habits in him. In a certain sense, then, the child through these processes gains mastery over those who are in authority above him.

Through the process of reaction formations in later life the ego is reinforced and the earlier anal sadistic traits are developed into more socially acceptable expressions, such as that of self-sacrifice, desire for justice, social improvement, meticulous attention to details,

a passion for orderliness and precision and other manifestations leading to an opinionated, rigid type of character. In many instances excessive thrift and parsimony is shown. The anal character of these obsessive neurotics shows decisive, aggressive trends against those individuals who are at variance with the inflexibility of the anal sadistic neurotic. He regards the genital impulse for coitus as being an excrementitious function and, therefore, a subject to be avoided as a dirty or filthy procedure. Such type of reaction from the earlier infantile high regard for excrement is, of course, a reaction formation. Regression to the early anal sadistic level, therefore, becomes frequent in these individuals. After regression takes place, the individual acts in a cruel manner toward the love object with the especial objective of debasing that love object, dominating, soiling, and physically abusing her. Fixation of the psychosexual development, however, occurs in the oedipal situation. The sadist constantly shows a tendency in a choice of sexual objects which have a symbolic significance or are unconscious representations of the mother. During this stage of his development the individual probably has lived in a relationship of infantile submission which is only lip service, so to speak, inasmuch as intense hatred toward the parents is unconsciously felt. Regression to the anal sadistic level reinforces this passive feminine relationship toward the paternal images. It conflicts with the aggressive tendencies of the individual toward active rivalry and with his passive submission. Thus, the sadist and the masochist are in the position of showing an ambivalence; namely, in quick swings toward one or the other manifestation. They may be aggressively violent toward the love object or suddenly yield to a feminine type of submission.

In the former instance the pervert adopts a virile, active attitude, often showing intense cruelty traits. In the latter instance there is considerable phantasy formation and the submissive act becomes symbolic of castration. Nevertheless, the masochistic attitude of entire submission may in itself be a very potent weapon of revenge for the phantasy castration because there is no real giving in to the lover and he never succeeds in actually obtaining possession of her. Thus, again masochism may be utilized and frequently is so utilized as a weapon of cruelty. Here again the inflexibility of the obsessive neurotic is clearly shown. Moreover, the fluctuating character exhibited by the obsessive neurotic in the manifestations of sadism or masochism leads to a vacillating, indecisive nature often incapable of strongly-drawn decisions.

The ego in its struggle against unconscious tendencies of the anal erotic stage finds that its best weapon of nullification is that of repression. These repressed instincts, of course, merely accentuate the genital conflicts which are the basis of the obsession neurosis. Another method is displacement toward insignificant acts which lead eventually into highly ritualistic procedures. Thus, the obsessive neurotic sets up routines of procedures or avoidances in which he lives psychically in an animistic world. A procedure of this nature is closely allied to the use of magic found in fetishism and other perverted acts. Through such ritualistic behavior the ego is enabled to neutralize some of the strong guilt feelings of the superego. The obsessive neurotic has a full understanding of his tendency toward vacillation, conflicts and doubts and learns through processes of isolation, nullification, denial of existence, and repression to avoid painful affects growing out of feelings of guilt. Thus, the desire to seek expiation may become so intense that the individual readily yields to physical abuse. Counterposed to this submissive attitude toward the superego is the intense ego striving to free itself of the repressive influence. This, of course, may break forth as an explosion of aggressive nature leading to highly sadistic acts. The aggression commonly takes as its purpose either the destruction of the object or its complete control. Thus, it will be noted that these tendencies revert directly back to the oedipus situation itself.

With respect to the application of the perversion of sadism toward the criminal, in all probability many sex crimes showing atrocious violence toward the love object often to the point of murder, have their source directly in this perversion. The body may be greatly mutilated. In many instances, the mutilation is self-inflicted, often in the form of attempted castration. It is a matter of common knowledge that many hold-ups are accompanied by intense sadism and that a great deal of unnecessary violence is perpetrated upon the victim. So prevalent is the sado-masochistic attitude that it pervades the very court itself. The attitude of the public in general and of some of the judiciary in particular is a direct expression of sadism toward the criminal. The history of the handling of criminals is replete with instances of the utmost cruelty at the hands of their captors. It is this element of sadism so prevalent in the community toward the criminal that is the most effectual check against intelligent and progressive advancement of penology. The science of penology has lagged perhaps more than any other type of human endeavor, particularly among the social sciences due directly to the sadistic attitude of the community as a whole.

Sodomy (Bestiality). The psychiatric acceptance of this term limits the field to the performance of sexual relations between human beings and animals. The law, however, takes a broader view of the matter and is inclined to consider that any person who has intercourse with another individual by means of the anus or mouth or submits to such deviated acts or has carnal knowledge with a dead body is guilty of sodomy. Thus, the legal definition includes the psychiatric conceptions of bestiality, fellatio, pederasty, and necrophilia. Bestiality is not uncommon among farm laborers in remote rural sections. Many of these individuals are feebleminded. The factors of low moral standards, lack of opportunity for indulgence in normal intercourse, narrow economic margins under which the individual lives, lack of opportunity for mingling with others in a community are probably more potent factors in inducing this type of perversion than are constitutional factors themselves.

The act of sodomy is viewed with considerable horror by the community. Some allowances are made legally by the court in the matter of sentencing individuals convicted of bestiality. The law as applied, however, to abnormal relationships between human beings as indicated by the law is treated most severely. A large number of states impose a penalty up to twenty years of servitude for the commission of such an act.

Toucherism. An irresistible impulse to touch the body of another person. Toucheurs are frequently encountered in large crowds. They obtain considerable sexual excitement by touching the breasts of women inadvertently or pinching of the buttocks or merely by casual contacts. If they rub against the other individual, they are known to be *frotteurs.* The condition is closely allied to that of fetishism and has strong, compulsive, obsessive trends. These individuals are psychopaths and may in many instances be suffering directly with a full-fledged neurosis. The law views them as misdemeanants, of an annoying character since the depredations are childish, but they are irritating to the victim herself.

Transvestism, the wearing of clothing of the opposite sex with the erotic desire of simulating attributes thereof. The practice is not uncommon among homosexuals and is seen in its full-fledged state in male individuals who make themselvxes up as females and parade the streets in open solicitation. In less public form homosexual parties may be devised, a portion of the members of which may dress themselves in female costumes and behave as females to other members of the party. Certain modified forms of this are seen on the stage as female impersonations. The law makes provision for the punishment of the wearing of clothing of the opposite sex but the law is not rigidly enforced. Male transvestists are well known to the police and are able to ply their trade upon the streets in a surreptitious manner only. They are not usually brought to judgment except in connection with other offenses.

Transvestism among females is very common and seems to be socially acceptable, the concept of the community being that it has no particular sexual significance from a perverted point of view and is more or less of a gay prank. Certainly the use of male attire by females does not possess the perverted interest that is shown by the male in such action. In this respect there is a parallelism in the perversion of exhibitionism. Trans-

vestism among females is often encountered among women who have an unusually large male component in their makeup. Such women dress mannishly, particularly in business pursuits and are usually frigid and unattracted by the opposite sex. Homosexuality in this group is proportionately less than might be assumed, but these personalities are rigid and without richness in emotion. The Law does not consider transvestism in the mannish woman as being punishable.

Uranism, the perversion of Homosexuality. The term was widely used a number of years ago but is rather infrequently encountered in present times.

Voyeurism (Peeping Tom) (Scoptophilia). The derivation of sexual excitement and satisfaction through viewing the genitalia or the nude body of an individual. The perversion is closely linked with that of exhibitionism. The exhibitionist exposes himself to view to another individual, whereas the voyeurer seeks gratification in looking at others. Usually, he prefers to remain unseen and gets especial delight in viewing the disrobing of women. The perverted interest shown by such individuals is really a fixation of an infantile curiosity instinct. The young child learns his relationship to other people sexually and socially through observation. He endeavors to learn the functions of his own body by observing those of other individuals. A certain amount of peeping is required for this. If such process becomes unduly emotionalized and remains of emotional interest to the individual in his adult years, he may find himself in the position of deriving his chief satisfaction through this infantile practice. The practice is frequently associated with masturbation.

Accommodations for scoptophiliacs are maintained in some special establishments in metropolitan areas, particularly on the Continent, for the unseen viewing of acts of defecation, masturbation and other procedures both normal and abnormal.

V. C. Branham, M.D.
Chief, Outpatient Section
Neuropsychiatric Division
Veterans Administration
Washington 25, D. C.

BIBLIOGRAPHY

Alexander, Franz and Staub, Hugo, *The Criminal, the Judge and the Public*. Translated from the German by Gregory Zilboorg, New York, The Macmillan Co.

Ellis, Havelock, *Studies in the Psychology of Sex*, Philadelphia, F. A. Davis Co.

Freud, Sigmund, *Three Contributions to the Theory of Sex*. Translated by A. A. Brill, New York & Washington, D. C., Journal of Nervous and Mental Disease Publishing Co., 1930.

Garma, Angel, M. D., *Sadism and Masochism in Human Conduct*, Translation from the Spanish by Samuel B. Kutash, Monograph No. 2, Journal of Clinical Psychopathology, Monticello, New York, Medical Journal Press, 1947.

Krafft-Ebing, Psychopathia Sexualis.

Moll, Albert, *Perversion of the Sex Instinct*, Translated by Maurice Popkin, Newark, The Julian Press.

PHOTOGRAPHY. Photography seems to be the perfect medium for the recording of facts. As a popular saying goes, "The camera cannot lie." Nothing is farther from the truth. For example, a witness to an automobile accident or a shooting is sitting in a parked car. There is at hedge between the occupant and the scene of the crime. If the photograph is taken at a level of 5′ 2″ which is the average level of the eyes of an individual sitting in a car, the true picture of the scene will be recorded. However, if the camera is placed at a higher level, the picture would indicate that that individual could see more of the crime than he actually did, while the reverse is true if the camera is set at a lower level. As a second example, a person at a certain vantage point claims that he saw a crime committed at the intersection of two highways. If a lens of long focal length is used to take a picture of the intersection from that vantage point, the resulting negative would seem to indicate that the individual is right on top of the intersection. If a lens of short focal length were used, he might seem to be, according to the picture taken, as entirely too far away to have witnessed anything happening at that point. While again certain evidence on the body of the car, which requires a slight amount of bas relief to bring out plastic qualities of the evidence, for example, mud or stain on the body of the car, requires

lateral lighting so as to throw the evidence into some relief. If the camera is set directly opposite the evidence to be photographed and flat lighting is employed, then the evidence will almost entirely be obliterated so far as the picture is concerned. All of these and a number of allied conditions may be unintentionally employed by the photographer so as to give a false picture of the actual scene required. In addition to this, it is possible through manipulations to falsify evidence. Thus, through retouching of the negative, montage, and other photographic trickery, entirely false impressions may be given. The photographer engaged in recording crime events, therefore, must be of honest integrity and have as his sole motto the slogan, "Does this represent the true picture of the crime?" Photography of this sort, therefore, is somewhat different than the demands of commercial photography.

In commercial photography the operator is more or less obliged to glamorize his subject. Thus, by the manipulation of light, the deepening of shadows, the throwing out into relief of prominent points, high-lighting, spot-lighting, the subject is given an art quality which is entirely out of keeping with requirements of photography in the criminalistic field. The chief requirements of such photography are depth of focus by which is meant that as many objects as possible behind and in front of the particular object upon which the lens is focused will be brought into sharp relief, clarity of detail (definition), coverage equivalent to the extent of vision of the average eye in a fixed position and the proper rendering of tone values through color-corrected lenses and the use of panchromatic film.

The photographing of the scene of the crime, whether it be an indoor or outdoor picture, requires primarily an over-all picture which has as its prime purpose the showing of the relationship of the object of investigation to fixed objects in the field. Thus, if an automobile is discovered on a side road leading from a main highway and a body is contained therein, the photograph will be made to show the distance of the car from the main highway, its relationship to the nearest fixed object, perhaps trees, and the general appearance of the landscape itself. This requires detail and proper perspective. In addition to this, all photographs should be supplemented by sketches in which distances shown upon the photographs are outlined after actual measurements of these distances have been made.

If the scene of the crime is an interior and the photographer has official standing so that he may be permitted to set up his apparatus without interference, he can accomplish a great deal more than is the case of the person who must work quickly and at sufferance with those in authority. In this case as in the outdoor picture, an over-all photograph of the entire scene must be obtained from the very start. Often the scene is a darkened corridor or a small cluttered-up room with inadequate lighting and with a body and other evidence jammed into one side of the room. The photographer will have difficulty in composing his picture but under all circumstances, the picture, if possible, should be composed on a ground glass screen.

If evidence cannot be removed to the laboratory for photography, a great deal of excellent close-up photography can be performed by the miniature camera with the use of a number of accessories. Thus, if it is required to photograph dusted thumbprints, jimmy marks on window sills, small objects up to the size of a small penknife, identification marks, scars on furniture or other objects, resort may be made to the miniature camera.

Macrophotography and so-called *Table-top Photography* is required from time to time in collecting police evidence. In macrophotography a very small object, such as a grain of wheat or several grains of sand or other extremely small objects may be photographed to a comparatively large size and then enlarged so as to assume magnification of 200 diameters or more, thereby enabling an analysis of structural material not possible in any other way short of the use of a microscope.

Many documents to be recorded are on colored paper and, therefore, require the use of filters.

The photographing of highly-polished objects, particularly the bodies of automobiles, can be much facilitated. Stains and markings which would ordinarily become neutralized by the glare of the highly-polished metal can be brought out readily by means of a polarizing screen over the front of the lens. The photographing of highly-polished table tops on which markings, such as thumbprints or other evidence, is much facilitated by the use of a polarizing screen over the lens. With respect to copying and reproduction work, both the lights and the lens should be screened with polarizing material. Frequently the material to be copied is on rough matte paper or again it may be on highly glossed paper surface. The correct rendering of texture with the elimination of glare in these cases is an absolute necessity. All paintings which might have to be reproduced for evidence can easily be recorded in this way, whereas it is extremely difficult without the use of polarizing screens. Glass surfaces, porcelain ware, reflections from waxed surfaces of any kind, such as those covered with blood or clinical specimens themselves will benefit greatly by the use of a polarizing screen.

Most of the work required by the criminal investigator with respect to the use of the microscope deals with the subject of ballistics and the comparison of documents or other objects requiring identification. A specially-devised instrument known as the *comparison microscope* is widely used in police science laboratories. This instrument consists essentially in two compound microscopes arranged in parallel and connected by a metal cross-beam in which are located right-angle prisms so that the separate images may be reflected through a single eye-piece. Each microscope has its own source of illumination with provisions for the adaptation of light filters, if necessary, and each stage is equipped with special holding apparatus so that bullets or other objects to be compared may be arranged in exact parallel and may be rotated simultaneously about their own axis or be manipulated separately. By this method each image of the object being viewed can be compared with the other and the images may be superimposed upon each other so that any likenesses or differences will be clearly brought out. Provisions are made for a double camera so that each image may be photographed simultaneously but separately for purposes of comparison. Through this arrangement, bullets, shells, fingerprints, handwriting, stains on fabric, etc., may be completely studied, analyzed, compared, and photographed. A series of ingenious apparatuses for holding various sized objects in different positions have been devised by police science laboratory technicians, and these may be made adaptable for use under the comparison microscope. In the case of photographing material for handwriting identification, small details are frequently required and these details in comparative form are enlarged and projected so that a complete analysis of the letter or phrase may be made.

Photographing of Prisoners for Identification. A direct outgrowth of the Bertillon System of identification of prisoners has been the use of photography showing a seated picture both front and profile views. The value of such photographs from the Bertillon point of view is obvious. For example, it has been said that the configuration of the shell of the ear presents so many different characteristics that a system can be devised whereby each individual can be classified by the conformation of his ear shell which will be as positive identification as that individual's fingerprints. The characteristics of the nose are most important and often are the most identifying feature of the face.

So-called "stand-up" pictures have come into increasing prominence in recent years. These stand-ups include the entire length of the individual who is dressed in ordinary civilian clothes. The idea is that in the event of escape or if the individual is wanted at a later time, he can be identified by having a view of him as he would actually appear walking along the street. In the event of escapes copies of these are made and distributed to sheriffs, police officers, and others in the vicinity so that identification can be made. Copies likewise may be multigraphed and distributed in poster form throughout the country.

The Use of Infra-Red Photography. Infrared photography depends on two main char-

acteristics of infra-red light; namely, the unusual ability to penetrate atmospheric haze and to render visible objects that would be ordinarily obscured to visible light and, secondly, the property by which certain objects reflect infra-red light without any particular reference as to their action to visible light itself. It is this second characteristic of infrared rays that is taken advantage of by the criminal investigator. Thus, altered documents or forgeries would show up under infra-red photography because of the difference in pigment used in the alterating fluid from the original ink. Infra-red light will likewise reveal lower layers of paint in suspected forgeries of paintings. Old documents which are either deliberately stained or deleted readily show up under infra-red photography which reveals the alterations made. This likewise appears on fabrics, parchment, wood, leather, and other objects. In photomicrography the use of infra-red emulsions will reveal hidden details in the structure of objects placed under the microscope.

Use of Ultra-Violet Photography. The ultra-violet photography is of great importance in criminal investigation. Radiations of this kind, of course, are not visible to the naked eye and, therefore, they will reveal through photography evidence that could not be otherwise noted. In general, the principle is that certain objects reflect ultra-violet radiations and others do not. If two given objects, perhaps differing slightly in color, reflect the ultra-violet radiations differently, this may be recorded on the photographic plate although the human eye cannot distinguish any difference in color between the two objects. Thus, if different inks have been used in a case of forgery, the inks may be apparently identical to the naked eye but the ultra-violet photography will record faithfully the difference in the two colors of ink, thereby uncovering a forgery. Chemicals that are used to erase ink are particularly susceptible to reflecting ultra-violet radiations and, therefore, ultra-violet photography of altered documents in which these bleaching chemicals have been used show up the places where the chemicals have been used with great fidelity. Many substances have the power of absorbing ultra-violet light and converting it into visible light in the form of efflorescence. The quality of fluorescence can be utilized to differentiate between substances that appear alike to the naked eye. Thus, in police work important ingredients can be separated out of a mass of material by means of this photography. A well-known example is the bright bluish fluorescence shown by quinine under ultra-violet radiation. Thus, the examination of hair may indicate by purple luminosity under the ultra-violet light showing the chronic use of aspirin. Various hair preparations may be differentiated by means of this method of photography through fluorescence. The detection of metallic poison, such as arsenic, copper, lead, and antimony, yield characteristic colors which, of course, can be checked by means of the spectroscope and by chemical analysis. Morphine fluoresces with a characteristic bright bluish color. Cocaine gives a white fluorescence, heroin shows up yellowish green, and aspirin purple. Of especial value is the matter of the examination of underclothing, bed linen, and other suspected garments for semen stains in suspected rape cases. Careful examination of all of this material by the naked eye is not only laborious but usually quite unfruitful, particularly if the stains have been of some duration. Under the ultra-violet radiation of semen stains, however, a bright blue fluorescence is clearly seen. This portion of the textile can be put aside and examined by other laboratory means, such as soaking the material in physiological salt solution and examining under the microscope for the microscopic appearance of spermatozoa as conclusive evidence. The red pigment of blood fluoresces strongly and this is likewise true of urine, milk, clear serum of blood, bones, and teeth. Fragments of teeth which might otherwise escape identification may be shown up under ultra-violet radiations by brilliant white fluorescence, whereas artificial teeth have a dull purplish or reddish appearance.

It has long been known that when any object is stamped with a die, molecular changes occur in the structure of the article stamped which penetrate far deeper into the substance than is apparent to the naked eye.

Advantage is taken of this by the police science laboratory in various ways. Thus, in stolen handbags or other leather articles where initials have been eradicated, it is possible by exposure to ultra-violet radiations to bring out clearly the original letters because of the molecular disturbance of the material beneath the erasure. This method has been used widely in bringing back numbers on engine blocks of stolen cars. Grinding, filing and otherwise machining out the numbers on an engine block with the stamping upon of a new number would seem to make it impossible to find out the original number put on by the factory. It is possible, however, by polishing down the metal to a plain surface and then exposing it to ultra-violet radiations to bring out the molecular changes induced into the metal at the time of the original stamping of the block by the die.

Ultra-violet photography, of course, is adaptable to use with a microscope. This is particularly true in the analysis of specimens brought from a suspected case of poisoning for the purpose of determining small amounts of alkaloidal poison. These give characteristic fluorescence when radiated with ultra-violet light as has been indicated in a paragraph above.

VERNON C. BRANHAM, M.D.
Chief, Out-patient Section
Neuropsychiatric Division
Veterans Administration
Washington, D. C.

BIBLIOGRAPHY

Clark, Walter, *Photography by Infra-Red*, New York, John Wiley and Sons, Inc., 1939.
Frapie, Frank R., and Morris, Robert H., *Copying Technique*, Boston, American Photographic Publishing Co., 1940.
Horgan, Stephen H., *Photoengraving in Black and Color*, Boston, American Photographic Publishing Co., 1938.
Snyder, Lemoyne, *Homicide Investigation*, C. C. Thomas, Baltimore, 1944.
Shank, W. Bradford, *Filters and Their Uses*, Little Technical Library, New York, Ziff-Davis Publishing Co., 1943.
Tobias, J. Carroll, *The Students Manual of Microscopic Technique*, J. Carroll Tobias, Boston, American Photographic Publishing Co., 1936.

POLICE ADMINISTRATION. The common meaning of the term police embraces the department of government charged with enforcing laws and ordinances and to provide for the collective internal security of the nation. Police agencies of varying types exist in all levels of government, federal, state, county, city, town and village. Specifically this article deals in the main with the representative organization which exists at municipal level and performs the general police function.

At federal level, several departments maintain their own investigative units which are charged with the investigation and enforcement of the particular laws over which the department has jurisdiction. Among these in terms of total number of investigative employees are the Enforcement Division, Alcohol Tax Unit, Treasury Department; Immigration Border Patrol of the Justice Department; Federal Bureau of Investigation of the Justice Department; Divisions of Investigation and Patrol, Bureau of Customs of the Treasury Department; Post Office Inspectors; Secret Service Division, Treasury Department; Bureau of Narcotics of Treasury Department; and Intelligence Unit, Bureau of Internal Revenue, Treasury Department.

At state level, a number of states maintain state police who have general police power throughout the state. In other states, a statewide organization for traffic patrol on the highways is charged with enforcement of motor vehicle laws. Some states have established state bureaus of identification which at state level are clearing houses for criminal identification and investigation. Other state departments maintain minor investigative agencies to investigate and enforce in a limited sense the particular laws with which the department deals.

County governments most commonly maintain sheriff's offices whose functions are both civil and criminal. The sheriffs' departments, one of the oldest forms of police power in the United States, do not generally maintain the high degree of organization found in the large cities. Some notable exceptions exist where the criminal branch of the sheriff's department will be found to have a large and all inclusive group of divisions specializing in all phases of law enforcement.

In villages and towns may be found a marshal or very small police department (ranging upward from one or two men). These units will be found to represent the law enforcement agency of the very small community.

The typical town or city police force is found in the towns and cities of the county and the degree of organization becomes more complex as the city grows in size. It is this typical town or city police force which is described in the following paragraphs. While it cannot be said to be typical of all of the police of the nation, it can be said to encompass the general methods and organization toward which the small municipal police force moves as communities grow.

The general functions of the modern municipal police department are prevention of crime, preservation of the peace, protection of life and property, enforcement of laws and ordinances (federal, state, county, and local) arrest and prosecution of offenders, and the rendering of miscellaneous services. These comprehensive activities are carried on under an oath to support the Constitution and enforce the laws of the United States, the Constitution and the laws of the state, and the laws and ordinances of the town or city. Under the authority of law, the functions of the police force are carried out by a group of officers, organized in branches or divisions of a department which is governed internally by specific rules of the department.

Organization Structure. The police organization is divided into major activities: General Administrative, Line Activities, and Service Activities.

Administrative activity is performed usually in the office of the Chief, or Superintendent of Police. The diversity of the democratic form of government as it appears in cities has led to at least four types of police control at the top. They are: Municipal Council, Board of Police Commissioners, Commissioner of Public Safety, or control by a police executive. The administrative unit has authority over the Line and the Service activities. The administrative unit may contain an Inspectional function which inspects the operations of all divisions.

The Line activities may consist of all, or a combination of these units: Patrol, Traffic, Detective or Criminal Investigation, Vice, and Crime Prevention.

The patrol unit, divided into three eight-hour watches in modern departments, is generally responsible for patrol of the city by uniformed officers who are charged with the general police function and for preliminary work in the specialties assigned to other divisions of the department. Usually the city is divided into patrol areas or beats which, depending upon the size and type of area, may be patrolled on foot or in an automobile.

The traffic unit is staffed by uniformed officers who are assigned to enforcement of traffic laws and duties related to pedestrian and vehicular safety. This duty may be performed on foot to aid in intersection or point control for the orderly and safe flow of traffic, with the added objective of reduction of congestion. It may be performed on motorcycle or by automobile with attention to enforcement of moving traffic regulation. And it may include squads assigned to investigation and analysis of traffic accidents, and maintenance of programs designed for traffic safety education.

The Detective or investigative unit is generally charged with the investigation of major criminal offenses. Detectives, in civilian clothes, may work singly or in teams. Frequently they conclude preliminary investigations undertaken by patrolmen. The detectives are commonly responsible for investigation of crimes, preservation of evidence, preparation of cases for prosecution, and the recovery of stolen property.

The Vice unit is concerned with control of prostitution, gambling, liquor and narcotics. Usually it is a specialized unit responsible directly to the head of the department or the head of the Detective Division.

The Crime Prevention Unit, or Juvenile Unit, is responsible for police attention to cases involving juveniles and cases involving women. Often this unit is charged with dealing both socially and legally with such cases. The principal objective is dealing with

cases which have occurred, and through them discovering factors which influence or cause such cases, with a view toward prevention.

The Service Activities, are those which provide services to the line units. Service Activities may consist of all, or a combination of these units: Personnel, Communications, Records and Jail, and Property Management.

The Personnel function may be carried on for a police force by a central personnel agency of a city. Many police departments maintain police personnel units which may be responsible for recruiting, promoting, and training of personnel. In a few departments these functions are highly developed.

Communications activity may consist of construction and maintenance, as well as operation of various communications systems. Of these, the outstanding modern development is the two-way or three-way police radio through which police cars are in instant communication with headquarters. Also supervised, may be the telephone systems, including police telephone extensions located on strategic street corners. Some cities maintain a light signal system by which officers may be signaled to telephone to headquarters in those circumstances where they are not available by police radio.

The Record Division is responsible for the maintenance of police records including officers' reports, statistics, and other police records. An identification unit maintains files of fingerprints of arrested persons. In the very large departments will be found crime detection laboratories, or at least technicians who preserve scientific evidence for laboratory analysis. In many organizations the jail operation is assigned to this division which entails security, housing, care, and feeding of prisoners, who may or may not serve jail sentences in city jails.

Property Management may be a separate unit which controls all police property and buildings including security, upkeep and repair, as well as alteration. This unit has custody of the property of jail inmates and of property held in evidence in criminal cases. It may be responsible for accounting and budget functions.

Common Characteristics. One common

characteristic of police departments in cities in the United States, is the wide variance in structural organization and in police practice. Notable exceptions to this generalization are fingerprint records (sponsored by the International Association of Chiefs of Police and now coordinated by the Federal Bureau of Investigation) and the operation of traffic accident prevention bureaus in many cities (where installations have been made by the Safety Division of the International Association of Chiefs of Police).

Normal growth of a city reflects these changes in police organization: the one-man department, then subdivision by levels of activity, then by kinds of activity, then subdivision of activity with attempt at specialization and finally by areas of activity. At any stage there may be subdivision by time of activity. Such growth brings problems of organization; particularly is this true of specialization, and subdivision by area.

Rules and Laws. The police organization which is designed to enforce a wide group of laws is governed also by Constitutions of the United States and of the States, and in some cases by Charters of cities, in addition to the laws of those political subdivisions and their ordinances, and, at local level, administrative rules.

Internally most police forces of any size are governed by rules and regulations of the particular police force. In the rules and regulations of some of the large cities are found specific and detailed rules or operation and of method.

The more complete rules and regulations may be divided into three sections. The functions and responsibilities of the functional divisions of the department may be detailed. The responsibilities of ranks and grades, and specific job assignment may be specified so there can be no question of responsibility for act or omission in all ordinary circumstances. Usually there is a section concerning conduct of police officers, and reference to charges, trials, and even penalties for unsatisfactory conduct or neglect of duty.

Duties of the Ranks. A typical department will have grades ranked in descending order.

The head of the department (variously a Chief, Superintendent, or Commissioner) is responsible to the administrative authority of the city and is responsible for the administration of the department.

An assistant head of the department may have line authority and be the actual operating head of the department, or may have a staff position exercising authority in the name of the head of the department.

Captains may be in charge of functional divisions of the department or territorial divisions of the department.

Lieutenants may be in charge of staff units of the department, assistants in charge of functional divisions or territorial divisions of the department.

Detectives, responsible for criminal investigation of major crimes, frequently do not have line authority but are responsible for supervision of investigations.

Sergeants may be in charge of functional subdivisions of divisions (usually squads or watches), or may supervise specific assignments of greater responsibility than that normally assigned patrolmen. **The most common** designations are Desk Sergeants or Field (or Patrol) Sergeants.

Patrolmen are responsible for beats or patrol areas. They may be assigned specialized duties especially at a station or headquarters.

In some departments there is a rank of Inspector, a staff position, where inspectional duties are performed on behalf of the administrative head of the department. The rank of Inspector in some large eastern departments (e.g., New York) may be used to designate the head of a major division of the department. Use of inspectors to perform an inspectional function as such is not yet widely developed.

The larger departments are characterized by variations of these ranks and by special assignments, and by the addition of "civilian" employees, who do not have peace officer powers. They are also characterized by expansion into precincts or districts, each of which may have its own complement of these ranks.

In all of these organizations, supervision flows downward and responsibility upward.

In some cases, certain officers may be assigned to staff functions and thereby removed from the line of command.

In a large department a Chief may have two assistant Chiefs, one in charge of line activities, another in charge of each division. In a department of moderate size, each division may have its own commanding officer, each of whom is directly responsible to the head of the department. In a smaller department, several divisions may be grouped under one commanding officer; and in a still smaller department these activities may all be performed by a few men. In a village, all functions may be performed by the marshal or constable.

One characteristic of the police patrolman is that generally he does not work under direct supervision and must often make his own decisions in emergencies promptly, without benefit of advice from higher authority. This responsibility basically differs from that of a fireman who usually works under more direct supervision of a company or platoon officer, and basically differs from that of a soldier in an infantry unit, for example, who fights under more direct supervision of a non-commissioned or commissioned officer.

Police Personnel. Police personnel is far from standardized in actual practice, but there is a growing tendency in recent years, especially in the larger cities, toward standardization and toward improved personnel.

Personnel recruited within the past few years tends to approach the recommendations of a committee of the International Association of Chiefs of Police. More and more police administrators are agreeing that there should be definite personnel standards approaching the following levels:

United States citizenship is invariably required within the past few years, particularly in the West. The rigid requirements of residence for a period of years in the city of appointment is being relaxed, so that some departments require only residence within the state, and a few have no residence requirement beyond citizenship. Age limits for recruiting are tending toward a minimum of 21 to 30 years of age, with mandatory retirement ranging from 60 to 70 years after appropriate years of service.

Height requirements tend toward a minimum of five feet eight inches or five feet nine inches. Weight in proportion to height is often required. Physical examinations often require evidence of no disabling defects. High school graduation or its equivalent is commonly required.

In many larger departments written examinations for recruits are held, some to measure abstract intelligence, others of general civil service design. Frequently recruits appear before an oral appraisal board where such personal characteristics as appearance, bearing, and personality are measured, and minimum qualifications must be met.

In most departments fingerprints are taken. In many, searching character investigations of applicants are conducted by competent investigators.

Training Programs. Notable advances in police training have taken place in American police departments during the past decade. There are two outstanding and nationally noted schools. One is the National Police Academy operated in Washington, D. C. by the Federal Bureau of Investigation. To this school each year are sent selected police officers from the United States and foreign countries for sixteen-week sessions in police investigation and methods. Invitations are sent to police departments to nominate students; selections must be approved by the FBI after qualifications are reviewed and character references investigated. After training, graduates are sent back to their own departments to teach police subjects to other members of the department. The other school is the Northwestern University Traffic Institute at Northwestern University. Scholarships are offered to in-service police officers for courses in traffic training of some months duration. This school, associated with the Safety Division of the International Association of Chiefs of Police, is firmly established as the leader in the traffic field. Other in-service training is offered in some junior colleges and colleges where institute-type short courses are held. Many short courses of general type, or on various specialties, have been given throughout the country with excellent results.

The Federal Bureau of Investigation has

sponsored, furnished instructors, and materials for zone schools set up throughout the country to teach institute-type courses of a few hours per week for a period of weeks or months.

Some medium size and large departments support departmental schools for recruit instruction lasting for periods of a week to three months, full time. Advanced courses are given in some of these schools for in-service officers.

Pre-entry training is offered in two types of police schools in some state or junior colleges, colleges or universities. The first of these is a two-year course leading to a certificate, or a four year course leading to a degree where technical police subjects are taught with a relative minimum of general subjects. The other type is found in some colleges and universities where the undergraduate course of study is primarily to provide a cultural background, with emphasis on basic courses in police organization and administration, the natural and social sciences, and other subjects providing a background for later technical police study when the individual attends an in-service school. In this type of program a faculty member may be appointed to advise students concerning courses of study and to advise individuals concerning possible future opportunity in the police field. Both types of college level courses are most successful where some selection can be made of students before they are encouraged to complete proposed courses of study.

Inspections, Measuring of Results. Recognized police standards have been developed to gauge results of police administration and to measure criminal activity. A system of Uniform Crime Reporting was sponsored by the International Association of Chiefs of Police about 1930, and tabulations and publishing of police statistics have since been taken over by the Federal Bureau of Investigation which publishes quarterly, semiannual, and annual Uniform Crime Reports. These reports provide comparisons on a time and geographical basis.

One measurement is a comparison of the numbers of police employees per thousand population between communities.

The most widely standardized inspectional procedure is the maintenance of police records. The compilation of those records gives an over-all picture of the volume of work, the manner in which it is being performed and the success of the police in meeting their responsibilities.

Comparisons are made with these measuring devices:

By recording "Major offenses known to the police per 100,000 population", the volume of major crime, trends, and the success of practical crime prevention methods are measured.

"Per cent of cases cleared by arrest" provides a comparative measure of the success of investigation.

For certain offenses "the number of persons charged by police" and the "percentage of convictions" are measures, usually in cases involving public morals.

Traffic Activity is measured by national police reports and by the National Safety Council in recording comparative statistics for "Injury Accident rate", "Traffic Accident Injuries, fatalities, and property damage." Between cities specific comparisons are made of motor vehicle deaths resulting from traffic accidents with ranking based on number of deaths per 10,000 registered vehicles and 100,000 population.

For internal comparisons on crime and traffic rates many departments use various forms of a Consolidated Daily Report, a Consolidated Monthly Report, and an Annual Report.

Many departments use a Monthly Platoon or Company Report to reflect for each individual patrolman the number of cases assigned and cleared, the number of cases originating with the individual officer, the number of traffic arrests made, the number of irregularities found by the patrolmen in routing patrol, particularly of business establishments, as well as the number of times he is called upon to correct or to complete work done.

Need for Crime Prevention. The greatest future opportunity for the police of the nation to be of service to the citizens of the country, lies in the field of Crime Prevention. Society will benefit most from police activity, not when repression is severe, not when apprehension and prosecution are most finely developed, but when underlying causes and influences are isolated, and techniques are applied to prevent crime from occurring. Practical crime prevention, properly applied will relieve human suffering and make American communities better places in which to live in years to come.

JOHN D. HOLSTROM
Chief of Police
Berkeley, California

BIBLIOGRAPHY

Federal Bureau of Investigation, Department of Justice, Washington, D. C., *Uniform Crime Reports* semiannual.
Gocke, Blye W., *A Police Sergeants Manual,* Los Angeles, O. W. Smith, 1944, 296 pp.
Gulick, Luther and Urwick, L., *Papers on the Science of Administration,* New York, Columbia University, 1937, 195 pp.
Institute for Training in Municipal Administration, *Municipal Police Administration,* Chicago, International City Managers Association, 1943, 531 pp.
Kreml, Lieutenant F. M., *Accident Investigation Manual,* Evanston, Northwestern University Traffic Institute, 1940, 231 pp.
Ridley, Clarence E., and Orin F. Nolting, eds., *The Municipal Yearbook,* Chicago, International City Managers Association Annual, 603 pp.
Smith, Bruce, *Police Systems in the United States,* New York, Harper Brothers, 1940, 384 pp.
Wilson, O. W., *Police Records: Their Installation and Use,* Chicago, Public Administration Service, 1942, 336 pp.

PREDICTION OF CRIMINAL BEHAVIOR. When human beings are able to predict future events with reasonable accuracy the way has been paved for the intervention of human intelligence in the control of those events. Planning for the future, if it is to be successful, is dependent upon knowledge of what is most likely to occur when a set of specific conditions are characteristic of a given situation. Such knowledge is extremely useful since its possession makes possible avoiding the waste of human effort and wealth.

The administration of criminal justice in the United States annually consumes a staggering sum of dollars, and a considerable portion of this wealth is spent in the treatment of those convicted of crime. The treatment process which is thus supported is expected to achieve a variety of objectives. Treatment is supposed to reform, punish, and rehabilitate the law breaker; to deter others from engaging in criminal activities; and finally to protect the great mass of law-abiding citizens from those who would prey upon them. To achieve these goals several treatment instrumentalities have been created. Jails, training schools, reformatories and penitentiaries have been constructed. Probation and parole systems have been established. Behavior clinics are supported. Recreational, character building, and educational programs are financed. In short, a multitude of activities and institutions are maintained so that society may deal in some fashion with those who deviate from the accepted norms. These deviates constitute a heterogeneous group. Its membership includes the habitual offender and the first offender; males and females; the young and the old; the rich and the poor; the good and the depraved; and it is the difficult task of those entrusted to administer criminal justice to choose from amongst the various treatment possibilities the one which best fits the personality and circumstances of the single offender. How well this choice is made determines to a considerable extent the effectiveness of the treatment technique used as well as the achievement of those ends of treatment deemed desirable by society. Anything, therefore, that will aid in making a more intelligent choice of treatment techniques will render more effective the administration of criminal justice. Such aid is available and can be secured from the work of investigators who have developed methods for predicting the most probable response of offenders to various treatment programs.

The first attempts to apply prediction techniques to aspects of criminal justice were made by E. W. Burgess, Sheldon and Eleanor Glueck in 1928 and 1929 respectively.[1] In

[1] Bruce, A. A., Harno, A. J., Burgess, E. W., and Landesco, J., *Parole and The Indeterminate Sentence.* Illinois State Board of Parole, 1928. Glueck, Sheldon and Glueck, Eleanor T., *500 Criminal Careers,* New York, Alfred A. Knopf, 1930. (The Gluecks discussed the feasibility of applying prediction techniques

1923, however, Hornell Hart, suggested that certain kinds of data pertaining to offenders' background could be used in predicting their response to parole.[2] Hart's suggestion in addition to the pioneering work done by Burgess and the Gluecks served to stimulate a number of other investigators, and as a consequence a number of studies exploring the feasibility of predicting criminal conduct have been made.[3]

The research of these scholars is predicated on the assumption that human beings can be subjected to scientific study and that such a study will lead to the classification of their characteristics into stable categories. It is further assumed that persons with a number of similar characteristics when placed in similar situations will act on the average in similar ways. The prediction of human behavior involves nothing esoteric or mysterious. Persons everywhere consciously or unconsciously engage in predicting human behavior every day. Whenever a motorist takes his car out of the garage and ventures on a public highway he engages in predicting the behavior of others. A moment's reflection will serve to convince the most skeptical that prediction of human behavior is an everyday occurrence. To be sure, errors are made and in some instances these errors lead to disasters but on the whole most predictions coincide with that which actually occurs. If this were not so, social life as we know it would be impossible. Prediction studies of criminal behavior involves much of that which is found in the predictions of the everyday world. They differ however, in the manner in which past experiences

are recorded and utilized in predicting the future. In scientific prediction an attempt is made to classify data pertinent to human experiences into stable and reliable categories. Data thus classified are summarized in some fashion so as to render them manipulatable in forecasting behavior. The end result of these two steps are expectancy tables or indices in which are found that which will most probably happen when specific types of humans are confronted with a given situation. In what follows the methods developed to construct such expectancy tables or indices will be discussed.[4]

As indicated above, E. W. Burgess published the first study in which a prediction table applicable to criminal behavior appeared. Burgess sought those factors in the pre-parole life of inmates of three Illinois penal institutions which were associated with success and failure of parole. The official files of 3000 paroled men from the Illinois State Penitentiary at Joliet, the Southern Illinois Penitentiary at Menard and the Illinois State Reformatory at Pontiac (the files of 1000 paroled men from the institution were examined) were scrutinized for such pre-parole information as criminal record, type of offense, national and racial origins, work history, family status, residence, etc. A total of twenty-one such categories of information were used and each of the men was classified in accordance with the data contained in the official files. An examination of the data gathered revealed striking differences between men who succeeded and men who failed on parole. It was found that differences in conduct of offenders on parole were associated with contrasting patterns of pre-parole characteristics of offenders.

In order to determine how closely associated with parole behavior each of the pre-parole items was Burgess compared the average parole violation rate for each of the institutions studied with the violation rates for each of the pre-parole factor in which the offender was classified. These comparisons revealed those factors in the pre-parole life of the offender which tended to facilitate or impede his successful response to parole. The following illustration

---

to aspects of criminal justice in an article which appeared in the *Harvard Law Review,* 42:300–329, January, 1929).
[2] Hart, Hornell, Predicting Parole Success, *Journal of Criminal Law and Criminology,* 14: 405–413, 1923.
[3] For a list of these studies see, *The Prediction of Personal Adjustment,* Social Science Research Council, Bulletin No. 48, New York, 1941.
[4] The limitation placed upon the length of this article has made it impossible to discuss all of the studies made in the prediction of criminal conduct. The studies reviewed were selected because it is believed that they contribute contrasting techniques for predicting criminal behavior.

TABLE I [5]

PRE-INCARCERATION WORK RECORD IN RELATION TO PAROLE VIOLATION

Previous Work Record	Violation Rate by Institution		
	Pontiac	Menard	Joliet
All persons (offenders)......................	22.1%	26.5%	28.4%
No previous work record....................	28.0%	25.0%	44.4%
Record of casual work......................	27.5%	31.4%	30.3%
Record of irregular work....................	15.8%	21.3%	24.3%
Record of regular work.....................	8.8%	5.2%	12.2%

should serve to make clear how the association between pre-parole factors and conduct on parole was determined. In Table I will be found the several parole violation rates associated with the pre-incarceration work records of offenders. An inspection of the data presented in this Table indicates that offenders with good work records are considerably better parole risks than offenders with no previous or casual work records. Thus the percentage of parole violators among offenders classified as having had a record of regular work was only 8.8 (Pontiac group) whereas the percentage of parole violators among offenders classified as having had no previous work record was 28.0. Each of the classificatory items in the pre-parole life of the offender was analyzed in this fashion and from these analyses was derived knowledge of those pre-parole factors associated with success or failure of parole.

In order to employ this knowledge in the prediction of parole conduct it is necessary to summate the effect of each pre-parole factor upon the parole conduct of the offender. Burgess achieved the summation by assigning the value of one to all of the pre-parole factors accompanied by parole violation rates less than the average parole violation rate for each group of 1000

[5] Bruce, A. A., Harno, A. J., Burgess, E. W., Landesco, J., op. cit., p. 229, Table XVIII.
[6] For a complete description of the technique see: Glueck, S., and E. T., 500 Criminal Careers, Alfred A. Knopf, New York, 1930. Chapter XVIII.

offenders studied. A prediction score for each offender was thus obtained. These prediction scores with their respective violation rates constitute the expectancy table of parole violation.

The Burgess method for constructing prediction tables is simple and requires no complicated calculations. Its use, however, raises some important questions. As already noted all factors in the pre-parole life of the offender are given equal weights regardless of how closely they are related to parole conduct. An examination of the data presented by Burgess will show that some factors are more closely related to conduct on parole while others show practically no relation to such conduct. Obviously, some way should be found to measure and to weigh the varying degrees of association of pre-parole factors with conduct on parole. Furthermore, a method which utilizes all factors or as many factors as the information in the official parole files makes available cannot but result in numerous inter-correlations of factors unless steps are taken to eliminate these inter-correlations. Such a factor as "economic status" is related in some degree to such factors as "work history," "dependency," "employment of mother," "residence," etc.

The technique developed by the Gluecks[6] for constructing prediction tables renders possible the weighting of factors as well as the utilization of only those factors closely related to predicted behavior. How each factor in the life of an individual is associated with aspects of conduct to be predicted is revealed by the coefficient of mean square contingency. This statistical device enabled the Gluecks to select out from a multitude of factors those which were closely related to behavior. The weighting of factors was accomplished by adding together the percentage of total failures for each sub-category of the categories of factors selected in which each of the individuals had been classified. Thus in the construction of a prediction table designed to aid judges six factors (pre-reformatory industrial habits, seriousness and frequency of pre-formatory crime, arrests for crimes preceding the offense which resulted in sentence to the reformatory, pre-reformatory penal experience, economic responsibility, mental status) were selected from a list of over fifty factors and the individual's score is a summation of the unfavorable items in pre-reformatory experiences weighted in accordance with their respective percentage values.[7]

Although the use of this method for constructing expectancy tables makes possible the weighting of factors as well as dealing with a few supposedly unrelated factors closely associated with conduct to be predicted, it involves a considerable amount of work. The nature of the computations it requires may tend to frighten those who have had little or no training in elementary statistics. The Gluecks have tried to remedy

this by eliminating the necessity of calculating the coefficients of mean square contingency. This modification in their technique appears in *Five Hundred Delinquent Women*.[8] There the reader will find a much simpler way to determine the degree of association between factors and conduct. All that is involved is the calculation of the maximum percentage difference between a specific sub-class of a factor category and the percentage of all individuals whose behavior places them in such factor category. The following illustration should make this clear. In Table II are presented the results of probation for 896 juvenile delinquents in relation to their age when probation was granted. An inspection of this table will show that the maximum percentage difference between any sub-class and the percentage of all delinquents who succeeded on probation is 2.6, the difference between 71.2 per cent and 73.8 per cent. Of how much significance is a maximum difference of 2.6 per cent? This question is answered by the Gluecks through the coefficient of mean square contingency. Their computations showed that a maximum difference of 3 or less indicated no relation between the factor and conduct; a maximum difference of 4 to 7 indicated a slight association; a maximum difference of 7 to 15 signified an appreciable association; a maximum difference falling

TABLE II [9]

AGE OF 896 JUVENILE DELINQUENTS AND OUTCOME OF PROBATION

| | | Outcome of Probation | | | |
| | | Non-Violators | | Violators | |
Age of Delinquents	Total N	N	%	N	%
10 years or less	42	30	71.4	12	28.5
11–12 years	115	83	72.1	32	27.8
13–14 years	196	136	69.3	60	30.6
15–16 years	325	228	70.1	97	29.8
17 years or more	218	161	73.8	57	26.1
Totals............	896	638	71.2	258	28.7

[7] Glueck, S., and E. T., *op. cit.*, pp. 280–289.

[8] Alfred A. Knopf, New York, 1934. Chapter XVII.

[9] From Monachesi, Elio D., *Prediction Factors in Probation*, Hanover, 1932. Table IV, p. 29.

within 15 and 26 is designated as an index of considerable association; and finally a maximum difference of more than 26 indicates a close association of the factor to conduct.[10] This table of values makes the task of selecting significant predictive factors comparatively simple. Once the factors which are to be used in predicting conduct have been selected the next step again involves totaling the percentage values attached to each of the sub-classes of the factors in which the individual is classified. The use of this method for constructing prediction tables reduces the work to an inspection and summation of percentages.

Another prediction device was developed by Argow.[11] His prognostic instrument is called a criminal-liability index which is to be used to determine the probability of rehabilitation or non-rearrest of first offenders. Argow examined the case histories of 563 inmates of Connecticut jails and tabulated the personal and social data therein contained in 31 classification categories (six categories were added later but were not used in scoring offenders). These personal and social data were the materials from which the index was created. The method employed by Argow in the construction of the index involves the following steps. First, the calculation of the percentage of first offenders and recidivists for each classificatory item. Second, the calculation of the ratio between the percentage of first offenders and the percentage of recidivists in each of the factor categories (the percentage of recidivists was used as the base). Third, the assignment to the ratios of a value on a scale of ten. Items which received a value below ten were considered as conducive to rearrest whereas those assigned a value above ten were designated as contributive to non-rearrest. Fourth, the scoring of each offender by utilizing the

values determined in the last step. The offender's final score is the average of all of the values assigned to each of the classification items. Fifth, the calculation of the mean scores for first offenders, recidivists and for the entire group of cases studied. Sixth and last, the division of the offender's score by the mean score of the group. The quotient thus obtained is the criminal-liability index. Argow's index thus indicates the rehabilitative possibilities of each offender by a score which is the summation of the varying effects on behavior of personal and social factors found to differentiate first offenders and recidivists.

In 1936, Laune's *Predicting Criminality*[12] was published, and with it came a new approach to the prediction of parole conduct. Laune's work represents an attempt to improve parole prediction by utilizing data which had not been employed in previous studies. He believes that an offender's adjustment to life after incarceration is dependent upon his attitudes. These attitudes undoubtedly are modified to a considerable degree by the experiences gained by the offender in the penal institution. It is therefore, necessary, when a decision is made regarding the parolability of an offender to take into account his attitudes. The problem, as Laune conceives it, is to devise a method for periodically determining an offender's attitudes so that parole officials may be reasonably certain as to when an offender is ready for release from the institution. A clue to an offender's attitudes is found, Laune believes, in the "hunches" of persons intimately acquainted with the offender. He further believes that fellow-inmates would be especially qualified to render valuable opinions as to another offender's parolability. "If these estimates or 'hunches' are valid, it follows that an analysis of the prisoners by an official, proceeding on the same basis as that which prompts the inmate's prediction, would place the authorities in possession of an excellent instrument for prediction."[13] Having made these reasonable assumptions Laune first addressed himself to the task of determining if such valid inmates' estimates exist. He asked two qualified inmates of the Illinois State Penitentiary at Joliet to rate

[10] Glueck, S., and E. T., *op. cit.*, p. 287.
[11] Argow, Walter W., "A Criminal-Liability Index for Predicting Possibility of Rehabilitation." *Journal of Criminal Law and Criminology*, 26: 561–577. Nov. 1935.
[12] Laune, Ferris F., *Predicting Criminality*, Northwestern University Studies in Social Sciences, No. 1, Northwestern University, Evanston, 1936.
[13] Laune, Ferris F., *op. cit.*, p. 9.

independently the parolability of 150 fellow prisoners. The ratings (predictions) of inmates X and Y were compared and an r of .6236 $\pm$ .0345 indicated a considerable amount of similarity in the two series. The comparison demonstrated that the raters apparently were utilizing somewhat similar data in arriving at their ratings, and as a result it seemed reasonable to ascertain the factors that entered into the estimates. "The method employed for the isolation and identification of the unit characters underlying 'hunches' may be termed the 'discussion method'."[14] Each inmate investigator discussed with the other the reasons which led him to assign certain ratings to each of the 150 inmates whom they had been asked to rate. These discussions led to the isolation of 42 unit factors which had formed the basis of the rater's estimates. The list contained such items as: excessive interest in clothes, stupidity, timidity, industry, sex cravings, lack of love for relatives, emotional stability, love of comfort, and wanderlust. An examination of the 42 so-called basic factors resulted in the addition of twelve more factors so that the final list contained 54 items. The scores made by each inmate on the final list were correlated with the initial ratings and coefficients varying from $+$.55 to $+$.83 resulted. Intercorrelations of factor scorings of different investigators ranged from $+$.68 to $+$.78. These coefficients tend to give a degree of reliability to the scoring technique.

Laune next attempted to devise some method for detecting the presence or absence of essential factors in the life of an offender without the aid of other inmates' "hunches." A questionnaire was developed which contained questions designed to yield information upon the basic factors and the answers to which indicated the parolability of the offender. The final form of the questionnaire which Laune employs as the basis of his expectancy table is the result of a great deal of experimentation and testing. It is an instrument designed to get to those attitudes

which are associated with views of life which impede or facilitate "normal" adjustment to everyday problems.

In spite of what one may think about the worth of the prognostic instrument created by Laune most persons will agree that an individual's attitudes toward life determine aspects of that individual's conduct. Laune's assumption that the attitudes of an offender undergo modification in accordance with his experiences within a penal institution is also reasonable. Therefore, an instrument which records these attitudes and their modification would prove to be of value in the treatment of offenders and in the prediction of the individual offender's response to treatment.

In "Predicting Juvenile Delinquency,"[15] Weeks presents the results of a study designed to explore the possibilities of predicting juvenile delinquency as well as types of delinquent behavior. Weeks compared 420 delinquent males with 421 non-delinquent males and found that the two groups differed in fourteen categories of social background factors. The significance of these differences was determined by calculating the critical ratios for each of the fourteen categories of social background information. In order to utilize the data thus derived in the construction of a prognostic instrument Weeks employed three methods. The first consisted of giving one point to the individual for every item of information significantly associated with delinquency. The second scoring method involves the assignment of critical ratio values to all factors found significantly differentiating between delinquents and non-delinquents. Both the positive and negative critical ratio were used in this scoring method although the annoyances consequent to dealing with negative numbers was eliminated by the addition of 50 points to each score. The scores thus derived were weighted scores. In the third method Weeks employed only the positive critical ratios. All three methods for scoring gave results which were found to be quite similar although "there seems to be a closer association between the series of scores in which weights were assigned than there is between the series in which one is weighted and the other is not."[16]

---

[14] Laune, Ferris F., *op. cit.*, p. 19.
[15] Weeks, H. Ashley, "Predicting Juvenile Delinquency." *American Sociological Review*, 8: 40–46, February, 1943.
[16] Weeks, H. Ashley, *op. cit.*, p. 44.

Weeks' work not only demonstrates that it seems possible to predict delinquency but also indicates that it would be feasible to predict types of delinquency. His data show that "there are some very pronounced differences in the distribution of scores for different types of delinquencies. The differences between the means will give some indication of this. The mean score for the property offender is 59.1 ± 1.3, for misdemeanants 49.9 ± 2.6, and for the traffic offenders 49.1 ± 2.2; whereas the mean score for the runaways, truants, and incorrigibles combined is 54.1 ± 2.0." [17] These differences in the social backgrounds of various categories of delinquents are sufficiently significant to warrant the construction of prognostic instruments which indicate the probabilities of specific types of delinquencies.

There is little need to discuss at any great length the value of Weeks study. All who are engaged in work designed to prevent delinquency will recognize how much aid could be derived from an instrument which would predict with a reasonable degree of accuracy who among a group of children would eventually become delinquent. Such an instrument would make possible taking remedial steps long before adjustment difficulties had become critically chronic.

All of the studies reviewed above indicate that it is possible to create prognostic devices which could be used to administer various phases of treatment programs for criminal offenders. Regardless of the methods used in the construction of such devices the primary objective to be achieved by the employment of such prognostic instruments in practice is the control of human behavior through the utilization of knowledge of the individual to be controlled. How this knowledge of the individual can be made useful is demonstrated by the studies herein reviewed.

The next step which must be taken in this field of predicting criminal conduct involves an extensive comparison of predicted behavior with actual behavior.[18] This next step is necessary if we are ever to discover the effectiveness of the factors chosen for prediction purposes. Furthermore, it is only through such comparisons that we shall be able to evaluate the merits of the several prediction methods proposed. The fact that prognostic instruments can be devised is well established but how well such instruments predict actual behavior remains for the most part unknown. Such knowledge is of utmost importance.

ELIO D. MONACHESI
Professor of Sociology
University of Minnesota
Minneapolis, Minnesota

BIBLIOGRAPHY

Note: The following list of titles are recommended in addition to those cited in the text of this article.

Attorney General's Survey of Release Procedures, Volume IV, *Parole*, Washington, D. C., U. S. Department of Justice, 1939.
Glueck, Sheldon and Eleanor T., *One Thousand Juvenile Delinquents*, Cambridge, Harvard University Press, 1934.
———, *Later Criminal Careers*, New York: The Commonwealth Fund, 1937.
———, *Juvenile Delinquents Grown Up.* New York: The Commonwealth Fund, 1940.
———, *Criminal Careers in Retrospect.* New York: The Commonwealth Fund, 1943.
Monachesi, Elio D., *Prediction Factors in Probation*, Hanover, N. H., The Sociological Press, 1932.
Tibbitts, Clark, Success or Failure on Parole can be Predicted. *Journal of Criminal Law and Criminology*, 22: 11–50, 1931.
Vold, George B., *Prediction Methods and Parole*, Hanover, N. H., The Sociological Press, 1931.
Prediction Methods Applied to Problems of Classification Within Institutions, *Journal of Criminal Law and Criminology*, 26: 202–209, 1935.

[17] Weeks, H. Ashley, *op. cit.*, pp. 45–46.
[18] Some work in this field has been done. See: Vold, George B., "Do Parole Prediction Tables Work in Practice?" *Publications of the American Sociological Society.* 25: 136–138, 1931. Sanders, Barkev S., "Testing Parole Prediction." *Proceedings of the Sixty-Fifth Annual Congress of the American Prison Association*, Atlanta, 1935. pp. 222–232. Monachesi, Elio D., "A Comparison of Predicted with Actual Outcome of Probation," *American Sociological Review.* 10: 26–31, Feb., 1945.

PREVENTION OF CRIME. Any discussion of crime prevention should be prefaced with a definition of terms: What do we mean by "crime"; at what stage in the development of a criminal episode are we interested in "preventing" it?

Crime or delinquency has at least two definitions. The legal view, shared by zealous advocates of rigid law enforcement, that it is a wilful act or omission forbidden and punishable by law, is the more popular. This proceeds from the theory that people are creatures of free will. But there is also the socio-criminologic view, that crime is an act symptomatic of something deeper, namely, of a person's basic inability to meet situations in a socially acceptable fashion. This proceeds from the theory of determinism—that crime is the result of a definite chain of causation in harmony with scientific laws and processes.

Under the legal definition, swift, certain and severe punishment of known offenders for crime is considered by many to act as a deterrent of unknown others from committing crimes, thereby preventing those as yet uncommitted crimes. Under the socio-criminologic definition, however, it is felt that to prevent crime the total person must be dealt with on all the levels (economic, social and psychological) and in all the places (home, school and community) which are likely to condition his personality or color his conscious and unconscious reaction to the many new situations he is likely normally to encounter in an average life-span.

Public and voluntary agencies engaged in some aspect of crime and delinquency preventive work are concerned primarily with (1) preventing anti-social behavior at its source, or (2) preventing its repetition (recidivism). As the prevention of recidivism involves the utilization of techniques of treatment, intra- and extra-murally, of the known and apprehended offender (a subject which is covered elsewhere herein) the context in which this discussion is formulated has been confined to those preventive efforts which have to do with anti-social behavior at its source. This is prevention in its purest sense.

Most modern criminologists have adopted the position that crime prevention entails dealing with people while they are yet young, before behavior patterns become fixed. This is derived from the increasingly

validated concept that in the commission of nearly every crime two sets of factors seem to operate simultaneously: (1) those called predisposing, existing in the past of the offender; and (2) those called precipitating, existing in the contemporary life of the offender.

Behavior scientists hold that the former dominate or control the offender's response to the latter; that, except for the accidental or situational offender, unless a predisposition or vulnerability to some anti-sociality exists, ordinary environmental precipitants will not attract a person to the commission of crime. In this sense crime, which is symptomatic of an infection of the personality structure, bears resemblance to the manifestations of somatic ills. These scientists argue further that if the prevention of crime is unrelated to its causes, the mere improvement of those conditions which merely precipitate crime would be as ineffective for its prevention as the use of aspirin for the prevention of the symptom of recurring headaches which have a deeper organic cause.

But the advocates of strict law enforcement interpret preventing crime as calling also for, among other things, increased police protection, better lighting on streets, additional locks on doors and automobiles, and forbidding the carrying of firearms. There is recurrent insistence upon lengthier prison sentences and less frequent resort to probation and parole. Criminologists concede that some of these measures, and others of a similar character, may be essential for the control of many known hopelessly habitual offenders. At the same time it is strongly felt that such measures do not deter or prevent crime at the hands of those whose predispositions may inexorably drive them, or whose vulnerability may lead them, into antisocial behavior. These repressive measures are at best regarded as protective expedients possessing only limited value; certainly they are not preventive in the sense in which the subject is here considered.

For a few hundred years there have been fully as many varieties of methods of crime prevention as there have been theories concerning the causes of crime. What is done in the name of repression of potential or known offenders, or as crime prevention, clings fairly closely to what is thought popularly to be the cause of crime. The claims made for the effectiveness of so-called preventive enterprises describe a wide arc, ranging from the assertion that rigid discipline and religious instruction of children are panaceas, to the theory that as crime may result from infected teeth or malfunctioning glands, dentistry and endocrinology are therefore among the crime preventive sciences. The list of factors which are thought to contribute to crime causation is almost interminable. Heredity and environment have been blamed, as have biological structure, climate, race, nativity and a host of other seemingly unrelated items.

Though still subjected to considerable disagreement, perhaps the most recently investigated concept of causation has to do with the role of mental and nervous disorders, and of mental deficiency. In this area is to be found a rich storehouse of valuable literature. In recent years the chief contribution of the psychological disciplines to the relentless search for clues to the mystery of why offenders offend is the doctrine that behavior is specially and specifically motivated; that crime is a symptom, actionally expressed, of internal maladjustment and conflict.

However, for these purposes a distinction must be drawn between those conditions which, like the foregoing, appear in the total constellation of positive and negative factors considered by behavior scientists to be contributive in crime causation, and those which are thought by the general public to dominate the causes of crime. On the whole, what is done in communities in the name of prevention comports generally to what is believed to be effective by that portion of the public which supports the enterprises financially. The current beliefs of the public are found to control the direction and philosophy of most preventive activities. Those activities, generally, proceed from the popular notion that crime stems from lack of religious training, broken home situations, poverty, slums, parental neglect, inadequate recreation facilities, comics, motion pictures and radio.

The concern of this discussion is not now to speculate which category—that of the behavior scientists or that of the lay public—is the more inclusive or conclusive. In each offender's history ingredients from each list may be found to exist, in greater or less degree. It is by this time no longer open to reasonable argument that in each case of known antisocial behavior the offender has been exposed to a hierarchy of influences. Ever since the aspiring science of criminology abandoned the archaic doctrine of single-causation in favor of the more modern doctrine of multiple-causation, it has become increasingly evident that no two offenders are motivated by the same set of factors. The question frequently arises, therefore, as to where the emphasis in preventive work should be placed.

This perplexing question cannot be simply answered. The utilization of any weapons to attack crime at its source should, of course, be related to our knowledge regarding the specific mechanisms of crime causation. This is as true of crime as it is of somatic disease. And, just as in the field of medicine the prevention of disease involves some awareness of cause, so the prevention of crime would be achieved more enduringly if activities calculated to produce that result operated in terms of those conditions—general and specific—which produce the phenomenon of antisociality, or even tend to do so. Although infinitely more study is yet required before those conditions, and their mysterious interaction, are fully known, the view has been expressed that our ignorance on the subject of crime causation may be exaggerated by some behavior scientists, perhaps as markedly as the extent and quality of our knowledge has been overestimated by the lay public. Although there is healthy uncertainty in the area of specific causation, and although entrenched notions of those anchored to the rigid law-enforcement theory and of those wedded to the emotional-volitional doctrine are probably as widely separated today as they ever were, there has nevertheless been elicited a modicum of agreement regarding the intimate, surrounding circumstances which contribute to crime and delinquency. Without their fully intending or realizing it, a few basic postulates have been wrought from exponents of extremist points of view. Following is a summary of those items upon which a minimum of disagreement occurs:

(1) That in a very high proportion of instances, adult criminals are persons who have been seriously disturbed, maladjusted, or delinquent children;

(2) That at least a small percentage of children who become delinquent, are mentally defective;

(3) That a larger percentage of them suffer from personality distortion, mental tensions and conflicts, and faulty habits;

(4) That an appreciable proportion of them, come from either definitely broken homes, or those in which the parents, by virtue of their mental makeup or conduct, are hardly competent to carry out successfully the duties of parenthood in modern society;

(5) That many delinquent children are to be found among those who have left school at a too early age, and had achieved neither sufficient academic education nor training in honest and useful trades or occupations;

(6) That the highest proportion of delinquent children spring from communities in which processes of deterioration and disintegration are marked, manifesting themselves (a) in certain cultural standards different from and in conflict with the standards followed by the majority of persons; (b) in conditions of poverty, undernourishment, overcrowding and squalor; (c) in inadequate social provision for wholesome (or at least not anti-social) recreational outlets; (d) in the presence of centers of anti-social attitude and behavior, such as gambling joints, poolrooms, improperly supervised dance halls and movie theatres, and the like.

It becomes important here, therefore, to evaluate the progress that has been made in thwarting criminal careers at their source by means of enterprises organized often in pursuance of the popular intuitive beliefs and, to a lesser degree, in pursuance of the beliefs of behavior scientists. At this juncture a dilemma exists. There is no well-defined catalogue of crime preventive activities. Except for the police, children's courts,

and reformatory institutions, public and private agencies are not organized primarily for the prevention of crime and delinquency. That function is considered to be an adjunct to or a by-product of their other related purposes. Direct services, designed mainly as crime preventives, are few; the indirect services are many. But both are equally important; for both—provided they are coordinated—are calculated to achieve the aim of modern society to reduce to an irreducible minimum the quantum of nonconforming behavior in an average community's stream of life. That they may fail in substantial measure to realize that aim will be the burden of a later portion of this discussion.

Examine some fairly typical indirect preventive services. Because wholesome recreation can contribute a vital and significant force in the lives of everyone, projects devoted to providing such recreation for young people have justifiably had claimed for them the function of contributing to delinquency and crime prevention.

Similarly, the replacement of slums and blighted areas with good housing make our cities and towns more attractive places in which families may live and work. Because a decent respect for the physical environment becomes an important element in preparing young people for law-abiding life, claims may also justifiably be made that housing projects contribute to the prevention of crime and delinquency.

Schools, because of their constant and intimate contact with all children in an effort to educate on an academic level and legitimately to develop cultural values, occupy a strategic role in the prevention of delinquency and crime.

In contrast to the foregoing examples of indirect services is the child guidance clinic, a direct service. This species of agency exists in many communities under various names: Bureau, or Institute, for Juvenile Research, or Child Guidance Center. These clinics may be found in hospitals, school systems, or juvenile courts. Their avowed purpose is to operate on a referral basis to provide the required clinical facilities for the early recognition, understanding and treatment of

children who manifest various types of behavior or personality disorders. The tools
they possess to carry out this purpose are
medical, psychiatric, psychological and social in character.

Before considering whether any of the
foregoing and other (later cited) services
operate to good effect in preventing crime
today, it might be well to remember that
basic to the activities of agencies which
operate to furnish direct and indirect preventive services are, or should be, certain
fundamental prerequisites. Upon these every
preventive effort is more or less dependent
for its direction and maximum benefit:

(a) the community must have a procedure for measuring the actual quantum
of pre-delinquent behavior;

(b) the community must have in hand
an inventory of its needs and resources as
related to the problem of crime and delinquency;

(c) the community must promote understanding by the public of the nature and
extent of that problem and of the manner
in which it is proposed that the problem
should be handled;

(d) the community must relate the problem of delinquency and crime to the existence of its other economic and social problems so that the public may be given proper
perspective;

(e) the community must be prepared to
act promptly and fully to correct those
conditions which are found to contribute to
delinquency and crime, and to integrate and
coordinate the service programs of all agencies dealing with children and youth into
a larger plan in which their total needs are
being dealt with.

In the past the word "coordinate" has
been exposed to awkward usage in connection with crime prevention. Every social
work or correctional conference and publication is devoted, at least in part, to an
exploration of the need for what is called
coordinated action. But words and phrases
sometimes lose their real meaning when
there is mistaken reliance upon the device
of their mere repetition. So it is with the

word "coordinate." It is all too often un-
defined for the uninformed public, who are
expected to resort to intuition to realize
its implication. Where crime and delinquency prevention are concerned, the heart
of coordination is the early recognitiy of
behavior problems, and prompt referral for
diagnosis and treatment. If the person or
agency recognizing or diagnosing a pre-
delinquent is not capable of affording the
therapy (of whatever form) that is needed,
the burden must be freely shifted to another
appropriate agency armed with the tools
with which that therapy might be given. To
bring this about sometimes involves legislative reforms; on other occasions it involves
local agreement for case allocations, the acceptance and discharge of responsibility. This
applies equally to schools, clubs, organized
recreation centers, police departments and
health agencies, transient aid services and a
wide variety of casework agencies which operate in rural and urban communities. In short,
the efficacy of any plan of coordination involves the essential requirement that all persons in the community that come in contact
with children who possess actual or potential
problems should have their own function
clearly defined and know how to bring into
play all of the other community resources
to pour on a given individual or family.
Under this blanket of responsibilitiy are
clergymen, teachers, union leaders, extension
workers, personnel department workers,
librarians, physicians, nurses, lawyers, staffs
of housing projects, operators of amusement
establishments, scout leaders, and the key
leaders among the youth themselves. No one
is exempt from responsibility in any plan of
coordination if the maximum effect is to be
given to activities for crime prevention.

A proper understanding of the setting in
which direct and indirect crime preventive
services function requires an examination of
the working relationships which should—but
unfortunately often do not—exist among
public and private agencies, the more effectively to accomplish the task they have set
for themselves. For it is a melancholy fact,
upon which most students of crime prevention agree, that in the absence of coordinated effort crime preventive activities in

the United States manifest their most obvious and fatal defects.

If it is criminologically accurate to say—as is being asserted with increasing frequency —that the delinquent and criminal are victims of avoidable harmful influences, found in their economic, social and psychological histories, then the prevention of delinquency and crime at their source necessarily involves a coordinated attack upon those conditions. But the accent of the attack is at least as important as the attack itself. In determining where the accent should be, there are at least two schools of thought in criminology today. There are those who believe that the approach should be of the shotgun variety, with its widespread attack based on the hope that a few of the pellets will hit the target. Another approach, to complete the simile envisages the use of a gun that shoots bullets accurately, aimed at a very specific bulls-eye.

These two philosophies seem on the surface to be antagonistic. In truth, they are—or can be—harmonious. As delinquency is a composite problem, it follows logically that it can be investigated and dealt with effectively only by the broadest kind of community approach. Every existing or created resource, designed to diagnose and offer therapeutic help to children who have betrayed symptoms of anti-social patterns, must be pressed into service at the earliest possible moment. The home, school, neighborhood, friends—in short, the whole physical environment of a person—constitute at least a part of the influence from which the virus of infection was derived. When, in the process of diagnostic investigation, a specific area of vulnerability is revealed and found to control the distorted behavior pattern of a child, then those tools which are usable profitably for the amelioration of that specific condition may concentratedly be employed. Because this formula or blueprint for action makes good sense in evolving techniques for the solution of any physical or social problems, it likewise makes good sense in crime prevention.

Despite the need for action in concert, it has long been felt that one of the evils inherent in current attacks upon delinquency and crime is the tendency of agencies to operate solo. They do so by functioning independently of the facts gathered by any other agency. For example, studies reveal the shocking circumstance that in a large community, about 85% of the families, some of whose members were involved in cases of delinquency coming before its children's court, were known to social agencies for a considerable period before the child first appeared in court. The underlying family situation had usually reached a very serious stage before that first contact.

It is not at all atypical for a child first charged with delinquency to be arraigned in children's court following a period during which he is well-known to several agencies in his community. A family service agency may know of him through the family's application for food, clothing or rent relief. A hospital may know of him through an ill parent's treatment at its clinic. The school may know of him as the result of truancy. The police may know of him because of his less-than-delinquent pranks in the neighborhood in which he lives. The welfare department may know of him because at one time he was a neglected child.

Yet, through what amounts to a conspiracy of silence or its equivalent, each knowing public or private agency refrains from apprising another until a serious eruption takes place in the behavior of the child. Normal family relationships may be disrupted for an appreciable time before the child blossoms from readily remediable, mild disturbance into violent anti-social action. Yet, in many places such would be the un-coordinated plan of agency relationship in the community that that vital fact does not become the occasion for treatment or referral until the disturbance flowers into crime.

In a large eastern city during a recent year, there were 10,374 children whose behavior had been labeled as delinquent. Of this number almost 7,100 of them were known to the Children's Court, 1,737 were known to the Police Department, 260 were known to the Board of Education, 120 to official institutions, and 1,165 to unofficial (voluntary) agencies and institutions, including the mental hygiene clinic. In one section of the city the delinquents known to Children's Court represented nearly 57% of the total; in another section of the same city they represented 76%, and in still another area 98%.

This leads to grave consequences. The work of private organizations cannot be controlled by public agencies; nor can voluntary agencies be depended upon to carry any definite proportion of a community's case load on a continuing basis. Hence, many vulnerable children who become known to private agencies may never be referred for further treatment until the child's subsequent behavior becomes serious enough to justify court intervention.

In the last analysis, what is needed to bring delinquency prevention at its source to its maximum efficiency is the earliest possible recognition of storm signals, or symptoms, by persons who make intimate contact with children in the home, school and community. Those symptoms describe a wide arc: they range from habitual lying, petty stealing, sexual irregularities, abusiveness, destructiveness, and general aggressiveness, to such less overt but equally significant signs as excessive shyness, periodic depression, anxiety or disproportionate fears, mental retardation, stuttering, bed-wetting. Yet, though the principle of early recognition has been adopted as a basis for the operation of the network of public and private agencies claiming to perform functions in that field, their most palpable defect is their failure to do just that. And any delay in setting into motion the machinery for reducing the severity of these or other symptoms by probing for their causes inevitably results in more overtly explosive behavior.

A few instances of that failure—the most notable of them—might be cited at this juncture. In default of the proper parental guidance which children should receive, schools should be prepared to furnish that essential service. Yet the majority of public and parochial schools in the United States possess no child guidance facilities. Indeed, as of May, 1946, in the entire United States there were only 688 mental hygiene clinics, of which 285 were for children. There were only 16 community clinics for school children, and but 9 which were found in divisions of state or county governments. Such clinics as do exist are clustered in large urban centers, while vast areas of the country remain untouched by clinical services. Indeed, the U. S. Children's Bureau reported recently that fully four-fifths of the counties of the nation are without family or guidance services of any kind.

Moreover, the acute shortage of psychiatrists has resulted in the creation of inordinately large caseloads in existing agencies; only a small portion can receive intensive treatment. This situation, in turn, results in discouraging referrals to these clinics by agencies which do succeed in identifying vulnerable children. The shortage of competent professional staffs for this type of service is due not alone to a need for more trained personnel, but also to the pitifully inadequate salaries offered to candidates for staff positions.

It has often been claimed that recreation is an effective crime preventive. In this category are to be found such agencies as camps, playgrounds, scout and ranger organizations, clubs, settlement houses, and the like. They promote the teaching of outdoor and athletic skills, arts and crafts, and otherwise provide leisure-time service for elementary and high school boys and girls. Most of them operate on the group-work principle, but some render casework services. There can be no doubt concerning the values inherent in wholesome recreation for the normally endowed youngster, or even—under proper supervision—for one suffering from a readily remediable personality defect. However, whether crime prevention is its avowed goal or merely one of its by-products, there are two manifest faults in this type of agency. The first is that most of them operate on the basis of somewhat rigid standards of membership which serve—directly and indirectly—to exclude large numbers of vulnerable children from a sharing of their otherwise salutary activities. The second resides in the lack of sufficiently perceptive personnel, capable of recognizing and properly evaluating the asocial or antisocial symptoms which many children are constantly throwing off—in their play, their work, their relationship with contemporaries,

their responsiveness to authority, and, perhaps most importantly, their attitude toward
their parents. To overlook these reactions
of children, observable in the course of their
participation (or non-participation) in recreational activities, is to ignore significantly
revealing danger signs.

One cannot comment on the rôle of recreation as a factor in crime prevention without
also mentioning the tendency of its proponents to over-simplify its effect upon a
deeply disturbed youngster whose antisocial
drive is dominantly internal rather than external. What is needed, more frequently than
recreational authorities are prepared to concede, is a means by which his emotional
energy—the hostilities, anxieties, and feelings
of rejection, among others—may be released
or re-directed. Such a child, to be sure,
needs outlets for his physical energy, and
can derive a modicum of satisfaction from
developing creative and competitive skills.
But, when all of that has been done (if it
can be done) there still remains in most
disturbed children a huge reservoir of un-
discharged, dynamic, underlying forces which
—in the traditional recreational facility—
remain undiscovered and unattended.

Another example of ineffectiveness in delinquency and crime prevention is to be
found in the mistaken reliance of the community upon its police department. Most
people, as has already been remarked, consider strict law enforcement an infallible
deterrent to further crime. But some go
farther. In a number of large urban centers
the police have, commendably enough, organized coordinating councils and what are
euphemistically called crime prevention
bureaus. The former consist of groups of
voluntary social agencies which already exist
in the community, whose stated purpose as a
council is to integrate diagnosis with treatment; to insure the location of those children
in the area who are in need of group-work
or casework, and to extend to them the type
of therapeutic service they most urgently
require. Were there a technique for enforcing the service contribution of agencies,
supported by public gifts and tax-exempted,
the measure of success of coordinating councils might be greater than it is. An outstand-

ing defect in the coordinating-council concept resides in the purely voluntary nature
of each agency's participation in the council.
Each tends to preserve its administrative
autonomy. In large part, following the initial
enthusiasm of an agency in promoting the
plan of coordination, the agency withdraws
or—because of the selectivity of its rigid intake policy—withholds its services from the
council.

The crime prevention bureau, on the other
hand, operates in relation to known casual
delinquents in the area who, having committed isolated acts of mild delinquency, are
made the beneficiaries of an uncommonly
benign attitude on the part of the police.
In some places the complaint is merely
registered in the files of the juvenile aid unit;
it is not made the occasion for court intervention. Restitution may be required. In
short, the complaint is adjusted, the child
is warned not to repeat the offense, parents
are cautioned to watch the child more carefully and (save in one or two exceptional
bureaus) there the matter usually ends, until
the child is heard from again in the form of
more serious anti-social behavior. The palpable defect of such a system rests in the
fact that the child has thrown off a symptom
which requires evaluation at the hands of
someone more competent to make proper
diagnosis than a well-intentioned policeman;
and, as a corollary, requires an awareness of
and willingness to refer the child to a treatment unit which will strive to adjust the
child. More often than not a disservice is
done to the community and to a child whose
seemingly casual delinquency results merely
in an adjustment of the complaint. Not
alone may such limited attention to the
offense be misinterpreted by the child; a significant symptom may be overlooked which,
later, can ripen into a more deeply rooted
pattern of behavior.

While the rôle of recreation as a preventive technique has been overestimated, what
has been said should not be construed as
meaning that community services calculated
to provide the children of an area with constructive leisure-time activities cannot also be
instrumental in a delinquency-preventive
sense. However, they must be related to

rather than independent of an integrated scheme of prevention. They must be one means, of which there are others, to a planned end.

Moreover, we have learned that such projects should not be organized primarily with the view to crime prevention. To so label them is to stigmatize their participants and restrict their otherwise salutary and diversified utility. An outstanding example of how such a project may be carried on successfully is to be found in the "Back-of-the-Yards" movement in Chicago. It is not, as opposed to the concept of a coordinating-council, primarily a crime preventive, though that is bound to be one of its by-products. The virtue of this plan—the organization of all the people of an area into a congress to find a common vital interest in the improvement of the neighborhood—is that it includes all creeds and varieties of people, young and adult. The only qualification for membership is that the person—of whatever age—reside in the area. It is a genuine "grass roots" movement. Its program revolves around health, child welfare, employment and housing. One of the characteristics of this plan is that the natural qualities of leaders in groups of young people are exploited. To be sure, there are some children who, because of their limited capacities, need a modicum of supervision, but often supervision has been carried to the extreme of becoming destructive of the child's personality and faculty for self-management.

The ideal neighborhood council, concerned with all aspects of community life, starts with the people of the area. Inspiration for its creation comes close to being spontaneous; and when that happens the enthusiasm is constant and genuine. This movement is distinguished from a project imported into the neighborhood under outside auspices. To conflict groups especially the police symbolize despised law and order; professional social workers represent abhorred supervised activity. And if we would deal constructively with conflict groups we ought to acknowledge that both of these are anathema to the very local elements whom the council is trying to reach. The secret, then, resides in the source from which the inspiration comes. At most,

the seed of the idea may be planted by others; the nourishment must be local. In that concept one will find the magical ingredient for success in this type of venture.

While there is a necessity for indigenously-inspired projects, not every community is equipped to or capable of conceiving, planning and operating them. Therefore, some states have organized Youth Bureaus, or Divisions of Community Services to give advisory service and financial grants to local communities to assist them in effectuating preventive programs. The underlying purpose of the promotional activities of official agencies is to stimulate an awareness of the special needs of young people, and to furnish advisory field staffs to counties and municipalities. They assemble research material, and confer with local official and unofficial agencies which are directly and indirectly related to the problem of crime in the community. They publish literature intended for distribution among professional and lay people who devote some part of their time to every aspect of crime, its control, prevention and treatment. And they assist in the development of a wide range of useful legislation through which the aims of crime prevention can be advanced.

However, such projects as those just above described have severely limited usefulness. To the extent that they closely integrate and unify the direction of the facilities—educational, medical, and law enforcement—for dealing wtih the individual problems of the maladjusted child, they perform a unique function. To the extent that they submerge the individual child in a system of social regimentation which ignores his special and personal background, in the home, the school and in the community, they serve to perpetuate the gross errors of their predecessors.

In summation, therefore, prevention of crime at its source, at least to the extent of reducing crime to its irreducible minimum, will be possible only when we embrace the dimension of individualization, dominated by a spirit of systematically applied scientific inquiry and treatment.

Moreover, no program calculated to prevent crime and delinquency holds the promise of a substantial measure of success unless the personnel administering it is in all respects trained, skilled, and warmly sympathetic to the needs of children and adults. Every preventive enterprise must maintain a program that is at least as attractive to youngsters with antisocial potentialities as it is to those who might spontaneously refrain from antisocial behavior.

EDWIN J. LUKAS
Executive Director
Society for Prevention of Crime
New York City

BIBLIOGRAPHY

Beeley, Arthur L., *Social Planning for Social Control,* University of Utah Press, 1935.
Burt, Cyril, *The Young Delinquent,* London, 1938.
Carr, Lowell J., *Delinquency Control,* Harper, 1940.
Glueck, Sheldon, and Eleanor, editors, *Preventing Crime,* McGraw-Hill, 1936.
Healy, William, and Bronner, Augusta, *New Lights on Delinquency,* Yale University Press, 1936.
New York Society for the Prevention of Crime, news releases, 1942.
Thurston, Henry W., *Concerning Juvenile Delinquents,* Columbia University Press, 1942.

PRIMITIVE SOCIETY, LAW AND ORDER IN.

Every human society is characterized by the adjustments of individuals toward each other and to the several groups which compose the society. Without a large measure of stability in institutions and behavior social order cannot be maintained. What makes social order possible?

Certain beliefs and customs are handed down from one generation to another and are thus accumulated and preserved in the form of institutional life. Each society shares certain values. These common value elements are expressed through ritual, ceremonies, art, religion, family experiences, social relations, economic and political activity, literature, and song. In other words, the attitudes, beliefs, and sentiments which people share in common reinforce and reflect the institutional framework which shapes their lives.

Social order is preserved because individuals can rely upon others acting in accepted and accustomed ways. Most of the time the expectations of the behavior of others as well as the required conduct of the

individual in any given situation can be relied upon. We are all conditioned by our environment to feel and act in accustomed common ways.

Individuals, however, differ from each other in certain respects. The environment is not identical for each member, it is similar. In addition, each person is endowed with native physiological and biochemical differences which, in part, determine the way in which the individual will react to and with his environment. The reaction of individuals, therefore, will inevitably modify the values held in common by the group. People share common values but they do not feel and behave identically. They are individuals, not robots.

How far can an individual deviate from accustomed ways of behavior without threatening the social order of the group? The question has little meaning apart from the specific context of a given culture. There are various levels of social order and wide margins to permissive behavior in every culture. Some forms of order are more important for the stability of the group than others. Some ways of behavior are rigidly enforced, others are left to personal taste. The minimum requirements for social stability will depend upon the particular cultural situation. (Mobility and size of population, technological advance, homogeneity of groups, political, social, and economic organization, religious beliefs, and so on).

In every society there are deviating types who depart from the accepted and expected standards of conduct. They threaten the orderly activities of the community. How shall they be dealt with and by whom? The answers to these questions also depend upon the particular society in which the disorderly behavior takes place.

The matter will be made clear if we first examine Western European culture. Briefly stated, our institutions, such as the religious, moral, economic, political and family organizations shape our lives. We acquire common patterns of conduct, attitudes, feelings, beliefs, and goals which make it possible to live together in relative peace. Common habits, shared sentiments, and our horizons of expectations make for stable social relations.

In some respects, at times, we kick over the traces. If our deviating behavior is no serious threat to society the criminal law does not interfere although one's parents or friends or business associates may. If our conduct is a serious threat to or an act affecting the person or property of another, the criminal law is used as a means of controlling such social disorder.

It will be recognized that our non-legal institutions provide the habits of conduct which make social *order* possible while the function of the criminal law is primarily to prevent certain forms of social *disorder*.

Today, we are so accustomed to the administration of criminal justice, i.e., the police, the courts, criminal procedure, criminal codes, jails and prisons, that we fail to realize that our criminal law agencies are the agencies of control developed in Western European culture. In fact, our police systems are approximately one hundred years old, the prison system about one hundred and thirty years old. The first systematized criminal codes of Western Europe are the French penal codes of 1791 and 1810. The modern trial jury is of relatively recent origin. The basic principles of Western European criminal law that (1) there be no crime without a law previously defining the act as criminal (2) there can be no punishment without law and (3) there can be no punishment without a crime are also of recent origin.

What has happened is that *in modern times the judicial and legal institutions of Western European Society have been detached from other instruments of government and society.* Persons have been selected exclusively to administer these legal agencies.

The particular historical development of the administration of criminal justice in Western Europe is another story. The reasons which determined why certain violations of customary behavior, although anti-social, should not be considered criminal while other anti-social behavior should be defined as criminal is also another interesting story. What is of interest in the present discussion is that Western European society has set the limits, shifting though they are, between customs, morals, and criminal law.

Strictly speaking, crime is a legal category. *Until a society has reached the point where there is a differentiation between legal and other social agencies, criminal law does not really exist as a body of distinct rules, procedures, and definitions of crime.* A crime is an act of omission or commission prohibited by the criminal law and for which violation the law provides some penalty or sanction.

In the strict legal sense, therefore, it can be said that crime and the administration of criminal justice do not exist in most primitive communities. There are no clear-cut legally constituted authorities in primitive societies declaring definite acts criminal, providing rigid procedures for ascertaining through trial proceedings the guilt or innocence of the accused, and legally sanctioning punishment.

The criminal law, as we understand it, does not exist in primitive communities but social disorder, defined in the context of primitive community life, does occur. The problem of dealing with individuals who threaten group solidarity must be met. How shall they be dealt with and by whom? Different primitive groups have developed their own peculiar agencies. Just as modern Western European criminal law is a function of a complex Christian, urban, industrial civilization and reflects its great emphasis upon property rights, so the techniques of controlling social disorder in any primitive society reflect the institutions and values of the given society.

It should be strongly emphasized, however, that few primitive communities make sharp distinctions between morals, manners, customs and legal obligations. Even those customs which are considered "quasi-juridical" are tied up with very complex psychological, social, religious, and magical elements. In other words, certain infractions of cusomary behavior are singled out for public censure. The criterion of selection is not to be found in a *legal rule* or definition but in the meaning the violation of customary behavior has in the *entire* structure of community activity. Similarly, the proceedings to discover guilt or innocence and the disposition of the case do not rest upon a series of fixed legal rules. They are compounded out of the religious beliefs of the group, their social organization, public opinion, prestige, a sense of obligation, fear of ridicule or social ostracism or magic and the like. Different elements enter, depending upon the cultural configuration of the society.

We now turn to a few illustrations. Our purpose is not to present a detailed account of law and order in any society. For that a detailed analysis of the specific culture would be necessary. We wish merely to illustrate generally the nature of "law and order" in primitive society.

The Trobriand Islands, north-east of New Guinea, are inhabited by a Melanesian community. Their economic and social life is closely organized into working teams. Fellow-villagers are bound to each other by mutual obligations. Thus, while fishing, the members of the crew are assigned definite tasks and assume definite obligations to each other. In return for a definite service each member of the crew receives a share in the catch. A member may surrender his share to a relative or friend. After the trip the fishermen turn over part of the catch to other villagers waiting on the shore. In return they receive vegetables. The exchange is accompanied by an elaborate ritual. The partners to the exchange are obligated to trade. The obligations are mutual. If one partner gives, the other must reciprocate and without too much delay.

Similarly, canoe trips are made by villagers between the several islands, in which ornaments are exchanged between partners (the "Kula ring"). If a partner from one village receives a gift he is obligated to return another.

Again there is a great deal of exchange of food gifts. These exchanges are carefully measured. Ceremonies accompany the transaction. The Melanesians are extremely vain about the amount of food they receive and can display. They are anxious to have the reputation of being generous in their gifts.

Now suppose some individual would like to escape his obligations? What keeps him in line? He fears loss of prestige, loss of later gain, public opprobrium. The sense of obligation to his partner insures order in the different series of exchanges. Any native who

dared flagrantly to violate his obligations would find himself outside of the social group. Thus, the "law" governing these transactions is not to be found in the legal elements of a contract or in a criminal code, but in the accepted pattern of privilege and responsibility inherent in the Melanesian system of reciprocal obligations. It is impossible to separate the Trobriand rules into "civil and criminal" regulations. The need for mutual service and assistance which is recognized and felt by the community binds the villages together and provides orderly activities.

If we turn to the Tlingit Indians of the American Northwest Pacific coast we find an altogether different configuration which determinates the way disorder in community life is checked. The relation of the individual to his clan is the deciding factor. Theoretically no individual can commit crime or be the victim of a crime. It is the clan which is responsible or the clan which is harmed. If property is stolen, or someone is murdered, it is a reflection on the clan, not on the individual thief or murderer. For example, if A, a member of low rank in clan X, killed B, a member of high rank in clan Y, A would not be punished but a fellow clansman in clan X of equal rank to B would be put to death. If B, the victim, was of lower rank than A, a payment of goods from clan X would satisfy clan Y.

The Tlingit clan was the unit of society, not the individual. *Within* the clan murder, adultery, or theft carried no penalty. But incest, witchcraft or marriage with a slave on the part of a member brought a death sentence because the clan's honor was put to shame.

If members of different clans got into a dispute during a potlatch (an inter-clan contest in which one clan attempts to gain greater prestige by destroying or giving away valuable possessions, thus humiliating the other clan) a chief of high rank would step between the parties holding aloft an important clan crest (token). The honor of the clans was at stake and no one would think of desecrating the crest by fighting.

The penalty for assault by a non-clansman was payment in goods by the clan of the assailant. The sovereignty of the clan and individual status in rank are characteristic of the social organization and entire culture of the Tlingit (and the entire Northwest Pacific coast area). This controlling pattern of Tlingit society also operates in settling interclan disputes.

The Eskimo live mainly on sea mammals. Without sufficient sea food famine quickly sets in. Heat and light for their snow huts are obtained from the blubber of the sea mammals. Since, in Eskimo mythology, the sea mammals were created from the finger joints of the sea goddess Sedna, the Central Eskimo are eager to propitiate her and to maintain her good will. The Eskimo have many Tabus whose observance protect Sedna. Any violation of the Tabus would incur her displeasure. The Eskimo believe that their periods of famine and starvation are caused by violations of the Tabus which remain undiscovered and unannounced. Contact with the unknown culprit is contaminating. Eskimo custom requires that such violations of Tabus be publicly confessed so that the offender atones and no longer threatens others. When the food supply is extremely low, the natives suspect a violation of Tabus. They enlist the aid of the Shaman, the *angakok*. He discovers there has been a transgression and the offender is sought for so that public confession might be made. If no confession is obtained, the offender would be put to death.

The confession of the Eskimo is thus one of the chief means of social control to insure a plentiful supply of food, an essential base for orderly community life. The Eskimo confession is hardly to be compared with what we understand by the administration of justice. Nevertheless, it does perform a function similar to that of our criminal law.

The danger of generalizing regarding law and order in primitive society can be illustrated by turning to the Bantu tribes in Africa. There we find some kind of legal system. Local chieftains head the "courts." Before appealing to the chief, however, the families involved in the disorder attempt to reach an amicable settlement privately. If there is no adjustment the matter is taken to the courtyard of the local chief. If the chief cannot reach an agreement between the parties the matter is referred to a district chief. If he cannot settle the matter the case is referred to a still higher "appellate" court.

Some of the Bantu tribes make a distinction between cases for which property payment is the judgment, and others which must be punished, usually by death, and which cannot be settled by property payments.

At the courts both parties and witnesses are given hearings. The chief sits on a stone surrounded by the elders of the kraal. The plaintiff presents his case. He may talk for hours without interruption. There is a great deal of irrelevant rhetoric. The defendant then starts palavering. Witnesses give their evidence. The old men of the kraal may ask questions. The parties may decide at any time to argue privately about the issues, in which case, no official notice is taken of the discussion. "Court is adjourned," we would say. When the private argument is finished the chief, again, pays attention. After arguments are heard the chief makes known his decision according to the customs of the community.

Sometimes a defendant will interrupt the hearing to ask permission of the chieftain to challenge the plaintiff to consult a diviner as to the former's guilt. The chieftain sends a representative to report on the outcome of the divination. If the defendant is divined to be guilty he pays a customary fine to the plaintiff. If innocent, the plaintiff must present an ox to the defendant for the false charge.

Serious antisocial acts (such as murder, witchcraft, and incest) endanger the whole society because the gods of the group are vexed. The offender must be killed or banished to propitiate the spirits and restore order. In less serious acts the offender can purge himself through medicinal herbs or by prescribed sacrifices to the deities or by property compensation to the victim or through public confession during which he partakes of a ritual meal.

Property compensation is permitted in such offenses as assault, adultery, and theft. The fine usually takes the form of surrendering a sheep, a goat, or cattle. The amount

OF CRIMINOLOGY

The Prison Chaplain

of the fine varies according to the rank of the offender and the gravity of the offense. (Cattle, which are the principal form of fines, play a very important rôle in the social and economic life of these natives.)

Village and district courts are also found among West African tribes and the natives of Uganda. The differentiation between custom and law as we understand "law" is not sharp. The proceedings to determine guilt are akin to the "courts" of the Barbarian tribes during the fifth to seventh centuries.

It is probable that were we able fully to comprehend the devices for preventing disorder among many African peoples we would discover that they are as complex as the legal institutions of Western Europe. In fact, just because so many different aspects of the several African cultures (religion, magic, custom, economic activity, ceremony, rank, status) are part of the way in which disputes are resolved, their devices are probably more complex than our own juridical arrangements and, in light of their own culture, just as logical.

Apart from African culture areas, the development of quasi-juridical agencies of controlling social disorder are generally not found among earlier non-European civilizations. Nevertheless, they have developed controls of one kind or another, such as have been described. Every society will inevitably number among its members some deviating individuals. The offender who deviates, nevertheless, shares the values and sentiments of his group. A sense of guilt will accompany a violation of group mores. Public opinion, religious belief, fear of magic, a sense of obligation, an awareness of losing the support of others upon whom one must depend, fear of social ostracism—such factors make for order in primitive society. Unlike Western European society with its highly differentiated legal institutions, the values of primitive peoples which make for order also prevent disorder, thus performing the functions of criminal law.

NATHANIEL CANTOR
Professor of Sociology
University of Buffalo
Buffalo, New York

BIBLIOGRAPHY

Dundas, C., Native Laws of Some Bantu Tribes of East Africa, *Jour. Anth. Inst.,* Volume 51, uu. 217–278.
———, The Organization and Laws of Some Bantu Tribes, *Jour. Anth. Inst.,* Volume 45, pp. 234–306.
Hogbin, H. I., *Law and Order in Polynesia: A Study of Primitive Legal Institutions,* 1934.
Lowie, R. H., *Primitive Society,* 1920.
Malinowski, Bronislaw, *Crime and Custom in Savage Society,* 1926.
Oberg, K., Crime and Punishment in Tlingit Society, *Amer. Anth., N. S.,* Volume 36, pp. 146–154.
Thomas, W. I., *Primitive Behavior,* Chapter XV, 1937.

THE PRISON CHAPLAIN. Evaluation of the chaplain's place in a prison program is a variable. Where the old idea persists that prison is a place of punishment, there the chaplain can be little more than a morale builder, trying to instill in his charges a faith in God which will help them bear their burdens and assist them in maintaining a good prison record. In the newer penology, by which the prison is operated as a place of rehabilitation, the chaplain has an important function and a wide field of service. Here he can use religion as a therapy. In cooperation with other phases of the rebuilding program, such as education, medical care, psychology, and trade training, religion becomes a means by which maladjusted lives can be made whole.

The work of the chaplain can indeed become the most valuable factor in a rebuilding program. Since new attitudes and new motives are usually dependent upon a change of heart, they can be achieved only by establishing a right relationship to God, which in turn will create a right relationship with men. In this program the chaplain will use every technique available for his purpose. Approach to the prisoner's problems will be made through worship services, religious education, directed reading, personal interviews, contacts with family and friends, and with the home church where such a relationship exists.

As a member of the prison staff, the chaplain can contribute valuable assistance to the total understanding of the individual prisoner. Prisoners will often confide information to the chaplain which they will not divulge to other staff members. By tradition, such confidences must be honored by the chaplain and cannot under any circumstances become a part of the case record. However, recommendations of the chaplain for classification and treatment purposes, will be largely dependent upon such personal knowledge and can assist the staff in evaluating progress of the treatment program.

Many prominent physicians attest to the value of prayer as a therapeutic. The patient who has a firm faith in Divine Providence stands a better chance of recovery than the patient who has no such faith. Doctor C. C. Jung, distinguished European psychologist, writes, after thirty year's practice, "Among all my patients in the second half of life, that is to say, past thirty-five, there has not been one whose problem in the last resort has not been that of finding a religious outlook on life. It is safe to say that every one of them fell ill because he or she had lost that which the living religions of every age have given to their followers, and not one of them has been really healed who did not regain his religious outlook." The same truth is experienced in cases of moral sickness and nervous disorders. Religion awakens in man a sense of guilt and wrongness. It opens the way by which he searches his heart and discovers his tensions and weaknesses. But it does not stop there. It offers release through confession of his sins and by the assurance that God is concerned with all of life and is ready to forgive and strengthen. It stresses the sacredness of all life. It seeks to put man right with God and his fellowmen.

The Bible is the Chaplain's chief working tool. His greatest responsibility lies in making the message of this Book real. Possibly only a very small percentage of men who enter prison have ever read the Bible in the free world. While it continues to be the world's best seller year after year, it is likewise the least read and used book. Bible illiteracy, even among college and university graduates, is alarming. But the usual statistics are reversed in prison. Here the Bible is read to a much greater extent than out in the world. If the chaplain can do nothing more than to encourage each inmate to accept the gift of a Bible and to use it in the privacy of his own cell, he has accomplished something of value. He will preach from this Book in his Sunday Chapel hours, interpret this Book in his week-day Bible Class groups and religious forums, and apply this Book to the individual lives of prisoners in his personal interviews.

The Chaplain's Vocation. The chaplain must have a very live sense of vocation. He must have the assurance that he has been called of God for the work that is his. He stands in the prison therefore, as the representative and spokesman of God and not of man. The message he gives must be God's message for man. He must know that while God hates sin, He does not hate the sinner. Therefore, the chaplain must receive all men in the spirit of compassion. While he must be a realist, not overlooking the sin that destroys men's lives, he must know that it is not the will of God that one should be lost but that all might come to have life. While rehabilitation may be the general aim of the prison program, the chaplain has a much higher one, the rebirth of the individual in the Kingdom of God.

The Chaplain's Appointment. How does one become a prison chaplain? By whom is he appointed or employed? The answers to these questions are rather difficult inasmuch as methods of appointment will probably vary in the different States. In most States chaplains receive their appointment by the Board of Prison Managers or Administrators. This is usually upon the recommendation of the Bishop of the Diocese in the case of Catholic Chaplains, and by recommendation of State or city Councils of Churches in cases of Protestant Chaplains. Federal Chaplains are appointed by the Commission on Prison Chaplains of the Federal Council of Churches of Christ in America. In prisons where no full-time chaplaincies are provided, interested local church groups supply religious services. Agencies such as The Salvation Army also are known for their prison work and their provision for visiting chaplains and religious advisers.

The Chaplain's Training. Most chaplains will readily admit their chief handicap to be lack of specialized training. While chaplains of most large prisons have received the required training of their Church and denomination which usually consists of four years collegiate and three years post-graduate study in the Theological Seminary, they will readily acknowledge that this job of being a prison padre is different. Here they deal chiefly with men and women who lack spiritual background, and who have had very little if any, religious training in either home or church. Here in prison the atmosphere is often unfriendly or antagonistic to religion. Many inmates hesitate to accept religion because of the ridicule of godless fellow-prisoners, or because they do not wish to have prison officials think they are using religion as a means to curry favor or to gain their release. Having never turned to God in the free world, many others wish to remain consistent. Again, there are others who became estranged to religion because of evident insincerity or actual hypocrisy of nominal church members, or because religion was forced upon them by harsh methods by cruel or tactless parents or guardians. And we must not forget too, that many men who come into prison associate whatever injustice or cruelty they may have experienced with the Church. The Church is, in their eyes, a part of that same system which brought them to this unhappy state. To deal with this kind of thinking requires an entirely different approach and treatment from that which the average minister uses in his parish. Here in prison religious platitudes cannot thrive. The approach to God and religious values must be simplified and made very real. Above all, the chaplain must love people, unlovely people, people with warped ideas, people who are antagonistic. He must be a master of patience and a student of human nature. He must be able to put himself into the place of the man who sits across the desk from him in an interview, while never once lowering his own standards of righteousness. This job, the chaplain soon learns, is a specialized ministry which requires skills, knowledge and insights which are not usually taught in theological schools and, which for the most part, must come to him as an endowment of Providence and usually through years of experience. Chaplains generally would accept any training opportunity which would fit them for greater efficiency and power in the difficult job they have undertaken.

The Council for Clinical Training is perhaps the only agency of its kind which provides a specialized post graduate training for prison chaplains. Chaplains of Federal Prisons are required to take this training which provides internships in general and mental hospitals, training schools and prisons. Director of the Council is the Rev. Frederick C. Kuether, 2 East 103rd Street, New York City 10, N. Y.

The National Chaplain's Association, an affiliate of the American Prison Association, offers an organized program for its membership. This Association meets annually with the American Prison Congress in a three-day conference in which problems are discussed and programs are compared for mutual helpfulness.

Objectives of the National Chaplain's Association are summed up in its Declaration of Principles: "In recognition of the vital importance of religious instruction, and of the right of all men, regardless of condition, to worship in accordance with the teachings of their chosen faith, the National Chaplain's Association adopts and urges these standards of religious work in penal and correctional institutions:

1. Chaplains, fully qualified and approved by established religious bodies, shall be appointed in every institution.
2. The Chaplain shall be a responsible member of the administrative staff, and accorded all professional privileges.
3. Appropriate facilities and equipment for the conduct of services of worship and other religious ministrations shall be provided.
4. The right of all inmates to attend services of worship, as arranged and determined by the chaplains, shall be recognized, and their attendance encouraged.
5. The right of all inmates to free counsel with their spiritual advisers shall be respected.
6. The right of all inmates to religious instruction shall be acknowledged, and suitable opportunities for such instruction be afforded.

7. The chaplain shall encourage the interest of religious and socially minded groups, and enlist their active support in the continued spiritual care and development of the inmate upon release.

Since officers of this association are elected annually, it is suggested that anyone desiring to contact the association may write to the secretary of the American Prison Association, 135 East 15th Street, New York 3, N. Y.

Federal Prison Chaplains are organized as an Association and also meet annually for conference. Other chaplain's associations are organized on a State-wide basis. All these groups have value in providing fellowship among men who are serving similar fields of work and in constantly encouraging improved methods and techniques.

THE CHAPLAIN'S RELATIONSHIP TO THE PRISONER

I. *Religious Services.* The prisoners whom the chaplain will reach by way of the chapel services will probably be only a fraction of the prison population. This is easily explained from a study of the prisoners' backgrounds. Most men and women who are so unfortunate as to be sentenced to incarceration have not been church people. Rarely do active church members come into the toils of the law. The usual story is that the prisoner may have been baptized in his infancy, attended religious instruction or Sunday School in early childhood, and possibly went to church services for a time with his parents. But this interest lapsed in the early teen years. A large percentage of inmates will report that they never became active members of any church, or if they did go to church, it was only upon special occasions such as Christmas or Easter.

These facts will be a challenge to the chaplain, for it will be difficult to interpret a new way of life to those who will not come within his hearing. Religion must be an elective. By its very nature it cannot be forced upon anyone. Its influence and value would be void unless it were voluntarily accepted. Even where chapel attendance is above average, there is usually the lack of program such as is found in churches outside the walls. In order to provide a program by which prisoners can be trained in church relationships and in which they may have opportunity to assume definite responsibilities, the writer ventured to organize a congregation among the Protestant men of Western State Penitentiary at Pittsburgh, Pennsylvania in October, 1942. Believing this to be one of the first of such programs to be organized in prison, and in the hope that the plan may be tried by other chaplains, a brief outline will be given of this program.

The Church of the Good Samaritan. The story really begins with the dedication of a chapel within the prison walls in June, 1942. Webster's Collegiate Dictionary defines the word chaplain as "a clergyman who has a chapel." By that definition there would probably be few who could call themselves by that title. Every prison has religious services of some kind, whether they be conducted by a resident chaplain or by visiting groups from churches of the community. But such services are generally conducted in the mess hall, or the auditorium where motion pictures and shows are presented, where band rehearsals are conducted, and where the general traffic of the prison constantly flows. American penology has been pathetically backward in recognizing the necessity for a place set apart entirely for religious purposes and dedicated wholly to the worship of God. In 1939 the first church within prison walls was dedicated at Clinton Prison, Dannemora, New York, through the grand work of Rev. A. R. Hyland, Catholic Chaplain. The Chapel of the Good Thief, dedicated to Saint Dismas, Patron Saint of Prisoners, was built by prison labor with funds contributed by interested individuals everywhere, and is a beautiful Gothic structure which would be welcome in any community.

In June, 1942, Father Hyland was the speaker for the dedication of the Church of the Good Samaritan at Western Penitentiary, Pittsburgh, Pa. A former hospital building was utilized and remodeled by the prisoners under supervision of the two chaplains. By telling the story of the needs of this prison chapel to individuals and to church and community groups, the chaplains secured funds with which the entire furnishings were purchased. There are thirty-three beautiful stained-glass windows in colors not usually known to prison—red, blue, lavender, green. Comfortable pews provide seating for three hundred. A completely furnished chancel, with choir stalls for two choirs. Central and the focal point of interest is the white marble altar. Off the vestibule at the front each chaplain has his office for private interviews and conferences. This has been a House of Prayer, a refuge in hours of loneliness, a meeting place for man with his God. Every prison should be so equipped. Even though institutional budgets cannot provide it, any prison administrator and his chaplains can solve the problem, once they realize the possibilities of such a chapel. There are always people in the churches who can be interested to support a program if it is worthy to be supported.

The Congregation is, of course, more important than the Chapel. When we first suggested our plan to organize a congregation among the Protestant men in prison, many friends, ministers and prison officials were skeptical. "You can't give any authority— even in minor matters—to inmates." "It won't work. They will come for a while because it's a novelty, but they won't stick to it. It will soon die." But others said, "It seems reasonable that if the congregational plan works out in the world, it ought to work in prison." So we tried it. In October, 1942, we organized the Church of the Good Samaritan with 126 charter members. For almost a year before this date we had conducted many group meetings to discuss the proposed congregation. A constitution and by-laws had been carefully drawn up which we called, "A Plan of Organization." A Council of twelve men had been appointed to serve temporarily until the first election could be held. Five years of trial prove that the plan works. More than 1500 men have become members in that time. Many of these have been released from prison or transferred to the minimum security prison. Our present membership tops six hundred, which represents 90% of the non-Catholic inmates.

The Congregational Plan has given the inmates a chance to participate. It is demo-cratic. The congregation meets four times a year to elect six members to the council, each to serve six-month terms. Groups are thus staggered so that there are always some experienced men on the council. Terms are short to permit more men to share the privilege of serving on the council. Council meetings are held regularly once a month and sometimes in special session. The Chaplain sits in at all meetings and acts as adviser. Council elects its own officers, appoints ushers, chancel and membership committees, and plans for the program of the chapel. New members are received into the congregation at any chapel service after having been interviewed by the chaplain. Each member is given an attractive membership certificate. The growth in membership can be attributed directly to the men themselves. A Membership and Attendance Committee is constantly at work to invite new members and to encourage the backsliders to "get on the ball." Attendance has been doubled and interest in the chapel services has been fairly constant. The Chaplain now has many assistants. Council members know prison life better than the chaplain can know it, and they are ready to advise what will work and what will not be popular.

It is a further aim of this congregational plan to associate men with churches of their own choice at the time of their release, so that the good beginnings which have been made in prison can be continued. It is highly important that the gain accomplished in individual lives be conserved and further developed if the prison program is really to have value. Insofar as it is possible, the chaplain tries to keep contact with these men, at least by correspondence and by occasional general letters reporting the progress of their church within the walls. A quote from one letter received from a former member will express the general attitude of many who are released to the world from this congregation: "I will never forget the Church of the Good Samaritan. I shall never let go the things I found there. This is the only nostalgic memory I have of that place. I wish that all the men could find in that sanctuary all that I did. There—it is as an oasis in the desert, offering the only haven where one can find peace and inner contentment. If all men had a sense of appreciation, then they could find an awareness of what you, as an emissary of God, are giving them." Such a letter should encourage any chaplain to give his best.

The ideal situation would, of course, provide a separate chapel for each of the three major faiths, Protestant, Catholic and Jewish. Each has different requirements for its worship of God. Each has different symbols which ought to be displayed. Each could operate its program simultaneously without conflict with the other groups. Misunderstandings could often be avoided. But inasmuch as most prisons are indeed fortunate to have one chapel, its use should be shared equally so far as possible. In fact, there is a value in sharing the same chapel. Inmates often bring prejudices with them from the outside world. Within prison walls these prejudices sometimes grow to alarming proportions. If men are to live together in harmony, they should learn to worship together the One God, and to hope together for the One Heaven. Proper cooperation of the chaplains, each respecting and honoring the other's approach to religion, will prove a good example for the prison population.

II. *Religious Education.* Another important function of the chaplain is teaching. Religious education is an important factor in the religious program. The prison population is usually a cross-section of community life. It will usually be found to be religiously illiterate. Whatever religious ideas the inmate may have, they will probably be only a residue of his childhood training—if any. He will probably not have advanced to adult knowledge and apprehension because he has neglected to further his spiritual life. His failure in life, as evidenced by his incarceration, may be a direct result of his failure to know or to appreciate the laws of God as they are related to his dealings with his fellowmen. Warped attitudes and wrong motives may have sprung from his misconceptions of God. Successful readjustment to community life may therefore be directly dependent upon his knowing God and the laws which govern life. This is the challenge of religious education. Each

prison chaplain must adapt his program to the prison schedule and the opportunities made available. It will be well to drop the much-used titles—Sunday School, Religious Education, etc. Many men think that Sunday School is for kids. Many do not want to be educated. Better call it Bible Discussion Group, Religious Forum, Bible Forum. The Bible is still the most interesting Book. Its stories and its lessons can be presented in popular ways so that men will respond to invitations to share in such discussion groups. There is a wealth of teaching material here that will never be exhausted. Programs can be changed from season to season to maintain interest. Such series as these are suggested: Books of the Old Testament, Books of the New Testament, Bible Heroes, Men Who Failed, Men Who Made Good, Parables of the Bible, Great Teachings of the Old and New Testament, The Life of Christ, The History of the Church as related in Acts and the Epistles, Men Who Found God. These series all suggested a popular presentation by the chaplain or guest teacher. Small groups are better adapted to a chapter-by-chapter study of Bible books. Such Bible discussion groups will reveal to the chaplain those men who have developed wrong conceptions about God and will give him opportunity to help them in his private interviews with them.

III. *Personal Interviews.* Possibly the most important relationship of the chaplain to the prisoner is in the personal interview. If the chaplain loves his God and his fellowmen, inmates will come to him freely for advice and counsel in their problems. In these personal contact with the inmates, whether it be at his desk in the chaplain's office, in the cell block, the hospital or the isolation cell, this is the chaplain's best opportunity to learn to know his men and to deal directly and honestly with their problems.

In the initial interview he will get acquainted with the new arrival and will interpret the prison program to him. Here he can provide counsel for the period of adjustment to this new and strange environment, and can provide counsel to encourage men to make proper use of their time by sharing

OF CRIMINOLOGY

The Prison Chaplain

in whatever opportunities for personal advancement the prison program affords.

Again, he will see the inmate just before his release from the institution, when he will have opportunity to advise him for his readjustment to the free world, and to encourage him to be faithful to whatever good he has accomplished for this new beginning.

But between the time of admission and the day of release, the chaplain will have hundreds of opportunities to meet the inmate, and each interview should strengthen the confidence and assurance of the inmate for the way of life which the chaplain represents by his preaching and his life. Every type of problem will be laid on the chaplain's heart. There will be family problems—concern for the welfare of his parents, worry about an estranged wife, or for proper material assistance to tide his family over the time of his imprisonment. Often there will be pleas in behalf of the inmate's children who are wayward or neglected. Parole problems will be presented. Men who have served long sentences have lost contact with the world outside. Where can they go at the time of their release? Can the chaplain suggest someone who will assist them with employment? Sometimes the inmate will bring his own personal worries. At the breaking point, he must talk with someone. Or, after years of burden hearing, he finally yields the truth about his life and wants to pour out to someone. The chaplain is the right man for such confidence. He must listen patiently. The most important part of any interview is listening. The chaplain will not be able to solve all the problems presented to him. Some problems will be outside his jurisdiction, but for these he can usually direct the inmate to the proper source of help. Some problems can be solved or at least lightened. Here the chaplain will cheerfully assist. Let me just say from personal experience that whatever you may promise to do—do it—and do it cheerfully and gladly. Only such service as is rendered with the whole heart can bring joy to the doer.

The Chaplain's Relationship to His Fellow Chaplains. Most large prisons will have, not one but three or more chaplains on the staff, Catholic, Protestant and Jewish. It is of

first importance that these should not be competitors, but co-workers in a most important job. There need be no conflict in their spheres of duty. It may seem to be out of place to even suggest that conflicts may occur. Yet it has happened that the disgruntled inmates of one group will apply to the chaplain of another group when they do not seem to gain their desires. In such cases the chaplains concerned should confer and work in harmony for the best interests of the inmate.

We are gradually overcoming prejudice and ill-will between the various church and social groups in the free world by interchange of pulpits and by participation in the Brotherhood program. We are learning that each individual has his place in the kingdom of God and that true religion nowhere permits hatred. Love to God and love for our fellowmen is the first and also the most important of the commandments. In the prison it is even more important that such cooperation be achieved between the various groups represented in its population. Here men live at close quarters and occasions for offense are more numerous. Here trifles can easily be enlarged and magnified until they can become major problems. The cooperation and the example of the chaplains can achieve a unity of purpose which will be valuable to the entire life of the prison.

Chaplain Rudolph I. Coffee of California State Prison at San Quentin has proposed a program for Interfaith Cooperation which deserves trial. (The Prison Chaplain, June 1947.) He suggests three approaches by which cooperation between the three major faith may be encouraged and fostered by the chaplains. I. By Inter-faith Meetings on Secular holidays such as Memorial Day, July Fourth, Thanksgiving Day. In such meetings the heroes of our country can be found among all faiths—serving a common cause. II. By Inter-faith Courtesies on Religious Days. He suggests that on Easter Day and Christmas the Jewish Chaplain may send or bear greetings from his group to the Catholic and Protestant chaplains. At Passover and Jewish New Year this courtesy can be returned. It is also suggested that each chaplain can explain the history of the ceremonials of his group to the other groups. Such visits would foster better understanding. III. By Inter-faith assemblies extolling great Americans. We may add also such opportunities as the School Commencement and Baccalaureate programs, the Educational Forum in which speakers are secured from the three faiths.

The same need as cited above is also evident in an effort to overcome racial prejudice. The personal attitude of the chaplains toward a cooperative program can be of great value. Certainly, we need to know each other better, and to try to build a greater appreciation for the viewpoints of those who believe differently from ourselves.

The Chaplain's Relationship to Other Staff Members. A similar need for cooperation is apparent in the chaplain's relationship with other members of the prison staff, administrative officers, and with all who have any contact with the inmate.

The chaplain is usually a member of the classification committee or sits as one of the members of the committee on parole applications. Here he can not only contribute to a better total understanding of the inmate, but he can also profit by the knowledge which other staff members may have of the inmate.

The chaplain will have opportunity to encourage the inmate to take the fullest possible advantage of the prison program. His word will often encourage men to apply for the courses offered in the educational program, or for correspondence courses when these are available. He can set men thinking about their future and suggest their participation in some form of trade-training to equip them for better living. In return, the doctor will often send inmates to the chaplain for spiritual guidance in their illness, or the psychologist will suggest to inmates that they see the chaplain.

The chaplain cannot interfere in areas which are outside his responsibility. He cannot, for instance, interfere with the disciplinary program of the institution. Yet it is often possible for him to mediate the inmate's cause in cases where he has intimate knowledge which will contribute to a better understanding of the inmate and his actions.

The Chaplain's Relationship to the Community. The chaplain's opportunity for service does not end at the prison doors. He can perform a valuable service by interpreting to the community, both the prisoner and the prison program.

Society in general has definitely warped ideas about prison. People think of a rock pile or the lash when you say prison. Even the honorable judges often sentence men to "years of hard labor" and send them to a prison where no such labor has existed for many decades. Ideas about inmates are likewise very unreal. Questions addressed to the chaplain by outside groups often indicate their lack of knowledge of prison life. "Do you carry a gun for self-protection?" "Do you always have guards with you when you meet with the prisoners?" People think of the men who live within prison walls, if indeed they ever think of them at all, as hardened beyond repair, as desperate and dangerous individuals. They get these ideas from the front-page stories of the newspapers, from fantastic radio serials, and from magazine gangster stories. While their idea about prisoners may be correct in some cases, it is not true of the large number of prison inmates. But it is easy to understand why parolees and discharged prisoners cannot find employment or a place to live in a world which knows so little about them and which mistrusts and fears them.

Even a decade ago "prison visiting" was a popular pastime. People went slumming to see what these queer men in prison might look like. Fortunately, most of that has been eliminated. Prison is not a place for the curious sight-seer. Prisoners should not be placed on exhibit if they are expected to maintain even a small degree of self-respect, and if they are expected to build their lives for a better future. Yet society has a right to know something about the institutions which are supported by their tax dollars. Penological progress can be furthered only by an intelligent public opinion. Progressive prison programs will gain the respect and win the approval of groups which are familiar with the purpose and the aim of prison administrators. And because restrictions for visiting forbid citizens going to the prison, the prison can go to them as administrative and staff members may have opportunity to bring the story to interested community groups. Because the work of redemption lies so close to the heart of the church, church groups will be especially interested to learn about programs of rehabilitation. They will want to know how the Gospel is preached to those in prison, and how it is received by the prison population. The chaplain will have no difficulty in securing invitations to speak of his work. His difficulty will rather lie in limiting those outside calls to the place where they will not drain both his time and his strength. Yet this is an important function in which the chaplain can serve a vital need. If the true story of sin and its consequences, of the possibilities of reformation and restoration, and of the value of the individual in the sight of God is to be told, it should be told by those who have seen with their eyes and heard with their ears and carried upon their hearts, the burdens of the imprisoned.

REV. A. W. STREMEL, D.D.
Protestant Chaplain
Western State Penitentiary
Pittsburgh, Pa.

BIBLIOGRAPHY

Annual Proceedings of The American Prison Association.
The Prison World, publication of American Prison Association.
The Prison Chaplain, published by National Chaplain's Association.
Journal of Clinical Pastoral Work, published by Council for Clinical Training.

PRISON INDUSTRIES. It is an objective and a responsibility of penal institutions to rehabilitate the prisoner if possible. Since one of the principal activities in attaining this goal is useful work, penal institutions must provide useful work for all prisoners able to work.

Useful work refers not only to the production of goods usable in the institution, or saleable on the market open to penal institutions but, it also refers to the benefits which accrue to the prisoner and which will enhance his chances for success upon returning to a free society. Useful work does not necessarily mean work of a kind which will permit the prisoner to master a trade. The ability to master a trade is limited to less than 50 per cent of the prisoners. Useful work does mean the prisoners will learn the desirable habits of industry and some of the skills which may be applicable on the job in a free society. About 80 per cent of the inmate population can profit from such training. For the remaining 20 per cent there is little that can be done for them through the development of work habits.

A program of useful work is essential to the smooth operation of an institution. It reduces or eliminates idleness, holds high the prisoners' morale and the morale of the staff, minimizes disciplinary problems, stimulates participation in other rehabilitative programs, and reduces the cost of operation to the taxpayer.

Few top-notch professional, skilled, semiskilled, or common laborers are found in the ranks of prisoners. Most prisoners have not learned what work is, how to work, and that work in itself is honorable. Many prisoners have the illusion only "suckers" work, the world owes them a living, and they can get that living for nothing.

Society probably does owe every individual the opportunity to learn what work is, to appreciate the value of work, to develop skills and to master techniques in the fields of labor for which the individual has aptitudes, and to earn a living. Most prisoners have yet to learn what work is, how to work in a manner acceptable to the industries in a free society, what constitutes a full day's work, and the value of work to the well-being of the individual. If the prison can teach the prisoner the desirable habits of industry and some of the skills applicable to jobs in a free society, it will have accomplished much toward the rehabilitation of the prisoner.

The stresses and strains which result from a lack of economic well-being or the inability to earn a livelihood are not the sole cause or even a major cause of misconduct and eventual imprisonment. However, economic insecurity does contribute pressures which result in misconduct and imprisonment. The occupational histories of many prisoners indicate they have held many jobs for short periods of time. Most jobs were blind-alley jobs. Few jobs required special training. Some jobs were seasonal. Most work periods terminated because the services of the individual were unsatisfactory and no longer desired or because the services of the individual were no longer needed. In some cases the individual tired of the work because it did not meet his needs, his aptitudes, or abilities. He, therefore, did not like it and desired a change.

The social conditioning from such job instability coupled with emotional immaturity and lack of adequate social values tends to develop into criminal action for both the first offender and the repeater.

Few experiences in life are repeated as easily, as readily, and with as much help from society as that of imprisonment. It appears the skid-ways are greased for the ex-convict's return to prison. This is partly due to the lack of training in preparation for life in a free society. During the period of confinement, little was done for the prisoner to enable him to cope with the demands of society more successfully than he was able to cope with them before his initial commitment. If all prisoners released from penal institutions were qualified to do some kind of common, semi-skilled, or skilled labor well, and that labor were in demand in a free society, much of the recidivism would disappear.

The long-range cost in the operation of penal institutions would be noticeably reduced if the State were to provide adequate training programs for the development of habits and skills in industry in accordance with the aptitudes of its prisoners and usable in the legitimate enterprises of a free society.

Prisoners trained in useful work habits and skills are less apt to repeat old offenses or to commit new ones after release. It is estimated that from fifty to eighty per cent of the prisoners in the institutions today are recidivists. It would be a tremendous savings to the State if this group were eliminated from institutional care because of training in work habits and skills suitable to the individual. Training of a suitable sort is less apt to be acquired by an ex-convict as a member in a free society than it is for him,

as a convict. Without training, without something really worth while to offer in the form of labor, his earning power is limited and with the limited earnings he must support himself and his family. It is more difficult for an ex-convict to pursue courses of training in a free society than it is for him, as a convict, to pursue similar courses during the period of imprisonment. The ex-convict, who is busily engaged in legitimate work, is both self-supporting and useful to society. He is not only less of a menace to society but with a little tolerance and understanding on the part of society he may become a worthy citizen.

Work programs in penal institutions are not a new idea in the United States. Such programs were inaugurated shortly after the prisons were started. But whereas today the objectives of labor in prison may be summed up as: (a) alleviation of the tedium of prison life; (b) repression of crime; (c) the production of economic commodities to decrease the cost of support; (d) prison discipline; and (e) reformation through useful work, in the recent past, prison labor was primarily a form of punishment. The offender upon receiving the judgment of the court, was sentenced to "imprisonment at hard labor." Society thought that prisoners should not merely work, but work hard since hard work to them was essentially a punishment.

Upon arriving in the prison, the offender found that prisoners were kept everlastingly busy. They were usually busy in the production of commodities which sold on the open market in competition with economic goods produced by free labor.

No thought was given to the training of prisoners except as such training enhanced the production within the shop and minimized the need of breaking in, instructing, and supervising new inmate help. Shop supervisors vied with one another in an attempt to secure long termers or lifers because an inmate personnel composed of long termers or lifers reduced the amount of effort the supervisor had to expend in order to achieve the production standard assigned. A new prisoner was sent to the shop requesting inmate help. Upon arriving at the shop he was taught the specific job in which there chanced to be an opening. If the shop chanced to be the tailor shop and the opening was among the group sewing on buttons, he was taught that particular task and he remained on that job as long as he stayed in the shop. Shop supervisors were more interested in developing good relations with the office of the deputy warden, the center from which work assignments were made, than they were in the well-being of the prisoners as a group or the individual prisoner. In many prisons in the earlier days, an outsider rented this prison labor, directed their work, and set the goals of production. This practice is now obsolete.

Apparently no attempt was made to ascertain the aptitudes of the prisoner, what kind of work he had been doing before his imprisonment, or what he hoped to do when released. The immediate responsibility of the work program was production, and work assignments were made on that basis. Whether the work experience enhanced the prisoner's possibility of adjustment upon return to a free society was immaterial. Incidentally, few work projects in the penal institutions were carried on in a manner resembling the practice observed in similar projects in a free society. The equipment was usually obsolete. Prisoners were indifferent respecting the quality and the quantity of the work done. They became very adept in the art of "soldiering" on the job. There were usually two or more inmates for each job in the shop. If the group in the shop was unable to meet the production standard set, more help was obtained and the shop supervisor was praised because he had helped reduce the number of inmates in idleness. Inmate morale was low. Their chief purpose, if it would be called such, was to struggle through another day with as little effort as possible and with no thought of accomplishment. The good records respecting absenteeism and prompt arrival on the job were not due to the initiative, drive, and ambition of the prisoners but they were the result of established prison routine.

Industry, in a free society, did not welcome the ex-convict into its labor ranks because he had little to offer and his habits of industry were bad. It is not to be inferred that the ex-convict did not want to work or that he could not work. Prison projects carried on in World War I and again in World War II demonstrated, beyond the shadow of a doubt, that prisoners want to work, can work, and are capable of producing high standard goods at a normal industrial pace under proper conditions and incentives.

The exceptional opportunities afforded during the two war periods usually do not obtain in times of peace when many prisoners are found to be in enforced idleness or sharing a job with several other prisoners. Prisoners do want to work and they can work. However, in times of peace there are not enough jobs to go around. Prison officials attempted to ameliorate the condition through the practice of over assignment and thereby defeated the primary purpose of the work program which is the rehabilitation of the prisoner. Under such a system it was not possible for the prisoner to do a full day's work, to acquire the desirable habits of industry, and to develop skills and to master techniques applicable to jobs in a free society.

Production is an important aspect of the work program. However, production as an objective in a program of rehabilitation, must be a secondary consideration. The purpose of a prison is to rehabilitate the prisoner if possible. Useful work is an important contribution in the program of rehabilitation because of the training it affords when it is properly managed. The prospect of training-on-the-job is a more positive incentive to do good work than is the practice of merely assigning a prisoner to a job just to give him a job; or, than is the practice of instilling fear in the prisoner, through punishment, if he fails to do a good job.

It has been observed that training-on-the-job tends to increase the per man out-put of work, the quality of the work, and the efficiency of the shop. The disciplinary problems, in the shop offering training-on-the-job, are reduced to a minimum. It is more difficult, it is true, to manage a shop with on-the-job training than it is to manage one with production as the principal objective. In the former, the superintendent and the foremen must be capable of teaching the techniques, skills, and methods to the prisoners in step with the progress of each prisoner. This may necessitate the frequent shifting about of the inmate personnel in the shop so that each prisoner may experience continued growth and progress according to his ability to absorb and to master that which is being offered in the on-the-job-training program. The superintendent and the foremen must be well qualified for their specific jobs, sincerely interested in and thoroughly understand the interests, aptitudes, and needs of the individual prisoner to the end that they may further and direct the prisoner's development in the best interests of society and the prisoner. Only in a few states today is rehabilitation the dominant purpose. For in about one half of the state prisons the main objective is still one of production in order that these prisons may become completely self-supporting.

In those prisons, however, where production is still dominant or the principal objective, the chief task is to instruct each prisoner on a specific operation and to drive him to the maximum limit in the repetition of that operation. Job assignments are based on production needs rather than on the prisoners' needs, aptitudes, and interests. Refusals to work are common and other disciplinary problems are numerous. The prisoner does not learn to do a full day's work, the desirable habits of industry, or skills applicable to a job in a free society. Production shops usually have two or more prisoners for each job. It is difficult to ascertain why superintendents require an over assignment of inmate personnel. It may be due to a personal inclination to enlarge upon the importance of their job by having a large number of prisoners under their supervision. It may be due to a natural development in an attempt to fortify their position by having a back-log of inmate help to fill the positions left open because of disciplinary action, parole, or the transfer of prisoners to another work project. In institutions operating under the policy that makes production of principal importance, thought respecting the prisoner's well-being, while in the prison or during the period of after care following

release from the institution, or rehabilitation, is at a minimum. Institutions dominated by the cry for production fail to meet the objective of penal institutions which is to rehabilitate the prisoner if possible. They fail to give society the protection it demands, pays for, and has a right to expect when the ex-convict returns to society.

Though rehabilitation through work adapted to the prisoners' aptitudes and abilities is the goal of the forward looking prisons of this era, numerous systems of employment have been and are still being used throughout the United States. Unfortunately, many of them were created in response to such terms as production, profit, punishment, and were indifferent to ideas of useful training habits of industry, and proficiency. In none of the systems were the work conditions proper or the incentives for work suitable. The prisoners were not looked upon as fellow members of society. They were looked upon as criminals, as undesirables, as persons who had forfeited the right to the consideration society might have given them.

The lease system removed the prisoner from the control of the state and placed him under the control of the lessee. Not only were all expenses for the prisoner cared for by the lessee and the state was saved the expense of building prisoners, hiring guards, and otherwise caring for the prisoner, but the lessee also paid a fee to the state in return for the services of the prisoner. It was a system of slave labor which stressed production, profit, and punishment. The apparent economy to the state was overshadowed by the increased danger and menace to society when those, who survived the system, returned to society.

The contract system of employment was somewhat better than the lease system in that the state retained control over the prisoners respecting housing, clothing, feeding, medical care, and discipline. The contractors furnished the materials and machines and they supervised the work of the prisoners. The contractors determined what the work assignment should be. The contractor paid the state a fixed sum for the daily work of the prisoner. In return, the contractor expected production and profit. Discipline (punishment) was in the hands of the prison officials who were eager to retain the good will of the contractors.

The piece-price system of employment placed the entire charge of the prisoners under the control of the prison officials. Interference of other than prison officials was removed. State officials determined the quantity, quality, and method of production. The state provided for the care of the prisoners, it owned the manufacturing equipment, and employed the supervisors of the work. The contractor furnished the material and paid the state an agreed amount for each finished item accepted. Production and profit were uppermost in the minds of the prison officials who were expected to make the institution self-supporting or as nearly self-supporting as possible. Usually, punishment was frequent, brutal, and harsh in response to the demands for production and profit. In some institutions prisoners received a stipend for the work done and they received a bonus if they did more than the assigned task for the day.

Under the lease, contract, and piece-price systems of employment the prisoner learns the meaning of "work" as "drudgery" and he probably learns to give a full day's work for a full day's time. He does not learn that work in itself is honorable. He probably did not learn the skills and master the techniques that were applicable on a job in a free society. He also developed adverse attitudes toward work and toward society. He becomes embittered because society allowed the kind of treatment he received. In many instances, the prisoner undoubtedly became more of a menace to society because of his incarceration and the kind of treatment he had received than he was at the time of his commitment. In none of the systems of employment cited above was there reasonable consideration in behalf of the prisoner and his preparation for life in a free society. Since protection to society under these types of prison systems is limited to the period of imprisonment, the prison officials perform this function very well.

The public account system of employment is one of production for the market. It differs from the piece-price system in that the state enters the manufacturing field on its own account. It buys the raw material, manufactures and puts the product on the market, and it assumes all the risk of conducting a manufacturing business. The state has the entire care and control of the prisoners.

The state-use system of employment is one in which the state carries on the manufacturing process and has entire charge of the prisoners. The manufactured products are not sold on the open market. The market is usually limited to the tax supported institutions of the state.

The states-use system of employment is a modification of the state-use system which makes it possible for the public or tax supported institutions in one state to purchase goods produced in the prisons of another state.

The public works and ways system of employment provides labor for the prisoners in the construction and repair of the prison or other public buildings, roads, parks, breakwaters, or other permanent public structures.

The public account, state-use, states-use, and public works and ways systems of employment represent legislative attempts to provide useful labor for the prisoners in minimum competition with free labor.

Society thinks the prisoner should work and work hard. However, the attempts, on the part of legislative bodies, state and federal, to provide work for the prisoners, have met with serious opposition from labor organizations and the manufacturers who employ free labor. The opposing forces contend the competition is unfair to the manufacturer because he cannot produce goods as cheaply as goods are produced with prison labor, since part of the cost of labor is paid by the state, that is, their food, clothing, and shelter are provided and the wages paid are far below that which free labor receives. Labor objects to prison-made goods because the manufacturer finds it necessary either to reduce wages or to stop production.

The objections offered by the forces opposed to prison-made goods have been somewhat nullified by the Prison Labor Authority regulations respecting the hours of labor for prisoners (not to exceed forty hours per week), the minimum price for which prison-made goods may be sold on the market, and the quantity of production according to the demands of the market. Today most states are not "dumping" cheap prison-made goods on the market.

Some of the systems of employment utilized in prison labor were less palatable than others to labor organizations and to the manufacturers. Among the systems found to be less acceptable were the lease, contract, piece-price, and public account systems. All of these provided for an open market in direct competition with the manufacturers and they did endanger private enterprise and the opportunities of free labor. Much of this threat to private enterprise and to free labor was due to poor management on the part of prison officials and to the greed of the manufacturers who employed free labor.

The forces (labor organizations and manufacturers employing free labor) opposing the manufacture of prison-made goods were successful in having Congress pass the Hawes-Cooper Act in 1929. This Act became effective in 1934 and it made it possible for any state legislature to bar prison-made goods from its state if shipped in from another state. The Ashurst-Sumner Act was passed by Congress in 1935. This Act prohibits transportation companies from accepting prison-made goods for transportation into any state in violation of the laws of that state, and it provides for the labeling of all packages containing prison products in interstate commerce. By 1940 every state in the Union had passed some legislation prohibiting the entrance of prison-made goods from other states or restricting the sale of prison goods on the open market. State legislation was necessary to make the Hawes-Cooper Act and the Ashurst-Sumner Act effective, since federal law cannot legislate for intrastate commerce.

In 1940 an Act was passed which excludes prison-made goods from interstate commerce with exceptions for farm machinery parts, farm commodities, goods made for the use of states and political subdivisions, and articles made in federal institutions for government use.

The changes in the system of prison labor due to the curtailment following restrictive legislation have resulted in an increasing amount of idleness in the prisons. The attempt to keep the prison inmates busy has failed. The attempt to produce as much as possible in order to lessen the expense of prisons to the taxpayer has failed. It has been estimated that the value of all prison-made goods for all penal institutions (state and federal) is a fraction of one per cent of the value of the goods produced on the outside.

More than $100,000,000 of the taxpayers' money is required annually for the custody and care of the inmates in the state and federal prisons. A large portion of this sum could be saved through the employment of the prisoners who are able to work. The training afforded the prisoner in a well planned work program would tend to rehabilitate the prisoner and to reduce the number of recidivists. Prison officials of the recent past were not fully aware of nor alert to the dangers which menaced the prison labor programs or they would have managed the operation of employment systems differently. The record of their resistance to the forces opposed to prison-made goods indicates they knew too little and they were too late. It will require the leadership of well qualified prison officials to regain the losses sustained in recent decades. The struggle will not be for a return of the systems of employment which have been abandoned because of legislative action. Modern penology could not accept them. The effort will probably center around an attempt to obtain the approval of a system of diversified employment and larger markets for the products of prison labor.

Diversified employment will provide more work for more prisoners. Diversified production by prison labor for government use does not compete unfairly with free labor. Diversified employment provides a wider range of opportunities for the training of prisoners in accordance with their aptitudes and interests. It provides for the training of small numbers of interested individuals in a variety of occupations under expert guidance. It permits the prisoner to explore and try out several kinds of work activities in an attempt to find that which is best suited to his abilities, interests, and needs. It can readily respond to the demands for labor in a free society. It is well suited to individualized instruction. It does prepare the prisoner for occupational participation in a free society and it does make an effective contribution toward the objective of penal institutions—the rehabilitation of the prisoner.

Some prisoners are not able to work. A few prisoners are unavailable for work even though they are able to work. Most prisoners are able and available for work. Prisoners do have individual differences in occupational interests and abilities as well as in other respects. The proper diagnosis of the prisoner's abilities, interests, and aptitudes is essential to that kind of study and understanding of the individual which will enable the prison officials to place him on a work assignment in terms of his best interests and the best interests of society.

Penal institutions in the more progressive states do have Classification Committees for the purpose of studying the individual prisoners. It is the purpose of the Committee to attempt to gain the information needed in order to make recommendations in behalf of the prisoner and to plan with the prisoner a program designed to meet his needs and to prepare him for life in a free society. All this is done in recognition of the demands of society.

Through the services of the Classification Committee, which has access to all available data pertaining to the prisoner, prison authorities find it possible to make more satisfactory job assignments for the prisoners in terms of physical fitness, past experiences, correctional effort, ability, interests, and training in preparation for life and occupational participation in a free society.

The services of the Classification Committee make it possible for prison authorities to know the degree of custody (maximum, medium, or minimum) recommended for each prisoner. With this information the prison authorities are in a position to consider job assignments to the honor camps and farms for the relatively new prisoners. Usually assignments of this nature are for prisoners who have served a reasonable portion of their sentences and who will soon become eligible for parole. Frequently, the change in work assignment from a job inside the institution to a camp or farm placement proves to be a detriment to the prisoner in that he must leave an on-the-job training opportunity in order to obtain the benefits that farm and camp placement offer. If relatively new arrivals in the prison were used to fill positions in the camps or on the farms, because they are well suited to that kind of work and have an aptitude for it, or because they are short timers who can be trusted, the inroads on the prisoners who are doing well on an on-the-job training program would be less devastating. It is no mere coincidence that the prisoners interested in self-improvement through training-on-the-job are frequently the very prisoners approved for camp and farm placement by the prison authorities.

Industrial employment of the kind found in a free society is desirable and it should be made available to prison labor whenever possible. However, any job in the institution can be utilized for training purposes if proper care is taken not to over assign prisoners to those jobs; if provision is made for a full day of work; if job placement is made with due care respecting the individual prisoner; if close supervision is provided to instruct, check, and stimulate the prisoner; if the techniques and skills of the job are mastered; and if the prisoner feels the job he is doing is useful.

Many of the maintenance jobs in the institution have their counterpart in society, and the prisoner who becomes proficient on the job in the institution is likely to find an opportunity for employment of a similar nature upon his return to society. If the ex-convict expects to hold a job following his release, he must do his job with greater proficiency than is expected of the man without a criminal record. This demand from society may appear to be unfair to the ex-convict. However, it is a part of the price he must pay for having transgressed the laws of society. The ex-convict may feel he has paid for his crime by serving "time." Seldom, if ever, is the price paid in full. By becoming proficient on a job in the institution, preferably the kind of job for which the prisoner has some aptitude and which offers employment on the outside, the prisoner enhances his chances for gainful employment following his release from the institution. Gainful employment could very well be the starting point in the program of successful adjustment to the demands of society.

It is unreasonable to expect prisoners to work with maximum drive and efficiency without the incentive of a wage, or the reduction of the sentence as a reward for good behavior and good work, or the granting of certain privileges. Yet, the success of the training program, achievement in the program of rehabilitation for the prisoner, the best interests of the state and the individual prisoner are served only when the prisoner does work with maximum drive and efficiency.

Prisoners should work. However, prisoners should not be required to work because work is looked upon as a form of punishment and society demands the offender should be punished. The prisoner should work because it improves his physical and mental well being if he is busy doing something useful. Prisoners should work because the product of their labor cuts down the cost of operation to the taxpayer. All able bodied prisoners, who would not be better engaged in educational activities, should work at something useful for the institution, for the state, and for themselves in terms of after care. They should work and thereby learn what work is, the value of work to their well-being, what constitutes a full day's work, and learn the desirable habits of industry, the skills and techniques employed, and the fact that work in itself is honorable.

CARL E. JOHNSON
Associate Professor
Department of Sociology
University of Wisconsin
Madison 6, Wisconsin

BIBLIOGRAPHY

Barnes, Harry Elmer and Teeters, Negley K., *New Horizons in Criminology,* Prentice-Hall, Inc., New York, 1943.
Gillen, John Lewis, *Criminology and Penology* (Third Edition) D. Appleton-Century Company, New York, 1945.
Robinson, Louis N., *Should Prisoners Work,* The John C. Winston Company, Chicago, 1931.
Sutherland, Edwin H., *Principles of Criminology* (Third Edition) J. B. Lippincott Company, Chicago, 1939.
Taft, Donald R., *Criminology,* The Macmillan Company, New York, 1942.
Manual of Suggested Standards for a State Correctional System, The American Prison Association, Committee on Model State Plan, Lewisohn, Sam A., Chairman, 135 East 15th Street, New York 3, New York, 1946.

PRISON MANAGEMENT. Until the turn of the century, prison management posed but one important problem: how to prevent escapes. And so long as inmates were securely locked in their cells, the warden had nothing to worry about. The concept of rehabilitation was completely frowned upon, except among progressive officials, and judging from the records there were far too few of them.

The policies of the "lock them up" school, of course, possessed a certain, simple and logical justification, for they grew out of the then prevalent theory that anyone who committed a crime was inherently evil. Men were born with criminal instincts or without them. That was all there was to it.

With the passage of years, however, science has shown that criminals are not born as such, but that definite causes so shape their lives that anti-social conduct is but a natural consequence. Prisons, therefore, must accomplish far more than incarcerating those men. They must transform them, if at all possible, into social assets.

Of course, the minds of some offenders have deteriorated to such an extent that it is impossible to do so. Such misfits should obviously be incarcerated for life and never allowed to molest the community again. But the vast majority of offenders can be turned into useful citizens. Granted that such is the goal of a prison warden, what does he require, and what are some of the basic problems that must be solved?

Personnel. No warden can be successful unless he has competent and adequate aids, whether they be uniformed guards, deputies, psychiatrists or teachers. These men, the backbone of an institution, should receive necessary instruction before assuming their duties, be paid adequate salaries, be protected by civil service, and promoted on the basis of merit. Subjecting employees to the whims of politicians, with dismissals after each election, hardly helps morale.

Segregation. In so many states today, all types of offenders are housed together. The young and the old, the feeble minded and the mentally alert, the hardened criminal and the beginner—a seething mixture of all the degenerative elements of society playing upon one another. How can inmates be rehabilitated in a clearing house for the worst forms of social experience? Prisons must provide for the segregation of the various types of lawbreakers. There should be separate institutions—not necessarily costly ones—for the psychopathic, for the feeble-minded, for the young offender, for the accidental offender, and for the habitual offender. And should all this prove too costly for some states, at least the young, and the mentally deficient should be segregated from the others.

Employment. Many people believe that prisoners are, as a rule, exceedingly lazy. "Jack could have worked instead of becoming a criminal," they say. Some offenders, of course, might not have been able to get jobs, but even if they could, it does not mean that they committed crimes because they were lazy. Many of them, I dare say, spent more time and effort in planning and committing their crimes than they would have, had they engaged in legitimate endeavors. The trouble was that such offenders did not like steady employment. They would work for a while, then loaf. Such men, in particular, must be given jobs that will enable them to acquire the habit of working every day. In fact, no man should be allowed to remain idle. Idleness demoralizes men and makes them physically and mentally sluggish. Realizing this, it is essential, now that victory against the Axis has been won, that institutions—which produced material during the war for the armed forces and thereby had no unemployment problem—be given other type of work. Jobs, involving the maintenance of an institution, cannot keep all inmates busy. Nor is it always possible to do so under the so-called "state use" system.

Rehabilitation. Regardless of the process, it is impossible to take a man who has been subjected to undesirable influences all through his growing years and, by waving over his head a magic word called rehabilitation, reform him. No one has performed such a remarkable feat.

But how can offenders be helped? Not by vicious methods, such as bullying, physical torture, and constant punishment. Men cannot be whipped into line. They must be inducted gradually into those patterns of behavior which society requires. Checkers, chess, music, stamp collecting, anything that can arouse some latent spark of interest other than his morbid pre-occupation with his past experiences is of value in effecting a criminal's reclamation.

With some the religious approach is necessary (full time chaplains should be available in all institutions); others can be aroused only through athletics (well-integrated athletic programs are also essential for reasons of health). Still others show an unsuspected inclination and aptitude for some trade which they were unable to develop outside. They should be instructed in that trade.

But while hundreds of inmates, no doubt, found themselves as a result of vocational education—one of the reasons why a first rate prison school with skilled teachers and librarian is a prime requisite for a rehabilitation program—it should be remembered that some are not capable of mastering a trade. In fact, a great number are illiterate—a serious handicap to a successful adjusting to community living. The removal of that handicap is therefore of paramount importance, together with education of an entirely different nature: character education.

But here again, wardens are beset with a maze of difficulties. For one thing, just how can a man's character be changed within the confines of a prison where society's misfits are congregated? There must of necessity be some outside influences, nebulous as they may be. They can well include outside lecturers who will discuss current topics, radio broadcasts, motion pictures and other forms of periodic entertainment. Furthermore, these diversions will also prevent inmates from becoming too institutionalized. For unless they keep pace with national and world affairs they will eventually return to the community complete strangers, incapable of adjusting themselves. Nor should we forget that receiving news about the "outside" gives them something constructive to think about —another essential element for rehabilitation.

Inmates. Those who need medical or psychiatric treatment should be cared for in a modern hospital, supervised by a physician, who should have competent aids, including nurses and a dentist.

Inmates should also be paid some wage for their work in prison, be allowed to receive visits and correspond with relatives and in special cases, friends. They should not wear a striped suit—or any uniform that is degrading—be subjected to a silent system or locked up in dungeon-like cells for infraction of rules. Disobedience should be punishable by loss of "good time," privileges, or placement in an isolation wing, that is habitable.

Coddling? Certainly not. Few, if any, inmates revert to crime because they are treated fairly and humanely. In fact, such treatment has reformed men—thousands of them.

But do we always release men who are reformed? This question poses a problem that troubles so many wardens. It involves the age-old system of imposing fixed sentences.

All of us know that some inmates leave prison although they are not the least reformed, and it is only a matter of time before they return for another term. On the other hand, there are other inmates who reform long before the expiration of their terms. Why should such men be kept behind bars needlessly? Obviously sentences should be measured to fit the criminal, not the crime.

Today a judge sentences a prisoner almost immediately after he has been found guilty. But how can the court predict how long it will take to reform that individual? It is a task beyond the power of anyone.

The court, therefore, should decide only the guilt or innocence of the prisoner. If found guilty, he should come under the jurisdiction of a sentencing board, composed of competent, fearless and non-political crimi-

nologists, psychiatrists, and others capable of dealing with behavior problems. That board shall not mete out a sentence until it has made a thorough study of the offender. But the sentence could be altered from time to time as he responds—or fails to respond— to correctional treatment. That would, of course, facilitate reclamation, particularly among the long term prisoners. For how in the world can wardens talk "reform" to those facing thirty, forty and fifty years. However, if prisoners knew that there was hope of eventually seeing the "outside," their frame of mind would change and they would be receptive to offers of help from penal officials.

The most serious objection to a sentencing board is that it might become corrupt or subject to political pressure. Naturally, this possibility exists, just as it does in all our branches of government. But because Judges have betrayed their office for personal gain should we abolish our judicial system? And because legislators have placed self-aggrandizement above the welfare of the community, should we abolish representative form of government?

There is no reason why honest and competent men cannot compose a sentencing board which represents the next logical step in the developing science of penology.

LEWIS E. LAWES
Former Warden
Sing Sing Prison

BIBLIOGRAPHY

Bates, Sanford, *Prisons and Beyond,* Macmillan, 1936.
Lawes, L. E., *20,000 Years in Sing Sing,* Long and Smith, 1932.
McKelvey, Blake, *American Prisons,* University of Chicago Press, 1936.

PRISON PERSONNEL. In an earlier day in this country, when State populations were small, money was hard to get, and man's understanding of offenders was limited, mass treatment was practiced. Little was done for the transgressor in an attempt to fit him for his return to society as a worthy, useful, and self-supporting member in the group of which he became a part. Imprisonment was for punishment on the theory that only punishment evened up the damage done and only punishment was effective in preventing the criminal from repeating his crime and in deterring others from crime. Every aspect of treatment was to be a part of the punishment. Thus the principle governing the administration was security for the protection of society for the duration of the sentence imposed upon the offender with minimum cost to the State. Under such conditions the chief problems of the warden were to prevent escapes, maintain discipline, avoid scandals, and manage the operation of the institution so that it would be self-supporting or as nearly self-supporting as possible. The warden who could show a profit above the cost of operation was considered to be successful.

The successful warden of that earlier day could not afford to be concerned about the improvement of the offender in health, in mind, in attitudes, or in habits. Rather the offender was fed the cheapest and coarsest food in minimum quantities. His work was designed to keep him everlastingly busy at tasks profitable to the institution, but not suited to an enterprise in a free society. Work was a form of punishment—the sentence specified hard labor as a part of the penalty—and no attempt was made to consider the inmate in terms of his fitness for the job or the value of the training and the development in the skills involved that might have a bearing upon the well-being of the inmate following his release from the institution.

There was a part time doctor but his chief duty was to limit the number on sick call, pass out a few pills, and remove himself from the scene. He did not dare to suggest a change in the work program for an inmate even though such a change would reduce the occupational hazard to the inmate's health. It was not his duty to inspect the food served to the inmates or to check the sanitary conditions within the institution. He was not encouraged to correct the physical defects of an inmate. He was expected to avoid all expense beyond that which was necessary to keep the inmate alive so that he could walk out of the institution upon release, and it was

not thought to be a serious matter if he failed in that respect.

There was no well developed educational program in that earlier period. The inmates were not taught how to make an honest living or how to live honestly. It was no concern of the prison personnel if an inmate were found to have been inadequately exposed to formal educational training. Prison personnel was resistant to educational endeavors because it was thought that such endeavors would pamper the inmates and eventually cause the inmates to become better informed than the personnel of the institution. Upon release from the institution, the inmate was on his own. What happened to him after he left the institution was of no concern or interest to the personnel of the institution until or unless the ex-convict were returned to the institution on another conviction as a repeater. The fact that the institution had done nothing to prepare the inmate for life in a free society was completely ignored but the repeater was constantly reminded that he had had his chance and that he had failed to make good. "Therefore, it must be that he likes the institution or he would have managed to remain out of it."

Recreational activities were unknown in the prison of yesteryear. Those unfortunates who were committed to prison were sent there for punishment. Imprisonment meant an opportunity for society to inflict corporal and other forms of punishment upon the offender. The provision of a recreational program in the weekly, monthly, or annual schedule of prison routine was completely ignored. Wide adverse publicity was given to the warden who first dared to let a group of selected inmates bask in the sun in the prison yard on a holiday. A prisoner was expected to be at work, locked in his cell, or in the hospital.

Appointments to positions on the institution staff were made, quite generally, on the basis of the political activity of the individual for the party in power. Every time the political complexion of the State changed, the personnel of the institution changed. No one knew how long he might be on the job and each attempted to make the most of it while he was there in so far as his personal interests were concerned. Thus, corruption and undesirable practices flourished.

Since few people knew anything about prisons in that earlier day, and the prison personnel was committed to the task of managing and operating the institution on a profit basis in excess of the cost of operation if that were possible, it was necessary to "cut the corners" where it would attract the least attention. Thus the hours of labor were long and salaries were too meager to attract qualified personnel. The employees worked in twelve hour shifts from 6:00 A.M to 6:00 P.M. or from 6:00 P.M. to 6:00 A.M. The staff was undermanned, overworked, and in constant danger. There was no tenure, no sick leave, no vacation with pay, and no plan of retirement.

The personnel was to govern and control. Discipline was obtained through the utilization of harsh measures which would instill the feeling of fear in the inmates. Corporal punishment was frequent. The inmates and the employees became harsh, brutal, and violent, with the result that members of society, not fully aware of the worthy achievements in the correctional field today, look askance upon anyone employed in the correctional field.

Offenders of all kinds, of all ages, first offenders, repeaters, sex offenders, murderers, thieves, arsonists, embezzlers, forgers, men and women, were thrown together under the management of a political henchman, surrounded with a personnel of the same ilk, insecure in their appointments, without qualifications for the job other than brawn, ignorance, and brutality. The personnel was deaf to the pleas of those under them and without feeling for another's well-being. The personnel did not understand the importance of training, education, good food, medical care, and mental development. Nor did they realize the need to cultivate desirable habits, wholesome attitudes, and hopeful outlooks on life. The personnel was filled only with a desire to display authority through corporal punishment and the practice of demeaning the inmate at every opportunity. It is probably true that the individual who entered the institution as an inmate felt he had

reached the end of the trail and he left all hope behind.

Since much of the clerical work as well as many of the skilled and semi-skilled jobs were performed by inmates assigned to do the work, the bulk of the personnel, known as guards, was for disciplinary and supervisory purposes. The guard in the earlier type prison had to be physically strong, above average height, alert, emotionally dull, fearless, obedient, adjustable to monotonous routine, not too intelligent or critically minded, ignorant of social science, amenable to political discipline, and reasonably honest.

There was no training for the guards. After taking the oath of office, the new guard was given an officer's handbook, an inmate's rule book, and a symbol of authority, usually a loaded cane or a loaded night stick, with the comment that so long as he met the requirements indicated in the officer's handbook he would have no trouble with the deputy warden, the chief disciplinary officer of the institution. The new guard was urged to study and become familiar with the contents in the officer's handbook and in the inmate's rule book. The rest of the information he gained from fellow employees, as they chanced to meet during the lunch hour or after working hours, or from inmates under his immediate supervision while on the job. Many a new guard or other employee was guided by inmates in their efforts to become established in prison routine, prison procedures, or even in the technical skills involved in the new responsibilities. There were a few exceptions to the generalizations indicated in the preceding paragraphs.

The statements in the preceding paragraphs do not reflect much credit upon the personnel of the penal institutions of an earlier day. However, the comments do reflect the popular attitudes and thoughts of the public respecting the inmate, prison administration, and the purpose of penal institutions. Prison administrators have been keenly aware of the shortcomings in the prison system and they have taken the initiative in seeking the assistance which would bring about the improvement needed for the accomplishment of the real purpose of penal institutions which is the rehabilitation of the inmate. Prison administrators were the first to recognize the inadequacies of prison practices and they were the first to recommend changes in those practices. The recommendations were based on first hand experience and they may be found in the Declaration of Principles adopted at the first National Prison Congress of 1870. Few of the principles adopted more than three quarters of a century ago have become a reality in prison practice today because the public's understanding of the penal problem has been inadequate, and out of step with the more recent findings. The public's attitude has been one of indifference toward financial support with which to implement the institutions in order that the work may be carried on with the improved methods and techniques.

Although the items enumerated above pertain more definitely to the old type prison, too many of the conditions mentioned are still to be found in penal institutions throughout the land.

A new philosophy relative to the care and treatment of individuals committed to penal or correctional institutions has developed in recent years. New objectives concerning care and treatment have been formulated. The changes in the methods and techniques of treatment and care have been noticeable. A change in the type of personnel employed to carry on the work has been inevitable. Additional institutional services have been found necessary to the successful accomplishment of those aims and objectives involved in the State's program for penal and correctional institutions.

Most progressive penologists are in agreement that the personnel is more important than the type of plant providing housing, for individuals committed. Contemplate the effect upon the inmate of the fortress like structure of the past when the chief responsibility was security—keeping the inmate safe. Today there is a new goal. Namely, the responsibility to redirect, restrain, re-educate, and rehabilitate the inmate, so that he may return to society, and there participate in the affairs of society, as a self-respecting, self-supporting, useful, and worthy member. An adequate plant with ample provisions for the care and treatment of the inmates is desirable and should be available. However, the most complete plant without adequate, well-trained, and highly qualified personnel is chiefly custodial in nature and thereby capable of meeting only the temporary responsibility of protecting society from its convicts during the period of their confinement.

It requires adequate well-trained, and highly qualified personnel to meet the responsibility of re-conditioning the inmate so that society may be protected from the depredations of convicts upon their release from the institution. About 97% of inmates return to society upon the completion of their sentences or on parole. They become neighbors in a community and enjoy many of the same privileges experienced by the non-criminal individual. If society is to enjoy the protection it has a right to demand and for which it pays, something more than merely locking men up and counting noses several times each day must be done.

In the new type prison, treatment and care are highly individualized because it has been discovered that mass treatment does not work. No two inmates are exactly alike. Each responds to a given form of treatment in a different manner. It is not humanly possible to treat all inmates alike. Some prisoners' attitudes may be changed and the effort to change them is worth while. The greatest stride forward in the history of penology could very well be the recent combined effort of the many services to individualize the treatment of each inmate. This shift from mass treatment to individualized treatment has necessitated, on the one hand, well trained and highly qualified specialists and, on the other, more qualified personnel in the established services and additional staff.

The new prison system in the progressive states with large populations and ample funds provides for the care of offenders on the basis of classification as to custody (maximum, medium, and minimum security), age, sex, offense, and treatment. The number of institutions in the State correctional system today is somewhat larger than the number of institutions found in the old State penal system and the average inmate population of an institution today is somewhat smaller. The services provided in each of the institutions are similar in kind, but differ in the application and purpose according to the needs of the respective institutions.

All institutions have disciplinary personnel, guards or custodial officers. Medical services are available to all institutions including dental, psychiatric, and psychological services. Educational, library, religious, and recreational services are included in the program designed to rehabilitate the inmate. Superintendents of departments and the foremen in the shops are selected with some consideration given to their ability to teach the skills involved in the work they supervise. The more recent additions in staff include the social case worker and the sociologist.

All personnel should be selected with care respecting the individual's fitness and training for the particular job and with proper consideration of the individual's personal qualities which foster cooperative effort, teamwork, and the ideals of service. Correctional work is a special field requiring personnel qualified by nature and training to deal with people who have failed under ordinary conditions and are in need of special treatment.

The bulk of the personnel is still composed of guards or custodial officers with higher standards and qualifications. It is probable that few guards are employed today who have not, at least, a high school education or its equivalent. It may be expected that the standards and qualifications will move upward as the working conditions improve, salaries become adjusted, and the real significance of correctional work is more fully realized. Some of the old standards, quite properly, continue to play an important role in the selection of personnel on the custodial staff. The new guard is expected to be physically strong, above average height, alert, courageous, obedient, and amenable to discipline. His loyalty to the administration is based on voluntary and enthusiastic cooperation in a difficult but absorbing constructive work. He is expected to be observing, intelli-

gent, and capable of making decisions. He is expected to carry out his decisions by force when necessary but by persuasion whenever possible. He is expected to possess good self-control and to be impartial, consistent, and objective. He is expected to be capable of inspiring confidence in inmates who are prejudiced against him. He is not expected to be tough and inconsiderate of the well-being of others, nor a tender-hearted sentimentalist. He is expected to have a wholesome respect for, and an acceptable recognition and working knowledge of the contributions of science and scientific workers in the correctional field. He is expected to preserve, amid discouraging difficulties, the belief that some prisoners' attitudes may be changed and that the effort to change them is worth while. He must be honest in all respects.

In some of the more progressive states, courses of training are being offered to the personnel of the correctional field. Institutes, lectures, correspondence study, and on-the-job training are some of the methods used in providing the information and understanding necessary for cooperative effort toward the achievement of the objectives in the penal program. Special emphasis has been given to the training and preparation of custodial officers. Unfortunately, welfare departments do not, as a general practice, look upon training courses as something that should be financed by the department, offered on state time, and made a requirement for every employee. This may be due, in part, to the fact that professional and skilled workers finance their training and the same may be expected of prison employees. It may be due, in part, to the fact that prison employee turn-over is large and there is a natural reluctance to finance the training of personnel which may not be on the job long enough to permit the department to utilize the benefits of such training. The prison employee turn-over is partly due to poor selection of personnel. Many individuals, who meet satisfactorily the qualifications indicated in a previous paragraph, are unable to measure up to the demands found in the institution. The work is distasteful to them. They cannot stand the sound of clanging iron doors and gates. It is not compatible with their natures to mingle with men who have transgressed the laws of society. The apparent hopelessness of the task may be too much for them or they may be fearful of the outcome if they remain.

The established services which have been carried over from the practice of mass treatment to individualized treatment have been improved, and numerous additional services have been added as the need for them became apparent and as funds became available. There has been noteworthy progress in the selection of personnel technically well trained, highly qualified, and thoroughly imbued with the ideals of service.

The department of medical services in the institution has made noticeable gains not only through the acquisition of psychiatric and psychological services, dental services, technicians and registered nurses but also in the nature and rôle of its services. No longer does the custodial officer, the superintendent of the shop, or other employees not in the department of medical services determine whether the inmate's request to see the doctor, to receive medical attention, is valid. That is strictly in the province of the medical department which has the responsibility to promote the well-being of each inmate in so far as the facilities and equipment available to the institution will permit, and the condition of each individual will warrant. The medical department is responsible for the provision of services in the fields of prevention, correction, and treatment for mental and physical health. It is natural, then, that the medical report on an inmate should have a significant rôle respecting such matters as job placement, corrective medical services, treatment, classification, pardon, and other forms of release from the institution.

The dental services, usually an arm of the medical department, care for the inmates in need of dental care through the services of one or more full-time dentists. The importance of proper dental care has long been recognized as a significant factor in the inmate's rehabilitation. The report of the dental service on the inmate may and should have a definite bearing on the plans formulated with the inmate relative to his program for rebuilding in preparation for his eventual return to society.

Progressive officials are giving increasing recognition to two other arms of the medical services, namely, the psychiatric and psychological services. These aid in obtaining a definite, thoroughgoing, and satisfying understanding of the individual inmate on the basis of scientific findings. The findings are particularly valuable respecting job placement, program planning, educational development, vocational training, recreational pursuits, camp or farm placement, discipline, classification, parole, pardon, and after care. The awareness of the value of these services in the institution has been more general than the utilization of them. This may be largely due to the fact that there are not enough qualified psychiatrists and psychologists to go around and funds have not been available in all instances for such services.

The educational services cut across each of the several other services within the institution. It is expected that the educational services will cooperate to the fullest extent with each of the other services. Educational training is not a panacea or cure-all for all the ills found in the population of an inmate body, but it does serve as a stimulating and motivating force in bringing about the reconditioning of an inmate. Educational training should have been an important part of the inmate's life in society. Educational training is partly to blame for his failure because it did not meet his needs. Education, within the institution, must strive to meet such specific needs. The need may be academic, vocational, social, cultural, physical, or the matter of accommodation to special factors such as limited mental ability, physical defects, or handicaps. The educational program should be flexible enough to meet the need of the individual. It must pick up the individual where it finds him and progress from that point onward as far as the ability of the individual will permit in the time allotted.

The educational services are expected to function in counseling and guidance work on the basis of the findings obtained through scientific aids such as psychological and achievement tests and other sources of information. The educational program, especially the vocational training program, should be flexible enough to meet the needs indicated by the current demands from free society.

Well trained, qualified civilian personnel is desirable for the staff of the educational service department, but prisoners can be used to advantage as teachers and instructors if placed under trained personnel and closely supervised. In a study of one state prison covering a period of eight years, it was found that less than ten per cent of those prisoners who had been employed as teachers failed to adjust in an acceptable manner upon their return to society. It is not known, but it is thought that the experience, of aiding others less fortunate than they may have had some influence in the development of more acceptable attitudes.

The institution personnel must be aware of the plan developed by the classification committee with the inmate, the current progress of the several services in carrying out that plan, and the inmate's needs, interests, and reactions of the moment. The civilian personnel of the educational staff should be qualified to adapt the techniques of their field to the needs of the individual and to interpret the individual problems of the inmates in the process of guidance and counseling. The staff must be constantly aware of the fact that the mere transfer of the patterns, methods, and techniques of the ordinary education program in society, to a penal institution gives no assurance of better results because of the new setting. It requires effort, interest, enthusiasm, sincerity of purpose, and courage to teach individuals rather than subject matter; to enjoy the relatively great progress of a few individuals rather than the comparatively feeble advances of large numbers of individuals; to avoid the tendency to make the job appear different from what it really is through the utilization of statistics which would lead one to think all or nearly all inmates within the institution were engaged in some feature of the educational program, when in reality less than 25% of the group were so engaged.

The value of library services, as an aid in rehabilitation, has long been recognized in theory. However, too many of the penal libraries are still merely storehouses for a miscellaneous collection of discarded books. The prison is a community of a peculiar kind. It needs a library suited to the needs of that kind of community. A good prison library must have a collection of books and periodicals that meet the needs and interests of those it serves, with adequate funds to regularly and systematically replenish it with new purchases. The work in the library should be supervised by a trained librarian, qualified to prepare the material for circulation, to stimulate prisoners in the use of the library, and to guide them in securing the material they want and need.

The work of the library should be closely allied with that of the educational department, and the librarian should be recognized for his contribution to the individualized study of prisoners. The trained civilian librarian should be a graduate from an accredited Library School, experienced in an administrative library position, and trained in adult education, sociology, psychology, and criminology. He should have a clear understanding of the institution's organization and of the rôle his work will have in it. He should develop a sympathetic understanding of institution life and inmates.

The preceding paragraphs suggest a picture quite different from that gained in visiting an institution. In response to a request to see the library, the custodial officer, with a record of many years of faithful service, sought for some time before he found the key to the library, a musty room, out of the way, with a few shelves on which were a few books, all of which was covered with a thick coat of dust and to which the officer offered the explanation, "This room is not used much."

In practice the library service is somewhere between the two extremes presented in the preceding paragraphs. Few penal or correctional institutions have adequate library facilities. Most of the libraries represent a collection of a lot of books most of which were donated. Seldom is there a provision in the budget for the purchase of new books. In most cases there is no provision for a trained librarian and much of the work is done by inmate help under the supervision of a civilian employee without library training.

The Federal Bureau of Prisons has made some very noticeable gains in the library service. In federal institutions all books are purchased. The library facilities are open to the inmates. There is a trained librarian on the job and the library has a place in the life of the inmate. Few State institutions in the correctional field have library facilities comparable to those found in the Federal correctional institutions. There is much room for improvement before institutional practices catch up with the recognition of the theoretical value of library services.

Transgressors of the laws of society committed to penal or correctional institutions may appear to be lacking in religious ideals. It may be thought that convicts give little promise of response to religious efforts. Few prisoners were religiously active at the time the offense was committed. It is probably true that most offenders had shied away from religious associates long before they transgresssed the laws of society. The religious activities experienced on the outside, in free society, did not meet the individual needs. The reasons for breaking away from religious activities, and religious associates may appear to be imaginary, false, and insignificant, but to the individual they are real, true, and important. Many prisoners are religious by nature. Many of them have been brought up in homes that are religious. Some of them have never had any religious belief. The prison population is a field of labor for a real chaplain who has had special training for the difficult tasks and who possesses qualities of personality that attract and inspire others. The successful chaplain must be sincere, understanding, tolerant, and approachable. He must be able in counseling individuals and in affording spiritual guidance. There are relatively few outlets in prison life for individual expression and the inmate is eager to make use of the few opportunities available to him. Religious participation is one of the few opportunities for individual expression and escape from prison atmosphere.

Freedom of worship implies permission to worship in accordance with personal be-

liefs and the opportuniy for such worship. There should be a chapel and a chaplain for each of the major religious faiths represented in the inmate population. If one chapel is used for all religious services, portable altars should be provided to meet the requirements of the different services. Many institutions have no chapel but utilize substitute structures. In such instances every effort should be made to give the substitute structure as much religious atmosphere as possible.

The chaplain's duties are limited to religious activities. He is a counselor. He affords spiritual guidance. If he is used for other duties, not within his religious field, in order to justify his retention on a full-time basis, his efforts, as a religious worker, are impaired. He has a full-time job in interviewing inmates, and inmate relatives who wish to see him, and in contacting religious organizations outside the institution. His presence is desired at the classification meeting and his success as a chaplain in the institution is determined in part by the cooperation he achieves with fellow staff members. The chaplain's job is a special field requiring personnel qualified by nature and training to deal with people who have failed under ordinary conditions and are in need of special treatment under the supervision of specialists who have been well trained and are peculiarly suited for the work.

Considerable effort is being made to train clergymen for the special jobs chaplains have to do in penal and correctional institutions. Prison administrators are more keenly aware of the need for chapels and office space for the chaplain to do a successful job, and they are attempting to provide these facilities. They are recognizing the importance of the rôle the chaplain plays in institutional work.

The objective of penal and correctional institutions is to rehabilitate the inmate, to prepare him for eventual return to society with minimum risk to society. The old type prison did not embrace this view nor could it have accomplished that objective, if such were its aim, because, among the many other defects in the system, it did not permit recreational activities. This may have been due, in part, to the fact that the prison administrators, in the old type prison, feared the public's criticism which accused them of "pampering the prisoner." It may have been partly the result of the fact that prison administrators were untrained for their jobs, were unaware of the valuable contributions derived from recreational activities, were more interested in holding their jobs by meeting the demands of a misinformed or ill-informed public than in helping the inmates, or lacked the understanding necessary to carry out a recreational program.

Today, though the public has little real understanding of the value of recreation in the institutional program, it is beginning to accept the idea that institutions exist primarily for the rehabilitation of the inmates, and the chances of success in accomplishing that end are enhanced when the health and morale of the inmates are properly considered.

With the better qualified and higher type of prison administrator found in the institutions today, the value of recreation in the prison program is being recognized. It is these leaders who struggle for organization, staff, equipment, and funds with which to carry on a suitable recreation program to the end that disciplinary control may be on a higher level than that of fear, that the mental and physical health of the inmates may be improved, that some outlet will be provided for the repressed energies, and that the ideals of fair play, cooperation, and teamwork may become established as a part of the mental and emotional equipment of the inmate about to be returned to society.

The director of recreation has a special job to do and he should be qualified by nature and training to deal with people who have failed under ordinary conditions and are in need of special treatment. He should be a graduate of an accredited Physical Education School and he should have those qualities of personality and character which will cause the inmates to accept his leadership readily and to profit by it. He must understand clearly the importance and place of his job in relation to the prison program as a whole. His success depends upon the cooperation he achieves with fellow staff members. The recreational services may be an arm of the department of education. Through the activities under his manage-

ment, the director of recreation would observe the progress of the individuals engaged in those activities and would report his findings to the director of education.

Formerly, the chief responsibility of the superintendents of departments and the foremen in the shops within the institution was production. Everything was subservient to the cry for production. Different systems of employment were utilized in the State penal systems, including lease, contract, piece-price, State use, public works and ways, and public account. All of them emphasized production. Some of the purposes of prison labor were (a) the alleviation of the tedium of prison life; (b) the repression of crime; (c) the production of economic commodities to decrease the cost of support; (d) reformation; and (e) prison discipline.

It is a responsibility of the State to provide work for all prisoners who are able to work. More than that, the kind of work provided for the prisoners must not only be profitable to the State but it also must provide opportunities for the prisoner to receive training of a kind suited to his abilities and capacities and which will enhance his chances for success in the program of after care following his release. The change in emphasis from production to training has necessitated a change in the selection of the personnel utilized in the supervision of the work projects. The personnel must know the specific job. They must also know how to teach the prisoners the necessary skills to carry on the work. They must have an acceptable working knowledge of the purpose of the institution respecting the efforts toward rehabilitation. Every shop or work situation within the institution is an opportunity for the training of prisoners in preparation for that eventful return to society.

Incidentally, it has been observed that the rate of production goes up as the opportunities and the facilities for training increase. This may be due to the improved morale which results as a prisoner recognizes the gains made toward becoming a skilled or semi-skilled worker in his chosen field of activity and realizes the value of such achievement in relation to his chances of making good upon his return to a free society. That system of training, through the work projects of the institution, which keeps pace with the current demands of free society most effectively enhances the chances of the prisoner to make good.

Two important recent additions to the staff of an institution are the social case worker and the sociologist. The sociologist is particularly important because he surveys the social environment in which the crime occurred and in which the criminal performed, and seeks to provide explanations of behavior originating in the social setting. This approach to the quest for information relative to the cause of the prisoner's behavior promises much toward the planning of a suitable program of adjustment for the prisoner and his eventual success in coping with the obstacles which caused him to violate the laws of society.

The social case worker or welfare officer of the institution is primarily concerned with the well-being of the individual prisoner while he is a ward of the State and during the period of after care following his release from the institution. He is interested in assembling information pertinent to the individual case in order that such information may be utilized in furthering the treatment administered to the prisoner in an attempt to rehabilitate him.

The warden of a modern institution with the new objectives, added services, and trained personnel still has the problem of preventing escapes, maintaining discipline, avoiding scandals, and managing the institution. His chief concern, however, is the rehabilitation of the inmates committed to the institution of which he is the head, and he must use every resource at his command to focus the efforts of the several services of the institution upon the individual inmates.

CARL E. JOHNSON
Associate Professor
Department of Sociology
University of Wisconsin
Madison 6, Wisconsin

BIBLIOGRAPHY

Barnes, Harry Elmer and Teeters, Negley K., *New Horizons in Criminology*, Prentice-Hall, Inc., New York, 1943.

Gillin, John Lewis, *Criminology and Penology* (Third Edition) D. Appleton-Century Company, New York, 1945.

Hopkirk, Howard W., *Institutions Serving Children*, Russell Sage Foundation, New York, 1944.

Lindner, Robert M., *Stone Walls and Men*, Odyssey Press, New York, 1946.

Manual of Suggested Standards for a State Correctional System, The American Prison Association, Committee on the Model State Plan, Lewisohn, Sam A., Chairman, 135 East 15th Street, New York 3, New York, 1946.

Reckless, Walter C. and Smith, Mapheus, *Juvenile Delinquency*, McGraw-Hill Book Company, Inc., New York, 1932.

Sutherland, Edwin H., *Principles of Criminology* (Third Edition) J. B. Lippincott Company, Chicago, 1939.

Taft, Donald R., *Criminology*, The Macmillan Company, New York, 1942.

Von Hentig, Hans, *Crime*, McGraw-Hill Book Company, Inc., New York, 1947.

PRISON SYSTEMS. Contrary to general impression the prison is a relatively modern invention, hardly more than a hundred and fifty years old. It is true that it had many antecedents, but the distinction between these earlier institutions and prisons is sharply defined. At the instigation of political authorities throughout the medieval ages men were often held, even for long periods of time, in castles or other fortress structures, but this incarceration was during the period of trial or preliminary to some punishment such as execution. There were exceptions, in the case of certain offenses, a limited number of fine cases, commutation of sentence, or in the instance of certain noblemen who might be confined for a brief time without other forms of punishment. While these places of confinement were, therefore, not primarily for the purpose of punishing by imprisonment, they must be regarded as contributors to the idea.

More directly connected was the church which was generally prohibited from using the death penalty. In the monasteries was practiced a withdrawal from society, much of the time being spent in cells. The church also maintained institutions in which all types of persons were confined, varying all the way from the sick, aged, crippled, and orphans to the insane, delinquents, and criminals. Ecclesiastical imprisonment sometimes was strict confinement in absolute solitude and at other times association with periods spent in a cell. One such institution, from which John Howard was supposed to have received some of the ideas which he later employed in England, was the house of correction for delinquent boys which was erected in 1703 as part of the Papal Hospice of Saint Michael in Rome. Work was done in common during the day, with separate cellular confinement at night. This institution used a system of cells for penitential reformation. In turn, some of the principles of reformation and the idea of cells and cellular confinement, however by day and night, was borrowed from Filippo Franci at the Hospice of San Filippo Neri in Florence, which was started in 1677.

Servitude in the galleys which was used extensively in many European nations, such as England, Spain, and France, from about 1500 until early in the eighteenth century, was a form of imprisonment by hard labor. It was also a forerunner of the modern prison as a form of punishment.

Houses of correction for penal treatment came into being in Europe during the sixteenth through the eighteenth centuries. They were places for the incarceration, often with labor, of minor offenders, such as vagabonds, family deserters, prostitutes, some juveniles, and other petty offenders. Such an institution, the London Bridewell, was founded in 1557. By act of parliament in 1576 and again in 1609 each English county was directed to establish a similar institution. By act of 1711 the maximum period of confinement was fixed at three years. Irons were used and the institutions were in general places of indiscriminate congregate confinement. Two famous institutions, the Hamburg workhouse and the Ghent house of correction, were established in 1669 and 1775 respectively. Jails and workhouses were established in America soon after settlement.

None of the houses of correction or other forms of imprisonment were used for more serious offenders, who were generally punished in some more severe fashion or executed. Besides the death penalty, common forms of punishment at the time were the galleys, physical torture, degradation by branding, maiming, the pillory, and transportation. These barbarous forms of punishment declined and were replaced by imprisonment not only on moral grounds but, as Sutherland has indicated, first because imprisonment on an extensive scale had previously been practically impossible, because of construction problems involved in the building of a secure institution and unsettled conditions of warfare in European countries. A second factor was the greater appreciation of freedom which arose with economic and cultural progress. Third, labor power was more important and could be utilized in prisons, as was shown in the houses of correction, and, finally, the distance between social classes being changed, the distinction was not as great between those who gave and received punishment, and the ruling classes could, therefore, also be punished by severe measures. In addition to these reasons, prisons also arose because of the need for greater security for long-term offenders than could be afforded in houses of correction and local jails.

In England the pioneer work of John Howard on local jails and the abandonment of transportation to America had great effect on the development of imprisonment. Some writers feel that the immediate forerunner of the Pennsylvania System in America was, in fact, the Wymondham Jail, Norfolk, England, built in 1784 to develop certain theories of John Howard's. As a result of wide surveys of contemporary penal conditions, Howard suggested the idea of solitary confinement of hardened offenders to aid penitence and reform. This jail provided for the separation of confirmed criminals from less hardened offenders, and of men and women. Later leaders like Sir William Blackstone and Sir William Eden drafted a comprehensive bill for a national penitentiary system providing for solitary cell confinement by night and close supervision by day while at work and at other activities. Passed in 1779, the law was never put into effect because of the American Revolution. Fifteen years later the government made a contract with Jeremy Bentham for the building of a large national prison called a Panopticon which was never built. In 1791 Parliament passed the first

General Prisons Act to set up national prisons throughout England and Wales, although nothing was immediately done. England, to accommodate the thousand or so prisoners formerly sent to the United States, used ship hulks for some eighty years, even after national prisons were established, and also transportation to Australia. In 1816 England finally erected at Millbank a central prison. In 1832 William Crawford was directed by the government to study the prison systems in the United States, out of which visit several institutions were erected modeled after the Pennsylvania system described below. In 1839 a law was passed making possible separate instead of congregate confinement in local prisons. Pentonville Prison, on the cellular plan, was opened in 1842 and, similar to the Pennsylvania system, separate confinement was required for the first period of sentence. This, however, was followed by employment on public works.

Transportation to Australia, which was used as a third stage of imprisonment, was in effect until abolished in 1853. In 1857 a system of four separate stages of imprisonment was provided. The first nine months were passed in solitary followed by three progressive stages, dependent upon conduct. This system was derived from that introduced into Ireland by Sir Robert Crofton in 1854, which became known as the Irish, or progressive stage, system. In turn, the fundamental elements of the Irish system had been developed in the indeterminate sentence, mark system, and parole of Maconochie in the English penal colony at Norfolk Island in Australia. Since 1850 convict prisons have been under a national commission, and by an act of 1877 all local jails were also put under a central commission. In 1898 these two boards were merged into one system with considerable control by the home secretary. The progressive stage system was extended in 1891 to those serving less than three years. Corporal punishment in 1898 was restricted only to special cases, and during this same year the crank and the treadmill were eliminated as methods of prison labor. By 1913 mental deficients were segregated in separate institutions. The forerunner of the Borstal system of semi-reformatory treatment for young adult offenders was the Prevention of Crimes Act of 1908.

In America at the time of the Revolution there were still the common jails, various harsh punishments, but rarely imprisonment for serious offenders. At the instigation largely of the Quakers, the Pennsylvania legislature in 1786 decided to take steps to reduce capital crimes and to punish criminals in other ways. Capital punishment was restricted to treason, murder, arson, and rape. For other crimes imprisonment, whipping, and hard labor in public were used. In 1790 the Walnut Street prison in Philadelphia was set aside for prisoners. Here the more serious offenders were confined to solitary cells, while the less hardened were kept in large rooms and allowed to work during the day. No irons or chains were used; there was a rule of silence in the shop and at the tables. Small wages were paid and the hours of work were not excessive.

The Walnut Street Prison is generally acknowledged as the beginning of the modern prison. Most U. S. prisons were patterned after it for almost half a century. While it worked reasonably well when it had a small number of prisoners, it later deteriorated due to a number of conditions. Newgate prison in New York City, 1797, and Charlestown at Boston, 1805, were later established along the same pattern.

The failure of Walnut Street prison led the Philadelphia Society for Alleviating the Miseries of Public Prisons to work for new types of institutions, the first being the Western Pennsylvania Penitentiary of 1818 where prisoners were confined in solitary confinement and were not given employment of any kind. In 1821 a law was passed for an Eastern Penitentiary, also with solitary confinement. This building was not occupied by prisoners until 1829, by which time the Western system without work was modified so as to provide solitary confinement with labor in the cells. Under the Pennsylvania system as practiced in the Eastern Penitentiary each prisoner was entirely isolated from others. Physical arrangements were such that, except for sickness or death, the prisoner was confined throughout the length of his sentence, sometimes several years, without seeing or communicating with another inmate. The only persons who could see him were the warden, guards, chaplain, and official visitors of Philadelphia organizations. The only reading material was a Bible. No letters could be written to anyone. Only labor and exercise in solitude relieved the monotony. The philosophy was that this system kept the less hardened away from the hardened, would enable a prisoner to think out his own reformation, and the labor would contribute to his support and reformation.

Prisoners in the Pennsylvania system suffered horribly from solitary confinement. The Auburn, New York prison of 1821 sought to correct this fault. Prisoners were originally classified into three grades. The first class were the most hardened, and, on the Pennsylvania pattern, were confined to their cells without work twenty-four hours a day. The second class, which were less incorrigible, spent part of the time in solitary and part in labor as a recreation. The third class, who were the most reformable, were confined alone at night but could work together during the day, but under the silent system. By 1823 the method of treating the third group was extended to all prisoners. The Pennsylvania system can be thought of as solitary and silent, while the Auburn was partially solitary but also silent. Discipline was harsh and no rewards were given for good behavior.

These two systems became models for prisons both in Europe and America, the Pennsylvania for the former and the Auburn for the latter. England, Germany, and Scandinavia adopted the Pennsylvania system and continued many of its features almost down to the present. Denmark, for example, still has the solitary system. In many ways, however, the two systems were similar, both preventing communication among the prisoners and both using cell confinement. In the Pennsylvania system the prisoners never knew each other, even by face, a feature that was later carried over into Europe in an extreme fashion by face masks. It was felt that this was an excellent feature, for it prevented a man being possibly injured by a prison record. The Auburn system, while not allowing communication, at least afforded recog-

nition. No communication was allowed with relatives or friends. Gillin has cited several reasons for the greater American adoption of the Auburn system. It was more economical to build, since more men could be housed than under the Pennsylvania's larger cells and peculiar construction. With its shops, Auburn was also more productive industrially than the Pennsylvania solitary work system. The exceptional leadership at Auburn was also significant. Both institutions, however, failed to achieve any marked degree of reformation, but the same can be said of the most modern present day systems.

Although Connecticut had a prison in an abandoned copper mine as early as 1773, it was not actually a real penitentiary, so that the distinction for the first state prison is usually given to Pennsylvania's Walnut Street jail of 1790. Other states followed in this order: New York, 1796; New Jersey, 1798; Virginia and Kentucky, 1800; Massachusetts, 1805; Vermont, 1809; Maryland and New Hampshire, 1812, and Ohio, 1816. Several of the original structures in these prisons, with improvements, of course, are still in operation. Relying heavily on transportation, Great Britain, aside from Millbank prison, completed in 1821, had no developed central prison until 1842.

While the essential features of the Auburn system of imprisonment have largely remained to the present day, many states have pioneered experiments in modification. Most important was Massachusetts in 1826, authorizing Boston to send juvenile delinquents to the House of Correction. In 1844 this state also permitted the transfer of insane prisoners from the state prison to the state mental hospital. Massachusetts state prison also had the first prison library and orchestra. In the Connecticut prison of 1827 was introduced a preliminary honor system with certain prisoners allowed to go outside the wall for certain duties. Maryland prison introduced the first school for all the inmates in 1829, and by 1833 had 211 literate inmates who originally had been illiterates. Georgia in 1832 instituted a system of rewards for good conduct. Tennessee Penitentiary in 1833 started a system of good time by which two days in every month were deducted from the sentence for good behavior and five added for every day of punishment. Vermont about 1831 allowed writing letters to friends and frequent visitors. The Massachusetts state prison on July 4, 1864 was one of the first to allow prisoners to assemble together on a holiday. Allowed only one hour, the men, previously under the silent system, were reported to have shaken hands, danced, shouted, and cried. The Illinois state prison experimented with the same plan in 1877.

The lock step, introduced in Auburn about 1821, was done away with at Sing Sing prison in 1900. The strict rule of silence gradually is fading out. Instead of prisoners being fed in their cells, as was customary at first and still general in Europe, a common dining room has been introduced. Silence at meals is still the general rule, except in our most progressive institutions. Work camps have grown up, particularly in southern institutions after the Civil War. A system of prison grades is now common. Experiments made in the classification of inmates according to custodial difficulties and possibility of reformation have resulted in the development of diversified institutions and maximum, medium, and minimum confinement institutions to care for various classes of offenders. A system of inmate self-government was developed by Thomas Mott Osborne at Auburn prison in 1913.

The actual function of prisons today in the minds of the public is in a state of confusion. Most people maintain that the function of a prison is to keep criminals from doing further injury to society. Another purpose is that of retribution or punishment, namely that the offender should suffer for his crime. To some the purpose of the latter is to deter not only the criminal but others from committing similar crimes. Finally, there is the belief of a considerable number of persons, particularly social scientists, that the exclusive purpose of the prison is to bring about reformation.

All of these purposes need to be examined. In the case of security the prison is relatively successful for a while, but it is a mistake to think that this situation continues for any length of time, for most all prisoners are released within five years time, many in probably a worse social situation than when they entered. There is little evidence of the deterrent effects of imprisonment. As for punishment, it is essentially based on a doctrine of free will rather than social causation. Punishment and reformation are entirely opposite procedures, and the two cannot be accomplished simultaneously.

If we assume that the function of a prison is to reform, which is the modern scientific approach, then imprisonment must be thought of in relation to a theory of criminal behavior. Such a theory holds that personality consists of general reaction patterns or psychogenic traits and attitudes. The former are probably the result of experiences during the early formative period of life and the latter of all social experience. Criminal behavior is human behavior, and the basic processes are consequently the same as for non-criminal behavior. Rather than any distinction in kind, the explanation of criminal behavior differentiates only between criminal and non-criminal behavior. Since essentially all that criminal behavior represents is a criminal attitude, reformation should be directed toward changing these attitudes and bringing about better adjustment in psychogenic traits. Unfortunately, in those rare places where advanced prison techniques are employed, so many negative factors are present, including the artificiality of prison life and the stigma of society, that reformation in this theoretical sense appears to be impossible to achieve to any marked degree within a prison system. This is demonstrated by the fact that 40 to 70 percent of the men in most prisons have been incarcerated before. Even though the records were incomplete, 56.5 percent of the prisoners committed to state and federal prisons and reformatories in the United States in 1936 had previous commitments to such institutions.

While imprisonment is the generally recognized procedure for dealing with crime, there is considerable variety in types of prisons and procedures used in connection with it. For short term offenders and misdemeanants there are municipal jails, county jails, county farms and chain gangs, and state farms for misdemeanants. Jails are also used for the detention of those awaiting trial or transfer to some other penal institution. Then there are, in our larger cities, many city and county work houses and houses of correction for certain types of offenders. Reformatories, usually for younger offenders but sometimes for first offenders, constitute another group which in reality are usually only modified prisons. Then there are the prisons, state and federal, to which persons are committed usually for the more serious offenses or for longer terms, generally in excess of one year. Finally, there are specialized institutions, industrial training schools for boys and girls, for women, for certain classes of young adult offenders, and for the criminal insane, epileptics, and mentally deficient.

The approximate number of penal and reformatory institutions in the United States is 4,400. Of these 1,500 are municipal jails, work houses, farms and stockades for offenders convicted of misdemeanors, 2,500 are county jails, workhouses, farms, and chain gangs for misdemeanants, 112 are state prisons, state farms and state chain gangs, 30 are state reformatories, 29 are federal prisons, reformatories and camps under the direction of the Federal Bureau of Prisons, and 23 prisons under the War and Navy Departments, 177 are juvenile reformatories, of which 2 are federal, 117 state, 30 county or municipal, and 25 private.

Approximately 3,000,000 persons, some of them more than once, are committed annually to jails and detention centers in the United States. The county and city jail population at a given time is estimated at about 60,000, and the population of juvenile institutions at about 35,000. Total prisoners present in state and federal prisons and reformatories of the United States in 1940, a typical pre-war year, numbered 171,626, of whom all but 6,352 were males. Of the state prisoners, 34.2 percent were in southern institutions, 33.1 percent in north central, 21.4 percent in northeastern, and 11.3 percent in western institutions. Total admissions during the year numbered 84,450, those received from the court numbering 73,456, and the remainder being returned escapees, parole violators, and other admissions. Discharges amounted to 90,287, and of these

40.3 percent were released unconditionally by expiration, pardon, or commutation. Escapes were 1,482, while deaths were 1,022, and executions in these institutions 86. During this year the median age of all male felons committed during the year was 27.8 years.

New York had 15,353 inmates in their state penal institutions in 1940, Illinois 11,374, Ohio 8,758, while Nevada had 255, New Hampshire 262, and Rhode Island 308. The largest institutions in 1940 were the Illinois Penitentiary at Joliet with 5,719, the Michigan prison with 5,356, and California state prison at San Quentin with 5,127. The smallest men's prison was the 214 in the Rhode Island state prison. In England in 1939 the average daily population of all correctional institutions was 10,326.

Considering the results, the cost of maintaining penal institutions is a heavy financial burden. The annual cost of operating our state and federal prisons and reformatories for its more than 170,000 inmates is at least $125,000,000. The budget of the U. S. federal institutions is about $18,000,000 annually. The cost of New York institutions in 1945–46 was $13,380,597, and California in 1945–46 was $4,050,966. England spent 1,798,561 pounds on her correctional institutions during the year 1942–43. Per capita annual costs in 1945 for keeping a person in prison vary from $172 in Arkansas, $220 in Texas, and $250 in Mississippi to $1890 in one California institution. The national average is well over $600 a year. Similar costs are found in Canada. Institutions for women and juveniles are rarely even partially self-supporting. In the case of men's institutions the restrictions placed on prison-made goods, the methods of industrial production, and the numerous correctional and educational functions in the more advanced make nearly all costly to operate. To make them self-supporting, which some prison administrators regard as a sign of efficiency, is usually at the expense of improved reformation procedures. Such costs and human misery raise the question of whether more feasible methods of crime treatment, such as the wider use of probation and parole and the development of more crime prevention programs, such as local community projects, cannot be devised at far less cost to society.

Generalizations about American prisons are difficult. With each county and state having its own system and reflecting independently its attitude toward progressive correctional policies, there is enormous diversity. Some American prisons are the most advanced in correctional theory and some are the most backward in the world. In many, conditions of treatment, both physical and mental, are little improved over a century ago. There can be found institutions in which there is no classification system, untrained political appointees as officers, rigid discipline, including some physical tortures, idleness, little vocational, or other education, and no psychiatric or other special services.

One significant trend in nearly all states has been toward increasing specialization of prisons. Originally all types of prisoners were kept in the same institution regardless of sex, age, or condition. The purpose of specialization is to prevent one type having a harmful effect on another and to provide for specialized care and treatment facilities. In the United States the federal government maintains its own system of 29 units of different types, having approximately 19,000 inmates. Each state has usually a separate juvenile institution for boys and one for girls; one or more reformatories for young men; a separate institution for women; at least one penitentiary and sometimes two for men; and sometimes specialized institutions, although sometimes in name only, for the criminal insane, the defective, the sick, alcoholic, narcotic addict, or sex offender. While Oregon has only three institutions, New Jersey has eight, California fifteen, and New York sixteen. Some institutions in the south maintain separate industrial schools for whites and Negroes. In Arkansas the per capita cost for the white boys is over twice that of the Negroes. Other southern institutions largely segregate Negroes and whites in separate cell blocks.

Classification by institution has reached a high degree of development in the U. S. federal institutions. Besides two institutions for juvenile delinquents and one for women, there are eight for short-term offenders, five

minimum custody for improvable offenders, one agricultural type, and three others for younger improvable offenders, three for older improvable, two for habitual (Atlanta and Leavenworth) and one for intractable offenders (Alcatraz). In addition, the federal prison system has available a New York City institution chiefly for those awaiting trial, an institution for physically and mentally maladjusted offenders, and it sends narcotic addicts to the United States Public Health Service Hospital at Lexington, Ky.

The British system is divided into local provincial prisons, London Area prisons, training centers, convict prisons, preventive detention prisons, and Borstal institutions. The local provincial prisons are those to which prisoners of all classes, convicted or unconvicted, whether sentenced to imprisonment, penal servitude, or Borstal detention are committed directly from the courts. They may either serve their sentences in these prisons, or be transferred by the prison commissioners to other appropriate institutions. The London Area prisons are a self-contained group. A training center is a regional prison to which are transferred all prisoners with normally sentences of not less than 12 months nor more than three years who are of sufficiently good character to offer hope of reformation and cooperation. Convict prisons are for those sentenced to penal servitude, although usually those with less than three years serve in the local prison. Preventive detention prisons are for a small group of habitual prisoners. Borstal institutions are for young persons of 16 to 21 sentenced to Borstal detention.

In general, the care of women prisoners in this country is better than the treatment of men. In half of the states, however, women prisoners are still confined within sections of the state prisons for men. Because they are simply an adjunct to the men's prisons, in general their care is less adequate and they are restricted far more than the men. While Indiana was the first state, in 1873, to segregate women from men by building a separate institution, this movement for separate institutions, however, has primarily developed in the period since 1910. A number of states have constructed separate institutions for women, variously known as reformatories, industrial institutions, houses of refuge, farms, homes and prisons, since the idea is to get away from terms which would stigmatize the offenders. Twenty-four states and the federal government have such separate institutions, although the latter had none until 1927. In general, they are small minimum security cottage plan institutions, although a few are still prison-like structures, employing rehabilitation procedures superior to most men's institutions. In Europe there has been less development in women's institutions than in the United States. Most of them, while separate, are parts of men's prisons. Soviet Russia has a mixed system in some institutions. There are separate departments for women, but they work with the men in the shops.

In addition to these state institutions, nearly all states have provisions which permit placing women prisoners in private institutions where feasible. In some instances, states contract with another state for the care of their women offenders. In others the age limit of the girls' industrial school is raised to permit the entrance of some older women rather than to build a separate institution. While individual classification is extensively used in women's institutions, segregation, where practiced, is limited to cottage residence. Although available evidence indicates that the record of success by women's institutions is better than that of those for men, there is a considerable percentage of failures. The condition and stigma of imprisonment by society, as well as confinement with others, could lead to no other expectation.

Institutions are frequently distinguished by the designation prison or reformatory. Elmira Reformatory, established in 1876, is considered the first institution of its type. Its immediate forerunner was the Irish system of graded institutions, indeterminate sentence, a mark system, and parole for progressive advancement, which was developed by Sir William Crofton and originally in Australia by Maconochie. At Elmira the attempt was to get away from repressive imprisonment. Prisons at the time were harsh disciplinary places with severe labor and no classification, and first and repeated offenders, old and

young, were confined together. Prisoners under the reformatory system were to be first time offenders from 16 to 30 years of age, there was a limited indeterminate sentence, a classification or grading of prisoners, a mark system, and emphasis on education and parole. Instrumental in the development of this institution were E. C. Wines and Zebulon R. Brockway, its first superintendent. It was enthusiastically received as a new prison system and was later adopted in England in a modified form as the Borstal system.

The results of the reformatory system in America, except for the initial period at Elmira, have been generally disappointing. Essentially, the form on paper remained, but the spirit became that of the old repressive prison. One of the most serious difficulties has been that personnel were usually those with prison type of training. Another has been that age or number of incarcerations does not indicate necessarily the degree of criminal development of a man. The original high figures of success at Elmira, estimated at 85 to 90 percent, have since been questioned in the light of more scientific evidence of the difficulty of measuring successful reformation. The more recent study, after a five-year period of release, of inmates of the Massachusetts Reformatory by the Gluecks showed 80 percent unreformed. Even though this included minor offenses it still indicates that there is not much reform in reformatories.

In America, some fifty years later, less than one-half the states have reformatories. Ten of the 23 men's reformatories, in 21 states, in 1943 were built over 30 years ago. Most of them do not differ from prisons; they are actually junior prisons. Practically all are walled institutions and the personnel of many is inefficient. The institutions have generally the same features of repression and regimentation. There is considerable overlapping in age of offenders with prisons; 64 percent of reformatory commitments in 1930 had previously been committed to correctional institutions. Their size is about the same as prisons, over half being more than 1,000 population. Education in general is as inadequate as in prisons. The reformatory is generally a reformatory in name only, with a few notable exceptions such as the revised program at Elmira, the California institution at Chino, New Jersey's reformatory at Annandale, and the federal institutions. Most should be regarded as prisons and new types of institutions erected with radically different programs.

England does not have an institution exactly like our reformatories for young adults. The Borstal system, adopted in 1909, has been devised for a selected group of juvenile adult offenders between the ages of 16 and 21. Young adults are sent to them for periods of not less than two or more than four years. The average number received for Borstal detention in recent years is annually about 1,800. In all, there are nine such institutions, each with a small population and classified as to type. Inmates are given vocational training, divided into smaller groups, and given considerable personal attention by the officials. The staffs are highly trained and wear civilian clothes. While the recidivism rate is estimated as high as 30 to 40 percent, there is evidence that the record is considerably better than most American institutions of similar type. With the exception of Sweden, continental Europe does not have special reformatory institutions for young adults.

The California Institution for Men at Chino, a new type of reformatory, has recently attracted considerable comment. Opened in 1941 and located on a ranch of several thousand acres, its inmates are carefully selected minimum security risks. There are no walls or guns, and the men are housed in both open dormitories and individual unlocked cells. The custodial staff is ununiformed. The men take an extensive educational and vocational program. There are considerable inmate privileges, including an inmate council and the privilege of frequent visits and picnics with their families and friends.

With the original objectives of the reformatory system in mind, a far-reaching revision of our present correctional system is the recent Youth Correction Authority plan developed by the American Law Institute. This plan, undoubtedly influenced by the British Borstal treatment of young offenders, proposes that the sentencing of a convicted offender should cease to be a court function and that a board or commission should have full responsibility for prescribing the care and treatment of an offender up to 21 years of age on probation, in an institution, or on parole, from the time he is convicted until released. The offender can be released at any time the Authority feels such action is consistent with the protection of the public. The proposed Authority may make use of "law enforcement, detention, probation, parole, medical, educational, correctional, segregative, and other facilities, institutions and agencies, whether public or private, within the state." This plan has been adopted in a slightly modified fashion by California (1941), Minnesota (1947), Wisconsin (1947), and Massachusetts (1948). Sweden has now a somewhat similar plan in operation for most offenders, regardless of age.

In California the Youth Authority is a three member board appointed by the governor which has responsibility for the classification, care, and treatment of all cases committed to it by the juvenile courts of the state, and such other youthful offenders up to 21 as may be accepted for treatment by the Youth Authority from the criminal courts of the state. Offenders are not sentenced by a judge to an institution but to the Youth Authority. Superintendents of institutions for youths and juveniles are appointed by the director of the Youth Authority from civil service, as are other employees. Other institutions are under the jurisdiction of an Adult Authority. In Wisconsin the Youth Service Act operates in much the same fashion, except that its board does not have direct control over the institutions. It is hoped that other states will adopt this plan and that it may be extended to all offenders regardless of age or conditions.

The administration of prisons in the United States is divided between the federal government and the 48 states. In addition there are numerous municipal and county systems. The Federal Bureau of Prisons, a part of the Department of Justice, administers a large variety of Federal institutions ranging from California to New York and from Washington to Florida. The Judge Advocate General of the War Department administers a large number of institutions for general prisoners. These range from small medium security disciplinary barracks to large maximum security institutions, such as Fort Leavenworth. The Corrective Services Division of the Bureau of Naval Personnel handles naval prisoners in retraining commands, disciplinary barracks, and the U. S. Naval prison at Portsmouth. The State Department administers certain consular prisons abroad. British prisons are administered in England and Wales by a prison commission and in Scotland by a director of the prison division. They have direct control over all English correctional institutions. In Canada the superintendent of penitentiaries in the Department of Justice has supervision over all federal institutions.

Among most of the states local institutions are autonomous, contributing to the confusion of standards and administration. County institutions are administered by county sheriffs or commissions. The states of Indiana, New York, New Jersey, Minnesota, Wisconsin, and Oklahoma now have regular supervision of jails and some states inspect them when complaints arise. In the case of Indiana a state work farm for misdemeanants has taken over the function of imprisoning most jail type offenders.

There are various types of organization in penal administration. The two most common systems, each used in eleven states, is the control of institutions by separate local boards of trustees, or the management of all prisons by a state prison commission or similar agency. Other systems which are widely employed are the ex-officio, where the governor and two or more state officials constitute the board as in the smaller states, the administration by a state board of control, administration by a state department where the individual is a member of the governor's cabinet as in New York, and the non-political type. The latter is sometimes known as the New Jersey type, where the administration of all correctional and charitable institutions is centered in a single state board of nine members. One member is appointed by the governor each year for eight years. Boards or commissions vary in size and authority, are sometimes appointed and in other instances elected, and while in some states they receive a salary in others they do not. The boards usually have a free hand, except where there is civil service, in appointing personnel. State juvenile institutions are frequently managed by a separate board or by some other agency separate from adults.

In general, there is a tendency toward centralization or administration in correctional institutions which, to some, appears to make possible greater political interference and too great mechanical uniformity. On the other hand, others maintain it offers more professional control and administration, more efficient personnel, less local graft and saves state expense. Some states confine the board to correctional functions, whereas in others correctional work is a separate part of a broader department dealing with all welfare activities. This is considered a better organization because it emphasizes that the correctional system is a part of the welfare program. It also facilitates the coordination of the prison program with other health and welfare services. Moreover, such a program lends more professionalization to the correctional program and usually assures better budgetary treatment. On the other hand, those who believe in a separate department of correction feel that it emphasizes the importance of this work and that the independence makes possible more rapid changes. Wisconsin furnishes an example of a fully coordinated correctional system within the state department of public welfare. The division of corrections has jurisdiction over both adult and juvenile institutions and includes a bureau of probation and parole whose agents supervise both probationers and parolees. The parole board is appointed by the department of public welfare. The division of corrections has responsibility for a psychiatric field service and inspection of city and county correctional institutions. Recently a Youth Services division was added to the department which also has responsibility for stimulating programs of delinquency prevention.

California now has a unique administrative

set-up, the Prison Reorganization Act of 1944 having provided basic changes in over-all administration. Its purpose was a unified statewide organization of correctional activities under a state department of corrections. The new department includes the director of corrections appointed by the governor, the board of corrections, the board of trustees of the women's institution, the Adult Authority (including the bureau of paroles) which has wide discretion over all adult male institutions, and the Youth Authority which exercises similar functions for juveniles and young adults. The Adult and Youth Authority boards each have three members, one of whom serves as director. The members of the Youth Authority are not responsible to the director of corrections but to the governor. Under the law one member of the Adult Authority is to be an attorney, one with practical experience in prison work, and one a sociologist.

Civil service status rather than political patronage is indispensable to the proper functioning of a prison system. No matter how good the system is on paper or how high the salaries, if the proper personnel are not selected the system will be inefficient. In most European countries, and in the United States federal system, nearly all prison officials are civil service employees who are appointed by a competitive examination, make a career out of their work, and are reasonably immune from political pressures. In 1939 only ten states had Civil Service Commissions and of these states only four or five had complete powers. There is great variation in examinations for correctional staff in the relative weight given training, experience, and personal interviews. Most state boards have a definite age limit and a standard of height and weight for guards. The standards even under civil service are not high. Maryland, Wisconsin, and New Jersey, for example, require only an elementary school education or its equivalent.

There are great variations in the salary and training given to correctional officers. Most wardens and considerable other prison personnel in the United States are political employees, and with little scientific training in their work, their previous experience often having been police or army work. Annual salaries in some states for correctional officers amount to less than $1,200, while in federal prison service the minimum salary is approximately $2,700. Some states now give in-service training to their employees such as the federal program where it amounts to fifteen weeks. A lecture course for prison officers in Massachusetts in 1921 was followed by similar programs in New York City and New Jersey. In a great number of institutions a man receives no formal training and must pick up what he can while on the job. The Universities of Wisconsin, Ohio State, and Notre Dame have recently begun offering a training program in correctional administration leading to a degree in this subject.

There have been various types of prison architecture. Many think the cell prison had its origin in the monastic system of the medieval church and some of the first forerunners of prisons were correctional quarters maintained by religious organizations. The Panopticon of Jeremy Bentham, designed about 1787, was an ingenious building which created great interest. It was to have been a circular building where every prisoner could be under continuous observation. It was adopted a century ago by Holland and Switzerland. The Eastern state penitentiary in Pennsylvania served as a model for prisons in all parts of the world, the main features being the radiating cell blocks, like the spokes of a wheel, with cells next to the outer walls and a corridor in the center. The design of the building facilitated the keeping of each inmate in solitary confinement, and the cells were fairly large, outside, and light. There was no chapel, school house, or dining hall, and no work place except in the cells. Each prisoner originally had a little yard outside his cell for exercise.

The Auburn or congregate prison system was only a modification of the Pennsylvania or separate system and became the model of most American prisons. Of the 100 institutions for long-term offenders in the United States, at least 80 are of the Auburn or fortress type. Eight prisons still in use are more than 100 years old. Over one-third were built over seventy years ago. The Auburn system, which was generally adopted in America, provided for a fortress-like inside cell block in separate oblong buildings with little sunlight, tiny cells, and workshops. Narrow passageways led past the cells, and catwalks for guards were provided. The Auburn type, still the most common type in prison structure, has been modified by modern devices to make escape more difficult, such as improved machine guns, higher walls, special steel bars and electrically controlled doors, and electric eyes for contraband. Other improvements include modern dining rooms, chapels, outside cell blocks, larger cells, windows in cells, and cell doors are no longer solid but barred. Some institutions have single cells while in others four or more men may be found in a cell.

A modification of the Pennsylvania and Auburn plans, in 1898, was completed at Fresnes near Paris. It was a prison built on a telegraph pole plan, substituting for the radiating Pennsylvania type by placing the buildings on either side of a central corridor which connects nearly all buildings. This plan is also utilized in Stillwater, Minnesota and Guelph, Ontario, and in modified form in the Lewisburg federal prison.

Modern prison methods have made it necessary for architects to turn their attention to new prison designs which are more functional and spend far less on outside facades and heavy walls. The most marked change in prison design has come through the erection of cottages, dormitories, and prison camps, largely to replace fortress prisons. These generally have no locked cells, no walls, no machine guns, but rely instead on classification and the development of proper inmate attitudes. Copied after European institutions, the first cottage type institution in this country was the Ohio School for Boys in 1865. Most women and many juvenile institutions, and the men's reformatories at Annandale in New Jersey and Chino in California, are examples of the newer types of cottage institutions. The Borstals of England for youthful offenders are also of this type. Despite the fact that erection costs have been estimated at $3,000 per inmate for the fortress type and only $600 to $800 for the more socially efficient type, most prisons still are as they were over one hundred years ago. Most penal institutions are far too large for effective personal guidance, some in fact running to several thousand inmates. Sweden is now extending virtually to all her penal system the idea of small, open institutions with not more than 40 to 100 inmates.

Today the trend is toward diversified institutions representing maximum, medium, and minimum security, according to individual needs. Maximum security generally means a walled institution with the majority of the inmates occupying inside cells, at all times surrounded by a high wall manned by armed guards. Medium security means an institution with no wall but perhaps a wire fence like factories, outside cells and dormitories, employment outside as well as inside the fence, and less physical features directed toward escape. Minimum security means an open institution, usually of the cottage, farm, or camp style, with the inmates not surrounded by either a wall or fence, working outdoors or in ordinary unlocked buildings without armed guards but only with persons who oversee the work. Smaller prisons, partially to accomplish this objective, are now establishing work farms and forestry camps in conjunction with a maximum security institution.

While prisoners who are feeble-minded, mentally ill, alcoholic, drug addicts, and sex offenders are still confined in with other prisoners in some states, there is a tendency now where possible to confine such offenders in other institutions or to build separate buildings with appropriate facilities for them. Some of the most advanced correctional systems have a separate receiving and classification institution or diagnostic center for prisoners newly received.

One of the major distinctions between prison systems can be found in the composition of their staffs. Some prisons, as the federal, have diversified, professionally administered programs, including classification, social work, vocational training, education, library, recreation, psychology, psychiatry, and health. At present, there is a tendency in most institutions for psychiatrists and psychologists to deal almost exclusively with the analysis of the behavior of inmates.

There is, however, increasing recognition that it is equally important to employ sociologists trained in analyzing the degree of criminal development as well as the social world of the offender. Other institutions have very few technical programs and in many instances are administered by inadequate and untrained personnel.

The development of classification is probably the most significant recent trend in prison work. Some early prison reformers were much disturbed by the fact that all classes of prisoners were being thrown together and having a mutual influence on one another. The Pennsylvania system, by separating offenders, was supposed to solve this problem as was the later proposal at Auburn for separate classes of offenders. Classification of prisoners, according to detailed sociological, psychiatric, psychological, educational, and medical examinations, has become a recognized part of a prison system in a number of states, although not in all. It involves individualization of treatment and was pioneered in New Jersey in 1917 and Belgium in 1920. The federal prisons have been the leaders in this work, as have also some states. In foreign countries Belgium and Sweden have particularly developed this approach. The classification committee may be located in each institution, in one or more designated institutions or may be located in a separate diagnostic depot independent of local administration, as in Illinois. Many feel that the classification committee should be an integral part of the prison staff, while others do not. In some, classification is used only to help eliminate custodial problems, in others it is the basis for a continuous individualized integrated program of reformation. In a few states which have the facilities not only are these two purposes incorporated, but classification also determines the type of institution to which a man will be sent. Classification without diversified types of programs and diversified institutional facilities is inadequate. In New Jersey, which has a highly developed central classification center, no two institutions serve the same purpose. The state prison, a walled institution, serves as an adult reception center and for prisoners whose records are poor. Bor-

dentown prison farm, an unwalled institution, is for medium and minimum security prisoners. Leesburg prison farm, an institution without cells, bars, or even a fence, is particularly used for men about to be released. Rahway reformatory is a walled institution for men 16 to 30 years of age. Annandale is a cottage type minimum security and, finally, Clinton reformatory for women is a cottage type. In all, about half the adult offenders are in institutions without walls. While classification seems to offer much hope for reformation, there are no statistics available to indicate any marked reduction in recidivism as a result.

Prison education has become increasingly important in most prison systems and has progressed far beyond the religious instruction of former days. Behind education lies the philosophy of reformation, and, particularly through vocational training, of improved economic livelihood. While statistics show the education of prisoners to have been only a few years, it must be realized also that the educational level of the general population is not high and that many persons with considerable education violate the law. While progress has been made, in 1941 only about one-fourth of the population of 44 state prisons and less than one-half of a group of state reformatories were in school. Federal penitentiaries and reformatories and only a handful of states have good educational systems. While most prisons have a nominal director of education, most prison schools are markedly inferior to the outside in the number and quality of personnel, books, and equipment. In general, the program is arranged to interfere with routine prison activities as little as possible. In 1940, exclusive of industrial work, there were only 296 full-time and 46 part-time teachers in all the United States prisons and reformatories, and as a consequence many have been forced to use inmate personnel as teachers. Prison education should be individualized, broadly inclusive in its offerings and, above all, should emphasize social integration. In some states the direction of prison schools is under the direct supervision of state departments of education and in Wisconsin even under the state university.

Almost all prisons have a library. Most of them are inferior, containing old discarded books and a large proportion of a religious type. In general, there are practically no professional prison librarians, since usually the prison chaplain is in charge. If prisons are to be important in reformation there must be a carefully selected useful library and aid given the individual inmate in selecting his reading program. Two national associations have recently prepared a prison library manual.

Productive work for prisoners has become a cardinal point of modern correctional work, although there is still considerable idleness in many prisons, amounting in the United States in 1940 to 56 percent as compared with 25 percent in 1885. Many feel that industry has become an over-emphasized feature of prison work in some, and that the needs of prison industries have taken precedence over individual reformation. Among the most important systems of prison labor are the piece price, lease, contract, public account, public works, prison farm, and state use systems. The trend has been the substitution of public for private systems of labor, only one percent of prison labor being the latter in 1940. State account systems have been decreasing until in 1940 88 percent of employed prisoners were working under either the state use or public works systems. The Hawes-Cooper Act of 1929 and the Ashhurst-Summers Act of 1935, by placing restrictions on goods in interstate commerce, have seriously restricted prison industries. The Prison Industries Reorganization Administration, in existence for a while after 1935, made studies to assist in the development of prison labor. Prison labor systems should be judged from the standpoint, primarily, of the welfare of the prisoner, training and reformation, competition with free labor, and ease of management. Prisoners in general receive wages of a few cents to forty cents a day, in the United States federal prisons some receive slightly more, while in many others they are paid nothing at all. In the Soviet Union many prisoners receive approximately the same wage as free labor, and in Sweden they receive a fairly good wage. The practice in Wisconsin and Michigan of expanding their workmen's compensation laws to include inmates should be taken over by other states. There is a slight tendency now to go beyond the industrial prison to a more rehabilitative type of institution with the industrial features subordinate. Sweden now permits many prisoners to work outside the institution in gainful employment and return to the institution each night.

While many prisons are still inadequately staffed, have little equipment, and often not even a separate hospital, medical facilities have probably improved more than any other feature of correctional systems. In 1940 there were 370 full-time physicians and surgeons directly connected with prisons and reformatories, besides many part-time. Most prisons have separate hospitals, and some may take their inmates to outside hospitals for special care. The interest in such services has broadened in many institutions far beyond simply caring for illness, but is now engaged in preventive and corrective services. Where the system is large enough there may be a medical center as has the federal prison system. Practically no institution yet meets the recommended standard of 100 beds per 1,000 inmates with a professional staff of fifteen. Psychiatric services are now recognized as an indispensable part of the medical and social service, although in 1940 there were still 77 full-time psychiatrists, which is far less than one per institution.

Recreational activities are also now considered not luxuries but essential to the development of a sound prison program. Not only is recreation looked upon as a health program but it is also felt to develop group participation. In contrast to the rigid exercise pens of many European prisons with walking the chief function, many modern prisons have varied physical education programs. In some, weekly motion pictures and plays have been added and the radio is general, although not always furnished free by the state. A large number of institutions have prison papers published by inmates as compared to official papers which are common in Europe. Prisoners confined in jails get very little recreational features.

Prisons constitute separate societies or,

more accurately, communities. Each is held together with a common series of meanings not only often peculiar to it but shared by other penal institutions. Social stratification ranges through a hierarchy of officers down through a hierarchy of prisoners. The absence of the two sexes and free communication with the outside world makes it an unusual community. Customs which were borrowed from other similar institutions or arose in the distant past are continued after their original function has disappeared. The beliefs of a prison are supported by a complex series of rationalizations which are extremely resistant to change, as those who have tried to modify prison practices have learned.

Most prisoners are divided into various grades and receive promotions or demotion according to the behavior they exhibit in an institution. The grades are usually three, and sometimes four. Each of the grades permit certain privileges or represent the loss of privileges. Good conduct while in an institution generally has an effect on the method of release and time served. There is evidence to indicate that model prisoners are often some of the worst reformation possibilities. The granting of privileges and their withdrawal if behavior does not warrant, rather than harsh measures, is in line with the most advanced methods of prison discipline.

Prisons are generally characterized by exaggerated discipline. Nearly all institutions have a large number of rules and regulations which more or less completely circumscribe the behavior of the individual. Detailed rules exist for the caring of cells, respect for officers, prompt obedience, boisterous conduct, and other similar prohibitions. Some states have large rule books with sometimes seventy or more rules which inmates must obey. Most rules are petty. Some are necessary for the maintenance of order in the institution, while most are rules which were introduced for rigid discipline, coercion, or because of some peculiar situation which may have long since disappeared. The presence of a large number of rules which do not exist in a free society and could not be enforced there, interferes seriously with reformation. Guards sometimes display authority by forcing rigid compliance with regulations. Classification by institutions should help greatly to keep rules at a minimum over persons who do not need them. Many institutions are either overly severe or overly lax. Corporal punishment was in practice in 1939 in at least 26 states and 12 states permitted whipping with a strap. Other institutions use force, such as beating with fists or clubs, spraying with a stream of water under high pressure, stringing up by the wrists, exposure to extremes of heat and cold or to electric shock, confinement in stocks or cramped sweatboxes, handcuffing to cell doors, and other forms of punishment. Canada and Great Britain make more frequent official use of flogging than the United States. Infractions are dealt with in the most progressive institutions by the removal of privileges or the use of carefully regulated isolation by segregation. In the south many restrictions are fewer and privileges are greater than other places in the United States. When prison rules are broken, however, punishment is likely to be more severe.

It is increasingly recognized that the artificiality of prison systems is the greatest bar to the reformation of a human being. Although the old Pennsylvania method of solitary confinement and the subsequent congregate silent system have given way in most institutions throughout the world, there is much in social participation that needs to be done. To change attitudes we need to encourage cultural assimilation and group contacts. The disadvantages of confinement with only infrequent outside social contacts have only been met by some self-government, infrequent rigidly supervised visits, limited letter writing privileges which are censored, restricted personal reading materials, and sometimes, as in England, by official visitors. Serious attempts have been made to modify this system at Chino, California by permitting Sunday family picnics and other contacts and in Sweden by granting frequent furloughs, employment outside the prison and encouraging extensive social relations with relatives and friends and other social participation. Also efforts to provide more social participation have been made at the Massachusetts State Penal Colony, the German Thüringian prisons, some Soviet institutions, and the English Borstal institutions. Mexico, Guatemala, and Soviet Russia also allow conjugal visits, largely, however, to control the sex problem in prison, which is universally one of its most serious and demoralizing features. Until such time as prison systems in general allow the maintenance of more normal social relations with the outside world they cannot hope to achieve changes in the attitudes of offenders or more satisfactory emotional adjustment.

A prisoner may be sentenced under a variety of different procedures largely dependent upon the type of sentence and the administrative procedures of the various states. Most prisoners receive a definite sentence. In 1940 some 40 percent of all commitments, however, were under an indeterminate sentence wherein an administrative board fixes the sentence and the judge merely sets the maximum and minimum provided by the legislature. Actually no sentences are completely indeterminate. Thirty-five states have such laws. The federal government has not yet passed such a procedure. This procedure became known in the United States about the time of the Civil War after its use in Australia and in the Irish system, and was an essential part of the Elmira Reformatory of 1869. In 1889 a general indeterminate sentence law was passed in New York.

Parole which is now used extensively, an outgrowth of the Irish system, in its first developed form was adopted in New York in the law of 1869 establishing the Elmira reformatory. All states now have parole laws, the last being enacted by Mississippi in 1944. Some prison systems use parole more than others. In 16 states more than three-fourths of all releases from state prisons and reformatories in 1940 were by parole while in 10 states less than one-fourth were by parole. It is used most extensively in the north and east and least in the south. Eligibility for parole is dependent upon a number of factors, including good time credits. The latter procedure was first put into law in New York in 1817 but apparently was not used, the first effective law being that of Tennessee in 1833. Such good time laws have been criticized as being simply automatic deductions without reference to a study of the offender. Parole has also been criticized, but most of such criticisms are not due to the principle of parole but are essentially caused by the improper selection of parolees, inefficient and inadequately trained staffs, political influence, and lack of flexibility in the administration of the parole laws.

While a considerable number of prisons have come a long way since the Pennsylvania and Auburn days of over a century ago, there are still too many backward institutions utilizing few modern correctional methods. Some of the major accusations against these institutions are social psychological. Punishment, which is still the common attitude toward prisoners, cannot possibly bring about internal reform in attitudes, and the stigma of imprisonment is a typical effect which obviates reform. Specific criticisms of most prisons are that they lack modern scientific social treatment, the prison officials are untrained and inefficient, the discipline rigid and brutal, and the prison through its general atmosphere, artificiality, and lack of sympathetic understanding between officials and inmates makes for increased social isolation rather than integration into society. There is ample evidence on this score from ex-inmates, prison officials, and scientific observers.

The predominance of these bad features in our prisons today raises questions about the future of prisons. Unfortunately it appears that with our present antiquated criminal laws and society's attitude toward the offender prisons will continue to exist for a long time. It should, then, be our purpose to bring all correctional institutions up to modern standards so as to do the least possible injury to those incarcerated in them. With our present prison systems it is surprising that even as many as one-fourth of the inmates of our prisons do not return. It is possible that a further increase can be made in this figure if the advanced procedures which have been discussed are generally adopted. These features of a modern prison system include the wide use of (1) carefully supervised probation rather than imprisonment, (2) central administration of the state correctional system, (3) professionally trained personnel under civil service, (4) small diversified institutions mainly of the minimum security type, (5) classification of the rehabilitative type, (6) adequate educational, library, employment, recreational and medical programs, (7) only such discipline as is absolutely necessary for ordinary social life, (8) an indeterminate sentence with (9) an adequate parole system having broad discretionary powers, such as proposed in the Youth Authority Act, and, (10) most important of all, extensive social participation in the form of communication with normal society through furloughs, receiving frequent visits and letters, as well as similar methods not as yet developed. Almost all of these features have been incorporated into the Swedish Prison Act of 1945.

As advanced and logical as these modern methods seem, we are faced with the fact that there is as yet no definite evidence to indicate that where some improved techniques have been tried crime has been materially reduced. Back of this difficulty in applying advanced prison methods lies the still existent struggle between the punitive and reformative approach to crime. If instead of punishment, imprisonment is regarded as merely indeterminate commitments for rehabilitative treatment, where all our knowledge of human behavior may be applied and where generally normal social relationships without social stigma may be maintained, it might be possible to develop and use prisons constructively. This calls for as great changes in free society's attitude toward crime as in improvements in the prison world. It is conceivable, however, that if prisons were not the kinds of places they are society's attitude toward the offender might change. Society stigmatizes a man not for the crime but for the imprisonment.

Prisons and other methods, however, constitute simply defenses against crime. The only really effective way to deal with crime is through prevention. This means that we must deal with the social situations which produce crime. This means community prevention in both general behavior patterns and attitudes, such as has been launched in the Chicago Area projects. The people themselves in their families and neighborhoods, and not well-intentioned outsiders or more and better formal agencies, must in the end deal effectively with crime and delinquency. We must prevent the development of criminal attitudes rather than try to change them by imprisonment.

MARSHALL B. CLINARD
Associate Professor of Sociology
University of Wisconsin
Madison, Wisconsin

BIBLIOGRAPHY

Attorney General's Survey of Release Procedures, Vol. V, "Prisons," 1940.
American Prison Association, *Manual of Suggested Standards for a State Correctional System,* New York, 1946.
Barnes, H. E., *The Evolution of Penology in Pennsylvania,* Indianapolis, 1927.
Barnes, H. E., and Teeters, N. K., *New Horizons in Criminology,* New York, 1943.
Brockway, Z. R., *Fifty Years of Prison Service,* New York, 1912.
Clemmer, D., *The Prison Community,* Boston, 1940.
Gillin, J. L., *Criminology and Penology,* 3rd ed., New York, 1945.
——, *Taming the Criminal,* New York, 1931.
Haynes, F. E., *The American Prison System,* New York, 1939.
Howard, J., *The State of the Prisons in England and Wales,* Warrington, 1777 and Dutton, New York, 1929.
McKelvey, B., *American Prisons,* Chicago, 1936.
Osborne Association, *Handbook of American Prisons and Reformatories,* New York.
Radzinowicz, L., and Turner, J. W. C. (ed.), *Penal Reform in England,* (2nd ed.), London, 1946.
Reckless, W. C., *Criminal Behavior,* New York, 1940.
Rusche, G., and Kirchheimer, O., *Punishment and Social Structure,* New York, 1939.
Sellin, T., *Recent Penal Legislation in Sweden,* Stockholm, 1947.
Sutherland, E. H., *Principles of Criminology,* 4th ed., New York, 1947.
Sutherland, E. H., and Sellin, T., "Prisons of Tomorrow," *Annals of the American Academy of Political and Social Science,* Vol. CLVII, Sept., 1931.
Taft, D. R., *Criminology,* New York, 1942.
Tannenbaum, F. R., *Crime and the Community,* Cincinnati, 1938.
Teeters, N. K., *World Penal Systems,* Philadelphia, 1944.
U. S. Bureau of the Census, *Prisoners in State and Federal Prisons and Reformatories* (annual).

U. S. Bureau of Prisons, *Federal Prisons* (annual).

Wood, A. E., and Waite, J. B., *Crime and Its Treatment*, Cincinnati, 1941.

Correctional reports published annually by various states and foreign countries.

PRISON VISITING. Inmates in jails and penitentiaries have as a rule been permitted to receive visitors as far back as the memory of man runneth. References to such visiting go back several centuries. Certainly, the records indicate this activity early in the history of American penology. Today such visiting is a common practice in the institutions in Europe, South America and North America. Visitors include friends and relatives, so-called "lay visitors", and representatives of the legal profession, the clergy and social organizations.

Prison inmates are, of course, primarily interested in receiving visits from friends and relatives, people whom they have known before they were incarcerated. These bring the outside world into the prison and form the connecting link with the free world.

Official attitude toward such visiting varies. There are those who regard the custom as a necessary evil. The thought is that if there were no visiting, there would be fewer institutional problems; it would be easier to guard against the smuggling in of contraband and prevent a number of other situations about which prison officials must be on the alert. Generally, however, and particularly among the more progressive of penologists, visits from friends and relatives are regarded as desirable as a source of benefit to the inmate, and therefore to be encouraged.

However, it is undoubtedly true that administrators of penal institutions have not exhausted the therapeutic value which lies in prison visiting. Such visits should aid the prisoner in solving his problem and help bring about a satisfactory adjustment to the outside world when once he is released. The family too should be given a clearer conception of the inmate's needs and be prepared for his ultimate return. If such program is to be carried out, institutions should have a trained member of their staff in charge of inmate visiting. All visitors to prisoners should be interviewed by this officer on the initial visit. While it is true that visits on the part of some individuals may be helpful to the inmate, it is also true that such contacts with others may be harmful. It is desirable that an inmate keep his contacts with the outside world but only if such contacts are beneficial. It may be preferred that upon release the inmate sever the ties which bind him to his relatives. Prison and parole officials should know these things. Such information cannot be secured unless someone in official position learns to know the family and the family relationships. Again, no benefit can be gained from the visit of any unstable parent who does nothing but sympathize with the inmate and blame law enforcement officials. It would be better if such visits were discontinued, and a substitution be made for a more stable relative. Further, visitors should be informed as to the inmate's attitudes and needs, so that if they are inclined to be helpful, they may govern their conversation accordingly. All of this planning is very desirable but it can be done only by an official who can devote sufficient time and thought to the activity.

Because of the fear which prison officials have (and such fears are not without foundation) that prison visitors may smuggle in contraband or plot with the inmate against the welfare of the institution, or in other ways disturb its peace and quiet, prison visits have been hemmed in with a number of regulations and restrictions. Usually there are limitations as to frequency, varying throughout the country from one visit a week to one a month. Usually such visits are limited to members of the immediate family with the provision that all of the relatives who expect to visit the inmate within a stated period must come in a group. Not infrequently the inmate is asked to list the names of the relatives with whom he would like to visit. These individuals are then investigated as to character and reputation. If the officials find that visits from some of these individuals would be undesirable, their names are removed from the list. Occasionally, provisions are made that visitors to prisoners shall be fingerprinted on the initial visit so that check can be made as to possible criminal record. Almost without exception prisons bar those having criminal records. Some institutions exclude girl friends from the visitors list.

The length of the visit varies from fifteen minutes to an hour or more. Some institutions permit longer visits in cases where relatives have traveled a long distance. At least one prison permits visiting time to accumulate up to twelve hours; if an inmate has not had a visitor for a number of months, he is granted more time on the occasion of the next visit. Fairly general is the requirement that visits be supervised by one of the custodial officers. Rules usually provide that the visitor submit to search, that he establish his identity, and that he refrain from calling on an inmate while the latter is passing through the quarantine period. Permission from the warden or his deputy is usually required if exceptions are to be made to established rules. The visitor is warned that violation of rules may lead to withdrawal of the privilege of visiting.

Rules governing prison visits naturally vary greatly. Many of the smaller institutions make very little restriction as to the length or frequency of the visits. Practically anyone may visit provided he knows on whom he wishes to call. Penal institutions with a large population must perforce make such limitations because of the size of the facilities, since it is impossible to handle more than a definite number of visits a day. Interesting are such variations as the following: One institution permits visitors to bring in certain foodstuffs which may be eaten with the inmate, while another forbids bringing in or consuming food in the visiting room. In some instances number and length of visits are determined by the conduct record of the prisoner. Those in solitary confinement, for instance, may have no visit; while others who are under a lesser degree of discipline may receive some visits, but not as many as are allowed those in good standing.

Observers have asked why prison visiting is hemmed in with so many restrictions which create an unnatural atmosphere and remove a great deal of the therapeutic value of the occasion. Why should intimate family affairs have to be discussed in the presence of a guard? Why should there be screens and other physical barriers to make discussions more difficult?

The fact is that particularly in the larger prisons experience has shown that unsupervised visits facilitate smuggling in contraband or plotting escapes, or create other situations inimical to the well-being of the institution. Certain it is that prison officials would not place these restrictions and thereby make handling of the visitors more difficult, if they did not regard such procedures as necessary. It is true, however, that instances occur in which these restrictions might well be waived. There are inmates who will not plot, and there are relatives who will not be party to violation of institution rules. If the visitors have been carefully investigated and their integrity has been established, and if, moreover, the inmate himself can be relied upon, it would seem that the meeting could take place without supervision and without the screen barrier. If, on the other hand, trust cannot be placed in the visitors, the usual restrictions can be enforced. There are institutions, particularly those which house the less serious type of offender which permit family gatherings without supervision and even allow the visitors to bring in food so that the family may have a picnic on the lawn. Such privileges would be an incentive to good conduct. A program of this type would, of course, require additional personnel to investigate and make decisions, and, unfortunately, appropriations are frequently insufficient to permit such additions.

Professional visitors usually consist of clergymen, attorneys, and representatives of social agencies. Prison officials as a rule admit such freely. Visits of this type are not deducted from the number which an inmate is allowed during a stated period. Penologists recognize the value of religion in the program of rehabilitation and encourage clergymen to visit such of their flock as may be in prison. Similarly, prisoners are allowed to consult with their attorneys. Occasionally institutions have the rule that a visiting attorney must either be the attorney of record, or must have evidence to show that the inmate has sent for him. This provision is made to prevent unscrupulous lawyers from building up a prison practice by persuading inmates that they have a case and soliciting retainers. Reputable men of the law have no difficulty seeing their clients. Representatives of social agencies are also allowed to visit such inmates as they wish to see. Modern classification committee programs seek the cooperation of social agencies and secure from them a great deal of valuable information. The progressive penologist welcomes the assistance of social workers, and such folk are readily admitted.

"Lay visitors" is a term applied to interested citizens representing no particular agency, who have become interested in prison inmates, are sympathetic with their plight and are intent on doing what they can for the welfare of these unfortunates. Names of these persons, such as Elizabeth Frye of England, loom large in the story of prison reform. The early history of the penal institutions of Pennsylvania reveals extensive use of the lay visitor. Not much has been done in the United States in modern times to exploit the value which may accrue from the lay visitor. Certainly there are sterling citizens in every community who could be prevailed upon to visit prison inmates, particularly those who have no friends or relatives and therefore rarely or never receive a visit. Relationships could be established which would be of value to the man while he is in the institution and immensely helpful in the adjustment which he must make when he is set at liberty. Obviously, if such program is to be of any value, the lay visitors must be carefully selected and must be given at least some training before they begin their work.

A topic of interest in connection with prison visiting is that of the conjugal visit. Proponents of such visits argue that all, or practically all of the prison situation is an unnatural one, particularly that of deprivation of companionship with members of the opposite sex. It is maintained that much of homosexuality in prisons would be prevented if such visits were allowed. The penal institutions of Mexico permit wives to visit their husbands in prison under certain conditions, and to spend the night with them. In Colombia inmates may leave the institution under guard to meet their wives at some designated places, or go to a licensed house of prostitution. Brazil permits wives unsupervised visits with their husbands, but will not allow visits from prostitutes. Although this question has been much discussed by American penologists, there is as yet no institution in the United States where officials permit such visits.

Garrett Heyns
Member, Michigan Parole Board
Lansing 13, Michigan

BIBLIOGRAPHY

Barnes, H. E., and Teeters, N. K., *New Horizons in Criminology,* Prentice-Hall, 1946, Chapter XXX.
Bates, Sanford, *Prisons and Beyond,* Macmillan, 1938, Ch. XIV.
Gardiner, Gordon, *Notes of a Prison Visitor,* Oxford University Press, 1938.
Hayner, Norman S., Recent Observations of Mexican Prisons, *Proceedings of the American Prison Association,* 1941, pp. 121-130.
Jorns, Auguste, *The Quakers as Pioneers in Social Work,* Macmillan, 1931.
McGee, Richard A., Controlling the Visiting Privilege, *Jail Assoc. Journal,* July-August, 1939.
Teeters, Negley K., The Role of Prison Visiting in the Penal Program, *Journal of Criminal Law and Criminology,* Nov.-Dec., 1939.
———, *Penology from Panama to Cape Horn,* Univ. of Pennsylvania Press, 1946.

PROBATION. Probation, as the name of an official correctional service, commonly denotes the dual functions of the system, that of the investigation of offenders prior to sentence in order that the Court may have detailed information concerning the history of the offender and the etiology of the offense, and the control and treatment of offenders conditionally released on probation.

Its roots can be traced back to the middle ages, when through "benefit of Clergy" and through invoking the law of "sanctuary" punishment was avoided or deferred. Modern probation legislation in this country is generally traced to the common law practice of suspending sentence which had its foundation in the practice of English Courts, and early statutes which authorized courts to suspend either the imposition or the execution of sentence.

Derived from the Latin word Probatio, a testing, Probation was the name given to this treatment of offenders by John Augustus, a shoemaker of Boston who, in 1841, through his interest in drunkards confined in that City's jail, became the first volunteer probation officer. Another Bostonian, Rufus W. (Father) Cook, and in Philadelphia William J. Mullen, who later became a prison agent for the Philadelphia Prison Society were among the first volunteers to engage in probation work.

From 1861 to 1867 Chicago had the services of a Commissioner to hear cases of delinquency among boys, a procedure in which a form of probation was utilized. In 1869 Massachusetts authorized the placement of juvenile offenders in private families, another early use of probation.

Massachusetts, which is regarded as the birthplace of probation in 1878 passed the first law authorizing the employment of a publicly paid probation officer, and this law further authorized the Municipal Court to place offenders on probation. In 1891 a second law was passed requiring the Superior Courts to appoint probation officers. Up to 1900, however, only six states had passed laws recognizing probation.

The creation of the juvenile court in Chicago, in 1899 was one of the most important factors in establishing probation. In 1899 the Legislature of Colorado established the Juvenile Court of Denver. This Court was an aggressive pioneer in the development of probation and specialized procedures for the treatment of juvenile offenders.

In 1861 England made provisions for the granting of probation in disposing of persons charged with some crimes, and in 1876 probation officers who were known as "missionaries" and were employed by social service agencies, functioned in some of the Police Courts. The Probation of Offenders Act in 1907 established publicly salaried probation officers. Belgium in 1888 provided for adult probation, and France established similar provisions in 1891. In the various countries of Europe, where probation has been written into the law, the service has generally been administered by volunteers or by social service agencies which have provided the means for supervising persons placed on probation.

In the Federal Courts, prior to 1916, some judges placed offenders on probation by suspending sentence indefinitely by filing, or by deferring the case. This method had been in use for over sixty years, when the Supreme Court of the United States held that a district judge was without power to suspend or defer sentence indefinitely. As a result of this decision, Congress passed the Federal Probation Act in 1925, but it was not generally used by the Federal Courts until 1930.

Up to 1940, 42 states, the District of Columbia, Alaska, Hawaii and Porto Rico, and the United States Congress, had provided for the use of probation. The six states which have not established probation services have suspension of sentence laws, but these are restricted to specific offenses. All states have established some form of probation treatment or specialized procedures for juvenile offenders. The Federal Government in 1938 passed a Juvenile Delinquent Act which provides for probation and special procedures for the treatment of juvenile offenders.

In some states all courts may place offenders on probation; in others it is limited to courts of record, or to courts having juvenile jurisdiction. Six states place no restrictions whatever upon offenses subject to probation; others prohibit its use for certain crimes, but there is no uniformity in the crimes prohibited. In three states the only offenses in which probation is prohibited are those in which the death penalty or life imprisonment is the prescribed punishment.

Development and Organization. When first established, probation was administered by volunteers. Probation Officers were sometimes recruited from Police Departments and other public agencies, but in the main they were humane persons interested in developing this new system, or they were the representatives of social service agencies. In some states this condition still exists, even where limited provision has been made for publicly salaried probation officers. Considerable experience with volunteer probation officers has demonstrated that probation work should be administered by paid officers, who can be assisted in some phases of treatment by volunteers working under their direction.

The Probation Officers Directory of the National Probation Association shows that there were 3975 paid probation officers in the United States in 1941. There are no reliable statistics as to the number of volunteer probation officers engaged in work in this field. In the majority of the states and their sub-divisions, the appointment of paid and volunteer probation officers rests solely in the discretion of the judges. In a very few instances, the administrators of departments have concurrent power with the Judge to make appointments.

In the last twenty-five years there has been a concerted drive toward the recruitment of properly trained personnel and for the establishment of social case work standards to govern probation work. In 1923 the U. S. Children's Bureau and the National Probation Association proposed the following minimum qualifications for probation personnel:

A. Education—preferably graduation from college or its equivalent or from a school of social work.

B. Experience—at least one year in case work under supervision.

C. Good personality and character, tact, resourcefulness and sympathy.

Only a limited number of Probation Departments have adopted these standards or similar qualifications recommended by the U. S. Department of Justice for the Federal Courts in 1938, and the New York State Division of Probation in 1943, although it is generally acknowledged that those engaged in probation work must be equipped for it by education and that probation officers should be competently trained social workers.

There has been an aggressive movement to place all workers in probation departments in the competitive civil service classification, and it has been strongly urged that every probation service should be regarded as a career service. In some jurisdictions judges are free to pick their own probation officers without Civil Service tests, on the theory that the probation officer stands in such a confidential relationship to the judge that the choice should not be subjected to outside control. Appellate Courts have ruled that the confidential relationship can be maintained even though probation officers are appointed from Civil Service lists. The large probation departments, with the exception of the Federal Service, are under Civil Service Control.

Probation agencies have developed in accordance with the needs and the social vision of the communities which they serve. They can be loosely classified as centralized state probation departments, some of which also administer parole, centralized county organizations, city and federal agencies, and divisions of courts. Some states have set up commissions to supervise the work of the Probation departments. Others have vested supervision in Departments of Welfare or other State agencies.

There is no centralized authority for the gathering of statistics with reference to the number of persons investigated, or annually placed on probation. Data gathered by the Bureau of the Census for the year 1939, which represented only twenty-five states and covered offenses disposed of in various county courts, shows that of the 54,929 defendants sentenced, 33.4% were placed on probation or received a suspended sentence. There was great variation in this disposition of cases among the states, the percentages ranging from 60.3% placed on probation in Rhode Island, to 14% placed on probation in North Dakota and Montana. The offenses in which probation was granted ranged from Murder 0.5% to Stolen Property, 44.5%.

The U. S. Attorney General's Report on Release Procedures states that, on the average, about one-third of the offenders sentenced by the State and Federal Courts of general jurisdiction are placed on probation or are released on suspended sentences. No complete statistics are available with reference to the use of probation in the lower courts.

In the Federal system, there were 4281 persons on probation in 1930. In 1931 the number had jumped to 11,273. In 1943 there were 24,521 persons under probation supervision.

In the State of New York, from 1933 to 1942 inclusive, 195,815 persons were placed on probation.

Investigation of Offenders. In two-thirds of the thirty-eight jurisdictions which have legislation on the subject of adult probation, the statutes give some consideration to the investigative process, although many of these jurisdictions do not indicate what the scope of the contemplated investigation shall be. Pre-sentence investigations of those considered for probation are mandatory only in California, Illinois, and New York.

To secure individualized treatment of offenders, judges must have reports which present complete and comprehensive investigations into the past history of the offender and the causes of his physical, mental, and social maladjustment. Proper selection of offenders for probation treatment makes such investigations imperative. In addition, institutions are helped to develop their programs of treatment through the information contained in such reports, and parole departments and cooperating social agencies are aided in a similar manner.

These investigations embrace the circumstances of the offense, the family history, the school record, the work record, the economic status and competency of the offender, his health, his recreational habits, associates, affiliations, previous delinquencies, an evaluation of the psychiatrist's report, and other pertinent data. In departments which conduct individualized studies in accordance with established probation techniques, this objective information is evaluated in relation to the personality of the offender and his reactions to his whole situation.

Some states have made provision for physical, mental, and psychiatric examinations as a part of the probation investigation. Massachusetts has given greater recognition to psychiatric and psychological examinations than any other state. The law requires that any person indicted for a capital offense or for any second offense, or who is convicted of a felony, must be the subject of such an examination.

Only a limited number of Probation Departments dealing with adults have full time psychiatric service. Rarely is there routine psychiatric study of every convicted offender. In most instances such study is made only of those who are considered abnormal. The majority of departments are unable to afford psychiatric service.

Psychiatric service has been more extensively used in the behavior studies of juvenile offenders. In some Children's Courts, psychiatrists function on a full-time basis. In others, the Probation Departments obtain psychiatric service either on a fee, or volunteer basis.

To supplement the investigation and study of the maladjustment of children, Children's Courts have integrated their services with those of Child Guidance Clinics. In some jurisdictions, intake bureaus have been set up in the Children's Courts, to which probation officers are assigned and where, as a part of the investigation process, they are engaged in weeding out cases which can be handled without formal arraignment.

Probation officers generally engage in both investigation and supervision of probationers. In a few larger departments there is a division of staff into investigation and supervision units.

Supervision and Rehabilitation. The individual who has committed a criminal act has indicated that he has failed to make a proper social adjustment. The mechanics of placing him on probation do not bring about any magical changes in his personality, his behavior patterns or his sense of social responsibility. His arrest, incarceration and his reaction to the formalisms of the law may create in him a sense of temporary fear, but such an element unless transmitted into a conscious and ungrudging respect for authority, is a very poor influence through which any permanent change of character can be effected. Changes in personality and in social attitudes must be predicated upon more constructive and lasting influences.

A constructive administration of probation envisages a period of social treatment designed to develop the best potentialities of the probationer. It is predicated upon an individualized study which will sharply bring into relief the conditioning influences responsible for his anti-social behavior. It requires the development of practical plans which will change him from a social liability into a social asset.

Two approaches are utilized; the first is legalistic and entails oversight of the probationer's activities insofar as they relate to community safety through his avoidance of further delinquent behavior. This involves personal reports by the probationer, checking home conditions, verification of employment, investigations into habits and associates and returning to the Court as probation violators those who by their conduct and refusal to participate in plans for their rehabilitation, indicate that they are in danger of reverting to anti-social conduct.

The second approach is through the application of social case work principles and techniques, for the adjustment of the individual within himself, his relation to those groups which are primary, and to society as a whole.

A sound philosophy of probation rejects the concept of mere custodial care during the period of probation. To have constructive value, treatment must be based upon insight into the personality and environment of the offender. The problems he presents must be set forth, and there must be an evaluation of the problem in terms of his social liabilities and assets. There must be an analysis of the causal factors, a definite evaluation of the probationer's needs and the practical and workable means that are to be used to influence him toward a higher level of responsibility and social consciousness. The plan must envisage the development of discipline and self-control, and wherever necessary, emotional adjustment and physical rehabilitation. It must apply itself also to academic and vocational education and religious development, and must portray the means that are to be used for the development of new resources and outlets.

The treatment process must further envisage the broadening of social relationships, family adjustment, an improvement in the physical conditions under which the probationer lives, and bring about the development of a measure of economic efficiency, and some financial security through a thrifty disbursement of earnings.

In the well organized and properly administered probation departments, the process of readjusting persons on probation is a cooperative effort through the enlistment of the aid of community agencies and, wherever they can be helpful, of volunteer workers.

In too many probation departments, properly planned social case work treatment cannot be used because of the lack of adequate financial support by the fiscal authorities. Departments which are understaffed are burdened with a case load of probationers which make it physically impossible for them to give any constructive treatment. It has been stated time and again at social work and probation conferences that a case load of not more than fifty probationers is all a probation officer can carry if he is to meet adequate standards of social case work planning and treatment. If the Probation Officer is also making pre-sentence investigations for the Court, his supervision case load should be much lower. Few, if any probation departments in this country have been able to maintain such a case load for probation officers.

Advantages, Success and Failure, Costs. Probation affords a basic approach to the individualization of crime treatment through the application of modern social case work methods. It permits the offender to continue living and working under improved normal conditions, but it presupposes a high degree of selectivity, and it cannot be used effectively for the treatment of every criminal offender.

It avoids the stigmatization of the offender and it is a means of developing his potentialities so that he can grow as an individual and develop the capacity to adjust to society. It keeps the family intact, and places responsibility for their care upon the probationer, instead of forcing them to become the recipients of charity.

Probation enables the person injured through the criminal act to be compensated for his loss or injury through restitution or reparation paid by the probationer, from his own earnings.

It affords an opportunity for a manipulation of cultural and physical factors in the environment in contrast to the rigidity of mass controls in a prison or reformatory.

Through its individualized studies of the personality of offenders and their motivations, and through its searching for the contributing factors of criminal behavior, probation is developing an informed public opinion with reference to the whole problem of crime.

It presents an opportunity for using all of the social resources of the community which can benefit the probationer and his family, and which will be helpful in enlarging their social attitudes and ethical concepts.

The probation system, by focusing attention on the failure of old methods of dealing with criminal offenders, and stressing the need for individualized study, has contributed to the establishment of socialized approaches to the treatment of crime. The inauguration of new methods in Children's Courts and the modern procedure in the treatment of youthful offenders, such as the creation of Youth Parts in Criminal Courts, where through specialized procedures, youthful offenders can be investigated prior to adjudication, are some of its contributions. The techniques which it has developed for the use of social case work in the readjustment of persons charged with anti-social acts, have been adopted in other fields.

The criteria for success and failure are set up by the various agencies which administer probation. These standards range from very good to very poor, and are governed by the quality of the leadership and the amount of public support given to the probation system in each locality. Authorities agree that many probation failures could be avoided if sufficient funds were provided by fiscal authorities to recruit an adequate number of properly qualified personnel to staff all departments, and to administer probation in accordance with the best techniques which have been developed in that field.

The U. S. Attorney General's Survey of Release Procedures in 1939 reported an analysis of 19,256 cases of persons placed on probation. 61% revealed no recorded violations during the probation period. 18% committed new offenses, and 21% had in some manner violated the conditions of release. In only 19% was it found necessary to revoke probation.

The New York Division of Probation in its Annual Report for 1942 stated that 18,437 persons had been discharged from probation that year. 74.2% had been discharged with improvement and 6.9% had been discharged without improvement.

Probation Departments throughout the United States have, in their annual reports, shown that probation achieves success in more than 70% of the cases entrusted to their care for supervision and rehabilitation.

In New York State, where the largest number of publicly salaried probation officers are employed, 506 in 1943, the average per capita cost for the administration of probation in 1939 was $51.90. In sharp contrast, the per capita cost for the care of persons in prisons and reformatories was $569.04, and in Institutions for delinquent children it was $861.

The low per capita cost of administering probation is responsible for many of the failures for which that system must assume responsibility. If Departments were adequately financed and properly staffed, the per capita cost would be much greater, but it would still fall far short of the cost of prison confinement.

Probation has had a rapid growth. It has had an uneven development and theory has outstripped practice. It has, however, in spite of the limitations imposed upon it, demonstrated its effectiveness as a socially valuable corrective treatment, and is generally regarded as the most constructive method of dealing with offenders whose attitudes and behavior patterns can be moulded by guidance and control.

IRVING W. HALPERN
Chief Probation Officer
Court of General Sessions
New York City

BIBLIOGRAPHY

Administrative Office of the U. S. Courts, *Federal Probation.*
Attorney General's Survey of Release Procedures, Probation, Volume II, U. S. Department of Justice.
John Augustus, First Probation Officer; Yearbooks; Adult Probation Laws of the U. S., National Probation Association.
Barnes and Teeters, *New Horizons in Criminology.*
Court of General Sessions, *A Decade of Probation,* New York City.
Glueck, Sheldon, Editor, *Probation and Criminal Justice.*

National Commission on Law Observance and
Enforcement, Report on Penal Institutions,
Probation and Parole.
Reckless and Smith, *Juvenile Delinquency.*
Sutherland, Edwin H., *Principles of Criminology.*

PSYCHIATRY AND THE LAW. Legislation was proposed in 1921 by the late Dr. L. Vernon Briggs, a prominent Boston psychiatrist, in his volume entitled, *The Manner of Man That Kills,* to provide for the automatic reference to the State Department of Mental Health for mental examination of persons held for trial who fall in certain specified legal categories. Doctor Briggs pointed out the necessity of such a provision in order to be fair to the defendant accused of serious crime, and also as a practical means of correcting the abuses of expert testimony in criminal trials, and he was successful in securing the passage in 1921 (Ch. 415, Acts of 1921) of a bill which he wrote and which has since generally been known as the Briggs Law.

The elements of the act were that any person indicted for a capital offense, or any person known to have been previously indicted more than once, or previously convicted of a felony, should be examined by the Department of Mental Diseases, "with a view to determining his mental condition and the existence of any mental disease or defect which would affect his criminal responsibility." It was also provided that this report of the Department should be accessible to the court, the district attorney and the attorney for the accused, and should be admissible as evidence on the mental condition of the accused. No fee was provided in the original act, but the local psychiatrists readily agreed, at Doctor Briggs' suggestion, to make the examination without compensation as a public service until such time as a fee could be provided.

Two years later (1923, Ch. 331), upon the recommendation of the Commissioner of Mental Diseases, Dr. George M. Kline, a fee was authorized by the general court—four dollars for each examination plus 20¢ per mile one way—a fee hardly large enough to warrant a charge of venality against the physicians! In 1925 (Ch. 169) on the recommendation of the Attorney General, the provision relative to the admissibility of the report was stricken out, and at the same time a penalty for wilful noncompliance by the clerk of court was added.

Despite the penalty, it continued to be self-evident that many defendants were not being reported for examination who should be. Fortunately the Commonwealth had a well organized central record system in the Board of Probation, a probation officer in every court, and a provision of law requiring the probation officer to ascertain the previous record of every defendant prior to his being granted bail by the court. It was a simple matter to integrate this system with the operation of the Briggs Law by securing an amendment to provide that the probation officer should report to the clerk if he had information indicating that a defendant fell within the provisions of the Briggs Law, and further requiring the clerk to act on this information (Mass. Acts of 1927, Ch. 59). Immediately a decided increase in the number of cases reported was noted. In 1929 (Ch. 105) a further amendment made the report of the examiners available to the probation officer—a logical step, since the probation officer is charged with the duty of advising the court as to pertinent facts to be considered in imposing sentence.

All of these amendments were enacted by the General Court as proposed and no opposition was voiced; with the exception of the admissibility provision, all were procedural. A proposal by the Commissioner of Mental Diseases that the scope of the law be extended to apply to defendants indicted for offenses punishable by life imprisonment, failed of passage in 1930 and again in 1931. The only other amendment (1941, Ch. 194, Sec. 11) inserted the new name of the Department, namely Department of Mental Health.

The statute [1] now reads as follows:

"Whenever a person is indicted by a grand jury for a capital offense or whenever a person, who is known to have been indicted for any other offense more than once or to

[1] Mass. Ann. Laws (Michie, 1933), c. 123, § 100 A, as amended by St. 1941, ch. 194, Sec. 11.

have been previously convicted of a felony, is indicted by a grand jury or bound over for trial in the superior court, the clerk of the court in which the indictment is returned, or the clerk of the district court or the trial justice, as the case may be, shall give notice to the department of mental health, and the department shall cause such person to be examined, with a view to determine his mental condition and the existence of any mental disease or defect which would affect his criminal responsibility. Whenever the probation officer of such court has in his possession or whenever the inquiry which he is required to make by section eighty-five of chapter two hundred and seventy-six discloses facts which if known to the clerk would require notice as aforesaid, such probation officer shall forthwith communicate the same to the clerk who shall thereupon give such notice unless already given. The department shall file a report of its investigation with the clerk of the court in which the trial is to be held and the report shall be accessible to the court, the probation officer thereof, the district attorney and to the attorney for the accused. In the event of failure by the clerk of the district court or the trial justice to give notice to the department as aforesaid the same shall be given by the clerk of the superior court after entry of the case in said court. Upon giving the notice required by this section the clerk of a court or the trial justice shall so certify on the papers. The physician making such examination shall, upon certification by the department, receive the same fees and traveling expenses as provided in section seventy-three for the examination of persons committed to institutions, and such fees and expenses shall be paid in the same manner as provided in section seventy-four for the payment of commitment expenses. Any clerk of court or trial justice who wilfully neglects to perform any duty imposed upon him by this section shall be punished by a fine of not more than fifty dollars."

The three essential features of the Briggs Law in such combination remained unique until 1938, when Kentucky[2] enacted a statute largely copied from the Massachusetts legislation; Michigan[3] followed suit in 1939, but no other State has adopted similar legislation. First, the reference of the case is automatic, that is, it is not dependent upon the

introduction of a plea of insanity, or upon an alleged "recognition" of mental disorder by the probation officer, judge, jail official, or some other nonpsychiatrist. Every defendant within the legal classes defined in the statute is examinable before trial, whether or not mental disease is alleged or suspected. If any distinction between "more serious" and "less serious" offenders is warranted, the "more serious" may be expected to be found in the groups designated in the law. (As a practical matter, the number of available psychiatrists and the demands of the court machinery would not permit the examination of *all* defendants, even of all accused of felony.) There have been instances in which a defendant has been found to be seriously disordered mentally whose condition had not been suspected by the jail officials, probation officer, or even his own attorney.

In the second place, the examination is made by impartial examiners. The request is made by the clerk of court, not by the district attorney or defense counsel, and the examiners are beholden to neither party, being expected only to make a clear and conscientious report.

In the third place, the selection of the examiners is made by a professional department in the administrative arm of the government, the Department of Mental Health, not by the judge or district attorney. It seems safe to say that the professional qualifications of psychiatrists may better be determined by psychiatrists than by non-medical persons.

The following table shows in summary form the development of the use of the Briggs Law. I am deeply indebted to Prof. Sheldon Glueck of the Harvard Law School, whose figures regarding the earlier years of the Briggs Law I have incorporated.[4] It is to be regretted that the only subsequent figures available are to be found in published

---

[2] Ch. 1, Second Special Session, 1938, §17.
[3] St. 1939, Public Act. 259.

[4] Glueck, S. Sheldon, State legislation providing for the mental examination of persons accused of crime. Bull. Mass. Dept. of Mental Diseases, 7:16–26, Oct. 1923 (No. 4). See also, for detailed study of the Briggs Law, with full bibliography, Overholser, W., The Briggs Law of Massachusetts: A Review and an Appraisal, 25 Journ. Crim. Law & Criminology, 859–883 (March-April, 1935).

reports of the Massachusetts Department of Mental Health; they indicate that in 1935 and the three following years the numbers of prisoners examined were, in order, 767, 817, 745 and 685. No detailed study of the operation of the law has appeared covering the period since 1934.

It will be noted that whereas the yearly average number of cases referred during 1921–26 was only 73.2, a startling increase occurred, beginning in 1927 (the year of the amendment requiring the probation officer to report to the clerk) and reaching a peak in 1932 of 909—an increase of 1140%! It will also be observed that the number of defendants not examined fell markedly. This fact was undoubtedly due to the cooperation of the justices of the Supreme Courts, who adopted the policy of postponing the disposition of cases known to come within the provisions of the Briggs Law until an examination could be completed. This policy seemed to be clearly intended by the wording of the law, even though it was held in the Vallarelli case [5] that non-compliance with the statute does not invalidate the trial. Many of the defendants missed were out on bail; a considerable number reported when requested, and the justices were inclined to indicate their expectation that this would be done, although recognizing that probably the court has no right to *compel* such an examination.[6]

Another point of interest is that the proportion of defendants reported to be abnormal mentally was not great. Some ill-informed persons have feared that psychiatrists, if given a free hand, would find practically *all* defendants insane. These figures show, however, that during a period of 14 years (1921–1935) only 15.8% of all defendants examined were reported to be either definitely abnormal mentally or in such condition that observation in a mental hospital was deemed advisable.

Under the Massachusetts statutes, the court

[5] Comm. v. Vallarelli, 273 Mass. 240, 173 N. E. 582 (1930).

[6] This point has not been decided. The court at least has no power to order a physical examination. Stack v. N. Y., N. H. & H. R. R. Co., 177 Mass. 155, 58 N. E. 686 (1900).

Year (Ending Oct. 15)	Cases Reported	Cases Examined	Percent Not Examined	Insane	Observation Advised	Mentally Defective	Other Mental Abnormalities	Percentage Reported Abnormal
1921–1926 (5 yrs.)	367 (av. 73.2)	295 (av. 59)	19.6	26	7	25	11	23.4
1927	138	87	37	5	1	9	1	18.3
1928	239	179	25.1	6	6	21	13	25.7
1929	370	283	23.5	4	16	27	11	20.1
1930	654	521	20.3	8	23	44	10	15.7
1931	766	703	8.2	6	27	87	10	17.9
1932	909	817	10.1	6	26	68	19	14.5
1933	818	725	11.3	3	23	55	15	13.2
1934	911	782	14.1	5	20	52	6	10.6
Total	5,172	4,392	....	66	143	388	96	....

Not examined, 780, or 15.5% of all cases reported. Total, all classes, 693, or 15.8% of all cases examined.

[396]

may commit a defendant to a mental hospital [7] as insane or for a period of observation, without a jury trial and indeed without medical evidence. In other words, there would seem to be little or no excuse for the court to fail to commit a defendant when reliably informed that there is doubt about his mentality. As a matter of fact, the courts have usually acted properly in this regard; in some instances the report may have arrived too late, or the facts as adduced by the examiners may have been insufficiently convincing. The results of a special study on this point are presented in the following table, covering four years (October 15, 1930–1934):

Commitment for Observation Recommended	Committed	Per Cent Committed
1931 21	13	62.8
1932 26	16	61.5
1933 23	16	69.6
1934 20	14	70.0

The law has been generally accepted in practice by the district attorneys and by lawyers for the defense. Very rarely indeed has the State or defense attempted to contest the findings of the examiners, recognizing them to be neutral and competent. If the report is "insane," the district attorney has usually asked for a directed verdict of "not guilty by reason of insanity" [8] or else arranged (more often) for the defendant's commitment without court appearance or trial. If the report is "observation advised," the practice has been generally in accord with that advice. Less predictable has been the action in the case of other reports, such as "mentally defective." Massachusetts has a defective delinquent law,[9] but the facilities have been overtaxed, and the law has had some defects which have made district attorneys cautious in invoking it. The savings in cost of trials have been great, and the public has been spared frequent "battles of experts," with the resulting distrust created by these spectacles. In the rare event of an attempt

by the defense to introduce contradictory testimony, the tendency has been for the jury to accept the views of the Briggs Law examiners.

In a number of cases carried up on appeal, the Supreme Judicial Court has interpreted certain aspects of the Briggs Law. The first case was that of Commonwealth v. Devereaux (257 Mass. 391, 152 N. E. 380), decided in 1926. In that case the court commented:

"The examination is required in order that no person so indicted may be put upon his trial unless his mental condition is thereby determined to be such as to render him responsible to trial and punishment for the crime charged against him, and that he has no mental disease or defect which interferes with such criminal responsibility. It is the duty imposed by the statute upon these doctors and others similarly assigned by the Department of Mental Diseases to say what is the mental condition of an accused and whether he has any mental disease or defect affecting his criminal responsibility. . . . It is a necessary deduction from all the circumstances that the defendant was put upon trial on the indictment because the report of the Department of Mental Diseases upheld his criminal responsibility. He would not have been brought to trial without evidence of his mental condition if that report had not been to the effect that he was of sufficient mental power to be criminally liable for his act and was not insane. . . . Doubtless the judge knew of this report at the trial. . . . He was justified in considering it in connection with the motion for a new trial in the circumstances here disclosed. . . . The judge had a right to examine the cause suggested in the motion for a new trial in the light of the contents of this report, in order to aid him in ascertaining whether justice required that there be a new trial."

In another part of the same decision the impartial nature of the report was emphasized as follows:

"It is a matter of general knowledge that there are in the service of the Commonwealth under this department persons eminent for special scientific knowledge as to mental diseases. The examination under the statute, therefore, may fairly be assumed to have been made by competent persons, free from any disposition or bias and under every

[7] Mass. Ann. Laws (Michie 1933) c. 123, §100.

[8] Id. §101.

[9] Id. §§113–124.

inducement to be impartial and to seek and ascertain the truth."

Judicial notice, then, is taken of the competence and impartiality of the examiners, and it is clearly indicated that the district attorney is not expected to bring to trial a defendant who is not pronounced to be sane and responsible. The figures already cited indicate that the district attorneys have followed the general lines laid down above. The expectation is further expressed that the trial judge will be guided by the report.

In other cases coming before the same court it has been held (1) that non-compliance with the provisions of the Briggs Law does not invalidate the trial as a matter of law;[10] (2) that having been examined by impartial experts under the Briggs Law the defendant is not entitled *as of right* to a further examination at the public expense;[11] and (3) that the examination does not compel the defendant to give evidence against himself in violation of his constitutional rights.[12] No cases involving the Briggs Law have been so far considered in the federal courts. The constitutionality of the law has never been directly passed upon, but there seems to be no good reason to question it.

The Briggs Law has amply proved its value as a practical means of reducing the opportunity for "battles of experts," of saving expense of trials and improper disposition, of assuring justice to the mentally ill defendant, and above all of assuring more effective protection to society. Many groups and individuals have studied its practice and approved; two States have adopted it. The law is not susceptible of transplantation in toto to any State, but depending upon local administrative organization and interest, the general plan is adaptable to other jurisdictions. To date, it has amply demonstrated that something *can* be done effectively about

[10] See Comm. v. Vallarelli, Note 5 *supra.;* Comm. v. Soaris, 275 Mass. 291, 175 N. E. 491 (1931); Comm. v. Gray, 49 N. E. (2nd) 603, 1943 Mass. Adv. Sheets 951.
[11] Comm. v. Belenski, 276 Mass. 35, 176 N. E. 501 (1931).
[12] Comm. v. Millen *et al.* 289 Mass. 441, 194 N. E. 463 (1935). Comm. v. Frank di Stasio, 294 Mass. 273, 1 N. E. (2nd) (1936) 189.

the expert testimony problem in criminal cases.

In this sense the Briggs Law can serve as a clear illustration of the general relationship between Psychiatry and the Law.

WINFRED OVERHOLSER, M.D.
Superintendent
St. Elizabeth's Hospital
Washington, D. C.

PSYCHOANALYSIS AND CRIMINOLOGY. That Freud discovered the unconscious has been mistakenly asserted many times; that Freud's true discovery was that the unconscious has dynamic power, that it possesses a force to make man act unwittingly and unwillingly, has not been asserted often enough. The crux of every psychological problem which is investigated by means of the psychoanalytic method is the bringing into light of the unconscious *motivations*; here the term "motivations" is used rather in its etymological sense of motive powers, of emotional or affective sources of actions, and not in the sense of conscious deliberations or deliberate, consciously constructed reasons. That Freud's discovery of the dynamic power of the unconscious should have deeply affected our traditional views on crime, criminology, and penology was inevitable; that the influence of psychoanalytic theory on criminology in all its facets—psychological, administrative, punitive, judicial and juridical—has not yet attained its full value is natural.

It is natural, because the immense popularity which psychoanalysis attained during the last quarter of a century has made us forget that it is only fifty years old, that there are still less than a thousand properly trained psychoanalysts in the whole world, and that the influence of psychoanalysis in many fields of human behavior has been more intensive than extensive. As far as criminology is concerned, the above statement would appear quite inaccurate unless properly qualified. As far as problems of delinquency and crime are concerned, a few psychoanalysts and psychoanalytically-minded social scientists have attempted to "invade" the field of criminology with zeal, conviction, considerable industry, and eloquence. The success of their self-assigned task is still un-determined, although they may be considered as very successful pioneers in the field (William A. White, Bernard Glueck, and the Sheldon Gluecks in the United States; Franz Alexander and Hugo Staub, to a lesser degree and of rather fleeting force, in Germany). On the other hand, the criminalists, from the lawyer to the judge and the prison warden, are still either entrenched in or enchained by centuries-old traditional misconceptions and formalities, and little if anything of the psychoanalytic impact has thus far been felt in the machinery of justice.

Lest the above appear unjust and untrue, one might observe that of recent years some courts and prisons and probation officers have begun to show the influence of psychoanalysis—but it is an indirect and almost remote influence. One might add further that the less cruel, and even more understanding, treatment of homosexual offenders in the Army and Navy of the United States during the last war might conceivably have—and probably has—developed under the influence of the psychoanalytic concepts of the sexual origin of neuroses and of sexual neuroses. The fact remains, however, that only the Chief of the United States Army's Neuro-psychiatric Services happened to be a trained analyst; the corresponding Chief in the Navy was an opponent of psychoanalytic theory, and the overwhelming mass of medical officers had not even a tangential relationship to psychoanalysis.

In other words, while some credit is due to psychoanalysis for its influence on the administration of justice today, it is primarily psychiatry (and particularly American psychiatry) that has been responsible for the major reforms in this field during recent years. (Examples: the Briggs Law in Massachusetts; the Joint Committees of the American Psychiatric and the American Bar Associations; the various attempts to permit consultations between the psychiatrists of the court, the defense, and the prosecution).

It would be interesting, of course, but not exactly in place here, to investigate the reason why psychoanalysis has thus far failed to exert on criminology the influence it should have and deserved to have exerted. It is perhaps more important, and certainly more practical, to trace the positive contributions of psychoanalysis to the field, even though these contributions may as yet be in the domain of observational synthesis and theory only.

Psychoanalytic reflection upon the nature of crime and the criminal proved at first rather incomprehensible—if not shocking—to the traditional world, lay and professional. It began with Freud's outline of the theory of sex and of the rôle of that which has become known as the Oedipus Complex. In accordance with these, Freud found that immorality and criminality are far from being contrary to human nature, as people were wont to believe, but are on the contrary attributes of human nature. One might add that the common meaning of the words "human nature" usually represents a semantic aberration, in so far as the words seem always to imply an unstated "better" or "good," or "not so good but pardonable," human nature. The ancient and pessimistic *homo homini lupus* has not been entirely forgotten or disregarded, but superficial and moralistic self-adulation still makes the average man speak of human nature as of something incipiently or actually good. Freud stated that this was not the case, that the child is "polymorphous perverse," and that man is primarily a being of immoral propensities and of criminal inclinations. This was mistaken by many as a stark, pessimistic view. That Freud in this view considered our immoral and criminal propensities and proclivities primarily atavistic expressions of man's failure to develop normally, and that this failure led to the development of or was the manifestation of neuroses of varying degrees, was at first overlooked. Had this point not been missed, Freud's fundamental faith in man would not have been overlooked, in so far as he considered human troubles—from perversions to kleptomania, arson, and murder—expressions of human frailty, of human ills which could be treated, perhaps cured, prevented, or otherwise humanely neutralized.

It is this humanistic and optimistic aspect of psychoanalysis that the average man fails to notice when he quotes Freud as having said that neither morality nor the law ever forbids that which is foreign to human nature; that the injunctions against murder, theft, lying, and incest were developed and established by our cultures as brakes and barriers against the universal tendency to kill, to steal, to lie, and to be sexually promiscuous. Viewed from the angle of this observation, which was arrived at not by inventive hypotheses and postulates but through many empirical, clinical studies, man's transgressions are neuroses of behavior. If they are not accompanied by any subjective symptoms such as headaches, for instance, or compulsion neurotic ceremonials, they may be considered as a special form of asymptomatic neuroses (known also under the less correct name of "neurotic characters"), the major manifestations of which are acts contrary to public morality and to written laws.

As the body of psychoanalytic knowledge grew in scope and depth, Freud, almost casually at first, pointed out the existence of individuals who seek (unconsciously) various manners of self-defeat, and who while consciously seeking all that is good and right seem to get into various troubles as if with uncanny fatality—the trend toward these troubles and the art of drifting into them unfailingly stemming from a neurotic (unconscious, of course) sense of guilt. Social transgressions—from petty thievery to automobile speeding, grand larceny, manslaughter, or murder—all of these may be committed in search for punishment; all sorts of punishment are sought by these people, from repeated imposition of fines and prison sentences, to the unconscious suicide by means of being judicially murdered at the hands of the state executioner.

This new conception of the psychology of many if not most minor and major delinquencies in children and adults required a reorientation in our thinking about crime and punishment. The first result of the reorientation was a deepening of the studies of the "criminal" nature in children and in criminals whose good fortune it was to be studied by psychoanalysts or psychoanalytically-minded psychologists, as well as more detailed studies of cases of criminals which had been variously adjudicated.

The reader is advised to consult the various analytical descriptions and authenticated studies of criminals such as the case of Father Schmidt (by William A. White), or the case of the suicide pact (by Alexander and Staub), or the case of a fourteen-year-old boy accused of murder (an article by this writer), or the detailed histories by Ben Karpman and the Gluecks, and many others which are scattered throughout the psychoanalytic and psychiatric literature, and which still await the day when they will be finally brought together, a systematic synthesis achieved, and a true psychoanalytic criminology formulated.

To date we seem to be still far from that day. We have a mass of data; an almost inexhaustible amount of material exists in the thousands of volumes of court records which could be made available to the detached psychological scholar. And a yet greater living mass of vibrant, dynamic material is concealed behind the walls of many prisons in which prisoners live without any true understanding of how they and life itself got them there, and less understanding of how to get out and stay out. True, many prisons in the United States today have psychiatrists, but the job and function of psychiatry in prisons seem not to have changed during the last two decades. It seems to justify the melancholy observation of Bernard Glueck that prison psychiatry seeks to make the prisoner a better prisoner and not a better citizen. Psychiatry in prisons tries, we might say, to be an efficient adjuvant to the business of prison management, and not an agency of psychodynamic studies of the individual prisoner.

The reasons for this as yet deficient state of affairs are many and complex, and they are rooted in centuries of tradition in the business of the administration of justice. That major and far-reaching reforms are needed is recognized by psychiatry and by many groups of the legal profession, as well as by many organizations which are working for prison reform, for the liberalization of the traditions limiting the scope of psychiatric expert testimony, for the better management of delinquent children, etc.

Psychoanalysis cannot directly be concerned with these practical reforms—not because it has nothing to contribute to them, or because for some reason it does not desire them, but because psychoanalysis can do nothing more than state its observations and conclusions and point the way. As has been said, there are as yet so few trained psychoanalysts that the world must wait until others, inspired by the findings of psychoanalysis, will help to push the machinery of human justice and penology along a new path of psychological light.

In the meantime, the issues can be formulated as clearly as possible, since deeper understanding of the whole psychology of judical justice is required. Such a deeper understanding was impossible without a clear knowledge of the unconscious forces which are released and set into play each time a crime is detected, the transgressor apprehended, indicted and tried, the verdict rendered, the sentence pronounced, and "justice" carried out. Society as a whole, the jury as its psycho-moral microcosm, the judge, the prosecutor, the attorney for the defense, the policeman, and the jailer are all involved in a complex psychological (i.e., emotional), mostly unconscious play of many unrecognized trends, prejudices, passions and impulses of which one must render oneself a clear account before one is able to understand the gigantic complexity in the center of which, in some spot of conspicuous obscurity, the criminal himself is woefully lost. The contribution of psychoanalysis to the understanding of this problem has been invaluable.

Psychoanalysis has not concerned itself with the justice of justice, either in the abstract or in the formalistic sense. In this field, as in the field of psychopathology, psychoanalysis posed the question in the following terms: Here is a phenomenon, a psychological, individual, or social phenomenon, purely personal or cultural. It expresses itself by means of symptoms, by means of "states of mind" said to be normal or abnormal, by means of specific behavior said to be good or bad, by means of cultural and legal traditions said to be moral and just. Let us set aside for a moment all evaluative implications, inferences, or assertions. Let us for a moment disregard the question of whether a given act is normal or abnormal, just or unjust, moral, unmoral, or immoral. Let us merely look into the emotional and ideational content of the phenomenon; that is to say, let us examine the unconscious motivations, the affective, instinctual forces which in a multitude of constellations produce this phenomenon of individual and/or social behavior, personal and/or institutional principles. After we have examined these forces, we might then be able to return to the business of appraising them, and we shall be able to make this appraisal from two points of view. First, we shall be able then to establish whether the given phenomenon actually tries to achieve, and succeeds in achieving, that for which it seems to strive. In other words, we shall be able to see whether the behavior examined is realistic or not. Second, we shall be able to establish whether the given set of forces—in their organized expression which is called neurotic, normal, or judicial procedural behavior—whether this set of forces serves or does not serve the good of the person and of the community, or whether instead it serves some purely instinctual, irrational, egoistic, non-social if not antisocial, urge or purpose. That is to say, we shall then be able to see whether this behavior is good or bad, just or unjust.

In its search for the answers to these many vexing questions, psychoanalysis—after it discovered the universality of what we usually call "immoral" and "criminal" impulses—turned its attention to the fact that the very concept of crime as it exists in the mind of the average man and in the spirit of the law is not a definite one; it is neither precise nor specific; it is rather something fluid and unclear. We might dismiss the whole problem by a purely formalistic statement that crime is a violation of the law as it exists. This is true—yet so very insufficient, for did not the law "decide" to consider theft or perjury a crime only *after* the community itself established its attitude toward theft and perjury and had fully condemned them as crimes in substance if not as yet in formal law? We shall seek in vain for a satisfactory, conclusive definition of crime, or for a differentiation between a moral crime or sin and a legal crime. Instead let us examine some simple psychological chain such as the willful or deliberate alteration of truth so characteristic of man.

The child supplies himself with what he wants and does not possess merely by the fantastic assertion that the wooden block *is* a house or a train. He tells a lie called a fantasy. He may go further and fantasy aloud and invent stories; he still lies by means of fantasy and daydreaming. He may grow up and continue to "lie" by creating poetry, Or he may become a pathological liar ,a perverter of truth. No one could then be certain as to the veracity of what he would say, and everyone would distrust him and be angry at him for trying to mystify, "to fool," to pull the leg of so many people. He, this grown-up who lies and believes his own fantasies like a child, even though with malice aforethought, is not yet considered a criminal, however. Only if and when he commits a fraud or perjures himself will he be officially called a criminal. We might say that he will then be considered a criminal precisely because he violated the written laws, but this is really not enough. Let us not overlook the fact that fraud and perjury are not mere acts against the public weal and therefore crimes, for plain lying and deceiving are also acts both antisocial and immoral. What makes that type of deceit called fraud and perjury a crime seems to be the element of egoistic aggression against others, for one does not commit fraud or perjury for the fun of it but for the purpose of acquiring something that would otherwise not be given or granted, for the purpose of increasing one's possessions or power. In other words, fraud and perjury are acts of aggression. It is a consummated act of aggression against others that actually makes fraud or perjury a crime in the eyes of the public as well as of the law. The same element of aggression could be found in theft and in counterfeiting, in assault, battery, manslaughter and murder. Whenever aggression, which must be repressed and "socialized" (sublimated), steps beyond the boundaries of sublimation, it becomes a crime. The whole mass of aggressive instincts known as infantile and archaic continues to live in us and seek expression and self-assertion. If and when they assert themselves in their direct form without any disguises and ambiguities, and if and when they become coupled with other infantile, instinctual reactions—sexual, in the narrow sense of the word, or such drives as are known as "partial sexual" drives—and come to light in the form of avariciousness, for instance, or gluttony (of which alcoholism may be a manifestation), they produce criminal behavior of great variety: from sexual transgressions to the gangster life of burglary and murder.

It is easily seen that criminal behavior is not a rational process. It has little to do with intellect, and less with that deliberate ill will which the law usually ascribes to criminals without any sense of psychological discrimination. Crime is deeply rooted in the instincts of man, and it is usually an act of the instinctual, impulsive life of the criminal individual.

We are not concerned now with a closer examination of the causes of crime. Suffice it here to say that, with the exception of a very few cases indeed, criminal behavior might be considered a special, antisocial if you will, elaborated extension of the neurotic behavior which is rooted in the aberrations, developmental and accidental, of the instinctual growth and integration of man. From this point of view, one cannot *measure* crime; one may only try to understand it. Nor can one prevent it by mere intimidation or punishment, as centuries of criminal history prove, any more than one can cure a neurosis by these means (there were times, long ago, when we attempted to cure the neurotic with intimidation and punishment). Therefore, one cannot establish a scale of punishments—a dosage of punitive measure to fit the given scale of crimes—without violating the fundamental principles of human psychology. Since the punishment and intimidation of the criminal do not cure him, or prevent others from becoming criminals, they serve no purpose; or rather, they do not serve the purpose which they are purported to serve. So it does not matter whether small or large doses of punishment are administered, since neither the small nor the large doses produce the effect which we expect and say they do. Hence the principle of "the punishment must fit the crime" never works, for the punishment cannot fit the crime from the standpoint of realistic goals, nor from the standpoint of justice—unless something else is meant by justice than mercifully to lead the criminal into the path of social rehabilitation and help him not to commit another crime.

Yet it is not difficult to see that our judicial punishments, from hard labor to execution or solitary confinement, are seriously considered just by the greatest majority of people; the average man experiences a sense of fitness when a thief is sent to prison and a murderer to the gallows. From where does this sense of fitness come? The reader is referred to the writings of William A. White, and to the chapter on Crime and Punishment of this writer's "Mind, Medicine and Man," for the examination of the historical, psychological, and cultural mass of evidence which leads an observer to the conviction that the real motive behind punishment is the principle of revenge, the old, primitive, even though highly modified and elaborated, talion principle of an eye for an eye and a tooth for a tooth. That sense of fitness which the average man feels when formal justice is done, and when the law demands that the punishment should fit the crime, comes from the sense of satisfaction that the criminal act was properly avenged. "Properly" means in proportion to the revengeful anger the average citizen and the law experience when confronted with a given crime.

What the psychology of this revengefulness is is another, although very important, matter. Suffice it to be said here, rather briefly and perhaps dogmatically, that the unconscious aggression and the unconscious criminality which is in us—unconscious but alive and restless—cannot help but be tempted by every crime committed within the scope of our vision or hearing—tempted, aroused, disturbed, stimulated. We could all easily become "infected" by any crime, become actors in an "epidemic" of crime, if it were not for the fact that there lives within us a force, as eager and as strong and as primitive as any instinctual force, called the Super-Ego.

This force has its developmental history and *should not be confused with our conscience,* although unfortunately it has been so confused by many psychoanalysts, and by Freud himself most of the time. It is this Super-Ego that demands that our inner aggressions and criminal drives be stilled by "proper punishment" of those whose aggressions break out into socially or morally noxious action. It is this archaic Super-Ego, which is unconscious and elemental in its demands, that makes us feel the sense of fitness when justice is done in accordance with a definite scale of revengeful punishment.

Were the whole psychological process as simple as has just been outlined, the whole problem of criminology would disappear. Men would do things which other men disapproved, and these other men would either kill off the so-called wrongdoers, or the wrongdoers would kill them off; the problem, as well perhaps as the future of our culture, would be solved by one brief period of internecine carnage. But the inner processes of justice are not solved so easily. Opposing the elemental, raging Super-Ego are many forces, which sometimes demand (unconsciously) the approval of the transgressor, and again (also unconsciously and by way of vicarious experiences) demand that the wrongdoer be pitied. Other forces, by way of a fusion of many ethical and religious, conscious and unconscious, but mostly unconscious, drives, demand that the transgressor be forgiven and set free—and let him who is without crime be the first to cast the noose around the neck of the accused. And there are still other forces which cause us to be frightened of our own merciful propensities and make us run to cover, straight into the maze of revengeful harshness—as if to say: "To forget and to forgive? Does it then mean that I would forget and forgive my own (unconscious) wish to steal or to kill? Would not then my friends, my neighbors, my teachers, and the newspapers have a right to say, and would they not say, that I actually *condone* larceny and murder? No—a thousand times. The accused is guilty; he must be pronounced guilty, and he must suffer proper punishment."

This is in brief the actual unconscious,

and even almost conscious, inner struggle that every juryman experiences as he sits in silent judgment, looking with a furtive and troubled conscience onto the dock, the judge's bench, and the defense and prosecuting attorneys. He sits there in silent and troubled communion with his conscience, but also in unwelcome and anxious communion with his unconscious welter of instinctual forces—of which he knows nothing and whose voice his conscious ear does not hear, but whose drives his own voice speaks. The juryman's burden is greater than that of the psychiatrist, or of any other scientific investigator who is burdened with the need to solve an intricate scientific problem, because the juryman has no other means than his own conscious and unconscious anxiety to guide him.

Theoretically, one may assume that trial by jury is after all the fairest and most just and honest trial since, out of the inner ordeal to which the juryman is subjected in his box, various opposing forces will be equalized and justice will prevail—for does not man's better nature always prevail? First, it is doubtful whether it does; second, it is doubtful whether this can be scientifically verified; and third, where great pressure is exerted on the unconscious, instinctual forces of man, there is always great danger that these unconscious forces, neurotic drives, will at least leave a heavy tinge of their work on the decision of the juryman. This being the case, it should appear clear that on the question of the transgressor's responsibility, especially when there is doubt as to his full sanity (and there should always be doubt on this point), the juryman is scientifically impotent and emotionally powerless inevitably to arrive at a correct decision, for it is a decision as to fact that is required, a decision which only psychological science can properly make.

The whole machinery of justice appears to most psychoanalytical students as a complex dramatization of many of the mutually opposed forces within us which, in the persons of the judge, the defense and the prosecuting attorneys, proceed to stage with the confusing panoply of technicalities the struggle for the possession and the disposal of the accused. The results, in cases of severe crimes against property and in cases of capital crimes, are more confusing and more deficient than it appears in the passionate neatness of the legal structure of criminal justice. Since the criminals who are removed from society, particularly those who are executed, are not available for detailed psychological study, the machine of penology can but proceed along age-long lines of artificialities and formalities which hide the true substance of many burning issues. Thus, the famous "test of insanity" is totally devoid of any psychological meaning as modern psychological science sees it. It stems from the sixteenth and seventeenth centuries, which knew no scientific psychology. Even the concept of "legal insanity" is only a legal concept which does not correspond to any clinical condition, or any human condition either, for that matter. It stems from centuries of human errors and prejudices which developed in the soil of the passions and blind instinctual forces of man, and these were investigated and brought to scientific light by psychoanalytic psychology only in the course of the past fifty years. The famous "right and wrong" test, a sort of test of responsibility of the accused, is strictly speaking a philosophical monstrosity which time and again has proved to have no empirical basis.

In brief, we deal here with formalisms and philosophical abstractions which are arranged in rows of penological paragraphs in a manner to avoid any and all psychology of man. The psychological motivations which underlie this restriction or exclusion of the role of living psychology are not difficult to find. They are deeply rooted in the obscure strata of human sadism which we are loathe to give up, regardless of how high the level of our cultural, technological development. Born in and out of the very womb of primitive human sadism, modern penology has not yet been able to extricate itself from its soil, which it claims to have abandoned in favor of higher justice. It has not yet been able to extricate itself, because until very recently it did not have at its disposal any true working psychology of human behavior. Penology had merely to adjust its revengeful sadism to certain demands of culture, ethics, and religion, and it did so in the usual manner of a violent and irrepressible instinctual drive which, when it meets an obstacle, is willing to disguise itself but not resign; it escaped into conceptual abstractions and formalistic technicalities, which are more symbolic than pragmatic and more conservative as to tradition than creative as to justice.

This is why the psychoanalytically oriented penologists have for some time been thinking of the future penal institution as a special type of hospital where the delinquent, the minor and the major criminal might be cared for and studied and reeducated in accordance with modern principles. Such a method of treatment would lead to the acquisition of new knowledge, to new understanding of the problems involved, and to more frequent and more thorough rehabilitation of the criminal—let alone the possibilities of preventive measures which such horizons offer.

However, these visions and hopes are far from true fulfillment yet, because the instinctual forces of hatred and revenge are not easy to still in the average man, or in the written laws at his command. One might recall in this connection that even the humanization of the care of the mentally ill by the simple act of breaking their chains, originated by Philippe Pinel at the end of the eighteenth century, aroused the harsh opposition not only of the average Frenchman but of the leaders of the Revolution, whose flag bore the slogans of liberty and equality. Dr. Pinel almost lost his head on the guillotine after his hospital (the Salpêtrière) was visited by the President of the Assembly, the famous Couthon. Pinel didn't lose his head on the guillotine merely because he didn't lose his head at the sight of the formidable, sadistic Couthon. He went to the Assembly and spoke to its members as a simple doctor, as a man who cared more about the human patient than an abstract political principle or conceptually formal slogans. He freed "those beasts," and the true psychiatrist has been treating them as human beings ever since, although it has required struggle and sacrifice, and although in many respects we are still far from the complete realization of that which is envisaged by psychiatry.

That which is envisaged by psychoanalytic psychology with regard to criminology might

have an even more arduous struggle ahead, and the outcome of this struggle is not quite certain at this writing. Certain it is that—no matter how slowly—the older conceptions of penology, with their vested interests in the service of hatred and revenge, will ultimately have to give way.

GREGORY ZILBOORG, M.D.
Psychiatrist
885 Park Avenue
New York 21, N. Y.

BIBLIOGRAPHY

Alexander, Franz, and Staub, Hugo, *The Criminal, the Judge, and the Public*, New York, The Macmillan Company, 1931, (English translation).
Glueck, Bernard: See articles in *The Journal of the American Medical Association, The New York State Journal of Medicine*, etc.
Glueck, Sheldon, *Mental Disorder and the Criminal Law*, Boston, Little Brown, 1925. *Crime and Justice*, Boston, Little Brown, 1936. *Criminal Careers in Retrospect*, New York, Commonwealth Fund, 1943.
Glueck, Eleanor and Sheldon, *Five Hundred Criminal Careers*, New York, Knopf, 1930.
Karpman, Benjamin, *The Individual Criminal; Studies of the Psychogenetics of Crime*, Washington, D. C., Nervous and Mental Disease Publishing Company, 1935.
White, William Alanson, *Crimes and Criminals*, New York, Farrar and Rinehart, 1933. *Twentieth Century Psychiatry*, New York, W. W. Norton, 1936.
Zilboorg, Gregory, *Mind, Medicine and Man*, New York, Harcourt Brace, 1943. Murder and Justice, *Journal of Criminal Psychopathology*, Vol. V, no. 1, pp. 1-25, July, 1943.

PSYCHOLOGICAL SERVICES IN PRISONS. The first instance of a psychologist operating in a penal institution in the United States is noted in Rowland's report of some experiments at the women's reformatory at Bedford Hills, New York, in 1913. This was at the very beginning of clinical psychology in America. Binet's last scale had come out but two years previously; only a year before Terman and Childs had produced the first Stanford revision of the Binet; Stern had not yet introduced the concept of the I.Q.; the Army Alpha and Beta were yet to come.

Fifteen years later, in 1928, Overholser surveyed the field and reported that 33% of the correctional institutions in the United States employed psychologists, making a total of 85 correctional psychologists. In 1941 Marquis reported the total number of correctional psychologists to have been 96. In 1944 the number was below that of 1928, or a total of 80 psychologists. The total in 1948 is unknown, but it is quite possible that the total number is still below the figure of twenty years before.

The figure of 80 correctional psychologists in all types of correctional institutions; courts, juvenile institutions, reformatories, penitentiaries, and prisons, indicates that there is about one psychologist to every four or five of these institutions. It also means one psychologist to every 2500 to 3000 inmates of correctional institutions. The ratio of psychologists to institutions and to inmates is poorer at the present time than it was twenty years ago although the total number of all psychologists in the United States has more than quadrupled. As a science, psychology has emerged from its infancy into a lusty adolescence. In the public mind psychology has gained great prestige, nevertheless, we find that the prisons in comparison with other agencies were far ahead 20 years ago and are far behind as of today in their employment of psychologists.

The reasons for this are complex and it is necessary to discover what the causes are for this regression. This same phenomenon is probably true also for psychiatry in prisons.

Present Status of Prison Psychology. It is important at this stage in the development of newer ideas in penology, to evaluate prison psychological services. It is necessary to confess that it is not possible for any one person to present a fair and complete evaluation of prison psychological services. However, information gained from personal experience and from various publications, leads to the conclusion that the quality of prison psychology, in general, and with a few rare exceptions, is below average.

An honest appraisal of the many factors involved may assist in the correction of those elements which are responsible for poor psychological services in prisons as well as other professional services which suffer from the same handicaps.

Of all the areas in which clinical psychologists work, none has a higher rate of personnel turn-over than do the prisons. None have so few academically well-trained people; often men not trained to the extent of even a master's degree in psychology are functioning as psychologists. To the writer's own personal knowledge there have been no fewer than three guards and two inmates who have been "psychologists" in penal institutions. In one "progressive" penal system which employs six psychologists, only two of them have master's degrees, none of them belongs to a psychological organization, none of them has ever attended a psychological conference.

Since services in prisons cannot be any better than the personnel involved, it is of value to discover why the more alert and advanced members of this profession use prisons for "experience," going to "better positions" as soon as possible.

The inferior "psychological climate," of the prison stems, in the first place, from the attitude of the warden, who is usually completely uninformed about the functions of psychologists, thinking that the sole purpose of the psychologist is to get IQ's and help eliminate defectives, just as he may think the sole function of the psychiatrist is to weed out the insane. This unfortunate attitude is echoed and intensified by the lower echelon.

A second reason related to the first, is the generally poor salary paid to prison psychologists—as well as to other professional personnel. In one of the richest and most progressive states the wages of psychologists and guards on an hourly basis are almost identical, although the guards make more per week since they work more hours!

A third reason refers to the general inflexibility of the prison. A prison psychologist finds that he is not encouraged—even discouraged—to write articles, to do research, to take more advanced work, to attend psychological conferences and the like. He finds he is regimented.

The fourth reason refers to the more-or-less defeatist, drab, sordid, and repressive attitude that permeates the usual prison with its venal and petty intrigues. Possession of a social conscience and an enlightened humanitarian optimism are often held as foolish consequences of youth and an impractical education.

Psychological services in prisons vary tremendously—in some cases a conscientious psychologist does a fair job, in most cases, a pedestrian job. Not until prisons set up and maintain high standards for personnel; pay salaries that will attract first rate men; adopt a philosophy of rehabilitation will psychologists function effectively in prisons.

A survey of services performed by prison psychologists revealed the fourteen following functions arranged in order of time spent. (1) Personality evaluation; adjustment counseling; interviewing. (2) Mental test administration and interpretation. (3) Administration and supervision (other than research). (4) Vocational counseling. (5) Individual research. (6) Teaching. (7) Non-psychological duties. (8) Educational Counseling. (9) Remedial teaching. (10) Personnel work. (11) Research direction and supervision. (12) Editing or writing. (13) Test construction. (14) Other duties.

Personality. The psychologist is rightfully considered as a specialist in evaluating personality in the broadest definition of the meaning—that which distinguishes and sets apart one man from all others. By means of interviews and psychometric techniques, the psychological clinician is able to report in a concise and pertinent manner those characteristics of temperament and character as well as motivations and abilities that will point out most effective ways of handling a man in terms of the interests of the institution, society, and himself. In the cases of men whose personality characteristics are warped by various pathological or affective disorders, the psychologist serves as an aide of the prison psychiatrist, with whom he works closely.

In the area of adjustment counseling, the psychologist handles the more difficult adjustment problems of the neurotic type which do not succeed with the rational direct methods used by other personnel. Therapeutic work is often done under the direction of a psychiatrist. Methods of counseling and psychotherapy vary with the psychologist. Perhaps most do not follow any definite school of thought, being eclectic, although hypno-

therapy and non-directive counseling have been reported in prisons. Counseling is perhaps the most important work the prison psychologist does and is particularly difficult due to the peculiar structuring of relationships. A therapeutic relationship is not compatible with the authoritative relationship that is the reality of a prison. Brancale doubts the feasibility of effective penal psychotherapy under the present system. For this reason, Zilboorg has suggested the employment of outside professional personnel for psychotherapy in prisons.

Psychotherapy, or adjustment counseling, in prisons is difficult to do for many reasons. One is the fact that approximately 50 to 75% of men in a prison fall into the so-called psychopathic group. They are resistant, have no insight at all into their problems, and do not desire help from a psychologist or a psychiatrist. The man with insight, who wants to see the "bug doctor" is often an inadequate individual, who does not have much to build on. The neurotic individual who benefits most from counseling is relatively rare in a prison and he finds that his fellow inmates will pick on him if he asks for therapy. It is very rare to find a case where good rapport can be established. The dynamics of the situation between an officer or an official of a punitive institution and an inmate is such that rapport, even if made, is not maintained. For this reason, it is the writer's opinion psychotherapy in an institution cannot hope, under present conditions, to go deep into the fundamental personality to uncover the dynamics but must be content to treat the individual on a superficial level.

The non-directive counseling method appears to be most favorable in this respect. It does not appear too formidable to the inmate, is not time consuming and allows the prisoner to discuss his problems without being pressed or directed.

Mental Testing. Although mental testing now has been relegated to second place in the duties of prison psychologists it still is the unique contribution of the psychologist. As an indication of the change in trend, we see that in penal jurisdictions the term "psychometrist" has yielded to "psychologist." By psychometrics is meant the administration of standardized instruments, the interpretation of the scores both as entities and in terms of each other and in terms of the individual as a unique person with individual problems. The psychologist is prepared to give routine information in five general areas: intelligence; achievement, both scholastic and job; interests and attitudes; aptitudes for clerical, sales, mechanical, stenographic, and other fields; and indices of personality. Far more important than the raw scores, "t" scores, percentiles et. al., resulting from the tests, are the necessary integrated interpretations of the test results in terms of the individual.

The value of psychological testing, whether it be a minimum battery of two or three tests, given in a group, and averaging ten minutes of the psychologist's time per man, or whether it be an intensive comprehensive individually-oriented plan, is that the results, when interpreted, are objective and accurate indications of important aspects of the individual. In essence, they are a quick, impartial and inexpensive manner of finding out things about people. The caution must be stated here, in view of the violations of sound principles found in some institutions, that psychological tests are just as delicate and dangerous instruments as surgical tools, and neither type of instrument should be handled by the unskilled. Properly used, in conjunction with an effective classification and guidance service, mental testing is of unique value.

Feebleminded prisoners are generally segregated from other men, either by being kept in special wings, or by transference to other institutions, either in the same or different state departments. This latter generally calls for a commitment procedure involving a special examination and a special report. The standards for the feebleminded vary, but the best procedure would appear not to depend on any definite numerical figure, such as an I.Q. of 70, but to leave the determination of mental incompetency to the experts in mental deficiency. The use of a definite I.Q. criterion such as is the procedure in some jurisdictions, is unwise, since the I.Q. is not constant but variable, uniformly decreasing the older the individual becomes;

thus, in the age range 17-19 only approximately three percent are defectives by the I.Q. 70 standard, while in the age range 50-59, 25% are defective using this same standard for tests that do not correct for age drop. This mechanical type of picking defectives is the result of setting of standards by people who do not understand the nature of mental loss in advanced ages, or by the mechanical administration of tests by unqualified people.

In one prison the author discovered that a "psychologist" had assigned some 800 men I.Q.'s based on dividing the raw score of the test by 180 months! In another prison, the "psychologist," a reconverted prison guard, had given the Otis SA test exclusively, but although he gave the test with the time limit of 30 minutes, he used the 20 minute norms!

It is in this area that most mistakes are made, since tests appear to be deceptively easy to administer. When an institution cannot find a psychologist, either an inmate clerk or a guard is often pressed into service with weird results.

While good testing may appear to be but a technical specialty, actually it calls for the highest type of judgment in the selection of tests, and the final interpretation which depends not only on the scores, but the reasons behind the scores, and the break-down of the elements of the tests, and the complex inter-relationships between the various test scores.

We have noted that psychological testing in prisons is generally of a low order. Often an inflexible battery is administered, sometimes by inmates, to all comers, and results are either not interpreted, or briefly summarized. This might be called static testing, in contrast to "dynamic" testing, which is done in terms of the individual's needs, and which is interpreted in terms of the subject rather than in terms of normative groups. Individual testing of the careful type is usually reserved for special cases, and is usually routinely done for the feeble-minded. It is not more testing that is needed, but better testing.

Administrative Duties. A good part of the psychologist's time is spent in administrative and supervisory duties. The extent of supervision depends on the unit. Minimal supervision usually implies the services of a civilian clerk, one or more inmate clerks, and a stenographer. Maximal supervision may mean the running of an entire institution such as a classification center or an institution for mental defectives where the psychologist coordinates the activities of all the personnel for diagnostic and therapeutic purposes.

Vocational Counseling. Most of the contacts between psychologists and prisoners, which are initiated by the latter, are primarily for the purpose of guidance in the selection of vocations. Confronted by the possibility of learning various occupations, or taking various courses leading to vocational skills, the inmate who hesitates to ask for emotional counseling readily avails himself of vocational guidance.

Vocational guidance is a specialty in itself, calling for a psychologically trained person with special skills and knowledge. Such guidance in prisons calls for a maximum of ability, due to emotional factors on the part of the inmates. One of the problems is the disinclination of men to achieve the basic information requisite for trade training. Convicts generally want to begin directly with fixing cars, or wiring buildings rather than going through the rigorous theoretical training required in achieving mastery of these fields. Relatively few of the men appear to have the emotional stability to begin at the bottom and to prepare themselves thoroughly, even if they have the requisite amount of intelligence and aptitude for success in chosen fields. Common also is the desire for a man to attain competence in areas far beyond him. One of the duties of the prison psychologist is to be tough-minded and realistic in this area. Experience in institutions where the men are permitted to pick their own areas shows high percentages of failure, high percentage of turn-over, dissatisfaction, and disruption of training.

One of the relatively few bright points found in psychological work in prisons is the satisfaction obtained when a good counseling job has been done. An example of such a case is cited:

A asked for vocational guidance. He was working as a barber, was rated as an excellent man with the razor and shears, had worked on the outside as a grocery clerk. He was twenty-seven years old, married, and had a high school education. Test results showed he had a very high intelligence, scholastic ability superior to education received, very high aptitude for both clerical and mechanical work. Interests appeared to be working in areas requiring precision and control. Personality seemed relatively normal with a strong feeling of personal inferiority. He had served one year in prison as a second offender and had two and a half years before meeting the parole board. He was advised to try blue-print courses, and he registered for a blue-print reading course. Completing this, he began to take advanced courses in draftsmanship with a correspondence school as well as advanced mathematics and engineering courses. By the time of his release he had attained exceptional skill as a draftsman and by sending out his drawings obtained a job offer from an engineering concern paying four times his previous maximum salary. At the same time that he was studying, in the last year and a half, he was teaching elementary draftsmanship to other inmates and succeeded in developing some other good men, some of whom had been referred to the drafting class by the psychologist. The effect on his general adjustment and personality was marked; he went out of the gates a new man, confident and eager, rather than afraid and beaten.

Vocational guidance is important to inmates; it is one of the things most on their minds, yet relatively few inmates appear to benefit much from prisons in this regard. One of the reasons may be that in some institutions, placement in the various shops is on the basis of time waited to get in the particular shop, or previous claimed experience in the trade, or the conformance of the inmate rather than by reason of his basic psychological abilities, interests and aptitudes. Properly developed, a strong vocational guidance program can be one of the major factors in rehabilitation.

Research. From the point of view of penology and of society in general, the major contribution of the psychologists is in basic research. However, it is evident that this research does not benefit the institution immediately and directly, and therefore is not always appreciated, and is rarely encouraged.

In terms of the wealth of data available, the constant population, the research problems that present themselves even on superficial consideration, it is discouraging that there is so little basic criminologic research. European psychologists appear to be far in advance in penal research. Few foundations have seen fit to subsidize investigations in this area, even though, apart from research into disease, there is probably no other kind of investigation that would repay scientific study more than those possible in prisons. Whatever else we can say about crime, we can always say that it is expensive; it is a cancer composed of living units on our social body, and we must learn how to cope with it psychologically since repression, terror, punishment, imprisonment and death do not appear to be effective as deterrents.

Although individual research is fifth in order in terms of time spent in various activities, it appears safe to say that we have not yet scratched the surface of research in prisons.

Teaching. The teaching done by the psychologist is usually in his field; courses on mental hygiene or elementary psychology are given to selected groups of inmates; group lectures to men awaiting release; sessions devoted to group therapy, comprise the greater number of his appearances before groups. Occasionally, a psychologist, desiring to make contact with those he sees rarely, may speak to larger assemblies of inmates, on psychological topics. The second aspect of teaching is lectures to the personnel on the same topics given to the inmates. This is an extremely important liaison between guards and the psychologists. Much more of it is desirable, since it serves some important ends; it gives guards the mental hygiene approach, the philosophy of human value and of rehabilitation; it enables the guards to obtain much needed insight into the abilities and the limitations of the psychologist. Not as many of these sessions as might be desirable are held—the reason being the question of schedule. If the guards gather on the institution's time, the prison activities must stop; inmates must be locked in. If they are done on the personnel's time, the attitude of the audience is distinctly unfavorable.

Educational Counseling. This area should probably be classed with vocational counseling since they usually go together. Most of the educational counseling is ordinarily done by the head school teacher, but the psychologist does some either routinely, by request of an individual inmate or by referral from the school.

Educational counseling problems fall into a number of categories. In the first case fall the illiterates. These are usually of two classes; those who can learn to read easily and those who have reading defects. In the first case the expected level of maximal reading ability is readily estimated by performance or group non-language tests, and teaching is given with periodic follow-up achievement tests. In the second case careful diagnosis of the case must be made, and in some instances, as explained in the next section, remedial work is done by the psychologist.

Another type of educational problem concerns the individual who is desirous of entering some trade or other specialty which will require a minimal amount of academic knowledge. As stated above, there is often a strong desire to enter a field immediately rather than take theoretical training. This is especially a problem when an individual has sub-normal intelligence, but insists that he is a competent worker in that field. The use of standardized employment questionnaires usually gives the psychologist insight into the degree of ability possessed by the claimant. Usually, minimum academic ability at the sixth grade level is demanded before permission to enter vocational shops is given.

A frequent problem is the individual who wishes to take the equivalent of high school or college courses, who has not even an elementary school diploma. If mental ability is high, permission may be granted. It is possible in some states for an alert, self-educated man to obtain a high school diploma in far less time than it ordinarily takes in the high schools. When the individual does not have the mental ability to profit from higher academic work, a problem arises, since he will feel that he is being discriminated against. Standards are essential so as to have effective homogeneous teaching groups.

"An interesting experience which had satisfactory results occurred when the head teacher of an institution sent a student for evaluation for high school work. The student made an excellent impression, was quite a convincing and able speaker. He easily gave the impression of superior intelligence on a subjective basis. A series of careful examinations showed that the inmate passed intelligence roughly equal to that of thirteen year old children, but that he had about ninth grade achievement in school work. The interpretation was that this youth, due to strong motivations, had managed to learn ninth grade work, which was maximal in terms of altitude. This interpretation was doubted by the head teacher, who felt the youth had unusual abilities, and as a result a friendly wager was made between the head teacher and the psychologist in terms of the future progress. At the end of every semester, for two years, this youth who pursued a half-day educational program with zeal was retested. At the end of four semesters, his achievement grades had remained constant, he had received failing marks in roughly half of the advanced courses he had taken, and had passed only one out of ten regents examinations. This series of events appeared to indicate a clear-cut vindication of psychological testing."

This case is cited because often institutional school teachers are out of touch with the latest developments in education. In contrast to the public schools, which put pressure on teachers to continue graduate work under the title of "Alertness" courses, in some prisons further theoretical work is practically forbidden.

The psychologist's value in regards to educational counseling benefits both the man, who is shown his potentialities and/or limitations, and the school which is permitted more effective groupings of students. The alternate to a scientific method of selection is dependence on the subjective opinion of one man who may not be in position to make competent judgments. When an educator possesses minimal knowledge of psychometrics, he can make effective use of test results for this purpose.

Remedial Work. The type of remedial work, which is usually remedial reading, depends on the character of the institution. Remedial education should be a specialty, requiring people trained in the various techniques. In prisons and reformatories, clinical psychologists are usually best equipped not only to diagnose the nature of the reading defect, but to decide what method would achieve success in the particular case and to apply these methods.

The importance of remedial education has been overlooked. It probably is one of the great contributing causes for juvenile delinquency, as a specific entity. We know that the average delinquent is a failure and a truant in school, even though he may be bright. It is precisely when we have an otherwise normal child, who can not read well, and who does poorly in school which creates conflict in the home, that we have the potential delinquent. The teaching of remedial reading is another of the infrequent bright spots in penal work, since success is usually immediate and apparent, and the gratefulness of the inmate in finally being able to conquer his dyslexia is heart-warming. The value of remedial reading in reformation and other juvenile correctional institutions should be the subject of extensive research.

The psychologist comes into face-to-face contact with other prison officials by means of board meetings, be they evaluation, assignment, screening, classification or any other kind of board. Whatever the functions of the board may be, he presents his opinion of the man and then participates in the vote. Board meetings present the psychologist an opportunity to indicate to the other members the purpose of psychological work, but often due to the press of cases that must be seen, board meetings are perfunctory affairs. Lindner has aptly satirized such meetings.

Personnel Work. A prison is a little self-contained community. It is self-sustaining to a large degree and there are many jobs for inmates; some attractive, others unattractive; some calling for skill, others requiring muscle; some offer training, others are routine; some offer desired privileges, others are shunned. The power of allocation of men to these positions is one of the Principal Keeper's strongest weapons to enforce discipline. Jobs are usually promised to one man when the incumbent leaves, if the applicant behaves himself. The question of the suitability of the man to the job, the matter of whether or not the man can benefit from the job, are both often subordinated to the problem of orderly control of the institution. In some cases psychologists are asked to decide which of several inmates are most likely to succeed in a particular opening. The psychologist usually functions in the matter of personnel placement of inmates on a classification or assignment board.

Research Direction. The type of research that a psychologist directs others in is usually the annual report. This is a routine gathering of facts, directing the computation of statistics, and planning the reports. Often the psychologist will summarize various findings.

Infrequently, large-scale psychological investigations are made, where the psychologist directs others in doing the routine work.

Writing. This area overlaps practically all of the other areas covered so far. Practically everything that the psychologist does requires some sort of note or report. This paper-work is required for the records, and the more complete a man's dossier, the better able is a subsequent worker to evaluate the individual.

Test Construction. This probably best fits under the heading of research. More frequent than the actual construction of new tests is re-norming a standard test in terms of the population of the institution. Sometimes the types of norms differ greatly. Each has a separate meaning to the psychologist.

Other Duties. The psychological duties of the penal psychologist not so far covered, are probably relatively rare. A notable exception is the necessity for testifying in court concerning the degree of intellect of an inmate who has been held in an institution for defectives past his maximal term on the ground that he has criminal tendencies and so low a degree of intellect as not to be able to restrain his criminal impulses.

Structure. The psychologist either functions as a separate individual, responsible to the warden, or he may function within a classification unit. In larger systems, there may be a Senior Psychologist who has responsibility for all psychological work in a system.

The Psychologist in a Classification Center. In recent years a new kind of penal institution has evolved—a vestibule institution—called variously Guidance, Reception, Classification Center. The functions of these centers is to receive sentenced men, to evaluate them and to 1. Transfer them to the various other institutions in terms of the final appraisal of the man. 2. Diagnose and prescribe for the individual, and 3. To actually treat the man.

In view of the diversity of evaluation procedures, the director of such an institution is generally not a prison man, in the general sense. Dr. Glenn M. Kendall at the Elmira Reception Center is primarily an educator, Dr. Norman Fenton, former head of the Guidance Center at San Quentin is a psychologist, and Dr. Henry W. Rogers, present head of the San Quentin Guidance Center, is a psychiatrist. Also, in view of the functions of the classification center, the proportion of evaluative experts rises sharply. The psychologist, who must function more or less in isolation in the typical prison, now finds that he is a member of a team of specialists: psychiatrists, vocational counsellors, educational counselors, recreation directors and sociologists. While in a prison the psychologist touched in the areas of all those specialists, he now has the possibility of limiting his services in a narrower area, and generally concerns himself with the psychometric program, personality evaluation by means of interviews and psychotherapy.

Because of his broad training, more than any other specialist, he finds that his duties overlap. Indeed, the psychologist finds that he is a general clinical psychologist, while the other workers are more-or-less psychologists also, who specialize in narrower areas. The last word can not be written in this matter, since the enormous growth of the ramifications of applied and clinical psychology makes the situation unclear.

Future Indications. It must be clearly borne in mind that psychology in terms of its basic thoeries and philosophies is in many respects in opposition to the universal practices of penology today. While it is universal prison practice to stamp down individuality, to impose discipline and restraint from above by sheer force and to attempt to negatively condition inmates against prisons by making prisons unpleasant places, the psychologist deplores the handling of men as though they were all alike and equally capable of improvement by any universal scheme of handling. The institutionalization of prisoners by removing all decisions from them and the consequences of the deadly monotony are considered to be evil and against mental hygiene principles. The psychologist by virtue of his training takes a more enlightened view of human nature, contending that human actions are often the results of unconscious forces, personality quirks which can only yield to deep therapy of the psychoanalytic type rather than to direct negative conditioning.

For this reason the psychologist (like the social worker, sociologist, psychiatrist, psychosomatic physician and others) cannot feel comfortable in the traditional prison. He must either give in, by becoming a mental tester, minding his business, and avoiding all issues; or be in continual theoretic opposition to prison policies.

The pattern of the future in regard to the new penology, which is more consistent with the theoretical beliefs of psychology, does not appear too clear. Men such as Fenton in California, Yepsen in New Jersey and Lindner in Maryland appear to be spearheading effective changes in penal practices. The Reception Center at Elmira, the penal reorganization in Michigan, the Guidance Center at San Quentin, are further indications of the putting into practice of scientific methods of dealing with prisoners. But not until a whole system is geared to operate for the effective treatment of criminals will psychologists be able to function effectively.

The march of progress has been slow, and developments have been neither evolutionary nor revolutionary but, rather have been saltatory. It seems imperative that critical experiments in penology be made, as suggested by the writer elsewhere. Not until we leave the realm of speculation and are able to prove the contentions of the social scientists with respect to their ability to rehabilitate criminals can psychology and the associated disciplines ask for complete power.

In such a treatment set up, the psychologist will play a major role, setting the theoretical tone of a system, continually evaluating and treating the individual. It does no good to punish the individual if the punishment does not reform.

RAYMOND CORSINI
Senior Psychologist
Guidance Center
San Quentin, California

BIBLIOGRAPHY

Brancale, R., Psychotherapy of the Adult Criminal, *J. Crim. Psychopath.*, 1943, 4, 472-483.
Corsini, R. J., A note towards penal experimentation, *Prison World*, Nov.-Dec., 1945.
———, Non-directive vocational counseling of prison inmates, *J. Clin. Psychol.*, 3, 1, 96-100.
Giardini, G. I., The Place of Psychology in Penal and Correctional Institutions, *Federal Probation*, April-June, 1942, 29-33.
Jackson, J. D., The Work of the Psychologist in a Penal Institution—A Symposium, *Psychological Exchange*, 1934, 3, 53-55.
Lindner, R. M., *Rebel Without a Cause*, Grune and Stratton, 1944.
———, *Stone Walls and Men*, Odyssey Press, 1946.
Marquis, D. C., The Mobilization of Psychologists for War Service, *Psychol. Bull.*, 1944, 41, 469-473.
Overholser, W., Psychiatric Services in Penal and Reformatory Institutions and Criminal Courts in the United States, *Mental Hyg.*, 1928, 12, 801-838.
Rowland, E., Report of Experiments at the State Reformatory for Women at Bedford, N. Y., *Psychol. Rev.*, 1913, 20, 245-249.
Shartle, C. L., Occupations in Psychology, *Amer. Psychol.*, 1946, 1, 559-582.
Zilboorg, G., (quoted in *J. of Crim. Law and Criminol.*, July-Aug., 1942, p. 67.

PSYCHOPATHIC PERSONALITY. According to official standards of nomenclature the term *psychopathic personality* applies to a large group of disorders generally regarded as not sufficiently severe to constitute psychosis. This group does not include the psychoneuroses or those static limitations of capacity referred to as mental deficiency. Within the category, at least for academic or statistical purposes, are placed patients handicapped by schizoid traits, by affective fluctuations beyond an ordinary range, by paranoid tendencies, but who are not so drastically disordered to be diagnosed as schizophrenia, manic-depressive psychosis or paranoia. All types of serious deviation of the sexual impulse are also included. The term then, in its currently accepted meaning, implies a personality disorder of limited degree and refers to widely varying types.

In ordinary practice, *psychopathic personality* is probably seldom used to designate the large and heterogeneous group so classified in books but, unless further qualified, implies a specific disorder well known clinically but not yet honored by a distinguishing term. The more or less equivalent and much more widely used designation, *psychopath*, particularly suggests to most psychiatrists not all the disorders formally merged, but primarily a large group of patients whose reactions are clinically familiar but whose official status is blurred by our current standards of classification.

It is this group, rather than the several border-line states, which constitutes the chief problem of psychiatry and of society in dealing with patients now classified under the ambiguous and somewhat evasive term *psychopathic personality*. Patients in this group are clinically distinct, behave in a recognizable and predictable pattern and could be dealt with consistently and to better practical advantage if they were regarded on the basis of their own specific limitations and deviations instead of, as is now done, on generalizations drawn from a large and widely mixed aggregation of types with dis-similar characteristics.

The disorder which all or nearly all psychiatrists today would probably agree on as representing the nucleus of what is designated by *psychopathic personality* and which the writer believes should without further delay be separated from all the other disorders now arbitrarily classified under a common term can be briefly outlined:

1. The so-called psychopath is ordinarily free from signs or symptoms traditionally regarded as evidence of a psychosis. He does not hear voices. Genuine delusions can not be demonstrated. There is no valid depression, consistent pathologic elevation of mood or irresistible pressure of activity. Outer perceptual reality is accurately recognized, social values and generally accredited personal standards are accepted verbally. Excellent logical reasoning is maintained and, in theory, the patient can foresee the consequences of injudicious or anti-social acts, outline acceptable or admirable plans of life and ably criticize in words his former mistakes. Psychoneurotic symptoms and conflicts are usually not demonstrable. There is no intellectual deficiency, in the ordinary sense, but at least average and frequently superior "intelligence" as determined by scientific tests or by the capacity to excel temporarily in business or studies when the abilities are so employed.

2. Despite this external appearance of a "normal" or superior person, the subject shows in the practical test of behavior, in the actual living of his life, gross incapacity and incompetence. His ethics as given in a verbal statement are often flawless; but he steals, lies, betrays and commits every breach of integrity known to man. Despite any punishment, however often repeated, he continues his ways unchanged. In abstract tests his judgment is good, but it is not applied in his own behavior. His anti-social acts involve him in what is regarded by others as disaster, and what he himself says he recognizes as disaster; but he is not deterred. His conduct, however damaging to himself and to those he impressively claims to care for, is furthermore often lacking in any discernible motive and, even if a slight motive can be inferred, it is vastly inadequate. In short, despite his superficial appearance of technical sanity, he behaves psychotically.

3. Though his explanations of, or excuses for, his mistakes are often ingenious and convincing and imply good insight, his persistent failure to utilize what he formulates in words makes almost inescapable the conclusion that his apparent insight is only verbal, that he, himself, is not in any real or practical sense affected by what, on the surface, looks like insight and understanding. In any sense worth considering except theoretically, he lacks insight to a degree not suggestive of psychoneurosis but of psychosis.

4. Though he expresses "normal" affective attitudes toward sweetheart, wife, children, parents, friends, and towards ordinary social goals and deterrents, and often in moving and superior language, his behavior strongly implies, if it does not virtually prove, an astonishing lack of true concern, an almost total failure of such things to matter to him. The extent of this deficiency is more in keeping with psychosis than with lesser personality deviations. In his acts he seems callous, cruel and faithless to an extreme degree, and those who persist in appraising him by his verbal responses and superficial appearance are likely to become vindictive or contemptuous towards him instead of evaluating him in terms of his serious personality disorder.

5. Unlike the ordinary criminal, he does not, despite an abundance of lawless and predatory acts, pursue any consistent scheme of gain or, apparently, seek goals that bring him advantage. His uninviting, inopportune and anti-social conduct is, in general, self-destructive and can be seen and described by him as such; but nevertheless he pursues it.

6. In his emotional relations with others he apparently forms no deep or lasting attachments and his sexual impulses, though expressed without inhibition, involve little or no personal involvement and do not seem strong or meaningful. The well-formulated and consistent deviations of sexual drive (sadism, homosexuality, etc.), though not rarely associated with the essential qualities of the *psychopath*, are by no means usual in such cases. Patients with true sexual deviations but without the other characteristics of the psychopath should not be identified with this group. The true psychopath is characterized not so often by a strong or consistent deviation as by a lack of formulation and seriousness in his sexuality. In him, neither heterosexuality nor homosexuality constitutes a serious aim or leads to a personal relation of any importance. Though sadism is sometimes found in a psychopath, most of the group do not experience specific and intense sexual pleasure from inflicting gross physical violence. On the other hand, it is probable that the true sadist, particularly the perpetrator of torture and murder

for sexual satisfaction, could not so conduct himself were it not for either callousness towards the victim consistent with specific deficiencies of the true psychopath, or emotional detachment consistent with schizophrenia. There is no doubt that tendencies of the sort discussed primarily here are sometimes found in conjunction with consistent and organized sexual deviations or perversions. Schizoid and cyclothymic disorders also are found in conjunction with sexual deviation. In the typical psychopath, however, in what is nearest the pure type, one finds not a distinct deviation with strong and consistent drive but an immature, superficial sexuality, most often directed towards the opposite sex but incapable of affording the subject much satisfaction or of influencing his conduct in any persistent aim.

This type of disorder, like paranoid or schizoid disorders, can be found in varying degrees, sometimes contituting merely a personality limitation or defect, sometimes disabling the subject to a point where he cannot satisfactorily live in freedom among others and attempt to manage his affairs. Many such patients who are entirely free of symptoms indicating psychosis by the theoretical standards show themselves far less fitted for unrestricted life in the social group than schizophrenic patients who are hallucinating and delusional. The fact that, according to our present official standards of classifications, patients disordered in this particular way must be diagnosed as *psychopathic personality* brings about regrettable and sometimes farcical confusion, since this diagnosis, by definition, whatever the facts of conduct may be, establishes the patient as free from psychosis and usually forces the courts to pronounce him as legally sane and competent.

Patients repeat apparently purposeless thefts, forgeries, bigamies, swindlings, distasteful or indecent acts in public, scores of times and, because the official medical category in which they are placed makes them, according to the books and tradition, sane and competent, they cannot be committed to psychiatric institutions for medical care or for protection of themselves and others. If, by any chance they are committed, which is exceptional, their "sanity" is soon reestablished by a staff of able psychiatrists at the institution to which they are sent, who correctly diagnose them as cases of *psychopathic personality*. This, however genuine their real disorder, frees them as legally competent persons from control or supervision.

On the other hand, these patients frequently, and in most courts usually, are able to evade prison sentences for their anti-social acts. Their lawyers are able to point out the obviously incompetent features in their careers and the jury, despite expert psychiatric testimony to the contrary, is unwilling to punish persons whose conduct shows such plain evidence of mental abnormality.

Such patients, then, so long as our present standards are maintained, cannot be given either medical care and supervision or be controlled otherwise by legal penalties and provisions. Many of them are arrested no less than a hundred times within a few years, are sent to psychiatric institutions dozens of times, but gain freedom to return and continue in conduct seriously damaging to themselves and to others.

If these patients, who are readily distinguishable, could be removed from the official medical classification where they are for purposes of diagnosis identified with dissimilar conditions, it is probable that their status could in time be considered in relation to facts rather than theories and that, when incompetent, they could be so pronounced medically and legally. They could then be protected and dealt with by medical procedures as are other patients affected by personality disorders.

The subtle nature of the so-called psychopath's disorder, as well as psychiatry's traditional refusal to consider him separately and on the basis of his own pathologic functioning, has perhaps contributed to the present confusion of his status. Unlike the long-recognized types of psychosis, his is a disorder that cannot usually be detected in a psychiatric interview or demonstrated objectively in a court. However plainly his disability and incompetency show up in the conduct of his life, he is able to manipulate words in such a way as to give a perfect appearance or mimicry of sanity. The true dis-

order is a central one which leaves the outer mechanics of logic and reasoning functionally intact. The *psychopath* can perceive consequences, formulate in theory a wise course of conduct, name and praise what is regarded as desirable or admirable; but his disorder is, apparently, such that he does not *feel* sufficiently and appropriately about these things to be moved and to act accordingly. What matters to other people does not, it seems, really matter very much to him, despite his ability to talk correctly about it.

If this hypothesis, which can fairly well account for the objective behavior of such a patient, is correct, one might properly term the disorder a semantic disability and, in severe cases, a semantic psychosis. As in the familiar instance of the language disability, semantic aphasia, the peripheral functioning is well preserved but the significance of this functioning is small, its relation to the subject's meaning and intentions and to his human reactions as a total organism, seriously impaired.

HERVEY CLECKLEY, M.D.
Professor of Neuropsychiatry
University of Georgia Medical School
Augusta, Georgia

BIBLIOGRAPHY

Cleckley, Hervey, *The Mask of Sanity*, C. V. Mosby & Co., St. Louis, 1941.
———, The Psychosis That Psychiatry Refuses to Face, *Journ. Criminal Psychopathology*, 6:117-130, July, 1944.
Henderson, D. K., *Psychopathic States*, W. W. Norton, N. Y., 1939.
Kahn, Eugen, *Psychopathic Personalities*, Yale University Press, 1931.
Karpman, Ben, *The Principles and Aims of Criminal Psychopathology*, *Journ. Criminal Psychopathology*, 1:187, 1940.
Korzybski, Alfred, *Science and Sanity*, The Science Press Printing Company, Lancaster, Pa., 1941.
Lindner, Robert, *Rebel Without a Cause*, Grune & Stratton, N. Y., 1944.
Maughs, Sydney, A Concept of Psychopathy and Psychopathic Personality—Its Evolution and Historical Development, *Journal Criminal Psychopathology*, 2:329-356, Jan., 1941, 2::465-499, Apr., 1941.
———, A Concept of Psychopathy and Psychopathic Personality, *Jour. Criminal Psychopathology*, 3:494-516, Jan., 1942, 3:664-714, Apr., 1942.
Statistical Guide, State Hospitals Press, Utica, N. Y., 1934.

R

RAPE. Rape may be defined as sexual intercourse with a female, not one's wife, by force and against her will. An important aspect of this crime is the fact that under a specified age a female is held by law as incapable of giving her consent. Consequently, if in New York where the *age of consent* is 18, a young woman of 17 voluntarily has intercourse with a man, he is guilty of rape, since the law says that she is incapable of giving her consent. As it was held in the State of California (People vs. Vann, 129 Cal., 118), "In such case the female is to be regarded as resisting, no matter what the actual state of her mind may be at that time. The law resists for her." Recognition of the lesser seriousness of technical rape has led in some states to a division of this crime into degrees.

The New York statute considers that rape has been committed when a person perpetrates an act of sexual intercourse with a female not his wife, against her will or without her consent; or (1) when she is incapable of giving consent because of idiocy, imbecility, or any unsoundness of mind, either temporary or permanent; or, (2) when she does not offer resistance because of mental or physical weakness, immaturity, or bodily ailment; or, (3) when she offers resistance and is forcibly overcome; or, (4) when her resistance is prevented by fear of immediate and great bodily harm which she has reasonable cause to believe will be inflicted upon her; or, (5) when her resistance is prevented by stupor, or weakness of mind produced by an intoxicating, narcotic or anaesthetic agent; or, when she is known by the defendant to be in such a state of mind from any cause; or, (6) when she is unconscious of the nature of the act and this fact is known to the defendant; or, (7) when she is in the custody of the law or of any officer of the law or in any place of lawful detention; or, (8) when she is under the age of 18 years.

Any sexual penetration, no matter how slight, is sufficient to complete the crime. A boy under the age of 14, however, cannot commit rape unless the prosecution can prove his physical ability to accomplish penetration. No conviction for rape may be had upon the testimony of the female defiled unless supported by other evidence.

Most men convicted of rape are normal in their sexual desires. However, there are also pathological rapists who specialize on young girls or even elderly women. These are more in the need of psychiatric than penal treatment.

BIBLIOGRAPHY

Gilbert, F. B., *Criminal Law and Practice of the State of New York*, Matthew Bender and Co., 1935.
Pollens, B., *The Sex Criminal*, Emerson Books, Inc., 1938.

RELEASE PROCEDURES. Release from prison is the dominant desire of prisoners. Only in very rare instances are cases found where an offender prefers prison custody to the "free world." There are more devices for prison release than there are for prison commitment. The only way to get into prison is by court order. An exception to this rule, if it may be called that, is the temporary confinement of persons, suspected of crime, either for their safety or for prevention from probable escape, where local jails are inadequate.

The procedures discussed in the following paragraphs will relate primarily to state and federal prisons and not to city and county jails where persons suspected of crime are held awaiting trial or where they may be confined to serve a short sentence. Release procedures from military prisons and from detention camps, also, are not included.

The release procedures of juvenile offenders in most jurisdictions are different from the procedures relating to adult offenders. Authorities are inclined to be more lenient toward juvenile offenders and probation is granted more freely to them. Prison officials in institutions for juveniles more frequently have wider authority for release of their charges than do prison officials in institutions for confinement of adults. In those institutions where both juvenile and adult offenders are confined the procedure is usually the same for both.

Release procedures are often governed by prevailing theories of the cause of crime and the treatment of offenders. Modern devices for release from prison have been delayed where there is a lag in public opinion toward crime and its treatment.

Types of Release. Release from prison may be obtained by a variety of methods. We will not include among them, except to mention, release by death or execution. Less than three per cent of the prison population die while in prison. The percentage is low partly because many are released by parole and pardon to avoid the stigma of death in prison. Escape, also, will not be included because the liability of imprisonment still hovers over the offender as long as he remains away from legal custody. Leaves of absence, or temporary release, are frequently granted, usually for not more than sixty to ninety days and in some states for as long as six months. Leaves are granted mostly for illness either of the offender or members of the family, care for dependents, and to attend to important business matters. Trips away from prison under guard to attend funerals of relatives or for medical treatment and for other purposes should not be included as a leave of absence.

Habeas corpus, a common law writ of ancient origin, has been recognized and preserved by constitutional provisions in the United States. Since it is designed to bring about the liberation by the courts of persons illegally imprisoned it will not be included

here among the list of procedures for prison release. We are proceeding on the assumption that the imprisonment of the offender is legal and will confine the discussion to procedures for the release of those so confined.

Methods of prison release may be divided into two broad classifications: unconditional release and conditional release. Unconditional release includes expiration of sentence, pardon and commutation of sentence. Conditional release includes parole, conditional pardon and other forms of conditional release.

Release from prison is an executive function of government, and the methods listed above come under this head. Probation is a judicial function of government. Probation is sometimes confused with parole by the uninformed. They are two different methods of dealing with delinquents. Parole is granted after the offender has served a portion of his sentence. The offender is placed on probation by the court before serving time in prison and may never go to prison as long as the rules laid down by the court are observed. "Bench parole," as pointed out by the Attorney General's *Survey of Release Procedures*, "is nothing more than a suspension of sentence without supervision (and) is not a parole at all, but a form of probation; the use of the word parole in this connection is improper and misleading, and should be eliminated."

The Attorney General's *Survey of Release Procedures* quotes Wilcox's *Theory of Parole* in making the distinction clear between parole and pardon:

"Pardon involves forgiveness. Parole does not. Pardon is a remission of punishment. Parole is an extension of punishment. Pardoned prisoners are free. Parolees may be arrested and reimprisoned without a trial. Pardon is an executive act of grace; parole is an administrative expedient."

There is no uniform terminology among the states relating to prison release procedures. For example, in Kansas if an offender has been on parole for one year and has a good record he may advertise for and receive a "conditional pardon." Under terms of the conditional pardon he is restored to his civil rights. When an offender has been granted a "citizenship pardon" his civil rights are restored and the state has no further jurisdiction and control over him. The difference between the conditional pardon and the citizenship pardon is, according to the Kansas law, the conditional pardon may be revoked if the subject violates the law and that he is required to make quarterly reports to the governor. Actually, the conditional pardon is a form of parole where supervision has been relaxed after the parolee has complied with certain provisions of the law. In those states where "conditional pardons" are granted and where the subject is under no supervision whatever, then it cannot be consistently said that he has been paroled. This is, in fact, a conditional pardon. The only similarity between pardon and parole is that in both instances the offender has been released from prison.

Probation. It was mentioned in a previous paragraph that probation is a function of the court and is not to be confused with executive acts relating to prison release. In Wisconsin and in a few other states probationers and parolees are supervised by the same agency, so therefore, it is necessary to make further mention of it.

Probation was practiced during colonial times and in 1836 Massachusetts gave statutory recognition to it. All states except Wyoming had probation laws by 1933. The federal probation act was passed in 1925.

When the courts were granted power to suspend the penalty for law violation, probation came into general use. Its application has become more general as the public has grown more enlightened with reference to treatment of offenders, and it is one of the chief devices in attempting to reclaim social deviates for society.

The extent of skill and care exercised by the courts or other agencies in their supervision of probationers is the principal factor in determining the efficiency of probationary practices. In order for probation to become really effective the courts must exercise careful judgment in selecting offenders to be reclaimed. Sympathy and sentiment should not enter into considerations relating to probation.

Probation at the present time, as in the past, has been applied more to juvenile and first offenders than to adults or to juveniles with criminal records. It has greater chance for success in communities where the people have included among their mores a respect for their promise and keeping their word.

Parole agencies in areas where probation is not generally practiced sometimes give paroles soon after imprisonment of the offender, where under other circumstances he would likely have been placed on probation. Also, parole authorities sometimes have granted paroles to offenders when doubt has arisen as to their guilt because of evidence not obtainable at the time of trial.

"Good-Time" Laws. "Good-time" is prison slang for the reduction of sentence for good behavior while in prison. The New York legislature passed the first good-time law in the United States in 1817. Connecticut passed one in 1821 and in 1836 Tennessee enacted a good-time law. These laws, like other rules relating to release from prison, are not uniform among the states as to the amount of time reduced for good behavior or as to administration of the law.

Congress passed an act in 1930 providing for additional deductions from sentences of prisoners employed in industries and camps. Congress, in 1947, made provision for extension of the act to apply to prisoners performing exceptionally meritorious or outstanding services in institutional operations. This act also provided for additional compensation out of the prison industries fund to prisoners rendering outstanding institutional services.

Good-time laws in some states with indeterminate sentence laws serve to reduce the time of the minimum sentence. Parole authorities object to these laws not because they reduce the minimum sentences and frequently hasten eligibility for parole, but because they often interfere with individualized parole selection.

The purpose of good-time laws, as their name implies, is to encourage good conduct in prison by offering as a reward a reduced sentence. These laws are of little value as a device for rehabilitating prison inmates. It is frequently the case in prison that the most hardened criminals maintain the most exemplary conduct in order to obtain an earlier release, while boys serving their first terms and with some possibility of being restored as useful citizens to society, violate prison rules with reckless abandon in order to gain prestige among their fellow inmates.

The objections to good-time laws may be summarized as follows: They are mechanical and often times poorly administered; the administration of good-time laws interfere with the administration of parole because they may operate to hasten or delay eligibility for parole. They may serve to reduce the time for parole supervision and thereby prevent necessary social treatment. Good-time laws are intended to improve prison conduct. An efficient parole system would be more effective.

The Attorney General's Survey stated that good-time laws are not likely to be eliminated until there is an ideal prison and parole system and that the prerequisites for these are a flexible parole law, a well administered parole board, and a modern prison system.

There is a lag of from fifty to a hundred years in public opinion in the United States toward the treatment for crime and for this reason it is not likely that all the states will have modern parole and prison systems within the immediate future. Until that time comes good-time laws will remain on the statute books. The chances are strong it will be a long time before scientific parole systems will make them unnecessary.

Pardon. The use of pardon is a part of the institutional structure of our society. Its roots are embedded in our social origins. The history of pardon varies according to the social history of the country. It was practiced among the ancient Hebrews, Greeks, Romans, Germans, English and other early European people.

Pardon is a function of the executive branch of government in the United States. However, there are limitations placed on the executives in the exercise of this power. The governor in about one half of the states are not permitted to pardon for treason and in more than forty states they are not allowed to grant pardons to persons convicted of impeachment. The president of the United States cannot grant a pardon for civil contempt of court because the punishment for this offense is remedial, that is, for the benefit of the complainant. The president may, however, issue a pardon for indirect contempt of court. He does not have the power of pardon in cases of impeachment. There is also a question of doubt whether the executive can pardon for legislative contempt. The pardoning powers vary from country to country. In some countries it is largely a legislative function and the pardoning power of the chief executive is restricted.

Unless a pardon has been delivered to and accepted by the person concerned it has no effect in the United States. The commutation of sentence is different in this respect from the pardon because it is effective without acceptance. Conditional pardons may be revoked but an unconditional pardon which has been delivered and accepted cannot be revoked unless it is proved in a court of equity the pardon was obtained through fraud.

Although the unconditional pardon restores to the subject his former civil rights, it does not restore everything. It does not restore offices which were forfeited and property interests others have acquired because of the conviction of the subject. Receipt of a pardon does not restore to the subject the license to practice his former profession, because in many instances the association of the members of the profession to which he belongs must pass on his permit to re-engage in the profession. The circumstances involved in the case will largely determine whether or not a pardon will remove the stigma of guilt.

A pardon is not a right to be claimed by the offender because it presumes his guilt. If the individual is not guilty he has recourse in the courts to set aside the verdict. If the case has passed out of the jurisdiction of the court then the next step is to apply for pardon.

Pardon is associated with clemency. As pointed out below, parole has no connection with clemency. Pardons are justified where the penalty is too severe or where there is a doubt as to the guilt of the offender. The number of pardons is usually in the inverse ratio to the number of paroles. In jurisdictions where parole is seldom granted the tendency is for the number of pardons to be relatively high. The procedure at hearings for pardons varies greatly. The hearings are mostly informal. In some cities in the United States the mayor has the authority to pardon persons convicted of violating municipal ordinances.

It is the opinion of many students of pardon and parole that the administration of each should be separated. The functions of pardon and parole should be clearly defined and differentiated, however, before this can be done. Conditional pardons should be abolished. The administration of pardon and parole in the federal government is separated. They are both in the Department of Justice. Pardon applications are handled by the pardon attorney who makes recommendations to the president through the attorney general. Parole matters are handled by a board of three members.

A large part of the pardons granted by the states come within the legitimate field of parole. Where the power of parole is restricted, resort is made to conditional pardon, commutation of sentence and reprieve. The right to pardon should not be abolished. Pardon should be reserved for its historical use for providing justice where the prevailing legal systems cannot do it in any other way. There are those who believe that if the legal system functions perfectly the need for pardons will be eliminated. Legal systems do not function that way, therefore machinery for pardons must be maintained.

In those states where boards have been established to deal with pardons they fall within one of three classifications: (a) Boards before whom applications must be brought, but the governor may, after receiving the board's recommendations, take any action he wishes; (b) boards whose favorable recommendations are necessary before the governor may issue a pardon; and, (c) where the pardoning power rests in the board in which the governor may be a member and have one vote, or he may have the power of veto over the board's recommendation.

It is not a good policy for the pardon board to have prison officials and other state officials as ex-officio members of the board. The relationship between prison official and inmate is such as to afford too great an advantage over the prisoner. The recommendations of prison officials, however, should be carefully considered but not necessarily followed. Other state officials are sensitive to public opinion because of their official position and for this reason might not be as objective in forming an opinion as they otherwise might be.

The Attorney General's *Survey of Release Procedures* states that pardon procedure should be simple, thorough, public, free of charge, and adversary rather than ex parte in nature.

The procedure should be simple enough for the average offender to understand it and to present his case without a lawyer; thorough enough for the decisions to be based on a careful investigation of the case; public so that the case may have full publicity in order that the public interest may be represented; free of charge because the case is not of interest to the offender alone, but to the public and the charge should not be borne by him; the procedure should be free to insure justice to all prisoners; adversary proceedings means that the state is present to represent public welfare.

The pardon board should not sit as a court to again try the applicant. It should confine its proceedings only to consideration of those matters that have to do with the granting of clemency. Attorneys should be permitted to appear before the board either with or without the applicant. Some prison officials object to permitting the prisoner to appear before pardon boards because they say it interferes with prison discipline and disrupts prison routine.

The pardon board's powers would be more effective if it is granted the authority to subpoena witnesses and require testimony under oath. Opinion is divided in regard to requiring the publication of notice of application for pardon. Those who are opposed say the requiring of publication of notice is a relic from the horse and buggy days and that no one reads the notices anyway. The argument for the publication of notice is to give probably interested persons information and to prevent or reduce the chances for the approval of an undeserved application.

Amnesty. Amnesty is the act of a sovereign power granting general pardon. Pardon as it is generally applied, refers to granting clemency to a person. Amnesty is wholesale pardon and has to do with granting clemency to a group or class of persons without reference to a particular individual. Although amnesty, like pardon, has an ancient origin, it has been seldom used in the United States. It is more common in countries torn with political turmoil. The purpose of amnesty is to restore general order. It is effective only in those countries with strong governments and is of little value where the governments are insecure. Amnesty is the same in its general effect as a single pardon in that it releases the individual as a member of a group from prison.

The courts is the United States have never made a legal distinction between amnesty and individual pardon. It is generally understood and accepted that the power to pardon includes the power to grant amnesty. Since the power to grant amnesty has not been given a thorough test in our courts it generally is thought that the power lies both in the president and the congress. Amnesty has never been used to any extent except during the Civil War and the years immediately following.

The doctrines regarding amnesty vary among European and other countries. The doctrine that prevails in each country is largely the product of the political history of that country. Amnesty in recent years, historically speaking, has been used more frequently for giving freedom to political prisoners. It has been the custom in the past to grant amnesty to persons convicted of crimes by the crown to commemorate some special event like accession to the throne, a royal wedding, or some other significant event of special interest to the royal family. In France, the power of granting general amnesty lies only in the legislative branch of government. The president of France may grant individual pardons.

The procedure for amnesty requires further clarification for applying the general proclamation to special cases. A sufficient body of law has not yet developed so as to afford the specific answer for individual cases. It was pointed out above, that a pardon must be accepted before it is effective. If amnesty is a pardon then it must be accepted to apply. There may be persons who come under the general blanket of amnesty who are not guilty and by accepting it would automatically put the stamp of guilt on them. The remedy in situations of this kind is to ask for trial. Amnesty, in contrast to pardon, may apply to cases that have not been tried and for which no conviction has been imposed.

Definition and Theory of Parole. Parole is differentiated from probation in that the offender to be released on parole must be incarcerated in a penal or correctional institution. Probation is granted by the court. Parole is granted by an agency of the executive department of government. The parolee is in continued custody of the state until final discharge or returned to prison for violation of parole rules and regulations.

Parole is differentiated from pardon in that it is not associated, if correctly interpreted, with executive clemency. Pardon is an act of executive clemency. Parole is not based on clemency but is intended to assist the offender in readjusting himself to normal life in the community. Technically, the parolee is still a prisoner with a wider area in which to live, and work in more nearly a normal environment. In brief, parole is a conditional release from prison for the purpose of restoring the offender to normal life in society.

There is no uniformity and meaning of parole as applied among the various states. In some states the law refers to parole as an act of clemency. Sometimes it is difficult to distinguish between conditional pardon and parole. Parole, in the strict meaning of the word is a conditional release. But when an offender is released automatically for good behavior at the expiration of his minimum sentence, this release should not be classified as a parole but considered an act of clemency. Under the Georgia law offenders who are discharged from prison by order of conditional release remain under the jurisdiction of the Board of Pardons and Paroles and are subject to rearrest and other rules governing parole until the maximum sentence date.

Reclaiming a person for society is entirely a different thing from releasing a criminal to society. For this reason, parole should be a supplement to and not a substitution for imprisonment. Parole should be rehabilitative rather than a clemency matter. It is most difficult to separate parole from clemency and it will continue to be that way as long as the courts, public officials, prisoners, the general public and the language of some of the state statutes confuse the terms. The assumptions underlying the theory of parole are by no means the same as those underlying the theory of pardon.

History. Parole came into general practice as the shift from punishment to reformation in the treatment of crime became more pronounced. The governors in some states suspended the sentence of offenders before the states established machinery for granting paroles and supervising parolees. These suspensions of sentences, however, were acts of clemency more than of parole but they carried with them an intention to rehabilitate and restore the offender to society. It was due to the absence of an adequate theory of parole and machinery for that purpose that the governors granted the suspension of sentence.

Modern parole is probably an outgrowth of the early conditional pardon, although conditional pardon is common today. Conditional release was probably first used extensively in the ticket-of-leave system in the early Australian penal colonies. Various forms of conditional release have been in use in Great Britain and on the continent for a century or more.

When the Elmira Reformatory was established soon after the Civil War in 1869 parole was incorporated in the law creating the institution. Elmira Reformatory was opened in 1876, which year really marks the beginning of modern parole in the United States. Since that date the administration of parole has gradually grown with varying results until 1947 when every state in the Union has a parole law of some kind.

Parole, like every other social institution, is the product of evolutionary growth. There is no uniform application of parole among the states and each law is a product of the evolution of treatment of crime in the respective states.

The Indeterminate Sentence. Parole and the indeterminate sentence are closely associated. As the indeterminate sentence came into more general use parole came into more general use also. It has long been recognized as the function of the court to decide on the innocence or guilt of persons charged with committing crime. The legislatures prescribe the penalty to be applied. The laws usually are elastic as to penalty and leave it to the discretion of the court. There are those who question the general competence of the court, or the legislature, to judge what treatment should be applied to offenders except, probably, in extreme cases. There are states, however, that have abolished the death penalty. They believe that the treatment of crime should be left to a special agency of government manned by personnel experienced and skilled in this work. The parallel development of parole and the indeterminate sentence conforms to this theory.

Parole laws and the indeterminate sentence are based on the theory that there is a difference in criminals. They also conform to the theory that crime is a social product. Offenders are encouraged to have less respect for the law when unequal sentences for the same offense are imposed and where there is no uniformity and consistency of parole policy. It is recognized that there are other factors to be considered when persons are sent to prison for committing the same offense that would justify separate treatment of the offenders.

Most indeterminate sentence laws are actually indefinite sentence acts. In 1935 the State of Washington repealed what was called an indeterminate sentence law and wrote in its place an "indefinite" sentence law. An indeterminate sentence really is a sentence with no minimum or maximum limit. The application of the indeterminate sentence is not in use anywhere in the United States today. Many states, however, have laws which provide for sentences with maximum or minimum terms, or both.

The federal government has a parole system but no indeterminate or indefinite sentence law. States with the so-called indeterminate sentence laws do not apply them to all cases or to all types of offense. Approximately three-fourths of the sentences in state and federal courts are definite sentences. The indefinite and indeterminate sentence should be an important factor in the parole system because it is impossible to determine at the beginning of the sentence the most favorable time to release the offender for parole treatment.

The indeterminate, or indefinite, sentence did not, like parole, have its origin in Europe. It is primarily an American institution and had its genesis in the early laws of Connecticut, New York, Ohio and Tennessee which provided for sentence reduction for good behavior in prison. Michigan passed the first indefinite sentence law in 1869. Minnesota has had an indefinite sentence law for juveniles since 1887 and for adults since 1893.

There were in 1944, according to the Bureau of Census in federal and state prisons in the United States, except Georgia, Michigan and Mississippi, 24,842 prisoners with definite sentences and 16,216 serving indefinite sentences. Less than one-half of the prisoners received by state institutions had definite sentences. Almost all those received at federal prisons had sentences of this type. That year 45.9 per cent of the federal and 26.9 per cent of the state prisoners, committed under definite sentences, received terms of less than two years. Eight states have no indefinite sentence laws. Indefinite sentence laws tend to lessen the number of pardons. The percentage of pardons tends to be higher in those jurisdictions where the penalty is severe and non-flexible.

For more than a century there have been laws providing for increased penalties for offenders with previous prison records. Since World War I mandatory habitual criminal laws have increased in the statute books. These laws prevent courts and parole agencies from adjusting penalties to fit the case. The theory underlying mandatory habitual criminal laws is, they act as a crime deterrent. There are insufficient data to prove they have served this purpose. There is reason to believe, however, they have been instrumental in reducing charges to minor offenses.

It is likely that the habitual criminal laws will defeat the purpose for which they were designed. They will not restrain the hardened criminal, and when sent to prison for life, he will be, unless kept under careful scrutiny, a disturbing factor in the maintenance of prison discipline.

Pardon and Parole Administration. There is no uniformity in pardon and parole procedure among the states. Since laws and customs vary among the states according to prevailing social climate it is probably well that no attempt should be made to bring about uniformity. It is conceded by many students of prison release procedures that the theories of pardon and parole are sound and that the defects are those involved in administration.

The pardon and parole authorities are separate agencies within the Department of Justice. In some states these functions are separated. In most of them the pardon power rests with the governor. In many states the governor has the power of parole. However, the parole authority should not rest with the governor because governors are not elected on the basis of this qualification. In matters of parole it is not necessary to take the chief executive's time to approve or disapprove the recommendations of a parole board who are supposed to be qualified for this job.

Agencies set up for considering pardons are not by this token qualified for determining paroles for the reason, as pointed out above, the theory relating to pardon is not the same as the theory of parole. A separate set of considerations must be taken up in pardon cases from those involved in parole matters.

Parole authorities have two functions. The first function, a semi-judicial one, is to grant, or revoke paroles. The second one is administrative and has to do with directing the personnel on the staff. It is desirable that these functions not be divided between two independent agencies.

Parole boards, or commission in some jurisdictions may be divided into three general classifications: (1) local or institutional; (2) a division of the state correctional or welfare departments; and (3), independent boards. The administration of juvenile probation and parole is separate from adult authorities in some states.

The best results, it seems, are obtained where paroles are granted by a central agency established for this purpose. There may be some who will disagree with this conclusion. Parole officials should have close contact with prison officials but prison officials should not participate in parole determination because their powers of parole are likely to color their judgments in prison administration. It is better, also, for the parole authority to be an independent agency and not a part of another department.

Parole authority instead of being an independent agency of government in some states is included in the welfare department, the general department of corrections, the public safety department or others. Usually when the parole authority is a part of some other agency of government the pardoning powers rest with another board and the governor. It is more common, when the parole authority is an independent agency, for it to include activities relating to pardon. Minnesota changed its parole law in 1945 by removing the parole board from under supervision and control of the department of social welfare and set it up as an independent agency.

The argument for the pardon and parole board in the general correctional department is that its function is an integral part of the correctional system; that the offender on receiving a sentence from the court should be under the supervision of the same agency until finally released. There is merit to this argument. Since, however, the parole and, also, the pardon functions are partly judicial, it is best they be separated, administratively, from the correctional system.

The committee on the model state plan of the American Prison Association outlined in October, 1946, the essential elements of a good parole system as it should apply to adult offenders. The elements include the following:

1. Freedom from improper control or influence, political or otherwise.
2. Sufficient flexibility in the laws govern-

ing sentences and parole to permit the parole of an offender at the time when his release under supervision is in the best interests of society.

3. A parole board or paroling authority composed of members qualified by native intelligence, training, and experience to weigh the complex problems of human behavior involved in parole decisions, and having the freedom from interference, patience, and integrity required to render wise and just decisions.

4. A staff of supervisory and administrative personnel, and other personnel adequate in numbers to care for the case load of the parole system, composed of persons selected in accordance with high standards of ability, character, training, and experience, and appointed on a career-service basis.

5. An administrative structure within the framework of the state government as a whole that makes it possible for the parole system, without sacrifice of proper independence, to function in complete coordination with other departments and services, notably probation services, correctional institutions, and departments of health, mental hygiene and welfare.

6. A proper public attitude toward the parolee, so that he be accorded fair and helpful treatment in his efforts to make good, especially in the all-important matter of employment.

State Parole Compact. Cases frequently occur where it is to the parolee's interest and the interest of society for him to go to another state. The reasons are usually to rejoin the family, better opportunity for employment, and to get away from former associates and environment.

Congress passed the Crime Control Consent Act in 1934 whereby the consent of congress is given to any two or more states to enter into agreements or compacts for cooperative effort and mutual assistance in the prevention of crime and for other purposes. It is this act upon which thirty-six states as of November, 1942, were signatories to the interstate compact. Under this agreement the states agree to supervise the parolees from other states. In some states there are nearly as many parolees under supervision from other states as their own parolees. This is offset frequently by the state's absentee parolees which approximately equalizes the supervisory load in the respective states.

Cost of Probation and Parole. The difference in per capita cost of supervision of offenders on probation and parole and maintenance in prison should not be a primary consideration in placing persons under supervision of probation and parole agencies. Probation and parole are justified on an economic basis if other considerations warrant it. The cost of maintaining a person in prison in Missouri in 1946 was $1.50 per day compared to twenty cents per capita cost for those on probation and parole. In Utah during the fiscal year 1945–1946 the annual per capita cost for imprisonment was $588.47 compared to $73.00 annual per capita cost for supervision of probationers and parolees. The comparative annual costs in the state of Washington were $500.00 and $50.00, respectively and in South Carolina for 1946, $434.35 and $17.07, respectively. The figures serve as a sample from states across the continent to show the economy of a probation and parole system.

A survey of statistics on parole issued by the federal government and the various states reveals that the number of parole violators is relatively low and in some states the percentage of parole violators is no higher than the crime rate for the general population. The general impression is likely to prevail among the general public that the rate is high because of the publicity connected with cases of parole violation. Little or no publicity attends the parolee that makes good. In the first place, it is not advisable to publicize a parolee's prison record and, secondly, there is not so much publicity value attached to a person's living a normal life as there is in the dramatic action sometimes associated with parole violations.

The small number of parole violators in a jurisdiction may mean either one of two things: (1) the ultra conservatism of the parole agency which takes no risks; and (2), the efficiency of the agency in its parole supervisory program and the success with which it rehabilitates its parolees.

Prerequisites for Effective Parole. In order for parole to be effective there should be adequate facilities for pre-parole investigation. Consideration should be automatic, that is, each offender should be given consideration on becoming eligible on completion of the minimum time served. The prisoner should appear at the hearing. Some boards permit counsel to appear with them. Unless there are unusual exceptions both counsel and representatives of the press should be excluded from the hearings. The board should be competent and experienced. Finally there should be adequate and competent supervision of the parolees.

There should be no automatic parole laws, or laws releasing prisoners with good behavior after serving a minimum sentence. However, preparation of the offender for parole should begin the day he is convicted. It is in this part of the program where the cooperation of prison officials can be most effective. Staff workers should have not more than 75 cases, 50 is preferable, assigned to them if satisfactory results are to be obtained. Local, volunteer, parole supervisors are generally unsatisfactory and inefficient.

Skepticism toward parole is generally warranted because of inefficient methods of administration. Sometimes unsympathetic courts can defeat the intent of parole laws by giving minimum sentences nearly equal to the maximum. The principal defects found in parole agencies are confusing leniency with reform as the main objective. Parole sometimes fails because of faulty administration which more often than not is the product of political patronage. The lack of training of board members and staff are contributing causes. There is no school in the United States for the exclusive training of parole workers. Bribery and graft are evils easily associated with parole. A few years ago the governor of a southwestern state was impeached for accepting bribes for pardons and paroles. In a few states there have been in the past epidemics of issuing pardons and paroles by state executives at the end of their administrations. This practice has served to prejudice a part of the public against all pardon and parole programs.

There are no available data on the correlation between parole rates and criminality rates. In several states persons convicted of certain crimes are rendered ineligible for parole. In some they are ineligible for an indefinite sentence which indirectly makes them ineligible for parole for only offenders on indeterminate sentence are ineligible. There are only five states where there are no restrictions on the time an offender may become eligible for parole.

Some states follow the policy of refusing paroles to offenders with prior convictions. This policy is subject to criticism. If after investigation the offender with prior convictions proves that he may be rehabilitated to the point where he may become a useful member of society then his previous prison record should not automatically stand in the way. In other words, each case should be considered on its own merits.

Good conduct in prison should not be the only criteria for considering an applicant for parole. The primary consideration is the applicant's prospects for making good after release. Since the enactment of federal and state social security laws providing aid to destitute and dependent persons, the welfare of the offender's family is not as important a factor to be considered in granting parole as formerly.

The rules vary among the states as to the time when an offender may be eligible for parole consideration. He must have served one-third his sentence by the federal courts in order to be eligible for parole by federal authorities. In Massachusetts the offender is eligible after serving two-thirds of the minimum sentence.

Preparation for Parole. Relatively few prisons do much toward preparing their inmates for assumption of responsibilities in a free society. A few states have a pre-parole training program. This program is usually given by parole staff workers at the institution.

Pre-parole training is a very important part of prison release procedure because the offender who has served time in prison requires conditioning to adjust himself to society. During his stay in prison he has become more or less institutionalized and to overcome this, pre-release training is necessary.

Rules Regulating Parolees. The average prison makes the inmate more unfit than fit to participate in the life of the community after release. For this reason it is important that the parolee be under supervision and conform to certain rules and regulations. Rules governing parolees may be too strict. Some states have rules prohibiting the parolee from marrying when marriage might help, rules against divorce when divorce might be one of the solutions to his problem. In other words, rules governing parolees should be flexible and elastic enough to apply to each case.

When a parolee breaks the rules he should be entitled to a hearing so that all the facts in the case may be brought out and that he may feel that he has been treated fairly. In the supervision of parolees there needs to be close cooperation with the police. It is normal for prejudices to arise between police and parolees. This may be overcome whereby the police may be very helpful in assisting the parolee on his road to normal living.

Discharge From Parole. Duration of parole varies from state to state. In most cases final discharge is not earlier than the earliest expiration date of the sentence and later than the maximum expiration date. Kansas grants paroles for maximum periods of two years. At the expiration of the period the parole may be extended if the conduct and progress of the parolee permit. In general final discharge from parole has the same effect as expiration of sentence.

In some states, Oklahoma for instance, parolees may never be discharged and may be and have been returned to prison for parole violation many years after the date of the termination of the maximum sentence. The theory underlying this law is that the constant threat of return to prison will tend to make the parolee more law-abiding. Since most parole violations are within six months after release and since the parole authorities should be able to judge before the expiration of the maximum sentence as to the parolee's ability to make good the parole authority should either return the parolee to prison or give him a final discharge on or before the date of expiration of maximum sentence. Where the parole is subject to indefinite supervision the law is frequently used to railroad him back to prison when charged with another offense about which there is considerable doubt as to guilt.

LEONARD LOGAN
Professor of Sociology
University of Oklahoma
Norman, Oklahoma

BIBLIOGRAPHY

Annual Report of the Director of the Administrative Office of the United States Courts, 1946, Washington, D. C.
Attorney General's Survey of Release Procedures, Department of Justice, Five volumes, United States Government Printing Office, Washington, 1939.
Barnes, Harry Elmer and Teeters, Negley G., *New Horizons In Criminology,* Prentice-Hall, Inc., New York, 1945.
Cohn, Richard E., Wartime Acceptability of Probationers and Parolees for Employment, *1944 Yearbook,* National Probation Association, New York.
Ellis, William J., The Value of a State Supervising Agency in the Correctional Field, *Proceedings* of The American Prison Association, 1941, New York.
Federal Prisons, 1945 and 1946, *Reports* of the Work of the Federal Bureau of Prisons, U. S. Department of Justice, Washington.
Glueck, Sheldon and Eleanor T., *After-Conduct of Discharged Offenders,* Macmillan and Company, London, 1945.
Graham, Mary Ruth, *These Came Back,* Bureau of Public Administration, University, Alabama, 1946.
Handbook of Interstate Crime Control, prepared by the Interstate Commission on Crime, Chicago, 1942.
Judicial Criminal Statistics, 1945, U. S. Bureau of the Census, Washington, D. C., 1947.
Lamour, Victoria A., *Principles of Social Case Work Treatment as Applied to Problems of Parole Supervision,* Division of Parole, State of New York, Albany.
LaRoe, Wilbur, Jr., *Parole With Honor,* Princeton University Press, Princeton, New Jersey, 1939.
Manual of Suggested Standards for a State Correctional System, prepared by the American Prison Association, Committee on the Model State Plan, New York, 1946.
Moran, Frederick A., The Origins of Parole, *1945 Yearbook,* National Probation Association, New York.
Prisoners In State and Federal Prisons and Reformatories, 1944, U. S. Bureau of the Census, Washington, D. C.
State Reports of Pardon and Parole Boards and Departments of Correction, 1940-1946.

Shalloo, J. P., *Legal and Social Concepts of Parole,* Federal Probation, Vol. XI, No. 2, pp. 37-41, April-June, 1947, Washington, D. C.
Sutherland, Edwin H., *Principles of Criminology,* Fourth Edition, J. B. Lippincott Company, New York, 1947.

RELIGION AND CRIME. It is generally conceded that any basic study of crime must include the earliest known beginning of man's attempt to set up codes of behavior in order that there might be an orderly society. It is also generally admitted that the most basic and thorough-going, yet simple code, was the original ten commandments given to Moses over 4,000 years ago on Mt. Sinai. Its completeness and startling brevity encompasses the thinking and behavior of man for all time, despite the ever widening areas of modern thought. The instructions given in the ten commandments on acts of omission and commission are strikingly modern in the light of today's human experience.

The subsequent simplified code of Hammurabi, 2285 B. C., further indicates that the breadth of man's thinking in those early days was wide enough to include the idea that this code must be a basically moral one so as to guide, not only individuals but also nations, if there were to be peace and orderly development.

The instruction of the human race and the codifying of its legal and moral rules has been left in many cases to the great religious organizations of the world. When the solons planned their programs for the control and punishment of violators of the world's codes, little or no thought was given in the earlier stages of civilization to the juvenile element, especially those cases where children were the helpless victims of conniving or criminal parents. The lot of these children has been a sad and desperate one and their only salvation lay within the mercies of the church, which founded not only asylums for them, but the first reformatories for the correction of their already badly distorted minds and lives.

Crime being the antithesis of morality, it naturally followed that the organized church, as the teacher and guardian of morality, should come to have a large interest in all that has to do with the criminal and his criminal acts. Unfortunately, however, though the church has labored for the reformation and betterment of the environment in which the criminal lives while incarcerated, insisting on better food, adequate clothing, proper sanitation and the elimination of slave labor and brutality, it has fallen down badly on its continuation of personal interest in the offender upon his release. Although its prison welfare societies have provided a home, clothes, food, and even employment and a limited measure of guidance, the church has generally failed to welcome the criminal back into its fellowship or accept him as a God-forgiven individual and a citizen who has paid the price for his amoral conduct.

This criticism has been weakly answered by the church element in almost the same manner in which the employing public has met the prisoner's request for a position. The employer says in effect, "We are not against giving you a chance, but our non-law violators, once they learn of your past, will make strong objections to working with thieves, burglars, rapists and murderers. If we are forced to choose between you and non-law violators, it is obvious what choice we must make."

Such an attitude on the part of business may be understandable, for they do not preach a high moral code of ethics. But when an institution which preaches the universal love of God for all of His erring creatures closes its doors to the former law breaker, it denies its own teaching.

There is, however, no such policy or encumbrance in dealing with those who have broken the law, so far as The Salvation Army is concerned. Its very birth and early existence precludes any such attitude. The Salvation Army was never intended to be an orthodox church with forms and ceremonies, rites and sacraments. Its mission is to the great unchurched masses who, even though redeemed, would not be welcomed into the orthodox church congregation because of their abysmal ignorance and dire poverty, or a criminal past.

The Salvation Army was founded in the East End of London in 1865. It immediately discovered that among its first converts were scores of former men and women criminals. Some had long records of vicious crimes, while others were simply the helpless victims of alcoholism, which had led them to become petty criminals. The types of criminals represented by this constantly growing group ran all the way from the petty thief to the professional and habitual criminal. This posed a serious problem for the newly born and small Salvation Army organization with its limited group of untrained but fanatically zealous leaders, many of whom had little education. All lacked any academic knowledge of criminology or penology and none of them had any instruction in psychology or the mental intricacies of maladjusted humanity, with its countless variations of behavior and thought pattern. Yet these early Salvation Army leaders attempted the impossible and by sheer force and boundless faith admitted large numbers of converted thieves, murderers, harlots and criminals of every class. It accepted as a Christ-given duty the challenge of saving the criminal from his life of wrong. It made the need for material and spiritual aid for prisoners one of its cardinal obligations in establishing its program of practical Christianity and it soon developed the pattern for a new and positive school of treatment for criminals.

The police had adopted a passive attitude of leaving the hopeless mass of criminals strictly alone. They had no desire to change their ways of thinking and acting and even turned their backs upon the continual violations of the law in poverty-stricken areas. Sometimes, however, they were forced to enter these squalid districts, but safety demanded that they do so in pairs. There were crime areas so thoroughly controlled by the lowest and most vicious of criminals that no effort was made to bring the light of real religion into the midnight of their lives. Yet it was in these very cesspools of human degeneracy and crime that The Salvation Army held its meetings, preached is Evangel and snatched its converts from the sordid criminals who defied even the police.

The history of this early work of the Army describes the determined hatred and persecution of these early reformers by the inhabitants of these communities. Scores of the Army members and officers were brutally beaten, and many subsequently died.

One of the first unexpected phenomena appearing among these converted criminals was the desire to change their surroundings. Strangely enough, they did not want this change so much by environmental means, for they had been born and bred amid the sordidness of the East End. They felt it, good or bad, to be their home and they chose to stay among their own people. However, the physical change in the immediate home conditions; morally, hygienically, and economically was amazing. It could be traced to the modern miracle that had changed thieves to honest men and women. The greatest changes took place among the children of the converts. They formerly had been taught all the tricks of the street Fagin and often suffered brutal beatings at the hands of both father and mother for failure in the pursuit of the trade being taught them. Such punishment had made them hard and vicious in thought and actions. Now, with their parents changed by the force of their new-found religion, the children began their education in a new world of honesty and love.

Modern criminology is only now beginning to learn that in any well-developed therapeutic plan for changing criminals there must be a definite place for that greatest of all forces in human experience, the spiritual. Man can only be remade through spiritual changes. When this definitely takes place, then, and only then, will the stigma of crime and prison commence to fade; and only then can there be guaranteed protection for society.

It is always true that society can only enjoy protection when the former offender is ready and able to merge his new honest and honorable life into that of the community. If the offender does not change his thinking and living in accord with the universally accepted social and moral codes, neither prison nor physical punishment will change him, but will only arouse his greater anti-social resentment. Five hundred years of history in the treatment of the criminal bears out that statement.

It was the constant demands of regenerated groups that created the necessity for a new social approach to the problems presented by former criminals. This approach called for new homes for the homeless or those without family or friends. It called for hospitals for unwed mothers and the venereally diseased. It called for homes and settlement houses for children whose parents worked for a living. It called for a counseling service to help those whose past criminal activities had saddled them with unsatisfied law claims. It called for a social approach that analyzed a former criminal's problems, and helped to solve them. The records of such services, with their results, were sent to new countries where the Army was working, and this slow but determined world expansion soon developed a technique and a dynamic branch of Army welfare service.

Officers were trained in the handling of offenders and organized into small groups known as "The Prison Gate Brigades." The name was derived from the fact that in England at that time no outsider was allowed within the prisons of the Kingdom. The Army officers, therefore went, in the early morning when the prisoners were released, to meet them at the prison gate. They were taken to Prison Gate homes operated by the Army, where they were fed, given a change of clothing, and a clean bed. After a stay of a week or more, the released prisoner was taken to an employer to secure a job. The employer knew of his record and was asked to keep it confidential. When once employed, the ex-convict was escorted to work every morning by an Army officer and called for at the end of the day. After dinner the former criminal was invited to share a short period of worship and prayer with other inmates and the officers of the Home. These services were devoted to the spiritual reclamation of the offenders. When once converted he was trained daily with patient and sincere effort on the part of the officers in charge of the home. This basic foundation was the genesis of the present worldwide program of activities of the Army to help solve this greatest of social problems—the care of former criminals when released from prison.

The Army's entry into the after-care field of penology in this country began in the county jail at Hartford, Connecticut in 1885. Its recent activities have spread until the Army now regularly visits every Federal and State penal and correctional institution in the United States. The Salvation Army also works in civil and criminal mental hospitals, reformatories, training schools and most of the more important county jails and penitentiaries, as well as the larger city prisons.

The national policy of the Army is to reach the widest possible number of prisoners. There are no limitations as to age, color, religion, politics, or previous record. Indeed, the Army takes the stand that the worse the man's record (the more he needs its help. It recognizes that the criminal is not only the usual social case problem, needing the generally accepted form of treatment, but that he has needs beyond that.

As penology has become a more highly developed science in the United States, its system of treatment, control, after care and supervision has developed in proportion and brought many vexatious problems. The Army has tackled this maze of perplexities with abundant faith. Probation and parole have offered opportunities for a nationwide service given by nearly 6,000 officers of all ranks and in all fields of Army activity. Because of its wide coverage of male, female, juvenile and adult institutions throughout the country, The Salvation Army has become the outstanding organization to which criminologists and penologists have always been able to turn for help in the solution of their problems. The police courts, departments of correction, wardens, chaplains, and all others whose duties entail service to offenders of the law, are daily applicants for the Army's services.

The intra-mural program of the Army calls for spiritual services in every kind of penal and correctional institution at regular and specific times. Personal interviews, with classification material supplied by the officials, guides and informs the Army officer as he seeks to learn the problems of the prison inmate who desires help for himself and family.

Free bible correspondence courses for short, medium, and long term prison inmates are given and an intra-mural inmate organization known as the Brighter Day League, run by the prisoners under the leadership of the chaplain and the Salvation Army officer, provides a moral vehicle for social and cultural use of leisure time. The "Lifer's Club," an exclusive organization for those serving life sentences, gives to these most hopeless of all prison inmates a medium of exchange for ideas, news, and social intercourse, as well as spiritual contact through meetings under the guidance of an inmate leader and with the supervision of the chaplain and the Salvation Army officer. This club publishes a quarterly magazine with news from many institutions of the activities of other clubs. It also carries editorials by the officers of the club.

The pre-parole work of the Army in supplying home, family, and employment investigations by trained experts of Family Service Bureaus helps to pave the way for the release of the prison inmate. Another priceless service of the Army is helping him find the right kind of employment, one that is permanent and well-paid and with an employer who knows of his record. The Army helps released convicts, whose homes have been broken up by imprisonment, by providing furnishings from our Social Service departments which salvages articles from city homes. This makes it possible for the released prisoner to start life over in a new environment and with little cost to himself.

Another Salvation Army service of great help to the ex-convict is the removal of old warrants charging him with untried crimes committed before his present incarceration. The procedure followed in every case is as follows: The Salvation Army writes to the court or D. A. who filed the warrant, advising him of its interest in the man. The recall of the warrant is suggested, but not its complete removal, by keeping it on file pending the man's good behavior. This is with the understanding that, if he violates his parole, the warrant is to be put in immediate force. In this way the Army is not asking something for nothing, yet providing the parolee with an incentive for good conduct.

The prison inmates are not forgotten by the Army at those seasons of the year when the outside world is festive. At Christmas time he is provided with a colorful new calendar, which is a rare and prized gift in a cell. The inmate is provided with Christmas cards of remembrance and Army literature. His family, when desired, is provided with Christmas cheer in the form of a check with which to buy a bountiful Christmas dinner and toys for the children.

Another service which is the utmost an inmate can desire is the granting of a pardon upon completion of his sentence and the subsequent return of his voting franchise. This entails much work in the courts, with the police, and finally a presentation to the Governor of the state of an application for the pardon. It is, and should be, the happiest culmination of all rehabilitation work by the Army for a former inmate.

Many a man who goes to prison and who is without family or friends, loses all his personal belongings upon arrest, since he has nobody to collect and save them for the day of his release. This is another service the Army performs. The Salvation Army warehouses are the repository of the weirdest collection of property imaginable.

The outside provisions of the Army for the inmate covers a long list of services. The summer camp for his wife and children, away from hot city streets, is one which the criminal can and does appreciate. Maternity and general hospital clinics, dental and optical, as well as psychiatric and psychological services form a complete program for the entire family.

The great danger point and ever present peril in any program of therapy for the ex-criminal is the leisure time period. To fill this gap in a life that has had little social or scientific planning, available night school activities of either the academic or vocational variety are encouraged. The cultural side is provided for by suggesting visits to museums, art exhibits, radio broadcasts, vocal and instrumental concerts, social and religious clubs. The spiritual side of the criminal's leisure time is prepared for in supplying letters of introduction to churches of his own choice or faith.

One of the best indications of the success of the leisure time program is the creation of the small thrift bank account. When the former bank robber or thief can take a bank book from his pocket and display small but regular deposits and say with pardonable pride, "It's all honest money I worked hard for and saved," that is a piece of social reconstruction that no money can buy.

The greatest need of human beings everywhere is to have a real friend who can and will give counsel. This is one of the major activities of the Army's prison work. There is no substitute for this kind of human service. It often changes the entire trend of a person's life and saves many former inmates from becoming recidivists.

Quite frequently a criminal becomes a fugitive from justice and later in life suffers the pangs of a guilty conscience. He is too proud to admit remorse to his own kind and is too scared to go to the police. Often others are involved and he fears denouncing them as much as facing the normal course of justice. He will, however, seek out an Army officer in whom he has confidence, sure that he will not be betrayed, to pour out his problem and ask advice.

The social implications of the rehabilitation of the criminal are many and dynamic. First, we must remember he has been labeled a "social misfit" by society because of his first or repeated derelictions. As a juvenile he has been called a truant, or even an incorrigible. Society has sought to repress, or in a measure, to restrain, and re-educate him. Failure of these efforts is soon made apparent by his continued social deviations, which attract the attention of the police and courts. Repeated warnings by the police, minor court appearances, bail to keep the peace, followed by arrest for more serious acts and subsequent convictions may bring another social offer or a fresh opportunity by way of probation. If this fails, the offender finally becomes one of the great army branded as criminals for all time by the social attitudes of free society.

To a far greater extent than present day society appreciates, the criminal is almost a total social loss from an economic, domestic, cultural or tax-paying point of view. We repeat, the social implications of his crime and subsequent imprisonment are many and far-reaching. He has become a social liability. The only possible recovery from this heavy social loss begins and ends with his complete rehabilitation.

It is here that the world-wide activities of The Salvation Army in the allied fields of criminology and penology present its true and vital worth. The new social implications of his restoration through the work of the Army develops in facts of economic production; in family reconstruction and the criminal's resumption of its support; and in his assuming his share of the common load of maintaining the social life of the nation. From a loss he is changed into a social asset, with all that implies.

The general services of the Army, especially in the field of parole, are extended to any and every state in the Union. The Federal government, through the Department of Justice and the Bureau of Prisons, is constantly being served by the Army in this form of penal treatment. The Army service to the Federal Bureau of Immigration, in accepting on parole the alien deportee, is much appreciated by the government, for this service is available at a moment's notice. In cases warranting action, the Army has been successful in securing the recall of deportation proceedings, thereby permitting the alien to remain in the country and subsequently become a citizen.

One of the greatest problems in starting a new life after a prison term, from a social standpoint, is in the field of marriage. Few clergymen want to perform marriages for ex-criminals. Fewer still are interested in the christening of the children of ex-convicts. The matter of burial, should an inmate die, or be executed in prison, and his body brought home for burial, is another instance where the clergy are loathe to cooperate in conducting the funeral. It is difficult for the clergy to evade or ignore the criminal past, and at the same time comfort the bereaved ones. Also, the occasion often brings together, for the first time since the offender went to prison, members of the family who want nothing to do with him. Often there are regrettable scenes.

The Army prison officer is always ready to meet these human problems and only asks that all dealings be aboveboard and honest.

No dissertation on the work of the Army in the field of crime would be complete without the statement that there is a definite conflict between crime and religion. The innumerable influences that react upon the offender are not overlooked. Nor are the mental, neurological or emotional contributions to his delinquency discounted. Yet it is insisted that the majority of criminals face an intense spiritual conflict within themselves before they can achieve real peace of mind and happiness.

It has been the experience of The Salvation Army over its 82 years of history that, in order for an individual to become criminal in his thinking, he must violate some one or more of the basic ten commandments. The conflict that rages in the heart and mind of the criminal is, in the majority of cases, a fight against the better instincts and knowledge of what is right. The truthful criminal will, in a quiet, personal conversation, admit that his act was one of open defiance of what he knew to be right, yet he did it largely because he thought he could get away with it. The moral aspect of his offense against God troubled him very little. The ever-present, yet immeasurable, distance between him and an intangible creator led him to give little or no thought to the spiritual repercussions that might follow.

The highly-praised work of the French Division of The Salvation Army in the liquidation of the so-called "Devil's Island" penal colony in French Guiana is a lesson in the psychology of applied religion in the field of criminology. This victory proved the efficacy of religion in the battle against crime. It was positive evidence that real religion is the only known completely successful therapy to cure the former criminal. When an offender fully accepts religion, he immediately begins to change the social setting of which he has so long been a destructive part.

The Salvation Army is primarily a religious organization. It is not superficially interested in crime or criminals. It is interested in the offender as a human being, once made in the image of God. Few well informed criminologists or penologists would find fault with the statement that crime, in its human aspect, is the definite evidence of the universal weakness of man. The Salvation Army heartily agrees with this thesis, but still insists that as God made man, so He can remake him. Immutable evidence from a world-wide service, to governments and criminals alike, provides the Army with such an abundance of human experience to prove this that we seldom bother to ask ourselves what is the primary cause of criminal acts; for the human frailties of man encompass the gamut of psychiatric and psychological disorders, as well as the multitude of commonly known contributing influences.

The Salvation Army is interested in every social and scientific instrument to help man find a better and more practical understanding of God.

Envoy J. Stanley Sheppard
Director, Men's Prison Bureau
Salvation Army
New York 11, N. Y

BIBLIOGRAPHY

Booth, E., *Darkest England and the Way Out,* Funk and Wagnalls, 1890.
———, *The Duty of the Salvation Army Toward the Criminal Populations of the World,* Salvation Army Publication, 1912.
Hiltner, Seward, Standards for Protestant Prison Chaplains, *Prison World,* May-June, 1940.
Leuba, J. H., *The Belief in God and Immortality,* Sherman, French, Boston, 1916.
Milans, H. F., *God and the Scrap Heaps,* Salvation Army Publication, 1945.
Miller, Francis J., The Inmate's Attitude Toward Religion and the Chaplain, *Proceedings,* American Prison Ass'n, 1941.
Pean, C., *Devil's Island,* Hodder and Stoughton, 1939.
Salvation Army *Annual Prison Reports* and *Year Books.*
Sheppard, J. S., *Lectures,* Salvation Army Training College, New York, 1936–1946.
Steiner, Franklin, *Religion and Roguery,* The Truth Seeker, New York, 1924.

RIOT. Whenever three or more persons, having assembled for any purpose, disturb the public peace, by using force or violence to any other person, or to property, or threaten or attempt to commit such disturbance, or to do an unlawful act by the use of force of violence, accompanied with the power of immediate execution of such threat or attempt, they are guilty of *riot.* (Penal law of New York State.) The crime of riot is punishable as a felony in accordance with the extent of the offender's offense although it is not divided into degrees.

Unlawful Assembly is defined as one in which three or more persons assemble with intent to commit any unlawful act by force or carry out any purpose in such a manner as to disturb the public peace. Also, when three or more individuals being assembled attempt or threaten any act tending toward a breach of the peace or any injury to person or property, or any unlawful act, it is an unlawful assembly. Every person participating in an unlawful assembly by his presence, aid or instigation, is guilty of a misdemeanor. A person, remaining present at the place of an unlawful assembly or riot, after warning by a public officer, is also guilty of a misdemeanor. A person, present at the place of an unlawful assembly or riot, who, being commanded by a duly authorized public officer to act or aid in suppressing the riot, or in protecting persons or property, or in arresting a person guilty of or charged with participating in the unlawful assembly or riot, neglects or refuses to obey such command, is guilty of a misdemeanor (Penal Law of New York State).

BIBLIOGRAPHY

Gilbert, F. B., *Criminal Law and Practice of the State of New York,* Matthew Bender & Co., 1935.

ROBBERY. Robbery may be briefly defined as *larceny* from the person of another by means of force, violence and fear of injury. More specifically it is the unlawful taking of personal property *from the person* or *in the presence of another, against his will,* by means of *force* or *violence,* or in *fear of injury,* immediate or future to his person or property, or the person or property of a relative, or of anyone in his company at the time of the robbery. To constitute robbery, the force or fear must be employed either to obtain or retain possession of the property or to prevent or overcome resistance to the taking. If employed merely as a means of escape, it does not constitute robbery. To snatch an article from the person of another is not robbery for there is absent any struggle or resistance by the owner, or any force or violence by the thief. The person from whom the property is taken must be put in fear by reason of the use of force or violence.

In the crime of robbery there is lacking any element of consent to the taking of the property. The person parts with the property against his will while the actual fear of the force or violence which might be used against him, his relatives or some person in his company is present. Force or fear must be employed. The degree of force is immaterial.

In New York State and many other jurisdictions three degrees of robbery are distinguished by statute. Robbery, as defined above is in *the first degree* when committed by a person, armed with a dangerous weapon; or, aided by an accomplice actually present; or, aided by the use of an automobile or motor vehicle; or, when the offender inflicts grievous bodily harm or injury upon the person from whose possession, or in whose presence, the property is taken, or upon the wife, husband, servant, child, or inmate of the family of such person, or anyone in his company at the time, in order to accomplish the robbery. In New York State, robbery in the first degree is punishable by imprisonment for an indeterminate term the minimum of which shall be not less than ten years and the maximum of which shall be not more than thirty years.

Robbery *in the second degree* is robbery committed not under circumstances amounting to robbery in the first degree when accomplished by the use of violence; or, by putting the person robbed in fear of immediate injury to his person or that of someone in his company. It is punishable by imprisonment for a term not exceeding fifteen years. Any other robbery is in *the third degree* punishable by imprisonment for not more than ten years.

According to Haynes, robbery, with murder as a frequent incident, is the chief cause of the prevailing popular belief in the existence of a crime wave. It is not its frequency of occurrence, since it constitutes little more than one-third of the number of burglaries, but rather its sensational character that has given it its spectacular effect.

Kaufman has recently made a therapeutic survey of one hundred consecutive cases of robbery from the psychiatric point of view. He attempted to classify the offenders along the lines of accepted psychiatric entities in view of possible therapeutic procedures. He found that the majority of these offenders did not present so-called psychiatric entities. About one-fourth appeared to be primarily sociological problems because of the strong cultural background to their criminality. The other three-quarters, although poorly classified as psychiatric entities, were people whose criminal activity was nonetheless a reaction to inner psychic conflict. It is because this criminal activity was not constant but episodic that these individuals escaped psychiatric investigation and subsequent therapy, which in many cases would have been profitable to some degree.

BIBLIOGRAPHY

Gilbert, F. B., *Criminal Law and Practice of the State of New York*, Matthew Bender and Co., 1935.

Haynes, F. E., *Criminology*, McGraw-Hill Book Co., 1930.

Kaufman, S. H., A Therapeutic Survey of One Hundred Cases of Robbery, *Journal of Criminal Psychopathology*, 4, 629–638, April, 1943.

S

SCHIZOPHRENIA. In the United States the term schizophrenia is commonly considered to be synonymous with the term dementia praecox. Literally schizophrenia means a splitting of the mind, by which is meant a loss or diminution of orderly, rational thoughts and feelings, a fragmentation of the mind, so to say, a loss of synthesis. The disorderly arrangement of the mind almost always occurs without loss of the sense of time, space or person; because of correct orientation the fragmentation of the mind in schizophrenia is usually clearly distinguishable from that observed in patients who show fragmentation in consequence of organic brain dysfunction due to injury, disease (e.g. syphilis) or toxicity (e.g. alcohol and other drugs). In other words, fragmentation in an otherwise healthy mind and brain is usually of a schizophrenic nature.

Fragmentation and clarity of the senses are not, however, the sole distinctive features. The abandonment of reality, in part or whole, as it appears to the sound mind, is of central significance. The subjects of this distorted way of living withdraw from the environment as it is naturally constituted. Some of the patients, namely, those diagnosed as *simple schizophrenia*, shrink more or less completely from all varieties of environmental contact; it might be said that only their bodies live, the spirit to mix with others in work or play is gone or morbidly diminished. Other schizophrenics, notably those classed as catatonics and hebephrenics secede from the realities of life, but their minds are active in a primitive or early infantile way. Those in the fourth subdivision, namely, the paranoids, distort their current surroundings to the extent of believing that a certain section of society persecutes them.

An important consideration lies in the fact that while schizophrenic individuals know the nature of their real surroundings and know literally whether their thoughts, feelings and actions are concordant with the *mores* and organic laws of the State, their mental processes are essentially guided by irrational impulses. It is the lower, baser, animalistic self, so to say, that controls their thinking, feeling and behavior. They live in accordance with a delusional concept of themselves and of the society in which they live.

Schizophrenia is the cancer of psychiatry in many analogous ways. Usually it is slow in its development, taking years to come to its full-blown stage. It is a cancer of the personality in the sense that the real and wholesome traits of adaptation are replaced by delusions, hallucinations and asociability. While it is theoretically possible to discuss a schizophrenic subject from the organic point of view, it is not currently possible to state that organic processes are directly responsible for the clinical manifestations. From the practical viewpoint it may be said that schizophrenia represents a relinquishment of natural habits, a "habit-deterioration," as some express it.

The causative factors are unknown. It does not appear unlikely that the potentialities for the disorder are laid down in the germ plasm, that is, that there is a genetic and an hereditarial component. Nor does it appear unlikely that certain deviations of physical growth and development (namely, the aesthenic type of body build, the endocrine disorders, disturbances in the self-regulating, autonomic system, etc.) may be a reflection of germ plasm maldevelopment. But, these aspects of schizophrenia await further and more reliable conviction.

Somewhat more than half of the total number of schizophrenic individuals come from those, who, before the onset of schizophrenia, are "shut-ins" in the personality sense. They are quiet, seclusive, inadequately social, with inordinately close home ties; they are shy, over-sensitive and given to day-dreaming. Their phantasy life is richer than their reality life. In a word, they are called *schizoid* and their thinking is said to be preeminently dereistic (*de* = away from + *res* = reality). This state of personality, called schizoidism, is not regarded as a cause, but rather as a forerunner to schizophrenia, almost in the sense of being a continuum with it.

While schizophrenia may have its onset at any age, it is rare in childhood, more common in late adolescence and has its highest incidence between the ages 20–30. It is slightly more prevalent among males. Education, environment and economic status seem not to play an important role in a causative way, though each may facilitate the development of the disorder.

Accidents, injuries and diseases may also cause schizophrenia to appear in a predisposed person. Under such circumstances the accident, injury or disease appears to operate as a precipitating, not as a final, cause. As a rule, however, schizophrenia seems to grow more or less imperceptibly out of the schizoid personality without the intervention of essential external causes.

The nuclear symptoms of the four subdivisions of schizophrenia are as follows:

1. *Simple* form. Quietness, seclusiveness, indifference, mental and physical inertia. There is substantially no desire to do anything; in common parlance the patients are "lazy, good-for-nothings." They have no interest in their past, present or future. Occasionally they may experience short episodes of a delusional and hallucinatory nature. As a group they very infrequently come in conflict with the law.

It is not easy to distinguish the indifference of these simple schizophrenic individuals from that of another group called *psychopathic personality*. While the indifference *per se* may be indistinguishable in the two groups, the background against which it

appears is significant. In schizophrenia there is little or no background of anti-social conduct or irritation at the social order, whereas in psychopathic personality there is usually the history of disobedience to home and school discipline, of pugnacity, of lying and stealing and inconsideration of the rights of others.

The course of simple schizophrenia is chronic. Not all of the members of this group are fully apathetic; some have a low-grade type of personal and environmental interest; they may work at simple, menial tasks in a half-hearted, or should we say quarter-hearted way.

Irresponsibility, stemming, it is believed, from a sick personality and not from conscious design is the keynote of this disorder. From the standpoint of the M'Naghten (McNaughton) rule these individuals know intellectually "the nature and quality of the act" and they know intellectually that "the act was wrong." They ordinarily are "laboring under such defect of reason" as not to know right from wrong. They are laboring under morbid apathy, of which absence of or indifference to reasoning is a part.

2. *Hebephrenic* form. The symptoms of this subdivision usually begin in the adolescent period. Recession from reality is generally sharp, being more or less complete within several weeks. It is in hebephrenia that the substitution of a phantasy world for the world of reality is particularly well developed. The patient acquires from his inner, unconscious mind a wealth of delusions and hallucinations. He believes himself to be the world (cosmic identification) and exchanges communications, through thought transference and hallucinations, with all animate and inanimate things. He considers himself to be The Redeemer, assuming the powers of omnipotence, omniscience and ubiquity. By mere thinking or by a gesture he controls everything. He becomes both male and female and by magic union with himself he populates the world. He is timeless, spaceless.

Accessory symptoms are complete indifference to the world of reality and to his own personal needs, including eating, dressing, cleanliness, warmth, sanitation, etc. Silly grinning is usually noticed.

The course of the disorder is usually chronic, though there may be partial or complete remission of symptoms during the early months or years of the disorder. Some few hebephrenic patients recover more or less completely after one or two attacks, though usually the rest of their lives is punctuated here and there with an episode.

When the illness is established, irresponsibility is clearly shown. These patients are so engrossed in their phantastic ways of living that the world of reality means little or nothing to them. Whatever spontaneous activities they show are almost always in response to delusions or hallucinations.

Though criminal acts are relatively rare among the members of this group, they are known to occur. A hebephrenic patient, delusionally obedient to the will of God, gleefully murdered three people, because God had told him to "borrow the lives" of the three in order to become The Christ. He knew that the organic law of man forbade murder, but he also knew, and, moreover, he firmly felt, that God's order was the only and final order.

The claim to the Messiahship is not in and of itself a signal of a formally deranged mind. There have been and are many claimants who show no clear-cut delusions or hallucinations, but who, on the contrary, control groups of society through astuteness and who acquire real and tangible wealth. They delude others, not themselves.

3. *Catatonic form.* Some people "freeze" in mind and body when called upon to do something about an environmental or a personal urge to which they cannot respond within normal range. They get "scared stiff"; they stand there "like a monument." Catatonia is prolonged and severe "freezing"; it is characterized by immobility, mental and physical, and by a more or less complete shutting off of all environmental stimuli. In this stage they do not see their surroundings, for the eyelids are tightly closed; they do not hear, for plugs of cotton reenforce mental deafness; they do not taste, because the lips are tightly approximated; they do not feel, unless the stimulus is very pain-

ful; the nose is open for breathing and thus living. Thinking is immobilized in the sense that it is not communicated to the outside world, yet the patient registers mentally what is going on about him. In court language he is "standing mute."

The "freezing" stage of catatonia may be the only stage, though usually it is not. Generally the patient "thaws out" and when he does he is as receptive to stimuli as he was aversive to them. He may pass from active negativism (freezing) to hypersuggestibility (thawing out); in the latter condition he echoes or reproduces stimuli from without, he mirror-images the postures, gestures and movements of others; this is called echomimia or echopraxia, or echokinesis; he repeats parrot-like what others say—echolalia. All of this is automatic repetition (echomatism). Another manifestation is called *command automatism,* the patient auomatically carrying out orders given to him.

One might think that here is the golden opportunity to order a (catatonic) enemy to destruction of himself or of another. I know of no such cases in recorded history or in my own experience. For some unknown reason even the most deeply hypnotized person fails to carry out orders that are contrary to his morals, except in the "movies."

Sometimes a catatonic patient is in a stage of "passive negativism," by which is meant that he does not spontaneously move or speak.

There is a fourth stage, characterized by constant repetition in response to internal stimuli. The patient repeats his own ideas over and over again; this is called stereotyped language or verbigeration; he may perpetually repeat an hallucination—hallucinatory verbigeration. Gestures or movements may be stereotyped.

The course of catatonic schizophrenia is variable. Generally the patient recovers several months after the initial onset. A few never have a recurrence; a few have two or three attacks. But the vast majority have several attacks, each succeeding one longer than its predecessor until chronicity supervenes.

Anti-social acts are rare in this group,

though suicide or other acts of aggression against oneself are not rare. The latter is apt to occur, when it does occur, in the very early part of an attack, before the patient has fully prepared his defenses against what he considers to be the harmful environment. On rare occasions he becomes aggressive to the "hostile" environment. In either instance, he is to be looked upon as irresponsible mentally.

4. *Paranoid* form. This is the subdivision of schizophrenia that the public knows best, perhaps because the paranoid patient makes his presence keenly known to it. The paranoid patient does not like the environment and fights against it. He believes that the environment is against him, that it is trying to debase, degrade and persecute him. His persecutors make him think bad thoughts; they persecute him through the sense organs; they put bad odors about him (hallucination of smell); they put pioson in his food (hallucination of taste); they call him bad names (hallucination of hearing); they apply disagreeable stimuli to his skin areas (hallucination of touch). For some reason he seems to be spared from pornography.

Usually it takes a few years for the clinical picture to be fully established. It is during this period of growth that the patient fights against the environment, often showing a very threatening attitude. He is incessantly defending himself against alleged debasement. He feels certain that others are trying to get him discharged from employment, they allegedly charge him with acts of immorality, they pry into his personal life.

This persecutory phase may, and usually does, last for several years. It is in the nature of the illness that the persecutors are never wholly successful in luring the patient into acts of moral turpitude. He fends them off, though the struggle is difficult. Over the months or years his tireless defenses begin to reward him in the form of ever-increasing strength with which to fight alleged overtures to sin. The vigor that he thus gains goes into the service of righteousness, which steadily grows until it achieves the level of all-righteousness. By this time his strength assumes the stature of omnipotence. With

these two qualities—all-righteousness and omnipotence—he begins to identify himself with the role of Christ.

It is characteristic for paranoid patients as a group that not all of them evolve to the Christ stage. Some get "fixed," so to speak, at the early level of antagonism to their fellow men. They are quarrelsome and resentful, feeling that society is abusing them. They often seek redress through the courts. There are two main trends of interest shown by them in court fights.

The litiginous paranoiac tries to engage the services of courts to help him gain, for instance, an heirship from which he has been illegally deprived by persecutors. The inventive paranoiac seeks court action on the alleged theft of some highly important invention of his.

These and similar patients, whose feelings of persecution are hidden in real facts, though the real facts are irrelevant to the false premise, are given a special name by psychiatrists; they are patients with paranoia and are not classified under the heading schizophrenia.

The patient is not known as a paranoid schizophrenic individual until and unless he develops a delusional system that is more or less easily discernible. Some few do not go beyond this kind of delusional mentality; while today they are said to have schizophrenia, they used to be distinguished from the severer patients by the term *paraphrenia*.

When the patient becomes hallucinatory as well as delusional he is unqualifiedly schizophrenic. This name applies also to the patient whose condition has progressed to the Messiah stage.

The course of the paranoid form of schizophrenia is usually chronic, though it may not progress through the several stages just described. Some of these patients have episodes of a paranoid nature; in the interval between attacks they are regarded as peculiar or eccentric, but they are not formally described as "insane."

Some schizophrenic patients do not fall easily into one or another of the subdivisions. They may, for example, have a mixture of catatonic and hebephrenic symptoms. They are usually classified as schizophrenia, mixed form.

LELAND E. HINSIE, M. D.
Professor of Psychiatry
Columbia University
New York

BIBLIOGRAPHY

Cameron, N., The Functional Psychoses, Chapter 19 in Hunt, J. McV.: *Personality and the Behavior Disorders*, Ronald Press, 1944.
Haufmann, E., and Kasanin, J., *Conceptual Thinking in Schizophrenia*, Nervous and Mental Dis. Monogr., No. 68, 1943.
Meyer, A., Jelliffe, S. E., and Hoch, A., *Dementia Praecox*, Gotham Press, Boston, 1911.
White, W. A., *Outline of Psychiatry* (12th Ed.), New York, Nervous and Mental Disease Monographs, 1929.
Woods, W. L., Language Study in Schizophrenia, *Journal of Nervous and Mental Disease*, 1938, 87, 290–316.

SEDUCTION. Seduction is the offense of inducing a woman to surrender her chastity. It is specifically defined by statute as follows: A person who, under promise of marriage, or by means of a fraudulent representation to her that he is married to her, seduces and has sexual intercourse with an unmarried female of previous chaste character, has committed the crime of seduction, and is punishable by imprisonment for not more than five years, or by a fine of not more than one thousand dollars or both.

The promise to marry must be absolute so that if a female consents to sexual intercourse upon the man's promise to marry her in the event that she becomes pregnant as a result of that intercourse, the man cannot be convicted of seduction. The subsequent inter-marriage of the parties, or the lapse of two years after the commission of the offense before the finding of an indictment, is a bar to a prosecution for seduction (New York State Penal Law). No conviction can be had for seduction upon the testimony of the female seduced, unsupported by other evidence.

BIBLIOGRAPHY

Gilbert, F. B., *Criminal Law and Practice of the State of New York*, Matthew Bender and Co., 1935.

SEGREGATION. The concept of *segregation* has at least three major connotations in the field of criminology:

(1) It refers to a natural process operating in the community by which social types, groups, and institutions become localized, differentiated, and perpetuated. By this process criminals as social types, criminal groups, and criminal institutions such as characterize so-called "vice-areas," become differentiated spatially and culturally from non-criminal social types, groups and institutions.

(2) It refers to a positive social policy directed toward separation of those convicted or suspected of crime from the rest of the society.

(3) It refers to the official separation and differential treatment of prisoners and other persons in confinement, before and after conviction, on the basis of formal or informal systems of classification.

I. Segregation as a natural process in social interaction has been studied extensively by sociologists, especially by those interested in human ecology. Two types of segregation arising from different processes of interaction have been distinguished by Wirth: (1) "passive segregation," which is the non-directed result of the operation of the process of competition among human beings, results in the location of persons and groups spatially and occupationally; (2) "active segregation" is the deliberate allocation of certain persons or groups to certain locations or occupational positions as the result of conflict in the society. As Wirth points out, "In a given case one or the other of these two types may predominate at different periods of historical development. Thus segregated vice districts have generally come into existence spontaneously, have subsequently been confined within legally prescribed boundaries under public supervision and have finally persisted unofficially, although no less visibly, in much the same areas even after their formal abolition by ordinances." [1]

Every civilization has recorded evidence of the existence, not only of individuals who have deviated from the cultural norms or

[1] Wirth, Louis, "Segregation," *Encyclopedia of the Social Sciences* (New York: The Macmillan Company, 1934), XIII, 643.

who have been considered offenders against the society, but also of *groups* of such persons who have distinguished themselves from other groups in the society by illegal and immoral cultural norms and occupational activities. Such groups typically have been considered "outlaws" in a literal sense—not subjected to the law and hence to be exterminated by those who were within the law. Typically they lived apart from the law-abiding group, but they were definitely a part of the society ("inner enemies") as distinguished from members of different societies. In some situations they have lived on the physical margins of the main group—in forest, swamp, or desert wilderness from which they might prey upon the rest of the community. The Robin Hoods and the frontier outlaws of many countries are familiar characters in story and folklore of many peoples.

In other periods and situations, as large cities and urban differentiation developed, certain areas of the city become recognized as the locale of persons and groups whose occupations are primarily illegal and immoral. Every large city has its "underworld" made up of persons and groups who violate either the moral or criminal code and who constitute a distinctive element in the population. Certain parts of almost every community of any size are recognized by most residents as "vice sections" or "criminal sections" and are given local names which have these connotations. In some of the older cities such as Paris, London, and some Oriental cities, these areas have preserved their distinctive character for generations, even for centuries. In rapidly changing cities of industrial countries the areas tend to shift as the ecological pattern of the city changes, particularly in response to changing population and economic organization. For example, commercially organized gambling and vice in American cities formerly were almost exclusively concentrated in areas close to the center of the city. Now there are similar areas located on the outer fringe of the city, either in suburbs primarily characterized by these activities or along the main arterial highways radiating from the cities.

The underworld not only occupies a specific physical location in the community, but it also typically has culture patterns which distinguish it from the rest of the society. The existence of criminal slang as a specialized vocabulary has long been known. Greene's *Coney-Catching Pamphlets* exposed the criminal vocabulary and other culture patterns of the Elizabethan London underworld. Outsiders, however, rarely learn the meaning of the criminal argot until that meaning has disappeared among the criminals, to be replaced by other meanings and words limited to the criminal group. Some criminal and quasi-criminal groups have adopted distinctive types of dress, as typified by the famous French Apachés. Even more distinctive are the ingroup attitudes of the members of the underworld toward their own kind, contrasted with their general suspicion and wariness of "respectable" society. According to Sutherland, "Admission to this underworld is secured generally by personal introductions and can be secured only by those who are regarded as not dangerous to the criminals, quasi-criminals, and politicians who compose the underworld." [2] Fundamental in the social structure of the underworld are the patterns of crime, distinctive codes of conduct, and specialized institutions and social roles which go to make up a culture complex quite distinct from other social milieus. These patterns, which grow out of the differentiation of the criminal from the law-abiding society, tend to increase the isolation between the two elements.

With the development of the science of human ecology, there has been an increasing study of the "natural areas" of the city and of the "natural history" of the process through which these areas develop and change. Common sense observation has been replaced by careful observation, particularly through the use of statistical evidence of variation in certain characteristics in specifically delimited areas. The studies of Clifford Shaw and his collaborators are outstanding in their utilization of this approach in connection with juvenile delinquency.

[2] Sutherland, E. H., *Principles of Criminology,* Fourth Edition (New York: J. B. Lippincott Company, 1947), 203.

Statistical evidence from fifteen American cities, as presented in their most recent volume,[3] reveals not only that rates of delinquency vary widely in different neighborhoods of the same city but that the areas with high delinquency rates also have high rates of adult crime as measured by commitment to the county jail. The rates are generally highest in areas nearest the center of the city and these areas have maintained high rates for three decades, although in the meantime the nationality composition of the population of the areas has changed almost completely. These conclusions have been substantiated by studies in other localities by other authors. Comparison with European and Oriental cities indicates that there is also concentration of delinquency and crime in certain areas, but these areas do not have the same location in the city.

The statistical evidence of the concentration of crime and juvenile delinquency in certain areas has received two types of explanation. One explanation, held by a limited number of persons, is on the basis of selective migration. It is held that since the areas in which the rates of crime and delinquency are highest are also the ones in which there is the most poverty and in which rents are lowest, it is probable that there has been a selection of constitutionally inadequate persons from the general population who have become concentrated in these areas and that these weaker persons are those who are most likely to become involved in crime and delinquency. The objection to this argument which has been made by other students is that in these same areas there is typically a high turnover in the population and that some of the groups who are migrants into the city and live in or adjacent to these areas have a high delinquency rate during the first generation but as these groups move out into other areas of the city their delinquency and crime rates decrease, while the incoming groups in the delinquency area have rates corresponding to those of the earlier groups. It is conceded, however, that

[3] Shaw, Clifford R., McKay, Henry, and others, *Juvenile Delinquency and Urban Areas* (Chicago: The University of Chicago Press, 1942).

there is a certain residue of persons who do not become economically successful enough to move out of the areas and that there are some who accept a mode of life which is appropriate to the area and remain there.

The hypothesis of segregation which has been stated by Wirth, as mentioned above, is held more generally by sociologists. Segregation of criminal and quasi-criminal persons and groups seems to operate as a consequence of competition and conflict in human society. Competitive-cooperation among human beings develops a division of labor and a set of social and occupational roles which are socially approved and within which most persons find a legitimate place. Distribution of persons spatially in the community, in terms of residence and place of work, also develops essentially from the competitive order. Patterns of deviant behavior, however, also exist and certain groups and persons compete for existence by following these patterns of behavior, which may be in the form of vice or gambling, or by preying upon the law-abiding members of the community. The persons who follow these patterns of behavior tend to become located spatially in certain sections of the community because of a combination of social and economic factors. As they become concentrated in certain areas they become more and more isolated from other elements in the society and this social isolation becomes a factor in increasing the segregation of this element from others. The area, then, develops a distinctive character through both the negative factor of isolation and the positive factor of local tradition.

The process of segregation may, to a large extent, go on with little conscious attention from either the law-abiding or the non-law-abiding groups. But as each group becomes increasingly aware of the threat which the other constitutes to what it conceives to be its welfare, attitudes of conflict become increasingly prevalent. The law-abiding group may try to eliminate the other element. Failing that, they try to increase the physical and social separation of the "undesirable element." Segregation at this point becomes a conscious policy arising out of society's fear and hatred of its "inner enemies." The extent of the use of segregation varies with the attitudes of society toward the offenders. In some cases it may be primarily social ostracism, categorizing certain types of people without physically separating them from the main group. This has, at certain times, been characterized treatment of sex offenders. In other cases, the offenders may be restricted to certain streets or certain communities, as has been true of treatment of prostitution. At the same time, as the conflict between the two elements in the society becomes increasingly sharp, the criminal group may seek segregation as a form of self-defense, getting protection in certain areas by collusion with borderline elements in the "respectable" society, such as some types of politicians and business men.

II. Segregation as a positive social policy has developed as society has taken a concerted stand against violators of the legal and moral codes. Particular practices have emerged, some of which have been primarily for the purpose of segregation, while others have had the effect of segregating the offenders although that was not the explicit and conscious intent of the practice. Banishment, corporal punishment, and imprisonment as ways of dealing with offenders have all been utilized for various purposes and with various effects not always intended. Segregation has sometimes been one of the motives of some of these practices, along with securing retribution and attempting to reform the offenders or to deter others from becoming offenders. The banishment and confinement of criminals is in some respects very similar to the banishment of lepers and their confinement in leper colonies. However, in the case of the lepers, segregation has been used *primarily* as a means of self-protection on the part of the group; in the case of violators of the legal and moral codes, banishment and confinement have not been used solely as a means of social defense against these "inner enemies" but also, and sometimes primarily, in the attempt to secure retribution for society in the interest of "justice." In fact, the failure to distinguish clearly between the motive of defense and other motives has made the policy

largely ineffective as a means of social protection.

Banishment is one of the oldest forms of treatment of offenders. While it originally was used as a way of eliminating individual violators, generally on the basis of religious beliefs, it frequently resulted in the development of a segregated criminal group as those who were "cast into the wilderness" managed to survive and find others like themselves with whom they could carry on their existence. The most elaborate development of the principle of ejecting offenders from society came with the plan of transporting convicts to penal colonies—a plan which was used extensively by the major European nations during the colonization and settlement of non-European areas opened up during the period of the great explorations. The western European countries, with the exception of France, abandoned the plan by the middle of the nineteenth century. Russia has continued the use of this system in Siberia even under the Soviet régime and some other countries use it to a more limited extent. At times use of penal colonies has been merely a method of getting rid of undesirables, similar to the isolation of the diseased. At other times criminals have been transported to work in mines or other profitable enterprises or to open up new lands for an expanding empire. Segregation of criminals in penal colonies solely as a social policy for preventing them from committing further offenses against society has seldom been carried out. However, Soviet Russia and Mexico have both established convict colonies for "unreformable offenders" with the purpose of permanent segregation rather than of punishment or reformation.

Corporal punishment of criminals who were not literally "cast out," while generally directed at retribution, deterrence, or reform, has actually, in itself and quite incidentally, operated to segregate criminals by differentiating them publicly from the rest of the community and thus making them unwelcome in any groups except those of fellow offenders. Some early types of punishment such as branding, ear-slitting, and labelling especially had the effect of setting off the criminal from the non-criminal population. Thus, the criminals, while not physically separated, were socially isolated and what social contacts they had were among themselves and other members of an outcast group. This form of segregation into groups of their own kind, however, has notoriously failed to prevent these "marked" offenders from committing further acts against the law-abiding community. In fact, to the extent that it has increased the hatred of those punished for the punishing group it has increased the conflict between the two segments of society.

By and large the practice of physically removing convicted offenders from society and segregating them in certain areas or institutions, such as penal colonies and prisons, for stipulated periods of time, is comparatively recent in social history. Up until the eighteenth century, most punishment of ordinary criminals was by death, commitment to galleys, or by various kinds of corporal punishment. Confinement was used mainly for political or religious offenders, debtors, waifs and strays, or for persons awaiting trial. With the development of humanitarianism in the eighteenth and nineteenth centuries there was a great reduction in the use of the death penalty and corporal punishment. At the same time, but for different reasons, the use of the galleys and transportation to overseas penal colonies were disappearing. The prison system developed primarily for purposes of punishment and reform to replace older treatments of offenders. Segregation of criminals in prison was not an end in itself but a means to achieve the purposes of justice and reform. Actually, as it has worked out, it has operated as an institution for the maintenance and spread of a criminal culture among persons convicted of crime. The prison, together with the general social ostracism of the ex-convict from respectable society, continues the natural process of segregation although this is not the purpose of the social policy.

Permanent segregation of criminals who are considered non-reformable and a continuing threat to social welfare, even though the latest crimes of which they are convicted do not carry a penalty of life imprisonment, has been suggested and tried. Some of the

penal colonies of Soviet Russia, as mentioned above, are used for permanent segregation. In America "habitual criminal" laws have been passed in fourteen states providing for life imprisonment upon a stipulated number of repeated convictions. The laws, however, have been very unevenly enforced as courts have generally been unwilling to carry through the policy in the face of adverse public criticism.

According to Wood and Waite:

The idea of segregating known criminals from society as a primary purpose of the criminal law finds little support in legislative action or judicial decision. To some extent the imprisonment of persons who have committed crime does prevent further crime by making commission of crime impossible during the limited time for which they are actually secluded from society. This, however, is a mere by-product of the punishment idea. Nowhere in the actualities of the law do we find a real purpose thus to prevent crime. *The length of segregation is not made dependent upon likelihood of repetition by the individual but upon the nature of the offense committed.* Even parole boards persistently and consistently release prisoners into renewed opportunities, not because they no longer need segregation as a matter of social safety, but because they have now received punishment "adequate to the nature of their offenses." So, too, even laws which provide for life imprisonment after a third or fourth offense are commonly talked of, by lawyers and newspaper men alike, as being primarily for the purpose of more severe punishment, rather than as though they were for the purpose of more effective segregation. If prevention through segregation were a recognized purpose of the law, we would find some relation in the penal statutes between the periods of imprisonment therein stipulated and the length of time that criminal tendencies manifested by certain acts might reasonably be assumed to continue. *The duration of incarceration would depend upon the character of the criminal, rather than upon the character of the crime.* But there is nothing of the sort in the statutes.[4]

Segregation as a social policy is challenged by the philosophy of *probation* in which the

[4] Wood, A. E., and Waite, J. B., *Crime and Its Treatment* (New York: The American Book Company, 1941), 354-55.

emphasis is upon the re-integration of the offender into law-abiding society. It is contended that segregation is a very poor measure for social protection, except for those for whom permanent segregation is considered the only possible measure. Segregation is costly, it is usually only a stop-gap preventive measure, and in the long run, by increasing the social distance between the criminal and the non-criminal group it increases conflict and the likelihood of further offenses. Probation, on the other hand, is based upon the ideal of the re-integration of the offender into law-abiding society and the attempt is made to keep the offender in the community while working toward his readjustment. Even probation, however, is usually administered as a part of a system in which imprisonment remains as a possible alternative or as a certain outcome of the failure of the individual to meet the terms of his probation. A more advanced view with reference to the segregation of offenders is that it should be entirely limited to those utterly incapable of living in normal communities and that all other offenders should be handled on an entirely individual basis, without even the alternative of imprisonment.

III. Segregation as a systematic procedure in the separation and differential treatment of various types of prisoners developed late in the eighteenth century as a consequence of the prison reform movement. Prison visitors had long been concerned about the promiscuity of the jails and houses of correction, where all sorts of persons, of both sexes and of all ages and varieties of mental and physical condition, were congregated together to await release from debt, or to serve penal sentences. Waifs and strays, abandoned children, women and girls were placed, and sometimes forgotten, in company with adult male criminals and insane persons. The name of Bridewell has become a by-word for this type of institution, with all its connotations of corruption. This situation was aggravated by the crowding of such institutions consequent from the increasing use of confinement as punishment.

Early pioneers in prison reform, such as John Howard, Elizabeth Fry, and Hippolyte Vilain, turned their attention to this indiscriminate herding together of all types of offenders and social cast-offs. The obvious health and moral hazards of this system led to the development of programs for the separate confinement and treatment of various kinds of institutional inmates. At first, this separation of types was on the basis of a crude classification. There was a distinction made between criminals and non-criminals, such as debtors, and between convicted offenders and those awaiting trial. Later, there developed a distinction between persons mentally diseased and those presumably sane, and, later still, a distinction between various types of offenders, primarily on the basis of degrees of "viciousness" and habituation to crime.

One of the earliest institutions on the European continent based upon the ideas of segregation was that erected in 1773 by Hippolyte Vilain at Ghent, Flanders. Among other reforms Vilain made provision for the separation of different types of prisoners. Felons were separated from misdemeanants and vagrants; women and children were each given separate quarters. Vilain was a pioneer in developing a prison architecture suitable to such a separation of prisoners and the prison at Ghent had a great influence on John Howard when the latter promoted a prison reform movement in England. Howard's *The State of the Prisons* (1777) made one of the earliest pleas for the separate confinement, in "penitentiary-houses" of "old, hardened offenders, and those who have, as the laws now stand, forfeited their lives by robbery, house-breaking, and similar crimes . . ." In 1781, a gaol erected at Wymondham, Norfolk, England, embodied the features endorsed by Howard. Different types of offenders were kept in cells and the sexes were placed in different parts of the building. Actually, the separation of prisoners was carried beyond the segregation of the various types to the point of solitary confinement for each prisoner, day and night.

Howard, in turn, influenced the Philadelphia prison reformers who in 1787 formed "The Philadelphia Society for Alleviating the Miseries of Public Prisons." The Philadelphia reformers were primarily concerned with the development of more humane treat-

ment of offenders and especially with elimination of barbaric corporal punishment and
reduction of the death penalty. But they
recognized that substitution of imprisonment
for the more drastic punishments necessitated changes in the existing prisons, especially the segregation of offenders, the hardened criminal from the novice, the debtor
from the ordinary criminal, and one sex from
the other. The Walnut Street Penitentiary
in Philadelphia, converted by the statute of
1790 from a jail, was an innovation in America, providing for such segregation, as well
as for the separation of persons awaiting trial
from those already convicted.

The Walnut Street Penitentiary initiated
in America a movement to develop segregated facilities in county jails—a movement
which has progressed very slowly over the
last century and a half. In many jails special rooms and cell blocks have been set aside
for untried prisoners but the maintenance of
one institution for the two purposes of detention and "correction" in most counties of
the country has meant that segregation even
today in thousands of jails is incomplete and
subject to the limitations of inadequate
buildings and inefficient or corrupt officials.

However, aside from the county jails,
there has been a steadily increasing development of specialized institutions for various types of offenders. As the prison population in the various states has increased,
necessitating the enlargement of old buildings or the erection of new penal and correctional institutions, differentiation has increased, making possible more segregation
of convicted offenders according to types.

Separation of the sexes has been one of
the most continuously maintained forms of
segregation. In the early years of prison development there were generally special wings
or sections in the general prisons set aside
for women within the prison enclosure. In
1873, as a result of a movement initiated by
the Friends' Meeting in Indiana, the Indiana
Reformatory Institution for Women and
Girls (later the Reform School for Girls and
Women's Prison) was built and became the
first definitely specialized institution for the
segregation of female offenders. In Massachusetts the Reformatory Prison for Women

was erected in 1877 and it was in this institution, in the 1880's, that a program of classification and segregation of the women inmates was begun, although specialization of
treatment was difficult since the institution
housed both misdemeanants and felons. The
first specialized institution for women, a reformatory as distinct from a woman's prison,
was established in New York State at Bedford Hills in 1901. The growth of specialized institutions for women, however, has
not been rapid or uniform in the United
States. As late as 1939 the American Prison
Association listed only 24 specialized institutions for women, one operated by the Federal Government, the others by seventeen of
the states. All of the other states made provisions for both men and women in separate
sections of their various institutions.

Another basis for segregation of offenders
has been that of age, primarily for the separation of juveniles from adults. Again the
work of John Howard was influential in
stimulating the Philanthropic Society of London to become interested, as early as 1788, in
the field of delinquency. It established an
"asylum" for delinquents "who were willing
to abandon their vicious pursuits and learn
the way to earn an honest living." In 1817
an institution for juvenile offenders was established by the magistrates of Warwick-
shire. The movement for the separate treatment of juveniles led to the Parkhurst Act
passed by Parliament in 1838, authorizing
institutional care for "depraved and vagrant
boys and girls." Under this act a prison for
juveniles was established on the Isle of
Wight. A further development in the specialized treatment of juveniles came with the
Industrial School Act of 1857 permitting delinquent children to be placed in private industrial schools or to remain in their own
homes.

Similar developments were taking place
in continental Europe and in the United
States. The first specialized institution for
children in America was the New York House
of Refuge, opened in 1825, as a result of the
work of the Society for the Reformation of
Juvenile Delinquents. Previous to that time
juvenile offenders had been sent to the state
prison. In the 1820's similar institutions,

which, like the New York House of Refuge, were semi-private, were opened in Boston and Philadelphia. In 1854 the first industrial school for girls was established in Lancaster, Massachusetts. Subsequently, all the states have established institutions for juvenile offenders, in most cases separate ones for boys and girls. They are generally referred to as "reform schools" in contrast to penal institutions for adult offenders. However, many counties still use the common county jail for the incarceration of juvenile delinquents awaiting disposition by the courts. In some of these jails there is segregation by age, at least of the younger children, but many jails in the less populated counties have no facilities for such separation.

The development of the "reformatory" idea led to the establishment of separate institutions for young adult offenders, particularly those with no previous record of crime. This latter feature was one of the first developments in treatment which differentiated between offenders in other terms than age and sex. The reformatory system had as an intrinsic feature differentiation among prisoners on the basis of the prisoners' own behavior and characteristics. In England this has led to the establishment of the Borstal Institutions, which were consolidated in the Prevention of Crime Act of 1908 and have been subsequently modified.

The Borstal Institutions are outstanding in their use of segregation of different types of prisoners for purposes of specialized treatment and as yet nothing comparable to them have been established in America. The Borstal Institutions vary in physical structure and program. The essential feature of the system is the allocation of youthful offenders to institutions which are most appropriate to the offenders' characteristics and needs. The plants range from those walled or partially walled to those completely unwalled, and from those in which there is emphasis upon physical training and discipline to those in which the emphasis is upon vocational education and social development. Commitment to the Borstal Institution is made only after careful investigation by probation officers and police, and is an alterna-

tive to commitment to jail or prison. After commitment the youth stays for thirty days at an allocation center for observation and classification before assignment to one of the specialized institutions.

In America the reformatory movement as a system of specialized treatment for certain types of young adult offenders developed during the latter half of the nineteenth century. It has generally had a dual motive; the segregation of young and presumably reformable offenders from the association and influence of those considered "vicious and hardened in crime," together with the development of a program of treatment designed to return the offender to a law-abiding life. The first institution designated for this segregated group was the Elmira Reformatory in New York, opened in 1876. In 1938 twenty states maintained institutions with the name "Reformatory." In general, the reformatory system has not deviated from the prison in the treatment of inmates and is differentiated from penitentiaries and other prisons, if at all, only by differences in ages and crime records of the inmates. Even that type of segregation is not consistently maintained, so there is much overlapping among the types of prisoners in different institutions within many of the states.

In addition to the development of the foregoing specialized institutions, there has been an increasing differentiation and segregation of the physically and mentally ill, the mentally defective, alcoholics and drug addicts among the prison population. Several states, mostly in the South, segregate prisoners by race, carrying into their penal practice a general social policy of racial segregation.

In general, segregation of various types of prisoners in the penal system has been on the basis of a rule-of-thumb classification, based on common sense notions or the pressures and special interests of particular times and groups. To a large extent it has followed the growth of the prison population and has resulted in and been limited by the building of specialized institutions.

The differential treatment of prisoners within institutions has been refined and accelerated by the increasing use of careful classification of prisoners.

Almost every administrator of a penal institution has differentiated between prisoners in some fashion or other, but some administrators have been more deliberate and conscious in this matter than others. For some wardens of prisons the inmates have been largely classified into two types—the "trouble-makers" and those who conformed. In the vocabulary of many prison administrators *segregation* is a term which is used to apply to the treatment of the trouble-makers and it commonly refers to placing them in special punishment cells or blocks of the institution. "Segregation units" usually refer to sections of the institution designed for punishment of those who violate the prison rules or are in some way considered disturbing elements in the prison routine.

The policy of classification of prisoners, however, has within the last generation increasingly utilized and applied knowledge of human behavior developed from scientific study and social work procedures. In some prison systems, characteristics of prisoners have been taken into consideration not only in allocating them to certain types of institutions but also in assigning them to cells, to work, to educational classes, recreation groups, and other prison facilities.

Segregation is becoming more and more the process which carries into effect a classification procedure. As there is an increasing recognition of the various types of individuals who constitute the prison population, it becomes more clear that the population must be more carefully grouped for purposes of specialized treatment and control. The consensus among modern penologists seems to be summarized in this statement by Frank Tannenbaum:

A modern prison program requires a centralized receiving and classifying prison. It requires the temporary or permanent hospitalization and segregation of special problem groups. It then calls for the broad division of the prison population into three major groups for maximum, medium, and minimum security housing. Within these groups there should again be as many subdivisions as seem desirable—tentative and experimental in character. These three broad groups should be housed in broadly different types of buildings with decreasing disciplinary provision and increasing freedom as a means of preparation for release.
Crime and the Community, p. 363 (Boston, Ginn & Co., 1938).

New Jersey was one of the pioneer states in developing a prison program based upon modern classification and segregation systems. New York and Illinois have instituted similar programs. The Congressional Act of 1930 provided for a program of that type for the Federal prisons by stipulating:

It is hereby declared to be the policy of the Congress that the said institutions be so planned and limited in size as to facilitate the development of an integrated Federal penal and correctional system which will assure the proper classification and segregation of Federal prisoners according to their character, the nature of the crime they have committed, their mental condition, and such other factors as should be taken into consideration in providing an individualized system of discipline, care, and treatment of the persons committed to such institutions.
C, 339, sec. 7, 46 Stat. 390.

IV. *Conclusion*. Most persons are inclined to forget that the prison system which is the dominant feature of present-day treatment of criminals is actually only about two centuries old. It is relatively recent in terms of the total span of human culture and is related to profound changes in Western society. With urbanization and increasing mobility of individuals in an industrialized world human relationships have taken on a more and more anonymous character. The conditions under which communities could deal with their offenders have been radically disturbed. In the small, local social worlds of pre-industrial society it was not necessary to segregate offenders in any formal way. Violators were well known to all as not trustworthy and were treated accordingly. Within industrial society symbiotic relationships replace those based on intimacy and tradition. The criminal group in such a society becomes segregated through the impersonal processes which operate in a dominantly competitive order.

Imprisonment—a policy of "active segregation" arising from conflict between segments of society—developed as one of the measures in the control of offenders in this new social system. However, the same society which has undergone the changes that brought about the use of imprisonment has also developed scientific knowledge, including a science of man and of society itself. As this knowledge expands, there is the possibility of using it for control in place of cruder measures resorted to when such knowledge was lacking. These sciences have demonstrated their value by their increasing use within a system which is based on segregation, but they have also pointed out clearly the limitations inherent in such a system. They suggest the possibilities of alternative measures which in the long run would make possible, perhaps even require, the abandonment of segregation as a social policy.

CLARENCE E. GLICK
Professor of Sociology
Tulane University
New Orleans, Louisiana
and
DORIS L. GLICK
Lecturer in Research
School of Social Work
Tulane University

BIBLIOGRAPHY

Barnes, H. E., and Teeters, N. K., *New Horizons in Criminology*, New York, Prentice-Hall, Inc., 1945.
Clemmer, Donald, *The Prison Community*, Chicago, Christopher Press, 1940.
Clinard, Marshall B., The Process of Urbanization and Criminal Behavior, *American Journal of Sociology*, 48 (1942), 202–13.
Levin, Y., and Lindesmith, A., English Ecology and Criminology of the Past Century, *Journal of Criminal Law and Criminology*, 23 (1937), 801–816.
Shaw, Clifford R., and McKay, Henry D., *Juvenile Delinquency and Urban Areas*, Chicago, University of Chicago Press, 1942.
Sutherland, E. H., *Principles of Criminology*, Philadelphia, J. P. Lippincott Co., 1947.
Wood, A. E., and Waite, J. B., *Crime and its Treatment*, New York, American Book Co., 1941.

THE SENTENCING BEHAVIOR OF THE JUDGE.

For several decades there has been much discussion of the dual function of the judge in the American trial court. Actually he may be said to play three roles. In jury trials he acts primarily as an umpire to see that the lawyers representing the state and the defendant play the game according to established rules; the judge also acts as a mentor to the jury. In non-jury trials he acts as umpire as he does in jury trials, decides the guilt or innocence of the defendant and, if the defendant is found guilty, prescribes the sentence.

There has never been any serious question of the judge's right to perform the first two functions, that of umpire and of evaluator of evidence to determine the guilt or innocence of the accused. His training and experience fit him for these tasks. On the other hand, there has been much debate over the question of whether the judge should impose the sentence. It has been pointed out that because the judge's training is almost totally legal, he does not have the background, knowledge or skills to do the actual sentencing. Again, it has been pointed out that the information which the judge possesses at the time he imposes his sentence is inadequate. Finally, it has been pointed out that the judge's personality may enter into his sentencing behavior.

Several proposals have been made to overcome these objections. One has been that the judge act merely as the umpire in jury trials and in Special Sessions or non-jury cases as determiner of guilt. The actual sentencing would be done by a board of experts, the judge perhaps being one member of that board. Another has been the practice, found in many states, of limiting the judge's prerogative in sentencing by such techniques as the indeterminate sentence. Here the actual length of the penal sentence is determined by a sentencing board attached to the institution where the prisoner is incarcerated. Another alternative is the partially indeterminate sentence where the judge sentences a man for a term with prescribed minimum and maximum lengths, and the actual period of imprisonment is determined by a board of experts.

It should be pointed out, however, that these restrictions of the judge's sentencing behavior apply only to penal sentences. Since the judge commonly also gives suspended sentences, places guilty people on probation or fines them, his lack of training in problems in human delinquency and their treatment as well as his personal idiosyncrasies have a wide implication.

Because of the prestige with which the judiciary is held, the problem of individual differences in the behavior of judges has been given relatively little attention. It is true that we occasionally see newspaper stories of some judge's unusual behavior in sentencing some criminal, but the average layman thinks of this display of human motives as the unusual rather than the customary behavior of the judge. In fact, most laymen and many legal writers state, as was the case in some of our early state constitutions, that *we have a justice of laws, not of men.* More sophisticated scholars, however, agree with the assertion of Chief Justice Hughes that this is a fallacy and that instead of the dichotomy of laws versus men we should state it thus: *we have a justice of laws through men.* To put it another way, if part of the sentence a man receives is determined by our written laws and part by the "human equation" we should know how large a part this *humán equation* plays.

If this *personaltiy of the judge element* is present to a marked degree then we may assume that there are inequalities and even injustices in the administration of the criminal law. We have grown away from the old philosophy of the sentencing of crimes and now recognize that we sentence criminals. This implies that the sentence is partly determined by the seriousness of the crime and partly by the personality of the criminal. However, it is becoming increasingly apparent that the sentence given the criminal is determined by a third factor, the personality of the judge, and that we are unaware of the size or importance of this factor in the administration of the criminal law.

This is not merely a theoretical or scientific question. As Major Frank I. Hanscom, member of the Board of Parole of New York State has asserted:

"when . . . 202 judges . . . hand out sentences as widely variant as their personalities may be, it is not difficult to see why there is

unrest among prisoners and a feeling among the law-abiding members of society that justice is not the even-handed goddess that she is symbolized." [1]

Nearly everyone who has worked with prisoners has heard them blame their incarceration upon the fact that they were sentenced by Judge X, or has overheard them talking among themselves about the sentencing tendencies of certain judges. It is customary for most of us who are "on the outside" to interpret such statements as mere projections of the prisoners' guilt. Until we know, however, how great a factor the personality of the judge is in the sentencing of guilty men, our interpretation of such statements as psychological dynamisms rather than facts of observation is perhaps tenuous.

In Scotland this problem of individual differences in the sentencing tendencies of judges is recognized to such an extent that certain court practices are based upon this phenomenon of the *personal equation:*

"The prosecutor in moving for sentence may suggest the degree of punishment which he thinks the convicted person deserves. The judge is supplied with a list of any previous convictions and also with a list of the sentences imposed by other judges for similar offenses. The latter is for the purpose of securing uniformity of sentence." [2]

Again, the extent to which the personality of the judge enters into the administration of justice is important in any discussion of one of our current problems in the field of legal philosophy. That is the problem of whether law exists in the statutes or in the behavior of the judges. This question is allotted much space in present-day legal journals under such descriptive terms as fundamentalism, nominalism, functionalism, realism, "law in books" and "law in action."

Another criminological problem associated with the foregoing one is that of the predictive formulae used in determining the reformability of criminals. These formulae usually include such factors as intelligence of

[1] United States Daily, June 4, 1932, *quoting* (1932) XXIII (3) *J. Crim. L. and Criminol.,* 509.
[2] Keedy, Criminal Procedure in Scotland, (1912-13) III (6) *J. Crim. L. and Criminol.,* 844.

the criminal, age, education, type of home, social history of the parents and so forth. Most of these formulae also include the severity of the crime and frequently use as a measure of severity the sentence imposed by the judge. Certainly, if there are any considerable differences among judges in the severity of sentencing, such predictive formulae are considerably distorted if they are not corrected for this variable.

Finally, some investigators have suggested that the judges themselves might benefit from studies of the extent of influence of the human equation. Jerome Frank summarizes the discussion of one investigator of this problem in these words:

"Everson in his report on the statistics of the decisions by the judges of the City Magistrate's Court expressed the belief that the publication of those records would cause a better understanding by the judges of their own work and lead them to a 'viewpoint somewhat tempered by the knowledge of what other judges are doing and with a broader viewpoint of the problems before him. Each magistrate will come to recognize his own personal peculiarities and seek to correct any that cannot be justified in the light of the records of his associates.' " [3]

The earlier and more numerous studies of sentencing processes are broad surveys. The results of these studies show that in certain areas the sentences imposed are more severe than in others; for example, sentences appear to be more severe in rural areas than in urban areas for certain types of crimes.[4] Other studies have shown that there is a judicial lag between the changes which take place in the law regarding sentencing and the actual changes which occur later in the behavior of the judge.[5]

[3] Frank, Jerome, *Law and the Modern Mind,* New York, Brentanos, 1930, p. 115.
[4] See: (a) *Criminal Justice in Cleveland,* Cleveland Foundation, 1921. (b) *The Missouri Crime Survey,* New York, Macmillan, 1925. (c) Crime and the Georgia Courts, *J. Crim. L. and Criminol.,* XVI, p. 2. (d) *Reports of the New York State Crime Commission,* Albany, 1927ff.
[5] See: (a) Exner, Franz, *Studien Über die Strafzumessung - Praxis Deutscher Gerichte,* Leipzig, E. Wiegand, 1931, 119 pp. (b) Frankel, Emil, History of Punishment in New Jersey, *J. Amer. Prison Assoc.,* 1937.

These studies might be described as analyses of the process of administering our criminal law on a sociological level. However, if we wish to ascertain the influence of the personality of the judge in our criminal administration procedures, we must seek a deeper level which might be called the individual or psychological level. Everson[6] was the first to make such a study. He investigated the judicial process as it took place with minor offenders in the New York City Magistrate's Court. Typical of his findings are the differences in behavior of the magistrates in sentencing certain types of criminals. For instance, he finds that one judge found guilty 97% of the 546 persons who appeared before him charged with intoxication. Of 673 cases arraigned before another judge charged with the same offense only 21% were found guilty. In disorderly conduct cases one judge found 82% of the cases guilty, whereas another judge in the same court discharged 54% of such cases arraigned before him. In vagrancy cases the number discharged by the several magistrates in this court varied from 4.5% to 79%.

Considering cases of all types brought before these magistrates we find that one judge imposed fines upon 84% and gave suspended sentences to 7%. One of his colleagues in the same court and over the same period fined 34% and gave suspended sentences to 59%.

The most extensive study of the influence of the personality of the judge was based upon the records of the Court of Common Pleas of one county in New Jersey over a ten-year period. Six judges sat in this court during this period, three of whom were on the bench for most of the years covered by the study. These judges are appointed by the Governor "by and with the consent of the Senate" for a term of five years. The prisoners whom the judges received were assigned (on a rotational basis), by the prosecutor, according to one of the prosecutors who held this office during part of the period; and almost always on this basis by the other prosecutor. The rare exception occurred when there was some spectacular case

[6] Everson, George, The Human Element in Justice, *J. Crim. L. and Criminol.,* X, p. 90.

and the prosecutor wished to pass such a case to a particular judge. These instances, however, occurred so infrequently as to be negligible.

The crimes for which the men were found guilty were those which occur most frequently in these courts. They can roughly be divided into four categories: (a) crimes against property, (b) crimes against property accompanied by violence, (c) sex crimes, and (d) violations of the Hobart Act (New Jersey's prohibition law).[7] Only cases in which the prisoner had been indicted and found guilty either by the judge or by the jury were used.

Since cases were assigned on a rotational basis, it can be assumed that the same proportion of criminals who had committed severe or minor crimes would appear before each judge. A study of the percentage of recidivists and non-recidivists arraigned before each judge and the percentage of each of the four categories of crimes mentioned above appearing before each judge indicates that this assumption is probably correct.[8] It was true that there was a time trend in the type of cases appearing in this court over this ten year period, but this did not act as a selective

[7] The actual crimes which are included under each of these categories are: (a) Crimes against property: larceny; larceny from the person; larceny and receiving; embezzlement; entering; attempted breaking and entering; breaking, entering, and larceny; breaking, entering, larceny and receiving; robbery; and entering and robbery. (b) Crimes against property with violence: assault with intent to rob; assault and battery with intent to rob; assault, battery and robbery; assault, battery, breaking and entering. (c) Sex crimes: carnal abuse, adultery; rape; assault with intent to rape; assault with intent to abuse; assault and battery with intent to rape; assault and battery with intent to abuse; assault, battery and rape; assault, battery and abuse. (d) Crimes in violation of the Hobart Act: maintaining a nuisance; possession of liquor; sale and possession of liquor; maintaining a nuisance and possession of liquor; maintaining a nuisance and sale and possession of liquor; manufacturing and possession of liquor; possession of a still; transportation and possession of liquor.

[8] For the original data see: Gaudet, Frederick Joseph, Individual Differences in the Sentencing Tendencies of Judges, New York, 1938, Archives of Psychology, No. 230, 58 pp.

factor in the cases appearing before each judge.

Granting the original assumption, the data indicate that the sentencing behavior of these judges was by no means uniform. Table I shows these differences in terms of the type of sentence imposed by each judge.

Each judge presumably receives approximately the same proportion of persons indicted for severe crimes as for minor ones, and similarly the same proportion of individuals with poor records and backgrounds as those with desirable ones. However, it will be seen in Table I that of 100 prisoners appearing before Judge F for sentencing, 34 would go to penal institutions, whereas if they had been sentenced by Judge B, 57 would have been incarcerated. Does this mean that 34 out of this hundred went to jail because of the crimes they committed and their background, while if sentencing had been done by Judge B an additional 23 would have received penal sentences instead of the lighter ones they received due to Judge F's personality? Or does it mean that 23 men who should have gone to jail did not because of Judge F's personality? In either case, we see that the criminal law "passing through" these men is considerably influenced by the "human equation" of the judge. It will be noted that Judges A and F are the most lenient in their sentencing tendencies, while Judges C, B, and D are the most severe.

Certain crimes increased in frequency, while others became less frequent in the period studied. Therefore the sentencing tendencies of the judges were broken down by type of crime. These results are presented in Table II.

Insofar as crimes against property are concerned, we have the same general condition as shown in Table I. That is, Judges A and F are the most lenient, and Judges B, C and D the most severe. This same general grouping prevails in crimes against property accompanied by violence. However, this grouping no longer applies with regard to sex crimes. Judge F remains a lenient sentencer, but he is now accompanied by Judge D. Whereas Judge E had been in a middle position in the first two categories of crimes men-

TABLE I[a]

PERCENTAGE OF VARIOUS TYPES OF SENTENCES GIVEN BY EACH JUDGE

Sentence	Judge A		Judge B		Judge C		Judge D		Judge E		Judge F	
	Number	Percent	Number	Percent	Number	Percent	Number	Percent	Number	Percent	Number	Percent
N.J.R.[b]	121	9.6	263	18.2	273	14.5	102	16.1	38	8.4	174	8.9
S.P.[c]	138	10.9	241	16.7	241	12.8	39	6.1	55	12.1	175	8.9
C.P.[o]	203	16.1	315	21.8	479	25.4	181	28.5	100	24.3	305	15.6
S.H.[d]	5	0.4	3	0.2	5	0.3	2	0.3	3	0.7	2	0.1
C.H.[e]	5	0.4	8	0.5	1	0.0	1	0.2	3	0.7	0	0.0
Total Penal	472	37.4	830	57.4	999	52.9	325	51.2	209	46.1	655	33.5
Susp.[f]	382	30.2	289	20.0	469	24.8	99	15.6	115	25.4	689	35.3
Prob.[g]	380	30.1	290	20.1	387	20.5	199	31.3	120	26.5	557	28.5
Fines[h]	29	2.3	37	2.6	33	1.8	12	1.9	9	2.0	52	2.7
TOTAL Number	1263		1446		1888		635		453		1953	
Percent	100.0		100.1		100.0		100.0		100.0		100.0	

[a] This is Table III, Gaudet, *op. cit.*

[b] Sentences to the New Jersey Reformatories are indeterminate sentences. The time the individual is incarcerated in one of these institutions is not dependent upon the judge but upon a sentencing board which decides the "length of the sentence" some time after the individual has been institutionalized. It is apparent that in these cases we do not have a measure of the severity of the sentencing of the judge, except insofar as it is a penal sentence. It is of greater severity than the three other types of sentences, namely, suspended sentence, probation, and fines. The general impression among lawyers is that sentences to the New Jersey Reformatories are somewhat equivalent to the County Penitentiary although somewhat more severe than the latter.

[c] S. P. refers to State Prison and C. P. to County Penitentiary. The difference between the two is that the prisoners sentenced to eighteen months or less go to the County Penitentiary, while those going to State Prison are sentenced to hard labor or to more than eighteen months. There is some discretion allowed the judge in assigning place of imprisonment.

[d] S. H. means State Home, which may be considered a sentence approximately equal to N. J. R. or C. P.

[e] C. H. means County Home. These sentences are less severe than any other penal sentences.

[f] The term, "suspended sentence," in New Jersey is to be taken literally. The difference between suspended sentence and probationary sentence is that the individual does not have to report to judicial officials each week, nor does he have to pay a small sum each week as he usually does when on probation.

[g] Prob. means probation.

[h] The term "fine" means fine only. It is true that in certain cases, a fine is given in addition to a probationary or penal sentence. Such sentences in this and later tabulations are classed with probationary or imprisonment sentence.

tioned above, he now is very severe. Because of the scarcity of cases involving violations of the Hobart Act, conclusions which may be drawn from these data are probably unsound.

The problem of *why* these judges reacted so differently in their sentencing behavior is far from solved. A study of the six judges mentioned above indicates that the problem of experience as a criminal court judge was not a factor. Those who were severe, as measured by the percent of penal sentences handed down during the first year or two on the bench, remained severe; those who started as lenient judges remained so.

This consistency is not found when suspended sentences are considered, but there is no uniform trend related to length of experience on the bench. The situation for probationary sentences appears the same as for suspended sentences. The fines imposed were so few as to make a trend analysis useless.

Other analyses of such factors as imminence of the judge's reappointment or change in business conditions seems to have had no observable effect upon judicial behavior. One is forced to conclude that the differences among these judges in their sentencing behavior can probably best be accounted for by the use of the general term "personality."

Another question studied was whether the sentencing tendency of the judge depended upon the method by which the guilt was determined—by the judge or by jury. One might expect that if a judge disagreed with the finding of guilty by the jury, he might try to correct this situation by handing down a light sentence. We know that judges frequently disagree with juries, even to the extent of delivering a condemnatory lecture to the jury. Of course, if the judge disagrees with the jury when it acquits a man, he can do nothing about it in his sentencing. In this Court of Common Pleas trials by jury are called quarter sessions, while in the special session the judge determines the guilt as well as sentencing the offender. The data used for this study were based on approximately five-eighths of the same 7,638 cases on which the previous studies were based. Court records did not indicate the type of trial in the other cases.

The data indicate that all of the judges gave fewer penal sentences while sitting in quarter sessions than while holding special sessions. However, the percentage of probationary sentences is greater in the case of quarter sessions with every one of the judges than it is in the special sessions. The probationary sentences may be regarded simply as a form of, or a substitute for, penal sentences, in which case the two sets of statistics are not at variance with each other. In the case of fines, each judge gave a higher percentage of fines in quarter sessions than he gave in special sessions.

These data seem to uphold the hypothesis expressed above, namely, that in quarter sessions (jury trials) the judge injects, consciously or otherwise, his feelings of certainty or lack of certainty of guilt by giving more lenient sentences.[9] However, the crucial test of leniency is to be found in the suspended sentence, the lightest of all sentences. Each of the judges in the study, however, gave more suspended sentences when he met without a jury than in quarter session. Hence, it appears that the previously stated hypothesis is not true, or that the judge's feelings of uncertainty were mild ones which caused him to lighten the sentence to some degree but not to go to the extreme of giving suspended sentences.

A further analysis of 1,109 of these cases selected at random was made using the type of plea which the accused made.[10] These results are indicated in Table III.

It will be seen that there were many more pleas of "not guilty" in those cases appearing in quarter sessions than in special sessions. These data clearly indicate that there were differences in the types of criminals or in the

[9] Its implications in regard to the *dictum* of so many trial lawyers, namely, "If you have a good case (from the point of view of the defendant) try it before a judge, if you are in doubt of your case try it before a jury" are not so clear.

[10] These cases were selected by taking three handfuls out of the stack of cards. Because these cards happened to fall in the years three to seven of the ten-year period covered by the study only three judges (B, C and D) were represented. Purely by coincidence, they also happen to be the most severe of the six judges.

TABLE II a

PERCENTAGE OF VARIOUS TYPES OF SENTENCES BY TYPE OF CRIME FOR EACH JUDGE

Property

Sentence	Judge A		Judge B		Judge C		Judge D		Judge E		Judge F	
	Number	Percent	Number	Percent	Number	Percent	Number	Percent	Number	Percent	Number	Percent
Penal	417	37.3	635	57.4	821	53.3	286	58.1	150	43.4	555	33.9
Suspended	364	32.5	263	23.1	435	27.7	88	17.9	100	28.9	587	35.9
Probation	331	29.6	207	18.1	307	19.6	117	23.8	91	26.3	481	29.4
Fines	7	0.6	16	1.4	6	0.4	1	0.2	5	1.5	14	0.9
TOTAL Number Percent	1119	100.0	1141	100.0	1569	100.0	492	100.0	346	100.1	1637	100.1

Property and Violence

Sentence	Judge A		Judge B		Judge C		Judge D		Judge E		Judge F	
	Number	Percent	Number	Percent	Number	Percent	Number	Percent	Number	Percent	Number	Percent
Penal	17	47.2	104	92.9	65	82.3	13	81.3	16	69.6	41	36.7
Suspended	17	47.2	5	4.5	11	13.9	0	0.0	5	21.7	70	62.5
Probation	2	5.6	3	2.6	2	2.5	3	18.7	2	8.7	1	0.9
Fines	0	0.0	0	0.0	1	1.3	0	0.0	0	0.0	0	0.0
TOTAL Number Percent	36	100.0	112	100.0	79	100.0	16	100.0	23	100.0	112	100.1

(Table II cont'd)

TABLE II—(continued)

PERCENTAGE OF VARIOUS TYPES OF SENTENCES BY TYPE OF CRIME FOR EACH JUDGE

Sex

Sentence	Judge A		Judge B		Judge C		Judge D		Judge E		Judge F	
	Number	Percent	Number	Percent	Number	Percent	Number	Percent	Number	Percent	Number	Percent
Penal	32	47.8	68	47.6	97	52.7	25	26.0	41	59.4	45	33.8
Suspended	2	3.0	16	11.2	20	10.9	11	11.5	4	5.8	19	14.3
Probation	32	47.8	54	37.8	60	32.6	60	62.5	22	31.9	56	42.1
Fines	1	1.5	5	3.5	7	3.8	0	0.0	2	2.9	13	9.8
TOTAL Number Percent	67	100.1	143	100.1	184	100.0	96	100.0	69	100.0	133	100.0

Hobart Act

Sentence	Judge A		Judge B		Judge C		Judge D		Judge E		Judge F	
	Number	Percent	Number	Percent	Number	Percent	Number	Percent	Number	Percent	Number	Percent
Penal	6	13.3	3	6.0	16	28.6	1	3.2	2	13.3	15	20.8
Suspended	3	6.7	5	10.0	3	5.4	0	0.0	6	40.0	13	18.1
Probation	15	33.3	26	52.0	18	32.1	19	61.3	5	33.3	19	26.4
Fines	21	46.7	16	32.0	19	33.9	11	35.5	2	13.3	25	34.7
TOTAL Number Percent	45	100.0	50	100.0	56	100.0	31	100.0	15	99.9	72	100.0

[a] This is Table IV, Gaudet, *op. cit.*

TABLE III [d]

PERCENTAGE OF DIFFERENT TYPES OF PLEAS ENTERED IN QUARTER AND IN SPECIAL SESSIONS

Plea	Judge B		Judge C		Judge D	
	Quarter Session	Special Session	Quarter Session	Special Session	Quarter Session	Special Session
Guilty [a]	9.3	40.0	15.1	37.0	6.2	26.0
Not guilty	4.4	3.0	19.1	10.4	9.7	10.3
Non vult [b]	10.7	42.2	9.0	43.4	17.7	48.7
Retracted [c]	75.5	14.8	56.8	9.2	66.4	15.1
TOTAL	100.0	100.1	100.0	100.0	100.0	100.0

[a] It is impossible for an individual to plead guilty and to come before the court in quarter session. According to the Recorder's Office, these are individuals whose pleas were later changed in court but not on the records. Hence, they should always be considered as retracted pleas, but are tabulated here as "guilty" since this is the way they appear on the records.

[b] The plea of *non vult* is considered to mean "throwing oneself on the mercy of the court."

[c] A "retracted plea" means that the prisoner first pleaded one way and later changed it; for instance, if he first pleaded not guilty and then changed to *non vult* or guilty."

[d] This is Table VIII, Gaudet, *op. cit.*

behavior of the criminals appearing in the two courts. However, if one remembers that all of these individuals were found guilty, the differences indicated in Table III do not appear to be great enough to explain the differences in the types of sentences given by the judges in the two courts. Table III shows that there was a greater percentage of pleas of *non vult* in special sessions than in quarter sessions. These are probably individuals who were hopeless of acquittal, and who threw themselves upon the mercy of the court. The higher percentage of retracted pleas in quarter sessions is probably due to the greater proportion of accused represented by lawyers in this court.

Discussions of data with lawyers practicing in this court brought forth the explanation cited before as their *dictum* that the cases appearing in special sessions were offenders who either did not have a lawyer or did not have bail. Hence, the offender preferred a special session trial to waiting in jail until the next quarter session.

A study of the Hobart Act violators showed that they appeared in quarter sessions much more frequently than in special sessions.

Probably most violators of this law had the means to hire lawyers to defend them, as well as to furnish bail until such time as the quarter sessions convened. These data regarding the behavior of judges in the two types of trials indicate that while the personality factors of the judges did account partially for differences in both types of trials, these sentencing differences were in part due to other factors.

Another study [11] of these same judges indicates that they differed as much in the length of penal sentences they imposed upon the guilty as they did in the frequency with which they gave different types of sentences. It was also found that these judges gave most of their penitentiary sentences in terms of three or multiples of three months.[12]

[11] Gaudet, Frederick J., Harris, George S., and St. John, Charles W., Individual Differences in Penitentiary Sentences Given by Different Judges, *J. Applied Psychology*, XVIII (5) Oct., 1934.

[12] Gaudet, Frederick J., Harris, George S., and St. John, Charles W., Individual Differences in the Sentencing Tendencies of Judges, *J. Crim. Law and Criminol.* XXIII (5), Jan.–Feb., 1933.

A similar tendency was observed in longer sentences in New York State,[13] where sentences were very frequently given in terms of five or multiples of five years.

Another factor which should be considered in studying the sentencing tendencies of judges is the influence of the probation officer. It is generally recognized that the probationary system was introduced into our courts so that sociology, psychology and penology might contribute to the sentencing procedure. The probationary system is frequently described as the most scientific of our sentencing techniques. However, it should be recognized that the influence of the probation officer or department is much greater in some jurisdictions than in others. Even in the same court the rôle of the probation officer will vary from judge to judge. In some administrations, his contribution is so insignificant that no change may be expected in the sentencing behavior of the judge. In other courts, or with certain judges, this contribution is a real one. The influence of the probation officer upon the sentencing behavior of a particular judge will depend upon the amount of information which the criminal law requires of judges before sentencing, as well as the extent to which each individual judge is willing to accept the aid provided by the probation officer.[14]

A serious difficulty was encountered in ranking the severity of the probationary sentences passed out by each judge. This was the fact that many of the sentences were in two or even three dimensions, such as "two years plus $1.00 a week, and obey parents." The chief problem was to determine the relative weight to be given to the length of the probationary period, to the weekly sum of money to be paid to the probation office, and to such admonitions as "obey parents," "attend mass regularly," or "keep away from evil companions."

It was arbitrarily decided to rank all pro-

[13] Report of the Crime Commission, State of New York,, Legislative Document, No. 23.

[14] In the data to be cited, the cases all came from one court. Hence, the information which the judge must have does not vary with individual judges, nor does the personality of the probation officer who talks over the cases on the day preceding sentencing day.

bationary sentences on the basis of length. For instance, in the case of Judge C his three most severe sentences were "five years plus 50 cents weekly;" "five years plus 25 cents weekly;" and "four years plus $4.00 weekly." The problem here was whether the third sentence might not actually be more severe than the other two. Where the admonitions were added to probation sentences, they were considered as a third subdivision in the ranking, and such a sentence as "two years plus 50 cents weekly plus make restitution" was considered one degree more severe than "two years plus 50 cents weekly," but less severe than "two years plus 75 cents weekly."

The severity of each of the six judges in terms of the length of his probationary sentences is indicated in Table IV.

The most impressive fact in these data is that, with the exception of Judge B, the probationary sentences given by these judges were very similar. For instance, the median sentence for all except Judge B was three years and varied only in the amount of monetary assessment. The upper quartile is also very similar for these five judges, and it is only in the lower quartile that we can detect any appreciable degree of variation from judge to judge.

The deviate, Judge B, is a judge who gives fewer probationary sentences and more penal sentences than his colleagues. This may mean that because he committed such a large proportion of his cases to penal institutions, those prisoners whom he placed on probation had committed relatively lighter offenses than those placed on probation by the other judges. An analysis of the frequency with which he placed offenders upon probation (see Table I) does not uphold this hypothesis, however.

Another check of this hypothesis was made by tabulating the types of crimes which those who received probationary sentences committed. If the above hypothesis were correct, we should expect Judge B to have given probationary sentences far less frequently in the more serious types of crimes than did the other judges. Obviously, "crimes against property accompanied by violence," and "sex crimes" are offenses of greater enormity than are mere "property crimes" or liquor law

TABLE IV [b]

VARIABILITY AND SEVERITY OF PROBATIONARY SENTENCES GIVEN BY EACH JUDGE [a]

Judge	Upper Quartile	Median	Lower Quartile	Range	Number
A	3 yr. plus $1.00	3 yr. plus 50c	3 yr. plus 25c	5 yr. plus $1.00 to 1 yr.	380
B	2 yr. plus 50c	2 yr. plus 25c	1 yr. plus 50c	3 yr. plus $2.00 to 6 mos. plus 50c	290
C	3 yr. plus 50c	3 yr. plus 50c	3 yr.	5 yr. plus 50c to 1 yr.	387
D	3 yr. plus 50c	3 yr. plus 25c	2 yr. plus 50c	3 yr. plus $1.00 to 1 yr. plus 25c	199
E	3 yr. plus 50c	3 yr.	2 yr. plus 50c	3 yr. plus $1.00 to 1 yr. plus 25c	120
F	3 yr. plus 50c	3 yr. plus 50c	2 yr. plus $1.00	5 yr. plus $1.00 to 6 mos. plus 50c	557

[a] The sentences refer to the duration of the penalty and the amount to be paid per week. In some cases the judges added further conditions; for example, Judge E's median sentence was actually "3 years probation and follow advice."
[b] This is Table IV from Gaudet, Frederick Joseph, The Differences Between Judges in Granting of Sentences of Probation, *Temple Law Quarterly*, XIX, (4), April, 1946, 471-484.

(Hobart Act) violations. These results are presented in Table V.

Before considering these data, it should be remembered that the types of crimes committed by those who were found guilty by this court changed over the years covered by the original study. There was an increase in crimes against property, a decrease in crimes

TABLE V [a]

DISTRIBUTION OF THE PROBATION SENTENCES OF EACH JUDGE BY TYPE OF CRIME

Types of crime	A	B	C	D	E	F
			Judges			
Property	86.6	70.5	79.3	61.0	76.5	86.3
Property and violence	0.5	0.7	0.5	1.5	1.7	0.2
Sex	8.9	17.3	15.5	28.8	17.6	10.5
Hobart Act	3.9	11.5	4.7	8.8	4.2	3.3
Total percent	100.0	100.0	100.0	100.0	100.0	100.0
Total number	381	295	387	205	119	553

[a] This is Table V from Gaudet, *Temple Law Quarterly, op. cit.*

against property accompanied by violence and a decrease in sex crimes. Violations of the Hobart Act remained constant over the period covered by this investigation. However, a comparison of these time trends with the data in Table V reveals that the original hypothesis on Judge B is not upheld. He evidently did not give shorter probationary sentences because he gave probationary sentences to offenders who had committed less serious crimes than the other judges.

Another comparison of the percentage of types of sentences given by each judge (see Table I) with the proportion of cases placed on probation for each type of crime by judges neither upheld nor contradicted the hypothesis regarding Judge B as a deviate in Table IV.

A comparison of the difference in severity of penitentiary sentences with differences in severity of probationary sentences presents a more meaningful measure of the influence of the probation officer in this court. The lengths of penitentiary sentences are shown in Table VI. These data show that the similarity observed in the length of the probationary sentences given by these judges is not found in the length of their penitentiary sentences. It should also be observed that there is no apparent relation between frequency and length of penal sentences assigned by the judges. The rank difference correlation between frequency and median length of penitentiary sentences given out by these judges is plus .34.

It is also interesting to observe that Judge

TABLE VI [a]

AVERAGE LENGTH OF JAIL OR PENITENTIARY SENTENCES GIVEN BY ALL

Judge	Judges					
	A	B	C	D	E	F
Upper Quartile	18 mos.	15 mos.	18 mos.	12 mos.	12 mos.	12 mos.
Median Sentence	12 mos.	9 mos.	10 mos.	6 mos.	9 mos.	6 mos.
Lower Quartile	6 mos.	6 mos.	6 mos.	6 mos.	4 mos.	3 mos.
No. of jail and Penitentiary Sentences	170	330	455	171	104	230
Percentage of imprisonments	35.6%	57.7%	53.3%	50.0%	45.0%	33.6%
Total number of cases, sentences of all kinds	1235	1489	1869	676	480	1693

[a] This is a modification of Table 1, Gaudet, Harris and St. John, J., *Appl'd Psychol., op. cit.*

B, who was the most lenient in length of probationary sentences, also gives short penitentiary sentences.

A final observation is that lawyers who practice in this court are able to anticipate the leniency or severity of the judges but cannot do so with any accuracy with others.

Before considering the implications which one might draw from these studies, it should be pointed out that they were not done in an attempt to "muck-rake" this court or the judicial system. In fact, the reputation of the judges who sat in this court as obtained from

conversation with scores of lawyers in the county is that they were above the average of judges in intelligence, knowledge of law and in general integrity on the bench.

It is probable that we can draw the following conclusions or speculations from these data:

1. That the influence of the "human equation" is as great in the sentencing tendencies of judges as it is in the other fields of human judgment which have been studied.

2. that legal nominalism as expressed by Blackstone ("the judgment though pro-

nounced or awarded by the judges, is not their determination or sentence, but the determination and sentence of the law"),[15] is one of the most fallacious of all types of legal fiction.

3. that the whole question of whether judges should be allowed to determine the length of sentence is still undecided. Although we know very little of the relative efficacy of different types of sentences or different lengths of sentences, it is certainly true that the personal idiosyncrasies of judges should be reduced to a minimum. Whether training in fields associated with the reformation of criminals would tend to reduce these differences in judges' sentencing tendencies is a problem worthy of investigation. In several European countries court officials usually receive special training in sentencing.

4. that although experience on the bench might conceivably be considered training for sentencing, the influence of this experience as measured by changes in sentencing tendencies appears to be negligible. In other words, experience probably does not change the personality factors which determine whether a judge will be more lenient or more severe than his colleagues.

5. that the regard with which the administration of criminal justice is held by lawyers, prisoners and laymen is lowered because of their belief that sentences are in part determined by the judges' personality.

6. finally, that the studies which have been made of judges' behavior are on a purely explanatory basis. Certainly, to ascribe the problem of the differences in judges' sentencing behavior to the vague term *personality* is merely an invitation to investigate the problem more thoroughly. Of equal urgency is the need to verify the assumption that individual differences in judges' sentencing tendencies are undesirable, and, if this is proved, to study its effects.

Associate Professor of Psychology
Director, Department of
Psychological Studies,
Stevens Institute of Technology,
Hoboken, New Jersey

[15] Robinson, E. S., *Law and the Lawyers,* New York, Macmillan, 1937, p. 10.

BIBLIOGRAPHY

Poffenberger, A. T., *Principles of Applied Psychology,* New York, Appleton-Century, 1942.
Gaudet, Frederick J., *Individual Differences in the Sentencing Tendencies of Judges,* New York, 1938, Archives of Psychology, No. 230, 58 pp.
Glueck, Sheldon, *Crime and Justice,* Boston, Little, Brown & Co., 1936.

SENTENCING PROCEDURES. Originally, at common law, when the death penalty followed a conviction of any felony, the sentencing procedure did not present serious problems. With the gradual abolition of the death penalty for practically all crimes, except for treason, murder and rape, and the consequent expansion of judicial discretion in the imposition of sentences, questions gradually developed as to the best method of determining the penalty to be inflicted and the manner in which sentence was to be pronounced.

Ordinarily the maximum penalties which may be imposed for specified crimes, and at times also the minimum penalties, are fixed by statute. Within the range specified by the Act of the Legislature, the judge has unlimited authority to decide what the sentence should be. The usual practice has been for the judge to determine what sentence should be imposed and to pronounce it immediately or shortly after conviction, whether the conviction was by plea of guilty, by the verdict of a jury, or a finding by the court.

The customary procedure in imposing sentence is to bring the defendant before the bar of the court and to inquire of him whether he has anything to say why sentence should not be pronounced against him, or words to that effect. This procedure is sometimes technically referred to as the allocution. The defendant or his counsel is then permitted to make an informal statement of whatever mitigating circumstances they desire to bring to the attention of the court as having a bearing on the sentence to be imposed. Some courts at times take formal testimony on the pertinent matters in connection with the imposition of sentence, while others do not. Generally rules of evidence do not prevail at such hearings. The court in its discretion accepts any information which it may deem helpful. In some courts it is customary for the prosecuting attorney to make a statement of facts from the standpoint of the prosecution, while in others this is not done. In some jurisdictions the prosecuting attorney also makes a definite recommendation to the court as to what the sentence should be. In many others, this practice is not followed as the sentence is there regarded as a matter solely and entirely within the discretion of the court. At the conclusion of the hearing, the judge orally pronounces sentence, which is later embodied in a formal written judgment, or is noted in the clerk's minutes.

A characteristic formulation of the procedure is found in Rule 32 (a) of the Federal Rules of Criminal Procedure, which sets forth the practice followed in the United States District Courts, and reads as follows:

(a) *Sentence.* Sentence shall be imposed without unreasonable delay. Pending sentence the court may commit the defendant or continue or alter the bail. Before imposing sentence the court shall afford the defendant an opportunity to make a statement in his own behalf and to present any information in mitigation of punishment.

(b) *Judgment.* A judgment of conviction shall set forth the plea, the verdict or findings, and the adjudication and sentence. If the defendant is found not guilty or for any other reason is entitled to be discharged, judgment shall be entered accordingly. The judgment shall be signed by the judge and entered by the clerk.

Generally the sentence imposed by the judge is not subject to appellate review, provided the sentence is within the limits prescribed by law. In this respect the trial judge's authority over sentences radically differs from his power to rule on questions of law, since rulings on questions of law are usually appealable. England is an exception, in that the Court of Criminal Appeals has jurisdiction to entertain appeals from the sentence itself, as well as from the judgment of conviction, and on an appeal from the sentence, may either decrease or increase the sentence originally imposed by the trial judge. In this country very few States confer such authority on appellate tribunals, Nebraska being a noteworthy exception, as in that State sentences imposed by a trial

judge are also subject to revision on appeal. Several years ago, the Attorney General of the United States, Honorable Homer Cummings, recommended enactment of legislation to confer power on the United States Circuit Courts of Appeals to review sentences imposed by the United States District Courts, but this proposal failed of adoption. Consequently, it may be said that the authority to impose sentence is perhaps the greatest power wielded by a judge of a criminal court, since his action in fixing what the sentence should be is ordinarily not subject to review, provided it is within the range prescribed by statute. There are some States, however, principally in the South, in which the sentence is fixed by a jury, in case the defendant is tried by a jury.

In some jurisdictions, the imposition of the death penalty in capital cases lies in the discretion of the jury. For example, in the Federal courts the death penalty is imposed for transporting a kidnaped person in interstate or foreign commerce, if the verdict of the jury so recommends and if the kidnaped person has not been liberated unharmed; while in cases of murder in the first degree and in cases of rape, the death penalty is imposed unless the jury qualifies its verdict by adding thereto "without capital punishment." In the District of Columbia the death penalty is imposed in rape cases if the jury expressly so specifies, otherwise not.

Experience has led many to the view that at the conclusion of the trial, or upon receiving a plea of guilty, the judge at times lacks sufficient information on which to make a determination as to what the sentence should be. It has come to be recognized more and more that a sentence should not be measured merely by the facts of the crime of which the defendant has been convicted and his prior criminal record. It is the general view that it is desirable to consider his family and social background, and other similar factors, in order to reach some estimate as to his chances of rehabilitation. Some study of the defendant's family and social background, education, employment record, mental development and character, is desirable in order to appraise the defendant's possibility or likelihood of becoming a law abiding member of society. With the gradual recognition of the importance of these considerations, the practice has grown of postponing the imposition of sentence for a period sufficient to make it possible to make an investigation and study of the factors which should be weighed in determining the sentence. The custom has gradually developed of appointing officers, generally known as Probation Officers, to make such presentence investigations and to prepare and submit to the trial judge a report on the results of such inquiry prior to imposition of sentence. Among the many States which have adopted this procedure, Massachusetts, New York and New Jersey may be regarded as outstanding.

By the Federal Probation Act, which became law in 1925, United States District Courts were authorized to appoint Probation Officers, one of whose functions is to make presentence investigations whenever requested by the court. Gradually most of the District Courts have adopted the practice of appointing Probation Officers and of referring specific cases to them for presentence investigation. The Probation Officers also perform the important function of supervising defendants who have been placed on probation. While Federal Probation Officers are appointed by the individual courts, they are subject to the supervision of the Administrative Office of the United States Courts located in Washington, as well as to the control of the court to which they are attached.

The extent to which presentence inquiries are undertaken and actually utilized necessarily depends on the individual judge. In the Federal Probation System, the use of presentence investigations has grown very rapidly. The Federal Rules of Criminal Procedure, which were adopted in 1946, require a pre-sentence investigation to be made in every case, unless the court otherwise directs. Rule 32 (c) provides:

(1) The probation service of the Court shall make a presentence investigation and report to the court before the imposition of sentence or the granting of probation unless the court otherwise directs. The report shall not be submitted to the court or its contents disclosed to anyone unless the defendant has pleaded guilty or has been found guilty.

(2) The report of the presentence investi-

gation shall contain any prior criminal record of the defendant and such information about his characteristics, his financial condition and the circumstances affecting his behavior as may be helpful in imposing sentence or in granting probation or in the correctional treatment of the defendant, and such other information as may be required by the court.

In many jurisdictions, the judge is authorized to suspend the execution of a sentence imposed by him, or to suspend the imposition of sentence. The practice of suspending sentences was also at times followed in the Federal courts, until in the case of *Ex parte United States,* 242 U. S. 27, the Supreme Court of the United States held that Federal courts did not have such authority.

As a result of enlightened legislation enacted from time to time, the practice of placing defendants on probation in cases in which such treatment appears useful and profitable, has gradually developed in many jurisdictions. Many offenders against the criminal law have been reclaimed to society by the use of probation as a substitute for incarceration. The Federal Probation Act of 1925 conferred on United States District Courts the authority to suspend the imposition or the execution of sentence and to place the defendant on probation. Thus, while the Federal courts may not suspend sentence without at the same time placing the defendant on probation, they have the power to grant probation. The use of probation by the Federal courts has been gradually increasing with good results, as the percentage of probation failures is comparatively small.

At times the use of probation has been criticized as a form of coddling the criminal. If used improvidently or recklessly, this undesirable result may indeed occasionally follow. On the other hand, in the hands of prudent and careful judges, probation has borne good fruit, particularly if probationers are closely supervised by competent and well-trained probation officers.

Many penologists have expressed the view that a system of imposing fixed sentences by the court at the time or shortly after conviction has a number of disadvantages. First, it leads to a great many inequalities and discrepancies between sentences, due to varying points of view on the part of different judges. Thus, the sentence imposed on a defendant depends not only on the facts of the case and the pertinent circumstances, but also on the fortuitous circumstance of what judge has jurisdiction of the case. While obviously it is not practicable or desirable to mete out the same sentence for the same offense in every case, since the surrounding circumstances and the personaltiy of the offender must be taken into account and the sentence adjusted according to his needs, nevertheless equality of treatment as distinguished from equality of sentence, is much to be desired. This result is not always attained under a system of imposition of sentence by individual judges within the rather elastic range fixed by statute. Several Attorneys General of the United States, among them Homer Cummings, Frank Murphy and Robert H. Jackson, have pointed out inequalities of sentences imposed in the Federal courts and have urged some modification of the present system.

Second, it is at times argued that it is not practicable even with all the information then available to impose a definite sentence at the time, or shortly after conviction, any more than it is practicable for a physician at the beginning of his patient's illness to determine how long his patient shall remain in a hospital. It has been urged that the sentence imposed by the court should be flexible and that the determination when the defendant should be released should be made at a later date when it is more practicable to ascertain whether he is likely to become a law abiding member of society.

These objections have led to the enactment of indeterminate sentence laws in their various forms. They originated about 1875 in the State of New York, when the so-called "Elmira Reformatory" was established for youthful offenders. Defendants sentenced to the reformatory were sentenced for an indefinite period with a specified maximum. They were released whenever the managers of the institution reached the conclusion that it was safe to set the prisoners at liberty. This determination was made on the basis of the training of the defendant, his attitude toward society and the development of his character.

During the past fifty years many States have gradually enacted indeterminate sentence laws, under which the sentence imposed by the court is for an indeterminate period and the exact time of the defendant's release is decided upon at a later date by an administrative board. Among the many States that have adopted indeterminate sentence laws in one form or another are California, Illinois, Massachusetts, New York, New Jersey, Washington, as well as many others. In some of the States in which such laws have been enacted, these provisions do not apply to all defendants, but only to those convicted of certain crimes, or those who are first offenders. As a result of the enactment of such statutes, a very large percentage of persons convicted of crime and sentenced to imprisonment are nowadays sentenced to indeterminate terms of incarceration.

Indeterminate sentence laws are of two general types. One class comprises laws under which the trial judge, in pronouncing sentence, fixes a minimum and a maximum term of imprisonment. The discretion of the administrative board ranges between these two poles. A characteristic statute of this type is found in the District of Columbia. The Indeterminate Sentence and Parole Act of the District of Columbia applies to all felonies, other than capital crimes. In imposing sentence in such cases the trial judge fixes a minimum and a maximum period of incarceration. The minimum sentence must be not more than one-third of the maximum sentence, but may be less. If the maximum sentence is for a life term, then the minimum sentence must be fifteen years. The defendant becomes eligible for parole after serving the minimum term. An administrative body, known as the Indeterminate Sentence and Parole Board, has authority to parole a defendant any time between the expiration of the minimum and the termination of the maximum sentence. If the board deems the defendant unworthy of parole, he is required to serve his maximum sentence less any commutation that he may earn for good behavior.

The second type of indeterminate sentence acts comprises statutes under which the judge does not impose any minimum sentence, but fixes only the maximum period of confinement. The administrative board having authority over such matters in due course makes a final determination as to when the defendant should be released. An advanced statute of this kind is to be found in California.

The advocates of indeterminate sentence laws claim many advantages for this new method of administering criminal justice. They urge that administrative boards, not being compelled to make decisions immediately upon conviction, are in a position to make a detailed inquiry into all of the factors that should enter into the determination of the question, as to when the defendant should be released from confinement. Some of the boards are equipped with a staff of psychiatrists, psychologists, social workers and experts of other types, who make exhaustive individual studies of each prisoner and make the results of their investigations available to the Board. Members of such boards themselves become expert in the field of penology and are therefore able, so it is argued, to make appropriate and well-founded decisions. The principal argument, however, in favor of indeterminate sentence laws, is that it is not desirable to decide at the outset how long a person should remain in confinement, but that it is advantageous to watch the development of his personality, his adaptability to training, and his desire and will to become rehabilitated, and to reach a decision as to when his release date should come on the basis of the progress of events. On the other hand, it is argued that the trial judge, having before him all the facts of the case and the surrounding circumstances, gathered not only from the evidence but also from the presentence investigation report, and knowing the needs of the community, is better equipped to determine a suitable sentence, than is an administrative board, at some later date and possibly located far away from the community.

The real test of the desirability of indeterminate sentence laws would lie in ascertaining whether they have reduced the percentage of recidivism and have led to a greater percentage of reformation and rehabilitation of criminals than has been the case under the system of fixing definite sentences in the original judgment of the court. Unfortunately, sufficient data are not available, or else have not been collated and classified, making it possible to give a definite answer to this question. The matter still remains in the realm of debate and discussion. From a theoretical standpoint, there appears to be a great deal of merit in indeterminate sentence laws.

The American Law Institute has made some exhaustive studies in this field. Its work has culminated in the formulation and recommendation for enactment by several of the States of a model statute providing for the creation of an indeterminate sentence system in a somewhat extreme form. Under this proposal, every sentence of imprisonment for a serious offense would be for a maximum term, the exact time of release to be fixed later by an administrative board. An unusual feature of this proposal is that it would permit the administrative board to continue a defendant's imprisonment indefinitely if it is deemed that he would be likely to resume his criminal career if set at liberty. The only limitation on this power would be that at periodic intervals the question of continuing the defendant's imprisonment would have to be submitted to the court for its approval, which would be empowered to overrule the board's decision in that respect. There has been considerable criticism of this aspect of the proposal, because conceivably it would permit life imprisonment in the discretion of an administrative board for any offense whatever, even one of a comparatively minor character, if the Board found that the defendant was likely to commit other crimes if set at liberty and if the court approved its conclusion. It seems to many that this feature of the model Act is extreme and even dangerous, in view of the possibility of miscarriage of justice, as well as of mistakes of judgment. The California indeterminate sentence law is to some extent patterned on the proposal of the American Law Institute, although it omits the drastic feature to which reference has just been made.

The Federal judicial system, except in the District of Columbia, which as stated above has a local indeterminate sentence law, still adheres to the system of fixed sentences imposed by the court. The Federal judiciary, however, has given considerable attention to the possible desirability of modifying the present mode of imposing sentences. Several years ago, the Conference of Senior Circuit Judges, which is presided over by the Chief Justice of the United States, and which is the governing body of the Federal judiciary from an administrative standpoint, appointed a committee to study this subject. The committee, after conducting exhaustive investigations and holding hearings, recommended legislation to provide for the creation of an administrative board to deal with sentences. The proposal was to the effect that a trial judge, if he determines to impose a sentence of imprisonment for more than a year, should sentence the defendant for the maximum term prescribed by statute for the offense of which he was convicted, and that the board should thereafter fix the actual sentence that the defendant should serve. This proposal did not meet with favor on the part of many Federal judges, some of whom felt that it would be unwise to withdraw from the court all control over the length of imprisonment to be suffered by the defendant. Further studies on the part of the committee appointed by the Conference of Senior Judges led to the formulation of a modified proposal. Under this plan the judge originally is to impose a tentative sentence for the maximum term prescribed by statute for the offense of which the defendant stands convicted. An administrative board appointed by the President is to make a study of the matter and then, within a specified time, is to submit a recommendation to the judge as to what the actual sentence should be. After receiving this recommendation, the judge is to impose a final sentence. If, however, he fails to take any action, then the sentence recommended by the board is to become the actual sentence in the case. The virtue of this plan is that it retains in the hands of the court the ultimate control over the sentence. This committee also proposed the creation of a special system in the Federal courts for

the treatment of youthful offenders, under twenty-four years of age. The proposed measure would authorize the judge in his discretion to commit youthful offenders to the custody of an administrative body to be known as The Youth Authority, for a term of five years. During this five-year period, the Youth Authority is to have control over the defendant. It is to be clothed with power to confine him for treatment or training at any institution of the penal, correctional or other type, or to place him on probation. If he is imprisoned, then the Youth Authority is to be empowered to release him on parole at any time within the five-year period. If the trial judge deems a youthful offender unsuitable for treatment of this kind, he may deal with him as he would in the case of any adult defendant. These proposals have been endorsed by successive Attorneys General of the United States, and hearings have been held thereon before Congressional Committees, at which the enactment of the legislation was urged by Bar Associations and organizations of lawyers and other persons interested in criminology and penology. These measures, however, have not as yet been acted upon by the Congress, but are still under consideration.

Hon. Alexander Holtzoff
United States District Judge
Washington 1, D. C.

BIBLIOGRAPHY

American Law Institute *Code of Criminal Procedure* and Notes thereto.
Federal Rules of Criminal Procedure.
The Presentence Investigation published by the Administrative Office of the United States Courts.
Numerous articles in *Federal Probation* a magazine published by the Administrative Office of the United States Courts.
U. S. Code, Title 18, Sections 724 et seq.
Various State statutes.

SOCIAL DISORGANIZATION AND CRIME. In keeping with its general development, sociology has been inclusive in the treatment of the subject of crime. Investigations have covered the racial-physical, the individual-psychological, and in a narrower sense, the sociological approaches. Criminology has discarded a racial explanation as insufficient to explain variation in amount and type of crime within racial categories. The Lombrosian concept of a criminal physical type received recent support from Earnest Hooton, but this hypothesis is not generally accepted by American criminologists. The differences between the criminal and non-criminal are slight, if existent at all, and in any case they can be explained by the social class to which most criminals belong.

Some investigators have maintained that crime may be understood best through the individual-psychological approach. Psychological and psychiatric researches have proved tremendously rewarding from the original and continued encouragement by Dr. William Healy. Two sorts of questions can be raised in this individual frame of reference. First, through what unique experiences and mental processes has a given individual become antisocial? This can be answered only by the method of individual case study, which leads to diagnosis, prognosis, and treatment of the criminal as a unique entity. Second, what general conditions, both mental and social in so far as they are experienced by the individual, are associated with criminal behavior? Here, researchers must change their frame of reference from an individual to individuals—from a criminal to criminals. The aim is to generalize about criminals as distinguished from noncriminals. It is in this field that the psychologist and psychiatrist may aid the sociologist in analyzing the relationship between various social conditions and the mental processes leading to criminal behavior.

The more specific sociological approach asks the general question, what social conditions are related to high crime rates. The logic of this frame of reference has been difficult to accept for those who insist that criminal behavior can be understood only through knowing the individual subjective factors. For instance, individuals often respond differently to the same social stimulus. Therefore, the sociological approach necessarily posits two assumptions. The first is that there are commonly held folkways and socially defined goals which produce some uniformity of individual actions in a social group. This is everywhere granted as valid, and, if it were questionable, it is method-

ologically valid to hold it as a hypothetical assumption. The second assumption, closely related to the first, is that the societies, communities, or groups being discussed are large enough to cancel out individual differences in responses to stimuli. This is largely a statistical problem when comparing differential crime rates, solved by testing the significance of difference. The method here is to correlate the variation in crime rates of social groups with particular social conditions.

Another method of isolating etiological factors in criminal behavior is to match individual criminals with noncriminals on as many factors as possible, such as age and sex; and then to compare the two populations with respect to a single uncontrolled variable. Both methods have been used to advantage, but too many of the earlier studies failed to use research controls by comparing criminals with the noncriminal population.

Investigators of the relationship between *social disorganization* and *crime* have had to define these two terms. Crime, legally defined as behavior contrary to law, suffers two drawbacks. First, an unknown amount of such behavior necessarily remains unrecorded. Statistics on offenses known to the police, published by the United States Department of Justice, are now considered most accurate for comparative purposes. However, here it is impossible to know the characteristics of the criminal and, furthermore, these figures are recorded neither by small units of the population nor by place of residence of the criminal. Therefore, convictions for felonies are considered the best available data for many purposes. The second drawback is the fact that the law itself is sometimes not indicative of public opinion. There are outmoded laws on the statute books as well as acts generally considered wrong which as yet have not been put into law. Thorsten Sellin has suggested that a more sociological concept of conduct norms be substituted for the legal definition. The point should certainly be considered in the analysis of minority-group crime and violations of liquor laws, but this definition is not subject to statistical computations. Furthermore, the major felonies are generally considered crimes in the civilized countries in both law and conduct norms and their incidence can be used for comparative purposes.

Social disorganization has often been used as a value judgment—as a term synonymous with what a particular writer considered undesirable. On the other hand, crime rates themselves have sometimes been considered indices of social disorganization or even identical with disorganization itself. Value judgments and this circular reasoning are to be avoided in this connection. One solution is to analyze the relationship of specific social conditions to crime without reference to such general concepts. However, without question there are some general social conditions best identified as social disorganization from which high crime rates emerge as one of the possible results.

Much of the earlier work done in the United States on the sociology of crime used the method of ecology to demonstrate the wide variation in crime rates for different areas of the country. Clifford Shaw's *Delinquency Areas* (1929), showing that crime rates tend to decrease radially from the center of Chicago, soon became a classic in this field. Further investigation has demonstrated that all deteriorated areas near the center of cities and industrial locations—slums—have high truancy, delinquency and crime rates. The *interstitial* areas, areas between well-established business and residential districts with mobile populations, and some urban isolated areas with deteriorated social conditions, have the highest rates. These studies have served to make definite and well-known the facts, even though they are now obvious and taken for granted. None the less, these studies do not go far enough to indicate specifically what slum conditions are related to high crime rates. All slum-dwellers, of course, do not commit crimes, even though the crime rates for these areas are sometimes twenty-five times those for other sections.

We have some studies which attempted to use research controls to indicate the relevant factors in the urban slums: notably by Cyril Burt in London (1925), New York State Crime Commission in New York City (1928 and 1930), and Shaw and McKay in Chicago (1931). Two points of agreement are that

dilapidated housing conditions, and inadequate and commercialized recreation are common to the delinquency areas. But one wonders how directly these are related to crime. Rural areas, especially European peasant communities, and less civilized peoples had primitive dwellings without the accompanying delinquency problem. Also, it is a queer logic which supposes that the game of pool and playing in streets are specific causes. Studies disagree on whether broken homes and congested populations are significant factors. This is to be expected since complete families may have adverse influences on children and it is difficult to understand why mere population per acre is an essential factor. The hypothesis of poverty as a general cause of crime brings the same disconcerting conclusions. Poverty in historic times and in modern rural areas does not produce the crime problem of urban conditions. Furthermore, there are the problems of white-collar criminality and political connivance with the criminal world; and there is the fact that only predatory crimes are correlated with economic conditions.

The welter of contradictory results in the search for specific social causes of crime led to the conclusions that there is no one cause; that there is multiple causation; or that cause must be found in the configuration of many functionally related factors. Although this interpretation is not completely misleading, it tends to leave unanswered the problem of evaluating the relative influence of the various factors. Some have concluded that it is fruitless to look for social causes —that the etiology of criminal careers can be meaningfully understood only in the analysis of the individual subjective factors. It is true that the individual case can only be analyzed in this way, however, this leaves unexplained the significant variation in delinquency and crime rates for peoples of different areas.

The fact is that the conclusions of many studies searching for correlations between specific objective indices of social conditions and crime are crude empirical findings. That is, granting that the correlations are statistically significant, little attempt has been made to specify within what broader social system the findings are valid and to determine whether the correlative factors are to be considered directly related to crime causation or related, in common with crime, to some more general factors. It would indeed be naive to look for a single generalization which would explain why each individual either did or did not commit crime. On the other hand, it is not unreasonable to believe that there are some broad conditions of the social structure which everywhere cause a disproportionately large number of people to deviate from the norms of their society. And if less limited generalizations are to be found, it is logical to look for them in the social and cultural system which is less removed from the subjective reactions of people than conditions of the physical environment. Physical things such as housing take on social meanings, but they take on different meanings to different peoples.

The studies mentioned above give other traits strikingly characteristic of urban crime. Contrasted with the rural criminal, the urban criminal is more professional and more recidivistic and he is more likely to commit crimes in groups and to belong to gangs. Criminal cultures, where the pattern of crime is passed on from one generation to another, as are folkways and mores, exist in some urban areas. These facts show that urban criminals tend to be qualitatively different. Their organization and opposition to prevailing social norms must be indicative of some peculiarity of the urban culture. It should be noted, however, that as a whole the American cities of 25,000 to 100,000 population have a higher criminality than those over 100,000.

Relevant to the production of criminal careers, the urban social-cultural milieu may be broadly characterized in the following terms. The city lacks strong local codes of behavior enforced by tradition and public opinion—it must rely upon the less efficient method of law enforcement. The heterogeneity, mobility and anonymity of urban people has broken down the social control of primary groups of personal relationships so that the individual is thrown back on his random impulses. Urban culture accentuates the motive of individual economic gain with

a minimum of moral sanctions. Because of economic insecurity, it is not surprising that the urban population is characterized by a disproportionately large amount of predatory crime. It is, without doubt, these broad social-cultural conditions of the urban community, exaggerated in slum areas, which more generally account for the extreme crime rates of the interstitial and isolated sections of the city.

The variable criminality of minority groups gives additional insight into the problem of social disorganization and crime. The foreign-born United States population, the resident Orientals, and the Jews tend to have relatively low crime rates while the Negro, the American Indians, and some second-generation immigrants have higher rates than the native-born white population. Although these are the general tendencies, statistics on particular nationality-group populations and case studies of particular communities indicate significant variations within these categories. These studies confirm what has already been said; namely, that a racial hypothesis of crime causation is difficult to support and that poverty alone cannot be considered a complete explanation. Positively, the most important sociological finding seems to be that an integrated community of minority peoples can maintain a relatively low crime rate in spite of their inferior status and unfavorable economic position. Integration here refers to the existence of community-wide participation in group activities of various kinds and loyalty to the minority-group as an in-group. Where such strong integration exists, hostility toward the minority-group probably has the effect of lowering the crime rate by creation of group morale.

The crime rate of those who leave the ethnic community tends to increase and approximate that of the majority population, even though they are able to better their economic position. Moreover, the type of crime committed also becomes similar to that of the majority-group, which in the United States means a predominance of predatory crime. The minority culture groups having the highest crime rates tend to be those which have become acculturated to the majority-group patterns of behavior, but due to hostility toward them they have failed to succeed in competition for social status. As a result certain minority populations such as the American Negro and Indian have failed to acquire respect for the values of private property and human life which accompany the prevailing folkway patterns. Under these conditions of demoralization, an undue number of crimes of violence might be expected.

The general thesis of the sociology of crime has been stated in its broadest terms as less a problem of abnormal individuals and more a problem of abnormal situations. This is not to gainsay that delinquency may be the out-growth of mental frustrations as Dr. William Healy has so well demonstrated. There are mentally diseased and deficient criminals, but, also, there are those with emotionally balanced personalities who have assumed unacceptable social roles; and there are mentally abnormal individuals who do not commit crimes. Furthermore, there is a great deal of evidence to indicate that many of the mental abnormalities find their origins in social situations. One task for the study of social disorganization and crime is to describe the general social situation which produces an excessive amount of criminal behavior in terms of individual social roles which constitute the social system. At the present state of our knowledge only the crudest outline can be sketched.

The social structure may be thought of as a system of behavior patterns—folkways and mores—which describe the correct ways of attaining socially defined ends—both immediate and long run life goals—all of which is sanctioned by ultimate values in the accepted philosophy. When this system works, that is when most people are able to attain their ends in socially acceptable ways or justify their nonattainment, the social structure is said to be integrated. Under conditions of rapid social change and population increase, immigration, and war this social structure may become disintegrated. The disintegration is a condition where the mores and folkways fail to satisfy many people as effective means of attaining their socially defined ends.

For example, the American economic patterns of getting jobs and promotions, and achieving security as well as our mores of hard work, thrift and honesty have failed to bring to many individuals fulfillment of their ambitions. The *standard* of living is a great deal higher than the *level* of living. Furthermore, the American emphasis on a social philosophy of individualism has tended to ignore the mores which recognize the rights of others and culturally sanctioned ends. The result is random behavior according to the immediate whims of the individual which increases dissatisfaction by deflating the individual ego. Most individuals are able to accept some failure; they rationalize their position in terms of bad luck, or their own inability, or they project their ambitions into their children's careers. Others commit suicide, experience mental breakdowns, live Bohemian lives, turn revolutionaries, or more frequently become criminals, except where the reactions mentioned above are culturally acceptable. The analysis of why individuals have one or another of these reactions requires further sociological and psychological investigation.

The above theory of social disorganization, defined as disintegration of the social system of behavior patterns, relates crime as a kind of socially defined behavior to the objects of the physical and social environment, bearing in mind the meanings which culture places upon them. This provides a theoretical framework for the valuable statistical findings concerning broken homes, poor housing, recreational needs and poverty. It provides an explanation for the high crime rates in some urban areas and their wide variation among minority groups. The theory suggests that crime is potentially possible in any society—at least to the extent that it is difficult to imagine a system of folkways and mores so well integrated with the culturally legitimate goals that no personality becomes frustrated. From the sociological as well as from the psychological point of view, it may be said that the possibilities of crime are implicit in social life The anthropologist, Bronislaw Malinowski, found that even in the well integrated primitive societies crime was not unknown, though it is significant that crime is rare in these societies. The theory of cultural integration also helps to resolve the disconcerting fact that some nonreligious groups have unusually low crime rates, as in the case of the nonaffiliated population of Netherlands where such official statistics are recorded; and the fact that some religious minority groups have high rates. It is quite evident that these cases are better explained on the basis of the social position of the group than on their particular religious beliefs and practices.

A sociological study of crime causation has practical significance for ameliorative programs. It suggests that a plan for individual treatment under social conditions conducive to criminal behavior is likely to have limited effect. The theory of cultural disintegration further suggests that an improvement of a single factor of the social conditions may be insufficient to overcome generally adverse cultural conditions. This statement may be applied to any one of the many social conditions statistically correlated with crime. For instance, Frederic Thrasher discovered that the influence of a boys' club and an elaborate recreational program in a delinquency area of New York City had little or no effect. However, it is more encouraging to find that some programs in Chicago and Los Angeles which have sought wider support from the various community agencies and which have used youthful indigenous leadership in their organizations have had somewhat greater success. Nevertheless, the directors of these projects have been among the first to recognize the difficulties of reorienting the peoples of these areas without more basic change in the American urban cultural patterns. It is believed that greater *social* integration may be brought to the populations of these areas by way of organized activities. How much the crime rates can be decreased without a change in the more basic folkways of making a living and their relationship to American high standards of living remains to be seen.

ARTHUR LEWIS WOOD
Associate Professor of Sociology
Bucknell University
Lewisburg, Pennsylvania

BIBLIOGRAPHY

Burt, Cyril, *The Young Delinquent,* 1925.
Cantor, Nathaniel F., *Crime and Society,* 1939.
New York State Crime Commission, *Crime and the Community,* 1930.
Ploscowe, Morris, *Report on the Causes of Crime,* Vol. 1, National Commission on Law Observance and Enforcement, 1931.
Reckless, Walter C., *Criminal Behavior,* 1940.
Sellin, Thorsten, *Culture Conflict and Crime,* 1938.
Shaw, Clifford R., and McKay, Henry D., *Report on the Causes of Crime,* Vol. II, National Commission on Law Observance and Enforcement, 1931.
Tannenbaum, Frank, *Crime and the Community,* 1938.

SOCIOLOGICAL ASPECTS OF DELINQUENCY AND CRIME. A modern society such as ours is composed of many different social groups, which attempt regulation of the behavior of individual members. The rules and regulations of such groups may be formal or informal, written or unwritten, numerous or sparse, tightly drawn or loosely enforced. The family has such rules. So does the church, the sect, the school, the labor union, the office, the professional society. Such rules for behavior are conduct norms. They define what should be done and what should not be done.

The adult criminal code and the juvenile court acts are just two sets of rules in our society. They are the legal rules which have been inscribed on the statute books. In many instances, the criminal and juvenile codes overlap the regulations and rules of the family, school, church, and other social groups attempting regulation. A person guilty of malpractice not only violates the criminal code but also the ethical code of the medical associations. However, a physician who advertises is not a violator of the criminal code but only the code of medical ethics.

The picture which should be carried in mind is one of several concentric circles. The largest circle contains the violations of all rules of all groups of society. This widest circle would circumscribe most of us, since most of us violate some rules of some groups during any given time interval. Some of our transgressions run afoul of the criminal or the juvenile code. But just what the proportion of violations of the criminal and juvenile code is to the total infractions of all rules of society is not known. The suspicion is that it is very small. So we move to circle number two which represents the violations of the criminal and juvenile codes. Within this small circle is a smaller circle of crimes known to the police, including juvenile cases. This circle of crimes known to the police is the circle of reported and recorded fact.

If a criminologist had to answer the question today, "When is crime," he would have to say that crime exists when it is reported and hence "known." The unreported violations of the criminal and juvenile codes as well as the unrecorded violations of codes of various social groups in our society are a very important area of study. They are the stratosphere of criminal and delinquent behavior but are not the circle of reported criminal and delinquent behavior.

The reporting of crime and delinquency depends upon many realistic factors, the most important of which is the unwillingness of victims or of observers of offenses to report to official sources, namely the police and the law enforcement agents. Moreover, some offenses may be of a private nature, known only to the violator himself or to the violator and the victim, such as sex crime, abortion, blackmail, attempted suicide, carrying concealed weapons, drug addiction.

Police experience has shown that there are certain kinds of offenses which are likely to be reported and hence "known to the police." These offenses include, homicide, rape, robbery, aggravated assault, burglary, larceny, and auto theft. Other assaults, forgery and counterfeiting, embezzlement and fraud, carrying and possessing weapons, sex offenses (not rape), offenses against family and children, violating drug laws, driving while intoxicated, violating liquor laws, drunkenness, disorderly conduct and vagrancy, gambling, violating traffic and motor vehicle laws, are offenses which have much less likelihood of being consistently reported to the police.

Even in the first group of offenses, those most consistently known to the police, there is only a small percentage of the total crimes known which leads to arrest. Here we have a small circle within the crimes known circle, which is called clearance by arrest. But the main types of crimes listed in the first group have varying degrees of liability for being cleared by arrest. If a pre-war year is taken as an example, the 1938 percentages of offenses cleared by arrest of offenses known to the police as reported by the Federal Bureau of Investigation were: 89.5 for murder; 87.1, manslaughter; 82.5, rape; 42.5, robbery; 77.3, aggravated assault; 34.7, burglary; 25.3, larceny; 22.3, auto theft. One notes that the chances of being acted upon officially for auto theft, larceny, burglary, and robbery are quite small, considering the high reportability of such offenses. It appears that the major crimes against the person have a high arrest liability whereas the major crimes against property have a very much lower arrest liability. This in part reflects the scale of values in American society, namely the very high importance attached to the sacredness and inviolability of the person. The arrest differential also reflects the greater ease of finding the offenders.

Within the very small circle of offenses cleared by arrest are the still smaller concentric circles of persons charged by police, of judicial prosecutions, of convictions, and of prisoners received from courts by correctional institutions. The innermost circle, namely, prisoners received from courts, is a mere fly speck in the circle of violations of the criminal code and is less than a fly speck in the widest of all circles, namely, violations of all codes of behavior. Van Vechten discovered that in the state of Minnesota and in the District of Columbia, where reporting at all stages of the legal procedure in handling offenders is in operation, there were 3.4 and 3.6 prisoners received from courts by correctional institutions out of every hundred crimes classified under group one (those consistently known to the police). Thirty five point seven and 34.8 cases out of every 100 group one crimes were cleared by arrest, while 5.9 and 6.4 cases out of a hundred in Minnesota and D. C. respectively were convicted.

One should understand the point that an increase in arrests or an increase in convictions out of every 100 cases of crime in the group one type of offenses does not reflect anything about the real volume of criminal behavior. Such an increase would reflect increased police efficiency and increased activity of the court system, supported by public opinion. The machinery for reporting crime, for arresting offenders, and for prosecuting them is not a constant throughout the years. Consequently, arrests, convictions, and prisoners received cannot be used as an index of the volume of crime but merely as indicators of policies and efficiency of law enforcement. Crimes known to the police as covered in the group one type of offenses would make the best indicator of the volume of crime. At the point of being known they are not subject to influence of law enforcement policies. They reflect the willingness of persons to report offenses and the efficiency of police science in covering and detecting crime.

There are two points in the circles of legal procedure against offenders at which a record of personal information is made in the United States. The one is clearance by arrest and the other is reception from courts by correctional institutions. In the case of juvenile offenders, personal information on individual cases is recorded at the court level. This is not true in adult cases, except in some instances where courts have a probation service to investigate probationable cases. Usually speaking the information obtained by the correctional institution is more verified than that obtained by the police at the arrest level.

Such recorded information at arrest or reception indicates that there are categoric risks for getting involved in the legal processing of crime—that is, for being arrested and being admitted to a correctional institution. Differential risks appear when any phenomenon is recorded on an individual basis for a heterogeneous population. There are mortality risks, accident risks, unemployment risks, credit risks, and so forth.

Risks for being arrested or received by a correctional institution are not pure mathematical chances for being involved in crime. They merely indicate the liability certain classes of individuals have, under a system of crime control at any given period, for being caught by the police or sent to an institution for offenders. Risks for being arrested

or received by a correctional institution indicate the differential chance that persons in various subcategories of population will become so involved. For example, occupation is a category of population and unskilled, semi-skilled, skilled, professional, etc., are subcategories under the main category. If we may suppose that unskilled persons in our society get arrested more than all other subcategories of occupation, then this subcategory of unskilled worker represents a high differential liability.

It is strongly suspected that, in spite of its not being recorded on arrest data and reception data of offenders, social class is one of the most important categoric risks for involvement. Several years ago Bonger gathered data from European cities to show that persons coming from the lower classes were disproportionately involved in crime. Law enforcement agencies have acted more rigorously in lower class cases than in upper class cases. Most criminologists would admit also that the lower classes are exposed to more demoralizing and disorganizing conditions of living also.

But it is suspected also that the upper classes are differentially immune to arrest and reception in prison. Evidence is accumulating to the effect that crime is prevalent in the upper class but that the deeds of the upper class are not acted upon officially. By the upper class here is meant persons in the professions, in administrative government positions, and in business management. If and when the public insists that law enforcement acts rigorously on the violators of trust, misusers of funds, the falsifiers of reports, the evaders of taxes, then it is logical to expect that the upper class will represent a high liability for crime involvement, mainly because of its exposure to money, contracts, and accounts. The middle class would then be the class in our society which is the freest of crime involvement. It is the forthright class, the class most interested in morals, welfare, decent standards of living, security, and law observance.

Males get arrested and received by institutions for offenders very much more than females. At the level of the juvenile court, boys' cases outnumber girls' cases 6 to 1 in pre-war years. During the war, this ratio was 5 to 1. In pre-war years, the ratio of males to females arrested, fingerprinted, and reported to the F.B.I. ranged from 10 to 1 to 13 to 1. During the war, this ratio declined to 5 to 1. The sex ratio of prisoners admitted to correctional institutions in the U. S. was approximately 19 to 1 in pre-war years.

Law enforcement in our society is supposed to be much more lenient on females than on males. Victims of offenses are more likely to report males than females. On the other hand, males have more opportunity to get involved in trouble in our society. And they are also supposed to be more active biologically.

The differential sex risk extends to certain types of offenses. It seems that there are offenses in which males are involved to a much greater extent than expected from the general sex ratio of arrest, such as rape (an all-male offense), auto theft, burglary, robbery, driving while intoxicated, and so on. And there are offenses in which females are arrested to a greater extent than expected from the general sex ratio, such as prostitution, other sex offenses, disorderly conduct, and vagrancy. Females appear not to get so heavily involved in technical offenses which require skill or in offenses requiring daring and strength.

The age distribution of officially recorded offenders is much different than the age distribution of the general population. Old persons are not much of a risk for crime involvement and neither are young children. In the United States, post adolescence and young adulthood appear to be the age period for greatest risk for arrest and admission to a correctional institution. Crime involvement reaches its peak at this point and slowly declines with increasing age. Such a trend might partly be explained by the sociological factor of settling down with age and by the biological factor of the general winding down of the organism. Auto theft, robbery, larceny, vagrancy, and rape appear to be offenses with a greater concentration of younger persons than expected, while driving while intoxicated, drunkenness, gambling, offenses against family and children have the greatest concentration of older persons.

Violation of drug laws, assault, criminal homicide, and embezzlement and fraud show only a somewhat older distribution of persons than expected from the age distribution of arrested persons generally.

If one examines the offenses in which young persons concentrate, it appears as if they involve activities which call for daring, energy, and courage. If one examines the offenses for which older persons are most reported, they seem to involve habit systems that are more likely to be pronounced in older than in younger persons.

In the United States, the colored population has much greater liability to be arrested and admitted to correctional institutions than the white population. For the most part this differential is a social class risk, since the Negro in America is more abundantly in the lower classes than the white man. The Negro is exposed to poorer living conditions and more demoralizing circumstances. He has more limited opportunity. He is acted upon more rigorously by law enforcing agencies. In addition, allowance needs to be made for the differential patterns of life which have characterized Negro history and living in the United States, which in turn permeate their family life, leisure time, and religious activity. Such patterns of life can have a direct effect upon exposure to arrest and involvement in crime.

The colored man was arrested somewhat more than twice as much as the white man in proportion to respective population during pre-war years. His arrest rate in comparison with the white arrest rate is several times as high for homicide, assault, carrying and possessing weapons, receiving or buying stolen property, gambling, and violation of liquor laws and is somewhat lower than general for driving while intoxicated, auto theft, forgery and counterfeiting, sex offenses, drunkenness, embezzlement and fraud. Actually the white man outdoes the Negro in skilled crimes, which fact suggests that the Negro has not had the experience with checks, automobiles, tools and dies, property that the white man has had. The great involvement in aggressions against the person suggests the operation of special patterns of living as well as a factor of frustration. Greater involvement in gambling, drunkenness, and receiving stolen goods is likely to reflect mainly differential police action.

Sociologists have called attention to area and regional risks in crime and delinquency. Generally speaking in the United States, crime and delinquency, both by residence of offender and reported place of the deed, declines in incidence away from the center of the city and increases in incidence as we approach the center of the city. Area risks are not limited to arrest data or data obtained at reception in the institution. They can be worked out from crime and delinquency which is known and reported. Even certain types of offenses have their peculiar ecological distribution in the American city and presumably in other cities, as Calvin Schmidt has so well shown for Minneapolis and Saint Paul. While the general distribution of crime and delinquency, follows the paths of disorganized areas, at the same time certain types of offenses may assume special distributions, such as jack rolling, holding up street cars and taxi cabs, pickpocketing, bank robbery. Such special distributions in the city represent the tendency for a certain type of activity to gravitate to the place where it can best be conducted.

Although there are some exceptions, rural districts as compared with urban communities have generally a much lower rate of reported crimes. One reason for the lower rate is underreporting, since the rural districts have poor facilities for police reporting of crimes known. On the other hand, rural areas are not an encouraging field for criminal activity, especially of the predatory type. And finally rural districts do not present the demoralizing conditions which urban communities present to their respective populations.

On the basis of crimes known to the police and reported to the F. B. I., the New England and Middle Atlantic states of the United States are lowest in reported crime and the southern states are the highest. Strangely enough, if we can accept this fact, it presents us with a paradox. Reported crime is lowest where it is expected to be the highest (greater urbanization and industrialization) and is highest where it should be

lowest (least industrialized and urbanized). It may be that the eastern states' greater orderliness and more established community organization can account for the paradox. The southern states are presumably a haven for more rugged, individualistic living, in which a tradition of orderliness and strong community organization has not developed. Hence, crime can be more rampant in the southern states.

The study of categoric and area risks is not a study of causes of criminal and delinquent behavior. Risks are liabilities within a certain framework. They are related to reported or observed incidence of a phenomenon. Causes are presumably related to the explanation of the phenomenon. Risks are objective and determinable. Causes of a phenomenon such as criminal behavior are not as determinable. The main factor which limits the study of risk is the reportability of data on the individual occurrences. The factor which limits the study of causes is the uncontrollability of the ingredients of behavior.

Most research in the study of criminal and delinquent behavior has attempted to shed light on causative factors. An overview of all the important work in this field leads to the statement that more is known as to what is not so about crime and delinquency than what is so. Criminologists must be prepared for the eventuality of abandoning the whole idea of discoverable causation and of following more promising leads. From a sociological standpoint certain clearings in the jungle of criminological study are appearing.

In the first place, it is becoming understood that criminal and delinquent behavior is a variable in its own right apart from the tendencies of the individual (not that the tendencies and traits of the individual do not make an individual susceptible to crime and delinquency). It is now recognized that crime and delinquency are definitions of behavior and what is crime and delinquency at any time or place depends upon the set of definitions of behavior. Generally speaking, society at any time or place attempts to preserve its important values in life by defining behavior as ill mannered, indecent, sinful, delinquent, criminal, and so forth and by attempting to bring infractions of rules under some sort of control. In addition, as we have already seen, behavior of any individual which runs counter to the established set of definitions (the code) must be interpreted as wrong, awful, serious, harmful by the victims of the aggression or by the observers of the infraction for behavior to be dealt with officially. Consequently, what passes for crime and delinquency at any time and place must be socially defined as such by society and interpreted as serious in order for the behavior to become crime officially. These two items alone make criminal and delinquent behavior a variable independent of the proclivities, traits, and tendencies of persons. A variable so constituted is a difficult one to control from the standpoint of establishing causation. Because of this fact also, it will probably be necessary for criminologists of the future to study delinquent and criminal behavior as behavior in its largest frame of reference, namely, infractions of all sorts of codes of conduct, and to cease confining themselves to the study of those who get caught officially.

In the second place, it is becoming increasingly clear that violating behaviors circulate in society as do any other patterns of behavior, approved or disapproved, and that many patterns of violations accumulate techniques for their performance as well as certain reenforcing attitudes and philosophy of life. The average boy in our society comes into a society of boys who practice masturbation and have certain attitudes toward it. In rare instances, the boy may discover masturbation for himself. But it is more likely that he finds the pattern already in circulation. The same line of thought follows for drugs, alcohol, stealing, vagrancy, begging, counterfeiting, horsetrading, suicide, murder, rape, and so on.

Some of the patterns which fall into our legal definitions of crime assume complicated proportions and have to be learned or acquired through studied practice. Take for example a card sharp or a confidence man. Some of the patterns of behavior which are outlawed as criminal take the form of an ancient trade, such as prostitution, gambling, confidence game, counterfeiting, criminal

fence, and have collected a rich tradition around themselves. Such patterns of activity attract persons who want to follow a trade of this sort and the successful operators become professional with high status in the criminal world. Still further some of the very lucrative patterns of predatory activity become the object of considerable organization for the fostering of the business of crime and we have organized crime. And lastly, new patterns of defined criminal activity arise from time to time, such as racketeering and blackmarketing, and add their contribution to a rich lore of patterns of activity which have from time to time been considered pariah, taboo, delinquent, or criminal. All these patterns constitute the criminal culture which exists and persists alongside the approved patterns of conduct. The patterns of criminal and delinquent culture are there for the individual of our society just as much as the Ten Commandments, approved marriage, respectable work, wholesome leisure.

In the third place, it is now apparent that the crux of the problem of causation from a sociological point of view is to discover why some individuals adopt or respond to certain patterns of behavior and not to others. Patterns of all kinds, good and bad, confront the person in our society. Why does he take up with shyster law practices? Why does he adopt drugs instead of chewing gum? Why does he steal instead of asking for the object or working for it?

The patterns are there and there are many subtle carriers of patterns: associates, books, hangouts, movies, pennyarcades, newspapers, magazines, radio. The most effective carrier of pattern as far as criminal and delinquent behavior is concerned is the human carrier—associates and especially those with prestige in our eyes. Sometimes it looks as if the companionship factor as the conveyor of pattern is almost self compelling. It looks as if there is always someone who can make us succumb, who can make the "preacher lay his Bible down," who can wean us from a happy marriage or from a good job, who can sell us a bill of goods when we have had high sales resistance up to now.

It is best to assume, however, that there is

a differential response factor. A person was in a state of readiness to be sold and that is why he bought. One is discontented with his job and that is why he succumbed to the false business venture. The same sort of thing applies to response elsewhere. It can be assumed that those who overtly responded to the Orson Welles war of the planets episode were already disturbed persons. Bargain sale advertisements have a way of getting favorable response from already prepared soil. No one knows at present how much the conveyor, the salesman, the companion prepares the soil, so that the person can respond to overtures or exposures.

But differential response to patterns of delinquency and crime can go deeper than the mere readiness to respond to overtures. It may be conditioned by attitudes toward life, by frustration and blockage, by emotional instability, by character traits, by psychopathic tendencies, and by unconscious drives. The absence of such conditions in the individual makes it easier for the person to reject truancy, alcohol, sex promiscuity, theft, cheating, and so forth, when presented to him by carriers.

Coming at the matter from the other angle, it is not enough to say that the psychopathic person, the emotionally disturbed person, the person of any assumed hereditary weakness or blemishes finds his way to crime as a lower level of adjustment, when adjustment cannot be made at better levels. There are too many psychopaths who do not take to drugs, to vagabondage, to sex aggressions, and so on. The point is that there must be a concatenation of confronting pattern and differential response to this specific pattern, assisted usually by carriers or purveyors of the pattern.

The job before the criminologists of the future is to discover the atomic strength of the carrier of patterns and the explosive charge of differential response. This can be done most readily by attempting to get tests which can measure the amount of emotional instability a person has, the amount of emotional disturbance, the amount of tension, the amount of perverseness. Just how to measure the compellingness of the pattern presented by such and such carrier or car-

riers is a task which must face the sociological researcher just as the former task faces the psychological workers in criminology.

WALTER C. RECKLESS
Professor of Sociology
Ohio State University
Columbus, Ohio

BIBLIOGRAPHY

Reckless, Walter C., *The Etiology of Delinquent and Criminal Behavior*, Social Science Research Council, Bulletin 50, New York, 1943.
——, *Criminal Behavior*, New York, 1940.
Schmid, Calvin F., *Social Saga of Two Cities*, Minneapolis, 1937.
Sellin, Thorsten, *Research Memorandum on Crime in the Depression*, Social Science Research Council, New York, 1937.
——, *Culture Conflict and Crime*, Social Science Research Council, Bulletin 41, New York, 1938.
Sutherland, Edwin H., *Principles of Criminology*, Chicago, 1939.
Taft, Donald, *Criminology*, New York, 1942.
Uniform Crime Reports, Federal Bureau of Investigation, United States Department of Justice, Washington, D. C., vol. 1–15.
Van Vechten, Courtland C., Differential Criminal Case Mortality in Selected Jurisdictions, *American Sociological Review*, Vol. 7, 1942, pp. 833–39.
Warner, W. Lloyd and Lunt, Paul S., *Social Life of a Modern Community*, New Haven, 1941, pp. 373–77.

SODOMY. Kraft-Ebing, the distinguished authority on sex, used the term *sodomy* to cover: (1) *bestiality*, the crime against nature, the "unnatural" crime of intercourse with an animal; and (2) *pederasty* or *buggery*, which signifies anal coitus between men. The Penal Law of the State of New York provides that, "A person who carnally knows in any manner any animal or bird; or carnally knows any male or female person by the anus or by or with the mouth; or voluntarily submits to such carnal knowledge; or attempts sexual intercourse with a dead body is guilty of *sodomy* and is punishable with imprisonment for not more than twenty years." Any sexual penetration, however, slight, is sufficient to complete this crime.

Sodomy is very often practised in prisons when the inmates denied contacts with persons of the opposite sex, turn to homosexual practices and other sexual perversions.

Besides sodomy, there are many other perversions for which a person may be arrested and sentenced to prison. These include various forms of sexual *sadism* and *masochism*, *indecent exposure* or *exhibitionism*, *incest*, and the various forms of sexual behavior which fall into categories considered abnormal, if not psychopathic.

BIBLIOGRAPHY

Gilbert, F. B., *Criminal Law and Practice of the State of New York*, Matthew Bender and Co., 1935.
Krafft-Ebing, R., *Psychopathia Sexualis*, F. A. Davis Co., 1893.
Pollens, Bertram, *The Sex Criminal*, Emerson Books, Inc., 1938.

STATISTICS OF CRIME.

The Value of a Comprehensive System of Criminal Statistics

The availability of official and trustworthy statistics of crime, criminals, criminal courts and penal and correctional institutions, is the beginning of wisdom in the administration of criminal justice, in the opinion of the National Commission on Law Observance and Enforcement.[1] The value of criminal statistics in society's struggle with crime is compared by the Commission with that of the balance sheet and profit-and-loss statement in a corporation's struggles for profits. Neither the balance sheet nor the profit-and-loss statement show why the business has been successful, yet no corporation would think of operating without them. The balance sheet and the profit-and-loss statement are for the corporation the indispensable tools of knowledge for any community that is attempting to reduce its crime and improve its administration of criminal justice.

Three functions have been assigned to criminal statistics by the Commission:

1. To provide the basic data for estimating the prevailing volume and trends of criminality. How much crime is there? What is its character? Is crime increasing or decreasing? What particular types of crime show increase or decrease?

2. To serve as an accounting system for all the governmental processes called into being by the phenomenon of crime. The whole process of governmental reaction to an illegal act from the time of arrest to committal to an institution and eventual liberation must be conceived in its entirety and all its operations must be recorded statistically in order to give a basis of judgment on the effectiveness of any part. The functioning of an institution involved in one phase of the process finds its reflection in the character of the work of an agency performing a different phase. Consistent and accurate records of the entire process would allow responsibility for failure to function properly to be correctly allocated.

3. To indicate broadly some of the causative factors productive of delinquency and provide a composite picture of the types of individuals who become delinquent; and to point out significant tendencies as to the general lines of investigations of nonstatistical character which must be made in order to determine the precise importance of these factors.

Principal Objectives of Criminal Agencies Statistics

Preliminary to delineating in the briefest manner possible the principal objectives of criminal agencies statistics, it may be opportune to recall what Dr. Leon C. Marshall has said in this connection: "There is, of course, no possibility of thinking through in advance all the problems which will arise on such a task. And, of course, there is no possibility whatever that such a task can be performed and then stand for all time—or even for any great length of time. The details should be worked out, not only in terms of its purposes, but also in full recognition of the character of the operation concerned and the personnel available. The objectives must continually be re-defined, and the details of any such system must change as social goals change and as social organizations to accomplish those goals change." [2]

[1] *Report on Criminal Statistics*, National Commission on Law Observance and Enforcement, Washington, 1931.

[2] In this connection see the following: *Instructions for Compiling Criminal Statistics—A Manual for the Use of Penal Institutions, Police Departments, Courts, Prosecutors, and*

With this in mind we present here only in broad outlines the chief purposes of statistics in the different fields of the administration of criminal justice.

Police. Statistics on the work of the various police agencies are extremely important because they constitute the primary source of information concerning the extent and nature of delinquency in any community. Statistics of the number of offenses known to the police and other crime detective agencies are regarded as the best-known index of the changing crime situation. Statistics of the initial process of law enforcement—complaints, investigations, arrests, prosecution, etc.—makes it possible to follow the cases "through all the intricacies of the later procedure so as to obtain a dynamic record of the work of all the agencies involved."

In addition police statistics will allow an evaluation of the effectiveness of the organization of the apprehending units.

Prosecution. Statistics concerning the prosecution of offenders should reveal the number and character dealt with by the prosecution, distinguishing between those in which prosecution was instituted and those on which no action was taken and the reasons why they were eliminated. Statistics of prosecution will afford a picture of the kind of law enforcement a particular community is obtaining.

Courts. Statistics concerning the courts should account for the general work and

Parole and Probation Agencies, U. S. Bureau of the Census, Washington, 1927; *Developments in Criminal Statistics in the Past Decade* by C. E. Gehlke and *State Bureaus of Criminal Statistics* by Thorsten Sellin, both printed in the Proceedings of the American Prison Congress, 1931; *Ohio Criminal Statistics, 1931—An Experiment in Methods and Techniques of State Reporting* by an associated group from the Institute of Law and the Ohio Institute, Alfred Bettman, W. C. Jamison, L. C. Marshall and R. E. Miles, The Johns Hopkins Press, Baltimore, 1932; and *A System of Criminal Judicial Statistics for California* by Ronal H. Beattie, University California Press, Berkeley.

See also the stimulating chapter on *The Blindness of Justice* in *Crime and Justice* by Sheldon Glueck, Professor of Criminology, Harvard Law School, Little, Brown, and Company, Boston, 1936.

practices of the various courts in the disposition of criminal cases who are before the courts on indictment, information, or affidavit for trial, and the penal treatment accorded.

It will thus be possible to have a statistical record of the number found not guilty and found guilty and the type of sentence imposed upon the latter. Questions such as these might be answered: "How many defendants were tried by jury, or by the court without a jury, and with what result? How many defendants were convicted? Were convictions on plea of guilty or by means of trial? What type of sentence was imposed on the convicted offender?"

Probation. Statistics on probation should show the number and proportion of individuals before the courts who are placed on probation; and should illuminate the whole probation procedure under which the execution of the sentence is deferred; and control over the convicted offender continued, making the final disposition dependent upon the outcome of the probationary period.

Jails and Workhouses. Statistics on local penal and correctional institutions are of considerable importance because of the strategic place which the jail and workhouse occupy in the penal system and the enormous numbers that pass through their gates. Statistics should show the number of persons detained, the reason for their detention, and the length of time they are incarcerated. These figures would reveal much concerning delays in justice, over-crowding, the practice of punishing those unable to pay a fine and the unsatisfactory procedure of keeping witnesses imprisoned for extensive periods.

State Penal and Correctional Institutions. Statistics on state penal and correctional institutions will reveal the facts concerning the sentencing practices in relation to time served, methods of release, and afford a general insight into penal administration.

Statistics on the commitments to state penal and correctional institutions measure the number of crimes punished by imprisonment or death within the period covered; and special commitment tabulations with reference to geographic distribution, sex, age, race, etc., indicate the relative extent to which members of various communities and classes have committed those offenses which were followed by convictions and imprisonment.

Through the classification system now in vogue in penal and correctional institutions of progressive states a great amount of social, medical, psychological and psychiatric data is becoming available on the personal and social characteristics of the individual delinquent, and causative factors in antisocial and criminal behavior.

Parole. Parole statistics should permit an evaluation of the functioning of this method of penal treatment. Freedom on parole provides an adjustment period for the prisoner after his release. The purpose of such adjustment period is to facilitate his return to normal community life. Parole is granted on the supposition that the parolee can properly be submitted to this regime of supervised freedom without reverting again to crime. Parole statistics should then inform us how far this supposition is realized and what proportion and types of individuals on parole do and do not achieve adjustment under parole supervision.

Juvenile Delinquents. Statistics on juvenile delinquents should receive separate consideration in the general program of criminal statistics since the present tendency is entirely to separate juveniles from adult offenders in court proceedings, to provide distinct institutions for them and to devise newer and more informal methods of dealing with the individual juvenile delinquent.

The statistics of the juvenile court and other unofficial agencies dealing with juvenile delinquents, as well as institutions for juvenile delinquents, should show the extent and nature of the problems of the individuals dealt with, the volume and kinds of services rendered as a part of the treatment process, and the extent to which these efforts have been effective.

Statistics compiled should further point out significant factors which contribute to the causation of juvenile delinquency and throw light upon the possibilities of applying corrective and preventive measures.

STATISTICS IN PREDICTION OF PAROLE AND PROBATION OUTCOME

The quest for knowledge regarding the personal behavior and social adjustment of individuals in the community subsequent to penal and related treatment has been of long standing. In such studies statistics play a very important part, of course.

The fundamental questions for which reliable answers are being sought include: "What happens to the former inmates of our prisons and reformatories? What percentage of them become law-abiding citizens? How many return to a life of crime and vice? What portion of them change from aggressive and dangerous criminals to misdemeanants, vagrants, chronic alcoholics and the like? What types of offenders persist in serious criminality, what types become minor offenders, what types give up their lives of crime? And at what ages do these changes occur? Is imprisonment a preventive of recidivism? How, in the light of human grist and human product of the mills of justice can we improve our methods of peno-correctional treatment?" [3]

Extensive work on the prediction of criminal behavior has been done by doctors Sheldon and Eleanor T. Glueck. "Not only are correlations of the make-up and early conditioning of different classes of offenders with their reaction to various types of treatment, of general scientific interest in gauging the efficacy of various corrective regimes, but they serve as the basis of prognostic instru-

[3] See *After-Conduct of Discharged Offenders* by Doctors Sheldon and Eleanor T. Glueck, Macmillian and Company, London, 1945.
See also article on Testing the Work of the Prison, by Dr. C. E. Gehlke in *Prisons of Tomorrow, The Annals of the American Academy of Political and Social Science,* September, 1931; article on Prediction of Criminality, by Michael Hakeem in *Federal Probation,* July-September, 1945; and paper on Evaluating the Results of Probation, by Bennet Mead, Annual Conference of National Probation Association, May, 1932.
Exhaustive statistical material on the parole conduct of nearly 60,000 individuals conditionally released from state penal and correctional institutions during the period January 1, 1928 and December 31, 1935, will be found in Volume IV, Parole, *The Attorney General's Survey of Release Procedures,* Washington, 1939.

ments that give promise of usefulness in the administration of criminal justice. We have evolved a method of doing this which we believe to be reasonably calculated to replace guess-work with sound knowledge, in the sentencing and releasing procedures of courts and parole boards."

Efforts Toward Standardization of Criminal Statistics

It may not be amiss to sketch very briefly efforts to standardize crime statistics that have been made in the United States during the last three decades or so.

The American Prison Association has had continuously functioning Committees on Statistics of Crime in its long career. At the annual meeting held in Indianapolis in October, 1913, the Chairman of the Committee on Statistics of Crime rendered an unusually able and incisive report on the subject under the title "The Ideals of Prison Reports."

At the annual meeting of the American Institute of Criminal Law and Criminology held in Indianapolis in September, 1920, Dr. Horatio M. Pollock as Chairman of the Committee on Statistics presented a report entitled "A Statistical System for the Use of Institutions for Criminals and Delinquents." The Committee remarked that "the lack of standard classification of crimes and of criminals has been one of the primary obstacles in the way of good statistics in criminology." The Committee felt that it had made a somewhat new approach as may be seen from the following: "In attempting to classify criminals the committee asked itself this question: What characteristics of the criminal are of most importance from the standpoint of prison administration and the welfare of the prisoner? There could be but one answer. The mental status is the primary consideration. This fact has been recognized in numerous special studies made in prisons and correctional institutions, but prior to this year had not formed a part of any statistical system dealing with criminals or delinquents." In 1924, Sam Bass Warner and Sanford Bates published their pamphlet "Information Concerning Adult Male Criminals Which Should Be Published by Reformatories, Penitentiaries, and State Prisons."

In order to secure comparable figures for its statistical reports on the police work in the United States, the Federal Bureau of Investigation of the United States Department of Justice has published a "Uniform Crime Reporting Handbook" for the use of law-enforcement officials and agencies containing suggestions for the preparation of uniform crime reports.

Standard Classifications of Offenses and Prisoners

An important conference to consider the feasibility of a standard classification of offenses for nation-wide use in the entire field of criminal statistics was held by leaders in this field in Washington, D. C., in December, 1931, and in its report to the Bureau of Investigation of the Department of Justice and to the Bureau of Census of the Department of Commerce it stated that the offense classification presented "may with propriety be termed the basic classification in all three branches of criminal statistics, police, judicial, and penal. A standard offense classification will not only make possible integration of these three branches of criminal statistics; it will also facilitate comparability of data from state to state, eventually promoting the national publication of comprehensive criminal statistics."

The standard classification recommended was adopted by the two Federal agencies mentioned above, and is used consistently throughout the Federal reports in which criminal statistics appear and has found general acceptance by state and local agencies compiling criminal statistics.[4]

Because of the continued interest for statistical information on the mental characteristics of delinquents the Committee on Classification of the American Prison Association issued a "Classification Handbook and Statistical Guide" which provided for a uniform "classification for the diagnosis of offenders on the basis of personality and behavior reaction together with intellectual de-

[4] *A Standard Classification of Offenses for Criminal Statistics. Adopted in 1932 for Use in the Bureau of the Census of the Department of Commerce, and the Bureau of Investigation, of the Department of Justice,* Washington, 1933.

viation, neurological and seriological abnormality; with the further provision for its adaptability to court and institutional statistical purposes."

CRIME CONFERENCES AND CRIMINAL STATISTICS

The subject of Criminal Statistics has been a topic which appeared at practically every crime conference, of which quite a few have been held in recent years, both nationally and locally.

A great deal of attention to criminal statistics was paid at The Attorney General's Conference on Crime, held in Washington, D. C. in December, 1934 and the gist of the thinking was incorporated in a paper entitled the "Importance of Criminal Statistics" by Professor Thorsten Sellin of the University of Pennsylvania.

At the most recent national crime conference—The National Conference on Prevention and Control of Juvenile Delinquency— held in Washington, D. C. in October 1946, the importance of "Statistics" in efforts to prevent and control juvenile delinquency was clearly recognized.[5]

The Conference saw the need "for the over-all planning of recording and reporting procedures so as to facilitate the correlation of police, juvenile-court, probation, and other delinquency statistics and also to make it easier to interrelate delinquency statistics with other social, economic, educational, and health statistics."

The report endeavored to classify delinquency statistics into three groups: 1. Data on the numbers and characteristics of children dealt with as delinquents; 2. Data on the character of and circumstances surrounding delinquent acts; 3. Data on socioeconomic and psychological factors involved in delinquency.

The Conference concluded that "in view of the lack of correlation between the statistical activities of the many groups active in the field of juvenile-delinquency procedures, and the areas and fields still inadequately covered, the report recommends that a Fed-

[5] The National Conference on Prevention and Control of Juvenile Delinquency. *Summary of Recommendations for Action,* Department of Justice, Washington, 1947.

eral inter-agency committee be created to study, in cooperation with appropriate State and local governmental agencies and voluntary associations, the statistics now being prepared by such agencies and associations, and to make concrete recommendations in connection therewith."

CRIME COMMISSIONS AND CRIMINAL STATISTICS

Crime Commissions early realized that "statistics regarding crime and criminals were difficult to obtain and were not centralized." [6]

The crime-commission movement, which, starting in Chicago in 1917, has led to the establishment in several cities and in some States of citizen's crime commissions, consisting of representative citizens working with private nongovernmental funds to maintain law-enforcement standards at a high level, has also contributed to the development of uniform crime statistics. These commissions have found it necessary to integrate statistics from police, courts, and correctional institutions and agencies in order to obtain a complete picture of crime problems and their treatment. Their studies of crime conditions have added greatly to information of the subject and have pointed clearly to the need for having access to reliable, officially compiled uniform crime statistics.

CRIMINAL JUSTICE AGENCIES COMPILING STATISTICS

The work of compiling comprehensive criminal statistics in the United States has been carried furthest by the Federal Government, although considerable progress in developing adequate crime statistics programs has also been made in several states and in some subordinate governmental units.

Police. A nationally-centralized system of police statistics has been carried on by the Federal Bureau of Investigation, United States Department of Justice since 1930, the reporting system having been originally formulated by the Committee on Uniform Crime Records of the International Association of Chiefs of Police.

[6] *Crime Commissions in the United States* by Virgil W. Peterson, Chicago Crime Commission, 1945.

The statistical information published in "Uniform Crime Reports for the United States and its Possessions, covers offenses known to the police, offenses cleared by arrest, and persons found guilty, persons released, data compiled from fingerprint cards as to sex and age, police employee data, etc. The latest report for the year 1946 contains figures on the police activities of 1,078 cities or towns with a population of more than 62,000,000. As to coverage the report states that "in addition to the 3,168 city and village police departments which forwarded crime reports during 1946, one or more reports were received during the year from 2,319 sheriffs and State police organizations and from 12 agencies in Territories and possessions of the United States, making a grand total of 5,499 agencies contributing crime reports to the FBI during 1946."

Criminal Courts. The formation of a competent system of judicial criminal statistics was one of the endeavors of the Institute of Law of Johns Hopkins University, under the direction of Leon C. Marshall. The results of these endeavors were embodied in a series of publications, including "Comparative Judicial Criminal Statistics: Ohio and Maryland—A Comparison of Trial Court Statistics for 1930;" "Ohio Criminal Statistics, 1931—An Experiment in Methods and Techniques of State Reporting;" "Comparative Judicial Criminal Statistics: Six States, 1931—The Courts of General Criminal Jurisdiction of Ohio, New Jersey, Iowa, Maryland, Rhode Island and Delaware;" and "Judicial Criminal Statistics in 43 Ohio Counties, 1937—The Ohio Experiment in Individual Case Reporting of Criminal Dispositions in Common Pleas Courts."

The collection of judicial criminal statistics on a national scale began to be undertaken by the United States Census Bureau in 1931. The annual reports contain statistical information concerning defendants eliminated without conviction and defendants convicted, method of disposition, and method of conviction, type of sentence, etc.

State statistics on the current work of the criminal courts, usually those of general criminal jurisdiction, are being compiled by judicial councils, now established in one form or another in a number of states.[7]

Criminal court statistics will also be found in the reports of the various crime surveys made in various sections of the country between 1920 and 1932, such as The Cleveland Crime Survey, The Missouri Crime Survey, The Report of the Minnesota Crime Commission, the Illinois Crime Survey and Crime and the Georgia Courts.[8] As stated by the United States Census Bureau, "these surveys served as the developing and testing ground for statistics on criminal administration. They demonstrated that by accounting methods much could be learned about the administrative agencies enforcing the criminal law, the allocation of responsibility for the various dispositions made of criminal cases, and the relative efficiency of their work."

Penal and Correctional Institutions. Among the most important publications giving the results of statistical inquiries on a national scale are those issued by the United States Bureau of the Census. Statistics of some sort relating to crime or criminals have been collected by the Bureau since 1850, dealing largely with the population of penal and correctional institutions, however. As explained by Dr. Leon E. Truesdell, of the Census Bureau, this may have been partly the result of historical accident, but made fundamentally because "the facts set forth in the prison records were simpler and more definite than most of the others. A man is committed to prison on a certain date, for a certain crime, under a specific sentence, remains a certain time, and is discharged on another certain date. By contrast, a case entered on a court docket may travel any one of a dozen paths before it is finally disposed of, many of which admit of vague and indefinite recordings and present unexpected combinations."[9]

[7] See Review of Judicial Council Reports in *Journal of the American Judicature Society,* August, 1938.
[8] For details see Criminal Justice Surveys Analysis, by Alfred Bettman in the *Report on Prosecution,* National Commission on Law Observance and Enforcement, 1931.
[9] The Problem of Collecting and Standardizing Statistics of Crime in 48 Sovereign States, *Proceedings of the American Statistical Association,* March, 1928.

The publications of the United States Census Bureau include:

"The Prisoners Antecedents—Statistics Concerning the Previous Life of Offenders Committed in 1923 to State and Federal Prisons and Reformatories; Supplementary to 'Prisoners: 1923,'" containing data on the place where the crime occurred; residence of prisoner and in relation to place of crime; time in state and county; educational status; age and marital condition; family status; age of leaving home; earnings; employment status; institutional history and war service.

"County and City Jails—Prisoners in Jails and Other Penal Institutions Under County or Municipal Jurisdiction, 1933—Statistics of Prisoners Present January 1, 1933, and Prisoners Received and Discharged from January 1 to June 30, 1933.

"Prisoners in State and Federal Prisons and Reformatories, 1944."

Federal Crime Statistics. During the last few years the Federal Bureau of Prisons, under the direction of the late Bennet Mead, has developed a body of important statistical information bearing on the federal system of criminal justice, including: An individual reporting system in the federal courts; a case-record system in federal penal and correctional institutions which will ultimately be utilized to evaluate the effectiveness of institutional treatment; probation statistics based upon the individual reports of probationer received for supervision and passed from supervision to know the number and types of investigations made by probation officers, the number and types of contacts of probation officers and their charges, and handicaps to rehabilitation which affect probationers.[10]

Juvenile Delinquents. Statistics concerning juvenile delinquents are compiled principally by the United States Children's Bureau. Beginning in 1927 efforts have been directed

[10] See *Federal Prisons 1944—A Review of the Work of the Federal Bureau of Prisons During the Year Ending June, 1944, including Statistics of Federal Prisoners and of Federal Parole Selection and Probation,* 1945.

toward the development of uniform juvenile court statistics on a nation-wide basis. In the early years of the activity individual courts were admitted to the reporting area without regard to the size of the community served. As the program developed, however, the expense of direct federal contact with small courts handling only a few children's cases during the year came to be disproportionately great, and the policy was adopted of gradually limiting direct reports to the Children's Bureau to courts serving areas of 100,000 or more population; and of cooperating with state agencies which would assume responsibility for collecting statistics from all courts within their states and send summarized reports to the Bureau.

The latest published report is: "Juvenile-Court Statistics 1945" containing statistical information on the number of juvenile delinquency-cases disposed of by 374 juvenile courts in the United States.

Statistics on the institutional care of the juvenile delinquents in the United States have been compiled by the United States Census Bureau. A fairly recent report, is entitled "Children Under Care of the State Training Schools for Socially Maladjusted Children."

An interesting study on "Institutional Treatment of Delinquent Boys" was published by the United States Children's Bureau in 1935. It was undertaken because "it is agreed that the primary objective of institutional treatment for delinquent boys is so to reeducate and redirect those boys as to enable them to return to normal social living free of supervision, it becomes pertinent to inquire to what degree existing institutions are achieving success in approaching that goal. A need to appraise the results of institutional treatment of delinquent boys in terms of fact exists."

A number of studies of delinquency areas concerned with the geographic distribution of the individual juvenile delinquents, by place of residence within the city, have been made during the last few years. Such data are regarded as important to localize the delinquency problem and to serve as a basis for further analysis of the relationship between types of community situations and juvenile delinquency.[11]

STATE INTEGRATION OF CRIMINAL STATISTICS

Crime has been regarded as predominately a state problem, and it is of paramount importance, therefore, that each state know the magnitude of the crime problem within its border and the methods of dealing with it. The protection of individual interests in life and physical integrity, in property, and in freedom; the ordering of human conduct so that it least infringes on social security; the protection of various social interests, are primarily objects of state concern.

Since there is general recognition that it is desirable to bring within the covers of a single state report the statistics of all the state's agencies of criminal justice requisite to the presentation of a thoroughly integrated picture of the administration of criminal justice as a whole, it would seem that the first step would be to induce each state body supervising a given branch of criminal justice to concentrate its efforts in having the individual agency extend and perfect its statistical work to conform to nationally agreed-upon standards in the collection procedure, the use of offense classification and statistical methods employed.

Such a program of integration is proposed in the report on "A State System of Criminal Statistics and Information" issued by The Ohio Institute in 1932, which, "is offered as a contribution toward the development of a more accurate and adequate system of state criminal statistics. While consideration is given primarily to Ohio, many of the problems involved arise also in other states, to the solution of which it is hoped that the present discussion will prove helpful. In the present stage of comparatively rapid development in this field in this country, further advances will doubtless before long supersede some of the views and suggestions herein set forth; toward some of these ad-

vances, however, this report may serve as a stepping stone." [12]

The experience of the two States—Massachusetts and New York—which have done more than any others to compile uniform statistics concerning crime problems within their own borders, might well be reviewed in connection with the establishment of uniform crime statistics on a State-wide basis.

The oldest State program for the uniform reporting of crime statistics is that carried on in Massachusetts. Some phases of this program date back to Colonial times. It has been carried on in substantially its present form, with reports being furnished by local police, jails, prosecuting agencies, courts, and correctional institutions and agencies, for nearly 70 years. The Massachusetts reports probably constitute the best source of over-all information as to crime and its treatment over a prolonged period of any data available in an American State. Moreover, for most of the past two decades, the annual compilations have been supplemented by a commentary written by the distinguished criminologist Dr. Sam Bass Warner.

The other major State-wide experiment in uniform crime statistics is that being conducted by the New York State commissioner of correction. The New York statute requiring the collection of crime statistics differs from the proposed Uniform Criminal Statistics Act chiefly in the fact that the administrative responsibility rests with the commissioner of corrections rather than with the attorney general and in a few other technical details.

The New York law calls upon the "division of criminal identification records and statistics" of the department of correction to prepare an annual report "which shall set forth the number and nature of all crimes reported or known to the police, of persons arrested, of persons tried by the criminal courts, and the action taken with relation thereto," together with a long catalog of other types of information about crime, criminals, and the treatment of offenders.

[11] For details concerning such studies see *Social Factors in Juvenile Delinquency*, by Clifford R. Shaw and Henry D. McKay, in *Report on the Causes of Crime* (vol. II), National Commission Law Observance and Enforcement, 1931.

[12] *A State System of Criminal Statistics and Information—Consideration of technical problems involved with special reference to Ohio*, The Ohio Institute, Columbus, Ohio, 1932.

AGENCIES OF CRIMINAL JUSTICE CONCERNED IN COMPILATIONS OF CRIME STATISTICS

Agencies of Criminal Justice		Municipal	County	State	Federal
POLICE		Local Police Constables	Sheriffs County Police	State Police Agencies for Enforcement of Special Criminal Statutes	U. S. Marshals Federal Bureau of Investigation Other Departmental Enforcement Units
PROSECUTION		Municipal Attorneys	County Prosecutors	Attorneys General	U. S. Attorney General U. S. Attorneys
CRIMINAL COURTS	Arraignment and Trial	Police Courts Recorders Courts Justices of Peace Magistrates Courts	Courts of General Criminal Jurisdiction	Circuit Courts	U. S. Commissioners U. S. District Courts
	Appeals	None	Courts for Appeals from Municipal Courts	Courts for Appeals from County Criminal Courts and Courts of Last Resort	U. S. Circuit Courts of Appeals
JUVENILE COURTS AND AGENCIES		Municipal Courts with Juvenile Jurisdiction Municipal Children's Bureaus	County Juvenile Courts	State Juvenile Commissions	U. S. District Courts District of Columbia Juvenile Court
PROBATION		Municipal Probation Departments	County Probation Departments	State Probation Departments	Federal Probation System under the Administrative Office of the U. S. Courts
PENAL AND CORRECTIONAL INSTITUTIONS—ADULTS		Municipal Jails and Lockups	County Jails County Workhouses County Penitentiaries	State Penal and Correctional Institutions	Federal Detention Headquarters, and Penal and Correctional Institutions
INSTITUTIONS—JUVENILE		Municipal Detention and Child Study Centers Training Schools	County Detention and Child Study Centers Training Schools	State Child Study Centers Training Schools	Federal Juvenile Training Schools
PAROLE		Municipal Parole Departments	County Parole Departments	State Parole Boards and Departments	U. S. Board of Parole

UNIFORM CRIMINAL STATISTICS ACT

One of the latest efforts in the direction of securing uniform criminal statistics is a proposal made in the fall of 1944 by a Special Committee on Uniform Criminal Statistics of the National Conference of Commissioners on Uniform State Laws embodied in "An Act Concerning Criminal Statistics and to Make Uniform the Law with Reference Thereto." [13]

The proposed Act provides for the establishment of a State bureau of criminal statistics. One of the bureau's prime duties would be to prepare an annual report containing statistics showing (1) the number and the types of offenses known to the public authorities, (2) the personal and social characteristics of criminals and delinquents, and (3) the administrative action taken by law-enforcement, judicial, penal, and correctional agencies in dealing with criminals and delinquents. It is expected that the report will "include statistics that are comparable with national criminal statistics published by federal agencies. . . ."

It would be the duty of the director of the bureau to "so interpret such statistics and so present the information that it may be of value in guiding the legislature and those in charge of the apprehension, prosecution and treatment of criminals and delinquents, or those concerned with the prevention of crime and delinquency."

Difficulties in the Way of Uniform Crime Statistics. Many difficulties have to be overcome before a uniform crime statistics program can be set in motion. These difficulties stem from the doctrine of "separation of powers" which has made the American system of criminal justice extremely complex. To be successful, a plan to unify crime statistics must take all these obstacles into account. It must deal with all the individual agencies which take part in the administration of justice without superimposing any new forms of control which may conflict with the conceptions of the administrative heads

[13] For details see *Report of the Special Committee on Uniform Criminal Statistics including Tentative Draft (of Uniform Criminal Statistics Act),* Kingsland Van Winkle, Chairman, September, 1944.

of the agencies expected to provide statistical information. It must achieve uniformity in statistical reporting without arbitrary regulations which fail to recognize legitimate differences in administrative procedure and public policy.

The chart on page 486 listing the major types of agencies which constitute sources of criminal statistics illustrates the complexity of the task of unifying criminal statistics on a State-wide basis. Comparatively few of these agencies are closely related to one another in the structure of government. Some agencies are parts of the executive branch of government, others are attached to the judiciary. Of the county and local agencies, comparatively few have ties to any State supervisory department and, when State supervision is involved, the relationship is to different State departments. Experience has shown the impracticability of assigning responsibility for the collection of statistics on crime and delinquency to a central statistical agency remote from the administrative agency directly responsible for the operations to which the statistics relate.

Compilation of statistics is intimately tied up with administration. If an advanced administrative and preventive program is to be drawn up and carried out, it must be based upon information gathered in the day-by-day experience of the operating agency itself.

The compilation of criminal statistics definitely requires specialized knowledge of the actual practices of the agencies administering criminal justice, not mere knowledge of statistical problems applying to the field of criminal justice; therefore, individual agencies must continue to compile and interpret statistics. The research personnel who compile and interpret the data possess the requisite familiarity with the tangible and intangible elements which cause variations in statistical findings or which conceal compensating differences.

Moreover, the administrator, having the responsibility under the law to manage the affairs of his department, must have supervision over the compilation of statistics so as to secure quickly and comprehensively the statistical tools he needs. He cannot be put into the position of having to explain his needs to an outside agency, and await its pleasure in compiling and interpreting the statistics he needs immediately.

Organizing a Uniform Crime Statistics Program. To achieve complete unity in the compilation of statistics dealing with crime and criminals in the broadest sense within the State and in relation to other States and the Federal Government, and to bring within the covers of a single State report the statistics of all the State's agencies of criminal justice requisite to the presentation of a thoroughly integrated picture of the administration of criminal justice as a whole, it would seem advisable that the task be assigned to a State board or commission independent of all existing State departments. Members of the board or commission would be representative of the leaders in the field of criminal justice and the public generally and appointed by the Governor with the consent of the Senate to serve long, overlapping terms.

This type of interdepartmental board or commission has been successfully used in other types of public service where the functions to be performed cut across conventional lines of departmental authority. Recent illustrations include the recommendations made by Governor Dewey to the New York legislature calling for the establishment of this type of youth service council to combat juvenile delinquency and the proposals pending in the New Jersey legislature to provide for the regulations of problems arising from the importation of migrant labor into the state.

Experience has shown that statistics on crime and delinquency must be built from the ground up. The agencies which administer criminal justice will inevitably require statistics for their own use. They will compile these statistics themselves and use them in their own day-to-day operations. The development of a uniform system depends upon awakening the appreciation of these agencies of the value of being able to compare their statistics with those of similar agencies or to see how their operations fit into the total process of criminal justice.

Included in the working plan of the State board or commission on crime statistics con-

ceived as a service agency, would be the development of the basic records to yield the standard statistical data requisite for the particular agency of criminal justice, including the formulation of standard classifications of offenses, procedural steps, sentences, and dispositions, and concerning the characteristics of persons dealt with by agencies of criminal justice. It would also involve the development of means of collecting statistical information from the basic records as maintained by the participating agencies, determining their relationship to one another, and suggesting analytical procedures so that the unified reports will be meaningful and significant to the participating agencies, to policy-making bodies, and to the public in general.

One of the first steps of the board or commission might well be to induce each State body supervising a given branch agency of criminal justice to concentrate its efforts in having the individual agency extend and perfect its statistical work to conform to nationally agreed-upon standards in the collection procedure, the use of offense classifications, and statistical methods employed.

Along with the efforts of the various State supervisory organizations to standardize and improve the existing record keeping and statistical system of its component agencies, definite plans should be made for a systematic discussion as to how we may best obtain the necessary interrelationship between the different agencies compiling criminal statistics.

The board or commission would have authority to appoint a director, chosen on the basis of professional qualification as determined by the State civil service commission, who should hold office at the pleasure of the State board or commission on crime statistics. The director should have thoroughgoing training in statistics, extensive specialized experience in the compilation of crime statistics and in criminological research, and have proved administrative and executive ability. He must be a man of first-rate abilities. He must have vision and capacity for translating his understanding of crime problems into practical methods of compiling and interpreting statistics, and be able to instill confidence among the agencies which provide the raw data used in the central bureau. If the person engaged as director does not have these qualities, the resulting compilations will all too likely be lifeless and devoid of any practical value as a guide to the better handling of crime problems.

A staff sufficient in number to carry on the duties assigned to the commission should be appointed by the director, subject to authorization by the commission and in compliance with State civil service procedures. Aiding the board or commission would be a technical advisory committee composed of representatives of all the agencies expected to compile and furnish criminal statistics. The function of the technical advisory committee would be to help the director set up an organization and formulate procedures which would lead to the presentation of a thoroughly integrated statistical picture of the administration of justice as a whole.

This proposal outlines a series of steps by which uniform criminal statistics can be assembled by the autonomous collaboration of the State, county, and local agencies which are responsible for the administration of criminal justice. It provides safeguards to assure technical competence on the professional side and able direction through interdepartmental cooperation.

International Criminal Statistics. The problem of securing international agreement on statistics on crime had been taken up by the International Penal and Penitentiary Commission as early as 1915. The mixed commission for international criminal statistics appointed by the International Statistical Institute and the International Penal and Penitentiary Commission presented a Model Plan in 1932 which was considered necessary "in the interest of a gradual harmonization of the criminal statistics of the various countries" to include the items to be considered in the international inquiry and the manner in which the statistics were to be presented. "For this purpose, the publications on criminal statistics in 40 countries were subjected

to a thorough examination, with the assistance of official information and private publication, in respect of the statistical units and the more or less numerous objects of the inquiry (in particular, the individual characteristics of the condemned persons)." [14]

EMIL FRANKEL, *Director*
Division of Statistics and Research
Dept. of Institutions and Agencies
Trenton, New Jersey

SUICIDE. Suicide is defined as the intentional taking of one's own life. At common law suicide was a crime, and the consequence was the forfeiture of the real and personal property of the person who committed suicide. However, most modern statutes do not impose any forfeiture for suicide because of the impossibility of reaching the successful perpetrator. The law nevertheless regards suicide as a grave public wrong. For example, in New York State, suicide is not a crime although attempted suicide is. Thus a court ruled that in the case of an insurance policy, which is void if the insured dies in the commission or attempted commission of a crime, the policy is enforcible where the insured commits suicide.

According to the Penal Law of the State of New York, "a person who wilfully, in any manner, advises, encourages, abets, or assists another person in taking the latter's life, is guilty of *manslaughter* in the first degree." Abetting and advising *an attempt* at suicide, is a *felony.* It is no defense to a prosecution under either of the above provisions, that the person who took, or attempted to take his own life, was not a person deemed capable of committing crime.

BIBLIOGRAPHY

Gilbert, F. B., *Criminal Law and Practice of the State of New York,* Matthew Bender and Co., 1935.

[14] *Proceedings of the International Penal and Penitentiary Commission,* Session held in Berne, August, 1946, Staempfli & Cie., Berne, 1946.

T

THERAPY. When one considers the appalling cost in lives and money and effort which society each year dedicates to the psychopath, it becomes a matter for amazement to discover how little of all the voluminous writing and research has been devoted to the treatment of these difficult, deviating personalities. Most of the work in the past has been concerned with the delicate task of separating the disorder from other psychiatric diagnostic groups; this requiring precise if boresome delineation of its characteristics along the classical lines of etiology, symptomatology, typology, incidence, course and prognosis. Moreover, the diagnosis has been a fertile field for verbal battles relating to its distinctness as a clinical entity, its status as a diagnostic class, and its phenomenological relationships. Lacking, until recently, a substantive core of hard, unalterable facts upon which to procede with objectivity in solving the riddle of psychopathy, it has been difficult for investigators and practitioners to grip the problem in such a way as to subject it to experimental or clinical manipulation.

Fortunately, we no longer need be troubled by the tiresome question, Who or what is a psychopath? We have come a long way from the obtuse kraepelinian formulations of an earlier day; and the emergent concept of psychopathy as a "respectable" division of the so-called mental disorders undergoes commendable clarity as we trace it from the adjectivally oriented followers of Kahn through to the depth psychologists and the recording-instrument-cum-test-tube experimentalists.

This is not to say, of course, that an era of complete agreement upon any single tenet of the psychopathic concept has matured. It is still more than likely that this writer and the psychiatrist at your local state hospital will dispute violently each facet of the entity. But our differences will, on the whole, be more apparent than real. The important thing is that we shall be discussing within the same psychosocial area. We will agree at once that psychopathy is a disorder of behavior that is manifested particularly in the social sphere, and that its effects are directed outwardly, away from the self. We will concur in the opinion that there is something episodic, almost convulsive-like about the expression of psychopathic behaviorisms. We will find ourselves in harmony also as to its compulsive-obsessive nature. We will be mutually impressed with the typical life-course and pattern of psychopathic existences. Finally, our experiences and ideas will tally when we compare the main symptomatic constellations presented in all psychopathic cases. On the other hand, our concord will rapidly disrupt when we approach the matter of therapy.

II

The treatment of the psychopath has by and large consisted of his removal from the community as an irritant and possible source of infection. *Positive* therapy, aiming at the goal of a radical alteration of the psychopath's own personality, is a novel endeavor, only hesitantly embarked upon by a handful of investigators. This has been due both to the general haziness and ill-defined nature of the disorder as well as to the peculiarity of the psychopathic syndrome with its overtones of hostility, changefulness, emotional superficiality and other treatment-deflecting characteristics. As a matter of fact, so many and so varied have been the obstacles to the handling of psychopathic personalities beyond the level of pure management that Chornyak (1941) undoubtedly reflected a considerable body of opinion when he declared that ". . . Just as the rest of medicine recognizes inoperable carcinoma and nobody feels disgraced about it, so we must learn to face the fact . . ." that psychopathy is untreatable.[1]

It is fortunate that such pessimism has not led to the complete abandonment of all efforts to subject the psychopath to treatment-methods. But the challenge of psychopathic personality is so persistent, and the need for therapy of such persons so acute, that the clinically courageous (or perhaps foolhardy) find it difficult to resist. Added to this—and enlarging immeasurably the scope of the field—is the usually unphrased but almost universally apprehended realization of the terrible social (and perhaps even political) import of psychopathy.[2]

Consideration of therapeutic attempts with this disorder can be subsumed under three general headings: the sociological, the biological, the psychological. The first deals with the manipulation of the environment; the second with the manipulation of the body; the last with the manipulation of those factors and functions comprehended by the loosely-used term "mind."

Our survey of sociological treatment-techniques reverts primarily to the antique method of restraint under institutionalization. Aberrant, disruptive, aggressive and hostile personalities, upon providing evidence that their presence in the free community was opposed to its best interests, were forcefully removed and confined until, with age, the disorder had spent itself. Classically, the first and only consideration was custody. Following the humanitarian 18th and enlightened 19th centuries, this notion of the efficacy of removal alone was transformed by the gradual evolution of the psychological and social sciences. The institution as such came to be conceived of as a center for treatment; and its very physical arrangement was predicated upon the thesis that a "climate" for therapy could be arranged.

As late as 1923, Barrett felt that institutionalization was the only solution to the problem of psychopathy and went no further than to prescribe confinement for long periods for "the protection of the social order." [3] He would have had psychopaths managed as mentally abnormal persons and, depending upon their mental status, kept in suitable institutions. That special institutions —and herein we see an early intimation of the notion of "climate"—more aptly suited the character of the psychopath was recognized abroad, especially in England, Belgium, France and Germany. Abély and Abély [4] (1934) recommended that such places be connected with mental hospitals rather than with prisons. For England, the Borstal system apparently serves the function of providing therapeutic removal and special "climate," although it is not known whether psychopaths are included in such projects.[5] In our own country, perhaps the most comprehensive development of the notion of institutional therapeutic "climate" has been provided by the U. S. Public Health Service attached to the Federal Bureau of Prisons.[6-9] The essence of the newer therapeutic institutionalization is the employment of "shotgun" psychiatric methods under a controlled at-

[1] Chornyak, J., Some Remarks on the Diagnosis of the Psychopathic Delinquent, *Amer. J. Psychiat.*, 97, 1941, 1326-40.
[2] Lindner, R. M., *Rebel Without A Cause,* Grune and Stratton, New York, 1944.

[3] Barrett, A. M., The Psychopathic Personality, *Med. Clinics of North Amer.*, 6, 1923, 1165-77.
[4] Abély, X., and Abély, P., L'enternment des Arriérés Socioux (Pervers Constitionnels), *Amer. Med.-Psychol.*, 92, 1934, 157-83.
[5] Healy, W., and Alper, B. S., *Criminal Youth and the Borstal System,* The Commonwealth Fund, New York, 1941.
[6] King, M. R., The Incarcerated Psychopath (paper presented at Annual Meeting of the American Psychiat. Ass'n, Chicago, May, 1939), Abs. in Cason, H., Springfield, Mo., 1942 (Mimeo.).
[7] King, M. R., Tentative Outline of Policies and Plans for the New Constitutional Psychopathic Unit of the Medical Center for Federal Prisoners, Springfield, Mo., (unpublished) 1939, Abs. in Cason, H. (ed.), *Summaries of Literature on Constitutional Psychopathy,* 5 vols., Springfield, Mo. (mimeo.).
[8] King, M. R., *Fourth Progress Report of the Psychopathic Unit,* Medical Center for Federal Prisoners, Springfield, Mo., June, 1941 (mimeo.).
[9] Fuller, J. K., Disciplining the Psychopath, *Proc. Warden's Conference, Fed. Pris. Serv.,* 1939 (mimeo.).

mosphere which acts to encourage and aid treatment. It co-exists with psychotherapy and occupational therapy, and has as its aim to cause "an extensive and profound alteration in the psychobiologic functioning of the patient." [10]

The success of the "climate" or sociological method of treatment cannot accurately be gauged, since no statistics appear in the literature. It is an admittedly apriori technique and, further, is dependent upon special institutional characteristics such as personnel, specialized services provided, and the myriad imponderables of any social atmosphere. It rests primarily on gestalt premises, and awaits further clarification by sociologists and psychologists of the subtleties of the concept of social "climate." The remainder of its principles borders upon and utilizes other treatment-techniques.

The biological types of therapy of psychopaths utilize pharmicology, surgery and the shock therapies. They presume organic malor dysfunctioning within the organism and seek to follow the traditional emphasis of medicine. Basic to the rationale of such methods is the proposition that the biological endowment of the psychopath is deficient or disturbed. Attempts to utilize such techniques date hardly more than a decade.

Cutts and Jasper (1941) and Lindsley and Henry (1942) reported upon the beneficial effects of benzedrine sulphate on behaviorproblem children; the latter study stressing the excellent results obtained with sodium dilantin.[11, 12] Davidoff and Goodstone (1942) were able to show improvement in many conditions including psychopathy following the administration of combined amytal and benzedrine.[13] In 1944, Silverman submitted evidence, obtained both clinically and by

way of the electro-encephalograph, that the only known drug to accomplish any marked changes in psychopaths for the better was sodium dilantin.[14] With benzedrine sulphate, Silverman observed no constant changes in EEG and disappointing clinical effects: phenobarbital yielded no consistent EEG changes and no clinical improvement: amytal and benzedrine was likewise non-rewarding: petit-mal shock therapy gave non-impressive clinical results and no major EEG changes. This author has most succinctly expressed the philosophy of the chemotherapy group. He believes that because of its relationships to the convulsive states, psychopathy is associated with organic brain disease . . . "The first consideration, then, in the handling of a case of psychopathic personality might be the use of special diagnostic procedures for the detection of cerebral lesions. If one cannot be found, or if the lesion is unamenable to other therapy, sodium dilantin might then be tried . . . Comprehensive treatment . . . should provide (also) for psychotherapy."

Only two instances of surgical interference in psychopathy have come to this writer's attention. Watts and Freeman (1938) report some evidence of improvement subsequent to bilateral prefrontal lobotomy in at least one case (#18) which bears a family resemblance to the disorder which is our topic.[15] This heroic method was also employed by Banay and Davidoff (1942) with a middle-aged sex psychopath who regained some insight, underwent improvement so far as his ethical sensibilities were concerned, and seemed to be "socially recovered." [16] It is obvious that the use of this therapeutic avenue has been too limited to permit of estimating its value.

Summing up regarding the biological varieties of treatment for psychopathy, we can say only that their argument rests upon the assumption of fundamental physical differences between psychopaths and other per-

[10] Cleckley, H., *The Mask of Sanity*, C. V. Mosby, St. Louis, 1941.

[11] Cutts, K. K. and Jasper, H. H. Effects of Benzedrine Sulphate and Phenobarbital on Behavior Problem Children with Abnormal Electro-Encephalograms, *Arch. Neurol. and Psychiat.*, 41, 1939, 1138–45.

[12] Lindsley, D. B., and Henry, C. E., The Effect of Drugs on Behavior and the Electroencephalograms of Children with Behavior Disorders, *Psychosom. Med.*, 4, 1942, 140–49.

[13] Davidoff, E., and Goodstone, G. L., Amphatamine-Barbiturate Therapy in Psychiatric Conditions, *Psychiat. Quart.*, 16, 1942, 541–8.

[14] Silverman, D., The Electroencephalograph and Therapy of Criminal Psychopaths, *J. Crim. Psychopathol.*, 5, 1944, 439–65.

[15] Watts, J. W., and Freeman, W., Psychosurgery, *J. Nerv. & Ment. Dis.*, 88, 1938, 589–601.

[16] Banay, R. S., and Davidoff, L., Apparent Recovery of a Sex Psychopath After Lobotomy, *J. Crim. Psychopathol.*, 4, 1942, 50 ff.

sons, an assumption for which there is considerable evidence.[17-20] Therefore their application (consequently their successes) has been most restricted.

Psychological treatment-techniques that have been used with success run the range from such simple psychotherapy as vocational guidance and orientation after Visher's (1922) suggestion;[21] through group therapy by way of the open forum after Mangun (1942);[22] non-Aristotelian personality reorientation by Korzybski's method of general semantics as reported by Lynn (1935);[23,24] to psychoanalysis.[25,26]

Among the treatment techniques for psychopathy which are psychological in nature, psychoanalysis is the most prominent and, it would seem, the most rewarding. However, it has been confined to private practitioners, for the most part, and its temporal interminability appears to constitute an irremovable barrier to wide-scale employment.

The creed of analysis in its approach to psychopathy has been expressed best by Alexander and Staub (1931).[27] It rests first upon a whole-hearted rejection of punishment. These authors decry the restraint practices still in evidence on the ground that it is ludicrous to cause suffering for an act over which the psychopath has no control. They show that he cannot be intimidated by primitive measures since he unconsciously feels the need for punishment, seeks it, even welcomes its severity . . . "To punish such individuals is psychologically meaningless and sociologically harmful." As for the ends of analysis, ". . . We aim to bring his expansive, active behavior under the control of his conscious personality." Psychoanalysis alone can do this and is successful because it "is able to remove the results of pathogenic influences of early life."

Dooley[28] (1924) expressed considerable doubt as to the efficacy of psychoanalysis with psychopathic women. "Attempts at psychoanalysis of the psychopathic woman have met with little success. She is seldom sincere in her wish for the re-education and transformation inevitable in a thorough analysis, and she is so frequently a liar that the work of sifting out the truth is a slow and often helpless undertaking. Her overwhelming desire for sympathy and petting leads her far in confession, but again interferes with her truthfulness. She makes but a weak and fluctuating transference and constantly seeks to use the analysis and the analyst himself to further her quite unregenerate purposes. The analysis becomes a disguised sort of flirtation, as she constantly brings up new 'resistances' to tempt the analyst on by challenging his skill and curiosity."

The foregoing statement by Dooley not only presents—between the lines—an excellent description of the psychopath, but highlights the paramount technical obstructions to the analysis of such difficult personalities. At the same time, this account is dated: our present knowledge of the intricacies of such mechanisms as the transference and resistance is far more complete and exact than it

[17] Lindner, R. M., Experimental Studies in Constitutional Psychopathic Inferiority, *J. Crim. Psychopathol.*, Part I, 4, #2, 1942, 252–76; Part II, 4, #3 1943, 484–500.
[18] Silverman, D., Clinical and Electroencephalographic Studies on Criminal Psychopaths, *Arch. Neurol. & Psychiat.*, 50, 1943, 18–33.
[19] Ingham, S. D., Some Neurologic Aspects of Psychiatry, *J. A. M. A.*, 111, August, 1938, 665–68.
[20] Jasper, H. H., Solomon, P., Bradley, C., Electroencephalographic Analysis of Behavior Problem Children, *Amer. J. Psychiat.*, 95, 1938, 641–58.
[21] Visher, J. W., A Study in Constitutional Psychopathic Inferiority, *Ment. Hyg.*, 6, 1922 729–45.
[22] Mangun, C. W., Group Psychotherapy, *Sixth Progress Report of the Psychopathic Unit*, Med. Center for Fed. Prisoners, Springfield, Mo., 1942, 63 ff. (mimeo.).
[23] Lynn, J. G., Preliminary Report of Two Cases of Psychopathic Personality with Chronic Alcoholism Treated by the Korzybskian Methods, (presented) First American Congress of General Semantics, 1935.
[24] Korzybski, A., *Science and Sanity*, Int. Non-Aristotelian Pub. Co., Lancaster, Pa., 1933.
[25] Diethelm, O., *Treatment in Psychiatry*, Macmillan Co., New York, 1936, 398 f.
[26] Alexander, F., and Healy, W., *Roots of Crime*, Knopf, New York, 1935.
[27] Alexander, F., and Staub, H., *The Criminal, the Judge, and the Public*, (tr. G. Zilboorg), Macmillan Co., New York, 1931.
[28] Dooley, L., The Psychopathic Woman, (in) Symposium on the Psychopathic Individual, *Ment. Hyg.*, 8, 1924, 192–6.

was at the time Dooley submitted this opinion. Psychoanalysis, in the 30's and 40's, has become more precise, pliable and adept; and the psychopath has been among those who have benefited from such an intellectual sharpening of an already potent weapon.[29-31] But even Wittels (1938) considered that attempts to analyze psychopaths are short-lived, because they tend to break away "before any transference worthy of the name can be established."

It seems to be generally held, as indicated above, that the major obstacles to successful analysis of the psychopath are (1) the time factor; (2) his inaccessibility as reflected in an unstable transference; and (3) the questionable validity of his productions under analysis, a problem concerning resistance on the various levels of awareness. To circumvent these hazards to therapy, however, it has been found feasible to resort to a technique of treatment that, while it is not specific for psychopathy alone, has been used with signal success in this disorder by the present writer.[32, 2] Believing that psychopathy is a disorder of personality which, while it may be based upon an individual's predisposing biology, is actually precipitated by analytically-determined traumata of early life, he finds in an analytic method the only avenue to exposure of and re-orientation toward such significant events of development. In essence, he argues that in respect of the psychopathic manifestations, it is the precipitant that must be uncovered; and that once this is done, the predisposing *anlagen* can be left in a relatively pure state for the further concern of medicine or surgery.[33] It will be seen by students of psychopathy that such a viewpoint constructs a compro-

mise between the various schools of thought on the subject, and provides a working hypothesis for treatment.

Hypnoanalysis is the therapeutic tool which this author regards as the most potent weapon in the entire psychological armamentarium for the dynamic treatment of the psychopathic personality. It is an avenue of approach compounded of psychoanalysis—from which it extracts the dynamic, interpretive core—and the art of hypnosis—divorced from its esoteric connotations. As a unique method it can be traced to the dawn of psychoanalysis, following which—as a result of certain objections which do not seem tenable any longer—it suffered abandonment in favor of unaided free-association. An occasional instrument at the service of clinicians and practitioners, its basic tenets were never formalized; and its status as a singular technique never recognized. In spite of the injunction of silence and disrepute leveled against the use of hypnosis in analysis, confessions of its worth as an adjunct to free-association not infrequently appeared; while even the more orthodox of the Freudians had at least to take cognizance of it.[34-36]

As for the technique of hypnoanalysis itself, the systematization which this writer has tried to give to it in order to establish it as a formal instrument for research and treatment has been detailed elsewhere.[37, 32, 2] Here it must suffice only to sketch the method briefly. Let it also be understood that other, similar work with it has been carried on elsewhere.[38, 39]

[29] Wittels, F., The Criminal Psychopath in the Psychoanalytic System, *Psychoanal. Rev.*, 24, 1937, 276–91.
[30] Wittels, F., Die Libidinöse Struktur des Kriminellen Psychopathen, *Int. Zeit. f. Psychoanal.*, 23, 1937, 360–75.
[31] Wittels, F., The Position of the Psychopath in the Psychoanalytic System, *Int. J. Psycho-analysis*, 19, 1938, 471–88.
[32] Lindner, R. M., Hypnoanalysis in a Case of Hysterical Somnambulism, *Psychoanal. Rev.*, 32, 1945, 325–339.
[33] Lindner, R. M., A Formulation of Psychopathic Personality, *Psychiatry*, 7, 1944, 59–63.

[34] Ferenczi, S., The Role of Transference in Hypnosis and Suggestion, (in) *Contributions to Psychoanalysis*, (tr. E. Jones) R. G. Badger Co., Boston, 1916.
[35] Freud, A., *The Ego and the Mechanisms of Defense*, Hogarth Press, London, 1937.
[36] Stekel, W., *Technique of Analytical Psychotherapy*, Norton, New York, 1940.
[37] Lindner, R. M., The Equivalents of Matricide, *Psychoanalytic Quarterly*, 17, 4, 1948.
[38] Gill, M. M., and Brennan, M., Treatment of a Case of Anxiety Hysteria by an Hypnotic Technique Employing Psychoanalytic Principles, *Bull. Menninger Clinic*, 7, 1943, 163–71.
[39] Erickson, M. H., and Kubie, L. S., The Successful Treatment of a Case of Acute Hysterical Depression by a Return Under Hypnosis to a Critical Phase of Childhood, *Psychoanal. Quart.*, 10, 1941, 583 ff.

The initiation of hypnoanalytic therapy or investigation consists in the training of the patient or subject first in achieving the so-called trance state with a minimum of effort on the part of both clinician and patient; subsequently of accustoming him to utilize such a state for the recall of early memories. An overwhelmingly important by-product of this stage in the work is the development of a manipulable transference, hereinafter to be exploited by the clinician and utilized in the manner so well described by the psychoanalysts. Following this period of schooling, free association is employed, deep hypnosis being resorted to when resistances *of the kind which do not originate from the transference* are encountered. Validity of production is insured by repetition of hypnotic periods; or, if crucial material appears first in free-association, it is repeated in the trance state.

A word needs to be said here concerning the uniqueness of hypnoanalysis in disintegrating resistances, a special phenomenon which alone is responsible for the greater share in reducing total treatment-time from years to three or four months at the outside. Since the transference is, in a very basic sense, the reflectance of resistance; when patients succumb to the clinician to the extent of entering the trance state—indicative of a real and durable transference-relationship—resistance literally ceases to exist. And when the material toward which intense resistance has been demonstrated is once produced under hypnosis, there is apparently a carry-over into the waking state to the place where there is no longer any hesitation in reproducing that same material. This "melting" of resistance takes place throughout the analysis, allowing the crucial developmental features to be handled in both hypnotic and waking states, thus assuring validity of repressed and significant memories. Further to insure against memorial carry-over from trance-state productions to waking association, amnesia is induced post-hypnotically after each session in which memories have been evoked hypnotically.

Along with the provision of a worthy transference, the more satisfactory management of resistance and the surety of absolute validity, another advantage of hypnoanalysis relates to the actual memorial matter which appears in the course of work. With the orthodox analytic technique, screen-memories often obscure the picture and delay the course of treatment: in hypnoanalysis such a beclouding becomes impossible. Further, two memorial types appear, the *regressive* and the *revivified*, which allow the clinician an enlarged opportunity for viewing analytic productions with far greater facility and objectivity. In the trance-state, when memories are evoked, they appear—or even more significantly, they can be made to appear—either as a reflection of the patient's present attitude towards past events, or *as if the patient is now living again the experience he relates*. Such an accomplishment of the method is invaluable in treatment. It enables an exact approximation of the present emotional and intellectual attitudinal complexion; and it provides a candid, first-hand accounting of the impact of traumatic episodes as they were actually experienced. More; the clinician, by observing motor behavior at such times, can—by comparing it with developmental norms such as Gesell's—accurately determine the date of each crucial occurrence.

When the material is exhausted, *i.e.*, when the clinician perceives that he has obtained information enough upon which to proceed with the re-educative phase of treatment, and when he has been assured that abreaction to the crises of developmental history is complete, reorientation is accomplished with the aid of the transference *and* posthypnotic suggestion. The new attitudes and patterns of behavior are literally grafted into the now receptive and prepared personality. They become encapsulated with ease and dispatch. Finally, the transference is dissolved by redirection of its energies and displacement into such productive paths as are prescribed by the newly-acquired insights.

So it becomes evident that hypnoanalysis functions to realize the ends of therapy while obviating the principal objections to the more orthodox methods of analysis. It consumes far less time and thus its benefits can be distributed more widely. It is—in this writer's view—applicable to all disorders of behavior which by present knowledge appear to be psychogenic. Because of its peculiar characteristics, it seems eminently suitable to psychopathy.

IV

While hypnoanalysis is not specific for psychopathic personality, it is the treatment of choice—so far as this investigator is concerned—since it comprises certain features which naturally conform to the disorder and compensate for the deficiencies of other treatment tools. In its heroic stamp it resembles the shock method; it is psychotherapeutically founded and includes continuous guidance.

The supreme virtue of hypnoanalysis in psychopathy is that it proceeds upon the basis of a firmly-entrenched transference relationship. No one of this writer's patients has ever broken away. In one case where a psychopath's behavior in the early stages of treatment gave indication that he wished to be relieved of therapy, a series of firm injunctions to continue were given under hypnosis, and the problem was solved. This has now become standard in the handling of psychopaths, a matter of routine before concluding the trance.

The method has yet to meet with failure, although the abandonment of therapy was enforced on two occasions when patients were released (from a penal institution). This writer, furthermore, has found that all patients can be trained in hypnosis so long as the effort is continuous and not too soon abandoned, and so long as the countertransference is firmly maintained at the level of objective sympathy and understanding.

The objections of Dooley, Wittels (cf. above) and others are met satisfactorily by hypnoanalysis in a way in which no other current therapeusis can claim. Validity is the core of the method, with the clinician in control at all times to check and recheck patients' productions. Resistances are disintegrated serially as they are encountered; while the curious—and not yet fully understood—phenomenon that leads to the dissolution of waking resistance routinely, following disclosure of resistance-matter under hypnosis, abets the rapid course of therapy. Conjointly with those attributes already sketched is the salient feature that in hypnoanalysis, because of its unique methodology, *the ego participates fully in the therapeutic process.* In other words, the entire personality partakes of treatment; and the full effect of the cathartic working-through is provided for by the simple device of assuring that the emotions evoked by crucial developmental events are experienced not alone under the trance but in the waking state as well. Now, with full participation in treatment by all facets of the personality, the splendid aims of analysis—to remove the unhealthy results of pathogenic early influences, and to bring behavior under "conscious" control—are realized.

Hypnoanalysis has provided novel evidence that the psychopathic personality is the resultant of a concatenation of precipitating crucial events harking back to the first years of life. Very briefly, it appears that the hostility of the psychopath is analytically determined by a failure properly to introject the father-image (hence, later, society), such a failure conditioned upon non-resolution of the oedipus struggle based, apparently, upon conflict resulting from the mis-interpretation of the primal scene. The lack of insight shown by psychopaths is traced to this selfsame source as an energetic, sub-liminal attempt to avoid recognition that it is the mother who is pre-eminently desired. This accounts, too, for his chaotic sexuality, even for his nomadism. Intimately related to the oedipal feature is a deeply-nourished fear of castration when his integrity is attacked. Sharing also in this formulation of precipitation for psychopathy are intensive inferiority convictions (and their well-known reaction-formations), in origin founded upon the apprehension of rejection by the father.

Since these dynamisms are familiar to almost all psychological disorders, it may be questioned why they give the picture of psychopathy in certain cases. The answer is sought among the predisposing conditions of physical endowment. The inter-relationships of disruptive, crux-like, traumata appear to act upon a biology more than likely of the same cast as that observed among various conditions similar to the epilepsies, organic brain lesions, choreas and encephalidities.

The geometrical resultant is the psychopath who lacks the determination to follow through a deliberative course of action to its socially acceptable conclusion; who points all his behavior to satisfy his immediate wishes and whims of the moment; who cannot use his intelligence as a governor upon behavior; who randomly exploits everyone and everything; who is burdened with guilt and seeks punishment which is both expensive and debasing to the community; who cannot comprehend or appreciate the rights of others nor his obligations to society; who, in short, represents not only a burden but even a threat to our civilization. . . .

ROBERT M. LINDNER
Chief Psychologist
Haarlem Lodge
Catonsville, Maryland

TRAFFIC VIOLATOR. Some new aspects of criminology have arisen because of the need for regulating the behavior of drivers. In spite of the fact that drivers can commit the equivalent of criminal offenses from homicide to minor property damage, the general tendency on the part of the public has been not to consider illegal or antisocial driving as criminal but to take the attitude that the violation of traffic laws as "something that anybody is likely to do." Nevertheless, traffic laws and ordinances are established through the same governmental channels as are the other criminal laws and they arise in response to the same social demands.

Traffic laws are regulatory to prevent property damage, injury, and also loss of life although they have the secondary purpose, which apparently is more obvious to the casual driver, of making the act of driving easier. If traffic were to become too snarled; if it were too difficult to use the speed possibilities of the motor car to a reasonable extent, the value of driving would be extremely limited.

From the standpoint of antisocial behavior, violation of those regulations which have to do with safety are much more important than those having to do with efficiency of movement, but the two cannot be separated. A law which has for its purpose the granting of a clear view to a driver who is approach-

ing a corner makes it possible not only for the driver to cross the intersection quickly but also safely.

Although engineering factors have been much more important to legislators in connection with safe driving, bad engineering has been from time to time recognized as criminal behavior. But no systematic group of laws had been predicated upon mechanical construction or the use of knowledge of engineering. Both engineering and human behavior lie behind traffic laws which differentiate criminality in traffic from other types of criminal behavior, and it is just as antisocial for the driver to neglect the care of his car, to fail to provide adequate lights, and not to have his brakes well adjusted as it is for him to carry concealed weapons. In both instances homicidal potentialities exist.

It must not be forgotten that driving is a privilege and not a constitution-given right, although the attitude of most drivers is that the Constitution grants them the driving privilege. The idea of freedom to behave as one wants, regardless of the rights of others calls in the police power of the state which curtails the freedom of drivers, for without such limitation of who shall drive and the curbing of bad driving in cities and even on country roads a holocaust would result. Hence by virtue of police power, driving is a privilege, the accession to which is granted only upon assurance that the driver will not be a menace to others.

The unscientific attitudes taken by police officials, legislators, and others who are not acquainted with modern psychiatry and medicine placed unnecessary limitations on drivers. Various driver's licensing plans were set up, at the same time certain broad aspects of the danger of driving were entirely neglected. The loss of a limb, mild paralyses, color blindness and deafness were assumed to be limitations which would justify the restriction of driver's licenses, but in studies of accident-prone individuals, particularly by the Psychopathic Clinic of the Recorder's Court in Detroit, it was found that most dangerous drivers were accident-prone because of a psychological attitude rather than because of any physical limitation. Color blind persons were found to be able to distinguish between signal lights although they could not sort colored yarns. Partially paralyzed persons or individuals with crippled limbs were found to be safe drivers in many instances as soon as their cars were properly equipped to compensate for the missing or ineffective member. Deaf individuals as a group have a two per cent better traffic record than drivers as a whole because drivers, when their car windows are shut, are deaf to outside sounds for all practical purposes.

There are five specific limitations which are quite obvious. (1) Persons with complete lack of mechanical aptitude due either to organic illnesses, such as crippling, paralysis, nervous system defects who cannot have a broad enough range of vision by virtue of stiff muscles in the neck and shoulders or who cannot manipulate the pedals and levers of a car by virtue of such handicap are seldom able to compensate for their physical deficiencies.

2. Persons with marked vision defects of certain types are not safe drivers, but the visual defect may be much more serious than safety "experts" originally believed before driving is rendered unsafe. Because of the large size, i.e., high visibility of vehicles and objects in the highway, low visual acuity does not necessarily affect judgment of speed and distance or the ability to drive safely. However, this deficiency may become more significant at night. There have been many truck drivers whose Snellen visual acuity rating has been as low as 20/200, or partial blindness, yet have excellent driving records.

3. The insane obviously should not drive for, although it is probably true that there are many insane persons operating motor cars on the streets of any city, many persons with serious mental illnesses have delusions that some people are trying to harm them and so may deliberately drive into innocent persons who are identified with their persecutors. In other cases, the judgment may be impaired and is often so affected that the mental state is not compatible with safe driving.

4. The feebleminded whose judgment is impaired ought to be restricted, but there are many many millions of high-grade mental defectives who are perfectly safe to

operate a motor car as long as their attitude toward driving and their alertness and mechanical reactions enable them to compensate for such judgment defects as they may have. It must not be forgotten that in most instances it takes two people to make an accident, but the alertness of the normal driver and the fact that traffic is becoming more and more channelized frequently prevents the impact of two motor vehicles when the defective makes a wrong decision. Habituation to routes and thorough learning of traffic laws decreases the number of opportunities that render a decision necessary on the part of the defective driver.

5. Epileptics offer a marked problem in the enforcement of traffic laws and the maintenance of safe driving. Certainly anyone who has lapses of consciousness, who suffers from any of the convulsive states where he loses control of himself for short periods or long periods is automatically likely to have an accident through no volition of his own. Some epileptics claim that their aura gives them a prescience of the convulsion and that they have sufficient time to park their cars before losing consciousness. Even with such persons the potentiality of an accident still remains because they may be in such a situation in traffic that they cannot park their cars, or stop without causing rapidly moving vehicles to hit them from behind. Nocturnal epileptics who claim they have no diurnal fits are still dangerous because they may, even after many years of not having them, have a convulsion in the daytime. Epileptics under treatment may go for a long period of time without convulsions, but they still may break out from under the influence of their medication or may neglect it.

The most important general cause of traffic violations and their consequent accidents is bad attitude on the part of the driver. Their attitudes may be permanent and may be a part of the personality of the driver or they may be transient. In either instance they cause aggressive behavior, indifference to the traffic law, a tendency or desire to run as close to regulations as possible, with the result that oftentimes these drivers run too close and violate the law.

Permanent attitude changes that are important are those which had their inception in the individual's childhood. The individual with psychoneurotic tendencies who has a hatred for his father and for law and order which the father symbolizes may become a "cop-hater" or an individual who resents being regulated. The overprotected child may have the attitude that he can get away with violations because he feels that his family will get him out of trouble. The child who has been pampered because of physical defects may hope to use these disorders to secure legal sympathy before the court, yet these same physical disorders may make him a mechanically incompetent driver. The prescription of medication to heal persons is not in itself a defense for traffic violations. Prescription of narcotics or sedative drugs by a physician should be prescribed in such a way that the effects will wear off before the individual has to drive a motor car. If the man is ill or under medication he should not drive, and his physician should so warn him, however, as yet physicians are not considered criminally negligent if they do not.

Another group of traffic law violators are those who have lost their emotional stability and violators who satisfy their feelings of inferiority.

The speeder who speeds for the sheer love of speeding may have the belief that his car is under control, although engineers may have studied the safe speeds for the roads where he is operating, which speeds are very much under his operating speed.

All of the childhood neurotic patterns, overprotection, and similar training errors which are considered as behavior disorders of childhood by careful study reveal themselves to be important in the traffic violation picture.

Transient attitudinal changes can arise from friction in the home, business, preoccupation with financial matters and the other causes which can make people more tense, more preoccupied, more indifferent to the rights of others, or even depressed or exhilarated.

Alcoholism is perhaps an over-rated cause of accidents, but the habitual alcoholics constitute the chief group of serious violators. A study of accidents shows that there are many more alcoholics in an accident-prone group of drivers, than there are insane, feeble-minded or physically unsound. The lack of coordination, judgment and even fatigue which accompany late evening drinking all play a part in accidents. The symptoms of alcoholism are not particularly important, particularly when an arrest is made by a police officer. If proof of alcoholism is needed, scientific standardized tests of blood, breath, and urine alcohol concentration should be used. If these are not available, the examination at the time of the arrest by a physician who has observed and studied the psychiatry of alcoholics is a relatively safe criminological procedure. There are too many objections to justify the use of the staggering gait, knee jerks or pupillary changes as observed by the policeman to permit this type of test to be considered as valid. Although moving pictures of the conduct of the alleged alcoholic at the time of the arrest should be valuable, they have not yet been accepted by courts.

Most of the criminological findings that are becoming more and more important with driving will find an expression in flying as the operation of aerial vehicles is approaching the significance of the operation of motor cars, and the general principles which are being developed in traffic court clinics for motorists should be strongly significant in the field of flight regulation, also.

LOWELL S. SELLING, M.D.
Former Director
Psychopathic Clinic
Recorder's Court
Detroit, Michigan

BIBLIOGRAPHY

Selling, Lowell S., Personality Traits Observed in Automobile Drivers, *Journal of Criminal Psychopathology*, 1:258, 1940.
———, A Preliminary Report Concerning Mental Pathology Found in Automobile Drivers, *Journal of Criminal Psychopathology*, 1:254, 1940.
———, The Psychopathology of the Hit-and-Run Driver, *The American Journal of Psychiatry*, 98:93, 1941.

TREASON. The definition of treason as a crime has been gradually narrowed down from seven forms of high treason under the

British Statute of Treasons of 1351, to two specific acts outlined in the Constitution of the United States. Article III, Section 3 of the Constitution provides that: "Treason against the United States shall consist only in levying war against them, or in adhering to their enemies, giving them aid and comfort." It is usually punishable by death.

Treason can also be committed against any state of the United States and so each state has its own statutes against treason. In New York, treason against the people of the state consists in: "(1) levying war against the people of the state, within the state; or, (2) a combination of two or more persons by force to usurp the government of the state, or to overturn the same, shown by a forcible attempt, made within the state, to accomplish that purpose; or, (3) adhering to enemies of the state, while separately engaged in war with a foreign enemy in a case prescribed in the Constitution of the United States, or giving to such enemies aid and comfort within the state or elsewhere." A

warrant for treason must set forth specifically the treasonable acts charged. Delivering up prisoners and deserters to the enemy is adhering to them and giving them aid and comfort, and is therefore treason.

To constitute levying war against the people of the state, an actual act of war must be committed. To conspire to levy war is not enough. Treason against the state is punishable by death.

Where persons rise in insurrection with intent to prevent in general by force and intimidation, the execution of a statute of this state, or to force its repeal, they are guilty of levying war. But an attempt, even though by numbers and force of arms, to resist the execution of a law in a single instance, and for a private purpose, is not levying war.

BIBLIOGRAPHY

Constitution of the United Sttaes.
Gilbert, F. B., *Criminal Law and Practice of the State of New York,* Matthew Bender and Co., 1935.

U

UNIVERSITY TRAINING FOR THE POLICE PROFESSION.

UNIVERSITY TRAINING FOR THE POLICE PROFESSION. Research here and abroad has thrown new light on delinquency, and it is known now to those who have followed this research that the attack upon crime and dependency must be begun in the plastic period of childhood. The policeman, not less than the workers in other fields concerned with the health, happiness, and welfare of children, has an important part to play in the formulation of those qualities which make for self-reliant and self-respecting citizens. Handicapped by the fact that the municipal, county and state police are untrained in the fundamental principles of crime prevention, these public services, well-meaning though they may be in the great majority of cases, are ill-equipped to deal with the problem that is so vital to the welfare of the people of this country.

Higher intellectual, moral, physical and training standards are an essential prerequisite for successful performance of all duties associated with police administration. Thousands of lives are needlessly lost through accidents on the streets and highways. Although many of the factors responsible for these accidents are known to specialists, comparatively few of them are used by the men who are directly responsible for the regulation and control of traffic.

Without scientific training and without the application of synthesis and analysis by the men engaged in the solution of these problems, we cannot hope to reduce the accidents that are responsible for the death of nearly fifty thousand people every year and the injury of approximately a million persons annually.

The transportation problem can never be solved by amateurs. The need is for experts trained in the dynamics of modern high-speed and heavy-volume traffic control. Only through this avenue of approach may the police traffic budgets be expended intelligently in the attack upon the social and economic losses of traffic accidents, retarded traffic flow and congestion.

Similarly, the vice problems associated with prostitution, gambling and narcotics beset police officials on every hand. The principles involved in the solution of these problems have never been thoroughly understood nor applied, and only through a professionalization of the police can these principles be made known and given effective expression.

Major riots, capital and labor relations, clashes of political ideals and other social phenomena must be studied and thoroughly understood by every person charged with the responsibility of protecting life and property and the preservation of the peace. An incipient riot may be quelled promptly by the sympathetic, understanding policeman, or it may be fanned into a volcanic eruption by the ignorant minion of the law.

Attention is directed to the fact that criticism of the police in the United States is universal. This criticism is but a reflection of the incompetency of our citizenship as a whole because it is generally understood that the people of a community get the kind of enforcement that they deserve. Not until the public as a whole are informed can they know what is best to do. A professionally trained police force would bring to the citizens of their communities a better understanding of the police problems and would convey to them information helpful in the solution of many difficulties. Evidence of this fact may be found in selected communities where attention has been given to the quality of the police personnel.

Police organization and administration,

police records administration, personnel administration, patrol and communications, criminal investigation and identification, crime prevention, and traffic regulation and control are professional activities of a high order. Every phase of the police enterprise is as technical as medicine and engineering, and it must be apparent to all thoughtful persons that the same training disciplines are required in the preparation of men and women for this strategic field.

The superb training resources of major universities and colleges in the United States can be applied with telling effect to the professional training requirements of police service. Experience has demonstrated that from the standpoint of academic organization, it is a comparatively simple matter to institute a professional police training program embracing four years of preparation at the university level.

An inspection of the current catalogs of all major institutions reveals that they already include among their regular offerings the collateral subjects such as sociology, psychology, economics, political science, public administration and others, that should be geared into a professional police training program. Approximately ninety per cent of the course materials that should be included in the police curricula are now a part of the regular offerings of these institutions. It only remains to superimpose upon these courses in an integrated program the necessary technical police subjects, in precisely the same manner as we have been doing for years in law, engineering, medicine and the other professions. Actually, it has been determined that four years represent too short a time in which to train a man for police service, and the program should include a fifth year at the graduate level to accommodate advanced study and research leading to the Master's degree in this technical field.

In-service training is not the answer to the training requirements of police service. It can only serve as a stop-gap until professionally trained men become increasingly available. In-service training is indispensable but its objective must be held clearly in mind. It was never designed to provide professional training but, on the other hand, to keep

trained men abreast of new developments in their field.

The application of university disciplines to the immediate problems of police administration is a matter of considerable importance. For illustration, it is generally recognized by the men who have studied police organizations that one of the chief defects is the absence of competent records. The police record system is indispensable to the intelligent control of operations, yet it is well known in police circles that few departments are adequately equipped for the discharge of this important function.

This subject is accorded a prominent position in established police curricula. The aspiring police officer receives thorough instruction in the mechanics and functions of the police record system, and the use of this important facility in the diagnostic approach to problems encountered by the police. He learns that the department and its administrators must have the facts concerning the character, extent and distribution of crime and delinquency in the community before operations can be intelligently planned and executed.

The student learns that an efficient police record system is a prerequisite to the intelligent control of operations and the measurement of the results of those operations. He discovers that it is an accounting system for the police business. He is taught how to secure the data, and how to compile and evaluate it. Instruction is given in the use of records for identification purposes, and for implementing investigative procedure. He obtains information concerning the use of records for administrative purposes, and how from an administrative point of view the general operations of the department as a whole may be strengthened and improved.

The utility of records in measuring the individual officer or groups of police personnel is demonstrated. He learns that in complex undertakings performed by many men, precision and certainty in action and control over far-flung operations can be achieved only with the assistance of record controls. In the analysis of emerging situations and in the measurement of departmental performance, the strategic position of the record system becomes apparent. Finally, and none the less important, it becomes evident to him that when the records are competently kept, they will identify the points where the preventive work of the police department may be focused. Factors contributory to crime and delinquency may be analyzed in every aspect.

The technical police courses in a university program embrace all of the requirements of the police recruit training school. In addition, these technical subjects are superimposed upon collateral offerings in connecting scientific fields, and inter-related with them so that the four-year program is an integrated preparation for the young man who aspires to a professional career in the police service.

Reference has been made to records in their application to crime prevention, but these records would be of little avail if the policeman had not the fundamentals necessary for an attack upon the problem. The student gains through the required courses an appreciation of the biological, physiological, psychological, sociological, pathological, economic and legal aspects of crime and delinquency. He becomes familiar with the therapeutic measures that may be invoked in behavior problem cases and is instructed in the techniques that he as an individual officer, and later as an administrator, must use in the police approach to delinquency prevention. Through the courses that are offered in Child Psychology, Mental Hygiene, Mental Measurements, Educational Psychology, Abnormal and Experimental Psychology, the student's thoughts are directed toward the action he must take to assist other officials and agencies in forming the character traits which are demanded of good citizens today.

He is taught how attitudes, good and bad, are formed and how to distinguish at the infantile level the elements that contribute to the development of unwholesome and unsocial attitudes, and the means that may be employed to counteract them. He learns to know during his student years the need for distinguishing between those behavior characteristics which are produced by pathological or biological defects from those that are the result of the child's contact with his environment.

He is shown how important it is to give attention to the factors in the home, in the school, in the neighborhood and even in the church, that produce mental conflicts, repressions, complexes and frustrations, and how they may be responsible for unwholesome habits of thinking, feeling and acting that lead to delinquency and crime. His attention is directed toward the positive approach to character formation and how he may participate in the general plan to teach children to develop self-control, self-reliance, self-direction and self-initiative.

Emphasis is placed upon the cooperating role of the police, court, probation, school, church, welfare, health and civic-minded organizations in the total community program. He learns the essential procedures by which leadership and resources of the community may be coordinated into an organized effort for promoting youth welfare. He is impressed in this disciplinary period with the importance of inculcating sound personal, social and spiritual ideals so that before the child has an opportunity to become delinquent, he is fortified with personality traits that may even, in fact, neutralize a defective inheritance.

Nor is the other aspect of police work neglected. It will be recognized that there will always be defective individuals. Animal breeders have exercised control over their stock extending over many generations. They study with care the pedigrees of their stock. Nevertheless, in spite of all the care exercised, there are occasional runts, throw-backs or defective offspring. Seemingly, notwithstanding the preventive work which may be done by the future policeman, we must reckon with the fact that there will always be deviates. Jennings, noted biologist, has estimated that even though we had full control over the heredity of human beings, it would take three thousand years to breed out feeblemindedness. Accordingly, the investigation of crime and the identification of criminals must go on, and these techniques receive appropriate attention in the university training of the future police officer.

Not only are the sciences useful in criminal investigation made a part of the program, but the art of criminal investigation is also introduced to the students. Deception detection techniques with the use of psychographs and other psychological devices, the spectrograph and other tools of the physics laboratory, the use of chemistry and biochemistry for the detection of suspected elements, all play their part in preparing the young man to serve in his community.

All the principles of successful criminal investigation are presented by technical experts who have had considerable field experience. What the student must do at the scene of the crime; what detection and interrogation methods he must employ; application of the principles and techniques of police interrogation; how to use photography; how to procure, preserve and present evidence, loom large in the practical aspects of the training program.

Similarly, criminal identification is presented not only from its scientific point of view but also as seen by the technician working in the police laboratory. This course is concerned with the critical examination of hairs, bones, physiological fluids, debris, fragments; traces of tools, teeth, fibre, feathers, dust, ash, vehicles; handwriting, typewriting, papers, inks and other suspected materials in the solution of criminal cases.

The suggestive biological significance of fingerprint patterns is thoroughly explored. The technical aspects comprehend the classification, filing and identification of fingerprints, and the development of latent fingerprints at the scene of the crime.

Reference has been previously made to traffic regulation and control. Here too, the scientific courses offered in an institution of higher learning may be effectively integrated with the technical aspects. Under the supervision of experienced technicians, the embryo officer gain an understanding of the factors contributory to accidents, as well as the means through which a smooth flowing traffic stream may be produced without increasing the chances of death and injury on the streets and highways. The educational process that must be employed to produce within the individual pedestrian or driver an awareness of danger that exists on the streets

as well as a conscious responsibility for the more courteous use of the highways, is a part of the program of indoctrination. Traffic engineering, education and enforcement go hand in hand in the curriculum, so that the young student who is exposed to this information leaves the college fully prepared to play his part in approaching a solution to this problem. The total scope of the departmental program includes specialized training for every branch of the police service.

Full and complete programs for the university training of police officials have been developed in various colleges such as State College of Washington, Michigan State College, University of California at Berkeley, University of Southern California, and other institutions.

The objectives of these programs are (a) to give students a broad liberal education in conjunction with intensive professional training for the police services; (b) to prepare them for a career in the police profession; (c) to develop the qualities of leadership and (d) to foster ideals of professional achievement in the public service.

The resources of the State College of Washington are geared to a training program that gives the ambitious student the diversified and rigorous training he needs for a career in the police field. Through the facilities of this Department, the future police officer embarks upon a training course comparable in scope and severity to the university curricula of other professions. By four years in a collegiate school of police training, the young man or woman acquires a knowledge of the various aspects, of modern police administration that could otherwise be obtained, if at all, only through decades of experience. In addition, the student enjoys the benefits of a cultural education necessary for ultimate advancement to positions of responsibility in the service.

Based upon the Vollmer system of police administration, tested procedures are taught and demonstrated in the specialized fields of police organization and administration, personnel administration, police records administration, patrol systems, criminal investigation and identification, delinquency and crime prevention, and traffic regulation and control. Supporting the technical police subjects and integrated with them in a balanced training program are the collateral courses in other arts and sciencec directly related to the problems of modern police administration.

The General Police Administration Course is intended for students who desire a comprehensive understanding of the police field as a whole and who are interested primarily in the administrative aspects of police service. The basic elements of this curriculum also serve as a foundation for the more specialized courses.

The Freshman and Sophomore years are devoted to basic work in the physical and social sciences, along with foundational courses in the police major. During this time the student gains a broad perspective and understanding of the relationship of the sciences to the problems of modern police administration. The Freshman and Sophomore program includes courses in Sociology, Political Science, Psychology, Chemistry, Physiology, Biology, Economics, English, Public Speaking, Typing, Military Science and Physical Education. These subjects are closely related to the major police courses taken during this period, which include the General Administration of Justice, Police Organization and Administration, Police Personnel Administration, and the Police Records System.

Advanced study characterizes the Junior and Senior years. Police courses taken during this period include the Police Communications System, the Police Patrol System, Criminal Investigation, Identification Systems, Criminal Law and Procedure, Law of Arrest, Law of Evidence, Delinquency and Crime Prevention, and Traffic Regulation and Control. Collateral work in the Junior and Senior program embraces advanced study in Urban Sociology, Criminology, Sociology of Adjustment, Group Behavior, Introduction to Social Work, Genetics, Problems of Child Welfare, Social Statistics, Methods of Social Research, Applied Psychology, Social Psychology, Abnormal Psychology, Psychology of Adolescence, Public Administration, Community Organization, Juvenile Delinquency, Parole and

Probation and Introduction to Penology. *Wherever circumstances permit, the student is encouraged to take at least one year of graduate work.*

Applicants for admission to the police curriculum are selected with considerable care. In addition to the general requirements for police service, and for College entrance, the student must possess certain basic qualifications for police service, including a commendable scholastic record in high school, robust health and mental balance plus the intelligence and aptitude required for success as a police officer. At the time of admission, the prospective student is required to take a comprehensive entrance examination and pass with a superior score. This battery of tests is the equivalent of police entrance examinations in the best American police departments. A rigid character investigation is made of all applicants. Each year of the four year professional training program may be considered as part of a screening process. A student may be disqualified at any time for further study in the police major if he fails to meet the standards of scholarship and performance prescribed by the department. All applicants admitted to the police curriculum must present to the Head of the Department a letter of recommendation from the Chief of Police in their home town.

Police Research. Research in the police arts and sciences must be considered as an integral part of a university police training program. The opportunities now presented for major research contributions in this field are calculated to challenge the interest of educational administrators in institutions of higher learning.

It will be recognized at the outset that to carry on the training program without also engaging in research would be placing a considerable limitation upon its advancement. There is an important need for comprehensive texts, reference works and treatises in all the subjects that should be taught in police schools, such as, for illustration, a text on the General Administration of Justice. A Patrolman's Manual covering every phase of the patrol function as the basic element of modern police service, is another major requirement which should receive early attention. Those who have studied the work of the police know that the individual patrolman on the beat is society's first line of defense against criminal attack, and that in the exercise of the preventive functions of police service, he may ultimately mark the turning point toward effective crime control.

Job analyses of patrol service already available further demonstrate that the area of performance is so comprehensive that nothing short of a manual to describe patrol duties will satisfy the need. However, it is a fact that up to the present time there are no existing manuals worthy of the name that will materially assist the patrolman in performing all those duties that are required of him by rules and regulations, and by law. He must look for guidance to general orders of the department and to special orders issued from time to time.

Similarly, there is up to the present moment no complete Sergeant's Manual, nor is there an officer's manual for the instruction and guidance of Lieutenants and Captains. These critical defects must of necessity be remedied. Further, strange as it may seem to the layman, there is no Manual on Police Tactics which may be used for instructional purposes, or that is available to administrators in directing the operations of their department. There is not in existence any work that deals with the principles of police organization and administration which can be recommended for general use or which may be employed as a text for police training.

There is at present available a Manual on Police Records by O. W. Wilson. This can be and is used for teaching purposes, as well as for use by officers in the field. This work needs to be supplemented, however, by a treatise that covers the whole field of records in the various police departments in this country and throughout the world.

There is as yet no work dealing exclusively with police statistics, and since the police problems differ from all other fields of activity, it is now imperative that some attention be given to this subject. We should know not only the extent of crime in the community but comparative studies must be made. Monthly variations and annual vari-

ations of specific offenses should be studied in addition to ratio of crimes against property to that of persons; ratio of crimes against persons to offenses against property; the relation of crimes to other social and economic data, so that an effort will be made to learn whether or not there is any correlation between crime and political shifting, economic oscillations or social fluctuations.

There is so much that is false circulating concerning crime that the time is now at hand to apply to each aspect of police work all the disciplines associated with the highest development of statistical analysis. We need to know, so far as it is possible, how the crime was committed, when committed, where committed, how committed and why it was committed. We need to know all that we can possibly know about the individual who committed the offense, including the factors that first contributed to that individual's delinquency and later, to his criminality and recidivism. The efficiency of the courts, prosecutor, police department and individual policeman should be studied and the ultimate disposition of each individual case should be carefully recorded so that the records will reflect what has happened to the individual from the date of his arrest until the case has been finally disposed of by the courts and penal or correctional institutions.

What is the story on crime and delinquency? What is the actual nature of the problems in connection with traffic regulation and control that confront the modern police department? What are all the details connected with vice in the community? These are the stories that have yet to be told in the scientific language of the statistical expert. Here is an opportunity for a monumental contribution to the policeman's art and science.

Research should also be focused upon a treatise dealing with personal identification. Every aspect of identification should be embodied in the work, including the contributions that are to be found in the volumes already published in the fields of Anatomy, Anthropology, Physiology, Histology, and other sciences, embracing every item that is useful to the police in the identification of individuals. There should also be included the description of the more than sixty criminal identification systems that are used throughout the world today. Genetic studies, biological studies, occupational studies and all other scientific inquiries made in connection with identification should be included in such a treatise. This may more than likely reach the proportions of an encyclopedia before the work is completely done.

The police of this country today recognize in a general way the promise of preventive tactics in the approach to crime control. However, surrounded by a maze of suggested panaceas for the solution of this problem, they are admittedly in the dark with respect to procedures thus far confirmed by research. There is an expressed desire on their part for a police crime prevention manual which in the language of the police officer, will place this information at their disposal and enable them to give expression to those techniques which they are in a position to apply. It is mandatory that they know how to participate in the total community program as a part of the coordinated effort by which leadership and resources in the community may be focused upon the discovery of the individual developing problem case, its diagnosis and readjustment.

Because report writing plays such a significant part in the policeman's life and because it will be increasingly important when the work of the police officer is placed on a professional plane, it will be worth the time expended to prepare a complete volume on this subject. What Gaum and Graves have done for the general fields, needs to be done in particular for the police field on a more elaborate basis. The examples of report devices should be included which will show the forms that are used in the different countries and in the different cities; the forms that are used for the several types of offenses; the simple forms used in small departments as well as the more elaborate forms to be found in such departments as the City of Los Angeles.

Gross in his Criminal Psychology has suggested some of the values of the application of psychology to investigation. Since the publication of his work, other books have been published in this and other countries. The works of Burtt, McCarty and others are suggestive of the ground that is to be covered. This is a rich and virgin field for psychological research. The European countries have given this matter wider attention than we have in the United States; therefore, publications in Europe must first be consulted before the research is instituted here. Translation projects would place this significant material at our disposal in further developing this field of inquiry.

A new traffic officers' Manual is also a requirement. Taylor's work was excellent for its period but this is out of print and needs to be rewritten. Further, as yet we have no work dealing with the history of the police beginning with the police practices of primitive people up to the completion of the proposed study. More details are needed concerning the Egyptian, Babylonian and Chinese police services. What was it that Confucius did twenty-five hundred years ago that completely altered the behavior of the people in the community he served when he was Minister of Crime? What in truth did the Praetorian Guards do? How effective were the early continental police? The history of police service up to the present needs to be written without further delay. Existing publications indicate that the material is voluminous, especially since it is necessary to study the history of all police services throughout the world.

There is an immediate need for the study of departments in other countries. For example, how do the police function in Asia? It is possible that police experts in Asiatic countries may be induced to prepare contributions as an integral part of the program. It is believed, for example, that Dr. Frank Yee, close friend and professional associate of a number of American police leaders, who received his Doctorate in this country and who is now Commissioner of Police Planning in China, may be induced to prepare a volume on the Police in China.

Honorable Yukon Feng, Chief Police Administrator, attached to the office of the Minister of Interior of China, who received his training in the United States, England and on Continental Europe, is a scholar of considerable note. Since he is the national administrative head of police service, there are substantial reasons for believing that he can be urged to make significant contributions, provided only that he can be assured that his efforts will not be wasted, and will be published in this country. Dr. Yusai Takahashi, formerly Police Secretary in the Home Office of Japan and a writer of demonstrated ability, and Dr. Matsui, Vice President of the Police and Fire organization of Japan and reputable author, may be contacted at this time and urged to prepare a volume on the subject of the Japanese Police. Several writers in Africa who have contributed to English police journals and in professional police circles in the United States could be induced to write the story of the African police. Certainly Europe offers many expert police administrators. The work of Dr. Arnold Lichem, "Die Kriminalpolizie," is illustrative of the type of police books that should be made available to the American policeman.

Especially important in the future, because of the intimate relationship that must of necessity exist between this country and Latin-American countries, is the study of the various police systems in those regions.

There are also a number of police scientists in the various Latin-American countries who have written extensively in this field and who, with some encouragement, would be more than willing to prepare volumes on the subject of the police in their several countries.

With much of our political, social, economic and cultural history springing from Mexico and Latin-America, the opportunity is herein presented to further strengthen the cultural linkage between two great civilizations in the Western Hemisphere. In addition to collaboration with Latin-American scholars in extending the range of police literature, those countries should be encouraged to send selected young men to this country for police training. Subsequently, the way may be prepared for the exchange of police officers between countries north and south of the equator.

Police Personnel Administration is another subject that is worthy of the best scientific research. What are the personal character-istics which peculiarly qualify a man for police service? How does it happen that some men have all the apparent qualifications and yet lack the ability to perform successfully the duties of a policeman? This entrancing subject in all of its details, including the application of scientific testing principles for the selection of recruits, rating systems to determine their efficiency in the various branches of police service, merit systems of all kinds, methods of dealing with personnel, personnel records and every other factor associated with the administration of personnel must of necessity receive the attention of research experts who are trained not only in the sciences that are applicable in this field but who also know something about police requirements and have had actual experience in police service.

Note will be made in the foregoing that research is directed toward the publication of volumes that are non-existent at the present time. Other basic research, as for illustration, the application of the principles of physics and chemistry to investigation, the application of biology and other principles to identification, and the application of sociological, biological and psychological principles to the project of crime prevention also merit attention at the research level.

Another important aspect of research which is also related to the literary field is the translation into English of important works now available in all the languages of the world. French, German, Italian and Russian scholars, among others, have been prolific contributors to modern police literature. Many of the finest contributions to scientific police procedure are yet to be translated into English. The works of Locard of France; Schneickert, Philipp, Mayer of Germany; Grassberger and his associates in Austria; Carrarra and Ottolenghi of Italy; Gambara of Spain and countless others are much too valuable not to be made available to the American policeman and student of police science and administration. In fact, this might be made a major project because much has been written in these European countries that is of great value to us. Niceforo, Reiss, Bertillon and others have written on some of the aspects of police science and much that they have included in their works has immediate applicability in this country. Reference has been previously made to Takahashi and Matsui, but there are other Japanese writers who have contributed to the field of police science and administration, whose works should be translated and made available.

Finally, it must be said that no one can possibly foresee the social and political changes that may take place in our structure during the decades of reconstruction and social readjustment that will follow the end of the present World War. Institutions of higher learning have a peculiar responsibility in the program of preparedness for any type of social or economic change which may transpire in the important years ahead.

Sufficient has been said to draw in broad outlines the opportunities that are now presented to the educational institutions of this country, with their magnificent resources for training and instruction. It is hoped that the administrators of these institutions will recognize their responsibilities to the public service in this respect and undertake the organized training of men and women for one of the most important of all governmental services. Few, if any, difficulties are presented. A baccalaureate program embracing four years of systematic instruction and leading to the Bachelor of Science degree can be inaugurated that will meet the highest academic standards in the educational field.

Considerable care must be exercised in the selection of the man who will be placed in charge of the program. He should possess the necessary academic background (preferably a Master's degree) and should be a man with extended police experience covering a period of not less than ten years. In connection with the availability of men for these positions, complete information may be obtained from Mr. August Vollmer, head of the National Association of University Police Training Officials. This organization maintains a directory of qualified men in this field and is in a position to make suitable recommendations.

The full implications of professional police training at the university level in terms of sound public policy can be best understood from the standpoint of results. As these men, university trained for a technical job, move upward on the scale of management to positions where they can influence policy and administration, the cities of this nation will begin to receive the caliber of police service to which they are entitled.

V. A. Leonard
Professor and Head
Dept. of Police Science and
   Administration
State College of Washington
Pullman, Washington

BIBLIOGRAPHY

Public Personnel Problems, by L. Meriam, Brookings Institution, Washington, D. C.
Government of Cities in the United States, by Zink, Public Administration Service, Chicago, Illinois.
The Police and Modern Society, by August Vollmer, University of California Press, Berkeley, California.
Crime and the State Police, by Vollmer and Parker, University of California Press, Berkeley, California.
Police Communication Systems, by V. A. Leonard, University of California Press, Berkeley, California.
Survey and Reorganization of the Seattle Police Department, by V. A. Leonard, 1947, Seattle, Washington.
Survey and Reorganization of the Dallas Police Department, by August Vollmer, Berkeley, California.
Survey and Reorganization of the Syracuse Police Department, by August Vollmer, Berkeley, California.
Principles of Criminology, by E. H. Sutherland, J. B. Lippincott, New York.
Principles and Methods in Dealing with Offenders, by Helen D. Pigeon, Public Service Institute, Philadelphia, Pa.
The Biological Basis of Human Nature, by H. S. Jennings, W. W. Norton & Co., N. Y.
Traffic Officer's Training Manual, by Clarence P. Taylor, National Safety Council.
Report Writing, by Carl G. Gaum and Harold F. Graves, Prentice-Hall, Inc., N. Y.

UNLAWFUL ENTRY. This crime is a misdemeanor and is a form of *burglary.* To commit unlawful entry there must be an entry in a building which is already opened. The offender does not break into or open the building. The entry must be for the purpose of or with the intention of committing a felony, a larceny, or a malicious mischief (willful destruction of property) inside the building.

USURY. Usury may be defined as the charging of an unconscionable or exorbitant rate or amount of interest. Specifically, it is interest in excess of a legal rate charged to a borrower for the use of money. The charging of interest for the use of money is allowed in all civilized countries, but in many places there are statutory prohibitions of unconscionable or iniquitous bargains as in England (since 1854) and in parts of the United States. In various states of the United States, there are legal restrictions to some legal rate of interest.

In New York State, the taking of security upon certain property for loans with rates of interest greater than six per centum per annum, is a misdemeanor.

BIBLIOGRAPHY

Gilbert, F. B., *Criminal Law and Practice of the State of New York,* Matthew Bender and Co., 1935.
Weber, M., *General Economic History,* New York, 1927.

W

THE WHITE COLLAR CRIMINAL. The white collar criminal is defined as a person with high socio-economic status who violates the laws designed to regulate his occupational activities. These laws include, in addition to certain sections of the regular penal code, the following trade regulations of the federal government and analogous laws of the several states: the antitrust law, the Federal Trade Commission law, the Interstate Commerce Commission law, the Securities and Exchange Commission law, the National Labor Relations law, the laws regulating advertising, patents, trademarks, and copyrights, and some of the special war regulations.

The white collar criminal should be differentiated, on the one hand, from the person of lower socio-economic status who violates the regular penal code or the special trade regulations which apply to him; and, on the other hand, from the person of high socio-economic status who violates the regular penal code in ways not connected with his occupation. The person of high socio-economic status who commits crimes such as murder or adultery in ways not connected with his occupation is excluded from the class of white collar criminals because he is not different in any significant respect from the person of lower socio-economic status who commits the same crimes.

The hypothesis on which this concept of white collar crime is based is that white collar crime differs from other crimes in the manner in which the law is implemented, but is cognate with other crimes in the genetic processes by which the behavior originates.

Several questions arise in regard to this concept of white collar crime: Is white collar crime "really" crime? In what respects is white collar crime different from other crimes and how are these differences explained? How extensive is white collar crime? What is the significance of white collar crime for theories of criminal behavior? An answer to each of these questions will be presented.

1. White collar crime is "really" crime. The laws which define the behavior under consideration have the two criteria of criminal laws which are used to differentiate criminal law from other law, namely, legal definition of an act as socially injurious and legal provision of a penalty for the act. That the behavior is defined as socially injurious is shown by the words which are used in the laws, such as "crime," "misdemeanor," "unfair," "discrimination," and "infringement." More fundamental evidence that the behavior is defined as socially injurious is found in the legislative debates and the other circumstances of the enactment of the laws. These circumstances demonstrate that the laws were enacted in order to protect competitors, customers, investors, inventors, wage-earners, and other classes of persons from injuries, and also to protect the system of free enterprise and other social institutions. In this respect, the general objectives of these special trade regulations are the same as the general objectives of the penal code. None of these regulations is arbitrary in the sense in which the law which requires automobiles to drive on the right side of the street rather than the left side is arbitrary. Furthermore, the special trade regulations are adaptations of the principles of the penal code and of the common law to modern social conditions. The laws regarding advertising are adaptations of the common law of fraud; the laws regarding infringement are adaptations of the common law of larceny; the prohibition of interference with collec-

tive bargaining in the National Labor Relations law has the same logical basis as the common law prohibitions of interference with freedom in the form of false imprisonment or extortion. The second criterion of the criminal law is the penal sanction. This is found in all of the laws under consideration, although, as will be elaborated below, the penal sanction is kept in the background in most of these trade regulations.

The objection is sometimes made that these laws are not criminal laws because they do not require that criminal intent be demonstrated. This objection is not warranted for the reason that criminal intent is not required in all sections of the regular penal code and the number of exceptions to this requirement is steadily increasing. The relaxation of this requirement that criminal intent be demonstrated is explained in part by the trend away from punitive methods, in part by the increased difficulty of proving criminal intent in the increasingly complex social life of modern times, and in part by the development within the law of a more behavioristic psychology as a substitute for the mentalistic and hedonistic psychology of the earlier generations.

While white collar crime is real crime in that it is a violation of laws which have the general characteristics of criminal laws, not all actions under those laws are concerned with criminal behavior. The Interstate Commerce Commission devotes much of its time to rate-making, and the Securities and Exchange Commission to appraisal of plans for financing. Moreover, some of the suits under these laws, especially regarding patents, raise no questions regarding criminality.

2. The laws which define white collar crime are characteristically implemented in a different manner than the ordinary penal code. Although the penal sanction is always present, it is kept in the background to be used as a last resort. Persons accused of white collar crimes are seldom arrested, fingerprinted, tried in criminal courts, or committed to prison. On the contrary, they are summoned to appear before a commission or a court operating under civil or equity jurisdiction; when decisions are rendered

against them, the orders are generally in the form of injunctions or cease-and-desist orders. These variations in procedures for protecting society against social dangers have the function of reducing or eliminating the stigma of crime. An analysis of the Sherman antitrust law will make this interpretation more clear. This law was enacted in 1890, with only one dissenting vote in Congress, as the result of many expressions of antagonism against "the trusts" which had been developing during the preceding decade. These trusts were regarded as doing great injury to their competitors, as raising prices to consumers, and as resulting in a concentration of wealth and power which endangered the system of free enterprise and the institution of democracy. Congress was compelled to take action to protect American society against this danger. The Sherman antitrust law was a declaration that restraint of trade was a crime and it provided a penalty of fine or imprisonment for the crime. Thus this antitrust law was indubitably a criminal law. The unique characteristic of this law, as contrasted with earlier criminal laws, was that it did not stop with the definition of the behavior as socially injurious and with the provision of a penalty. It went on to authorize two procedures as alternatives to prosecution under the criminal jurisdiction.

First, the attorney general was authorized to petition a court of equity for an injunction against the person or corporation alleged to be in restraint of trade; a violation of this injunction was punishable as contempt of court by a fine or imprisonment. This equity procedure was a distinct departure from previous law which had held that, except in emergencies, an injunction could not be used to enforce a criminal law. In the Sherman antitrust law the use of the injunction to enforce a criminal law was authorized and this modification of the law in adjustment to persons of high socio-economic status may be regarded as a legal invention.

Second, persons who were injured by violations of the antitrust law were authorized to sue for damages in a court of law and the damages to be awarded, in case of a decision for the plaintiff, were required by law to be triple the damages actually suffered.

These damages were designed to repair the injury which had been done and also to punish the offender, but the punitive aspect of the award was concealed in the form of damages. The significant point, however, is that these alternative procedures could be used only if the antitrust law had been demonstrated to be violated and, by definition, a violation of the antitrust law was a crime. Consequently, the violation of the law was a crime regardless of whether the decision was under criminal, civil, or equity jurisdiction, just as tuberculosis is tuberculosis regardless of whether the method of treatment is blood-letting, poultices, or streptomyocin. The criterion of criminal law is not found in the procedure used in a specific case but in the procedure which is authorized as a potential procedure: a thief is no less a thief when placed on probation than when committed to prison.

The antitrust law became a precedent in formulating trade regulations in later decades. In most of them the punishment was kept in the background and thus the stigma of crime was avoided. This objective was found also in the enactment of juvenile court laws but has not been realized so completely in regard to juvenile delinquents as in regard to white collar criminals. Despite the formal jurisdiction and the legal terminology, the juvenile delinquent continues to be regarded by the public as a criminal; likewise the criminologists have developed most of their theories of criminal behavior from the study of juvenile delinquents. On the other hand, the general public seldom regards business men who violate the trade laws as criminals, and the criminologists have practically never taken this behavior into account in the development of their theories of criminal behavior.

3. The different implementation of the laws which apply to white collar criminals is explained principally by the high socio-economic status of the criminals. This is shown by the fact that, while 71 per cent of the decisions under the antitrust law against trade unions in the period 1890–1929 were made under the criminal jurisdiction, only 27 per cent of the similar decisions against business concerns were made under criminal

jurisdiction. The legislatures authorize and the administrative and judicial agencies use these different procedures when dealing with business men partly because of fear of reprisals by the powerful business groups, but principally because of admiration for and confidence in business men. Legislators have believed that these violations will cease when they are called to the attention of these respectable persons, that these persons do not conform to "the criminal type" and should not be treated as criminals. Experience has demonstrated that this confidence in business men has not been justified, for white collar criminals have a much higher rate of recidivism than other criminals, as a class. The enactment of the antitrust law did not stop restraint of trade, but the trend toward monopoly continued and perhaps increased its pace after that behavior was defined as criminal.

The high status of the business men is not the only factor in the differential implementation of the law. A second factor is the relative lack of support of the laws by the mores, due in part to the recency of the laws, and in part to the control of the agencies of public communication by the business men who violate the laws. A third factor is the trend away from punitive methods of social control in the home, the school, the church, and the State. The dependence on non-punitive methods is greater in all areas of crime than in earlier generations, and it is relatively much greater in white collar crime than in other crime because the trade regulations are relatively new and therefore less affected by the traditional punitive procedures.

4. White collar crime, as defined, is very prevalent in American society. This has been demonstrated by many Congressional and other investigations in many areas of business, such as public utilities, banking, insurance, real estate, manufacturing, and merchandising. The investigations of the last century made the American public acquainted with the robber barons of that period; the later investigations present criminals whose methods are more suave but whose respect for law is no greater and whose determination to realize their own

objectives regardless of the law is no less than those attitudes of the robber barons.

In order to secure more precise evidence regarding the prevalence of white collar crime than is provided in such general investigations, an examination has been made of the legal records of the seventy largest industrial and merchandising corporations in the United States (excluding financial, public utility, and petroleum corporations). These records include the subsidiaries as well as the main corporations and cover the life careers of the corporations, which average about forty years.

These records show that every one of the 70 corporations has violated the laws enumerated above, according to official decisions of courts or commissions, with a range from 1 to about 40 adverse decisions per corporation and an average of about 14 per corporation. Of the 70 corporations, 58 have 252 adverse decisions on charges of restraint of trade; in many cases the decisions show that the corporation has carried on its illegal policy throughout its entire career. These decisions justify a conclusion that the large corporations, with few exceptions, oppose a system of free competition and free enterprise and have been attempting to substitute a system of private collectivism. Again, of the 70 corporations 44 have 144 adverse decisions under the National Labor Relations laws during the decade since the enactment of that law in 1935. Thus, approximately two-thirds of the large corporations are so strenuously opposed to collective bargaining that they violate the law in order to prevent its use in their industries. Thus, in general, the official record of decisions demonstrates with great certainty that every one of these large corporations has violated these trade regulations and that some of them violate them with great frequency. The "habitual criminal" laws of some states use three or four previous convictions as the dividing line between habitual and occasional offenders. If this criterion be used, approximately three fourths of the large corporations are habitual white collar criminals. Moreover, this enumeration of official decisions is far from complete.

5. If the preceding definitions of white collar crime and the arguments regarding it are justified, the concept of white collar crime has great significance from the point of view of theories of criminal behavior, due to the fact that it calls attention to a large area of criminal behavior which has been neglected by criminologists. The criminologists have placed great emphasis on poverty and on the social and personal pathologies which are customarily associated with poverty. They have placed their emphasis on such factors because they have confined their studies to criminals of the lower socio-economic class and have, therefore, based their theories on a biased sample of all criminals. Respectable business men who violate the law are seldom in poverty and seldom manifest the social and personal pathologies. The General Motors Corporation does not violate the law because of an Oedipus complex, the General Electric Company because it is emotionally unstable, the Anaconda Copper Company because of bad housing conditions, Armour & Company because of a broken home, the Standard Oil Company because of lack of recreational facilities, or any of them because of poverty as ordinarily understood. Such explanations do not apply to these violations of law, whether the violations be considered as behavior of corporations or as behavior of the persons who direct and manage the corporations.

If personal and social pathologies do not explain the behavior of white collar criminals, they presumably do not explain the behavior of other criminals, since white collar criminals constitute a type in terms of the manner of implementation of the law. The personal and social pathologies of lower class criminals may be incidental, just as "night air" was incidental in the causation of malaria. We should attempt to explain white collar crimes and other crimes in terms of processes which are common to both of them. These common factors are to be found in the "laws of learning" and in the modern social organization, with its specificity of cultural relations.

If this concept of white collar crime is justified, it has implications, also, from the point of view of treatment and prevention of criminal behavior. The re-distribution of wealth may be highly desirable for other reasons but presumably not as a means of control of crime. Similarly, it may be highly desirable for other reasons to correct or prevent emotional conflicts, but this will presumably have little effect on the prevention or correction of delinquent behavior.

EDWIN H. SUTHERLAND
Professor of Sociology
Indiana University

BIBLIOGRAPHY

The principal original sources of information on white collar crime are the official reports of federal commissions, especially the Federal Trade Commission, the National Labor Relations Board, and the Securities and Exchange Commision. Federal and state investigating committes, too numerous to mention, have made reports on different areas of business and many of these reports contain reliable information on white collar crimes. The following articles attempt to analyze such original materials from the point of view of criminology.

Barnes, Harry Elmer, and Teeters, Negley K., *New Horizons in Criminology*, Chap. 3, New York, 1943, Prentice-Hall.
Sutherland, Edwin H., White Collar Criminality, *Amer. Sociol. Rev.*, 5:1–12. February, 1940.
———, Crime and Business, *Annals of Amer. Acad. of Pol. and Soc. Science*, 217:112–18, September, 1941.
———, Is 'White Collar Crime' Crime? *Amer. Sociol. Rev.*, 10:132–39, April, 1945.

WORLD PENAL SYSTEMS.

At first glance, a world-wide view of penology, including such elements as architectural plant and equipment, management and reformative programs would give the impression of wide diversity. Yet to the trained observer who looks closely there is a certain sameness about all the systems of penal treatment. This is certainly true of countries of the western world. Even Oriental philosophies of dealing with the wayward bear a close resemblance to European and American penology. And there are valid reasons for this wide similarity.

While there was some incipient penal reform prior to the heroic age of Beccaria and Howard, much of it was restricted to the regeneration of delinquent youth. The fascinating pioneering of Filippo Franci in Florence in 1667, enthusiastically described by Mabillon, the French Benedictine, and of Pope Clement XI in his Hospice of St. Michele at Rome in 1703, were only flashes of insight in a world in which the attitudes toward the wrongdoer were exceedingly grim and brutal. Imprisonment had been introduced for the chastisement of vagrants and sturdy rogues in the Houses of Correction in London (1557) and a few years later all over western Europe but, aside from these experiments, adult felons were doomed to the galleys, the gibbet or to sundry physical tortures, many of them highly refined. As early as 1619 Britain resorted to transporting many of her criminals to the American colonies which came to a halt with the beginning of the American revolution.

During the eighteenth century a penal renaissance slowly evolved led by Beccaria who, in turn, had been strongly influenced by the French physiocrats. Thus was brought into being theoretical principles based on human justice and honest decency. John Howard's volumes based on his many visits to the jails and prisons of Europe also exercised a great effect on the thinking of kindly disposed men and women in all walks of life and even permeating the realm of nobles and princes. And the citizens of the newly-formed American state were likewise influenced by both reformers.

It is to America that the student of penology turns for information on the modern era of penal treatment. The philosophy of imprisonment is deeply steeped in the monastic features of the church as we may see from the seeds of the philosophy as practiced in San Michel and in the writings of Mabillon. But credit must also be given to the work of the burghers of Amsterdam who, as early as 1596, established a systematic institution for dealing with vagrants and to Hippolyte Vilain who organized his *Rasphuys* for the same class of delinquents at Ghent in 1773. Howard was impressed with these experiments and advocated them in spite of their severity, judged by present day standards. The Philadelphia reformers were also impressed so, in 1790, they saw to it that their Walnut Street Jail was renovated and a régime set up that called for imprisonment with productive labor, instruction and religious instruction.

This institution was the forerunner of the Pennsylvania System of separate confinement, later inaugurated in the Eastern Penitentiary at Philadelphia. A few years prior to this, however, the Auburn System was developed in New York state which emphasized the rigid rule of silence with productive labor in association. Under the cruel lash of Elam Lynds this system appealed to penologists in the United States but visitors from abroad, both from Europe and South America, were more favorably impressed with the Philadelphia system. Thus we see the world divided on penal treatment during the nineteenth century, with both systems vying for adoption and expansion.

All of the above is well-known to penologists and, sketchy as it is, it represents a necessary background in order to understand modern penal treatment throughout the world.

World penal philosophy and current institutional practices are similar in their larger elements for another reason. The eleven International Penitentiary Congresses, held from 1872 to 1935 at approximately five year intervals, have played an important role in synthesizing thought and practice dealing with architecture, management and program. Delegates from the Orient attended as well as those from Latin America, the Near East, Australia and South Africa. Certainly the picture of penal systems today reflects in large measure the results of these deliberations.

At these meetings discussion centered around the progressive stages system introduced into Ireland by Sir Joshua Jebb and expanded by Sir Walter Crofton, the reformatory movement in the United States which capitalized on Crofton's genius and added the indeterminate sentence, the revolutionary philosophy of probation which grew out of the venerable suspended sentence and added the essential feature of supervision, and parole which dignified the bare essentials of conditional release. Here, then, is the framework of modern penology.

Today we see little that is bizarre and not much that is novel in the treatment of

criminals. Nor do we see the sterility of the British treadmill, crank or other infernal machines that made useless drudgery for prisoners during the nineteenth century. We do, however, see much idleness in prisons; not much physical brutality but a great deal of psychological badgering. There is an almost universal apathy as to the basic needs of the prisoner, aside from his physical maintenance, and a lack of disciplined imagination in dealing with such important problems as prison labor, classification and education. Substitutes for imprisonment lag in the thinking of many who realize the shortcomings of the prison but who do not have the will to crusade for the more realistic and fruitful results that are bound to follow.

In such a short review as this must necessarily be, it is impossible to point out the features of penal management of the various countries of the world. Only a few remarks can be made concerning European countries, the Far East, India and Latin America. Following these a short resume of some of the more progressive measures of dealing with prisoners now being carried out somewhere throughout the world will be briefly discussed.

THE EUROPEAN SCENE

Aside from Russia and perhaps a few other Balkan countries, the philosophy underlying European penal treatment stem from the workhouse era and the later experiments formulated in the United States. Separate confinement, known throughout Europe as the cellular system, was adopted in practically every country and is still maintained in many, although in a much diluted form. The proceedings of the International Congresses are replete with descriptions of systems which featured isolation of individual prisoners for varying periods of time.

As time went on and new ideas were conceived by realistic students of the problems of penology, many of whom were prison wardens of vision, penitentiary management and program changed materially. Most of these innovations were developed during the last third of the nineteenth century and the first part of the twentieth. For many years regimentation, expiation, atonement, were all emphasized by the administrators and law makers of all countries. Some countries, notably England, France, Russia and Italy resorted to transporting criminals to distant lands. Russia and France have persisted in this longer than any other country although Italy's modern system features penal colonies off the mainland in the Tuscan archipelago.

Space forbids an analysis of the systems in operation in individual countries of Europe. Each country has made definite contributions to modern penal procedure. Few, except, perhaps, Sweden, have broken definitely with the past so far as treatment of adults is concerned. Interesting experiments have been made with minors. Perhaps the most significant are the Borstal System as developed in Britain, Observation Centers of Belgium and the "prison schools" of Sweden, similar to the British Borstals.

None of the European countries have had a dearth of penal reformers who were not only scholars but men of vision as measured by the political and social philosophy current during the times they lived. Britain may well be proud of her long list of prison reformers including Bentham, Romilly, Peel, Buxton and Elizabeth Fry, as well as less known toilers in the field such as John Bellers, Thomas Shillitoe and Sarah Martin. It would consume too much space to record the names of those who modified the brutality and apathy found in prisons throughout Europe, but no country from Turkey to Spain, from Italy to Scandinavia has been totally lacking in courageous leadership in this field. Many persons well-known in the literature of Europe are practically unknown to those living in the United States.

PENOLOGY IN THE FAR EAST

Japan. Penal reform in Japan is alleged to have begun following surveys made by a stalwart missionary, Dr. John C. Berry, in 1873. Governor Kanda was much impressed with the candor of these reports and set in motion certain reforms which vastly improved the condition of the prisons and their occupants. The penal code drawn up at that time forms the basis of the present penal system.

Japan has copied extensively from British methods. There are four types of prisons:

(1) those reflecting penal servitude; (2) for imprisonment—that is, for less serious offenses; (3) houses of detention, for minor infractions; and (4) confinement, for those awaiting trial. Separate, and even solitary confinement, forms the basis of Japan's system but only for temporary periods. The length of time depends on the law and the discretion of the warden.

One interesting feature of Japan's prisons is the garb worn by the inmates. It is dark red and, since there is no heat in the prisons, is heavily padded. Insignias denoting the type of crime committed, length of sentence and status of the prisoner are sewed on the clothing.

Disciplinary measures are archaic, such as the strait jacket, fetters, handcuffs, chains and ropes. One redeeming feature of Japan is that as early as 1888 a course in guard training was inaugurated. In this she deserves distinction.

Japan has been represented at some of the International Penitentiary Congresses, so she has not been totally ignorant of the status of penal treatment in western countries.

China and the Philippines. The year 1902 marks the beginning of the movement to improve the prisons of China. In that year it was decreed that workhouses should be established for all prisoners sentenced to "exile and imprisonment." In 1909 a model prison was erected in Peking and before the Revolution other prisons were erected in some of the other provinces.

Since the founding of the Republic the construction of penal establishments took on significance so that by 1918 there were more than thirty modern prisons. The system of separate confinement was formally introduced in 1922. In that same year reformatories were created for juveniles.

China's convicts have the privilege of working at productive employment with compensation. There is an excellent course in guard training.

Modern China operates under the penal code of 1935. Among its features are special sections dealing with the treatment of children, classification of adult criminals, prison labor and education, the last being an attempt to mitigate the "awful isolation" of prisoners.

The war has disrupted China's prisons to an alarming degree. Most of the cities in which the prisons are located were under the domination of Japan. Some of China's penal administrators functioned under Japanese rule while others left for free China. One of the big tasks in China's post-war era will be to develop her penology.

Prisons in the Philippines, prior to the war, were noted for their industry. There were three large institutions and fifty-two provincial jails under the centralized supervision of the Insular Director of Prisons. The prisons are: Bilibid, a great industrial prison in Manila accommodating 2,000 convicts; Iwhig penal colony with 1,500 prisoners; and San Ramón Prison Farm, set aside primarily for native Moros.

India's Prison System. Prior to 1704, when the East India Company, under authority of the British government established western concepts of law and order in India, those who violated the law were beheaded or were trampled to death by elephants at the whim of native rulers. By 1836 a large number of jails had been erected throughout the country and road making by convicts was abandoned due to the high mortality rate.

While many penal reforms were made in 1836, the real starting-point of modern reform is dated from 1919–20 when a report on Indian jails envisaged a realistic plan of penal treatment. The Borstal system, probation and other such innovations from Britain were slowly introduced in the various provinces.

Prison management in India must square with the conditions peculiar to this heterogeneous and perplexing country. Dietary rules, preparation of food, prison architecture, institutional discipline—all must be adapted to the nature of the disposition of the various religious groups. This is the most perplexing feature of Indian penology. Another serious problem to be dealt with in India is that of the wandering criminal tribes. The number of these tribes alone is in the thousands. Some measures have been adopted to cope with this menace, but there is much even yet that is necessary before

some control of these millions of professional criminals will be effected.

LATIN AMERICAN PENOLOGY

It is but natural that the status of scientific and progressive penology in the various countries of Latin America would depend on the degree of economic, social and political development attained since the revolutions that threw off the yoke of Spanish exploitation. Thus, in the areas of both Central and Latin America, as well as the Caribbean district are to be found systems of penology that range from the most backward and benighted to those characterized by progressive insight and social understanding.

But even in the most progressive countries one finds vestiges of the Spanish epoch—for example, in the architecture and administration of the jails (*carceles*) and also in many of the penal codes. The penitentiaries, however, follow the architectural motif of the Philadelphia prison and the philosophy of separate confinement took root to the same degree as in Europe.

Only within recent years have any of the countries built new prisons. The National Penitentiaries, located in the capitals, were erected from 1840 up to 1890 and most of them are in a sorry state of disrepair. New construction of significance may be found in Colombia, Argentina and Brazil. Peru has developed an ambitious project of construction to make up for the lag in penology that has permeated the country for so many years. There is a tendency to erect small institutions with a combination of Spanish architecture and the "telephone pole" type of construction.

Several of the Latin American countries are resigned to a do-nothing policy, and in these there is little hope of anything emerging for many years.

The diagnostic clinic has been developed to a high degree in such countries as Colombia, Ecuador, Chile and Argentina. It must be remembered that the first such clinic was conceived by José Ingenieros in Argentina. Some of the South American countries have done remarkable things in the field of juvenile treatment. Chile has only recently opened its colorful and progressive *Ciudad del Niño* in which sound case work methods have been devised; Argentina has long possessed several highly successful *Colonias Hogares* for both boys and girls; and the cities of São Paulo and Rio de Janeiro are pioneering in child care.

Criminal causation in all Latin America is studied primarily from the biological approach rather than the sociological. This is due to the continental influence, primarily from France, Italy and Spain. However, there are several students of the problems of crime who are rapidly pointing out the fallacies inherent in this approach, so it is quite possible that the environmental school will be much better represented in the near future.

A NEW DAY IN PENAL TREATMENT

As we survey the world today we find that no country has yet freed itself completely from the retributive philosophy that made penal treatment so barbaric in the past. Here may be seen a flash of progressive insight; there may be witnessed reaction of the worst sort. It is a fair conclusion to assert that only by the interplay of ideas and methods existing throughout the world in specific countries can reform of lasting significance be realized in this dismal sphere of human relations. There is no country so enlightened that it cannot learn from others.

Nevertheless, there are obvious limits to what nations can learn from one another in this field. Many methods and techniques which seem to work admirably in some countries might completely fail in others where the essential material and ideological prerequisites do not exist. However, no country can afford to repudiate the concepts developed elsewhere without a fair trial, or, at least, without an honest consideration.

The thesis is gaining strength that the criminal is a human being and that he is a victim of either biological handicaps or social maladjustment, or both, rather than being a perverse creature who wrongs society because he is just perverse by choice. Classification procedure as developed first in Argentina and Belgium, and later in the United States, is a distinct advance over the older methods of placing the prisoner in categories based on his crimes. The full man must be understood through scientific tests in the various fields dealing with human nature.

And the treatment, recommended by those who make these examinations should be as individualized as possible. It may be medical, psychological, or industrial; it may well be a combination of all types. Rehabilitation through the prison process is the objective. It is doubtful, however, that this can be realized since the prison is obviously an outmoded institution. Yet it represents society's only major technique of handling those who are convicted of major offenses. It is recognized by more and more penologists that prisoners should be released from the institution as rapidly as possible and placed under restraint in the community where more normal facilities, as well as richer, are present. It is too much to expect a normal person to emerge from the abnormal atmosphere of a prison no matter how meaningful his program there was.

Some innovations practiced throughout the world can be of service in the new penology which is definitely emerging and which will be accelerated undoubtedly in the post-war world. Some of the most fruitful of these follow.

The Use of Prison Labor Outside Penal Establishments. Here is an interesting departure from tradition but one that may be much abused unless resorted to with great caution. No prison can productively employ all its inmates. Hence, measures should be taken to permit as many as possible to work away from the prison. Some may even live in the community, reporting at stated intervals to the prison authorities. Canada, Italy and Czechoslovakia have already done much along this line. Some South American countries, especially Colombia, have done this for years. Agriculture especially lends itself to this practice.

Work Camps. There is nothing new or unique with work camps. Many prison systems are based primarily on such a system. Again, much abuse can spring from these camps but there is no reason why brutality should be a part of any system. Australia, New Zealand, Switzerland, at its famous camp at Witzwil, and Belgium, at Merxplas, have developed the camp idea to an amazing degree.

The Wider Use of Leaves or Furlough. Weekend visits, furloughs at Christmas and on other holidays, visits home once a month or more frequent, could be granted on the basis of good work or on some other basis determined by the classification clinic. There are thousands of prisoners who could be depended on to return to the prison after they had been accorded a visit home. Russia has gone in for this sort of procedure in a big way. It is a healthy practice because it keeps up the morale of both the man in prison and the members of his family. This can be expanded by permitting inmates to have conjugal visits as is practiced in Mexico, for instance, or in Colombia, where the inmates leave the prison for sexual gratification. Other South American countries, notably Brazil, permit the inmate's wife to come to the prison for a conjugal visit.

The Abolition of Flogging in Children's Institutions. Unfortunately, Britain and the United States lead the world in the practice of flogging children. In many countries it is never resorted to. France abolished the practice in 1899. It is not even contemplated in South American countries. The practice has no bearing on progressive treatment of juveniles and should be abolished everywhere. Our own country has much to learn along this line.

The Scrupulous Segregation of Those Awaiting Trial. This presupposes the erection of special houses of detention for those unable to furnish bail. Scandinavia has led the way in providing these special quarters. Many countries, especially the United States, has a long way to go in separating this group of persons from the misdemeanants and other types of offenders found in our crude county jails. A man is not guilty until he is proved so. Hence, the present system is patently unfair and discriminatory.

The Wider Use of Female Police. Many of the larger cities of the world have female police but none has as many as are needed. As a system it is nowhere developed except in Austria. This is a development that must come in the near future.

Preventive Detention. This system is in operation in Britain and other countries in Europe, notably Italy. It calls for an extra sentence for habitual and professional criminals after they have served their regular sentence. It is frankly a method of keeping under restraint that class of criminals that persists in living by crime. Australia's penal code permits her courts to place "persistent misdemeanants" in what is termed "reformative detention." This is analogous to preventive detention except for chronic minor offenders. Until a realistic indeterminate sentence is developed a measure of this sort has possibilities. It is limited, however, to possible constitutional rights of citizens.

Restitution for Crime. Many countries, especially some in Latin America, maintain a realistic system whereby the offender must make restitution to his victim. It is interesting to note that this question was debated in several of the International Prison Congresses. It cannot be denied that there are possibilities in this practice which should be explored. There is almost universal agreement on the desirability of developing such a system; the controversy arises on the methods of securing the indemnity.

Miscellany. Many additional practices which have for their objective the ultimate reformation of the criminal can be listed. All are important and call for serious consideration. All are being used in some countries throughout the world. They are as follows: the development of hobbies—Spain and Latin American countries have developed this interesting phase of treatment. They include sculpture, painting, the keeping and selling of pets by prisoners, ceramics, weaving of blankets, raising of vegetables and flowers for sale—in Colombia's prison at Bogotá prisoners cultivate cut flowers for florists; the use of community volunteers as developed on such a large scale in English prisons; also in Czecho-slovakia where over 8,000 private individuals work with immured prisoners; officer training on a scientific basis such as has been developed in our own country, Sweden, Belgium, Japan and Argentina; biological laboratories and observation clinics where emphasis is placed primarily on crimino-biological investigation as in Belgium, Argentina and Brazil; permission for prisoners to wear their own clothes, as in Holland; the installation of theatres such as is found in the Hungarian prison at Vac; the expansion of prison education, meaningful religious instruction, more adequate supervision of prisons—all of these and many more call for examination and adoption where practicable.

Penal philosophy and practice are dynamic; they are constantly in a state of flux. Penal programs everywhere are theoretically attempting to cope with the crime problem. Discipline, training, productive work, religion, therapy—all have a place in the modern penal program. What is needed is realism and vision. A bird's eye view of world penology can supply much that is good for the

new age in penal procedure if leaders will but look.

NEGLEY K. TEETERS
Professor of Sociology
Temple University
Philadelphia, Penn.

BIBLIOGRAPHY

Annals of the American Academy of Political and Social Science, *Prisons of Tomorrow,* September, 1931.
Barker, F. A., *The Modern Prison System of India,* Macmillan, 1944.
Gillin, John L., *Taming the Criminal,* Macmillan, 1931.
Teeters, Negley K., *World Penal Systems,* Philadelphia, 1944.
———, *Penology from Panama to Cape Horn,* Philadelphia, 1946.

Y

THE YOUTH CORRECTION AUTHORITY PLAN.

In 1940 a committee of the American Law Institute, after study and discussion over a two-year period, recommended a widely discussed plan for meeting the youth crime situation. The recommendation was in the form of a model bill for state legislatures, with the title, Youth Correction Authority Act. The committee, which had been selected to represent all pertinent professions, was composed of the following specialists: Curtis Bok, E. R. Cass, Sheldon Glueck, Leonard V. Harrison, William Healy, Edwin R. Keedy, Austin H. MacCormick, William E. Mikell, Thorsten Sellin, Joseph N. Ullman, and John B. Waite. Their proposal focused attention upon two specific phases of youthful crime: the process of sentencing convicted offenders and the process of treating or correcting them. Directly, in California, and indirectly, in New York, the proponents of the plan have succeeded in effecting substantial reforms in the handling of young offenders against the law. In both these programs, however, and in the case of the correction bills considered by congressional committees (S. 677 and H. R. 2445, 79th Congress, 1st Session), two significant divergences have been made from the original plan: the sentencing power and the control of probation have been left substantially undisturbed, and would not, as in the original plan, be transferred to an executive board.

The original plan provided in general:

(1) that when a youth between the ages 16 and 21 has been convicted of a violation of law for which the maximum penalty prescribed is less than death or imprisonment for life, and is more than 60 days, the court shall commit him to a three-member Youth Correction Authority appointed by the governor;

(2) that the Authority shall set up detention and diagnostic centers for making an individualized study of each person committed to it, and that the specialized personnel of the diagnostic centers shall recommend the type and length of treatment needed in each case;

(3) that the Authority may place a youth on probation, release him on parole, order his confinement in existing institutions, or use and devise new methods of treatment. The Authority would be unhampered in making prompt modification of any course of correctional treatment whenever a youth should show need of it.

In substance, then, it was proposed that, for those between 16 and 21 found guilty of serious but not the most serious offenses, the procedures of sentencing, probation, correction, parole, and discharge would be conducted by one agency instead of dozens. The result at which the plan has always aimed is unification into one course of treatment of all procedures in the handling of youthful offenders so that the widest possible flexibility and the closest possible individualization of treatment might be effected. Youth was selected for this new program because of its susceptibility to correctional treatment and in the trust that criminal careers could be forestalled.

Support for the plan came at once from those organizations and individuals who were ready for a radical attack upon the problem and who had rejected the principle of retributive punishment. Opposition came principally from those judges, lawyers, probation officers, and others who believed that the courts could not relinquish the right to pro-

OF CRIMINOLOGY

Youth Correction Authority Plan

nounce sentence and to administer the work of probational supervision.

The Sentencing Power. The question of shifting the sentencing power from the courts to a board, which had often been debated in the past, was at the center of much of the discussion stimulated by the Youth Correction Authority Plan. Warner and Cabot in their *Judges and Law Reform*, 1936, had argued for a "disposition tribunal," and listed earlier proposals to this end. Leonard V. Harrison, one of the authors and leading proponents of the plan, in his *Preventing Criminal Careers*, 1941, quotes affirmations of the principle of the sentencing board from Alfred E. Smith, Paul V. McNutt, and Lewis E. Lawes. One of the chief features of the wide-spread discussion over the plan is that the principle of the sentencing board has been brought into open popular debate, with attention focussed upon a specific application of it.

On this most debatable characteristic of the plan important comments were made at the hearings in Washington of the House Committee on the Judiciary held in May and June, 1943, to consider a bill incorporating a federal form of the plan. At those hearings Hon. John J. Parker, Senior Circuit Judge, appeared as Chairman of the Committee on the Punishment of Crime of the Conference of Senior Circuit Judges, and testified in support of the bill. This bill, like all other forms of the plan which have been put forward, differs in several ways from the model bill, but the discussion of the sentencing power has been fundamentally the same in all cases.

Judge Parker averred that there are three defects in the present system of sentencing in the federal courts (defects which other advocates of change have alleged to be even more noticeable in other jurisdictions): lack of sufficient knowledge on the part of some judges, diversity in length of sentences, depending on the judge, and lack of coordination between the sentencing and the paroling authorities. With regard to the latter point, the Youth Correction Authority plan would make these two authorities identical for that group of offenders which the plan would affect.

"The real objection to the bill on the part of some judges," in an opinion expressed by Judge Parker and by other advocates of the plan, "is that they think that sentences should be handled like awards of damages, i.e., measured by what they conceive to be the prisoner's culpability, and are unwilling to accept the modern view that punishment must be reformative as well as retributive."

It should be added and noted that neither Judge Parker nor most of the other critics of the sentencing procedure have argued for the complete shift of sentencing power from the courts, but only for a further shift than has already been made in many jurisdictions through the development in combination of indeterminate sentencing and parole. The federal bill, for example, provides for an original sentence by the court of the maximum term allowed by law to be modified or affirmed as a definite sentence on the basis of recommendations as to length of treatment by a board; the board would have entire jurisdiction as to type of treatment and would have the responsibility for conducting the treatment. The proposed board, which would have divisions for both youth and adults, would also take over all federal parole functions.

A clear-cut statement of the sentencing problem from the point of view of the new plan was made at the House hearings by Hon. Sanford Bates, then Parole Commissioner of New York State and later Commissioner of Institutions and Agencies for New Jersey. Commissioner Bates remarked that judges should not be expected to be experts in law and at the same time "humane scientists," that there are "two jobs to be done and that they need two sets of experts to do it. . . . Justice may decide what he did, but science has to decide who he is and what is going to be done to him."

Opposition to the Youth Correction Authority plan in all of its four major forms, the original, the federal, the California, and the New York forms, has usually centered on this issue of the sentencing power. Professor Jerome Hall of the Indiana University Law School, writing in the American Bar Association Journal of May, 1942, expressed the fear that under the plan "the judge will be reduced to the status of a clerk to enter pleas of guilty, or in the minority of contested cases to that of an umpire of the legal contest." Professor Hall argued that most judges do know enough to pronounce correct initial sentences to be modified later by parole boards, and that the imposition of sentences by judges is "an integral characteristic of the judicial office and a valuable symbol of law enforcement."

Correctional Treatment. The second general question raised by the projection of this new attack upon the youth crime problem revolves around methods of correction. An extended discussion of the rôle of punishment in the administration of justice and the rehabilitation of offenders has been maintained by the advocates and opponents of the plan. It has been provided in all forms of the bill that the proposed authority should have power not only to use existing correctional institutions but also to establish and use new facilities for treatment, such as work camps, hostels, foster homes, and institutions of all degrees of security. The authority would be given power also to make arrangements for cooperative use of private agencies. The thinking that underlies this emphasis upon new methods, as stated in *Youth and Crime*, a pamphlet with which the American Law Institute announced its new program, is that:

"(1) Retributive punishment as a method of dealing with criminals is not sufficiently effective for the proper protection of society.

"(2) The punitive method has in fact already begun to give place to practices based on other ideas.

"(3) Methods of treatment based on the characteristics of the offender and other causal factors of his conduct can and should be devised."

The correctional procedures most often referred to by advocates of the plan are those of the English Borstal system and the experimental program of the New Jersey reformatory at Annandale. Critics of the plan have asserted that to carry too far the individualization of treatment is to encourage that same diversity of sentences which offenders resent as unfair. Some critics have insisted on the importance of the offender's learning,

through the experience of punishment, that justice is the law. Advocates of the individual treatment plan have replied that the fact of conviction is often punishment enough, and that the purpose of confinement and of other corrective measures is not to match a specific offense with an equal weight of punishment, but to prevent criminal careers, an endeavor in which punishment would certainly have place as a part of education in realism.

The compulsory character of rehabilitative correction and the danger to civil liberties which would be entailed by any unrestricted application of it are recognized in all forms of the plan by limitations upon the length of control which the authority could maintain. In the New York bill, for example, though discharge of a youth by the authority is required only "as soon as in its judgment further control of such youth is no longer required in the public interest," still, depending on the case, he must be discharged before he is 21 or 25, or within three years. In cases where longer control might be considered to be in the public interest the authority would make an order to extend the period of control and apply to the supreme court for review of such order. If confirmed, the extension of control would be for two or five years, depending on the type of commitment.

It has been argued that these limitations upon the power of the authority are inconsistent with the flexibility of sentencing at which the plan aims and for which it generally provides. But defenders of the plan do not by any means wish to confer dictatorial authority upon any agency. The bill is inevitably a compromise between the individual's rights to liberty under law and the state's authority to protect society by the individualized treatment of offenders (which would require longer and shorter periods of control, in some cases, than the maximum and minimum terms prescribed for violations of law).

The two chief areas of disagreement over the plan, sentencing and correcting, are, of course, closely related. For one of the strongest contentions of advocates of the plan is that there has been a significant development in very modern times of a science of psychiatry and a profession of social work, and of a collaboration between the two in the field of probation and correction. So long as the old methods of merely custodial detention are the only ones available, it matters little who decides to what institution a youth be sent.

Only in conjunction with new possibilities of correctional treatment, fully devoted to a program of individualized re-education, do the recommendations of a sentencing board have all the pertinence which they would have under the Youth Correction Authority plan.

State Programs. California adopted the plan in 1941, with changes fitted to particular conditions. During its first two years the agency was hampered by lack of funds, and, at the discretion of the authority, as provided for in all forms of the bill, few youths were committed to it. In 1943, however, it was for the first time given an adequate appropriation. The word "correction" was dropped from its title, in recognition of the fact that it had become increasingly active as an agency for prevention as well as correction. Most of the commitments to the California Youth Authority have been from the juvenile courts, a possibility provided for in the New York bill as well, at the discretion of the courts. The mandatory provision that courts commit all youthful offenders to the authority has not always been adhered to. The outstanding fact, however, in the history of the California Youth Authority is the development of new methods of correction. Forestry camps have been organized, in which youths lead an active, educative life. In contract with the army the authority has opened work camps in connection with arsenals. Under army supervision the boys repair military equipment. They have their own shops, dormitories, living quarters, and recreation facilities, and are paid prevailing wages.

One of the most important developments in California has been the successful recruitment of new and well-qualified personnel, attracted by the spirit and possibilities of the new program for preventing criminal careers. Leaders who are personally qualified to teach and guide young persons are of crucial importance in any such program, and for this reason, among others, the authority has in nearly all cases been proposed as a separate agency of the state, rather than as a part of the correction department. Any bias in favor of old routines of custodial punishment would, in the eyes of proponents of the plan, seriously disqualify a person for leadership in the newer methods of correction.

The latest development is that in January, 1944, the California Legislature passed an act creating an Adult Authority, applying the same program to adult offenders, and integrating the two authorities in a new Department of Correction.

Another version of the plan was drafted in New York State in 1941 and introduced in the State Legislature and reintroduced in subsequent years until 1945. It was supported from the beginning by the Community Service Society of New York, the Society for the Prevention of Crime, and other groups. A state-wide committee of civic leaders coordinated the support for the bill under the chairmanship of Hon. Austin H. MacCormick, director of the Osborne Association and formerly Commissioner of Correction for New York City.

The bill was at first identical in all significant features with the American Law Institute's model. Later it was amended to leave undisturbed the court's powers of granting and administering probation. The bill provided for an independent authority having undivided jurisdiction over diagnosis, classification, sentence, correction, parole, and discharge, with the limitations already described over length of control. In addition, the authority as well as the courts would have probation functions. It was thought that in cases of doubt whether to grant probation, the courts would commit to the authority and let it decide, after more thorough study of the youth than the court had been able to make.

The bill won stronger support each year, until near the close of the 1944 session it passed the Senate, though with the tacit knowledge that there was not time for the Assembly to act upon it. During the 1945 session, though popular support for it was stronger than ever, the bill was not reported out of committee.

However, during the 1945 session a report was issued by an Interdepartmental Committee on Delinquency composed of the heads of the state departments concerned, and a series of bills was introduced and passed to carry out the recommendations of the committee. No mention was made in the report of the Youth Correction Authority idea, but the program put into law contained some of the features of it and clearly had been worked out in response to the demand for a modern approach to the problem of youth crime.

The most significant features of this program are a Youth Service Commission to coordinate local delinquency-preventing activities, and a classification center in the Department of Correction. One of the new laws provides, for those male offenders between 16 and 21 convicted of offenses punishable by imprisonment in institutions under the Department of Correction, except those sentenced to death, that:

(a) a reception and classification center shall be established by the Department of Correction;

(b) youths affected by the law shall be sentenced to an institution of the department without designating its name and be committed to the reception center for classification;

(c) there shall be no other change in the sentencing power of the court;

(d) the director of the reception center may return a youth to the county from which he was committed to be re-sentenced and to be dealt with in all respects as though he had not been committed;

(e) a classification board, composed from the staff of the reception center, shall recommend the institution best suited to receive the offender, the type of program to be followed, and the approximate length of treatment.

This program, while moving in the same direction as the Youth Correction Authority plan, gives little power to the classification board, and changes in methods and spirit of correction are left entirely to the administrative discretion of the Commissioner of Correction. The likelihood of the present department's developing new methods (and, consequently, of the sentencing procedure's becoming inadequate) may be judged from the following passage in the report of the interdepartmental committee: "No better plan than is represented by the objectives and procedures of the best institutions has yet been proposed for reclaiming delinquents and criminals to a law-abiding life. There should be, and probably is, a better answer to delinquency and crime than institutionalization, but to date no such plan is available." That such a plan is available has been the contention of the proponents of a Youth Correction Authority. They can be expected to continue to press for radical modernization in methods of dealing with youthful offenders. Movements in support of the proposal are under way in several other states. Mr. John R. Ellingston, special advisor for the American Law Institute, is actively assisting groups throughout the country to draft legislation and to organize backing for it. The institute is carrying on educational work with the support of a special fund collected for the purpose. In 1944, at the request of the Rhode Island Department of Social Welfare, Mr. Ellingston drafted an act for the integration of all prevention and correction activities for all age groups along the lines of the Youth Correction Authority Act. The Wisconsin bill applies to all offenders under thirty, and is supported by the governor and the Department of Public Welfare, to which the bill would give the powers of the authority. The end of the war, with the expected rise in the incidence of crime, has seen a renewal of interest in the plan in all states.

SEN. THOMAS C. DESMOND
94 Broadway
Newburgh, New York

BIBLIOGRAPHY

California Youth Authority and New York State Department of Correction, Various publications.

Harrison, Leonard V., Preventing Criminal Careers, Community Service Society of New York, 1941.

Harrison, Leonard V., and Grant, P. M., Youth in the Toils, Macmillan, New York, 1938.

Healy, William, and Alper, Benedict S., *Criminal Youth and the Borstal System,* The Commonwealth Fund, New York, 1941.

House of Representatives, 78th Congress, *Hearings Before Committee on the Judiciary on H. R. 2139 and 2140,* Government Printing Office, Washington, 1943.

Law and Contemporary Problems, *The Correction of Youthful Offenders,* Entire issue, Duke University School of Law, Durham, N. C., Autumn, 1942.

Sellin, Thorsten, *The Criminality of Youth,* The American Law Institute, Philadelphia, 1940.

Social Work Yearbook, 7th and 8th issues, Various articles and bibliographies, Russell Sage Foundation, New York, 1943 and 1945.

Warner, S. B., and Cabot, H. B., *Judges and Law Reform,* Harvard University Press, Cambridge, 1936.

Stellin, Thorsten, The Criminality of Youth, The American Law Institute, Philadelphia, 1940.

Social Work Yearbook, 7th and 8th issues, Various articles and bibliographies, Russell Sage Foundation, New York, 1945 and 1945.

Warner, S. B., and Cabot, H. B., Judges and Law Reform, Harvard University Press, Cambridge, 1936.

Healy, William, and Alper, Benedict S., Criminal Youth and the Borstal System, The Commonwealth Fund, New York, 1941.

House of Representatives, 78th Congress, Hearings Before Committee on the Judiciary on H. R. 2139 and 2140, Government Printing Office, Washington, 1943.

Law and Contemporary Problems, The Correction of Youthful Offenders, Entire issue, Duke University School of Law, Durham, N. C., Autumn, 1942.